Dalal

The SAGE Handbook of
Family Business

Editorial Board Members

The SAGE Handbook of
Family Business

Edited by
Leif Melin, Mattias Nordqvist
and Pramodita Sharma

Los Angeles | London | New Delhi
Singapore | Washington DC

Los Angeles | London | New Delhi
Singapore | Washington DC

SAGE Publications Ltd
1 Oliver's Yard
55 City Road
London EC1Y 1SP

SAGE Publications Inc.
2455 Teller Road
Thousand Oaks, California 91320

SAGE Publications India Pvt Ltd
B 1/I 1 Mohan Cooperative Industrial Area
Mathura Road
New Delhi 110 044

SAGE Publications Asia-Pacific Pte Ltd
3 Church Street
#10-04 Samsung Hub
Singapore 049483

Editor: Delia Martinez Alfonso
Assistant editor: Colette Wilson
Production editor: Sushant Nailwal
Copyeditor: David Hemsley
Proofreader: Derek Markham
Indexer: Gary Birch
Marketing manager: Alison Borg
Cover design: Wendy Scott
Typeset by: C&M Digitals (P) Ltd, Chennai, India
Printed in Great Britain by Henry Ling Limited, at the
Dorset Press, Dorchester, DT1 1HD
Printed on paper from sustainable resources

First edition published 2014

Library of Congress Control Number: 2013935403

British Library Cataloguing in Publication data

A catalogue record for this book is available from the British Library

ISBN 978-0-85702-363-6

Contents

Notes on Editors and Contributors

EDITORS

Leif Melin, PhD, is Professor of Strategy and Organisation and the Hamrin Professor of Family Business Strategy at Jönköping International Business School (JIBS). He is the founding and past Director of Center for Family Enterprise and Ownership (CeFEO). He has served as Dean and Managing Director for JIBS. He was a founding researcher of the STEP project (Transgenerational Entrepreneurship Practices) and has served as member for the Global STEP Project Board. In 2012, he was honored with the International award at the 26th anniversary conference of the Family Firm Institute, and was also selected as a Family Owned Business Institute Scholar. He is the founder and annual co-chair of the EIASM Family Firm Research Workshop. He has published in international journals and book volumes, including *Strategic Management Journal*, *Journal of Management Studies*, *Strategic Organization*, *Long Range Planning* and *Family Business Review*. He serves on the editorial board of several international journals.

Mattias Nordqvist, PhD, is Professor of Business Administration and the Hamrin International Professor of Family Business. He is the Director of Center for Family Enterprise and Ownership (CeFEO) and on the faculty of Jönköping International Business School (JIBS) in Sweden, where he has also served as an Associate Dean. Mattias is a former Co-Director of the Global STEP Project and Visiting Scholar at Babson College, USA, University of Alberta, Canada and Bocconi University, Italy. He was selected as a Family Owned Business Institute Scholar in 2007–2008 and 2011–2012 by the Seidman College of Business, Grand Valley State University, Grand Rapids, USA, and has won the Family Firm Institute (FFI) Award for Best Unpublished Research Paper twice, in 2005 and 2011. Mattias is a recipient of the Young Entrepreneurship Researcher Award 2006 from the Swedish Entrepreneurship Forum and the Swedish Agency for Economic and Regional Growth. He is a co-founding Associate Editor of the *Journal of Family Business Strategy*.

Pramodita Sharma, PhD, is the Sanders Professor for Family Business at the School of Business Administration, University of Vermont. Prior to this appointment, she was the CIBC Distinguished Professor of Family Business at the John Molson School of Business, Concordia University in Montreal. She is a visiting scholar at Babson College, where she serves as the Academic Director of the Global Successful Transgenerational Entrepreneurship Practices (STEP) project. In 2011, she was honored with the prestigious Barbara Hollander award at the 25th anniversary conference of the Family Firm Institute. In addition to two co-authored books, she has published about 50 scholarly articles and book chapters on family business studies. She serves as the Editor-in-Chief of *Family Business Review*, and is the co-founder of the Family Enterprise Research Conference and the founding Chair of the Annual Global Family Enterprise Case Competition.

CONTRIBUTORS

Sondos G. Abdel Gawad is Assistant Professor in the Entrepreneurship Department of IE Business School, Madrid, Spain. She holds Bachelor degree of Business Administration, with high honors, from the American University in Cairo, Egypt. She received her Master of Research degree in Management Science from ESADE. Her research interest includes entrepreneurial capabilities, strategic entrepreneurship and organizational learning. She is a member of the Academy of Management and serves as a reviewer for its Entrepreneurship division. Her research has been presented in several academic conferences. Her research has also appeared in several journals.

Howard E. Aldrich received his PhD from the University of Michigan and is Kenan Professor of Sociology, Chair of the Sociology Department, Adjunct Professor of Business at the University of North Carolina, Chapel Hill, and Faculty Research Associate at the Department of Strategy & Entrepreneurship, Fuqua School of Business, Duke University. His 1979 book, *Organizations and Environments*, was reprinted in 2007 by Stanford University Press in its Business Classics series. His book *Organizations Evolving* (Sage, 1999) won the George Terry Award from the Academy of Management and was co-winner of the Max Weber Award from the OOW section of the American Sociological Association. In 2000, he won the Swedish Foundation on Small Business Award for his research on entrepreneurship. In 2002, he won the Sitterson Award for Excellence in Freshman Teaching at UNC-CH. His latest book, *An Evolutionary Approach to Entrepreneurship: Selected Essays*, was published by Edward Elgar in 2011.

Raphael (Raffi) Amit is the Robert B. Goergen Professor of Entrepreneurship and a Professor of Management at the Wharton School. Dr Amit founded and leads the Wharton Global Family Alliance (WGFA), a unique academic-family business partnership established to enhance the marketplace advantage and the social wealth creation contributions of global families through thought leadership, knowledge transfer and the sharing of ideas and best practices among influential global families. Dr Amit holds BA and MA degrees in Economics, and received his PhD in Managerial Economics and Decision Sciences from Northwestern University's Kellogg Graduate School of Management. Dr Amit's current research and teaching interests center on family business management, governance and finance, on venture capital and private equity investments, on the design of business models and on business strategy. He has published extensively in leading academic journals and is frequently quoted in a broad range of practitioner outlets.

Pascual Berrone is Associate Professor of strategic management and holder of the Schneider Electric Chair of Sustainability and Business Strategy at IESE Business School. He is also vice-president of the Iberoamerican Academy of Management. He received his PhD from Carlos III University. His work focuses on corporate governance, family firms, sustainable innovation and corporate social responsibility. His studies have been published in the *Academy of Management Journal*, *Administrative Science Quarterly*, *Strategic Management Journal*, *Human Resource Management*, among many others, and he has received several prestigious 'best paper' awards. He currently acts as an associate editor for *Family Business Review*.

Anna Blombäck has a PhD in business administration and currently works as assistant professor at Jönköping International Business School (JIBS) in Sweden where she is also a member of the Center of Family Enterprise and Ownership (CeFEO). Blombäck primarily does research in the areas of corporate marketing and corporate social responsibility and has several publications in international journals on the topics. She takes particular interest in exploring these topics in the family business context; for example how the entwinement of family and business history influences corporate identity, brand management and corporate image.

Rhonda S. Breitkreuz, PhD, is an Associate Professor of Gender, Family, and Policy Studies in the Department of Human Ecology at the University of Alberta. Her current research interests include the integration of work and family, gender and family, and the impact of social policy on family well-being. Her research on the gendered nature of welfare-to-work, the work-family integration of those in marginalized employment, and program implementation in family support centres has been published in a variety of leading inter-disciplinary social science journals. Rhonda is a member of the Research Advisory Committee for a granting agency called The Alberta Centre for Child, Family, and Community Research.

Ethel Brundin is Professor in Entrepreneurship and Business Development at Jönköping International Business School. She is affiliated with the Center of Family Enterprise and Ownership, a member of the global family business research project of STEP (Successful Transgenerational Entrepreneurship Practices), permanent visiting professor at the Witten Herdecke University in Germany and at the University of the Western Cape, South Africa. The focus of her research interest is micro processes in family businesses including emotions, entrepreneurship and strategic leadership – often in combination. She is currently studying the meaning, practices and implications of ownership in family firms during ownership transfers. Together with Professor Charmine Härtel, she has recently received a grant for a project about 'Advancing emotions in family firms'. She has published in international journals such as *Journal of Business Venturing* and edited books about emotions in strategic and entrepreneurial leadership as well as about immigrant and social entrepreneurship.

Michael Carney is a Professor and Senior Concordia University Research Chair in Management at Concordia University. He received his PhD from University of Bradford. Carney has published extensively on the corporate and organizational strategies of Asia's family-owned business groups and on the development of the global institutional environment of international aviation. His research focuses on entrepreneurship and the comparative analysis of business, financial and governance systems and their influence upon the development of firm capabilities and national competitiveness. Carney is editor in chief of the *Asia-Pacific Journal of Management*. He is a member of the editorial boards of the *Journal of Management Studies, Family Business Review* and *Journal of Family Business Strategy*. He has published in journals such as the *Academy of Management Journal, Asia Pacific Business Review, Asia Pacific Journal of Management, Entrepreneurship: Theory and Practice, Family Business Review, Journal of Management Studies, Management and Organization Review, Organization Studies* and *Strategic Management Journal*.

Jon C. Carr is currently an Associate Professor of Management at the Neeley School of Business, Texas Christian University. In 2001, he was a NASA-ASEE Faculty Fellow, where he worked on projects related to technology transfer, remote-sensing applications and organizational development. Dr Carr has published research on entrepreneurship, family business and organizational behavior topics in numerous journals, to include the *Academy of Management Journal, Organizational Behavior and Human Decision Processes, Strategic Entrepreneurship Journal, Journal of Applied Psychology* and *Journal of Management and Entrepreneurship Theory & Practice*. Jon's research interests include workplace attitudes and cognition, and their impact on family business and entrepreneurship contexts.

James J. Chrisman, PhD, is Professor of Management and Director of the Center of Family Enterprise Research at Mississippi State University. He also holds a joint appointment as a Senior Research Fellow with the Center for Entrepreneurship and Family Enterprise at the University of Alberta. He currently serves as a Senior Editor for *Entrepreneurship: Theory and Practice*. His research interests include the strategic management of family business, entrepreneurship and economic development.

Andrea Colli is Professor of Economic History at Bocconi University, Milan. His research and publication activity concerns the evolution of modern business in a comparative and historical perspective. He has written extensively about small firms and industrial districts, about internationalization strategies and big business transformation. A substantial section of his activity has been devoted to the study of family firms and their evolutionary patterns. Recent books include *Business History: Complexities and Comparisons* (2011), with Franco Amatori, and *Mapping European Corporations: Strategies, Structures, Ownership and Performances* (2011), with Abe De Jong and Martin Iversen.

Guido Corbetta is a Professor of Strategic Management and AIdAF-Alberto Falck Professor of Strategic Management in Family Business at Bocconi University, Milan. He is also senior faculty member of the SDA Bocconi Business School and member of the editorial committee of *Entrepreneurship: Theory and Practice* and *Family Business Review*. He is a Fellow of IFERA (International Family Enterprise Research Academy).

Justin Craig, is an Associate Professor of Entrepreneurship at Northeastern University in Boston. He serves as an Associate Editor of the *Family Business Review* and on the editorial board of the *Journal of Family Business Strategy* and *Journal of Management and Organizations*, as well as on the global board of the Successful Transgenerational Entrepreneurship Practices (STEP) international research project.

Allan Discua Cruz is a Lecturer of Entrepreneurship and member of the Centre for Family Business at the Institute for Entrepreneurship and Enterprise Development in the Lancaster University Management School. He received his PhD from Lancaster University concentrating on collective approaches to portfolio entrepreneurship. His current research focuses on family entrepreneurial teams and entrepreneurial dynamics of families in business. His work has been published in the *Journal of Family Business Strategy*, *Business History*, *Entrepreneurship & Regional Development* and *Entrepreneurship Theory & Practice*.Allan is a member of the STEP project team at Lancaster University and a visiting professor in Honduras, where he contributes to national research initiatives in entrepreneurship and family business.

Cristina Cruz is Professor of Entrepreneurship and Family Business at IE Business School. She also holds the Bancaja Chair for Young Entrepreneurs at IE University. Her research interests are in corporate governance and entrepreneurship in the context of family owned companies. Her work has been published in academic journals such as the *Academy of Management Journal, Administrative Science Quarterly* and *Journal of Business Venturing*.

Sharon M. Danes is a Professor in the Family Social Science Department at the University of Minnesota and one of the authors of the Sustainable Family Business Theory. She has authored over 160 refereed research articles, book chapters and outreach publications emphasizing the intersection of economic and social decision-making. She has received over $1,050,000 of research and educational grants in recent years; the most recent grant was from National Science Foundation. She is an IFERA (International Family Enterprise Research Academy) Fellow. She has been a Juran Faculty Scholar, Juran Center for Leadership in Quality, Carlson School of Management, University of Minnesota. She is a Past-Chair of the Family Business Section of the US Association for Small Business and Entrepreneurship. She serves on several editorial boards of research journals.

Alexandra Dawson, PhD, is an Assistant Professor of Management at Concordia University's John Molson School of Business in Montreal, Canada. Her research, on the growth and entrepreneurial behavior of family firms, has appeared or is forthcoming in *Journal of Business Venturing, Family Business Review, Entrepreneurship: Theory and Practice, European Journal of Work and Organizational Psychology* and *Journal of Family Business Strategy*.

Keith Duncan is Professor of Accounting and Finance and the Director of the Executive MBA program at Bond University. His research covers financial reporting and decision making, corporate governance and control, family business, resource and asset valuation, takeover and distress analysis, strategy, and accounting education. He has also co-authored books and chapters on company accounting, educational and curriculum design, case studies and financial reporting. In addition to his extensive teaching and research experience at leading institutions in the USA, New Zealand, South Africa and throughout East Asia, he has consulted to and conducted executive development for government and commercial organizations including family businesses.

W. Gibb Dyer, PhD, is the O. Leslie Stone Professor of Entrepreneurship and the Academic Director of the Ballard Center for Economic Self-Reliance in the Marriott School of Management at Brigham Young University. Professor Dyer is a recognized authority on family business and entrepreneurship and has been quoted in publications such as *Fortune, The Wall Street Journal, The New York Times* and *Nation's Business*. In 2007 he received the faculty teaching award from Brigham Young University's division of continuing education, and in 2008 received the outstanding faculty award from the Marriott School at BYU. He was recently ranked one of the top 10 researchers in the world in the field of family business. He has published over 45 articles and 7 books, which have been cited over 4,000 times. He has had visiting appointments at IESE (Spain), the University of Bath (England) and the University of New Hampshire (USA).

Kimberly A. Eddleston is an Associate Professor of Entrepreneurship & Innovation at the D'Amore-McKim School of Business Northeastern University, where she holds the Walsh Research Professorship, and the Daniel and Dorothy Grady Research Fellowship. She is also a research fellow at the University of St Gallen. Professor Eddleston received her PhD from the University of Connecticut and her graduate degree from Cornell University and ESSEC. She has won multiple awards for her research including best paper awards from the Family Firm Institute, The Diana Conference on Women's Entrepreneurship, USASBE, the *Journal of Small Business Management* and the Academy of Management. Her research has appeared in journals such as the *Academy of Management Journal, Journal of Applied Psychology, Academy of Management Perspectives, Journal of Business Venturing, Entrepreneurship: Theory and Practice, Journal of International Business Studies* and *Journal of Management Studies*.

Neus Feliu is a Senior Associate at Lansberg, Gersick and Associates LLC, and a PhD Candidate in Management Science at ESADE Business School (Barcelona, Spain). At LGA she advises family enterprises primarily in Europe and North and South America, on governance and continuity in family companies, offices and foundations. Her current research focuses on family social capital, based on her background in economics and organizational psychology.

Paloma Fernandez Perez, PhD, is currently Professor of Economic and Business History at the Faculty of Economics and Business from Universitat de Barcelona in Spain. Her research interests are family businesses in a long term comparative perspective. She has published several books, the most recent being *La ultima globalizacion y el renacer de los grandes negocios familiares en el mundo* (Bogota, Catedra Corona and Uniandes, 2012), and articles in leading business history journals such as *Business History Review* and *Business History*. She coordinates a team of 22 researchers from 11 countries in a joint study of the history of the largest family businesses in Latin America, Spain and Portugal.

Zulima Fernández is Professor of Strategic Management at the Universidad Carlos III de Madrid, where she is also Director of the Institute of Entrepreneurship and Family Firms. She is President of the Spanish Association of Business Administration (ACEDE), Spain. Her research interests include internationalization strategies, innovation and family firms. She has published in journals such as *Journal of International Business Studies*, *Family Business Review*, *Technovation* and *Journal of World Business*, among others.

Denise Fletcher is Professor of Entrepreneurship and Innovation at the University of Luxembourg. Her research centres on developing sociological understandings of entrepreneurial forms of work. Her work starts from the premise that a high proportion of entrepreneurial endeavours begin in relationships within households, families or couples as economic and social assessments are made about the ways in which household productive capacity, along with individual life orientations, can be translated into commodities that have market value. Combining theories from management and sociology, her work examines how emotions, boundaries, roles and resources are negotiated within entrepreneurial work. She has published in a number of the leading small business/entrepreneurship journals. She is also editor of the research monograph *Understanding the Small Family Business* (Routledge, 2002).

Peter Foreman is Associate Professor of Management at Illinois State University. His research encompasses a range of topics related to managerial and organizational cognition, with particular attention to organizational identity, identification, image, and reputation. His work has appeared in internationally recognized outlets such as *Academy of Management Review*, *Organization Science*, and *Organizational Behavior and Human Decision Processes*... He has been particularly interested in examining hybrid identity organizations and the inherent issues of managing multiple identities and complex identifications. This research program has spanned a wide array of industries – including healthcare, insurance, cooperatives, sporting events and higher education – and a variety of locations throughout the USA, Canada and Europe. Much of this work has been conducted in family-owned businesses, particularly in agricultural-related contexts such as crop farming, ornamental horticulture, meatpacking, winemaking and agritourism.

Eric Gedajlovic is the Beedie Professor of Strategy and Entrepreneurship at the Beedie School of Business at Simon Fraser University. He received his PhD from Concordia University. Much of his research focuses on entrepreneurship, family business and the comparative analysis of business, financial and governance systems and their influence upon the development of firm capabilities, strategic assets and national competitiveness. Eric works with co-authors on three continents and has conducted empirical research on companies in various parts of the world. He is currently working on several studies of firms in Southeast Asia, Japan and Europe. His research has been published in leading international management journals including the *Academy of Management Journal, Strategic Management Journal, Journal of Management Studies, Organization Science, Journal of Business Venturing* and *Entrepreneurship: Theory and Practice.* He sits on the editorial boards of the *Journal of Management Studies* and the *Asia Pacific Journal of Management.*

Kelin Gersick, PhD, is co-founder and a Senior Partner of Lansberg, Gersick & Associates. He is also a Management Fellow at the Yale School of Organization and Management, and Professor Emeritus of Organizational Psychology at the California School of Professional Psychology. Kelin is the lead author of *Generation to Generation: Life Cycles of the Family Business* (Harvard Business School Press, 1997), *The Succession Workbook: Continuity Planning in Family Foundations* (Council on Foundations, 2000), *Generations of Giving: Leadership and Continuity in Family Foundations* (Lexington Books, 2004), and many articles, cases, columns and other publications. He has served as Co-Editor-in-Chief of *Family Business Review,* and is currently Chair of the Research Board for the International Institute for Family Enterprise.

Sanjay Goel, PhD, is an Associate Professor of Strategic Management and Entrepreneurship at University of Minnesota Duluth, USA. His current research interests include entrepreneurship theory, governance and strategy in family business firms, and conceptual issues in developing theories in family business field. He is the President of International Family Enterprise Research Academy (IFERA).

Luis R. Gomez-Mejia Professor of Management at University of Notre Dame. Before that, he was the Benton Cocanougher Chair in Business at the Mays College of Business, Texas A&M University and a Regents Professor at Arizona State University. He has held prior positions at University of Colorado and University of Florida. He has published more than 140 papers, many of those appearing in the best journals of the field such as *Administrative Science Quarterly, Academy of Management Journal, Academy of Management Review* and *Strategic Management Journal.* He has also received numerous awards for his research. During the past 12 years he has devoted much of his efforts to research dealing with the special issues affecting family firms.

Charmine E.J. Härtel, PhD, is Head of Management and Chair of Human Resource Management and Organisational Development at UQ Business School, The University of Queensland, Brisbane, Australia. Charmine is Fellow and President of the Australian and New Zealand Academy of Management, Fellow of the Australian Institute of Management, Fellow of the Australian Human Resource Institute, Lifetime Honorary Member of Psi Chi and current Program Chair for the Academy of Management's Gender and Diversity in Organization's Division. She is a leading expert in the areas of emotions and workplace wellbeing and her publications appear in leading journals such as the *Academy of Management Review, Journal of Management, British Journal of Industrial Relations, Journal of Applied Psychology* and *The Leadership Quarterly.* She is co-editor of the Research on Emotion in Organizations book series and primary author of the original textbook, *Human Resource Management,* which approaches the topic from a well-being perspective.

Daniel T. Holt is currently an Assistant Professor of Management in the College of Business at Mississippi State University. He received his PhD in management from Auburn University. Prior to joining the faculty at Mississippi State University, he served in the US Air Force, serving as an engineer in Central America, Asia and the Middle East. Daniel's research interests include family business, entrepreneurship, measurement methods and organizational change. His work has been published in numerous journals to include *Family Business Review*, *Entrepreneurship Theory & Practice*, *Journal of Applied Psychology* and *Journal of Management Studies*.

Carole Howorth is Professor of Entrepreneurship and Family Business at Bradford University School of Management. She was Founding Director of the Centre for Family Business at Lancaster University Management School, England. Her research focuses on entrepreneurship and the performance of family businesses. She has completed a number of studies examining the implications of family businesses balancing the competing objectives and values of family and business, particularly stewardship, trust and governance. In 2010 and 2012 she was Toft Visiting Professor at Jönköping International Business School. She chairs the IFB Research Foundation Academic Council and has been a member of the global board of the STEP Project for Family Enterprises.

Frank Hoy is the Paul R. Beswick Professor of Innovation & Entrepreneurship at Worcester Polytechnic Institute in the United States where he also serves as Director of the Collaborative for Entrepreneurship and Innovation. He and Pramodita Sharma are co-authors of *Entrepreneurial Family Firms* (Pearson Prentice Hall, 2010). Hoy served as vice president of the Family Firm Institute (FFI), as past president of the United States Association for Small Business and Entrepreneurship (USASBE), and is currently president of the Family Enterprise Research Conference. He is a Fellow of FFI, the International Council for Small Business, the International Family Enterprise Research Academy, and USASBE.

Tuuli Ikäheimonen, MSc, is a doctoral student of Management and Organization at the Lappeenranta University of Technology (LUT) School of Business, Finland. She also works as a Training Manager in the LUT Centre for Training and Development. Her research interests include family business governance, especially boards of directors, and succession.

Albert E. James earned his MBA and PhD from the University of Alberta School of Business. His dissertation topic focused upon why non-family managers choose to stay employed in family firms. Prior to pursuing his doctorate, Albert had a 20-year career with a variety of family firms. He began his academic career in the summer of 2012 as an Assistant Professor of Entrepreneurship at Bishop's University in Sherbrooke, Quebec. Albert has previously published on women's entrepreneurship and family business, with his articles featured in the 25th Anniversary special issue of *Family Business Review* and the special issue on family business in *Family Relations*.

Jennifer E. Jennings, PhD (formerly Cliff), is an Associate Professor within the Department of Strategic Management and Organization at the University of Alberta. Her research has been published within several leading journals including the *Academy of Management Annals, Academy of Management Journal, Academy of Management Review, Entrepreneurship: Theory and Practice, Family Business Review* and *Journal of Business Venturing*. The recipient of several Best Paper Awards, and co-author of one of the 25 most influential family business articles (Aldrich & Cliff, 2003), Jennifer is currently a Field Editor at the *Journal of Business Venturing*.

Iiro Jussila, DSc, is a Professor of Management and Organization at the School of Business in Lappeenranta University of Technology (Finland). His research is focused on collective entrepreneurship including family businesses and co-operatives from both strategic and humanistic perspectives. He is a Board Member of the International Family Enterprise Research Academy (IFERA) and of the Co-operative Network Studies university network.

Franz W. Kellermanns is the Addison H. & Gertrude C. Reese Endowed Chair in International Business und Professor of Management at the Belk College of Business at the University of North Carolina - Charlotte. He holds a joint appointment with the INTES Center at the WHU -Otto Beisheim School of Management (Germany). He received his PhD from the University of Connecticut. His research interests include strategy process and entrepreneurship with a focus on family business research. He has published in journals such as *Organization Science, Journal of Management, Journal of Management Studies, Journal of Organizational Behavior, Journal of Business Venturing, Entrepreneurship Theory and Practice*, and *Academy of Management Learning and Education*, among others. He is a Co-Editor of the *Entrepreneurship Theory and Practice and* serves on the editorial boards of *Family Business Review, Journal of Business Venturing, Journal of Management, Journal of Management Studies, Journal of Family Business Strategy and Strategic Entrepreneurship Journal*. He is a co-editor of the recent books, *Handbook of Strategy Process Research* and *Innovating Strategy Process*.

Rania Labaki, PhD, is Associate Professor of Management Sciences at the University of Bordeaux IV, France. She teaches and conducts research on finance and family business, especially corporate governance and financial policies, family relationships, and emotions in decision-making. She is a former Visiting Scholar at Baruch College – The City University of New York, where she was involved in research projects and invited lectures relative to family business topics. She is member of the Family Business Research Centre and INSEEC Research Centre. Rania also serves as Academic Director of the Family Business International Foundation. She is guest editor for *Entrepreneurship Research Journal*, reviewer and editorial board member for several academic journals in management and family business. She is a recipient of several international awards recognizing her contribution to research in the family business field, such as the FFI Best Unpublished Paper Award in 2012, IFERA Best Research Paper Award in 2011 and 2005, and Emerald LiteratiNetwork Outstanding Reviewer Award in 2011.

Rebecca G. Long, PhD, is an Associate Professor of Management and Director of Graduate Studies for the College of Business at Mississippi State University. She serves on the editorial review board of *Family Business Review* and her research has appeared in academic journals such as the *Journal of Management, Human Relations, Academy of Management Journal, Business Ethics Quarterly* and *Entrepreneurship Theory & Practice*. Her research interests revolve around social exchange and the development of social capital within the family firm.

G.T. (Tom) Lumpkin is the Chris J. Witting Chair of Entrepreneurship at the Whitman School of Management at Syracuse University in New York. His primary research interests include entrepreneurial orientation, social entrepreneurship, family business and strategy making processes. He is a globally recognized scholar whose research has been published in the *Academy of Management Review, Academy of Management Journal, Journal of Management Studies, Strategic Management Journal, Journal of Management, Strategic Entrepreneurship Journal, Entrepreneurship Theory & Practice* and *Journal of Business Venturing*. Tom is a Co-Editor of the *Strategic Entrepreneurship Journal* and serves on the editorial boards of the *Academy of Management Journal, Entrepreneurship Theory & Practice, Journal of Business Venturing* and *Family Business Review*.

D'Lisa N. McKee is an Assistant Professor of Management in the College of Business and Management at the University of Illinois Springfield. She holds an MBA from Drury University and is currently completing her dissertation in Management in the College of Business at Mississippi State University on the topic of visible body modification in organizations. Her research interests include counter-normative behavior, social identity, trust, commitment, turnover and family business, with a particular interest in the intersection of OB/HR concepts with entrepreneurial questions. She has publications in the *Journal of Managerial Issues*, the *Journal of Family Business Strategy* and the *Journal of Behavioral and Applied Management*, as well as eight refereed management conference presentations, three of which won best paper awards.

Alexander McKelvie, PhD, is an Associate Professor of Entrepreneurship at the Whitman School of Management at Syracuse University. Alex's research concerns how and why firms grow, and how entrepreneurs and entrepreneurial firms pursue opportunities. He serves on the review board for *Family Business Review*, among other journals. He received the NFIB Best Doctoral Dissertation award in Entrepreneurship and has twice won the Research Promise Idea award from the Entrepreneurship Division of the Academy of Management. He has also received multiple teaching awards. His work appears in a number of journals, including *Journal of Business Venturing*, *Strategic Entrepreneurship Journal* and *Entrepreneurship Theory & Practice*.

Aaron F. McKenny is a doctoral candidate in the division of management and entrepreneurship at the University of Oklahoma. His current research interests center on the intersection of strategic management and entrepreneurship. He currently serves on the review board for *Family Business Review* and his research has appeared in several scholarly journals, including *Journal of Business Venturing*, *Organizational Research Methods*, and *Journal of the Academy of Marketing Science*.

Timothy M. Madden is an Assistant Professor of management at Old Dominion University in Norfolk, Virginia. He received his PhD from the University of Tennessee. In addition to his research on conflict within the family firm, his current research focuses on organizational ambidexterity, not-for-profit performance and management education. His research has been published in the *Academy of Management Review*, *Organizational Research Methods*, *Journal of Business Ethics* and the *International Entrepreneurship and Management Journal*.

Martha Martinez is an Associate Professor at DePaul University Department of Sociology. She concentrates her work on the areas of work, organizations, markets and political economy. Her publications have analyzed how the organizations of the apparel and real estate industry interact with both demand and supply issues and have consequences for the creation of inequality among individuals and families. She is also interested in the social analysis of how firms are formed, how they evolve and how they manage to survive. Since both markets and organizations are affected by public policies, she incorporates the role of government in a globalized context into her research. Her publications include 'Networking strategies for entrepreneurs: managing cohesion and diversity' in the *International Journal of Entrepreneurial Behavior*, 'The housing crisis and Latino home ownership in Chicago: mortgage applications, foreclosures, and property values' for the Institute of Latino Studies of University of Notre Dame and 'Torreón: the new blue jeans capital of the world' in *Free Trade and Uneven Development: The North American Apparel Industry after NAFTA*.

Ken Moores, AM, is Emeritus Professor and was the Founding Director in the Australian Centre for Family Business at Bond University, Australia, where he had previously served as

Professor of Accounting, Dean of Business and Vice-Chancellor and President. His research in accounting, education, management and family business has been published in a wide range of international refereed journals. His co-authored books include *Learning Family Business*: *Paradoxes and Pathways* (Ashgate, 2002; Bond University Press, 2010); *Daughters on the Stage: Leadership Roles of Women in Family Businesses* (Edward Elgar, 2009); and *Understanding Family Enterprise* (Bond University Press, 2011). A member of the advisory board of *Family Business Review* and the editorial board of *Journal of Small Business Management*, Ken is a Fellow of the International Family Enterprise Research Academy. Ken serves the family business community in a variety of different capacities including as a Company Director, a regular speaker at family business conferences, a consultant to family businesses and professional advisory firms, a judge of the annual Australian Family Business Awards, and recently concluded 12 years as a member of the board of directors of Family Business Australia (FBA) Ltd.

Miriam Muethel, BSc, MSc, PhD, holds the Chair of Organizational Behavior at the WHU–Otto Beisheim School of Management. Her research interests comprise international management (particularly Confucian Asia), organizational behavior and business ethics. Since 2011 she has been a member of the Global Economic Fellow Program, where she contributes in the area of ethics. She has published (among others) in the *Journal of International Business Studies*, *Journal of International Management*, *Journal of World Business*, *Human Resource Management Journal* and *MIT Sloan Management*. Before joining WHU, Dr Muethel worked for over two years as a business consultant at Volkswagen in the area of international project management.

Nigel Nicholson started his career as a journalist before becoming a business psychologist. At London Business School he divides his time between research, writing, executive teaching, public presentations, media work and business advising. His expertise is diverse, but he is most active currently in the areas of leadership and family business. He is well known for his pioneering application of the ideas of evolutionary psychology to business. He has published over 20 books and 200 articles. His latest book, *The 'I' of Leadership: Strategies for Seeing, Being and Doing*, is published in 2013 by Jossey-Bass. He runs two highly successful and innovative leadership programmes at London Business School, *High Performance People Skills for Leaders* and the legendary *Proteus Programme*, as well as customized executive programmes. He has strong personal and professional links with the African and Indian business communities.

María Jesús Nieto is Associate Professor of Strategic Management at University Carlos III of Madrid (Spain), where she is Director of the Master in Entrepreneurship and Co-Director of the Master in International Business Administration. Her current research interests include internationalization strategy and innovation management, with particular focus on small and medium enterprises and family firms. Some of her recent papers have been published in journals such as the *Journal of International Business Studies*, *Research Policy*, *Technovation*, *Journal of Small Business Management*, among others.

G. Tyge Payne is an Associate Professor of Strategic Management and holder of the Jerry S. Rawls Endowed Professorship of Management at Texas Tech University. His research generally examines strategic fit and interorganizational relationships across multiple levels of analysis and within various contexts. Specifically, organization-environment fit/misfit, organizational virtue, social capital, firm-level entrepreneurship and venture capitalism are primary subjects of interest. Dr Payne has authored or co-authored over 40 peer-reviewed publications appearing in such outlets as *Business Ethics Quarterly, Entrepreneurship: Theory and Practice, Family Business Review, Health Care Management Review, Journal of Business Ethics, Journal of Management, Journal of Management Studies, Journal of Product Innovation Management, Journal of Small Business Management* and *Organization Science*, among others. Currently, he serves as a review board member for *Family Business Review, Journal of Small Business Management* and *Journal of Management*.

Allison Pearson is the Jim and Julia Rouse Professor of Management in the College of Business at Mississippi State University. She is also a W.L. Giles Distinguished Professor and a John Grisham Master Teacher. She received her PhD in organizational behavior from Auburn University. Her research has been published in *Journal of Applied Psychology, Journal of Management, Decision Sciences, Entrepreneurship Theory & Practice, Journal of Business Venturing, Journal of Business Research* and *Family Business Review*, and has been featured in *Worth Magazine* and the NBC Today Show. She is an Associate Editor for *Family Business Review.*

Sabine Rau (formerly Klein) is Professor of Family Business at WHU-Otto Beisheim School of Management. Before returning to academia, Dr Rau founded her own business and then joined her family's business. She re-started her academic career as a Research Fellow at INSEAD in 2001. In 2003 Professor Rau took over the presidency of the international family business researchers, ifera (www.ifera.org), which she led until 2007. Professor Rau has published in various journals such as *Strategic Management Journal, Family Business Review, Journal of Business Research, Entrepreneurship, Theory & Practice, Small Business Economics, Entrepreneurship and Regional Development* and others. She wrote one of the first textbooks on family business, which is now in its third edition. Her research focus is on the influence of family onto the business and vice versa. Topics such as succession, governance, and family-specific resources and its influence on performance are central to her research.

Trish Reay is Associate Professor in the Department of Strategic Management and Organization at the University of Alberta School of Business. She is actively engaged in qualitative research addressing topics related to institutional and organizational change, organizational learning and identity. She is currently an Associate Editor at *Family Business Review*.

Peter Rosa holds the George David Chair of Entrepreneurship and Family Business at the University of Edinburgh, where he is the Head of the Entrepreneurship and Innovation Group. He has a specialist interest in habitual and portfolio entrepreneurship both in individual and family contexts, and has contributed to leading entrepreneurship journals. He currently leads the University of Edinburgh's participation in the STEP Family Business Project, and is conducting research on trans-generational entrepreneurship processes in Scotland and Uganda. He holds posts as a Visiting Professor at the University of Witten/ Herdecke in Germany, at the Makerere University Business School, Uganda and at the Uganda Management Institute.

Carlo Salvato is an Associate Professor of Strategic Management at the Department of Management & Technology, Bocconi University, Italy, where he collaborates with the AIdAF-Alberto Falck Chair in Strategic Management in Family Business. He is also an Associate Editor of the *Family Business Review*.

Arist von Schlippe is Chair in Leadership and Dynamics in Family Business and academic director of the Witten Institut for Family Business (WIFU) at the Faculty of Management and

Economics, Witten/Herdecke University, Germany. Professor Dr von Schlippe holds a PhD in psychology, specification in family therapy and family psychology, a postdoctoral lecture qualification in clinical psychology and psychotherapy, and is a licensed psychological psychotherapist. He has authored numerous publications about clinical and family business issues, including *Teaching Book for Systemic Family Therapy and Counseling*, which is now in its 11th edition and has been translated into seven languages.

Klaus A. Schneewind is former head of the research and teaching unit, Personality Psychology, Psychological Assessment and Family Psychology, Department of Psychology, Ludwig-Maximilians-University, Munich, Germany. Presently he is professor of family psychology at the Psychological College Berlin. He is a founding member of the International Academy of Family Psychology and the European Society on Family Relations and has undertaken several longitudinal research projects on the development of couples, families and parent–child relations. He is head of the European research consortium FamWork (Family Life and Professional Work: Conflict and Synergy) and has authored numerous publications relating to the field of family psychology, including the German textbook *Familienpsychologie* (Family Psychology) and the interactive DVD parent training program *Freiheit in Grenzen* (Freedom within Limits) for parents with children aged 3 to 18 years.

Salvatore Sciascia is Assistant Professor at IULM University, Milan (Italy). He got his PhD at Università Cattaneo (Italy) after visiting the Jonkoping International Business School (Sweden) and the University of Lugano (Switzerland). His research interests include entrepreneurship and family business. He is a member of the editorial review board of *Family Business Review* and serves as reviewer for several academic journals. Salvatore has authored papers appearing in journals such as *Family Business Review, Entrepreneurship Theory & Practice, Strategic Entrepreneurship Journal, Journal of Business Research, Small Business Economics, Journal of Small Business Management* and *Entrepreneurship & Regional Development*. He recently received the following recognitions: inclusion in the Academy of Management Best Paper Proceedings (2011); best paper on Entrepreneurship and Family Businesses at the 6th EIASM Workshop on Family Firms Management Research (2010); best paper presented at the 9th IFERA World Family Business Research Conference (2009); best article in *Family Business Review* (2008).

Jeremy C. Short is the Rath Chair in Strategic Management in the division of management and entrepreneurship at the University of Oklahoma. His research focuses on multilevel determinants of firm performance, strategic decision processes, entrepreneurship, research methods, franchising and family business. He currently serves as an Associate Editor for the *Journal of Management* and *Family Business Review*, and he is also on the review boards for *Journal of Business Venturing* and *Organizational Research Methods*. His research has appeared in a number of journals including the *Strategic Entrepreneurship Journal, Strategic Management Journal, Organization Science, Organizational Research Methods, Organizational Behavior and Human Decision Processes, Journal of Management, Personnel Psychology, Academy of Management Learning and Education, Entrepreneurship Theory & Practice, Journal of Management Education, Journal of Vocational Behavior, Business Ethics Quarterly* and *Family Business Review*. He has also published graphic novels on entrepreneurship (*Atlas Black: The Complete Adventure*) and family business (*Tales of Garcón: The Franchise Players*).

Prashant Shukla is a PhD student in the strategy area at the Beedie School of Business at Simon Fraser University. He holds an MS in Economics from the W. P. Carey School of Business at

Arizona State University. His current research focuses on alternative corporate governance regimes around the world and the role of institutions, in conjunction with ownership structure and owners identities, in determining firm performance and strategies. Aside from family firms, Shukla is also interested in the business groups in emerging markets. In particular, he is interested in innovation, entrepreneurship and strategies within these groups and the subsequent impact of these choices on national competitiveness. He has presented his work at the Academy of Management Conference and is a reviewer for the *Journal of Small Business Management*.

David G. Sirmon is an Associate Professor of management in the Foster School of Business at the University of Washington. He received his PhD from the W. P. Carey School of Business at Arizona State University and has previously served on the faculty at Texas A&M University and Clemson University. His research, which focuses on resource orchestration, firm governance, family business and strategic entrepreneurship, has appeared in journals such as the *Academy of Management Journal*, *Academy of Management Review*, *Strategic Management Journal*, *Journal of International Business*, *Journal of Management* and *Entrepreneurship: Theory & Practice*, among others. He was awarded the 2012 SMS Emerging Scholar Award.

Ritch L. Sorenson is the Opus Chair in Family Business and the Director of the Family Business Center at the University of St Thomas, Minneapolis. Dr Sorenson developed concentrations in family business at two universities. At the University of St Thomas, Dr Sorenson has sponsored three conferences that bring scholars and family business owners and advisors together to confer about family business. The papers presented at the conference are published in a special issue of *Family Business Review*, a book titled *Family Business and Social Capital* and in a forthcoming book about the landscape of family business outcomes. Dr Sorenson has been an Associate Editor for *Family Business Review* and has published research in a variety of journals, including *Entrepreneurship: Theory and Practice*, *Journal of Business Venturing*, *Group and Organization Studies*, *The Leadership Quarterly*, *Academy of Management Learning and Education* and *Academy of Management Executive*.

Lloyd Steier is a Professor in the Department of Strategic Management and Organization at the University of Alberta School of Business. He holds a Distinguished Chair in Entrepreneurship and Family Enterprise and is the Academic Director of both the Centre for Entrepreneurship and Family Enterprise and the Alberta Business Family Institute. Lloyd is an active family business researcher with extensive experience in teaching and program development at the undergraduate, MBA, PhD, executive and family outreach levels. He has also co-edited a number of special issues devoted to family enterprise including *Entrepreneurship: Theory and Practice*, *Journal of Business Venturing* and the *Strategic Entrepreneurship Journal*.

Alex Stewart is the Coleman Foundation Chair in Entrepreneurship at Marquette University. His four degrees, all from York University in Toronto, are in business, political science and social anthropology. He has been Chair of the Entrepreneurship Division of the Academy of Management, and Program Chair of both the Organization Science Winter Conference and the Family Enterprise Research Conference.

Belén Villalonga is an Associate Professor of Management and Organizations (with Tenure) at New York University's Stern School of Business. Between 2001 and 2012 she was on the faculty at Harvard Business School.

Professor Villalonga's teaching, research, and consulting activities are focused on family enterprise governance, strategy, and finance. She has developed and taught family business courses or programs for graduate and undergraduate students at both universities as well as for executives and business families. Her award-winning research has been published in top academic journals, has been cited over 800 times in academic publications, and has been featured in the leading international business media outlets.

She also serves as an independent director on the boards of two family-controlled public companies, Acciona and Grifols. Professor Villalonga has a PhD in Management and an M.A. in Economics from the University of California at Los Angeles, as well as a second PhD in Business Economics from Complutense University of Madrid. She is fluent in Spanish, English and French, and conversant in Portuguese and Italian.

David A. Whetten is the Jack Wheatley Professor of Organizational Studies and Director of the Faculty Center at Brigham Young University. Prior to joining the Marriott School of Management in 1994 he was on the faculty at the University of Illinois for 20 years. He also serves as a visiting professor at Xi'an Jiaotong University in China, National Chengchi University in Taiwan and Oxford University. He has served as editor of the *Foundations for Organizational Science* book series and the *Academy of Management Review*. He received the Outstanding Educator Award from the Organizational Behavior Teaching Society in 1992 for his pioneering work in management skills education. He is an active member of the Academy of Management and was elected an Academy Fellow in 1991; in 1994 he received the Academy's Distinguished Service Award, he served as President in 2000, and in 2004 he received the OMT Division Distinguished Scholar Award.

Miles A. Zachary is a doctoral student in the department of management at the Rawls College of Business Administration at Texas Tech University. His research interests include competitive dynamics, macro-entrepreneurship, and issues of temporality and time. He is currently an ad hoc reviewer for *Family Business Review* and the *International Small Business Journal*. His research appears in a variety of management and interdisciplinary journals including *Strategic Entrepreneurship Journal, Family Business Review, Journal of the Academy of Marketing Science, Business Horizons, Journal of International Business and Cultural Studies* and *Journal of the Academy of Business and Economics*.

Shaker A. Zahra is the Department Chair and Robert E. Buuck Chair of Entrepreneurship in the Strategic Management and Entrepreneurship, Carlson School of Management, University of Minnesota, USA, where he is also the Academic Director of the Gary S. Holmes Center for Entrepreneurship. Widely published in leading academic journals, he has received several research, teaching and service awards. Shaker has served on the boards of over 25 academic journals, as the Chair of the Entrepreneurship Division of the Academy of Management, and as Director of the Babson Entrepreneurship Research conference, among others.

Thomas Zellweger holds the family business chair at the University of St Gallen, Switzerland. He holds an MBA from the University of St Gallen. After two years in banking with Derivative in Brussels (Belgium), he received his PhD at the University of St Gallen in 2006. Thomas is founding associate editor of the *Journal of Family Business Strategy* and serves on the editorial board of *Family Business Review*. He was a research fellow at Babson College, USA, visiting professor at the University of British Columbia, Sauder School of Business, Canada, and is a permanent visiting professor at the University of Witten/Herdecke, Germany. His research has been published in academic journals such as *Organization Science*, *Journal of Business Venturing*, *Entrepreneurship Theory & Practice*, amongst others. Thomas is member of two supervisory boards of medium-sized family firms in Switzerland and regularly consults to owners of mid-sized to large family firms.

Zhen Zhang is a doctoral student in the department of Strategic Management and Organization at the University of Alberta School of Business. Her research interests focus on identity construction, narrative analysis and immigrant entrepreneurship in family businesses.

Introduction: Scope, Evolution and Future of Family Business Studies

Pramodita Sharma, Leif Melin
and Mattias Nordqvist

THE SCOPE AND POSITION OF FAMILY BUSINESS STUDIES

'Family business studies' is a multidisciplinary field of research that 'is distinguished from its sister disciplines by its singular focus on the paradoxes caused by the involvement of family in business' (Sharma et al., 2012: p.1). The overarching aim of this field of study is to build knowledge on one specific type of organizations – the family enterprises. These are the most prevalent form of business organizations in the world. In these organizations, the overlap between family and work systems is such that family members significantly influence the key decisions and direction of an enterprise, and vice versa.

Scholars from varied disciplinary backgrounds, theoretical perspectives, and methodological orientations are drawn to family business studies by their unified quest to understand the determinants and consequences of variations of family involvement in business. Research is directed to understand how such involvement influences the formation and evolution of family enterprises over time (e.g., Aldrich and Cliff, 2003; Chua et al., 2004; Hoy and Sharma, 2010). Similarities and differences of values, goals, resources, strategies, and performances of family firms from their non-family counterparts are studied as evident from several chapters in this *Handbook* (e.g., Amit and Villalonga, 2014; Rau, 2014; Salvato and Corbetta, 2014; Sorenson, 2014). Attempts are made to understand psychological and behavioral issues such as emotions, identity, trust, and conflicts within different categories of family firms (in this *Handbook*, e.g., Brundin and Härtel; 2014; McKee et al., 2014; Steier and Muethel, 2014; Whetten et al., 2014). In terms of age, size, scope, and legal form, the heterogeneity of family enterprises is large, necessitating and challenging authors to clearly define the segment of these enterprises under investigation in a study (e.g., Melin and Nordqvist, 2007).

Sharma et al. (2007) traced the practice driven evolution of family business studies. In doing so, it becomes evident that the seedlings of family firm research were sown in the early 1950s with Calder's (1953) dissertation on the problems of small manufacturing family firms. The establishment of the first Family Business Center in 1962 by thoughtful practitioners – Léon and Katy Danco in Cleveland, Ohio – provided a means for interested practitioners and scholars to connect with each other. Individual efforts to understand the unique dilemmas and challenges of family enterprises continued for the next few decades (e.g., Donnelley, 1964; Ewing, 1965; Levinson, 1971; Davis, 1982). However, it was the appearance of the special issue of *Organizational Dynamics* in 1983 that further triggered interest in research on family firms. The establishment of *Family Business Review* (FBR) in 1988 – the first journal devoted solely to publishing research on family firms – further fueled this interest as it provided a reliable venue for interested scholars and practitioners to share ideas and knowledge on issues important to family enterprises and key stakeholders therein. The opening paragraph of the first issue of FBR pinpointed some key questions for the study of family firms:

> What is a Family Business? People seem to understand what is meant by the term *family business,* yet when they try to articulate a precise definition they quickly discover that it is a very complicated phenomenon. Consider the following situations: A business is owned by a family but run by non-family managers. A business is owned by a large, multi-national corporation but run by a local family. A business is jointly owned by two unrelated partners, each of whom has a son in the business. Are these all family businesses? (Lansberg et al., 1988: p. 1) (case modified)

Challenged by these questions and retaining a close link with practice, much research on family firms during the late 1980s and early 1990s focused on defining 'a family business' and understanding leadership succession in these firms (e.g., Handler, 1989; Litz, 1995). Most contributions were made by scholars who came from within the world of family businesses, that is, those who were interested in understanding

family firms as their prime subject of study (Gedajlovic et al., 2012).

Since the mid-1990s there has been a significant momentum in research on family enterprises. The debate of whether the pursuit of research on family enterprises is a phenomenon, a discipline, or a field continues in some quarters. Increasingly, however, scholars are referring to the 'field of family business studies' indicating 'a clear need to focus research efforts on the uniqueness of family firms which differentiates them from other organizational forms' (Gomez-Mejia et al., 2011: p. 695). While concurring with this argument, we also posit that in addition to understanding the difference between family and non-family enterprises, it is equally important to understand the significant heterogeneity within the population of family firms (e.g., Sharma et al., 1996; Melin and Nordqvist, 2007). Furthermore, it is essential to keep the multi-disciplinary nature of the family business studies to draw insights from and give back to other fields of study (Zahra and Sharma, 2004). Along these lines, focusing on the interaction between the family business studies and the broader discipline of management and organization, Gedajlovic et al. (2012) recently concluded:

> Our view is that future progress in the field will require important contributions from both family business 'specialists' as well as 'generalists' from traditional disciplines in the organizational sciences. For family business specialists, the primary challenge will be to widen their focuses to address questions that range beyond the narrow confines of the field as it is presently constituted. To those scholars who frame their research domains in more generalist terms, more frequent incorporations of the ubiquitous family firm into their theoretical frameworks and research designs would strengthen the validity and generalizability of their findings. (p. 1030)

The legitimacy and importance of family business studies in relation to other scholarly fields is on an upswing (Pérez Rodríguez and Basco, 2011; Craig and Salvato, 2012 and Sirmon, 2014 in this *Handbook*). Several factors have contributed to this trend. Since early 2000s, articles on issues and topics central to family enterprises have appeared with some regularity in leading management and finance journals. Examples include Gomez-Mejia et al. (2001) in the *Academy of Management Journal*; Lee et al. (2003) in the *Academy of Management Review*; Schulze et al. (2001) in *Organization Science*; and Anderson and Reeb (2003) in the *Journal of Finance*. Second, several leading journals have commissioned special issues on family enterprise research. Just a few examples include special issues of *Corporate Governance: An International Review*, *Entrepreneurship and Regional Development*, *Entrepreneurship Theory & Practice*, *International Small Business Journal*, *Small Business Economics*, *Journal of Business Research*, *Journal of Business Venturing*, *Journal of Management Studies*, and the *Strategic Entrepreneurship Journal*. These thematic issues introduce the regular readers of a journal to the ubiquity of and the unique dynamics of family enterprises, at times attracting leading scholars from disciplines such as anthropology, entrepreneurship, strategic management, international business, industrial psychology, human resource management, sociology etc., to conduct research on family enterprises. Further, the organizers of the annual Theories of Family Enterprise Conference, originally launched by the Universities of Alberta and Calgary in 2001, have regularly invited established scholars in related fields to develop and present papers on family business topics. The important role of this conference in building the field's legitimacy cannot be overestimated.

As these scholars get more engaged in family enterprise research, their scholarly conversations even when contributing to their primary field of study are modified to reflect this new understanding of family firms. While family firm research may not yet have become 'fully integrated into mainstream conversations in the organizational science' (Gedajlovic et al., 2012: p. 1011), increased scholarly interaction with other disciplines has helped to strengthen the legitimacy of family business

studies as an independent field of study. Consequently, today, virtually all journals and conferences in management or business and finance are encouraging research on family enterprises.

The field's original journal, *Family Business Review*, has rapidly moved from being a venue primarily for the sharing of best practices to become a highly regarded scholarly journal with a strong and growing impact on the theoretical and empirical development of knowledge on family firms. In addition to FBR, today there are two other journals exclusively focused on publishing research on family enterprises – the *Journal of Family Business Strategy* launched in 2010 and the *Journal of Family Business Management* launched in 2011. Senior scholars predict a strong future for family business studies and applaud the performance of the field's own journals. However, they encourage researchers to not only publish in the field journals but also in general outlets. Such diversification strategy is likely to expand knowledge on family enterprises while enhancing the field's legitimacy and impact. In the words of Michael Hitt:

> [F]amily business research is going to blossom! … it is blossoming right now and that will increase … the field is at a precipice of the next step … the future is very bright … family business studies have been published more broadly now (not only in entrepreneurship but also in management and social science journals) which serves as delivering legitimacy to the field … having publications in broader journals enhances the legitimacy in the eyes of many stakeholders … disciplines or sub-disciplines need to be able to publish in specialized journals but also need to publish in more general outlets to increase their overall status and legitimacy. (Hitt, quoted in Craig and Salvato, 2012: p. 113)

Another important development in relation to the scope and position of family business studies is the skew of the field towards business rather than towards the family system or a balanced perspective. Perhaps, this fact is most strikingly highlighted by James et al. (2012). Based on a review of 2240 articles on family enterprises published between 1985 and 2010, these authors observe that:

> The analysis vividly illustrates not only the increased dominance of publication outlets and theoretical perspectives associated with business but also the near disappearance of those associated with family. (p. 87)

James et al. (2012) join the growing coterie of scholars from economics (Bertrand and Schoar, 2006), sociology (Aldrich and Cliff, 2003), management (Dyer Jr., 2006; Litz et al., 2012), entrepreneurship (Nordqvist and Melin, 2010), and family science (e.g., Heck and Trent, 1999; Rogoff and Heck, 2003 and Danes, 2014) arguing in favor of focusing more attention on the family variable in family business research. Many of these perspectives are reviewed and elaborated upon in this *Handbook* (e.g., Jennings et al., 2014; Martinez and Aldrich, 2014; Nicholson, 2014; Rosa et al., 2014; von Schlippe and Schneewind, 2014; Shukla et al., 2014; Stewart, 2014).

In terms of the level of analysis, thus far scholars have focused largely on firm level of analysis, as opposed to individual/s or groups within a firm,[1] or multiple firms run by an enterprising family (e.g., Habbershon and Pistrui, 2002; Sharma, 2004). In other words, research has focused 'on a family business' and not 'in a family business' or 'on the business family'. Evidence of this focus is seen in studies aimed to understand the impact of family firms on an economy (e.g., Shanker and Astrachan, 1996), the success rate of family firms over generations (e.g., Ward, 1987), and even in topics such as financial performance, governance, and succession that have dominated the literature. For reviews on these topics, see Amit and Villalonga (2014), Gersick and Feliu (2014), Goel et al. (2014), and Long and Chrisman (2014) in this *Handbook*. To study the financial success or longevity of a firm is a different concern than understanding the entrepreneurial behaviors of an enterprising family or the overall success of a family enterprise group (Colli, 2012). It was only recently that the focus of

the field has been redirected towards the portfolio of enterprising family, also referred to as, family business groups in some contexts, as it became clear that a majority of enterprising families launch, grow, and shed multiple firms over time (Carney et al., 2011; Zellweger et al., 2012; Rosa et al., 2014).

Great promise lies in understanding the change and renewal processes over generations of enterprising families – a core focus of the global Successful Transgenerational Entrepreneurship Practices (STEP) project (Habbershon et al., 2010). How do long-lived dynastic families maintain their entrepreneurial spirit over generations? How do they acquire and shed resources over time? If patient or survivability capital is integral to the success of family enterprises, how do they determine when it is time for organic growth and when the best course of action is aggressive acquisition based growth? Or, when is it time to engage in incremental efficiency focused innovations instead of the rapid path-breaking innovations? And, what type of leader is suited for each stage of evolution of an enterprise? Are family or non-family CEOs better suited to run family enterprises? How might each unit controlled by the enterprising family be governed? Research explorations along these process dimensions have only just begun, leaving ample opportunities for future knowledge explorers (e.g., Sirmon and Hitt, 2003; Sharma and Manikutty, 2005; Hall and Nordqvist, 2008; Bergfeld and Weber, 2011; Colli, 2012; Salvato et al., 2012).

Later in this chapter, we discuss a few potentially impactful opportunities related to family enterprise research. But, first, let's step back and view family business studies from an overarching perspective to elaborate on what distinguishes this field of study from others. The tenacious definitional issues and the related topic of performance are discussed next. This is followed by a reflection on the field's evolutionary journey thus far, and the few major trends that have emerged and are likely to guide its development over the next few decades. Next, we reflect on a few opportunities and challenges for family business studies. In the concluding section, we briefly share the vision guiding this *Handbook* and the process used to bring this project to fruition.

DISTINGUISHING FEATURE OF FAMILY BUSINESS STUDIES

Family business scholars have always maintained that family involvement in business or the reciprocal influence of family and business distinguishes family business studies from other disciplines (e.g., Astrachan, 2003; Rogoff and Heck, 2003). For example, the domain of family sciences is to understand the issues within the family system and factors affecting this system. On the other hand, for fields such as entrepreneurship and strategy focused on the business system, the core interest lies in understanding factors that influence the formation of organizations, their strategies, or the performance of enterprises. Perhaps, the distinction between family business studies and its sister fields is most vividly illustrated by Yu et al.'s (2012) study aimed to understand the variables of interest to family business scholars. By identifying and classifying the dependent variables used in 257 empirical studies on family business published between 1998 and 2009, this study shows that family business researchers are using only a handful of independent variables related to family involvement in business. However, these scholars aim to understand the impact of these variables on 327 different dependent variables. This finding lead Yu et al. (2012) to conclude that:

> unlike many established business disciplines that tend to investigate how an array of independent variables are related to a few dependent variables, the family business discipline seems to be focused on how a few independent variables are related to many dependent variables. (Yu et al., 2012: p. 45)

Since the 1980s, family business researchers have reported the pursuit of a multiplicity of goals by family enterprises (e.g., Ward, 1987; Taguiri and Davis, 1992). Using somewhat different terminology, two recent reviews reinforce this idea arguing that this multiplicity distinguishes family from non-family firms. Gedajlovic et al. (2012) refer to the 'mixed managerial motives' of owner managers. Gomez-Mejia et al. (2011: p. 656) discuss the 'affective utilities and non-financial goals', arguing that 'major managerial choices will be driven by a desire to preserve and enhance the family's socio-emotional wealth apart from efficiency or economic instrumentality considerations'. The socio-emotional wealth (SEW) perspective has quickly become an important theoretical framework to understand the behavioral choices of family firm managers and owners (for a review, see Berrone et al., 2012 and in this *Handbook*, Berrone et al., 2014). It has even been argued that SEW can be considered an emerging unifying theoretical canon for the field of family firm studies as it addresses the core issues that make family firms unique and is built on and draws from the family firm research itself and not only on insights from other fields (e.g., Gomez-Mejia et al., 2011; Berrone et al., 2012). However, the extent to which SEW will play the role of a unifying theoretical perspective for the field, or when such unification is possible, or even desirable, remains to be seen. As the field is still young, we expect to see additional and complementary theoretical frameworks to emerge over the next five to ten years.

For instance, Gedajlovic et al. (2012) suggest that owners and managers have diverse and mixed sets of personal motives, some economic and some noneconomic, that drive their decision making in family firms. Researchers in family business studies have known and taken into account these mixed motives for a long time, while it is something that most general organization and economic theorists have tended to neglect. Thus, this central and distinguishing factor of family firm offers scholars 'an opportune context in which to develop and test theories of how executives manage the tradeoff between multiple and mixed goals and also how they identify, evaluate, and marshal resources to exploit opportunities in pursuit of those goals' (Gedajlovic et al., 2012: p. 1027).

The notions of SEW and mixed motives surely help to identify the uniqueness of family firm studies. However, while the domain of the field is becoming clearer and more focused, its breadth is large enough to make it attractive to investigators from multiple disciplinary, theoretical and methodological traditions, and geographic regions. Perhaps, both the focus and the breadth of the field are natural given the central characteristics of the phenomenon it is attempting to investigate and understand. As an organizational form, the 'family firm' is certainly enough specific to deserve focused attention of scholars. However, as a large variety of organizations can be classified as family firms, scholars must remain cautious of this diversity when designing their research studies (e.g., Melin and Nordqvist, 2007; Westhead and Howorth, 2007; Amit and Villalonga, 2014). Admittedly, although the focal clarity has been helpful in building a community of scholars and the field's legitimacy (Craig and Salvato, 2012), it has also caused some persistent issues to deal with. Examples include the definitional and performance issues discussed next.

DEFINITIONAL AND PERFORMANCE ISSUES

Since the first few lines of FBR, shared earlier in this chapter, family business scholars have been engaged in a definitional debate. Over the years, several definitions of family business have been proposed and efforts made to reconcile different views (e.g., Handler, 1989; Litz, 1995; Westhead and Cowling, 1998). This scholarly conversation has settled into a general agreement of a more inclusive theoretically focused 'essence based' definition and a sharper focused operational definition that relies on the 'components of involvement' in business

(Chua et al., 1999). Based on research interests, the business unit focused essence approach is further bifurcated to understand firm behavior (Chua et al., 1999) or the consequences of this behavior on resources often expressed as 'familiness' (Habbershon and Williams, 1999). The following essence based definition is often used to conceptually distinguish family from non-family firms:

> The family business is a business governed and/or managed with the intention to shape and/or pursue the vision of the business held by a dominant coalition controlled by members of the same family or a small number of families in a manner that is potentially sustainable across generations of the family or families. (Chua et al., 1999: p. 25)

Definitions using the components approach often employ the extent of family involvement in ownership, management, and governance. For example, the F-PEC scale that has been developed and refined over the years aims to measure the extent and nature of family involvement in and influence on a business unit (Klein et al., 2005; Holt et al., 2010). Arguing against a dichotomized view of what is or is not a family firm, this continuous scale assesses family influence on three dimensions of power, experience, and culture. In this *Handbook*, Pearson et al. (2014) trace the development of F-PEC scale as they provide a compendium of all scales available in the field along with their reliability measures.

Thoughtful operationalization of the 'family firm' variable is critical as significant variance in empirical results has been reported based on the definition of family firm employed. For example, by using broad, mid-range, and narrow definitions[2] of family firm, Shanker and Astrachan (1996) found that the number of family businesses in the United States ranges from 20.3 million to 4.1 million, as does their collective impact on the economy. Similarly, Westhead and Cowling (1998) found that the number of family firms in the UK varied from 80% of all firms to 15%, depending on the used combination of the generational involvement of family in ownership and management, and the self-perception of the firms' leaders on whether a firm is a family firm or not.

Research comparing the financial performance of family and non-family firms further confirms the key role of definitions used. Both the direction and valence of results vary significantly depending on how 'family firm' is defined (e.g., Miller et al., 2007; Sciascia and Mazzola, 2008). In this *Handbook*, Amit and Villalonga (2014) provide a comprehensive review[3] of research focused on the financial performance of publicly held family firms, clearly demonstrating the significant impact of the definitions used on results obtained. These studies illustrate the critical impact of operational definitions on empirical results and remind researchers to be mindful of the heterogeneity of family firms when building theory or designing empirical research. The overarching guidance from these reviews is to use multiple definitions of family firm to understand how the empirical findings change based on the extent and nature of family involvement in business. With the hope of inspiring future research related to definitional and performance issues, we make a few observations below.

The 'Family' as a Variable and Unit of Analysis

Despite several articles that have focused on clarifying the definition of a family firm and developing scales to measure the extent of family influence in a firm, hardly any efforts have been directed to either define or measure the 'family' variable (Pearson et al., 2014). Even in scales aimed to measure the family climate or family harmony or family influence, the task of defining the 'family' is left to the respondent, leaving open the possibility of multiple interpretations of a key term in the same data set. This is especially important given the significant heterogeneity in family structures in today's society where simultaneously multiple variations of family co-exist (e.g., Walsh, 2003; McGoldrick et al., 2010).

While the 'family' variable is important when we discuss the firm level of analysis, it becomes even more critical when designing studies using family as a unit of analysis. Examples include research on habitual or portfolio entrepreneurship by enterprising families (e.g., Zellweger et al., 2012; Rosa et al., 2014). As a social institution, family shapes the values of its members. In turn, these values influence the attitudes and behavioral choices of family members. It should be noted that 'family' as the unit of analysis does not imply unified or harmonious families. As with all social settings, conflicts are a natural part of family (McKee et al., 2014, in this *Handbook*). Yet another reason for considering the 'family' as the unit of analysis is the growing interest in the potential of family as a carrier of different forms of capital, such as social, cultural, financial, and human (in this *Handbook*, e.g., Danes, 2014; Sorenson, 2014).

In terms of defining and developing measures of the 'family' variable, some green shoots of ideas are emerging in the literature. For example, Sharma and Salvato (2013) propose the adoption of essence and component based approaches for defining the family variable. They suggest that the components of consanguinity, cohabitation, legal status, generations, gender, and birth-order may be used to operationalize the family variable. Data collected on these component dimensions can help to determine the heterogeneity of families within a study. The essence of family firm has been described in a few different ways. For example, Nordqvist and Melin (2010) note that 'a key attribute of the family is its tendency to perpetuate its existence by ensuring its integration' (p. 223). Based on joint emotional and cognitive aspects that shape an 'adhesion that is vital to the existence of a family group and its interest', families produce and reproduce rites that may bind them together (Bourdieu, 1996: p. 22). Others view family as 'a group of people affiliated through bonds of shared history and a commitment to share a future together while supporting the development and well being of individual members' (Hoy and Sharma, 2010: pp. 49).

Given the strong case made by several recent authors in the 25th anniversary issue of FBR of a critical need to focus more attention on the 'family' variable in family business research (e.g., James et al., 2012; Litz et al., 2012), great promise lies in devoting efforts to design studies based on the family as the unit of analysis and to define and develop valid and reliable measures for the family variable. In undertaking this task, it will be important to be mindful of the multiplicity of the concept of family across cultures and time (e.g., Hoy, 2014, in this *Handbook*).

Goal–Performance Linkage

Significant efforts have been devoted to compare the financial performance of family and non-family firms (Yu et al., 2012). It is somewhat surprising that despite the long-term orientation often attributed to family firms (e.g., Miller and Le-Breton Miller, 2005) and survival goals often superseding the short-term performance goals (e.g., Colli, 2012), most research on performance is either cross-sectional or spans a narrow time frame. Reviews and meta-analyses of research on financial performance of family firms indicate insignificant and inconsistent findings that vary based on definitions used and contextual factors such as generation and institutional environment (Stewart and Hitt, 2012; Amit and Villalonga, 2014).

Since the 1980s, the pursuit of multiple goals by family firms has been known. It is also clear that while some desired goals are firm centered, others are family centered (e.g., Ward, 1987; Tagiuri and Davis, 1992). More recent empirical studies confirm this trend as family firms espouse and aim to attain multiple goals (McKenny et al., 2012). Although most firms find the simultaneous attainment of family and business centered goals to be a challenging task, those who successfully accomplish it do well on both dimensions (e.g., Basco and Pérez Rodriguez, 2009).

While several measures have been employed to gauge the financial performance of a firm, efforts are being devoted to develop reliable measures for non-economic performance. For example, Berrone et al. (2012) have proposed a five-dimensional measure of the socio-emotional wealth of a family firm that they label as FIBER. The five dimensions are *family* control and influence, family *identification* with the firm, *bonding* social ties, *emotional* attachment, and *renewal* of family bonds to the firm through dynastic succession. Björnberg and Nicholson (2007) have presented a validated scale to assess the family climate. Further testing and refinement of such scales is likely to help researchers to measure performance on multiple dimensions as strongly advocated by Colli (2012).

Performance is an outcome measure. A firm's 'success' can only be assessed against its desired goals. So, if a researcher is interested in gauging the level of a firm's success, it becomes necessary to also understand its goals, necessitating a nuanced comparison of firms with similar goals. Even if a researcher is not interested in a firm's success per se but in understanding the factors that lead to high financial performance at a point in time, desired goals must still be incorporated in the study, along with other theorized factors.

For future studies, when it comes to understanding family firm performance, three directions appear promising: (i) to view both goals and performances as multi-dimensional constructs and employ measures that capture these dimensions related to the family and the business system; (ii) to juxtapose measures of goals and performances to better understand firm success; and (iii) to employ research designs and methods that capture evolution of goals and thus performances over time.

Unit Versus Group Level of Analysis

Efforts must continue to build robust measures to capture the extent and nature of family involvement at the business unit level.

However, research from different parts of the world is revealing that most enterprising families are involved in multiple enterprises either simultaneously or serially (e.g., Au et al., 2013; Orozco and González, 2014; Zellweger et al., 2012). This suggests the need to develop an understanding of such portfolio and serial entrepreneurship activities of enterprising families (Rosa et al., 2014). For example, following research conducted under the rubric of strategic business units, it would appear that at times resources may be transferred from one unit to the other depending on the nature of competition and the competitive advantages (e.g., Dess and Robinson, 1984; Govindrajan, 1986). It would be interesting to investigate if this holds for family enterprises as well. If so, how must researchers interested in understanding performance and success of firms design studies to incorporate such within group relationships and resource transfers? A design with different levels of analysis such as the sub-unit level, firm level, and group level seems appropriate.

The level of analysis issue is not only important in studies focused on the performance variable, but also for two other widely studied topics of succession and governance of family enterprises. Reviews on both these topics point in the same direction of the need to incorporate multiple levels of contexts and develop more nuanced situational understanding (in this *Handbook*, McKenny et al., 2014). The following statements from chapters in this *Handbook*, made after thorough reviews of succession and governance, are indicative of this future promise:

> [W]ithout a broader multi-level context, these theories can do little to help us understand the origins of these social facts, the development of the succession process, or the impact of that process on the future of the firm. (Long and Chrisman, 2014)

> More authors are moving away from a blanket endorsement (or critique) of independent-director-dominated boards for all family businesses, and advocating the need to be situational, concluding that not one board style fits all ... for the more complex family enterprises, the questions of board

structure, composition, and size need to take into account the overall organizational structure. ... Which board? Serving what governance purpose?

> Actually, the list of potential boards in the complex, later-generation family enterprise is longer, including the family office board, the family foundation board, the boards of subsidiaries and joint ventures, and the 'pseudo-board' created by interlocking groups of trustees. The relationships among all of these family business boards within the same family enterprise raise many interesting questions. (Gersick and Feliu, 2014)

In short, great promise lies in developing definitions and measures of family, incorporating this variable better in family business studies, juxtaposing studies on firm performance or success with desired goals, and focusing research at different levels of analysis not only in terms of business units and groups, but also in terms of topics such as governance and succession. Before we further comment on trends and promising future directions related to family enterprise research and education, let's pause briefly to reflect on the field's evolution.

EVOLUTION OF FAMILY BUSINESS STUDIES

Tracing the roots of family business studies since the first dissertation by Calder (1953) focused on the management problems of small family firms, Sharma et al. (2007) observed the practice driven evolution of the field. Institutions such as Family Business Centers and professional associations have played an integral role in building this field of study. Close interactions between scholars and family business leaders formed the basis of some of the field's classic books,[4] such as Gersick et al. (1997), Miller and Le-Breton Miller (2005), and Ward (1987). Scholars and practitioners were eager to build a venue for sharing ideas on how to better understand and serve family enterprises. Most Centers and Chairs were supported by sponsorship from the business community, thereby providing avenues for maintaining close association between scholars and practitioners.

Several management scholars lament the growing gap between research and practice, expressing disappointment at the 'negligible gains in usable knowledge' (Starbuck, 2006: p.1) and lack of research that is 'really interesting' (Bartunek et al., 2006: p. 9). Against this backdrop, how is family business study evolving as a field? Given its strong roots in practice, how is the fast pace of its growth impacting the relationship between theory and practice? In this section, we reflect on this issue and three major trends observed as a consequence of the high pace of growth of family business studies over a remarkably short time frame.

Clock Builders and Time Tellers

The foundation of family business studies lies in a close interaction and mingling of practitioners and scholars. Fortunately for this field of study, *clock builders*[5] – individuals who set up institutions and means for *time tellers* to contribute effectively – continue to build the field and opportunities within it (cf. Collins and Porras, 1997). Efforts of both types are necessary to continue building the depth, breadth, growth, and legitimacy of a field. In other words, while some efforts must focus on deepening the research rigor, others must continue to expand its reach into scholarly, practitioner, and student communities. In addition, vigilance must be maintained to ensure relevant usable knowledge is being created and disseminated effectively into scholarly as well as practitioner communities around the world.

Viewing the field from this multi-dimensional perspective, it is evident the pluralism of contributions continues as the field grows (Boyer, 1990; Sharma, 2010). A few examples of work targeted to retain the relevance of research while growing its reach and rigor are shared below.

(a) Applied research projects such as the Global STEP Project that develop longitudinal in-depth comparative case studies from multiple countries and have institutionalized mechanisms to continue increasing the rigor of work while providing opportunities for regular interactions between scholars and practitioners to share ideas and co-create knowledge.

(b) Journals such as the *Family Business Review* have a dedicated editor who compiles practical implications of articles published in FBR and employs different ways to disseminate this knowledge in usable forms to the practitioner communities. Starting with the March 2013 issue, through FBR's 'Call for Research' section, a mechanism has been established for practitioners to share ideas on topics they encounter in practice but feel there is not enough scientifically generated usable knowledge.

(c) Family Business Centers, often supported by sponsors from family enterprises, further help maintain a close interaction between research and practice. Research conducted in Centers and through family business associations is often shared with practitioners in the form of conferences, workshops, and/or reports. Examples include research commissioned by the Family Firm Institute and presented in scholarly journals (e.g., Zellweger et al., 2012), and conferences such as *Transitions* in the USA that are jointly hosted by *Family Business Magazine* and Stetson University's Family Enterprise Center, and the Witten Congress for Family Businesses, hosted by the Witten Institute for Family Business at Witten/ Herdecke University in Germany.

(d) Annual research conferences such as EIASM Workshop on Family Firm Management Research, EURAM's family business track, Family Enterprise Research Conference (FERC), the Family Firm Institute (FFI), and the International Family Enterprise Research Academy (IFERA) are intended to facilitate interactions between scholars as well as between scholars and practitioners.

(e) Active involvement of some scholars in practitioner forums such as Family Business Networks, Young Presidents Organization, Family Business Australia, Canadian Association of Family Enterprises, FDC Brazil's programs for Business Families are but only a few examples of opportunities for researchers and practitioners to interact and learn from each other.

In short, while family enterprise research is now regularly making its way to top-tier journals (e.g., Villalonga and Amit, 2006; Miller et al., 2007; Chrisman and Patel, 2012; König et al., 2013), and editors of premier journals are noticing increased rigor in family business scholarship as indicated by the comment below from the past editor of the *Academy of Management Journal*, parallel efforts are being devoted to grow the reach and maintain the relevance of research.

In editorial capacities, my experience indicates that family firm scholars are strongly committed to designing and completing high quality research studies. Because of this, I anticipate that increasingly impactful scholarship will flow from scholars' efforts to study significant questions. (Ireland, quoted in Craig and Salvato, 2012: p. 112)

Given the time demands of publishing and of advising or running family enterprises, efforts must continue to maintain the delicate balance between research and practice. At an individual level, scholars will need to determine their own ways to ensure their work does not become insignificant (cf. Vermeulen, 2007, and in this *Handbook*, Dawson, 2014). Collective efforts towards this end must also continue.

From Generalization to Specialization

The pioneers in the field played multiple roles in building and disseminating knowledge on family enterprises. They simultaneously taught, conducted research, and advised family enterprises. Some continue to maintain this multiplicity of roles. However, with the growing demands of rigor in advising, research, and education, and the geometric increase in opportunities on all three dimensions, the trend is moving from generalization to specialization.

Advisors often find it helpful to collaborate with others from different backgrounds as they devise ways to understand the core issues and develop solutions for enterprising families. Generalization is giving way to specialization at individual level. This is being combined with integration of expertise at team or group levels. Similarly, researchers are becoming more focused on the particular topics and sets of issues they investigate.

Mastering the ins and outs of any one journal takes significant time and effort. Thus, researchers tend to select a handful of target outlets for their work and then build a mastery of the conversations in that outlet so as to position their research and contributions to add value to those scholarly conversations (cf. Huff, 1999). In some instances, seemingly parallel to the strategy followed by advisors, individual scholars are focusing on building their own brand for excellence in some theory, method, or topic, and then combining forces with other scholars to build competitive advantage when it comes to publishing – a trend reminding us of an African saying: 'If you want to travel fast, travel alone. If you want to travel far, travel together'. A quick review of the chapters in this *Handbook* or author listings of family business research articles will indicate this trend towards specialization of expertise and integration of forces, where co-authorship has become steadily more common.

Centers established during the early years of the field focused mostly on outreach activities. To varying degrees, these Centers also served the internal constituents of the institutions that housed them, by developing courses and supporting research. Family Business Centers housed at the Kennesaw State, Loyola, and Oregon State Universities are among the oldest in the field. Over time, while outreach has remained the primary mission of some of these Centers, others have evolved to more deeply support the research and teaching missions of their institutions. For example, Kennesaw State University's Cox Family Business Center was instrumental in the launch of the EMBA program for 'Families in Business' and is home to the *Journal of Family Business Strategy*. Loyola University's Family Business Center has continued to develop innovative programs for business families. Some examples include the Next Generation Leadership Program established in 1995 and the Family Business Stewardship Institute launched in 2008.

Since these early pioneers, new Centers have emerged all around the globe with singular or multiple missions. Stetson University has a strong focus on family business education, while the Centers at Jönköping International Business School, University of St Gallen, University of Alberta, and Mississippi State University are largely research oriented, with varying degrees of focus on teaching and outreach. Of the newer initiatives, perhaps the Family Business Australia Network and the programs at the FDC in Brazil and ITESM in Mexico are moving at the fastest pace with regards to thinking of programs and opportunities for continuing education of the enterprising families. Several others are joining this task, including on-line education providers like the Business Families Foundation and the Family Firm Institute.

As reminded by Steier and Ward (2006), the nature of programs and deliverables focused on by different Centers will continue to vary depending on the mission of the institutions in which they are housed. Following the trend from generalization to specialization in research and advising, perhaps the next stage for Family Business Centers will also involve choosing a focal domain and then employing all resources to build excellence in that domain. Ample work is needed on dimensions of building leading edge research, educational programs, and tools to support and build an advising practice. The field is still small enough to provide opportunities for all Center Directors or scholars from different disciplines to congregate in meetings, and this is likely to continue in the near future. However, parallel to the integration in scholarly teams and advisors, alliances and co-operation between Centers trying to accomplish similar goals is likely to be helpful.

Globalization of Family Business Studies

While the seeds of family business research and education were sown in the 1950s, 1960s, and 1970s in a limited number of places, it was in the 1980s that these seeds seemingly spread on a broader scale across the world. For example, the first Chair in family business in the

USA was established at the Baylor University in 1978, the first European Chair in this area was about ten years later at IESE in Spain in 1987. Australian presence in this area started in mid 1990s with the establishment of the Australian Family Business Center at the Bond University. Institutions in Africa, Asia Pacific, Latin America, and the Middle East joined in their quest for research and family business education a bit later as the awareness of the significant role of these enterprises to the social and economic landscapes of different countries became evident. But, the catch up is happening quickly as is evident from the growing demand for summits and workshops focusing on family enterprises.

Where there is humanity, there are family enterprises. And, curious scholars are devoting their attention to understanding the dilemmas faced by these enterprises with the hope of creating usable knowledge. Even when efforts at institution building are localized, with the ease of travel and technology, attendees at family business research events, such as the Annual IFERA Conference, tend to come from around the world. For example, while the EIASM Family Firm Management Workshop and EURAM's family business track were originally launched to serve the community building needs of European scholars interested in family enterprise research, their annual conferences attract scholars from around the world. Similarly, while FERC was envisioned as a North American conference, even in its inaugural year attendees came from different continents. The most recent example indicating the globalization of the field is the Family Enterprise Case Competition (FECC) launched by the University of Vermont in 2013. The inaugural competition attracted 16 teams from 10 countries in North America, Latin America, Europe, and Asia, further reinforcing the global interest in family business education and research.

The increased globalization of family firm studies also means new research opportunities. Gedajlovic et al. (2012) observe that investigating the role of different institutional environments and family firm performance is one important area where family firm studies can contribute to the more general disciplines of management and economics. They argue that family firm's 'distinctive characteristics and ubiquity provide an opportune basis for exploring how various institutional variables influence the value firms may obtain from particular types of capabilities as well as the consequences of their particular disabilities' (Gedajlovic et al., 2012: p. 1024). In other words, while family firms represent the most common organizational form across the globe, these firms also face different challenges and opportunities depending on the institutional environments in which they are embedded. A global approach to research on family firms is thus needed to fully embrace the potential in this field of study and its opportunity to enrich other fields and disciplines.

The growth and expanding interest in the field is good news for interested practitioners and scholars. This growth has been marked by three trends that are likely to continue over the next few decades: (i) continued efforts to build institutions and excellence simultaneously; (ii) moving the field from generalization to specialization on all its dimensions; and (iii) the global interest in research, education, and advising focused on family enterprises. Next, we discuss the opportunities and challenges posed by these major trends on research and education related to family enterprises.

CHALLENGES AND OPPORTUNITIES FOR RESEARCH

The authors of each chapter in this *Handbook* provide ample guidance on trends related to the topics reviewed, the current status of knowledge, and pending interesting research questions. In this section, we share some overarching observations related to family enterprise research based on our work with authors of this *Handbook* and other experiences in the field.

Nature of the Questions Explored

Overall, a continual increase in research sophistication can be observed in terms of questions asked as scholars are coming to grips with the heterogeneity of organizations that fall under the domain of family business studies. The broad spectrum questions that fascinated researchers during the early stages of the field's evolution are being supplemented by those aimed to develop a finer grained understanding of the phenomenon of interest (Zahra and Sharma, 2004; Salvato and Aldrich, 2012). For example, instead of asking what proportion of family firms have non-family CEOs, or whether or not family members form better CEOs, recent scholarly investigations have turned their attention to the *why* and *how* questions, such as why family or non-family CEOs are appointed and how some career trajectories lead to the CEO suite (e.g., Salvato et al., 2012). Future research might take the next step to understand the factors that lead to effectiveness of a CEO or leadership team in family enterprises that are characterized by different core goals and performance aspirations on multiple dimensions.

Similarly, research on innovation has progressed from whether family or non-family firms, or family or non-family CEOs are more innovative, to investigating conditions that lead to varied degrees and types of innovation by firms and leaders (e.g., Bergfeld and Weber, 2011; Huybrechts et al., 2013; and in this *Handbook*, McKelvie et al., 2014; Zahra et al., 2014). In another line of research, scholars are challenging the notion of assuming that family members or family firms are less professional than their non-family counterparts (e.g., Hall and Nordqvist, 2008). Instead multiple dimensions of professionalization are being explored (e.g., Stewart and Hitt, 2012; Dekker et al., 2013).

Virtually all chapters in this *Handbook* encourage research questions and designs aimed to build a nuanced understanding of family enterprises. The exciting research questions following such an ambition will incorporate both studies of causal factors explaining the *why* or the *how* underlying the phenomenon of interest, and in-depth studies aimed at generating theories on why and how families and family firms shape their futures.

Zahra and Sharma (2004) observed the wide and shallow nature of family business studies as the literature covered a lot of ground in terms of topics studied but lacked depth of understanding on any particular topic. This is further reinforced by Yu et al. (2012) review, which revealed 327 different dependent variables used in the field. Although a lot has been written on some topics, such as succession, governance, and performance, as is evident from review chapters in this *Handbook* (Amit and Villalonga, 2014; Gersick and Feliu, 2014; Goel et al., 2014; Long and Chrisman, 2014), even in these topics future opportunities lie in digging deeper to develop a nuanced understanding of the issues of interest (Nordqvist et al., 2009). Towards this end, not only will researchers benefit from asking interesting research questions (Salvato and Aldrich, 2012), but also employing multiple methods towards this end (Sharma and Carney, 2012).

Methods

As evident in this *Handbook* the field attracts and enjoys a diversity of methodological perspectives that help to deepen understanding of family firms (elaborated in chapters by Colli and Fernández Pérez, 2014; Fletcher, 2014; Pearson et al., 2014; Reay and Zhang, 2014; McKenny et al., 2014). While cross-sectional studies have been the most frequently employed methods in family enterprise research, it is encouraging to notice that longitudinal studies are beginning to emerge (e.g., Salvato et al., 2010; Sieger et al., 2011; Wennberg et al., 2011). Furthermore, it is exciting to see an increase in usage of diversity of methods being adopted in family business research. Some examples include simulations (Chirico et al., 2012), content analysis (McKenny et al., 2012), interpretive approach (Nordqvist et al., 2009), narrative analysis (Dawson and Hjorth, 2012), and experimental design (Hatak and Roessl,

in press). As proposed in the chapter by Fletcher (2014), critical analysis that involves problematizing accepted knowledge and exposing taken-for-granted assumptions, is likely to widen the structural, political, and ethical aspects of family businesses and enterprising families. Topics such as gender issues, locating gender relations in wider social structures and dominant discourses, await attention. At this time, analysis based on critical theory is virtually non-existent in the field of family business. Interested scholars could draw on different streams of critical social science research and methods in use in critical research.

Regardless of the chosen method, the expected rigor has been on a continuous upswing (Sharma et al., 2012). These high expectations are going to necessitate more efforts from authors to master one or a few methods, and stay at the forefront of new knowledge and scholarly discussions related to those methods. Thoughtful scholars remind us to:

> get a deep grounding in a substantive discipline, such as sociology, as well as becoming proficient in at least understanding if not using the state-of-the-art research methods in the field. (Aldrich, quoted in Craig and Salvato, 2012: p. 111)

Theoretical Perspectives

The volume of family business research is continually increasing. De Massis et al. (2012) report 734 articles published in 47 different journals in the 15-year time period from 1996 to 2010. In contrast, the 25-year period from 1971 to 1995 produced almost the same amount of articles on family firms in fewer journals (Sharma et al., 1996). While broad based reviews continue to appear (e.g., De Massis et al., 2012), it will become evident from the chapters in this *Handbook* that a thorough literature review of topics that have received significant attention is a demanding undertaking. With the increase in the volume of literature, we expect the trend towards increased specialization of topical expertise to continue.

Several theoretical perspectives from varied disciplinary backgrounds are reviewed in this *Handbook*. Some of these perspectives, such as agency and resource-based views of the firm, have been frequently used in past research (see reviews by Shukla et al., 2014; Rau, 2014). Others, such as stakeholder and socio-emotional wealth, are gaining rapid momentum (Berrone et al., 2014). Also reviewed in this *Handbook* are theoretical perspectives that have a great potential for informing family business studies but have not yet been used much in the literature. Examples include family therapy and psychology (von Schlippe and Schneewind, 2014), anthropology (Stewart, 2014), sociology (Martinez and Aldrich, 2014), evolutionary theory (Nicholson, 2014), emotion theory (Brundin and Härtel, 2014), organizational identity theory (Whetten et al., 2014), paradox theory (Zellweger, 2014), family science (Danes, 2014; Jennings et al., 2014), and critical social science (Fletcher, 2014). As will become evident in going through each of these chapters, promising research awaits attention. This is also the case in traditional management areas such as accounting and marketing, as evidenced by the chapters in this *Handbook* by Duncan and Moores (2014) and Blombäck and Craig (2014). As rich insights can be gained from diversity, we expect to see a multiplicity of theoretical perspectives being adopted to strengthen and deepen our understanding of the heterogeneity within the family businesses and building the usable knowledge on these enterprises (Melin and Nordqvist, 2007). As scholars, however, we will need to constantly remind ourselves to familiarize ourselves with the classic works that inform these perspectives. In doing so, the importance of contextualizing family business studies must be kept in mind.

Incorporating Context

Management scholars have noticed the powerful impact of context on research findings, arguing that ignoring the surroundings associated with the phenomenon of interest leads to within-study variations and conflicting results (e.g., Cappelli and Sherer, 1991; Johns, 2006). Although calls are frequently made to incorporate context in research, the actual task of doing so in research designs has proven to be challenging. In family business studies, the effect of ignoring the context is most evident in the inconsistent results of studies directed to understand whether family or non-family firms are financially better performers (e.g., Stewart and Hitt, 2012). In this *Handbook*, Amit and Villalonga (2014) illustrate how contextual factors such as location, industry and external environment impact the research findings of studies focused on financial performance.

Family business scholars have incorporated context in theoretical as well as empirical studies. Examples include understanding survival versus demise of family enterprises in hostile environments (e.g., Hatum, 2007; Orozco and González, 2014), the role of institutions on shaping the values of family enterprises (Parada, Nordqvist, and Gimeno, 2010), portfolio entrepreneurship (Sieger et al., 2011), principal–principal conflicts (Sauerwald and Peng, 2013), succession (Saxena, 2013), and the role of location and number of owners on innovation output (Deng et al., 2013). In this *Handbook*, the chapters on internationalization (Fernández and Nieto, 2014) and social innovation (Zahra et al., 2014) stress the critical role of context in family business research.

Over the last few decades, most regions in the world, including Asia Pacific, Europe, and Latin America have experienced rapid contextual changes. Responding to the challenges of family enterprises to understand the pathways likely to lead to success amidst changing institutional environments, researchers have designed studies to develop this understanding. Examples include the STEP books on Transgenerational Entrepreneurship in Asia Pacific (Au et al., 2011), Europe (Nordqvist and Zellweger, 2010), and Latin America (Nordqvist et al., 2011). In addition, a recent issue of *Asia Pacific Journal of Management*, on Strategic Management in Asian Family Enterprises (Sharma and Chua, 2013), included several interesting articles on research designed to deepen the understanding of family enterprises with contextual changes in this region. This new and important stream of research is likely to trigger more research studies, both in the regions already receiving scholarly attention as well as in others in which family business research is needed (e.g., Africa and the Middle East). Such research will not only contribute to the understanding of family enterprises around the world, but its findings are likely to contribute to mainstream management, responding to the challenge of 'giving back to sister disciplines' (Zahra and Sharma, 2004; Craig and Salvato, 2012).

GUIDING VISION AND THE MAKING OF THIS HANDBOOK

This *Handbook* was envisioned to provide both a retrospective and prospective on family business studies. Our desire was to create a rich tapestry by weaving together the current knowledge on topics studied by family business researchers from varied theoretical and methodological perspectives. Not only did we want each chapter to provide a reflective overview of the current status of the field on the focal topic, we hoped it would stimulate future research. Our *Handbook* was aimed to guide and frame future research, deepening understanding on topics already part of family business studies, opening new avenues and alternative perspectives not yet explored in the literature. In other words, we wanted to take stock of what we know, while reflecting how we might deepen understanding on topics already part of the literature and others we might explore.

Creation of this *Handbook* has been a long and pleasant journey extending over two years. It started with the development and presentation of a proposal with a list of possible topics and authors for the consideration of Sage Publishing. A systematic and thorough review process by the publisher provided excellent feedback on our proposal and resulted in revisions leading to the addition of new topics while dropping some others in our original list. Once the topics were decided, the best possible authors for each were identified and invitations to develop chapter proposals extended. We reached out to the best, and thus busiest scholars. We were simultaneously delighted and humbled by the excellent response of the scholarly community to our invitations.

Authors were asked to submit a brief proposal of their ideas for each chapter. After an initial round of feedback from editors on these proposals, authors were asked to submit a full draft of their chapters to be presented at a three-day *Handbook* conference. Each chapter was presented and discussed at length at this conference aimed to provide developmental feedback to authors. A member of the international editorial board of this *Handbook* discussed each presented chapter. After the reviews and conference feedback, each chapter has been resubmitted at least twice, with intermediate feedback from the editors.

Our desire was to engage with as many notable scholars in the field as possible. With 74 contributing authors and 14 distinguished members of our international editorial board, this *Handbook* is the product of excellent collaboration between the contributors, the editorial board members, and the editors. Twenty-nine chapters reviewing different theories, methods, and issues follow this introductory chapter. Five reflective essays round off this *Handbook*. It is our hope that it adds value to our collective pursuit to create usable knowledge on family enterprises around the world.

NOTES

1 Exceptions include founders and to a much lesser extent the next generation members.
2 Broad definition required the family to have some degree of effective control over the strategic direction of the business and an intention for business to remain in the family.
    Mid-range definition included all the criteria in the broad definition and further required the founder or a descent to run the company.

Narrow definition required multiple generations of the family to be actively involved in the daily operations of the business and more than one family member to have significant management responsibility.

3   Stewart and Hitt (2012) provide another review on family firm performance in both private and publicly listed firms. De Massis et al.'s (2012) annotated bibliography of the 215 most cited articles published 1996–2010 is another valuable resource.

4   See Hoy (2012) for reviews of these books incorporating reflections from authors.

5   Having a great idea or being a charismatic visionary leader is 'time telling'; building a company that can prosper far beyond the presence of any single leader and through multiple product life cycles is 'clock building' … builders of visionary companies tend to be clock builders, not time tellers. (Collins & Porras, 1997: pp. 23)

REFERENCES

Aldrich, H.E. and Cliff, J.E. (2003). The pervasive effects of family on entrepreneurship: Towards a family embeddedness perspective. *Journal of Business Venturing*, 18: 573–596.

Amit, R. and Villalonga, B. (2014). Financial performance of family firms. In *SAGE Handbook of Family Business*. Edited by Melin, L., Nordqvist, M., and Sharma, P. London: Sage.

Anderson, R.C. and Reeb, D.M. (2003). Founding-family ownership and firm performance: Evidence from the S&P 500. *The Journal of Finance*, 58(3): 1301–1328.

Astrachan, J.H. (2003). Commentary on the special issue: The emergence of a field. *Journal of Business Venturing*, 18: 567– 572.

Au, K., Craig, J., and Ramachandran, K. (2011). *Family Entrepreneurship in Asia Pacific: Exploring Transgenerational Entrepreneurship in Family Firms*. Cheltenham, MA: Edward Elgar.

Au, K., Chiang, F.T., Birtch, T.A., and Ding, Z. (2013). Incubating the next generation to venture: Case study of a family business in Hong Kong. *Asia Pacific Journal of Management*.

Bartunek, J.M., Rynes, S.L., and Ireland, D. (2006). What makes management research interesting, and why does it matter? *Academy of Management Journal*, 49: 9–15.

Basco, R. and Pérez Rodriguez, M.J. (2009). Studying the family enterprise holistically: Evidence for integrated family and business systems. *Family Business Review*, 22(1): 82–95.

Bergfeld, M. and Weber, F. (2011). Dynasties of innovation: Highly performing German family firms and the owners' role for innovation. *International Journal of Entrepreneurship and Innovation Management*, 13(1): 80–94.

Berrone, P., Cruz, C., and Gomez-Mejia, L.R. (2012). Socioemotional wealth in family firms: Theoretical dimensions, assessment approaches, and agenda for future research. *Family Business Review*. 25(3): 258–279.

Berrone, P., Cruz, C., and Gomez-Mejia, L.R. (2014). Family-controlled firms and stakeholder management: A socioemotional wealth preservation perspective. In *SAGE Handbook of Family Business*. Edited by Melin, L., Nordqvist, M., and Sharma, P. London: Sage.

Bertrand, M. and Schoar, A. (2006). The role of family in family firms. *Journal of Economic Perspectives*, 20: 73–96.

Björnberg, Å. and Nicholson, N. (2007). The family climate scales: Development of a new measure for use in family business research. *Family Business Review*, 20(3): 229–246.

Blombäck, A. and Craig, J. (2014). Marketing from a family business perspective. In *SAGE Handbook of Family Business*. Edited by Melin, L., Nordqvist, M., and Sharma, P. London: Sage.

Bourdieu, P. (1996). On the family as a realized category. *Theory, Culture and Society* 13(3):19–26.

Boyer, E.L. (1990). *Scholarship Reconsidered: Priorities of the Professoriate*. Princeton, NJ: The Carnegie Foundation for the Advancement of Teaching.

Brundin, E. and Härtel, C.E.J. (2014). Emotions in family firms. In *SAGE Handbook of Family Business*. Edited by Melin, L., Nordqvist, M., and Sharma, P. London: Sage.

Calder, G.H. (1953). Some management problems of the small family controlled manufacturing business. Doctoral dissertation, School of Business, Indiana University.

Cappelli, P. and Sherer, P.D. (1991). The missing role of context in OB: The need for a meso-level approach. *Research in Organization Behavior*, 13: 55–110.

Carney, M., Gedajlovic, E.R., Heugens, P.P.M.A.R., Van Essen, M., and Van Oosterhout, J. (2011). Business group affiliation, performance, context, and strategy: a meta-analysis. *Academy of Management Journal*, 54(3): 437–460.

Chirico, F., Nordqvist, M., Colombo, G., and Mollona, E. (2012). Simulating dynamic capabilities and value creation in family firms: Is paternalism an 'asset' or a 'liability'? *Family Business Review*, 25: 318–338.

Chrisman, J.J. and Patel, P.C. (2012). Variations in R&D investments of family and non-family firms: Behavioral agency and myopic loss aversion perspectives. *Academy of Management Journal*, 55: 976–997.

Chua, J.H., Chrisman, J.J., and Chang, E.P.C. (2004). Are family firms born or made? An exploratory investigation. *Family Business Review*, 17(1): 37–54.

Chua, J.H., Chrisman, J.J., and Sharma, P. (1999). Defining the family business by behavior. *Entrepreneurship Theory & Practice*, 23(4): 19–39.

Colli, A. (2012). Contextualizing Performances of Family Firms: The Perspective of Business History. *Family Business Review*, 25: 243–257.

Colli, A. and Fernández Pérez, P. (2014). Business history and family firms. In *SAGE Handbook of Family Business*. Edited by Melin, L., Nordqvist, M., and Sharma, P. London: Sage.

Collins, J. and Porras, J.I. (1997). *Built to Last: Successful Habits of Visionary Companies*. New York: Harper Collins.

Craig, J.J.B. and Salvato, C. (2012). The distinctiveness, design, and direction of family business research: Insights from management luminaries. *Family Business Review*, 25(1): 109–116.

Danes, S.M. (2014). The future of family business research through the family scientist's lens. In *SAGE Handbook of Family Business*. Edited by Melin, L., Nordqvist, M., and Sharma, P. London: Sage.

Davis, J.A. (1982). The influence of life stage on father–son work relationship in family companies. Doctoral Dissertation. Harvard University.

Dawson, A. and Hjorth, D. (2012). Advancing family business research through narrative analysis. *Family Business Review*, 25: 339–355.

Dawson, A. (2014). A look into the future: What is the next generation of family business scholars focusing on? In *SAGE Handbook of Family Business*. Edited by Melin, L., Nordqvist, M., and Sharma, P. London: Sage.

De Massis, A., Sharma, P., Chua, J., and Chrisman, J. (2012). *Family Business Studies: An Annotated Bibliography*. Northampton, MA: Edward Elgar.

Dekker, J.C., Lybaert, N., Steijvers, T., Depaire, B. and Mercken, R. (2013). Family firm types based on the professionalization construct: Exploratory research. *Family Business Review*, 26(1): 81–99. doi:10.1177/0894486512445614

Deng, Z., Hofman, P.S., and Newman, A. (2013). Ownership concentration and product innovation in Chinese private SMEs. *Asia Pacific Journal of Management*.

Dess, G.G. and Robinson, R.B. (1984). Measuring organizational performance in the absence of objective measures: The case of the privately held firm and the conglomerate business unit. *Strategic Management Journal*, 5(3): 265–273.

Donnelley, R. (1964). The family business. *Harvard Business Review*, 42(3).

Duncan, K., and Moores, K. (2014). Accountability and stewardship of family business. In *SAGE Handbook of Family Business*. Edited by Melin, L., Nordqvist, M., and Sharma, P. London: Sage.

Dyer, G.J. (2006). Examining the 'family effect' on firm performance. *Family Business Review*, 19: 253–273.

Ewing, D.W. (1965). Is nepotism so bad? *Harvard Business Review*, 43(1): 22.

Fernández, Z. and Nieto Jesús, M. (2014). Internationalization of family firms. In *SAGE Handbook of Family Business*. Edited by Melin, L., Nordqvist, M., and Sharma, P. London: Sage.

Fletcher, D. (2014). Family business inquiry as a critical social science. In *SAGE Handbook of Family Business*. Edited by Melin, L., Nordqvist, M., and Sharma, P. London: Sage.

Gedajlovic, E., Carney, M., Chrisman, J.J., and Kellermanns, F.W. (2012). The adolescence of family firm research: Taking stock and planning for the future. *Journal of Management*, 38(4): 1010–1037.

Gersick, K.E., Davis, J.A., Hampton, M.M., and Lansberg, I. (1997). *Generation to Generation: Life Cycles of the Family Business*. Boston, MA: Harvard Business School Press.

Gersick, K.E. and Feliu, F. (2014). Governing the family enterprise: Practices, performance, and research. In *SAGE Handbook of Family Business*. Edited by Melin, L., Nordqvist, M., and Sharma, P. London: Sage.

Goel, S., Jussila, I., and Ikäheimonen, T. (2014). Governance in family firms: A review and research agenda. In *SAGE Handbook of Family Business*. Edited by Melin, L., Nordqvist, M., and Sharma, P. London: Sage.

Gomez-Mejia, L.R., Nunez-Nickel, M., and Gutierrez, I. (2001). The role of family ties in agency contracts. *Academy of Management Journal*, 44: 81–95.

Gomez-Mejia, L.R., Cruz, C., Berrone, P. and De Castro, J. (2011). The bind that ties: Socioemotional wealth preservation in family firms, *Academy of Management Annals*, 5(1): 653–707.

Govindrajan, V. (1986). Decentralization, strategy, and effectiveness of strategic business units in multi-business organizations. *Academy of Management Review*, 11(4): 844–856.

Habbershon, T. and Williams, M. (1999). A resource-based framework for assessing the strategic advantage of family firms. *Family Business Review*, 12(1): 1–125.

Habbershon, T.G. and Pistrui, J. (2002). Enterprising families domain: Family-influenced ownership groups in pursuit of transgenerational wealth. *Family Business Review*, 15(3): 223–237.

Habbershon, T.G., Nordqvist, M. and Zellweger, T. (2010). Transgenerational Entrepreneurship. In

Transgenerational entrepreneurship: Exploring growth and performance in family firms across generations. Edited by Nordqvist, M. and Zellweger, T. Cheltenham, MA: Edward Elgar.

Hall, A. and Nordqvist, M. (2008). Professional Management in Family Businesses: Toward an Extended Understanding. *Family Business Review*, 21(1): 51–69.

Handler, W.G. (1989). Methodological issues and considerations in studying family businesses. *Family Business Review*, 2(3): 257–276.

Hatak, I. and Roessl, D. (in press). Relational competence-based knowledge transfer within intra-family succession: An experimental study. *Family Business Review*.

Hatum, A. (2007). *Adaptation or Expiration in Family Firms: Organizational Flexibility in Emerging Economies.* Northampton MA: Edward Elgar Publishing.

Heck, R.K.Z. and Trent, E. (1999). The prevalence of family business from a household sample. *Family Business Review*, 12: 209–224.

Holt, D.T., Rutherford, M.W., and Kuratko, D.F. (2010). Advancing the field of family business research: Further testing the measurement properties of the F-PEC. *Family Business Review*, 23(1): 76–89.

Hoy, F. (2012). Book reviews: Ward, J.L., Keeping the Family Business Healthy (1987/2011), Gersick et al., Generation to Generation (1997), and Miller and Le-Breton Miller, Managing for the Long Run (2005). *Family Business Review*, 25(1): 117–120.

Hoy, F. (2014). Entrepreneurial venturing for family business research. In *SAGE Handbook of Family Business.* Edited by Melin, L., Nordqvist, M., and Sharma, P. Sage: London, UK.

Hoy, F. and Sharma, P. (2010). *Entrepreneurial Family Firms.* New York: Pearson Education.

Huff, A.S. (1999). *Writing for Scholarly Publication.* SAGE Publishers, CA.

Huybrechts, J., Voordeckers, W., and Lybaert, N. (2013). entrepreneurial risk-taking of private family firms: The Influence of a non-family CEO and the moderating effect of CEO tenure. *Family Business Review*, 26(2): 161–179.

James, A.E., Jennings, J.E., and Breitkruz, R. (2012). Worlds apart? Re-bridging the distance between family science and family business research. *Family Business Review*, 25(1): 87–108.

Jennings, J.E., Breitkreuz, R.S., and James, A.E. (2014). Theories from family science: A review and roadmap for family business research. In *SAGE Handbook of Family Business.* Edited by Melin, L., Nordqvist, M., and Sharma, P. London: Sage.

Johns, G. (2006). The essential impact of context on organizational behavior. *The Academy of Management Review*, 31(2): 386–408.

Klein, S., Astrachan, J.H., and Smyrnios, K. (2005). The F-PEC scale of family influence: Construction, validation, and further implication for theory. *Entrepreneurship: Theory and Practice*, 29: 321–339.

König, A., Kammerlander, N., and Enders, A. (2013). The family innovator's dilemma: How family influence affects the adoption of discontinuous technologies by incumbent firms. *Academy of Management Review*, 38(3): 418–441.

Lansberg, I., Perrow, E.L., and Rogolsky, R. (1988). Editors' notes. *Family Business Review*, 1(1): 1–8.

LaPorta, R., Lopez-de-Silanes, F., and Shleifer, A. (1999). Corporate ownership around the world. *Journal of Finance*, 54: 471–517.

Lee, D.S., Lim, G.H., and Lim, W.S. (2003). Family business succession: Appropriation risk and choice of successor. *Academy of Management Review*, 28(4): 657–666.

Levinson, H. (1971). Conflicts that plague family business. *Harvard Business Review*, 49(2).

Litz, R.A. (1995). The family business: Toward definitional clarity. *Family Business Review*, 8(2): 71–81.

Litz, R.A., Pearson, A.W., and Litchfield, S. (2012). Charting the future of family business research: Perspectives from the field. *Family Business Review*, 25: 16–32.

Long, R.G. and Chrisman, J.J. (2014). Management succession in family business. In *SAGE Handbook of Family Business.* Edited by Melin, L., Nordqvist, M., and Sharma, P. Sage: London, UK.

Martinez, M. and Aldrich, H. (2014). Sociological theories applied to family businesses. In *SAGE Handbook of Family Business.* Edited by Melin, L., Nordqvist, M., and Sharma, P. Sage: London, UK.

McGoldrick, M., Carter, B., and Garcia-Preto, N. (2010). *The Expanded Family Life Cycle: Individual, Family, and Community Perspectives*, 4th edition. New York: Pearson.

McKee, D., Madden, T.M., Kellermanns, F.W., and Eddleston, K.A. (2014). Conflicts in family firms: The good and the bad. In *SAGE Handbook of Family Business.* Edited by Melin, L., Nordqvist, M., and Sharma, P. London: Sage.

McKelvie, A., McKenny, A., Lumpkin, G.T., and Short, J.C. (2014). Corporate entrepreneurship in family businesses: Past contributions and future opportunities. In *SAGE Handbook of Family Business.* Edited by Melin, L., Nordqvist, M., and Sharma, P. Sage: London, UK.

McKenny, A.F., Short, J. C., Zachary, M.A., and Payne, G.T. (2012). Assessing espoused goals in private family firms using content analysis. *Family Business Review*, 25(3): 298–317.

McKenny, A.F., Payne, G.T., Zachary, M.A., and Short, J.C. (2014). Multilevel analysis in family business studies. In *SAGE Handbook of Family Business*. Edited by Melin, L., Nordqvist, M., and Sharma, P. Sage: London, UK.

Melin, L. and Nordqvist, M. (2007). The reflexive dynamics of institutionalization: The case of the family business. *Strategic Organization*, Vol 5(3): 321–333.

Miller, D. and LeBreton Miller, I. (2005). *Managing for the Long Run: Lessons in Competitive Advantage From Great Family Businesses*. Boston, MA: Harvard Business School Press.

Miller, D., Le Breton-Miller, I., Lester, R.H., and Cannella, A.A. (2007) Are family firms really superior performers? *Journal of Corporate Finance*, 13(5): 829–858.

Nicholson, N. (2014). Evolutionary theory: A new synthesis for family business thought and research. In *SAGE Handbook of Family Business*. Edited by Melin, L., Nordqvist, M., and Sharma, P. London: Sage.

Nordqvist, M., Hall, A., and Melin, L. (2009). Qualitative research on family businesses: The relevance and usefulness of the interpretive approach. *Journal of Management and Organization*, 15: 294–308.

Nordqvist, M. and Melin, L. (2010). Entrepreneurial families and family firms. *Entrepreneurship & Regional Development*, 22(3): 211–239.

Nordqvist, M. and Zellweger, T. (2010). *Transgenerational Entrepreneurship: Exploring Growth and Performance in Family Firms Across Generations*. Cheltenham, MA: Edward Elgar.

Nordqvist, M., Marzano, G., Brenes, E.R., Jimenez, G., and Fonseca-Paredes, M. (2011). *Understanding Entrepreneurial Family Business in Uncertain Environments: Opportunities and Resources in Latin America*. Cheltenham, MA: Edward Elgar.

Orozco, L.E.C. and González, G.C. (2014). Family firms and entrepreneurial families as breeding ground for virtues. In *Exploring Transgenerational Entrepreneurship: The Role of Resources and Capabilities*. Edited by Sharma, P., Sieger, P., Nason, R., Gonzalo, A.C., and Ramachandran, K. Cheltenham, MA: Edward Elgar.

Parada, M., Nordqvist, M., and Gimeno, A. (2010). Institutionalizing the family business: The role of professional associations in fostering a change of values. *Family Business Review*, 23(4): 355–372.

Pearson, W.A., Holt T.D., and Carr, C.J. (2014). Scales in family business studies. In *SAGE Handbook of Family Business*. Edited by Melin, L., Nordqvist, M., and Sharma, P. London: Sage.

Pérez Rodríguez, M.J. and Basco, R. (2011). The cognitive legitimacy of the family business field, *Family Business Review*, 24(4): 322–345.

Rau, S.B. (2014). Resource-based view of family firms. In *SAGE Handbook of Family Business*. Edited by Melin, L., Nordqvist, M., and Sharma, P. London: Sage.

Reay, T. and Zhang, Z. (2014). Qualitative methods in family business research. In *SAGE Handbook of Family Business*. Edited by Melin, L., Nordqvist, M., and Sharma, P. London: Sage.

Rogoff, E.G. and Heck, R.K.Z. (2003). Evolving research in entrepreneurship and family business: Recognizing family as the oxygen that feeds the fire of entrepreneurship. *Journal of Business Venturing*, 18: 559–566.

Rosa, P., Howorth, C., and Cruz, A.D. (2014). Habitual and portfolio entrepreneurship in the family context: longitudinal perspectives. In *SAGE Handbook of Family Business*. Edited by Melin, L., Nordqvist, M., and Sharma, P. London: Sage.

Salvato, C., Chirico, F., and Sharma, P. (2010). A farewell to the business: Championing exit and continuity in entrepreneurial family firms. *Entrepreneurial and Regional Development*, 22(3/4): 321–348.

Salvato, C. and Aldrich, H.E. (2012). 'That's interesting!' in family business research. *Family Business Review*, 25(2): 125–135.

Salvato, C., Minichilli, A., and Piccarreta, R. (2012). Faster route to the CEO suite: Nepotism or managerial proficiency? *Family Business Review*, 25(2): 206–224.

Salvato, C. and Corbetta, G. (2014). Strategic content and process in family business. In *SAGE Handbook of Family Business*. Edited by Melin, L., Nordqvist, M., and Sharma, P. London: Sage.

Sauerwald, S. and Peng, M.W. (2013). Informal institutions, shareholder coalitions, and principal–principal conflicts. *Asia Pacific Journal of Management*.

Saxena, A. (2013). Transgenerational succession in business groups in India. *Asia Pacific Journal of Management*.

Sciascia, S. and Mazzola, P. (2008). Family involvement in ownership and management: Exploring nonlinear effects on performance. *Family Business Review*, 21(4): 331–345.

Schulze, W.S., Lubatkin, M.H., Dino, R.N., and Buchholtz, A.K. (2001). Agency relationships in family firms: Theory and evidence. *Organization Science*, 12(2): 99–116.

Shanker, M.C. and Astrachan, J.H. (1996). Myths and realities: Family businesses' contribution to the US economy. A framework for assessing family business statistics. *Family Business Review*, 9(2): 107–123.

Sharma, P., Chrisman, J.J., and Chua, J.H. (1996). *A Review and Annotated Bibliography of Family Business Studies*. Norwell, MA: Kluwer Academic Publishers.

Sharma, P. (2004). An overview of the field of family business studies: Current status and directions for future. *Family Business Review*, 17(1): 1–36.

Sharma, P. and Manikutty, S. (2005). Strategic divestments in family firms: Role of family structure and community culture. *Entrepreneurship: Theory and Practice*, 29(3): 293–312.

Sharma, P., Hoy, F., Astrachan, J.H., and Koiranen, M. (2007). The practice driven evolution of family business education. *Journal of Business Research*, 60(10): 1012–1021.

Sharma, P. (2010). Advancing the 3Rs of family business scholarship: Rigor, Relevance, Reach. Volume 12 of *Advances in Entrepreneurship, Firm Emergence and Growth*. Edited by Stewart, A., Lumpkin, G.T., and Katz, J. 12: 383–400.

Sharma, P. and Carney, M. (2012). Value creation and performance in private family firms: Measurement and methodological issues. *Family Business Review*, 25(3): 233–242.

Sharma, P., Chrisman, J.J., and Gersick, K.E. (2012). 25 years of Family Business Review: Reflections on the past and perspectives for the future. *Family Business Review*, 25(1): 5–15.

Sharma, P. and Chua, J.H. (2013). Strategic management in Asian family enterprises. *Asia Pacific Journal of Management*.

Sharma, P. and Salvato, C. (2013). Family firm longevity: A balancing act between continuity and change. In *A Global Revolution: The Endurance of Large Family Businesses in the World*. Edited by Pérez. P.F. and Colli, A. Cambridge: Cambridge University Press.

Shukla, P., Carney, M., and Gedajlovic, E. (2014). Economic theories of family firms. In *SAGE Handbook of Family Business*. Edited by Melin, L., Nordqvist, M., and Sharma, P. London: Sage.

Sieger, P., Zellweger, T., Nason, R., and Clinton, E. (2011). Portfolio entrepreneurship in family firms: A resource based perspective. *Strategic Entrepreneurship Journal*, 5: 327–351.

Sirmon, D.G. and Hitt, M.A. (2003). Managing resources: Linking unique resources, management and wealth creation in family firms. *Entrepreneurship: Theory and Practice*, 27: 339–358.

Sirmon, D.G. (2014). Developing the field of family business research: Legitimization, theory, and distinctiveness. In *SAGE Handbook of Family Business*. Edited by Melin, L., Nordqvist, M., and Sharma, P. London: Sage.

Sorenson, R.L. (2014). Values in family businesses. In *SAGE Handbook of Family Business*. Edited by Melin, L., Nordqvist, M., and Sharma, P. London: Sage.

Starbuck, W.H. (2006). *The Production of Knowledge: The Challenge of Social Science Research*. Oxford: Oxford University Press.

Steier, L. and Ward, J.L. (2006). If theories of family enterprise really matter so does change in management education. *Entrepreneurship Theory & Practice*, 30(6): 887–895.

Steier, L. and Muethel, M. (2014). Trust and family businesses. In *SAGE Handbook of Family Business*. Edited by Melin, L., Nordqvist, M., and Sharma, P. London: Sage.

Stewart, A. and Hitt, M. (2012). Why can't a family business be more like a non-family business: Modes of professionalization in family firms. *Family Business Review*, 25(1): 58–86.

Stewart, A. (2014). The anthropology of family business: An imagined ideal. In *SAGE Handbook of Family Business*. Edited by Melin, L., Nordqvist, M., and Sharma, P. London: Sage.

Tagiuri, R. and Davis, J.A. (1992). On the goals of successful family companies. *Family Business Review*, 5(1): 263–281.

Vermeulen, F. (2007). I shall not remain insignificant: Adding a second loop to matter more. *Academy of Management Journal*, 50(4): 754–761.

Villalonga, B. and Amit, R. (2006). How do family ownership, control and management affect firm value? *Journal of Financial Economics*, 80: 385–417.

Von Schlippe, A. and Schneewind, K.A. (2014). Theories from family psychology and family therapy. In *SAGE Handbook of Family Business*. Edited by Melin, L., Nordqvist, M., and Sharma, P. London: Sage.

Walsh, F. (2003). Normal Family Processes: Growing diversity and complexity. 3rd edition. The Guilford Press: NY.

Ward, J. (1987). Keeping the family business healthy: How to plan for continuing growth, profitability, and family leadership. San Francisco, CA: Jossey-Bass.

Wennberg, K. Hellerstedt, K., Wiklund, J., and Nordqvist, M. (2011). Implications of Intra-Family and External Ownership transfer of family firms: Short-term and Long-term performance Differences. *Strategic Entrepreneurship Journal*, 5(4): 352–373.

Westhead, P. and Cowling, M. (1998). Family firm research: The need for a methodology rethink. *Entrepreneurship: Theory and Practice*, 23(1): 31–56.

Westhead, P. and Howorth, C. (2007). Types of private family firms: An exploratory conceptual and empirical analysis. *Entrepreneurship and Regional Development*, 19: 405–431.

Whetten, D., Foreman, P., and Dyer Jr, G.W. (2014). Organizational identity and family business. In *SAGE Handbook of Family Business*. Edited by Melin, L., Nordqvist, M., and Sharma, P. London: Sage.

Yu, A., Lumpkin, G.T., Sorenson, R.L., and Brigham, K. H. (2012). The landscape of family business outcomes: A summary and numerical taxonomy of dependent variables. *Family Business Review*, 25: 33–57.

Zahra, S.A., Labaki, R., Gawad, S.G.A., and Sciascia, S. (2014). Family firms and social innovation: Cultivating organizational embeddedness. In *SAGE Handbook of Family Business*. Edited by Melin, L., Nordqvist, M., and Sharma, P. London: Sage.

Zahra, S. and Sharma, P. (2004). Family business research: A strategic reflection. *Family Business Review*, 17(4): 331–346.

Zellweger, T.M., Nason, R.S., and Nordqvist, M. (2012). From longevity of firms to transgenerational entrepreneurship of families: Introducing family entrepreneurial orientation. *Family Business Review*, 25(2): 136–155.

Zellweger, T.M. (2014). Toward a paradox perspective of family firms: The moderating role of collective mindfulness in controlling families. In *SAGE Handbook of Family Business*. Edited by Melin, L., Nordqvist, M., and Sharma, P. London: Sage.

PART I

Theoretical Perspectives in Family Business Studies

Theories from Family Science: A Review and Roadmap for Family Business Research

Jennifer E. Jennings, Rhonda S. Breitkreuz
and Albert E. James

INTRODUCTION

A startling trend is evident within the past 25 years of family business research. What began as a field informed by theories of both business *and* family has become a domain weighted heavily towards the former. Consider these findings from our comprehensive bibliographic analysis of 2240 scholarly articles published on the topic of family enterprise between 1985 and 2010 (James et al., 2012). In 1985, less than 1 in every 5 articles published (18 percent) drew primarily upon theories of business; by 2010, the proportion had jumped to almost one half (49 percent). In sharp contrast, while almost one third (29 percent) of the articles published in 1985 drew primarily upon theories of family, 25 years later that proportion had fallen to less than 1 in a 100 (under 1 percent).

In our view, the decreased usage (if not virtual disappearance) of family-oriented theories is not only noteworthy but also lamentable, contributing to a sense of 'lopsidedness' within recent family business research (Dyer, 2003;

Dyer and Dyer, 2009). Indicators of this asymmetry include the fairly limited range of topics studied relative to those deserving of scholarly attention, the tendency to adopt an insufficiently differentiated view of family firms, and an over-emphasis on the family enterprise – rather than the enterprising family (Moores, 2009) – as the unit of analysis (Melin et al., 2014). The consequence is a field that has perhaps strayed a bit too far from its distinctive focus; that is, from building knowledge about the '*reciprocal* influence of family and business' (Zahra and Sharma, 2004: 333; emphasis added).

In light of these drifts, the overarching purpose of this chapter is to demonstrate how the resurrection of theories from family science can further the distinctive focus of family business research: first, by enriching current understanding of how family affects business; and second, by stimulating lesser-asked questions about how business affects family. Restoring a greater sense of balance at this juncture is important not merely for broadening the scope of future research but also, and more importantly, for ensuring the most beneficial implications of that research in practice. This is because a lack of attention to either domain – business *or* family – is likely to trigger a negative spiralling effect that exacerbates or creates problems within both over time. Moreover, inadequate attention to the family sphere is likely to be especially problematic given that good business performance is rarely sufficient for overcoming poor family relations, which, if left unaddressed, can subsequently interfere with the long-term survival of family firms (Ward, 1997; Olson et al., 2003 and Sharma, 2004).

To demonstrate the value of re-integrating family theories more firmly within family business research, we have structured our chapter as follows. We start by delineating the domain of family science and explaining why we selected the five focal theories. In our ensuing coverage of each theory, we first summarize its intellectual roots, core constructs, central premises, and fundamental questions. We then offer examples of how the theoretical perspective has been explicitly or implicitly invoked within extant research. Following this, we demonstrate the theory's promise for future research, paying especial attention to how it can be integrated with a prevailing business-oriented perspective to generate exciting new questions worthy of examination. Finally, in the spirit of both informed pluralism (Willmott, 2008) and giving back to the discipline from which we have borrowed (Zahra and Sharma, 2004; Sharma et al., 2007), we reflect briefly upon how the selected theories from family science can themselves be enriched when considered within the context of family enterprise.

OVERVIEW OF THE SELECTED THEORIES FROM FAMILY SCIENCE

Family science is an applied, interdisciplinary field of study. Scholarship in this discipline tends to focus on family relationships, processes, communication, wellbeing and experiences in various socio-cultural, economic, and political contexts. Prominent conferences such as The National Council on Family Relations and Community, Work and Family regularly feature leading-edge research and discourse on these topics. The field's top scholarly publication outlets include the *Journal of Marriage and Family*, *Journal of Family Issues* and *Family Relations.* For more comprehensive reviews of the theories covered in this chapter (and others), we encourage interested readers to consult recently published handbooks by Bengtson et al. (2005), White and Klein (2008), and Smith et al. (2009).

Although numerous other foundational theories used in family science could potentially be drawn upon to inform and enrich understanding of family enterprise, we decided to focus upon systems theory, life course theory, social exchange theory, structural functionalism, and symbolic interactionism. The main reason is that these are widely considered to constitute the major traditions within family scholarship (Dilworth-Anderson et al., 2005). Indeed, a recent study revealed that all but symbolic interactionism were among the top ten theoretical frameworks utilized within the *Journal of Marriage and Family* over the last decade (Taylor and Bagdi, 2005). Additional reasons specific to each theory also informed our choices.

For instance, we chose systems theory and life course theory because they are the perspectives that have been most obviously applied within the family business literature thus far. These theories are implicit in such popular analytic tools as Lansberg's (1983) two-circle model, Tagiuri and Davis' (1982) three-circle model, and Gersick et al.'s (1997) three-dimensional developmental framework. In contrast, we chose social exchange theory not because it is already highly salient within the family business literature, but because it shares a number of assumptions with what Chrisman et al. (2010) identified as the dominant perspective in contemporary research on family firms – agency theory. Because of this overlap, social exchange theory possesses considerable potential for extending agency research without contesting its key assumptions and central premises.

The final two family theories, structural functionalism and symbolic interactionism, were chosen because they are arguably the most enduring in family scholarship. Although the former is sometimes critiqued as outdated, it continues to be a dominant approach – particularly in empirical research that does not explicitly identify a guiding theoretical perspective, but implicitly uses neo-structural functionalist assumptions to identify research problems and questions (for elaboration of this argument see Lempert and DeVault, 2000; Kingsbury and Scanzoni, 2004; MacDermid et al., 2005). Symbolic interactionism is even older, yet is still considered instructive for understanding the importance of meaning and interaction within the family (LaRossa and Reitzes, 2004); moreover, core concepts from symbolic interactionism are evident in some of the newer family theories.

A condensed comparison of the five theories appears in Table 2.1. It should be noted that the relatively clear-cut manner in which we describe and distinguish each doesn't necessarily happen in practice, particularly at the level of model development and testing. We encourage readers to consult the illustrative set of papers listed within row 7 of the table for examples of the methodologies utilized within recent empirical work associated with each approach.

SYSTEMS THEORY

Summary of the Theoretical Perspective

Family systems theory is derived from general systems theory, which was developed to explain the behaviour of complex, organized systems. General systems theory is considered by some to be more of a worldview than a theory – one that incorporates 'a way of looking at the world in which objects are interrelated with one another' (Whitechurch and Constantine, 2004: 325). Systems theory emerged in family scholarship in the late 1950s, burgeoned in the 1980s, and remains prominent in family therapy and communication research in particular (Smith et al., 2009).

Family systems theorists tend to look at family *as* a system, rather than examining family *within* a larger macro-system context (Whitechurch and Constantine, 2004). In family systems theory, the family is viewed as a relatively closed system of interactions between individual members (Albanese, 2010). The focus is not so much on input variables such as the personalities of individual members, or output variables such as the outcomes of family interactions, but on the *interactions* themselves. As such, it is interested in intra-family processes such as family functioning, conflict, cohesion, and communication. Recent examples include Doherty and Craft (2011) and Garrett-Peters et al. (2011).

Several key assumptions of systems theory are used in family scholarship. Perhaps the most important is that a family system must be understood as a whole. In other words, the behaviour of individual members, when looked at separately, will not provide an accurate picture of what is occurring (Whitechurch and Constantine, 2004). Because of the interconnectedness between different components of the family system and the individuals within, the system looked at holistically is something different than separate individuals co-existing. Given this focus on the whole, pathology within families is not seen as attributable to single individuals but rather as a dysfunction of the entire system (Albanese, 2010).

Systems theorists also assume that humans, and thereby the systems in which they live, are capable of self-reflexivity. The self-reflexivity of a family system is facilitated through communication between individuals, creating an opportunity for the joint creation of meaning (Whitechurch and Constantine, 2004). In addition, because of this unique

Table 2.1   Summary of selected foundational theories predominant within the family science literature

	Systems	Life course	Social exchange	Structural functionalism	Symbolic interactionism
Intellectual roots	Emerged in the late 1950s; derived from general systems theory; early theorists include Bateson et al. (1950) and Kantor and Lehr (1975).	Emerged in the 1960s; derived from family development theory; early theorists include Hill and Rodgers (1964) and Elder (1974).	Emerged in the late 1950s; derived from market concept of exchange; early theorists include Homans (1961) and Thibaut and Kelly (1959).	Emerged in the post-war era; derived from American functionalism; early theorists include Parsons (1951).	Emerged in the 1920s; derived from American pragmatism; early theorists include Mead (1934), Cooley (1956) and Blumer (1969).
Core constructs	Interaction patterns within the whole family system (e.g., conflict, communication); self-reflexivity.	Life events, transitions, and pathways; historical context; linked lives between family members.	Resource exchange; social rewards and costs; self-interest; rationality; reciprocity; interdependence.	Normative and non-normative family compositions; spousal roles; child socialization; stability; equilibrium.	Symbols; values; behavioural norms; shared meanings; family identity; self-concept.
Central premises	The interconnections between family members impact the functioning of the family system.	The life pathways of individuals are influenced by the social ecology and historical context in which they live.	Family relationships entail a rational exchange of resources (social and economic) to maximize rewards and minimize costs.	Specified, gendered roles within normative family structures provide greater stability for family members and society.	Interactions between family members create shared identities through common symbols (e.g., situations and values).
Key assumptions	Individual behaviour is best understood through an analysis of the family system.	The timing and context of key events and transitions throughout an individual's life course are important.	Individuals are rational and motivated by self-interest in relationships.	The normative family unit best maintains equilibrium in the family and society.	Individuals develop concepts of self and identity primarily through interactions in the family.
Level of analysis	Family	Individual in social context	Individual	Family	Individual within family
Fundamental question	What are the processes or interactions within families that impact the overall functioning of the family system?	What are the implications of an individual's family context, and the timing of key events and transitions, on his or her life course?	What are the rewards and costs of family relationships for a particular individual in the family – and how do these influence his or her behaviour?	What are the effects of stability and instability in family structures on family members and other institutions?	How do a family's symbolic meanings and interaction patterns affect how individual family members think, feel and act?

	Systems	Life course	Social exchange	Structural functionalism	Symbolic interactionism
Recent work within the family science literature[a]	Doherty and Craft (2011); Garrett-Peters et al. (2011)	Kennedy et al. (2010); Rauscher (2011)	Donnelly and Burgess (2008); Nakonezny and Denton (2008)	Potter (2010); Zeiders et al. (2011)	Powell (2011); Sykes (2011)
Illustrative work within the family business literature	Davis and Stern (1981); Tagiuri and Davis (1982); Beckhard and Dyer (1983); Kepner (1983); Lansberg (1983)[b]; Hollander and Elman (1988); McCollom Hampton (1988); Whiteside and Brown (1991); Olson et al. (2003); Dyer (2006)[b]; Bjonberg and Nicholson (2007); Pieper and Klein (2007); Lumpkin et al. (2008); Distelberg and Blow (2011)	McGoldrick (1992); Kaye (1996); Gersick et al. (1997); Owens (2002); Klein (2008)[c]; Hoy and Sharma (2010)	Kellermanns and Eddleston (2007); Ward et al. (2007); Leaptrott and McDonald (2008)	Curimbaba (2002); Sharma and Manikutty (2005)[d]; Klein (2008)[c]	Lansberg (1983)[b]; Bertrand and Schoar (2006); Dyer (2006)[b]; Hall and Nordqvist (2008); Sharma and Manikutty (2005)[d]; Milton (2008); Sharma and Nordqvist (2008); Shepherd and Haynie (2009); Smith (2009)

[a] The studies included in this row are not about business-owning families per se. for examples of such studies see Table 2.2

[b] This article was classified as representative of both systems theory and symbolic interactionism; the former because of the conceptualizing of families as systems and the latter because of its focus upon behavioural norms and/or values.

[c] This article was classified as representative of both life course theory and structural functionalism; the former because of the use of life stages in its conceptualization, and the latter because of the reliance on structural characteristics to delineate family types.

[d] This article was classified as representative of both structural functionalism and symbolic interactionism; the former because of its frequent use of the term 'family structure' and the latter because of the specific manner in which the term was conceptualized, which focuses upon behavioural norms.

ability of humans to self-reflect, families are able to make plans and to establish goals for themselves. Inherent in the concept of self-reflexivity is the assumption of fluidity in interactions. The self-reflexivity of a family system enables a family to reflect upon and adapt previous transactions, therefore changing family interactions and processes. Family systems theory is therefore a dynamic rather than static theory of family processes.

In sum, systems theory looks at families as a whole, focusing on the interactions between members and how these contribute to the functioning of the entire system. The overarching question addressed by this approach is: *What are the processes or interactions within families that impact the overall functioning of the family system?*

Illustrative Work within the Family Business Literature

As indicated by the illustrative work listed within the bottom row of Table 2.1, systems theory is by far the most commonly and explicitly utilized approach within family business research of the five perspectives selected for this chapter. Much of this work, however, tends to invoke systems theory quite differently than the approach adopted within family scholarship. The most striking departure is the tendency of family business scholars to consider the family system as primarily open rather than closed; that is, as an entity that both influences and is influenced by others (especially the business system). Moreover, considerably more emphasis has been placed to date on how the family system negatively (or positively) impacts the business system rather than vice versa. Lansberg's (1983) discussion of how family norms create human resource problems in family firms represents a widely-recognized example of the former. McCollom Hampton's (1988) case study provides an important illustrative counterpoint, revealing not only how family systems can sometimes provide the coordination and control mechanisms missing within an organization – but also how a business can

sometimes provide family members with a means of individuation.

The 'dual system' approach to family enterprise research has been critiqued in several ways. One criticism is that it neglects other influential subsystems – a critique that contributed to the development of multi-system models incorporating ownership (Tagiuiri and Davis, 1982) and, more recently, the individual as well as the environment (Pieper and Klein, 2007). A second criticism is that the dual system approach tends to de-emphasize differences among family firms (Melin and Nordqvist, 2007). This critique has been partially addressed within more complex frameworks such as Gersick et al. (1997) three-dimensional developmental model. A third criticism is that the dual system approach has diverted attention away from understanding the family enterprise 'supra system' as a whole (Whiteside and Brown, 1991) – especially those pertaining to 'the functional interweaving of family and business' (Hollander and Elman, 1988: 161; see also Kepner, 1983). The sustainable family business model developed by Stafford et al. (1999) represents a noteworthy response to this third critique.

For further details on the above-noted and related work we encourage readers to consult the comprehensive reviews by Pieper and Klein (2007) and Sharma and Nordqvist (2008), which trace the evolution of systems-based research within the family business field. We conclude our own review by briefly summarizing three recent articles not included in theirs. Dyer (2006), for example, suggested that enhanced understanding of why certain family firms enjoy comparative advantage whereas others suffer comparative disadvantage might result from examining the effects of family systems deemed to be closed, random, open or synchronous based on characteristic interaction patterns and values. Bjornberg and Nicholson (2007) recently introduced the Family Climate Scales questionnaire, which they describe as 'a self-report measure of whole-family functioning formulated for the field of family business'

(p. 220) that is 'based on or compatible with family systems theory' (p. 231). Similarly, Lumpkin et al. (2008) proposed a multidimensional means of determining an individual's *family orientation*; that is, the extent to which family involvement is perceived and valued as a potential determinant of processes and outcomes in family firms. As a final recent example, Distelberg and Blow (2011) offer an intriguing extension to the 'supra system' approach in particular, demonstrating that family business systems characterized by either extremely rigid or extremely diffuse boundaries are non-optimal; instead, those with permeable boundaries offer the fewest challenges.

Potential New Directions for Family Business Research

Other extensions can be derived by re-visiting how systems theory tends to be invoked within family scholarship, identifying core constructs that have not yet been widely utilized within the family business literature, and then considering how these constructs can be integrated with the field's prevailing perspectives. As an illustration, consider family system theory's untapped potential to extend an approach that Chrisman et al. (2010) recently demonstrated to be predominant within contemporary family business research – the resource-based view (RBV). To demonstrate this potential, we apply constructs from systems theory that have been relatively under-examined by family business scholars to date; namely, a family's capacity for self-reflection and self-correction. Although Butler and Ko (2009) discussed the self-regulating and goal-adjusting behaviour of families in a paper presented at that year's *Theories of Family Enterprise* conference, which we expanded upon in a commentary upon their work (Jennings and James, 2009), these constructs have not yet been integrated with RBV research in particular.

We wonder whether a relationship exists between a family's capacity for self-reflection and self-correction and the focal RBV constructs of familiness and sustainable competitive advantage (Habbershon and Williams, 1999; Sirmon and Hitt, 2003). More specifically, does the intensity with which a business family engages in self-reflexivity influence the degree to which their firm can be deemed as possessing distinctive versus constrictive familiness? We might hypothesize, for instance, that those families which engage in more frequent self-reflection will be the ones that demonstrate distinctive, rather than constrictive, familiness within their firms. It may be, however, that the frequency with which a family engages in self-reflection may be less important than the quality of their reflexivity. This then raises questions about the preconditions that enable family members to engage in proactive and meaningful reflection upon how the family itself might be contributing to constrictive familiness within the firm and/or deviations from prior or desired levels of competitive advantage. Insights into questions like these may be gleaned from family systems research focused upon interaction patterns such as communication styles, decision-making practices, and approaches to conflict resolution.

LIFE COURSE THEORY

Summary of the Theoretical Perspective

Life course theory is a dynamic, contextual theory that seeks to understand the continuity and change of families over time and across generations. It is a theory that developed partly in response to changing family demographics in contemporary society, and partly as a response to critiques of family development theory (Bengston and Allen, 2004). Family development theory, which was originated by Hill and Duvall (1948), posited that families go through distinct stages of development, with specific tasks at each stage (courtship, marriage, childrearing, etc.). It was critiqued for having static and normative assumptions about universal family trajectories and for discounting the life experiences of individuals (Bengston and Allen, 2004).

In contrast, life course theory examines the experiences of individuals, while factoring in the importance of the social context in which the lives of individuals are embedded. In addition, it explicitly recognizes and addresses the heterogeneity of families. Therefore, life course theory marks a significant departure from family development theory in that it stresses the importance of looking not only at normative patterns and processes in the development of individuals and families, but also at their inherent diversity (Bengston and Allen, 2004). For recent examples of studies using a life course approach, see Kennedy et al. (2010) and Rauscher (2011).

Life course theory focuses on a few key concepts: context, time, and life pathways. The context, or social ecology, of an individual's life course is of particular interest. In understanding the social ecology of a person, life course theorists consider the broader social context of an individual's life, the social creation of meaning within the various life transitions that occur, and the inevitable changeability of the social environment. This perspective is thus dynamic, recognizing themes of continuity and change in an individual life course. In addition, this theory recognizes the dynamic agency of the individual who is not only influenced by the social ecology of his or her world, but also influences the family and social structures within which he or she is embedded (Bengston and Allen, 2004).

Also integral to life course theory are the life events and life transitions that occur through the passage of time. Bengston and Allen (2004) argue that a life course perspective in family science must include three key temporal dimensions: ontogenetic time (specific events in an individual lifetime that change interactions or individuals); generational time (life events or family transitions that change interactions or individuals); and historical time (life events in the larger social context that change individual and/or family values and roles). As such, the intersections between one's personal life story and social-historical time – life pathways (MacMillan and Copher, 2005) – are important in a life course perspective.

Life course theorists also examine 'linked lives' (Elder, 1994), or the interconnections between the life pathways of different individuals, especially family members. The premise here is that an individual's pathways influence another's experiences over the life course. For example, a significant job change (life transition) of one spouse will impact the life experience of the other. The notion of linked lives also extends across generations. For instance, the serious illness of a parent (life event) is not only likely to impact the day-to-day childhood experience of his or her children but also to shape their future life experiences.

To summarize, life course theory considers how social context, the timing of transitions, and the life pathways of individuals shape a particular life course. A central question derived from this perspective is: *What are the implications of an individual's family context, and the timing of key events and transitions, on his or her life course?*

Illustrative Work within the Family Business Literature

Family theorists would likely point out that much of the extant work within the family business literature that focuses on life stages is more appropriately characterized as having adopted a 'family development' rather than a 'life course' perspective. We nevertheless summarize this work here because of its distinct focus on the passage of time, which is shared with life course theory and is not as prominent within any of the other perspectives reviewed for this chapter. One noteworthy exception to this disclaimer is Owens' (2002) historical analysis of the relationship between a critical life event – the death of a family business owner – and the subsequent longevity of his or her firm under different forms of inheritance. We see this study as most reflective of the life course perspective because of its emphasis on the 'linked lives' between, in this case, a major life transition within the business family and the 'life pathway' of the family firm. Indeed, it is the only article in the dataset compiled for our bibliographic analysis (James et al., 2012) with an abstract containing the term 'life course'.

The following articles were identified within our dataset through the search term 'life cycle'. As a result, they collectively draw attention to the importance of a business family's developmental stage. Davis and Tagiuri (1989), for instance, investigated how different combinations of a father and son's life stages affected the quality of their working relationship within a family firm. And although not about business families per se, McGoldrick's (1992) article was published in the *Family Business Review* as a 'classic' – likely to remind readers of the complexity inherent in family, particularly when ethnicity is considered in concert with developmental phases. In contrast, Kaye's (1996) essay is firmly situated in the family firm context, but the causality between family and business dynamics is opposite to that in Davis and Tagiuri (1989). More specifically, Kaye argued that, in some instances, family businesses can interfere with the healthy life stage development of family members. Most recently, Klein (2008) utilized the concept of life stages to extend Milton's (2008) work on identity confirmation in family firms (which we summarize later in this chapter), suggesting that the effects of this process are likely to differ depending on the successor's stage of development.

Finally, it would be remiss of us not to include Gersick et al.'s (1997) widely-known three-dimensional developmental model as another illustrative example. Although this work does not appear within the dataset compiled for our bibliographic analysis (because it was published as a book rather than a journal article), the authors explicitly stated that they drew upon 'the many fine theorists studying family life cycles' (1997: 19) when constructing their model. As such, it is not surprising that one of the three axes delineates distinct stages in the development of business families – i.e., the young business family, entering the business family, working together family and passing the baton family – each with its unique set of challenges. Similarly, Hoy and Sharma's (2010) more recently published book also adopts a life cycle approach to understanding entrepreneurial family firms.

Potential New Directions for Family Business Research

Because family business scholars have primarily applied the construct of life stages in their work thus far, considerable potential exists to extend the field by invoking more contemporary concepts from the family life course perspective. We draw attention to three such constructs here: life transitions, linked lives, and historical time. Although we illustrate how these could be invoked to extend just one stream of family business scholarship – the RBV approach discussed previously – we encourage others to consider pairings with other prevailing perspectives and research topics.

In our view, the notions of life transitions, linked lives and historical time suggest interesting extensions to the fundamental question underlying the RBV approach to family enterprise, which pertains to the origins and effects of 'familiness'. For example, are there certain points in a family's life course that are more conducive to starting a business with greater potential to develop distinctive (rather than constrictive) familiness? We also wonder whether and how familiness is affected if major transitions in the 'linked lives' of the business family and the family business are experienced sequentially versus contemporaneously. Do families and businesses that weather crises within their separate spheres at the same time – such as a death in the former and an economic downturn in the latter – tend to experience an increase or decrease in familiness? And how are these dynamics affected by broader contextual events in historical time? For example, if a family business was founded during (or has previously survived) an economic recession, does this tend to engender a stronger sense of familiness?

SOCIAL EXCHANGE THEORY

Summary of the Theoretical Perspective

Emerging in the late 1950s, social exchange theory uses a market concept of exchange to explain the glue that maintains human relationships. Sociologists began to use the theory to examine how people use exchanges such as status, love and attractiveness to get their wants and needs met. Among others, George Homans (1961) is credited with bringing the theory to general sociology, suggesting that human behaviour is greatly influenced by reinforcement and punishment. As such, individuals negotiate with one another to maximize their gains (Smith et al., 2009). Other early social exchange theorists posited that 'every individual voluntarily enters and stays in any relationship only as long as it is adequately satisfactory in terms of his rewards and costs' (Thibault and Kelly, 1959: 37). Social exchange theory is premised on the notion that human social relationships are connected to the exchange of resources. See Donnelly and Burgess (2008) and Nakonezny and Denton (2008) for recent examples.

There are four key assumptions in this theory. The first is that individuals are motivated by self-interest (White and Klein, 2008). To this end, social relationships are often described as a kind of market. In this 'market', each individual behaves in a self-interested way in order to maximize his or her individual gains. Homans for instance, states that 'the open secret of human exchange is to give the other man behaviour that is more valuable to him than it is costly to you and to get from him behaviour that is more valuable to you than it is costly to him' (1961: 62). The

second key assumption is that individuals are constrained by their choices. In the attempt to maximize their gains and limit their losses, individuals use past experiences to make choices about the future (Smith et al., 2009). In this light, individual behaviour is understood through the actor's motivations, not by external factors. This is therefore a highly individualist theory. The third key assumption is that individuals are rational. Because humans are capable of rational thought, they will make decisions based on the least cost and most benefit to them. However, exchange theorists recognize that the perceived costs and benefits of particular decisions will vary over time, and between individuals. So, what seems like a rational choice to one person may be perceived differently by another. The fourth key assumption is that social relationships entail interdependence and reciprocity. Reciprocal gains must therefore be experienced by both individuals in any particular relationship. Related to this reciprocity is the expectation of fairness. That is, both parties must perceive the relationship to be beneficial in order to continue in the exchange (Smith et al., 2009).

In sum, social exchange theory views families as a social institution that entails both rewards and costs to the individual. According to this theory, then, a relationship will likely be maintained so long as the rewards to each member are greater than the costs to the individual. A central question for family scholars derived from this theoretical framework is: *What are the rewards and costs of family relationships for a particular individual in the family – and how do these influence his or her behaviour?*

Illustrative Work within the Family Business Literature

To locate illustrative work within the family business literature, we searched the 2240 articles constituting the dataset for our bibliographic analysis for those that contained the term 'exchange' in their abstract. Culling papers on stock exchange measures or ownership exchange left only a handful that could be deemed representative of the social exchange perspective from family science. We summarize the three articles published within business-oriented journals here, noting that others have been published in the family science literature (e.g., Gudmunson et al., 2009).

Kellermanns and Eddleston (2007) drew explicitly upon social exchange theory to offer a more nuanced view of the relationship between conflict and the performance of family firms. More specifically, they proposed that this relationship is likely to be moderated by 'family member exchange'; that is, by the level of reciprocity among family members. The findings from their survey of 51 family firms revealed that while a high level of family member exchange had the expected effect of attenuating the negative performance impact of process conflict, it had the unexpected effect of exacerbating the negative performance impact of cognitive conflict.

Ward et al. (2007) also focused upon social exchanges within family firms, but their emphasis was more on the nature of reciprocal obligations between employees and the firm – i.e., psychological contracts – than the level of reciprocity among family members. These scholars asserted that studying the former type of reciprocal obligations possesses considerable potential for developing a more comprehensive understanding of the complex human resource issues within family firms. One of their key illustrative propositions is that family employees are more likely than non-family employees to form relational or balanced contracts than either transactional or transitional contracts.

Leaptrott and McDonald (2008) applied a social exchange perspective to the creation of new family businesses. More specifically, they investigated the extent to which an adult child's decision to join his or her parents in starting a business venture is dependent upon the potential to establish reciprocal relationships rather than perpetuate historical attachment-based and/or hierarchy-based relationships between the two generations. Their survey findings revealed that adult children possess a clear preference for starting a venture that would create a reciprocal arrangement with their parents (i.e., as co-owners) over one that would continue arrangements based on attachment and/or hierarchy (i.e., as subordinates).

Potential New Directions for Family Business Research

Each of the articles summarized above draws attention to the same core construct from social exchange theory: the notion of reciprocal relationships. As such, in our ensuing discussion of potential new directions for family business research, we focus upon a different fundamental concept: the notion that relationships among family members involve resource exchanges that are social as well as economic in nature. In particular, we demonstrate how this notion can be utilized to extend work within the dominant paradigm underlying contemporary family firm research – agency theory (Chrisman et al., 2010) – even though the two perspectives share a number of basic assumptions.

As elaborated more fully elsewhere (James et al., 2012), we consider much agency-oriented research to be preoccupied with the central question of whether agency costs tend to be lower or higher in family firms relative to non-family firms and the consequent implications for comparative organizational performance. As such, considerable agency-oriented research examines the types of employment contracts that possess the potential to reduce agency costs. Much of this research tends to assume, however, that the 'agents' (i.e., managers) in family firms are not members of the owning family. In our view, one of the most intriguing potential extensions stems from questioning this basic assumption.

More specifically, what are the implications for agency-oriented research if more explicit attention was paid to the fact that many agents in family firms are actually members of the owning family? Although such family managers may not yet be owners (i.e., principals), it seems that they represent a distinct class of agent – one that could perhaps be labelled 'latent principals'. Given their intermediate status somewhere between pure agents and pure principals, we wonder about the implications for the employment contracts of these managers. For instance, are the family's social exchange principles (such as equality or need) or the firm's economic exchange principles (typically merit or equity) more important to the design of such contracts? We also wonder about the implications across different types of employment contracts. Are social exchange considerations more important for family versus non-family agents working within family firms – or are they less so? It would be interesting if researchers were to discover, for example, that economic rather than social contract breaches are reacted to more by family members, possibly because of the potential to repair the latter type of breach within the family sphere. These are but a handful of illustrative ways in which we can envision the social exchange perspective from family science extending extant work within only the agency-oriented stream of family business research. We encourage others to consider its potential contributions to other dominant paradigms and core topics. Pairing social exchange theory with resource dependence theory in future research on family firms seems particularly germane and potentially informative.

STRUCTURAL FUNCTIONALISM

Summary of the Theoretical Perspective

Structural functionalism became an especially important theory of family sociology in the postwar era, dominating research from the early 1940s to the mid 1960s (Mann et al., 1997). It arose as a response to one of the pressing questions of the time: How could citizens be assured stability and safety within a post-industrial, post-war society? Talcott Parsons (1951), the founder of this

theory, suggested that the answer lay in the construction of a normative family unit that would be the foundational social building block of society. This family unit would provide two important social functions: the socialization of children and a place where adult personalities could be developed in a stable environment.

A few key assumptions shape structural functionalist theory. For one, the societal context is acknowledged to exert external forces upon families. These outside forces are often viewed as threats, and the role of the family unit is to serve as a buffer between them and the wellbeing of family members. Central also to structural functionalism is the assumption that families socialize children, and that this function provides the stability essential for the maintenance of society (Smith et al., 2009). In addition, structural functionalists assume that this stability is achieved when there is equilibrium, or balance, in the family. Balance is best maintained through compliance with a narrowly defined notion of family; i.e., the traditional structure consisting of husband, wife, and children (Kingsbury and Scanzoni, 2004).

Spousal roles are very clearly delineated within this traditional family structure. The husband plays the 'instrumental' role of the breadwinner and serves as the bridge between the family and the outside world, his purpose being to maintain economic viability within the home as well as protecting the family from the hazards of the outer world. In turn, the wife plays the 'expressive' role, with a focus on maintaining relationships within the family, and providing a safe haven where the family can develop emotional relationships and maintain equilibrium. Finally, structural-functionalists assume interdependence between the different roles: although distinct and differentiated by sex, they both serve vital functions within the family (Kingsbury and Scanzoni, 2004).

Today, structural functionalism continues to be a predominant theory in family scholarship, although it is often implicitly rather than explicitly acknowledged as a theoretical perspective (Stacey, 2000). Implicitly, structural functionalist assumptions often influence the kinds of questions family scholars ask, underlying those dealing with stability, structure and adjustment to non-normative family formations (Kingsbury and Scanzoni, 2004; MacDermid et al., 2005). See Potter (2010) and Zeiders et al. (2011) for recent examples. Given that a key theoretical outcome of structural functionalism is that diversions from traditional family forms promote instability in other social groups, the fundamental question within this paradigm can be expressed as follows: *What are the effects of stability and instability in family structures on family members and other institutions?*

Illustrative Work within the Family Business Literature

To date, very little family business research has drawn explicitly upon structural functionalism. A search of the articles included within our bibliographic analysis, for instance, revealed very few published within business-oriented journals that even mention the term 'family structure' in their abstracts. Those that do, however, offer provocative glimpses into the potential of a structural-functional lens for deepening the field's understanding of how family can affect processes and outcomes within family firms.

Curimbaba (2002) is one illustrative example. This study examined how a key structural feature of families – the gender composition and ordering of children – influences the experiences of daughters working within their family's business. The findings revealed stark differences between the experiences of daughters with older brothers and those who were either the eldest of their siblings or from families with only female offspring. This structural feature of the business-owning family shaped not only the daughter's socialization towards business in general, but also perceptions of her role within the family firm and her consequent visibility as a manager and potential successor. In particular, daughters with older brothers tended to be viewed by themselves and others as

'invisible' heiresses whereas those from other family structures tended to be viewed as either 'professional' or even 'anchor' heiresses.

Sharma and Manikutty's (2005) article also emphasizes the term 'family structure', but both the conceptualization of this term and the discussion of associated effects differ considerably from Curimbaba (2002). With respect to the notion of family structure, for instance, Sharma and Manikutty (2005) invoked Todd's (1985) typology, which classifies families into four broad types based on values and norms regarding inter-generational authority versus liberty and intra-generational equality versus inequality. The authors then developed a series of propositions delineating how these family 'structures' differentially impact the speed with which strategic divestments are implemented in family firms. Such decisions are expected to take longest within firms run by families that uphold norms of both parental authority and sibling equality.

Finally, a structural functional lens is implicit within one of Klein's (2008) key extensions of Milton's (2008) work on identity confirmation in family firms. Klein suggested that the role of identity confirmation in such firms is likely to depend upon the type of business-owning family. Structural characteristics such as the number and diversity of family members are utilized to derive four types of increasingly complex family structures: (1) *core* families comprised of parents and their direct offspring living in the same household; (2) *extended* families consisting of that core family's direct relatives; (3) *patchwork* families that contain step-children; and (4) *multigenerational kinship* families 'with more than 50 or 100 members' (Klein, 2008: 1085).

Potential New Directions for Family Business Research

Given the paucity of family business research conducted to date from a structural-functional lens, numerous opportunities exist for future work. Given that we discussed potential integrations with agency theory and the resource-based view elsewhere (James et al., 2012), here we focus on how it might fruitfully extend another increasingly-utilized perspective: stewardship theory. As described by Le Breton-Miller and Miller, the stewardship approach views individuals within family firms as not only motivated by self-interest but also 'driven by higher-level needs such as self-actualization, social contribution, loyalty and generosity' (2009: 1171). The fundamental question within this and other work (e.g., Eddleston and Kellermanns, 2002; Eddleston et al., 2012; Miller and Le Breton-Miller, 2006) seems to be: How do individuals develop a sense of stewardship towards a family business – and with what consequences for the firm?

In our view, one of the key potential contributions of structural functional theory for stewardship research involves explicating the conditions within the family that are more or less likely to foster such a mentality. Illustrative research questions can be derived from the theory's emphasis on spousal roles and child socialization. For instance, how do the career choices of parents – especially with regards to actively participating (or not) in the family business – influence whether their children think and act like stewards of the firm? We would hypothesize that a sense of stewardship is more likely to be fostered when *both* parents play significant roles in the family business. Our reasoning is that in such situations, children are less likely to vicariously develop a sense of entitlement by observing one parent benefit financially from the firm without being actively involved within it. We note the irony of such an arrangement, however, which would be deemed a departure from the traditional spousal roles espoused by early structural functionalists.

SYMBOLIC INTERACTIONISM

Summary of the Theoretical Perspective

Symbolic interaction theory, a perspective associated with scholars such as Cooley (1956), Mead (1967 [1934]), and Blumer (1969), seeks to understand the behaviours of individuals through the creation of meaning that comes through interactions with others. The primary interest of symbolic interactionism is to understand 'how humans in concert with one another create symbolic worlds and how these worlds, in turn shape human behavior' (LaRossa and Reitzes, 2004: 136). Given its name, it is perhaps unsurprising that the constructs central to understanding this theory consist of *symbols* and *interactions*. Symbols refer to the shared meanings attributed to particular objects, situations, or values. Interactions refer to the social exchanges and connections that individuals have with other key people in their lives. Together, symbols and interactions create an understanding of shared meaning that facilitates the development of individual and family identities. See Powell (2011) and Sykes (2011) for examples of recent studies.

Three key assumptions shape the symbolic interactionist perspective. The first is that the development of a *self-concept* is very important for individuals (Smith et al., 2009). The self, according to Mead (1967 [1934]), is developed through a continual interaction between 'I' and 'me'. In this conceptualization, the 'I' represents the spontaneous self, whereas the 'me' represents the social self that learns how to behave through interaction with others. Similarly, Cooley (1956) discussed the concept of the 'looking-glass self', in which individuals develop their identity through interactions with, and responses from, others. Through this process of interactions, individuals attain feedback about their behaviours, most often from their primary social groups such as the family (Smith et al., 2009).

Another key assumption of symbolic interactionsim is that human behaviour can be understood through gaining insight into the *meaning* that individuals attribute to particular objects, events, or situations. These meanings vary according to an individual's context, life experience, and value base. According to symbolic interactionist theory, the meaning we attribute to symbols is developed through our interactions with other influential individuals, and through the feedback received in our interactions (LaRossa and Reitzes, 2004).

The third key assumption in symbolic interactionism is that the environment into which an individual is born is filled with values and symbols that influence his or her development. According to symbolic interactionists, families are the key social groups in an individual's environment contributing to identity development. Through interactions with other family members, values are attained and appraised (Burgess, 1926; Handel, 1985). Individual family members align their behaviours within meanings held by others within their family, and each family and its members ultimately develop behavioural and role norms (LaRossa and Reitzes, 2004; Smith et al., 2009). Individual identity is thus shaped within the context of families and the meaning of the interactions occurring within them.

To summarize, symbolic interactionism seeks to understand how individual behaviour is moulded through interactions with others and the meaning that results from common understandings of particular social worlds. The fundamental question for family scholars working within this paradigm can be expressed as follows: *How do a family's symbolic meanings and interaction patterns affect how individual family members think, feel and act?*

Illustrative Work Within the Family Business Literature

Our bibliographic analysis revealed only one article published within a family business journal that explicitly mentioned the term 'symbolic interactionism' in its abstract. Hall and Nordqvist drew upon this theory to argue that effective professional managers within family firms need to be 'sensitive to the owner family's values and norms as well as to their goals and meanings of being in business' (2008: 56). Indeed, the primary

conclusion drawn from their comparative case analysis is that CEOs who do not possess this type of cultural sensitivity are likely to fail in their role despite possessing impressive formal qualifications.

A handful of family business articles can be deemed as having implicitly adopted a symbolic interactional lens even though this term was not explicitly mentioned in their abstracts. Of these, most have focused on family values. At the macro level, for example, Bertrand and Schoar (2006) demonstrated how national-level differences in the importance attached to family values contribute to cross-country differentials in a wide variety of economic outcomes (GDP, self-employment rates, proportion of total market value controlled by families, etc). At a more meso level, Lansberg (1983) detailed how contradictions between normative family and organizational principles create problems for effective human resource management in family firms. Adopting a more positive stance, Sharma and Nordqvist (2008) argued that the performance of different types of family firms depends upon the fit between the guiding values of the family and the governance structures instituted within the business. And at a more micro level, Smith (2009) used qualitative interview data to demonstrate how family stories – or 'familial fables' – act as transmitters of family and business values to next-generation members.

Articles emphasizing the concepts of family/self identity rather than family values can also be considered as having implicitly drawn upon symbolic interactionism. Shepherd and Haynie's (2009) essay is a case in point. Recognizing the tension that often arises between a business-owning family's identity and that of the firm, these scholars introduced the notion of a 'family-business meta-identity' as a potential means of resolving such conflict. Milton (2008) called attention to self rather than family identity, arguing that the confirmation of an individual's identity within a family firm can act as a competitive resource. Finally, the articles by Sharma and Manikutty (2005) and Dyer (2006) summarized previously could also be considered reflective of a symbolic interactionist perspective because of their emphasis on a family's behavioural norms.

Potential New Directions for Family Business Research

Given that an emergent body of family business research is starting to coalesce around the constructs of family norms, values and identity, here we raise potential new directions suggested by two lesser-utilized concepts from symbolic interactionism: shared understandings and symbols. In each case, we illustrate how these constructs can be invoked to develop extant work from the stewardship perspective in particular (for potential integrations with agency and RBV approaches, see James et al., 2012). When doing so, we consider the possibility that these shared understandings and symbols exist and are utilized not only *within* a business-owning family (see the articles by Micelotta and Raynard, 2011, and Parmentier, 2011, on building a family brand) but also *between* the members of this family and the non-family members who work within the family's firm.

One such extension involves exploring whether stewardship attitudes and behaviours are more prevalent amongst non-family employees when there is a greater shared understanding amongst family members (especially those working within the business) that the firm exists for reasons beyond maximizing the wealth of the owning family. This type of enquiry is consistent with the more general question of whether certain types of shared understandings are especially effective at fostering stewardship within family firms. Other interesting extensions flow from the notion of symbols. For instance, what sort of symbols do owning families use to create a sense of stewardship amongst organizational members? Although Smith (2009) has called attention to the symbolic potential of familial narratives, we wonder about the relative prevalence, salience, and

impact of other forms, such as visual artefacts and/or dramatic events. We also wonder if ambiguity within these symbols can unintentionally foster *non*-stewardship attitudes and behaviours. For instance, is it possible for members of owning families to use symbols in such a patently instrumental manner that they provoke non-family employees to think and act more like agents? One business family that we are aware of, for example, gave event tickets to its non-family employees – but only when they had received the tickets for free themselves from suppliers. Over time, this gesture came to be resented, as it was viewed as a further symbol of the owning family's lack of genuine generosity towards its non-family employees.

CONCLUSION

We started this chapter by calling attention to a rather startling observation and by articulating a rather lofty objective. The starting observation was the steady decline – and now near disappearance – of family-oriented theories relative to business-oriented theories over the past 25 years of family business research (James et al., 2012). Our lofty objective was to join others seeking to stimulate a reversal of this trend (Aldrich and Cliff, 2003; Dyer, 2003; Rogoff and Heck, 2003; Sharma et al., 2007; Dyer and Dyer, 2009), by demonstrating the value of resurrecting family scholarship to a more prominent position within the field's future research agenda. Through the process of summarizing five of the most enduring and influential theoretical perspectives within family science, and reviewing how each has been applied within the family business literature thus far, two additional observations became salient.

The first can be expressed as follows. Although the relatively small corpus of work drawing upon family theory has undoubtedly contributed interesting and insightful understandings to the phenomenon of family enterprise, we couldn't help but notice that family business scholars have tended to utilize select

Table 2.2   Potential extensions of family theory and research suggested by scholarship on family enterprise

	Systems	Life course	Social exchange	Structural functionalism	Symbolic interactionism
Fundamental question within focal family-oriented perspective	What are the processes or interactions within families that impact the overall functioning of the family system?	What are the implications of an individual's family context, and the timing of key events and transitions, on his or her life course?	What are the rewards and costs of family relationships for a particular individual in the family – and how do these influence his or her behaviour?	What are the effects of stability and instability in family structures on family members and other institutions?	How do a family's symbolic meanings and interaction patterns affect how individual family members think, feel and act?
Illustrative work within family scholarship examining business families and their firms	Matheny and Zimmerman (2001); Lee et al. (2006)	Paul et al. (2003); Glauben et al. (2004)	Gudmunson et al. (2009)	Kaslow (2005); Guttman and Yacouel (2007)	Haugh and McKee (2003); Philbrick and Fitzgerald (2007)
Potential extensions of existing family-oriented theory and research	*From RBV:* Are the interaction patterns within business-owning families influenced by their firms' degree of distinctive familiness – and with what consequences for the functioning of the overall family system?	*From RBV:* How does the nature and timing of major changes in a firm's comparative advantage influence the life pathways of individuals within a business-owning family?	*From agency:* Are the rewards and costs of family relationships calculated differently for individuals who are 'principals' or 'latent principals' of a family business?	*From stewardship:* To what extent is stability (or instability) within business-owning families associated with a stewardship mentality towards the business (or lack thereof)?	*From stewardship:* What sort of symbols and rituals do business-owning families utilize within the family setting to foster a sense of stewardship towards the firm amongst next-generation members?

aspects of the various perspectives – and not always those considered most central within the field of family science. Instead of viewing this observation as a critique we prefer to portray it as an opportunity, for it implies that a great deal of richness inherent in the original family theories remains untapped. Indeed, the illustrative new directions associated with each perspective that we presented within this chapter barely scratch the surface of this untapped potential.

The second emergent observation also stems from the predominant manner in which the family theories have been invoked within family business research to date. Much (if not most) of the extant work has primarily drawn upon these theories to explain how family (often negatively) impacts business.

In contrast, comparatively few studies have examined either reciprocal relationships between the two domains or how business impacts family (see also Yu et al., 2012). While the previously mentioned studies by McCollom Hampton (1983) and Olson et al. (2003) represent notable examples of the former, Kaye's (1996) essay, which we also summarized earlier, represents an intriguing example of the latter. So, too, does Mehotra et al.'s (2010) analysis, which demonstrates how succession decisions within Japanese family firms can sometimes change the composition of business-owning families through the addition of adopted sons.

In Table 2.2, we offer a 'mini-roadmap' for furthering research related to lesser-asked questions about the impacts of business on family. Following the tenets of informed pluralism (Wilmott, 2008), in this final summary table we re-state the fundamental questions underlying the major traditions within family scholarship selected for this chapter, recognize extant work within this sister discipline that has examined business-owning families, and raise potential extensions for that field by reversing the causality of the same family and business theory pairings invoked earlier. In other words, we consider the potential of constructs from the business-oriented paradigms to inform family-oriented questions, rather than vice versa.

We expand much more fully upon the implications of business ownership for family scholarship in a special issue of *Family Relations* (Jennings et al., 2013). We hope this chapter inspires others to not only borrow from the rich, rigorous, and relevant field of family science but also give back to this sister discipline. We also hope it renews interest in furthering what several prominent scholars (e.g., Astrachan, 2003; Zahra and Sharma, 2004; Pieper and Klein, 2007) see as the family business field's most distinctive focus – the reciprocal influence of family and business.

NOTE

This chapter benefited greatly from the detailed, knowledgeable, and encouraging feedback provided by the reviewer and our handling editor, Pramodita Sharma. We would also like to acknowledge the research assistance provided by Laura Wunderli, as well as the financial support provided by SSHRC Grant No. 410–2009–0321 awarded to the first author.

REFERENCES

Albanese, P. (2010). Introduction to Canada's families: Historical and recent variations, definitions, and theories. In D. Cheal (ed.), *Canadian Families Today: New Perspectives* (2nd edn, pp. 2–26). Don Mills, ON: Oxford University Press.

Aldrich, H.E. and Cliff, J.E. (2003). The pervasive effects of family on entrepreneurship: Towards a family embeddedness perspective. *Journal of Business Venturing*, 18, 573–596.

Astrachan, J.H. (2003). Commentary on the special issue: The emergence of a field. *Journal of Business Venturing*, 18, 567–572.

Bateson, G., Jackson, D., and Weakland, J. (1950). Toward a theory of schizophrenia. *Behaviour Science*, 1, 251–264.

Beckhard, R. and Dyer, W. (1983). Managing continuity in the family-owned business. *Organizational Dynamics*, 12(1), 4–12.

Bengtson, V., Acock, A., Allen, K., Dilworth-Anderson, P., and Klein, D. (2005). Theory and theorizing in family research. In V. Bentsong, A. Acock, K. Allen, P. Dilworth-Anderson, and D. Klein, *Sourcebook of Family Theory and Research* (pp. 3–14). Thousand Oaks: Sage.

Bengtson, V. and Allen, K. (2004). The life course perspective applied to families over time. In P. Boss, W. Doherty, R. LaRossa, W. Schumm, and S. Steinmetz, *Sourcebook of Family Theories and Methods: A Contextual Approach* (pp. 469–499). New York: Springer.

Bertrand, M. and Schoar, A. (2006). The role of family in family firms. *Journal of Economic Perspectives*, 20(2), 73–96.

Bjornberg, A. and Nicholson, N. (2007). The family climate scales-development of a new measure for use in family business research. *Family Business Review*, 20(3), 229–246.

Blumer, H. (1969). *Symbolic Interactionism*. Englewood Cliffs, NJ: Prentice Hall.

Burgess, E. (1926). The family as a unity of interacting personalities. *The Family*, 7, 3–9.

Butler, J. and Ko, S. (2009). Family systems, family business system, and system dynamics, Presented at the 2009 Theories of Family Enterprise Conference, Boston, MA.

Chrisman, J., Kellermanns, F., Chan, K., and Liano, K. (2010). Intellectual foundations of current research in family business: An identification and review of 25 influential articles. *Family Business Review*, 23(1), 9–26.

Cooley, C. (1956). *Social Organisation*. Glencoe, IL: Free Press.

Curimbaba, F. (2002). The dynamics of women's roles as family business managers. *Family Business Review*, 15(3), 239–252.

Davis, P. and Stern, D. (1981). Adaptation, survival, and growth of the family business: An integrated systems perspective. *Human Relations*, 34(3), 207–224.

Davis, J. and Tagiuri, R. (1989). The influence of life stage on father–son work relationships in family companies. *Family Business Review*, 2(1), 47–74.

Dilworth-Anderson, P., Burton, L., and Klein, D. (2005). Contemporary and emerging theories in studying families. In V. Bengston, A. Acock, K. Allen, P. Dilworth-Anderson, and D. Klein (eds), *Scourcebook of Family Theory and Research* (pp. 37–50). Thousand Oaks, CA: Sage.

Distelberg, B. and Blow, A. (2011). Variations in family systems boundaries. *Family Business Review*, 24(1), 229–246.

Doherty, W. and Craft, S. (2011). Single mothers raising children with 'male-positive' attitudes. *Family Process*, 50(1), 63–76.

Donnelly, D. and Burgess, E. (2008). The decision to remain in an involuntary celibate relationship. *Journal of Marriage and Family*, 70(2), 519–535.

Dyer, W. (2003). The family: The missing variable in organisational research. *Entrepreneurial Theory and Practice*, 401–416.

Dyer, W. (2006). Examininig the 'family effect' on firm performance. *Family Business Review*, 19(4), 253–273.

Dyer, W. and Dyer, W. (2009). Putting family into family business research. *Family Business Review*, 22(3), 216–219.

Eddleston, K. and Kellermanns, F. (2002). Destructive and productive family relationships: A stewardship theory perspective. *Journal of Business Venturing*, 22, 545–564.

Eddleston, K., Kellermanns, F., and Zellweger, T. (2012). Exploring the entrepreneurial behavior of family firms: Does the stewardship perspective explain differences? *Entrepreneurship Theory & Practice*, 36(2), 347–367.

Elder, G. (1974). *Children of the Great Depression: Social Change in Life Experience*. Chicago, IL: University of Chicago Press.

Elder, G. (1994). Time human agency and social change: Perspectives on the life course. *Social Psychology Quarterly*, 57, 4–15.

Garrett-Peters, P., Mills-Koonce, R., Zerwas, S., Cox, M., and Vernon-Feagans, L. (2011). Fathers' early emotion talk: Associations with income, ethnicity, and family factors. *Journal of Marriage and Family*, 73(2), 335–353.

Gersick, K., Davis, J., McCollom Hampton, M., and Lansberg, I. (1997). *Generation to Generation: Life Cycles in Family Business*. Boston, MA: Harvard University Press.

Glauben, T., Tietjc, H., and Weiss, C. (2004). Intergenerational succession in farm households: Evidence from upper Austria. *Review of Economics and the Household*, 2(4), 443–462.

Gudmunson, C., Clinton, G., Danes, S., Werbel, J., and Loy, S. (2009). Spousal support and work – family

balance in launching a family business. *Journal of Family Issues*, 30(8), 1098–1121.

Guttman, J. and Yacouel, N. (2007). On the expansion of the market and decline of the family. *Review of Economics of the Household*, 5(1), 1–13.

Habbershon, T. and Williams, M. (1999). A resource-based framework for assessing the strategic advantages of famly firms. *Family Business Review*, 12(1), 1–25.

Hall, A. and Nordqvist, M. (2008). Professional management in extended family business: Toward an extended understanding. *Family Business Review*, 21(1), 51–69.

Handel, G. (1985). *The Psychosocial Interior of the Family* (3rd edn). New York: Aldine de Gruyter.

Haugh, H. and McKee, L. (2003). 'It's just like family'–shared values in the family firm. *Community, Work & Family*, 6(2), 141–158.

Hill, R. and Duvall, E. (1948). *Families Under Stress*. New York: Harper.

Hill, R. and Rodgers, R. (1964). The developmental approach. In H. Christensen, *Handbook of Marriage and the Family* (pp. 171–211). Chicago, IL: Rand McNally.

Hollander, B. and Elman, N. (1988). Family owned business: An emerging field of enquiry. *Family Business Review*, 1(2), 145–164.

Homans, G. (1961). *Social Behaviour: Its Elementary Forms*. New York: Harcourt, Brace & World.

Hoy, F. and Sharma, P. (2010). *Entrepreneurial Family Firms*. Upper Saddle River, NJ: Pearson Education.

James, A., Jennings, J., and Breitkreuz, R. (2012). Worlds apart? Re-bridging the distance between family science and family business research. *Family Business Review, 25th Anniversary Special Issue*, 25, 89–110.

Jennings, J., Breitkreuz, R. and James, A. (2013). When family members are also business owners: Is entrepreneurship good for families? *Family Relations*, 62, 472–489.

Jennings, J. and James, A. (2009). Strengthening the loops: Extending Butler & Ko (2009) general systems perspective on family business. *Theories of Family Business Conference*. Boston, MA.

Kantor, D. and Lehr, W. (1975). *Inside Family: Toward a Theory of Family Process*. San Francisco, CA: Jossey-Bass.

Kaslow, F. (2005). Maternal mentoring: A relatively new phenomenon in family business. *Journal of Family Psychotherapy*, 16(3), 11–18.

Kaye, K. (1996). When the family business is a sickness. *Family Business Review*, 9(4), 347–368.

Kellermanns, F. and Eddleston, K. (2007). A family perspective on when conflict benefits family firm performance. *Journal of Business Research*, 60(10), 1048–1057.

Kennedy, A., Agbenyiga, D., Kasiborski, N., and Gladden, J. (2010). Risk chains over a life course among homeless urban adolescent mothers: Altering their trajectories through formal support. *Children & Youth Services Review*, 32(12), 1740–1749.

Kepner, E. (1983). The family and the firm: A coevolutionary perspective. *Organizational Dynamics*, 12(1), 57–70.

Kingsbury, N. and Scanzoni, J. (2004). Structural-functionalism. In P. Boss, W. Doherty, R. LaRossa, W. Schumm, and S. Steinmetz (eds), *Sourcebook of Family Theories and Methods: A Conceptual Approach* (pp. 195–217). New York: Springer.

Klein, S. (2008). Commentary and extension: Moderating the outcome of identity confirmation in family firms. *Entrepreneurship Theory & Practice*, 32(6), 1083–1088.

Lansberg, I. (1983). Managing human resources in family firms: The problem of institutional overlap. *Organizational Dynamics*, (Summer), 29–38.

LaRossa, R. and Reitzes, D. (2004). Symbolic interactionism and family studies. In P. Boss, W. Doherty, R. LaRossa, W. Schumm, and S. Steinmetz (eds), *Sourcebook of Family Theories and Methods: A Conceptual Approach* (pp. 135–162). New York: Springer.

Le Breton-Miller, I. and Miller, D. (2009). Agency vs. stewardship in public family firms: A social embeddedness reconciliation. *Entrepreneurship Theory & Practice*, 33(6), 1169–1191.

Leaptrott, J. and McDonald, J. (2008). Entrepreneurial opportunity exploitation and the family: Relationship based factors that affect the adult child's decision to jointly participate with parents in a new venture. *Entrepreneurial Executive*, 13, 63–100.

Lee, Y., Danes, S., and Shelley, M. (2006). Work roles, management and perceived well-being for married women within family businesses. *Journal of Family and Economic Issues*, 22(3), 523–541.

Lempert, L. and DeVault, M. (2000). Guest editor's introduction: Special issue on emergent and reconfigured forms of family life. *Gender & Society*, 14, 6–10.

Lumpkin, G., Martin, W., and Vaughn, M. (2008). Family orientation: Individual level influences on family firm outcomes. *Family Business Review*, 21(2), 127–138.

MacDermid, S., Roy, K., and Zvonkovic, A. (2005). Don't stop at the borders: Theorizing beyond dichotomies of work and family. In V. Bengston, A. Acock, K. Allen, P. Dilworth-Anderson, and D. Klein (eds),

Sourcebook of Family Theory and Research (pp. 493–616). Thousand Oaks, CA: Sage.

MacMillan, R. and Copher, R. (2005). Families in the life course: Interdependency of roles, role configuration, and pathways. *Journal of Marriage and Family*, 67, 858–879.

Mann, S., Grimes, M., Kemp, A., and Jenkins, P. (1997). Paradigm shifts in family sociology? Evidence from three decades of family textbooks. *Journal of Family Issues*, 18, 315–349.

Mathenay, A. and Zimmerman, T. (2001). The application of family system theory to organizational consultation: A content analysis. *American Journal of Family Therapy*, 29(5), 421–433.

McCollom Hampton, M. (1988). Integration in the family firm: When the family system replaces controls and culture. *Family Business Review*, 1(4), 399–417.

McGoldrick, M. (1992). Ethnicity and the family life cycle. *Family Business Review*, 5(4), 437–459.

Mead, G. (1967 [1934]). *Mind, Self and Society*. Chicago, IL: University of Chicago Press.

Mehrotra, V., Morck, R., Shim, J., and Wiwattanakantang, Y. (2010). Apoptive expectations: Rising sons in Japanese family firms. *Western Finance Association Conference*. Victoria, Canada.

Melin, L. and Nordqvist, M. (2007). The reflexive dynamics of institutionalization: The case of family business. *Strategic Organization*, 5(3), 321–333.

Melin, L., Nordqvist, M., and Sharma, P. (2014). Introduction: Scope, evolution and future of family business studies. In L. Melin, M. Nordqvist, and P. Sharma (eds), *The Sage Handbook of Family Business*. London: Sage.

Micelotta, E. and Raynard, M. (2011). Concealing or revealing the family?: Corporate brand identity strategies in family firms. *Family Business Review*, 24, 197–216.

Miller, D. and Le Breton-Miller, I. (2006). Family governance and firm performance: Agency, stewardship, and capabilities. *Family Business Review*, 19(1), 73–87.

Milton, L. (2008). Unleashing the relationship power of family firms: Identity confirmation as a catalyst for performance. *Entrepreneurship Theory & Practice*, 32(1), 1063–1081.

Moores, K. (2009). Paradigms and theory building in the domain of business families. *Family Business Review*, 22(2), 167–180.

Nakonezny, P. and Denton, W. (2008). Marital relationship: A social exchange theory perspective. *American Journal of Family Therapy*, 36(5), 402–412.

Olson, P., Zuiker, V., Danes, S., Stafford, K., Heck, R., and Duncan, K. (2003). The impact of the family and the business on family business sustainability. *Journal of Business Venturing*, 18, 639–666.

Owens, A. (2002). Inheritance and the life-cycle of family firms in the early industrial revolution. *Business History*, 44(1), 21–46.

Parmentier, M. (2011). When David met Victoria: Forging a strong family brand. *Family Business Review*, 24, 217–232.

Parsons, T. (1951). *The Social System*. New York: Free Press.

Paul, J., Winter, M., Miller, N., and Fitzgerald, M. (2003). Cross institutional norms for timing and sequences and the use of adjustment strategies in families affiliated with family owned businesses. *Marriage & Family Review*, 35(1), 167–192.

Philbrick, C. and Fitzgerald, M. (2007). Women in business-owning families: A comparison roles, responsibilities, and predictors of family functionality. *Journal of Family and Economic Issues*, 28(4), 618–634.

Pieper, T. and Klein, S. (2007). The bulleye: A systems approach to modeling family firms. *Family Business Review*, 20(4), 301–319.

Potter, D. (2010). Psychosocial well-being and the relationship between divorce and children's academic achievement. *Journal of Marriage and Family*, 72(4), 933–946.

Powell, H. (2011). Letters to Louis: Marital dissolution through the social construction of lived experience. *Journal of Divorce & Remarriage*, 52(1), 19–32.

Rauscher, E. (2011). Producing adulthood: Adolescent employment, fertility, and the life course. *Social Science Research*, 40(2), 552–571.

Rogoff, E. and Heck, R. (2003). Evolving research in entrepreneurship and family business: Recognizing family as the oxygen that feeds the fire of entrepreneurship. *Journal of Business Venturing*, 18, 559–566.

Sharma, P. (2004). An overview of the field of family business studies: Current status and directions for the future. *Family Business Review*, 27(1), 1–36.

Sharma, P. and Manikutty, S. (2005). Strategic divestments in family firms: Role of family structure and community culture. *Entrepreneurship Theory & Practice*, (May), 293–311.

Sharma, P. and Nordqvist, M. (2008). A classification scheme for family firms: From family values to effective governance to firm performance. In J. Tapies and J. Ward (eds), *Family Values and Value Creation: The Fostering of Enduring Values Within Family-owned Businesses* (pp. 71–101). New York: Palgrave Macmillan.

Sharma, P., Hoy, F., Astrachan, J., and Koiranen, M. (2007). The practice-driven evolution of family business education. *Journal of Business Research*, 60, 1012–1021.

Shepherd, D. and Haynie, J. (2009). Family business identity, conflict, and expedited entrepreneurial process: A process of revolving indentity conflict. *Entrepreneurship Theory & Practice*, 33(6), 1245–1264.

Sirmon, D. and Hitt, M. (2003). Managing resources: Linking unique resources, management, and wealth creation in family firms. *Entrepreneurship: Theory and Practice*, 27(4), 339–358.

Smith, R. (2009). Mentoring and perpetuating the entrepreneurial spirit within family business by telling contingent stories. *New England Journal of Entrepreneurship*, 12(2), 27–40.

Smith, S., Hamon, R., Ingoldsby, B., and Miller, J. (2009). *Exploring Family Theories* (2nd edn). New York: University of Oxford Press.

Stacey, J. (2000). Family values forever. *Nation*, 273, 26–29.

Stafford, K., Duncan, K., and Winter, M. (1999). A research model of sustainable family businesses. *Family Business Review*, 12(3), 197–203.

Sykes, J. (2011). Negotiating stigma: Understanding mother's responses to accusations of child neglect. *Children & Youth Services Review*, 33(3), 448–456.

Tagiuri, R. and Davis, J. (1982). Bivalent attributes of the family firm. Working paper, Harvard Business School, Cambridge MA, Reprinted 1996. *Family Business Review*, 9(2), 199–208.

Taylor, A. and Bagdi, A. (2005). The lack of explicit theory in family research: A case analysis of the Journal of Marriage and Family 1990–1999. In A. Bengtson, K. Cook, K. Allen, P. Dilworth-Anderson, and D. Klein (eds), *Sourcebook of Family Theory and Research* (pp. 22–29). Thousand Oaks, CA: Sage.

Thibault, J. and Kelly, H. (1959). *The Social Psychology of Groups*. New York: Wiley.

Todd, E. (1985). *The Explanation of Ideology, Family Structures and Social Systems*. Oxford: Basil Blackwell.

Ward, J. (1997). Growing the family business: Special challenges and best practices. *Family Business Review*, 10(4), 323–337.

Ward, S., Envick, B., and Langford, M. (2007). On the theory of psychological contracts in family firms. *Entrepreneurial Executive*, 12, 37–50.

White, J. and Klein, D. (2008). *Family Theories*. Thousand Oaks, CA: Sage.

Whitechurch, G. and Constantine, L. (2004). Systems theory. In P. Boss, R. Doherty, R. LaRossa, W. Schumm, and S. Steinmetz (eds), *Sourcebook of Family*

Theories and Methods: A Contextual Approach (pp. 325–352). New York: Plenum.

Whiteside, M. and Brown, F. (1991). Drawbacks of dual systems approach to family firms: Can we expand our thinking? *Family Business Review*, 4, 383–385.

Willmott, H. (2008). For informed pluralism, broad relevance and critical reflexivity. In D. Barry, and H. Hansen (eds), *The Sage Handbook of New Approaches in Management and Organization* (pp. 82–83). London: Sage.

Yu, A., Lumpkin, G., Sorenson, R., and Brigham, K. (2012). The landscape of family business outcomes: A summary and numerical taxonomy of dependent varriables. *Family Business Review*, 25, 33–57.

Zahra, S. and Sharma, P. (2004). Family business research: A strategic reflection. *Family Business Review*, 17(4), 331–346.

Zeiders, K., Roosa, M., and Tein. J. (2011). Family structure and family processes in Mexican-American families. *Family Process*, 50(1), 77–91.

3

Theories from Family Psychology and Family Therapy

Arist von Schlippe and Klaus A. Schneewind

INTRODUCTION

It has long been evident that the way the overlap between family and business is managed is crucial in understanding success or failure in family businesses. Finding a conclusive theory of family firms that is able to take into account the reciprocal relationships between both systems, as well as integrating organizational theory and family systems theory, can be seen as the 'ultimate aim of the field of family business studies' (Sharma, 2004, p. 24). Such a theory would have to include the individual level, as well as the interpersonal and organizational levels, and explain how family firms are distinct from other companies. Of course, such an endeavor requires a broad scope of different disciplines to bring their knowledge together (see Fig. 3.1). Yet many authors, such as Zahra and Sharma, complain that 'the family business field still lacks coherence' and that 'family firm research remains fragmented in its focus and findings' (2004, p. 333).

This might have to do with the fact that the multiplicity of theories from different disciplines which are involved is difficult to handle: 'The field of family business studies has borrowed heavily from other disciplines, including psychology, sociology, economics, law, and family systems' (Zahra and Sharma, 2004, p. 336). On the other hand, there is still seen to be a predominance of economic theories in the field. Two recent reviews see agency or stewardship theory and/or the resource-based view as the most prominent paradigms: Chrisman et al. (2010) analyzed 25 of the most frequently cited family business (FB) research articles; Siebels and zu Knyphausen-Aufseß (in press) reviewed 235 publications. Though Sharma sees it as encouraging that other theoretical perspectives are gaining impact – '[approaches] such as behavioral agency, configurational approach, socio-emotional wealth, social identity theory, and stakeholder theory are beginning to surface as well' (2011, p. 6) – an integration of these perspectives is still a long way off.

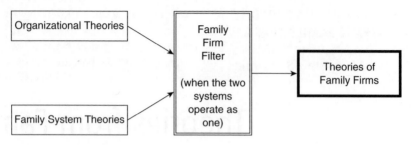

Figure 3.1   The aim of family-business studies (Sharma, 2004, p. 25)

So there still is a gap between the emphasis that is put on psychological issues in the FB literature and the actual application of these theories. Approaches to integrate psychological theories in understanding family businesses are to be found but are still not very common. To give some examples: Sharma et al. (2003) use the 'theory of planned behavior' to explain succession. Davis and Herrera (1998) suggest making better use of social psychology when starting FB research in general (theories of group cohesiveness, social comparison, conformity, etc.). Gordon and Nicholson (2008) use the psychology of conflict to understand severe conflicts in FB families. Kellermanns and von Schlippe (2011) explain the intensity of conflict in family businesses by taking into account psychological mechanisms such as fundamental and hostile attributional errors. Kets de Vries (1996) analyzed the deeper level of protagonist behavior in family businesses under a psychoanalytical lens. The role of emotions is addressed in the concept of 'emotional messiness' (Brundin and Sharma, 2012; see also Chapter 27 on emotions in this book, Brundin and Härtel, 2014), as well as in 'emotional ownership' (Zellweger and Astrachan, 2008). At the same time the importance of family dynamics is highlighted again and again (e.g., Dyer, 2003; Dyer, 2006; Dyer and Dyer, 2009; Zachary, 2011). Lansberg (1992) discussed the family side of family businesses with one of the founding figures of family therapy (S. Minuchin),

and Lansberg and Astrachan (1994) explored succession in family businesses by applying the 'circumplex-model of family relationships' (e.g., Olson and Gorall, 2003, see below).

Constructs which are explicitly related to that field such as the 'family embeddedness of any entrepreneurial action' (Aldrich and Cliff, 2003), 'familiness' (Habbershon und Williams, 1999; Weismeier et al., 2013) or 'family orientation' (Lumpkin et al., 2008) remain rare. Scholars complain about the trend 'to neglect the family as a variable', assuming this might be related to the fact that most researchers come from management or related disciplines (Dyer and Dyer, 2009, pp. 216–217). Hence, this chapter will elaborate on the potential benefits of theoretical and conceptual frameworks rooted in family psychology and family therapy that might be useful in FB research.

Before embarking on the task of exploring theories about families, we would like to propose a definition: 'Families are biologically, socially or legally related units of persons which – in whatever composition – comprise at least two generations in pursuing certain goals' (Schneewind, 2010, p. 35). As to the kind of goals that families are striving for, Cherlin (2005) introduced a rough distinction between public and private goods. Families qualify as producers of public goods that are deemed of societal relevance (e.g., having and raising children) as well as producers of private goods (e.g., providing security and intimacy). In the case of family businesses, the interplay between families as producers of public and private goods becomes particularly evident.

THEORIES IN FAMILY PSYCHOLOGY AND IN SYSTEMIC FAMILY THERAPY

Family Psychology and Systemic Family Therapy – The Two 'Unequal Siblings'

Family psychology and family therapy arose independently of each other, even though they share not only the 'subject' but also many sources and ideas. The link between the two approaches remains rather weak to this day. The first is deeply rooted in academic psychology, research and theory, being thus an approach within the context of science. The other emerged from clinical practice when courageous psychotherapists began to cross the boundaries of strictly individual psychoanalytical settings and started to work with families – an approach within the context of profession (Buchholz, 1999). As both approaches are of interest in stimulating ideas and building concepts, the focus will be placed on issues within the different theories which might be of interest for use in FB research.

Family psychology emerged in the early 1980s, and soon became a dynamic research field (Liddle et al., 2006; Bray and Stanton, 2009; Schneewind, 2010). Crossing the boundaries between traditional disciplines, it is closely related to pedagogy, medicine, laws and sociology, and also imbues traditional subjects of psychology such as developmental, differential, social, clinical psychology, etc. Family psychology covers a broad territory, going beyond questions of mental health, involving family and marital issues, developmental issues in relation to the family lifecycle (the contextual dimension of human development) and parental styles, as well as issues relating to health, gender and counselling, etc.

Systemic family therapy, on the other hand, emerged from clinical practice and psychotherapy starting in the 1950s (e.g., Hoffman, 1981; Simon et al., 1985; Winek, 2010). Starting from the theory of family systems (Hoffman, 1981) and communication theory

(Watzlawick et al., 1967), the discussion moved forward. Today contemporary systemic therapy can be seen as being based on three theoretical foundations: the theory of social systems (Luhmann and Bednarz, 2005); the theory of complex dynamic systems (Haken, 1992); and narrative theory, which looks at how social realities are jointly constructed by the way stories are told within specific systems (e.g., Bruner, 1991).

Theories in Family Psychology and Family Business Research

A recent review of current theories in family psychology (Crosbie-Burnett and Klein, 2009) enumerates 12 distinct theories plus the notion of theoretical eclecticism. A closer look will now be taken at the most prominent of these: (a) family systems theory; (b) attachment theory and ecological theory of development including family development theory; (c) social conflict and family stress theory; and (d) family communication theory.

Family Systems Theory

Fundamental to family systems theory is a paradigmatic as well as programmatic shift from an individualistic to a systemic approach. Stanton (2009, p. 9) pointed out:

> If we want to understand and treat individuals, couples, families, and larger social groups effectively, we need to conceptualize cases within the system in which they exist (the context and the meaning attributed to the context), assess the salient factors in the system, and intervene at identified points across the system.

It is difficult to speak about 'the' systems theory, as there are many different approaches and traditions, which are hard to compare. Family systems theory presents a holistic framework focusing on mutual relationships within families.

It took some time to disengage personality psychology from a static trait-oriented approach, suggesting that a trait such as agreeableness or emotional instability resides as a context-free determinant of observable behavior within the person. Instead, a systemic approach conceives of an individual's personality as a concept that may vary across contexts or interpersonal conditions as the person develops. Such a systemic view of an individual's personality and its development has been suggested by Andersen et al. (2007, p. 177) using the concept of 'personality signature'. Their conceptualization of personality also includes the idea that individuals – more or less consciously – self-select into specific and also diverse situations and interpersonal circumstances that might contribute to the stability of their internal responses and behavioral tendencies: you might feel like being 'somebody else' experiencing yourself in different circumstances. This fact might be quite important in looking at processes in family businesses, especially severe conflicts such as 'family wars' (Gordon and Nicholson, 2008), where people act in a way that they never would have imagined being able to: the context brought out these specific aspects of their 'personality signature'.

The crucial point is that, from a systemic stance, human beings are not only characterized by the present status, former development and anticipated future of their individual features (e.g., personality variables, physical health, etc.) but also by their interpersonal relations (e.g., couple, family and intergenerational relations) as well as the macro-systemic and environmental factors that influence the life of individuals and their interpersonal relationships (e.g., opportunity structures comprising cultural, socio-economic, communal support, education, work conditions, etc.). There are several specific concepts that underlie the theoretical framework of family systems theory (Whitchurch and Constantine, 2009). In the following the more prominent of them are briefly reviewed.

Holism This is a core concept in any systems theory: a system must be seen and understood as a whole, and cannot be understood by dividing the elements into single units (nonsummativity).

Goal orientation Families organize their common life according to more or less explicit goals, which are supposed to provide their coexistence as a family with a sense of meaning and continuity.

Equifinality and multifinality Equifinality means that a system might achieve a certain goal via different activities. By contrast, multifinality denotes the idea that a specified family activity might lead to different consequences. So, the question of how the 'ideal' successor might be brought up, for example, turns out not to be answerable (Erdmann, 2010).

Regularity, rules and patterns Upon observing families over a longer period of time it becomes evident that the relationships among family members are 'patterned' in such a way that they can be characterized by certain rules and routines (Fiese, 2006).

Circular causality In contrast to linear causality, which rests on the assumption that an event A causes a consequence B, circular causality conceives of ongoing interactions among family members as a reciprocal influence (Watzlawick et al., 1967).

Positive and negative feedback Generally speaking, feedback is a process initiated by someone with the intention of either destabilizing or restabilizing an initial situation or set point. With respect to interaction among family members, positive feedback is principally change-oriented, whereas negative feedback aims at returning to the initial situation.

Homeostasis vs heterostasis Closely related to the preceding point is the concept of homeostasis, which refers to the maintenance or balancing of the equilibrium of forces within the family system. On the other hand, heterostasis can be conceived of as the opposite of homeostasis: the process of disbalancing a family system's structural features that might finally lead to new relationship patterns.

Boundaries An important aspect when dealing with families is looking at the boundaries among the members within the family. This might be the boundary of each family member related to his or her individual privacy, or the boundaries governing the relations among family subsystems.

Self-organization and self-reference

An important feature of living systems is that – within certain limits – they are endowed with the potential for self-development and self-preservation – a feature that has been called 'autopoiesis' by Maturana and Varela (1980; see also Haken, 1992). An autopoietic system continuously reproduces the elements that it consists of, balancing out top-down and bottom-up processes.

Internal model of experience A 'system' is not a 'thing' that can be touched. It refers to a particular point of view of conceiving relationships within families. This holds for outsiders (e.g., external managers) as well as for insiders (i.e., family members). Hence, it does not suffice to conceive of family relationships from an outsider perspective (e.g., by only observing family interactions). In addition, it is indispensable to also know what kind of internal representations family members have (Schneewind, 2010).

Concerning FB research Many research questions might be derived from different models of social systems, such as how the mutual influences between family and business can be identified, and how the joint reality, the 'family paradigm' (Reiss and Olivieri, 1983) of a business family might differ from that of others. It might be a challenge to understand any behavior of a person as a function of the wider context and the way he/she ascribes meaning to the context. The patterns and rules that evolved between family and business and vice versa can be constructed in a circular pattern of mutual influence. An interesting question might also concern gender-specific questions:

how can gender roles be described in FB families, what specific 'gender-role strain' is put on male/female successors (Levant and Philpot, 2006)?

Family Development Theories

From a developmental perspective, an individual's potential for establishing positive relationships with other people is deeply rooted in his/her early relationship experiences, which are usually played out in the family context via specific attachment processes (Bowlby, 1969). Moreover, attachment processes operate across an individual's complete lifespan (Johnson and Bradley, 2009). Bowlby's attachment theory and its refinements have spawned a vast amount of conceptual and empirical studies (Cassidy and Shaver, 2008). At the core of all these studies are universal attachment needs, which require the attention and responsive action of an attachment figure (e.g., mother or spouse) to ensure safety and comfort along with positive or at least less negative emotions vis-à-vis the person in need (e.g., child or partner). In the long term this will contribute to a secure attachment style on the part of the person in need. On the contrary, if the attachment figure is perceived as inaccessible or unresponsive, particular attachment behaviors will be activated to elicit responses from the attachment figure that reduce the pain of discomfort.

To assure the development of a secure attachment style, the attachment figure has to demonstrate what Ainsworth et al. (1978) have called sensitivity, i.e., noticing, interpreting accurately, responding promptly and interacting appropriately when dealing with distressed behavior. Moreover, it has been shown that specific attachment styles are at least partially transferred across generations (Cowan and Cowan, 2009). However, looking at close personal relationships solely from an attachment point of view would miss other relationship qualities such as specific patterns of parenting or types of partner relationships that might be either enhancing or detrimental to relationship development. Also, the quality of the couple relationship has been found to be predictive of successful developmental outcomes – also in family businesses.

The findings from several studies that confirm an at least partial transgenerational transmission of attachment styles bring theories of family development onto the scene.

One of the most often cited sources on psychological aspects of family development is the concept of the family lifecycle (Carter and McGoldrick, 1980). It also has broadly been paid regard to in the FB literature (see Gersick et al., 1997; Lansberg, 1999). At the core of this approach is a description of normative and non-normative transitions of families across their lifespan. Concerning normative transitions, they range from leaving the family of origin, founding a family, living with young children and subsequently with youths, and transitioning to the postparental phase and into the late period of life.

Lasloffy (2002) has developed a systemic family development model for training purposes that incorporates systems theory, family stress theory and a multigenerational perspective of family development theory. In a similar vein, Klein and White (2008) proposed a process-oriented approach to family development instead of a phase-specific normative sequence of developmental stages.

The most prominent approach that has been developed to meet this requirement is associated with the legacy of Bronfenbrenner (2005). Particularly noteworthy is his theory-driven process-person-context-time (or PPCT) model (Bronfenbrenner and Morris, 1998; see also Lerner, 2005). At the heart of Bronfenbrenner's theoretical model are the individual person and the relational character of his/her development that becomes evident in what he calls *proximal processes*, i.e., a person's transactions with his/her immediate external environment.

Concerning the *person* the PPCT model distinguishes (a) dispositions to actively initiate and continue proximal processes, (b) resources to actively shape proximal processes and (c) demand characteristics fostering or disrupting the operation of proximal processes (Bronfenbrenner and Morris, 1998).

The *context* components in the PPCT model are located at four ecological levels that are conceived as nested systems, i.e., the micro-, meso-, exo- and macrosystem. In its last version Bronfenbrenner conceived of the microsystem as a person's transactions with his/her immediate environment including the semiotic system. The *mesosystem* denotes a set of interrelated microsystems containing the developing person at a particular point of his or her life (e.g., family, school, work environment). By contrast, the *exosystem* consists of contexts that a person is not directly involved in though this person's development is nevertheless influenced by the impact these contexts have on other persons with whom the target person is in direct contact. Finally, the *macrosystem* is conceived of as the superordinate level of a person's ecology of development comprising such patterns of influence as cultural, political, economic or legal conditions of his or her life.

The last concept of Bronfenbrenner's PPCT model is *time* as an indispensable ingredient of a developmental approach to the four ecological levels just mentioned. Based on the concept of *chronosystem,* Bronfenbrenner and Morris (1998) developed a refined conceptualization of time within their bio-ecological model of human development emphasizing the importance of proximal processes.

Concerning FB research Aspects of developmental approaches are of interest to family businesses throughout the lifecycle. For example, specific aspects of constructive parenting (e.g., fostering children's self-efficacy by providing and supporting appropriate learning opportunities) have been shown to contribute to successful entrepreneurship in subsequent generations (Schmitt-Rodermund, 2004). Danes et al. (2010) showed that, among other predictors, couples living in a strong and committed relationship were more successful in the venture creation process. This finding also extends to a transgenerational perspective of self-employment suggesting that – particularly for male offspring – their parents' successful self-employment serves as a role model for choosing self-employment as a career (Mungai and Velamurni, 2011).

The PPCT model in particular provides an integrative and useful theoretical platform for work-family research in the context of family businesses. Attachment patterns and proximal processes might be intensely modulated by the presence of the FB. Parental sensitivity in particular might be influenced by specific strain stemming from the need to put business demands first. Specific attachment style patterns might be identified in the FB context that govern the relationships between parents and children as well as between spouses. Other questions might relate to the kind and quality of proximal processes contributing to family strengths and to what extent FB families differ when operating small vs large family businesses in terms of their integration and participation in their social ecology.

Social Conflict and Family Stress Theory

Generally speaking, conflict thrives on scarce resources and the inequality of access to these resources (e.g., amount of love and appreciation, money and time, level of power and influence, privilege of engaging in specific activities, etc.; see also Chapter 26 on conflicts in this book, McKee et al., 2014). Hence, at the base of conflict within or between families there is a confrontation over having control of scarce and highly valued resources (cf. Ingoldsby et al., 2004). A key issue within families is who has the power to assert his or her interests. Power struggles might also arise between families concerning scarce or critical resources. In particular, prevalence of conflict within and between families when operating a family business might be especially challenging in terms of the allocation of time, money and strategic decisions in both short- and long-term perspectives (e.g., balancing work and family life, allocation of responsibilities,

appointing successors, etc.), which usually causes stress.

The birth of family stress theory goes back to 1949. In Hill's 'ABC-X model' (Hill, 1949), A refers to the stressor event (e.g., economic difficulties in a family business), B designates the family resources (e.g., availability of financial aid from a close friend) and C the family's perception or attribution of relevance concerning the event (e.g., optimism about breaking the financial bottleneck). If the family is not able to adequately cope with and solve the event this will lead to a crisis (e.g., inability to surmount the financial difficulties), which is the X component in Hill's stress model (cited by Schneewind, 2010).

McCubbin and Patterson (1982) developed an extension by introducing a pre-crisis and post-crisis phase, which caused them to label their model the Double ABC-X model. The pre-crisis phase consists of Hill's three A, B, C components. Persistence of the original crisis into the post-crisis phase eventually leads to new stressor events which contribute to what is called the double A factor. Hence, the new stressor might exacerbate the problem (e.g., serious illness of a family member besides the threat of insolvency). In addition, attempts at coping with the new situation might trigger existing and new resources, which contribute to what McCubbin and Patterson have called the double B factor (e.g., getting help from a doctor with whom the family is on friendly terms in addition to the loan from a close friend). Depending on how the family handles the more complex challenges of the new situation, the ensuing adaptation might either turn out to be positive (a process called 'bonadaptation' by McCubbin and Patterson) or else it might aggravate the overall situation by putting more strain on the family, which might finally result in the family's maladaptation (e.g., if the family business falls into insolvency).

In a similar vein, Patterson (2002) has tried to explain familial adaptation processes in her 'Family Adjustment and Adaptation

Response' or FAAR model with a particular emphasis on family resilience, i.e., a construct that refers to 'the phenomenon of doing well in the face of adversity' (Patterson, 2002, p. 350). Borrowing from Antonovsky's (1987) individual resiliency concept, family resiliency refers to two aspects, i.e., family resiliency as a capacity and as a process, which provides the FAAR model with the flavour of a dynamic developmental approach. In short, the FAAR model emphasizes four central concepts, i.e., 'families engage in active processes to balance family demands with family capabilities as they interact with family meanings to arrive at a level of family adjustment or adaptation.' (Patterson, 2002, p. 350). The Double ABC-X and the FAAR model both have their merits for gaining a better understanding of the processes and the development of family businesses.

Concerning FB research   The experience of specific scarcity of resources (e.g., appreciation, time, attention) might be evaluated differently by family members. These processes might be connected to power struggles that are less likely in non-FB families. It might be a challenge to apply the ABC-X model to analyze specific conflict situations, to identify specific stressors and their accumulation over time. And of course the strategies that are applied in FB families to ensure work–family integration with as little stress as possible as well as specific processes that contribute to strengthening family resiliency are of significant interest.

Family Communication Theory

Many different family communication theories have been described (e.g., Vangelisti, 2004; Braithwaite and Baxter, 2006; Segrin and Flora, 2011). Here we will concentrate on a general theory of family communication developed by Koerner and Fitzpatrick (2002), which stresses the importance of family relationship schemas. The theory builds on Baldwin's (1992) general model of relationship schemas, which is based on relational

knowledge and comprises three subsets of knowledge, i.e., self-schema, other-schema and schema on interpersonal scripts. A relational schema contains one's knowledge about him/herself, others and relationships, and about how to interact in relationships – it is a kind of 'map', which guides behavior in different contexts. Koerner and Fitzpatrick (2002, p. 83ff) contend, 'family relationship schemas contain knowledge that is both experiential and prescriptive and that is central to all relationships with family members.' An important axiom in their theory assumes that 'relational schemas affect relational communication through their influence on automatic and controlled cognitive processes' (2002, p. 82). By referring to an influential earlier contribution by McLeod and Chaffee (1972) on 'the construction of social reality', Ritchie and Fitzpatrick (1990) introduced the concept of family communication patterns, which are based on two fundamental orientations making up a family's communication climate. The two orientations are called 'conformity orientation' and 'conversation orientation'.

By cross-tabulating high and low values of both dimensions, families can be classified according to four types that have been labelled pluralistic (high conversation, low conformity), consensual (high conversation, high conformity), laissez faire (low conversation, low conformity) and protective (low conversation, high conformity). In the meantime, a series of studies summarized in a meta-analysis (Schrodt et al., 2008) has shown that these family communication patterns are predictive of psychosocial outcomes (e.g., relational health, mental well-being), behavioral outcomes (e.g., conflict management skills) and information processing outcomes (e.g., informational reception apprehension). To illustrate, Schrodt (2009, p. 182) concluded that young adults who experienced a pluralistic family communication climate (i.e., high conversation and low conformity orientation) seem to be 'better equipped to generate solutions to problems and to adapt to times of stress and adversity than those from consensual families' (i.e., high conversation and high conformity orientation). By contrast, the laissez-faire and protective family communication climates are inversely related to family strength and satisfaction. Similarly, another study arrived at the conclusion that the ingredients of a pluralistic family communication climate may equip young adults with the 'communication and cognitive processing skills necessary to solve personal problems, cope with stress, and to make healthy lifestyle decisions' (Koesten et al., 2009, p. 91).

Concerning FB research Based on the theoretical grounds and empirical findings of Koerner's and Fitzpatricks's (2002) general theory of family communication it may be concluded that this approach has great potential for adaptation to FB research. Moreover, it should be kept in mind that family communication patterns – although there is some intergenerational transmission of such patterns (cf. Whitton et al., 2008) – are not written in stone. Thus it would seem obvious to offer and eventually apply appropriate professional family-oriented interventions to the benefit of FB families (cf. von Schlippe and Klein, 2010).

There might be specific relational schemas that are learnt in FB families. Fertile questions might be how these schemas govern the (conformity-oriented vs conversation-oriented) communication patterns, and whether coincide with family satisfaction or dysfunction, as well as to what extent FB families draw on different communication patterns depending on the topics being discussed (e.g., family or business-related issues)?

Theories from Systemic Family Therapy and Family Business Research

Family therapy emerged from clinical practice and developed into a 'systemic' approach during the 1980s. Of course this is not the place to provide an overview of therapeutic models (see Winek, 2010). Instead, we will focus on specific theoretical aspects of selected models so as to derive research questions for family businesses. We shall present four models of the founder's generations: Satir, Minuchin, Selvini Palazzoli, Boszormenyi-Nagy/Stierlin; and two models that represent the systemic tradition: the narrative and linguistic approaches.

Self-esteem and Communication-clarity: Experiential Family Therapy

Virginia Satir was one of the pioneers in the evolving field of family therapy. Her ability in 'disentangling people from mystifying communicational traps' (Hoffman, 1981, p. 221) was famous. Her core concept is the self-esteem of persons, their ability to value their own self and to stay in a friendly and loving relationship with themselves. The way a person is able to do this is responsible for the way he/she communicates. Processes in the family of origin and with significant others strongly affect one's sense of self. Low self-esteem needs to be protected and covered by the individual, who thus starts to communicate in an incongruent way.

Satir saw four main patterns of incongruent communication (Satir et al., 1991):

- blaming (attack as a way of protection);
- placating (actively going into 'one-down-position');
- irrelevant (distracting to avoid confrontation);
- computing (avoiding any feelings).

'Congruence' means that the self-esteem of a person does not need to be protected and thus he/she is able to communicate clearly, openly and directly, expressing their own needs and interests without expecting immediate fulfilment, and listening to those of the others.

Concerning FB research Satir was a charismatic practitioner; her concept was generated out of practice and is less deeply involved in theory (Banmen, 2002). Nevertheless her approach offers a range of stimulating questions as regards FB families.

Being part of a FB family might affect the self-esteem of the family-members and thus the way of communicating in a specific way. This concept had already been picked up by FB research: Lansberg (1999, p. 161) described the relevance of *congruent* communication between generations in FB families: 'Children are very attentive to the contradictions between parents' words and their deeds ... In some families, the clash of powerful and contradictory messages ... can trap children in a double-bind' (see also Litz, 2008; 2012). FB families might differ in the openness/congruency or rigidity/incongruency of their communication patterns. The 'congruence-scale' (Lee, 2002), based on the Satir model, might be a good instrument to generate exciting data.

Boundaries and Boundary Ambiguity

The model of Salvador Minuchin, that of 'structural family therapy', was the main concept in use till the 1980s. His core concept was 'family boundaries'. This term describes the more or less symbolic marks between a family and its environment as well as among its members. They aren't necessarily physical (although the parents' bedroom door might be one) but they rather determine how subsystems mark their communication boundaries. So the term 'boundary', for example, describes the way in which a couple handles its privacy towards the rest of the family (without children interfering day and night or the grandparents interfering in the children's education), or how distinctions are drawn between males and females or between members of different generations: can mother and daughter have a 'very special' relationship without other family members interfering, will a secret be kept, will private information (such as partnership issues) be shared inappropriately (e.g., by a parent with a child)? Boundaries can be roughly classified as clear, rigid or diffuse (Minuchin, 1974). If they are too weak, diffuse boundaries bring the family into a degree of closeness which makes it difficult to experience individuality, as

uniqueness is not tolerated ('enmeshment'). If they are too strong, rigid boundaries create great emotional distance between family members and fail to convey the feeling of being related to the family members, resulting in 'disengagement' (e.g., see Simon et al., 1985, p. 27; Olson and Gorall, 2003; Liddle et al., 2006). Clear boundaries create the 'matrix of identity' by balancing the sense of belonging and the experience of being a separate individual.

Families frequently have to deal with triadic interactions. Can boundaries be managed without constant interference or will 'pathological triangles' (Haley, 1977) arise when the generation boundary is secretly crossed and cross-generational alliances and secret coalitions occur (e.g., a child is drawn into the conflict as the 'best friend' of a parent)?

Boundaries change over time as every family has to balance different steps of the lifecycle differently. Boundaries also are handled markedly different in diverse cultures, as they reflect core values of a culture (Liddle et al., 2006, p. 335). Boss and Greenberg introduced the concept of 'Family boundary ambiguity' (e.g., 1984), which refers to a lack of clarity as to who is 'in' and who is 'out' of the family system, and who is performing what roles and tasks. Originally developed in the context of severe chronic illness (is a paralyzed patient still 'in' although not taking part in communication or 'out'?), the concept helps understand problems of (dis-orientation in different kinds of families (e.g., in step-families).

Concerning FB research The structural model attracted the interest of FB research quite early on (Lansberg, 1992). The term 'boundary' in particular leads to interesting questions (e.g., Distelberg and Blow, 2011). The presence of the company 'within' the family adds complexity in handling boundaries. To many business families, the question 'Who is in?' is crucial, as the answer might have tremendous influence on the company (e.g., who takes part in shareholder meetings, are spouses admitted to ownership, how to deal with homosexual relationships?).

The FB might create a certain form of boundary ambiguity, experienced in the separation between operative members/ shareholders and others. The question as to which issues might be discussed with whom might lead to confusion about one's own identity. Finally, founder and successor working in the company could create a close subsystem that might affect boundary management and the relationships between the other family members.

Paradox and Counterparadox

The group of Mara Selvini Palazzoli created the 'Milan model' (Selvini Palazzoli et al., 1978) working with families with severely disturbed members (anorectic, schizophrenic). Based upon the work of Bateson (1972) they tried to realize a purely 'cybernetic' model, concentrating only on observable interaction patterns, ignoring all ideas about 'inner processes'. The Milan team explained schizophrenic behavior as an attempt to communicate within a context of many contradicting and paradoxical communications. The members avoid conflicts by avoiding clear definitions of relationships. They fight secretly over control and definition of relationship. Thus a 'game' is created which brings about the feeling of 'damned if you do and damned if you don't'. The communication is not open, incongruent messages are given. Given the intense nature of the relationships within a family this can bring the members into states of feeling disoriented, irritated and confused. An atmosphere of 'double-bind' communication arises (Watzlawick et al., 1967), which is associated with stress (Roy and Sawyers, 1986) and with psychic illnesses, as 'crazy' behavior might be a way out of this trap.

Concerning FB research Paradoxes in the FB context might occur due to the presence of two different social systems (business and family) with contradicting logics. The contradicting expectations of both systems are inevitable and continuously present (von Schlippe and Frank, 2013): 'Whereas a family exists to facilitate the development and growth of its members, a business exists to serve the needs of its customers' (Litz, 2012). Litz suggests that double-bind theory may play a special role in 'unravelling enigmas' of certain business families (see Kaye, 1996), he assumes that 'double binds would be more likely to occur in firms operating in cultures characterized by greater power distance, insofar as children would be more likely to defer to parental hierarchy' (Litz, 2012, p. 23). So this aspect deserves attention in research (Schuman et al., 2010).

The communication patterns in business families need to be precisely described and distinguished in order to find out if double-bind communication can be identified. Case studies might reveal specific paradoxes that FB families find themselves in. Traditions of family management rules might be analyzed within the framework of this theory: family strategies that had been developed over years can be examined under this perspective, possibly showing how leaders over generations intuitively had managed paradoxes by establishing intelligent rules (Groth and von Schlippe, 2012).

Invisible Loyalties and Premises of Justice

An approach that explicitly takes up hypotheses concerning the inner life of individuals is adopted by Boszormenyi-Nagy and Spark (1973) and Stierlin (2007). They put emphasis on unconscious assumptions of unsolved emotional issues of previous generations. A person born into a family enters a 'multiperson loyalty network' and experiences the demands of complying with values, expectations and obligations of the group: 'Things such as trust, merit, legacy, and fulfilment are far more important than the "psychological" functions of "feeling" and "knowing"' (Simon et al., 1985, p. 217). So the family sets up a frame of expectations. A person takes over this frame and the psychic structures of the individual reflect the internalization of expectations. Loyalty-bonds may be experienced as 'being in debt' towards the family, towards the suffering of parents or grandparents and their legacy. The concept of delegation means that a family member might take over a certain task from one person from the previous generation, which might be unconscious, so as to live out a dream that an ancestor never dared to realize. Experiencing family loyalty 'is less like a high-minded moral choice than a submersion in a soup of less noble motives, like guilt, anxiety, inertia. Resembling a blind, compelling instinct, it is an allegiance no more chosen than hunger or the need to sleep' (Wylie, 1999, p. 23). And missions can be in conflict; they may bring the person into a double-binding legacy of split loyalty (e.g., 'live out the emancipatory side, that mother never dared to show' and 'be the well-behaving daughter'). Missions can be more or less outspoken, this may lead to certain forms of dependency: nothing binds more than a vaguely given promise, 'maybe, one day, you will inherit …' (Simon, 2002).

Important issues in this field are questions regarding the (unconscious) premises of justice and fairness that count in a family. Members internally process a kind of 'accounting system', counting the 'debits and credits' towards the family. One might feel proud of accomplishments achieved, or burdened with guilt and feelings of worthlessness – according to the 'premises of justice' of the family-system one is connected to (Stierlin, 2007, S. 43). A kind of 'multigenerational account book' is kept, multigenerational obligations including the expectations of debts being repaid over time ('Some day I'll be recompensed for my suffering'). Problems arise when compensation for personal suffering comes too late (or never) or is insufficient. Then it shows that family members kept their 'accounts' in a highly diverging way. 'Statements of account' do not come in written form as from the bank, but rather in the form of feelings of being 'right' (loyal to the family-values) or 'wrong' (not

keeping up with the family's standards). So massive emotions may arise of feeling betrayed by the accumulation of injustices: being hurt in core values, feeling betrayed by someone you love triggers intense negative emotions (including the urge for revenge).

Concerning FB research   Justice is definitely a topic in business families (Van der Heyden et al., 2005). Succession in particular might bring about these feelings, as this is a point where no 'consensus-fiction' can be upheld any longer: when the last will is opened, it shows who is awarded and who has been apportioned the blame. Many of the extreme emotions in FB families become understandable by applying the question of how members keep the 'private accounting system' of their obligations and award-expectations towards the family. Research on 'multigenerational account books' within FB families might be a difficult but rewarding endeavor. The clarity of expressing and negotiating expectations might differentiate between functional and dysfunctional business families.

Coming down to the basic feeling of betrayal due to expected and never cashed 'cheques' might help understanding highly escalated FB conflicts. And some strange behavior in families may be seen as an attempt to create equalization: 'Some of the fiercest succession battles are fought over titles and what they connote to different people' (Lansberg, 1999, p. 214). This might widen the concept of 'psychological contracting' into a transgenerational perspective, to understand the open and covert promises that are given or expected – and the intense emotions after an experienced breach of contracts (Rousseau, 2004).

The Power of Stories: Narrative Approaches in Family Therapy

Anyone asked about a topic of personal interest will usually start to tell a story: this happened then, and afterwards that happened, and that is why things are now as they are. The narrative approach in family therapy is connected closely to the names of the Australian therapists White and Epston (1990). In psychology, Bruner (e.g., 1991) and Gergen (2001) can be seen as the central figures. The approach follows constructivist philosophy by seeing the reality of mental (Bruner) and social (Gergen) worlds as a result of social construction. It puts emphasis on the way in which these realities are constructed: by means of stories. Any experience that someone lives through is immediately gone, experience must therefore be 'storied', 'and it is this storying that determines the meaning ascribed to experience' (White and Epston, 1990, p. 10). Experience thus becomes subject to 'narrative thinking' (Bruner, 1991). And in this way a poetic, a narrative aspect emerges: as an author, the person creates a 'plot' around which he/she builds the story (see Fig. 3.2). Without this process the event will be forgotten: what is not structured in a narrative way gets lost to the memory (Bruner, 1991). Stories are the way our memory is constructed. They are of course not sheer invention, but one has to take into account 'that the meanings that people derive in these acts of interpretation are determined by the interpretive resources that are available to them, and further, that these meanings are negotiated in communities of people and within the various terms and institutions of culture' (White, 2000, p. 9).

And stories are not told on one's own; there is no independent author. A person by birth enters a 'micro-universe of stories' coming into contact with the family's reality. The 'memory of the family' contains a set of stories, and after years and decades of telling, these stories have become strong 'sense-attractors' (Kriz, 2001). Persons 'become' what they are by stories ('Nobody ever likes me!'), and also the identity of a family ('We have always been the best') or of subgroups ('They betrayed our great-grandfather so he changed his last will') is what the stories tell.

Concerning FB research Although this approach is already widely used in organization research (e.g., Czarniawska, 1998; Brown et al., 2009; Zwack and von Schlippe, 2011) little research has yet been done on the meaning of stories and the tradition of storytelling in family businesses (e.g., McCollom, 1992). Von Schlippe and Groth (2007) differentiate between centripetal stories such as founder's myths that enhance the feeling of connectedness, and centrifugal stories such as stories about conflict or a lack of justice that tend to split up relationships. Zwack and von Schlippe, 2011 showed how

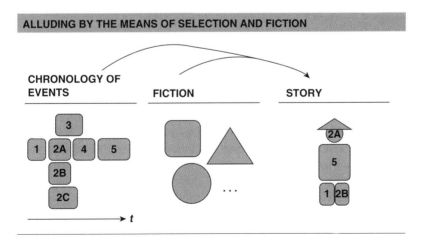

Figure 3.2 Turning the event into a story

Source: Zwack and von Schlippe (2011)

stories are used in FB families to transfer values to the next generation.

So the field is open to explore stories and their meanings in research. Stories of the same event might differ tremendously between different branches of the family. Some stories may support centripetal processes in the family, while others rather may deepen the feeling of distance. The essential plot that a story conveys may differ from story to story and from person to person. This 'volatility' is difficult to handle in research: how can objects that are fragile and constantly in motion like a butterfly be fixed? But it would be a mistake not to trace stories for such reasons as stories are surely highly meaningful when it comes to the transmission of tacit issues.

Human Systems as Linguistic Systems: Problem-determined Systems

Quite a challenging approach was proposed by Harry Goolishian and Harlene Anderson. Their theoretical considerations are close to the narrative theory, seeing human systems as systems, which generate language and meaning: 'Systems can be described as existing only in language and communicative action' (Anderson and Goolishian, 1988, p. 372). Communication is 'the system', it is not the 'product', 'attribute' or 'result' of a system, which consists of people. It's rather the opposite: a social system comes into being through communication. A problem, then, is not the result of critical interactions in a system: a system in therapy rather has coalesced around 'something' (whatever it is) that has been marked as a 'problem' by significant participants. Anderson et al. (1986) created the term 'problem-determined system' to describe this process. Membership is gained by taking part in specific communicative actions: defining something as a 'problem' and developing ideas of the causes of the 'problem' as well as possible ways to solve them. Therapy consequentially does not seek out structures and conflicts any more but rather focuses on how meaning is generated, how stories and narratives are developed. The task of therapy shifted from intervention to the question of how constructive dialogues might be installed. Misunderstandings and conflicts are viewed as differing ideas and understandings of the meaning of events and behaviors. In their understanding of a system they are quite close to the 'theory of social systems' of Luhmann (2012) who explicitly sees communication, not human beings, as elements of a social system. The theory cannot be described here in detail (Wimmer et al., 2005; von Schlippe and Frank, 2013).

In this context another term is of interest: as a 'problem-determined system' is created by specific communications surrounding the 'problem', it becomes the 'organizing principle' of the communication. More and more topics that are usually talked about are 'taken over' by problem-communication. Luhmann (2012) sees this kind of communication as a 'parasite', conquering more and more areas of everyday communication. The capacity of family members to engage in a communicative system around other topics is diminished, and communication becomes impoverished. This kind of process might be illustrated by imagining a family with an alcohol-addicted member: sooner or later a problem-determined system will become established. The family communication will be impoverished by the 'parasite', as interaction is organized 'around the bottle' (Steinglass et al., 1987): the problem-determined system shifts from sobriety cycles to intoxication cycles, and the communication patterns grow in intensity as the family cannot talk about anything else but 'the problem'.

Concerning FB research   If we replace the words 'problem' or 'bottle' by 'business' these ideas might be quite exciting. What would it mean to look at a social system that 'consists' of communication surrounding the company, and find out that ordinary 'bonding communication' that usually characterizes families (von Schlippe and Klein, 2010; Groth and von Schlippe, 2012) is 'conquered' by business communication? Can we find families where communication about business has become a 'parasite', an 'organizing principle' of family communication, and how can they be differentiated from families who manage to maintain relationship-related communication? Can we speak of family businesses as a 'sickness' (Kaye, 1996) when we see family communication being centred more and more exclusively on business questions, and might we find an indicator of the degree of (a lack of) well-being and happiness of the FB family members?

ASSESSING FAMILIES IN FAMILY PSYCHOLOGY AND THERAPY

As it would go beyond the scope of this chapter to describe the many instruments that are being used in family psychology and family therapy, the reader is referred to the three volume handbook on family measurement techniques by Touliatos et al. (2001). Although in need of being updated, this handbook is still an excellent resource covering a large number of assessment tools. In addition, several other books provide a broad array of family assessment techniques that might be seminally used in family business research (e.g., Jordan, 2003; Hertlein and Viers, 2005; Williams et al., 2011; Sperry, 2012).

Beyond the instruments referring to different devices of family assessment there are a variety of approaches to studying family processes based on qualitative and quantitative methodologies which it is likewise not possible to discuss in detail in this chapter (however, see the chapters pertaining to Part VI of this handbook). In the present context it may suffice to point out some publications which cover in some detail not only practical competencies such as assessment and intervention competencies when dealing with families (e.g., Stanton and Welsh, 2011), but also highly sophisticated approaches to designing and evaluating empirical studies in the field of family psychology and family

therapy (e.g., Sprenkle and Piercy, 2005; Daly, 2007) that might also provide fertile ground for research in the field of family business.

CONCLUSION

The present chapter has tried to pull together a variety of theoretical approaches derived from the two 'unequal sisters' of family psychology and family therapy. Upon closer inspection it might become evident that under the overarching umbrella of an approach based on the general assumptions of systems theory, there are more common 'genes' than one might perhaps have expected. Although the various theoretical approaches differ in breadth and specificity concerning the topics they are dealing with, they have great potential to draw on another 'unequal sister' under a common umbrella: the field of family business. We have tried to demonstrate possible inferences and applications derived from family psychology and family therapy that might be useful in generating new questions and conducting the corresponding research to answer these questions. In fact, we would be pleased to see a fruitful triangulation of the three 'unequal sisters' under one umbrella – and we are quite sure that this would add to the healthy growth and productivity of all three siblings.

REFERENCES

Ainsworth, M.D.S., Blehar, M.C., Waters, E. and Wall, S. (1978). *Patterns of Attachment: A Psychological Study of the Strange Situation*. Hillsdale, NJ: Erlbaum.

Aldrich, H.E. and Cliff, J.E. (2003). The pervasive effects of family on entrepreneurship: Toward a family embeddedness perspective. *Journal of Business Venturing*, 18, 573–596.

Andersen, S.M., Thorpe, J.S. and Kooij, C.S. (2007). Character in context: The relational self and transference. In Y. Shoda, D. Cervone and G. Downey (eds), *Persons in Context: Constructing a Science of the Individual* (pp. 169–200). New York: Guilford.

Anderson, H. and Goolishian, H.A. (1988). Human systems as linguistic systems: Preliminary and evolving ideas about the implications for clinical theory. *Family Process*, 27, 371–393.

Anderson, H., Goolishian, H.A. and Winderman, L. (1986). Problem-determined systems: Towards transformation in family therapy. *Journal of Strategic and Systemic Therapies*, 5, 1–14.

Antonovsky, A. (1987). *Unraveling the Mystery of Health: How People Manage Stress and Stay Well*. San Francisco, CA: Jossey-Bass Publishers.

Baldwin, M.W. (1992). Relational schemas and the processing of social information. *Psychological Bulletin*, 112, 461–484.

Banmen, J. (2002). The Satir model: Yesterday and today. *Contemporary Family Therapy* 24, 7–22.

Bateson, G. (1972). *Steps to an Ecology of Mind*. Chicago/London: University Press.

Boss, P. and Greenberg, J. (1984). Family boundary ambiguity: A new variable in family stress theory. *Family Process* 23, 535–546.

Boszormenyi-Nagy, I. and Spark, G. (1973). *Invisible Loyalties: Reciprocity in Intergenerational Family Therapy*. New York: Harper and Row.

Bowlby, J. (1969). *Attachment and Loss: Vol. 1. Attachment*. New York: Basis Books.

Braithwaite, D.O. and Baxter, L.A. (eds) (2006). *Engaging Theories in Family Communication: Multiple Perspectives*. Thousand Oaks, CA: Sage.

Bray, J.H. and Stanton, M. (eds) (2009). *The Wiley-Blackwell Handbook of Family Psychology*. Chichester: Wiley-Blackwell.

Bronfenbrenner, U. (ed.) (2005). *Making Human Beings*. Thousand Oaks, CA: Sage.

Bronfenbrenner, U. and Morris, P.A. (1998). The ecology of developmental process. In W. Damon and R.M. Lerner (eds), *Handbook of Child Psychology: Vol.1. Theoretical Models of Human Development* (5th edn, pp. 993–1028). New York: Wiley.

Brown, A., Gabriel, Y. and Gherardi, S. (2009). Storytelling and change: An unfolding story. *Organization* 16, 323–333.

Brundin, E. and Härtel, Ch. (2014). Emotions in family firms. In Melin, L., Nordqvist, M. and Sharma, P. (eds), *SAGE Handbook of Family Business*. London: Sage.

Brundin, E. and Sharma, P. (2012). Love, hate, and desire: The role of emotional messiness in the business family. In Carsrud, A. and Bännback, M. (eds), *Understanding Family Businesses: Undiscovered Approaches, Unique Perspectives, and Neglected Topics*. Berlin/Heidelberg/New York: Springer.

Bruner, J. (1991). The narrative construction of reality. *Critical Inquiry*, 18, 1–21.

Buchholz, M. (1999). *Psychotherapie als Profession* [Psychotherapy as profession]. Gießen: Psychosozial.

Carter, B. and McGoldrick, M. (1980). *The Family Life Cycle*. New York: Gardner.

Cassidy, J. and Shaver, P.R. (eds) (2008). *Handbook of Attachment* (2nd edn). New York: Guilford.

Cherlin, A.J. (2005). *Public and Private Families: An Introduction* (4th edn). Columbus, OH: McGraw-Hill.

Chrisman, J.J., Kellermanns, F.W., Chan, K.C. and Liano, K. (2010). Intellectual foundations of current research in family business: An identification and review of 25 influential articles. *Family Business Review*, 23, 9–26.

Cowan, P.A. and Cowan, C.P. (2009). Couple relationships: A missing link between adult attachment and children's outcomes. *Attachment and Human Development*, 11, 1–4.

Crosbie-Burnett, M. and Klein, D.M. (2009). The fascinating story of family theories. In J.H. Bray and M. Stanton (eds), *The Wiley-Blackwell Handbook of Family Psychology* (pp. 37–52). Chichester: Wiley-Blackwell.

Czarniawska, B. (1998). *A Narrative Approach to Organization Studies*. London: Sage.

Daly, K.J. (2007). *Qualitative Methods for Family Studies and Human Development*. Thousand Oaks, CA: Sage.

Danes, S.M., Matzek, A.E. and Werbel, J.D. (2010). Spousal context during the venture creation process. In A. Stewart, G.T. Lumpkin and J.A. Katz (eds), *Entrepreneurship and Family Business*, 12 (pp. 113–161). Bingley: Emerald Group.

Davis, J.A. and Herrera, R.M. (1998). The social psychology of family shareholder dynamics. *Family Business Review*, 11, 253–260.

Distelberg, B.J. and Blow, A. (2011). Variations in family system boundaries. *Family Business Review*, 24, 28–46.

Dyer, W.G., Jr. (2003). The family: The missing variable in organizational research. *Entrepreneurship: Theory and Practice*, 27, 401–416.

Dyer, W.G., Jr. (2006). Examining the 'family effect' on firm performance. *Family Business Review*, 19, 253–273.

Dyer, W.G., Jr. and Dyer, W.J. (2009). Putting the family in family business research. *Family Business Review*, 22, 216–219.

Erdmann, Ch. (2010). Unternehmerfamilien und Nachfolgebereitschaft [Business families and readiness for succession]. *Familiendynamik* 35(1), 40–48.

Fiese, B.H. (2006). *Family Routines and Rituals*. New Haven, CT: Yale University Press.

Gergen, K. (2001). *Social Construction in Context*. London: Sage.

Gersick, K., Davis, J., Hampton, M. and Lansberg, I. (1997). *Generation to Generation: Life Cycles of the Family Business*. Boston, MA: Harvard.

Gordon, G. and Nicholson, N. (2008). *Family Wars: Classic Conflicts in Family Business and How to Deal With Them*. London: Kogan.

Groth, T. and Schlippe, A. von (2012). Die Form der Unternehmerfamilie – Paradoxiebewältigung zwischen Entscheidung und Bindung [The form of business family: Coping with paradox between deciding and attachment]. *Familiendynamik*, 37(4), 268–280.

Habbershon, T., and Williams, M. (1999), 'A resource-based framework for assessing the strategic advantages of family firms', *Family Business Review*, 12(1), 1–22.

Haken, H. (1992). Synergetics in psychology. In W. Tschacher, G. Schiepek, and E.J. Brunner, (eds), *Selforganization and Clinical Psychology* (pp. 32–54). Berlin: Springer.

Haley, J. (1977). Towards a theory of pathological systems. In P. Watzlawick and J.H. Weakland (eds), *The Interactional View* (pp. 94–112). New York: Norton.

Hertlein, K.M. and Viers, D. (2005). *The Couple and Family Therapists's Notebook*. Binghamton, NY: Haworth.

Hill, R. (1949). *Families Under Stress: Adjustment to the Crises of War Separation and Reunion*. New York: Harper and Brothers.

Hoffman, L. (1981). *Foundations of Family Therapy: A Conceptual Framework for Systems Change*. New York: Basic Books.

Ingoldsby, B.B., Smith, S.R. and Miller, J.E. (2004). *Exploring Family Theories*. Los Angeles, CA: Roxbury.

Johnson, S.M. and Bradley, B. (2009). Emotionally focused couple therapy: Creating loving relationships. In J.H. Bray and M. Stanton (eds), *The Wiley-Blackwell Handbook of Family Psychology* (pp. 402–415). Chichester, Wiley.

Jordan, K. (2003). *Handbook of Couple and Family Assessment* (2nd edn). New York: Nova Science.

Kaye, K. (1996). When the family business is a sickness. *Family Business Review*, 9, 347–368.

Kellermanns, F. and Schlippe, A. von (2011). Konflikte in Familie und Unternehmen erkennen und vermeiden [Identify and avoid conflict in family and business]. In Koeberle-Schmid, A., Fahrion, H.-J., Witt, P. (eds), *Family Business Governance. Erfolgreiche Führung von Familienunternehmen* (2nd edn, pp. 429–441). Berlin: Schmidt.

Kets de Vries, M.F.R. (1996). *Family Business. Human Dilemmas in the Family Firm*. London: Thomson.

Klein, D.M. and White, J.M. (2008). *Family Theories* (4th edn). Thousand Oaks, CA: Sage.

Koerner, A.F. and Fitzpatrick, M.A. (2002). Toward a theory of family communication. *Communication Theory*, 12, 70–91.

Koesten, J., Schrodt, P. and Ford, D.J. (2009). Cognitive flexibility as a mediator of family communication environments of young adults' well-being. *Health Communication*, 24, 82–94.

Kriz, J. (2001). Self-organization of cognitive and interactional processes. In: Matthies, M., Malchow, H. and Kriz, J. (eds), *Integrative Systems Approaches to Natural and Social Dynamics* (pp. 517–537). New York: Springer.

Lansberg, I. (1992). The family side of the family business: A conversation with Salvador Minuchin. *Family Business Review*, 5(3), 59–73.

Lansberg, I. (1999). *Succeeding Generations*. Boston, MA: Harvard.

Lansberg, I. and Astrachan, J. (1994). The influence of family relationships on succession planning and training. *Family Business Review*, 7(1), 39–60.

Lasloffy, T.A. (2002). Rethinking family development theory: Teaching with the systemic family development (SFD) model. *Family Relations*, 51, 206–214).

Lee, B. (2002). Development of a congruence scale based on the Satir model. *Contemporary Family Therapy*, 24, 217–239.

Lerner, R.M. (2005). Urie Bronfenbrenner: Career contributions of the consummate developmental scientist. In U. Bronfenbrenner (ed.), *Making Human Beings* (pp. ix–xxvi). Thousand Oaks, CA: Sage.

Levant, R. and Philpot, C. (2006). Conceptualizing gender in marital and family therapy: The gender role strain paradigm. In Liddle, H. et al. (eds), *Family Psychology. Science-based Interventions* (2nd edn, pp. 301–329). Washington, DC: APA.

Liddle, H.A., Santisteban, D.A., Levant, R.F. and Bray, J.H. (eds) (2006). *Family Psychology: Science-based Interventions* (2nd edn). Washington, CA: APA.

Litz, R. (2008). Two sides of a one-sided phenomenon: Conceptualizing the family business as a Mobius strip. *Family Business Review*, 21, 217–236.

Litz, R. (2012). Double role, double binds? Double bind theory and family business research. In Carsrud, A. and Bännback, M. (eds), *Understanding Family Businesses: Undiscovered Approaches, Unique Perspectives, and Neglected Topics*. New York: Springer.

Luhmann, N. (2012). *Introduction to Systems Theory*. New York: Wiley.

Luhmann, N. and Bednarz, J. (2005). *Social Systems*. Palo Alto, CA: Stanford University Press.

Lumpkin, G.T., Martin, W. and Vaughn, M. (2008). Family orientation: Individual-level influences on family firm outcomes. *Family Business Review*, 21(2), 127–138.

Maturana, H. and Varela, F. (1980). *Autopoiesis and Cognition*. Boston, MA: Riedel.

McCollom, M. (1992). Organizational stories in a family-owned business. *Family Business Review*, 5, 3–24.

McCubbin, H.I. and Patterson, J.M. (1982). Family adaptations to crisis. In H.I. McCubbin, A.E. Cauble and J.M. Patterson (eds), *Family Stress, Coping, and Social Support* (pp. 26–47). Springfield, IL: Charles C. Thomas.

McKee, L., Madden, Th., Kellermanns, F., Eddleston, K. (2014). Conflicts in family firms: The good and the bad. In Melin, L., Nordqvist, M. and Sharma, P. (eds), *The SAGE Handbook of Family Business*. London: Sage.

McLeod, J.M. and Chaffee, S.H. (1972). The construction of social reality. In J. Tedeschi (ed.), *The Social Influence Process* (pp. 50–59). Chicago, IL: Aldine-Atherton.

Minuchin, S. (1974). *Families and Family Therapy*. Cambridge, MA: Harvard University.

Mungai, E. and Velamuri, S.R. (2011). Parental entrepreneurial role model influence on male offspring: Is it always positive and when does it occur? *Entrepreneurship: Theory and Practice*, 35, 337–357.

Olson, D.H. and Gorall, D.M. (2003). Circumplex model of marital and family systems. In F. Walsh (ed.), *Normal Family Processes* (3rd edn, pp. 514–547). New York: Guilford.

Patterson, J.M. (2002). Integrating family resilience and family stress theory. *Journal of Marriage and Family*, 64, 349–360.

Reiss, D. and Olivieri, M. (1983). Family paradigm and family coping. In Olson, D. and Miller, B. (eds), *Family Studies Review Yearbook I* (pp. 113–126*)*. Beverly Hills, CA: Sage.

Ritchie, L.D. and Fitzpatrick, M.D. (1990). Family communication patterns: Measuring interpersonal perceptions and interpersonal relationships. *Communication Research*, 17, 523–544.

Rousseau, D.M. (2004). Psychological contracts in the workplace: Understanding the ties that motivate. *Academy of Management Executive*, 18 (1), 120–127.

Roy, L. and Sawyers, J. (1986). The double bind: An empirical study of responses to inconsistent communications. *Journal of Marital and Family Therapy*, 12, 395–402.

Satir, V., Banmen, J., Gerber, J. and Gomori, M. (1991). *The Satir Model: Family Therapy and Beyond*. Palo Alto, CA: Science & Behavior.

Schlippe, A.v., Frank, H. (2013). The theory of social systems as a framework for understanding family businesses. *Family Relations* 62(3), 384–398

Schlippe, A. von and Groth, T. (2007). The power of stories – zur Funktion von Geschichten in Familienunternehmen [About the function of stories in family businesses]. *Kontext*, 38, 26–47.

Schlippe, A. von and Klein, S. (2010). Familienunternehmen – blinder Fleck der Familientherapie? [Family businesses – blind spot of family therapy?]. *Familiendynamik*, 35, 10–21.

Schmitt-Rodermund, E. (2004). Pathways to successful entrepreneurship: Parenting, personality, early entrepreneurial competence, and interests. *Journal of Vocational Behavior*, 65, 498–518.

Schneewind, K.A. (2010). *Familienpsychologie* [Family psychology] (3rd edn). Stuttgart: Kohlhammer.

Schrodt, P. (2009). Family strength and satisfaction as function of family communication environments. *Communication Quarterly*, 57, 171–186.

Schrodt, P., Witt, P.L. and Messersmith, A. (2008). A meta-analytical review of family communication patterns and their associations with information processing, behavioral, and psychosocial outcomes. *Communication Monographs*, 75, 248–269.

Schuman, A., Stutz, S. and Ward, J. (2010). *Family Business as Paradox*. New York: Palgrave.

Selvini Palazzoli, M., Boscolo, L., Cecchin, G. and Prata, G. (1978). *Paradox and Counterparadox*. New York: Jason-Aronson.

Segrin, C. and Flora, J. (eds) (2011). *Family Communication* (2nd edn). New York: Routledge.

Sharma, P. (2004). An overview of the field of family business studies: Current status and directions for future. *Family Business Review* 17(1), 1–36.

Sharma, P. (2011). Editor's notes: 2010 – A year in review. *Family Business Review*, 24(1), 5–8.

Sharma, P., Chrisman, J.J. and Chua, J.H. (2003). Succession planning as planned behavior: Some empirical results. *Family Business Review*, 16(1), 1–16.

Siebels, J. and zu Knyphausen-Aufseß, D. (in press). A review of theory in family business research: the implications for corporate governance. *International Journal of Management Review*.

Simon, F.B. (ed.) (2002). *Die Familie des Familienunternehmens* [The family of family business]. Heidelberg: Carl Auer Systeme.

Simon, F.B., Stierlin, H. and Wynne, L. (1985). *The Language of Family Therapy: A Systemic Vocabulary and Sourcebook*. New York: Family Process.

Sperry, L. (ed.) (2012). *Family Assessment* (2nd edn). New York: Routledge.

Sprenkle, D.H. and Piercy, F.P. (eds) (2005). *Research Methods in Family Therapy* (2nd edn). New York: Guilford.

Stanton, M. (2009). The systemic epistemology of the specialty of family psychology. In J. H. Bray and M. Stanton (eds), *The Wiley-Blackwell Handbook of Family Psychology* (pp. 5–20). Chichester: Wiley-Blackwell.

Stanton, M. and Welsh, R. (2011). *Specialty Competencies in Couple and Family Psychology*. New York: Oxford University.

Steinglass, P., Bennett, L.A., Wolin, S.J., Reiss, D., (1987). *The Alcoholic Family*. New York: Basic Books

Stierlin, H. (2007). *Gerechtigkeit in nahen Beziehungen* (Justice in close relationships). Heidelberg: Carl Auer Systeme.

Touliatos, J., Perlmutter, B.F. and Straus M.A. (2001). *Handbook of Family Measurement Techniques* (3 vols). Thousand Oaks, CA: Sage Publications.

Van der Heyden, L., Blondel, C. and Carlock, R.S. (2005). Fair process: Striving for justice in family business. *Family Business Review*, 18 (1), 1–21.

Vangelisti, A.L. (ed.) (2004). *Handbook of Family Communication*. Mahwah, NJ: Erlbaum.

Watzlawick, P., Beavin, J.H. and Jackson, D.D. (1967). *Pragmatics of Human Communication: Study of Interactional Patterns, Pathologies and Paradoxes*. New York: Norton.

Weismeier, D., Frank, H., Schlippe, A.v. (2013). Untangling 'familiness'. A literature review and directions for future Research. *Entrepreneurship and Innovation* 14(3), 165–177.

Whitchurch, G.G. and Constantine, L.L. (2009). Systems theory. In P.G. Boss, W. Doherty, R. LaRossa, W.R. Schumm and S.K. Steinmetz (eds), *Sourcebook of Family Theories and Methods: A Contextual Approach* (pp. 325–352). New York: Springer.

White, M. (2000). *Reflections on Narrative Practice*. Adelaide, Australia: Dulwich Centre

White, M. and Epston, D. (1990). *Narrative Means to Therapeutic Ends*. New York: Norton.

Whitton, S.W., Walding, R.J., Schultz, M.S., Allen, J.P., Crowell, J.A. and Hauser, S.T. (2008). Prospective associations from family-of-origin interactions to adult marital interactions and relationship adjustment. *Journal of Family Psychology*, 22, 274–286.

Williams, L., Edwards, T.M., Patterson, J. and Chamow, L. (2011). *Essential Assessment Skills for Couple and Family Therapists*. New York: Guilford.

Wimmer, R., Domeyer, E., Oswald, M. and Vater, G. (2005). *Familienunternehmen – Auslaufmodell oder Erfolgstyp?* [Family business – expiring or successful types?]. Wiesbaden: Gabler.

Winek, J.L. (2010). *Systemic Family Therapy*. Beverly Hills/London: Sage.

Wylie, M.S. (1999). The ties that define. *Family Therapy Networker*, May-June, pp. 21–31.

Zachary, R. (2011). The importance of the family system in family business. *Journal of Family Business Management*, 1(1), 26–36.

Zahra, S. and Sharma, P. (2004). Family business research: A strategic reflection. *Family Business Review*, 17, 331–346.

Zellweger, T. and Astrachan, J. (2008). On the emotional value of owning a firm. *Family Business Review*, 21, 347–363.

Zwack, M. and Schlippe, A. von (2011). The transmission of values in family businesses – stories as a form of communicating cultural values. Paper presented at the 7th Workshop on Family Firm Management Research of the European Institute for Advanced Studies in Management (EIASM), May 2011, Witten, Germany.

4

The Anthropology of Family Business: An Imagined Ideal

Alex Stewart

INTRODUCTION

Anthropology: An Underutilized Resource

Cultural and social anthropology can advance family business studies thanks to well developed literatures in three areas: kinship theory, relevant research, and ethnography (up-close field research using participant observation). Despite these potential benefits, the discipline remains an 'unutilized resource for advancing the field of family business studies' (Stewart, 2003, p. 383). Although it shares central interests with family business scholars (Rutherford, 2010; Stewart, 2008) it has not been widely utilized (Wigren, 2007). Searching the abstract of family business journals (largely *Family Business Review*) for a variant of 'anthropology' uncovers just one article. Searching the full text uncovers 21, largely incidental, references. More generally, anthropologists and business scholars have, since the 1960s, largely ignored one another (Jordan, 2010; Rosa and Caulkins, 2013; Sunderland and Denny, 2007, pp. 28–32).

How to Make Progress

How could the promise of the anthropology for family business be better fulfilled? For scholars brave enough to take on this task, two prerequisites stand out. First, they should familiarize themselves with anthropological findings and concepts. They should learn kinship theory and study relevant ethnographic works. They should then adapt this knowledge to family business by asking fundamental questions about kinship in connection with business. This would require attention to sources of solidarity and conflict, to cultural variation, and to the lived experience of kinship. Such a preparation is the subject of Part 1 of this chapter.

Second, family business scholarship should be methodologically sound and suited to family business studies. Methodology in anthropology is less well understood than in, say, economics or psychology. Therefore,

Part 2 addresses this concern. It focuses on five 'tactics' for ethnographic method in Stewart (1998), applying them to issues in the family business field. It also addresses the need for cross-disciplinary study.

Business school researchers with these competencies could make outstanding scholarly contributions. Their writings could also unveil real-world details to capture the imagination of practitioners. These points are related. Up-close field research explores in depth the lived world of practitioners, uncovering the 'complex and tacit processes' of family firms (Nordqvist et al., 2009, p. 295) that often go unnoticed in our journals. Examples discussed below include 'betrayal as a force of production' (Yanagisako, 2002), 'strategies of heirship' (Goody, 1976), and behind-the-scenes roles of women in apparently male dominated cultures (Hamabata, 1990). These examples apply to Italy and Japan, reminding us that anthropology's cross-cultural perspective militates against ethnocentrism. Moreover, anthropological findings about kinship complement the strength of family business research, which is more discerning about business than family matters (Stewart, 2008; Stewart and Hitt, 2012).

PART 1: PREPARING TO CONTRIBUTE

Before launching into anthropological research in family business, scholars will also need a thorough preparation in the relevant literatures. How should they begin this preparation?

Familiarity with Relevant Ethnographies

Preparation could start with readings in the most developed, closely relevant field in anthropology. However, much of this field – kinship theory – would appear too opaque and exotic on first exposure (Patterson, 2005; Peletz, 1995). If scholars began instead with

relevant ethnographies they would simultaneously start to learn kinship theory. These texts could also fire their ambitions and suggest possibilities for their own work (Van Maanen, 2011).

Unfortunately, I know of no book-length ethnographies of family business at the firm level. This contrasts with ethnographies of non-family firms (Hodson, 1998; Morrill & Fine, 1997). Particularly lacking are in-depth scholarly studies on both kinship and business within individual firms (Nordqvist et al., 2009). Ram (1994) and Helin (2011) are qualified exceptions; they studied more than one firm but focused on one in each case. Family business ethnographies typically focus on multiple firms in industry clusters. These include Italian footwear (Blim, 1990) and silk (Yanagisako, 2002) clusters, and emigrant Chinese in the leather goods (Oxfeld, 1993), textiles (Wong, 1988) and take-away restaurant trades (Song, 1993).

Ram (1994) and Yanagisako (2002) are relatively attentive to business issues, and highly recommended. Yanagisako conducted high quality fieldwork, reflected in compelling accounts of several family firms. She is insightful on notions like 'the conundrum of the second-generation self-made man' (pp. 90–92) and 'betrayal as a force of production' (chap. 4). By the latter she means familial creative destruction (see also Goody, 1996, pp. 141–145, 155, 203; Kasdan, 1965):

> In later years, as the firm matures and begins to bring in members of the second generation, limitations to firm growth and expansion fuel sentiments of distrust and suspicion, which operate as forces for the division of the firm, the diffusion of technology, and the destruction of families. Out of these processes emerge new firms, new families and new solidarities. (Yanagisako, 2002, p. 115)

Two books about Japanese family businesses by Japanese-American scholars, Hamabata (1990) and Kondo (1990), are more typical of ethnographies of family firms, because neither offers much insight into business as such. Their focus – Hamabata's especially – is on the family. Nonetheless, both demonstrate the value of studies that examine businesses from the family perspective. They reveal a complex 'set[s] of mutual connections' between 'market [and] family' (Davidoff and Hall, 1987, p. 32). Hamabata, for example, found that wealthy Japanese women conducted economic transactions through their natal kin. This was interesting and unexpected in a strongly patrilocal society; i.e., brides leave the geographic area of their families of orientation and affiliate with their husband's kindred instead (1990, p. 28).

A widespread finding in historical and ethnographic studies is that while women apparently play only private, domestic roles, they nonetheless influence business and public affairs, often through female only networks (Davidoff and Hall, 1987, pp. 202, 227; also Bruun, 1993, p. 22; Colli et al., 2003; Farrell, 1993, chap. 4; Lomnitz and Pérez-Lizaur, 1987, p. 118; Ram, 1994, pp. 132–136; Robertson, 1991, p. 41). These findings offer insights into the linkages of business and kinship. Unfortunately, few studies examine the kinship–business connection in depth for the implications of this connection for the business itself.

Knowledge of Kinship Studies

'Kinship', 'Family', 'Household'

Making sense of kinship writings requires an understanding of the relationships between 'family', 'kinship', and 'household'. 'Kinship' can be defined as 'the network of genealogical relationships and social ties modeled on the relations of genealogical parenthood'(Holy, 1996, p. 40), 'as culturally defined by the society involved' (Good, 1996, p. 312). The 'systems' formed in this way 'divide people into categories of kin, and then define marriageability in terms of these categories. They define descent, if you like, and legislate alliance' (i.e., marriage); they are thus 'the assortive mating systems of the species' (Fox, 1983, pp. 2, 1).

A universally applicable definition of 'family' is elusive (Creed, 2000). 'People

know what they mean when they use the word family, and the meaning is usually clear to others by the context ... but most would find it difficult to define [the word] precisely' (Pine, 1996, p. 223). Its meanings are variable and often fuzzy (Davidoff and Hall, 1987, pp. 31, 216; Stafford, 2000). With these qualifications, the effort by Harrell (1997) is helpful. He sees the family as a subset of kinship: 'kinship principles have ramifications beyond the family ... The family is a special type of kinship group, one consisting of close relatives in close cooperation in daily life' (1997, p. 5).

'Households' have been proposed as more useful alternative than 'families' for family business scholarship (Aldrich and Cliff, 2003). Certainly, the physical and human arrangements of households are important variables (Blim, 1990; Bruun, 1993; Yanagisako, 1979). Unlike families, however, households are not subsets of kinship systems but, being defined by function and by residence, include such non-kin as servants and boarders, and comprise overlapping subsets within (extended) families (Brettell, 2002).

Cross-cultural Variation

Ethnographies are more entertaining than kinship theory, but there is no escaping the constructs of the field (e.g., 'affinity': ties through marriage). Moreover, familiarity with kinship theory alerts us to the range of human variation. Kinship systems share commonalities and universal constraints (e.g., the length of the human lifespan; Harrell, 1997; Sangren, 2009), but they vary in many ways, even in the same country at the same time (Yanagisako, 1978). This variance can help family firm scholars to minimize ethnocentric assumptions about human possibilities. For example, family business scholars almost never study the practices of marriage 'payments': neither 'dowry' nor 'brideprice' are found in the full texts of journals with 'family business' in their names (ProQuest (TM) search, 5/24/2012). Yet these practices involve 'substantial' transfers of wealth and are current in both India and China (Anderson, 2007; Brown et al., 2011, p. 140).

Other variable properties of kinship systems affect family firms. Examples include the modes of transmitting property or office, the cultural understanding of 'family' itself (Shimizu, 1991), rules of marriage and affinity (Shapiro, 1997; Stockard, 2002), and gender and sex role expectations (Ortner, 1996; Stone, 2010). Crucially for entrepreneurs, the potential for discretion in treatment of kin also varies (Scheffler, 2001; Stewart, 2010). Little wonder that we find that family firms vary across multiple dimensions (Goody, 1996; Stewart and Hitt, 2012; Yanagisako, 2002).

Old' Scientific and 'New' Humanistic Kinship Studies

A source of confusion for newcomers to kinship theory is disagreements between the 'old' and 'new' kinship studies. This distinction parallels older and newer modes of anthropology. Although these distinctions are not clear-cut they are widely encountered. The 'old' kinship studies tend to adopt what Van Maanen (2011) termed 'realist tales' while the 'new' ones adopt such experimental modes as 'confessional', 'impressionist', 'critical', and 'literary tales'.

These distinctions center on the tension within anthropology between science and humanism (Eriksen, 2006, pp. 13, 25, 32–34; Johnson and Johnson, 1990; Malkki, 2007). Stereotypically, social scientific ethnography pursues naturalist documentation; on the other hand, humanistic ethnography pursues cultural critique or art, or both (Armstrong, 1971, pp. 80–100; Lett, 1997, pp. 1–19; Mulligan, 1987). Scientific ethnography aims to be objective, comparative, realist, and focused on social processes; humanistic ethnography to be subjective, particularistic, interpretive, and focused on lived experiences (Patterson, 2005; Peletz, 1995). This distinction is demonstrated by quotes from two recent ethnographies, both of which concern inter-connections between local and global economic forces:

Artesanías can be lucrative. A sweater wholesaler generally makes a profit of $1 per sweater, and some make twice that, selling 5,000 to 250,000 sweaters annually. This is impressive in a country where the average annual per capita income has hovered around $1,100 since the end of the 1980s according to World Bank statistics. (Meisch, 2002, p. 78)

The universal bridge to a global dream space still beckons us. The bridge might take us out of our imagined isolation into a space of unity and transcendence: the whole world. We find ourselves like a man looking out from his parochial island toward the vast but hazy world of the mainland. The bridge of universal truths promises to take us there. Yet ... we become hardened, or, alternatively, we are overcome with grief and anger. (Tsing, 2005, p. 85)

This latter passage (clearly) reflects a humanistic anthropology and is reminiscent of an early vision of such an anthropology by Wagner (1979, p. 10), who called for 'appreciating our species quest for meaning and all the elusive ghosts – responsibility, empathy, justice, awe, creativity, beauty, the numinous – that go with it, and identifying *ourselves* with that quest'.

These distinctions are not always so apparent; many ethnographies have elements of science and of art (Wagner, 1979). Some 'old' kinship studies include excellent treatments of 'new' kinship issues (compare Fortes, 1949), and Geertz, the most influential advocate of humanism (Kuper, 1999, chap. 3), was skeptical about postmodernism and adamant that his approach was scientific (Geertz, 1973, pp. 15, 24). Further, 'new' kinship studies are heterogeneous and some current kinship theory is avowedly scientific. An example of the latter is the network analysis of kinship by White and his colleagues (e.g., White and Johansen, 2006).

However, the differences between humanistic and scientific approaches are not merely rhetorical, nor do they affect only extreme advocates of one approach or another. Questions about the purpose of scholarship divide important kinship scholars. For example, should scholars aim to approximate 'truth', or is that a naive goal? What role, if any, should data, or non-anthropological theories, play in kinship studies? Thus, the field includes lively debates by proponents of one persuasion or the other (Holy, 1996, chap. 7; Scheffler, 2010).

Partisanship can roughly be inferred by the critique or approbation of the work of David Schneider. His work was an influential precursor of the new kinship studies (Feinberg, 2001; Shimizu, 1991). Schneider was a student of Parsons, whose own work sought to untangle the relationships between four 'system levels': culture, social relationships, psychology and biology (Parsons, 1951). However, Schneider reduced the anthropological study of kinship to culture *sui generis* (Godelier, 2011 [2004], pp. 19–22, 69, 104; Kuper, 1999, chap. 4). The implication was that central issues for family business, connections between business and kinship (both of which involve culture but also personality and social relationships) were out of bounds. Schneider also combined a sweeping rejection of prior ethnographies as projections of western presumptions, with a disregard for evidence in his own work (Schneider, 1995, pp. 209–212). His later writings helped persuade many anthropologists (except in France; Patterson, 2005) to abandon kinship as a topic of inquiry (Carsten, 2000).

Focus on Important Questions

Preparation Specific to Family Business

A relevant anthropology of family business asks fundamental questions. Why does kinship exist; how does this generate ambivalence in relationships; how does this affect family firms? (Stewart and Miner, 2011). What is the relationship between kinship and other relations, such as economic, religious or political (White and Jorion, 1996)? These questions have long been debated. Some have argued that kinship relations are merely epiphenomena or idioms about something else. A prominent example was a book about 'the relation between land use and kinship within [a particular] territorial framework',

in which Leach (1961, pp. 299, 305) announced 'that kinship systems have no "reality" at all except in relation to land and property. What the social anthropologist calls kinship structure is just a way of talking about property relations which can also be talked about in other ways'.

As Godelier cautioned, 'this was a provocation of the sort Leach was fond of launching' and it led, with other writings of the era, to further discussion of 'the links between kinship and economy, power, religion, etc.' (2011 [2004], pp. 16, 19, also 485). Godelier's own efforts to answer this question are worth an effort at a précis. In his view:

> Leach missed the essential point. The language of kinship is inevitable in so far as, from a person's birth, kinship relations are a source of right and obligations that precede any contract ... The great strength of kinship is that it embeds these rights and obligations in relationships ... which, for some, are nurturing, protecting, and which provide the primary material and social support that greets the person at his or her birth. (p. 314)

In short, there are reasons that kinship *and not something else* provides the idiom for the most valued obligations in a culture (Bloch, 1971; Bloch and Sperber, 2002; Stewart and Miner, 2011). Godelier does not, however, infer that kinship plays a preeminent role amongst the other 'practices and areas of life' (Godelier, 2011 [2004], p. 72), nor that kinship can itself be the basis for the organization of a territorial group. Such a role can only be played by relationships that cut across all its members, and these relationships in his view are political and religious. These latter two 'co-opt' (p. 82) or 'come to reside' (p. 480) 'in a given kinship relation and make all kinship relations serve their own functioning and reproduction' (p. 480; alternatively political-religious relations 'take over', pp. 481, 483: 'investissent', p. 646 of the French edition). Only these non-kinship relations 'have the capacity to create a *general state of interdependence* between all of the groups and individuals ... and which make the society into a *whole* ... This is something kinship *per se* ... is precisely incapable of doing' (p. 483).

Godelier's thesis holds more than theoretical interest. 'Kinship relations everywhere' he claims 'can and especially must support' those political-religious relations that have infiltrated them (p. 496; we must ask again why it is *kinship* and not something else that must do this). The consequence, he argues, is that non-kinship (or akinship) social relations are transformed into:

> the stuff of kinship. And everything that falls under kinship is transformed into relations between the sexes in the first place and then between parents and children. And finally everything having to do with kinship is imprinted into sexed bodies from birth and becomes an attribute of a person's sex ... [and are] metamorph[ized into] *'gender' differences'* that are perceived to characterize 'not only men and women but myriad beings that populate the universe. (p. 496)

It follows (pp. 496–497), that revolutions in the domain of sex roles must be fought primarily on the terrain of politics and also of religion.

The Kinship–Business Interface

A related question for family business scholars is explaining the process by which entrepreneurial opportunities derive from the kinship–business interface (Johannisson, 2002). Anthropological answers to this question require assumptions about the ways the 'domains' of kinship and business are distinct. They also require reference to foundational work in the anthropology of entrepreneurship, according to which entrepreneurs find value from creating bridges between different spheres of exchange (Barth, 1967). As Stewart and Hitt elaborated McDonough (1986), (2012, p. 72):

> Discrepancies in evaluation can arise because of constraints on exchange – in an obvious example, familial love is not widely regarded as saleable. They can also arise simply from differing perspectives. For example, impecunious noble families may enter into marital exchanges with the newly wealthy, trading prestige for commercial opportunities or capital, and vice versa.

Numerous ethnographies have contributed to our understanding of this process at the business-kinship interface (Bruun, 1993; de Lima, 2000; Lomnitz and Pérez-Lizaur, 1987; Marcus and Hall, 1992; McDonough, 1986; Ram, 1994).

Attention to Lived Experiences

Exploring the business-kinship interface requires attention to everyday experiences of kinship. For this, the 'new' kinship studies are more attentive, examining emotional qualities like ambivalence (Lambek, 2011; Peletz, 1995). A proponent argues, 'To understand relatedness, and to understand the place of relatedness in dynamic relationships that converge in the domestic arena yet extend beyond it, requires detailed analysis of spoken and unspoken meanings, the micropolitics of interactions, and historical structurings of power in particular places at specific moments' (Van Vleet, 2008, p. 195; also Godelier, 2011 [2004], p. 78). Compared with the focus in the 'old' kinship studies on structure, function and 'the politico-jural aspect of kinship' (Holy, 1996, p. 51), more focus is on human agency (willfulness and strategizing: Viazzo and Lynch, 2002) and 'everyday cooperation, negotiation, and competition' (Yan, 2001, p. 239).

An exemplar of the focus on lived kinship is Stafford's paper on 'the processual and creative aspects of Chinese kinship and relatedness' (2000, p. 38). He argues for four inter-connected and *'equally* forceful ... systems of Chinese relatedness': not only patriliny and affinity (the 'old' kinship topics), but also '"the cycle of *yang*" (which centers mostly on parent–child relationships) and "the cycle of *laiwang*" (which centers mostly on relationships between friends, neighbours, and acquaintances' (as above). These latter two systems are ignored in formalist analyses that render the familial and domestic as separate from kinship. Moreover, these two systems – and *laiwang* in particular – are important for understanding the opportunities for discretion facing Chinese entrepreneurs.

Attention to general patterns at the expense of everyday, 'domestic' kinship misses vital concerns in family firms. For example, Hamabata found that the wife of a Japanese company president believed that 'for their household [i.e., their *ie*] ... the objective was to bring in talent through marriage and adoption' (1990, p. 44). These are typical Japanese 'strategies of heirship' (Goody, 1976), amenable to analysis from afar. However, Hamabata's fieldwork in the domestic realm led him to an observation attainable only that way: her daughter strongly objected to becoming, effectively, a household head – 'a man in the guise of a woman' – wishing instead to be 'a true *hana-yome* (a newlywed bride)' (p. 45). Both aspects of this vignette, the pattern of discretion in Japanese family firms of incorporating adopted sons-in-law into the *ie*, and the way it played out in action, are needed for an understanding of these family firms.

Alertness to Sources of Solidarity and Conflict

For the entrepreneur, kinship can be a resource, a hindrance, or irrelevant (Wallman, 1975). Relatives can be the most reliable, long-term sources of support (Bloch, 1973); they can be the most insidious of foes (Gordon and Nicholson, 2008). Relationships with kin can be infused with deeply felt obligations, or entirely instrumental (Stewart, 2003). How can we explain the way the range of possibilities plays out on the ground? The answer depends on the context, so a first step is attentiveness to ethnographic detail. For example, Peletz urged us to learn 'more about how and why Chinese [family firms] are able to overcome familial ambivalence in the context of economic cooperation when many other groups (e.g., Malays, Javanese, and Thais) are not' (1995, p. 355).

Peletz speaks to a core question for family firms: how and why can kinship be a source of solidarity but also of conflict (Stewart, 2003). We have noted the role of differential growth in kin compared with wealth

(Yanagisako, 2002). As this implies, the answer requires understanding of the links between kinship and property, of succession and inheritance (dowry, bridewealth), and of formal and realized law (Anderson, 2007; Hann, 2005). Overarching all of these topics is differential power in sex roles (Godelier, 2011 [2004], pp. 74, 80–85, 483, 496–497).

Ethnographic studies of the role of property include the example of 'betrayal as a force of production' (Yanagisako, 2002) noted above. Another is Greenhalgh's (1994) article on power differentials within the family. Another is Goody's (1976) works on 'strategies of heirship' or ways to cope with a shortage of heirs. Strategies include marital choices (e.g., serial monogamy, polygyny) and incorporative practices such as adoption (Stewart, 2010). A related topic is the process of entrepreneurs who dis-embed from kinship obligations at one stage of building their ventures, but re-embed as honored community leaders later on (Hart, 1975; Stewart, 1990).

PART 2: WELL-EXECUTED ETHNOGRAPHY

Criteria for Ethnographic Method

Having prepared themselves with their readings, anthropologists who study family business also need to prepare methodologically. Ethnography, or inquiry based on participant observation, is the core method of social and cultural anthropology. Perhaps I should say *set of methods*, plural, due to the medley of approaches (Adler and Adler, 2008; Malkki, 2007). Anthropological ethnographers lack a consensus on, or even an interest in, the criteria and standards for appraising these productions (Briggs, 2007; Werner, 1998; Wigren, 2007). In an effort to fill this void, I have proposed that ethnography should be judged by three epistemic values or criteria, provided that the ethnography aims to approximate scientific truth (Stewart, 1998, p. 14; my editors believed that these criteria apply equally to 'postmodern, poetic, and other nonscientific ethnographies', p. v).

The three criteria are (1) descriptive truth (or 'veracity'); (2) transcendence of perspectives – i.e., relative impartiality – (or 'objectivity'); and (3) specifying the applicability of its insights to other settings (or 'perspicacity'). Their 'quantitative' equivalents are validity, reliability and generalizability. In Stewart (1998), I noted the challenges in research that make the criteria hard to satisfy, and the most effective 'tactics' that help to overcome these challenges. Here, our focus is on the latter.

Veracity (Akin to Validity)

Validity seems an innocuous criterion for ethnography. However, I agree with Wolcott (1994) that the term is too colored by connotations of psychometrics and propose the alternative term 'veracity' (Stewart, 1998, pp. 14–15). By this I mean descriptive truth. This goal is never fully achieved, but attempts to attain it are critical. Without some success in this direction no other criteria need concern us (p. 18). Due to the challenges confronting its attainment, both in the field setting and in the person of the researcher (pp. 19–20), I propose several 'tactics', of which the most crucial are prolonged fieldwork, good participative role relationships, and the search for reorienting observations.

Tactic One: Prolonged Fieldwork

Most 'qualitative' studies in management conform to publish or perish norms by adopting 'rapid appraisal' approaches (Stewart, 1998, p. 20; also Morrill and Fine, 1997). This is unfortunate (Werner, 1998). Prolonged fieldwork of 12–18 months or more 'is the single most potent tactic that ethnographers have to enhance veracity' (Stewart, 1998, p. 20). Without it, researchers miss witnessing cultural and interpersonal subtleties. They miss chances to get 'sufficiently 'behind the scenes' in, for example, succession processes (Lam, 2011) where they might witness discrepancies between actions and words (Hodson, 1998, p. 1191). They miss chances to notice disconfirming observations and multiple perspectives. For example, Chagnon (1968) and Godelier (2011 [2004], chap. 2) misunderstood kinship systems early in their fieldwork.

Tactic Two: Helpful Participative Roles

Another reason to persist in fieldwork is that ethnographers often need to assume a sufficiently 'active' or 'complete' membership role (Adler and Adler, 1987). The role of 'researcher' is insufficient to 'generate opportunities for inquiry ... [that provides] exposure to interactions and performances, in a wide variety of naturalistic, backstage social contexts [preferably with] access to a wide variety of actors' (Stewart, 1998, pp. 23–24; also Mosse, 2006). Some sort of 'apprenticeship' role is ideal (Coy, 1989), though access to such roles may be difficult.

Difficulties with access may account for the dearth of ethnographies of family firms. Access into any organizational sites can be challenging (Feldman et al., 2003). Access into family firms is particularly challenging. Families themselves often maintain 'relatively closed and highly protected boundaries' (Daly and Dienhart, 1998, p. 102). Gatekeepers of family firms may be accustomed to privacy, and concerned that sensitive family matters could be publicized if they granted researchers up-close, long-term access.

Opportunistic use of pre-existing connections such as consultancy roles may be needed, as it was for Dalton and other organizational ethnographers (Dalton, 1959; Helin, 2011). One such form of access that suits family business research is native or auto-ethnography, such that insiders study their own firms (Jackson, 2004; Jacobs-Huey, 2002). Learned's dissertation (1995, pp. 49–55) is an example (e.g., Learned painfully dismissed his father from the board of directors). Another possible design is the study of family firm individuals, not firms, along the lines of Harper's (1987) photo-ethnographic study of a mechanic, or Keesing's (1978) oral history of a Melanesian entrepreneur.

Tactic Three: Search for Reorienting Observations

'Longer periods of fieldwork ... increase variation in what could be observed and in the capacities to notice' (Stewart, 1998, p. 21). Therefore, prolonged fieldwork enables another tactic, that of good membership roles, and also a third tactic, that of seeking reorienting observations (Campbell, 1975). This latter tactic relies on the persistent 'suppositional work' of recognizing one's emerging expectations and seeking to discover surprises or reorientations in our developing understandings (Locke, 2011a, p. 631). It is a comprehensive search for comparisons and connections among phenomena. In Mills' terms (2000 [1959], p. 200), the scholar puts 'together hitherto isolated items, by finding unsuspected connections.'

Implementing this tactic is difficult, due to our inclination to notice 'confirming rather than disconfirming evidence' (Creswell and Miller, 2000, p. 127). It is facilitated by habits such as rendering observations explicit, by using photographs (Collier and Collier, 1986; Harper, 1987) or (more commonly) fieldnotes (Emerson et al., 2011; Sanjek, 1990a). The search for reorienting observations may also be enabled, post-fieldwork, by in-depth indexing of data in computer retrieval programs (Friese, 2012; Stewart, 1998, p. 53).

Objectivity (Akin to Reliability)

Once you have stayed long enough in appropriate roles, noting many reorienting observations, you launch your 'write-up', presenting the perspectives of insiders from whom you have learned. At this point, the criterion of objectivity poses a question: which perspectives? Have you depicted, for example, only the views of 'key informants' among the leaders (Aunger, 2004)? Or only the views of disenchanted branches of the family? Or only the views of males, or females? Or only family and not non-family, members? A study that is 'more objective ... [is] less dependent on a singular perspective' (Hegelund, 2005,

p. 663). It 'transcends' the perspectives of just the researcher and just of (certain) informants (Hunt, 2003, chap. 8; Stewart, 1998, p. 16). You cannot depict all perspectives equally. But you can sample multiple perspectives from multiple informants (Goldthorpe, 2000, pp. 74–79; Heider, 1972). You can try systematically to cover the 'range of variation' amongst them (Werner, 1998; Werner and Bernard, 1994, p. 9).

Tactic Four: The Ethnographer's Path

You can also reveal for readers which perspectives you have encountered and represented. You do so by depicting what Sanjek (1990b, pp. 398–400) calls 'the ethnographer's path', the network of informants that the researcher engages' (Stewart, 1998, p. 34; also Werner, 1998). This depiction can be implicit in your account; explicit discussions are unusual (Moffat, 1992). The way you represent the path is certainly less important than the path itself. But only if you make it transparent can others evaluate the biases that affect yours or any ethnography. Only then can they learn 'the *range of variation in perspectives* that were witnessed' (Stewart, 1998, p. 35). Only then can they evaluate your study's objectivity.

Perspicacity (Somewhat Akin to Generalizability)

Perspicacity is the closest analogue to external validity or generalizability that ethnographers can aim for. But it is not the same. It has two elements: (i) the generation of insights that (ii) can be utilized in studies in different spatial, temporal and cultural contexts. In short, it 'is the capacity to produce applicable insights' (Stewart, 1998, p. 47). The primary goal is generation of insights, and a secondary goal is their representation so as to help others to develop insights of their own. The first, primary, goal is the object of tactic five: 'exploration.'

Tactic Five: Exploration

'Exploration' is a process of discovery. It 'is a quest; it is not a technique that lends itself to tidy or comprehensive prescriptions' (Stewart, 1998, p. 57). To the contrary, it calls for 'imagination' (Locke, 2011a, p. 614; Stebbins, 2001, p. 230). Mills (2000 [1959], p. 201) expressed it this way: 'Imagination is often successfully invited by putting together hitherto isolated items, by finding unsuspected connections'. He recommended disconnecting and reconnecting theories. Besides creativity and imagination, then, the key construct here is 'connections.'

Connections are of two types. In one type, a modal observation of a cultural object, say, a post-marital residence rule, is connected with another observation as a matter of *comparison or contrast*. In the other type, it is *placed in a wider context*, another aspect of social life that impinges on the modal object, such as patterns of inheritance. Both of these connections are needed to answer Becker's question 'What is this a case of?' (Ragin, 1992, p. 6). And as Locke (2011b, p. 89) argues, to answer this question we need a wide range of 'data and ... cycles of generating and trying out ideas against them.' We need to make multiple connections with comparisons and contexts.

Why this should be stems from the way ethnographers make sense of observations. As Geertz (1974) demonstrated, we have to consider multiple examples of a cultural object to discern what it is, how it compares with similar cultural objects and how various instances compare with one another (see also Urban, 1999). These comparisons derive from within-site observations, ethnographies about other cultures, and personal experiences and preconceptions (Barth, 1999; Godelier, 2011 [2004], pp. 12; 70–72; Mills, 2000, p.195). The need for connections also derives from the nature of an insight, in the sense the word is used here.

Middle Range Theories

An insight is not an observation pure and simple. It is not a mere social 'fact'. It is an 'unexpected', non-trivial patterned set of social facts or observations that can fruitfully be compared with observations in other times and places (Arnould et al., 2007, p. 107). Ethnographic insights of this sort tend to be middle-range theories. An example is Goody's conception of 'diverging devolution' (bilateral inheritance: inter-generation transmission of property to both sexes), which he associates with 'dowry, with monogamy, with in-marriage of various sorts, and with kin terms that differentiate the nuclear family from more distant kin' (Goody, 1969, p. 55; also 1976; Hann, 2008). Goody's theory was developed from the systematic comparison of multiple ethnographies, using the Human Relations Area Files (see Ember and Ember, 2009). Other examples of middle range theories derived from localized fieldwork include Yanagisako's (2002) betrayal as a force of production, and Barth's (1967) entrepreneurship as the bridging of spheres of exchange. The example I used in Stewart (1998, pp. 48–51, 62, 82–83), is Aubrey Richard's (1950) 'matrilineal puzzle', which holds that matrilineal systems have structural challenges requiring resolution.

For reasons of space and readers' interests, ethnographers rarely spell out the connections that generated their concepts. However, Yanagisako hints about how she recognized 'betrayal as a force of production' (2002, chap. 4). She asked herself comparative questions. Which informants tended most to use the common phrase '*parenti, serpenti* [relatives are snakes]' (p. 110). Who tended to deny that kinsfolk are relatives? Who was depicted as a non-relative in one context but as a relative in another? What level of wealth among family firms characterized those who most used this expression? As these examples demonstrate, comparative questions lead to contextual questions. The syndrome she depicted was most pronounced amongst those firms lacking the wealth to provide venture opportunities for all descendants and that 'relied on relatives for technical labor rather than financial capital' (p. 116).

Contexts

Whenever the topic of kinship is explored, comparisons lead to other contexts. Family business researchers should be alert to the possibility that any set of observations – whether categorized as a matter of ritual and ideology, politics and law, ecology, labor needs, and so on – might prove important for explaining the family (Yanagisako, 1979). Kinship is notoriously inter-connected with other social and cultural topics (Creed, 2000; Godelier, 2011 [2004]; Peletz, 1995). For example, a study of 'the function of kinship in politics' concluded that understanding requires attention to 'other social categories' such as factionalism, religious affiliation, class and ethnicity' (Buessow, 2011, p. 108). Not every connection will be illuminating, but certain connections, as those with demography, sex roles, and modes of access to property and other rights should be entertained (Scheffler, 2001; Yanagisako, 1979).

Consider the example above from Hamabata (1990, pp. 41–46), in which a president's daughter resisted marrying a *muko-yooshi* (male bride) to succeed to her father's status, her only brother being indulged and incapable. Among the comparisons needed for explicating this incident, we would need to know (as Yanagisako did) the level of wealth of the firm. Only those successful enough to attract a capable son-in-law might also be able to provide for the independence displayed by the daughter. We would have to ask about the daughter's gender ideology, in which she saw the burdens of an *oyome-san* (bride), under the thumb of a mother-in-law in a stranger's household, to be less than those of a 'household headship in the guise of the household wifeship ... [and] denying the very essence of femininity' (p. 45). We would have to make comparisons with other potential brides as well as forms of gender ideology. We would also consider the implications for 'strategies of heirship' (Goody, 1976). We would need to bear in mind the relative power of marriageable daughters as well as available sons-in-law.

An Insight Should be Useful for Others

As this example suggests, perspicacious middle range theories are amenable to disconfirmation or reconfiguration because they allow for corollaries. In the example of the matrilineal puzzle, one could propose that matrilineal systems are relatively unstable given certain residential patterns and contingencies; in the case of betrayal as a force of production, that later generation offshoots of family firms tend to be involved in disputes over intellectual property; in the case of Barth's theory of entrepreneurship as the crossing of spheres of exchange, that entrepreneurs are especially likely to be aware of more than one such sphere. The capacity of insights to be useful for later development has implications for how ethnographies should be reported. They should report sufficient detail for this purpose, ideally (perhaps) idealistically, enough that 'all the contingencies that inhere in or affect their proffered constructs and theories [can be considered for] the potential reconstruction or disconfirmation [of your insight] by other scholars' (Stewart, 1998, p. 63).

Research Tradeoffs

Perspicacity is the closest that ethnography comes to generalizability, but it is not the same. We learn about the actual behaviors and cultures of others using ethnography as our lens. However, we learn about the distribution and variance of behavior and culture with surveys as our lens. We cannot do both at once; surveys and fieldwork pull in incompatible directions (Van Maanen, 1975). Efforts have been made to merge the approaches (Aunger, 2004; Gravlee et al., 2009) but it is hard to overcome the tradeoffs of research. In Brinberg and McGrath's terms, only one of the goals of 'generalizability, precision and realism can be maximized' (1985, p. 43). In Weick's (1979, pp. 35–36) terms, we can maximize only two amongst the goals of being general, simple or accurate.

The core of ethnography – up-close, unobtrusive observation, and situated learning – does not generate generalizability. For example, the qualities that make for an excellent informant do not make for repre-sentativeness (Spradley, 1979, pp. 47–54). Moreover, 'standardization of techniques' (Cohen, 1977, p. 245) would be needed for cross-cultural comparisons, if one were to directly feed data from various cultures into the same algorithms, without the need for another level of interpretation. The reason ethnographic standardization is a quixotic goal is the 'complex relationships between indicators [which need to be 'locally applic-able'] and variables' (Cohen, as above). The former are often culture-specific, defying read-ily comparable measures. 'Anthropology has not standardized its techniques ... precisely because it values its own holistic richness and therefore requires culture-specific indicators, not cross-culturally applicable instruments' (as above).

Improvization

For the problem of within-site variation, the solution in principle is random sampling of informants (Heider, 1972; Johnson and Johnson, 1990). However, this solution does violence to the character of participant observa-tion. Ethnographers who were in some sense insiders but who treated people randomly would soon lose their credibility. They also could not pursue disconfirming observations without prioritizing theoretically useful, not random, comparisons. The ethnographic 'strat-egy' in fieldwork should be *'seeking out diversity'* (Barth, 1999, p. 82), not randomness. Further, this seeking must be opportunistic, given fieldwork realities. As Malkki (2007, p. 180) argues about the improvisational charac-ter of ethnography, the reason there is no 'stable tradition with a fixed battery of methods ... [is that] improvisation *is* the tradition'. Improvisa-tion is a reason there can be no fixed, singu-lar ethnographic method, but rather 'an open, flexible, context-dependent, and time-sensitive *repertory* of possibilities' (as above).

Triangulate, if You Seek Generalizability

Goldthorpe (2000, p. 70) believes that eth-nography can test 'explanatory accounts' at the level of 'the social processes through which ... relations among variables are actu-ally generated and sustained' – something surveys cannot accomplish. However, he holds that none of the ethnographic approaches to the 'problems of variation across locales' (p. 79) is adequate. Sociology simply has not produced law-like theories that will, once observed in one locale, 'necessarily be found [to apply] in all comparable locales' (p. 81). Therefore, theories produced from ethnogra-phies must be tested with other means. Should you wish to learn about variability and distribution, non-ethnographic methods are needed (Werner and Bernard, 1994). Ethnographers seeking generalizability need to triangulate (Scandura and Young, 2000). Examples of triangulation, with representative surveys to test the external validity of ethnographic findings, include Hollos and Larsen (2004) and Ryan and Bernard (2006).

Cross-disciplinarity

For these methodological reasons, a robust anthropology of family business does not rely only on ethnography. Moreover, this anthro-pology does not rely only on anthropology. It uses sociology, history, and possibly law and psychology (Godelier, 2011 [2004], p. 522; Stewart, 2008). Comprehensiveness and con-textualization draw us to questions best stud-ied in other disciplines (Malkki, 2007; Mills, 2000 [1959], p. 224). For example, 'history and anthropology are in fact closely related' (Brettell, 2002, p. S46) and many relevant works cross across these two disciplines (e.g., Goody, 1996; Jones, 2006; Kuper, 2009; McDonough, 1986; Segalen, 1986; Watson, 1985). Of course, the business dis-ciplines are also needed, because the family business field lies at the margins of kinship and business.

WHAT CAN WE HOPE FOR?

This chapter has offered an 'imagined ideal' for the anthropology of family business. Scholars who follow its suggestions will make outstanding contributions, whether they are business school scholars who learn anthropology, or anthropologists who learn about business (Rosa and Caulkins, 2013). Family business is a boundary-crossing field that calls for expertise in both familial and commercial domains. Family business research has been much stronger about business than it has about kinship (Stewart and Hitt, 2012). Skewing away from kinship is particularly notable at the level of detail of a good ethnographic study. These details could refer to important business issues (e.g., the example of a daughter's unwillingness to marry a successor to her father). Sadly, few ethnographic studies of family firms have been very alert to business domain. Ideally, ethnographic writings would have the depth of real-world detail on both domains, so as to inform and to resonate with family business members as well as with scholars. Nordqvist et al. argued that interpretive research has the 'practical ... goal' of helping practitioners to manage in their dynamic, 'complex' worlds (2009, p. 306). This is the ultimate goal, the imagined ideal, for an anthropology of family business.

REFERENCES

Adler, P.A. and Adler, P. (1987). *Membership Roles in Field Research*. Newbury Park, CA: Sage.

Adler, P.A. and Adler, P. (2008). Of rhetoric and representation: The four faces of ethnography. *Sociological Quarterly*, 49, 1–30.

Aldrich, H.E. and Cliff, J.E. (2003). The pervasive effects of family on entrepreneurship: Toward a family embeddedness perspective. *Journal of Business Venturing*, 18, 573–596.

Anderson, S. (2007). The economics of dowry and brideprice. *Journal of Economic Perspectives*, 21(4), 151–174.

Armstrong, R.P. (1971). *The Affecting Presence: An Essay in Humanistic Anthropology*. Urbana, IL: University of Illinois Press.

Arnould, E.J., Price, L., and Moisio, R. (2007). Making contexts matter: Selecting research contexts for theoretical insights. In R.W. Belk (ed.), *Handbook of Qualitative Research Methods in Marketing* (pp. 106–128). Northampton, MA: Edward Elgar.

Aunger, R. (2004). *Reflexive Ethnographic Science*. Lanham, MD: AltaMira.

Barth, F. (1967). Economic spheres in Darfur. In R. Firth (ed.), *Themes in Economic Anthropology* (pp. 149–174). London: Tavistock.

Barth, F. (1999). Comparative methodologies in the analysis of anthropological data. In J.R. Bowen and R. Peterson (eds), *Critical Comparisons in Politics and Culture* (pp.78–89). New York: Cambridge University Press.

Blim, M.L. (1990). *Made in Italy: Small-scale Industrialization and its Consequences*. Westport, CT: Praeger.

Bloch, M. (1971). The moral and tactical meaning of kinship terms. *Man (N.S.)*, 6, 79–87.

Bloch, M. (1973). The long term and the short term: The economic and political significance of the morality of kinship. In J. Goody (ed.), *The Character of Kinship* (pp. 75–87). London: Cambridge University Press.

Bloch, M. and Sperber, D. (2002). Kinship and evolved psychological dispositions. *Current Anthropology*, 43, 723–748.

Brettell, C.B. (2002). Gendered lives: Transitions and turning points in personal, family, and historical time. *Current Anthropology*, 43(Supplement), S45–S61.

Briggs, C.L. (2007). Anthropology, interviewing, and communicability in contemporary society. *Current Anthropology*, 48, 551–580.

Brinberg, D. and McGrath, J.E. (1985). *Validity and the Research Process*. Thousand Oaks, CA: Sage.

Brown, P.H., Bulte, E., and Zhang, X. (2011). Positional spending and status seeking in rural China. *Journal of Development Economics*, 96, 139–149.

Bruun, O. (1993). *Business and Bureaucracy in a Chinese City: An Ethnography of Private Business Households in Contemporary China*. Berkeley, CA: Institute of East Asian Studies, University of California, Berkeley.

Buessow, J. (2011). Street politics in Damascus: Kinship and other social categories as bases of political action, 1830–1841. *The History of the Family*, 16(2), 108–125.

Campbell, D.T. (1975). Degrees of freedom and the case study. *Comparative Political Studies*, 8, 178–193.

Carsten, J. (2000). Introduction: Cultures of relatedness. In J. Carsten (ed.), *Cultures of Relatedness* (pp. 1–36). New York: Cambridge University Press.

Chagnon, N.A. (1968). *Yanomamo: The Fierce People*. New York: Holt, Rinehart and Winston.

Cohen, R. (1977). Comment on 'Standardization and measurement in cultural anthropology: A neglected area'. *Current Anthropology*, 18, 235–258.

Colli, A., Fernández Pérez, P., and Rose, M.B. (2003). National determinants of family firm development? Family firms in Britain, Spain, and Italy in the nineteenth and twentieth centuries. *Enterprise and Society*, 4, 28–64.

Collier, J. Jr. and Collier, M. (1986). *Visual Anthropology: Photography as a Research Method*. Albuquerque, NM: University of New Mexico Press.

Coy, M.W. (1989). Being what we pretend to be: The usefulness of apprenticeship as a field method. In M.W. Coy (ed.), *Apprenticeship* (pp. 115–135). Albany, NY: State University of New York Press.

Creed, G.W. (2000). 'Family values' and domestic economies. *Annual Review of Anthropology*, 29, 329–355.

Creswell, J.W. and Miller, D.L. (2000). Determining validity in qualitative research. *Theory into Practice*, 39, 124–130.

Dalton, M. (1959). *Men Who Manage: Fusions of Feeling and Theory in Administration*. New York: Wiley.

Daly, K. and Dienhart, A. (1998). Navigating the family domain: Qualitative field dilemmas. In S. Grills (ed.), *Doing Ethnographic Research: Fieldwork Settings* (pp. 97–120). Thousand Oaks, CA: Sage.

Davidoff, L. and Hall, C. (1987). *Family Fortunes: Men and Women of the English Middle Class, 1780–1850*. Chicago, IL: University of Chicago Press.

de Lima, A.P. (2000). Is Blood thicker than Economic Interest in Familial Enterprises? In P.P. Schweitzer (ed.), *Dividends of kinship: Meanings and uses of social relatedness* (pp. 151–176). London: Routledge.

Ember, C.R. and Ember, M. (2009). *Cross-cultural Research Methods*, 2nd edn. Lanham, MD: AltaMira.

Emerson, R.M., Fretz, R.I., and Shaw, L.L. (2011). *Writing Ethnographic Fieldnotes*, 2nd edn. Chicago, IL: University of Chicago Press.

Eriksen, T.H. (2006). *Engaging Anthropology: The Case for a Public Presence*. New York: Berg.

Farrell, B. (1993). *Elite Families: Class and Power in Nineteenth Century Boston*. Albany, NY: State University of New York Press.

Feinberg, R. (2001). Introduction: Schneider's cultural analysis of kinship and its implications for anthropological relativism. In R. Feinberg and M. Ottenheimer (eds), *The Cultural Analysis of Kinship: The Legacy of David M. Schneider* (pp. 1–31). Urbana, IL: University of Illinois Press.

Feldman, M.S., Bell, J., and Berger, M.T. (eds) (2003). *Gaining Access: A Practical and Theoretical Guide for Qualitative Researchers*. Lanham, MD: AltaMira Press.

Fortes, M. (1949). *The Web of Kinship among the Tallensi*. London: Oxford University Press.

Fox, R. (1983). *Kinship and Marriage: An Anthropological Perspective*. New York: Cambridge University Press.

Friese, S. (2012). *Qualitative Data Analysis with ATLAS. ti*. Newbury Park, CA: Sage.

Geertz, C. (1973). Thick description: Toward an interpretive theory of culture. In C. Geertz, *The Interpretation of Cultures* (pp. 3–30). New York: Basic Books.

Geertz, C. (1974). 'From the native's point of view': On the nature of anthropological understanding. *Bulletin of the American Academy of Arts and Sciences* 28, 26–45.

Godelier, M. (2011 [2004]). *Métamorphoses de la parenté*. Paris: Fayard. Translated (2011) as *The Metamorphoses of Kinship* (N. Scott, Trans.), London: Versa.

Goldthorpe, J.H. (2000). *On Sociology: Numbers, Narratives, and the Integration of Research and Theory*. New York: Oxford University Press.

Good, A. (1996). Kinship. In A. Barnard and J. Spencer (eds), *Encyclopedia of Social and Cultural Anthropology* (pp. 311–318). London: Routledge.

Goody, J. (1969). Inheritance, property, and marriage in Africa and Eurasia. *Sociology*, 3, 55–76.

Goody, J. (1976). *Production and Reproduction: A Comparative study of the Domestic Domain*. Cambridge: Cambridge University Press.

Goody, J. (1996). *The East in the West*. Cambridge: Cambridge University Press.

Gordon, G. and Nicholson, N. (2008). *Family Wars: Classic Conflicts in Family Business and How to Deal With Them*. London: Kogan Page.

Gravlee, C.C., Kennedy, D.P., Godoy, R., and Leonard, W.R. (2009). Methods for collecting panel data: What anthropology can learn from other disciplines. *Journal of Anthropological Research*, 65, 463–483.

Greenhalgh, S. (1994). Deorientalizing the Chinese family firm. *American Ethnologist*, 21, 746–775.

Hamabata, M.M. (1990). *Crested Kimono: Power and Love in the Japanese Business Family*. Ithaca, NY: Cornell University Press.

Hann, C. (2005). A new double movement? Anthropological perspectives on property in the age of neoliberalism. *Socio-Economic Review*, 5, 287–318.

Hann, C. (2008). Reproduction and inheritance: Goody revisited. *Annual Review of Anthropology*, 37, 145–158.

Harper, D. (1987). *Working Knowledge: Skill and Community in a Small Shop*. Chicago, IL: University of Chicago Press.

Harrell, S. (1997). *Human Families*. Boulder, CO: Westview.

Hart, K. (1975). Swindler or public benefactor? – The entrepreneur in his community. In J. Goody (ed.), *Changing Social Structure in Ghana* (pp. 1–35). London: International African Institute.

Hegelund, A. (2005). Objectivity and subjectivity in the ethnographic method. *Qualitative Health Research*, 15, 647–668.

Heider, E.R. (1972). Probabilities, sampling, and ethnographic method: The case of Dani colour names. *Man (N.S.)*, 7, 448–466.

Helin, J. (2011). Living moments in family meetings: A process study in the family business context. Unpublished doctoral dissertation, Jönköping International Business School.

Hodson, R. (1998). Organizational ethnographies: An underutilized resource in the sociology of work. *Social Forces*, 76, 1173–1208.

Hollos, M. and Larsen, U. (2004). Which African men promote smaller families and why? Marital relations and fertility in a Pare community in Northern Tanzania. *Social Science and Medicine*, 58, 1733–1749.

Holy, L. (1996). *Anthropological Perspectives on Kinship*. London: Pluto.

Hunt, S.D. (2003). *Controversy in Marketing Theory: For Reason, Realism, Truth, and Objectivity*. Armonk, NY: M. E. Sharpe.

Jackson, J.L. Jr. (2004). An ethnographic *film*flam: Giving gifts, doing research, and videotaping the native subject/object. *American Anthropologist*, 106, 32–42.

Jacobs-Huey, L. (2002). The natives are gazing and talking back: Reviewing the problematics of positionality, voice, and accountability among 'native' anthropologists. *American Anthropologist*, 104, 791–804.

Johannisson, B. (2002). Energising entrepreneurship: Ideological tensions in the medium-sized family business. In D. Fletcher (ed.), *Understanding the Small Family Business* (pp. 46–57). London: Routledge.

Johnson, A. and Johnson, O.R. (1990). Quality into quantity: The measurement potential of fieldnotes. In R. Sanjek (ed.), *Fieldnotes: The Makings of Anthropology* (pp. 161–186). Ithaca, NY: Cornell University Press.

Jones, A.M. (2006). Culture, identity, and motivation: The historical anthropology of a family firm. *Culture and Organization*, 12, 169–183.

Jordan, A.T. (2010). The importance of business anthropology: Its unique contribution. *International Journal of Business Anthropology*, 1, 7–17.

Kasdan, L. (1965). Family structure, migration and the entrepreneur. *Comparative Studies in Society and History*, 7, 345–357.

Keesing, R.M. (ed.) (1978). *Elota's Story: The Life and Times of a Solomon Islands Big Man*. New York: St Martin's Press.

Kondo, D.K. (1990). *Crafting Selves: Power, Gender, and Discourses of Identity in a Japanese Workplace*. Chicago, IL: University of Chicago Press.

Kuper, A. (1999). *Culture: The Anthropologists' Account*. Cambridge, MA: Harvard University Press.

Kuper, A. (2009). *Incest and Influence: The Private Life of Bourgeois England*. Cambridge, MA: Harvard University Press.

Lam, W. (2011). Dancing to two tunes: Multi-entity roles in the family business succession process. *International Small Business Journal*, 29, 508–533.

Lambek, M. (2011). Kinship as gift and theft: Acts of succession in Mayotte and ~~ancient~~ [sic] Israel. *American Ethnologist*, 38, 2–16.

Leach, E.R. (1961). *Pul Eliya: A Village in Ceylon: A Study of Land Tenure and Kinship*. Cambridge: Cambridge University Press.

Learned, K.E. (1995). The creation of firm resources: A native ethnography. Unpublished doctoral dissertation, Texas Tech University.

Lett, J. (1997). *Science, Reason, and Anthropology: The Principles of Rational Inquiry*. Lanham, MD: Rowman & Littlefield.

Locke, K. (2011a). Field research practice in management and organization studies: Reclaiming its tradition of discovery. *Academy of Management Annals*, 5, 613–652.

Locke, K. (2011b). Looking for what we have a case of. *Qualitative Research in Organizations and Management*, 6, 88–92.

Lomnitz, L.A. and Pérez-Lizaur, M. (1987). *A Mexican Elite Family, 1820–1980: Kinship, Class and Culture*. Princeton, NJ: Princeton University Press.

Malkki, L.H. (2007). Tradition and improvisation in ethnographic field research. In A. Cerwonka and L.H. Malkki (eds), *Improvising Theory: Process and Temporality in Ethnographic Fieldwork* (pp. 162–187). Chicago, IL: University of Chicago Press.

Marcus, G.E. and Hall, P.D. (1992). *Lives in Trust: The Fortunes of Dynastic Families in Late Twentieth Century America*. Boulder, CO: Westview.

McDonough, G.W. (1986). *Good Families of Barcelona: A Social History of Power in the Industrial Era*. Princeton, NJ: Princeton University Press.

Meisch, L.A. (2002). *Andean Entrepreneurs: Otavalo Merchants and Musicians in the Global Arena*. Austin, TX: University of Texas Press.

Mills, C.W. (2000 [1959]). *The Sociological Imagination*. New York: Oxford University Press.

Moffatt, M. (1992). Ethnographic writing about American culture. *Annual Review of Anthropology*, 21, 205–229.

Morrill, C. and Fine, G.A. (1997). Ethnographic contributions to organizational sociology. *Sociological Methods and Research*, 25, 424–451.

Mosse, D. (2006). Anti-social anthropology: Objectivity, objection, and the ethnography of public policy and professional communities. *Journal of the Royal Anthropological Institute (N.S.)*, 12, 935–956.

Mulligan, T.M. (1987). The two cultures in business education. *Academy of Management Review*, 12, 593–599.

Nordqvist, M., Hall, A., and Melin, L. (2009). Qualitative research on family businesses: The relevance and usefulness of the interpretive approach. *Journal of Management & Organization*, 15, 294–308.

Ortner, S.B. (1996). *Making Gender: The Politics and Erotics of Culture*. Boston, MA: Beacon Press.

Oxfeld, E. (1993). *Blood, Sweat, and Mahjong: Family and Enterprise in an Overseas Chinese Community*. Ithaca, NY: Cornell University Press.

Parsons, T. (1951). *The Social System*. New York: Free Press.

Patterson, M. (2005). Introduction: Reclaiming paradigms lost. *Australian Journal of Anthropology*, 16, 1–17.

Peletz, M.G. (1995). Kinship studies in late twentieth century anthropology. *Annual Review of Anthropology*, 24, 343–372.

Pine, F. (1996). Family. In A. Barnard and J. Spencer (eds), *Encyclopedia of Social and Cultural Anthropology* (pp. 223–228). London: Routledge.

Ragin, C.C. (1992). Cases of 'what is a case?' In C.C. Ragin and H.S. Becker (eds), *What is a Case? Exploring the Foundations of Social Inquiry* (pp. 1–17). New York: Cambridge University Press.

Ram, M. (1994). *Managing to Survive: Working Lives in Small Firms*. Oxford: Blackwell.

Richards, A.I. (1950). Some types of Family Structure among the central Bantu. In A.R. Radcliffe-Brown and D. Forde (eds.), *African systems of Kinship and Marriage* (pp. 207–251). London: Oxford University Press.

Robertson, A.F. (1991). *Beyond the Family: The Social Organization of Human Reproduction*. Berkeley, CA: University of California Press.

Rosa, P. and Caulkins, D.D. (2013). Entrepreneurship studies. In D.D. Caulkins and A.T. Jordan (eds), *A Companion to Organizational Anthropology* (pp. 98–121). New York: Wiley.

Rutherford, D. (2010). Kinship, capital, and the unsettling of assumptions: Contemporary anthropology and the study of family enterprise and entrepreneurship. In A. Stewart, G.T. Lumpkin, and J.A. Katz (eds), *Entrepreneurship and Family Business* (pp. 277–283). Bingley, UK: Emerald.

Ryan, G.W. and Bernard, H.R. (2006). Testing an ethnographic decision tree model on a national sample: Recycling beverage cans. *Human Organization*, 65, 103–114.

Sangren, P.S. (2009). 'Masculine domination', desire and Chinese patriliny. *Critique of Anthropology*, 29, 255–278.

Sanjek, R. (1990a). The secret life of fieldnotes. In R. Sanjek (ed.), *Fieldnotes: The Makings of Anthropology* (pp. 187–270). Ithaca, NY: Cornell University Press.

Sanjek, R. (1990b). On ethnographic validity. In R. Sanjek (ed.), *Fieldnotes: The Makings of Anthropology* (pp. 385–418). Ithaca, NY: Cornell University Press.

Scandura, T.A. and Williams, E.A. (2000). Research methodology in management: Current practices, trends, and implications for future research. *Academy of Management Journal*, 43, 1248–1264.

Scheffler, H.W. (2001). *Filiation and Affiliation*. Boulder, CO: Westview.

Scheffler, H.W. (2010). Kinship and gender. In A. Stewart, G.T. Lumpkin, and J.A. Katz (eds), *Entrepreneurship and Family Business* (pp. 285–290). Bingley, UK: Emerald.

Schneider, D.M. (1995). *Schneider on Schneider: The Conversion of the Jews and Other Anthropological Stories as told to Richard Handler*. Durham, NC: Duke University Press.

Segalen, M. (1986). *Historical Anthropology of the Family*. New York: Cambridge University Press.

Shapiro, W. (1997). Marriage systems. In T. Barfield (ed.), *The Dictionary of Anthropology* (pp. 304–307). Oxford: Blackwell.

Shimizu, A. (1991). On the notion of kinship. *Man (N.S.)*, 26, 377–403.

Song, M. (1999). *Helping out: Children's Labor in Ethnic Businesses*. Philadelphia, PA: Temple University Press.

Spradley, J.P. (1979). *The Ethnographic Interview*. New York: Holt, Rinehart & Winston.

Stafford, C. (2000). Chinese patriliny and the cycles of *yang* and *laiwang*. In J. Carsten (ed.), *Cultures of Relatedness* (pp. 37–54). New York: Cambridge University Press.

Stebbins, R.A. (2001). *Exploratory Research in the Social Sciences*. Thousand Oaks, CA: Sage.

Stewart, A. (1990). The bigman metaphor for entrepreneurship: A 'library tale' with morals on alternatives for further research. *Organization Science*, 1, 143–159.

Stewart, A. (1998). *The Ethnographer's Method*. Newbury Park, CA: Sage.

Stewart, A. (2003). Help one another, use one another: Toward an anthropology of family business. *Entrepreneurship: Theory and Practice*, 27(4), 383–396.

Stewart, A. (2008). Who could best complement a team of family business researchers, scholars down the hall or in another building? *Family Business Review*, 21, 279–293.

Stewart, A. (2010). Sources of entrepreneurial discretion in kinship systems. In A. Stewart, G.T. Lumpkin, and J.A. Katz (eds), *Entrepreneurship and Family Business* (pp. 291–313). Bingley, UK: Emerald.

Stewart, A. and Hitt, M.A. (2012). Why can't a family business be more like a non-family business: Modes of professionalization in family firms. *Family Business Review*, 25, 58–86.

Stewart, A. and Miner, A.S. (2011). The prospects for family business in research universities. *Journal of Family Business Strategy*, 2, 3–14.

Stockard, J.E. (2002). *Marriage in Culture: Practice and Meaning Across Diverse Societies*. New York: Wadsworth.

Stone, L. (2010). *Kinship and Gender*, 4th edn. Boulder, CO: Westview.

Sunderland, P.L. and Denny, R.M. (2007). *Doing Anthropology in Consumer Research*. Walnut Creek, CA: Left Coast Press.

Tsing, A. (2005). *Friction: An Ethnography of Global Connection*. Princeton, NJ: Princeton University Press.

Urban, G. (1999). The role of comparison in the light of the theory of culture. In J.R. Bowen and R. Peterson (eds), *Critical Comparisons in Politics and Culture* (pp. 90–109). New York: Cambridge University Press.

Van Maanen, J. (1975). Police socialization: A longitudinal examination of job attitudes in an urban police department. *Administrative Science Quarterly*, 20, 207–220.

Van Maanen, J. (2011). *Tales of the Field: On Writing Ethnography*, 2nd edn. Chicago, IL: University of Chicago Press.

Van Vleet, K.E. (2008). *Performing Kinship: Narrative, Gender, and the Intimacies of Power in the Andes*. Austin, TX: University of Texas Press.

Viazzo, P.P. and Lynch, K.A. (2002). Anthropology, family history, and the concept of strategy. *International Review of Social History*, 47, 423–452.

Wagner, J. (1979). The humanistic perspective in anthropology: A brief overview. In B.T. Grindal and D.M. Warren (eds), *Essays in Humanistic Anthropology: A Festschrift for David Bidney* (pp. 3–12). Washington, DC: University Press of America.

Wallman, S. (1975). Kinship, a-kinship, anti-kinship: Variations in the logic of kinship situations. *Journal of Human Evolution*, 4, 331–341.

Watson, R.S. (1985). *Inequality Among Brothers: Class and Kinship in South China*. New York: Cambridge University Press.

Weick, K.E. (1979). *The Social Psychology of Organizing*, 2nd edn. Reading, MA: Addison-Wesley.

Werner, O. (1998). Do we need standards for ethnography? *Field Methods*, 10(1), 1–3.

Werner, O. and Bernard, H.R. (1994). Ethnographic sampling. *Cultural Anthropology Methods*, 6(7), 7–9.

White, D.R. and Johansen, U.C. (2006). *Network Analysis and Ethnographic Problems: Process Models of a Turkish Nomadic Clan*. New York: Lexington.

White, D.R. and Jorion, P. (1996). Kinship networks and discrete structure theory: Applications and implications. *Social Networks*, 18, 267–314.

Wigren, C. (2007). Assessing the quality of qualitative research in entrepreneurship. In H. Neergaard and J.P. Ulhøi (eds), *Handbook of Qualitative Research Methods in Entrepreneurship* (pp. 383–405). Northampton, MA: Edward Elgar.

Wolcott, H.F. (1994). *Transforming Qualitative Data*. Thousand Oaks, CA: Sage.

Wong S.-L. (1988). *Emigrant Entrepreneurs: Shanghai Industrialists in Hong Kong*. Hong Kong: Oxford University Press.

Yan, Y. (2001). Practicing kinship in rural north China. In S. Franklin and S. McKinnon (eds), *Relative Values: Refiguring Kinship Studies* (pp. 224–245). Durham, NC: Duke University Press.

Yanagisako, S.J. (1978). Variance in American kinship: Implications for cultural analysis. *American Ethnologist*, 5, 15–29.

Yanagisako, S.J. (1979). Family and household: The analysis of domestic groups. *Annual Review of Anthropology*, 8, 161–205.

Yanagisako, S.J. (2002). *Producing Culture and Capital: Family Firms in Italy*. Princeton, NJ: Princeton University Press.

5

Sociological Theories Applied to Family Businesses

Martha A. Martinez and Howard Aldrich

INTRODUCTION

Sociological and family business studies have consistently found that family businesses are a sizable component of the economy, although estimates of their impact depend on which definition a researcher adopts. Defined in terms of who they employ, we know that many entrepreneurs rely on family members, whether paid or unpaid (Aldrich et al. 1998; Heck and Trent 1999). Using data on tax returns for the year 2000 and information from the US Census, Astrachan and Shanker (2003) provided a stringent definition in which only businesses with high family involvement can be called family firms; such firms have employees and multiple generations of a family are involved. By this definition, family businesses constitute 54 percent of all business with employees. In a representative national sample of nascent entrepreneurs in the United States, Ruef et al. (2003) examined patterns of equity ownership and found that spouses form a majority of entrepreneurial teams. Whether defined by employment or ownership, family businesses thus comprise a sizable share of the business population and play an important role in capitalist economies.

Sociology has long recognized the importance of families as entities in modern capitalist societies. Structural-functionalists see the nuclear family, for example, as the key to the social and geographical mobility undergirding a universalistic, achievement-based occupational system, while at the same time socializing and nurturing children and adults (Parsons and Bales 1955). From this perspective, researchers have argued that family businesses expand opportunities to people from humble origins (Lippmann et al. 2005). Capitalist societies provide many opportunities for people to obtain the capital required to start businesses and families provide resources, among them free labor, helping them survive.

In contrast to structural functionalists, Marxists see the family as the mechanism through which hegemonic relations of production are reproduced over time (Yanagisako and Collier 2004). In particular, they argue that family businesses perpetuate inequality because entrepreneurial parents imprint entrepreneurial values in their children (Miller and Swanson 1958), reinforce those values during adolescence, and provide financial and other support during adulthood (Aldrich and Kim 2007). Furthermore, families with wealth possess an important business resource: capital. Some researchers have asserted that liquidity constraints inhibit start-ups (Blanchflower and Oswald 1998; Fischer and Massey 2000), although others have disputed that assertion (Kim et al. 2003). Empirical studies have found no consistent relationships between levels of household wealth and a propensity to create businesses (Kim et al. 2003), although the opposite is true: many families become wealthy because of family-owned businesses (Keister 2000). Families can have a major effect on social inequality because of their potential impact on the intergenerational transmission of wealth and the uneven distribution of opportunities between and within families, stemming, in part, from the particularistic loyalties engendered by family ties.

Despite the recognition of the intimate relationship between social and economic organization, sociologists have tended to separate the study of production, mostly performed through firms in capitalist society, from the study of reproduction, involving studies of the family as a socializing and stabilizing institution (Yanagisako and Collier 2004). Obviously, there are exceptions to this dichotomy, such as the literature on family/work spillover (Glass and Estes 1997) or the more comprehensive frameworks of family businesses discussed elsewhere in this volume. However, as a general rule, sociological theory has separated the study of families and of firms.

As this volume is about 'family firms' rather than about families with firms, we will concentrate on sociological theories that deal with what we consider key issues in the study of firms: survival and growth. We explore how three sociological theories of organizational survival and growth can be integrated within a family firms' framework: network theory, new institutional theory, and evolutionary theory. All three treat 'organizations' as their unit of analysis, viewing firms as bounded social entities interacting with their social contexts. These theories emphasize structural constraints and opportunities created by environments and families, contrasting with more atomistic views of family firms that concentrate on individuals' strategic choices.

NETWORK THEORY

We chose network theory because it provides a systematic framework for examining relations between individuals and groups and takes account of the content of relations as well as the surrounding context (Kadushin 2012). Originating in anthropological studies of natural groups and their contexts, network analysis has evolved into an analytic framework with a highly sophisticated vocabulary for describing relationships and their dynamics. It has contributed two ways of conceptualizing family business networks. First, a family itself can be seen as a network of internal relationships within a firm. Second, the patterns of relationships held by family members can be seen as a network connecting family firms to external organizations and entities. We take up each view, in turn.

Within-family Networks

Network theory explores the unique contributions of families and their cohesive relationships to firm creation and performance. Network analysts contrast the cohesive networks formed by relatively homogeneous strong ties, such as family members and close friends, with the less cohesive networks formed by relatively diverse weak ties, such as acquaintances. Relationships within networks and the resources they bring are conceptualized as a form of social capital that is invested in improving economic outputs. The term 'capital' implies that social connections benefit business activities, but the theory recognizes the possibility of both positive and negative effects. Social capital theory posits that if family businesses enjoy higher levels of cohesion, they will benefit from enhanced performance. For example, transactions costs may be lower in family firms because of decreased costs of communication and coordination between like-minded people (Steier 2001). This benefit helps us understand why family firms are so prevalent, as individuals constructing organizations tend to rely on their strong ties when forming entrepreneurial teams (Ruef et al. 2003). Groups built on strong ties tend to have advantages when environments place a premium on group solidarity and unified action in the face of competition and uncertainty.

Network theory also considers the possible disadvantages created when firms rely on family capital rather than on social capital from more diverse sources. For example, family firms tend to have restricted network reach (Kadushin 2012), are less likely to include members of the business elite (Sirmon and Hitt 2003), and may have limited capabilities for developing strong ties with non-family individuals (Chrisman et al. 2005). Cohesive family relations can endow businesses with the advantages of solidarity and commitment but at a potential cost of suppressing diverse points of view, thus creating a homogeneous outlook. In general, firms headed by entrepreneurs that have developed mainly strong, cohesive connections – either family or non-family – tend to be less innovative (van Geenhuizen and Soetanto 2012). Some have noted that the family, as a pre-capitalistic form of organization based on cohesion and solidarity, could undermine the instrumental, rationalized, merit, and competition-based functioning of firms (Whyte 1996).

In contrast to closed networks of family members, diverse networks that include non-family members can facilitate access to wide-ranging sources of information and alternative viewpoints. Granovetter's theory of the strength of weak ties posited that such ties connected people to information sources they would otherwise never hear about, because their strong ties typically rely on the same sources (Granovetter 1974). However, diverse networks may create problems of governance because heterogeneity creates conflict and undermines entrepreneurial efficiency (Martinez and Aldrich 2011). But, it is also possible that family networks provide solutions to the weaknesses of bureaucracies and markets, creating competitive advantages and facilitating survival and growth (Dyer and Handler 1994; Whyte 1996).

Network theory's identification of a tension between cohesion and diversity has spawned a rich empirical tradition regarding families and entrepreneurship. First, family firms can serve as incubators for other firms. Some studies have found a relationship between having entrepreneurial parents and an increased propensity toward self-employment (Scott and Twomey 1988; Matthews and Moser 1996; Arum and Mueller 2004). Cohesion within entrepreneurial families can encourage individuals to develop attitudes, habits, and perceptual models that make them more likely to become entrepreneurs (Kolvereid 1996). Second, supportive strong ties also increase people's motivations to start a business (Sequeira et al. 2007). Research indicates that women benefit less from this process; Aldrich and Kim (2007) noted that sons were much more likely to work in their parents' businesses than daughters. Not coincidentally, sons of entrepreneurial parents are also more likely than daughters to become entrepreneurs (Matthews and Moser 1996). We speculate that women with entrepreneurial backgrounds may be more aware of the time and energy demands of entrepreneurship through their family experience and may be unwilling to adopt such a demanding lifestyle.

Several characteristics of cohesive family businesses may limit their ability to innovate. Ventures starting with networks centered around strong identity ties, such as those found in families, tend to reproduce already existing business models (Sequeira and

Rasheed 2006), whereas diverse ties (weak or strong) tend to promote innovation (Julien et al. 2004). Cohesion may thus cause reproduction rather than innovation because of direct social pressures (i.e. the pressure to create a business similar to the family business), and lack of innovativeness might also stem from the cognitive consequences of strong cohesive communities (Liao and Welsch 2003). However, family firms might be able to overcome the disadvantages of their homogeneity by purposely developing alliances with non-family firms (Sirmon and Hitt 2003).

With regard to financial capital, nationally representative data as well as community studies show that – with the possible exception of spouses – only family firms from a handful of ethnic minority groups can count on financial support from family members (Zimmer and Aldrich 1987; Bates 1994; Aldrich et al. 1996). However, even if family networks cannot provide money directly, they nonetheless can offer alternative means for solving problems. Family members are most helpful when their support is role-appropriate, such as in providing personal services (Kim et al. 2007). In normal business situations, family ties appear to help only when they supply information and resources that correspond with their areas of competence (Renzulli and Aldrich 2005). Money saved by family assistance can then be funneled to other areas of financial need. In particular, strong ties benefit firm performance by allowing strategies such as withholding salaries from family members and cross-subsidizing businesses from other family enterprises (Jones and Jayawarna 2010). Family networks are most beneficial when they provide resources, information and business opportunities, while at the same time not binding their members in terms of industry, geography, strategies, or adoption of new ideas (Wu 1983; Kristiansen and Ryen 2002).

Network ties can provide advantages to family businesses with regard to the cost of labor. Family members usually have higher levels of commitment to a business, and long-serving members may have extensive tacit knowledge of the industry. They tend to be more reliable and willing to make sacrifices in terms of time, money, and effort with long-term goals in mind (Stewart 2003; Anderson et al. 2005). However, using strong family contacts as employees may cost family firms dearly with regard to acquiring information from external sources. Generally, employees are instrumental in providing information, especially market information (Jack 2005), but family employees may provide more limited information when they are distracted by issues involving family dynamics. Moreover, family considerations may undermine or preclude the development of systems linking performance and rewards (Ram and Holliday 1993). By favoring family, business owners may also create conflict between kin and non-kin employees (Whyte 1996).

External Networks

When studying relationships between organizations, analysts distinguish between embedded and arms-length/market relationships. The degrees or levels of embeddedness depend on the percentage of transactions carried out with particular firms on a sustained basis versus those performed with firms on the basis of pure market considerations, such as price. Bringing families into the study of inter-firm relations raises the question of whether the study of family connections across organizations really belongs to the realm of 'family business studies.' The organizations involved could be family-based or not. However, there are certain obvious cases in which studying interorganizational relations clearly requires that analysts study family firms. Habbershon and Pistrui (2002) argued that enterprising families, in their efforts to create transgenerational wealth, behave more like family business groups. Consider, for instance, conditions under which the boundaries between organizations and other entities become blurred. In their sample of Scottish family firms, Anderson et al. (2005) found that a quarter of firm ties with external organizations were family based, providing material and affective resources without the hazards traditionally involved with external relationships.

Families can offer access to opportunities because of particularistic ties to resource providers and especially government officials and agencies. During market transitions in China and Eastern Europe, former government officials and their relatives were able to leverage their connections with the state into successful contracts (Rona-Tas 1994; Clark 2000; Tsai 2005). The combination of weak capitalist institutions and well-connected firms created what some researchers called 'network capitalism' (Boisot and Child 1996; Puffer and McCarthy 2007). Some theorists argue that this combination created a distinctive market-based system that was neither socialist nor capitalist.

In applying network theory to family business, analysts must be careful not to assume that all families are the same. Families may differ on a wide range of dimensions and our theories should reflect this diversity, perhaps by using the concept of 'family capital' (see Chapter 31 in this volume; Danes, 2014). Although some scholars have defined family capital as a special form of social capital – more intense, enduring, and immediately available than other forms (Hoelscher 2002) – we believe that a more general definition can help measure how families are different from each other. Danes et al. (2009) defined family capital as the sum of human, social, and financial capital resources possessed by a particular family. They found that within family businesses, the different types of family capital explained variations in business success. In another example, Mustakallio et al. (2002) found that family size and the level of interaction in the family affected the quality of governance in family firms.

Applying sociological network theory to family firms thus yields a number of insights. First, network theory reminds us that the founding and operation of business firms depends upon relations between many people, not just the actions of solo and independent entrepreneurs. Second, a network perspective highlights the embeddedness of family members in sets of ties within and across firms that both facilitate and constrain economic actions. For example, strong ties can reduce transactions costs but also block innovation. Third, the concepts of direct and indirect ties and strong and weak ties point out the tension between cohesion and solidarity versus innovation and efficiency. Family cohesion and solidarity may result in an insular culture that may hinder the development of universalistic standards for evaluating employees. Cohesion may also favor traditional rather than innovative strategies, thus impeding chances for growth, but solidarity may enable family firms to survive crises that doom other types of firms.

NEW INSTITUTIONAL THEORY

We chose new institutional theory because it is now the dominant sociological perspective on organizations and provides a set of principles for understanding the socio-cultural context of human behavior, as well as a framework for explaining how people come to interpret the world in a certain way. New institutionalism or new institutional theory (NIT) was born as a reaction against rational theories of organizations which assumed that the pursuit of efficiency explains most organizational behavior and structure (Selznick 1996). In contrast, NIT focuses on the objectified and taken for granted nature of organizations and organizational environments; it emphasizes the effects of value-laden institutions and the way in which actions are legitimated when cloaked in institutionally accepted rhetoric. NIT views institutions as patterned behavior infused with meaning by normative systems and perpetuated by social exchanges facilitated by shared cognitive understandings. It posits that organizations' survival depends on their compliance with institutional requirements that may have little to do with efficiency (Aldrich and Ruef

2006) and also posits that the quest for legitimacy can cause organizational inertia. For example, many companies in America feel the need to make extraordinary efforts to hire minority candidates to avoid criticisms from the government, the media, consumers, and society in general, regardless of the fact that those efforts imply an additional expenditure of money and effort.

NIT helps us put the evolution of family firms in historical context. Theorists often assume that the business and family spheres are separate domains, with distinct cultural requirements. In traditional societies, work and family structures were part of the same integrated web of cultural norms (Rapoport and Rapoport 1965). In these societies, things did not require an explanation other than social convention or 'we have always done it that way.' Modernity and industrialization brought two transformations that apply both to family and work. First, they created a separation between work and family structures. As a result, in modern society, production and reproduction take place in different spheres and are often perceived as separate arenas of social life. The second transformation was the expansion of instrumental rationality to all areas of life. Although the spread of instrumental rationality has strongly affected the family (by pushing for greater gender equality, for example), its effects have been even stronger in the workplace because of the expansion of innovations like scientific management, Total Quality Management, and the digital revolution. Therefore, theorists as well as observers often assume that business and family spheres are separate domains, with distinct cultural requirements: the workplace emphasizes rationality and the family emphasizes relationships and emotions. We believe the demand for logically coherent and rational explanations for actions is stronger within the economic sphere occupied by firms than in the more traditional one occupied by families. Some have described these domains as separate institutional fields (Melin and Nordqvist 2007). However, the two fields intersect at many levels.

The existence of family and business institutions as separate entities means that family firms, from the perspective of NIT, take into account not only the functional efficiency of actions but also how such actions would affect the solidarity of the family. Carney (2005) argued that, in general, the family firm embodies incentives, authority patterns, and norms of legitimation that create a propensity for actions that favor parsimony, personalism, and particularism. In contrast, the business environment rewards behaviors that are based on standardization, short-term efficiency, and an entrepreneurial orientation. People in family firms must thus simultaneously deal with two distinct culturally legitimate frames of action.

Many researchers have recognized the inherent tension between the institutional arrangements in which families are embedded and those surrounding business enterprises (Reid et al. 1999), possibly leading to role conflicts for family business members (Deacon 1996). Businesses' needs for efficient and rationalized systems of work often stand in direct conflict with family needs and responsibilities, but they both can also be in conflict with the entrepreneurial spirit that emphasizes risk-taking, opportunity detection, and change. For example, in family firms, institutional forces supporting rationalization and professionalization may clash with forces supporting a more entrepreneurial and emotional orientation (Johannisson 2002).

Does that mean that institutional theory predicts that family firms will be less efficient and perform more poorly than other types of firms? Not necessarily. The outcome depends upon the relative balance between forces pressing for technical competence versus those concerning institutional norms and practices. An important component of institutions in business fields is that they are rationalized, or explained in ways that specify the design of procedures to attain specific objectives, providing acceptable 'reasons' for behaviors. However, a key tenant of new institutional theory is that what appears to be based on rational considerations may simply be culturally appropriate and ceremonial in nature (Meyer and Rowan 1977). Institutional forces are sometimes confused with technical or competitive causes of organizational behaviors because of their 'apparent' rationality. Thus, empirical studies in NIT try to separate behaviors that are motivated by technical competence from those that are the product of institutional pressures (Carruthers 1995; Roberts and Greenwood 1997; Westphal et al. 1997).

For example, for public companies facing low stock values, a well-known strategy is to downsize, thus often increasing stock prices. However, for many companies, their low performance has nothing to do with their labor costs and everything to do with their strategy. Downsizing has become not a tool for efficiency, but rather a cultural marker of potentially better future outcomes that can be symbolically displayed to outside observers. From this point of view, behaviors that appear to fulfill the rational requirements of the business environments are not necessarily any more technically appropriate than those motivated by the cultural influences of values held by families. In fact, the cultural elements of the family and the behaviors that it promotes may be the source of a competitive advantage in specific environments, particularly in those where resources are scarce (Carney 2005).

NIT researchers have developed categories of the content of institutions and also the mechanisms through which institutions influence organizational behavior. In terms of content, institutions are social structures that have attained a high degree of resilience and are composed of cultural-cognitive, normative, and regulative elements. Such elements are readily apparent in the case of family firms. Cultural-cognitive elements are the shared conceptions constituting the nature of social reality and providing meaning; people comply with these conceptions because it would be inconceivable to do otherwise. For example, many cultures have strict cultural codes defining the composition of a 'legitimate' family. This institutional element becomes relevant when families battle over whether in-laws have the same rights of access to business resources as blood relatives. Normative systems comprise values and norms that specify how things should be done, defining goals and objectives and appropriate ways to pursue them. For example, cultural values may create expectations that family members will deal with each other without regard to instrumental ends. Finally, regulatory elements concern rule setting, monitoring, and sanctioning activities (Ram and Holliday 1993; Scott 2001). For example, government regulations may strictly limit the number of hours per day that young family members can work, even though such regulations are 'irrational' from the point of view of the family's needs.

The interaction between culture and organization is mediated by the socially constructed habitual patterns of perception and evaluation that people develop in all societies (Selznick 1996). Cultural pressures are inescapable, especially because the external presence of cultural elements becomes institutionalized in organizational routines. Over time, institutions acquire an exterior, objective, and non-personal character (Zucker 1987). Subsequently, cultural elements, such as symbols, norms, and rules, play a constraining role in decision making. We could ask whether a family's contributions to the socialization of its members triumphs over higher-order institutional elements. The family has an early advantage in the formation of cognitive filters because homogeneity within families exerts stronger conforming pressures than institutional forces originating externally (Leaptrott 2005). Thus, members have difficulty escaping the iron cage of the family, both in terms of its influence on cognition and on internal pressures to conform.

Institutional theory therefore helps us understand why the cultures of family firms are different in key aspects from that of other firms, having different repertoires of strategic choices. Because of institutional arrangements, family firms tend to have different relationship to stakeholders (Vallejo 2008), are less likely to take entrepreneurial risks (Naldi et al. 2007), and have longer investment and ownership horizons (James 1999). Furthermore, family firms must be cautious when dealing with issues where taking account of family relations can be seen as illegitimate. For example, family owners often care more about their reputations for responsibility than their counterparts, and are therefore less likely to downsize by firing employees. By contrast, owners of other firms can use downsizing as an almost automatic response to certain types of organizational crises (Deacon 1996).

Institutional Isomorphism

One of the main insights of NIT is that institutional forces tend to make organizations more similar to each other. DiMaggio and Powell (1983) identified three types of mechanisms that created uniformity in organizational behaviors and organizational forms: coercive, mimetic, and normative. A few studies of family firms have found examples of each.

Coercive isomorphism is the result of formal and informal pressures exerted on organizations by other organizations on which they depend. Governments generate the most important and common source of these pressures by creating legal environments affecting many aspects of organizational behavior and structure. In fact, governments can be powerful enough to change the involvement of families in firms. For example, after the currency crisis in Asian markets in 1997, the government of Singapore forced family-owned Chinese banks to relinquish control of their organizations to professional managers (Tsui-Auch and Lee 2003).

Mimetic isomorphism, a response to uncertainty in environments, describes how organizations imitate other organizations that they consider more successful or legitimate. Parada et al. (2010) identified a case of mimetic isomorphism in which the owner of a pharmaceutical firm, following

the example of his friends and their firms, decided to pass on his firm to all four sons rather than only the first born, as his family had done in the past. NIT posits that the practices of highly visible firms that are perceived as successful will be copied, regardless of whether the imitator has any direct evidence that the practices actually produce positive outcomes. In this regard, members of firms are doing what they perceive as 'appropriate,' rather than acting on the basis of evidence. Arregle et al. (2007) theorized that because family firms are highly dependent on their owners' families for key resources, they face both mimetic and coercive pressures to develop similar structures.

Normative isomorphism is a result of professionalization, in which professional associations create normative pressures as they struggle to homogenize the conditions of their work. In the case of family business, the pressure of consultants, family business networking organizations, and university-based family business centers have created normative pressures for family firms to adopt family councils as a form of governance (Melin and Nordqvist 2007). Family councils are forums in which family members can articulate their values, needs and expectations in relation to the business (Gersick et al. 1997). NIT predicts that family firms will adopt such forms without regard to their own unique circumstances, possibly ignoring technical and instrumental considerations.

Given this complexity, we agree with Melin and Nordqvist (2007) that it is myopic to assume all family firms have similar institutional elements and belong to the same organizational field. Families in different countries are different, and there are variations even in what appear to be homogenous fields. The effect of institutions on family firms depends, in part, on the vision or mission created by a dominant coalition of members (Habbershon et al. 2003), and that may include non-economic goals (Chrisman et al. 2003). Understanding interactions between families and businesses thus requires that we attend closely to the institutional conditions in which they are embedded. For example, certain types of family firms are predominant in some organizational fields but not in others. In Chicago, the dry cleaning industry is dominated by small family businesses owned by Koreans, whereas the restaurant population is characterized by a myriad of organizational forms, varying from small family firms to large franchises. These complexities in both NIT and the study of family firms can be addressed by an evolutionary framework, which looks at the interactions between strategies and environments. We will explore evolutionary theory in the next section.

We believe that a sociological approach using NIT provides additional insights into family firms beyond those of network approaches. First, NIT is particularly useful in studying patterns of family business dynamics across cultures, because it deals with the macro level imposition of cultural elements and the micro-level use of norms and cultural values as cognitive filters for actions (Zucker 1991). Second, it helps us appreciate that family business structures and cultures vary across societies in part because of national differences in political, economic, social, and cultural institutions (Colli et al. 2003). Third, it provides a powerful counterweight to theories of management that emphasize rational and instrumental reasons for business practices. NIT posits that people in family businesses often do things because they are culturally appropriate, given the circumstances, rather than because they are the most technically efficient (Meyer and Rowan 1977).

EVOLUTIONARY THEORY

As NIT has begun paying more attention to humans' capacities for enacting change, both alone and in cooperation with others, evolutionary theory has become more popular. Although some authors have argued for a systems approach to modeling family firms (Pieper and Klein 2007), we believe an evolutionary approach is more comprehensive. Whereas NIT provides the family business literature with a generalized awareness of cultural, social and political environments, evolutionary theory brings together environments and organizations, as well as structure and agency.

Evolutionary theory studies the processes of variation, selection, and retention in the context of a struggle to secure scarce resources, physical, social, and cultural (Campbell 1969). This struggle is characterized by competition among social actors to obtain resources ahead of their competitors or to avoid competition altogether (Barnett et al. 1994). Variation, selection and retention occur simultaneously rather than sequentially and are linked in continuous feedback loops and cycles based on the interaction between organizations and their environments. Variation generates the organizational structures, strategies, and routines that are to be selected, with selection criteria set by environmental or internal forces; retention processes preserve the selected variation. Retention processes also restrict the kinds of variations that may occur, as similar or compatible strategies to those already established are more likely to be designed. However, environments evolve with organizations, as competitive struggles as well as cooperative alliances can change the character of selection criteria (Aldrich and Ruef 2006). Driven by competitive struggles and cooperative actions, the processes of variation, selection, and retention jointly shape the course of evolution.

The two final components of evolutionary theory are the ideas of *contingency* and *fit*. Evolutionary analyzes posit that outcomes result from interactions between organizations and environments, rather than being attributable to either organizations or environments, taken separately. Every explanation is thus contingent. The effect of organizational properties depends upon environmental contexts and the effects of contexts are unknowable until organizational properties are specified. Understanding how a 'fit' arises between organizations and their environments is therefore key to comprehending trends in organizational change. Scholars usually evaluate 'fit' in terms of outcomes like survival, profitability, and growth. A fit need not be perfect, but rather just the best fit, under the circumstances.

From an evolutionary perspective, family ownership can be both a survival advantage and a disadvantage. For example, many family firms combine ownership and control, changing the nature of agency costs because responsibility is not delegated to a hired manager but rather retained by the owners, who are the people with the greatest stake in having the business succeed (James 1999). Although this unity of ownership and control can be a survival advantage, it poses a problem when one generation of owners wishes to retire from management and turn the business over to the next generation. They must find ways to transfer leadership from one generation to another (Handler and Kram 1988), which implies they face an additional survival hurdle. The location of family firms may be tied to the residential location of the family, which may mean that firms are created in environments that may not be ideal in terms of resource availability and competition levels (Westhead and Cowling 1998). Being tied to a location for non-business reasons may also make it difficult for the family firm to adapt to changing external circumstances. In addition, smaller organizations, such as the typical family business, have difficulty raising capital, dealing with government regulation, and attracting talent away from larger organizations (Aldrich and Auster 1986).

Regardless of environmental constraints and additional difficulties, as the literatures on strategy and family businesses demonstrate, family firms often have choices and some are able to adapt as their environments change (Gallo 1995; Naldi et al. 2007). The family firm literature could benefit by borrowing the concept of co-evolution from the evolutionary approach. Theorists now recognize that families, organizations, populations, and communities and their environments can co-evolve (Kepner 1983). For example, at the organizational level, co-evolution occurs within a population of heterogeneous firms when organizations with adaptive learning capabilities are able to interact and mutually influence each other (McKelvey 2002; Volberda and Lewin 2003). Particularly in the case of new organizational forms, interaction between firms shapes the structure of emerging industries (Haveman and Rao 1997; Djelic and Ainamo 1999; Lampel and Shamsie 2003). Co-evolution between firms and institutions is also possible. Organized actors with sufficient resources can collectively reshape institutions by attempting to select, modify, or create them in ways that favor their interests, especially when they work purposefully together (DiMaggio 1988; Leca and Naccache 2006). Several studies have shown how family firms have successfully used lobbying and political connections to transform institutional environments (Fogel 2006; Dieleman and Sachs 2008).

Family business theorists recognize the need to emphasize performance outcomes as an ultimate measure of the fit between environment and strategy (Habbershon and Williams 1999). They also recognize that the advantages and disadvantages of family influence depend on specific environments (Habbershon et al. 2003). A handful of studies have made a connection between different family characteristics, strategic orientations, and outcomes like growth (Casillas et al. 2010) and financial performance (Bennedsen et al. 2005; O'Boyle et al. 2010). The role of the family in creating a new entrepreneurial venture is usually explored by the entrepreneurial rather than family business literature (Nordqvist and Melin 2010). However, family business scholars have shown great interest in variations in entrepreneurial orientation, which refers to an entrepreneur's capabilities in responding to opportunities created by external environments. Zahra (2005) found that family ownership and involvement promote entrepreneurship in general in already established firms, whereas the length of tenure of CEO founders has the opposite effect. Zahra et al. (2004) also found that culture is a more significant predictor of entrepreneurial orientation for family firms than for non-family ones.

Evolutionary theory is concerned with organizations over their entire life course and thus can easily incorporate family business research that focuses on family life cycles and family characteristics, particularly issues of ownership and managerial succession (Cabrera-Suarez et al. 2001; Chua et al. 2003; Cater and Justis 2009). In general, succession is seen as a multistage process involving a sequence of steps (Gersick et al. 1997). However, studies of succession tend not to include environmental variables, thus offering an incomplete view of the succession process (Le Breton-Miller et al. 2004). Combining the life cycles of families with life cycles of organizations and populations can produce greater insight in how external environments affect the succession process. For example, Chua et al. (2004) distinguished between organizations that are born as family firms and those that become family firms later in their organizational life cycle. The authors hypothesized that the institutional pressures created by families are different in the two types of organizations, and that firms born as family enterprises are designed with the founding family's needs in mind. In contrast, families must simply adapt to organizations that become family firms later in their life cycle. Although such studies represent a move toward an evolutionary approach, they could place more emphasis on how adaptation and learning depend on external environments.

Adaptation and learning by family firms, in response to long-term changes in environmental conditions, can be analyzed in evolutionary terms. In one of the most quoted articles in family business research, as noted by Chrisman et al. (2010), Aldrich and Cliff (2003) advised analysts to study changes in the structure of the family during the last hundred years, as well as changes in norms and expectations regarding families and their economic activities. They suggested that investigators should devote more attention to

the learning that occurs in the interaction between strategies and family structure. For example, research could examine how family firms adapt to local, regional, and national conditions when they expand or move to other countries. This issue is particularly interesting in the context of different ethnic groups expanding into the global economy through family firms. Some small steps in this direction have been made, for example, by recognizing that both family and organizational characteristics determine outcomes (Sharma 2004).

Thus, an evolutionary approach contributes additional sociological insights into family firms, particularly because it is an encompassing perspective that makes good use of the other theories we have reviewed, as well as other social and behavioral science theories. First, it directs our attention to the historical and comparative conditions under which family firms arose and have changed over time. Second, it is inherently process oriented, demanding that we follow firms and families over time to understand their co-evolution at multiple levels of analysis.

CONCLUSION

Each of the sociological theories explored in this chapter has something to offer for the study of family firms. All of them propose a view of family involvement in business whose results are contingent on environmental conditions, organizational structures, and family characteristics.

The Three Theories and their Methodological Implications

Of the three theories we have reviewed, network theory offers concepts that highlight the advantages and disadvantages families bring to the business environment. The theory differentiates between social capital created by cohesion and social capital created by diversity (Kadushin 2012). Its biggest insight, that families bring cohesive social relationships to business environments, also represents its greatest weakness, as it clusters all families and family structures into a single category. To go beyond general statements, researchers should stop assuming all families are the same. Researchers need to distinguish between different family configurations inside firms and the advantages and disadvantages associated with each. 'Family businesses' where only husband and wife work together should not be treated the same as 'family businesses' involving brothers, uncles, and cousins (Salvato 2004). Network theories of family business need to categorize firms according to the types of families involved and explicitly measure the family-based resources provided.

Methodologically, analysts applying network principles need micro-level data not only on the presence of ties between people and organizations but also on the content of those ties. Network theory has moved away from the old assumption that ties were simple and reciprocated and toward a conception of them as multiplex and directed. Many of the methodological advances in network analysis require that analysts have data not only from the focal people involved but also from all other people in a particular context. Network statistics such as centrality and closure are best calculated from complete matrices of connections between all the people potentially connected within a domain (Burt 2005). Accordingly, traditional fieldwork-based approaches to studying ties within and between family firms must be supplemented with comprehensive surveys, although the development of new network sampling methods has somewhat eased the burden (Borgatti and Halgin 2011).

New institutionalism, the second theory we reviewed, has informed family research about the importance of institutional structures, cultural norms and values, and the way in which people's interpretations of their experiences are affected by what they have learned to take for granted in a society. The challenge for future researchers will be to explore the conditions under which firms buffer or integrate the demands of the external environment to satisfy both the requirements of families and external institutional environments. Furthermore, researchers must remember that because the family is a societal institution, it does change over time as societies evolve. We need to further explore how changes in cultural expectations regarding families have affected family businesses and their relationships with the rest of society.

Methodologically, institutional theorists now work across multiple levels of analysis, ranging from agent-based to historical and comparative approaches (Powell and Colyvas 2008; Scott 2008). With its sweeping reach, institutional theory defies easy categorization with regard to its associated methodological tools. Cliometrics, which is sometimes called the 'new economic history,' can help us understand the historically shifting role of family firms in capitalist societies, but it must be carried out by people with deep substantive knowledge about the phenomena (Boldizzoni 2011). Similarly, micro-level interpretive accounts of how family firms understand and act on their environments must be sensitive to the dangers of ignoring the larger collective context in which family members actions are embedded (Aldrich 2011).

The third sociological approach, evolutionary theory, offers the greatest possibilities for integrating and synthesizing research on family firms. It builds on trends in institutional theory that compel researchers to analyze the dynamic complexity of institutions and environments. Furthermore, evolutionary theory integrates the study of organizational environments with organizational strategy, one of the strong areas of research in the field of family firms (see Parts II and III in the present volume). Using selection logic, evolutionary theory emphasizes the constraining influence of environments on which organizations and organizational practices survive. However, evolutionary theory also emphasizes the learning opportunities provided by environmental diversity and change. We have suggested that more attention be paid to the role of environmental contingencies in understanding the ways in which family firms adapt and change.

Methodologically, evolutionary theory is the most eclectic of the approaches we have reviewed. In drawing on institutional theories about historical and comparative forces affecting family firms, evolutionary theory calls for research designs that cover decades and even centuries, as well as regions and entire continents (Aldrich 2009). Models of co-evolutionary change depend upon complex research designs that allow analysts to associate particular organizational forms with specific patterns of institutional and environmental change (Carney 2007). Evolutionary theory posits that selection and adaptation go hand-in-hand, but testing this idea requires that analysts measure specific environments as well as use longitudinal data to follow complex recursive processes. A consistent theme throughout evolutionary models is the need for data on dynamic processes, whether the unit of time is a day, year, or decade.

Final Thoughts

We believe our review shows that family firms are not just remnants from a bygone era, but rather evidence of the continuing importance of kinship ties in modern capitalist societies. Regardless of which sociological perspective we adopt, we find evidence of a significant role for families and family members in a nation's commercial sector. Social capital within family networks often facilitates interorganizational relations, although it occasionally disrupts them. Families in business keep alive some traditional business practices that efficiency-oriented firms would otherwise push to the periphery. Diversity across economic entities within business populations stems, in part, from diverse family traditions. Finally, from an evolutionary perspective, family businesses co-evolve with other societal institutions and may indirectly reveal a great deal about social trends.

REFERENCES

Aldrich, H.E. 2009. 'Lost in space, out of time: How and why we should study organizations comparatively.' In *Studying Differences Between Organizations: Comparative Approaches to Organizational Research*, edited by B. King, T. Felin and D.A. Whetten, 21–44. Bingley, UK: Emerald Group.

Aldrich, H.E. 2011. 'Heroes, villains, and fools: Institutional entrepreneurship, NOT institutional entrepreneurs.' *Entrepreneurship Research Journal*, 1 (2):1–3.

Aldrich, H. and E.R. Auster. 1986. 'Even dwarfs started small: Liabilities of age and size and their strategic implications.' In *Research in Organizational Behavior*, edited by B.M. Staw and L.L. Cummings, pp. 165–198. Greenwich, CT: JAI Press.

Aldrich, H.E. and J.E. Cliff. 2003. 'The pervasive effects of family on entrepreneurship: Toward a family embeddedness perspective.' *Journal of Business Venturing*, 18 (5):573–596.

Aldrich, H.E. and P.H. Kim. 2007. 'A life course perspective on occupational inheritance: Self-employed parents and their children.' In *Research in the Sociology of Organizations*, edited by M. Ruef and Michael Lounsbury, 33–82. Oxford: JAI Press Elsevier.

Aldrich, H.E., and M. Ruef. 2006. *Organizations Evolving*, 2nd edn. London: Sage Publications.

Aldrich, H.E., A. Elam, and P.R. Reese. 1996. 'Strong ties, weak ties, and strangers: Do Women business owners differ from men in their use of networking to obtain assistance?' In *Entrepreneurship in a Global Context*, edited by S. Birley and I.C. MacMillan, 1–25. London: Routledge.

Aldrich, H.E., L. Renzulli, and N. Langton. 1998. 'Passing on privilege: Resources provided by self-employed parents to their self-employed children.' In *Research in Social Stratification and Mobility*, edited by K. Leicht, pp. 291–318. Greenwich, CT: JAI.

Anderson, A.R., S.L. Jack, and S.D. Dodd. 2005. 'The role of family members in entrepreneurial networks: Beyond the boundaries of the family firm.' *Family Business Review*, 18 (2):135–154.

Arregle, J-L., M.A. Hitt, D.G. Sirmon, and P. Very. 2007. The Development of Organizational Social Capital: Attributes of Family Firms. *Journal of Management Studies*, 44(1): 73–95.

Arum, R. and W. Mueller. 2004. *The Reemergence of Self-employment: A Comparative Study of Self-employment Dynamics and Social Inequality*. Princeton, NJ: Princeton University Press.

Astrachan, J.H. and M.C. Shanker. 2003. 'Family businesses' contribution to the US economy: A closer look.' *Family Business Review*, 16 (3):211–219. doi: 10.1177/08944865030160030601.

Barnett, William P., Henrich R. Greve, and Douglas Y. Park. 1994. "An Evolutionary Model of Organizational Performance." *Strategic Management Journal*, 15, S (Winter): 11–28.

Bates, T. 1994. 'Social resources generated by group support may not be beneficial to Asian immigrant-owned small businesses.' *Social Forces*, 72 (3):671–689.

Bennedsen, M., K. Nielsen, F. Pérez-González, and D. Wolfenzon. 2005. *Inside the family: The Role of Families in Succession Decisions and Performance*. Copenhagen: Institute of Economics, University of Copenhagen.

Blanchflower, D.G. and A.J. Oswald. 1998. 'What makes an entrepreneur?' *Journal of Labor Economics*, 16 (1):26–60.

Boisot, M. and J. Child. 1996. 'From fiefs to clans and network capitalism: Explaining China's emerging economic order.' *Administrative Science Quarterly*, 41 (4):600–628.

Boldizzoni, F. 2011. *The Poverty of Clio: Resurrecting Economic History*. Princeton, NJ: Princeton University Press.

Borgatti, S.P. and D.S. Halgin. 2011. 'On network theory.' *Organization Science*, 22 (5):1168–1181. doi: 10.1287/orsc.1100.0641.

Burt, R.S. 2005. *Brokerage and Closure: An Introduction to Social Capital*. Oxford: Oxford University Press.

Cabrera-Suarez, K., P. De Saa-Parez, and D. Garcia-Almeida. 2001. 'The succession process from a resource- and knowledge-based view of the family firm.' *Family Business Review*, 14 (1):37–46. doi: 10.1111/j.1741-6248.2001.00037.x

Campbell, Donald T. 1969a. "Variation and Selective Retention in Socio-Cultural Evolution." *General Systems*, 14:69–85.

Carney, M. 2005. 'Corporate governance and competitive advantage in family-controlled firms.' *Entrepreneurship: Theory and Practice*, 29 (3): 249–265. doi: 10.1111/j.1540–6520.2005.00081.x.

Carney, M. 2007. 'Minority family business in emerging markets: Organization forms and competitive advantage.' *Family Business Review*, 20 (4):289–300. doi: doi:10.1111/j.1741–6248.2007.00097.x.

Carruthers, B.G. 1995. 'Accounting, ambiguity, and the new institutionalism.' *Accounting, Organizations and Society*, 20 (4):313–328. doi: 10.1016/0361–3682(95)96795-6.

Casillas, J.C., A.M. Moreno, and J.L. Barbero. 2010. 'A configurational approach of the relationship between entrepreneurial orientation and growth of family firms.' *Family Business Review*, 23 (1):27–44. doi: 10.1177/0894486509345159.

Cater, J.J. and R.T. Justis. 2009. 'The development of successors from followers to leaders in small family firms.' *Family Business Review*, 22 (2):109–124. doi: 10.1177/0894486508327822.

Chrisman, J.J., J.H. Chua, and R. Litz. 2003. 'A unified systems perspective of family firm performance: An extension and integration.' *Journal of Business Venturing*, 18 (4):467–472.

Chrisman, J.J., J.H. Chua, and P. Sharma. 2005. 'Trends and directions in the development of a strategic management theory of the family firm.' In *Entrepreneurship: Theory & Practice*: Wiley-Blackwell.

Chrisman, J.J., F.W. Kellermanns, K.C. Chan, and K. Liano. 2010. 'Intellectual foundations of current research in family business: an identification and review of 25 influential articles.' *Family Business Review*, 23 (1):9–26.

Chua, J.H., J.J. Chrisman, and P. Sharma. 2003. 'Succession and nonsuccession concerns of family firms and agency relationship with nonfamily managers.' *Family Business Review*, 16 (2):89–107. doi: 10.1111/j.1741–6248.2003.00089.x.

Chua, J.H., J.J. Chrisman, and E.P.C. Chang. 2004. 'are family firms born or made? An exploratory investigation.' *Family Business Review*, 17 (1):37–54. doi: 10.1111/j.1741–6248.2004.00002.x.

Clark, E. 2000. 'The role of social capital in developing Czech private business.' *Work Employment Society*, 14 (3):439–458. doi: 10.1177/09500170022118518.

Colli, A., P. Fernandez-Perez, and M.B. Rose. 2003. 'National determinants of family firm development.' *Enterprise and Society*, 4 (1):28–64.

Danes, S.M. 2014. 'The future of family business research through the family scientist's lens.' In *SAGE Handbook of Family Business*, edited by L. Melin, M. Nordqvist, and P. Sharma. London: Sage.

Danes, S.M., K. Stafford, G. Haynes, and S.S. Amarapurkar. 2009. 'Family capital of family firms.' *Family Business Review*, 22 (3):199–215. doi: 10.1177/0894486509333424.

Deacon, S.A. 1996. 'Utilizing structural family therapy and systems theory in the business world.' *Contemporary Family Therapy*, 18 (4):549–565.

Dieleman, M. and W.M. Sachs. 2008. 'Coevolution of institutions and corporations in emerging economies: How the Salim Group morphed into an institution of Suharto's crony regime.' *Journal of Management Studies*, 45 (7):1274–1300.

DiMaggio, Paul J. and Walter W. Powell. 1983. 'The Iron Cage Revisited: Institutional Isomorphism and

Collective Rationality in Organizational Fields.' *American Sociological Review*, 48, 2 (April): 147–160.

DiMaggio, P.J. 1988. 'Interest and agency in institutional theory.' In *Institutional Patterns and Organizations: Culture and Environment*, edited by L.G. Zucker, 3–21. Cambridge, MA: Ballinger Publishing Company.

Djelic, M-L. and A. Ainamo. 1999. 'The coevolution of new organizational forms in the fashion industry: A historical and comparative study of France, Italy, and the United States.' *Organization Science*, 10 (5):622–637.

Dyer, W.G. and W. Handler. 1994. 'Entrepreneurship and family business: Exploring the connections.' *Entrepreneurship: Theory & Practice*, 19 (1):71–83.

Fischer, M.J. and D.S. Massey. 2000. 'Residential segregation and ethnic enterprise in US metropolitan areas.' *Social Problems*, 47 (3):408–424.

Fogel, K. 2006. 'Oligarchic family control, social economic outcomes, and the quality of government.' *Journal of International Business Studies*, 37 (5):603–622.

Gallo, M.A. 1995. 'Family businesses in Spain: Tracks followed and outcomes reached by those among the largest thousand.' *Family Business Review*, 8 (4):245–254.

Gersick, K.E., J.A. Davis, M. McCollom Hampton, and I. Lanberg. 1997. *Generation to Generation: Life Cycles of the Family Business*. Boston, MA: Harvard Business School Press.

Glass, J.L. and S.B. Estes. 1997. 'The Family responsive workplace.' *Annual Review of Sociology*, 23:289–313.

Granovetter, M. 1974. *Getting a Job: A Study of Contacts and Careers*. Cambridge, MA: Harvard University Press.

Habbershon, T.G. and J. Pistrui. 2002. 'Enterprising families domain: Family-influenced ownership groups in pursuit of transgenerational wealth.' *Family Business Review*, 15 (3):223–237. doi: 10.1111/j.1741-6248.2002.00223.x.

Habbershon, T.G. and M.L. Williams. 1999. 'A resource-based framework for assessing the strategic advantages of family firms.' *Family Business Review*, 12(1):1–25. doi:10.1111/j.1741–6248.1999.00001.x.

Habbershon, T.G., M. Williams, and I.C. MacMillan. 2003. 'A unified systems perspective of family firm performance.' *Journal of Business Venturing*, 18 (4):451–465.

Handler, W.C. and K.E. Kram. 1988. 'Succession in family firms: The problem of resistance.' *Family Business Review*, 1 (4):361–381. doi: 10.1111/j.1741–6248.1988.00361.x.

Haveman, H.A. and H. Rao. 1997. 'Structuring a theory of moral sentiments: institutional and organizational coevolution in the early thrift industry.' *The American Journal of Sociology*, 102 (6):1606–1651.

Heck, R.K.Z. and E.S. Trent. 1999. 'The prevalence of family business from a household sample.' *Family Business Review*, 12 (3):209–224.

Hoelscher, M.L. 2002. 'The relationship between family capital and business performance.' Doctoral dissertation, Texas Tech University.

Jack, S.L. 2005. 'The role, use and activation of strong and weak network ties: A qualitative analysis.' *Journal of Management Studies*, 42 (6):1233–1259.

James, H.S. 1999. 'Owner as manager, extended horizons and the family firm.' *International Journal of the Economics of Business*, 6 (1):41–55.

Johannisson, B. 2002. 'Energizing entrepreneurship: ideological tensions in the medium-sized family business.' In *Understanding the small family business*, edited by D. Fletcher. London: Routledge.

Jones, O. and D. Jayawarna. 2010. 'Resourcing new businesses: Social networks, bootstrapping and firm performance.' *Venture Capital*, 12 (2):127–152.

Julien, P-A. E. Andriambeloson, and C. Ramangalahy. 2004. 'Networks, weak signals and technological innovations among SMEs in the land-based transportation equipment sector.' *Entrepreneurship & Regional Development*, 16 (4):251–269.

Kadushin, C. 2012. *Understanding Social Networks: Theories, Concepts, and Findings*. New York: Oxford University Press.

Keister, L. 2000. *Wealth in America: Trends in Wealth Inequality*. Cambridge: Cambridge University Press.

Kepner, E. 1983. 'The family and the firm: A coevolutionary perspective.' *Organizational Dynamics*, 12 (1):57–70.

Kim, P.H., H.E. Aldrich, and L.A. Keister. 2003. 'Does wealth matter? The impact of financial and human capital on becoming a nascent entrepreneur.' Paper presented at the Academy of Management annual meeting, Seattle, WA.

Kim, P.H., K. Longest, and H.E. Aldrich. 2007. 'Can you lend me a hand? Social Support, network structure, and entrepreneurial action.' Working paper. Madison, Wisconsin: University of Wisconsin.

Kolvereid, L. 1996. 'Prediction of employment status choice intentions.' *Entrepreneurship: Theory & Practice*, 21 (1):47–57.

Kristiansen, S. and A. Ryen. 2002. 'Enacting their business environments: Asian entrepreneurs in East Africa.' *African & Asian Studies*, 1 (3):165.

Lampel, J. and J. Shamsie. 2003. 'Capabilities in motion: New organizational forms and the reshaping of the Hollywood movie industry.' *Journal of Management Studies*, 40 (8):2189–2210.

Leaptrott, J. 2005. 'An institutional theory view of the family business.' *Family Business Review*, 18 (3): 215–228. doi: 10.1111/j.1741–6248.2005.00043.x.

Le Breton-Miller, I., D. Miller, and L.P. Steier. 2004. 'Toward an integrative model of effective FOB succession.' *Entrepreneurship: Theory & Practice*, 28 (4):305–328. doi: 10.1111/j.1540–6520.2004.00047.x.

Leca, B. and P. Naccache. 2006. 'A critical realist approach to institutional entrepreneurship.' *Organization*, 13 (5):627–651.

Liao, J. and H. Welsch. 2003. 'Social capital and entrepreneurial growth aspiration: A comparison of technology- and non-technology-based nascent entrepreneurs.' *The Journal of High Technology Management Research*, 14 (1):149–170.

Lippmann, S., A. Davis, and H.E. Aldrich. 2005. 'Entrepreneurship and inequality.' *Research in the Sociology of Work*, 15 (1):3–31.

Martinez, M.A. and H.E. Aldrich. 2011. 'Networking strategies for entrepreneurs: Balancing cohesion and diversity.' *International Journal of Entrepreneurial Behaviour and Research*, 17 (1):7–38.

Matthews, C.H. and S.B. Moser. 1996. 'A longitudinal investigation of the impact of family background and gender on interest in small firm ownership.' *Journal of Small Business Management*, 34 (2):29–43.

McKelvey, B. 2002. 'Model-centered organization science epistemology.' In *Companion to Organizations*, edited by J.A.C. Baum, 752–780. Thousand Oaks, CA: Sage Publications.

Melin, L. and M. Nordqvist. 2007. 'The reflexive dynamics of institutionalization: The case of the family business.' *Strategic Organization*, 5 (3):321–333.

Meyer, J.W. and B. Rowan. 1977. 'Institutionalized organizations: Formal structure as myth and ceremony.' *American Journal of Sociology*, 83 (2):340–363.

Miller, D.R. and G.E. Swanson. 1958. *The Changing American Parent; A Study in the Detroit Area*. New York: Wiley.

Mustakallio, M., E. Autio, and S.A. Zahra. 2002. 'Relational and contractual governance in family firms: Effects on strategic decision making.' *Family Business Review*, 15 (3):205–222. doi: 10.1111/j.1741–6248.2002.00205.x.

Naldi, L., M. Nordqvist, K. Sjåberg, and J. Wiklund. 2007. 'Entrepreneurial orientation, risk taking, and performance in family firms.' *Family Business Review*, 20(1):33–47. doi: 10.1111/j.1741–6248.2007.00082.x.

Nordqvist, M. and L. Melin. 2010. 'Entrepreneurial families and family firms.' *Entrepreneurship and Regional Development*, 22 (3–4):211–239. doi: 10.1080/08985621003726119.

O'Boyle, E.H., M.W. Rutherford, and J.M. Pollack. 2010. 'Examining the relation between ethical focus and financial performance in family firms: An exploratory study.' *Family Business Review*, 23 (4):310–326. doi: 10.1177/0894486510375412.

Parada, M.J., M. Nordqvist, and A. Gimeno. 2010. 'Institutionalizing the family business: The role of professional associations in fostering a change of values.' *Family Business Review*, 23 (4):355–372. doi: 10.1177/0894486510381756.

Parsons, T. and R.F. Bales. 1955. *Family, Socialization and Interaction Processes*. Edited by T. Parsons. Glencoe, IL: Free Press.

Pieper, T. and S. Klein. 2007. 'The bulleye: A systems approach to modeling family firms.' *Family Business Review*, 20 (4):301–319.

Powell, W.W. and J.A. Colyvas. 2008. 'Microfoundations of institutional theory.' In *The SAGE Handbook of Organizational Institutionalism*, edited by R. Greenwood, C. Oliver, K. Sahlin, and R. Suddaby, 276–298. London: Sage.

Puffer, S.M. and D.J. McCarthy. 2007. 'Can Russia's state-managed, network capitalism be competitive?: Institutional pull versus institutional push.' *Journal of World Business*, 42 (1):1–13.

Ram, M. and R. Holliday. 1993. 'Relative merits: Family culture and kinship in small firms.' *Sociology*, 27 (4):629–648. doi: 10.1177/0038038593027004005.

Rapoport, R. and R. Rapoport. 1965. 'Work and family in contemporary society.' *American Sociological Review*, 30 (3):381–394.

Reid, R., B. Dunn, S. Cromie, and J. Adams. 1999. 'Family orientation in family firms: A model and some empirical evidence.' *Journal of Small Business and Enterprise Development*, 6 (1):56–67.

Renzulli, L.A., and H. Aldrich. 2005. 'Who can you turn to? Tie activation within core business discussion networks.' *Social Forces*, 84 (1):323–341.

Roberts, P.W. and R. Greenwood. 1997. 'Integrating transaction cost and institutional theories: Toward a constrained-efficiency framework for understanding organizational design adoption.' *The Academy of Management Review*, 22 (2):346–373.

Rona-Tas, A. 1994. 'The first shall be last? Entrepreneurship and communist cadres in the transition from socialism.' *The American Journal of Sociology*, 100 (1):40–69.

Ruef, M., H.E. Aldrich, and N.M. Carter. 2003. 'The structure of founding teams: Homophily, strong ties, and isolation among US entrepreneurs.' *American Sociological Review*, 68 (2):195–222.

Salvato, C. 2004. 'Predictors of entrepreneurship in family firms.' *Journal of Private Equity,* 7 (3):68–76.

Scott, M.G. and D.F. Twomey. 1988. 'The long-term supply of entrepreneurs: Students' career aspirations in relation to entrepreneurship.' *Journal of Small Business Management,* 26 (4):5–13.

Scott, R.W. 2001. *Institutions and Organizations.* Thousand Oaks, CA: Sage Publications.

Scott, W. 2008. 'Approaching adulthood: The maturing of institutional theory.' *Theory and Society,* 37 (5):427–442. doi: 10.1007/s11186-008-9067-z.

Selznick, P. 1996. 'Institutionalism "old" and "new".' *Administrative Science Quarterly,* 41 (2):270–277.

Sequeira, J., S.L. Mueller, and J.E. McGee. 2007. 'The influence of social ties and self-efficacy in forming entrepreneurial intentions and motivating nascent behavior.' *Journal of Developmental Entrepreneurship,* 12(3):275–293.

Sequeira, J.M. and A.A. Rasheed. 2006. 'Start-up and growth of immigrant small businesses: The impact of social and human capital.' *Journal of Developmental Entrepreneurship,* 11 (4):357–375.

Sharma, P. 2004. 'An overview of the field of family business studies: Current status and directions for the future.' *Family Business Review,* 17 (1):1–36. doi: 10.1111/j.1741-6248.2004.00001.x.

Sirmon, D.G. and M.A. Hitt. 2003. 'Managing resources: Linking unique resources, management, and wealth creation in family firms.' *Entrepreneurship: Theory & Practice,* 27 (4):339–358.

Steier, L. 2001. 'Family firms, plural forms of governance, and the evolving role of trust.' *Family Business Review,* 14 (4):353–368. doi: 10.1111/j.1741-6248.2001.00353.x.

Stewart, A. 2003. 'Help one another, use one another: Toward an anthropology of family business.' *Entrepreneurship: Theory & Practice,* 27 (4):383–396.

Tsai, K.S. 2005. 'Capitalists without a class: Political diversity among private entrepreneurs in China.' *Comparative Political Studies,* 38 (9):1130–1158. doi: 10.1177/0010414005277021.

Tsui-Auch, L.S. and Y-J. Lee. 2003. 'The state matters: Management models of Singaporean Chinese and Korean business groups.' *Organization Studies,* 24 (4):507–534. doi: 10.1177/0170840603024004001.

Vallejo, M. 2008. 'Is the culture of family firms really different? A value-based model for its survival through generations.' *Journal of Business Ethics,* 81 (2):261–279. doi: 10.1007/s10551-007-9493-2.

van Geenhuizen, M. and D.P. Soetanto. 2012. 'Open innovation among university spin-off firms: What is in it for them, and what can cities do?' *Innovation: The European Journal of Social Science Research,* 25 (2):191–207. doi: 10.1080/13511610.2012.660328.

Volberda, H.W. and A.Y. Lewin. 2003. 'Guest editors' introduction: Co-evolutionary dynamics within and between firms: From evolution to co-evolution.' *Journal of Management Studies,* 40 (8):2111–2136.

Westhead, P. and M. Cowling. 1998. 'Family firm research: The need for a methodological rethink.' *Entrepreneurship: Theory & Practice,* 23 (1):31–56.

Westphal, J.D., R. Gulati, and S.M. Shortell. 1997. 'Customization or conformity? An institutional and network perspective on the content and consequences of TQM adoption.' *Administrative Science Quarterly,* 42 (2):366–394.

Whyte, M.K. 1996. 'The Chinese family and economic development: Obstacle or engine?' *Economic Development and Cultural Change,* 45 (1):1–30.

Wu, Y-L. 1983. 'Chinese entrepreneurs in Southeast Asia.' *The American Economic Review,* 73 (2):112–117.

Yanagisako, S.Y. and J.F. Collier. 2004. 'Toward a unified analysis of gender and kinship.' In *Kinship and Family: An Anthropological Reader,* edited by R. Parker and L. Stone. Oxford: Blackwell Publishers.

Zahra, S.A. 2005. 'Entrepreneurial risk taking in family firms.' *Family Business Review,* 18 (1):23–40. doi: 10.1111/j.1741-6248.2005.00028.x.

Zahra, S.A., J.C. Hayton, and C. Salvato. 2004. 'Entrepreneurship in family vs. non-family firms: A resource-based analysis of the effect of organizational culture.' *Entrepreneurship: Theory & Practice,* 28 (4):363–381.

Zimmer, C. and H. Aldrich. 1987. 'Resource mobilization through ethnic networks: Kinship and friendship ties of shopkeepers in England.' *Sociological Perspectives,* 30 (4):422–445.

Zucker, L.G. 1987. 'Institutional theories of organization.' *Annual Review of Sociology,* 13:443–464.

6

Economic Theories of Family Firms

Prashant P. Shukla, Michael Carney
and Eric Gedajlovic

INTRODUCTION

Across time and place, family owned and controlled firms (FFs) are a ubiquitous organizational form (Arregle et al., 2007). In addition to the countless numbers of small to medium-sized FFs, many of the world's largest firms are family owned and controlled. The thriving businesses of the Tatas and Ambanis in India, the Waltons and Fords in the USA, and the Toyotas and Mitsubishis in Japan are indicative of the importance of FFs in generating economic wealth. As Schulze and Gedajlovic (2010) point out, the prevalence of FFs is indicative of two characteristics. First, from an economic viewpoint, the prevalence of FFs implies their ability to survive, for economic theory predicts that organization forms are subject to competitive selection mechanisms that extinguish inefficient organizational forms. Second, the ubiquity of FFs also suggests an inherent capacity for adaptation to a multitude of environments, differing in terms of history, culture, and institutional development.

Yet, it is only recently that FFs have begun to receive significant scholarly attention. The emergent consensus of recent work suggests FFs share several unique and bivalent traits. Due to their inherently contradictory traits (Tagiuri and Davis, 1996), a broad range of economic theories have been advanced to explain the functioning and performance of FFs. In this chapter, we survey literature spanning four decades from economics, finance, entrepreneurship, and management journals to arrive at a list of theories that have been used in investigating FFs. To obtain the list of relevant papers we manually searched journals of these disciplines using search words such as 'family firms,' 'performance in family business,' etc. Having collected more than a hundred papers for review, we categorized them based on the theoretical lens used in the inquiry; this led us to the most important and oft-used economic theories of FFs. In our review, we provide general overviews of these theories and discuss how they have been employed or used to explain aspects of FF behavior and in turn how family firm research has contributed to development of these theories.

Economic theories of the firm are concerned with the interaction of economic agents, contract designs, and providing incentives to generate and distribute rent. Rent creation is the value in excess of that required to compensate suppliers of factors of production (labor, capital, knowledge, etc.) needed to produce a good or service (Amit and Shoemaker, 1993). To generate economic rents a firm must combine and integrate resources acquired from factor markets into capabilities or strategic assets (Amit and Shoemaker, 1993). Using slightly different terminology, Makadok (2001) proposes two rent-creation processes, 'resource picking' and 'capability building,' the former consists of the exercise of skill in identifying appropriately priced resources, while the latter corresponds to the idea of resource combination to produce capabilities as discussed by Amit and Shoemaker (1993). A failure to create rents from their resources constitutes failure since the resources acquired by the firm in competitive factor markets cannot be retained unless the firm's owners are able to compensate them at prices prevailing in factor markets. In undertaking the task of rent creation, FFs are sometimes advantaged by the synergistic interaction of their acquired resources and their unique self-supplied strategic assets, and at other times disadvantaged by constraints inherent in their identity. The prevailing methodology used in the literature to establish whether FFs generate rents is to compare their financial performance with other, non-family, types of firm. Accordingly, in our survey we adopt a firm-level analysis to examine how economic agents interact within the context of the family firm to organize rent-generation processes, compared with other types of firms.

We begin by considering three branches of agency theory. We first consider 'classic' agency theory, which highlights the conflict of interest between a firm's principals, the firm's owners, and agents, executives who control the deployment of resources in the firm (Jensen and Meckling, 1976). Second, we consider principal-principal agency theory, which is concerned with conflicts of interest between different types of owners, namely majority and minority shareholders in publicly listed family firms. We then consider the third variation of agency theory – the behavioral agency model – which represents a synthesis of agency and prospect theories to illustrate that the owners of FFs will hold different risk preferences compared with diversified investors in other types of firms, and hence tend to be loss averse with respect to investment preferences and be motivated by different goals than the diversified owners of other types of firm (Wiseman and Gomez-Mejia, 1998).

Fourth, we consider the resource-based view of rent creation. This stream of literature identifies a range of self-supplied rent-generating resources that are unique in family firms including tacit knowledge, social capital, and patient capital, while simultaneously also identifying several self-imposed constraints on the effective use of resources, including factors such as financial capital constraints, nepotism, and other human capital constraints. Finally, we consider two prominent economic theories, transaction cost (Coase, 1937; Williamson, 1981) and property rights theory (Alchian and Demsetz, 1972), that we suggest are underemployed by scholars in addressing certain facets of family firm functioning and performance. Transaction cost theory (TCT) is concerned with the comparative cost of conducting a transaction within firms and markets and with the need to develop the most efficient forms of contracts to engage factors of production. Property rights theory (PRT), shares a similar concern for the design of efficient contracts and is additionally concerned with the efficient allocation of property rights and decision-making rights within the firm (Mahoney, 2005). Table 6.1 summarizes the focal arguments for each theory, their current usage in the context of FFs, and the potential for extending them. We conclude the chapter with a discussion of

Table 6.1 Current and potential usage of economic theories in family firms

	Theory	Focal issue	Existing use in the context of FFs	Potential avenues for extension
1	**Agency theory**			
1(a)	Principal-agent	Conflict in goals of principals and agents, difficulty in observing the agent's actions; leading to costs in governance.	Family ownership mitigates the classic PA problems of a corporation but gives rise to unique PP problems.	Delineate across which governance structures, resources, environments, do benefits of low PA costs exceed the disadvantages of PP?
1(b)	Principal-principal	Principal's actions – affectively motivated and self-interested – are not in best interest of the firm or the minority shareholders.	Majority shareholders expropriate financial benefits from minority shareholders and make affective decisions w.r.t. inheritance, managerial appointments, etc.	Use multiple theories to investigate how do FFs compensate for the negative effects of PP problems – resources, lower governance costs, social networks?
1(c)	Behavioral agency model	Decisions based on non-economic reference points such as SEW, inconsistent preferences, and loss-aversion.	Family's decisions w.r.t. firm diversification and growth strategies can harm the firm when these decisions are geared toward protecting SEW rather than maximizing profits.	Combine BAM with other theories to explore when SEW-based decisions are financially beneficial for FFs, and how FFs overcome the downsides of SEW-based decisions?
2	Resource-based view	VRIN resources as a means of rent generation, gaining sustainable competitive advantage and Ricardian rents.	FFs are inherently endowed with resources such as social, human, patient capital etc. that facilitate rent creation.	Explore the bottlenecks and the subsequent negatives of family resources, using RBV in conjunction with other theories. Explore the development of dynamic capabilities in FFs.
3	Transaction costs theory	Existence of firms; coordination of resources and economic activity at minimum costs via contracting or integration.	**Pros:** Lower governance costs for hiring and training; production of GNTs. **Cons:** Same governance decisions also bring resource bottlenecks.	Blending RBV, PRT, and TCT considerations to explain the pros and cons in one framework. Explore portfolio entrepreneurship in FFs using a TCT lens.
4	Property rights theory	Defining residual claims and decision-making rights in the firm to minimize conflicts and costs.	**Pros:** Lower costs of preparing, enforcing, and resolving contracts. **Cons:** Exploitation of incomplete contracts, lack of transparency in firm, leading to lower firm value and performance.	Blending RBV, TCT, agency, PRT, and institution-based considerations to explain the pros and cons in one framework. Explore franchising using TCT and PRT perspective.

Fig. 6.1, which offers a prototype framework of an integrated economic perspective on the family firm and the potential for these theories to further gain from family firm research.

PRINCIPAL AGENCY THEORY

Principal agency theory is one of the most often applied theories in the social sciences with applications in economics, political science, law, and finance. Principal agency theory predicts that due to information and goal asymmetries, conflicts of interest will arise whenever a principal hires an agent to perform a task on his or her behalf (Eisenhardt,1989).

In their seminal paper, Jensen and Meckling (1976) identify three major agency costs: (1) costs incurred while monitoring the agents' activities; (2) costs incurred to align an agent's incentives with a principal; and (3) the residual loss incurred by the incongruity in principal agent (PA) goals even after the aforementioned efforts to mitigate the problems. Jensen (1986) suggests that an important PA problem concerns the utilization of free cash flows: principals prefer that free cash be returned to them as dividends but managerial agents may prefer to retain the cash within the firm to invest in activities that serve their own purposes. Finding and implementing solutions to such agency problems is costly to the firm and diverts attention away from efficient resource accumulation and capability building, both crucial for sustained rent creation (Makadok, 2001). Much of the principal agency theory literature is concerned with the study of mechanisms that may mitigate the costs arising from PA conflicts. Some PA costs are averted in family firms because ownership and managerial control are combined in the family's hands. Principal agency theory predicts that the combination of ownership and control mitigates PA problems because family owners are more involved in managing the firm where they are effective 'monitors-in-place' who are both motivated and well positioned

to discipline executive behavior (Anderson and Reeb, 2003a, 2003b). Traditional PA reasoning suggests that FFs exercise greater diligence in managing costs (Brickley and Dark, 1987), avoid allocating free cash flow to low return projects (Carney, 2005), and are more effective and motivated at monitoring salaried managers (Anderson and Reeb, 2003a, 2003b). Accordingly, principal agency theory hypothesizes that the monitoring and incentive structures found in family firms will provide them with relative advantages over firms whose owners are highly dispersed. Adherents of principal agency theory can point to a large body of evidence to support the hypothesis (Anderson and Reeb, 2003a, 2003b).

Though there is considerable theory to support the principal agency hypothesis, the balance of the evidence is mixed. This mixed effect of the combination of separation and ownership on performance in FFs has been documented in studies such as Carney and Gedajlovic (2002). The authors showed that combination of ownership and control in FFs has positive as well as negative outcomes. In their study of listed firms in Hong Kong, the authors conclude that while coupled ownership is negatively related to investments in capital expenditure, it is positively related with dividend payment, liquidity, and profitability. A series of studies in the finance literature also provides contrasting conclusions about the efficiency of FFs from a principal agency viewpoint. Anderson et al. (2003) document the inherent lower agency costs of debt in FFs, which by virtue of undiversified and concentrated shareholders are able to circumvent the conflict between shareholders, who want to invest in risky projects, and bondholders, who demand higher premiums in turn. Similarly, in investigating agency conflicts between minority shareholders and concentrated owners, Anderson and Reeb (2003a) find that FFs outperform non-FFs, while Anderson and Reeb (2003b) show that minority shareholders are not exploited by concentrated family shareholders but in fact benefit from family ownership. However, the advantages of unification of ownership and control are accompanied by disadvantages. Anderson et al. (2008) conclude that large publicly-traded FFs in the USA tend to be more opaque – about 5% more – than non-FFs. More opaque FFs are more prone to conflict between controlling and minority shareholders leading to a devaluation of firms with a family member at the helm. Complementing these findings, Villalonga and Amit (2006) find evidence of costs of conflict between family and non-family shareholder in FFs. However, in the presence of a founder-CEO or Chairman, these costs are still lower than those found in firms with dispersed ownership. This helps increase firm value and lends more support from the principal agency perspective of FFs.

Minority-majority stakeholder agency conflict are manifest in several other facets of FFs governance structures such as dual class shares (Tinaikar, 2008; Villalonga and Amit, 2009), voting rights, pyramids (Villalonga and Amit, 2008), and dividend payout (Carney and Gedajlovic, 2002). While, dual class structures are found to be negatively associated with performance (Tinaikar, 2008), the proclivity of FFs for increasing the wedge between cash flow and control rights nullifies incentives for private benefits and increases regulation and monitoring (Tinaikar, 2008; Villalonga and Amit, 2009). Similarly, pyramids and voting agreements have been found to be positively related with firm value (Villalonga and Amit, 2008).

A stream of principal agency theory research has distinguished between FFs that are headed by founders and those headed by heir. Several studies find that founder managed firms outperform firms managed by heirs. For example, Villalonga and Amit (2008) find that while FFs are geared toward creating wealth for the firm, FFs with founders are more likely to create wealth for themselves as well as the shareholders. In this scenario, minority investors in FFs headed by founder families will be better off relative to investors in non-FFs. But once again findings

are mixed. While FFs headed by a founder may do a better job of mitigating agency issues, Anderson et al. (2009), find that both founder- and heir-controlled family firms exhibit preferences for investing in riskier R&D projects, notwithstanding the negative effect of such actions on the shareholders and the firm. Furthermore, FFs also exhibit a long-term orientation and risk-averse behavior by investing in purchase of physical assets, which require about 6% longer to depreciate.

In sum, the extant literature documents the positive qualities of FFs in their mitigation of traditional PA costs, but it also provides evidence for FFs as a setting that facilitates agency issues between minority-majority shareholders. Based on the ubiquity, the overall success of FFs, and the evidence, one could argue that the benefits of combining ownership and control outweigh the costs (Anderson et al. 2003; Anderson and Reeb 2003; Villalonga and Amit 2009; and others). However, the prevalence and persistence of FFs remains an open question (Schulze and Gedajlovic, 2010). Thus, we believe that the landscape of FFs continues to present challenges and opportunities for scholars. FFs provide natural settings for testing predictions of traditional agency theory as well as extending the theory's scope. As we note in Table 6.1, delineating the situations where the positives of combined ownership and control outweigh the negatives, and vice-versa, is a natural direction for future research. Alvarez and Barney (2004) draw attention to this point and call for more investigation of the rent-generation process to identify the governance structures that are most efficient in generating and sustaining rents. FFs offer the perfect setting to further our understanding of rent-generating and rent-sustaining governance mechanisms.

PRINCIPAL-PRINCIPAL AGENCY THEORY

Given the mixed support for the hypotheses that FFs mitigate PA costs, one cannot conclude that FF governance is always more efficient than alternative forms of governance desirable. Indeed, research on FFs in a variety of institutional settings has contributed to the extension of agency theory by illuminating the potential negative effects of combined ownership and control. A new branch of agency theory identifies problems arising from the combination of ownership and control: principal-principal (PP) agency theory. As summarized in Table 6.1, PP agency costs arise from two sources: the conflicts between controlling family shareholders and the minority shareholders (Morck and Yeung, 2003; Cheung et al., 2006) and the family members' affectively motivated actions (Schulze et al., 2003; Gomez-Mejia et al., 2007), which can harm the economic interests of both family members and minority investors.

PP conflicts between controlling and minority shareholders begin with managerial entrenchment (Gomez-Mejia et al., 2001; Morck et al., 2005), which is the capacity of a controlling shareholder to hold senior executive office for an extended period regardless of his or her performance. Extended executive tenures can have negative effects on a firm's performance as managerial entrenchment facilitates the adoption of devices such as pyramiding, characterized by ultimate ownership of a firm via ownership of a chain of organizations (Morck and Yeung 2003), tunneling, expropriating cash benefits between subsidiary organizations (Bertrand, Mehta, and Mullainathan, 2002), and connected party transactions (Cheung et al., 2006). Each of these devices relies on the capacity of an ultimate or controlling shareholder to expropriate value from minority shareholders. For example, Cheung et al. (2006) find that the likelihood of connected-party transactions among firms in Hong Kong increases when ultimate ownership is traced to firms located in mainland China. The announcements of connected-party transactions result in, on average, excess negative returns compared with firms' announcements of arms-length transactions. Similarly, the

existence of control rights in excess of cash flow rights commonly found in family firms indicates an expropriation risk and is 'priced in' to the firm's market value. Claessens et al. (2002) find that firm value increases with cash flow ownership of the majority shareholder but when the control rights of the largest shareholders exceed the cash-flow rights, the firm value declines.

The intersection of PP agency theory and institutional theory has produced several insightful insights. First, scholars have begun to examine moderating role of underdeveloped institutions in enabling expropriation (Dharwadkar et al., 2000; Young et al., 2008; Peng and Jiang, 2010). In advanced economies, minority shareholders are compensated for bearing expropriation risk but in underdeveloped markets there is no such premium (Faccio et al., 2001). Second, in addition to the direct negative effects of concentrated ownership and firm value, recent research finds that the concentrated ownership of the firm dampens innovation and skews public policy, producing a cumulative negative effect on economic development (Morck et al., 2000; 2005). Third, research on the interaction of agency dynamics, institutional conditions, and economic development suggests that concentrated family ownership is beneficial in the context of well-developed institutions (Peng and Jiang, 2010). In such well-developed institutional environments FFs adopt value enhancing strategies such as hiring professional managers and relinquishing majority ownership (Burkart et al., 2003). Contrarily, the apparently opportunistic behavior of FFs in less developed institutional environments raises pressing questions about the role of FFs as the engines of economic development, as they are sometimes portrayed (Khanna and Palepu, 1999). These unanswered questions open up continuing research opportunities aimed at delineating the different behavior patterns of FFs operating in different types of institutional environment.

The second type of PP issues underscores the tendency for FFs to make economically inefficient decisions (see row 1(b), Table 6.1). Family members at the helm have been shown to make decisions detrimental to firm's resources, incentive structure, capability building processes, and governance. The concentration of executive control in FFs can reduce motivation and initiative-taking behavior of non-family members (Burkart et al., 1997). To avoid the dilution of their control families can be reluctant to award stock options to non-family members, an act that decreases their incentive (McConaughy, 2000). Similarly, FFs' tendency towards nepotism and favoritism can deplete human capital, leading to negativity and disloyalty among non-family employees, which in turn can lead to shirking and free-riding problems (Schulze et al., 2003). Furthermore, the perception of favoritism and weak incentives in FFs can be a significant barrier to recruiting and retaining talented human capital (Schulze et al., 2001), which is a significant constraint on a FF's abilities in cultivating high-quality human capital. Inevitably, the accumulation of PP agency issues run counter to efficient capability building in organizations and sustained rent creation (Amit and Shoemaker, 1993; Makadok, 2001). Moreover, predispositions toward affect-influenced decision making not only handicaps FFs resource acquisition activities, but also harms their ability to combine resources effectively.

Furthermore, driven by nepotism and legacy norms, FFs appoint relatives in important positions even when they are cognizant of the sub-par abilities to the appointees (Bertrand and Schoar, 2006). While any succession within the family has a negative impact on firm performance (Bennedsen et al., 2007), primogeniture-based inheritance, also a common phenomenon in FFs, has additionally been found to be associated with the retention of obsolete management practices (Bloom and van Reenen, 2007). Finally, even in the absence of affective decision making and active expropriation of minority shareholders, FFs human and financial constraints can limit FF growth beyond a threshold level (Gedajlovic et al., 2004). In a nutshell, PP agency theory suggests FFs are handicapped in their resource acquisition and rent-creating capabilities which inevitably harm their financial performance.

BEHAVIORAL AGENCY MODEL

While classical PA theory emphasizes the potential benefits arising from combined ownership and control and PP agency theory emphasizes the costs, the emergence of the third variant of agency theory, the behavioral agency model (BAM) points FF scholars in a completely new direction. Wiseman and Gomez-Mejia (1998) argue that classical agency theory is deficient in its assumption that manager risk preferences are constant across the full spectrum of risk-return choices. Borrowing from prospect theory (Kahneman and Tversky, 1979), Wiseman and Gomez-Meija (1998) relax the assumption of constant risk preference and introduce the idea of dynamic decision making – which suggests that prior risk decisions can inform future behavior. This new assumption provides for more refined predictions of agents' risk preferences and decisions. Borrowing from prospect theory, BAM incorporates the idea of loss-aversion (see row 1(c), Table 6.1) – which suggests self-interested individuals are more likely to prefer the minimization of current losses over maximizing future gains. Importantly, agents may retain a preference for loss aversion even if it entails accepting higher risk; risk preference, thus, becomes a pivotal determinant of agent behavior. Based upon these focal points, BAM sheds light on decision-making processes in FFs which have previously puzzled scholars. Our discussion of BAM, however, is concise on purpose: Berrone et al. (2014) have discussed it at length in this handbook so we recommend interested readers to continue on to Chapter 10.

Applying BAM precepts, Gomez-Mejia et al. (2007) show that the primary reference point for families governing FFs is maintaining socio-emotional wealth (SEW), which they define as non-economic satisfaction derived from firm ownership (Berrone et al., 2012). Numerous factors, including control, influence, community reputation, emotional attachment, social ties, and family image have been advanced as the non-economic reference points FFs apply in their decision-making processes. Several studies bolster BAM-driven decision making in FFs. Gomez-Mejia et al. (2007) in a study of Spanish olive oil mills over a period of 54 years conclude that when faced with a decision of becoming a part of a cooperative, FFs were less likely to join than NFFs – even though remaining independent meant incurring significant risks to their financial performance. The results suggest loss aversion has a strong impact in FFs decisions making processes. Similarly, Gomez-Mejia et al. (2010) find that FFs are less diversified with respect to both product-markets and geography compared to non-FFs, even when diversification is financially rewarding for the firm. Thus, when faced with the trade-off between SEW preservation via independence and prestige and wealth generation, FFs prefer to preserve SEW, exhibiting loss-aversion with respect to SEW. However, although large, publicly-traded FFs diversify less than NFFs, their acquisition tend to be unrelated to the main business of the firms and hence more risky from a traditional economic standpoint (Miller et al., 2010). Though more risky, such unrelated acquisitions, however, allow FFs to leverage their unique resources such as networks and reputation and diversify the wealth of the family while allowing them to maintain control of the business. As we explain later under our discussion of transaction cost theory, viewed in this regard, such 'unrelated' diversification does not seem that unrelated or risky for FFs.

As one can surmise, FFs preference for SEW may counteract the valuable rent-creating processes inside a FF. However, if loss aversion is so endemic in FFs and if it were highly detrimental to firm performance, FFs would not be as prevalent as they evidently are. We conjecture that there is a

tipping point between the opposite forces of economic and affective motivations; and FFs are able to realize when it is absolutely imperative to use an economic frame of reference to make a decision as opposed to an affect driven decision. It has been shown that FFs make tough decisions about CEO tenure based on firm performance and business risks involved even when a family member occupies the top position in the firm (Gomez-Mejia et al., 2001), and in fact the human capital and talent of family members supersedes any agency biases in CEO appointments in FFs (Salvato et al., 2012). In addition, SEW also motivates lower cash compensation for CEOs in FFs; yet, family CEOs are compensated for their pay discount via better protection against systematic and uncontrollable risks in the business environment (Gomez-Mejia et al., 2003). Such a decision cumulatively has the possibility of freeing up financial resources in FFs that can possibly be used for building rent-creating capabilities such as SEW-driven human capital accumulation and enhancement (Cruz et al., 2011).

The application of BAM to the FFs suggests that greater attention needs be given to research that explores the contingencies and managerial functions that enable FFs to alternate between affective and economic frames of reference. Such an exploration is likely to be prolific for family firm scholars. However, BAM does not explain how FFs manage to free themselves from the grip of loss aversion and the attendant harmful economic decisions that follow, nor does BAM offer an explanation of when and why SEW-based decisions can produce benefits to FFs (row 1(c), Table 6.1). We propose orienting research along a route that promotes the development of BAM within its agency theory origins while simultaneously improving our understanding of FF governance and rent-generation processes. Like other variants of agency theory, we propose that BAM should be applied in concert with other theoretical perspectives such as institutional theory, which reinforces SEW logic seeking reputation and bolsters FFs strategies that are driven by environmental concerns as much by financial motives (Berrone and Gomez-Mejia, 2009). Such theoretical fusion would better enable scholars to chart out contingencies and managerial functions when FFs use either SEW or economic benefits as their point of reference in their decision making and how FFs are able to overcome the negative financial repercussions of certain SEW-based decisions.

RESOURCE-BASED VIEW

Popularized by Barney (1991), the resource-based view (RBV) of the firm is one of the most dominant paradigms in strategic management. The RBV underscores the fact that resources, are heterogeneously distributed across firms and that firms gain sustained competitive advantage by accumulating resources that are valuable, rare, inimitable, and non-substitutable (VRIN) (Barney, 1991). Amit and Shoemaker (1993) also corroborate this viewpoint by acknowledging that it is the decisions made by management in accumulating and deploying firm resources that lead to organizational rent creation. In addition to resource accumulation, RBV scholars have also underscored the importance of developing organizational and technological capabilities to exploit these resources as an important part of the process that leads to rent creation (Mahoney, 2001) (row 2, Table 6.1).

An emerging body of research suggests that certain qualities inherent in families furnish them with the unique resources that can be leveraged by FFs to attain competitive advantage (van Essen et al., 2013). Habbershon and Williams (1999) first pointed out that familial advantage is formed through the interaction of the tripartite forces of the family, business, and the family members leads to distinctive familiness, which is in fact the true VRIN resource in FFs. However, as we summarize in row 2 of Table 6.1, we do not believe that the availability of these unique resources always produce a net benefit for FFs. This is because FFs enjoy advantages of leveraging

some kind of resources but are disadvantaged in acquiring and leveraging others. In terms of advantageous resources, the single most important one is the availability of family social capital (FSC), which is inextricably tied to organizational social capital (OSC) (Arregle et al., 2007), human capital, and management (Sanders and Nee, 1996; Sirmon and Hitt, 2003; Zahra, 2010). When FSC is endowed with positive attributes, such as stability, closure, and frequent interactions, the OSC developed is likely to be a positive resource for the firm as well (Arregle et al., 2007). As illustrated by Sanders and Nee (1996), in immigrant diasporas, a family's social capital can enable family members to engage in entrepreneurial ventures as they value their relatives' and friends' foreign education, which is often undervalued by local employers.

FFs may also be advantaged in acquiring certain types of resources because they can apply particularistic decision criteria in their decision making with employees and business associates (Carney, 2005). In transitional economies, where there is considerable uncertainty regarding the reliability of business partners, particularistic norms of mutual commitment among affiliates of family business groups can facilitate relational contracting (Gilson, 2006) and reduce firms restructuring costs (Luo and Chung, 2005). Gilson (2007) reasons that the strong incentive in FFs to refrain from expropriating minority shareholders because of the probability of detection and incurring a reputation penalty that will increase the costs of transacting in other domains also curb agency costs. Indeed, long-lived FFs who vigilantly monitor their reputation for honoring contracts may find themselves in a virtuous circle of resource acquisition. It is no surprise then that studying the oldest FFs in the world, Micelotta and Raynard (2011) find that these firms project their familial trait, albeit in different ways, to create a lasting corporate brand or reputation, an integral part of their SEW. In BAM vernacular, FFs that are motivated to protect their SEW, and where family members perceive themselves as stewards or caretakers for the firm (Zahra, 2003; Miller et al., 2008), their stewardly and altruistic actions can drive down the relational contracting costs and build goodwill among stakeholder groups. Thus, in this virtuous circle perspective, firms attract resources on more favorable terms, while further burnishing the family's reputation in stakeholder communities by their stewardly actions and in turn improve financial performance (Miller et al., 2008).

Because they are not subject to norms of shareholder wealth maximization, FF decision-makers have greater leeway in projecting their personal values into the firm's decision-making processes. Carney (2005) describes this freedom to impress oneself on the firm as personalism. Extending this logic further, Sirmon and Hitt (2003) presents an analysis based on the synergy of affective logics such as stewardship and personalism. The authors contend that FFs are better equipped to cultivate intangible resources such as that contained in human and social capital. Yet other forms of governance advantages include community-level shared knowledge among FFs for problem solving, establishing values and norms, etc. (Lester and Cannella, 2006). Thus, FFs can invoke unified strategies to cope with the problems. Furthermore, FFs enjoy enhanced performance when they are led by lone-founders (Miller et al., 2007) through more entrepreneurial and growth-driven strategies (Miller et al., 2011).

Notwithstanding their advantages in cultivating and acquiring rent-generating resources, family influence can also have a negative impact on resource acquisition. For instance, family conflicts can spillover into the firm operations with negative consequences (Lester and Cannella, 2006). PP agency issues can manifest in multiple ways (Gilson, 2006, 2007), and the affective reference point for firm decisions can economically harm the firms (Gomez-Mejia et al., 2007). Similarly, leadership succession in FFs can bring severe destruction of the VRIN resources accumulated over the years and a

loss in dynamic capabilities required to manage these resources. Succession is also accompanied by expropriation risk if the FF appoints an external manager to the senior executive position (Lee et al., 2003). Alternatively, the appointment of a family member can result in poor quality management (Bloom and van Reenan, 2007) and a decline in firm value (Bennedsen et al., 2007).

In sum, while FFs are benefited by their endowment of unique resources, they are also limited by constraints on their human and social capital as well as the negative spillover of family on to the business. Furthermore, we have seen that the interaction of agency and RBV considerations sometimes complement one another and at other times they contradict each other to eliminate idiosyncratic resources and firm value. Nevertheless, RBV has made valuable contribution to our understanding of the functioning and performance of FFs. In turn, studying FFs has proved to be fertile territory ground for theorizing and testing RBV inspired hypotheses. However, there is much yet to be done to explore the resource constraining and generating effects of family influences on their unique family resources (see row 2, Table 6.1). In addition to understanding both the positive and negative effects of family resources on FFs, we suggest that the possibility of efficient succession remains an open question for the field. We know little of the circumstances where succession leads to the preservation or destruction of heterogeneous and idiosyncratic firm resources that have been associated with rent creation. Furthermore, ascertaining which resources and/or capabilities become positive or negative under what institutional and agency conditions also merit further research.

TRANSACTION COST THEORY

Transaction cost theory (TCT) addresses one of organization theory's most ontological questions: Why do firms exist? In his seminal work, Coase (1937) addresses this question by reasoning that markets and vertically integrated hierarchies represent alternative ways of governing transactions necessary for production of goods and services. Several decades later Williamson (1975) revisited the question and offered a theory of the advantages and disadvantages of markets and hierarchies. Williamson (1981) suggests that hierarchy is efficient under the conditions of asset specificity, that is when investments in assets and dedicated to firm specific tasks and cannot be redeployed to other transactions. Conversely, markets are comparatively more efficient transactions requiring generic assets and for those involving intermediate levels of asset specificity (row 3, Table 6.1). However, sometimes, due to the cost of operating a bureaucracy, hierarchies can be expensive modes of transactional governance.

A natural extension of the transaction cost logic is to ask why FFs exist. TCT has been applied to explain a variety of firm behaviors such as the extent of vertical integration (Monteverde and Teece, 1982; Hart and Moore, 1990), contracting structure (Joskow, 1985), and internal corporate structures, such as the conglomerates and multidivisional form. Given the global prevalence of FFs it is somewhat surprising that TCT has not been much applied to explain the unique features of FF governance. We reason that FFs have inherent advantages in development and maintenance of certain kinds of assets and it is these advantages that are crucial in explaining the existence as well as governance of FFs.

In their application of TCT to FFs, Gedajlovic and Carney (2010) distinguish assets along two dimensions: tradability, the extent to which an asset can be bought and sold in the markets, and specificity, the extent to which the development and utilization of an asset is tied to an organization. Assets such as office supplies that are easily tradable and are generic in application are transacted through markets; whereas firm-specific and non-tradable assets such as reputation, networks, etc. are developed and handled in an organization. The authors contend that FFs enjoy governance advantage at producing and leveraging value from generic non-tradable assets 'GNT' (2010: 1148). The key insight presented is that GNTs such as reputation, tacit knowledge, etc. are non-tradable so are developed within a firm but are generic in application, i.e., they could be developed and utilized in a variety of product market settings. For example, a reputation for honoring contracts is as valuable in selling insurance as it is in manufacturing automobiles.

GNT assets offer a simple but cogent explanation of phenomena such as serial and portfolio entrepreneurship. From a Rumeltian point of view, the entrepreneurial ventures of these types of FFs might seem unrelated, and hence more risky, but the FFs' diversified portfolio of businesses may represent the coherent application of GNTs across multiple product markets. Indeed, this TCT reasoning, coupled with the affective decision-making reference points, may jointly explain the unrelated portfolio entrepreneurship in FFs identified by Miller and his colleagues (Miller et al., 2010). Moreover, the prevalence of diversified family business groups in emerging markets is frequently explained with reference to their abilities in closing institutional voids (Khanna and Palepu, 1997, 1999). For instance, by developing GNTs assets such as social capital and reputation, FFs can enable relational modes of contracting in jurisdictions with weak commercial law. In contrast, the contracting routines of multinational enterprises from more advanced economies are more dependent upon the existence of strong commercial law and they are comparatively disadvantaged in emerging markets. Therefore, FFs, investing in generic assets such as information and reputation so as to minimize search costs for their potential trading partners (Ben-Porath, 1980) are a superior organizational structure in these conditions.

Furthermore, FFs also seem to be advantaged in terms of executive search, a time-, effort-, and resource-intensive process for firms. Due to economic as well as affective motives, such costs are mitigated in case of

FFs when they appoint family members as successors. First, in addition to the desire to appoint family members in managerial positions, risk of appropriation by outside managers once they are privy to the FF's stock of tacit knowledge provides impetus to keep the management within the family. Second, appointment of family members in key positions will be favored by the existence of complex inheritance legal structures. Bjuggren and Sund (2002) illustrate this point in case of Sweden, but it is high likely that such analysis is generalizable to many countries. Thus, as Lee et al. (2003) illustrate, when faced with possible performance setbacks because of risks of appropriation by an outside manager or the appointment of low-ability offspring in key position, driven by both governance as well as environmental forces, FFs can bypass market transaction costs while making managerial decisions by passing down the reign to their offspring.

However, as Gedajlovic and Carney (2010) point out, FF governance advantages come with their associated resource-based limitations such as constrained skilled professional resources, restricted access to financial resources, etc. that hinder performance and growth (Gedajlovic et al., 2004). In addition, family conflicts can easily spill over onto firm operations and low ability family personnel can further have a negative impact on firm performance (Pollak, 1985). Thus, from a TCT viewpoint, FFs do not seem to be clearly advantaged across the two important components of rent creation: resource picking and capability building (Makadok, 2001). Rather, TCT approach delineates both the positive and the negative aspects of FFs. We see this mix of transaction cost efficiencies and the concomitant, self-imposed resource-based constraints as an intriguing facet of FFs and as reasons to employ more TCT logic in the context of FFs.

As we summarize in Table 6.1, an explicit exploration of the interaction of the opposing forces in FFs to uncover the net outcome is an exciting avenue for future research. In light of our discussion explicating the linkages between transaction cost advantages and resource-based disadvantages, we reason that future research should seek to build upon this theoretical opposition. We suggest that the employment of integrated TCT and RBV reasoning may offer insights into the rent-generating capabilities of both FFs and other types of firms and offers a promising perspective for researchers. In addition, an exciting avenue for FF research would also be to utilize TCT logic to better understand franchising decisions under family management. Given that FFs typically prefer to retain control of the firms (McConaughy, 2000), we reason that franchising represents a preferable organizational form for the FFs since it offers the means of overcoming resource constraints as well as enjoying administratively efficient governance arrangements (Carney and Gedajlovic, 1991).

PROPERTY RIGHTS THEORY

In their seminal paper, Jensen and Meckling (1976) laid down the foundation for property rights theory (PRT) as a potential link between transaction cost and agency theory. While TCT provides an efficiency account for the existence of the hierarchical firm, agency theory emphasizes misalignments in the goals of managers and owners and identifies costs inherent in the hierarchical PA relationship (Fama and Jensen, 1983; Bertrand and Schoar, 2006). PRT provides a bridge for the two paradigms by emphasizing (1) the careful alignment of individual rights to costs and rewards and (2) the contracting of all resource owners with a central hierarchical authority. By advocating the use of central contracting, i.e., contracts between the resource owners and a central authority in the hierarchical firm instead of designing individual contracts between each of the resource owners, PRT establishes an efficient mechanism to minimize agency costs, which are a source of inefficiency in firms according to agency theory (Alchian and Demsetz, 1972).

PRT also notes that hierarchical contracts with resource providers can be poorly designed, leading to misaligned objectives and damp-ened incentives. In such circumstances, more careful allocation of contractually enforceable property rights can realign objectives and sharpen incentives. For example, in vertically integrated retail chains, the goals of retail unit management, hired on standard employment contracts, are not closely aligned with the goals of the firm, and retail unit managers have little incentive to exercise effort or inge-nuity in the performance of the tasks. In contrast, franchising contractually and delib-erately allocates specific tasks and investment responsibilities to the franchisor and fran-chisee as well stipulating the rights to residual returns to be incurred by each party. Com-pared with the pure hierarchy, franchising curbs the stifling control of HQ executives and reduces agency costs related to ownership of residual rents in organizations (Brickley and Dark, 1987). It is also a means to sur-mount resource constraints and grow faster without ceding control for FFs (Carney and Gedajlovic, 1991). A synopsis of positives and negatives in FFs from a PRT perspective is presented in row 4 of Table 6.1.

FFs are home to several interesting impli-cations for the property rights allocation and contractual norms in the organizations. FFs frequently engage in relational contracting where formal and legally binding contracts are absent. Owner-managers, leveraging their personal social networks, can engage in 'handshake deals' (Steier, 2001) and commit to long-term and unspecified trading obliga-tions (Park and Luo, 2001). On one hand, relational contracting avoids extensive for-mal contracting costs and expensive legal recourse implied in court-arbitrated dispute resolutions (Gulati, 1995). On the other hand, however, FFs can be burdened by extensive unwritten liabilities to business partners, which are difficult to value on objective criteria. Uncertainty about the true value of a firm's assets and liabilities creates difficulties with the transfer of assets to new owners – a possible source of a negative impact on firm evaluations. Thus, FFs seem to have a proclivity to simply by-pass

defining proper contracts (Gomez-Mejia et al., 2001), which has mixed effects on the firm. The literature is largely silent on the cumulative effect of such contracting in FFs. The question 'Can (and when do) the positives of particularistic relations com-pensate for the negatives of ambiguous or absent contracts?' is still open for future investigation.

An ambiguous or incomplete property rights structure has been associated with sev-eral other negatives in FFs as well. Literature on FFs documents the lack of transparency in their operations (Anderson et al., 2009), which allows the controlling families to expropriate wealth from minority shareholders using a variety of tactics such as pyramids (Morck and Yeung, 2003), tunneling (Bertrand et al., 2002, etc. Thus, when the primary motive is extracting benefits for private uses, PRT logic suggests that the employees and minority shareholders, without any residual claims, would be discouraged from making any firm-specific investments as these may also be used by controlling families for their own benefit (Grossman and Hart, 1986). Furthermore, the perceived inequity and misallocated property rights provide disincentive for employees and managers to put effort in performing their tasks (Bennedsen et al., 2007).

FF literature is also replete with exam-ples of studies documenting the advantages FFs have during market transitions due to their informal sources of networks (Luo and Chung, 2005), and capacities for deploying reputation-based relational con-tracting (Gilson, 2006, 2007). However, a PRT-oriented investigation of FFs in transi-tioning markets is still missing in the literature. Logically, PRT would suggest that as market institutions supporting prop-erty rights evolve, the FF advantages with relational contracting should diminish. But how exactly do FFs adapt their contracting practices when the quality of commercial law is improving? What other organiza-tional practices and processes does such institutional change affect in their property rights structures? Such questions are vitally relevant to scholars interested in the intersection of PRT and institution-based theory (Peng, 2002). In addition, given the prevalence of FFs in emerging economies (Morck and Yeung, 2003; Morck et al., 2005), investigations motivated by these questions would be extremely pertinent to economic development scholars as well.

Notwithstanding the mixed performance effects of ambiguous and incomplete property rights, FFs have managed to survive and thrive in a wide array of environments (Arregle et al., 2007). Can we then presume that FFs more than compensate for their poor property rights deficiencies through their resource acquisition advantages? After all, without net-positive rent-creating abilities FFs should not be expected to survive. As summarized in Table 6.1, we propose that scholars adopt multi-theoretical lenses to investigate FF's complex rent-creating dynamics. Recent investigations of the competitive and collaborative dynamics of FFs in emerging markets hint at the efficient use of relational contracting (Chen, 2001) to preserve their reputation and attain competitive advantage. Thus, we expect that the application of PRT in conjunction with theories of competitive dynamics in the context of family firms can mutually improve both theories. In sum, the underrepresentation of property rights perspective in the FF literature coupled with the evident ramifications of these structures on a firm's internal abilities and its environmental fit, present scholars with new opportunities for theory building and simultaneously improves our understanding of FFs.

TOWARD AN ECONOMIC THEORY OF FAMILY FIRMS

We began this chapter with the goal of surveying major economic theories as they have been applied to FFs. In doing so, we have suggested how studies of the family firm can contribute to the development of these theories. The focus of this contribution is to describe how economic theories inform our understanding of rent-creating and rent-destroying mechanisms in FFs. We have also identified under-studied questions and pinpointed several promising avenues for future research (see Table 6.1). At this concluding point in our exposition, we pose one final question: is there a general or unified economic theory of FFs? Is it possible to integrate these diverse economic theories, each offering distinctive insights, into a holistic and fundamental economic understanding? We believe that an economic theory of FFs should address the inherently bivalent characteristic implied in the combination of family and firm. Doing so yields the basic understanding that FFs simultaneously embody advantageous and disadvantageous qualities with regard to rents. Each of the theories we have reviewed in this paper tends to emphasize one side of the equation to the neglect of the other. Accordingly, the application of a single economic theory is likely to provide only a partial account. For this reason, we advocate the adoption of multiple-theoretical perspectives to capture the complexities of FF competitive advantage and rent creation.

Before the recent acceleration of research, economic understanding of the firm was focused exclusively on the costs arising from the separation of ownership and control in the classic corporations. FFs, by combined ownership and control, provided the perfect context to check whether the traditional agency costs vanish when we do away with such a separation. These inquiries lead researchers to discover that while traditional PA problems might be mitigated in FFs, the combined ownership and control leads to different kinds of agency costs. Corroborating the symbiotic relationship of FF research and theory development, two other variants of agency theory were born out of this inquiry: principal-principal agency theory (Burkart et al., 1997; Anderson and Reeb, 2004) and the behavioral agency model (Wiseman and Gomez-Mejia, 1998). However, none of these three variants of agency theory provides a holistic framework for FFs. While principal agency theory underscores the rent-creating abilities of FFs due to unification of ownership and control, it ignores the negative aspects of FFs; PP agency theory, in turn, does just the opposite. Similarly, the BAM explains the non-economic motivations behind decisions, which often destroy rent-creating opportunities in FFs, but does not address the mechanisms behind economically sound decisions that enable FFs to survive.

Similarly, other economic theories surveyed in this chapter lack the holistic framework we believe is needed to capture the bivalent qualities of family firms. The resource-based view articulates the FFs capacities with unique resources, family social capital (Arregle et al., 2007). Yet, RBV scholars typically overlook the negative impact of resource constraints on a FF's rent-generating abilities. We propose that two under-utilized economic theories, namely TCT and PRT, can fill an important role the development of a holistic economic framework for FFs. As discussed above, both TCT and PRT focus upon FFs' advantages and disadvantages with respect to rent creation (see rows 3 and 4, Table 6.1). Moreover, when coupled with other paradigms such as RBV, agency, or institutional theory, both TCT and PRT have the capability to provide the foundation for a much more comprehensive framework of FFs. For instance, TCT identifies family firm advantages with respect to leveraging rents from generic and non-tradable assets, but simultaneously also highlights resource constraints arising from family governance Likewise, PRT hails the advantages of the FF property rights structure in the lower costs for personnel, trading partner search, and contract writing and enforcement. However, these benefits are counterbalanced by inefficiencies arising from incomplete contracting.

Thus, we see TCT and PRT as two foundational theories underpinning a comprehensive economic framework of FF rent creation. As a starting point, we recommend developing taxonomy of rent-generating advantages and disadvantages in respect to FFs' internal and external governance mechanisms. In Fig. 6.1, we offer a preliminary version of such a taxonomy based upon the theory surveyed in this chapter. The figure also contains a preliminary taxonomy of potential moderating effects, such as the level of institutional development, founder/heir leadership, or succession processes, on the family firm governance–rent creation relationship. Whether these moderating effects positively or negatively impact the family firm governance–rent creation relationship remains a task for future research. We note the potential impact of the level of development of an economy's market supporting institutions as a fruitful area for future research. Indeed, the fact that FFs coexist with other types of firms in highly varied institutional environments (North, 1990) raises intriguing questions about the direction and strength of these potentially moderating effects. Notwithstanding the empirical difficulties in multi-country studies, we believe it will be important to control for these variegated institutional effects. Therefore, we also advocate the use of more advanced and cutting-edge methodologies like meta-analysis (cf. van Essen et al., 2013) to answer questions that address both the specific moderating effects of environments as well as those that concern the cumulative performance effects of FFs across various contingencies.

Thus, family firms are not all alike nor are they all uniquely different. In a maturing field of research a primary goal for economically inclined scholars is to identify more comprehensive mid-range economic theory that can account for the evident difference between types of family firms in the different economic institutional circumstances and their rent-generating consequences. We have attempted to provide a prototype of such a framework and we hope that we have been successful in taking the next steps toward an economic theory of FFs. As illustrated by the development of the BAM, FFs have continually catalyzed theory development. We see the possibility of a similar synthesis in the future. Just as the intriguing non-economic decision making in FF catalyzed the fusion of agency theory and prospect theory and resulted in the BAM, so it is likely that the unexplained facets in FFs facilitate a larger synthesis, resulting

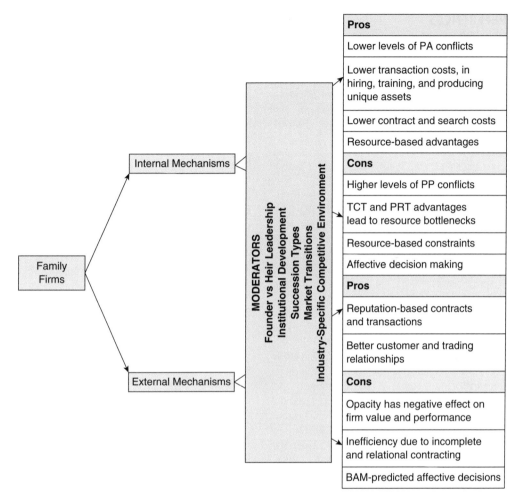

Figure 6.1   An integrated economic framework of FFs – a prototype

in a more comprehensive economic framework of not just FFs but perhaps lead to the development of a new paradigm.

However, we do acknowledge that our framework seeks to explain the existence and performance of FFs from an economic viewpoint. As we have seen, FFs can exist because of non-economic motives such as emotional attachment (Gomez-Mejia et al., 2007), voids in the institutional environment (Khanna and Palepu, 1999), lack of employment opportunities (Sanders and Nee, 1996), etc., and can survive, by virtue of their endowments of survivability and patient capital (Arregle et al., 2007), even when they don't have an economic advantage of NFFs. Thus, the fact that

our framework does not incorporate evidently strong psychological and sociological reasons for the existence and persistence of FFs, can be viewed as its boundary condition. We choose to leave these considerations untouched as we are certain that such considerations are being dealt with elsewhere by scholars who have both interest and expertise in the areas. Despite its boundaries, the pursuit of an economic theory of FFs promises to be a rewarding journey, one that could not only provide us an indispensible toolkit in analyzing the numerous economic facets of FFs, but also possibly beget new paradigms in strategic management. We hope FF researchers share our viewpoint and consider venturing down this avenue.

REFERENCES

Alchian AA, Demsetz H. 1972. Production, information costs, and economic organization. *American Economic Review* 62: 777–795.

Alvarez SA, Barney JB. 2004. Organizing rent generation and appropriation: toward a theory of the entrepreneurial firm. *Journal of Business Venturing* 19(5): 621–635.

Amit R, Shoemaker PJT. 1993. Strategic assets and organizational rent. *Strategic Management Journal* 14(1): 33–46.

Anderson RC, Duru A, Reeb DM. 2008. Founders, heirs, and corporate opacity in the US. Working Paper.

Anderson RC, Duru A, Reeb DM. 2009. Family preferences and investment policy: evidence from capital expenditures and R&D spending. Working Paper.

Anderson RC, Mansi SA, Reeb DM. 2003. Founding family ownership and the agency cost of debt. *Journal of Financial Economics* 68(2): 263–285.

Anderson RC, Reeb DM. 2003a. Founding-family ownership and firm performance: evidence from the S&P 500. *Journal of Finance* 58(3): 1301–1328.

Anderson RC, Reeb DM. 2003b. Founding-family ownership, corporate diversification, and firm leverage. *Journal of Law & Economics* 46(2): 653–683.

Anderson RC, Reeb DM. 2004. Board composition: balancing family influence in S&P 500 firms. *Administrative Science Quarterly* 49: 209–237.

Arregle JL, Hitt MA, Sirmon DG, Very P. 2007. The development of organizational social capital: attributes of family firms. *Journal of Management Studies* 44(1): 73–95.

Barney J. 1991. Firm resources and sustained competitive advantage. *Journal of Management* 17(1): 99–120.

Bennedsen M, Nielsen KM, Perez-Gonzalez F, Wolfenzon D. 2007. Inside the family firm: the role of families in succession decisions and performance. *Quarterly Journal of Economics* 122(2): 647–691.

Ben-Porath Y. 1980. The F-connection: families, friends, and firms and the organization of exchange. *Population and Development Review* 6 (1): 1–30.

Berrone P, Gomez-Mejia LR. 2009. Environmental performance and executive compensation: an integrated agency-institutional perspective. *Academy of Management Journal* 52(1): 103–126.

Berrone P, Cruz C, Gomez-Mejia LR. 2012. Socioemotional wealth in family firms: a review and agenda for future research. *Family Business Review* 25(3).

Berrone P, Cruz C, Gomez-Mejia LR 2014. Family-controlled firms and stakeholder management: a socioemotional wealth preservation perspective. In Sharma P, Melin L, Nordqvist M. (eds), *SAGE Handbook of Family Business*. London: Sage.

Bertrand, M., Mehta, P., & Mullainathan, S. (2002). Ferreting out Tunnelling: an Application to Indian Business Groups. *Quarterly Journal of Economics,* 117(1): 121–148. doi:10.1162/003355302753399463

Bertrand M, Schoar A. 2006. The role of family in family firms. *Journal of Economic Perspectives* 20(2): 73–96.

Bjuggren P-O, Sund L-G. 2002. A transactions cost rationale for transition of the firm within the family. *Small Business Economics,* 19: 123–133

Bloom N, van Reenan J. 2007. Measuring and explaining management practices across firms and countries. *Quarterly Journal of Economics* 82(4): 1351–1408.

Brickley J, Dark F. 1987. The choice of organizational form: the case of franchising. *Journal of Financial Economics* 18: 401–420.

Burkart M, Gromb D, Panunzi F. 1997. Large shareholders, monitoring, and the value of the firm. *Quarterly Journal of Economics* 112(3): 693–728.

Burkart M, Panunzi F, Shleifer A. 2003. Family firms. *Journal of Finance* 58(5): 2167–2201.

Carney M. 2005. Corporate governance and competitive advantage in family-controlled firms. *Entrepreneurship: Theory and Practice* 29(3): 249–265.

Carney M, Gedajlovic E. 1991. Vertical integration in franchise systems: agency theory and resource explanations. *Strategic Management Journal* 12: 607–629.

Carney M, Gedajlovic E. 2002. Coupled ownership and control and the allocation of financial resources: evidence from Hong Kong. *Journal of Management Studies* 39(1): 123–146.

Chen M-J. 2001. *Inside Chinese Business: A Guide for Managers Worldwide.* Cambridge, MA: Harvard Business Press.

Cheung YL, Rau PR, Stouraitis A. 2006. Tunneling, propping, and expropriation: evidence from connected party transactions in Hong Kong. *Journal of Financial Economics* 82(2): 343–386.

Claessens S, Djankov S, Fan JPH, Lang LHP. 2002. Disentangling the incentive and entrenchment effects of large shareholdings. *Journal of Finance* 57: 2741–2771.

Coase, RH. 1937. The Nature of the Firm. *Economica,* 4(16): 386–405. doi:10.1111/j.1468-0335.1937.tb00002.x

Cruz C, Firfiray S, Gomez-Mejia LR. 2011. Socioemotional Wealth and Human Resource

Management (HRM) in Family-Controlled Firms. *Research in Personnel and Human Resources Management, 30*: 159–217. doi:10.1108/S0742-7301(2011)0000030006

Dharwadkar R, George G, Brandes P. 2000. Privatization in emerging economies: an agency theory perspective. *Academy of Management Review* 25(3): 650–669.

Faccio M, Lang LHP, Young L. 2001. Dividends and expropriation. *The American Economic Review,* 91(1): 54–78.

Fama EF, Jensen MC. 1983. Separation of ownership and control. *Journal of Law and Economics* 26: 301–326.

Eisenhardt KM. 1989. Agency theory: an assessment and review. *Academy of Management Review* 14(1): 57–74.

Gedajlovic E, Carney M. 2010. Markets, hierarchies and families: toward a transactions cost theory of the family firm. *Entrepreneurship: Theory and Practice* 34(6): 1145–1172.

Gedajlovic E, Lubatkin MH, Schulze WS. 2004. Crossing the threshold from founder management to professional management: a governance perspective. *Journal of Management Studies* 41(5): 899–912.

Gilson RJ. 2006. Controlling shareholders and corporate governance: Complicating the comparative taxonomy. *Harvard Law Review* 119(6): 1641–1679.

Gilson R. 2007. Controlling family shareholders in developing countries: anchoring relational exchange. *Stanford Law Review* 60(2): 633–635.

Gomez-Mejia LR, Haynes K, Nunez-Nickel M, Jacobson K, Moyano-Fuentes J. 2007. Socioemotional wealth and business risks in family controlled firms. *Administrative Science Quarterly* 52(1): 106–137.

Gomez-Mejia LR, Larraza-Kintana M, Makri M. 2003. The determinants of executive compensation in family controlled public corporations. *Academy of Management Journal* 46(2): 226–237.

Gomez-Mejia LR, Makri M, Larraza-Kintana M. 2010. Diversification decisions in family-controlled firms. *Journal of Management Studies* 47(2): 223–252.

Gomez-Mejia LR, Nunez-Nickel M, Gutierrez I. 2001. The role of family ties in agency contracts. *Academy of Management Journal* 44(1): 81–95.

Grossman SJ, Hart OD. 1986. The costs and benefits of ownership: a theory of vertical integration. *Journal of Political Economy* 94: 691–719.

Gulati R. 1995. Does familiarity breed trust? The implications of repeated ties for contractual choices in alliances. *Academy of Management Journal* 38(1): 85–112.

Habbershon TG, Williams M. 1999. A resource-based framework for assessing the strategic advantages of family firms. *Family Business Review* 12(1): 1–25.

Hart O, Moore J. 1990. Property rights and the nature of the firm. *The Journal of Political Economy* 98(6): 1119–1158.

Jensen M. 1986. Agency costs of free cash flow, corporate finance, and takeovers. *American Economic Review* 76(2): 323–329.

Jensen MC, Meckling WH. 1976. Theory of the firm: managerial agency costs and ownership structure. *Journal of Financial Economics* 3: 305–360.

Joskow PL. 1985. Vertical integration and long term contracts: the case of coal burning electric generating plants. *Journal of Law, Economics, and Organization* 1(1): 33–80.

Kahneman D, Tversky A. 1979. Prospect theory: an analysis of decision under risk. *Econometrica* 47: 263–290.

Khanna T, Palepu K. 1997. Why focused strategies may be wrong for emerging markets. *Harvard Business Review* 75: 41–51.

Khanna T, Palepu K. 1999. The right way to restructure conglomerates in emerging markets. *Harvard Business Review* 77: 125–134.

Lee K, Lim G, Lim WS. 2003. Family business succession: appropriation risk and choice of successor. *Academy of Management Review* 28(4): 657–666.

Lester RH, Cannella AAJ. 2006. Interorganizational familiness: how family firms use interlocking directorates to build community level social capital. *Entrepreneurship: Theory and Practice* 30: 756–775.

Luo X, Chung CN. 2005. Keeping it all in the family: the role of particularistic relationships in business group performance during institutional transition. *Administrative Science Quarterly* 50(3): 404–439.

Mahoney JT. 2001. A resource-based view of sustainable rents. *Journal of Management* 27: 651–660.

Mahoney JT. 2005. *Economic Foundations of Strategy*. Thousand Oaks, CA: Sage.

Makadok R. 2001. Toward a synthesis of the resource-based and dynamic-capability views of rent creation. *Strategic Management Journal* 22(5): 387–401.

McConaughy DL. (2000). Family CEOs vs. Nonfamily CEOs in the Family-Controlled Firm: An Examination of the Level and Sensitivity of Pay to Performance. *Family Business Review* 13(2): 121–131. doi:10.1111/j.1741-6248.2000.00121.x

Micelotta ER, Raynard M. (2011). Concealing or revealing the family? Corporate brand identity strategies in family firms. *Family Business Review* 24(3): 197–216.

Miller D, Le Breton-Miller I, Lester RH. 2010. Family ownership and acquisition behavior in publicly-traded companies. *Strategic Management Journal* 31(2): 201–214.

Miller D, Le Breton-Miller I, Lester RH. 2011. Family and lone founder ownership and strategic behavior: social context, identity and institutional logics. *Journal of Management Studies* 48(1): 1–25.

Miller D, Le Breton-Miller I, Lester RH, Cannella AA Jr. 2007. Are family firms really superior performers? *Journal of Corporate Finance* 13(4): 829–858.

Miller D, Le Breton-Miller I, Scholnick B. 2008. Stewardship versus stagnation: an empirical comparison of small family and non-family businesses. *Journal of Management Studies* 45(1): 51– 78.

Monteverde K, Teece DJ. 1982. Supplied switching costs and vertical integration in the automobile industry. *The Bell Journal of Economics* 13(1) L 206–213.

Morck R, Stangeland DA, Yeung, B. 2000. Inherited wealth, corporate control, and economic growth: the Canadian disease. In R. Morck (ed.) *Concentrated Corporate Ownership*. National Bureau of Economic Research Conference Volume. Chicago, IL: University of Chicago Press.

Morck R, Wolfenzon D, Yeung B. 2005. Corporate governance, economic entrenchment, and growth. *Journal of Economic Literature* 43: 655–720.

Morck R, Yeung B. 2003. Agency problems in large family business groups. *Entrepreneurship: Theory and Practice* 27(4): 367–383.

North D. 1990. *Institutions, Institutional Change and Economic Performance*. Cambridge: Cambridge University Press.

Park SH, Luo Y. 2001. Guanxi and organizational dynamics: organizational networking in Chinese firms. *Strategic Management Journal* 22(5): 455–477.

Peng MW. 2002. Toward an institution-based view of strategy. *Asia Pacific Journal of Management* 19: 251–267.

Peng MW, Jiang Y. 2010. Institutions behind family ownership and control in large firms. *Journal of Management Studies* 47(2): 253–273.

Pollak RE. 1985. A transactions cost approach to families and households. *Journal of Economic Literature*, 23(2): 581–608.

Salvato C, Minichill A, Piccarreta R. 2012. Faster route to the CEO suite: nepotism or managerial proficiency? *Family Business Review*, doi:10.1177/0894486511 427559

Sanders JM, Nee V. 1996. Immigrant self-employment: the family as social capital and the value of human capital. *American Sociological Review* 61(2): 231–249.

Schulze W, Gedajlovic E. 2010. Whither family business? *Journal of Management Studies* 47(2): 191–204.

Schulze W, Lubatkin M, Dino RN. 2003. Exploring the agency consequences of ownership dispersion among the directors of private family firms. *Academy of Management Journal* 46(2): 179–194.

Schulze W, Lubatkin MH, Dino RN, Buchholtz AK. 2001. Agency relationships in family firms: theory and evidence. *Organization Science* 12(2): 99–116.

Sirmon DG, Hitt MA. 2003. Managing resources: linking unique resource management and wealth creation in family firms. *Entrepreneurship: Theory and Practice* 27(4): 339–358.

Steier L. 2001. Family firms, plural forms of governance, and the evolving role of trust. *Family Business Review* 14(4): 353–367.

Tagiuri R, Davis J. 1996. Bivalent attributes of the family firm. *Family Business Review* 9: 199–208.

Tinaikar S. 2008. Voluntary disclosure and ownership structure: an analysis of dual class firms. Working paper.

van Essen M, Carney M, Gedajlovic E, Heugens P. 2013. Do US publicly listed family firms differ? Does it matter? A meta-analysis. *Strategic Management Journal* (forthcoming).

Villalonga B, Amit R. 2006. How do family ownership, control, and management affect firm value? *Journal of Financial Economics* 80(2): 385–417.

Villalonga B, Amit R. 2008. Family control of firms and industries. Working paper.

Villalonga B, Amit R. 2009. How are US family firms controlled? *The Review of Financial Studies* 22(8): 3047–3091.

Williamson OE. 1975. Markets and hierarchies: some elementary considerations. *American Economic Review* 63(2): 316–325.

Williamson OE. 1981. The modern corporation: origins, evolution, attributes. *Journal of Economic Literature* 19(4): 1537–1568.

Wiseman RM, Gomez-Mejia LR. 1998. A behavioral agency model of managerial risk taking. *Academy of Management Review* 22(1): 133–153.

Young M, Peng M, Ahlstrohm D, Bruton GD, Jiang Y. 2008. Corporate governance in emerging economies: a review of the principal-principal perspective. *Journal of Management Studies* 45(1): 196–220.

Zahra SA. 2003. International expansion of US manufacturing family businesses: the effect of ownership and involvement. *Journal of Business Venturing* 18(4): 495–512.

Zahra SA. 2010. Harvesting family firms organizational social capital: a relational perspective. *Journal of Management Studies* 47(2): 345–366.

7

Evolutionary Theory: A New Synthesis for Family Business Thought and Research

Nigel Nicholson

INTRODUCTION

Family business brings together two fundamental institutions of human existence: the family and work organization. Throughout human history these have coexisted – in earlier times inextricably intertwined, and in modern times often quite separated, except in the family firm. This makes family firms of special interest. Their distinctiveness, advantages, and risks present a challenge to business research.

In this chapter I have several goals. First, I shall consider the status of evolutionary theory as having very general integrative scope, for it pertains not just to this topic, but in its modern formulation to all aspects of human society and endeavor. Second, we will consider the family as a key social entity in biology, and especially for humans, where co-evolutionary logic applies. That is, family forms are adaptive to a historical and regional contexts. Third, I will seek to show how evolutionary theory has the capacity to provide an overarching integration of

current more middle-range formulations, specifically agency, resource-based, and stewardship theories. Fourth, we will examine what light evolutionary thinking sheds on common features of family firms. Fifth, we look more particularly at the interior dynamics of families in business, illustrating how universal forms of primate conflict and cooperation are readily observable in the family firm sector. The chapter concludes by considering the uniqueness of human families, and the contributory role to their configural dynamics of gender, age spacing, and heritable individual difference factors.

THEORY AND FAMILY BUSINESS

What is the purpose of theory in general and specifically in the family business context? One can require that theory supply a unifying explanatory framework for extant knowledge within the domain of its chosen range; achieving this with maximum parsimony; explaining more than the phenomena it originally sought to explain; and pointing the way toward new knowledge and hypotheses to be tested (Godfrey-Smith, 2003). Theory has also to be internally consistent as well as externally congruent with what we know about the world, i.e., empirical knowledge and other established theory. In the family business context we are confronted with a phenomenon that has many forms and expressions; that is replete with complex causal sequences that have major psychological consequences for the actors involved and major economic consequences for firms, sectors and national economies (Sharma, 2006).

The question this raises for the field is the well-known problem of the trade-off of specificity for completeness in explanation (Weick, 1969). So-called 'grand theories' can function as broad explanatory umbrellas under which shelter more phenomenon-specific models. In this sense evolutionary theory is not just another competing theory.

In a field where there are a small number of middle level theoretical positions and a predominance of atheoretical empirical studies, or studies that are 'eclectic' in their use of concepts, the evolutionary perspective offers an overarching organizing framework for thought (Wilson, 1998).

The current disposition of theory and empiricism in the field arguably makes it ripe for such integration. With this in mind I wish to assert that evolutionary theory is less a set of a contested set of propositions, but a 'fact' (Smith, 2011). The biological process of evolution is verifiably visible all around us, thus the theoretical challenge is to apply its tenets to yield (a) new insights and (b) parsimonious integration of existing theory and knowledge. In this chapter I shall be seeking to show how it fulfills both of these objectives.

Box 7.1 shows the essential principles of evolutionary theory which will guide my discussion.

Box 7.1   Nine Key Principles of Evolutionary Theory

1 **Modification by descent**. This was Darwin's phrase to denote the core principle that features that allow or do not hinder an organism from passing them on to the next generation are retained as part of the phenotype of the succeeding generation. By this recursive process over generations features that impair reproduction are successively winnowed (Dennett, 1995).

2 **The dynamics of selection**. This proceeds by a biological algorithm of variation-selection-retention. The variation is in the characteristics of the phenotype, which we now know to be encoded in the DNA of the genotype, caused by the mixing of genetic profiles in sexual reproduction, random mutation, and epigenetic processes. The selection arises from the impact of the environment on the phenotype. Retention is also an environmental contingency, for it depends on the ability of the organism to reproduce (Barrett et al., 2002).

3 **Reproductive fitness**. This is the contingent relationship between the ability of the organism to reproduce and its environmental context. It is key to understanding how species arise and become extinct, as well as how an organism's phenotypic characteristics do not have a constant value in the game of evolutionary survival (Draper and Harpending, 1988).

4 **Forms of selection**. There are three. (1) Natural selection consists of direct environmental impacts on the fate of the phenotype, such as predators, pathogens, and impairments to the organism. These can also occur inter-utero, e.g., sperm competition (Baker and Bellis, 1989). (2) Sexual selection is the process by which mating opportunities are allocated by the preferences of organisms. This is driven by the process by which individuals signal their value as potential partners and parents, by behaviors or attributes that reliably reflect 'good genes' (Miller, 2000). (3) Kin selection is the process by which one organism can achieve reproductive fitness indirectly, by supporting the reproduction of others who share their genes (Hamilton, 1964).

5 **Sex differences and individual differences**. The mechanisms described above that produce variation do so by systematic and random processes. Systematic processes are those that follow patterned forms, the most notable of which are sex differences, on which we shall say more later. Random variations create the spectrum of phenotypes that enable assortative mating and the economy of comparative advantage. One element of this is frequency dependent selection – the idea that features can gain or lose value by their scarcity or frequency in a population (Nettle, 2006).

6 **Multi-level selection**. At the frontier of evolutionary thought is analysis of how communities are shaped and themselves shape the course of selective processes. These ideas have been called dual inheritance theory (DIT), which shows how genotypic variation is group context dependent, for example the emergence how the shift to agrarian living 10,000 years ago led to the ability to absorb lactated non-human milk (Feldman and Cavalli-Sforza, 1969).

7 **Co-evolution**. This implies that cultural and genetic evolution are subject to historical change (Sober and Wilson, 1998). Co-evolution is the interdependence of species' evolution, and between species and changing features of their environments. Co-evolution recognizes that the criteria for reproductive fitness are not constant, but change over time and context (Henrich, 2004; Richerson and Boyd, 2005).

8 **Consilience**. This term was coined by the biologist and father of what used to be called 'sociobiology', E.O. Wilson, to denote the unity of knowledge (Wilson, 1998). It is an-ultra-realism that says that all forms of human knowledge and invention, including the arts, can in principle be integrated and explained by a common set of principles.

9 **Evolved mind**. The development of Darwinian thought since the publication of *On the Origin of Species* over 150 years ago has in recent decades come to be known as evolutionary psychology. This amounts to a project by scholars from many disciplines across the social and life sciences to account for and describe the contents of the evolved mind (Barkow et al., 1992). The presumption is that human needs, cognitive biases, social preferences, group behaviors, and the like, were as much shaped by evolution for fitness in our environment as were our bodies. The same selective processes have shaped what modern Darwinians call mental 'modularity' – specific neurocognitive processes and biases that confer fitness advantages on the organism (Barrett and Kurzban, 2006).

These are the ideas that form the basis for an account I shall seek to provide to explain the character, processes and variations in family firms.

THE FAMILY AS A PRIMAL ENTITY

The family is a fundamental biological entity. It can be defined as members of a species who interact and often co-reside for the purposes of procreation and the nurturing of offspring (Davis and Daly, 1997). In many species this is a highly transient association, but in others – many birds, mammals, and some reptiles – the care of the young and mutual provisioning require more prolonged co-residence (Emlen, 1997). Among primates the family assumes even greater significance as a building block in complex

social organization, reaching its most refined form in the clan whose structure comprises interlocking family groups (Harcourt and Stewart, 2007; Meder, 2007). Families take many different forms. Among primates one finds a variety of communal structures, with collective and reciprocal care for offspring and interbreeding among both related and unrelated group members (Imanishi, 1960; Hrdy, 2009).

These kinship systems are closely coupled with the environmental niches and challenges species face, i.e., they are adaptive to contexts and the cycles of change that recur predictably within them, thereby constituting solutions to the problem of maximizing reproductive fitness over a range of recurrent circumstances (Megarry, 1995). Kinship systems are born of multi-level selection processes. At the individual level, sexual selection, natural selection, and kin selection (sometimes called inclusive fitness; see Box 7.1) direct the drives and orientations of individuals towards specific social forms, including mating preferences, nurturance of the young, competition, status seeking, display, and social preferences (Tudge, 1998; Cummins, 2005).

These preferences shape social structure, including familial forms, which also are units of selection and socialization (Keesing, 1975), i.e., at the heart of the recursive processes of co-evolution (Boyd and Richerson, 1985). Culture is the highest manifestation of co-evolution: a set of social conventions that help subgroups adapt to changing local environmental conditions whilst satisfying the needs and impulses of a relatively unchanging evolved human nature.

Cultures frame and are regulated by systems of rules that govern how people work and live together, in the form of marriage laws, moral codes, inheritance rules, courtship customs, and various taboos. These forms differ widely, and contemporary evolutionary anthropologists identify both the selective pressures that give rise to these variations, and their residue in human culture and history (Cronk and Gerkey, 2007). Peoples of the desert, mountains, and rivers have evolved distinctive conventions of kinship and sociality that reflect the constraints of their environments – natural hazards, food supply, resources, competition, threat, warfare, and the like (Low, 2007).

Although the contingent link between environments and cultures is strong (Sperber, 1996; Wilson, 1998) it is not determining. As Richerson and Boyd (2005) show, there is a degree of arbitrariness, or rather willed choice, to the systems we adopt. The authors present examples of tribes living under identical conditions who having adopted different marriage, inheritance, and property laws experience quite different outcomes, to the degree that the more successful are able to colonize the less successful and thereby spread their practices. Such assimilation is a major engine of cultural evolution. Richerson

and Boyd argue that the norms of former cultures persist as residues in conditions where they no longer have relevance. They cite the culture of honor that persists in the southern USA as a relic of their southern European origins, in contrast to the cooler and more rational ethos of the northern states, populated by the descendants of more austere Scandinavian, German, and English settlers. One may reflect that such cultural echoes play a part in the cross-cultural variation to be found in family firms around the globe and even within polyglot economies (Loomis and McKinney, 1956; Yan and Sorenson, 2006).

Families persist because they remain highly efficient, adaptive, and satisfying institutions (Becker, 1981). Yet, cultural evolution is changing the shape, structure, and functioning of the family. As societies develop, the strategy of maximizing fitness by maximizing one's family size (spreading the risk and sharing the labor) has shifted decisively to concentrating parental investment in fewer offspring (due to reasonably assured longevity and increased resource competition) (Lancaster and Lancaster, 1987; Mace, 2007). Thus one sees the amorphous large family clan being supplanted by the 'beanpole' family structure – height from increasing numbers of generations co-locating, and a lack of width from few offspring (Markson, 2004). This structural trend has profound implications for the shape of family business.

FAMILIES IN BUSINESS: TOWARDS THEORETICAL INTEGRATION

In this section I shall consider the first purpose in the review – its ability to integrate other perspectives. Subsequently we will look at how this provides a fresh perspective on family dynamics.

Since the beginning of time families have been units of production as well as reproduction, i.e., kinship groups have always engaged in shared enterprise. It is only in the last few thousand years that distinctions have been institutionalized between work and leisure.

In primitive societies there are tasks that have to be shared and executed for the community to survive, and voluntary activities conducted for pleasure, adornment, education, and entertainment (Coon, 1979; Boehm, 1999; Whiten, 1999).

Family businesses were among the first business organizations, and have remained a consistent presence in markets, arguably for the reason that they represent one of the prime remaining examples of how work and love – two fundamental needs according to Freud and evolutionary theory – can be reconciled (Babcock, 1998). Expressions of positive sentiments and shared goal-directed activity – work + love – are central to the continuing appeal of family firms.

From an economic standpoint they also solve an important agency problem: uniting accountability with ownership (Jensen and Meckling, 1976). They raise other issues, which we shall explore subsequently, but it does appear from an evolutionary perspective that they are the form of business that it appeals to our nature, satisfying our preference for high trust exchange within a communal structure, with permeable and flexible boundaries between economic and social interests (Stewart, 2003; Nicholson, 2008a).

The family business literature has been dominated by mainly descriptive empiricism, though, as is evident in this volume, a number of theoretical perspectives have received attention. Principal-agent theory is one of them, which, from a position of economic rationality, asks the question of how the divergent or convergent interests of actors bound together in formal and informal contracts incentivize them to behave (Gomez-Mejia et al., 2001; Schulze et al., 2001). This is a perfectly sensible question, though it has been sharply criticized by sociologists and others (Nilakant and Rao, 1994; Ghoshal, 2005), mainly for its rationalist materialist assumptions. Evolutionary theory has no quarrel with these. It takes a goal-driven view of human behavior, appreciating how many human motives are both self-oriented and material. This is the area in which evolutionary theory can provide a science-based integration of agency theory – by providing a nuanced account of 'interests' as nested hierarchies of goals – from their proximate manifestation (impulses, wants, reactions) to their distal origins (fitness-enhancing goals).

The notion of interests can prove quite problematic, inasmuch as it suggests that these may be defined externally to the person and in multiple contested ways. Moreover interests often go way beyond easily calculable utilities. The evolutionary perspective notes (a) that there are a number of species universal 'interests' that are not so easily calculable (we shall look at these in more detail shortly as they apply to family business dynamics, for they readily explain many of the commonly observable problems and benefits of the family business model); and (b) that these are widely subject to individual differences, and that outcomes become more predictable to the degree that one has knowledge of actors' unique dispositions.

A second recurrent theoretical stream is resource-based theory, which also has an underlying presumption of interests, though in this case, linked to the centrality, relevance, and scarcity of resources relevant to the firm's economic and social outcomes (Tokarcyzyk et al., 2007). Evolutionary theory does not demur from the logic of this formulation, but rather helps to elaborate the nature and value of what family capital contributes to business success. This resides in the genetic common interests of kinship groups and how certain kinds of working structures may help their value to be realized (Stewart, 2003). Evolutionary theory is also mindful that family interests are divided at the same time as they united. It shows how the disposition of resources may prove a source of unique disadvantage to family firms, where resource-based theorists tend only to stress the upside (Habbershon and Williams, 1999).

A third theoretical view, one that departs from the utilitarian model, is stewardship theory (Davis et al., 1997; Eddleston and Kellermans, 2007). This emanates from humanistic assumptions about people's needs for growth, self-actualization, and belonging, which find fulfillment in shared enterprise. The firm embodies this wider set of collective interests, within which leaders become 'stewards' or even 'servants' of the greater good of the business. Evolutionary theory agrees that individual interests may become subsumed under the wider interests of the collective, but adds the biological criterion of relatedness as making this especially compelling in the family firm. Humanistic perspectives can be reconciled with evolutionary theory to the degree that the abstract goals they identify as motivators of behavior draw their psychic energy from deeper, often subconscious fitness goals which they indirectly serve (Mayr, 1988; Buss, 2004).

THE EVOLUTIONARY VIEW OF HUMAN NATURE AND ITS RELEVANCE TO FAMILY FIRMS

In this and the next section, I shall seek to show how ideas derived from the evolutionary perspective apply to family firms – first, in this section, in relation to their general properties, and, later in this chapter, to more specific features of family dynamics.

The core of the evolutionary perspective is adaptation to environmental demands, and the organism is fitted for this purpose through its goals, guided by a range of cognitive mechanisms around attention, perception, and control, and supported by a repertoire of culturally supported behaviors and abilities. We are fitted for survival and reproduction in three major ways that correspond to this tool kit.

First is the nested nature of goals (Carver and Scheier, 1998). As noted above, at base these are largely unconscious distal goals; served by the superficial, local, and largely conscious proximate goals. Evolutionary psychologists are particularly interested in the relationship between these levels of goals, and especially in the mechanisms of self-deception, whereby our deeper goals of self-interest are achieved partly by

virtue of our ignorance of them (Trivers, 2000; Kurzban and Aktipis, 2006).

The nature of human goals therefore combines universals with local variation. The source of the variation is a mix of culture and individual differences, to which we shall return subsequently. The universals that affect family firms are concentrated in the area where parents seek to enhance the fitness of themselves and their relatives by selective benefits, i.e., nepotism (Bellow, 2003; Neyer and Lang, 2003). Status and reputation are key values in human groups and therefore nepotism takes the form not just of material favor but the advancement of offspring within society and its institutions, including the firm (Henrich and Gil-White, 2001). The principle of kin selection (see Box 7.1) – individual self-sacrifice on behalf of the kinship gene pool – provides a powerful dynamic for the sustenance of multi-family clans.

A unique feature of family firms is that the firm's assets are passed on through generations. This, in effect, makes them part of parental investment. In mature firms ownership can be regarded as genetic shareholding. The firm is looked at less as a bundle of assets but as part of a bloodline. Evolutionary theory thus provides a more parsimonious explanation of 'stewardship' than the imprecise concepts of humanistic psychology.

Second, cognitive scientists have over recent decades documented quite comprehensively the suite of systematic biases that affect our attention, judgment, and decisions at every level and stage of our responses to the world (Piattelli-Palmarini, 1994). They affect how we selectively attend to incoming data, how we process information, and how we psychologically adjust ex post. They include over-confidence; illusions of control; biased appraisal of value according to prominence; time discounting of value; the endowment effect (overvaluing possessions); steeper utility curves for losses than gains (loss aversion); conformational bias; asymmetries of choice and the like. Many of these are shared with other sentient species (Arkes and Ayton, 1999; Nettle, 2004). Much of this work has examined these as atomized phenomena, without paying attention to their origins as fitness-enhancing mechanisms. It is only recently that scholars have started noting the evolutionary adaptive foundation of these biases and processes. The theoretical link is clear with what evolutionists call the EEA – the environment in which we evolved – around 200,000 years of clan dwelling, hunting and gathering in deforested savannas and tundra (Hasleton and Nettle, 2006).

Our cognitive adaptations are fitted to short-range quick decision-making to minimize risk and overcome significant obstacles in pursuit of our goals (Pinker, 1997). In the contemporary environment of highly rational data-rich decision-making our biases, helpful to us in the EEA, become a liability and a source of continual errors in strategy, probabilistic calculation, decision-making and risk taking (Evans and Cruse, 2004). Many of the control mechanisms in organizations are designed to counter human intuition, instinct and reactivity, but they do so imperfectly.

It is well known that family firms have a strong preference for informality (Neubauer and Lank, 1998). The bonds of loyalty and affection lessen the need for controls that apply in situations where trust cannot be assured, so family firms are often able to use their intuitions and informality to good effect – making decisions fast and collegially (Tagiuri and Davis, 1992). But when this generalizes to an aversion for governance mechanisms they are unprotected from the runaway irrational passions of family members (Gordon and Nicholson, 2008). This explains the bivalent character of family firms (Tagiuri and Davis, 1996) – wonderfully capable of connecting and fluidly improvising whilst maintaining strong ties, yet vulnerable to control failures when emotions intrude. As the agency theorists point out, altruism is one of these hazards (Schulze et al., 2003).

Evolutionary theory has devoted much attention to the origins of altruism since it would appear to contradict the tenets of self-interest (Sober and Wilson, 1998; Gintis

et al., 2003). As we have seen nepotistic altruism poses no theoretical problem – it is completely explained by the principle of kin selection – but it is a hazard if it leads to inequitable rewards and benefits between family members and between family and non-family employees. Reciprocal altruism with non-kin is an adaptive feature of communities, i.e., where one is likely to have repeated encounters with other members, and is not exclusive to humans. Perhaps the hardest to explain is non-reciprocated altruism in one-shot encounters (e.g., giving to beggars in a strange city). This reflects a variety of human instincts, which are plugged into our need to achieve and sustain reputation in the human community, by conducting acts that sustain our model of ourselves as principled actors in a world where we can make a difference (Frank, 1988). It is clearly one of the most important building blocks for competitive advantage in family firms that create a family climate embracing kin and non-kin alike (Nicholson, 2008b).

The third area, human behaviors and abilities, is the most varied. The earliest hominid species, from around 7 million years ago, were marked out by (a) their bipedalism and (b) tool use (Barrett et al., 2002). Subsequently language became a third source of distinction (Pinker, 1994). Bipedalism was a condition that created many new possibilities, such as long-distance hunting, leaving the hands free for a variety of skills. It also created a demand for extreme sociality, since an anatomical consequence of the adaptation of bipedalism is the need for the infant cranium to grow outside the womb, requiring social structures and instincts to support communal living and child care. Language and subsequently the development of self-consciousness and control – the ego functions – enable ever more sophisticated forms of mimesis and learning (Tomasello, 1999). Thus did a weak, vulnerable furless biped come to conquer the world.

The two sources of our advantage, which together are the key tools of cultural evolution, are 'mind-reading', i.e., the ability to infer variations in others' motives and interests, and innovation, in tool making and use, weaponry, and in social institutions. The 'natural' size of the human group is 150 – called 'Dunbar's number' after the evolutionary scientist who discovered that there was a direct correlation between the size of a primate's prefrontal cortex and the size of their group (Dunbar, 1992). This number represents the human network capacity, though of course we readily scale up to more impersonal multiples and down to more intimate teams. The preference among family firms for relatively small scale enterprises achieves advantage through the bonds and informality that this facilitates. The ability of family firms to integrate successfully non-family is aided by a biology that renders human paternity uncertain, enabling adoptive and affinal (non-kin) affiliations to bind people into coalitions of multiply overlapping interests (Strassmann, 1981; Hrdy, 2009).

The new frontier of evolutionary thought is how cultures evolve and adapt to meet the needs of human nature and a changing environment, with game-changing consequences for fitness criteria, i.e., different sets of qualities gain evolutionary advantage with culture change. This is the central idea of what is called dual inheritance theory (Richerson and Boyd, 2005; McElreath and Henrich, 2007).

The relevance for family businesses is that all social institutions, including family firms, have to be adaptive to their internal and external contexts. The external include national culture, the business context and temporally varying factors. The internal are goals and motives of the stakeholders and agents involved in the enterprise. Together these constitute a set of forces to be accommodated, though they are also factors that can be sometimes shaped by the will of family agents and others. This recursive cycling between innovation and adaptation is what has driven human cultural evolution over the millennia. We don't just adapt to environmental niches, we create them (Laland, 2007).

Family businesses have not only been adapted to their context and their members, but they have played a significant role in the evolution of business cultures around the world (Landes, 2006). Their adaptive fitness is the cause of their success or failure. This is a very general statement, so let us drill down into the dynamics that determine these outcomes.

THE INNER LIFE OF FAMILY FIRMS: AN EVOLUTIONARY PERSPECTIVE

Consilience among disciplines and fields of knowledge – one of the principles of Darwinian thought (Wilson, 1998) – is especially appropriate for such a multidisciplinary field as family business. Yet at the heart of the field, and much on the minds of family business leaders and their advisors, lies family dynamics, for it is implicated in many of the classic dilemmas and problems faced by family firms such as leadership succession, ownership disputes, leadership problems, and variations in firm performance.

There is a large literature on marriage and the family that seeks to elucidate the inner dynamics of families, but almost exclusively from a therapeutic perspective (Broderick, 1993). The theories that are applied are usually psychoanalytically oriented, focusing on the diagnosis, description, and possible responses to how pathological dramas are played out. Theorizing is low level, and because of its fragmentation psychoanalytic theory offers no consistent interpretive framework for the study of co-working families (Macmillan, 1997). The evolutionary perspective can do much better in providing general explanatory propositions; pointing to the causes of local dynamics.

Let us start with the general principles before moving on to consider variations in patterns of family adaptation and response. Evolutionary research notes the following about families among primates in general and humans in particular:

1   Strong and weak ties of genetic relatedness sustain a structure of clans, tribes and social elites (Hrdy, 2009).

2 The rearing of offspring requires the investment of multiple adults (male parental investment and 'alloparenting').

3 Various social instincts help facilitate gene pool diversification and incest avoidance.

4 Sexual dimorphism (physical contrast between the sexes) is positively correlated with polygyny and, more rarely, polyandry (multiple sexual partners of either sex).

5 Sexual selection leads to competition for fitness advantage through mate choice, among choosy females and competing males (Miller, 2000).

Tolstoy's much quoted opening to the novel *Anna Karenina*, that happy families are alike while each unhappy family is unhappy in its own way, is only half right. Both happiness and unhappiness – amity and conflict – spring from species general universal forces, and find unique expression according to a range of situation-specific inputs that we shall briefly review. Before embarking on this discussion we should note, as developed in the chapter in Part V of this volume, that conflict has creative as well as destructive potential (Kellermans and Eddlestone, 2004). As we have remarked it comes from this bivalence (Tagiuri and Davis, 1996): cultural advantage and risk disadvantage; the splitting force of conflict and the binding force of love. Family firms outperform their non-family competitors by harnessing the creative possibilities of difference through a sustainable dialectic; especially if productively embedded in communities of entrepreneurship (Aldrich and Cliff, 2003).

There are five universals that emerge from evolutionary analysis that relate to family business functioning: kinship bonds; gender differences; affinal bonds; parent–offspring relations; and sibling competition.

Kinship Bonds

This can be briefly discussed, since we have already noted how nepotism is a universal feature of all familial species (Neyer and Lang, 2003). This is a key driver of every family firm – how the enterprise's existence serves the shared interests of related individuals. It is a threat where it results in inequities and

biased decisions, as noted by agency theorists (Schulze et al., 2003).

Gender Differences

Sex differences in humans stem from their distinctive strategic role in securing the reproductive fitness of the next generation, through sexual selection and social role differentiation/division of labor (Ridley, 1993; Geary, 1998). Primate studies have noted the critical role of females in the politics of dominance and succession (De Waal, 1982; Goodall, 1986). Human patterns are much more varied and culturally conditioned, yet similar politics are discernible. In the family business literature, variations in the role of women in family firms have been observed and discussed, not least their role in the politics of succession, which is often subtle and 'backstage' (Brush, 1992; Danes and Olson, 1993; Cole, 1997; Jimanez, 2009). Women are often central actors in relationships that drive the family firm, and function unofficially as 'chief emotional officer' to compensate for the single-minded task focus of their male partners (Westhead and Cowling, 1998).

Indeed one can argue that co-evolutionary forces make female leadership well suited to this networked era of multiplex inter-business relationships, requiring skills of coordination, emotional intelligence, and multi-tasking (Nicholson, 2012). Anecdotal evidence seems to indicate that family businesses were among the first to realize the advantages that women leaders bring to enterprises, though always hampered by the persistence of unequal burdens in the domestic division of labor and primary responsibility for child rearing. Copreneurs, for example, often fall foul of incommensurate expectations about workload and division of labor (Fitzgerald and Muske, 2002; Marshack, 1993).

Affinal Bonds

The convention of pair-bonding with unrelated or distantly related members of the opposite sex is a primary defense of the human immune system, by maximizing genetic variation (Ridley, 1993). This also represents a risk, for only the biochemistry of love and attachment holds couples together until they have the powerful shared genetic interest of offspring (Buss, 2000). Thus a first line of potential vulnerability to family firms are these 'affinal' bonds, though a partnership of diverse talents is clearly also a potential platform for business success (Kaye, 1999; Cole and Johnson, 2007). So it is that families, and their firms, are vulnerable to conflicts arising in this bond, though in general the benefits of smoothing over the cracks in family business marriages is a preferred option when there are substantial material investments in the commonwealth of the family firm.

Parent–Offspring Relations

The nepotistic instinct ensures that parents love their children and nurture them. Children, in their dependency, experience a reciprocal intimate attachment, if they have successfully bonded (Mercer, 2005). This has been claimed to be reflected in different 'attachment styles' among leaders and followers (Popper et al., 2000; Shalit et al., 2010). It would seem that attachment is not unqualified or invariant, and indeed evolutionists have drawn attention to the universality of the phenomenon of parent-offspring conflict. This stems from the fact that the preferences of parents for the ultimate destiny of their transmitted genes often diverges from the preferences of the bearers of those genes, their children (Trivers, 1974). Parents wish is to direct their children towards ends that constitute best bets for their genes' future prosperity, including mate choices. Parents themselves may have differing views of those interests, but the offspring are even more likely to diverge in their view.

Children develop their own conceptions of their 100% genetic self-interest, which outweighs the 50% interest of the parent. The resultant tug of war between parents too slow to relinquish control of their children, and the children with premature drives for autonomy, is a drama that is widely experienced in many

family firms. Where parents command substantial resources they may achieve greater docility from children than where there is less materially at stake (Gersick et al., 1997). Such conflicts create major challenges for succession, where parents are reluctant to let go, or children decide quite early in adulthood that their desire for autonomy can never be realized within the family firm (Lansberg, 1999).

Sibling Competition

Every parent of multiple children knows this is a source of distress, for of course the parents' genetic interests are equal in offspring. Parents overriding interest lies in maximizing the fitness of all their offspring. They want what the Talmud calls 'peace in the house'. This genetic democracy has two qualifications. One is gender. Since boys' status is more transmitted inter-generationally, females deriving status from their out-marriage, there is a marked inclination in some cultures to favor males (Wrangham, 1987). For example, Sharia inheritance law stipulates that males should receive twice the share of females.

Another qualifier is favoritism. This is less simple. There are various reasons why one or more children may be favored over others (Hrdy, 2001). First, is to concentrate investment in the fittest offspring (Trivers, 1972; Zervas and Sherman, 1994). Second, is to compensate the weaker offspring with greater investment (Suitor and Pillemer, 2000). Third, is to favor one child over others because they conform to parental wishes. Parents may also be apt to favor those that they perceive as more similar to themselves (Platek et al., 2002). There is evidence that all these occur, and indeed, behavior genetics research shows that parental warmth is a heritable property of *the child* (Plomin, 1994), i.e., some children are genetically more 'lovable' than others.

The first strategy – investment in strength – is optimal when resources are scarce or when the viability of the offspring is marginal, as has been demonstrated in an observational study parental attention to pre-term twins (Mann, 1992). The second strategy – compensation – is likely when the family is resource-rich and there are multiple opportunities for breeding. The third option – favoring conformity – is especially relevant to family firms, where there is often a large bundle of assets (the firm) and positions (succession) which may not be readily divisible. Dividing shares of course is possible, but parents are likely to want that to be correlated with the promise of commitment and competence in the child to put resources to good use.

This brings us to birth order, primogeniture, and the gene politics of the family, which, it has been argued, is acted out as a mini-evolutionary drama within each family (Sulloway, 2001). This sees the family as an ecosystem with finite parental resources and attention to which offspring successively lay claim. In this drama the firstborn has exclusive access to this commonwealth, to which parents will allow conditional access. The enacted strategy by firstborn and only children is thus one of conformity and achievement, calibrated via exchange with the regime of controls and goals enacted by parents (Hertwig, Davis and Sulloway, 2002). The practice of primogeniture in family firms is undoubtedly based upon the expectation of firstborn conformity (Bennedsen et al., 2007).

The arrival of the secondborn creates a challenge for all parties. For the firstborn the laterborn bring a dilution of attention and resources, which were formerly theirs exclusively. This may trigger a redoubling of efforts to extract favor, and strategies to deny the sibling equal access. Because the older sibling has the advantages of age and experience, laterborns compete on different criteria – strategies that make them innovative, rebellious, or deviant. Research also shows that middleborns, having neither first nor most recent claim on parental attention, consequently have weaker parental bonds (Salmon, 1999). However, these strategies are not dispositions – hence they are not inevitable. Heritable stable individual difference factors will exert a more determining influence on the family ecosystem, as we shall see below.

These five issues do not inevitably disrupt family firms, for several reasons. One is the countervailing priority of kin selection, and the desire to help and support those who share your genes, whether they be siblings, parents, or offspring. The other factors are the unique contingencies in the field – individual differences and contextual factors, to be discussed in the next section.

Two further key issues are relevant in family firms: relationships among cousins and more distant relatives; and cooperation between kin and non-kin executives. Both are essential to the long term survival of the family firm.

First, we know that the G1–G2 transition is fraught with difficulties for the reasons we have reviewed above (Davis and Tagiuri, 1989). The G2–G3 transition to the cousin consortium can be analyzed by the same logic (Gersick et al., 1997). Here is where the family firm divides into branches, creating the politics of cousins with weaker genetic ties and divided interests. The family business literature rightly portrays this as the phase where good governance becomes imperative to avoid the inter-branch feuds that historically have destroyed many viable firms (Gordon and Nicholson, 2008).

The second challenge, the integration of non-kin into the family firm, is essential to enable any firm except the very largest to move beyond a very constrained form. In the absence of genetic ties, special steps have to be taken to avoid 'tissue rejection' and nepotistic allocation of rewards, power, and opportunities often deter non-family talent from joining the business. The answer, as I have argued elsewhere, resides in building an inclusive culture (Nicholson, 2008b). Evolutionary theory shows that coalitions between kin and non-kin are common features of many social entities, and that human sociality makes such associations an essential feature of extended clans.

Yet, as research shows, all of these tensions have been potentially lethal to the survival of family businesses. Let us now consider how.

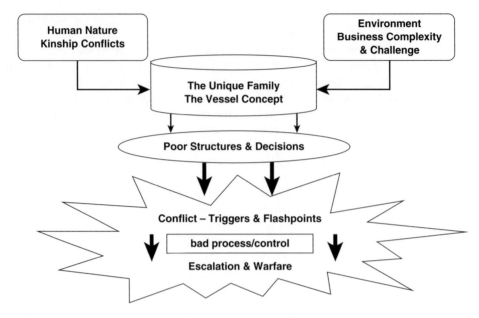

Figure 7.1   Vessel concept view of family business conflict

THE UNIQUE FAMILY – THE VESSEL PRINCIPLE

Figure 7.1 illustrates a principle that can help to elucidate the special risks that family firms face. It uses the analogy of a clay pot which, barring accidents, functions reliably to carry the water of life. This vessel represents the normal human family. Now you take a high pressure hose and fire a powerful jet into the pot. Pretty soon, any incipient flaws or weak spots will be found and the vessel will shatter. This high pressure is the additional load a family has to bear in running a business (Gordon and Nicholson, 2008).

The model suggests that not every family is fit to run a firm. Difficult relationships which can be managed under normal circumstances fracture when placed under the amplified pressure of running a business. Is it possible to predict which families will struggle? The answer is broadly affirmative. The model depicts the unique family – the vessel – as receiving and having to accommodate two sets of inputs. First are the universal sources of intra-familial tension we have reviewed, to which is added the unique burden of any

particular business and the issues it presents. How these are played out depends on the nature of the family vessel.

This is the structure and dynamics of the unique family. There are innumerable factors but let us concentrate on the main ones, as shown in Fig. 7.2.

At any point in time the family has a particular size and membership. Size, we know, has an effect on the dynamic of the family (Wagner et al., 1985). One can anticipate that conflict will be less intense the larger the family, with more scope for coalitions of mutual aid, and that the presence of females will have a moderating effect on the family climate. However, so much depends on the unique configural dynamics of personalities and other variables that no reliable trends of these kinds are to be found (Boer and Dunn, 1992; Black et al., 2005). Second are the personalities and other individual difference attributes of members. Behavior genetics shows us that many of these are heritable but do not run in families (Lykken, McGue, Tellegen and Bouchard, 1992). This apparent paradox derives from that many individual qualities are determined by

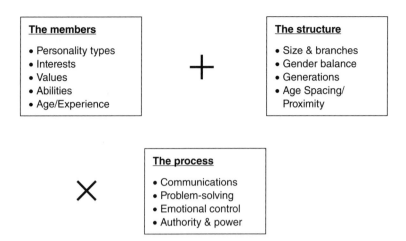

Figure 7.2 The unique family

unique combinations of expressed gene (called non-additive causation in behavior genetics). The outcome is that although siblings share on average 50% of their genes with each other (unless they are identical twins) and with their parents, there is a close to zero correlation between siblings, or between children and their parents on many qualities, especially personality (Plomin, 1994). Of course parents are apt wishfully to make attributions about similarities and differences – 'you are just like your mother' – that have no empirical foundation.

The configural dynamics of the family are thus due largely to what I have elsewhere called the 'gene lottery' (Nicholson, 2001). A family that contains several high achievement-striving extraverts will develop a quite different climate to one containing creative or nurturing types. Yet we can predict that conflict is more likely with similarity in age and gender. Closely age-spaced boys are especially prone to conflicts, as are family firm with fathers and sons who are close in age (Tagiuri and Davis, 1996). Together these factors create what can be called family climate, which can predispose members to make poor decisions and fail to exercise self-control (Björnberg and Nicholson, 2007). These are the processes indicated in Fig. 7.2. Without them, as shown

in Fig. 7.1, the family and its firm is vulnerable to inadequate reactions to the flash points that may occur in any dynamic situation.

One final element that may be noted is leadership. Within family firms this is also subject to the gene lottery, and a cause of special challenge at the point of leadership succession (Nicholson, 2001). Even with the most carefully groomed family business succession, the gene lottery dictates that there is more likely to be a radical shift in leadership style as one moves between generations than there is in the public company where leaders can be selected from a much wider pool to preserve the status quo (Gordon and Rosen, 2004). This leads to a special liability and perhaps source of innovation as family firms progress through the generations – they have greater likelihood of radical change in style through the transition process (Lansberg, 1999; Miller et al., 2003).

At the same time it may be noted that siblings, cousins, parents, and children are able to forge remarkable partnerships in the conduct of their enterprises. One can say that it requires some luck from the invisible hand of the gene lottery to deal a family a set of relationships where conflicts lack intensity, and are a source of creative energy to provide the spirit of flexibility and renewal that exemplifies so many successful family firms

(Denison et al., 2004; Miller and Le-Breton-Miller, 2005).

Clearly this is an area where further research is needed – a combined quantitative/qualitative methodology – to evaluate which elements mitigate or amplify inputs to produce the wide range of outcomes we see in family business. The inputs include the factors we have considered: a configural assessment of individual differences, such as recommended by Moynihan and Peterson (2002); measures of family size and structure (Nicholson and Björnberg, 2004); and measures of the levels of demand, complexity, and market position of the firm. This is not an exhaustive list, but these could be seen as chief amongst those that expose families to the risks we have reviewed. Mediating outcomes, such as conflict, are structure and process, represented by governance mechanisms and leadership. As other chapters in this volume elaborate, it is the role of governance to anticipate and neutralize destructive conflicts and bring parties together to make strategy and solve problems. Likewise, leadership has a key role in setting the framework and driving the process. Multi-level comparative case study research can elucidate these relationships. They might even prospectively foretell the dynamic combinations that prefigure success and failure.

CONCLUSION

This review has attempted to show the breadth and depth of evolutionary theory to explain not only many key phenomena in family firms, but also, as a science-based approach to the unity of knowledge, to encompass other theoretical perspectives. It is on this basis that one can assert that evolutionary theory has potentially a special status as a paradigm to guide family business researchers from all disciplinary orientations.

Specifically it draws attention to the following:

- Evolutionary theory can supply explanatory content to the concept of interest in agency theory, to the

notion of family capital in resource-based theory, and to the source of values that are central to stewardship theory.
- The institution of the family is a biological universal, and not just for our species, which exhibits certain regularities that are discernible in contemporary family firms. There are also visible cultural variations in family firm functioning that can be explained using co-evolutionary concepts and analytical tools.
- Nepotism is a human universal, as specified by the idea of parental investment in evolutionary theory. Inherent processes of bonding, communication and co-action within kinship groups confer special advantages and risks on to family firms.
- Human biology and sexual reproduction encourage 'affinal' bonds to be strong within families and other social groups, enabling kin and non-kin to cooperate intimately, though not without risks.
- The family business derives unique strength from the co-existence of kinship bonds + potential sources of creative conflict, but affinal (non-kin) bonds are a source of vulnerability to the cohesion of family firms.
- Parent–offspring and sibling divisions are biogenetic sources of conflict that need to be managed. Behavior genetics also indicates that favoritism may be a persistent threat within family firms.
- Birth-order effects have the potential to shape the strategic orientation of family leadership. The fact that heritable individual differences do not run in families (because they are the result of non-additive genes) implies a predictable risk of discontinuity through inter-generational successions.
- Evolutionary theory and behavior genetics underscore the uniqueness of family structure and culture, making them differentially 'fit' to run a business. The adaptive and successful family firm will, according to this analysis, be the one that has a manageable set of human inputs (individual differences, family structure) and business pressures, and which is guided by sound structure and process in governance and leadership.

So, to conclude, evolutionary theory has something special to bring to the family business field in three ways. First, it derives from first principles of biological science and thus provides a platform of secure knowledge for more domain-specific theory and research. Second, it provides an integrating explanatory framework for many highly visible phenomena in family firms, as well as reconciling various current theoretical perspectives. Third, it supplies a range of analytical tools and insights for the diagnostic analysis of specific firms, types of firms, and cross-cultural variations in firm behavior.

REFERENCES

Aldrich, H.E. and Cliff, J.E. (2003). The pervasive effects of family on entrepreneurship: Toward a family embeddedness perspective. *Journal of Business Venturing*, 18: 573–596.

Arkes, H.R. and Ayton, P. (1999). The sunk cost and Concorde effects: Are humans less rational than lower animals? *Psychological Bulletin*, 125: 591–600.

Babcock, C.R. (1998). PsychoDarwinism: The new synthesis of Darwin and Freud. In C. Crawford and D. Krebs (eds), *Handbook of Evolutionary Psychology*, pp. 457–583. Mahwah NJ: Lawrence Erlbaum.

Baker, R.R. and Bellis, M.A. (1989). Number of sperm in human ejaculates varies in accordance with sperm competition theory. *Animal Behaviour*, 37: 867–869.

Barkow, J.H., Cosmides, L., and Tooby, J. (eds) (1992), *The Adapted Mind: Evolutionary Psychology and the Generation of Culture*. Oxford: Oxford University Press.

Barrett, H.C. and Kurzban, R. (2006). Modularity in cognition: Framing the debate. *Psychological Review*, 113: 628–647.

Barrett, L., Dunbar, R., and Lycett, J. (2002). *Human Evolutionary Psychology*. Basingstoke: Palgrave.

Becker, G.S. (1981). *A Treatise on the Family*. Cambridge, MA: Harvard University Press.

Bellow, A. (2003). *In Praise of Nepotism: A Natural History*. New York: Doubleday.

Bennedsen, M., Nielsen, K.M., Perez-Gonzales, F., and Wolfenzen, D. (2007). Inside the family firm: The role of families in succession decisions and dynamics. *The Quarterly Journal of Economics*, 122: 647–691.

Björnberg, A. and Nicholson, N. (2007). The family climate scales: Development of a new measure for use in family business research. *Family Business Review*, 20: 229–246.

Black, S.E., Devereux, P.J., and Salvanes, K.G. (2005). The more the merrier? The effect of family size and birth order on children's education. *The Quarterly Journal of Economics*, 120: 669–700.

Boehm, C. (1999). *Hierarchy in the Forest: The Evolution of Egalitarian Behavior*. Cambridge, MA: Harvard University Press.

Boer, F. and Dunn, J. (1992). *Children's Sibling Relationships: Developmental and Clinical Issues*. Hillsdale, NJ: Lawrence Erlbaum.

Boyd, R. and Richerson, P.J. (1985). *Culture and the Evolutionary Process*. Chicago, IL: University of Chicago Press.

Broderick, C.B. (1993). *Understanding Family Process*. Thousand Oaks, CA: Sage.

Brush, C.G. (1992). Research on women business owners: Past trends, a new perspective and future directions. *Entrepreneurship: Theory and Practice*, 16: 5–30.

Buss, D.M. (2000). *The Dangerous Passion: Why Jealousy is as Necessary as Love or Sex*. London: Bloomsbury.

Buss, D.M. (2004). *Evolutionary Psychology: The New Science of Mind*. Boston, MA: Pearson.

Carver, C.S. and Scheier, M.F. (1998). *On the Self-regulation of Behavior*. Cambridge: Cambridge University Press.

Cole, P.M. (1997). Women in family business. *Family Business Review*, 10: 353–371.

Cole, P.M. and Johnson, K. (2007). An exploration of successful copreneurial relationships postdivorce. *Family Business Review*, 20: 185–198.

Coon, C.S. (1979). *The Hunting Peoples*. New York: Penguin.

Cronk, L. and Gerkey, D. (2007). Ecological and socio-cultural impacts on mating and marriage systems. In L. Barrett, (ed.), *Oxford Handbook of Evolutionary Anthropology*, pp. 463–478. Oxford: Oxford University Press.

Cummins, D. (2005). Dominance, status and social hierarchies. In D.M. Buss (ed.), *The Handbook of Evolutionary Psychology*, pp. 676–697. New York: Wiley.

Danes, S.M. and Olson, P.M. (2003). Women's role involvement in family businesses, business tensions, and business success. *Family Business Review*, 16: 53–68.

Davis, J.N. and Daly, M. (1997). Evolutionary theory and the human family. *Quarterly Review of Biology*, 72: 407–425.

Davis, J.A. and Tagiuri, R. (1989). The influence of life-stage on father-son work relationship in family companies. *Family Business Review*, 2: 47–74.

Davis, J.H., Schoorman, F.D., and Donaldson, L. (1997). Toward a stewardship theory of management. *Academy of Management Review*, 22: 20–47.

Dennett, D.C. (1995). *Darwin's Dangerous Idea: Evolution and the Meanings of Life*. New York: Simon & Schuster.

De Waal, F. (1982). *Chimpanzee Politics*. Baltimore, OH: Johns Hopkins University Press.

Denison, D., Lief, C., and Ward, J.L. (2004). Culture in family-owned enterprises, Recognizing and leveraging unique strengths. *Family Business Review*, 17: 61–70.

Draper, P. and Harpending, H. (1988). A sociobiological perspective on the development of human reproductive strategies. In K. MacDonald (ed.), *Sociobiological Perspectives on Human Development*, pp. 340–372. New York: Springer Verlag.

Dunbar, R.I.M. (1992). Neocortex size as a constraint on group size in primates. *Journal of Human Evolution,* 20: 469–493.

Eddleston, K.A. and Kellermans, F.W. (2007). Destructive and productive family relationships: A stewardship theory perspective. *Journal of Business Venturing,* 22: 455–565.

Emlen, S.T. (1997). Predicting family dynamics in social vertebrates. In J.R. Krebs and N.B. Davies (eds). *Behavioral Ecology: An Evolutionary Approach*, 4th edn, pp. 228–253. Oxford: Wiley-Blackwell.

Evans, D. and Cruse, P. (eds), (2004). *Emotion, Evolution, and Rationality*, pp. 193–208. Oxford: Oxford University Press.

Feldman, M.W. and Cavalli-Sforza, L.L. (1989). On the theory of evolution under genetic and cultural transmission with application to the lactose absorption problem. In M.W. Feldman (ed.), *Mathematical Evolutionary Theory*, pp. 145–173. Princeton, NJ: Princeton University Press.

Fitzgerald, M.A. and Muske, G. (2002). Copreneurs, An exploration and comparison to other family businesses. *Family Business Review*, 15: 1–15.

Frank, R. (1988). *Passions Within Reason*. New York: Norton.

Geary, D.C. (1998). *Male, Female*. Washington, DC: American Psychological Association.

Gersick, K.E., Davis, J.A., Hampton, M.M., and Lansberg, I. (1997). *Generation to Generation: Life Cycles of the Family Business*. Cambridge, MA: Harvard Business School Press.

Godfrey-Smith, P. (2003). *Theory and Reality: An Introduction to the Philosophy of Science*. Chicago, IL: University of Chicago Press.

Ghoshal, S. (2005). Bad management theories are destroying good management practices. *Academy of Management Learning & Education*, 4: 75–91.

Gintis, H., Bowles, S., Boyd, R., and Fehr, E. (2003). Explaining altruistic behavior in humans, *Evolution and Human Behavior*, 24: 153–172.

Gomez-Mejia, L.R., Nunez-Nickel M., and Gutierrez, I. (2001). The role of family ties in agency contracts. *Academy of Management Journal*, 44: 81–95.

Goodall, J. (1998). *The Chimpanzees of Gombe: Patterns of Behavior*. Cambridge, MA: Harvard University Press.

Gordon, G. and Nicholson, N. (2008). *Family Wars*. London: Kogan Page.

Gordon, G.E. and Rosen, N. (2004). Critical factors in leadership succession. *Organizational Behavior & Human Performance*, 27: 227–254.

Habbershon, T.G. and Williams, M.L. (1999). A resource-based framework for assessing the strategic advantages of family firms. *Family Business Review*, 12: 1–25.

Hamilton, G.D. (1964). The genetical evolution of social behaviour. *Journal of Theoretical Biology*, 7: 1–16, 17–52.

Harcourt, A.H. and Stewart, K.J. (2007). *Gorilla Society: Conflict, Compromise, and Cooperation*. Chicago, IL: University of Chicago Press.

Haselton, M.G., and Nettle, D. (2006). The paranoid optimist: An integrative evolutionary model of cognitive biases. *Personality and Social Psychology Review*, 10: 47–66.

Henrich, J. (2004). Cultural group selection, coevolutionary processes and large-scale cooperation. *Journal of Economic Behavior & Organization*, 53: 3–35.

Henrich, J. and Gil-White, F.J. (2001). The evolution of prestige: Freely conferred deference as a mechanism for enhancing the beneits of cultural transmission. *Evolution and Human Behavior*, 22: 165–196.

Hertwig, R., Davis, J.N. and Sulloway, F.J. (2002). Parental investment: How an equity motive can produce inequality. *Psychological Bulletin*, 128: 728–745.

Hrdy, S.B. (2001). *Mother Nature: A History of Mothers, Infants, and Natural Selection*. New York: Pantheon Books.

Hrdy, S.B. (2009). *Mothers and Others: The Evolutionary Origins of Mutual Understanding*. Cambridge, MA: Harvard University Press.

Imanishi, K. (1960). Social organization of subhuman primates in their natural habitat. *Current Anthropology*, 1: 393–407.

Jensen, M.C. and Meckling, W.H. (1976). Theory of the firm: Managerial behavior, agency costs and ownership structure. *Journal of Financial Economics*, 3: 303–360.

Jimanez, R. (2009). Research on women in family firms: Current status and future directions. *Family Business Review*, 22: 51–64.

Kaye, K. (1999). Mate selection and family business success. *Family Business Review*, 12: 105–115.

Keesing, R.M. (1975). *Kin Groups and Social Structure*. New York: Holt, Rinehart and Winston.

Kellermans, F.W. and Eddleston, K.A. (2004). Feuding families: When conflict does a family firm good. *Entrepreneurship: Theory and Practice*, 29: 209–228.

Kurzban, R. and Aktipis, C.A. (2007). Modularity and the social mind: Are psychologists too self-ish? *Personality and Social Psychology Review*, 11: 131–149.

Laland, K.N. (2007). Niche construction, human behavioural ecology and evolutionary psychology. In R.I.M. Dunbar and L. Barrett. *The Oxford Handbook of Evolutionary Psychology*, pp. 35–48. Oxford: Oxord University Press.

Lancaster, J.B. and Lancaster, C.S. (1987). The watershed: Change in parental-investment and family formation strategies in the course of human evolution. In J.B. Lancaster, J. Altmann, L. Sherrod, and A. Rossi (eds), *Parenting Across the Life Span: Biosocial Dimensions*, pp. 187–206. New York: De Gruyter.

Landes, D.S. (2006). *Dynasties: Fortunes and Misfortunes of the World's Great Family Businesses.* New York: Viking.

Lansberg, I. (1999). *Succeeding Generations.* Boston, MA: Harvard Business School Press.

Loomis, C.P. and McKinney, J.C. (1956). Systemic differences between Latin-American communities of family farms and large estates. *American Journal of Sociology*, 61: 404–412.

Low, B.S. (2007). Ecological and socio-cultural impacts on mating and marriage systems. In L. Barrett, (ed.), *Oxford Handbook of Evolutionary Anthropology*, pp. 449–462. Oxford: Oxford University Press.

Lykken, D.T., McGue, M., Tellegen, A., and Bouchard, T.J. (1992). Emergenesis: Genetic traits that may not run in families. *American Psychologist*, 47: 1565–1577.

Mace, R. (2007). The evolutionary ecology of human family size. In R.I.M. Dunbar and L. Barrett. *The Oxford Handbook of Evolutionary Psychology*, pp. 383–396. Oxford: Oxford University Press.

Macmillan, M. (1997). *Freud Evaluated: The Completed Arc.* Boston, MA: MIT Press.

Mann, J. (1992). Nurturence or negligence: Maternal psychology and behavioral preference among preterm twins. In J.H. Barkow, L. Cosmides, and J. Tooby (eds), *The Adapted Mind: Evolutionary Psychology and the Generation of Culture.* Oxford: Oxford University Press.

Markson, E.W. (2003). *Social Gerontology Today: An Introduction.* Los Angeles, CA: Roxbury.

Marshack, K.J. (1993). Coentrepreneurial couples: A literature review on the boundaries and transitions among Copreneurs. *Family Business Review*, 6: 355–369.

Mayr, E. (1988). *Toward a New Philosophy of Biology: Observations of an Evolutionist.* Cambridge, MA: Harvard University Press.

McElreath, R. and Henrich, J. (2007). Dual inheritance theory: The evolution of human cultural capacities and cultural evolution. In R.I.M. Dunbar and L. Barrett (Eds), *Oxford Handbook of Evolutionary Psychology*, pp. 555–570. Oxford: Oxford University Press.

Meder, A. (2007). Great ape social systems. In W. Henke, I. Tatersall, and T. Hardt (eds), *Handbook of Paleoanthropology, Vol. 2*, pp. 1235–1271. New York: Springer-Verlag.

Megarry, T. (1995). *Society in Prehistory: The origins of human culture.* London: Macmillan

Mercer, J. (2005). *Understanding Attachment.* New York: Praeger.

Miller, D., Steier, L., and Le Breton-Miller, I. (2003). Lost in time: Intergenerational succession, change, and failure in family business. *Journal of Business Venturing*, 18: 513–531.

Miller, G.F. (2000). *The Mating Mind, How Sexual Choice Shaped the Evolution of Human Nature.* London: Heinemann.

Miller, D. and Le Breton-Miller, I. (2005). *Managing for the Long Run: Lessons in Competitive Advantage from the Great Family Businesses.* Cambridge, MA: Harvard Business School Press.

Moynihan, L.M. and Peterson, R.S. (2002). A contingent configuration approach to understanding the role of personality in organizational groups. In B.W. Staw and R. Sutton (eds), *Research in Organizational Behavior.* Greenwich, CT: JAI Press.

Nettle, D. (2004). Adaptive illusions: Optimism, control and human rationality. In D. Evans and P. Cruse (eds), *Emotion, Evolution, and Rationality*, pp. 193–208. Oxford: Oxford University Press.

Nettle, D. (2006). The evolution of personality variation in humans and other animals. *American Psychologist*, 61: 622–631.

Neubauer, F. and Lank, A.G. (1998). *The Family Business, Its Governance and Sustainability.* London: Macmillan.

Neyer, F.J. and Lang, F.R. (2003). Blood is thicker than water: Kinship orientation across adulthood. *Journal of Personality and Social Psychology*, 84: 310–321.

Nicholson, N. (2001). Gene politics and the natural selection of leadership. *Leader to Leader.* No. 20, Spring, pp. 46–52.

Nicholson, N. (2008a). Evolutionary psychology and family business: A new synthesis for theory, research and practice. *Family Business Review*, 21: 103–118.

Nicholson, N. (2008b). Evolutionary psychology, corporate culture and family business. *Academy of Management Perspectives*, 22: 73–84.

Nicholson, N. (2012). The evolution of business and management. In S.C. Roberts (ed.), *Applied Evolutionary Psychology*, pp. 16–35. Oxford: Oxford University Press.

Nicholson, N. and Björnberg, A. (2004). Evolutionary psychology and the family firm: structure, culture and performance. In S. Tomaselli and L. Melin (eds), *Family Firms in the Wind of Change.* Research Forum Proceedings. Lausanne: IFERA.

Nilakant, V. and Rao, H. (1994). Agency theory and uncertainty in organizations: An evaluation. *Organization Studies*, 15: 649–672.

Piattelli-Palmarini, M. (1994). *Inevitable Illusions*. New York: Wiley.

Pinker, S. (1994). *The Language Instinct*. New York: Morrow.

Pinker, S. (1997). *How the Mind Works*. New York: Norton.

Platek, S., Burch, R., Panyavin, I., Wasserman, B., Gallup, G. (2002). Reactions to children's faces: Resemblance affects males more than females. *Evolution and Human Behavior*, 23: 159 –166.

Plomin, R. (1994). *Genetics and Experience: The Interplay between Nature and Nurture*. Thousand Oaks, CA: Sage.

Popper, M., Mayseless, O., and Castelnovo, O. (2000). Transformational leadership and attachment. *Leadership Quarterly*, 11: 267–289.

Richardson, P.J. and Boyd, R. (2005). *Not by Genes Alone: How Culture Transformed Human Evolution*. Chicago, IL: University of Chicago Press.

Ridley, M. (1993). *The Red Queen: Sex and the Evolution of Human Nature*. New York: Viking.

Salmon, C.A. (1999). On the impact of sex and birth order on contact with kin. *Human Nature*, 10: 183–197.

Schulze, W.S., Lubatkin, M.H., Dino, R.N., and Buchholtz, A.K. (2001). Agency relationships in family firms: Theory and evidence. *Organization Science*, 12: 99–116.

Schulze, W.S., Lubatkin, M.H., and Dino, R.N. (2003). Toward a theory of agency and altruism in family firms. *Journal of Business Venturing*, 18: 473–490.

Shalit, A., Popper, M., and Zakay, D. (2010). Followers' attachment styles and their preference for social or for personal charismatic leaders. *Leadership & Organizational Development Journal*, 31: 458–472.

Sharma, P. (2006). An overview of the field of family business studies: Current status and directions for the future. In P.Z. Poutzouris, K.X. Smyrnios, and S.B. Klein (eds), *Handbook of Research on Family Business*, pp. 25–55. Cheltenham: Edward Elgar.

Smith, C.M. (2011). *The Fact of Evolution*. New York: Prometheus Books.

Sober, E. and Wilson, D.S. (1998). *Unto Others: The Evolution and Psychology of Unselfish Behavior*. Cambridge, MA: Harvard University Press.

Sperber, D. (1996). *Explaining Culture: A Naturalistic Approach*. Oxford: Blackwell.

Stewart, A. (2003). Help one another, use one another. Toward an anthropology of family business. *Entrepreneurship: Theory and Practice*, 27: 383–396.

Strassmann, B.I. (1981). Sexual selection, paternal care, and concealed ovulation in humans. *Ethology and Sociobiology*, 2: 31–40.

Suitor, J.J. and Pillemer, K. (2000). Did mom really love you best? Developmental histories, status transitions, and parental favoritism in later life families. *Motivation & Emotion*, 24: 105–120.

Sulloway, F.J. (2001). Birth order, sibling competition, and human behavior. In H.R. Holcomb III (ed.), *Conceptual Challenges in Evolutionary Psychology: Innovative Research Strategies*, pp. 39–83. Studies in cognitive systems, Vol. 27. Dordrecht, the Netherlands: Kluwer.

Tagiuri, R. and Davis, J.A. (1992). On the goals of successful family companies. *Family Business Review*, 5: 43–62.

Tagiuri, R. and Davis, J.A. (1996). Bivalent attributes of the family firm, *Family Business Review*, 9: 199–208.

Tokarczyk, J., Hansen, E., Green, M., and Down, J. (2007). A resource-based view and market orientation theory examination of the role of 'familiness' in family business success. *Family Business Review*, 20: 17–32.

Tomasello, M. (1999). *The Cultural Origins of Human Cognition*. Cambridge, MA: Harvard University Press.

Trivers, R.L. (1972). Parental investment and sexual selection. In B. Campbell (ed.), *Sexual Selection and the Descent of Man*. Chicago, IL: Aldine.

Trivers, R.L. (1974). Parent-offspring conflict. *American Zoologist*, 14: 249–264.

Tudge, C. (1998). *Neanderthals, Bandits and Farmers*. London: Wiedenfeld & Nicolson.

Wagner, M.E., Schubert, H.J., and Schubert, D.S. (1985). Family size effects: A review, *Journal Genetic Psychology*, 146: 65–78.

Weick, K.E. (1969). *The Social Psychology of Organizing*. New York: McGraw-Hill.

Westhead, P. and Cowling, M. (1998). Family firm research: The need for a methodological rethink. *Entrepreneurship Theory & Practice*, 23: 31–56.

Whiten, A. (1999). The evolution of deep social mind in humans. In M. Corballis and S.E.G. Lea (eds), *The Descent of Mind* (pp. 155–175) *Mind*. Oxford: Oxford University Press.

Wilson, E.O. (1998). *Consilience, The Unity of Knowledge*. New York, Vintage Books.

Wrangham, R.W. (1987). The significance of African apes for reconstructing human social evolution. In W.G. Kinzey (ed.), *The Evolution of Human Behavior: Primate Models*. Albany, NY: SUNY Press.

Yan, J. and Sorenson, R. (2006). The effect of Confucian values on succession in family business. *Family Business Review*, 19: 235–250.

Zervas, L. and Sherman, M. (1994). The relationship between perceived parental favoritism and self-esteem. *The Journal of Genetic Psychology*, 155: 25–33.

8

Family Business Inquiry as a Critical Social Science

Denise Fletcher

INTRODUCTION

As stated in the introduction to this handbook and evidenced in its various critical contributions, family business as a field of inquiry has significantly advanced in volume and variety of perspectives, theories and methods. The field has come a long way since rationalist and normative principles dominated the field and advocated the need to isolate family from business issues to ensure the effective working of a business (see Calder, 1961; Donnelley, 1964). In addition, recognition of the unhelpful theoretical polarity that this thinking caused in the field in the perpetuation of business vs family 'systems' or domains (Habbershon and Pistrui, 2002), has helped to give a research response to the complexity and contradiction of family business activity. Furthermore, the inclusiveness of wider theoretical perspectives from resource-based analyses (Chrisman et al., 2003), field theory (Riordan and Riordan, 1993), agency theory (Daily and Dollinger, 1993; Schulze et al., 2003), stewardship theory/altruism (Davis

et al., 2010), family business systems (Zody et al., 2006) and family-embeddedness (Aldrich and Cliff, 2003), to name a few, have helped to broaden the theoretical landscape of this sphere of study and furnish critical explanations from sociology, anthropology, psychology and economic theory etc.

All of this is positive development for a growing field of inquiry but especially for establishing that family firms are a significant empirical phenomenon in the world economy and society, constituting a prominent organisational form. In spite of this, however, theorising remains at the level of insight, exposure and illumination of family business issues/problems, rather than at the level of critique. This relates in part to the prevailing rationalist and modernist discourse that continues to influence family business inquiry and a lack of critical reflection on the relationship between family firms and wider institutions, discourses and ideologies. In scholarly activity, criticism is concerned with exposing and challenging that which is taken for granted, critiquing extant literature, ensuring rigour of method, moving from description to explanation, demonstrating an evidence base, displaying audit trails and so forth. All of these critical tasks are important to scholarly inquiry, but as Alvesson and Aschcraft (2000 p. 61) argue, 'typically, critical studies place a local object of study in a wider cultural, political, and economic context relating a focused phenomena to broader discursive and material formations (such as class, late capitalism, affluent/post scarcity society and male domination etc.)' This means that critical studies in terms of social science analyses also have wider structural, political and ethical implications. Furthermore, through critique, scholars also question the ontological and epistemological bases of socially scientific knowledge/understanding.

Different critical orientations can be found in the application of various methodological and theoretical approaches – all of which inspire some form of critique, i.e., critical ethnography (Thomas, 1993); critical realism (Reed, 2009); critical methodology (Alvesson and Ashcraft, 2009); critical contexts of research (Buchanan and Bryman, 2007); feminist analyses (Calas and Smircich, 2009); the 'doing' of critical management research (Alvesson and Deetz, 2000; Alvesson and Skoldberg, 2000); and the application of pragmatic realism to advocate an analytical-critical means of understanding the realities of human resource management (Watson, 2010).

In family business inquiry, however, the meaning and implications of a critical tradition have not been widely addressed and it is rare to see such analyses being developed for critiquing family business practices. There is also an absence of reflections on how the specificities of family business contexts can potentially contribute to a critical social science. This lack of critical reflection is explained in more detail below by referencing Alvesson and Deetz's (2000) notion of a 'consensus' discourse (p. 23), which is a term they use to denote the relation of research practices to dominant social discourses.

Although Alvesson and Deetz (2000) state that researchers in organisation and management studies came to critical theory and postmodern writings relatively late, it is argued here that such ideas are later still in reaching into family business studies. It is widely reported how family firms are ever present and visible in all spheres of the economy from the home-based business to the large multinational with family owners. And yet we have little understanding of how family businesses structures, settings and practices produce relations of power or asymmetry. It is more than timely, therefore, to consider what a critical social science means for family business inquiry. At the same time, there is also scope to consider how family business inquiry can contribute to advancing a critical social science. As Jones (2005, p. 276) states, 'the position of family firms in the economic realm is [to say the least], "complicated", and although we understand some of this complicatedness there is scope to take our critical analyses a step further'.

In the first section below, I discuss the need for critique-inspired analyses of family businesses research. Second, the topic of leadership in family business research is reviewed in order to demonstrate the absence of (and yet potential for) critical 'readings'. In this section also, gender issues in family business research are discussed to explain the meaning and purpose of critique. Third, I outline what is meant by a critical tradition by relating this to critical theory and postmodernist ideas. To conclude this part, a summary is provided of the main themes underlining a critical tradition. Finally, at the close of the chapter, some synthesising themes, issues and tasks that characterise critical research are then drawn out to provide a critique-inspired agenda for research action in family business. These critical tactics are elaborated with reference to an illustrative account of family business philanthropy where it is demonstrated how critical themes can be applied and drawn out in family business research.

THE DOMINANCE OF A 'CONSENSUS' DISCOURSE AND THE NEED FOR A CRITICAL STANCE IN FAMILY BUSINESS

In order to emphasise the need for critique-inspired analyses of family businesses, reference is made to Alvesson and Deetz's (2000) notion of a 'consensus' discourse (pp. 23–24). They introduce this notion (in contrast to the notion of dissenus) to denote the relation of research practices to dominant social discourses. Their aim is to create some analytic distinctions upon which to contrast different research perspectives based on the extent to which certain research practices either 'work within' (consensus discourse) or 'disrupt' (dissensus discourse) 'a dominant set of structurings of knowledge, social relations, and identities' (p. 24). Although one could easily think about consensus and dissensus in terms of agreement and disagreement, the authors' intention is to see the two discourses as 'the presentation of unity or of difference; and the continuation or disruption of any prevailing discourse' (p. 25). A detailed review of the four analytic distinctions that Alvesson and Deetz (2000) put forward as an alternative to Burrell and Morgan's (1979) analysis is not the main priority here, however. What is important is to stimulate critical reflection within the family business field on the relationship of particular research practices to a dominant social discourse of 'consensus'. This notion of consensus is now elaborated.

A consensus discourse signals the preoccupation of particular research practices with the preservation of unity where 'the primary goal of research is to display a discovered order with a high degree of fidelity or verisimilitude … and where existing orders are treated as unproblematic' (Alvesson and Deetz, 2000, p. 26). It is characterised by a lack of openness to:

the significance of random events and [where] deviance [is] played down in the search for norms and descriptions that are thought to mirror entities that exist in the external world in a relatively fixed state. In research practices reflecting a consensus discourse, attention is usually given to processes reducing deviance, uncertainty and dissonance. (Alvesson and Deetz, 2000, p. 26)

Also, language within the research process is treated as a system of representations, to be neutralised and made transparent. Such research practices contribute to the 'continuation of a dominant and prevailing discourse' (Alvesson and Deetz, 2000, p. 25) that overprivileges normative unity and integration (Ainsworth and Cox, 2003) at the expense of evaluating difference, dissensus and fragmentation.

In the extant family business field of inquiry, a consensus orientation can be observed in several ways. First, it can be seen in an over-reliance on the robustness of empirical data and an uncritical tendency to privilege the confirmation of theory and empirical data, rather than disputing or disrupting what is known in order to search for alternative (or pluralistic) ways of understanding the world. Second, it is evidenced in the preoccupation with essences, elements and components of family business where the research task is concerned with revealing the intrinsic qualities or core essences that underlie or shape particular organisational phenomena (such as leadership or culture). Here, the researcher starts from an assumption that various essences/components 'exist' and are fixed within the organisation independently of the researcher's interaction there and these essences constitute an underlying order or structure that can be discovered through the probing of research tools. This contrasts with alternative research perspectives that give attention to the on-going co-construction and production of meanings, attributes and configurations of family business practice. Third, a consensus orientation can be noted in the lack of consideration to the 'local and temporal conditions of production' of insights and meanings (Alvesson and Deetz, 2000, p. 29) and inattention to the contextualised multivoicedness of research accounts. Fourth, it is reflected in the insufficient attention awarded to the various discourses and linguistic, narrative or story-telling devices that are used to create meaning and which often produce asymmetrical relations (some exceptions to this are McCollom, 1992; Hamilton, 2006; Helin, 2011). Fifth, a consensus orientation can be seen in the uncritical acceptance of the freely acting autonomous family business owners or successors and their stewardship, agency or decision-making efforts and the scarcity of consideration to the struggles, conflicts and tensions experienced in these processes.

An appropriate topic in family business to discuss in relation to a consensus discourse and associated research efforts that treat the research phenomena as fixed and unproblematic, is that of leadership. In spite of being one of the most frequently discussed topics in organisation theory, in family business, it is largely taken for granted subject. This is partly explained by the fact that leadership in family business settings is sometimes overshadowed by issues of ownership, succession or governance – topics which have been widely and usefully discussed in the family business literature. However, this means that there is still limited understanding about leadership in family business contexts (Dyer, 1994; Thomas, 2002a, 2002b). Furthermore, there is little depth of understanding 'as to what levels of influences and processes are most critical to understanding leadership' (Mumford et al., 2009, p. 123).

A further problem is that the literature on family business leadership is strongly influenced by what von Krogh et al. (2012) refer to as 'old leadership' assumptions and ideas. Studies that adopt 'old leadership' consider leadership styles in terms of 'possessive individualism' (Dachler et al., 1995), which means that organisational processes are directly related to the attributes or competencies of special individuals or personalities. As a result, studies emphasise the significance of role modelling, strategic leadership and leader–follower or transactional styles of leadership that privilege the centrality of a figurehead leader (Pearson and Marler, 2010). Family firm studies reflecting 'old leadership' would, for example, signal problems with the

willingness of CEOs to relinquish their leadership roles (Aronoff and Ward, 1992), or the importance of successor selection and planning in relation to birth order/best candidate (Ward, 1987), integrity and commitment (Chrisman et al., 1998, p. 28). In addition, 'old leadership' styles of study would categorise different 'types' of leadership (as participative, autocratic, laissez-faire, expert and referent; Sorenson, 2000) from complex organisational processes that are treated as universal, unproblematic, discoverable and reifiable.

The problem, therefore, with 'old leadership' perspectives for family business settings is that they are, as Mumford et al. (2009, p. 113) argue, based on an idealised model of leader behaviour. But 'leadership cannot be reduced to an individual social actor or to discrete relations amongst social actors. Rather, it is a freely interpenetrating unlocalisable process (Wood, 2005, p. 1105) – a *relation* of almost imperceptible directions, movement and orientations, having neither beginning nor end (Wood, 2005, p. 1115). Furthermore, as Mumford et al. (2009, p. 115) argue, leadership is not, a 'neutral' phenomena and 'most organisations seek to train central aspects of leadership and [have] … explicit and implicit policies in place intended to improve employee and "follower" satisfaction'. These contextual factors are mostly overlooked in 'old leadership' perspectives and they are not always accounted for in studies that profess to move beyond 'old leadership' thinking. More specifically, they neglect to examine how leadership is a skilful process of reality construction and shifting influence (Hosking, 1988; Wood, 2005; Uhl-Bien, 2006) involving power, conflict and emotions. Furthermore, in the extant family business literature, the dominance of a consensus discourse means that there is an uncritical acceptance of what form leadership takes in family business contexts and the struggles, conflicts and tensions that are inevitably involved in leadership processes (especially with historical patterns of family interactions) are often glossed over.

To break out of this dominant set of social relations, research practices and 'structurings of knowledge' (Alvesson and Deetz, 2000, p. 24) and develop critically oriented analyses of family businesses, certain steps are necessary. At the very least, our research inquiry would be concerned with what Levin (1993) helpfully argued for almost two decades ago – that is, moving from a close and non-problematised view of family to one which tries to accommodate the complex issues drawn from the everyday experience and interpretations of family business members and employees. This means problematising what is known/accepted, exposing what is taken for granted, searching for alternative meanings, drawing attention to context, issues of power or conflict and the struggles that go on as organisational activities are realised. Critical analyses would also emphasise process rather than 'possessive individualism'; they would avoid reification and the affirmation that there is a stable and existent 'order' in organisations that is discoverable through the research process. All of these are central to critical analysis but going further into critique, however, it is important to accommodate a more political and ethical stance as the researcher becomes concerned with how deep social formations constrain human behaviours, affect autonomy and decision-making, which often lead to a 'freezing of social reality' for certain groups of people producing asymmetrical relations of power (Alvesson and Deetz, 2000, p. 9). A case in point here is the study of gender in relation to family business – a review of which is now outlined in order to further illustrate the need and potential for a critical stance.

A common approach to the study of gender in family business situations is to consider 'gender as a variable' in shaping organisational life. Here studies consider gender in family business settings to report what happens to men/women in these contexts by comparing masculine/feminine experiences, values, styles of managing, ethics and motivations (e.g., Loscocco and Leicht, 1993;

Kaslow & Kaslow, 1993; Danes et al., 2007; Bjorkhaug and Blekesaune, 2008; McCollom-Hampton, 2009; Barrett and Moores, 2009). In addition, many analyses addressing gender focus on 'standpoint positions' that give voice to women's unique experiences. Here, gender is important for demonstrating that women are carriers of particular insights and meanings (Alvesson and Billing, 1997, p. 52) – insights that warrant research attention in their own right. This could be seen, for example, in the case of family studies that draw attention to the previously 'invisible' role of women in business-owning families (Gillis-Donovan and Moynihan-Bradt, 1990; Dumas, 1998; Nelton, 1998; Danes and Olson, 2003; Hamilton, 2006). Furthermore, some studies focus on the family or household unit as a means to highlight the multiple formal/informal work and 'third shift' family roles/responsibilities that women have in business-owning families (Baines and Wheelock, 2000; Baines et al., 2002; Lee et al., 2006; Philbrick and Fitzgerald, 2007).

All of these are worthy and important areas of study. These studies (rightly) privilege gender in order to identify inequalities, promote feminine qualities, diminish patriarchy and male domination, and to enable justice, emancipation and equality for women. Often in family business inquiry, however, the dominant approach is to conceive of gender in terms of limited male/female distinctions rather than reframing family business through critical positions such as 'liberal feminist' (Calas and Smircich, 2009) or 'feminist-sociological' (Alvesson and Skoldberg, 2000). In critical positionings, the analytical aim is to inspire reflection and sensitivity towards gender issues in terms of 'the socially constituted patterns that are produced *through* male/female, masculine/feminine distinctions' (Alvesson and Billing, 2009, p. 1, referring to Acker, 1992, p. 250) rather than emphasising male/female differences. Thus, a stronger critical (ethical and political) dimension is important for family business inquiry, not only to highlight the specificities of women in business, but also to reveal (and reduce) the barriers that inhibit female participation in family business and to demonstrate the production of gendered patterns.

Furthermore, a critical reading would challenge how, in many ways, arriving at gender issues through units of analysis (such as family or household) is problematic in that it appears that it is only where attention is given to the role of spouses or the domestic partners of business owners, that gender issues and relationships are acknowledged as significant. This seems to signify (unhelpfully) that gender relations become more pertinent when women come into view, either to partner with men in business or to support men informally from the side-lines. At best, an association of business with households or spouses/families in business is significant for encouraging a 'feminine sociology' (Kanter, 1977, p. 14), where an analysis of women's centrality in economic roles contributes to the feminisation of workplace practices. At worst, the association of family business with the domestic/feminine/household realm means that such activities are categorised as 'informal' economic activities that are secondary or subordinate to mainstream economic activity. Jones (2005) makes this point with reference to family firms where he is critical of the lack of status of family businesses research in management inquiry because of its association with the domestic (rather than productive) realm.

When linking issues of family and gender, therefore, researchers face a number of analytical and epistemological challenges. One can expand traditional liberal/sociological feminist perspectives that begin with male/female distinctions or gender differences to inspire social change. Alternatively, one could challenge male/female distinctions as valid points of departure (Alvesson and Billing, 1997) and work towards an alternative conceptualisation that sees 'men/women categories as ambiguous, arbitrary and contradictory, indeterminate and dynamic ... and having a temporal, precarious meaning – a meaning which is tied to context' (p. 41).

Instead of male/female categories, this alternative perspective would locate gender relations in social structures, institutions, cultural processes and dominant discourses. With reference to gender and family business, critical perspectives would, therefore, not only attempt to challenge dominant discourses about the invisible women of family business but would also examine more closely how family business contexts are sites for the production of gender relations (Alvesson and Billing, 1997, p. 11; Bruni et al., 2004; Katila, 2010). An example of this is Mulholland's (2003) study of the ways in which women contribute to the wealth of family firms and how their efforts are ultimately appropriated and marginalised by male family members. This study portrays how the enactment of family business practice is imbued with gender relations. This is because in practising family business work, men and women exhibit a range of gendered practices; 'they recast their understanding of their situation ... in relationship to those with whom they interacted and their contingent gendered performance contributes to redefining in each situation what kind of gender relations are possible' (Bruni et al., 2004, p. 561).

Critique is concerned, therefore, with understanding how social structures and patterns of relationships constrain human behaviours in family firms and explaining how issues such as leadership and gender (or alternatively culture, governance, ownership, succession etc.) are connected to power issues and/or asymmetrical relations. A useful generic definition of critique that has relevance and transferent possibilities for family businesses inquiry is suggested. This 'refers to the examination of social institutions, ideologies, discourses (ways of constructing and reasoning about the world through the use of a particular language) and forms of consciousness in terms of representation and domination' (Alvesson and Deetz, 2000, p. 8). To move from criticism to critique, however, it is necessary to take account of various streams of thought that have contributed to a 'critical tradition' in social science inquiry. In the limited space of a book chapter, however, it is impossible to examine all intellectual streams. It is intended, therefore, to discuss the critical tradition from two particular (but interrelated) intellectual streams of thought: critical theory and postmodernism.

Noting Alvesson and Deetz (2000, p. 1), each of these streams of thought has, albeit in different ways, a concern with 'questioning established social orders, dominating practices, ideologies, discourses and institutions'. Furthermore, it is important to observe that each set of ideas provides something similar and yet different to our understanding of social science inquiry. They also contribute to each other. Without considering postmodern themes, Alvesson and Deetz (2000) claim that critical theory becomes unreflective with regard to cultural elitism and pessimistic about the potentialities for change. Without critical theory, postmodernism becomes 'esoteric' and relativist. In short, both intellectual streams provide unique and important ways to understand organisations and their management (Alvesson and Deetz, 2000, p. 10). These are now reviewed in order to signal the value/significance of these ideas for family business inquiry. At the same time, in view of the complexity and breadth of ideas, it is also necessary to draw out some synthesising features as we contemplate family business as a critical social science.

A CRITICAL TRADITION FROM TWO PERSPECTIVES: CRITICAL THEORY AND POSTMODERNISM

Critical Theory

In the context of business and management, critical theory (CT) is a broad set of intellectual resources for critiquing received wisdom and knowledge about society, the economy and the various organisational, institutional and managerial practices that constitute the socio-economic world. In so far as a definition of CT is possible, it may be defined as a

self-conscious social critique that is directed at social change and emancipation through enlightenment and which does not cling dogmatically to its own doctrinal assumptions (Horkheimer, 1972 [1937]). Unlike other theories that we see in family business such as stewardship, agency or resource-based theory, CT is not a theory that can be easily recognised for signifying a unified position or standpoint. It is not characterised by a set of unified principles. Nor, do the ideas of CT cohere into a clear blueprint for research action. Instead, as aptly asserted by (Willmott, 2008), CT is a 'refreshing reservoir of ideas … drawn from sociology, philosophy, economics, psychology' (p. 66). This is because CT – or, more accurately, the body of work associated with a group of critical theorists – was inspired by an intellectual movement known as the Frankfurt school (involving people such as Horkheimer, Adorno, Marcuse, Erich Fromm, Habermas and many others[1]). Although these various theorists did not use the term itself, the term 'Frankfurt School' arose informally to describe the thinkers affiliated or associated with the Frankfurt Institute for Social Research (*InstitutfürSozialforschung*), which was founded in 1923. They had in common concerns with how economic and social systems produced oppression, exploitation, repression, unfairness and asymmetrical power relations through hierarchical positions and asymmetry involving class, gender or ethnicity (Alvesson and Deetz, 2000).

Ironically, the creation of the Frankfurt Institute of Social Research was itself a critical act of the time, in that funding for the institute came from wealth generated by industrial practices of a multi-national grain/cereal family business which began in 1896 (Weil, Hermanos and Cia[2]). In the section that follows, a summary of the account of this family business in Adorno (2008) is given. The founder-owner of this company, entrepreneur-merchant Hermann Weil (born in 1868 in rural Steinsfurt, Germany), was highly critical of the exploitative practices of industrial capitalism. He regarded these as a 'source of justified indignation on the part of exploited workers' (Adorno, 2008, p. 81). As a result, it was his wish to aid scientific progress and it was the money from the family business that enabled the creation of the Institute for Social Research, which became the focal point of an independent intelligentsia known later as the critical theorists.

The account goes on to report that Herman Weil was the tenth child of a German-Jewish family whose father had taken him out of school to become an apprentice in the grain trade with the Mannheim firm 'Isitor Weismann and Co'. As a result of his lost schooling, Herman Weil had an unsatisfied hunger for education and a need for recognition. Herman rose quickly through the company to become the youngest chief clerk in the grain trade in Germany. At that time Mannheim, having inland port facilities, was an important centre for the European grain trade and its grain exchange mediated deals between the great European cereal-growing areas and overseas markets. In addition to his thirst for knowledge and recognition, he also wanted to seek a fortune on his own. He studied Spanish, worked for Danone in Antwerp and opened the Argentine branch of Danone (of which he negotiated a share of 20%). He saw Argentina as the grain-exporting country of the future. He left Danone and, together with his older brothers, established Weil Hermanos and Cia in 1896, which became a transnational business for growing and exporting grain.

In the same year that the business was created, Adorno (2008) reports that Herman and his wife, Rosa, had a son Felix (1896–1975). Felix initially lived in Argentina with his parents, but his father wanted him to have the benefits of a humanist education in Germany. Thus, at the age of 9, Felix was returned to Germany to study at the Goethe Gymnasium in Frankfurt. However, it was always Herman's intention for his son to join the family business, but after one year working in Argentina in the grain business, Felix demonstrated that he had limited talent for the wheat trade. Felix was more interested in revolutionary ideas and he

eventually became the financial founder of the Institute. In addition, Felix's father had a strong belief in scientific progress and believed that such phenomena as Russian Bolshevism, German Marxism, German social democracy, anti-Semitism, trade unionism and labour law should merit scientific study (as opposed to research by political parties). Collectively, these interests and motivations encouraged a social change initiative that not only produced institutional outcomes (in the form of the Frankfurt Institute for Social Research but also other centres/institutes that built upon these ideas in later years). In the actions and behaviours of this family business, therefore, we can see the motives and stirrings of a critical tradition – the (ethical and social) necessity 'to critique, and challenge the basis, of contemporary forms of alienation and oppression' (Willmott, 2008, p. 66). In addition, it stimulated an intellectual movement of ideas that had in common the following interests (adapted from Alvesson and Deetz, 2000, p. 84):

1 The reproduction/challenging/reformulation of beliefs, consent and identity.
2 The naturalisation of social order, or the way a socially/historically constructed world would be treated as necessary, natural, rational and self-evident.
3 The universalisation of managerial interests and the suppression of conflicting interests.
4 The domination by instrumental, and eclipse of competitive, reasoning processes.
5 Hegemony, the way consent becomes orchestrated.

To help explain these themes, Willmott (2008) identifies four points of critique that characterise CT: the critique of positivist science; the critique of technocracy; a critique of one-dimensionality and consumerism; and an emphasis on communicative action. These critiques are now briefly reviewed to explain the dominant themes of CT.

The first critique, which has shaped critical theory, is the 'critique of positivist science'. Willmott (2008) refers to Horkheimer and Adorno (2002) to review an argument about the way in which 'modern civilisation has become ... mesmerised by a one-sided means-ends (instrumental) conception of reason ... whereby science becomes an ideology that operates as a force for domination' (Willmott, 2008, p. 67). Furthermore, in a quest for quantification, measurement and impartiality, the rational pursuit of factual truth means that questions of meaning or value are stripped away in order to codify facts or data about phenomena into tidy units which can be verified (Clegg, 2008). The purpose of stripping out subjective meaning or personal values, from a positivist point of view, is that factual truths or sense data can be revealed which can then be scientifically verified through the application of repeatable methods. However, once we lose sight of how scientific knowledge is connected to an interest in emancipation from asymmetrical power relations, Willmott (2008) argues that 'science becomes an ideology that operates as a force of domination' (p. 67).

The second critique is a 'critique of technocracy', which is characterised by its denial of the role of moral-practical concerns in processes of social development and the presumption that the ends of human existence are self-evident (Willmott, 2008, p. 67). He argues that the formation of managerial elites that are not accountable to subordinates is an example of technocracy at work where non-experts are disenfranchised and technocratic systems are developed to strengthen such purposive-rational action (p. 67). Alvesson and Deetz (2000) also refer to this problem by making reference to the dominance of 'elite' or 'a priori' research practices. This signals the tendency of some research programs 'to privilege the particular language system of the researcher and the expertise of the research community' (p. 28). As these authors go on to say, 'in most cases these research approaches follow an Enlightenment hope for producing rational knowledge not constrained by traditions or the particular belief system of the researcher or the researched' (p. 29). Furthermore, 'the more functionalist (or normative) versions openly

proclaim "objectivity" and value neutrality based on the shared language game and research methods that tend to overlook the positions of their own community ... and the temporal conditions of production' (Alvesson and Deetz, 2000, pp. 28–29).

The third critique is a critique of 'one-dimensionality and consumerism' (Willmott, 2008, p. 68). This critique emerges from the work of Marcuse (1964) who highlights how the organisation of economic systems and societies has the potential to create forms of social repression and the blocking of revolutionary (or emancipatory) potential. It was Marcuse's argument that trends towards bureaucracy and efforts in advanced industrial societies to create new structures of stabilisation (through the media, advertising, management systems and contemporary discourses), have the effect of drawing in and integrating individuals into existing systems of production and consumption. In particular, it was his argument that such systems produce 'false needs' and deflect peoples' emancipatory impulses as they become passive, unreflective consumers.

The fourth critique according to Willmott (2008) that characterises critical theory emphasises the importance of communicative action (Habermas, 1984). Communicative action is based on the notion of communicative rationality, which in contrast to instrumental (goal-oriented) rationality, is concerned with encouraging greater democratisation and the reduction of barriers to participation in public discourses through the medium of language. In this, it acknowledges that the 'frustrations and sufferings [which] manifest as communicative distortions ... operate as recurrent and potent sources of motivation for emancipatory change, critical reflection and self-determination' (Willmott, 2008, p. 67). Through dialogue and argumentation, which encapsulates objective and subjective worlds (and their social interrelationship), space for self-reflection is created as well as the opportunity for exposing propositional truths, subjective experiences and interpretations. Thus, communicative action is a critique underlying

CT and becomes important for encouraging research efforts that help to 'clarify meanings through critical scrutiny in dialogue form' (Alvesson and Ashcraft, 2009, p. 64). This is seen as important as it is through dialogue and argumentation that a path for social action is enabled.

Having reviewed the core ideas underlying critical theory, it is appropriate at this juncture to turn to the second intellectual movement that has contributed to a critical tradition: postmodernism.

Postmodernist Thinking

As with critical theory, the ideas labelled 'postmodern' cannot be captured into a single perspective or discipline. It is impossible to do justice to the wealth of ideas and debates that explore this complex term and which reach into all forms of expression, whether artistic, literary or academic. Relating again to Alvesson and Deetz (2000) and Smircich and Calas (1987), I summarise their arguments about a postmodern discourse in an effort to honour the key points, but an effort which also risks a 'boiling down' of their rich and complex analyses.

In common with critical theory analyses, postmodernist ideas stem from a need to differentiate from modernist ideas, assumptions and ways of thinking. By 'modernist', in a management and organisation context, Alvesson and Deetz (2000):

> draw attention to the instrumentalisation of people and nature through the use of scientific-technical knowledge (modelled after positivism and other rational ways of developing safe, robust knowledge) to accomplish predictable results, measured by productivity, and technical problem solving leading to the 'good' of economic and social life, primarily defined by accumulation of wealth by production investors and consumption by consumers. (p. 13)

The movement of ideas labelled postmodernist are, therefore, an experimental and reactionary movement against the perceived excesses of modernism with its underpinning rational and reductionist logic of representation – a problem that was referred to earlier in relation to CT. As Chia (2000, p. 162) puts it, postmodern ways of thinking, 'aim to restore to the world that which modernity took away and give epistemological legitimacy to forms of knowing and being which are usually glossed over or taken for granted'. In this sense, we can highlight what Smircich and Calas (1987) refer to as a 'reactionary postmodernism', where these intellectual ideas were reacting to the overconfidence in positivist science's acceptance of the robustness of empirical data and a preoccupation with confirmation of empirical regularities and data.

As with CT, the underlying problematic in postmodernist thinking is a concern with research processes and theories that attempt to 'order, dissect and represent fluid living experiences in order to make them ... more amenable to instrumental control and manipulation' (Chia, 2000, p. 162). Also, in line with CT, postmodern projects are concerned with 'non-enlightened voices [and] the human possibilities that are suppressed' (Alvesson and Deetz, 2000, p. 15). Unlike critical theory, however, the postmodern discourse is concerned with 'the end of the historical discourse of progress and emancipation and its endless deferral of social promise or social change – whereby more technology, more knowledge and more dialogue are seen as being somehow ... [able] to accomplish the promise ...' (p. 15). Furthermore, postmodern ideas challenge 'the human subject as a coherent entity with natural rights and potential autonomy'.

> In his place is 'the decentred, fragmented, gendered, classed subject' [and where] the grand narratives of theory and history are replaced by disjoined and fragmented local narratives, potentially articulated and sutured; [here also] ... metaphysics, with its philosophies of presence and essence, [loses] ... terrain to the celebration of multiple perspectives and a carnival of positions and structurings ..... [Here], resistance and alternative readings (rather than reform or revolution) become the primary political posture'. (Alvesson and Deetz, 2000, pp. 15–16)

Here also, we can speak of a more 'post-modernism of resistance' (Smircich and Calas, 1987).

The details of these complex philosophical ideas are not our main focus here, and, helpfully, Alvesson and Deetz (2000, pp. 95–96) draw out a set of common themes that characterise a postmodernist intellectual movement and are useful for our purpose:

1 The centrality of discourse – textuality – where the constitutive power of language is emphasised and 'natural' objects are viewed as discursively produced.
2 Fragmented identities – emphasising subjectivity as a process and the 'death' of the individual, autonomous, meaning-creating subject where the discursive production of the individual replaces the conventional 'essentialistic' understanding of people.
3 The critique of the philosophy of presence and representation where the indecidabilities of language takes precedence over language as a mirror of reality and a means for the transport of meaning.
4 The loss of foundations and the power of grand narratives where an emphasis on multiple voices and local politics is favoured over theoretical frameworks and large-scale political projects.
5 The power/knowledge connection where the impossibilities in separating power from knowledge are assumed and knowledge loses a sense of innocence and neutrality.
6 Hyper reality (simulcra) replace the 'real world' where simulations take precedence in contemporary social order.
7 Research aimed at resistance and indeterminacy, where irony and play are preferred to rationality, predictability and order.

Having reviewed some of the key ideas and premises of critical theory and postmodernism, I will shortly turn to the task of providing a synthesis of these ideas in order to provide a frame of reference and agenda for critical inquiry in family business research. Before this, a conclusion of the preceding discussion is provided to summarise what has been addressed in this analysis.

SUMMARY OF PRECEDING ANALYSIS

In this chapter the key priority has been to review the main ideas shaping a critical tradition so as to stimulate more critique-inspired analyses of family businesses. It was argued that, in spite of a rich theoretical landscape, there is a lack of critical reflection in family business inquiry and this, added to the legacy of a rationalist and modernist discourse, means that critical theories have been slow to influence family business research. In order to progress a dialogue about the need for critique-inspired analyses of family businesses, reference is made to Alvesson and Deetz's notion of a 'consensus' discourse (2000, pp. 23–24) to explain the dominance of certain assumptions and prevailing practices that inhibit critique. To illustrate this, the topic of leadership in family business settings is reviewed in order to highlight the absence of (and yet potential for a critical 'reading'). From this, some preliminary critical constituents of a critically inspired analysis are identified. These centre on problematising what is known/accepted, exposing what is taken for granted, searching for alternative meanings, drawing attention to context, issues of power, conflict and highlighting the struggles that occur in daily organisational life. In addition, critically inspired research is not concerned with affirming that there are stable and existent 'orders' in organisations that are discoverable through the research process. In contrast, the researcher focuses on organisational processes as they come into being with all the messiness, conflict and struggles that are involved in securing consent for decisions, actions and strategies. In addition, with reference to an account of research on gender aspects in family business research, it is argued that critique also has a political and ethical stance as the researcher becomes concerned with how deep social formations constrain human behaviours, and affect autonomy and decision-making.

In order to elucidate further the notion of critique, the third part of the chapter provided an overview of the roots of a critical tradition.

This was done by reviewing the two intellectual streams of thought associated with critical theory and postmodernism. To help with this task, I also made reference to the role of a nineteenth century family business whose global economic organisation, wealth-value creation and concern about the exploitative nature of industrial capitalism, produced an institutional response in the form of the Institute for Social Research. In the philanthropic actions of this family business, the motives and stirrings of a critical tradition are identified. These embrace CT's interest in the historical discourse of emancipation, progress and more enlightened processes of communicative action to alleviate discrimination, exploitation and alienation. They also incorporate postmodernist thinkers' opposition to essentialism/universalism and instead promote interests in the discursive production of social phenomena, acts of resistance, dissensus, local understandings and pluralities.

Having reviewed these two intellectual streams, the final section of this chapter draws out the synthesising themes and issues that characterise critical research in order to progress a critique-inspired agenda for research action in family business. After outlining the six main dimensions of critical inquiry, I demonstrate how critical themes can be applied to family business accounts by further reference to the illustrative account of family business philanthropy. From this analysis, it is illustrated how family business inquiry can potentially contribute to a critical social science.

MOVING FORWARD: CRITICAL RESEARCH TACTICS FOR PROGRESSING FAMILY BUSINESS INQUIRY AS A CRITICAL SOCIAL SCIENCE

Based on the previous analysis, some generic themes for progressing family business as a critical social science are outlined. These have been adapted from Alvesson and Deetz (2000) and Alvesson and Sköldberg (2000)

and they synthesise some of the interlinking features of CT and PM that have just been discussed. These features centre on CT and PM's common interest in the social, historical, political construction of knowledge, people and social relations (and how these are 'represented'). They also centre on their joint vocation in taking account of domination and asymmetrical power relations. In addition, both intellectual streams are concerned with the connection between knowledge and power, attention to local particularities and a challenging of the fixed 'being' state of individuals and efforts to capture/mirror such entities. All of these themes demonstrate consideration for the ethical and political aspects of knowledge creation.

A CRITICAL SOCIAL SCIENCE IN SIX MAIN DIMENSIONS

A critical social science can, therefore, be captured in six main dimensions (the first four are from Alvesson and Deetz, 2000, p. 8). To this I add a further two which are addressed more directly in Alvesson and Ashcraft (2009). The themes also connect to many of the points outlined earlier in this chapter. It should be noted that these are generic themes or questions that can be applied to evaluate most topics and issues in organisational and family business research related to human behaviour. This is because critique, as noted earlier, is concerned with how social formations, patterns, institutions and practices constrain human behaviours and produce asymmetrical relations of power that affect autonomy and consent. However, in the subsequent analysis they are discussed in the context of family firms.

1   Identifying and challenging the assumptions behind ordinary ways of perceiving, conceiving and acting.
2   Recognising the influence of history, culture and social positioning on beliefs and actions.
3   Imaging and exploring extraordinary alternatives, ones that may disrupt routines and established orders.

4 Being appropriately sceptical about any knowledge or solution that claims to be the only truth or alternative.
5 Consideration for the ethical and political aspects of knowledge creation.
6 Giving attention to local particularities and the social production of acts of resistance or forms of consent.

Implications for Family Business Research

To give an illustration of how these generic dimensions relate to family business, I refer once again to the initiative to create the Institute for Social Research by the Weil family. It was noted above how the initiative was evidence of an unease or discomfort with the effects of industrial capitalism and a desire to challenge its accepted outcomes by supporting the academic scrutiny of alternative progressive ideas. In this, illustrating points 1 and 3 above, there was therefore a political agenda to produce dissensus in the established norms, routines, structures and systems which perpetuated dominant interests and which kept people from genuinely understanding, expressing themselves or acting upon their own interests (Mumby, 1988; Alvesson and Willmott, 1992, 1996).

Critically inspired family business research, whether the focus is on governance, strategy, succession or internationalisation should, therefore, endeavour to 'defamiliarise' the family business unit and problematise what appears to be self-evident, natural and unavoidable into something that is strange and unfamiliar (Alvesson and Deetz, 2000). This enables research attention to be drawn to alternative viewpoints or perspectives and routines/practices that do not affirm what is known about family firms but which focus on efforts to circumvent, disrupt or destabilise. In so doing, this does not mean taking an 'anti' family business stance. Nor does it mean being atheoretical. The trick with critical social science research, Alvesson and Deetz (2000, p. 9) claim, is to 'create a balance between a basic critical

orientation, being informed with theoretical ideas and a political agenda – and an open, empirically sensitive interest in discovering themes of repression'.

When developing critique, it is also important, as noted in the second dimension above, to take account of the historical context within which the researched phenomena is situated. For example, turning back to the example of the Frankfurt Institute, supporting the emergence of an intellectual movement which was concerned with challenging the very practices and structures of industrial capitalism that had enabled the Weil family business to become successful, seems a counter-intuitive exercise on their part. Placing the creation of the Institute, however, in an historical context with other acts of benevolent acts helps to explain the philanthropic behaviour. To demonstrate this critical point in relation to the Weil family business, it is noted how, along with many other nineteenth-century industrialists, Weil senior was reportedly critical of what he saw as the exploitative practices of industrial capitalism. In many ways, such feelings of social responsibility were not unique to the period and family capitalism spurred many philanthropic or social/community initiatives that had a concern for the welfare and moral education of their workers. In contrast to the militarist nature of early factory life, many prominent industrialists were keen to develop a cooperative attitude among the workers (Wilson, 1995). The emergence of the Cooperative Society in the UK (around 1858) was initiated by industrialists who had grouped together in the cause of temperance and reform to provide better access to quality food for their workers (Leeman, 1963). Wilson (1995) comments how whole communities and infrastructures were built up for workers by family capitalism (such as housing, churches, schools, shops and recreational facilities). In many ways, therefore, the behaviours of the Weil family reflect the paternal capitalist discourses of the late nineteenth century. Such discourses were very prevalent and demonstrated in the 'roll-call of industrial giants of industrial revolution' who exhibited benevolent and philanthropic concern for the welfare of their workforce (Pollard, 1965, pp. 232–6).

A focus on critique, therefore, rather than merely demonstrating the stated philanthropy of family firms, would examine in a detailed way how family business practices and their owners are discursively produced/shaped by such social/economic/political discourses. We know, for example, that family firms sometimes actively resist participation in the symbolically potent space of public finance and capital markets (Jones, 2005, p. 276), but we do not fully understand what ideologies, discourses and reasonings contribute to this and how such behaviours produce consequences for the functioning of family organisations (see Fletcher, 2002). To address such contradictions and complexities would mean projecting outwards from the family firm to wider institutions, ideologies and discourses that contribute to the knowledge and inquiry of the 'family firm'. Then the analysis would demonstrate how the broader cultural, economic or political context (in terms of particular cultural patterns, historical processes or institutional practices) are both shaping (and being shaped by) family business activities.

More specifically for the Weil account, a critical orientation might also examine how industrial paternalism was merely another means by which employers were able to nurture particular values into their workers (Wilson, 1995), thus diverting social responsibility (and with it power) away from the home and family into corporate structures. A critical commentary would also question the taken for grantedness of how, over a period of time, such a family business account becomes reported and formalised into an historical memoir and where the conflict, tensions and obligations central to family business organisation are glossed over to produce a sanitised account of 'what was'. Such a critical commentary might also question the absence of other voices (in particular women) in the account in the centrality of

the father–son dyad. In so doing, analysis would, relating to point 4 above, become sceptical about any knowledge claims that purport to be the only truth and to take account of the ethical and political aspects of knowledge creation (point 5). Furthermore, the research process, as discussed earlier, would view organisational activities such as governance, innovation or marketing as shifting, multivoiced and continuously shaped by various struggles and conflict.

Illustrating point 6, critique is also concerned with analysing the local particularities, and more importantly, the social construction of various acts and behaviours that demonstrate relations of power. At the level of the father–son dyad, for example, it is reported how the son, Felix, was able to break away from the family business obligations and what was, for him, a restrictive and unfulfilling occupation. The father's (apparent) acceptance of this is also acknowledged perhaps related to the orchestrating of his own consent to fulfil the occupational obligations to his father which meant a shortening of his own education. Equally for Herman Senior, we can see how the social structures of the time meant that he had little freedom other than to become an apprentice in his father's business, which influenced his developing identity. However, although we are encouraged to 'read' from the above account the father's willing acceptance of the son's inaptitude for business and wish to work in the scholarly/academic realm, a critical analysis would note that such issues of hereditary management, succession and the need to (presumably) find alternative non-family members to take over the business, are complicated processes involving emotions, conflict, tensions, values, expectations, duty and obligations. Ainsworth and Cox (2003) make a similar point where with reference to two case studies in which they examine how the dynamics of control, compliance and resistance demonstrate how the notion of 'family' has symbolic, material and ideological significance. Central to the more observable issues in family firms, therefore, there are also (less observable) issues of repression, unfairness and asymmetrical power relations that are generated through family hierarchies, relationships and values. The task of critical research then, is not to merely describe and explain but to engender social change by challenging these asymmetries.

The various dimensions of critical research suggest that interpretive research techniques are best suited to doing critical research. Interpretivist philosophies such as pragmatism, phenomenology, hermeneutics, symbolic interactionism and ethnomethodology, followed by social constructionism and post-structuralism, are research traditions that are concerned with the scientific inquiry of the human/social world. As is explained in more detail in Chapter 29 of this book (Reay and Zhang, 2014), interpretive philosophies stress that human behaviour/interpretations/social processes and interactions have a significant scientific role to play in the construction of social reality. Instead of stripping out the subjective, the value laden, the ethical, the negotiated and the taken for granted, interpretive inquiry privileges the interpretation processes that are central to meaning-making, sense-making, interactivity, reflexivity, storying, language, discourse, narration and social reality construction processes. This contrasts with positivist thinking as was mentioned earlier in the context of critical theory, which advocates the need to strip away questions of meaning and value in order to codify facts or data about phenomena into tidy units which can be verified (Clegg, 2008). Interpretive research techniques are best suited, therefore, for understanding themes of repression or relations of asymmetry and for producing socially oriented and context-sensitive scientific methodologies for examining the human/social world.

Finally, to close this chapter, it is argued that the six dimensions outlined are not only helpful for guiding us into critique but also, with such questions in mind, we can begin to examine how family business activities constitute more than a site or context for social science research. To sharpen our engagement with these kinds of critical questions, Alvesson and Deetz (2000) and Alvesson and Aschcraft (2009) encourage us to think about these processes not only in terms of *insight and critique* but also in terms of *transformative redefinition*. The first of these, as has been discussed, addresses how, through interpretation, it is possible to become aware of the less-explicit aspects of social life. The second addresses how the problematic nature of these dimensions and how issues of domination and repression contribute to the freezing of social reality in a certain 'ideological and institutionalised order' (Alvesson and Deetz, 2000, p. 21). Third, transformative redefinition is concerned with the signalling of 'alternative ways of thinking, relating and acting within and against this order' (p. 21).

With critical theories in hand, we have the potential to argue that family businesses have an important role to play in advancing a critical social science. They also help us to examine and understand the ideologies, discourses and reasonings about the world that produce perceptions of family firms as 'anachronistic oddities' (to use a term adopted by Nicholson, 2003, p. 1). Ensuring that these critiques are central to our dialogue and discourses around family business is essential for the continued growth of the field.

NOTES

1 *Theodor W. Adorno, One Last Genius*, by Detlev Claussen, translated by Rodney Livingston, Harvard University Press, 2008. Originally published as *Theodor W. Adorno: Einletztes Genie*, Frankfurt am Main: S. Fischer VerlagGmbh, 2003.

2 From *Theodor W. Adorno, One Last Genius*, by Detlev Claussen, translated by Rodney Livingston, Harvard University Press, 2008. Originally published as *Theodor W. Adorno: Einletztes Genie*, Frankfurt am Main: S. Fischer VerlagGmbh, 2003.

REFERENCES

Acker, S. (1992) 'Gendering organizational theory', in A.J. Mills and P. Tancred (eds), *Gendering Organizational Analysis*, London: Sage (pp. 248–260).

Ainsworth, S. and Cox, J.W. (2003) 'Families divided: culture and control in small family business', *Organization Studies*, 24(9):1463–1485.

Aldrich, H. and Cliff, J. (2003) 'The pervasive effects of family on entrepreneurship: toward Sa family embeddedness approach', *Journal of Business Venturing*, 18(5):573–597.

Alvesson, M. and Ashcraft, K.L. (2009) 'Critical methodology in management and organization research', in D. Buchanan and A. Bryman (eds), *The Sage Handbook of Organizational Research Methods*, London: Sage.

Alvesson, M. and Billing, Y.D. (1997) *Understanding Gender and Organizations*, London: Sage.

Alvesson, M. and Deetz, S. (2000) *Doing Critical Management Research*, London: Sage.

Alvesson, M. and Sköldberg, K. (2000) *Reflexive Methodology: New Vistas for Qualitative Research*, London: Sage.

Alvesson, M. and Willmott, H. (1992) *Critical Management Studies*, London: Sage.

Alvesson, M. and Willmott, H. (1996) *Making Sense of Management: A Critical Introduction*, London: Sage.

Baines, S. and Wheelock, J. (2000) 'Work and employment in small businesses: perpetuating and challenging gender traditions', *Gender Work and Organization*, 5(1):45–55.

Baines, S., Wheelock, J. and Oughton, E. (2002) 'A household approach to the small business family', in D. Fletcher, *Understanding the Small Family Business*, London: Routledge (pp.168–179).

Barrett, M. and Moores, K. (2009) 'Spotlights and shadows: preliminary findings about the experiences of women in family business leadership', *Journal of Management and Organization*, 15(3):363–377.

Bjorkhaug, H. and Blekesaune, A. (2008) 'Gender and work in Norwegian farm businesses', *SociologicaRuralis*, 48(2):152–165.

Bruni, A., Gherardi, S. and Poggio, B. (2008) 'Gender and entrepreneurship: an ethnographic approach', *Gender, Work & Organization*, 15(6):672–674.

Buchanan, D. and Bryman, A. (2007) 'Contextualising methods choice in organizational research', *Organizational Research Methods*, 10(3):483–501.

Burrell, G. and Morgan, G. (1979) *Sociological Paradigms and Organisational Analysis*. Aldershot: Gower.

Calas, M.B. and Smircich, L. (2009) 'Feminist perspectives on gender in organizational research: what is and is yet to be', in D. Buchanan and A. Bryman (eds), *The Sage Handbook of Organizational Research Methods*, London: Sage.

Calder, G.H. (1961) 'The peculiar problems of a family business', *Business Horizons* 4(3):93–102.

Chia, R. (2008) 'Postmodernism', in R. Thorpe and Robin Holt (eds), *The Sage Dictionary of Qualitative Management Research*, London: Sage.

Chrisman, J.J., Chua, J.H. and Sharma, P. (1998) 'Important attributes of successors in family businesses: an exploratory study', *Family Business Review*, 11(1):19–34.

Chrisman, J.J., Cchua, J.H. and Steier, L.P. (2003) 'An introduction to theories of family business', *Journal of Business Venturing*, 18(4):441–8.

Clegg, S. (2008) 'Positivism and post-positivism', in R. Thorpe and Robin Holt (eds), *The Sage Dictionary of Qualitative Management Research*, London: Sage.

Dachler, H.P., Hosking, D.M. and Gergen, K.J. (1995) *Relational Alternatives to Individualisation: Management and Organisation*, Aldershot: Avebury.

Daily, C.M. and Dollinger, M.J. (1993) 'Alternative methodologies for identifying family versus nonfamily managed businesses, *Journal of Small Business Management,* April. 79–90.

Danes, S and Olson, P.D. (2003) 'Women's role involvement in family business, business tensions and business success', *Family Business Review*, 16(1):53–68.

Danes, S.M., Stafford, K. and Loy, J.T.C. (2007) 'Family business performance: the effects of gender and management', *Journal of Business Research*, 60(10):1058–1069.

Davis, J.H., Allen, M.R. and Hayes, H.D. (2010) Is Blood thicker than water? A study of stewardship perceptions in family business, *Entrepreneurship: Theory and Practice*, 34(6):1093–1116.

Donnelley, R.G. (1964) 'The family business', *Harvard Business Review*, 42(Mar-Apr):93–105.

Dumas, C. (1998) 'Women's pathways to participation and leadership in the family-owned firm, *Family Business Review*, 11(3):219–228.

Dyer, W. G. Jr. (1994) 'Toward a theory of entrepreneurial careers', *Entrepreneurship: Theory & Practice*, 19(2):7–21.

Fletcher, D.E. (2002) 'Family as a discursive resource for understanding the small family business', in D.E. Fletcher, *Understanding the Small Family Business*, London: Routledge.

Gillis-Donovan, J. and Moynihan-Bradt, C. (1990) 'The power of invisible women in the family business', *Family Business Review*, 3(2):153–167.

Habbershon, T.G. and Pistrui, J. (2002) 'Enterprising families domain: family-influenced ownership groups in pursuit of transgenerational wealth', *Family Business Review*, XV(3):223–237.

Habermas, J. (1984) *The Theory of Communicative Action, Vol. 1: Reason and the Rationalization of*

Society. Translated by T. McCarthy. Boston, MA: Beacon Press.

Hamilton, E. (2006) 'Whose story is it anyway? Narrative accounts of the role of women in founding and establishing family businesses', *International Small Business Journal*, 24(3):253–271.

Helin, J. (2011) 'Living moments in family meetings: a process study in the family business context', PhD Dissertation, Family Business Research Centre, Jonkoping Business School, Jonkoping, Sweden.

Horkheimer, M. (1972 [1937]) *Traditional and Critical Theory.* Selected Essays. Trans. Matthew J. O'Connell et al. New York: Herder and Herder.

Horkheimer, M. and Adorno, T. (2002) *Dialetic of enlightenment: philosophical fragments*, edited by Gunzelin Schmid Noerr, translated by Edmund Jephcott, CA: Stanford University Press.

Hosking, D.M. (1988) 'Organizing, leadership and skilful process', *Journal of Management Studies*, 25(2): 147–166.

Jones, A.M. (2005) 'The elementary structures of the family firm: an anthropological perspective', *Human Organization*, 64(3):276–285.

Kanter, R.M. (1977) *Work and Family in the United States: A Critical Review and Agenda for Research and Policy*, New York, Russell Sage Foundation.

Kaslow, F. W., & Kaslow, S. (1993). The family that works together: Special problems of family businesses, *in* S.Zedeck *(Ed.), Work, families, and organizations,* pp. 312–351. *San Francisco: Jossey-Bass.*

Katila, S. (2010) 'Negotiating moral orders in Chinese business families in Finland: constructing family, gender and ethnicity in a research situation', *Gender, Work & Organization*, 17(3):297–319.

Lee, Y.G., Rowe, B.R. and Hong, G.S. (2006) 'Third shift women in business-owning families', *Journal of Family and Economic Issues*, 27:72–91.

Leeman, F.W. (1963) *Cooperation in Nottingham*, Manchester: The Cooperative Press Ltd.

Loscocco, K.A. and Leicht, K.T. (1993) 'Gender, work-family linkages and economic success among small business owners', *Journal of Marriage and the Family*, 55(4):875–887.

Marcuse, H. (1964) *One-dimensional Man: Studies in the Ideology of Advanced Industrial Society*, Boston, MA: Beacon Press.

McCollom, M.E. (1992) 'Organizational stories in a family owned business', *Family Business Review*, V(1):3–23.

McCollom-Hampton, M. (2009) 'Women in family business leadership roles: daughters on the edge', *Family Business Review*, 22(4):366–369.

Melin, L. and Nordqvist, M. (2010) Entrepreneurial families and family firms, *Entrepreneurship and Regional Development*, 22(3–4):211–239.

Mulholland, K. (2003) *Class, Gender and the Family Business*, Basingstoke: Palgrave MacMillan.

Mumby, D. (1988) *Communication and Power in Organizations: Discourse, Ideology and Domination*, Norwood, NJ: Ablex.

Mumford, M.D., Friedrich, T.L., Caughron, J.L. and Antes, A. (2009) 'Leadership research traditions, developments and current directions', in D.A. Buchanan and A. Bryman, *The Sage Handbook of Organizational Research Methods*, London: Sage.

Nelton, S. (1998) 'The rise of women in family firms: a call for research now', *Family Business Review*, 11(3):215–218.

Nicholson, N. (2003) 'Understanding the family firm: a new framework for theory and research', London Business School Working papers, Spring, pp. 1–46.

Pearson, A.W. and Marler, L.E. (2010) A leadership perspective of reciprocal stewardship in family firms, *Entrepreneurship: Theory and Practice*, 34(6): 1117–1124.

Philbrick, C. and Fitzgerald, M. (2007) 'Women in business-owning families: a comparison of roles, responsibilities and predictors of family functionality', *Journal of Family and Economic Issues*, 28(4):618–634.

Pollard, S. (1965) *1990 Industry Management*, London: Edward Arnold.

Reay, T. and Zhang, Z. (2014) 'Qualitative methods in family business research', in L. Melin, M. Nordqvist and P. Sharma (eds), *The Sage Handbook of Family Business*, London: Sage.

Reed, M. (2009) 'Critical realism: philosophy, method or philosophy in search of a method?', in D. Buchanan and A. Bryman (eds), *The Sage Handbook of Organizational Research Methods*, London: Sage.

Riordan, D.A. and Riordan, M.P. (1993) 'Field theory: an alternative to systems theories in understanding the small family business', *Journal of Small Business Management*, April: 66–78.

Schulze, W.S., Lubatkin, M.H. and Dino, R.N. (2003) 'Toward a theory of agency and altruism in family firms', *Journal of Business Venturing*, 18(4):473–490.

Smircich, L. and Calas, M. (1987) 'Organizational culture: a critical assessment', in F. Jablin, L. Putnam, K. Roberts and L. Porter (eds), *Handbook of Organizational Communication*, Newbury Park, CA: Sage.

Sorenson, R.L. (2000) 'The contribution of leadership style and practices to family and business success', *Family Business Review*, 13(3):183–200.

Thomas, J. (1993) *Doing Critical Ethnography*, Newbury Park, CA: Sage.

Thomas, J. (2002a) 'Freeing the shackles of family business ownership', *Family Business Review*, 15(4):321–336.

Thomas, J. (2002b) 'The emergence of leaders in family business', in D.E. Fletcher, *Understanding the Small Family Business*, London: Routledge.

Uhl-Bien, M. (2006) 'Relational leadership theory: exploring the social processes of leadership and organizing', *The Leadership Quarterly*, 17(6): 654–676.

von Krogh, G., Nonaka, I. and Rechsteiner, L. (2012) 'Leadership in organizational knowledge creation: a review and framework', *Journal of Management Studies*, 49(1):240–277.

Ward, J.L. (1987) *Keeping the Family Business Health: How to Plan for Continuing Growth, Profitability and Family Leadership*, San Francisco, CA: Jossey-Bass.

Watson, T.J. (2010) 'Critical social science, pragmatism and the realities of HRM', *The International Journal of Human Resource Management*, 21(6): 915–931.

Willmott, H. (2008) 'Critical theory', in R. Thorpe and R. Holt (eds), *The Sage Dictionary of Qualitative Management Research*, London: Sage.

Wilson, J.F. (1995) *British Business History (1720–1994)*, Manchester: Manchester University Press.

Wood, M. (2005) 'The fallacy of misplaced leadership', *Journal of Management Studies*, 42(6): 1101–1121.

Zody, Z., Sprenkle, D., MacDermid, S. and Schrank, H. (2006) 'Boundaries and the functioning of family and business systems', *Journal of Family and Economic Issues*, 27:185–206.

Major Issues in Family Business Studies

9

Financial Performance of Family Firms

Raphael Amit and Belén Villalonga

INTRODUCTION

Family business is one of the fastest growing areas of research within management and related fields such as finance. The main reason for this growth is the increased realization among the academic community that most companies around the world are family controlled, that they are systematically different from other firms, and that those differences are manifested in the relative performance of both groups of firms. In other words, family businesses matter – very much, and to very many people.

Until recently, however, family business research was perceived as a niche topic affecting a small group of companies, published by a small group of researchers in an even smaller set of specialized outlets, and therefore of limited interest to the academic community at large. It wasn't until a few studies put family businesses in the broader business context by presenting rigorous empirical evidence about the prevalence and performance of family businesses relative to non-family

businesses that top academic journals opened their doors to family business research, giving it the visibility it deserves.

In this chapter we review the evolution of this research, from its antecedents to its current state. Based on our review, we identify what we see as the main drivers of variation in the cumulative evidence about family business financial performance. We then proceed to analyze the challenges associated with the measurement of performance in family businesses, and propose feasible ways to address some of those challenges.

HOW PREVALENT ARE FAMILY BUSINESSES?

Villalonga and Amit (2006) find that the empirical relation between family ownership, control, or management and firm performance is entirely contingent on the definition of family business used, not just in the magnitude of this relation but even in its sign, which switches from positive to negative if founder-led firms are excluded from the definition. Before discussing family business performance, it is therefore important to discuss the relative prevalence of family and non-family businesses in the economy under different definitions.

Many family business articles begin with the assertion – sometimes even a statistic – that most businesses around the world are family owned or controlled. Until recently, however, there was little empirical evidence to substantiate these assertions or numbers, for the simple reason that no corporate census or database keeps track of whether businesses are family-owned or not for a large and representative sample of companies.[1] Moreover, most businesses around the world are either privately held or owned indirectly through investment vehicles that are themselves privately held. Thus it is typically very difficult, when not impossible, to determine who the ultimate owners of a firm are – let alone whether those owners are family related. Shanker and Astrachan (1996) carefully survey the existing research on this question and reach the same conclusion.

The earliest reliable estimates of the prevalence of family businesses are those provided for Fortune 500 firms by Sheehan (1967) and Burch (1972), who respectively reported 30 per cent and 42 per cent of the largest publicly listed firms as family businesses, based on a definition of family business as one where an affluent individual or a family or group of families owns 4–5 per cent or more of the voting stock or has board representation. Burch also reported an additional 17 per cent in the 'possibly family-owned category'.

Several later studies have added to the body of evidence about the prevalence of family ownership or control among large US firms. In 1986, Shleifer and Vishny examined the identity of the largest shareholders in the 1980 Fortune 500 and found that 33 per cent of them were families represented on the boards of directors; an additional 22 per cent included other corporations or family holding companies not represented on the board – i.e.,

possibly family owned as well. McConaughy (1994) reports that 21 per cent of the companies on the Business Week 100 list had a direct descendant of the founding family as CEO, president or chairman. Jetha (1993) found that 37 per cent of the 1992 Fortune 500 firms had a descendant of the founding family as a key officer, director, or owner. Anderson and Reeb (2003) found that founders or their families were key officers, directors, or owners in one-third of the S&P 500 corporations during 1992 to 1999. Closer to Anderson and Reeb's estimate, in Villalonga and Amit (2006) we found that 37 per cent of the Fortune 500 firms between 1994 and 2000 had founders or their families as key officers, directors, or owners. We also found that these estimates are highly sensitive to the definition used; Table 9.1, which is based on the results in that paper, reports estimates of the prevalence of family businesses under nine alternative definitions. Under the most restrictive one, which incorporates the additional conditions that the family be the largest vote holder, have at least 20 per cent of the votes, have family officers *and* family directors, and be in the second or later generation, the percentage goes down to 7 per cent.

It is important to emphasize that Fortune 500 or S&P 500 firms are the largest firms in the USA and, as such, not a representative sample of companies around the world or even within the USA. In fact, they are not even a representative sample of US *publicly listed* firms. In Villalonga and Amit (2010) we assembled a random sample of public US firms and found that, using the same definition of a family business as Anderson and Reeb (2003) and Villalonga and Amit's (2006) primary definition, 55 per cent of the sample are family businesses. If non-founding families are also counted in, the percentage rises to 71 per cent. These findings confirm that, as can be expected, family businesses are significantly more prevalent among smaller firms, and suggest that these percentages would be even higher if the entire population of US firms – public and private – were considered.

Table 9.1   Effect of the definition of 'family firm' on the relative prevalence and value of family firms

Definition of family firm	Proportion of family firms in the sample	Regression-adjusted difference in Tobin's q between family and non-family firms	
1. One or more family members are officers, directors, or blockholders	37%	0.23	*
2. There is at least one family officer and one family director	26%	0.29	*
3. The family is the largest voteholder	20%	0.29	
4. The family is the largest shareholder	19%	0.32	*
5. One or more family members from the 2nd or later generation are officers, directors, or blockholders	19%	−0.13	
6. The family is the largest voteholder and has at least one family officer and one family director	14%	0.33	
7. The family is the largest shareholder and has at least 20% of the votes	12%	0.15	
8. One or more family members are directors or blockholders, but there are no family officers	8%	0.06	
9. The family is the largest voteholder, has at least 20% of the votes, one family officer and one family director, and is in 2nd or later generation	7%	−0.28	**

Note: This table is based on the results in Villalonga and Amit (2006) and reports, for different definitions of a family firm, the coefficient of a family firm dummy variable in multivariate OLS regressions of Tobin's q on that dummy and on several control variables. The family refers to the founder or a member of his/her family by either blood or marriage. Blockholders are owners of 5% or more of the firm's equity, either individually or as a group. Tobin's q is measured as the ratio of the firm's market value to total assets. For firms with non-tradable share classes, the non-tradable shares are valued at the same price as the publicly traded shares.

The control variables are: governance index (number of charter provisions that reduce shareholder rights); non-family blockholder ownership; proportion of non-family outside directors, market risk (beta); diversification; R&D/sales; CAPX/PPE; dividends/book value of equity; debt/market value of equity; log of assets; log of age; sales growth; and year and Fama-French industry dummies.

The sample comprises 2,808 firm-year observations from 508 Fortune 500 firms listed in US stock markets during 1994–2000.

Asterisks denote statistical significance at the 1% (***), 5% (**), or 10% (*) level, respectively.

Unfortunately, there is no equally reliable evidence about the prevalence of family businesses in such a population. Nevertheless, Shanker and Astrachan (1996) develop a careful methodology to come up with estimates of the impact of family businesses on the US economy based on the legal form of organization of business taxpayers. They conclude that, using a broad definition of family business which, similar to the one used most widely for public businesses, calls for family involvement in either ownership or management, 100 per cent of all sole proprietorships and about 60 per cent of all partnerships and private corporations can be deemed family businesses. Aggregating across all businesses in the economy, the resulting estimate is that 92 per cent of all US businesses can be considered family businesses. Astrachan and Shanker (2003) provide an updated figure of 89 per cent based on year 2000 data. The empirical evidence about the prevalence of family businesses around the world remains limited to public company data, with the exception of a few isolated countries like Denmark for which there is evidence from private companies as well (Bennedsen et al., 2007). La Porta et al. (1999) examine the ownership and control structures of the 20 largest publicly traded firms in each of the 27 richest economies, as well as ten smaller firms in some of these countries. To establish who controls the firms, they look at the identities of the ultimate owners of capital and voting rights. They find that 30 per cent are controlled by families or individuals. For the smaller firms and using a less restrictive definition of control (a 10 per cent threshold as opposed to 20 per cent), the fraction of family-controlled firms in their sample rises to 53 per cent. Claessens et al. (2000) examine 2,980 public corporations in nine East Asian countries and find that over two-thirds of the firms are controlled by families or individuals. Faccio and Lang (2002) analyze the ultimate ownership and control of 5,232 public corporations in 13 Western European countries and find that 44 per cent of the firms are family controlled, and 34 per cent are widely held. There have been many subsequent studies reporting on the prevalence of family businesses in individual countries, but these three remain the most comprehensive (even within individual countries, in the case of the latter two). In the introduction to this book, Sharma et al. (2014) review some of the possible explanations to the varying prevalence of family businesses around the world.

DO FAMILY BUSINESSES PERFORM BETTER OR WORSE THAN NON-FAMILY BUSINESSES?

Having empirically confirmed that family businesses matter (a great deal) in terms of their prevalence, a natural question arises about whether the distinction between family and non-family businesses matters for firm performance.

Theoretical Frameworks

From a theoretical standpoint, the answer to this question is not clear, even within a given theoretical framework or disciplinary approach. One such approach is provided by agency theory in financial economics. On the one hand, the classic agency theory of Berle and Means (1932) and Jensen and Meckling (1976) suggests that ownership concentration alleviates the conflicts of interest between owners and managers. In particular, higher managerial ownership should align the incentives of owners and managers, while ownership concentration in the hands of outside blockholders should increase owners' incentives to monitor managers. Either way, the prediction is that ownership concentration should lead to increased corporate performance. This prediction particularly applies to family owners, who often not just hold large stakes in their companies but also occupy top management positions in them. The family business literature, as reviewed elsewhere in this book, has also offered a number of arguments that would lead us to expect family businesses to perform better than non-family businesses.

On the other hand, several counterarguments to this point have been made, even within an agency-theoretic perspective. Demsetz (1983) argues that ownership concentration is the endogenous outcome of profit-maximizing decisions by current and potential shareholders, and should thus have no effect on firm value. Stulz (1988) argues that managers can become entrenched if their ownership is too high. Shleifer and Vishny (1997) argue that high degrees of ownership concentration in the hands of outside blockholders can create a new agency problem, between large (controlling) shareholders and small (minority) shareholders. Either way, ownership concentration facilitates the appropriation of what Grossman and Hart (1986) label 'private benefits of control' by managers or large shareholders, at the expense of minority shareholders, and can lead to reduced firm value. This argument once again applies particularly well to family shareholders, who unlike the ultimate owners behind a large institutional shareholder, are the ones who directly enjoy these benefits. Burkart et al. (2003) propose a theoretical model of family business that trades off these agency benefits and costs of family control.

In addition to using agency theory to explain performance differences between family and non-family firms, Chrisman et al. (2005) indicate that the resource-based view is another theoretical perspective that is useful in explaining these performance differences (see Sabine Rau's chapter in this book as well; Rau, 2014). Their central argument is that family involvement enables the firm to accumulate unique resources and capabilities that allow them to develop family-based competitive advantages. Family firms enjoy long-term relationships with external stakeholders and using these external relationships enhances the performance of family firms (Carney, 2005; Chrisman et al., 2009). In addition, Chrisman et al. (2008) suggest that family and non-family firms differ from each other with respect to strategic behaviors, such as strategic response to the threat of imitation or strategic flexibility, and such differences create variation in firm performance.

The chapters in Part II of this book review other theoretical perspectives in family business studies that are rooted on a variety of disciplines, including psychology, sociology, and anthropology. A review of these different streams of literature further supports the view that the relationship between family involvement and performance remains somewhat ambiguous from a theoretical standpoint.

Empirical Studies of Family Business Performance

Whether family businesses perform better or worse than non-family businesses is thus an empirical question, and one that remained unresolved when we began our research on this subject, which would ultimately be published as Villalonga and Amit (2006).

At the time, the empirical evidence about this question was scant and conflicting, even within a single country – the United States. Holderness and Sheehan (1988) had found that firms that were majority-owned by individuals or families had a lower Tobin's q (the ratio of a firm's market value to the replacement cost of its assets, which is often used as a size-adjusted measure of firm value). Morck et al. (1988) had found that the effect of having the founding family among the top two officers was contingent on the firm's age: the effect was positive for firms incorporated after 1950, but negative for older firms. The findings of Smith and Amoako-Adu (1999) and Pérez-González (2006, first draft 2001) that CEO successions by family members had a negative impact on performance were consistent with Morck et al.'s result. On the other hand, McConaughy et al. (1998) and Anderson and Reeb (2003) found that family businesses outperformed non-family businesses, especially when family members served as CEOs.

McConaughy et al. (1998), who define family businesses as family-managed businesses (those with a founding family member as CEO), also found significant differences between founder-managed and descendant-managed family businesses, although the sign of the differences they found was contingent on the methodology they used. When they analyzed separately the subsamples of founder-managed and descendant-managed family businesses using a matched-pairs univariate comparison to non-family businesses, they found that descendant-managed firms outperformed founder-managed firms in terms of market-to-book equity value, sales growth, and cash flow per employee. However, when they pooled together the two groups of family-managed businesses and compared them to non-family businesses in a multivariate regression framework, they found that founder-managed firms outperformed non-family managed businesses by a wider margin than descendant-managed businesses (which also outperformed non-family businesses, however).

Besides this direct evidence about our research question, several streams of literature provided related evidence.

First, there were many empirical studies about the relation between ownership and performance. Demsetz and Lehn (1985) had found a significant linear relation between ownership concentration and profitability but, more importantly, they also found that, in support of Demsetz's (1983) argument, the relation disappeared after controlling for the endogeneity of ownership concentration. Later, Morck et al. (1988) examined the association between managerial ownership and Tobin's q, and found a non-monotonic relation between the two: q increased with managerial ownership up to a certain point, beyond which it began to decline. This result is consistent with Stulz's (1988) argument that managerial entrenchment limits the incentive-alignment benefits of managerial ownership. McConnell and Servaes (1990) found similar results using a different regression specification (quadratic instead of piece-wise), as did many subsequent studies (for a review see Demsetz and Villalonga, 2001). However, none of those studies controlled for the endogeneity of ownership like Demsetz and Lehn (1985) had done. Himmelberg et al. (1999) and Demsetz and Villalonga (2001) did, replicating Demsetz and Lehn's (1985) original two-stage analysis on the measures of ownership and performance that were used in the later studies, and found that the relation (monotonic or not) between managerial ownership and Tobin's q also disappeared.

Second, several working papers had picked up on Morck et al.'s (1988) less-publicized finding that young firms managed by their founding families had a higher q, and confirmed that founder-CEO firms traded at a premium relative to all other firms: Palia and Ravid (2002), Adams et al. (2009), and Fahlenbrach (2009). The latter two studies also showed that the 'founder-CEO premium' was robust to endogeneity concerns.

Third, there was an ongoing debate about the performance of business groups around the world. Khanna and Palepu (2000) had found that group affiliation was associated with superior performance, whereas Bertrand et al. (2002), using the same Indian data, had found evidence of what Johnson et al. (2000) refer to as 'tunneling' – the transfer of assets and profits out of firms for the benefit of their controlling shareholders. Although the debate had originally been framed as a comparison between group-affiliated firms and stand-alone firms, or between diversified and focused firms (given the parallel debate about the conglomerate discount), the evidence provided by La Porta et al. (1999), Claessens et al. (2000), and Faccio and Lang (2002) that most firms around the world are controlled by large shareholders soon shifted attention to the ultimate ownership and control issues in business groups.

A fourth stream of empirical research that bridged the first and third thus emerged showing that the 'wedge' between cash-flow and control rights created by control-enhancing mechanisms such as pyramids and dual-class stock has a negative impact on firm performance: La Porta et al. (2002) first found this result in their global sample, as did Claessens et al. (2002) in East Asia, and Lins (2003) in 18 emerging markets. Morck et al. (2005) reviewed this literature and concluded that, in countries where a few families end up controlling considerable proportions of their countries' economies through these means, the resulting corporate governance problems can attain macroeconomic importance – affecting rates of innovation, economy-wide resource allocation, and economic growth.

A fifth stream of research that we considered relevant was the literature about dual-class stock. Although dual-class firms had a long history in the United States, a change in regulation in the mid-1980s triggered a flurry of dual-class recapitalizations and, with them, a flurry of academic research, mostly in the form of event studies. Most of these studies, such as Jarrell and Poulsen (1988), found a negative stock market reaction to announcements of such recapitalizations. Others like Partch (1987) found a positive reaction. More recently, some countries have experienced the opposite trend – dual-class unifications – and several studies provided evidence of a positive market reaction to those unifications: Amoako-Adu and Smith (2001) for Canada; Hauser and Lauterbach (2004) for Israel; and Pajuste (2005) for seven European countries. Other studies of dual-class stock had focused on the voting premium at which superior voting shares typically trade relative to the inferior voting shares in the same company. These included Levy (1982), Lease et al. (1983, 1984), and Zingales (1995) for the United States; Zingales (1994) for Italy; and Nenova (2003) for 18 countries.

In Villalonga and Amit (2006), we brought these five literature streams to bear on our research question, which we framed in terms of firm value: 'Are family businesses more or less valuable than non-family businesses?' The first two were directly related to our question. The third and fourth did not specifically focus on family businesses; however, La Porta et al. (1999), Claessens et al. (2000), and Faccio and Lang (2002) had shown that most controlling shareholders around the world were individuals and families (with much greater prevalence than the State, financial firms, or other owner types), which suggested that family businesses might have driven many of these results. Likewise, the fifth stream of research, about dual-class stock, had traditionally been studied in the context of insider holdings, not of family ownership. However, DeAngelo and DeAngelo (1985) and Nenova (2001) had looked into the identity of those insiders and shown that the primary beneficiaries of dual-class stock were in fact founding families: Nenova reported that this was the case for 79 per cent of the dual-class firms in her comprehensive international sample, and for 95 per cent of US dual-class firms. Their results implied that the separation of ownership and control enabled by dual-class stock was in fact a manifestation of the agency problem between large (family) shareholders and small (non-family) shareholders, rather than of the agency problem between owners and managers, as the dual-class literature had typically been framed.

To bridge these different streams of research and bring them to bear on our research question, we concluded it was important to distinguish among three elements in the definition of a family business: ownership, control (in excess of ownership),

and management. We used this approach to test our research question empirically using all non-financial firms that were in the Fortune 500 at any point between 1994 and 2000 as our sample. Consistent with several of the research results described above, we found that family ownership per se on average created value, and that family control in excess of ownership (achieved through mechanisms such as dual-class stock) destroyed value, although not enough to offset the positive effect of ownership. On the other hand, the performance effects of family management were large enough to overpower those of the other two elements, but their sign was entirely contingent on the CEO or chairman's generation: relative to non-family businesses, founder-led firms outperformed, while descendant-led firms underperformed. These results were robust to the inclusion of multiple control variables (including age, sales growth, and a number of financial characteristics and corporate governance measures), and remained significant after controlling for the endogeneity of family ownership, control, and management.

As a result of these effects, we found that the answer to the question 'are family businesses more or less valuable than non-family businesses?' was contingent on the definition of family firm used. We considered nine alternative definitions, as we did when we examined the question of family business prevalence. Table 9.1, which is based on the results in our 2006 article and cited earlier in this chapter, also shows the multivariate q results under the nine definitions. When family businesses were broadly defined, as in Anderson and Reeb (2003), to include all those firms in which the founder or a member of his or her family by either blood or marriage was an officer, director, or blockholder, we found that family businesses traded at a significant premium relative to non-family businesses. However, results changed significantly when we restricted our definition by requiring minimum thresholds for family control (e.g., 20 per cent of all shares or votes), that the family be the largest shareholder or voteholder, that there be family officers or directors, or that the firm be in second or later generation. Using our most restrictive definition, which incorporated all of those conditions, we found that family businesses traded at a significant discount relative to non-family businesses. As suggested above, the 'deal-breaker' – the factor that turned the premium into a discount – was whether or not founder-controlled firms were included in the sample.

Miller et al. (2007) replicated some of the analyses and findings of Villalonga and Amit (2006) on a broader cross-section of US firms (the Fortune 1000 and a random sample of 100 smaller public firms). Specifically, they found confirmation for Villalonga and Amit's finding that the estimated value of family businesses relative to non-family businesses is contingent on the definition used, and particularly on whether or not founder-controlled firms are included among family businesses.

While Miller et al. (2007) suggest that Villalonga and Amit (2006) did not distinguish between founder-led and descendant-led firms, we note that the distinction between founder-led and descendant-led firms is one of the main findings of Villalonga and Amit (2006), which is also articulated in the abstract, and is substantiated by five tables which depict rigorous empirical analyses. Miller et al. also highlight the concept of 'lone founder firms' as distinct from first-generation family firms (the difference being that in first-generation family firms there can be more than one member of the founder's generation; there are no subsequent generation members in either case). They find that, in their sample, only lone founder firms significantly outperform non-family firms. (Other) first-generation family firms also outperform, but not significantly so. It is unclear whether the lack of statistical significance of the latter result is driven by economic reasons or by the scarcity of first-generation firms once the 'lone founder' firms are excluded from the group. Therefore the reasons that make founder-led firms outperform and later-generation firms

under-perform also remain unclear: are they the benefits that founders bring with them (e.g., vision, dedication, entrepreneurial culture); the costs that later generations bring with them (e.g., regression to the mean in management skills, maturity of the business); or the higher coordination costs of having multiple family members involved in the business? Perhaps further research can help us untangle these different possibilities.

One caveat to the founder-led firm results in all of these studies is that the samples in these studies are always relatively large, publicly listed firms. Thus, there is an inherent survivor bias in that, for young, high-growth firms to have reached their large, public status while still under founder management or control, these firms must really be the very top performers among their peers. Given the natural attrition in family firms as they age and Pérez-González's (2006) and Villalonga and Amit's (2006) finding that family firms performance declines after the founder's generation, however, one could argue that the survivor bias might even be greater in second- and later generation firms, which would imply that the existing estimates of a founder premium are in fact conservative.

DRIVERS OF VARIATION IN THE CUMULATIVE EVIDENCE ABOUT FAMILY FIRM PERFORMANCE

After Anderson and Reeb (2003) and Villalonga and Amit (2006), the literature about family business has burgeoned, including a large number of studies that have provided further evidence about the performance of family businesses. Table 9.2 reports the main results of these studies.

The cumulative evidence suggests that family businesses significantly outperform their non-family-owned peers. However, as Table 9.2 suggests, there is significant variation in results across studies. Four factors appear to drive this variation: family business definition, geographic location, industry

Table 9.2 Summary of studies of family business performance

			Measure				Main Results						
Authors	Year	Journal	Family ownership	Family control	Family management	Succession	Effect of family ownership	Effect of family control	Effect of family management	Effect of management succession	Performance measure	Country sample	Time period
Adam et al.	2009	*Journal of Empirical Finance*			Founder CEO				Positive		Tobin's *q*, ROA	USA	1992–1999
Allouche et al.	2008	*Family Business Review*		Dummies for strong control (family ownership and management) or weak control (family ownership or management)			Positive		Positive		ROA, ROE, ROIC	Japan	1998 and 2003
Ali et al.	2007	*Journal of Accounting Economics*	Dummy for family firm				Positive				ROA	USA	1998–2002
Anderson et al.	2003	*Journal of Financial Economics*	Dummy for family firm		CEO-family	CEO-descendent	Positive (negative to the DV in the paper)		Negative (positive to the DV in the paper)	Negative (positive to the DV in the paper)	Corporate yield spread	USA	1993–1998
Anderson and Reeb	2003	*Journal of Finance*	Dummy for family firm and family ownership stake		Family CEO		Inverted U-shape		Positive		Tobin's *q* and ROA	USA	1992–1999
Anderson and Reeb	2003	*Journal of Law and Economics*	Dummy for family firm	Percentage of family ownership stake	Founder CEO	Descendent-CEO	Positive		Positive (marginal)	Negative (marginal)	Excess value, economic value added	USA	1993–1999

(Continued)

Table 9.2 (Continued)

Authors	Year	Journal	Measure				Main Results					Country sample	Time period
			Family ownership	Family control	Family management	Succession	Effect of family ownership	Effect of family control	Effect of family management	Effect of management succession	Performance measure		
Anderson and Reeb	2004	*Administrative Science Quarterly*	Dummy for family firm	Board representation			Negative	Negative (moderator)			Tobin's *q*	USA	1992–1999
Barontini and Caprio	2006	*European Financial Management*	Dummy for family firm	Dummy for family firm	Family CEO	Next generation CEO or non-executive		Positive	Positive	Depends on whether descendent assume CEO or non-executive director	Tobin's *q* and ROA	Continental West Europe	1999–2001
Basu et al.	2009	*Journal of Banking and Finance*	Family ownership stake				U-shape				Acquiring firm's CAR	USA	1993–2000
Ben-Amar and Andre	2006	*Journal of Business, Finance and Accounting*		Ultimate voting block held by a family	Family CEO			Positive	Positive		Acquiring firm's value: Abnormal return	Canada	1998–2002
Bennedson et al.	2007	*The Quarterly Journal of Economics*			Family CEO				Negative	Negative	ROA	Denmark	1994–2002
Berrone et al.	2010	*Administrative Science Quarterly*	Dummy for family firm		Family CEO		Positive		Insignificant		Environmental performance	USA	1998–2002
Bloom and Van Reenen	2007	*Quarterly Journal of Economics*	Dummy for family firm			CEO is chosen by primogeniture (the eldest male child)	Positive however insignificant			Negative	Management practice (z-score)	US, France, Germany and UK	2004–2005
Boubaker	2007	*Multinational Finance Journal*		Excess voting right				Negative			Tobin's *q*	France	2000
Bozec and Laurin	2008	*Journal of Business, Finance and Accounting*	Dummy for family firm	Cash-flow right/ voting right			Positive	Negative			Tobin's *q*, ROI, ROA, ROE	Canada	1999

			Measure			Main Results					
Authors	Year	Journal	Family ownership	Family control	Family management Succession	Effect of family ownership	Effect of family control	Effect of family management succession	Performance measure	Country sample	Time period
Chang et al.	2010	*British Journal of Management*		Board control/voting right > 20%/voting right – cash flow right			Negative		Innovation announcement-period abnormal return	Taiwan	1999–2005
Chen et al.	2010	*Journal of Financial Economics*	Dummy for family firm			Positive			ROA	USA	1996–2000
Ding and Pukthuanthong-Le	2009	*Journal of Enterprising Culture*	Family ownership stake	Percentage of non-family directors		Negative	Positive		IPO pricing	Taiwan	1997–2004
Driffield et al.	2007	*Economics of Transition*		Excess voting right			Positive		Tobin's *q*	Indonesia, Korea, Malaysia and Thailand	1994–1998
Dyer and Whetten	2006	*Entrepreneurship: Theory and Practice*	Dummy for family firm			Mixed			Corporate social performance	USA	1991–2000
Gomez-Mejia et al.	2007	*Administrative Science Quarterly*	Dummy for family firm			Positive/depends			Socioemotional wealth/risk	Spain	1944–1998
Guedri and Hollandts	2008	*Corporate Governance: An International Review*		Two family directors + 5% ownership			Insignificant		ROI and Tobin's *q*	France	2000–2006
Heaney and Holmen	2008	*Applied Financial Economics*		Excess voting right			Negative		Cost of under-diversification	Sweden	1988–1991
Hillier and McColgan	2009	*Journal of Business, Finance and Accounting*			Family CEO			Negative (family CEO turnover has positive effect)	Cumulative Abnormal Return	UK	1992–1998

(Continued)

Table 9.2 *(Continued)*

Authors	Year	Journal	Measure			Main Results			Performance measure	Country sample	Time period
			Family ownership	Family control	Family management Succession	Effect of family ownership	Effect of family control	Effect of family management succession			
Holmen and Nivorozhkin	2007	*Applied Financial Economics*	Dummy for family firm	Dual class of share		Positive (partial)	Negative		Tobin's q and ROA	Sweden	1985–2001
Jara-Bertin et al.	2008	*Corporate Governance*		Contestability of control among shareholders			Negative		Tobin's q	Europe	1996–2000
Jiraporn and DaDalt	2009	*Applied Economics Letters*	Dummy for family firm			Positive			Abnormal accruals (earning management)	USA	1992–1999
Klein et al.	2005	*Corporate Governance: An International Review*	Dummy for family firm			Mixed			Tobin's q	Canada	2002
Lee	2004	*SAM Advanced Management Journal*	Dummy for family firm			Mixed			Profitability, operation, and financial	USA	2002
Lin and Hu	2009	*Corporate Governance: An International Review*			Family CEO			Depends	Tobin's q, ROA	Taiwan	1991–2000
Luo and Chung	2005	*Administrative Science Quarterly*			Percentage of family members in inner circle			Positive	ROA	Taiwan	1973–1996
Martikainen et al.	2009	*The Quarterly Review of Economics and Finance*	Dummy for family firm						Productivity	USA	1992–1999

			Measure				Main Results						
Authors	Year	Journal	Family ownership	Family control	Family management	Succession	Effect of family ownership	Effect of family control	Effect of family management	Effect of succession	Performance measure	Country sample	Time period
Miller et al.	2007	*AoM Proceedings*	Dummy for family firm			Next generation ownership and CEO	Negative		Positive	Negative	Growth and shareholder return	USA	1996–2000
Miller et al.	2007	*Journal of Corporate Finance*	Dummy for family firm				Depend (lone founder FF or not)				Tobin's *q*	USA	1996–2000
Nelson	2003	*Strategic Management Journal*			Founder CEO				Positive		IPO premium	USA	1991
Oswald et al.	2009	*Journal of Small Business Management*	% of family-owner employees		Percentage of family-owner top management team members		Negative		Negative		Sales growth, revenue, capital structure	USA	1997
Perez-Gonzalez	2006	*The American Economic Review*				Next generation CEO				Negative	ROA, Tobin's *q*	USA	1994
Perrini et al.	2008	*Corporate Governance*	Dummy for family ownership				Insignificant				Tobin's *q*	Italy	2000–2003
Sciascia and Mazzola	2008	*Family Business review*	Percentage of family ownership		Percentage of family members among top managers		Insignificant		Negative quadratic		Survey measure of performance relative to competitors, based on 7 accounting items	Italy	2000

(Continued)

Table 9.2 (Continued)

Authors	Year	Journal	Measure				Main Results				Performance measure	Country sample	Time period
			Family ownership	Family control	Family management	Succession	Effect of family ownership	Effect of family control	Effect of family management	Effect of family management succession			
Sirmon et al.	2008	Entrepreneurship: Theory and Practice	Dummy for family ownership								Value added	France	
Sraer and Thesmar	2007	Journal of the European Economic Association	Dummy for family firm		Family CEO	Heir CEO	Positive		Positive	Positive	ROA, ROE, Tobin's q and dividend to profit	France	1994–2000
Villalonga and Amit	2006	Journal of Financial Economics	Dummy for family firm and family ownership stake	Control-enhancing mechanism and family excess vote-holding	Family CEO	Next generation chairman or CEO	Positive	Negative	Depends	Negative (for the second generation)	Tobin's q	USA	1994–2000
Villalonga and Amit	2009	The Review of Financial Studies		Family excess vote-holding	Founder CEO			Mixed	Positive		Tobin's q	USA	1994–2000
Viviani et al.	2008	Journal of Private Equity	Dummy for family firm				Insignificant				Buy-and-hold abnormal return	Italy	1995–2005
Wang	2006	Journal of Accounting Research	Dummy for family firm and family ownership stake		Family CEO	Descendent CEO	Negative	Negative		Negative	Earning quality (abnormal accruals)	USA	1994–2002
Zhao and Millet-Reyes	2007	Journal of International Financial Management and Accounting	Family ownership stake				Negative				Content of accounting information	France	1994–1998

affiliation, and intertemporal variation in economic conditions.

1 *Family business definition.* As Villalonga and Amit (2006) show, the answer to the question of whether family firms are better or worse performers than non-family firms is contingent on how family businesses are defined, and in particular how family ownership, control, and management enter the definition. Decomposing family firm definition in this way allows them to find a positive performance effect of family ownership per se, a negative effect of family control in excess of ownership, and an effect of family management that is entirely contingent on the family's generation (positive for founders, negative for subsequent generations). Table 9.2 shows whether and how different empirical studies of family business performance have incorporated these three elements into their operational definition of a family firm, and what the resulting impact has been on their findings about family firm performance.

2 *Geographic location.* As Table 9.2 shows, there is also geographical variation in these results. For instance, Barontini and Caprio (2006) followed our family ownership-control-management decomposition and found that, in Western Europe, the effects of family ownership and control are exactly as we found for the United States, as is the existence of a significant founder-CEO premium. However, they found no significant descendant-CEO discount. Maury (2006) found similar results for Europe, including a premium for family management, although they did not distinguish among generations. In Amit et al. (2010) we found a negative association between family firm's relative performance and the degree of institutional development of different regions within China.

3 *Industry affiliation.* Several studies have shown that there is significant variation across industries in the prevalence of family businesses (Anderson and Reeb, 2003; Villalonga and Amit, 2006; Miller et al., 2007). In Villalonga and Amit (2010), where we examine what drives family control of firms and industries, we further find that the value of family control – the value premium or discount of family firms relative to non-family firms – also varies significantly across industries.

4 *Intertemporal variation in economic conditions.* Villalonga (2010) examines whether and how the value of family control changes with economic conditions. Using a sample of US and European companies, she finds that the difference in value between family and non-family businesses changed significantly from before to after the 2007–2008 financial and economic crisis. The differences are attributable to differences in structural characteristics between the two groups of firms, rather than to differences in their response to the crisis. Consistent with the view that families 'manage for the long run' and strive to maintain control of their firms, family firms have more conservative financial and strategic management policies, which benefits both family and non-family shareholders during economic downturns. These findings suggest that the value of family control is countercyclical, making family businesses more stable and longer-lived than non-family businesses even if after the founder's generation their performance levels are lower. They also help understand the puzzle of how family firms can survive as publicly traded entities beyond the founder stage, given the evidence about later-generation firms' underperform, and the finding that families as controlling shareholders often appropriate private benefits of control.

CHALLENGES OF MEASURING PERFORMANCE IN FAMILY BUSINESSES

It is important to note that these and all other empirical studies of the performance of family firms rely exclusively on financial performance measures – i.e., accounting profitability or market value. Demsetz and Villalonga (2001) compare the adequacy of accounting profits and market value (or Tobin's q, which is the ratio of market to book value of assets) in the context of the relationship between corporate ownership and firm performance. As they note, there are two important respects in which these two measures differ. One is in time perspective, backward-looking for accounting profits and forward-looking for market-based performance measures. Whether one wants to look at an estimate of what management has accomplished or at an estimate of what management will accomplish is clearly a choice; thus, one cannot say that one approach is better than the other; they are just different. The second difference is in who is actually measuring performance. For the accounting profit rate, this is the accountant constrained by standards set by his profession. For market measures, this is primarily the community of investors constrained by their acumen, optimism, or pessimism. Again, it is not clear which of the two is preferable or more subject to behavioral biases.

Moreover, business families often think of performance in a broader sense, including both pecuniary and non-pecuniary benefits. For instance, Gómez-Mejía et al. (2007) use a catch-all construct *socio-emotional wealth* (SEW) as a label for all non-economical, non-financial performance objectives of family-controlled firms. Presumably these objectives may include such factors as the protection of the family brand, its heritage, its legacy, its reputation, and its political influence. Berrone et al. (2010) establish that family-controlled, publicly traded firms protect their SEW by having superior environmental performance relative to non-family firms. Gómez-Mejía et al. (2007) show that families are willing to take on more business risk in order to protect their SEW (see Berrone et al., 2012, for a review of their work on SEW). McKenny et al. (2012) propose the use of content analysis as a way to incorporate families' multidimensional performance objectives into empirical studies of private family firm performance. Likewise, Basco and Pérez-Rodríguez (2009) use a survey measure of family success that captures 13 different items, including time to be with the family, family loyalty and support, and the generation of possibilities for the children among others.

While we fully appreciate and acknowledge the complexity and multidimensionality of family business success, we argue that defining performance in such a broad way is a dangerous proposition, since almost any decision can be justified on those grounds. Moreover, non-pecuniary benefits are difficult, when not impossible, to measure. Nevertheless, it is important to keep these aspects

in mind to understand decision-making at family businesses.

To complicate matters further, it is often unclear for whom the family seeks to optimize performance, however defined: for the family itself, for all of the firm's shareholders, for all stakeholders, or for society at large? The longstanding debate about whether firm owners and managers should protect the interests of shareholders or a broader base of stakeholders takes on special relevance in the family business context, since of all shareholder types, founding families are arguably the most likely to take some of those other constituencies into account.

Even if we as researchers agree to focus on financial performance, its measurement raises special challenges in the context of family business. To begin with, most family firms are private. As a result, their financial accounts are rarely available to researchers. Even when they are, they are not subject to the same disclosure and auditing requirements as those of publicly listed firms and as a result are typically less reliable. Moreover, family business owners might want to prioritize asset growth over profitability and to do so in such a manner that minimizes taxes and increases value transferred across generations – for example, by reducing profits in a senior generation business to an entity owned by a subsequent generation – which begs the question of how to measure the value of a family's broad holdings and not of any particular asset. The unavailability of a stock price that is readily available to measure private firms' market value forces researchers to estimate it. Another implication of these firms' private status is that the value estimates from standard valuation methods like DCF and multiples need to be adjusted to account for the illiquidity or lack of marketability of the stock.

In addition, the value of a share depends on who holds it. For instance, a share is worth more in the hands of a controlling shareholder than in the hands of a minority shareholder, because control is valuable in itself. Hence a controlling interest in a firm is worth more on a per share basis than a minority interest. Another way to say this is that the value of a share depends on how many additional shares the holder – and other shareholders – own and control. For example, a share representing 1 per cent of a company is worth a lot more to a shareholder who has 49.5 per cent than to one who has 48 per cent (or 51 per cent, for that matter).

A share can also be worth more for a founding family than for a non-founding family, due to emotional considerations – which are only partly subsumed in the value of control. It is also worth more to a diversified shareholder than to an undiversified shareholder (as business families often are), because the latter are exposed to idiosyncratic risk in addition to systematic risk. In summary, the value of the family firm is unlikely to be allocated among different shareholders in proportion to their ownership stakes, and the net effect on value of each shareholder's characteristics needs to be estimated. Villalonga (2009) describes how standard valuation methods can be adjusted to address the different performance measurement challenges mentioned above, and proposes a general valuation framework that can be used to value family businesses.

Finally, the measurement of performance in family business studies is also challenging because of the econometric issues involved. There is a voluminous literature in financial economics, starting with Demsetz and Lehn (1985), that has looked into the relation between corporate ownership and performance. Challenging the Berle and Means' (1932) thesis that ownership concentration should lead to increased corporate performance and supporting Demsetz's (1983) theoretical arguments to the contrary, Demsetz and Lehn (1985) found that, after correcting for the endogeneity of corporate ownership, ownership structure has no significant effect on performance. Morck et al. (1988) argued that Demsetz and Lehn's failure to find such an effect was due to their use of a linear regression model, and they found a significant effect of managerial ownership on performance

when using a non-linear (piece-wise) specification, as did McConnell and Servaes (1990) using a quadratic specification. Many subsequent studies of the ownership-performance relation have found significant effects on performance using similar quadratic specifications. However, Demsetz and Villalonga (2001) analyze the ownership-performance literature in detail and find that those studies failed to control for endogeneity as Demsetz and Lehn (1985) had in their seminal study; they further show, empirically, that after such endogeneity is controlled for, even the non-linear effects go away.

This finding has important implications for the literature on family firm performance, which can be framed as a specific case of the broader corporate ownership-performance literature where the identity of those owners are the firm's founding families. Some studies of family business performance, like Sciascia and Mazzola (2008), have used quadratic specifications and found significant effects of family ownership, control, or management on firm performance. As Demsetz and Villalonga show, however, the use of non-linear specifications for measuring ownership effects on performance adds little to our understanding of these effects unless researchers can further show that those effects are robust to endogeneity and sample selection biases. Unfortunately, few of the studies shown in Table 9.2 do this. However, Villalonga and Amit (2006) do devote careful attention to controlling for the endogeneity of family ownership, control, and management, and find that, unlike the broader results about ownership and performance, their findings about family business performance are robust to such controls.

CONCLUSION

This chapter has reviewed what we know and do not know about the performance of family businesses. The cumulative evidence at this point suggests that there is wide variation in performance within family business, which is why, when comparing them to non-family businesses, different studies have found apparently conflicting results. Our review has highlighted several drivers of variation in the cumulative evidence about family firm performance: family business definition, geographic location, industry affiliation, and intertemporal variation in economic conditions. Several results appear to hold quite universally, namely, the superior performance of founder-led firms over later-generation family firms and non-family firms, and the negative impact of performance of family's control over their economic ownership. The impact of second- and later generation family management on performance, however, has been found to be dependent on the time and geographic context.

This chapter has also discussed the theoretical and empirical challenges associated with measuring family business performance. We have centered our review on quantitative, objective financial measures, which apply to both family and non-family businesses. However, because of the interplay between family dynamics, family brand, family legacy, and business issues in family businesses, especially in multi-generational and multi-branch family businesses, we believe that there is room for researchers to develop new, integrated, and holistic performance measures which capture, in an objective and quantifiable manner, both the behavioral issues as well as the economic/financial issues that affect the performance of family businesses. While it is a challenging task, since the context and issues of every family are very different, we believe that the development of such performance measures would enable families and researchers alike to benchmark family business performance in a manner that captures the family dynamics issues that are so important in the context of family business.

NOTE

1   Even recently assembled databases that include corporate ownership information, like Amadeus or Osiris, only provide a crude and often inaccurate approximation of who ultimately controls a given company. A few countries such as the Nordic countries in Europe do collect sufficient taxpayer information to establish whether or not any firm in those countries – public or private – is family-owned. Still, a significant amount of work is required from researchers to arrive at a reasonable classification to distinguish family businesses from non-family businesses (see, e.g., Bennedsen et al., 2007; Sjögren et al., 2011).

REFERENCES

Adams, R., Almeida, H., and Ferreira, D. (2009) 'Understanding the relationship between founder-CEOs and firm performance', *Journal of Empirical Finance*, 16(1): 136–150.

Ali, A., Chen, T-Y, and Radhakrishnan, R.(2007) 'Corporate disclosures by family firms', *Journal of Accounting and Economics*, 44(1–2): 238–286.

Allouche, J., Amann, B., Jaussaud, J., and Kurashina, T. (2008) 'The impact of family control on the performance and financial characteristics of family versus nonfamily businesses in Japan: A matched pair investigation', *Family Business Review*, 21(4): 315–330.

Amit, R., Ding, Y., Villalonga, B., and Zhang, H. (2010) 'The role of institutional development in the prevalence and value of family firms', Working Paper.

Amoako-Adu, B. and Smith, B.F. (2001) 'Dual class firms: Capitalization, ownership structure and recapitalization back into single class', *Journal of Banking & Finance*, 25(6): 1083.

Anderson, R.C. and Reeb, D.M. (2003) 'Founding-family ownership and firm performance: Evidence from the S&P 500', *The Journal of Finance*, LV III(3): 1301–1328.

Anderson, R.C. and Reeb, D.M. (2003) 'Founding-family ownership, corporate diversification, and firm leverage', *Journal of Law and Economics*, 46(2): 653–684.

Anderson, R.C. and Reeb, D.M. (2004) 'Board composition: Balancing family influence in S&P 500 Firms', *Administrative Science Quarterly*, 49(2): 209–237.

Anderson, R.C., Mansi S.A., and Reeb, D.M. (2003) 'Founding family ownership and the agency cost of debt', *Journal of Financial Economics*, 68(2): 263–285.

Astrachan, J.H. and Shanker, M.C. (2003) 'Family businesses' contribution to the U.S. economy: A closer look', *Family Business Review*, 16(3): 211.

Barontini, R. and Caprio, L. (2006) 'The effect of family control on firm value and performance: Evidence from continental Europe', *European Financial Management*, 12(5): 689–723.

Basco, R. and Pérez-Rodríguez, M.J. (2009) 'Studying the family enterprise holistically: Evidence for integrated family and business systems', *Family Business Review*, 22(1): 82–95.

Basu, N., Dimitrova, L. and Paeglis, I. (2009) 'Family control and dilution in mergers', *Journal of Banking and Finance*, 33(5): 829–841.

Ben-Amar, W., and André, P. (2006) 'Separation of ownership from control and acquiring firm performance: The case of family ownership in Canada', *Journal of Business Finance & Accounting*, 33(3–4): 517–543.

Bennedsen, M., Nielsen, K.M., Perez-Gonzalez, F., and Wolfenzon, D. (2007) 'Inside the family firm: The role of families in succession decisions and performance', *Quarterly Journal of Economics*, 122(2): 647–691.

Berle, A. and Means, G. (1932) *The Modern Corporation and Private Property*. New York: Harcornt, Brace & World.

Berrone, P., Cruz, C., and Gomez-Mejia, L.R. (2012) 'Socioemotional wealth in family firms: Theoretical dimensions, assessment approaches, and agenda for future research', *Family Business Review*, 25(3): 280–297.

Berrone, P., Cruz, C., Gomez-Mejia, L.R., and Larraza-Kintana, M. (2010) 'Socioemotional wealth and corporate responses to institutional pressures: Do family-controlled firms pollute less?', *Administrative Science Quarterly*, 55(1): 82–113.

Bertrand, M., Mehta, P., and Mullainathan, S. (2002) 'Ferreting out tunnelling: An application to Indian business groups', *Quarterly Journal of Economics*, 117: 1047–1073.

Bloom, N. and Van Reenen, J. (2007) 'Measuring and explaining management practices across firms and countries', *The Quarterly Journal of Economics*, 122(4): 1351–1408.

Boubaker, S. (2007) 'Ownership-control discrepancy and firm value: Evidence from France', *Multinational Finance Journal*, 11(3–4): 211–252.

Bozec, Y. and Laurin, C. (2008) 'Large shareholder entrenchment and performance: Empirical evidence from Canada', *Journal of Business Finance and Accounting*, 35(1–2): 25–49.

Burkart, M., Panunzi, F., and Shleifer, A. (2003) 'Family firms', *The Journal of Finance*, 58(5): 2167–2201.

Burch, P. (1972) *The Managerial Revolution Reassessed*. Lexington, MA: D.C. Heath.

Carney, M. (2005) 'Corporate governance and competitive advantage in family-controlled firms', *Entrepreneurship: Theory & Practice*, 29: 249–265.

Chang, S.C., Wu, W.Y., and Wong Y.J. (2010) 'Family control and Stock Market reactions to innovation announcements', *British Journal of Management*, 21(1): 152–170.

Chen, S., Chen, X., Cheng, Q., and Shevlin, T. (2010) 'Are family firms more tax aggressive than non-family firms?', *Journal of Financial Economics*, 95(1): 41–61.

Chrisman, J.J., Chua, J.H., and Kellermanns, F. (2009) 'Priorities, resource stocks, and performance in family and nonfamily firms', *Entrepreneurship: Theory & Practice*, 33(3): 739–760.

Chrisman, J.J., Chua, J.H., and Sharma, P. (2005) 'Trends and directions in the development of a strategic management theory of the family firm', *Entrepreneurship: Theory & Practice*, 29(5): 555–575.

Chrisman, J.J., Steier, L.P., and Chua, J.H. (2008) 'Toward a theoretical basis for understanding the dynamics of strategic performance in family firms', *Entrepreneurship: Theory & Practice*, 32(6): 935–947.

Claessens, S., Djankov, S., and Lang, L.H.P. (2000) 'The separation of ownership and control in East Asian corporations', *Journal of Financial Economics*, 58(1–2): 81.

DeAngelo, H. and DeAngelo, L. (1985) 'Managerial ownership of voting rights: A study of public corporations with dual classes of common stock', *Journal of Financial Economics*, 14: 33–69.

Demsetz, H. (1983) 'The structure of ownership and the theory of the firm', *Journal of Law & Economics*, 26(2): 375–390.

Demsetz, H. and Lehn, K. (1985) 'The structure of corporate ownership: Causes and consequences', *The Journal of Political Economy*, 93(6): 1155.

Demsetz, H. and Villalonga, B. (2001) 'Ownership structure and corporate performance', *Journal of Corporate Finance*, 7(3): 209–233.

Ding, H.B. and Pukthuanthong-Le, K. (2009) 'Family firm IPO performance and market signals', *Journal of Enterprising Culture*, 17(1): 55–77.

Driffield, N., Mahambare, V., and Pal, S (2007) 'How does ownership structure affect capital structure and firm value? Recent Evidence from East Asia', *Economics of Transition*, 15(3): 535–573.

Dyer Jr, W. and Whetten, D. A. (2006) 'Family firms and social responsibility: Preliminary evidence from the S&P 500', *Entrepreneurship: Theory and Practice*, 30(6): 785–802.

Faccio, M. and Lang, L.H.P. (2002) 'The ultimate ownership of Western European corporations', *Journal of Financial Economics*, 65(3): 365.

Fahlenbrach, R. (2009) 'Founder-CEOs, investment decisions, and stock market performance', *Journal of Financial & Quantitative Analysis*, 44(2): 439–466.

Gómez-Mejía, L.R., Haynes, K.T., Núñez-Nickel, M., Jacobson, K.J.L., and Moyano-Fuentes, J. (2007) 'Socioemotional wealth and business risks in family-controlled firms: Evidence from Spanish olive oil mills', *Administrative Science Quarterly*, 52(1): 106–137.

Grossman, S.J. and Hart, O.D. (1986) 'The costs and benefits of ownership: A theory of vertical and lateral integration', *The Journal of Political Economy*, 94(4): 691–719.

Guedri, Z. and Hollandts, X. (2008) 'Beyond dichotomy: The curvilinear impact of employee ownership on firm performance', *Corporate Governance: An International Review*, 16(5): 460–474.

Hauser, S. and Lauterbach, B. (2004) 'The value of voting rights to majority shareholders: Evidence from dual-class stock unifications', *Review of Financial Studies*, 17(4): 1167–1184

Heaney, R. and Holmen, M. (2008) 'Family ownership and the cost of under-diversification', *Applied Financial Economics*, 18(21): 1721–1737.

Hillier, D. and McColgan, P. (2009) 'Firm performance and managerial succession in family managed firms', *Journal of Business Finance and Accounting*, 36(3–4): 461–484.

Himmelberg, P., Hubbard, R.G., and Palia, D. (1999) 'Understanding the determinants of managerial ownership and the link between ownership and performance', *Journal of Financial Economics*, 53: 353–384.

Holderness, C.G. and Sheehan, D.P. (1988) 'The role of majority shareholders in publicly-held corporations: An exploratory analysis', *Journal of Financial Economics*, 20(1–2): 317.

Holmen, M. and Nivorozhkin, E. (2007) 'The impact of family ownership and dual class shares on takeover risk', *Applied Financial Economics*, 17(10): 785–804.

Jara-Bertin, M., Lopez-Iturriaga, F., and Lopez-de-Foronda, A. (2008) 'The contest to the control in european family firms: How other shareholders affect firm value', *Corporate Governance: An International Review*, 16(3): 146–159.

Jarrell, G.A. and Poulsen, A.B. (1988) 'Dual-class recapitalization as antitakeover mechanisms', *Journal of Financial Economics*, 20: 129–152.

Jensen, M.C. and Meckling, W.H. (1976) 'Theory of the firm: Managerial behavior, agency costs and ownership structure', *Journal of Financial Economics*, 3(4): 305–360.

Jetha, H. (1993) 'The industrial Fortune 500 study', Unpublished Working Paper, Loyola University, Chicago.

Jiraporn, P. and DaDalt, P. (2009) 'Does founding family control affect earnings management?', *Applied Economics Letters*, 16(2): 113–119.

Johnson, S., La Porta, R., Lopez-de-Silanes, F., and Shleifer, A. (2000) 'Tunneling', *American Economic Review*, 90: 22–27.

Khanna, T. and Palepu, K. (2000) 'The future of business groups in emerging markets: Long-run evidence from Chile', *Academy of Management Journal*, 43(3): 268–285.

Klein, P., Shapiro, D., and Young, J. (2005) 'Corporate governance, family ownership and firm value: The canadian evidence', *Corporate Governance: an International Review*, 13(6): 769–784.

La Porta, R., Lopez-de-Silanes, F., and Shleifer, A. (1999) 'Corporate ownership around the world' *Journal of Finance*, 54(2): 471–517.

La Porta, R., Lopez-de-Silanes, F., Shleifer, A., and Vishny, R. (2002) 'Investor protection and corporate valuation', *The Journal of Finance*, 57(3): 1147.

Lease, R.C., McConnell, J.J., and Mikkelson, W.H. (1983) 'The market value of control in publicly-traded corporations', *Journal of Financial Economics*, 11(1–4): 439–471.

Lease, R.C., McConnell, J.J., and Mikkelson, W.H. (1984) 'The market value of differential voting rights in closely held corporations', *Journal of Business*, 57(4): 443–467.

Lee, J. (2004) 'The effects of family ownership and management on firm performance', *SAM Advanced Management Journal*, 69(4): 46–53.

Levy, H. (1982) 'Economic valuation of voting power of common stock', *Journal of Finance*, 38: 79–93.

Lin, S-H., and Hu, S-Y. (2007) 'A family member or professional management? The choice of a CEO and its impact on performance', *Corporate Governance: An International Review*, 15(6): 1348–1362.

Lins, K.V. (2003) 'Equity ownership and firm value in emerging markets', *Journal of Financial & Quantitative Analysis*, 38:159–184.

Luo, X. and Chung, C.N. (2005) 'Keeping It all in the family: The role of particularistic relationships in business group performance during institutional transition', *Administrative Science Quarterly*, 50(3): 404–439.

Martikainen, M., Nikkinen, J., and Vahamaa, S. (2009) 'Production functions and productivity of family firms: Evidence from the S&P 500', *The Quarterly Review of Economics and Finance*, 49(2): 295–307.

Maury, B. (2006) 'Family ownership and firm performance: Empirical evidence from Western European corporations', *Journal of Corporate Finance*, 12(2): 321–341.

McConaughy, D. (1994) 'Founding-family-controlled corporations: An agency-theoretic analysis of corporate ownership and its impact upon performance, operating efficiency and capital structure'. PhD Dissertation, University of Cincinnati.

McConaughy, D.L., Walker, M.C., Henderson, Jr., G.V., and Mishra, C.S. (1998) 'Founding family controlled firms: Efficiency and value', *Review of Financial Economics*, 7(1): 1.

McConnell, J.J. and Servaes, H. (1990) 'Additional evidence on equity ownership and corporate value', *Journal of Financial Economics*, 27(2): 595–612.

McKenny, A., Short, J., Zachary, M., and Payne, T. (2012) 'Assessing espoused goals in private family firms using content analysis', *Family Business Review*, 25(3): 298–317.

Miller, D., Le Breton-Miller, I., Lester, R.H., and Cannella, A.A. (2007) 'Are family firms really superior performers?', *Journal of Corporate Finance*, 13(5): 829–858.

Miller, D., Le Breton-Miller, I., and Lester, R.H. (2007) 'Divided loyalties: Governance, conduct and performance in family and entrepreneur businesses', *Academy of Management Proceedings*, 1: 1–6.

Morck, R., Shleifer, A., and Vishny, R. (1988) 'Management ownership and market valuation: An empirical analysis', *Journal of Financial Economics*, 20(1–2): 293–315.

Morck, R., Wolfenzon, D., and Yeung, B. (2005) 'Corporate governance, economic entrenchment and growth', *Journal of Economic Literature*, 43(3): 655–720.

Nelson, T. (2003) 'The persistence of the founder influence: Management, ownership, and performance effects at initial public offering', *Strategic Management Journal*, 24(8): 707–724.

Nenova, T. (2001) 'How to dominate a firm with valuable control: Regulation, security-voting structure, and ownership patterns of dual-class firms', Working Paper, Harvard University.

Nenova, T. (2003) 'The value of corporate voting rights and control: A cross-country analysis', *Journal of Financial Economics*, 68: 325–351.

Oswald, S., Muse, L., and Rutherford, M.W. (2009) 'The influence of large stake family control on performance: Is it agency or entrenchment?', *Journal of Small Business Management*, 47(1): 116–135.

Pajuste, A. (2005) 'Determinants and consequences of the unification of dual-class shares', *SSRN Working Paper Series*.

Palia, D. and Ravid, S.A. (2002) 'The role of founders in large companies: Entrenchment or valuable human capital?', Unpublished Working Paper, Rutgers University.

Partch, M.M. (1987) 'The creation of a class of limited voting common stock and shareholder wealth', *Journal of Financial Economics*, 18: 313–339.

Pérez-González, F. (2006) 'Inherited control and firm performance', *American Economic Review*, 96(5): 1559–1588.

Perrini, F., Rossi, G., and Rovetta, B. (2008) 'Does ownership structure affect performance? Evidence from the Italian market', *Corporate Governance: An International Review*, 16(4): 312–325.

Rau, S.B. (2014) 'Resource-based view of family firms', in L. Melin, M. Nordqvist, and P. Sharma (eds), *SAGE Handbook of Family Business*. London: Sage.

Sciascia, S. and Mazzola, P. (2008) 'Family involvement in ownership and management: Exploring nonlinear effects on performance', *Family Business Review*, 21(4): 331–345.

Shanker, M. and Astrachan, J. (1996) 'Myths and realities: Family businesses' contribution to the US economy – A framework for assessing family business statistics', *Family Business Review*, 9: 107–123.

Sharma, P., Melin, L., and Nordqvist, M. (2014) 'Introduction: Scope, evolution and future of family business', in L. Melin, M. Nordqvist, and P. Sharma (eds), *SAGE Handbook of Family Business*. London: Sage.

Sheehan, R. (1967) 'Proprietors in world of big business – There are more of them around than you think', *Fortune*, 75(7): 178.

Shleifer, A. and Vishny, R. (1986) 'Large shareholder and corporate control', *Journal of Political Economy*, 94: 461–488.

Shleifer, A. and Vishny, R. (1997) 'A survey of corporate governance', *The Journal of Finance*, 52(2): 737.

Sirmon, D., Arrgle, J. L., Hitt, M., and Webb, J. (2008) 'The role of family influence in firms' strategic responses to threat of imitation', *Entrepreneurship: Theory and Practice*, 32(6): 979–998.

Sjögren, H., Bjuggren, C.M., and Johansson, D. (2011) 'A note on employment and GDP in Swedish family-owned businesses: A descriptive analysis', *Family Business Review*, 24(4): 362–371.

Smith, B.F. and Amoako-Adu, B. (1999) 'Management succession and financial performance of family controlled firms', *Journal of Corporate Finance*, 5: 341–368.

Sraer, D. and Thesmar, D., (2007) 'Performance and behavior of family firms: Evidence from the french stock market', *Journal of the European Economic Association*, 5(4): 709–751.

Stulz, R. (1988) 'Managerial control of voting rights – Financing policies and the market for corporate control', *Journal of Financial Economics*, 20(1): 25–54.

Villalonga, B. (2009) 'Note on valuing control and liquidity in family and closely held firms', *Harvard Business School Cases*, February: 1–14.

Villalonga, B. (2010) 'Does the value of family control change with economic conditions? Evidence from 2007–2009', Working Paper, Harvard Business School.

Villalonga, B. and Amit, R. (2006) 'How do family ownership, control and management affect firm value?', *Journal of Financial Economics*, 80: 385–417.

Villalonga, B. and Amit, R. (2009) 'How are U.S. family firms controlled?', *Review of Financial Studies*, 22(8): 3047–3091.

Villalonga, B. and Amit, R. (2010) 'Family control of firms and industries', *Financial Management*, 39: 863–904.

Viviani, D., Giorgino, M., and Steri R. (2008) 'Private-Equity-Backed IPOs and Long-Run Market Performance Analysis of Italian Firms', *The Journal of Private Equity*, 11(3): 50–60.

Wang, D. (2006) 'Founding family ownership and earnings quality', *Journal of Accounting Research*, 44(3): 619–656.

Zhao, R. and Millet-Reyes, B. (2007) 'Ownership structure and accounting information content: Evidence from france', *Journal of International Financial Management and Accounting*, 18(3): 223–246.

Zingales, L. (1994) 'The value of the voting right: A study of the Milan stock exchange experience', *Review of Financial Studies*, 7(1): 125–148.

Zingales, L. (1995) 'What determines the value of corporate votes?', *Quarterly Journal of Economics*, 110(4): 1047–1073.

10

Family-controlled Firms and Stakeholder Management: A Socioemotional Wealth Preservation Perspective

Pascual Berrone, Cristina Cruz and
Luis R. Gomez-Mejia

INTRODUCTION

During the last decade, studying family firms and understanding the differences in their strategic decisions with respect to their non-family counterparts has nourished a relevant stream of research in the management field. Often relying on the important role family firms play in the global economy, both in terms of economic growth and employment (Oster, 1999) as the central motivational argument, this line of work has focused on strategic issues such as diversification (Anderson and Reeb, 2003; Gomez-Mejia et al., 2010), acquisitions (Miller et al., 2010), management compensation (Gomez-Mejia et al., 2003), board composition (Anderson and Reeb, 2004), innovation (Gomez-Mejia et al., 2011b) and environmental performance (Berrone et al., 2010), among other factors. Much of the research in this area has drawn from theoretical insights derived from agency theory (Morck and Yeung, 2003; Schulze et al., 2001), stewardship theory (Miller and Le Breton-Miller,

2006), or the resource-based view of the firm (Sirmon and Hitt, 2003).

Under the various rubrics listed above, family firms were assumed to be essentially homogenous and arguments were focused largely on how either the family's uniqueness or conflicts within the family affect internal decisions. As a result, investigation of how decisions in family firms affect external parties and stakeholders received relatively little attention. Indeed, in a review of stakeholder theory, Laplume et al. (2008: 1174) lamented that despite the fact that 'family firms offer a particularly interesting research context given the overlap between firm and family values ... [there is] a conspicuous absence of scholarship on stakeholder management of family firms'. This diagnosis was confirmed in the review of the family firm field by Gomez-Mejia et al. (2011a: 681), who noted that 'references to stakeholders in prior family work are rather indirect and often simplistic.' And despite the persuasive call made by Sharma (2004) in her review of the benefits of stakeholder theory in explaining the reality of family firms, with a few exceptions (e.g., Cennamo et al., in press; Mitchell et al., 2011; Zellweger and Nason, 2008), efforts in this direction have been rather tangential. This omission is notable considering that the assumption of profit maximization as the sole goal of the firm and the shareholder as the sole relevant actor, although widely used, has been challenged from theoretical (Harrison et al., 2010; Lan and Heracleous, 2010), empirical (Berrone et al., 2007), and practical stances (PricewaterhouseCoopers, 2011).

A wealth of studies suggests that some firms pursue a variety of objectives beyond the pursuit of profits and therefore act as a mediating hierarchy that balances and manages conflicting stakeholder interests. This raises the question of what happens when different owners have divergent motives for handling stakeholders' demands. In the particular case of family businesses, recent work has recognized that family firms are motivated by non-financial aspects and family owners are committed to the preservation of their socioemotional wealth (SEW) (see Gomez-Mejia et al., 2011a for a recent review). Yet we know very little about the impact of family-held firms' non-pecuniary objectives on the way they cope with external actors, what in this chapter we call stakeholder management (SM). Our aim in this chapter is to address that gap.

Consistent with prior literature and drawing on insights from institutional theory and stakeholder management approach, we develop the argument that family principals in general are guided by a strong drive to protect and enhance their socioemotional endowments (SEW). The notion of socioemotional wealth refers to the affective endowments that family owners consciously or unconsciously establish with the firm and impacts the way they make decisions (Gomez-Mejia et al., 2011a). Like non-family firms, we expect family firms to attend to the needs of those stakeholders believed to be economically beneficial. However, unlike non-family companies, needs from secondary or fringe stakeholders will be more salient to family

firms, even if responding to their needs is not economically attractive, since by doing so family owners obtain intangible benefits that enhance their SEW.

This chapter contributes to various streams of management literature. As Mitchell et al. (2011) recently stated: 'understanding how family firms prioritize the demands placed on them by various stakeholder groups has both theoretical and practical importance' (p. 236). First, by addressing the link between ownership and stakeholder management, we add to those studies which examine how the ability and motives of specific types of equity holders enable them to use their ownership position to pursue their particularistic agendas. We recognize non-financial objectives as an important influence in family-controlled firms and theorize about how stakeholder management may be affected by the strengths of these non-pecuniary objectives. We also enlarge institutional theory since the traditional institutional lens does not distinguish how different types of owners will address external normative forces.

Second, we contribute to the family business literature by suggesting that family-held firms differ in their approach to stakeholders and in their response to institutional pressures from non-family-held firms, since the family principals' SEW preservation objectives lead them to be more concerned about the needs of others, even if doing so is less appealing financially.

Finally, we contribute to the current literature by acknowledging that family firms do not operate in a vacuum and consequently, an analysis of their realities cannot be conducted in isolation from external elements.

CONCEPTUAL FRAMEWORKS

Traditionally, the family business field has been dominated by three well-established theoretical approaches: agency theory, stewardship theory and the resource-based view of the firm (see the chapters by Rau, 2014, and Shukla et al., 2014, in this book for a comprehensive review of these approaches). A common characteristic across these theoretical approaches is that they not only produce conflicting arguments fueled by mixed empirical evidence, but also that they focus almost exclusively on the internal issues that affect these firms' structure, process, and performance, with little or no attention to external elements, leading to incomplete and partial views about the firm's reality. However, social constraints outside the firm may influence the internal mechanisms used and these are particular to the institutional environment in which the firm finds itself.

This lack of consideration about how family firms deal with their external environment and their stakeholder networks leaves the field with a deep gap. This is worrisome since all these aspects are highly relevant in a context that is shifting from considering 'sustainability' merely as the idea of survival of individual firms to a more challenging concept that includes issues such as climate change, water stress, depletion of natural resources, pollution, shifting demographics, poverty, inequality, and so on. Many companies and scholars have condensed all these elements under a single heading called 'corporate social responsibility' or 'stakeholder management'. Regardless of the nomenclature, the scope and scale of these developments challenge market rules and create new success factors for the survival of individual companies. As a result, corporations are expected to develop new competencies for recognizing and addressing emerging threats and to leverage emerging opportunities to support society's quest for sustainability, even if doing so does not have a direct impact on financial performance.

Family businesses are not an exception to this trend. However, the traditional view that the family, as the family business's main stakeholder, is relatively insulated from the pressures that external stakeholders may exert on the firm has been challenged. As argued below, institutional theory and the stakeholder management approach are promising frameworks in this direction.

Institutional Theory

Institutional theory (DiMaggio and Powell, 1983; Meyer and Rowan, 1977; Scott, 1995, 2005) focuses its attention on the role of social stimuli in shaping an organization's actions. A central tenet of institutional theory is that when firms adopt strategies in adherence to institutional prescriptions, they reflect an alignment of corporate and societal values (Meyer and Rowan, 1977) and obtain external validation or legitimacy (Scott, 1995). In turn, legitimacy sustains organizational operativeness and survival (Aldrich and Fiol, 1994; DiMaggio and Powell, 1983; Oliver, 1991). Consequently, institutional theory supports the notion that concern over legitimacy influences firms by pushing them to adopt certain managerial practices that are expected to be socially valuable even if these practices do not yield an economic benefit. At the same time, it also implies that poor social performance risks social legitimacy and seriously hinders corporate prestige and image (Bansal and Clelland, 2004; Fombrun, 1996; Hart, 1995).

However, despite advancements in the field, we still don't have satisfactory answers about what type of firms are more prone to comply with institutional requirements, in spite of evidence that firms vary widely in this regard (Delmas and Toffel, 2008). This 'legitimacy seeking' perspective has overemphasized the blanket role of institutional forces but paid little attention to how organizational heterogeneity within the same institutional field may lead to unique and/or diverse responses. As Hoffman (2001: 138) notes, 'the form of the response from the organization is as much a reflection of the institutional pressures that emerge from outside the organization as it is the form of organizational structure and culture that exist inside the organization'. This suggests that if we consider organizations' unique aspects, we may be in a stronger position to predict and understand how they respond in a differential manner to institutional pressures.

In the context of family businesses, the few studies existing that deal with institutional theory are influenced by the dominant insider perspective of the family business. For instance, Nordqvist and Melin (2002) and Parada et al. (2010) used it as a framework for understanding how and why governance practices are introduced and changed in family businesses. In the same line, Reay (2009) examines how institutional pressures may influence family business identity over time and how they interact to shape responses to entrepreneurial opportunities. Despite the valuable contributions of these novel studies, it is still to be decided whether family firms are more responsive (or more sensitive) to external forces and if so, why this is the case.

Stakeholder Management

According to the stakeholder management approach, a firm's survival is a consequence of its capacity to establish and maintain a relationship with its network of stakeholders (Clarkson, 1995; Post et al., 2002). The principal owner or manager is responsible for supervising all stakeholders' claims and not just shareholders' welfare. These stakeholders are broadly defined as those affected directly or indirectly by the firm's actions (Freeman, 1984), including all those that suffer any form of pain as a result of such actions (Hart and Sharma, 2004).

The firm's stakeholder management approach is closely tied to the concept of social responsibility and entails the notion of corporate social responsibility. Firms that attend to the needs of consumers, employees, NGOs, government, the natural environment, and other societal groups are considered to perform in a socially responsible fashion. Companies can perform in terms of social responsibility by acts of commission or omission. In the former case, the company adopts a proactive stance to address a social concern (e.g., donations to eradicate hunger), while in the latter case, the firm is well regarded from a social standpoint if it avoids corporate wrongdoing (e.g., it does not pollute the environment).

While this approach is intellectually attractive, it is certainly challenging from a practical perspective as managers struggle to balance conflicting voices from different stakeholders. At the outset, one of the main barriers managers have to overcome is identifying who the firm's relevant stakeholders groups are (Sharma, 2001), also known as the 'identification problem'. Once identified, managers need to give priority to different stakeholder groups (and their claims) based on their degree of salience and importance (Mitchell et al., 1997). This is known as the 'prioritization' problem. More revealing is the fact that the notion that the stakeholder management approach leads to better financial performance, is dubious at best. From a theoretical standpoint, normative approaches to stakeholder theory (Donalson and Dunfee, 1994; Evan and Freeman, 1983; Philips, 1997; Rawls, 1971; Wicks et al., 1994), with strong emphasis on ethical and moral standards, argue that the interests of all legitimate stakeholders have an intrinsic value and no one interest should dominate over the interests of the other stakeholders. This implies that good stakeholder management is an end to itself regardless of the economic consequences for the firm.

Admittedly, instrumental approaches to stakeholder management (Berman et al., 1999; Donalson and Preston, 1995; Jones, 1995; Jones and Wicks, 1999) suggest that attending to different stakeholders is seen as a source of competitive advantage because when the firm meets the needs of a wide variety of stakeholders, it enjoys certain benefits – for instance, improvements in its reputation, increased trust in the communities in which they operate, access to superior resources, reduced exposure to liability, and enhanced social legitimacy, which are ultimately expected to contribute to the bottom line. However, even the most enthusiastic advocates of the instrumental approach recognize that the benefits of serving multiple constituencies are often intangible, distant, undefined and difficult to obtain (Harrison et al., 2010). The situation gets more complicated when one looks at the significant amount of research that has been devoted to understanding empirically whether or not social actions serve as a means to the end of corporate financial performance, which has yielded inconclusive results (Margolis and Walsh, 2003; Orlizky et al., 2003).

If the link between stakeholder management and firm performance is tenuous at best, one question that comes to mind is why do firms engage in social actions? More precisely, why do firms fulfill the needs of others when there is no clear reciprocity or direct economic exchange benefits provided by the stakeholders who are the recipients of the firm's actions?

In the context of family firms, attempts to answer this question were practically non-existent during the 1980s and 1990s when the popularity of the three overlapping circles model of family–business–ownership (Gersick et al., 1997; Tagiuri and Davis, 1992a) focused research efforts on understanding different goals and expectations of the various (internal) stakeholders of the system (Sharma, 2001). In line with this internal view of the family firm, two recent studies use stakeholder theory in the family business context. First, Zellweger and Nason (2008) explore how different (economic and non-economic) performance dimensions are interrelated in family firms and how these relationships impact organizational effectiveness through the satisfaction of multiple stakeholders. Mitchell et al. (2011) study the uniqueness of the concept of stakeholder salience in a family business context. Three main conclusions are shared by the two studies: (a) the importance of the family as a unique and distinct stakeholder; (b) the idea that the mix of economic and non-economic motives makes family firms naturally predisposed to satisfy the demands of multiple stakeholders; and (c) the fact that these two aspects make stakeholder management more complex for family owners. Unfortunately, the literature still lacks a satisfactory answer to the question of whether (and why) family firms are more inclined to attend to external stakeholders. The review showed that even though both

institutional theory and the stakeholder management approach are theoretically designed to address issues related to how firms interact with the external environment, when applied to the family business context, both approaches were biased towards analyzing internal issues and considered the family to be the main (and perhaps the only) salient stakeholder. However, there has recently been a shift toward a broader view of stakeholder management in family firms, one that accounts for the importance of institutions and external stakeholders, as evidenced from the increasing number of empirical studies devoted to this topic. These studies are reviewed in the next section.

DO FAMILY FIRMS CARE MORE ABOUT THEIR STAKEHOLDERS? – EMPIRICAL EVIDENCE

Although limited, some empirical research has examined stakeholder management and responses to institutional pressures in family firms. These studies are summarized in Table 10.1.

With almost no exceptions, family business studies support the notion that family firms have a natural tendency to be more predisposed to respond to stakeholder demands. For instance, regarding employee policies and practices, Stavrou and Swiercz (1998) report that family businesses tend to manifest a deep sense of personal responsibility towards their employees. Similarly, they are more likely to implement more 'care-oriented' contracts for external recruits (Cruz et al., 2010) and less likely to downsize (Block, 2010; Stavrou et al., 2007).

Evidence also suggests the family firms' greater concern to contribute to their communities' welfare. For example, family firms give significantly to philanthropic activities (Déniz-Déniz and Cabrera-Suarez, 2005) and often have charitable arms within their organizations (Danco and Ward, 1990). Dyer and Whetten (2006) reported that family firms pursue significantly fewer activities causing

Table 10.1   Summary of empirical evidence regarding stakeholder management in family firms

Authors	Variable of interest	Main findings
Covin (1994)	External stakeholders' perceptions	External stakeholders value the increased endeavor of family businesses toward social actions.
Stavrou and Swiercz (1998)	Employee policies and practices	Family businesses manifest a deep sense of personal responsibility towards their employees.
Déniz-Déniz and Cabrera-Suarez (2005)	Philanthropic activity	Family firms give significantly to philanthropic activities.
Dyer and Whetten (2006)	Corporate social responsibility	Family firms pursue significantly fewer activities causing concern regarding social responsibility and environmental management than non-family firms.
Chen et al. (2008)	Voluntary disclosure	Family firms on average provide less voluntary disclosure than non-family firms but they are more likely to give earnings warnings to preempt the negative publicity that may result from not issuing warnings.
Berrone et al. (2010)	Environmental performance	Family firms exhibit better environmental performance than non-family firms. This effect is greater when the firm has strong roots in the local stakeholder environment.
Bingham et al. (2010)	Social rating performance	Family firms exhibit a more relational orientation toward their stakeholders than non-family firms.
Block (2010)	Downsizing	Family businesses are less likely to downsize.
Chen et al. (2010)	Tax policy strategies	Family firms are less tax-aggressive than their non-family counterparts.
Cruz et al 2010	Executive compensation	more caring contracts to external recruits
Krappe et al. (2011)	External stakeholders' perceptions	Family businesses are valued for their long-term corporate philosophies and fair working conditions.
Martin et al. (2011)	Corporate social responsibility practices	Family firms are more likely than non-family firms to be confronted with more shareholder proposals that question the firm's social investments.

concern (i.e. negative activities) regarding social responsibility and environmental management than non-family firms. Similarly, a recent study by Bingham et al. (2010) demonstrates that family firms exhibit a more relational orientation toward their stakeholders than non-family firms, and thus engage in higher levels of CSP. Berrone et al. (2010), using panel data from 194 US firms operating in polluting industries, demonstrate that controlling families adopt environmentally friendly strategies more frequently than non-family firms. Moreover, they also show that this effect is greater when the firm has strong roots in the local stakeholder environment.

Martin et al. (2011) examined the extent to which dominant family principals in publicly held firms defend corporate social responsibility practices which may come into conflict with the desires of non-family shareholders. They treat shareholder proposals as indicative of disagreement between family principals and non-family shareholders and reported that family firms are more likely than non-family firms to be confronted with more shareholder proposals that question the firm's social investments and that the family generally chooses to take an antagonistic stance against those non-family shareholder proposals.

Consistent with family owners' concern for a better reputation and the avoidance of harm, Chen et al. (2008) found that although family firms on average provide less voluntary disclosure than non-family firms, they are more likely to give earnings warnings to preempt the negative publicity that may result from not issuing warnings. Similarly, Chen et al. (2010) demonstrated that family firms are less tax-aggressive than their non-family counterparts, *ceteris paribus,* suggesting that family owners are willing to forgo tax benefits in order to avoid the damage to their reputation resulting from tax avoidance activities.

Some studies performed both in the United States (Covin, 1994) and Europe (Krappe et al., 2011) show that overall, external stakeholders value the increased endeavor of family businesses toward social actions. In particular, Covin (1994) showed that people perceive family businesses to be more concerned about employee satisfaction than non-family firms. Interestingly, participants rated family businesses higher on commitment despite a perceived lower degree of formalization of processes and procedures. The study by Krappe et al. (2011) reported that family businesses are valued for their long-term corporate philosophies and fair working conditions. This positive self-perception of the family business leads the author to conclude that there exists a family brand effect in the sense that these organizations 'become a brand on their own' (p. 38). This family business brand effect seems to be corroborated by studies showing the preference of certain stakeholders for establishing relationships with family-owned businesses (Cooper et al., 2005; Orth and Green, 2009).

WHY DO FAMILY FIRMS CARE MORE ABOUT THEIR STAKEHOLDERS? – THEORETICAL EXPLANATIONS

The previous review represents an empirically contrasted body of knowledge that suggests that family firms, in general, have a natural tendency to be more predisposed to respond to stakeholder demands, at least when compared to non-family firms. Despite this, one position within the family business field advocates the idea that family firms may not be more socially responsible. The reason lies in 'amoral familism', a concept coined by Banfield (1958) which refers to the notion of family members' distrust of anyone who does not

have blood ties. Banfield studied this aspect in the context of Southern Italy during the 1950s and found that certain villages were severely affected by poverty, weak infrastructure and poor health conditions and blamed it on the lack of cooperation and trust between families. He found that families were overwhelmingly concerned with their own wellbeing and saw other families as potential enemies.

Using a similar argument, Fukuyama (1995) suggested that distrust of outsiders is the reason why family firms tend to be small, particularly in low-trust societies. He believed that family involvement – and its consequential lack of cooperation with strangers – is detrimental to the growth of firms. Fukuyama's argument was later empirically confirmed by LaPorta and his colleagues (1997), who showed that strong family ties are bad for the development of large firms.

Amoral familism may adopt different forms, from benevolent conceptions such as parental altruism (e.g., family-biased hiring decisions) to more harmful situations such as cronyism, inequality, and nepotism. Moreover, the notion of amoral familism is closely related with the idea that family firms are self-centric. Morck and Yeung (2004), for instance, suggested that the reason why they found that countries whose large firms are controlled by big mercantile families provide less public good, are poorer and less egalitarian is that influential family firms become 'political rent seekers' and engage in bribery and other corporate malfeasance practices to protect their interests at the expense of the broader society.

The idea that family firms may not be socially responsible can also be observed in the business press and the non-fictional literature. Perhaps the most celebrated work is the book by Matthew Josephson (1934), who used the pejorative term 'robber barons' to refer to powerful nineteenth-century United States businessmen and their families. He explained how leading industrialists and bankers belonged to families such as the Morgans, Schwabs, Rockefellers, or the Vanderbilts and used questionable business practices to become powerful and showed no appreciation for the general public. More recently, Walmart, perhaps the largest family-controlled firm in history, has come under intense fire for its employee practices, its relations with suppliers, and the company's impact on the natural environment. Anecdotally, the implication of the *Wall Street Journal* (acquired by Rupert Murdoch from the Bancroft family) in a phone-hacking scandal raised deep concerns about the integrity of families in businesses. In a similar vein, it is hard to forget that many of the financial scandals of the late 1990s and early 2000s occurred in publicly listed family-controlled firms, both in the United States and abroad. Together, these elements suggest that family firms might not have a sincere concern about different stakeholders. Rather, families may use their strong ownership position to build barriers that insulate them from the pressures that 'stranger' stakeholders might exert. However, the idea that family firms do not care about stakeholders seems to be an 'exception', as demonstrated by the overwhelming evidence reviewed in the previous section.

According to Miller et al. (in press): 'although all organizations must pursue some forms of legitimacy, there are particular contingencies that may make that quest more pressing and compelling … cases in which a family has an influential ownership stake and/or managerial role will fall into this category' (p. 8). Family firms are expected to be particularly concerned about legitimacy and reputational issues for several reasons. First, social punishments and reputational sanctions affect not only the company but also the family. If the company's image, which is the intentionally projected impression to outsiders, is condemned by the general public, it could be emotionally devastating for family members, who often work passionately for the admiration and glorification of the family's name and, in many cases, companies become 'family-branded' firms (Parmentier, 2011). Indeed, Dyer and Whetten (2006: 789) argued that most family firms would see 'negative press pertaining to a bitter labor

strike over health benefits, customers' complaints about faulty products, or legal suits following an ecological disaster, as indelible stains on themselves and as an extension on their company and their family name'. Thus, these firms have a special interest in being perceived as good corporate citizens, and they are rather cautious about the image they project to their customers, suppliers, and other stakeholders.

Related to the above, conforming to stakeholders' expectations may not *enhance* financial performance but it might be useful for *preserving* the organization's financial well-being. Even though good social performance may entail certain risks, taking part in social initiatives avoids being stigmatized as an irresponsible corporate citizen. A reputation for responsible behavior may serve as a form of social insurance, protecting the firm's assets in times of crisis (Godfrey, 2005), so that when damaging acts occur, stakeholders are more likely to give the firm the benefit of the doubt regarding intentionality. Reserves of 'goodwill' protect a firm's reputation in the marketplace, which may help sustain a more stable earnings stream (Fombrun, 1996; Roberts and Dowling, 2002). This mechanism of financial protection is particularly appealing to family firms, since family members tend to concentrate all of their capital in a single organization, so that the family's wealth largely depends on the long-term performance and survival of just one entity.

In addition, some scholars suggest that family businesses are characterized by altruism (Schulze et al., 2003a). This characteristic entails other-benefiting activities such as consideration of others' interests when important decisions are made, benevolence, non-reciprocal good deeds, and philanthropic giving in the community at large. At the family level, altruism is likely to not only affect relations between members within the firm (Cruz et al., 2010), but also to percolate outside the firm and affect relations with its stakeholders. Family leaders may behave as stewards committed to using their power for the good of the company and all those involved with it (Chua et al., 1999). As anecdotal evidence suggests, in many cases, family firms become deeply embedded in their communities and family members become active players. Employees are often friends and relatives who live in the same location where the business was originally founded. Relationships with vendors and suppliers are long-established and may involve family ties. Firms may sponsor community meetings and local teams. This suggests that family firms are likely to engage in social strategies believed to satisfy stakeholder demands, such as environmental conservation, and to avoid organizational actions that have an adverse impact on stakeholder groups, such as manufacturing operations involving noxious emissions (Berrone et al., 2010; Sharma and Sharma, 2011).

Lastly, attending to the societal demands of different constituencies requires a long-term vision and constant commitment to stakeholders (Aragon-Correa and Sharma, 2003; Hart, 1995). These requirements are likely to be met by family firms, whose long-term perspective, concern for business perpetuation, and willingness to make investments to benefit the future generation of owners (Schulze et al., 2003b) may prompt a 'generational investment strategy' that allows for the accumulation of patient capital (Sirmon and Hitt, 2003: 343). This aspect is reinforced by the fact that family executives and officers tend to enjoy long tenures and their welfare is not tied to short-term results (Gomez-Mejia et al., 2003), which allows them to engage in long-term projects with uncertain financial outcomes such as those related to social actions.

A recent study by Sharma and Sharma (2011) offers an integrated view of the antecedents of proactive stakeholder management (in the particular case of environmental strategies) in family firms. According to the authors, family owners possess five distinct characteristics that fortify their proactiveness toward adopting environmentally friendly strategies: (1) the family's significant and long-lasting influence on the dominant coalition;

(2) longer leadership tenures; (3) the desire to transfer the firm to future generations; (4) strong identification of the family with the firm; and (5) a desire to maintain a positive reputation for the firm and the family.

In short, theoretical explanations support the notion that family firms are more prone to respond to stakeholder demands and that they do so out of a combination of instrumental and normative motives that are linked to the unique identity of family owners. However, as it stands now, the literature on institutions and stakeholder management in family firms is highly fragmented. As argued below, we believe that the adoption of a SEW approach can best capture the family firms' uniqueness and serve as a unifying analytical perspective for investigating stakeholder management in family firms.

AN INTEGRATIVE APPROACH: A SOCIOEMOTIONAL WEALTH PRESERVATION PERSPECTIVE TO STAKEHOLDER MANAGEMENT IN FAMILY FIRMS

Table 10.2 summarizes the key aspects of the institutional theory and stakeholder management and how the socioemotional wealth integrates them to provide satisfactory answers to the gaps that these literatures show.

Although most of the papers reviewed so far do not formally refer to socioemotional wealth, all of them explain the family firm's substantial responsiveness to stakeholder needs as driven by non-economic utilities derived by dominant family owners. Concepts such as close identification of family members with the firm, preservation of a positive family image, concerns about the company's perpetuation, desires of family members to influence decisions, and care for acquaintances and community relations, among others, were collectively labeled 'socioemotional wealth' by Gomez-Mejia et al. (2007).

The SEW approach not only provides the field with an overarching construct to capture the uniqueness of family businesses, but it

Table 10.2   The SEW preservation perspective as an integrative approach to stakeholder management in family firms

Theory	Main propositions regarding stakeholder management	The research gap	The SEW preservation approach to stakeholder management in family firms
Institutional theory	Organizations need legitimacy to survive (Scott, 1995). Concern over legitimacy influences firms by pushing them to adopt certain managerial practices that are expected to be socially valuable even if these practices do not yield an economic benefit (Deephouse, 1999; Scott, 1995).	Why are some firms (e.g., family firms) more likely to respond to institutional pressures than others?	Variation in firm's responses to institutional pressures and stakeholders' needs is likely to be a function of who controls the organization and how much the controlling party values achieving social worthiness apart from any economic gains (Berrone et al., 2010).
Stakeholder theory	Firm has multiple goals in addition to maximizing shareholders' economic value, and should accordingly aims at satisfying the needs of multiple constituents (Donaldson and Preston, 1995; Freeman, 1984). Regardless of the approach (instrumental versus normative), the link between stakeholder management and financial results is unclear (Margolis and Walsh, 2003; Orlizky et al., 2003).	Why are some firms (e.g., family firms) more likely to attend to external stakeholder demands than others?	Family firms that use socioemotional criteria when making choices are more likely to engage in stakeholder management activities because by doing so they protect and enhance their socioemotional endowments (Berrone et al., 2012).

also offers a theoretical explanation for their distinct behavior (Berrone et al., 2012). Using the behavioral agency model (Wiseman and Gomez-Mejia, 1998) as theoretical anchor, proponents of SEW suggest that because the affective content often takes priority in family firms and they are typically motivated by, and committed to, the preservation of their socioemotional wealth, they will use non-economic goals as reference points. This means that strategic choices and policy decisions are primarily framed in terms of potential SEW gains or losses. Thus, in scenarios where the affective endowment is at risk, the SEW approach predicts that family firms will engage in actions that will preserve such endowments even if these actions are financially damaging. Recently, the SEW construct was disaggregated into a set of theoretical dimensions by Berrone et al. (2012), who developed the 'big five' FIBER

model. FIBER stands for **f**amily control and influence, **i**dentification of family members with the firm, **b**inding social ties, **e**motional attachment of family members, and **r**enewal of family bonds to the firm through dynastic succession.

The SEW formulation was first applied in the context of social issues by Berrone et al. (2010). These authors juxtaposed the traditional sociopolitical perspective of how firms respond to external pressures, in which parties often act as self-serving entities that overtly manipulate to gain personal advantages, with the socioemotional wealth approach, in which family owners are guided by the intrinsic value of affect-related motives. The authors sustain that family firms are more likely to engage in environmentally friendly activities, even if they involve costs and financial uncertainties, driven by a belief that such a risk is counterbalanced by non-economic gains.

Given that environmental strategies can help reduce social and reputational costs, secure the family's good name, guarantee its control, and contribute to the company's endurance, the authors argue that family firms are especially likely to see these strategies as valuable.

More recently, Berrone et al. (2012) not only argued that family firms are more inclined to respond to stakeholders' demands but they do so proactively. According to them, family firms are more prone to adopt proactive stakeholder engagement (PSE) activities – referring to those substantive actions intended to engage proactively with stakeholders and identify potential problems before they arise – because, by doing so, they preserve and enhance their socioemotional wealth (SEW). They further explore the impact of the different dimensions of SEW on PSE and identify distinctive logics that explain the adoption of such practices. They argue that family firms will proactively engage more primary stakeholders (those whose welfare is most directly affected by the firm's actions) as a way to strengthen relational trust, and gain endorsement for the firm's direction and management, and they will do so for instrumental reasons. This is most likely to occur when the primary reference point is driven by (a) a desire to maintain control and influence over the firm, (b) a sense of dynasty that implies a long-term orientation, and/or (c) a strong concern for the family identity. However, when the central SEW reference point is either (d) the presence of strong social ties or (e) the owner's emotional attachment to the firm, normative argumentation might dominate, and the firm is more likely to also attend to secondary stakeholders (those with a tenuous, ambiguous or more distant link to the firm). In these cases, since what is at stake is a 'sense of belonging' rather than control or identity, actions towards stakeholders are more unselfish as opposed to calculative or 'tit-for-tat'.

The SEW preservation approach to stakeholder management has recently received additional empirical support in the work of Miller et al. (in press). According to these authors, family firms will adopt strategic conformity as concerted efforts to achieve legitimacy in the eyes of external stakeholders. Their main reasoning is that family involvement in ownership and management will be viewed as suspicious by outside stakeholders. This suspicion may arise from the importance to many family owners of SEW preservation. To neutralize this effect, families exhibit visible conformity in the business practices that are important to these non-family stakeholders.

In short, the use of socioemotional wealth preservation as a primary driver of family-controlled firms goes beyond the general proposition of institutional and stakeholder theory – that the presence of influential stakeholders exerts pressures on firms' decisions – to suggest that family owners exert additional pressure on themselves to be held in high regard by internal and external stakeholders. They do so for a combination of instrumental and normative motives that are intrinsically tied to the preservation of the family's SEW.

CONCLUSION

This chapter provides an initial basis for understanding external pressures and stakeholder management in family firms. The evidence reviewed so far largely supports the notion that family firms do care about their stakeholders, at least to a greater extent than their non-family counterparts. They do so to preserve and enhance the family's socioemotional endowment. However, since family firms often need to satisfy simultaneously multiple stakeholders with financial and non-financial claims (Zellweger and Nason, 2008), there is a need to further investigate the intersection between stakeholder management and family firms. Augmenting knowledge in this area would be beneficial for academia as well as for the corporate world, since the latter is increasingly oriented to a stakeholder management approach. Specifically, we believe that the boundaries of this emerging field can be expanded by addressing three broad research questions: (a) how do family businesses prioritize the demands of different stakeholders?; (b) how does meeting multiple stakeholders' demands help the family to achieve performance goals?; and (c) how may stakeholders benefit from adoption by the family business of a SEW logic? These three research questions are developed in greater depth below. *Futur research* ①

How do Family Businesses Prioritize the Demands of Different Stakeholders?

Family businesses face a unique set of challenges in prioritizing which stakeholder group matters most and understanding how families give priority to competing stakeholder claims. This has both important theoretical and practical implications. As mentioned before, the study by Berrone et al. (2012) provides some interesting insights in this direction. By building on the individual dimensions of socioemotional wealth, the authors propose that the different weights that families place on these dimensions may account for family firms' heterogeneity in identifying, prioritizing and responding to different stakeholder groups. Their study broadly distinguishes between primary and secondary stakeholders. Empirical testing of this idea as well as a finer categorization of stakeholder groups are needed to capture differences in stakeholder salience or, in other words, 'who really counts' (Mitchell, Agle, and Wood, 1997) for family business owners.

Moreover, the uniqueness of family firms may alter the bases of stakeholder power, legitimacy and urgency that define stakeholder salience. Compared to non-family businesses, stakeholder power in family firms is more likely to be based on prestige and social symbols such as love or acceptance, legitimacy refers to status derived from birth and close relationships, and urgency is biased toward socioemotional wealth preservation goals (Mitchell et al., 2011). Additionally,

exploring this line of research can enlighten 'within' differences among family firms. Understanding varying levels of power, legitimacy, and urgency can be informative of why family firms are heterogeneous in the manner in which they view and respond to the claims and pressures of family and non-family stakeholders. Future research should address how these unique stakeholder salience issues impact family firms when adopting stakeholder management decisions.

Another valuable extension in this direction would be to analyze the extent to which the links between SEW and stakeholder salience are moderated by individual, organizational, and environmental conditions. Berrone et al. (2012) suggest that, for instance, it might be interesting to see how family firms prioritize stakeholders when resources are tight. The authors suggest that, in those cases, primary stakeholders will be favored since families would be guided more strongly by instrumental (as opposed to normative) motives. In a similar vein, we expect the industry in which the company operates to be an important moderator variable. Family firms competing in high technology-intensive industries would require highly technical industry-specific knowledge that would force them to look for highly specialized human capital, even when this implies jeopardizing their socioemotional wealth. Other moderators such as size, generational stage, board of director composition, and culture may be important catalysts on family firms' susceptibility to external pressures and stakeholders.

It is also expected that different generations would have different strategies for managing their stakeholders. Researchers generally agree that family identification, influence, sense of legacy, emotional attachment, regard for family image, and strength of social ties all change as the firm transitions from one generation to the next (Cennamo et al., in press). Collectively, they suggest that the emphasis on preserving the family's socioemotional wealth lessens as the firm moves through generations and that financial considerations become more important as a frame of reference (Gomez-Mejia et al., 2007). Future research should address how these changes in reference points affect the way families manage their stakeholder relationships.

How Does Meeting Multiple Stakeholders' Demands Help the Family to Achieve Performance Goals?

The family business literature no longer sees controlling families as being motivated by the pursuit of socioemotional goals alone and refrains from projecting the largely naïve picture of seeing families as selfless altruists who subordinate their own interests to the interests of their social context at any given time. Rather, the SEW approach to the family business accepts the view that family firms are motivated by the pursuit of a mix of financial and socioemotional goals (Berrone et al., 2012; Gomez-Mejia et al., 2007; Gomez-Mejia et al., 2011a). Given this mix of motives and the fact that family firms often wish to simultaneously satisfy multiple stakeholders with financial and non-financial performance demands, there is a need to comprehensively explore how different performance dimensions are interrelated and how they allow efficient satisfaction of multiple stakeholders.

Traditional views suggest that satisfying competing stakeholder demands involves important tradeoffs for controlling families and that, in most cases, family firms may be willing to trade economic performance for non-economic benefits (Gomez-Mejia et al., 2007; Gomez-Mejia et al., 2011a). However, the financial and socioemotional aspects of economic activity can be mutually reinforcing and have positive synergistic effects (Zellweger and Nason, 2008). For instance, environmental strategies can help the family firm to reduce social and reputational costs so family firms are likely to see these strategies as a valuable means for protecting and enhancing socioemotional wealth. At the

same time, they may be seen as a way to protect the organization's financial wellbeing since a positive reputation derived from responsible behavior creates a basis for developing a feeling of reciprocity with and trust in different stakeholders (Cennamo et al., in press). In turn, family businesses would gain flexibility in their contractual relationships with stakeholders, thereby increasing their efficiency (Cruz et al., 2010). This may serve as a form of social insurance, protecting the firm's assets in times of crisis (Godfrey, 2005). This efficiency-enhancing effect may explain why family firms are able to survive despite their growth constraints (Galve-Górriz and Salas-Fumás, 2004). Therefore, the analysis of synergistic performance effects provides an interesting opportunity for future research. Moreover, if family firms are more likely to satisfy multiple stakeholders, they should be more prone to measuring success by how well they satisfy their stakeholder base. This implies assuming that families are aware of the impact that their actions have on stakeholders' perceptions and how this awareness affects their strategies toward stakeholders (e.g., reactive vs passive). Relatedly, stakeholder engagement behaviors can be ordered along a continuum ranging from least to most involved (e.g., Morsing and Schultz, 2006; Pater and Van Lierop, 2006), but this variance has not yet been considered in extant studies. These issues represent important avenues for future research.

How May Stakeholders Benefit from Adoption by the Family Business of a Logic in Dealing with Stakeholder Relationships?

The literature has largely emphasized the tradeoffs between pursuing financial and non-financial goals in family firms in a negative sense, suggesting that the family may be pursuing non-financial interests that might put other stakeholders at a disadvantage (Morck et al., 2005). However, it could also be the case that the preservation of SEW by the controlling family may benefit other stakeholders for several reasons.

First, family enterprises have been reported to display strong community relations (Tagiuri and Davis, 1992b) and as being embedded in their societal context (Berrone et al., 2010). According to Zellweger and Nason (2008: 205), 'this allows these firms to establish more effective relations with support organizations (e.g., banks) while maintaining legitimacy with other constituencies'. Also, the existence of embedded ties makes it more likely that a firm in difficulties will be able to draw upon resources and, for example, attract business from partners to weather through challenging periods (Chua et al., 2011). A recent study by Sieger and colleagues (2011) shows that family firms that nurture embedded ties in their communities have access to business opportunities afforded by the joint family and business networks. Similarly, Miller and Le Breton-Miller (2005) show in a study of large, long-standing family firms that continuity and the power to institute changes without outside interference or control enable these firms to generate and make exceptional long-term use of patient strategies and relationships with stakeholders, resulting in the establishment of long-term relationships with clients, suppliers, and investors. Therefore, under certain environments, the family can be beneficial to other stakeholders by filling institutional voids, providing access to important networks and being an important source of patient and survivability capital. These positive effects remain largely unexplored both theoretically and empirically, so more research effort is needed to understand how stakeholders appropriate economic and non-economic benefits when dealing with family firms.

In conclusion, family firms are likely to pursue family-centered non-economic goals that create socioemotional wealth. Protecting this wealth may be the strongest motivation for family owners to attend to a broad set of stakeholders. And while family-centered non-economic goals and traditional business goals of profitability may on occasions be self-reinforcing, when they are conflicting, desires to preserve socioemotional wealth will often take precedence in family firm decision-making over economic wealth considerations. This explains the natural tendency in family firms to go beyond economically relevant stakeholders, addressing the needs of secondary or fringe constituencies affected by the company's actions.

ACKNOWLEDGEMENTS

The first author is indebted to the Schneider-Electric Chair in Sustainability and Business Strategy as well as to the Spanish Ministry of Economy and Competitiveness (ECO2012-33018) for providing financial support.

REFERENCES

Aldrich HE, Fiol CM. 1994. Fools rush in? The institutional context of industry creation. *Academy of Management Review* 19: 645–670.

Anderson RC, Reeb DV. 2003. Founding-family ownership, corporate diversification, and firm leverage. *Journal of Law and Economics* 46: 653–684.

Anderson RC, Reeb DV. 2004. Board composition: Balancing family influence in S&P 500 firms. *Administrative Science Quarterly* 49(2): 209–237.

Aragon-Correa JA, Sharma S. 2003. A contingent resource-based view of proactive corporate environmental strategy. *Academy of Management Review* 28(1): 71–88.

Banfield EC. 1958. *The Moral Basis of a Backward Society*. Glencoe, IL: Free Press.

Bansal P, Clelland I. 2004. Talking trash: Legitimacy, impression management, and unsystematic risk in the context of the natural environment. *Academy of Management Journal* 47(1): 93–103.

Berman SL, Wicks AC, Kotha S, Jones TM. 1999. Does stakeholder orientation matter? The relationship between stakeholder management models and firm financial performance. *Academy of Management Journal* 42(5): 488–506.

Berrone P, Cruz C, Gomez-Mejia L, Larraza-Kintana M. 2010. Socioemotional wealth and corporate responses to institutional pressures: Do family-controlled firms pollute less? *Administrative Science Quarterly* 55: 82–113.

Berrone P, Cruz C, Gomez-Mejia LR. 2012. Socioemotional wealth in family firms: Theoretical dimensions, assessment approaches and agenda for future research. *Family Business Review* 25(3):258–279.

Berrone P, Surroca J, Tribo J. 2007. Corporate ethical identity as a determinant of firm performance: A test of the mediating role of stakeholder satisfaction. *Journal of Business Ethics* 76(1): 35–53.

Bingham J, Dyer WG, Smith I, Adams G. 2010. A stakeholder identity orientation approach to corporate social performance in family firms. *Journal of Business Ethics* 99(4): 565–585.

Block J. 2010. Family management, family ownership, and downsizing: Evidence from S&P 500 firms. *Family Business Review* 23: 109–130.

Cennamo C, Berrone P, Cruz C, Gomez Mejia LR. in press. Socioemotional wealth and proactive stakeholder engagement: Why family controlled firms care more about their stakeholders. *Entrepreneurship Theory and Practice*: 1–40.

Chen S, Chen X, Cheng Q. 2008. Do family firms provide more or less voluntary disclosure? *Journal of Accounting Research* 46(3): 499–536.

Chen S, Chen X, Cheng Q, Shevlin T. 2010. Are family firms more tax aggressive than non-family firms? *Journal of Financial Economics* 45(1): 41–61.

Chua JH, Chrisman JJ, Kellermanns F, Wu Z. 2011. Family involvement and new venture debt financing. *Journal of Business Venturing* 26(4): 472–488.

Chua JH, Chrisman JJ, Sharma P. 1999. Defining the family business by behaviour. *Entrepreneurship: Theory and Practice* 23(4): 19–39.

Clarkson MBE. 1995. A stakeholder framework for analyzing and evaluating corporate social performance. *Academy of Management Review* 20(1): 92–117.

Cooper MJ, Upton N, Seaman S. 2005. Customer relationship management: A comparative analysis of family and nonfamily business practices. *Journal of Small Business Management* 43(3): 242–256.

Covin TJ. 1994. Perceptions of family-owned firms: The impact of gender and educational level. *Journal of Small Business Management* 32(3): 29–39.

Cruz C, Gomez-Mejia LR, Becerra M. 2010. Perceptions of benevolence and the design of agency contracts: CEO-TMT relationships in family firms. *Academy of Management Journal* 53(1): 69–89.

Danco LA, Ward JL. 1990. Beyond success: The continuing contribution of the family. *Family Business Review* 3(4): 347–355.

Deephouse DL. 1999. To be different, or to be the same? It's a question (and theory) of strategic balance. *Strategic Management Journal* 20: 147–166.

Delmas M, Toffel MW. 2008. Organizational responses to environmental demands: Opening the black box. *Strategic Management Journal* 29(10): 1027–1055.

Déniz-Déniz MC, Cabrera-Suarez K. 2005. Corporate social responsibility and family business in Spain. *Journal of Business Ethics* 56: 27–41.

DiMaggio PJ, Powell WW. 1983. The iron cage revisited: Institutional isomorphism and collective rationality in organizational fields. *American Sociological Review* 48(2): 147–160.

Donalson T, Dunfee TW. 1994. Toward a unified conception of business ethics: Integrative social contracts theory. *Academy of Management Review* 19(2): 252–284.

Donalson T, Preston LE. 1995. The stakeholder theory of the corporation: Concepts, evidence, and implications. *Academy of Management Review* 20(1): 65–91.

Dyer GW, Whetten DA. 2006. Family firms and social responsibility: Preliminary evidence from the S&P500. *Entrepreneurship: Theory and Practice* 30(4): 785–802.

Evan W, Freeman ER. 1983. A Stakeholder theory of the modern corporation: Kantian capitalism. In *Ethical Theory in Business*. Beauchamp T, Bowie N (eds), Englewood Cliffs, NJ: Prentice-Hall.

Fombrun CJ. 1996. *Reputation: Realising Value From the Corporate Image*. Boston, MA: Harvard Business School Press.

Freeman ER. 1984. *Strategic Management: A Stakeholder Approach*. Englewood Cliffs, NJ: Prentice Hall.

Fukuyama F. 1995. *Trust*. New York: Free Press.

Galve-Górriz C, Salas-Fumás V. 2004. Family ownership and performance: The net effect of productive efficiency and growth constraints. Working Paper, Universidad de Zaragoza.

Gersick K, Davis J, Hampton M, Lansberg I. 1997. *Generation to Generation: Life Cycles of the Family Business*. Boston, MA: Harvard Business School Press.

Godfrey PC. 2005. The relationship between corporate philanthropy and shareholder wealth: A risk management perspective. *Academy of Management Review* 30(4): 777–798.

Gomez-Mejia LR, Cruz C, Berrone P, De Castro J. 2011a. The bind that ties: Socioemotional wealth Preservation in family firms. *Academy of Management Annals* 5(1): 653–707.

Gomez-Mejia LR, Haynes K, Nuñez-Nickel M, Jacobson KJL, Moyano-Fuentes J. 2007. Socioemotional wealth and business risks in family-controlled firms: Evidence from Spanish olive oil mills. *Administrative Science Quarterly* 52(1): 106–137.

Gomez-Mejia LR, Hoskisson RE, Makri M, Campbell J. 2011b. Innovation and the preservation of socio-emotional wealth in family controlled high technology firms. Working Paper. Management Department, Mays Business School, Texas A&M University, College Station, Texas.

Gomez-Mejia LR, Larraza-Kintana M, Makri M. 2003. The determinants of executive compensation in family-controlled public corporations. *Academy of Management Journal* 46(2): 226–237.

Gomez-Mejia LR, Makri M, Larraza-Kintana M. 2010. Diversification decisions in family-controlled firms. *Journal of Management Studies* 47(2): 223–252.

Harrison JS, Bosse DA, Phillips RA. 2010. Managing for stakeholders, stakeholder utility functions, and competitive advantage. *Strategic Management Journal* 31(1): 58–74.

Hart SL. 1995. A natural-resource-based view of the firm. *Academy of Management Review* 20(4): 986–1014.

Hart SL, Sharma S. 2004. Engaging fringe stakeholders for competitive imagination. *Academy of Management Executive* 18: 7–18.

Hoffman AJ. 2001. Linking organizational and field-level analyses. *Organization & Environment* 14(2): 133–252.

Jones TM. 1995. Instrumental stakeholder theory: A synthesis of ethics and economics. *Academy of Management Review* 20(2): 404–437.

Jones TM, Wicks AC. 1999. Convergent stakeholder theory. *Academy of Management Review* 24(2): 206–221.

Josephson M. 1934. *The Robber Barons*. New York: Harcourt, Brace and Company.

Krappe A, Goutas L, von Schlippe A. 2011. The 'family business brand': An enquiry into the construction of the image of family businesses. *Journal of Family Business Management* 1(1): 37–46.

Lan LL, Heracleous L. 2010. Rethinking agency theory: the view from law. *Academy of Management Review* 35(2): 294–314.

Laplume A, Sonpar K, Litz RA. 2008. Stakeholder theory: Reviewing a theory that moves us. *Journal of Management* 34(6): 1152–1189.

LaPorta R, López-de-Silanes F, Shleifer A. 1997. Trust in large organizations. *American Economic Review* 87(2): 333–338.

Margolis JD, Walsh JP. 2003. Misery loves companies: Rethinking social initiatives by business. *Administrative Science Quarterly* 48(2): 268–304.

Martin G, Makri M, Gomez-Mejia LR. 2011. Shareholder proposals in family controlled firms. *IE Business School Working Papers Series.*

Meyer J, Rowan B. 1977. Institutional organizations: Formal structure as myth and ceremony. *American Journal of Sociology* 83: 340–363.

Miller D, Le Breton-Miller I. 2005. *Managing for the Long Run: Lessons in competitive Advantage From Great Family Businesses*. Cambridge, MA: Harvard Business School Press.

Miller D, Le Breton-Miller I, Lester RH. 2010. Family ownership and acquisition behavior in publicly-traded companies. *Strategic Management Journal* 31(2): 121–136.

Miller D, Le Breton-Miller I, Lester RH. in press. Family firm governance, strategic conformity and performance: Institutional versus strategic perspectives. *Organization Science.*

Miller D, Le Breton-Miller I. 2006. Family governance and firm performance: Agency, stewardship, and capabilities. *Family Business Review* 19(1): 73–87.

Mitchell RK, Agle BR, Chrisman J, Spence LJ. 2011. Toward a theory of stakeholder salience in family firms. *Business Ethics Quarterly* 21(2): 235–255.

Mitchell RK, Agle BR, Wood DJ. 1997. Toward a theory of stakeholder identification and salience: Defining the principle of who and what really counts. *Academy of Management Review* 22(4): 853–886.

Morck R, Wolfenzon D, Yeung B. 2005. Corporate governance, economic entrenchment, and growth. *Journal of Economic Literature* 43(3): 655–720.

Morck R, Yeung B. 2003. Agency problems in large family business groups. *Entrepreneurship Theory and Practice* Summer: 367–382.

Morck R, Yeung B. 2004. Family control and the rent seeking society. *Entrepreneurship Theory and Practice* 28: 391–409.

Morsing M, Schultz M. 2006. Corporate social responsibility communication: stakeholder information, response and involvement strategies. *Business Ethics: A European Review* 15(4): 323–338.

Nordqvist M, Melin L. 2002. The dynamics of family firms: An institutional perspective on corporate governance and strategic change. In *Understanding the Small Family Firm*. D. Fletcher (ed.), London: Routledge, pp. 94–110.

Oliver C. 1991. Strategic responses to institutional processes. *Academy of Management Review* 16(1): 145–179.

Orlizky M, Schmidt FL, Rynes SL. 2003. Corporate social and financial performance: A meta-analysis. *Organization Studies* 24(3): 403–441.

Orth UR, Green MT. 2009. Consumer loyalty to family versus non-family businesses: The roles of store image, trust and satisfaction. *Journal of Retailing and Consumer Services* 16: 248–259.

Oster SM. 1999. *Modern Competitive Analysis*. New York: Oxford University Press.

Parada MJ, Nordqvist M, Gimeno A. 2010. Institutionalizing the family business: The role of professional associations in fostering a change of values. *Family Business Review* 23(4): 355–372.

Parmentier MA. 2011. When David met Victoria: Forging a strong family brand. *Family Business Review* 24(3): 217–232.

Pater A, Van Lierop K. 2006. Sense and sensitivity: the roles of organisation and stakeholders in managing corporate social responsibility. *Business Ethics: A European Review* 15(4): 339–351.

Philips RA. 1997. Stakeholder theory and the principle of fairness. *Business Ethics Quarterly* 7: 51–66.

Post JE, Preston LE, Sachs S. 2002. Managing the extended enterprise: The new stakeholder view. *California Management Review* 45(1): 6–28.

PricewaterhouseCoopers I. 2011. Creating value from corporate responsibility: Does your reported data get the respect it deserves? In *Sustainability Reports*. Delaware.

Rau SB. 2014. Resource-based view of family firms. In *The Sage Handbook of Family Business*. Melin L, Nordqvist M, Sharma S (eds), Sage: London.

Rawls J. 1971. *A Theory of Justice*. Harvard, MA: Harvard University Press.

Reay T. 2009. Family-business meta-identity, institutional pressures, and ability to respond to entrepreneurial opportunities. *Entrepreneurship: Theory and Practice* 33(6): 1265–1270.

Roberts PW, Dowling GR. 2002. Corporate reputation and sustained superior financial performance. *Strategic Management Journal* 23(12): 1077–1093.

Scott WR. 1995. *Institutions and Organizations*. Thousand Oaks, CA: Sage.

Scott WR. 2005. Institutional theory: Contributing to a theoretical research program. In *Great Minds in Management: The Process of Theory Development*. Smith KG, Hitt MA (eds), London: Oxford University Press.

Schulze WS, Lubatkin MH, Dino RN. 2003a. Toward a theory of agency and altruism in family firms. *Journal of Business Venturing* 18: 450–473.

Schulze WS, Lubatkin MH, Dino RN. 2003b. Exploring the agency consequences of ownership dispersion among the directors of private family firms. *Academy of Management Journal* 46(2): 179–194.

Schulze WS, Lubatkin MH, Dino RN, Buchholz RA. 2001. Agency relationships in family firms: Theory and evidence. *Organization Science* 12(2): 99–116.

Sharma P. 2001. Stakeholder management concepts in family firms. *Proceedings of International Association of Business and Society (IABS)*: 254–259.

Sharma P. 2004. An overview of the field of family business studies: Current status and directions for the future. *Family Business Review* 17(1): 1–36.

Sharma P, Sharma S. 2011. Drivers of proactive environmental strategy in family firms. *Business Ethics Quarterly* 21(2): 309–334.

Shukla P., Carney M, Gedajlovic E. 2014. Economic theories of family firms. In *The Sage Handbook of Family Business*. Melin L, Nordqvist M, Sharma S (eds), Sage: London.

Sieger P, Zellweger T, Nason R, Clinton E. 2011. Portfolio entrepreneurship in family firms. *Strategic Entrepreneurship Journal* 5(4): 327–351.

Sirmon DG, Hitt M. 2003. Managing resources: Linking unique resources, management, and wealth creation in family firms. *Entrepreneurship Theory and Practice* 27(4): 339–358.

Stavrou E, Kassinis G, Filotheou A. 2007. Downsizing and stakeholder orientation among the Fortune 500: Does family ownership matter? *Journal of Business Ethics* 72(2): 149–162.

Stavrou E, Swiercz P. 1998. Securing the future of the family enterprise: A model of offspring intentions to join the business. *Entrepreneurship Theory and Practice* 23(2): 19–31.

Tagiuri R, Davis JA. 1992a. On the goals of successful family businesses. *Family Business Review* 5(1): 43–62.

Tagiuri R, Davis J. 1992b. Bivalent attributes of the family firm. *Family Business Review* 9(2): 199–208.

Wicks AC, Gilbert DR, Jr., Freeman ER. 1994. A feminist reinterpretation of the stakeholder concept. *Business Ethics Quarterly* 4: 475–498.

Wiseman RM, Gomez-Mejia LR. 1998. A behavioral agency model of managerial risk taking. *Academy of Management Review* 22(1): 133–153.

Zellweger T, Nason R. 2008. A stakeholder perspective on family firm performance. *Family Business Review* 21(3): 203–216.

11

Governing the Family Enterprise: Practices, Performance and Research

Kelin E. Gersick and Neus Feliu

INTRODUCTION

Organizational researchers are increasingly drawn to family businesses because they illuminate so many important models and theories: family dynamics and human development, theory of the firm, agency theory, economic development, labor market theory, social capital theory, and many others. Consultants and professional service providers are also attracted to family enterprises as clients. In fact, over the recent decades, there have been many more professionals working with family firms than studying them. As a field, our best opportunity to maximize our understanding of family businesses is to utilize both of these sources of data on family firms; that is, to integrate formal research and theory with documented implementation experience to build a platform for future development.

This is critically important in the area of governance. Research on corporate governance has proliferated in recent decades, generating a huge literature on the legal, financial, and strategic control of organizations. But a very small part of that research has taken into account family ownership and the special nature of family firm governance over time and across generations (Le Breton-Miller and Miller, 2009). In particular, only a few researchers have looked at governance systems as they are actually implemented in family firms, assessing their successes and failures in overseeing such core outcomes as ownership continuity, business performance, stakeholder benefits and satisfaction, emotional ownership, leadership development in sequential generations, and entrepreneurship.

Similarly, the primary interventions by consultants in the family business field over the past three decades have been in governance: family councils, family assemblies, boards of directors, family offices, family foundations, shareholders agreements, and financial planning tools such as trusts and limited family partnerships. However, publications based on that body of work very rarely go beyond the descriptive, and sometimes prescriptive. Consultants offer advice based on their experience, and rely on logic and common sense to persuade potential clients that they see the problem accurately and the solution clearly. Where there is research evidence some advisors make use of it, but many of our often-repeated 'best practices' are supported by face validity rather than empirical assessments. We have come to a moment of challenge to our understanding of governance in the field. If we are to move forward we need to consolidate the existing empirical work and integrate it with what has been learned from experience, to generate both a confident basis for our advice to families, and a comprehensive agenda for future research.

In this chapter we review the existing literature on governance implementation in family enterprise. The chapter begins with a brief discussion of the domain of governance, first in corporations in general, and then in family business in particular. Then we review the literature on governance implementation in the business, ownership, and family circles, sampling both the academic research literature and the reports of professionals in the trade and general press. We reviewed more than 400 articles and books, and have included over 200 in the bibliography, but this is only a sample. In making choices about which publications to include, we considered direct relevance in the practitioner articles, and research design, contribution, and cites by others for the academic papers. We have also relied heavily on our own professional experience with hundreds of business families over the past 30 years, which undoubtedly shapes our interpretations of the body of research and our proposals for filling gaps. Each section ends with suggestions about the most promising areas for future work, and the most interesting dilemmas for the continuing evolution of our research canon.

DEFINITIONS AND DOMAIN OF FAMILY BUSINESS GOVERNANCE

Pieper's (2003) excellent review reaches the conclusion that there is no consensus on the definition of governance, either in corporations in general or in family enterprise. Keasey et al. provide one often-quoted definition for corporate governance in general: 'Corporate governance is the process and structure used to direct and manage the business affairs of the company towards enhancing business prosperity and corporate accountability with the ultimate objective of realizing long-term shareholder value, whilst taking into account the interests of other stakeholders' (1997: 288). This is a somewhat different focus from the perspective of researchers in economics or finance: 'Corporate governance deals with the ways in which suppliers of finance to corporations assure themselves of getting a return on their investment' (Shleifer and Vishny, 1997: 737), or the law: 'Corporate governance refers to the monitoring and control over how the firm's resources are allocated, and how relations within the firm are structured and managed' (McCahery and Vermeulen, 2006:1).

In these professions, governance refers to ownership of business organizations (in fact, governance and ownership are often treated as synonymous) (Carney, 2005). In two ways, that is too limited for our purposes. First, ownership is a financial and legal reality; governance is an organizational one (Uhlaner et al., 2007: 227), including both structural and process components. In this review of governance practices in family enterprise, we are not only interested in ownership rights, but rather in how oversight and control are exercised, and in how governance contributes to firm performance.

Secondly, we are using governance in reference to all of the sub-sectors of a family enterprise, not just the business ownership, because what is being governed is the family capital in all its forms: financial, human, intellectual, social, and organizational (Hughes, 2004; Sharma, 2008). Family enterprise governance oversees all the collaborative operations of the family, including wealth management, philanthropy, and human development (Gersick, et al., 1997; Neubauer and Lank, 1998; Lansberg,

1999; Mustakallio et al., 2002). Goldbart and DiFuria give an example of a very different definition of governance, appropriate particularly for family business: 'Governance is the means of stewarding the multigenerational family organization ... [It] establishes the processes whereby: strategic goals are set, key relationships are maintained, the health of the family is safeguarded, accountability is maintained, and achievement and performance are recognized' (2009: 7). This chapter uses this broader definition as its domain for governance implementation, reviewing the research and professional literature on the practice of governance in family enterprises.

THEORETICAL MODELS FOR GOVERNING THE FAMILY ENTERPRISE

In contemporary organizational studies, the dominant theoretical foundation for research on corporate governance is agency theory. (For a full discussion of agency theory in family business governance see Goel et al., 2014, in this volume.) Agency theory focuses on the differentiated needs of two categories of stakeholders: principals (the owners) and agents (their employed managers) (Berle and Means, 1932; Jensen and Meckling, 1976; Fama and Jensen, 1983; Jensen, 1993). The goals of principals and agents are inherently different, and since the prime purpose of the corporation is to serve the economic interests of the owners, it falls upon them to design mechanisms (governance) to control the behavior of their agents so that the organization operates in service of the owners' interests. However, those control mechanisms come with costs. Minimizing agency costs is therefore an important contributor to organizational success, and a useful measure of governance implementation and effectiveness.[1]

However, the agency model is more complex in family-controlled companies with the addition of a third key stakeholder – the family – which creates additional demands for appropriately balanced and coordinated

governance procedures (Corbetta et al., 2002; Corbetta and Salvato, 2004; Braun and Sharma, 2007; Lambrecht and Lievens, 2008). With this elaboration, agency theory merges with the dominant conceptual model for family business, the Three-Circle Model. This model, first articulated by Tagiuri and Davis (1996) and elaborated into a three-dimensional developmental model by Gersick et al. (1997), conceptualizes family enterprise as a Venn diagram of three sub-systems – the owners, the business (or other operating organization[s]), and the family – each with its distinctive membership, agenda, and developmental processes. The Three-Circle Model helps clarify the tasks and purposes of governance in reference to each of the key subsystems – the essential work that governance must accomplish if the family enterprise is to succeed – and therefore the basis for evaluating governance implementation in research and practice.

In the **ownership circle**, the governance system must serve the actual equity owners of the enterprise (individual, partners, and/or shareholders). Its goals and obligations in this circle are to protect both the security of the asset base and the return on those assets. The specific tasks of governance include establishing and monitoring the structures that actually hold the owners' equity, guaranteeing compliance with all legal and accounting requirements, setting risk and return parameters and tracking all of the data on performance, generating capital from whatever sources are most advantageous, communicating effectively with current (and sometimes prospective) owners to minimize the cost of capital, determining the amounts and formats of distributions, and all other tasks that serve the owners as investors. These tasks are most often carried out by a board of directors, but that depends on the legal form of the organization – they can also be assigned to partners, trustees, or the sole or controlling owner as an individual. Governance failure in this circle risks *loss of capital* if owners lose confidence in the enterprise as an investment.

In the **business circle**, the governance system must serve the operating company, most often through its executives and managerial leadership. Here governance adds value by determining and enforcing standards for executive performance; articulating the core values and cultural norms that the governors expect managers to rely on in making choices and decisions; defining short- and long-term strategies; overseeing human resource management; and all other tasks of selection, supervision, assessment, and development of the senior operational executives that maximizes their performance in line with the overall objectives of the owners. Especially in closely-held businesses, well-functioning governance also helps to avoid destructive interference by individual owners into the domain of management, which if unchecked can undermine professional management as much as neglect. Once again, these tasks are most often assigned to a board of directors,[2] but the structure may vary. Governance failure here carries the risk of *loss of competitiveness*.

Those first two sets of governance tasks are generic to all corporations. It is the governance tasks in the **family circle** that are distinctive in family enterprise. Here the effectiveness of governance depends on its ability to serve the needs of the family, extending beyond current shareholders to include all those who are related by blood, adoption, or marriage and share a psychological sense of enterprise ownership – past, present, and future. The purposes of governance in this circle are to clarify the demands and rewards of family membership in relation to the business, to define and communicate the opportunities for involvement in all of the family's collaborative ventures, to facilitate information flow in ways that maximize trust and minimize manipulation, to establish and oversee the non-business/non-financial aspects of the enterprise (often including philanthropy), and most of all to enhance a sense of belonging throughout the extended family, across the subcategories of branch and generation. When governance in the family circle

is working well, it nurtures the emergence of the family's shared dream (Gersick et al., 1997; Lansberg, 1999), and then it structures the operationalization of that dream in organizational practice. Governance failure in this circle risks *loss of commitment* and, as a result, *loss of continuity*.

It is the effort to balance the agendas of these three classes of stakeholders – owners, managers and employees [agents], and family – that sets the agenda for governance, and the criteria against which research on governance implementation can be assessed. Therefore, we have organized this chapter around the Three-Circle Model, dealing in turn with governance implementation in ownership and the business, and then in the family.

RESEARCH ON GOVERNANCE IMPLEMENTATION IN THE OWNERSHIP AND BUSINESS CIRCLES

Although the purposes of governance are different when serving the needs of owners and managers, the governance structures and the literature about them are for the most part the same. Therefore, to avoid duplication in reviewing the body of research, we have combined the literature review for those two circles. We review the core research literature on boards of directors first, and then cover the much smaller body of work on other governance mechanisms: blockholding, dual stock classes, CEO/Chair duality, shareholder agreements, shareholder assemblies, and trusts.

Boards of Directors

In contemporary private-enterprise economies, nearly all legal systems specify some kind of board of directors as the ultimate governance authority in a corporation (Mintzberg, 1983; Fama and Jensen, 1983; Cadbury, 1992, 1999; Monks and Minow, 1996; Gomez and Moore, 2009). The literature on boards in general is large; the literature on boards in family businesses is still very small (Bettinelli's review concludes: 'Research on family business boards is almost nonexistent'; 2011: 152). Furthermore, most of the research on boards that does exist draws samples primarily from family-controlled, publicly-traded companies, rather than from the much larger group of privately-held family companies, despite the prevalent advice from practitioners that they too benefit from well-functioning boards (Teksten et al., 2005; Voordeckers et al., 2007).

A high percentage of the general organizational literature on boards of directors looks at the basic demographics and formal structure of the board, primarily the number and type of directors and the makeup of board committees. Some of the research is purely descriptive, while other studies look for associations between various characteristics and firm performance.

Board Size

The earliest and still most common research topic on boards of directors concerns the number of directors. Finegold and Lawler, in a recent survey of a sample of Fortune 1000 company directors, concluded that board size has been relatively stable in recent years, averaging just over 10 members, including the CEO and one or two other insiders (2009). The consensus is that smaller boards are more efficient, but in the extreme may limit the available range of skills and expertise among directors (Setia-Atmaja et al., 2009). Lane et al. (2006) summarize a group of studies and conclude that the optimal range for public, non-family firms is 5–9 directors, and 7–12 for family-controlled companies. There is some discussion of the special advantages of larger boards in family-controlled companies, in part to satisfy representational dynamics among family shareholder blocks (usually family branches) and in part because the concentrated authority of founders and large family blockholders is less dangerous within a larger group of directors. However, researchers in Europe have reported samples of family businesses with smaller boards than

their non-family counterparts (Navarro and Ansón, 2009). We found many suggestions from practitioners on the preferred size of a family business board (Ward, 1989, 1991), but no empirical findings on the consequences of board size for board performance in family firms.

Categories of Directors

No topic in the general governance literature has generated more heated debate than the optimal mix of directors from management, ownership, and outside the company (for example, Baysinger and Hoskisson, 1990; Judge and Zeithaml, 1992; Raheja, 2005). Practitioner and academic authors have traditionally favored strong, independent boards (Johnson, 1990; Pendergast et al., 2011), especially following the high-profile governance failures of the past decade, and the legislative responses such as Sarbanes–Oxley. In one of the few empirical studies, Millstein and MacAvoy review the recent history of boards from the legal perspective, and then test two measures of board professionalism, concluding that there is 'a statistically significant relationship between an active, independent board and superior corporate performance as measured by earnings in excess of costs of capital over the industry average' (1998: 1318). They also offer some hypotheses about why most research produces mixed results on the link between board structure and firm performance (complexity of the causal links, environmental events, and non-transparency).

In the family business literature, academics and practitioners alike have been nearly unanimous in endorsing the value of a strong board of directors with a presence, and often a majority, of independent outside directors (Zall, 2004; Brenes et al., 2011; Pendergast et al., 2011). This is one of the most frequently recommended governance 'upgrades' for family firms of all sizes, from small privately-held ventures to large traded firms (Jaffe and Lane, 2004). Sir Adrian Cadbury, commenting on the application of his influential report on family enterprise in the United Kingdom to family firms, summed up his conclusions with, 'the continuing success of a family firm is best assured if it is headed by an effective Board ... One with competent, independent-minded, outside directors on it' (Cadbury, 2000: 33). The most consistent and articulate academic voice for this view has been John Ward, who along with his colleagues, in numerous articles and presentations and more than a dozen books, has made the case for independent family business boards (Ward, 1988, 1991; Ward and Handy, 1988). Ward's recommendations are always well argued, and he has probably had more influence on the field's normative consensus on governance structure in family businesses than anyone else.

But the support for independent boards in the family business literature has not been unanimous. Ford (1988, 1989) raised a challenge to the assumption that outside directors add benefit: 'Unfortunately, there is a noticeable lack of empirical data to support the notion that outside directors actually make a difference on the boards of directors of privately-owned firms' (1988: 50). Ward's rejoinder was that, while the data on firm performance and board composition in family firms was still scarce, a purely financial assessment of the impact of non-family directors is only part of the story (1989). He and others argued that there are corollary benefits from a professional board that may not be picked up by traditional secondary analyses or surveys (most of which have extremely low return rates). The existence of a board, especially if it includes directors who are not employees or advisors of the controlling owners, leads to more transparency, more objective decision-making, more data-based evaluations and career oversight for family employees, more efficient use of executive time and meetings to accomplish governance tasks, and as an overall result, a higher probability of continuity. Reporting on the results from 360 responses to their Family Business Board Survey, Pendergast and his colleagues found that only 48 per cent of those family

companies self-define as having a 'functional board'; 67 per cent consider their board 'effective' or 'highly effective' with a steep curve from 54 per cent among those who have a family-only board, 83 per cent of those who have two or more independents, and 96 per cent of those who have a majority of independent directors (2011: 252). The self-report data is strong, and the data on board task activities and business performance may follow.

However, in both public and closely-held companies, whether or not family-owned, the research findings to date on independent directors are mixed. In the general corporate governance literature, research on the impact of independent directors on firm performance, share value, strategy, and operations most often finds little or negative impact (Agrawal and Knoeber, 1996; Coles et al., 2001; Daily et al., 2003; Bartholomeusz and Tanewski, 2006; Gordon, 2007; Finkelstein et al., 2009), and in some cases a decrease in firm performance when the percentage of independent directors goes up (Schulze et al., 2001). Other studies have reported a positive effect of independent boards under certain conditions (Baysinger and Butler, 1985; Filatotchev et al., 2005; Han and Celly, 2011), usually later in the firm's life cycle. Some studies, especially in non-US economies, find a positive impact of an independent board on firm value or lower cost of capital, while not measuring firm performance (for example, Yeh and Woidtke, 2005). Earlier work by Yeh and colleagues (Yeh et al., 2001) found that, in a Taiwanese sample, the combination associated with the highest firm performance was high family ownership and low family representation on the board – an intriguing finding that suggests important follow-up research to test its cultural specificity. Overall, for public corporations as a whole, the record is inconclusive. As Gordon (2007) put it, 'Independent directors – that is the answer, but what is the question?'

For large family-controlled corporations, the strongest data on this topic are the extraordinary findings of Anderson and Reeb (2003,

2004) on family control in S&P 500 firms. These researchers are best known for documenting that family-controlled publicly-traded companies outperform their non-family counterparts on a variety of profitability and market measures. However, they also looked deeper into the ownership and governance mechanisms that may lead to that advantage, and found a strong positive effect on firm performance in those family firms with greater board independence (they found no similar benefit from independent directors in non-family firms). Going further, they found a curvilinear relationship between board structure and firm performance:

> At low levels of family board representation relative to independent director representation, increases in the presence of family directors exhibit a positive relation to firm performance. But after the ratio of family board representation to independent director representation exceeds 0.50 (one family director to two independent directors), firm performance deteriorates. At higher levels of family representation relative to independent directors (beyond one to one), firm performance deteriorates even further. (Anderson and Reeb, 2004: 224)

They conclude that independent directors provide direct benefit in 'tempering agency problems between founding-family owners and outside shareholders' leading to 'performance premiums for family firms with greater levels of board independence relative to non-family firms or family firms with insider-dominated boards' (2004: 231). They do acknowledge that they are making causal inferences from correllational data, so they call for more detailed follow-up research on board structures, committees, nominating procedures, and the implications of these findings for smaller firms.

In both the general corporate governance literature and the work on family companies in particular, after several decades of inconclusive results looking at different percentages of directors from each category measured against a wide range of performance indicators, the tone of the research is changing. More authors are moving away from a blanket endorsement (or critique) of independent-director-dominated boards for all family businesses, and advocating the need to be situational, concluding that not one board style fits all (Corbetta and Salvato, 2004; Lane et al., 2006). They call for much more specific research linking board configurations to company lifecycle, industry, history, and particular task responsibilities (Sharma et al., 1997; Nicholson et al., 2009). For example, R&D firms may need more insiders who know the technology and the players; larger, diversified firms need a broader range of expertise, and therefore a larger board (Coles et al., 2001, 2008). Additionally, some authors suggest a transitional stage of an advisory board, to help overcome family fears about losing control. Lambrecht and Lievens (2008) see this structure as a way to introduce outsiders in a 'safe mode', as it has no legal status (the power remains in the hands of the owners) and it is easily dissolved.

There are also calls for clarifying the role of outside director in the family business board. Some writers suggest that for family companies, purely independent directors may not be as important as 'affiliate' directors, who are not family members or managers, but who come to the board with a prior business connection, professional service history, or investment link to the family or the company. Jones et al. (2008), for example, found that directors of this type have valuable information and familiarity with the family firm, and more at stake, than unaffiliated independents, and therefore offer specific value in encouraging product diversification, overcoming a family-firm bias toward persistence with over-mature product arrays. Practitioners are also calling for more specific guidance from outcome research so that they can design board development interventions and better orientation for new directors, helping them 'fulfill the functions they are uniquely positioned to serve within family companies that have public shareholders' (DeMott, 2008: 825).

In particular, it is vital to further investigate the suggestion from several key studies of a curvilinear relationship between family engagement in governance and performance (Anderson and Reeb, 2003). These studies suggest that for the first generation of entrepreneurial firms, focused on survival and growth, more family involvement is better, aiding capital retention, lowered costs of labor, and high energy and commitment. But as the firm matures, especially after the departure of the founder, less family involvement on the board may be correlated with better financial performance, more appropriately aggressive risk-taking and growth, and more accurate assessment of successor family managers. If those findings hold up across a variety of situations, it would be extremely valuable to practitioners as a guide to their advisory work with families on evolving the structure and membership of the board across time.

In addition, for the more complex family enterprises, the questions of board structure, composition, and size need to take into account the overall organizational structure (Jara-Bertin et al., 2008). Which board? Serving what governance purpose? For example, the owners/investors may form a holding company, a family partnership, or a private trust company, each requiring a separate governing board to oversee their asset-management and asset-allocation functions. At the same time, in the business circle each operating company may have its own board, also with governance responsibilities but for a different set of constituents, with very different demands.

Actually, the list of potential boards in the complex, later-generation family enterprise is longer, including the family office board, the family foundation board, the boards of subsidiaries and joint ventures, and the 'pseudo-board' created by interlocking groups of trustees. As a result, the questions of insider/outsider representation, or optimal number of directors and frequency of meetings, or transparency and information flow, have no general answer. The relationships among all of these family business boards within the same family enterprise raise many interesting questions about appropriate representation, optimal number and category of directors, legal and tax beneficial structures, required expertise, goal setting for return on assets, and liquidity and exit provisions.

Finally, regarding board structure, there are also interesting researchable questions about different skill sets required for directors at different levels, and the critical issue of the allocation of the family's human capital across governance roles in these organizational hierarchies. Is it beneficial for family members to follow a maturational progression from divisional board to operating company board to holding company board? Does it serve the family's interest for that to be an automatic sequence based on age or years of service, without consideration of competencies? What about branch representation on boards – is branch equality more relevant, or more tenacious, at one level than another, and with what consequence for both the financial and interpersonal well-being of the extended family? To date there is no broad-sample empirical data reported in the literature about the structure, function, or impact of these networks of boards in the increasingly complex structures of family-controlled enterprises.

Board Process

The literature on boards has been dominated by studies of board structure and demographics, with much less attention to board process and functioning (Forbes and Milliken, 1999; Ricart et al., 1999; Carver and Oliver, 2002). Zahra and Pearce in their excellent literature review conclude:

> There is a wide gap between the normative literature's recognition of these board roles and empirical documentation of the extent to which each is performed in reality ... There are countless lists of what boards should do. Yet, evidence on what boards actually do is not well documented. (Zahra and Pearce, 1989: 304, 325)

Some critics argue that, regardless of their makeup, boards are ill-equipped to accomplish the governance tasks that have been assigned to them, because of lack of time (corporate boards meet an average of 18 hours per year), lack of specific information (due to sheer volume and to willful withholding by managers), and lack of the full range of skills that are required (Eisenberg, 1976; Shleifer and Vishny, 1997; Baird and Rasmussen, 2007). It has been suggested that the gap between implementation and effective performance is even larger in family firms than in corporations in general, as the owners' ambivalence about board-dominated governance in general leads them to create boards and then ignore or circumvent them (Corbetta et al., 2002).

Forbes and Milliken studied boards as decision-making groups. They express a general negative view of the potential for boards, describing them as large, elite, and episodic decision-making groups – the kind of groups particularly vulnerable to 'process losses ... It is often difficult for the board to do these [control and service tasks], ... and on many boards the quantity and quality of substantive interaction are, in fact, minimal' (1999: 490). They posited that board functioning depends both on board demographics and on board processes such as conflict management, norms on levels of effort, and level of cohesiveness on the board. They offer a set of testable hypotheses about the direct and indirect impact of board process on firm performance. James (1999a) discusses the purposes and constraints on reciprocal relationships in governance, comparing family-based informal ties with formal contractual relationships. He generates hypotheses about the conditions that make one or the other more appropriate and effective, particularly in the extended time horizon of family continuity (James, 1999b). Neither set of hypotheses has been tested.

The interpersonal process in family business boards in particular has generated a very small literature, despite the opportunity to test many family dynamics models and theories in the working context of business governance (e.g., family lifecycle models, Bowenian theory, structural family analysis,

psychodynamic theories). Johnson (2004) presents a conceptual analysis of a case study, but few other articles go beyond pure description, with an emphasis on the drama of conflict. There is to date no significant empirical study relating board process (task clarity, conflict management, team development, leadership style, generational and branch collaboration and competition) to governance effectiveness (financial oversight, strategy formation and implementation, succession planning) in family companies.

Board Tasks of Special Importance in Family Business Governance

One of the board's tasks that has special meaning in family companies is determining appropriate distributions to owners (Easterbrook, 1984; Farinha, 2003). Distributions are an important governance responsibility in all corporations, affecting capital-raising and shareholder behavior in general, but in family-owned companies they take on special financial, lifestyle, and symbolic importance. Setting dividends serves the purpose of maintaining investor commitment and defusing anxiety about insider expropriation, even though in economic terms dividends are often a low-efficiency method for providing return on investment, particularly when they are paired with raising capital through debt (Shleifer and Vishny, 1986; Setia-Atmaja et al., 2009; Yoshikawa and Rasheed, 2010).

Some agency theorists argue that one of the purposes of dividends is to reduce the amount of free cash under the control of managers, in order to reduce Type 1 (owner-manager) agency risks and costs (Gugler, 2003). It is also hypothesized that dividends reduce Type 2 (owner-owner) agency costs by 'leveling the playing field' between insider shareholders (who may have a number of different financial perquisites and benefits that are not available to minority and non-managerial owners) and the shareholder group at large (Faccio et al., 2001; Setia-Atmaja et al., 2009: 864). Given the importance of financial rewards, it is surprising that there is not much literature on the particular meaning of dividends in family companies, particularly the impact of percent ownership, generation in control, family branch involvement in management, geography, and liquidity needs of the family members. There is also no empirical research exploring whether or not there are typically different levels of dividends between wholly-owned or closely-held family companies and family-controlled publicly-traded companies.

A second board governance task of particular importance to family businesses is succession planning. There is an extensive family business literature on succession planning; in fact, it is the most written-about topic in the field (Sharma et al., 1997; Chrisman et al., 2003). However, most of that research is on development and selection procedures, and the incumbent-successor relationship. Only a small number of studies address the governance aspects of succession: the organizational location of control over the succession process, the role of the board, and the performance outcomes of different succession procedures (Handler, 1994). A paper by Phan et al. (2005) offers an excellent review of the governance dynamics in succession planning. They find only one empirical study of 'the link between succession and firm performance'. That study (Morris, 1997) found that while the succession process can be enhanced through successor preparation, clarity on the decision-making procedures, and open communication, the relationship between the process and firm performance was mixed. Phan also found a negative correlation between the stakeholder satisfaction with the succession plan, and revenue growth; that is, the more the family liked the succession process and outcome, the less well the company performed after the transition. This is a provocative early finding on a very specific governance-succession dynamic, representing the great opportunity for interesting research on this topic.

In summary, there is no area of family business research more promising or consequential than empirical investigations of the governance performance of boards of directors in family-controlled companies. The descriptive practitioner literature is extensive, but outcome research is scarce. Huse (2000) identifies four seminal review papers on board performance and impact (not specifically on family company boards, but on SME boards, which overlaps significantly but not completely with the family-controlled territory): Zahra and Pearce (1989), Pettigrew (1992), Johnson et al. (1996), and Forbes and Milliken (1999). All four reviews suggest detailed and well-considered research agendas. More recent review articles have continued the call (Daily et al., 2003; Uhlaner et al., 2007). Most of the authors offer theoretical models or extensions of classical theory such as agency, stewardship, stakeholder analysis, behavioral economics, and all end their presentations of hypotheses and propositions with a call for empirical research. It is time for the field to catch up.

Other Mechanisms of Governance in the Ownership and Business Circles

In publicly-traded companies, families have other techniques in addition to board membership to exercise ownership control. Research on these ownership features has for the most part not been reported in the family business literature, even though the research samples heavily represent family-controlled, publicly-traded companies. We are including these ownership vehicles and processes in this review of the research on governance implementation, because they have a major impact on governance and are particularly important in family-controlled businesses.

Blockholding

This term refers to the concentration of ownership in the hands of individuals and voting blocks. The general rule is that any shareholder who owns directly or controls 5 per cent or more of the voting shares of a corporation is a 'blockholder'. This ownership concentration is the classic characteristic of family-controlled firms. In the general organizational literature, there are many warnings that this kind of concentrated ownership is a threat to rational governance, but in the growing number of published studies on the impact of organizational blockholders, the results are unremarkable. For example, Bozek and Laurin (2008) found that firm performance may be negatively affected when a blockholder has the incentive and opportunity to expropriate resources from minority shareholders, but that special voting rights, as in many family firms, does not itself lead to poorer performance. La Porta and colleagues (La Porta et al., 1999, 2000) analyze large samples of international data on ownership dispersal, generally finding that the weak regulatory and judicial conditions that exist in most non-US economies favor family consolidation of governance authority.[3] A fair summary of this literature would be that there is no strong evidence of a general detrimental impact of blockholding (Holderness, 2003; Ben-Amar and Andre, 2006), particularly in economies like the USA where there are strong legal and normative protections for the rights of minority shareholders (Burkart et al., 2003). Nevertheless, there is a need for more study of the power dynamics among large and small blockholders in family firms (Jara-Bertin et al., 2008), and in particular the governance consequences of various representation solutions.

Dual stock class systems

This is the second control mechanism often used by families at the point when they seek outside capital, and transition from a privately held to a traded company. In these companies one class of stock, widely traded or at least transferable, holds the majority of the equity of the firm; a second class of stock, very closely held (in these cases most often within the family, or even in one sector or generation of the family) controls the governance (voting) rights (Masulis et al., 2008). The most common ratio is 1:10; that is, each supershare carries 10 votes (Gompers et al.,

2007). It is estimated that 5–8 per cent of US publicly-traded corporations have more than one class of common stock. Economists who study corporate finance have suggested a negative impact of supershares on the ability to attract investment capital, and hypothesized Type II agency costs of expropriation of minority shareholder rights and benefits by the controlling elite (Harris and Raviv, 1988; Bebchuk et al., 1999; Bozec and Laurin, 2008). But other studies have found no overall detrimental effect in family companies (Grossman and Hart, 1988; Barontini and Caprio, 2005; Villalonga and Amit, 2008). The consensus is that dual-class stock structures are very effective at warding off potential hostile takeovers, and while they definitely carry some cost in the capital markets, that is often seen as worth it to insiders (Gompers et al., 2007). DeMott (2008) suggests that some wealthy owners will gladly sacrifice a marginal portion of share value to secure continued control. Nevertheless, there are situations where single-class, one-share-one-vote rules appear to lead to better choices and more merit-based decisions, particularly when assessing the performance of managers (Harris and Raviv, 1988). Studies on the impact of dual-classes of stock on generational dynamics among family branches, board performance, and succession planning in family firms has not been reported.

Chair/CEO role duality

One aspect of corporate structure that has generated some empirical research, concerns the advantages or disadvantages of the same individual serving as board Chair and CEO (duality). The US tradition has been to emphasize efficiency and alignment, leading to more frequent duality. In Europe and the old British Commonwealth, with a stronger tradition of checks and balances, the roles are rarely combined. But the situation may be different in family firms. Bartholomeusz and Tanewski (2006), for example, found that family firms in an Australian sample were four times more likely than non-family public firms to have one individual as CEO and

Chair; Navarro and Ansón (2009) found that 55 per cent of their sample of Spanish family businesses had one person serving in both roles. Kor (2006) found a similar percentage in Asian family firms.

For publicly-traded corporations in general, there are numerous studies testing the impact of duality or separation of the CEO and Chair roles on a number of organizational outcomes: performance, operations, strategy, conflict, liquidity, cost of capital, reputation in the market, and human resource management. However, as in the other topics of governance assessment, no conclusion seems to be very strongly supported. The trend in the USA over the past two decades has clearly been toward separation of the roles, as endorsed by the Sarbanes–Oxley requirements for publicly-traded companies (Braun and Sharma, 2007). However, there are a growing number of studies challenging the empirical justification for opposing duality in family firms (Boyd, 1995; Baliga et al., 1996; Coles et al., 2001; Daily et al., 2003; Kor, 2006; Braun and Sharma, 2007). For example, Braun and Latham (2009) found that in a recession, dual leadership companies recovered faster. Daily and Dollinger's early work (1992) on owner-managed and professionally-managed family companies found a small, non-significant advantage for duality. Westphal (1999) presents some interesting findings that even when the roles are split, strong social ties between CEOs and directors can actually improve board input in strategic decision-making, without an accompanying loss in board oversight. In contrast, there is a small literature on the entrenchment of owner-family CEOs in the face of poor performance. Hillier and McColgan (2004, 2009), for example, find that family CEOs are less likely to be fired after business downturns than non-family CEOs, independent of the CEO's personal shareholding. In addition, they report in a sample of UK listed companies (50 per cent with CEO/Chair duality) that stock prices, sales growth, and employment all climb following the departure of a family CEO, if the successor is not a family member (see also Pérez-González, 2001). It may be that, in good times, duality fosters efficiency and lowers agency costs, whereas in bad times, it insulates poor executive performance and slows needed change. There is clearly a need for more specific research on duality in family companies that takes into account industry, generation of the leader, board membership and activity, and capital structure.

Shareholder agreements

Shareholder agreements have been traditionally discussed in the literature as part of the legal and financial infrastructure of the business, but not as a governance tool. They are most often drafted to control the transfer of voting shares, in order to restrict dispersal, to retain desired balance among family branches through a sequence of rights of refusal for tendered shares, and/or to specify the process for valuation in an effort to reduce conflict in within-family transfers. The governance implications of these agreements are becoming better understood, alongside their tax and financial consequences (McCahery and Vermeulen, 2006), but the core governance questions have not yet been addressed. For example, what is the link between the terms of the share-transfer provisions and the engagement of branches in the succession process? Do liquidity options available to minority family shareholders affect the engagement of family members and branches in governance, and if so, with what consequences for process (board-manager cooperation or conflict) and outcomes (firm performance)? What difference does it make to governance if in-laws are permitted to be owners, either through inheritance, gift, or divorce?

A special subcategory of shareholder agreements with particular relevance to family companies is prenuptial agreements. Like all forms of shareholder agreement, these are designed in part to control the dispersal of ownership shares, in this case as a result of (usually later-generation) marriage. Once again, there is a fairly broad descriptive literature about prenuptial agreements (Estess,

1996), and some informal literature by legal and other advisors either advocating or opposing them in principle (Griffiths, 2011), but no systematic empirical research on their impact on governance process, firm performance, and ownership continuity, or on their effect on the process of sibling partnerships and cousin consortiums (for example, are talented and appropriate in-laws still eligible for board service if a prenuptial prohibits them from inheriting shares, and if so, are they entitled to distributions that may be available to other directors?).

Shareholder assemblies

The shareholder assembly is typically described as an expansion of the company's annual meeting, a standard in corporate governance. Well-designed shareholder assemblies are usually organized so that owners hear from business leaders about company performance, interact with the board of directors, and ratify (sometimes with discussion or even debate) the overall strategy and financial plans of company leadership. The shareholder assembly also typically elects the family directors.

Family business advisors have routinely advocated convening such meetings as high-involvement, face-to-face events, rather than relying on the proxy-based rituals that are common in traditional public companies. Consultants have written about the benefits of integrating geographically-dispersed family branches; highlighting company accomplishments in an effort to sustain long-term financial commitment; motivating potential next-generation members to be willing to participate in governance by filling family-designated seats on boards, councils, and committees; demonstrating family engagement to employees, managers, outside directors, and current and potential investors; and explaining or justifying decisions about distributions (Elstrodt, 2003; Poza, 2008). However, the impact of the design, attendance, and agenda of shareholder assemblies on the board and managerial behavior that follows, on relationships among shareholders, or on company performance in family firms remains to be studied.

Sometimes in the descriptive literature and in practice, shareholder assemblies are not clearly distinguished from family assemblies, which appropriately belong in a different circle with different membership, tasks, and sources of legitimacy. In first-generation controlling owner businesses, there may be no practical difference. However, as the company grows and there are both owners and non-owners in the expanding family, the distinction has important governance implications. For example, especially in families who have a newly formalized governance structure, the shareholder assembly may elect the family council, which may be a practical convenience but actually is not a shareholder responsibility. Alternatively, sometimes family assemblies take it upon themselves to select family directors, also a blurring of the circles unless the shareholders have formally delegated that task to the council. In either direction, this crossover can be a transitional step, when the family is too large for all members to participate actively in governance, but not large enough to support separate gatherings of current shareholders and the extended family. This illustrates a core gap in the governance implementation literature. Research on the optimal timing of a separation of ownership and family governance, and the performance and continuity consequences of being either 'too early' or 'too late', would be a significant contribution to the literature.

Trusts, private trust companies, estate planning, and other wealth transfer structures and mechanisms

Even further from the mainstream of governance research are the systems that families put in place to preserve and transfer wealth. These structures are discussed in the legal, financial, and business literature as financial entities, but they also have serious governance implications, both obvious and hidden. The use of trusts as estate planning tools, primarily to shield large inheritances from taxes, exploded in the second half of the 20th century. As state and federal laws permitted and encouraged a wide range of trust structures, clients turned to their legal advisors to suggest best practices. Hughes (2004) was one of the first voices to point out that the criteria that attorneys used to choose trustees and frame their roles – financial expertise, credibility, and dependability – were ignoring a critical part of the role. Trustees are governors. During the settlor's lifetime, they have ready access to his/her judgment and priorities. But what about subsequently? Trustees fulfill their fiduciary responsibility to the beneficiaries by making critical investment choices, and in many cases those choices have profound impact on strategy, financial structure and risk profiles, and viability of the companies – which often come to be owned not by the family descendants of founders, but by the trusts themselves. Some of the newer structures, such as private trust companies, may add even further to the governance complexity.

Professionals have begun to think and write more about the governance aspects of wealth transfer in families. However, a significant, formal research literature has yet to emerge testing the effectiveness of various solutions, such as the impact of the particular kind of trust (for example, revocable, irrevocable, GRATs (Grantor Retained Annuity Trust), GRITs (Grantor Retained Income Trust), generation-skipping, beneficiary-controlled) on performance in the owned companies. This is a great opportunity for legal scholars and family-business researchers to collaborate on investigating the consequences beyond tax minimization of trust design: for example, the policies for the selection of initial and successor trustees, the trustee-director relationship, the role and membership of private trust company boards, differences in the behavior of successor generations depending on whether they are outright inheriting owners or trust beneficiaries, consequences of the age at which the beneficiary has access to trust capital, and the impact on governance and strategy of different kinds of trustees (such as

institutional trustees, family trustees, and private trust companies). The number of significant family-controlled enterprises that will become trust-controlled in the coming decades greatly increases the urgency of generating good data and analyses as soon as possible.

Summary of Governance Implementation in the Ownership and Business Circles

A very high proportion of the published literature on governance concerns boards of directors. The practice literature is strongly supportive of independent boards for family enterprise. The research literature lags behind (true for non-family businesses as well). Correlational data on the relationship between board structure and firm performance is beginning to accumulate; data on board process is still rare.

We briefly summarized the literature on six other governance topics in the ownership and business circles that have particular importance for family enterprises: blockholding, dual class stock systems, CEO/Chair duality, shareholder agreements, shareholder assemblies, and trusts. For all of these topics, there is some research on their design and operation in corporations in general. What remains to be developed is a broad literature on their particular implementation in family owned and controlled companies, and the integration of financial, legal, business, and family variables in assessing their impact on governance and continuity in family enterprise.

GOVERNANCE IN THE FAMILY CIRCLE

We are stretching the traditional definition of governance when we include the family circle, because there are no 'owners' in a family. Nevertheless, families need governing as well – not only in the sense that all human systems may benefit from leadership and structure, but because business-owing families have organizational work to do *as families*, and their ability to do that work efficiently and effectively has material consequence for business and financial operations, and for the preservation of family wealth.

However, we are not proposing that all aspects of family process are usefully called governance. There is a difference between family relationships, harmony, or communication, and governance. Family governance is specifically concerned with enterprise goals. We consider the family to be engaged in governance only when they are attending to the financial and operational interdependence of family members in their businesses, foundations, offices, investment portfolios, and assets held in common. This distinction is important because it provides the justification for formalizing family governance, while freeing the family to think about its organizational control functions separately from its network of personal relationships.

Governance in the family circle, as in the business and ownership, is enacted through one or more organizational settings and procedures. We will review the literature on implementation of governance in family councils, family assemblies, family mission statements, family offices, and family foundations.

The Family Council

The family council is the board of directors for the family circle (Poza, 2009). It can be an all-inclusive, self-appointed, or elected workgroup of family members, whose main tasks are to make decisions about the business of the family and to educate families about the enterprise (Lansberg, 1999; Dickstein, 2003; Jaffe, 2005; Goldbart and DiFuria, 2009). Gersick et al. define the family council as 'a group who periodically come together to discuss issues arising from their family's involvement with a business. The fundamental purpose of a family council is to provide a forum in which family members can articulate their values, needs, and expectations

vis-à-vis the company and develop policies that safeguard the long-term interests of the family' (1997: 237).

Like boards of directors, family councils have been very widely advocated by family business advisors for decades (Ward, 1987; Lansberg, 1988, 1999, 2007; Herz-Brown, 1993; Aronoff and Ward, 1996; Gersick et al., 1997; Jaffe et al., 1998; BDO Center for Family Business, 2004; Jaffe, 2005; De Visscher, reported in Cruz, 2008; Poza, 2008, 2009; Parada et al., 2010). *Family Business Magazine* archives include almost 200 articles describing family councils. Most of the professional literature focuses on the general benefit of the council for both the family and the firm (Gray, 2009), particularly in later stages of family firm development (sibling partnership and cousin consortiums) (Lansberg, 2007; Moore and Juenemann, 2008). Advocated functions of the family council include:

- forging family consensus, and counteracting declining family bonds and low identification with the firm, as families grow and spontaneous social contacts among family members decrease (Kets de Vries, 1993; Mustakallio et al., 2002);
- articulating a family strategy for business and wealth management (Goldbart and DiFuria, 2009), including planning, rule setting, and collaborative asset allocation, which are 'not natural activities for families' (Dickstein, 2003);
- limiting family conflicts that could negatively affect the business (Benson et al., 1990; McManus, 1990);
- supporting succession planning (Handler, 1994; Leon-Guerrero et al., 1998; Lansberg, 1999), particularly in facilitating the family's exploration of their 'collective dream of continuity' (Lansberg, 1997), and in conveying a policy-driven, stewardship culture and enthusiasm for the business (Aronoff and Ward, 1996);
- educating and welcoming younger generations (Lansberg, 2007; Poza, 2009), as 'a forum for lifelong learning' (Aronoff and Ward, 1996: 282).

Many articles include case stories. For example, Lamp presented the case of the first six years of the Eddy Family Council. The Eddy Family framed the role of the Family Council as the caretaker of 'investors' relations'. They believe the family council has 'clearly strengthened the business … and the family' (2007: 5). The author concludes that the critical conditions for the family council to accomplish its tasks are education and socialization of new family council members, and an independent budget for funding its activities. Daugherty (2009) illustrates a case of a family council that led a transition in both the management and ownership of a family firm. This case portrays the governance functions of the council, fostering and enhancing ties among family members, allowing it to frame the policies of restructuring and redesign.

Nevertheless, after 25 years of both family firm research and extensive consulting interventions in business families, there is essentially no evaluative outcome research on family councils.[4] Many articles propose roles for the family council in key governance functions, and may provide case examples, but they do not present aggregate data on the councils' implementation or performance. As a result, there is no consensus as to the design details: the most effective size, composition, frequency of meetings, election process, roles, or specific tasks of the family council. And, most importantly, there is no longitudinal, controlled research to actually test the effectiveness of family councils at achieving their objectives.

Looking forward, a first step might be the creation of typologies, which will allow testing the impact of the different legal, financial, and organizational forms that family councils take. The interesting work will be in the details: Who pays for them? How are their budgets managed? Where does the membership come from – election, appointment, volunteerism, or some other process? For elected councils, are they at large or representative, and if the latter, representing what constituencies? What tasks tend to lead to experiences of success for council members, and what other tasks are experienced as frustrating or failed efforts?.

Second, research on the impact on council structure and process of specific family characteristics such as marital stability, variance in number of offspring across generations and branches, emigration and geographic mobility, traditions of inheritance, and gender dynamics, would add to our understanding of their governance functions. Researchers can also explore the impact of culture, geography, and ethnicity on council design (for example, Brenes et al. (2011) found that Latin American business families use Family Councils as communication facilitators, not governance tools).

Then, the most pressing need is for basic performance metrics for family councils. We need to build a body of research on the four main outcomes most commonly sought by family councils: (1) finding the family's 'common ground' on business values, business culture, philanthropy, and wealth management; (2) educating family members, particularly the rising generations, about the family enterprise; (3) facilitating communication between the extended family and the leaders in the ownership and business circles; and, as a result of the other three tasks, (4) enhancing the family's commitment to the enterprise. Impact studies are always difficult, requiring inspired selection of dependent measures, and most often multi-method longitudinal data gathering. But considering the extensive endorsement of this governance solution, it is clearly one of the topics most deserving of the effort.

Other Family Circle Governance Structures

Family assemblies

Family assemblies are the periodic (typically annual) gathering of an extended family. These events often include formal meetings where information is shared about investments and operating companies, speakers and facilitated discussions, and other recreational activities that are common in family reunions. Ward argues that 'the best practice' that is most important to long-term family business growth is the process of holding family meetings' (1997: 335). Other advisors suggest that family meetings can help families achieve consensus regarding family mission, family values, and the raison d'être for the sustainability of the family business over generations (Vilaseca, 2002; Jaffe and Lane, 2004; Montemerlo, 2005; Gimeno et al., 2006). Family Assemblies are often recommended as particularly useful in large family groups with broad geographic dispersal, highly diffused ownership, and a desire to sustain economic interdependence through subsequent cousin generations.

It is a reasonable hypothesis that shared experiences with the extended family will facilitate governance implementation: selection of directors, trustee-beneficiary relationships, capital retention, and broad support for investment and distribution policies. However, as for family councils, the overall impact of family assemblies, as well as specific operational questions such as the differentiation between family assemblies and shareholder assemblies, and the most effective frequency, agenda, and choices about who gets invited, are interesting and as yet unexplored research topics.

Family constitutions, protocols, and mission statements

Many advisors work with families on creating mission statements or family constitutions and protocols, beyond the shareholder agreements that govern ownership. The recent increase in interest in family constitutions may be in response to the maturation of a large cohort of entrepreneurial post-World War II nuclear families through sibling and multi-generational partnerships to complex, geographically-dispersed family networks (Gersick, 2002a, 2002b). In addition, popular culture presents young adults in these extended families with an unlimited array of alternative value systems and lifestyles. Senior generation leaders who are concerned about the continuity of the enterprise in this 'competitive market' for the family's attention, may use a constitution to articulate their values and culture, to formalize the 'rules of engagement', and to emphasize the obligations and

requirements for participation in the benefits of future ownership.

Family constitutions have been seen as a nice-to-have accessory in the USA, and more of a first-choice governance option in Latin America and parts of Europe. Brenes et al. (2011) found them to be very popular in concept in Latin America, although often not implemented or adhered to. In the USA, they received a flurry of attention after Covey identified mission statements as a habit of successful individuals and families (Covey, 1989; McClain, 2006).

So far the literature on family mission statements and constitutions is primarily descriptive; the value is seen as self-evident by the professionals who advocate them (for example, Hauser, 2003; Coombes and Wong, 2004). Some case studies conclude a benefit of formal statements (Lewine, 2006). Other authors discuss the value of protocols to promote particular outcomes, such as 'fair process' (Van der Heyden et al., 2005; Blondel et al., 2001), or the avoidance of later problems such as 'reputation exposure, wealth entropy, family division and legal costs' (Griffiths, 2011). We could not identify any formal study aggregating governance provisions from a large sample of family constitutions, or assessing the impact or specific benefit of family mission statements on governance or family firm performance.

Family offices

The term 'family office' is used to cover a very wide range of service centers, investment oversight functions, back office operations, and other support services for family members (Murray et al., 2002). Some family offices are closely linked to operating businesses, using company staff to provide financial and legal support for family members. Other family offices are actually just one individual or a collection of independent contractors from various professions, designed primarily to enhance coordination among investment, legal, insurance, and tax advisors. However, a growing number of families have created something much more formal: an independent partnership or corporation with a significant budget and staff who operate the business of the overseeing the family's private wealth. Professionals estimate that there are 3,000 family offices of this type in the USA, and the number is growing annually. The concept of governance is clearly relevant for these organizations.

Once again, most of the literature on family office governance is advice-giving from experienced professionals, and case examples (for example, Hauser, 2001; Families in Business, 2003 [brief articles by Maslinki, Youngman, Stern, Beyer and Brown, Patterson, and Ward]; Jaffe and Lane, 2004; Griffiths, 2011). Lansky and Pendergast (2010) offer some interesting observations that generate testable research hypotheses, such as that wealth management does not provide the same 'glue' for extended families as governing an operating company, that individual rights are more relevant in family office governance, and that the wide range of services make family office governance more complicated. Additional questions that are raised in case studies include: What constituencies have a legitimate right to governance authority in a family office: investor-funders, clients for services, or the entire family? What governance mechanisms work to integrate and balance the goals of these stakeholders? Can family councils effectively act as boards of directors for family offices, and if not, what structure is most effective?

The family office industry has matured well beyond its former preoccupation with service menus and the selection of money managers, and some aggregate data are emerging. The Wharton Global Family Alliance publishes results of their research program on family offices, concluding that 'family governance is key' (Amit et al., 2008: 31; see also Knowledge at Wharton, 2008; Amit and Liechtenstein, 2009). Their survey and interview data summarize both operational practices and governance structures.

However, family office research highlights one of the special features of the family business field: a significant amount of the research that is conducted is proprietary, available only to clients or members and subscribers of private associations. For example, the Family Office Exchange (www.familyoffice.com) publishes a number of survey reports, case studies, and papers by practitioners about family offices, but they are not published in the academic literature. They are available to fee-paying members or, in some cases, for purchase by the public. This blending of fee-for-service products with knowledge generation is complicated for the field. It is not peer reviewed like journal articles, but the work may represent the insightful conclusions of experienced professionals. For example, FOX publishes *50 Best Practices for an Enduring Family Enterprise*, described as 'a comprehensive guide to the proven strategies and approaches family offices have used to improve nearly all aspects of their operations ... It highlights proven governance and operational practices your management team and governing board can use' (Family Office Exchange, September 2008: list price, $4,500); or *How Wealth Owners Measure Value: Evaluating the Performance of Your Wealth Advisor or Family Office* (Family Office Exchange, October 2010: list price, $1,500). There are similar other sources. Campden (www.campdenresearch.com) publishes reports such as an annual European Family Office Survey (for 2011 entitled *Beyond Uncertainty: Family Offices Adapt to Unpredictability*: price, $3,140). The integration of valuable proprietary findings and data into the mainstream is a policy and professional challenge, and is discussed in more detail in the section on future research below.

Family foundations

The research literature on family foundation governance is even more limited than the work on family businesses. There are estimated to be more than 40,000 private foundations in the USA alone, and many more donor-advised funds and corporate giving programs in family-controlled companies. The Family Foundations division of the Council on

Foundations has been that organization's fastest growing sector over the past several decades. Philanthropy in general has benefitted from an enormous increase in attention to professionalism, transparency, fiscal accountability, strategic planning, impact assessment, and all aspects of organizational functioning. However, the focus of the literature in the field has been and continues to be on program – the work of grantmaking, analogous to operations in the family business – with much less attention to governance.

An early small-sample study of family foundations (Gersick et al., 1990) proposed a set of hypotheses for further study, but until very recently there had been few empirical studies of governance structure in family philanthropy. The publications that do address governance are almost exclusively case stories and best-practice suggestions written by experienced family participants in philanthropy or by professional advisors to foundations from a variety of disciplines (Esposito, 2002; Angus, 2004), or guides for regulation-compliant governance, written primarily by attorneys (McCoy and Miree, 2010). Examples of more formal research on family foundation governance include one study sponsored by the National Center for Family Philanthropy (Gersick et al., 2004), another by the Foundation Governance Project of the Center for Effective Philanthropy (CEP, 2004, 2005), and a recent study on the effects of governance on grantmaking strategy by Lungeanu and Ward (2012). The Gersick et al. (2004) study of governance and continuity in multi-generational family foundations found a range of governance practices that evolved through successor generations, but in general an under-investment in board structure and development, preparation of rising generations, and operational and financial oversight, when compared with grantmaking activities. The CEP study is straightforward in acknowledging that, 'given that there is no universal, comparable performance measure for foundations – no analog to a company's stock price or profitability, for example – it is difficult to connect governance practices to foundation performance' (Center

for Effective Philanthropy, 2005: 2). As a 'proxy' for direct measures, they rely on CEO and trustee perceptions of foundation board effectiveness.

Angus and Herz-Brown (2007) found in an online-based survey that most families are 'informal' in their governance structure and processes for philanthropy, and have not specifically discussed or chosen governance procedures. Nevertheless, most philanthropy consultants observe that family philanthropy has been dramatically professionalized in recent decades, and data on governance needs to catch up. Most of the governance implementation issues described earlier for the business circle are relevant for family foundations, in particular: (a) the correlates of governance behavior with foundation performance; and (b) the differentiation and integration of the different vehicles for family philanthropy, including corporate philanthropy in family-owned firms, family foundations, and personal and branch giving within philanthropic families. How are each of the streams governed to collectively reflect the family's philanthropic values, and how are the family's human capital resources most optimally allocated among them? The professional literature estimates that up to $6 trillion will be transferred in the United States through philanthropy over the next few decades (Havens and Schervish, 1999; Journal of Gift Planning, 2006). The need for more quality research on governance in this sector is urgent.

Summary: Governance Implementation in the Family Circle

There is a small but developing literature investigating more differentiated family governance roles across stages of development (Leon-Guerrero et al., 1998). In particular, governance can act as a counterbalance to the negative effects of increasing family and ownership complexity (Jaffe and Lane, 2004) as the ownership governance system evolves from a controlling owner to a sibling partnership and further to a cousin consortium

(Gersick et al., 1997; Lansberg, 1999; Steier, 2001). Some research addresses the consequences of increasing family complexity: decreases in entrepreneurship, capability development, business growth and family firm financial performance (Lambrecht and Lievens, 2008); a decline of family satisfaction regarding family-company relationships (Gimeno et al., 2006); a decrease in family interrelation and cohesiveness due to increasing differences in personal goals, values, and commitment to the business (Ward, 1997); and a rise in the agency cost of conflict (Schulze et al., 2001). These authors and others (Montemerlo, 2005; Vilaseca, 2002) conclude that family governance can diminish the de-stabilizing pressure of complexity and growth, and enhance the owing-family unity and commitment to the business by formalizing family-firm relationships and regulating the role of the family in the business.

But this optimistic hypothesis, endorsed in practice by most family business consultants, needs empirical testing (Astrachan, 2009). Future research can articulate the criteria that distinguish effective family governance from ineffective efforts, and to apply those criteria to both case examples and large samples to assess outcomes. This is a different task from the ownership and business governance circles, because in those cases there is an existing full literature on corporate governance, both theory and practice. The work in those arenas is to adapt, refine, and apply those theories and general hypotheses to family owned and controlled firms. In contrast, in the family circle, while there is plenty of work in print on family dynamics, relationships, roles, communication, and conflict, there is very little organizational literature on how those dynamics play out in family governance. The field is wide open for new empirical studies.

Summary: A Research Agenda for Family Enterprise Governance

New research over the past several decades on corporate governance in general, and the increasingly sophisticated studies on family business, are the foundation for a major leap forward in governance implementation research. The work of practitioners with family councils, boards of directors, family offices, succession planning, strategy, and corporate finance, has raised a clear and compelling set of hypotheses that need testing. In addition, leaders in the field are calling for research with practical implications – relevant works that reduce the knowing–doing gap (Sharma, 2010). New web-based techniques for broad sample data gathering are widely available. A very large population of senior and junior generation family leaders have participated in executive education, joined family business forums, and been introduced to scholarship and theory in graduate programs. They understand the value of research, and are eager for normative data. There is also a growing cadre of students at all levels of graduate and professional education who are more aware of family enterprise, and looking for interesting and consequential research topics. The opportunity is there to return to the theories and models that have been presented by academics, and the prescriptions and experience of consultants, and to use rigorous sampling, data-gathering, and data-analytic tools to look at what is actually in place in family business governance and how it is working. We do have some exemplary beginnings. The 2012 FFI Best Quantitative Dissertation award was for Memili's work in just this area: an extensive investigation of the impact of governance mechanisms on firm performance, and the link between family involvement, corporate governance provisions, and profitability in publicly-traded family firms (Memili, 2011). Her complex analysis is a major contribution, and should be emulated.

In each of the sections above, on business, ownership, and family governance, we have summarized ideas for further research that are suggested in articles in the existing literature. In addition to these specific topics, there are a few major themes in research on governance implementation that deserve attention from multiple studies and approaches.

1 *The development of governance through stages of formalization and growth.* As the level of expertise required to govern effectively increases, and the percentage of family members in each generation who can actively participate in corporate governance goes down, roles for family members must become differentiated. There is a pressing need for more research on the ways families govern over time (for example, how families evolve from selecting family directors as a symbolic or representational right of shareholding, toward choosing individuals who are prepared to be value-adding contributors to the bottom-line performance of the enterprise). There is also an immediate need for research on the governance role of non-director family owners, particularly in family businesses owned by second, third, and later generations.

2 After 30 years of intensive advice, education, and encouragement for governance implementation in family firms, how are families dealing with 'governance fatigue', later-generation leadership, and the threat of inadequate talent or interest in governance? Legal and financial advisors have done a powerful job in recent decades helping families secure their financial resources for current and future generations. Their success takes some of the pressure off rising generations to commit themselves to family governance, especially the most talented, who have other attractive and lucrative options. The family business is no longer the only, or even necessarily the best, game in town as it was for the founding generations. What rewards will be required to sustain governance implementation in the future?

3 *More cross-cultural and international research.* The bulk of research on agency theory and corporate governance has been conducted on the largest US corporations. Now there is a growing body of studies from other countries, many of which highlight the dominant role of family enterprise in their economies.[5] Some of the articles point out particular features of the legal system, capital market, or cultural traditions that affect governance structures in different economies (for example, the two-tiered board system in Europe, discussed in Huse, 1998; Licht et al., 2001, 2007; Tabalujan, 2002; Pieper, 2003; Filatochev et al., 2005). Others test key hypotheses in new settings, such as the relationship between family control and organization performance in Europe (Barontini and Caprio, 2005), or the effect of weak or strong legal protection for minority owners in various countries on the felt need of controlling shareholders to maintain voting control (Morck and Yeung, 2003). However, as in the US-focused writings, there is still very little empirical research on governance implementation that goes beyond case stories and general models. Many academics are calling for more focus on outcomes and for cross-cultural replication of promising research from one region to another (Uhlaner et al., 2007).

4 *Integrating research and practice.* The combination of research and practitioner experience provides an excellent platform for the next stage of knowledge generation. This goal has been put forward by Sharma and Nordqvist (2008) in their article on value creation within family-owned business. Their study makes an elegant case for the uniqueness of family governance for each family enterprise based on the underlying values that each family holds. We suggest that researchers follow their initiative and look closely at family heterogeneity (Davis, 1982; Hollander, 1983; Ward, 1987; Lansberg, 1988), identifying the core attributes of family business and relating them to different governance structures and designs.

But the integration of formal academic research and practice reporting will not come easily. In the section above on family offices, we mentioned the extensive research on governance sponsored by professional associations. While some of their work is understandably aimed at advocating for their constituents, emphasizing accomplishments and successes rather than rigorously testing hypotheses, they also conduct studies that document the prevalence of governance structures, and in some cases the demographics, typical budgets, and activities of boards, family offices, and foundations.[6] Much of this research on governance implementation is in the form of case studies and aggregated experience; there is little outcome or impact research concerning governance. Nevertheless, their work provides a very promising platform for the academic researchers to build on, to the extent that it is available to them.

The association-sponsored research issue is only a special case of a more general dilemma with two parts: constraints on sharing proprietary data, and on the best methods for investigating complex phenomena. Throughout its relatively short history, family business has been a practitioner-driven field. While the involvement of scholars from the relevant social and behavioral sciences has been accelerating, it is still primarily a guild of professionals delivering services to clients while building both a proprietary and a disseminated knowledge base. The bulk of our shared understanding at present about family enterprise governance has come from their careful observations, action research, case methods, and post-hoc analyses.

However, as in all professional fields, competitive success among providers is based in part on knowing more, and having better answers, than others. It is natural for practicing professionals to be prescriptive rather than equivocal, and there is little incentive to engage in rigorous research that would highlight variability,[7] or commoditize best practices. In contrast, academics have institutional and career-advancing incentives to challenge common knowledge, and a tradition that until something is true at least 95 per cent of the time it cannot be considered to be anything but chance. But they have their constraints as well. The more complicated, quantitative/qualitative designs are expensive and take too long for most academics. Longitudinal, intensive, multi-method data gathering in large samples of operating family enterprises is a dream design that will always be rare. So in a field like family business, with complex phenomena and little guiding theory, the practitioners tend to rely on untested conclusions on big questions, and the researchers focus on rigorous detail for manageable small ones. We need to find a way to capitalize on and integrate the best of both approaches.

In summary, we need more research addressed to the issues and fascinating unknowns of family enterprise governance in all three circles: the structure and process of boards; the fair, productive, and collaborative management of wealth; and the effective organization of families across time and generations. Governance implementation is a sector of our field that is hungry for well-designed studies and well-analyzed data. As we meet that need, it will help us to move beyond broadly-accepted 'common knowledge' about governance practice, and keep us focused on the core task at hand – discovering

what is really true so that we can intervene in ways that are truly helpful.

NOTES

1   A huge body of literature has developed to explore the conditions that either create or reduce agency costs and risks. Fama and Jensen (1983) suggested that family businesses minimize agency costs, since ownership and management are unified in the same individuals, which creates a significant advantage for family companies in the marketplace. That conclusion was challenged by other researchers, who countered that while some kinds of agency costs might be ameliorated (owner-manager costs, sometimes called Type I agency costs), a different set of costs (called Type II) were much higher – the split between those owners in control (through majority holdings, executive roles, or both), and more peripheral and minority owners (Burkart et al., 2003; Morck and Yeung, 2003; Morck et al., 2005).

2   The assignment of the board of directors to either the ownership or the business circle is arbitrary, but it illustrates an ambiguity in the Three-Circle Model that may actually be the best evidence of that model's conceptual usefulness. In fact, the board of directors must reside in both circles. How a board sorts out its different (and sometimes misaligned) obligations to the ownership and business circles on such issues as dividends, debt, risk, expansion, compensation, and career development for owner-employees, is exactly the kind of dilemma that the model illuminates.

3   There is a very large literature in corporate economics on the relationship between the level of regulatory and judicial protection of investors and the sources and cost of capital across regions and countries. This work suggests one very interesting explanation of the global prevalence and persistence of family ownership (as a capital-protection mechanism in economies with weak or unenforceable public policy), but it falls outside the domain of this chapter.

4   This may indicate that the professionals, associations, and scholars in the field have institutionalized the family council as a sign indicator that a family enterprise has been 'professionalized', without any requirement to assess its functioning or impact (Melin and Nordqvist, 2007). A recent study on family firm governance practices from an institutional theory perspective (Parada et al., 2010), pointed out the influence of collective norms, such as those that emerge in professional associations, on the establishment of formalized family governance systems. Families model other families in business in their responses to the challenges they face as family enterprises (mimetic forces), and family firm associations and professionals have identified a loosely-constructed set of best practices that are most frequently recommended to their clients (normative forces). Creating a family council is one of these practices. We agree with Parada et al. (2010) that

institutional pressures help organizations evolve, but sometimes the structures are endorsed without attention to specific content, tasks, authority, and functionality.

5   Exemplary articles include: Australia (Bartholomeusz and Tanewski, 2006; Setia-Atmaja et al., 2009), Europe (Corbetta and Tomaselli, 1996; Huse, 1998; Ricart et al., 1999; Klein, 2000; Gubitta and Gianecchini, 2002; Van den Berghe and Carchon, 2002; Barontini and Caprio, 2005; Bennedsen et al., 2006; Voordeckers et al., 2007; Jara-Bertin et al., 2008; Sciascia and Mazzola, 2008; Navarro and Ansón, 2009; Kowalewski et al., 2010; Bettinelli, 2011), Ghana (Abor and Biekpe, 2007), Indonesia (Tabalujan, 2002), Japan (Yoshikawa and Rasheed, 2010), Latin America (Brenes et al., 2011), Lebanon (Fahed-Srieh, 2009), Malaysia (Amran and Ahmad, 2009), and Southeast Asia (Suehiro, 1993; Chang, 2003; Filatochev et al., 2005; Peng and Jiang, 2010).

As would be expected given the development of the world economy in recent decades, there is a particularly active literature about Asian family enterprise (Khan, 1999; Faccio et al., 2001; Yeh et al., 2001; Yeh and Woidtke, 2005; Lee et al., 2008; Lee and Li, 2009; Shyu and Lee, 2009), with a focus on the cultural and economic characteristics of mainland and overseas Chinese family companies (Lawton, 1996; Carney and Gedajlovic, 2001; Filatotchev et al., 2005; Wu, 2006; Chen and Hsu, 2009; Lansberg and Gersick, 2009).

6   For example:

*   The National Association of Corporate Directors (NACD) publishes white papers and booklet series on leadership and governance, addressing specific challenges facing boards and directors from both public corporations and private and family owned business.
*   The *FFI Practitioner*, an electronic journal edited by the Family Firm Institute, provides practical advice on governance practices and professional interventions, with a cross-disciplinary perspective (it is published in both English and Spanish). Articles in the *Practitioner* have covered such topics as compensation (Schneider and Schneider, 2005), family member employment policies and procedures (Krasnow, 2005), innovation (Craig and Moores, 2009), wealth management (Greenberg, 2006), and consulting challenges (Ginsburg and Saunders, 2011).
*   The Family Office Exchange (FOX) Research Studies include numerous survey and data-based analyses of family office practices and wealth management activities of its member offices and, to some extent, of the broader population. While they have focused more on services than on governance, FOX Research Studies have addressed topics such as investment risk planning and management, wealth transfer, multi-family and family office sustainability and performance, selection and oversight of professional advisors, and development of successor generations.
*   In philanthropy, The Council on Foundations reports on governance and board composition in family foundations, and publishes case stories and common practice

written by participants and professionals in family philanthropy (for example, Stone, 1993). Similarly, the Association of Small Foundations publishes *The Essentials*, a quarterly publication that includes practical articles on governance practices, grant-making processes, and the management of small foundations. The National Center for Family Philanthropy (NCFP)'s newsletter, *Passages*, often presents case examples, survey results, and references to research literature. The NCFP Pursuit of Excellence Project is a specific effort to gather and disseminate implementation data on governance and operations to a broad audience of family foundations, particularly those not large enough to hire consultants and engage in their own more elaborate research and benchmarking efforts.

7   Researchers are happy to explain small percentages of the variance; clients expect a bit more.

REFERENCES

Abor, J. and Biekpe, N. (2007) 'Corporate governance, ownership structure, and performance of SMEs in Ghana: implications for financing opportunities', *Corporate Governance*, 7(3): 288–300.

Agrawal, A. and Knoeber, C.R. (1996) 'Firm performance and mechanisms to control agency problems between managers and shareholders', *Journal of Financial and Quantitative Analysis*, 31(3): 377–397.

Amit, R., Liechtenstein, H., Prats, M.J., Millay, T., and Pendleton, L. (2008) *Single Family Offices: Private Wealth Management in the Family Context*. Philadelphia, PA: Wharton Global Family Alliance.

Amit, R. and Liechtenstein, H. (2009) *Report Highlights for 'Benchmarking the Single Family Office: Identifying the Performance Drivers'*. Philadelphia, PA: Wharton Global Family Alliance.

Amran, N.A. and Ahmad, A.C. (2009) 'Family business, board dynamics and firm value: evidence from Malaysia', *Journal of Financial Reporting and Accounting*, 7: 53–74.

Anderson, R.C. and Reeb, D.M. (2003) 'Founding-family ownership and firm performance: evidence from the S&P 500', *The Journal of Finance*, 58(3): 1301–1328.

Anderson, R.C. and Reeb, D.M. (2004) 'Board composition: balancing family influence in S&P 500 firms', *Administrative Science Quarterly*, 49: 209–237.

Angus, P. (2004) *Family Governance: A Primer for Philanthropic Families*. Washington, DC: National Center for Family Philanthropy.

Angus, P. and Herz-Brown, F. (2007) *Family Governance Meets Family Dynamics: A Survey and Strategies for Successful Joint Philanthropy*. Washington, DC: National Center for Family Philanthropy.

Aronoff, C.E. and Ward, J.L. (1996) *Family Business Governance: Maximizing Family and Business Potential*. Marietta, GA: Family Enterprise Publishers.

Astrachan, J.H. (2009) 'Using and abusing family business research', *Family Business Magazine*, Autumn: 40–42.

Baird, D.G. and Rasmussen, R.K. (2007) 'The prime directive', *University of Cincinnati Law Review*, 75: 921–942.

Baliga, B.R., Moyer, R.C., and Rao, R.S. (1996) 'CEO duality and firm performance: what's the fuss?', *Strategic Management Journal*, 17: 41–43.

Barontini, R. and Caprio, L. (2005) 'The effect of family control of firm value and performance: evidence from continental Europe', *European Corporate Governance Institute*, 1: 1–53.

Bartholomeusz, S. and Tanewski, G.A. (2006) 'The relationship between family firms and corporate governance', *Journal of Small Business Management*, 44(2): 245–267.

Baysinger, B.D. and Butler, H.N. (1985) 'Corporate governance and the board of directors: performance effects of changes in board composition', *Journal of Law, Economics and Organizations*, 1(1): 101–124.

Baysinger, B. and Hoskisson, R.E. (1990) 'The composition of boards of directors and strategic control: effects on corporate strategy', *Academy of Management Review*, 15(1): 72–87.

BDO Centre for Family Business (2004) *Getting the Family to Work Together*. London: Institute for Family Business.

Bebchuk, L., Kraakman, R. and Triantis, G. (1999) 'Stock pyramids, cross-ownership and dual class equity: the creation and agency costs of separating control from cash flow rights', Harvard Law School John M. Olin Center for Law, Economics and Business Discussion Paper Series, Paper 249.

Ben-Amar, W. and Andre, P. (2006) 'Separation of ownership from control and acquiring firm performance: the case of family ownership in Canada', *Journal of Business Finance and Accounting*, 33(3–4): 517–543.

Bennedsen, M., Nielsen, K.M., Pérez-González, F., and Wolfenzon, D. (2006) 'Inside the family firm: the role of families in succession decisions and performance', European Corporate Governance Institute, Paper 132.

Benson, B., Crego, E.T., and Drucker, R. (1990) 'Calling the family to order', *Family Business Magazine*, February.

Berle, A. and Means, G. (1932) *The Modern Corporation and Private Property*. New York: Macmillan Press.

Bettinelli, C. (2011) 'Boards of directors in family firms: an exploratory study of structure and group process', *Family Business Review*, 24(2): 151–169.

Blondel, C., Carlock, R., and Van Der Heyden, L. (2001) 'Fair process: striving for justice in family firms', INSEAD Working Paper 2001/54/ENT, Fontainebleau, France.

Boyd, B.K. (1995) 'CEO duality and firm performance: a contingency model', *Strategic Management Journal*, 16(4): 301–312.

Bozec, Y. and Laurin, C. (2008) 'Large shareholder entrenchment and performance: empirical evidence from Canada', *Journal of Business Finance and Accounting*, 35(1–2): 25–49.

Braun, M. and Sharma, A. (2007) 'Should the CEO also be chair of the board? an empirical examination of family-controlled public firms', *Family Business Review*, 20(2): 111–126.

Braun, M.R. and Latham, S.F. (2009) 'When the big "R" hits home: governance in family firms during economic recession', *Journal of Strategy and Management*, 2(2): 120–144.

Brenes, E.R., Madrigal, K., and Requena, B. (2011) 'Corporate governance and family business performance', *Journal of Business Research*, 64: 280–285.

Burkart, M., Panunzi, F., and Shleifer, A. (2003) 'Family firms', *The Journal of Finance*, 58(5): 2167–2201.

Cadbury, A. (ed.) (1992) *Report of the Committee on 'The Financial Aspects of Corporate Governance'*. London: Gee & Co.

Cadbury, A. (1999) 'What are the trends in corporate governance? How will they impact your company?', *Long Range Planning*, 32(1): 12–19.

Cadbury, A. (2000) *Family Firms and their Governance*. London: Egon Zehnder International.

Carney, M. (2005) 'Corporate governance and competitive advantage in family-controlled firms', *Entrepreneurship: Theory and Practice*, 30: 249–265.

Carney, M. and Gedajlovic, E. (2001) 'Corporate governance and firm capabilities: a comparison of managerial, alliance, and personal capitalisms', *Asia Pacific Journal of Management*, 18: 335–354.

Carver, J. and Oliver, C. (2002) *Corporate Boards that Create Value*. San Francisco, CA: Jossey-Bass.

Center for Effective Philanthropy (2004) *Foundation Governance: The CEO Viewpoint*. CEP Foundation Governance Project No. 21.

Center for Effective Philanthropy (2005) *Beyond Compliance: The Trustee Viewpoint on Effective Foundation Governance*. CEP Foundation Governance Project No. 30.

Chang, S.J. (2003) 'Ownership structure, expropriation, and performance of group-affiliated companies in Korea', *Academy of Management Journal*, 46(2): 238–253.

Chen, H-L. and Hsu, W-T. (2009) 'Family ownership, board indepedence, and R&D investment', *Family Business Review*, 22(4): 347–362.

Chrisman, J., Chua, J., and Sharma, P. (2003) 'Current trends and future directions in family business management studies: toward a theory of the family firm', Coleman White Paper.

Coles, J.L., Daniel, N.D., and Naveen, L. (2008) 'Boards: does one size fit all?', *Journal of Financial Economics*, 87(2): 329–356.

Coles, J.W., McWilliams, V.B., and Sen, N. (2001) 'An examination of the relationship of governance mechanisms to performance', *Journal of Management*, 27: 23–50.

Coombes, P. and Wong, S.C. (2004) 'Why codes of governance work', *The McKinsey Quarterly*, 2: 48–53.

Corbetta, G. and Tomaselli, S. (1996) 'Boards of directors in Italian family businesses', *Family Business Review*, 9(4): 403–421.

Corbetta, G., Gnan, L. and Montemerlo, D. (2002) *Governance Systems and Company Performance in Italian SMEs*, Working Paper, ISEA, Bocconi University, Milan, Italy.

Corbetta, G. and Salvato, C.A. (2004) 'The board of directors in family firms: one size fits all?', *Family Business Review*, 17(2): 119–134.

Covey, S. (1989) *The Seven Habits of Highly Effective People*. New York: Free Press.

Craig, G.B. and Moores, K. (2009) 'Innovation is oxygen to families in business', *FFI Practitioner*, 5.

Cruz, E.S. (2008) 'Sustainable growth for family firms', Business World Publishing Corporation, July 29: 1–4.

Daily, C.M. and Dollinger, M.J. (1992) 'An empirical examination of ownership structure in family and professionally managed firms', *Family Business Review*, 5(2): 117–136.

Daily, C.M., Dalton, D.R., and Cannella Jr. A.A. (2003) 'Corporate governance: decades of dialogue and data', *Academy of Management Review*, 28(3): 371–382.

Daugherty, M. (2009) 'Our family's journey to a family council', *Family Business Magazine*, Winter.

Davis, J.A. (1982) *The Influence of Life Stage on Father–Son Work Relation in Family Companies*. Ann Arbor, MI: University Microfilms.

DeMott, D.A. (2008) 'Guests at the table? Independent directors in family-influenced public companies', *Journal of Corporation Law*, 33(4): 819–863.

Dickstein, S. (2003) 'The family council: a useful adjunct to the functions of the wealth management professional', *Journal of Wealth Management*, 5(4): 12–14.

Easterbrook, F.H. (1984) 'Two agency-cost explanation of dividends', *American Economic Review*, 74(4): 650–659.

Eisenberg, M. (1976) *The Structure of the Corporation*. Boston, MA: Little, Brown and Company.

Elstrodt, H.P. (2003) 'Keeping the family in the business', *McKinsey Quarterly*, (4): 94–103.

Esposito, V. (2002) *Splendid Legacy: The Guide to Creating Your Family Foundation*. Washington, DC: National Center for Family Philanthropy.

Estess, P. (1996) Yours, mine, and ours – prenuptial agreements in family businesses, *Entrepreneur Magazine*, November.

Faccio, M., Lang, L.H., and Young, L. (2001) 'Dividends and expropriation', *American Economic Review*, 91(1): 54–78.

Fahed-Sreih, J. (2009) 'An exploratory study on a new corporate governance mechanism', *Management Research News*, 32(1): 50–61.

Fama, E.F. and Jensen, M.C. (1983) 'Separation of ownership and control', *Journal of Law and Economics*, 26: 301–325.

Families in Business (2003) Business for Family Business: Family Office (contributions from M. Maslinski, I. Youngman, M. Stern, C. Beyer and T. Brown, R. Patterson, and J. Ward), 2(1): 72–85.

Farinha, J. (2003) 'Dividend policy, corporate governance and the managerial entrenchment hypothesis: an empirical analysis', *Journal of Business Finance and Accounting*, 30(9–10): 1173–1209.

Filatotchev, I., Lien, Y., and Piesse, J. (2005) 'Corporate governance and performance in publicly listed, family-controlled firms: evidence from Taiwan', *Asia Pacific Journal of Management*, 22: 257–283.

Finegold, D. and Lawler III, E. (2009) 'Behind the boardroom doors: changes underway in US corporate governance post Sarbanes-Oxley', in P.Y. Gomez Gomez and R. Moore (eds), *Board Members and Management Consultants*. Charlotte, NC: Information Age Publishers, pp. 3–25.

Finkelstein, S, Hambrick, D.C., and Cannella, A. (2009) *Strategic Leadership: Theory and Research on Executives, Top Management Teams, and Boards*. New York: Oxford University Press.

Forbes, D.P. and Milliken, F.J. (1999) 'Cognition and corporate governance: understanding boards of directors as strategic decision-making groups', *Academy of Management Review*, 24(3): 489–505.

Ford, R.H. (1988) 'Outside directors and the privately-owned firm: are they Necessary?', *Entrepreneurship: Theory and Practice*, 13(1): 49–57.

Ford, R.H. (1989) 'Establishing and managing boards of directors: the other view', *Family Business Review*, 2(2): 142–146.

Gersick, K.E. (2002a) 'Staying connected while growing apart', *Families in Business*, 1(2): 68–70.

Gersick, K.E. (2002b) 'Part II: Governance in the evolving family business', *Families in Business*, 1(3): 77–79.

Gersick, K.E., Lansberg, I., and Davis, J. (1990) 'The impact of family dynamics on structure and process in family foundations', *Family Business Review*, 3(4): 357–374.

Gersick, K.E., Davis, J., Hampton, M., and Lansberg, I. (1997) *Generation to Generation: Life Cycles of the Family Business.* Cambridge, MA: Harvard Business School Press.

Gersick, K.E., Stone, D., Desjardins, M., Muson, H., and Grady, K. (2004) *Generations of Giving: Leadership and Continuity in Family Foundations.* Lanham, MD: National Center for Family Philanthropy and Lexington Books.

Gimeno Sandig, A.G., Labadie, G.J., Saris, W., and Mayordomo, X.M. (2006) 'Internal factors of family business performance: an integrated model', in P.Z. Poutziouris, K.X. Smyrnios, and S.B. Klein (eds), *Handbook of Research on Family Business.* Cheltenham: Edward Elgar, pp.145–164.

Ginsburg, J.A. and Saunders, M.R. (2011) 'Who is the client: working with families in closely held business?', *FFI Practitioner*, 7.

Goel, S., Jussila, I., and Ikäheimonen, T. (2014) 'Governance in family firms: a review and research agenda', in L. Melin, M. Nordqvist, and P. Sharma (eds), *The SAGE Handbook of Family Business.* London: Sage.

Goldbart, S. and DiFuria, J. (2009) 'Money and meaning: implementation of effective family governance structures', *Journal of Practical Estate Planning*, 11(6): 7–9.

Gomez, P-Y. and Moore, R. (2009) *Introduction to Board Members and Management Consultants.* Charlotte, NC: Age Publishers.

Gompers, P.A., Ishii, J., and Metrick, A. (2007) 'Extreme governance: an analysis of dual-class firms in the United States', Rodney L. White Center for Financial Research, Working Paper No. 12–04.

Gordon, J.N. (2007) 'The rise of independent directors in the United States, 1950–2005: of shareholder value and stock market prices', *Stanford Law Review*, 59: 1465–1568.

Gray, L. (2009) 'The three forms of governance: the core element in asset protection', *Pitcairn Update*, Fall: 1, 3.

Greenberg, V. (2006) 'Investments in life settlements – producing returns with certainty', *FFI Practitioner*, 2.

Griffiths, C. (2011) 'Family value: how private clients filled the corp gap', *The Lawyer*, May 23: 12–13.

Grossman, S.J. and Hart, O.D. (1988) 'One share–one vote and the market for corporate control', *Journal of Financial Economics*, 20(1): 175–202.

Gubitta, P. and Gianecchini, M. (2002) 'Governance and flexibility in family-owned SMEs', *Family Business Review*, 15(4): 277–297.

Gugler, K. (2003) 'Corporate governance, dividend payout policy, and the interrelation between dividends, R&D, and capital investment', *Journal of Banking and Finance*, 27(7): 1297–1321.

Han, M. and Celly, N. (2011) 'Professional CEO, independent directors, innovation and family controlled firms' performance', Conference Proceedings, International Council for Small Business, World Conference.

Handler, W. (1994) 'Succession in the family business: a review of the research', *Family Business Review*, 7(2): 159–174.

Hauser, B. (2001) 'The family office: insight into their development in the US, a proposed prototype, and advice for adaptation in other countries', *Journal of Wealth Management*, Fall: 15–22.

Hauser, B. (2003) 'All in the family', *Chartered Secretary Focus*, September: 14–15.

Harris, M. and Raviv, A. (1988) 'Corporate governance: voting rights and majority rules', *Journal of Financial Economics*, 20(1): 203–235.

Havens, J. and Schervish, P. (1999) 'Millionaires and the millennium: new estimates of the forthcoming wealth transfer and the prospects for a golden age of philanthropy', Social Welfare Research Institute, Boston College.

Herz-Brown, F. (1993) 'Loss and continuity in the family firm', *Family Business Review*, 6(2): 111–130.

Hillier, D.J. and McColgan, P.M. (2004) 'Firm performance, entrenchment and managerial succession in family firms', *SSRN*, November, available at: http://ssrn.com/abstract=650161.

Hillier, D. and McColgan, P. (2009) 'Firm performance and managerial succession in family managed firms', *Journal of Business Finance and Accounting*, 36(3): 461–484.

Holderness, C.G. (2003) 'A survey of blockholders and corporate control', *Economic Policy Review*, 9(1): 51–63.

Hollander, B.S. (1983) 'Family-owned business as a system: a case study of the interaction of family, task, and marketplace components', paper presented at the Annual Meeting of the Academy of Management, Texas.

Hughes, J.E. (2004) *Family Wealth: Keeping it in the Family.* New York: Bloomberg Press.

Huse, M. (1998) 'Researching the dynamics of board-stakeholder relations', *Long Range Planning*, 31(2): 218–226.

Huse, M. (2000) 'Board of directors in SMEs: a review and research agenda', *Entrepreneurship and Regional Development*, 12: 271–290.

Jaffe, D.T. (2005) 'Strategic planning for the family in business', *Journal of Financial Planning*, March: 50–56.

Jaffe, D.T., Bork, D., Lane, S., Dashew, I., and Paul, J. (1998) 'We the people: to form a more perfect union', *Family Business Magazine*, Winter.

Jaffe, D.T. and Lane, S.H. (2004) 'Sustaining a family dynasty: key issues facing complex multigenerational business- and investment-owning families', *Family Business Review*, 17(1): 81–98.

James, H.S. (1999a) 'What can the family do for business? Examining contractual relationships', *Family Business Review*, 12(1): 61–71.

James, H.S. (1999b) 'Owner as manager, extended horizons and the family firm', *International Journal of the Economics of Business*, 6(1): 41–55.

Jara-Bertin, M., Lopez-Iturriaga, F.J., and Lopez-de-Foronda, O. (2008) 'The contest to the control in European family firms: how other shareholders affect firm value', *Corporate Governance*, 16(3): 146–159.

Jensen, M.C. (1993) 'The modern industrial revolution, exit, and the failure of internal control systems', *The Journal of Finance*, 48(3): 831–880.

Jensen, M.C. and Meckling, W.H. (1976) 'Theory of the firm: managerial behavior, agency costs and ownership structure', *Journal of Financial Economics*, 3: 305–360.

Johnson, E.W. (1990) 'An insider's call for outside direction', *Harvard Business Review*, 3: 46–55.

Johnson, J.L., Daily, C.M., and Ellstrand, A.E. (1996) 'Boards of directors: a review and research agenda', *Journal of Management*, 22(3): 409–438.

Johnson, P. (2004) 'Shared thinking and interaction in the family business boardroom', *Corporate Governance*, 4(1): 39–51.

Jones, C.D., Makri, M., and Gomez-Mejia, L.R. (2008) 'Affiliate directors and perceived risk bearing in publicly traded, family-controlled firms: the case of diversification', *Entrepreneurship: Theory and Practice*, 32(6): 1007–1026.

Journal of Gift Planning (2006) 'Wealth transfer: a digest of opinion and advice', *Journal of Gift Planning*, 10(2).

Judge, W.Q. and Zeithaml, C.P. (1992) 'Institutional and strategic choice perspectives on board involvement in the strategic decision process', *Academy of Management Journal*, 35(4): 766–794.

Keasey, K., Thompson, S., and Wright, M. (1997) *Corporate Governance: Economic, Management, and Financial Issues*. Oxford, UK: Oxford University Press.

Kets de Vries, M.F. (1993) 'The dynamics of family controlled firms: the good and the bad news', *Organizational Dynamics*, 21(3): 59–71.

Khan, H.A. (1999) 'Corporate governance of family businesses in Asia: what's right and what's wrong? Asian Development Bank Institute', Asian Development Bank, Working Paper No. 3, pp. 1–42.

Klein, S.B. (2000) 'Family businesses in Germany: significance and structure', *Family Business Review*, 13(3): 157–182.

Knowledge at Wharton (2008) 'SFOs in action: how the richest families manage their wealth', available at: http://knowledge.wharton.upenn.edu/article/1964.cfm

Kor, Y.Y. (2006) 'Direct and interaction effects of top management team and board compositions on R&D investment strategy', *Strategic Management Journal*, 27: 1081–1099.

Kowalewski, O., Talavera, O., and Stetsyuk, I. (2010) 'Influence of family involvement in management and ownership on firm performance: evidence from Poland', *Family Business Review*, 23(1): 45–59.

Krasnow, H.C. (2005) 'The hidden issue in firing family members', *FFI Practitioner*, 2005(1).

Lambrecht, J. and Lievens, J. (2008) 'Pruning the family tree: an unexplored path to family business continuity and family harmony', *Family Business Review*, 21(4): 295–313.

Lamp, C. (2007) 'The Eddy Family Council: meeting and eating since 2000', *Family Business Magazine*, Autumn.

Lane, S., Astrachan, J., Keyt, A., and McMillan, K. (2006) 'Guidelines for family business boards of directors', *Family Business Review*, 19(2): 147–167.

Lansberg, I. (1988) 'The succession conspiracy', *Family Business Review*, 1(2): 119–143.

Lansberg, I. (1997) 'The best investment a family will ever make: the creation of a family council is one way to restore the balance between business and family life', *Family Business Magazine*, Winter.

Lansberg, I. (1999) *Succeeding Generations: Realizing the Dream of Families in Business*. Cambridge, MA: Harvard Business School Press.

Lansberg, I. (2007) 'The best investment the family can make', *Family Business Magazine*, Winter.

Lansberg, I. and Gersick, K.E. (2009) *Tradition and Adaptation in Chinese Family Enterprises*. HSBC Suisse.

Lansky, D. and Pendergast, J. (2010) 'Is good governance different in the family office setting?', *Family Business Magazine*, Spring.

La Porta, R., Lopez-de-Silanes, F., and Shleifer, A. (1999) 'Corporate ownership around the world', *The Journal of Finance*, 54(2): 471–517.

La Porta, R., Lopez-de-Silanes, F., Shleifer, A., and Vishny, R. (2000) 'Investor protection and corporate governance', *Journal of Financial Economics*, 58(1): 3–27.

Lawton, P. (1996) 'Berle and Means, corporate governance and the Chinese family firm', *Australian Journal of Corporate Law*, 6: 348–379.

Le Breton-Miller, I.L. and Miller, D. (2009) 'Agency vs. stewardship in public family firms: a social embeddedness reconciliation', *Entrepreneurship: Theory and Practice*, 33(6): 1169–1191.

Lee, J. and Li, H. (2009) *Wealth Doesn't Last 3 Generations: How Family Businesses can Maintain Prosperity*. Hackensack, NJ: World Scientific.

Lee, S.-H., Phan, P., and Yoshikawa, T. (2008) 'The role of the board and its interaction with the successor's human capital in the Asian family enterprise', *Multinational Business Review*, 16(2): 65–88.

León-Guerrero, A.Y., McCann, J.E., and Haley, J.D. (1998) 'A study of practice utilization in family businesses', *Family Business Review*, 11(2): 107–120.

Lewine, E. (2006) 'Ratifying the family constitution', *The New York Times*, January 26.

Licht, A., Goldschmidt, C., and Schwartz, S. (2001) 'Culture, law, and finance: cultural dimensions of corporate governance laws', Discussion draft #CLF 6–SSRN.doc.

Licht, A., Goldschmidt, C., and Schwartz, S. (2007) 'Culture rules: the foundations of the rule of law and other norms of governance', *Journal of Comparative Economics,* 35: 659–688.

Lungeanu, R. and Ward, J. (2012) 'A governance-based typology of family foundations: the effect of generation stage and governance structure on family philanthropic activities', *Family Business Review*, 25(4): 409–424.

Masulis, R.W., Wang, C., and Xie, F. (2008) 'Agency problems at dual-class companies', European Corporate Governance Institute, Working Paper 209.

McCahery, J.A. and Vermeulen, E.P. (2006) 'Corporate governance and innovation: venture capital, joint ventures, and family businesses', European Corporate Governance Institute, Working Paper 65/2006.

McClain, L. (2006) 'Family constitutions and the (new) constitution of the family', *Fordham Law Review*, 75(2): 833–881.

McCoy, J.J. and Miree, K.W. (2010) *Family Foundation Handbook*. Chicago, IL: CCH Publications.

McManus, K. (1990) 'Whose company is this anyway?', *Family Business Magazine*, February.

Melin, L. and Nordqvist, M. (2007) 'The reflexive dynamics of institutionalization: the case of the family business', *Strategic Organization*, 5(3): 321–333.

Memili, E. (2011) 'Control-enhancing corporate governance mechanisms: family versus non-family

publicly traded firms'. PhD Dissertation, Mississippi State University, Mississippi State.

Millstein, I.M. and MacAvoy, P.W. (1998) 'The active board of directors and performance of the large publicly traded corporation', *Columbia Law Review*, 98(5): 1283–1322.

Mintzberg, H. (1983) *Power in and Around Organizations*. Englewood Cliffs, NJ: Prentice-Hall.

Monks, R. and Minow, N. (1996) *Watching the Watchers: Corporate Governance for the 21st Century*. Cambridge: Blackwell Publishers.

Montemerlo, D. (2005) 'Family ownership: boost or obstacle to growth?', paper presented at the FBN-IFERA World Academic Research Forum, EHSAL, Brussels.

Moore, J. and Juenemann, T. (2008) 'Good governance is essential for a family and its business', *Family Business Magazine*, Summer.

Morck, R. and Yeung, B. (2003) 'Agency problems in large family business groups', *Entrepreneurship: Theory and Practice*, 27(4): 367–382.

Morck, R., Wolfenzon, D., and Yeung, B. (2005) 'Corporate governance, economic entrenchment and growth', *Journal of Economic Literature*, 43(3): 655–720.

Morris, M., Williams, R., Allen, J., and Avila, R. (1997) 'Correlates of success in family business transitions', *Journal of Business Venturing*, 12(5): 385–401.

Murray, B., Gersick, K.E., and Lansberg, I. (2002) From Back Office to Executive Suite – the Evolving Role of the Family Office. *Private Wealth Management*. London: Campden Publishing Limited.

Mustakallio, M., Autio, E., and Zahra, S.A. (2002) 'Relational and contractual governance in family firms: effects on strategic decision making', *Family Business Review*, 15(3): 205–222.

Navarro, M.S. and Anson, S.G. (2009) 'Do families shape corporate governance structures?', *Journal of Management and Organization*, 15(3): 327–345.

Neubauer, F. and Lank, A. (1998) *The Family Business: Its Governance for Sustainability*. New York: Macmillan Press.

Nicholson, G.J., Kiel, G.C., and Hendry, K.P. (2009) 'Bounding the role of the director', in P.Y. Gomez and R. Moore (eds), *Board Members and Management Consultants*. Charlotte, NC: Information Age Publishers, pp. 89–108.

Parada, M.J., Nordqvist, M., and Gimeno, A. (2010) 'Institutionalizing the family business: the role of professional associations in fostering a change of values', *Family Business Review*, 23(4): 355–372.

Pendergast, J., Ward, J., and De Pontet, S. (2011) *Building a Successful Family Business Board*. New York: Palgrave MacMillan.

Peng, M.W. and Jiang, Y. (2010) 'Institutions behind family ownership and control in large firms', *Journal of Management Studies*, 47(2): 253–273.

Perez-Gonzalez, F. (2001) 'Does inherited control hurt firm performance?', Columbia University, Working Paper.

Pettigrew, A. (1992) 'On studying managerial elites', *Strategic Management Journal*, 13: 163–182.

Phan, P.H., Butler, J., and Lee, S.-H. (2005) 'Corporate governance and management succession in family businesses', paper presented at the First Haniel Foundation Entrepreneurship and Management Conference, Berlin.

Pieper, T.M. (2003) 'Corporate governance in family firms: a literature review', *IIFE Insead*, Working Paper No. 2003/97.

Poza, E.J. (2008) 'A guide for family businesses', *Bloomberg Businessweek*, April 16.

Poza, E.J. (2009) 'Rediscovering just how much patient family ownership matters', *Family Business Magazine*, Autumn.

Raheja, C.G. (2005) 'Determinants of board size and composition: a theory of corporate boards', *Journal of Financial and Quantitative Analysis*, 40(2): 283–306.

Ricart, J.E., Alvarez, J., and Gallo, M. (1999) 'Governance mechanisms for effective leadership: the case of Spain, *Corporate Governance*, 7(3): 266–287.

Schneider, F.S. and Schneider, M.K. (2005) 'Four ways of differentiating compensation in family business', *FFI Practitioner*, 2005(1).

Schulze, W.S., Lubatkin, M.H., Dino, R.N., and Buchholtz, A.K. (2001) 'Agency relationships in family firms: theory and evidence', *Organization Science*, 12(2): 99–116.

Sciascia, S. and Mazzola, P. (2008) 'Family involvement in ownership and management: exploring nonlinear effects on performance', *Family Business Review*, 21(4): 331–345.

Setia-Atmaja, L., Tanewski, G.A., and Skully, M. (2009) 'The role of dividends, debt and board structure in the governance of family controlled firms', *Journal of Business Finance and Accounting*, 36(7): 863–898.

Sharma, P. (2008) 'Commentary: familiness: capital stocks and flows between family and business', *Entrepreneurship: Theory and Practice*, 32(6): 971–977.

Sharma, P. (2010) 'Advancing the 3Rs of family business scholarship: rigor, relevance, reach', *Entrepreneurship and Family Business*, 12: 383–400.

Sharma, P., Chrisman, J., and Chua, T. (1997) 'Strategic management of the family business: past research and future challenges', *Family Business Review*, 10(1): 1–35.

Sharma, P. and Nordqvist, M. (2008) 'A classification scheme for family firms: from family values to effective governance to firm performance', in J. Tàpies and J.L. Ward (eds), *Family Values and Value Creation: The Fostering of Enduring Values within Family-Owned Businesses*. New York: Palgrave McMillan, pp. 71–101.

Shleifer, A. and Vishny, R.W. (1986) 'Large shareholders and corporate control', *Journal of Political Economy*, 94(3): 461–488.

Shleifer, A. and Vishny, R.W. (1997) 'A survey of corporate governance', *The Journal of Finance*, 52(2): 737–783.

Shyu, Y. and Lee, C.I. (2009) 'Excess control rights and debt maturity structure in family-controlled firms', *Corporate Governance*, 17(5): 611–628.

Steir, L. (2001) 'Family firms, plural forms of governance, and the evolving role of trust', *Family Business Review*, 14(4): 353–367.

Stone, D. (1993) 'Who is on the board?', *Foundation News*.

Suehiro, A. (1993) 'Family business reassessed: corporate structure and late-starting industrialization in Thailand', *Developing Economies*, 31(4): 378–407.

Tabalujan, S. (2002) 'Family capitalism and corporate governance of family-controlled listed companies in Indonesia', *University of New South Wales Law Journal*, 25(2): 1–39.

Tagiuri, R. and Davis, J. (1996) 'Bivalent attributes of the family firm', *Family Business Review*, 9(2): 199–208.

Teksten, E.L., Moser, S.B., and Elbert, D.J. (2005) 'Boards of directors for small businesses and small private corporations: the changing role, duties and expectations', *Management Research News*, 28(7): 50–68.

Uhlaner, L., Wright, M., and Huse, M. (2007) 'Private firms and corporate governance: an integrated economic and management perspective', *Small Business Economics*, 29: 225–241.

Van den Berghe, L.A.A. and Carchon, S. (2002) 'Corporate governance practices in flemish family businesses', *Corporate Governance*, 10(3): 225–245.

Van der Heyden, L., Blondel, C., and Carlock, R. (2005) 'Fair process: striving for justice in family business', *Family Business Review*, 18(1): 1–21.

Vilaseca, A. (2002) 'The shareholder role in the family business: conflict of interests and objectives between nonemployed shareholders and top management team', *Family Business Review*, 15(4): 299–320.

Villalonga, B. and Amit, R. (2008) 'How are US family firms controlled?', *Review of Financial Studies*, 22(8): 3047–3091.

Voordeckers, W., Gils, A.V., and Heuvel, J.V. (2007) 'Board composition in small and medium-sized family firms', *Journal of Small Business Management,* 45(1): 137–156.

Ward, J.L. (1987) *Keeping the Family Business Healthy.* San Francisco, CA: Jossey-Bass.

Ward, J.L. (1988) 'The active board with outside directors and the family firm', *Family Business Review,* 1(3): 223–229.

Ward, J.L. (1989) 'Defining and researching inside versus outside directors: a rebuttal to the rebuttal', *Family Business Review,* 2(2): 147–150.

Ward, J.L. (1991) *Creating Effective Boards for Private Enterprises.* San Francisco, CA: Jossey-Bass.

Ward, J.L. (1997) 'Growing the family business: special challenges and best practices', *Family Business Review,* 10(4): 323–337.

Ward, J.L. and Handy, J.L. (1988) 'A survey of board practices', *Family Business Review,* 1(3): 289–308.

Westphal, J.D. (1999) 'Collaboration in the boardroom: behavioral and performance consequences of CEO-board social ties', *Academy of Management Journal,* 42(1): 7–24.

Wu, C.-F. (2006) 'The study of the relations among ethical considerations, family management and organizational performance in corporate governance', *Journal of Business Ethics,* 68: 165–179.

Yeh, Y., Lee, T., and Woidtke, T. (2001) 'Family control and corporate governance: evidence from Taiwan', *International Review of Finance,* 2(1–2): 21–48.

Yeh, Y. and Woidtke, T. (2005) 'Commitment or entrenchment? Controlling shareholders and board composition', *Journal of Banking and Finance,* 29: 1857–1885.

Yoshikawa, T. and Rasheed, A.A. (2010) 'Family control and ownership monitoring in family-controlled firms in Japan', *Journal of Management Studies,* 47: 274–295.

Zahra, S.A. and Pearce, J.A. (1989) 'Boards of directors and corporate financial performance: a review and integrative model', *Journal of Management,* 15(2): 291–334.

Zall, R. (2004) *The Board of Directors in a Family-Owned Business. Director's Handbook Series.* Washington, DC: National Association of Corporate Directors.

12

Governance in Family Firms: A Review and Research Agenda

Sanjay Goel, Iiro Jussila and Tuuli Ikäheimonen

INTRODUCTION

It can be fairly said that family business research is perhaps first and foremost a study of a specific ownership and governance form. Over the past twenty years or so, governance of family business has been studied extensively, in management as well as economics, finance, and accounting areas, contributing largely to the definition of family business as a specific and distinctive field (e.g., Chen and Hsu, 2009; Daily and Dollinger, 1992; Habbershon and Pistrui, 2002; Sharma, 2004). An important realization in this discussion is that the distinctive and heterogeneous features of a family business also imply that governance in a family firm can potentially be a value-destroying (i.e., leading to loss of decision-making efficiency and financial performance) *or* a value-creating resource (i.e., ameliorating some of the agency problems of widely-held non-family firms, and families directly in control of the firm via a family CEO outperforming non-family firms (e.g., Anderson and Reeb, 2003; Carney, 2005).

In this review, we take stock of the progress made collectively so far in the scientific knowledge of this resource (or capability, as a more dynamic view would perhaps suggest). One caveat – the aim of this review is not to be a comprehensive and exhaustive compendium of all possible studies on family business governance. Rather we attempt to identify major themes in extant research and provide some fruitful directions for future research. (For a more practice-oriented review of governance in family firms, including implementation issues, see the chapter by Gersick and Feliu, 2014, in this volume.)

The chapter is organized as follows. First, we introduce the literature and methods used in this review, explaining our choices. Second, we set the stage with some important background notions. Next, we provide our review of the extant body of knowledge, identifying the dominant themes and emerging certainties. Finally, we discuss issues that future research on family business governance should address in order to shed light on the identified gaps as well as cover new ground.

LITERATURE AND METHODS

In our attempt to identify the major themes in family business governance, we searched for articles that would help us describe what has been done, find what the key directions of research are, and to highlight new and interesting directions. We excluded articles that covered purely ownership issues, without discussing any governance implications. (For a more complete review of the ownership literature to date, the reader is referred to Block et al., 2011, as well as Mazzi, 2011.) These eliminated a few articles that appeared in finance and accounting areas, for example, those that discussed family's financial ownership and its relationship to other owners. Table 12.1 summarizes our effort.

In our further analysis of the literature we asked the following questions: (1) what claims are emerging as accepted certainties in the field; (2) what interesting directions have been taken that need to be further explored; and (3) what questions of significant promise remain unexplored? While any review obviously is somewhat subjective in nature, we take comfort in the fact that the main conclusions of this review represent the consensus of the three authors of this review – this is no mean feat among even a small group of knowledgeable people in any field.

SETTING THE STAGE

Before moving to the discussion of the major themes in family business governance, let us point out something important to family businesses and their governance and the lenses that have been used in the extant studies.

Governance Issues Vary Across Family Firms

In general, governance systems in a firm play the role of keeping the firm's goals and actions in line with expectations of the firm's critical stakeholders via providing advice to and networking (service role), monitoring and aligning incentives of firm leadership (control role) (Hillman and Dalziel, 2003; Jaskiewicz and Klein, 2007; Walsh and Seward, 1990). As firms are not similar (e.g., in terms of *who* the critical stakeholders are), different aspects of governance are highlighted across firms.

There is considerable heterogeneity within family firms. For example, based on ownership within the family alone, family business literature describes various forms of ownership based on the stage of dispersion, such as sibling partnership and cousin consortium (Gersick et al., 1997). Therefore, governance issues in each of these family firms differ widely.

Theory is Elaborated Through the Use of Common Lenses

Congruence in the study of family business governance is achieved through the use of particular lenses across investigations. Two theoretical perspectives in particular have often been employed by family business scholars: agency and stewardship theory.

From agency theory perspective, each particular family firm type is characterized by a set of (contractual) agency relations within and between the family system, ownership system and the business system (Van den Berghe and Carchon, 2003). At the same time, differences in family leadership and values may yield differences in degree of stewardship behavior in family firms, with concurrent differences in governance issues.

For a while, these lenses (agency and stewardship) were used independently. This independence was driven by fundamentally different (contrasting) assumptions about family businesses, rather than being contingent on other aspects of the context. For example, some scholars using the agency theory lens argued that family businesses exist as instruments via which family owners pursue self-serving family utility at the expense of the company and its minority shareholders (Bertrand and Schoar, 2006; Claessens et al., 2002; Morck et al., 2005).

Table 12.1   Studies on governance in family firms

Author(s) and year	Research focus	Theoretical perspective	Empirical (sample)/ conceptual
Anderson and Reeb (2003)	The relation between founding-family ownership and firm performance in large public firms.	Agency theory	403 firms covering 1992 to 1999 for Standard & Poor's 500 firms (141 family firms)
Anderson and Reeb (2004)	Boards role in mitigating conflicts between opposing shareholder groups and their interests. Testing of board role as a balancing entity by investigating the relation between firm performance and board independence in the presence of founding-family ownership.	Agency theory, stewardship theory	2,686 Standard & Poor's 500 firms for the period 1992 to 1999 (876 family firms). In 141 firms the founding-family hold stakes
Anderson et al. (2003)	Impact of founding family ownership structure on agency cost of debt.	Agency theory	Large, publicly traded US firms (Fortune 500)
Bammens et al. (2008)	The influence of generational changes on governance needs and characteristics of family businesses board of directors, namely two main board task needs (advice and control) and its composition.	Resource-based view, agency theory	286 Belgian family firms
Bartholomeusz and Tanewski (2006)	Relations between family control and corporate governance structures.	Agency theory	100 listed companies (50 family firms and 50 non-family firms)
Bettinelli (2011)	The relationship between board composition and board processes.	Agency theory, stewardship theory, resource dependence theory	90 family business directors in Italy
Birley (2001)	Attitudes of owner-manager to both business and family decisions.	Unspecified/ no clearly identified theoretical perspective	16 countries: Canada, Denmark, Finland, Germany, Greece, Italy, Japan, Netherlands, Poland, Spain, Sweden, Switzerland, USA, Belgium, Ireland and UK
Block (2011)	Optimal compensation contracts of non-family managers employed by family firm and a comparison between the contracts of family and non-family managers. The problems arising from goals and time horizon that differ from those of owning family.	Agency theory	Conceptual paper
Blumentritt (2006)	Relationship between the existence of board of directors and advisory boards and the use of planning.	Agency theory, resource dependency	133 family firms in southeastern Wisconsin and northern Illinois
Blumentritt et al. (2007)	Key attributes of successful and unsuccessful relationships between a family and a non-family CEO.	Agency theory, stewardship theory	27 family business members (employer of non-family CEO) or non-family CEOs themselves
Braun and Sharma (2007)	Relationship between CEO duality and firm performance.	Agency theory, stewardship theory	84 family controlled public firms (FCPFs) in the US context
Brenes et al. (2011)	The impact of governance mechanisms, especially professional board of directors on firm performance.	Unspecified/ no clearly identified theoretical perspective	22 Latin American families who own businesses and who established family protocols

Author(s) and year	Research focus	Theoretical perspective	Empirical (sample)/ conceptual
Brunninge and Nordqvist (2004)	How ownership structure, especially family and/or venture-capital involvement, as well as entrepreneurial activities help explain the involvement of independent members of board of directors.	Unspecified/ no clearly identified theoretical perspective	1,026 Swedish private, independent SME (about half of the original sample of 2,455 firms)
Carney (2005)	The relation between organizational value-creating (or value-destroying) attributes and firms' system of corporate governance.	Agency theory, social capital theory	Conceptual paper
Chrisman et al. (2004)	Different nature of agency costs and relation to firm performance.	Agency theory	1,141 small privately held US family and non-family firms
Chrisman et al. (2007)	Incentive compensation of family managers.	Agency theory, stewardship theory	208 small privately held family firms in the USA
Chua et al. (2009)	How differences in goals, altruistic tendencies and strategic time horizons might affect performance evaluation and incentive compensation firms that employ both family and non-family managers. How these differences would affect the firm performance.	Agency theory	Conceptual paper
Corbetta and Montemerlo (1999)	Analyzing the structure and behavior of Italian firms. Compare them with those in USA in terms of family involvement, ownership and governance structures, top management teams, decision-making processes, strategic goals and succession.	Unspecified/ no clearly identified theoretical perspective	252 Italian family firms, 1,029 US family businesses
Corbetta and Salvato (2004)	Board roles and characteristics vary among national cultures and different company types. In contrast research dominated by standard prescriptions.	Various, e.g. agency theory, stewardship theory, resource dependence theory	Conceptual paper
Daily and Dollinger (1992)	Differences in structures, processes, and performance between family-owned and – managed and professionally-managed businesses.	Agency theory	486 small manufacturing firms
Enriques and Volpin (2007)	Differences in the ownership structure of companies in the three main economies in continental Europe with comparisons to the USA and UK. Corporate governance issues that arise in firms with a dominant shareholder.	Agency theory	Data from different sources and from UK, United States, France, Germany and Italy
Feltham et al. (2005)	The degree of dependence of family-owned business on a single individual decision-maker and the factors associated with this reliance.	Unspecified/ no clearly identified theoretical perspective	765 Canadian family-owned businesses
Filatotchev et al. (2005)	The effect of ownership structure and board characteristics on performance.	Agency theory, institutional theory	228 public Taiwanese multi-industry founding family controlled firms

(Continued)

Table 12.1   (Continued)

Author(s) and year	Research focus	Theoretical perspective	Empirical (sample)/ conceptual
Goel et al. (2013)	Whether highly empathetic family CEOs tend to over-emphasize the preservation of socioemotional wealth. The effect of external directors on CEO's emphasis.	Various, e.g. behavioral agency theory, institutional studies	180 Belgian and Dutch small and medium-sized independent family businesses with the family member CEO
Gomez-Mejia et al. (2003)	Determinants of CEO compensation.	Agency theory	253 family controlled firms
Gomez-Mejia et al. (2001)	Influence of family ties between principal and agent on agency contract.	Agency theory	Population of 276 firms composed of all daily newspapers published in Spain during the period 1966–1993
Gubitta and Gianecchini (2002)	Impact of non-family management on the corporate governance structure.	New theory of property rights, summary of agency, stewardship and resource dependency theories	83 small and medium-sized family enterprises in north-eastern Italy
Jaskiewicz and Klein (2007)	Effect of goal alignment between owners and managers on board composition and board size.	Agency theory, stewardship theory	548 non-quoted family businesses in Germany
Johannisson and Huse (2000)	How contrasting ideologies influence the selection process of outside directors.	Various e.g. agency, managerial-hegemony, resource-dependence, resource-based and power theories, and stakeholder approaches	In pilot study: 12 small family businesses in southern Sweden. In-depth case part, two different family businesses in southern Sweden
Johnson (2004)	Interaction amongst directors seeking to achieve agreement on a key strategic issue in quarterly board meetings.	Unspecified/ no clearly identified theoretical perspective	Board of one family business in UK, the whole board acted as informants
Jones et al. (2008)	Influence of affiliated directors in the diversification decision.	Social capital theory	403 firms (203 family businesses, and 200 non-family controlled)
Klein et al. (2005)	The influence of better governance practices (CG index) to firm value in developed market (Canada).	Agency theory	263 Canadian firms
Kotey (2005)	Differences between family and non-family SMEs in business goals, management practices and performance as they grow.	Unspecified/ no clearly identified theoretical perspective	233 small non-family and 362 small family firms, and 305 family and 341 non-family medium-sized firms in Australia
Kowalewski et al. (2010)	Influence of family involvement in terms of family ownership and family-connected management on firm performance.	Agency theory, resource-based view	217 firms in Poland
Krivogorsky and Burton (2011 current version)	Nature of dominant ownership and its impact on economic performance of the firm. Country effect influencing on dominant owners and the performance of their companies.	Agency theory, stewardship theory	1,533 publicly traded companies from continental Europe
Kuan et al. (2010)	Association between corporate governance and cash-policy.	Agency theory	1,164 family controlled firms in Taiwan

Author(s) and year	Research focus	Theoretical perspective	Empirical (sample)/ conceptual
Lane et al. (2006)	Significance and suitability of governance reforms and practices of publicly held large organizations for the closely held, family owned businesses. 'Comparison' of market model of CG and control model of CG.	Market model of corporate governance, control model of corporate governance	Conceptual paper
Lubatkin et al. (2007b)	Parental altruism and its relation to family firm governance.	Agency theory	Conceptual paper
Martinez et al. (2007)	Impact of family ownership on firm performance in Chile.	Unspecified/ no clearly identified theoretical perspective	Chile, 175 listed firms, 100 of them family controlled
McConaughy (2000)	CEO compensation in family firms.	Agency theory	82 founding-family-controlled firms
Miller and Le Breton-Miller (2006)	The nature of publicly traded family-controlled businesses (FCBs) in terms of four governance choices (level and mode of family ownership, family leadership, the broader involvement of multiple family members and the planned or actual participation of later generations) and their influence on the success or failure of companies.	Agency theory, stewardship theory	Conceptual paper
Miller et al. (2007)	Effect of family influence on firm performance.	Agency theory	Fortune 1000 and random sample of 100 smaller public companies
Miller et al. (2008)	Structure and behavior of family owned businesses compared to non-family owned businesses.	Stewardship theory, stagnation perspective	676 small founder-owned and -managed firms in Canada
Mishra et al. (2001)	The influence of founding family control on firm value and the impact of different corporate governance conditions to firm value.	Agency theory, others	120 Norwegian founding family controlled and non-founding family controlled firms
Mustakallio et al. (2002)	Developing and testing the model that explores the influences of contractual (formal control) and relational (social control) governance on strategic decision making quality.	Agency theory, social theories of governance	192 family firms in Finland
Pieper et al. (2008)	Relationship of goal alignment between owners and managers and the existence of a board of directors.	Agency theory, stewardship theory	714 family influenced businesses in Germany
Randøy and Goel (2003)	Influence of ownership structure on firm performance in small and medium-sized enterprises with and without founding family leadership.	Agency theory	68 public firms in Norway
Rautiainen et al. (2010)	Ownership as a phenomenon that connects families to business activities.	Modern portfolio theory, behavioral finance theory	Longitudinal case study of the Finnish family business

(Continued)

Table 12.1   (Continued)

Author(s) and year	Research focus	Theoretical perspective	Empirical (sample)/ conceptual
Sacristán-Navarro and Gómez-Ansón (2009)	Differences in family and non-family firm corporate governance structures. Whether different family ownership configurations affect governance structures.	Agency theory	132 non-financial Spanish listed firms
Sacristán-Navarro and Gómez-Ansón (2007)	The use of indirect ownership, pyramids, and cross-shareholdings. The extent to which cash-flow rights differ from control rights. The degree of the firm's professionalization according to type of owner category.	Agency theory	195 listed family firms in Spain
Sacristán-Navarro et al. (2011)	Influence of family ownership and control and the presence of a second significant shareholder on firm performance.	Agency theory	118 non-financial Spanish companies
Salvato and Melin (2008)	The process through which the family-controlled businesses access and recombine resources to match the evolving needs of their business.	Social capital theory	Four family controlled businesses (two from Italy and two from Switzerland)
Schulze et al. (2002)	Influence of altruism on agency relationships in family firms.	Agency theory	Conceptual paper
Schulze et al. (2003)	Dispersion of ownership and family firms' use of debt.	Agency theory, behavioral economics	1995 Arthur Anderson Survey of American family businesses, 1,464 family firms
Schulze et al. (2001)	Agency costs of family ownership.	Agency theory, economic theory of the household	1995 Arthur Anderson Survey of American family businesses, 1,376 family firms
Sciascia and Mazzola (2008)	If and how family involvement in ownership (FIO) and management (FIM) affect performance.	Agency theory, stewardship theory, social capital theory	620 Italian small and medium-sized firms
Selekler-Goksen and Yildirim Öktem (2009)	Impact of national and international pressures to improve corporate governance.	Institutional theory	Six Turkish Family Business Groups studied in three data points: 2002, 2004, 2006
Setia-Atmaja et al. (2009)	The use of dividends, debt and board structure for exacerbating or mitigating agency problems between controlling and minority shareholders.	Agency theory	316 firms in Australia (family and non-family controlled firms)
Silva and Majluf (2008)	The effect of family ownership on performance in an emerging economy basing on two dimensions of family ownership: ownership concentration and characteristics of family control. The effect of firm's institutional relatedness on performance.	Agency theory	331 firm-year observation from non-financial Chilean corporations
Steier (2001)	Understanding trust as a governance mechanism and source of competitive advantage within family firm.	Unspecified/ no clearly identified theoretical perspective	Three cases

Author(s) and year	Research focus	Theoretical perspective	Empirical (sample)/ conceptual
Steier (2003)	Primary rationalities governing the exchange relationships in family investment decisions during the early stages of new venture creation and their influence on governance structure.	Agency theory, venture capital theory	Four illustrative cases
Steier and Miller (2010)	Understanding governance philosophies (ownership, management and control) both before and after succession as well as related transformations between these periods.	Unspecified/ no clearly identified theoretical perspective	13 individuals from different companies
Steijvers and Voordeckers (2009)	Are agency costs of debt in private family firms higher or lower compared with private non-family firms.	Agency theory	US small businesses (fewer than 500 employees), sample of 443 lines of credit
Thomas (2009)	Shareholders views about the business and family business sustainability as the 'ownership tree' grows in multi-generational family business.	Stewardship theory	50 related family members of the multi-generational family business
Tsao et al. (2009)	The relationship between founding-family ownership and firm performance and the role of using HPWS as a mechanism to motivate and retain valuable employees.	Resource-based theory, agency theory, stewardship theory	91 Taiwanese public companies (64 family owned)
Van den Berghe and Carchon (2002)	Exploring relationship between ownership structure, board and management practices.	Agency theory, corporate governance	325 Flemish companies (154 family businesses)
Vilaseca (2002)	The elements that influence the conflict of interests and objectives between non-employed shareholders and TMT, and its impact on commitment to the family firm.	Agency theory, commitment theory, FB shareholders literature	Field study of the 156 shareholders and executives in 10 Spanish firms
Villalonga and Amit (2006)	The affect of family ownership, management and control to the value of the firm. Which of the two agency problems is more damaging to firm value - the conflict of interest with managers or the conflict with large controlling shareholders.	Agency theory	All Fortune 500 firms during the period 1994–2000 (primary industry of financial services, utilities, and government are excluded)
Villanueva and Sapienza (2009)	How outside investors are affected by the 'familiness' of the firm and whether embeddedness for goals other than the maximization of business outcomes lead to an attractive or unattractive option for outside investors.	Agency theory, stewardship theory	Conceptual paper
Voordeckers et al. (2007)	Determinants of board composition in small and medium-sized family firms.	Various, e.g., agency theory, stewardship theory, institutional theory, resource dependency theory, social network theory	211 Belgian small and medium-sized family firms

(Continued)

Table 12.1   (Continued)

Author(s) and year	Research focus	Theoretical perspective	Empirical (sample)/ conceptual
Westhead and Howorth (2006)	Association between ownership and management profiles and firm performance and objectives.	Agency and stewardship theories	272 private family businesses in UK, structured questionnaire
Westhead et al. (2002)	Differences between first-generation family companies and multi-generational family companies in terms of their selected ownership form and management structure.	Unspecified/ no clearly identified theoretical perspective	Random sample of family and non-family private limited liability unquoted companies in UK (272 family firms)
Yang (2010)	Relationship between insider ownership and earnings management in family firms and the impact of family versus non-family CEOs on earning management.	Agency theory	3,914 firm-year observation from Taiwanese listed firms
Zellweger and Nason (2008)	Financial and non-financial outcomes in family firm across multiple stakeholder categories.	Stakeholder theory	Conceptual paper

This stream of research conceptualized family business leadership as selfish and driven by expropriating benefits for the family from other systems. On the other hand, scholars employing the stewardship lens saw family businesses as model organizations, run by enlightened family owners driven by a broader purpose, who pursue social and self-actualization goals to the benefit of all stakeholders (Arrègle et al., 2007; Habbershon and Williams, 1999; Le Breton-Miller and Miller, 2006; Miller and Le Breton-Miller, 2005, 2006). This stream of research conceptualized family business leadership as driven by altruism toward all stakeholders, and family in particular, in pursuit of filial duty to provide for the next generation.

Other approaches incorporate social/ relational capital (Jones et al., 2008), or develop a contingent perspective on agency and stewardship behavior (Miller et al., 2011), where the contingencies come from the family (e.g., family structure or generation), the business, or the ownership subsystem. It is important to understand that if we choose to use a particular lens (those introduced or remaining to be introduced to the field), it will also color the questions and answers that would be salient to us.

AGENCY THEORY DOMINATES THE FIELD

Based on our review, it can be fairly said that agency theory has dominated the study of governance in family firms. Overall, representing a deductive approach, research in this vein has been used to test and support agency theory's key predictions in terms of agency, agency costs (incentives and monitoring), and performance.

Unification of Ownership and Control Leads to Performance Advantages

Daily and Dollinger (1992) were among the earliest to use the agency theory lens on family business governance. Their empirical study found that significant differences exist between family-owned and managed and professionally managed businesses in terms of both structural and process dimensions, and that family-owned and managed firms exhibit performance advantages resulting from unified ownership and control.

Family CEOs may also have better incentive alignment with family owners. McConaughy

(2000), for instance, found that compensation levels and incentive-based pay are relatively lower for family CEOs than for non-family CEOs. The differences stem from family CEOs having different and superior incentives than non-family CEOs. Work by Gomez-Mejia et al. generally supports this finding and provides more explanations. Family CEOs, who are typically also the dominant owners of family firms, may trade lower compensation for longer tenures. Family CEOs thus are protected in case of poor performance and high risks in family firms (Gomez-Mejia et al., 2001). Family CEOs trade use the security of tenure to make larger relative investments in R&D (risk-taking) (Gomez-Mejia et al., 2003).

External Directors are Functional

Agency theory predictions (and prescriptions) are also generally supported with respect to board composition, where the focus of research has been on controlling agency costs (Van den Heuvel et al., 2006), via the appointment of external/independent directors.

In the context of family businesses (FBs), one view is that a board of directors would be useful as monitors only in the context of relatively low levels of goal alignment between family owners and the managers (Pieper et al., 2008). Few outside influences have a voice in governing a family firm. Due to the FB's financial conservatism monitoring by debt-holders is less common (Anderson and Reeb, 2003; Gallo and Vilaseca, 1998). Thus, the composition of the family firm's board of directors is crucial in the quality of governance in family firms (Bammens et al., 2011; Corbetta and Salvato, 2004; Daily and Dalton, 1992; Forbes and Milliken, 1999; Lane et al., 2006).

While family control by itself has a mixed result on performance in different contexts, (Filatotchev et al., 2005), and even though family firms are generally more reluctant to appoint independent directors (Brunninge and Nordqvist, 2004), controlling family firms with greater board independence outperform non-family firms. Independent board members seem to mitigate potential opportunistic behavior by large, controlling shareholders (Anderson and Reeb, 2004; Filatotchev et al., 2005). They also reduce the behavioral tendencies of family leaders that may favor the family but hurt business goals (Goel et al., 2013). Overall, the professionalization of governance bodies helps the family firms (Martinez et al., 2007), and outside directors help to increase group effort and motivation to be active (Bettinelli, 2011). These studies support the notion that independent directors make the board better monitors of management, which can be interpreted as supporting agency theory.

STEWARDSHIP PERSPECTIVE CHALLENGES

Opposing observations to the above have also been made, even though not all evoke the stewardship perspective. For example, Klein et al. (2005) found that board independence was negatively correlated with a family firm's financial performance. Contrary to agency theory prescriptions, insiders and affiliated directors are argued to add significant value in a family firm.

Affiliated Directors Make a Valuable Contribution

Family directors on the board may be seen as serving several important functions. First, they can be seen as being used to continue the preservation of family values (Bammens et al., 2008; Randøy and Goel, 2003) and the founding values of the firm in successive generations. Second, 'affiliate' directors can provide the necessary relational resources (social capital and advice) to assist in product diversification (Jones et al., 2008), leading to a positive impact on firm performance (Arosa et al., 2010).

Martin-Reyna and Duran-Encalada (2012) investigate interesting issues related to the influence of *both* family ownership and governance on firm performance, contextualizing the degree of family ownership with governance. They find that while the relationship between ownership concentration and firm performance is positive in family firms, it is negative in non-family firms. In addition, relationships between the governance mechanisms (i.e., board composition and financial leverage) and firm performance is contingent on the nature of the owners. These results add new empirical evidence confirming prior literature that suggests that we cannot ignore the identity of the owners and their priorities and preferences. The identity of owners and their governing rationalities influences corporate conduct (Miller et al., 2010). Hence, family ownership negatively mediates the independent directors' and the financial leverage's influence on firm performance, while the opposite holds true for affiliate and inside directors. However, Anderson and Reeb (2004) found (under conditions of high levels of family board representation relative to independent directors) a significant and negative relationship between the presence of affiliated directors and a family firm's financial performance. These contrasting results lead us to suggest that institutional factors may account for the contrasting findings.

Overall, this collective body of research suggests that perhaps affiliated directors play a *subtler* role in family firm governance, and use the trust that the family reposes in them to shield the firm from dysfunctional influences of the family (e.g., sibling rivalry for control of the firm), and guide the decision making toward better financial performance. Collectively, these findings also suggest that modeling more contingencies arising from heterogeneity in the family, ownership, management, and business subsystems, as well as a wider variety of performance measures, could be usefully pursued to fully understand the value of affiliated directors in different kinds of family firms.

External Directors are an Important Resource

While external directors have a general 'monitoring' effect on family firm's management,

the directors are valued by the family CEOs more for their service role (Dumas et al., 2000; Van den Heuvel et al., 2006; Ward and Handy, 1988). In private FBs in particular, due to concentration of ownership and the large overlap between ownership and management, external directors are primarily hired for their service role (Andersen and Reeb, 2004; Bammens et al., 2008; Jones et al., 2008; Van den Heuvel et al., 2006).

Indeed, advice from external directors with functional skills and experiences that are lacking inside the family may be an essential element for FBs to bridge the skills gap (Bammens et al., 2011). Provision of resources has been found to be a very important role of boards in private family firms (Corbetta and Salvato, 2004; Voordeckers et al., 2007), including helping owner managers avoid decision pathologies such as escalation of commitment (Woods et al., 2012). Goel et al.'s (2013) study points the specific ways in which they may influence the context which CEOs use to make decisions – by influencing the degree of emphasis of the values and goals set by the CEO – in addition to performing their traditional roles of monitoring and mentoring.

Research on family business governance also points to the more subtle uses of external directors – that of providing objectivity and de-emotionalizing sometimes emotionally charged situations. These directors also have a personal, trust-based relationship with the family (Ng and Roberts, 2007) and can thus make the family more responsive to their advice and impose limits on the CEO's discretion (Chrisman et al., 2004; Combs, 2008; Jaffe, 2005; Johannisson and Huse, 2000; Schulze et al., 2001). External directors may, for example, advise the family on succession issues and make the decision-making process more rational (Van den Heuvel et al., 2006; Westhead, 2003) or control the degree of family influence in the firm (Basco and Perez Rodriguez, 2009).

Ng and Roberts' (2007) study of external directors in family firms indicated that external directors play a vital mediating role in a web of firm and family relationships *by protecting the firm* from the damaging intrusion of family altruism and managerial opportunism. For example, external directors are likely to have a restraining influence on a family CEO's tendency to place higher importance on family-directed goals. More generally, research has found that the objectivity that external directors provide in a variety of decision-making contexts is valuable to the family firm (Alderfer, 1988; Danco and Jonovic, 1981; Donckels and Lambrecht, 1999; Jonovic, 1989; Mueller, 1988). Finally, Johannisson and Huse (2000) suggest that non-executive directors may enable the balancing of the different demands of entrepreneurialism, paternalism, and managerialism.

Family Leaders' Possible Enlightenment and Reflectivity Deserves More Attention

Overall, the particularly nuanced relationship of the 'external' directors in family firms is in sharp contrast to the relatively clinical and arms-length detachment that is assumed, and indeed prized, in non-family and widely-held firms. In particular, the use of external/independent directors to protect the firm from the family CEO's nepotistic tendencies should be investigated further in the context of privately held family firms, since it is in these firms that the CEO, while under no obligation to appoint independent directors, may need the most restraint engendered by these directors. In these firms, the existence of independent directors may be a sign of enlightened family firm management by the family CEO, and a sound prescription coming out of family business research on governance.

Our overall conclusion on this issue is that, collectively, research on the role of external directors in family businesses has led to a more nuanced understanding of how family business leaders use external directors to control the former's own harmful nepotistic tendencies. This seems to indicate, on average, some degree of foresight and self-awareness among the family business leaders

regarding the utility of independent directors in the family firm.

SOCIAL CAPITAL THEORY PROMISES

We already discussed above some functions of social capital in family business governance. Overall, the use of relational governance lens offers a promising lens to study governance in family firm, although this has not been used extensively (e.g., Mustakallio et al., 2002; Nordqvist and Goel, 2008). It is also a natural lens to study family firm governance, since family firms have ample freedom and opportunity to rely on more informal governance structures (such as social control mechanisms through shared attitudes and values) than do non-family firms. Thus it has been said that family influence makes a difference not only in formal governance, but 'also in the *quality of relationships* and the *prevalence of informal control mechanisms*' (Astrachan, 2010, emphasis added).

External Directors' 'Affiliation' is Valuable

Although the appointment of external directors in FBs may be mainly driven by satisfying business needs (Ng and Roberts, 2007), the majority of them also have good social ties with the family CEO (Jones et al., 2008). This leads to a subtle change in the definition of 'externality' in family businesses – under such conditions it is more appropriate to consider the non-family directors as 'affiliated' rather than 'external'.

Among the few empirical studies using the relational view, based on the development of social capital and building on the notion of affiliated 'external' directors, Jones et al. (2008), argued that these 'external' ('affiliated' in our terms) directors stimulate family firms to pursue diversification strategies by sharing their knowledge and experience with family executives, and hence reducing the perceived risk. Thus the relational governance view is also supported by the social capital lens to emphasize the idea of external directors' service role.

Board Independence Works in Founder-led Contexts

There is also some empirical evidence supporting the affiliation perspective, at least in particular social contexts. For instance, in a sample of European family firms, Garcia-Ramos and Garcia-Olalla's (2011) findings contradict the widespread belief that smaller and more independent boards always lead to better firm performance. They found a positive effect of board size on business performance only in non-founder-led family firms and a negative effect of board size on founder-led family businesses. Interestingly, they also found that the presence of independent directors on the board has a positive effect on performance when a firm is run by its founder (corroborated by Arosa et al., 2010). However, when descendants lead the firm, the presence of independent directors has a negative effect on performance.

The findings of Garcia-Ramos and Garcia-Olalla (2011) and Arosa et al. (2010) complement Miller et al.'s (2011) study that provides a more nuanced understanding of agency relationships by incorporating the social context in which these relationships are embedded. Specifically, these authors argued for, and empirically supported, the notion that lone founders are embedded in constituencies that are emotionally detached and cater mostly to commercial logic, whereas a family firm that is a collective of individual family members as shareholders may be subject to affective logic and non-market rationalities typical of family relationships. Thus differing social contexts of the family decision makers may switch the dominant, driving rationality as emerging from the business or family subsystem.

The Identity of the Principal Makes a Difference

A possible explanation to explain the findings by Garcia-Ramos and Garcia-Olalla's

(2011), and Miller and Le Breton-Miller's (2011) study is that the commercial logic-driven founders perhaps appointed independent board members as a foil to keep family rationalities at bay. The descendants, driven by affective logic, inherited these independent directors. Since these directors were not personally chosen by the descendants, they lacked the trust-based authority and gravitas to have their voice heard, and the affective logic took over the firm, resulting in weaker financial performance.

Both these studies thus highlight the contribution of context in understanding who are the likely 'principals' in the relationship, and understanding their specific goals that the agents are likely to be asked to serve, and emphasize Randøy and Goel's (2003) findings that the efficacy of agency mechanisms is directly linked to the agency context of the firm, and that family firms should choose to protect themselves from 'unhealthy' monitoring which may destroy the family firm's competitive advantage.

These efforts and findings open up the possibility of contextualizing a wide array of possible agency relationships in family firms. They are consistent with previous research that suggests that agency and stewardship theories are not mutually exclusive (Astrachan, 2010). As agency theory and stewardship theory operate under different assumptions, each may be valid depending on the context to which it is applied (Shen, 2003). Agency assumes individualism (which may lead to goal heterogeneity among individual managers, family members, and other owners). The degree of agency costs is related to the degree to which the goals are different, since costs must be incurred to align the goals among different parties. On the other hand, stewardship assumes collectivism (or a concern for goals other than one's own, which could lead to shared goals, or goal convergence, among managers, family members, and other owners).

Formal or Informal? The Strength of the Informal Decreases the Need for Formal

Pieper et al. (2008) found that relatively high levels of family commitment to the business and overlap of values between the owning family and the management (which can be seen as indicative of an alignment of interests, or a collectivistic attitude descriptive of greater family cohesion) result in fewer formal governance structures, such as boards of directors (Astrachan, 2010). This is consistent with the line of thinking found in Mustakallio et al. (2002), who used the social capital lens to distinguish between contractual and relational governance. By demonstrating that informal (relational) governance mechanisms are important for family firms, they underlined their suggestion that family firm governance should be grounded on the unique characteristics of the family firms.

The call to use more such relational governance is welcome, because it may span a wider variety of institutional contexts – since there are some institutional contexts where formal contractual agreements, and thus governance, based on such agreements may not be salient. Recent work that investigates performance contracts for family and non-family managers (Block, 2011; Chua et al., 2009), for example, sheds implicit light on this issue – the contracts between the family and non-family managers could be different, because of differing degrees of enforceability, due to differing degrees of relationship specificity between the contracting parties. Even within families, Steier (2003) argued that the agency contracts of family businesses may show a wide variation, depending on whether the family or business rationalities predominate.

Search for a Richer Set of Contingencies

There are other studies that are good examples of finer grained modeling of family firm specific contingencies that are needed to advance the knowledge of governance in family firms. For example, Miller and Le Breton-Miller's (2006) study on family ownership, control, leadership, and family continuity offers these choices as contingencies that determine governance performance (e.g., when independent directors are useful), and what resources are created. Another interesting study looks at heterogeneity of outside investors' 'tolerance for family involvement' in the business – while some minority investors may have more narrow, financial goals, others may be more tolerant of a 'family agenda' (Villanueva and Sapienza, 2009). This suggests that some outside investors may actually exhibit a preference for family influence and family goals, which may explain why they may stick with the family firm.

INSTITUTIONAL CONTEXT MATTERS

Principal–Principal Issues are Important in Emerging Markets

Overall, we found that most studies in governance were conducted in the USA and Europe, with only a few studies from emerging markets (Filatotchev et al., 2005; Martínez et al., 2007). In developed economies, because ownership and control are often separated and legal mechanisms protect owners, the governance conflicts that receive the lion's share of attention are the principal–agent (PA) conflicts between owners (principals) and managers (agents) (Jensen and Meckling, 1976). However, in emerging economies, the institutional context generally makes the enforcement of agency contracts more costly (North, 1990; Wright et al., 2005). This results in the prevalence of a more concentrated firm ownership (Dharwadkar et al., 2000).

Concentrated ownership, combined with an absence of effective external governance mechanisms, is believed to result in more frequent conflicts between controlling and minority shareholders (Morck et al., 2005). This new perspective has come to be known as the principal–principal (PP) model of corporate governance.

Family Business May Thrive in the Presence of Institutional Weaknesses

The PP model centers on conflicts between the controlling and minority shareholders in a firm (cf. Dharwadkar et al., 2000). The overall assumption of this line of research is that the controlling shareholder uses its control to expropriate rent from minority investors (e.g., Morck and Yeung, 2003).

More recently, Aguilera and Crespi-Cladera (2012) offered an alternative, and positive, explanation of family firms in different institutional contexts. They argue that Family Business Groups (FBG) may represent a *relatively* efficient governance form to allocate capital and make the market for capital in the presence of the very institutional weaknesses identified by Morck et al. FBGs, in this view, may be a natural product of weaknesses in formal institutions, a view supported by Khanna and his colleagues (Khanna and Palepu, 1997, 2000a, 2000b). Thus, governance via FBGs may be relatively efficient, with the better alignment of incentives, relative to the high agency costs of widely-held firms.

Different Institutional Contexts Require Different Levels of Openness

The view that 'institutional context matters' is represented in extant family business research. For instance, it has been found that there are country differences in the degree to which family businesses involve outsiders (Corbetta and Montemerlo, 1999) due to higher ownership concentration in Europe (Enriques and Volpin, 2007), which in turn lead to differences in governance issues facing the firm and the family. For example, Dyer and Mortenson (2005) reported that founders use several strategies to ameliorate the risk, including the development of social capital and networks to garner political, human, and financial capital.

Cultural Differences Lead to Differences on the Firm-level

Astrachan (2010) asks a provocative question that suggests another kind of institutional variation – that of family cultures, which could be individualistic or collectivistic. These differences in individualistic and collectivistic cultures among families may in turn be partially nested in national or regional institutions, as they are shaped by forces of history, and may represent the evolutionary vestiges of quest for survival and permanence. A deep understanding of family cultures may require a deep understanding of these forces.

Institutional Environments Differ Because of Different Sets of Family Firms

Using a more macro-level performance construct, Lester and Canella (2006) describe how family firms use interlocking directorates to develop what they call 'interorganizational familiness'. It is these networks that help family firms mitigate some of their agency costs. Further, Lester and Canella (2006) also put forward that the social capital created through the interlocking can help family firms not only adapt to changes in the environment, but also shape that (e.g., political) environment. In other words, while Morck, Aguilera et al. explore the effect of family firms as a function of the institutional context, Lester and Canella (2006) explain how family firms may change the institutional contexts that they operate in. Macro-level studies like these are rare in the field of management, but are important to understand the ecological effects of the existence and behavior of family firms.

PROMISING CONTINGENCIES

A variety of contingencies have been outlined above. This section is devoted to other promising contingencies that can help us towards more finer-grained analyses of family business governance in the future.

Social Contingency

As Le Breton-Miller and Miller (2009) point out, agency assumptions have been viewed critically. Eisenhardt (1989), Granovetter (2005), and Hirsch et al. (1987) have argued that this economic perspective reduces organizational and social reality to rationales that 'ignore social forces and relationships', and view human nature only through the filters of economic rationality, self-interest, opportunism, and greed. More precisely, Le Breton-Miller and Miller (2009: 1170) argue that both these opposing family utility (i.e., agency as exhibited in principal–principal conflict) and stewardship views:

> have merit – but to different degrees under different circumstances – these being determined not simply by economic or psychological considerations, but sociological ones. Specifically, the more a business and its primary executive actors are socially embedded in a family, the more likely will agency-based rationales dominate those of stewardship.

Le Breton-Miller and Miller (2009) use the variety of family firms as defined by variations in familial ownership, management, and generational involvement to model the nature and extent of such embeddedness. The embeddedness perspective may be especially powerful in a family context, given that family relations are infused with deep emotional, biological, and complex social ties and moral obligations, reified by layers of social exchanges over time. These relationships, while likely to be highly idiosyncratic in a family, are also the 'ties that bind'. When ties cannot be broken with ease, people are likely to govern and be governed with a view toward self-preservation at one end, and 'making it work' at the other. Issues of co-alitions, sub-identities, and the psychological and emotional costs of withdrawal/engagements may become salient. These issues offer additional complexities that are assumed away

in relatively easy to define, and break, contractual relations that are modeled in mainstream economic perspectives.

Leadership Contingency

Self-control of the owner/family business leader has been investigated by Lubatkin et al. (2007a). Lubatkin et al. (2007b) evoke the degree of self-control exercised by controlling owners as a moderating variable that determines the extent of agency (due to parental altruism) that a family business may exhibit. By presenting the family ownership form as it is generally presented in the family business literature; i.e., 'neither as a panacea nor a pariah' (e.g., Chrisman et al., 2003; Greenwood, 2003; Steier, 2003; Zahra, 2003), Lubatkin et al. (2007a: 959) force the field to focus on the key contingency of family business leadership. This implies that family business leadership is endogenous to whether, and the degree to which, agency issues will be embedded in family business operations. By the same token, family business leadership can influence the adoption and permeation of stewardship values over time and across generations by exercising judicious self-control.

FUTURE RESEARCH

Based on our review of literature, we believe that a paradigmatic shift in knowledge about family business governance may need to encompass the following research questions. In turn these questions may lead to insights that lead to the development of family business governance as a theory of content.

Between-group Questions

This relates to the relative cost of agency in family versus non-family firms. While the extant research covered above has outlined agency costs in both family and non-family firms, future research is needed to flesh out the extent of such agency costs instead of assuming a broad equivalence. Specifically, models incorporating the limits of agency behavior in family firms, versus agency behavior in non-family firms (where managers may be concerned more about their own reputation, and their objectives may be more divergent from the objectives of the firm), would seem to be a worthwhile direction to pursue.

Future research should also focus on the qualitative differences in both the 'agents' and 'principals' in family and non-family firms. It has been established that the agents in family firms have more complicated 'contracts' with the owners. Governance research in family business has also acknowledged the role of competency of principals and agents, as well as the multi-faceted goals that family businesses pursue. However, governance issues that straddle these issues together are fertile areas of future research. In this vein, the work by Hendry (2002) on the issue of competency and difficulty in specifying goals would be an especially useful direction to pursue.

Within-group Questions

While research has conceptualized the 'agents' and 'principals', as well as variations in these contracts (e.g., Steier, 2003), deeper research in the contingencies within families that make these behaviors salient would be welcome. Beyond the contingencies of family structure and family identity, some of the contingencies that could be modeled are family cohesion, collective emotional harmony/conflict, family culture (including family values and socialization), and the absorptive capacity and collective memory of families. These contingencies, and therefore the resultant roles, are not static, but dynamic as families change over time in their structure, composition, identity, and leadership.

It has been recognized that family firms are embedded in social structures that differ substantially from those of non-family firms (Steier et al., 2009). However, the

embeddedness is not merely social. By applying a generic definition of 'agent', with its notion of time-dependent and arms-length contractual relations, family business research may be missing an opportunity to particularize the concept of an 'agent' to family firms. Agency relations in family firms may spill over outside the boundaries of contracts, may be of indefinite and long time horizons, and may be imbued with offsetting moral, social, and cultural considerations of duty and responsibility.

Longitudinal, Evolutionary Approaches

Building on Steier (2001) and Bammens et al. (2008), Ikäheimonen et al. (2013) bring together a variety of aspects from the family business context (e.g., a desire for continuity, intergenerational succession, growing complexity of the family business across generations, and variations in the degree of family influence over time) to suggest that family boards may need to evolve over time to preserve their effectiveness and relevance at any point of time. These longitudinal studies may be ideal to map the evolutionary changes in family business governance as the family business itself evolves over generations and across a variety of family business leaders and owners. More generally, longitudinal studies have the potential to thread a variety of theoretical lenses together in a contingent fashion, and prescribe specific governance changes depending on changes in underlying contingencies that determine the preponderance, for instance, of agency or stewardship driven thinking in family businesses.

CONCLUSION

Family business as a distinct organizational context offers unique governance issues. Research extending governance research from other contexts to family business has corroborated some conclusions from other contexts, but has also articulated some differences. These differences arise especially from the subtle changes in definitions-in-use in family business – e.g., definitions of externality and independence in the context of directors. Research has also begun making advances in using theoretical lenses other than agency and stewardship that may be more relevant for family business, and hold the promise of a more nuanced understanding of governance in family business – e.g., relational governance and social networks. While extant research has employed some contingencies (e.g., generation), a more comprehensive body of knowledge on governance in family firms would require modeling of additional contingencies to account for the heterogeneity of family firms. This in turn may lead to the development of a finer grained theory of content related to family business governance, rather than family business governance as a specific context among a variety of governance contexts. Overall, while we are heartened by the progress made so far in this area, we believe that family business governance research is in its infancy, and believe that scholars from a variety of perspectives could substantially enrich our knowledge in this area.

REFERENCES

Aguilera, R.V. and Crespi-Cladera, R. (2012) 'Firm family firms: Current debates of corporate governance in family firms', *Journal of Family Business Strategy*, 3(2): 66–69.

Alderfer, C.P. (1988) 'Understanding and consulting to family business boards', *Family Business Review*, 1(3): 249–261.

Anderson, R.C., Mansi, S.A., and Reeb, D.M. (2003) 'Founding family ownership and the agency cost of debt', *Journal of Financial Economics*, 68(2): 263–285.

Anderson, R.C. and Reeb, D.M. (2003) 'Founding-family ownership and firm performance: Evidence from the S&P 500', *The Journal of Finance*, 58(3): 1301–1328.

Anderson, R.C. and Reeb, D.M. (2004) 'Board composition: Balancing family influence in S&P 500 firms', *Administrative Science Quarterly*, 49(2): 209–237.

Arosa, B., Iturralde, T., and Maseda, A. (2010) 'Outsiders on the board of directors and firm performance: Evidence from Spanish non-listed family firms', *Journal of Family Business Strategy*, 1(4): 236–245.

Arrègle, J., Hitt, M.A., Sirmon, D.G., and Very, P. (2007) 'The development of organizational social capital: Attributes of family firms', *Journal of Management Studies*, 44(1): 73–95.

Astrachan, J.H. (2010) 'Strategy in family business: Toward a multidimensional research agenda', *Journal of Family Business Strategy*, 1(1): 6–14.

Bammens, Y., Voordeckers, W., and Van Gils, A. (2008) 'Boards of directors in family firms: A generational perspective', *Small Business Economics*, 31(2): 163–180.

Bammens, Y., Voordeckers, W., and Van Gils, A. (2011) 'Boards of directors in family businesses: A literature review and research agenda', *International Journal of Management Reviews*, 13(2): 134–152.

Bartholomeusz, S. and Tanewski, G.A. (2006) 'The relationship between family firms and corporate governance', *Journal of Small Business Management*, 44(2): 245–267.

Basco, R. and Pérez Rodríguez, M.J. (2009) 'Studying the family enterprise holistically', *Family Business Review*, 22(1): 82–95.

Bertrand, M. and Schoar, A. (2006) 'The role of family in family firms', *Journal of Economic Perspectives*, 20(2): 73–96.

Bettinelli, C. (2011) 'Boards of directors in family firms: An exploratory study of structure and group process', *Family Business Review*, 24(2): 151–169.

Birley, S. (2001) 'Owner-manager attitudes to family and business issues: a 16 country study', *Entrepreneurship: Theory and Practice*, 26(2): 63–76.

Block, J.H. (2011) 'How to pay nonfamily managers in large family firms: A principal-agent model', *Family Business Review*, 24(1): 9–27.

Block, J.H., Jaskiewicz, P., and Miller, D. (2011) 'Ownership versus management effects on performance in family and founder companies: A bayesian reconciliation', *Journal of Family Business Strategy*, 2(4): 232–245.

Blumentritt, T. (2006) 'The relationship between boards and planning in family business', *Family Business Review*, 19(1): 65–72.

Blumentritt, T.P., Keyt, A.D., and Astrachan, J.H. (2007) 'Creating an environment for successful nonfamily CEOs: An exploratory study of good principals', *Family Business Review*, 20(4): 321–335.

Braun, M. and Sharma, A. (2007) 'Should the CEO also be chair of the board? An empirical examination of family-controlled public firms', *Family Business Review*, 20(2): 111–126.

Brenes, E.R., Madrigal, K., and Requena, B. (2011) 'Corporate governance and family business performance', *Journal of Business Research*, 64(3): 280–285.

Brunninge, O. and Nordqvist, M. (2004) 'Ownership structure, board composition and entrepreneurship: Evidence from family firms and venture-capital-backed firms', *International Journal of Entrepreneurial Behavior & Research*, 10(1/2): 85–105.

Carney, M. (2005) 'Corporate governance and competitive advantage in family-controlled firms', *Entrepreneurship: Theory and Practice*, 29(3): 249–265.

Chen, H.L. and Hsu, W.T. (2009) 'Family ownership, board independence and R&D investment', *Family Business Review*, 22(4): 347–362.

Chrisman, J.J., Chua, J.H., and Litz, R. (2003) 'A unified systems perspective of family firm performance: An extension and integration', *Journal of Business Venturing*, 18(4): 467–472.

Chrisman, J.J., Chua, J.H., and Litz, R.A. (2004) 'Comparing the agency costs of family and non-family firms: Conceptual issues and exploratory evidence', *Entrepreneurship: Theory and Practice*, 28(4): 335–354.

Chrisman, J.J., Chua, J.H., Kellermanns, F.W., and Chang, E.P. (2007) 'Are family managers agents or stewards? An exploratory study in privately held family firms', *Journal of Business Research*, 60(10): 1030–1038.

Chua, J., Chrisman, J., and Bergiel, E. (2009) 'An agency theoretical analysis of the professionalized family firm', *Entrepreneurship: Theory and Practice*, 33(2): 355–372.

Claessens, S., Djankov, S., Fan, J.P.H., and Lang, L.H.P. (2002) 'Disentangling the incentive and entrenchment effects of large shareholdings', *The Journal of Finance*, 57(6): 2741–2771.

Combs, J.G. (2008) *Commentary: The Servant, the Parasite, and the Enigma: A Tale of Three Ownership Structures and Their Affiliate Directors*. Wiley-Blackwell.

Corbetta, G. and Montemerlo, D. (1999) 'Ownership, governance, and management issues in small and medium-size family businesses: A comparison of Italy and the United States', *Family Business Review*, 12(4): 361–374.

Corbetta, G. and Salvato, C.A. (2004) 'The board of directors in family firms: One size fits all?', *Family Business Review*, 17(2): 119–134.

Daily, C.M. and Dollinger, M.J. (1992) 'An empirical investigation of ownership structure in family and professionally managed firms', *Family Business Review*, 5(2): 117–136.

Daily, C.M. and Dalton, D.R. (1992) 'Financial performance of founder-managed versus professionally managed small corporations', *Journal of Small Business Management*, 30(2): 25–34.

Danco, L.A. and Jonovic, D.J. (1981) *Outside Directors in the Family Owned Business*. Cleveland, OH: The University Press.

Dharwadkar, R., George, G., and Brandes, P. (2000) 'Privatization in emerging economies: An agency theory perspective', *Academy of Management Review*, 25(3): 650–669.

Donckels, R. and Lambrecht, J. (1999) 'The re-emergence of family-based enterprises in East Central Europe: What can be learned from family business research in the western world?', *Family Business Review*, 12(2): 171–188.

Dumas, C., Goel, S., and Zanzi, A. (2000) 'Through the eyes of the beholder: Determinants of positive perception of board contribution in family-owned firms', *International Journal of Entrepreneurship and Innovation*, 1(3): 151–161.

Dyer, W.G. and Mortensen, S.P. (2005) 'Entrepreneurship and family business in a hostile environment: The case of Lithuania', *Family Business Review*, 18(3): 247–258.

Eisenhardt, K.M. (1989) 'Agency theory: An assessment and review', *Academy of Management Review*, 14(1): 57–74.

Enriques, L. and Volpin, P. (2007) 'Corporate governance reforms in continental Europe', *Journal of Economic Perspectives*, 21(1): 117–140.

Feltham, T.S., Feltham, G., and Barnett, J. (2005) 'The dependence of family business on a single decision-maker', *Journal of Small Business Management*, 43(1): 1–14.

Filatotchev, I., Lien, Y.-C., and Piesse, J. (2005) 'Corporate governance and performance in publicly listed, family-controlled firms: Evidence from Taiwan', *Asia Pacific Journal of Management*, 22(3): 257–283.

Forbes, D.P. and Milliken, F.J. (1999) 'Cognition and corporate governance: Understanding boards of directors as strategic decision-making groups', *Academy of Management Review*, 24(3): 489–505.

Gabrielsson, J. and Huse, M. (2005) '"Outside" directors in SME boards: A call for theoretical reflection', *Corporate Board: Role, Duties & Composition*, 1(1): 28–37.

Gabrielsson, J. and Winlund, H. (2000) 'Boards of directors in small and medium-sized industrial firms: Examining the effects of the board's working style on board task performance', *Entrepreneurship & Regional Development*, 12(4): 311–330.

Gallo, M.A. and Vilaseca, A. (1998) 'A financial perspective on structure, conduct, and performance in the family firm: An empirical study', *Family Business Review*, 11(1): 35–47.

García-Ramos, R. and García-Olalla, M. (2011) 'Board characteristics and firm performance in public founder- and nonfounder-led family businesses', *Journal of Family Business Strategy*, 2(4): 220–231.

Gersick, K., Davis, J., Hampton, M. and Landsberg, I. (1997) *Generation to Generation: Life Cycles of the Family Business*. Boston, MA: Harvard Business School Press.

Gersick, K. and Feliu, N. (2014) 'Governing the family enterprise: Practices, performance, and research', in *The SAGE Handbook of Family Business*. Melin, L., Nordqvist, M. and Sharma, P. (eds). Sage: London.

Goel, S., Voordeckers, W., Van Gils, A., and Van den Heuvel, J. (2013) 'CEO's empathy and salience of socioemotional wealth in family SMEs – the moderating role of external directors', *Entrepreneurship & Regional Development*, 25(3–4): 111–134.

Gomez-Mejia, L., Larraza-Kintana, M., and Makri, M. (2003) 'The determinants of executive compensation in family-controlled public corporations', *Academy of Management Journal*, 46(2): 226–237.

Gomez-Mejia, L.R., Nunez-Nickel, M., and Gutierrez, I. (2001) 'The role of family ties in agency contracts', *Academy of Management Journal*, 44(1): 81–95.

Granovetter, M. (2005) 'The impact of social structure on economic outcomes', *The Journal of Economic Perspectives*, 19(1): 33–50.

Greenwood, R. (2003) 'Commentary on: "Toward a theory of agency and altruism in family firms"', *Journal of Business Venturing*, 18(4): 491–494.

Gubitta, P. and Gianecchini, M. (2002) 'Governance and flexibility in family-owned SMEs', *Family Business Review*, 15(4): 277–298.

Habbershon, T.G. and Pistrui, J. (2002) 'Enterprising families domain: Family-influenced ownership groups in pursuit of transgenerational wealth', *Family Business Review*, 15(3): 223–237.

Habbershon, T.G. and Williams, M. (1999) 'A resource-based framework for assessing the strategic advantages of family firms', *Family Business Review*, 12(1): 1–25.

Hendry, J. (2002) 'The principal's other problems: Honest incompetence and the specification of objectives', *Academy of Management Review*, 27(1): 98–113.

Hillman, A.J. and Dalziel, T. (2003) 'Boards of directors and firm performance: Integrating agency and resource dependence perspectives', *Academy of Management Review*, 28(3): 383–396.

Hirsch, P., Michaels, S., and Friedman, R. (1987) '"Dirty hands" versus "clean models"', *Theory and Society*, 16(3): 317–336.

Ikäheimonen, T., Pihkala, T. & Ikävalko, M. (2013). The evolution of the family business board - a case study. In Smyrnios K.X., Poutziouris, P.Z. & Goel, S. (eds) (2013) *Handbook of Research on Family Business*, Second Edition. Edward Elgar Publishing Limited, Cheltenham UK.

International Family Enterprise Research Academy (IFERA) (2003) 'Family businesses dominate', *Family Business Review*, 16(4): 235–240.

Jaffe, D.T. (2005) 'Strategic planning for the family in business', *Journal of Financial Planning*, 18(3): 50–56.

Jaskiewicz, P. and Klein, S. (2007) 'The impact of goal alignment on board composition and board size in family businesses', *Journal of Business Research*, 60(10): 1080–1089.

Jensen, M.C. and Meckling, W.H. (1976) 'Theory of the firm: Managerial behavior, agency costs and ownership structure', *Journal of Financial Economics*, 3(4): 305–360.

Johannisson, B. and Huse, M. (2000) 'Recruiting outside board members in the small family business: An ideological challenge', *Entrepreneurship & Regional Development*, 12(4): 353–378.

Johnson, P. (2004) 'Shared thinking and interaction in the family business boardroom', *Corporate Governance: The International Journal of Effective Board Performance*, 4(1): 39–51.

Jones, C.D., Makri, M., and Gomez-Mejia, L. (2008) 'Affiliate directors and perceived risk bearing in publicly traded, family-controlled firms: The case of diversification', *Entrepreneurship: Theory and Practice*, 32(6): 1007–1026.

Jonovic, D.J. (1989) 'Outside review in a wider context: An alternative to the classic board', *Family Business Review*, 2(2): 125–140.

Kellermanns, F.W. and Eddleston, K.A. (2004) 'Feuding families: When conflict does a family firm good', *Entrepreneurship: Theory and Practice*, 28(3): 209–228.

Khanna, T. and Palepu, K. (1997) 'Why focused strategies may be wrong for emerging markets', *Harvard Business Review*, 75(4): 41–49.

Khanna, T. and Palepu, K. (2000a) 'The future of business groups in emerging markets: Long-run evidence from Chile', *Academy of Management Journal*, 43(3): 268–285.

Khanna, T. and Palepu, K. (2000b) 'Is group affiliation profitable in emerging markets? An analysis of diversified Indian business groups', *The Journal of Finance*, 55(2): 867–891.

Klein, P., Shapiro, D., and Young, J. (2005) 'Corporate governance, family ownership and firm value: The Canadian evidence', *Corporate Governance: An International Review*, 13(6): 769–784.

Kotey, B. (2005) 'Goals, management practices, and performance of family SMEs', *International Journal of Entrepreneurial Behaviour and Research*, 11(1): 3–24.

Kowalewski, O., Talavera, O., and Stetsyuk, I. (2010) 'Influence of family involvement in management and ownership on firm performance: evidence from Poland', *Family Business Review*, 23(1): 45–59.

Krivogorsky, V. and Burton, F.G. (2011) 'Dominant owners and financial performance of continental European firms', *Social Science Research Network*, available at: http://papers.ssrn.com/sol3/papers.cfm?abstract_id=1086469 13.4.2012.

Kuan, T.H., Li, C.S., and Chu, S.H. (2010) 'Cash holdings and corporate governance in family-controlled firms', *Journal of Business Research*, 64(7): 757–764.

Lane, S., Astrachan, J., Keyt, A., and McMillan, K. (2006) 'Guidelines for family business boards of directors', *Family Business Review*, 19(2): 147–167.

Lansberg, I. and Astrachan, J.H. (1994) 'Influence of family relationships on succession planning and training: The importance of mediating factors', *Family Business Review*, 7(1): 39–59.

Le Breton-Miller, I. and Miller, D. (2006) 'Why do some family businesses out-compete? Governance, long-term orientations, and sustainable capability', *Entrepreneurship: Theory and Practice*, 30(6): 731–746.

Le Breton-Miller, I. and Miller, D. (2009) 'Agency vs. stewardship in public family firms: A social embeddedness reconciliation', *Entrepreneurship: Theory and Practice*, 33(6): 1169–1191.

Lester, R.H. and Cannella, A.A. (2006) 'Interorganizational familiness: How family firms use interlocking directorates to build community-level social capital', *Entrepreneurship: Theory and Practice*, 30(6): 755–775.

Lubatkin, M.H., Durand, R., and Ling, Y. (2007b) 'The missing lens in family firm governance theory: A self-other typology of parental altruism', *Journal of Business Research*, 60(10): 1022–1029.

Lubatkin, M.H., Ling, Y., and Schulze, W.S. (2007a) 'An organizational justice-based view of self-control and agency costs in family firms', *Journal of Management Studies*, 44(6): 955–971.

Lubatkin, M.H., Schulze, W.S., Ling, Y., and Dino, R.N. (2005) 'The effects of parental altruism on the governance of family-managed firms', *Journal of Organizational Behavior*, 26(3): 313–330.

Martin-Reyna, J.M.S. and Duran-Encalada, J.A. (2012) 'The relationship among family business, corporate governance and firm performance: Evidence from the Mexican stock exchange', *Journal of Family Business Strategy*, 3(2): 106–117.

Martínez, J.I., Stöhr, B.S., and Quiroga, B.F. (2007) 'Family ownership and firm performance: Evidence from public companies in Chile', *Family Business Review*, 20(2): 83–94.

Mazzi, C. (2011) 'Family business and financial performance: Current state of knowledge and future research challenges', *Journal of Family Business Strategy*, 2(3): 166–181.

McConaughy, D.L. (2000) 'Family CEOs vs. nonfamily CEOs in the family-controlled firm: An examination of the level and sensitivity of pay to performance', *Family Business Review*, 8(2): 121–131.

Miller, D. and Le Breton-Miller, I. (2005) *Managing for the Long Run: Lessons in Competitive Advantage from Great Family Businesses*. Boston, MA: Harvard Business School Press.

Miller, D. and Le Breton-Miller, I. (2006) 'Family governance and firm performance: Agency, stewardship, and capabilities', *Family Business Review*, 19(1): 73–87.

Miller, D., Le Breton-Miller, I., Lester, R.H., and Cannella, A.A. Jr. (2007) 'Are family firms really superior performers?', *Journal of Corporate Finance*, 13(5): 829–858.

Miller, D., Le Breton-Miller, I., Lester, R.H., and Scholnick, B. (2008) 'Stewardship vs. stagnation: an empirical comparison of small family and non-family businesses', *Journal of Management Studies*, 45(1): 51–78.

Miller, D., Le Breton-Miller, I., and Lester, R.H. (2010) 'Family ownership and acquisition behavior in publicly-traded companies', *Strategic Management Journal*, 31(2): 201–223.

Miller, D. and Le Breton-Miller, I. (2011) 'Governance, social identity, and entrepreneurial orientation in closely held public companies', *Entrepreneurship: Theory and Practice*, 35(5): 1051–1076.

Miller, D., Le Breton-Miller, I., and Lester, R.H. (2011) 'Family and lone founder ownership and strategic behaviour: Social context, identity, and institutional logics', *Journal of Management Studies*, 48(1): 1–25.

Mishra, C.S., Randoy, T., and Jenssen J.I. (2001) 'The effect of founding family influence on firm value and corporate governance', *Journal of International Financial Management and Accounting*, 12(3): 235–259.

Morck, R., Wolfenzon, D., and Yeung, B. (2005) 'Corporate governance, economic entrenchment, and growth', *Journal of Economic Literature*, 43(3): 655–720.

Morck, R. and Yeung, B. (2003) 'Agency problems in large family business groups', *Entrepreneurship: Theory and Practice*, 27(4): 367–382.

Mueller, R.K. (1988) 'Differential directorship: Special sensitivities and roles for serving the family business board', *Family Business Review*, 1(3): 239–247.

Mustakallio, M., Autio, E., and Zahra, S.A. (2002) 'Relational and contractual governance in family firms: Effects on strategic decision-making', *Family Business Review*, 15(3): 205–222.

Nash, J.M. (1988) 'Boards of privately held companies: Their responsibilities and structure', *Family Business Review*, 1(3): 263–269.

Ng, W. and Roberts, J. (2007) "Helping the family": The mediating role of outside directors in ethnic Chinese family firms', *Human Relations*, 60(2): 285–314.

Nordqvist, M. and Goel, S. (2008) 'No family is an island: A social network approach to governance in family firms', in Phan, P.H. and Butler, J.E. (eds), *Information Age Press Series on Research in Entrepreneurship and Management*, 6th edition.

North, D.C. (1990) *Institutions, Institutional Change, and Economic Performance*. Cambridge: Cambridge University Press.

Pieper, T.M., Klein, S.B., and Jaskiewicz, P. (2008) 'The impact of goal alignment on board existence and top management team composition: Evidence from family-influenced businesses', *Journal of Small Business Management*, 46(3): 372–394.

Randøy, T. and Goel, S. (2003) 'Ownership structure, founder leadership, and performance in Norwegian SMEs: Implications for financing entrepreneurial opportunities', *Journal of Business Venturing*, 18(5): 619–637.

Rautiainen, M., Pihkala, T., and Ikävalko, M. (2010) 'Family business in family ownership portfolios', *International Journal of Entrepreneurial Ventures*, 1(4): 398–413.

Sacristán-Navarro, M. and Gómez-Ansón, S. (2007) 'Family ownership and pyramids in the Spanish market', *Family Business Review*, 20(3): 247–265.

Sacristán-Navarro, M. and Gómez-Ansón, S. (2009) 'Do families shape corporate governance structures?', *Journal of Management & Organizations*, 15(3): 327–345.

Sacristán-Navarro, M., Gómez-Ansón, S., and Cabeza-Garcia, L. (2011) 'Family ownership and control, the presence of other large shareholders and firm performance: further evidence', *Family Business Review*, 24(1): 71–93.

Salvato, C. and Melin, L. (2008) 'Creating value across generations in family-controlled businesses: the role of family social capital', *Family Business Review*, 21(3): 259–276.

Schulze, W.S., Lubatkin, M.H., Dino, R.N., and Buchholtz, A.K. (2001) 'Agency relationships in family firms: Theory and evidence', *Organization Science*, 12(2): 99–116.

Schulze, W.S., Lubatkin, M.H., and Dino, R.N. (2002) 'Altruism, agency, and the competitiveness of family firms', *Managerial & Decision Economics*, 23(4): 247–259.

Schulze, W.S., Lubatkin, M.H., and Dino, R.N. (2003) 'Exploring the agency consequences of ownership dispersion among the directors of private family firms', *Academy of Management Journal*, 46(2): 179–194.

Sciascia, S. and Mazzola, P. (2008) 'Family involvement in ownership and management: exploring nonlinear effects on performance', *Family Business Review*, 21(4): 331–345.

Selekler-Goksen, N.N. and Yildirim Öktem, Ö. (2009) 'Countervailing institutional forces: corporate governance in Turkish family business groups', *Journal of Management and Governance*, 13(3): 193–213.

Setia-Atmaja, L., Tanewski, G.A., and Skully, M. (2009) 'The role of dividends, debt and board structure in the governance of family controlled firms', *Journal of Business and Accounting*, 36(7): 863–898.

Sharma, P. (2004) 'An overview of the field of family business studies: Current status and directions for the future', *Family Business Review*, 17(1): 1–36.

Shen, W. (2003) 'The dynamics of the CEO-board relationship: an evolutionary perspective', *Academy of Management Review*, 28(3): 466–476.

Silva, F. and Majluf, N. (2008) 'Does family ownership shape performance outcomes?', *Journal of Business Research*, 61(6): 609–614.

Steier, L. (2001) 'Family firms, plural forms of governance, and the evolving of trust', *Family Business Review*, 14(4): 353–368.

Steier, L. (2003) 'Variants of agency contracts in family-financed ventures as a continuum of familial altruistic and market rationalities', *Journal of Business Venturing*, 18(5): 597–618.

Steier, L.P., Chua, J.H., and Chrisman, J.J. (2009) 'Embeddedness perspectives of economic action within family firms', *Entrepreneurship: Theory and Practice*, 33(6): 1157–1167.

Steier, L. and Miller, D. (2010) 'Pre- and post-succession governance philosophies in entrepreneurial family firms', *Journal of Family Business Strategy*, 1(3): 145–154.

Steijvers, T. and Voordeckers, W. (2009) 'Private family ownership and the agency costs of debt', *Family Business Review*, 22(4): 333–346.

Thomas, J. (2009) 'Attitudes and expectations of shareholders: the case of the multi-generation family business', *Journal of Management & Organization*, 15(3): 346–362.

Tsao, C.-W., Chen, S-J., Lin, C-S., and Hyde, W. (2009) 'Founding-family ownership and firm performance: The role of high-performance work systems', *Family Business Review*, 22(4): 319–332.

Van den Berghe, L.A.A. and Carchon, S. (2002) 'Corporate governance practices in Flemish family businesses', *Corporate Governance: An International Review*, 10(3): 225–245.

Van den Berghe, L.A.A. and Carchon, S. (2003) 'Agency relations within the family business system: An exploratory approach', *Corporate Governance: An International Review*, 11(3): 171–179.

Van den Heuvel, J., Van Gils, A., and Voordeckers, W. (2006) 'Board roles in small and medium-sized family businesses: Performance and importance', *Corporate Governance: An International Review*, 14(5): 467–485.

Vilaseca, A. (2002) 'The shareholder role in the family business: Conflict of interests and objectives between nonemployee shareholders and top management team', *Family Business Review*, 15(4): 299–301.

Villalonga, B. and Amit, R. (2006) 'How do family ownership, control and management affect firm value?' *Journal of Financial Economics*, 80(2): 385–417.

Villanueva, J. and Sapienza, H.J. (2009) 'Goal tolerance, outside investors, and family firm governance', *Entrepreneurship: Theory and Practice*, 33(6): 1193–1199.

Voordeckers, W., Van Gils, A., and Van den Heuvel, J. (2007) 'Board composition in small and medium-sized family firms', *Journal of Small Business Management*, 45(1): 137–156.

Walsh, J.P. and Seward, J.K. (1990) 'On the efficiency of internal and external corporate control mechanisms', *Academy of Management Review*, 15(3): 421–458.

Ward, J.L. and Handy, J.L. (1988) 'A survey of board practices', *Family Business Review*, 1(3): 289–308.

Westhead, P. (2003) 'Succession decision-making outcomes reported by private family companies', *International Small Business Journal*, 21(4): 369–401.

Westhead, P. and Howorth, C. (2006) 'Ownership and management issues associated with family firm performance and company objectives', *Family Business Review*, 19(4): 301–316.

Westhead, P., Howorth, C., and Cowling, M. (2002) 'Ownership and management issues in first generation and multi-generation family-firms', *Entrepreneurship and Regional Development*, 14(3): 247–269.

Woods, J.A., Dalziel, T., and Barton, S.L. (2012) 'Escalation of commitment in private family businesses: The influence of outside board members', *Journal of Family Business Strategy*, 3(1): 18–27.

Wright, M., Filatotchev, I., Hoskisson, R.E., and Peng, M.W. (2005) 'Strategy research in emerging economies: Challenging the conventional wisdom', *Journal of Management Studies*, 42(1): 1–33.

Yang, M.-L. (2010) 'The impact of controlling families and family CEOs on earning management', *Family Business Review*, 23(3): 266–279.

Zahra, S.A. (2003) 'International expansion of US manufacturing family businesses: the effect of ownership and involvement', *Journal of Business Venturing*, 18(4): 495–512.

Zellweger, T. and Nason, R.S. (2008) 'A stakeholder perspective on family firm performance', *Family Business Review*, 21(3): 203–216.

13

Management Succession in Family Business

Rebecca G. Long and James J. Chrisman

LR

Qual.

INTRODUCTION

Management succession is an important issue for all types of business, but those owned and operated by families face an additional set of challenges unique to their organizational form. Beyond the usual problems associated with ensuring competent leadership for the future (e.g., Finkelstein and Hambrick, 1996; Kesner and Sebora, 1994; Zajac, 1990), family firm transitions must be accomplished within the confines of restricted candidate pools, as well as the personal and often delicate relationship ties among incumbents, successors, and the family itself (De Massis et al., 2008; Le Breton-Miller et al., 2004). Given these challenges, it is not surprising that a large number of family businesses fail after a shift in intergenerational leadership, nor is it surprising that family business leaders consider succession to be of vital importance to the firm's future performance (Chua et al., 2003; DeMassis et al., 2008). The family business literature on the topic is plentiful but somewhat lacking in theoretical coherence. Recent efforts (e.g., Cabrera-Suárez, De Saá-Pérez, and Garcia-Almeida, 2001; De Massis et al., 2008; Le Breton-Miller et al., 2004), however, address a pattern of constructs and relationships that mirror more established work in the general CEO succession literature (Kesner and Sebora, 1994). These models, in part, answer Sharma, Chrisman and Chua's (1997) call for a strategic management approach to family business research and point toward the need for a more comprehensive and coherent theoretical framework.

Specifically, family business succession research to date falls short in at least two areas. First, although extant work explicitly acknowledges the multi-level nature of family business succession, few if any studies attempt to theorize or test multi-level relationships. Second, despite recognition of multi-level interactions and the process-oriented nature of family business succession, research has tended to ignore the benefits to be found in developing theory aimed at explaining not just the 'what' of family business succession but the 'how' as well as the 'why'. Thus, as noted by Handler (1992) over two decades ago, a good deal of the value in extant research is limited to its description of inputs into family business succession and not in its ability to explain, predict, or direct the process.

The purpose of this chapter then is not to provide a comprehensive catalog of the empirical and anecdotal works that make up the family business succession literature, but to discuss the current state of knowledge and offer a better perspective on the work to be done. To that end, our review of the literature employs a multi-level model of the succession process that includes constructs at the micro (individual attributes), meso (interpersonal/group relations), and macro (firm processes and strategies) levels of analysis. We follow our overview with thoughts on directions for future research and the further development of a theory of succession, organizing our discussion of gaps in the literature as well as avenues of possible resolution around a set of interrelated and cross-level theories we believe are particularly well suited to the unique demands and inner workings of family firms during the succession process.

LITERATURE REVIEW: SUCCESSION AS TRANSFER AND TRANSITION

Before proceeding to our review of the literature, it is important for purposes of clarity that we specify our methodology and the theoretical assumptions we have made in framing this review. First, with regard to our method, we focused almost exclusively on academic literature with theoretical and empirical content. This material came from previous reviews of the family business succession literature (Brockhaus, 2004; De Massis et al., 2008; Handler, 1994; Le Breton-Miller et al., 2004) and a thorough examination of the content of 20 management journals. We only deviated from this approach to the extent that we found a handful of relevant works in economics/

Table 13.1   Journals included in review with respective article counts

Family Business Review	60
Entrepreneurship Theory & Practice	10
Journal of Business Venturing	7
International Small Business Journal	7
Journal of Small Business Management	5
International Entrepreneurship Management Journal	2
Academy of Management Journal	1
Academy of Management Review	1
Administrative Science Quarterly	1
American Journal of Small Business	1
Entrepreneurship & Regional Development	1
Harvard Business Review	1
Journal of Business Research	1
Management Decision	1
Organization Science	1
Small Business Economics	1
The Journal of Finance	1
The Leadership Quarterly	1
The Quarterly Journal of Economics	1

finance journals or were able to uncover less rigorous papers that supported the larger academic literature. The journals searched as well as the articles underlying our review and how they fit into our classifying scheme can be found in Tables 13.1 and 13.2, respectively.

Second, we should clarify our analytical assumptions. In this chapter, we view the idea of levels of analysis as a powerful tool for understanding the web of social relations in which family business succession is embedded (Granovetter, 1973). It helps us to frame and unify our understanding of what motivates individual as well as group actions, the impacts of those actions on others in the firm, and the 'umbrella' structures those actions create over time (Berger and Luckmann, 1967). At the micro-level of analysis, we assume that the perceptions and behaviors of incumbents and successors are to a significant extent the product of their social interactions and their particular positions in the family and business context. Conversely, we also expect that incumbents and successors in turn impact other individuals and social structures through their interactions. At the meso-level

Table 13.2   Review articles by level of analysis

Level of analysis	Author(s)
Individual attributes	
Incumbent attributes	Barach and Gantisky, 1995; Cadieux, 2007; Dyer, 1986; Haberman and Danes, 2007; Handler, 1990, 1991; Harveston et al., 1997; Hubler, 1999; Kaye, 1996; Kelly et al., 2000; Lansberg, 1988; Marshall et al., 2006; McGivern, 1978; Pontet et al., 2007; Pyromalis and Vozikis, 2009; Rubenson and Gupta, 1996; Sharma et al., 2001; Venter et al., 2005; Zellweger et al., 2010
Successor attributes	Barach et al., 1988; Cabrera-Suárez et al., 2001; Cabrera-Suárez, 2005; Cater and Justis, 2009; Chrisman et al., 1998; Dumas, 1998; Dumas et al., 1995; Dyer, 1986; Fiegener et al., 1994, 1996; File and Prince, 1996; Garcia-Alvarez et al., 2002; Goldberg, 1996; Goldberg and Wooldridge, 1993; Haberman and Danes, 2007; Handler, 1991; Hubler, 1999; Keating and Little, 1997; Lambrecht, 2005; Morris et al., 1997; Pontet et al., 2007; Pyromalis and Vozikis, 2009; Royer et al., 2008; Sardeshmukh and Corbett, 2011; Sharma et al., 2001; Sharma and Irving, 2005; Sharma and Rao, 2000; Shepard and Zacharakis, 2000; Stavrou, 1999
Interpersonal/group relations	
Incumbent–successor relations	Cabrera-Suárez, 2005; Cabrera-Suárez et al., 2001; Dyck et al., 2002; Dyer, 1986; Goldberg, 1996; Haberman and Danes, 2007; Handler, 1990, 1992; Lansberg, 1988; Matthews, Moore and Fialko, 1999; Seymour, 1993
Family relations	Churchill and Hatten, 1987; Davis and Harveston, 1998; Dunn, 1999; Dyer, 1986; Handler, 1990, 1991; Hubler, 1999; Matthews, Moore and Fialko, 1999; Miller, 1998; Morris, Williams, Allen and Avila, 1997; Pyromalis and Vozikis, 2009; Swagger, 1991
Non-family stakeholders	Barnett, Long and Marler, 2011; Bruce and Picard, 2006; Dyck et al., 2002; Pyromalis and Vozikis, 2009
Firm processes and strategies	
Rational processes	Barnett et al., 2011; Churchill and Hatten, 1987; Dyer, 1986; Dyck et al., 2002; Handler, 1990; Harveston et al., 1997; Kirby and Lee, 1996; Lansberg, 1988; Lansberg and Astrachan, 1994; Malone, 1989; Marshall et al., 2006; Morris et al., 1997; Motwani et al., 2006; Murray, 2003; Pardo-del-Val, 2009; Pyromalis and Vozikis, 2009; Seymour, 1993; Sharma et al., 2003a; Sonfield and Lussier, 2004; Westhead, 2003
Ownership transfers	Bennedsen et al., 2010; Bjuggren and Sund, 2002, 2005; Burkart et al., 2003; Gersick, et al., 1999; Gersick et al., 1997; Gómez-Mejía et al., 2007; Perricone et al., 2001; Thomas, 2002; Ward and Dolan, 1998; Westhead, Howorth, and Cowling, 2002
External considerations	(Boards of Directors) Barach and Gantisky, 1995; Dyer, 1986; Handler, 1994; Lansberg, 1988; Malone, 1989; Sharma et al., 2001; Westhead, 2003
	(Culture/Ethnicity) Bachkaniwala et al., 2001; Bocatto et al., 2010; Brenes et al., 2006; Cabrera-Suárez, 2005; Chau, 1991; Chittoor and Das, 2007; Corbetta, and Montemerlo, 1999; Fahed-Sreih and Djoundourian, 2006; Howorth and Assaraf Ali, 2001; Janjuha-Jivraj and Woods, 2002; Kuratko et al., 1993; Lee and Tan, 2001; Nam and Herbert, 1999; Perricone et al., 2001; Santiago, 2000; Sharma and Rao, 2000; Tan and Fock, 2001; Tatoglu et al., 2008; Yan and Sorenson, 2006

we presume that social relations effect and are affected by the attitudes of the involved individuals. Finally, we assume that macro-level social processes and structures are manifested and maintained through the inter-action of individuals who also have the power to change those structures by changing their actions. Thus, our multi-level analysis of family business succession requires the use of theory or theories capable of explaining actions and outcomes at all three levels of analysis simultaneously.

Another set of assumptions relates to the process of family business succession.

Studies of family business succession view such transitions as a long-term process rather than a single event. An early model of this process (i.e., Longenecker and Schoen, 1978) proposed, for example, that succession parallels the life stages of the successor in a father-to-son succession. In this process, the successor is seen as moving through seven stages, from a dim awareness of the business in childhood (pre-business stage) through full-time employment in the firm (functional stage) to independent leadership of the family business (mature succession stage). Similarly, Churchill and Hatten's (1987) model of family business succession proposes a family firm life cycle model 'anchored' by succession and driven by a 'biological imperative'. In this classic model, Churchill and Hatten describe the father-to-son succession process in terms of four distinct stages: (a) owner management, (b) training/development, (c) cross-generational partnership, and (d) transfer of power. Handler (1990, 1994) elaborates these models by calling attention to the social identities and role transitions underlying each of these stages. She analyzes the succession process as a 'mutual role adjustment' in which the incumbent and successor proceed through a series of role changes 'central' to 'the transferral of leadership, experience, authority, decision-making power, and equity' (Handler, 1994: 136). Along with the recognition of family business succession's multi-level nature, we take these process models of knowledge transfer and role transition as the grounding assumptions underlying this review of the literature.

We begin our review with a look at the micro-level individual attributes that family business researchers have found to most strongly impact the succession process. Following our examination of both incumbent and successor characteristics, we consider meso-level research where interpersonal and group relations have been found to significantly influence both the choice of successor and the success of the process itself. We

complete our review by looking at the effect of a family firm's macro-level structures on the succession process.

INDIVIDUAL ATTRIBUTES

A large portion of the research on succession focuses on constructs at the micro-level of analysis. In general, it can be divided into studies addressing incumbent attributes or successor attributes, which we examine in turn.

Incumbent Attributes

An incumbent's reluctance or even inability to transfer control of the family firm to a successor is the most frequently referenced obstacle to succession (Sharma et al., 2001). Several studies have indicated the importance of an incumbent's ability to overcome personal fears of losing control or power as well as anxieties that may surround loss of social position, status, and identity (Dyer, 1986; Handler, 1990, 1994; Lansberg, 1988; Le Breton-Miller et al., 2004; McGivern, 1978). Some authors (e.g., Handler, 1994) have interpreted an incumbent's resistance to this sort of change as a denial of their mortality or an abiding belief in their own indispensability. Indeed, in a worst-case scenario, Kaye (1996) argues that the attachment of some incumbents (and families) to the firm is very much like that of an addiction, with all of the attendant negative consequences.

Thus, for potential successors to have an opportunity to develop properly and for the process to have a chance to work, it is argued that incumbents need to possess the ability to delegate authority to the successor when appropriate (Barach and Gantisky, 1995; Dyer, 1986; Handler, 1990; Le Breton-Miller et al., 2004). More specifically, evidence in the literature indicates that the current leader should be open and cooperative (Barach and Gantisky, 1995) as well as trusting and willing to share with the successor (Handler, 1990). Alternatively, Barach and Gantisky (1995) point out that micro-management, mistrust of subordinates, and dysfunctional aggression on the part of incumbent leaders, have a negative impact on the succession process.

In terms of Handler's 'mutual role adjustment' (1990) approach, we interpret the micro-level findings on incumbent attributes as examples of resistance to or acceptance of necessary role changes. That is, in cases where leaders are fearful of losing the power and social position role benefits they as owner-managers have come to enjoy, research (see, e.g., Leary and Tangney, 2002) shows that anxiety about such social identity threats is often expressed as aggression, threat rigidity, and mistrust of others. Conversely, in situations where incumbents recognize the need for succession or even initiate the process themselves (e.g., Cadieux, 2007), knowledge transfers and exchange of roles are enhanced by willingness to mentor, openness to new experiences, and enthusiasm for the transition. Indeed, in her study of five family firms involved in successful transitions, Cadieux (2007) found that incumbents were not only willing to invest time and effort in transferring leadership of the firm, but were willing to take on new roles such as serving as post succession advisors to the firms' new CEOs. Whether an incumbent chooses to continue as post-succession advisor or moves on to other pursuits, it seems that the important thing is that transition to new roles is a conscious and clearly defined choice (Dyer, 1986; Handler, 1990; Lansberg, 1988; Sharma et al., 2001).

Successor Attributes

Role changes are also in store for the family business successor and the literature shows that, along with commitment to the business, the willingness on the part of the successor is a precursor to succession (Barach and Gantisky, 1995; Chrisman et al., 1998; Sharma et al., 2001; Sharma and Rao, 2000). Chrisman et al.'s (1998) study of respondents at 485 family firms found that the most desirable successor characteristics, beyond even competency, are integrity and commitment to the

firm. Those positive traits are more likely to occur when the successor's own career and identity needs can be fulfilled within the family business (Handler, 1992, 1994). Such a fit between the needs of the individual and the features of the firm lead to a successor who is committed, enthusiastic, and ultimately satisfied (Barach and Gantisky, 1995; Handler, 1990; Le Breton-Miller et al., 2004).

In addition to personal motives and needs, the literature suggests successors also need to possess the sorts of human capital skills and experience perceived as necessary for leading the firm (Barach et al., 1988; Chrisman et al., 1998; De Massis et al., 2008). For example, in 485 firm manager rankings of important successor attributes, Chrisman et al., (1998) found interpersonal skills, decision-making skills, and experience to be among the most highly ranked. These sorts of skills can be established through career development inside the firm, outside work experience, and formal education. Time inside the family business allows a successor to develop skills specific to the firm, especially those that may be strategically important (e.g., Barach and Gantisky, 1995; Barach et al., 1988; Cabrera-Suárez et al., 2001; Goldberg, 1996). Moreover, it also allows the successor to become familiar with the firm's culture and employees, building relationships and credibility as he or she learns the ins and outs of the organization (Barach and Gantisky, 1995; Barach et al., 1988; Cabrera-Suárez, 2005; Dyer, 1986). Career development inside the firm also allows for the continuing development of the social capital that is so important in the transgenerational sustainability of family firms (Cabrera-Suárez, 2005; Pearson et al., 2008). Researchers also argue for the importance of gaining experience and credibility through work outside the firm as such experience provides the successor with opportunities to develop self-confidence and an independent social identity (e.g., Barach et al., 1988; Dyer, 1986). Finally, others (e.g., Dyer, 1986; Goldberg, 1996; Morris et al., 1997) argue for a relationship between the level of a successor's educational attainment and post-succession performance (cf. Cabrera-Suárez, 2005).

Thus, a successor's human capital and social capital, as well as a willingness and commitment to playing the role of family firm leader are vital to the succession process.

What We Don't Know

While succession research at the micro-level of analysis has afforded a great deal of insight into the individual motivations and skills that incumbents and successors require to successfully navigate the succession process, it has done little to explicate the social dynamics surrounding these attributes. For example, while the literature has recognized the consequences of role transitions for incumbents (Handler, 1990), we do not understand what factors may help incumbents in making those necessary transitions. Research could also be done to better understand how incumbents adjust their social identities and learn new roles. And, foreshadowing the next level of analysis, researchers should work to understand what can be done within the family to help or hinder the incumbent's transition process.

In a similar vein, relatively little attention has been given to how successors are prepared to assume command of the firm. For example, since integrity and commitment are seen as critical attributes (Chrisman et al., 1998), research examining the ways in which a successor demonstrates integrity and under what conditions others' perceptions of the successor's integrity may be altered would be useful. Equally useful are studies that help reveal what actions families should take or avoid to build successor commitment. Further, investigations into the possible bases for commitment and attitudinal changes over time are needed (Sharma and Irving, 2005).

As noted earlier, beyond the personal motives and attitudes of a potential successor, skills and experience also matter (Barach et al., 1988; Chrisman et al., 1998; De Massis et al., 2008) in explaining successful family business transitions. Investigations into what incentives are needed to encourage the development of appropriate skills would be beneficial as well as research into effective methods for monitoring the progress of potential successors. For example, studies examining the oversight and development of a successor's relational skills, credibility, and social capital would be invaluable to a better understanding of family business succession.

INTERPERSONAL/GROUP RELATIONS

Another common set of predictors are group or meso-level variables, particularly those associated with interpersonal relations among the participants. Researchers in family business succession, for example, recognize the pivotal value of trust and cohesion in developing a shared vision (Sharma et al., 2001). It has been argued as well (e.g., Bruce and Picard, 2006; Cabrera-Suárez et al., 2001; De Massis et al., 2008; Lansberg, 1988) that incumbent–successor commitment to the transfer of the knowledge and resources necessary for implementation of a shared vision are also vital. Beyond family relationships, the literature also indicates the important role other stakeholders such as non-family managers and key customers or suppliers can play in the succession process (e.g., Bruce and Picard, 2006; Cabrera-Suárez et al., 2001; De Massis et al., 2008; Lansberg, 1988).

Incumbent–Successor Relations

At the interface between individuals and the groups involved in the succession process is the interpersonal relationship between incumbent and successor and their satisfaction with that association. The quality of this interpersonal relationship has been consistently found to affect the succession process (Cabrera-Suárez, 2005; Cabrera-Suárez et al., 2001; Dyer, 1986: Goldberg, 1996; Handler, 1990, 1992; Lansberg, 1988). A relationship built on trust and respect is particularly necessary in transferring knowledge and social capital from one generation of family firm leaders to the next (Cabrera-Suárez, 2005; Cabrera-Suárez et al., 2001) and other researchers (e.g., Handler, 1990; Dyck et al., 2002) have suggested that a mentoring relationship of some duration is valuable in completing the succession process. In a study of seven family business successions, Cabrera-Suárez argues that the relationship between father and son is particularly complicated because of the multiple professional as well as personal feelings and experiences involved in their dealings with one another. Thus, the author asserts that this social capital transfer is more than just mentoring 'because the father influences his son's development and expectations during all their shared lifetime experience' (2005: 90).

Family Relations

The deep family relations Cabrera-Suárez (2005) notes in father–son successions exist to some degree among other members of a business family as well. Such intimate, long-term bonds help to establish the shared vision others (e.g., Barach and Gantisky, 1995; Chrisman et al., 1998; Dyer, 1986; Dyck et al., 2002; Sharma et al., 2001) have confirmed is so fundamental to succession. A shared vision of the ultimate purpose of the business and its future is built upon and supportive of family trust and harmony (Sharma et al., 2001), factors also determined to contribute to the success of the process (Churchill and Hatten, 1987; Dyer, 1986; Handler, 1990). In fact, Morris et al. (1997), using a sample of 209 family firms, found that family harmony is more critical than the development of the successor or the succession plan itself.

Non-family Stakeholders

Another set of relationships with potential to support or hinder family firm succession are those with non-family managers and key customers or suppliers (De Massis et al., 2008). In general, Bruce and Picard (2006) argue that conflicts with non-family managers can hamper the succession process. More specifically, in a model of the factors that prevent intra-family succession, De Massis et al. (2008) propose both lack of trust in and commitment to the potential successor on the part of non-family managers as a significant influence. Similarly, Cabrera-Suárez's (2005) study of seven family firm successions found that a completed transfer of leadership was characterized by loyal and collaborative non-family managers, implying that their supportive roles were in part the result of their empowerment and inclusion in decision-making. In contrast, she found that where succession process was only partly completed, non-family managers were limited in their development and acted as obstacles to successors.

While not directly a part of the family business and its day-to-day operations, we include here Lansberg's (1988) note that long-term customers and suppliers sometimes develop personal relationships with an incumbent and may resist extending that relationship to the successor (De Massis et al., 2008; Steier, 2001). In instances where such relationships are essential to firm survival, De Massis et al. (2008) remind us that they have the power to halt the succession process altogether. Conversely, in a study of 18 family owned businesses, Steier (2001) finds that it is also the case that some established relationships and the social capital they represent for the incumbent may be viewed by the successor as expendable.

What We Don't Know

Meso-level analyses reiterate the decisive impact of interpersonal and group relations in constructing family business succession. In particular, it has been argued that trust, cohesion, and a shared vision are imperative for the effective building and transfer of resources and relationships from incumbent to successor (e.g., Bruce and Picard, 2006; Cabrera-Suárez et al., 2001; De Massis et al., 2008; Lansberg, 1988). We do not have, however, any significant understanding of how these social assets are created nor of the process by

[Handwritten note: Answering the call to investigate the influence of family and non-family relationships in SP.]

which they are shifted from one generation to the next. Moreover, although some scholars (e.g., Cabrera-Suárez et al., 2001; Steier, 2001) have begun to look more closely at social capital transfers during family business succession and to differentiate those resources according to whether they lie inside or outside the firm, a better appreciation of the specifics of social capital creation and influence would be advantageous. For example, studies might inquire into the differences among social capital types (i.e., bonding versus bridging) and the differences in their impact on succession. More work also appears to be needed in understanding how trust and cohesion is transferred from the family to the firm.

Furthermore, little work is available that helps us understand how other family members and non-family employees contribute to the succession process. For example, while some scholars testify to the significance of family harmony in the succession process (Churchill and Hatten, 1987; Dyer, 1986; Handler, 1990; Morris et al., 1997; Sharma et al., 2001), others emphasize the consequences of conflict with non-family managers and some outside stakeholders (Bruce and Picard, 2006; Cabrera-Suárez, 2005; De Massis et al., 2008; Steier, 2001). Additional exploration of the sources of harmony and conflict and establishing how such relational properties can be encouraged or mitigated is also needed.

FIRM PROCESSES AND STRATEGIES

Finally, there are analyses of family business successions that can be classified loosely as macro-level. Among these accounts is succession planning (Dyck et al., 2002; Dyer, 1986; Handler, 1990; Lansberg, 1988, 1999; Malone, 1989; Sharma et al., 2001), process factors (De Massis et al., 2008), the impact of ownership changes, and the presence of such outside influences as boards of directors (Le Breton-Miller et al., 2004; Steier, 2001). Succession planning is most prevalent in articles

of this type and takes as its founding principle that succession is a process rather than a single event. As such, succession is a long-term undertaking that works best when it includes systematic training, mentoring, clearly stated criteria, and defined transitional roles for the participants. Below, we discuss the impact a planned succession process can have on stakeholder satisfaction as well as firm performance and follow with a review of the influence of external considerations in the firm's transgenerational survival.

Rational Processes

There is general agreement in the literature that planning succession as a long-term and systematic process is crucial to an effective transfer of the firm from one generation to the next (e.g., Dyck et al., 2002; Dyer, 1986; Handler, 1990; Lansberg, 1988; Le Breton-Miller, 2004; Sharma et al., 2001). In their analysis of obstacles to intra-family succession, De Massis et al. (2008) convey the details of what outcomes can be expected when family enterprises fail to rationalize eight different aspects of the process. Five of these factors deal with those parts of the process that involve the incumbent and successor. Specifically, it is essential that roles of both participants be clearly defined (Handler, 1990; Lansberg, 1988). Also of consequence is timely or adequate exposure of the successor to the firm in order to learn the business and develop relationships with stakeholders (Lansberg and Astrachan, 1994). While these factors relate to the more subjective aspects of early succession, the next three factors, (a) accurate evaluation of successor training needs, (b) development of formal training programs, and (c) sufficient timely feedback to the successor, all involve the more objective aspects of firm knowledge transfer (i.e., successor training). In this view, De Massis et al. (2008; see also Le Breton-Miller et al., 2004) argue that neglecting to establish objective criteria for selection of a successor along with failure to communicate to other stakeholders the who, what, and why of the process can lead to succession failure. Barnett et al. (2012) have proposed that such instances may create a procedural justice climate in which non-family managers see the process as being unfairly weighted in favor of family members and thus as a group may act to obstruct the succession process.

Ownership Transfers

Family ownership is a distinguishing characteristic of family firms (Chua et al., 1999) that has received considerable attention in the literature for two reasons. First, family ownership tends to lead to idiosyncratic decision making (Carney, 2005) based on a desire to preserve socioemotional wealth (Gómez-Mejía et al., 2007). Second, at least in the case of larger family firms, the decision rights of family owners may exceed their cash flow rights and encourage wealth expropriation (Bennedsen et al., 2010). However, despite the importance of ownership configurations in family firms, relatively little attention has been given to intra-family ownership transitions in general or how they influence intra-family management succession in particular.

The few studies that have been conducted provide some preliminary insights into the patterns, processes, and problems of ownership transitions. For example, Gersick et al. (1999) and the more extensive work of Gersick et al. (1997) have dealt with all three sets of issues as well as provided the dominant classification of ownership configurations in the literature: controlling owner, sibling partnership, and cousin consortium. Those authors argue that there are three primary patterns of ownership transitions: (1) recycles, which involve changes in the owners but no change in the ownership configuration; (2) devolutionary transitions, which involve a change from a more to less complex ownership configuration; and (3) evolutionary transitions, which involve a movement toward a more complex configuration. They also argue that ownership transitions generally include six stages – developmental pressures, trigger events, disengaging, exploring alternatives, choosing, and commitment – that can vary in sequence and in time span. Finally, Gersick et al. (1997, 1999) note the conflicts that occur among family members with different dreams, talents, and needs as well as the various financial, legal, and environmental issues that can make decision making more complex.

Among the few studies that complement Gersick et al.'s (1997, 1999) work, Ward and Dolan (1998) and Westhead et al. (2002) both suggest that in general, recycles and evolutionary transitions are more prevalent than devolutionary transitions, which seems to mean that the number of owners frequently increase but rarely decrease. Perricone et al. (2001) find age and gender remain important in the determination of who obtains ownership control in ethnic family firms, which suggests that in many instances outcomes are preordained. Furthermore, Thomas's (2002) study of ownership transitions in Australian family firms highlights the problems of inheritance, liquidity, financial factors, investment preferences, and emotions that must be dealt with. Her findings seem to support Bjuggren and Sund (2002) who, using a transaction cost perspective of ownership transitions, argue that the problems that family firms encounter fall into four primary categories: valuing the firm, financing the transfer, legal issues, and the potential for emotional conflicts.

External Considerations

Research addressing succession at the boundary of the family business and its external environment is limited, with a few studies considering the influence of boards of directors, relations with external groups, and culture/ethnicity.

Le Breton-Miller et al. (2004) and De Massis et al. (2008) both mention the need to rationalize the succession process and further support the idea of an active board of directors in succession. Given that the incumbent and others are willing to accept their contributions, establishment of a board of directors that includes a number of outside expert members can also be useful in initiating and carrying out a succession plan (Barach and Gantisky, 1995; Dyer, 1986; Handler, 1994; Lansberg, 1988; Malone, 1989; Sharma et al., 2001). Moreover, in his sample of wholesale lumber firms, Malone (1989) found a positive relationship between an outside board of directors and business continuity planning; continuity or firm sustainability planning was also significantly related to a firm's strategic planning.

Since Handler's (1994) call for additional research into ethnicity and family business succession, studies examining successions in countries from China (Yan and Sorenson, 2006), to Turkey (Tatoglu et al., 2008), to Spain (Bocatto et al., 2010), and back around the world to the Philippines and Singapore (Santiago, 2000; Tan and Fock, 2001) have flourished. Most of the differences found (if any) seem to be of degree rather than kind (e.g., Bocatto et al., 2010; Cabrera-Suárez, 2005; Fahed-Sreih and Djoundourian, 2006). For example, consistent with an earlier Canadian study (i.e., Chrisman et al., 1998), Sharma and Rao's (2000) study of desirable successor attributes among 98 Indian family business owners found that they rated integrity and commitment as the most important successor attributes. On the other hand, presumably reflecting differences in culture and values, Indians ranked blood and family relations higher than their Canadian counterparts. In other instances, similarities in the presence of planning and boards of directors have been found in different cultural contexts (Bocatto et al., 2010; Fahed-Sreih and Djoundourian, 2006).

What We Don't Know

Clearly, as others have noted (e.g., Le Breton-Miller et al., 2004; De Massis et al., 2008), there is a substantial amount of work left to be done at the macro or firm-level of analysis in family business succession.

Beginning with succession planning, although investigators place its absence among the top reasons for failed successions, little is known about why or how planning increases success. Questions regarding how much of its impact is a function of the quality of the actual plan, the learning that occurs through the process of planning, or the commitment to succession signaled to stakeholders by the fact that planning is attempted have yet to be answered. Moreover, there have been no investigations into how the planning process may differ depending upon the specific circumstance of the individual firm. For example, it seems likely that planning for succession from founder to second-generation successor would be substantially different from that involving succession in later family business iterations. Another area of interest would be the relationship between various aspects of succession planning and the loyalty/support of non-family managers. For instance, we might evaluate which aspects of the process are likely to promote or impede empowerment (Cabrera-Suárez, 2005) of non-family managers and thus influence their commitment to a successor (Barnett et al., 2012; De Massis et al., 2008).

Furthermore, the relevance to family business succession of ownership transfer needs more analysis. Very little is known about intra-family ownership transfer and even less has been done on how ownership transfer and manager succession interact. In this respect, investigations of two interrelated issues seem to provide a potentially fruitful path to improve our knowledge. First, ownership transitions can occur before, during, or after the management succession process (Westhead et al., 2002). Understanding the interactive affects of the timing of ownership and management transitions would add to our knowledge. For example, ownership transitions that occur before management successions could hinder or help the process as well as influence the criteria by which the effectiveness of the succession is judged depending on who gains ownership control. Likewise, if management succession comes first the possibility for owner–manager agency problems may be exacerbated.

Second, ownership transitions are not necessarily congruent with management successions in terms of the parties to whom ownership and management control are ceded. For example, if management control and only partial ownership control is passed to one family member, owner–owner agency issues are likely between the successor and other owners, especially if the latter included family members who are not otherwise involved in the business (cf., Gersick et al., 1997). Unfortunately, we know relatively little about how the timing of ownership transitions and the changes in ownership configurations that occur after the transition influence the management succession process or a manager's ability to effectively run the organization after assuming leadership of the firm.

Moreover, while we may be relatively knowledgeable about some of the relationships inside the family firm and the impact those connections can have on succession, we know much less about the particulars of other relations such as boards of directors. Although it is likely that the relationship between succession planning and the presence of a board of directors with some independent members (Lansberg, 1988) is related to a lack of family ties, future work needs to explain how these relationships develop and under what conditions they actually support effective transitions. In this respect, Steier's (2001) investigation into the significance of a successor maintaining, eliminating, and replacing relationships with external stakeholders (e.g., a firm's service providers, suppliers, advisors) during and after succession may be a useful point of departure for gaining a better understanding of the affect of boards of directors and other external relations. No matter the group under study, we would do well to develop our knowledge of how a family firm's passage through these transgenerational shifts can alter its relationship to the external environment.

With regard to cross-cultural studies of family business succession, as noted above, there has been a good deal of research examining family businesses operating within the borders of particular nations or operated by owners of particular ethnicities. However, little seems to have been done in the way of empirically or theoretically (cf. Yan and Sorenson, 2006) addressing how and why succession processes in different socio-cultural milieu vary, if indeed they do vary. For example, Sharma and Rao's (2000) study found that, beyond agreements on the importance of integrity and commitment to the business, Indian and Canadian (see also Chrisman et al., 1998) respondents differed significantly in the weight they attached to other successor attributes. Specifically, Indians favored family relations while Canadians valued a successor's skills and work experiences more. Research looking into the cultural values that may underlie these preferences would be helpful, as would studies examining how particular cultural values may impact a family's understandings and expectations of the succession process as well as its content. For example, it is possible that the very notion of planning holds a different place in the consciousness of various cultures and thus may also differ in the weight it carries. Similarly, as suggested by Sharma and Rao (2000), it also would be interesting to investigate the presence of culturally driven definitions of terms like 'integrity' and 'commitment', recognizing that such value-laden concepts are likely embedded in individual as well as socio-cultural histories.

FUTURE RESEARCH: THEORIZING A MULTI-LEVEL SUCCESSION PROCESS

It is clear to us that the approaches, constructs, and relationships that populate the succession literature are disconnected from one another yet not inconsistent with Handler's (1990) proposed explanatory frame of knowledge transfers and role transitions. The problem we believe lies in our failure to develop a meaningful explanation of how the various pieces of our knowledge fit together to produce effective succession and support transgenerational sustainability. To the extent that the family business succession literature fails to articulate a succinct explanation of not only the constructs involved but the how and why of their connectedness, then it is atheoretical. This is not to suggest that there is no theory in the succession literature, only that bits of established theories are mostly used in an atomistic fashion, restricted to a somewhat idiographic understanding of a particular sample or only carried through as the basis for a handful of studies. For example, beyond the general systems approach used by authors such as Stafford et al. (1999; see also Lansberg's 'overlapping institutions', 1983) and Handler's (1990) transition/stages model, the most often used approaches are agency theory, transaction cost, and the resource-based view (e.g., Bjuggren and Sund, 2002; Bocatto et al., 2010; Cabrera-Suárez et al., 2001; Royer et al., 2008). Researchers with a more behavioral bent have looked to Ajzen's (1991) theory of planned behavior (e.g., Carr and Sequeira, 2006; Sharma et al., 2003a), stakeholder theory (e.g., Sharma et al., 2001; Sharma et al., 2003b), and organizational commitment (Sharma and Irving, 2005). Despite their usefulness, none of these established management theories appear capable of providing an overarching theoretical framework of the succession phenomenon in its totality.

To accomplish that task requires a theoretical perspective or set of related theories that can be employed at more than one level of analysis. Coleman (1986) argues that such an approach must be able to explain (a) individual behavior (e.g., incumbents and successors), (b) how the actions of multiple individuals combine to create structure (e.g., norms, family capital), and (c) how these structures impact the behavior of individuals involved (e.g., the perceptions of non-family managers). In the next section, we introduce a set of interrelated theories that meet Coleman's criteria. We believe they can be useful in integrating our knowledge about family business succession and point the way to fruitful avenues for future research.

We have addressed the topic of family business succession with two fundamental assumptions in mind. First, we presume that the succession process is multi-level in nature and characterized by significant cross-level effects among individuals (e.g., incumbents and successors), groups (e.g., family, non-family managers), and structures (e.g., succession planning, successor training). Second, we assume that the succession process is largely one of resource flows and role transitions by mutual adjustment. Role transition in Handler's (1990) sense is an extended 'dance' between the incumbent and successor during which a transfer of the incumbent's role behaviors and firm-related social capital takes place. Thus, to understand more fully family business succession and leadership/management transfers in general we must be at a minimum able to answer three questions. First, what are the antecedents of the social capital available to affect intergenerational transfer? Second, what is the nature of that social capital? Third, how is it passed from incumbent to successor? We propose that social exchange theory (e.g., Blau, 1964; Coleman, 1986; Ekeh, 1974; Emerson, 1976; Homans, 1958; Kelley and Thibaut, 1978) will prove useful in addressing these questions. It is a well-established perspective on the study of social processes and structures that is broad enough to encompass such sister approaches as social capital, agency theory, and network analysis as well as many of the theories already present in the family business and general management literature. Thus, we suggest that social exchange theory has the capacity to (a) explain theoretically many of the elements found in the family business succession literature, (b) provide a theoretical point of departure for filling gaps in current knowledge, and (c) supply the basis for a comprehensive and coherent theory of family business succession.

Exchange Theory and What We Can Learn

Exchange theory's disciplinary foundations lie in economics, sociology, psychology, and anthropology. It recognizes that exchange of social and material resources is fundamental to human interaction at all levels and proposes that social regularities and structures are a natural result of the repeated interactions necessary to the exchange of these resources. Of primary interest to exchange theory is the relationship between interconnected actors (e.g., incumbents and successors). The allied agency, social capital, and network approaches proceed from exchange theory's focus on relationships and examine the character of those relationships (e.g., agency), the resources created and exchanged through those relationships (e.g., social capital), and the structures constructed from those relationships (i.e., networks). Thus, exchange theory and its ancillaries, offer a strong basis for understanding the process of family business succession.

All exchanges operate according to a set of exchange rules, framing a 'normative definition of the situation that forms among or is adopted by the participants in an exchange relation' (Emerson, 1976: 351). Normative definitions of particular exchange relations, of course, depend on the nature of the relationship, its participants, and the resources exchanged. However, the universal element of social exchange is the concept of reciprocity (see Janjuha-Jivraj and Spence, 2009, for a recent application of this construct to family business succession). Reciprocity, the notion that some complementary return is expected from exchange, varies in kind depending on the type of relationship (e.g., family versus non-family) and serves to distinguish two broad types of exchange content – generalized and restricted (Ekeh, 1974). Following Long and Mathews' (2011) discussion of these exchange types in explaining the development of family ethics and cohesion, we briefly outline generalized and restricted exchange and sketch out some of their links to other theories.

Long and Mathews (2011) state that restricted exchange is based on a norm of direct reciprocity and contractual responsibility in which exchange participants are motivated first by self-interest such as might exist between a non-family manager and family firm employer. The relationship between actors in restricted exchanges is formed as a means to specific ends, and based on expectations of an immediate or short-term return. Thus, there is a strong instrumental element to the relationships in restricted exchange that reduces and sometimes eradicates cohesion among participants, as the relations are characterized by a high level of individualism, competition, and impersonality. This kind of relationship may help to explain some instances noted by De Massis et al. (2008; see also Cabrera-Suárez, 2005) in which non-family managers refuse to support a successor or even obstruct the succession process. This type of exchange is implicit in the agency (e.g., Jensen and Meckling, 1976) and transaction cost (e.g., Williamson, 1981, 1991) approaches. It also furnishes a point of intersection with succession studies and other work such as Gomez-Mejia et al.'s (2001) study of the impact of relational ties in agency contracts or Bjuggren and Sund's (2002) transaction cost-based explanation of transitions and transfers. Moreover, agency theory can be seen as an attempt to explain and perhaps prevent the costly breakdown of restricted exchange relationships based on contracts. Indeed, as Chrisman et al. note, 'problems between the parent-owner, the progeny successor, and other stakeholders may have nothing to do with altruism, but everything to do with traditional problems of moral hazard or adverse selection' (2004: 350).

In contrast, Long and Mathews (2011) present generalized exchange as relations based on a norm of indirect reciprocity, in which no direct or immediate return is automatically expected from a partner to a particular exchange similar to that found in familial altruism. The relationship in generalized exchange is often based on friendship, kinship, or affection, developed over time, and valued as an end in itself. Obligation is not simply to a single exchange partner, but to the group as a whole (e.g., the family or family business) where reciprocity may be extended to any member. In the succession literature, for example, we find that it is important for successors to develop long-term supportive relations with family and non-family stakeholders as well as with the incumbent (e.g., Cabrera-Suárez, 2005). Ekeh labels this 'the law of extended credit' when he declares, '[a] breach of exchange rules … is regarded not just as the sole business of the cheated individual but of the group' (1974: 55). He further argues that this 'extended credit' reciprocity relies on group trust, and makes relations more cohesive, cooperative, and homogeneous – all factors essential to the creation of bonding social capital (Adler and Kwon, 2002; Arregle et al., 2007; Nahapiet and Ghoshal, 1998; Pearson et al., 2008).

This type of exchange is reflected in the theory of organizational commitment Sharma and Irving (2005) use to investigate the bases of successor commitment to the family firm. Generalized exchange can also be seen in Hall and Nordqvist's (2008) symbolic interaction article on family business transitions to professional management. It is also this sort of long-term normative exchange that supplies a partial basis for the theory of planned behavior underlying Sharma et al.'s. (2003a) model of succession planning activities in family firms (see also Carr and Sequeira, 2007; Zellweger et al., 2011). Finally, here is a most likely theoretical connection for family studies perspectives on family business succession. For example, the fundamental interpersonal relations orientation (FIRO) model introduced into the family business literature by Danes and her colleagues (2002) affords direct insight into the content of a family's interpersonal exchanges as well as those between incumbent and successor when change is initiated.

Rather than focus on the characteristics of individual exchange relations, exchange network analysis (Emerson, 1976) steps away from the actors involved and examines the form relationships take. Its focus is on nodes and ties, no matter whether those nodes represent individuals (e.g., incumbents and successors), groups (e.g., non-family managers or boards of directors), or organizations (e.g., the family firm and its suppliers), nor whether ties fall within levels of analysis or operate across levels. The important point in the study of exchange networks is not why actors participate (e.g., self-interest or altruism) or what that participation may produce (e.g., social capital) but, given that the relations exist, what is likely to happen to the relationship in the future. Thus, exchange network analysis examines such features as the strength of ties, reciprocity of ties, network bridges, brokerage, and centrality as well as whether relations are closed or open (see, e.g., Burt, 1992; Granovetter, 1973; Kelly et al., 2000). For example, Kelly et al. (2000) propose using a founder's centrality within the family firm's top decision-making team to predict such outcomes as the firm's financial performance and strategic behavior relative to its industry. Such a perspective positions family business researchers for a more complete understanding of macro family business transformations as well as organizational change generally.

While the above exposition stops short of directly addressing each of the gaps in our knowledge of family business succession, it should serve to indicate the broad range of social exchange theory's potential applications in succession studies. Specifically, social exchange theory and its associated perspectives allow for the fruitful study of events and processes at all levels of succession analysis. Moreover, this set of theories allows for analysis of the cross-level linkages that operate throughout the succession process and the family firm as a whole. Such underpinnings can supply a solid basis for reconciling extant succession literature by placing it within a working theory of family business succession.

CONCLUSION

Although somewhat fractured, the literature on family business succession is not incommensurable. Indeed, its focus on motives, experience, trust, relationships, and social process suggest an underlying awareness among researchers of the iterative and dual nature of socioeconomic life (Berger and Luckmann, 1967; Giddens, 1984). What is missing is a unifying theoretical explanation for the empirical relationships we have thus far established. While the social capital perspective (e.g., Pearson et al., 2008) and resource/knowledge-based views (Cabrera-Suárez et al., 2001; Steier, 2001) of the family firm help to explain some of the content of family business operations, their application in the realm of family business succession has been limited as have applications of several other established theories (e.g., FIRO, theory of planned behavior, organizational commitment, stakeholder theory, symbolic interaction). Moreover, without a broader multi-level context, these theories can do little to help us understand the origins of these social facts, the development of the succession process, or the impact of that process on the future of the firm. Such a step is necessary if we are to help family owners assess and successfully manage this crucial transition. In this chapter, we have suggested that social exchange theory (Coleman, 1986; Homans, 1958; Levi-Strauss, 1971; Mauss, 2000; Simmel, 1973) provides a basis for addressing these questions in a holistic way that can incorporate, integrate, and extend knowledge about family business succession (e.g., incumbent/successor relations, family social capital) and firm transformations more generally. This perspective can provide a framework for simultaneously modeling micro-, meso-, and macro-level constructs and cross-level interactions necessary for a more complete understanding of family business succession.

Thus, social exchange deals with the foundations and nature of the relationships between individuals and groups of individuals and how those relationships may be altered by the context and the changes in the context that govern the exchanges that occur. In this sense, it addresses the antecedents and nature of the social capital that is available to affect intergenerational transfer and helps us to understand how transfers from incumbent to successor might occur as well as to predict the effectiveness of such attempts. Furthermore, because human capital is to a large extent based on the nature and types of social exchanges that occur among individuals over time it can help us comprehend what incumbents and other stakeholders have available and are willing to give as well as the absorptive capacity and receptivity of potential successors. As a consequence, we encourage researchers to more fully embrace social exchange theory as an umbrella concept to guide future studies on management succession in family firms.

REFERENCES

Adler, P.S. and Kwon, S.W. (2002). 'Social capital: Prospects for a new concept', *Academy of Management Review*, 27(1): 17–40.

Ajzen, I. (1991). 'The theory of planned behavior', *Organizational Behavior and Human Decision Processes*, 50(2): 179–211.

Arregle, J., Hitt, M., Sirmon, D., and Very, P. (2007). 'The development of organizational social capital: Attributes of family firms', *Journal of Management Studies*, 44(1): 73–95.

Bachkaniwala, D., Wright, M., and Ram, M. (2001). 'Succession in South Asian family businesses in the U.K.,' *International Small Business Journal*, 19(4) 15–27.

Barach, J.A. and Gantisky, J.B. (1995). 'Successful succession in family business', *Family Business Review*, 8(2): 131–155.

Barach, J.A., Gantisky, J., Carson, J.A., and Doochin, B.A. (1988). 'Entry of the next generation: Strategic challenge for family business', *Journal of Small Business Management*, 26(2): 49–56.

Barnett, T.R., Long, R.G., and Marler, L.E. (2012). 'Vision and exchange in intra-family succession: Effects on procedural justice climate among non-family managers', *Entrepreneurship Theory & Practice*, 36(6): 1207–1225.

Bennedsen, M., Nielsen, K.M., Perez-Gonzalez, F., and Wolfenzon, D. (2007). 'Inside the family firm: The role of families in succession decisions and performance', *The Quarterly Journal of Economics*: 647–691.

Bennedsen, M., Pérez-González, F., and Wolfenzon, D. (2010). 'The governance of family firms', in K.H. Baker and R. Anderson (eds), *Corporate Governance: A Synthesis of Theory, Research, and Practice*. Hoboken: Wiley, pp. 371–390.

Berger, P. and Luckmann, T. (1967). *The Social Construction of Reality: A Treatise on The Sociology of Knowledge*. New York: Doubleday.

Bjuggren, P. and Sund, L. (2002). 'A transaction cost rationale for transition of the firm within the family', *Small Business Economics*, 19: 123–133.

Bjuggren, P. and Sund, L. (2005). 'Organization of transfers of small and medium-sized enterprises with the family: Tax law considerations', *Family Business Review*, 18(4): 305–319.

Blau, P. (1964). *Exchange and Power in Social Life*. New York: Wiley.

Bocatto, E., Gispert, C., and Rialp, J. (2010). 'Family-owned business succession: The influence of pre-performance in the nomination of family and nonfamily members: Evidence from Spanish firms', *Journal of Small Business Management*, 48(4): 497–523.

Brenes, E.R., Madrigal, K., and Molina-Navarro, G.E. (2006). 'Family business structure and succession: Critical topics in Latin American experience', *Journal of Business Research*, 59: 372–374.

Brockhaus, R.H. (2004). 'Family business succession: Suggestions for future research', *Family Business Review*, 17(2): 165–177.

Bruce, D. and Picard, D. (2006). 'Making succession a success: Perspectives from Canadian small and medium-sized enterprises', *Journal of Small Business Management*, 44(2): 306–309.

Burkart, M., Panunzi, F., and Shleifer, A. (2003). 'Family firms', *The Journal of Finance*, 58(5): 2167–2201.

Burt, R. (1992). *Structural Holes*. Cambridge, MA: Harvard University Press.

Cabrera-Suárez, K. (2005). 'Leadership transfer and the successor's development in the family firm', *The Leadership Quarterly*, 16: 71–96.

Cabrera-Suárez, K., De Saá-Pérez, P., and García-Almeida, D. (2001). 'The succession process from a resource- and knowledge-based view of the family firm', *Family Business Review*, 14(1): 37–48.

Cadieux (2007). 'Succession in small and medium-sized family businesses: Toward a typology of predecessor roles during and after instatement of the successor', *Family Business Review*, 20(2): 95–109.

Carney, M. (2005). 'Corporate governance and competitive advantage in family-controlled firms', *Entrepreneurship: Theory & Practice*, 29(3): 249–266.

Carr, J.C. and Sequeira, J.M. (2007). 'Prior family business exposure as intergenerational influence and entrepreneurial intent: A theory of planned behavior approach', *Journal of Business Research*, 60: 1090–1098.

Cater, J.J. and Justis, R.T. (2009). 'The development of successors from followers to leaders in small family firms: An exploratory study', *Family Business Review*, 22(2): 109–124.

Chau, T.T. (1991). 'Approaches to succession in east Asian business organizations', *Family Business Review*, 4(2): 161–179.

Chittoor, R. and Das, R. (2007). 'Professionalization of management and succession performance – a vital linkage', *Family Business Review*, 20(1): 65–79.

Chrisman, J.J., Chua, J.H., and Litz, R.A. (2004). 'Comparing the agency costs of family and non-family firms: Conceptual issues and exploratory evidence', *Entrepreneurship Theory & Practice*, 28(1): 335–354.

Chrisman, J.J., Chua, J.H., and Sharma, P. (1998). 'Important attributes of successors in family businesses: An exploratory study', *Family Business Review*, 11(1): 19–34.

Chua, J., Chrisman, J., and Sharma, P. (1999). 'Defining the family business by behavior', *Entrepreneurship: Theory and Practice*, 23 (4): 19–39.

Chua, J., Chrisman, J., and Sharma, P. (2003). 'Succession and nonsuccession concerns of family firms and agency relationship with nonfamily managers', *Family Business Review*, 16(2): 89–107.

Churchill, N. and Hatten, K. (1987). 'Non-market-based transfers of wealth and power: A research framework for family businesses', *American Journal of Small Business*, 11(3): 51–64.

Coleman, J. (1986). 'Social theory, social research, and a theory of action', *The American Journal of Sociology*, 91(6): 1309–1335.

Corbetta, G. and Montemerlo, D. (1999). 'Ownership, governance, and management issues in small and medium-size family businesses: A comparison of Italy and the United States', *Family Business Review*, 12(4): 361–374.

Danes, S., Rueter, M., Kwon, H., and Doherty, W. (2002). 'Family FIRO model: An application to family business', *Family Business Review*, 15(1): 31–43.

Davis, P.S. and Harveston, P.D. (1998). 'The influence of family on the family business succession process: A multi-generational perspective', *Entrepreneurship Theory & Practice*, 2: 31–53.

De Massis, A., Chua, J., and Chrisman, J. (2008). 'Factors preventing intra-family succession', *Family Business Review*, 21(2): 183–199.

Dumas, C. (1998). 'Women's pathways to participation and leadership in the family-owned firm', *Family Business Review*, 11(3): 219–228.

Dumas, C., Dupuis, J.P., Richer, F., and St.-Cyr, L. (1995). 'Factors that influence the next generation's decision to take over the family farm', *Family Business Review*, 8(1): 99–120.

Dunn, B. (1999). 'The family factor: The impact of family relationship dynamics on business-owning families during transitions', *Family Business Review*, 12(1): 41–60.

Dyck, B., Mauws, M., Starke, F.A., and Mischke, G.A. (2002). 'Passing the baton: The importance of sequence, timing, technique and communication in executive succession', *Journal of Business Venturing*, 17(2): 143–162.

Dyer, W.G., Jr. (1986). *Cultural Change in Family Firms: Anticipating and Managing Business Family Transitions*. San Francisco, CA: Jossey-Bass.

Ekeh, P. (1974). *Social Exchange Theory: The Two Traditions*. Cambridge, MA: Harvard University Press.

Emerson, R.M. (1976). 'Social exchange theory', *Annual Review of Sociology*, 2: 335–362.

Fahed-Sreih, J. and Djoundourian, S. (2006). 'Determinants of longevity and success in Lebanese family business: An exploratory study', *Family Business Review*, 19(3): 225–234.

Fiegener, M.K., Brown, B.M., Prince, R.A., and File, K.M. (1994). 'A comparison of successor development in family and non-family businesses', *Family Business Review*, 7(4): 313–329.

Fiegener, M.K., Brown, B.M., Prince, R.A., and File, K.M. (1996). 'Passing on strategic vision: Favored modes of successor preparation by ceos of family and non-family firms', *Journal of Small Business Management*, 34: 15–26.

File, K.M. and Prince, R.A. (1996). 'Attributions for family business failure: The heir's perspective', *Family Business Review*, 9(2): 171–184.

Finkelstein, S. and Hambrick, D. (1996). *Strategic Leadership: Top Executives and Their Effects on Organizations*. Minneapolis, MN: South-Western.

Garcia-Alvarez, E., Lopez-Sintas, J., and Gonzalvo, P.S. (2002). 'Socialization patterns of successors in first-to second-generation family businesses', *Family Business Review*, 15(3): 189–204.

Gersick, K.E., Davis, J.A., Hampton, M.M., and Lansberg, I. (1997). *Generation to Generation: Life Cycles of the Family Business*. Boston, MA: Harvard Business School Press.

Gersick, K.E., Lansberg, I., Desjardins, M., and Dunn, B. (1999). 'Stages and transitions: Managing change in the family business', *Family Business Review*, 12(4): 287–297.

Giddens, A. (1984). *The Constitution of Society: Outline of the Theory of Structuration*. Berkeley, CA: University of California Press.

Goldberg, S.D. (1996). 'Effective successors in family-owned business', *Family Business Review*, 9(2): 185–197.

Goldberg, S.D. and Wooldridge, B. (1993). 'Self-confidence and managerial autonomy: Successor characteristics critical to succession in family firms', *Family Business Review*, 6(1): 55–73.

Gómez-Mejía, L.R., Haynes, K.T., Núñez-Nickel, M., Jacobson, K.J.L., and Moyano-Fuentes, H. (2007). 'Socioemotional wealth and business risk in family-controlled firms: Evidence from Spanish olive oil mills', *Administrative Science Quarterly*, 52(1): 106–137.

Gómez-Mejía, L.R., Nunez-Nickel, M., and Gutierrez, I. (2001). 'The role of family ties in agency contracts', *Academy of Management Journal*, 44(1): 81–95.

Granovetter, M. (1973). 'The strength of weak ties', *American Journal of Sociology*, 78: 1360–1380.

Haberman, H. and Danes, S.M. (2007). 'Father-daughter and father-son family business management transfer comparison: Family FIRO model application', *Family Business Review*, 20(2): 163–184.

Hall, A. and Nordqvist, M. (2008). 'Professional management in family businesses: Toward an extended understanding', *Family Business Review*, 21(1): 51–69.

Handler, W. (1990). 'Succession in family firms: A mutual role adjustment between entrepreneur and next generation family members', *Entrepreneurship Theory & Practice*, 15(1): 37–51.

Handler, W. (1991). 'Key interpersonal relationships of next-generation family members in family firms', *Journal of Small Business Management*, 21: 21–32.

Handler, W. (1992). 'Succession experience of the next generation', *Family Business Review*, 5(3): 283–307.

Handler, W. (1994). 'Succession in family business', A review of the research. *Family Business Review*, 7(2): 133–157.

Harveston, P.D., Davis, P.S., and Lyden, J.A. (1997). 'Succession planning in family business: The impact of owner gender', *Family Business Review*, 10(4): 373–396.

Homans, G. (1958). 'Social behavior as exchange', *The American Journal of Sociology*, 63(6): 597–606.

Howorth, C. and Assaraf Ali, Z.A. (2001). 'Family business succession in Portugal: An examination of case studies in the furniture industry', *Family Business Review*, 14(3): 231–244.

Hubler, T. (1999). 'Ten most prevalent obstacles to family-business succession planning', *Family Business Review*, 12(2): 117–122.

Janjuha-Jivraj, S. and Spence. L.J. (2009). 'The nature of reciprocity in family firm succession', *International Small Business Journal*, 27: 702–719.

Janjuha-Jivraj, S. and Woods, A. (2002). 'Successional issues within Asian family firms: Learning from the Kenyan experience', *International Small Business Journal*, 20(1): 77–94.

Jensen, M.C. and Meckling, W.H. (1976). Theory of the firm: Managerial behavior, agency costs, and ownership structure', *Journal of Financial Economics*, 3: 305–360.

Kaye, K. (1996). 'When the family business is a sickness', *Family Business Review*, 9(4): 347–368.

Keating, N.C. and Little, H.M. (1997). 'Choosing the successor in New Zealand family firms', *Family Business Review*, 10(2): 157–171.

Kelley, H. and Thibaut, J. (1978). *Interpersonal Relations: A Theory of Interdependence*. New York: Wiley.

Kelly, L.M., Athanassiou, N., and Crittenden, W.F. (2000). 'Founder centrality and strategic behavior in the family-owned firm', *Entrepreneurship Theory & Practice*, 25(2): 27–42.

Kesner, I. and Sebora, T. (1994). 'Executive succession: Past, present and future', *Journal of Management*, 20(2): 329–372.

Kirby, D.A. and Lee, T.F. (1996). 'Research note: Succession management in family firms in the north east of England', *Family Business Review*, 9(1): 75–85.

Kuratko, D., Hornsby, J., and Montagno, R.V. (1993). 'Family business succession in Korean and U.S. firms', *Journal of Small Business Management*, 31: 132–136.

Lambrecht, J. (2005). 'Multigenerational transition in family businesses: A new explanatory model', *Family Business Review*, 18(4): 267–282.

Lansberg, I. (1983). 'Managing human resources in family firms: The problem of institutional overlap', *Organization Dynamics*, 12(1): 39–46.

Lansberg, I. (1988). 'The succession conspiracy', *Family Business Review*, 1(2): 119–143.

Lansberg, I., and Astrachan, J.H. (1994). 'Influence of family relationships on succession planning and training: The importance of mediating factors', *Family Business Review*, 7(1): 39–59.

Leary, M. and Tangney, J. (eds) (2003). *Handbook of Self and Identity*. New York: Guilford.

Le Breton-Miller, I., Miller, D., and Steier, L. (2004). 'Toward an integrative model of effective FOB succession', *Entrepreneurship Theory & Practice*, 28(4): 305–328.

Lee, S. and Tan, F. (2001). 'Growth of Chinese family enterprises in Singapore', *Family Business Review*, 14(1): 49–74.

Levi-Strauss, C. (1971). *The Elementary Structures of Kinship*. Boston, MA: Beacon.

Long, R.G. and Mathews, K.M. (2011). 'Ethics in the family firm: Cohesion through reciprocity and exchange', *Business Ethics Quarterly*, 21(2): 287–308.

Longenecker, J.G. and Schoen, J.E. (1978). 'Management succession in the family business', *Journal of Small Business Management*, 16: 1–6.

Malone, S.C. (1989). 'Selected correlates of business continuity planning in the family business', *Family Business Review*, 2(4): 341–353.

Marshall, J.P., Sorenson, R., Brigham, K., Wieling, E., Reifman, A., and Wampler, R.S. (2006). 'The paradox for the family firm CEO: Owner age relationship to succession-related processes and plans', *Journal of Business Venturing*, 21: 348–368.

Matthews, C.H., Moore, T.W., and Fialko, A.S. (1999). 'Succession in the family firm: A cognitive categorization perspective', *Family Business Review*, 12(2): 159–170.

Mauss, M. (2000). *The Gift: The Form and Reason for Exchange in Archaic Societies*. London: Routledge.

McGivern, C. (1978). 'The dynamics of management succession', *Management Decision*, 16(1): 32.

Miller, W.D. (1998). 'Siblings and succession in the family business', *Harvard Business Review*, Jan–Feb: 23–36.

Morris, M.H., Williams, R.O., Allen, J.A., and Avila, R.A. (1997). 'Correlates of success in family business transitions', *Journal of Business Venturing*, 12(5): 385–401.

Motwani, J., Levenburg, N.M., Schwarz, T.V., and Blankson, C. (2006). 'Succession planning in SMEs: An empirical analysis', *International Small Business Journal*, 24(5): 471–495.

Murray, B. (2003). 'The succession transition process: A longitudinal perspective', *Family Business Review*, 16(1): 17–34.

Nahapiet, J. and Ghoshal, S. (1998). 'Social capital, intellectual capital, and the organizational advantage', *Academy of Management Review*, 23(2): 242–266.

Nam, Y.H. and Herbett, J.I. (1999). 'Characteristics and key success factors in family business: The case of Korean immigrant businesses in metro-Atlanta', *Family Business Review*, 12(4): 341–352.

Pardo-del-Val, M. (2009). 'Succession in family firms from a multistaged perspective', *International Entrepreneurship Management Journal*, 5: 165–179.

Pearson, A., Carr, J., and Shaw, J. (2008). 'Toward a theory of familiness: A social capital perspective', *Entrepreneurship: Theory & Practice*, 32(6): 949–969.

Perricone, P.J., Earle, J.R., and Taplin, I.M. (2001). 'Patterns of succession and continuity in family-owned businesses: Study of an ethnic community', *Family Business Review*, 14(2): 105–121.

Pontet, S.B., Wrosch, C., and Gagne, M. (2007). 'An exploration of the generational differences in levels of control held among family businesses approaching succession', *Family Business Review*, 20(4): 337–354.

Pyromalis, V.D. and Vozikis, G.S. (2009). 'Mapping the successful succession process in family firms: Evidence from Greece', *International Entrepreneurship Management Journal*, 5: 439–460.

Royer, S., Simons, R., Boyd, B., and Rafferty, A. (2008). 'Promoting family: A contingency model of family business succession', *Family Business Review*, 21(1): 15–30.

Rubenson, G.C. and Gupta, A.K. (1996). 'The initial succession: A contingency model of founder tenure', *Entrepreneurship Theory & Practice*, 21: 21–35.

Santiago, A.L. (2000). 'Succession experiences in Philippine family business', *Family Business Review*, 13(1): 15–35.

Sardeshmukh, S.R. and Corbett, A.C. (2011). 'The duality of internal and external development of successors: Opportunity recognition in family firms', *Family Business Review*, 24(2): 111–125.

Schulze, W.S., Lubatkin, M.H., Dino, R.N., and Buchholtz, A.K. (2001). 'Agency relationships in family firms: Theory and evidence', *Organizational Science*, 12: 99–116.

Seymour, K.C. (1993). 'International relationships in the family firm: The effect on leadership succession', *Family Business Review*, 6(2): 263–281.

Sharma, P., Chrisman, J., and Chua, J. (1997). 'Strategic management of the family business: Past research and future challenges', *Family Business Review*, 10(1): 1–35.

Sharma, P., Chrisman, J., and Chua, J. (2003a). 'Succession planning as planned behavior: Some empirical results', *Family Business Review*, 16(1): 1–15.

Sharma, P., Chrisman, J., and Chua, J. (2003b). 'Predictors of satisfaction with the succession process in family firms', *Journal of Business Venturing*, 18: 667–687.

Sharma, P., Chrisman, J., Pablo A., and Chua, J. (2001). 'Determinants of initial satisfaction with the succession process in family firms: A conceptual model', *Entrepreneurship: Theory & Practice*, 25(3): 17–35.

Sharma, P. and Irving, P.G. (2005). 'Four bases of family business successor commitment: Antecedents and consequences', *Entrepreneurship Theory & Practice*, 29(1): 13–33.

Sharma, P. and Rao, S. (2000). 'Successor attributes in Indian and Canadian family firms: A comparative study', *Family Business Review*, 13: 313–330.

Shepard, D.A. and Zacharakis, A. (2000). 'Structuring family business succession: An analysis of the future leader's decision making', *Entrepreneurship Theory & Practice*, 24: 25–39.

Simmel, G. (1973). 'The problem of sociology', in Levine, D.N. (ed.), *Georg Simmel on Individuality and Social Forms: Selected Writings*. Chicago, IL: University of Chicago, pp. 23–35.

Stafford, K., Duncan, K.A., Dane, S., and Winter, M. (1999). 'A research model of sustainable family businesses', *Family Business Review*, 12(3): 197–208.

Stavrou, E.T. (1999). 'Succession in family businesses: Exploring the effects of demographic factors on offspring intentions to join and take over the business', *Journal of Small Business Management*, 37: 43–61.

Steier, L. (2001). 'Next-generation entrepreneurs and succession: An exploratory study of modes and means of managing social capital', *Family Business Review*, 14(3): 259–276.

Swagger, G. (1991). 'Assessing the successor generation in family businesses', *Family Business Review*, 4(4): 397–411.

Tan, W. and Fock, S. (2001). 'Coping with growth transitions: The case of Chinese family businesses in Singapore', *Family Business Review*, 13(2): 123–139.

Tatoglu, E., Kula, V., and Glaister, K. (2008). 'Succession planning in family-owned businesses: Evidence from Turkey', *International Small Business Journal*, 26(2): 155–180.

Thomas, J. (2002). 'Freeing the shackles of family business ownership', *Family Business Review*, 15(4): 321–336.

Venter, E., Boshoff, C., and Maas, G. (2005). 'The influence of successor-related factors on the succession process in small and medium-sized family businesses', *Family Business Review*, 18(4): 283–303.

Ward, J. and Dolan, C. (1998). 'Defining and describing family business ownership configurations', *Family Business Review*, 11(4): 305–310.

Westhead, P. (2003). 'Succession decision-making outcomes reported by private family companies', *International Small Business Journal*, 21(4): 369–401.

Westhead, P., Howorth, C., and Cowling, M. (2002). 'Ownership and management issues in first generation and multi-generation family firms', *Entrepreneurship and Regional Development*, 14: 247–269.

Williamson, O.E. (1981). 'The economics of organization: The transaction cost approach', *American Journal of Psychology*, 87: 548–577.

Williamson, O.E. (1991). 'Comparative economic organization: The analysis of discrete structural alternatives', *Administrative Science Quarterly*, 36: 269–296.

Yan, J. and Sorenson, R. (2006). 'The effect of Confucian values on succession in family business', *Family Business Review*, 19(3): 235–250.

Zajac, E. (1990). 'CEO selection, succession, compensation and firm performance: A theoretical integration and empirical analysis', *Strategic Management Journal*, 11(3): 217–230.

Zellweger, T., Seiger, P., and Halter, F. (2011). 'Should I stay or should I go? Career choice intentions of students with family business background', *Journal of Business Venturing*, 26(5): 521–536.

14

Business History and Family Firms

Andrea Colli and Paloma Fernández Pérez

INTRODUCTION: BUSINESS HISTORY: NATURE AND BOUNDARIES

Business history is mainly concerned with the historical development of business (Jones and Zeitlin 2007: 3). From the methodological point of view, it addresses general topics and issues, building on primary sources, and, in its best form, aims at interpreting the available evidence in the light of theory, challenging conceptual frameworks upon the basis of new historical evidence. Notwithstanding the recent diversification of their research, business historians remain predominately interested in the interaction between organisations and the 'rules of the game', to show that organisations both have been *and* still are heavily influenced by the institutional and economic environment, although it is also true that organisations sometimes anticipate or even precipitate institutional and economic change (Knutsen et al. 1999: 9). Within this general framework, business historians have studied the evolution in the forms of the business firm in

the long run, and in the variations in ownership patterns, organisational structures and the strategic orientations of companies across space and time (Amatori and Colli 2011). In this 'micro' approach lies the main difference between business history and economic history; the latter being basically interested in the 'macro' level of growth and development. However, this divide is more apparent than real. Taking the enterprise as its main unit of analysis, business history aims at providing 'micro' explanations of 'macro' issues, such as the economic growth of countries, globalisation, varieties of capitalism, and the divergence between the West and the rest of the world. Due to its hybrid origins, business history is naturally multi-disciplinary, and uses concepts and methods from history, organisational and network theory, entrepreneurship studies and economics. Current research on family businesses from a business-history scientific perspective is, thus, characterised by both a strong diversity and a wealth of approaches (Fernández Pérez 2003: 48; Colli and Rose 2007: 195).

In the following sections, this diversity is addressed, first, by presenting the key scholars and ideas that have developed the study of family firms and families in business from a business-history perspective. Then, a longer section is devoted to the contributions made by business historians to the understanding of general issues of the past which are of great interest for family-business researchers today: governance, succession, training, performance, relationship with the environment, survival and decline, gender, and networks. A third section evaluates the potential attractiveness of a historical approach in family-business studies. The final section examines the potential mutual fertilisation between business history and management studies, and the positive outcome of the rigorous application of historical research methods and techniques.

BUSINESS HISTORY AND FAMILY FIRMS: A HISTORICAL APPROACH TO KEY SCHOLARS AND IDEAS

The focus on the forms of enterprises and their ownership structures immediately brought business historians into contact with the issue of family firms and, more generally, of family capitalism – that is, a business system in which family-run businesses are a structurally relevant section of the industrial demography (Colli 2003). In its present form, business history originated at the beginning of the 1960s with the influential research of Alfred D. Chandler (Chandler 1977). With the aim of explaining the rise of the large managerial corporation, the great US historian considered the family as a (relevant) stage in the life of the modern enterprise, a necessarily transient ownership form to be dismissed when growth called for public listing and for the inclusion of skilled professionals in the management of the company.[1] More or less implicit was the assumption that the persistence of family ownership was an obstacle which hindered the efficiency of companies, limiting their natural

process of growth, a view shared by many other influential scholars, such as Edith Penrose (Penrose 1959).

During the 1960s and 1970s, three (disconnected) streams of research into family ownership and family business gained ground. The first was developed by historians interested in agrarian societies, who focused on the relationship between the accounts of rural farms, inheritance practices, the political rules of the game, and local or regional processes of economic decline or progress. The rapid industrialisation and the big migratory waves from the countryside to the cities in many countries in those decades stimulated an important academic interest in a world that was disappearing (Goody et al. 1976). The second stream (given that the first mainly developed in History Faculties and Departments) focused on pre-industrial societies and on the role of family ownership in the development of social classes and privileges (Butel 1974; Burguière 1976; Hareven 1977; Stone 1977; Socolow 1978). Finally, a third line of research, developed, above all, in Economics Faculties and Business Schools, which started to produce studies about entrepreneurial dynasties, mainly written by professional scholars, but also by journalists and consultants, frequently with a hagiographic approach aiming at celebrating the virtues of individuals and dynasties (Barker 1960; Carr 1965; Abels 1965; Church 1969; Chapman 1977; Ward 1978; and further references in Landes 2006). Implicit in this stream of research was the emphasis on the influence of family ownership on the strategic choices of the firm in terms of investment decisions, financing and delegation to managers. The internal dynamics between the business sphere and this type of kinship relations received far less attention.

Among business historians, a different attitude towards family firms started to emerge during the second half of the 1980s, due to factors which included the mounting criticism of large integrated organisations and, above all, the astonishing success of industrial districts and small firms – most of which were family-owned and managed – in Europe (Piore and Sabel 1984). The growing relevance of Asian economies was also a determining factor, in which a relevant role was historically played by large conglomerates and family-owned and managed business-groups (Amsden 1989, 2004; Colpan et al. 2010). The stubborn persistence of family ownership was also fascinating for historians, despite the claims of convergence towards the managerial public company in advanced economies, something which was also emphasised in the 'varieties of capitalism' debate, which emphasised the existence of multiple versions of capitalistic societies, each characterised by efficient forms of organisations and ownership structures (Whitley 1999; Soskice and Hall 2001).

All this made business historians realise that: (a) it was necessary to move one step beyond the idea of family business as a stage in the life-cycle of the modern enterprise; (b) a better contextualisation of the relative efficiency of family firms in different places and periods was needed; and (c) business history could provide a wide variety of longitudinal evidence to test existing theories and to inspire new ones (Jones and Khanna 2006). After some promising attempts (Ōkōchi and Yasuoka 1984), a new stream of business-history research started to be published from the beginning of the 1990s, explicitly emphasising the efficiency and comparative advantages of family firms. In 1993, Geoffrey Jones and Mary Rose edited *Family Capitalism* (Jones and Rose 1993), a collection of business-history essays on family firms from Asia to Europe and the USA across three centuries. In their introduction, the editors emphasised how business historians had surprisingly considered family firms as 'forces for conservatism and backwardness', instead of highlighting their vitality and endurance across space and time. All the essays in the collection provide a very positive vision of family firms, of their efficiency and capability to adapt, stressing the idea of the *relative efficiency* of family firms inside a particular environment, determined not only by

geography but also, from a longitudinal point of view, by cultural transformations which occurred over time. In this line, other studies started to be published during the 1990s, referring to family firms as sources of competitiveness in a historical perspective. Examples are abundant, but one is worth citing: in 1993, Mary Rose published her 'Beyond Buddenbrooks: the family firm and the management of succession in nineteenth-century Britain' (Rose 1993), in which a careful analysis of the management of succession practices was performed on British firms during the Industrial Revolution. In 1995, the same author edited one of the books in Edward Elgar Publishing's 'International Library of Critical Writings in Business History' series under the title *Family Business*, in which a number of articles addressed the relevance of family firms in the process of industrialisation and in the rise of modern economies (Rose 1995). Since then, a number of studies by business historians have been published, in which family firms are both considered as engines of growth and as relevant components of national business systems, and their internal dynamics are addressed in greater depth, also from a comparative perspective (e.g., Church 1993; Colli et al. 2003). In 1997, Youssef Cassis published a major analysis of the historical development of European big business explicitly emphasising the role played by family firms in the process (Cassis 1997). However, even though some early attempts to provide some synthesis of the debate have been made (Colli 2003), a critical evaluation of the contribution of family firms to the process of economic growth and development is still lacking.

Business historians, however, with some outstanding exceptions (Howorth et al. 2006), have tended not to develop their own specific conceptualisations and theoretical frameworks about family firms. What they did was to follow the suggestions deriving from other disciplines, largely from management studies which, in the same period, were focusing on specific research questions concerning both the endogenous aspects of family firms as well as their impact on the external environment. In doing so, business historians implicitly decided to frame their research in the broader field of family-business research, resorting to the same concepts being used by management scholars, offering a broad array of interesting evidence.

BUSINESS HISTORY AND FAMILY BUSINESS STUDIES

Business history is not simply a provider of evidence. Theories can be tested, and new hypotheses introduced, by critical analysis of historical facts. In this perspective, it stimulates further reflection about the possible forms of family capitalism, including the ways in which family firms reacted to the transformation in the external framework (institutional, technological and even cultural). Family-business histories have, in the last decades, been used not only for descriptive purposes, but also to understand and explain the relationship between family-business management and topics of great relevance in economics and management in general: efficiency, competitiveness, factors of failure and success due to changes in external environment, economic growth or decline, internationalisation, the resilient presence of some type of firms in specialised-market niches in some regions or in global markets, and the transformations in the training and professionalisation practices to adapt to changing market and institutional conditions (see Table 14.1 at the end of the chapter for some examples). The rest of this section will be dedicated to areas of family-business research in which the chronological dimension plays a relevant role.

Ownership and Governance

The issue of ownership and corporate governance in family firms is particularly interesting for business historians, from at least two perspectives. The first concerns the contribution of family firms *at the aggregate level* to economic growth in the long run. The second looks at the evolution, at the micro level, of the relationship between ownership and governance in the course of the firm's life-cycle.

As far as the first perspective is concerned, business historians have only recently started a systematic investigation of the topic. Given the quality and quantity of the available data, an even impressionistic estimate of the relevance which family firms held in the past within a given economic system is, at present, unthinkable. Aggregate data about the diffusion of family ownership were extremely scarce until very recently (after the 1980s) even for the most advanced economies. From a business-history perspective, the attempt to re-construct the ownership structures of the largest companies (normally for benchmark years) is more realistic, even though it requires an extremely time-consuming effort, given the absence or scarcity of information about ownership. Given this situation, it is only very recently that some projects which aim at re-constructing the ownership structures of the largest companies, have begun (see, e.g., Colli et al. 2011 and Fernández Pérez et al., 2011). These projects start to make available detailed information about the presence of family control in the long run, at least among the largest companies. These data could easily be joined with those produced by other cross-sectional research (e.g., Pavan 1973; Channon 1974; Rumelt 1974; Dyas and Tanheiser 1976, La Porta et al. 1999; Barca and Becht 2001; Faccio and Lang 2002; Anderson and Reeb 2003), in order to obtain an overview of the relevance of large family firms in the most advanced economies. The construction of longitudinal datasets in order to assess the impact of family firms in modern economies is still in its infancy, but is a relevant contribution to the field of family-business studies. Clearly, this raises a number of critical methodological issues, including that of the definition of family ownership and control, and the identification of the appropriate sources of data, including detailed information about ownership distribution, which are often retrievable only in company archives, which are not always accessible.

A second relevant area in which business history provides a relevant contribution is the analysis of ownership transformation during the process of the evolution of family firms. Business historians have at their disposal a vast array of cases and original narratives, solidly built upon the basis of primary, archival research, which serves to illustrate how family ownership evolves in the course of the enterprise's life, not necessarily in the direction of the dissolution of family ownership into a managerial public company. One example is Harold James' comparative study of three family dynasties (the *Falck*s, *Wendel*s and *Haniel*s) in the steel industry over two centuries, in which the persistence of long-term family ownership in the three companies is explained by the ability of the controlling families to manage the expansion process while maintaining control over the companies (James 2006: 379–380). Mats Larsson, Håkan Lindgren and Daniel Nyberg (Larsson et al. 2008) have examined the evolution of corporate governance practices in the long run in two multi-generational Swedish groups, the *Bonnier*s and the *Wallenberg*s. The reconciliation of expansion with personalised control without sacrificing efficiency has been studied by Emmanuel Chadeau with regard to large firms in twentieth-century France (Chadeau 1993), and by Sluyterman and Winkelman (1993) and Arnoldus (2002) for the Netherlands. Notwithstanding the availability of a number of case histories, a synthesis is still lacking here, as is an attempt to highlight the relationships between governance, value creation and competitiveness (Carney 2005).

Succession, Training and Education

Succession is a process which per se takes place in the long run. Inter-generational transition has been a favourite subject of business historians, who are interested in understanding not only the outcomes of the process, but

also how the process itself took place. Upon the basis of this research, experienced historians stress that the succession process, the way in which it is managed and its potential outcomes, is to be considered as relative to both time and space. Business histories of family firms often contain explicit reference to different ways of managing succession across time and generations, contextualising practices and modalities to specific cultures and periods. A good example of this is provided by the above-mentioned *Wallenberg* family. Lindgren (2002) has investigated the leadership transfer across five generations, analysing, at the same time, both training and the selection of potential leaders, as well as the relationships among the members of the incoming generations. This study shows how well the historical approach can not only help in identifying the long-term process of succession practices, but also in highlighting continuities in succession practices transmitted across generations in the same family firm. The longitudinal perspective provides a good ground for observing the transformation of succession practices over time, following social and cultural transformations, as well as their effectiveness in specific contexts, for instance, exploring the leader selection process among heirs (from primogeniture to competencies) or their formation and education (from practice to formal training). One way to re-read the business histories of family firms is to look at the ways in which the succession and training practices evolve over time, following, for instance, the transformations in the nature of the family in Western culture, and allow the long-term survival of family firms (Diaz Morlan 2002). Some research has examined the ways in which inheritance practices have successfully influenced the life-cycle of family businesses in the first industrial revolution (Owens 2002). In this field, historical research has a strong interpretative potential: current succession and training practices among Western family firms are very different from those in use a century ago (when the first male son was expected to inherit the leadership, and when training was a mixture of on-the-job experience and travel abroad), but are astonishingly similar to what is in use today in countries experiencing a fast industrialisation process, such as China and India.

Business history has also studied the relationship between the creation and expansion of formal education for business purposes, and the real training practices of senior and junior generations of different family businesses in different countries. Some recent research (Fellman 2001; Fellman and Leino-Kaukiainen 2006) challenges not only the idea of family managers as being oriented towards long-term planning and guided by stewardship purposes, but also negative views of family firms as being slow to adapt and susceptible to failure in terms of proper training practices. Forthcoming research into Catalan firms in the second half of the twentieth century clearly shows not only that the professionalisation of the management of middle-sized family-controlled businesses was based upon a combination of elements widely addressed by family-business literature (such as better education of family members, the hiring of outsiders, in-house selection and training, etc.), but also upon an original trust-based relationship among local firms, which allowed them to outsource professional services in other family firms, thereby providing the necessary support to solve the problems of succession, internationalisation and financing.[2]

Performance(s)

Historical research into the performances of family firms (per se and in comparison with non-family firms) is still in its infancy, and could benefit a lot of the quantitative cross-sectional research performed in management studies, in terms of inspiration and orientation towards the investigation of large aggregates of information about the long-term performances of family firms (Anderson and Reeb 2003; Villalonga and Amit 2006). This lack of analysis can be explained in two

ways. The first refers to the difficulties in finding reliable and comparable data in order to assess the financial performance. Apart from the availability and quality of data, accounting practices and disclosure requirements have varied enormously over time and among countries, making it difficult, if not impossible, to make long-term comparisons. At present, it is impossible (in the case of historical research) to compare the financial performances of single enterprises with those of the industry in a given period of time, due to the lack of aggregate data. As far as large companies are concerned, for which better information is available, some attempts have been made in the past, but without any distinction between family and non-family firms (Cassis 1997).

The second explanation refers to the concept of performance in business-history research. Business historians have tended to emphasise other typologies of performance than the financial one, thereby anticipating recent developments in family-business literature interested in developing the concept of socio-emotional wealth (Gomez-Mejia et al. 2007). Cassis (1997) explicitly suggests longevity and growth, together with profits and profitability, as performance measures. In the famous comparative analysis of British, German and American big business, Alfred Chandler considers market share (more than profits) as the ultimate measure of performance in order to judge the efficiency of the business enterprise (Chandler 1991). However, no clear distinction is made between family and non-family firms here. Notwithstanding these efforts, micro-level research is still extremely rare, even if some promising examples are available. Robin Mackie has been able to examine the relationship between family ownership and survival in the Scottish parish of Kirkcaldy over one century, finding consistent evidence of the positive impact of family ownership on the survival opportunities of companies (Mackie 2001).

The issue of performance measurement and analysis, from a historical perspective, is thus a particularly promising field in which collaborative research can flourish among historians and management scholars. Business historians can, in fact, address the issue of performance (both from the financial point of view and from the others highlighted above), thereby exploiting the existing databases or even creating new ones.

Stakeholder Management, Reputation and Corporate Social Responsibility

Another research area relevant for business historians concerns the relationship between the family firm and its stakeholders, including the local community in which it is embedded. Here, too, examples are abundant but general synthesis is absent or rare. Some cases are particularly telling. In early modern period and during the first phase of the industrialisation process, stakeholder relations were particularly important for the efficiency of firms, due to the high level of trust necessary in an uncertain environment. Family firms developed sophisticated stakeholder management models by leveraging on their 'familiness' – the unique set of resources generated by the interaction between the family sphere and that of business (Habbershon and Williams 1999). Ojala and Luoma-aho (2008) looked at stakeholder management in Finnish tradesmen family firms between the mid-eighteenth and nineteenth centuries, emphasising how relevant the role of personal reputation was in creating stable and enduring relationships. Stakeholder relations were considered absolutely strategic by entrepreneurial families during the first phases of the industrialisation process, when the concept of the 'extended family' was the most common solution to the lack of formal industrial relations. Thus, Harold James, in his comparative study of the *Falck*, *Wendel* and *Haniel* family histories, stresses the role played by the relationships with employees and stakeholders as a relevant goal for the leadership. At *Falck*, for instance, in 1931 – 25 years after its foundation – the family decided to put its name on the name of the enterprise (James 2006: 250), in order to emphasise its family quality, and, in the official speeches and documents, the leaders spoke of 'the large family of *Acciaierie e Ferriere Lombarde Falck*', referring to their employees.

As suggested by the Finnish example, reputation plays a relevant role in stakeholder management in family firms, which also has a relevant role in a context characterised by high uncertainty and risk. In the *Falck* case, the attachment to reputation was seen as a source of invaluable capital for the enterprise, something to preserve and enhance. This was made clear by the founder of the company, Giorgio Enrico Falck, in his will, which was opened and read in 1942:

> I do not know whether future events will allow the enterprise to be maintained and developed. Naturally, I hope so. In all things, act so as to create honour for its name and mine, which I tried to make esteemed. Above all, be honest, scrupulous and not be tempted by unclear dealings whose basis is speculation. (cited in James 2006: 258)

In a recent article published in the *Business History Review*, based upon primary sources and archival material such as correspondence and letters over three generations in a British merchant family firm from the 1870s to the 1950s, Gordon Boyce clearly describes the role of the inter-generational transmission of family values and culture, showing how much reputation was considered as a sort of 'immaterial asset' which was difficult to accumulate, important to preserve and extremely easy to ruin (Boyce 2010).

Examples of the relevance of immaterial, reputational capital are abundant in the history of banking, especially when family private banks are considered. Christopher Kobrak has clearly stressed the relevance of 'familiness' in private merchant banking, especially in high-risk transactions. He examines the cases of banking houses, such as the *Morgan*s and *Warburg*s, which were able to establish an international reputation which was strongly linked to their family nature, a competitive advantage which lasted until the regulatory 'revolution' of the 1930s, which often imposed public regulations over the banking system.

Survival, Success and Decline

Business historians have used historical archives to show how failure or success mainly depend on the ability of a family firm to adapt to changes in the external environment, in different historical, territorial and cultural settings. Disparate examples, from that of the *Bromley*s in the Philadelphia textile industry between 1850 and 1940 (Scranton 1993), to the case of the indigenous family firms in colonial Bombay in the eighteenth century (Smith 1993) to that of well-known dynasties such as the *Ford*s, *Rockefeller*s, *Agnelli*s, *Toyoda*s, *Peugeot*s, *Renault*s, *Citroën*s, *Guggenheim*s, or the *Morgan*s (Landes 2006) tend to support this perspective. Longevity – defined not only as the prolonged existence of a company, but also as the ability of a family to maintain its leadership position – has recently become a focus of historical analysis, even if there is no evidence of a quantitative, systematic longevity analysis similar to that reported in Goto (2006). However, business historians have addressed the issue of the resilience and longevity of family firms by analysing the impact of institutional factors (Colli et al. 2003) and changes in market dynamics and technology (Fernández Pérez and Puig 2007; Puig and Fernández Pérez 2009). Several examples can be found upon a country basis (e.g., Berghoff 2006 about German *Mittelstand*), or for industries characterised by diffused family ownership and management, such as paper and pulp (Gutierrez 1999; Ojala and Lamberg 2006), metals and shipping (Fernández Pérez 2007; Valdaliso et al. 2010; Lubinski 2011), alcoholic beverages (Da Silva Lopes 2007), and private banking and financial intermediation (Díaz Morlán 2002; Kobrak 2009).

Networks and Gender

Gender studies and networks have recently been among the research areas in which business historians in general, and family firms

in particular, have provided research and valuable evidence. Given the 'thickness' of the concept of the network – the fact that, under the same label, a number of different, but interconnected, meanings are collected – business historians have produced research in several directions, applying the idea in various ways and contexts (Fernández Pérez and Rose 2010). One promising area is the re-construction of the co-operative attitude among family firms. A significant example can be found in the history of associations of family firms which were organised in order to lobby at the governmental level, for which detailed studies are beginning to become available (Fernández Pérez and Puig 2009).

Another, more common, stream of research aims at re-constructing, through archival research and the analysis of internal documents, the extent and outcomes of network-building by family members, which resulted in a stable asset for the activity of companies, thereby explaining their efficiency, especially in humble environments. Examples range from British trading companies in India (Forestier 2010), to foreign activities in Spanish banking (López-Morell and O'Kean 2008), from Greek shipping companies (Harlaftis and Theotokas 2004) to publishing houses (Fernández Moya 2010). What makes business historical research particularly promising in this respect is the possibility of fruitfully employing its particular research methodology, based upon the analysis of primary sources – for instance, those available in family archives – in order to re-construct the network of relationships built by family members (James 2012).

Like networks, gender is another area in which business historians have been concentrating their efforts. The presence of women in particular market niches, such as the services sector, transport and communication companies, and industries linked to domestic consumption and activities controlled by women in the United States and in Europe, has been examined (Kowlek-Folland 2001; Kowlek-Folland and Walsh 2007). In some inter-disciplinary collaborative experiences, business historians and management scholars have established relationships between the invisibility of women in the documents about the ownership of businesses in the past, and the institutional rules of the game, while at the same time exploring the usefulness of concepts such as 'leadership' in order to appreciate and analyse more fully the important role of women in family businesses in a variety of sectors and activities in both past and present conditions (Fernández Pérez and Hamilton 2010).

DO WE NEED A HISTORICAL APPROACH?

Challenging Abstractness

Why is history relevant? One advantage of the historical approach is the possibility of coupling comparative and longitudinal perspectives. History has its own methodology (see the last section) but it is not a technique; it is a scientific discipline that analyses the influence of time and space in order to explain the diverse pathways and evolution of humankind. It deals with success. Yet, in historical sources, historians more commonly find evidence about the failure and decline of social groups and institutions, and, sometimes, about Darwinist processes of adaptation and survival to new conditions. In a-historical approaches, family firms are all too often considered to be something homogeneous over space and time, but this is clearly not the case when historical evidence is taken into account.

Recently, and after decades of never-ending debates, a widely-accepted definition of what a family business is has been released. According to the European Commission (2009), a firm can be considered as a family business if some precise conditions apply with regard to the possession of voting rights and to the involvement of family members in the governance of the firm itself. The result of a successful collective-lobbying effort, it has been welcomed by both scholars and researchers, because it undoubtedly solves many problems of a statistical nature as well as those emerging from the wide range of definitions adopted in different studies, which hindered the possibility of comparing valuable research efforts. However, business historians feel relatively uncomfortable with such a precise definition. The reason is quite obvious: more than other social scientists, historians are aware of the changing nature of the topics of their studies, both in geographical and chronological terms, and tend to avoid 'conceptual cages'. In the existing business histories of family firms (including those mentioned in the previous paragraphs), it is practical and empirical definitions of family firms that prevail. Bearing in mind how much the nature of the family itself has changed in the medium to long term, it is not easy to accept clear-cut definitions. The same can be said when comparing the notion of the family, and hence the nature of the family firm, across different cultures (Colli 2003 and Fernández Pérez et al. 2011).

Undoubtedly, under certain conditions, the family firms of the present reveal outstanding similarities with those of the past. Historical research has demonstrated that strategies of survival and success in the industrialising states of Europe anticipated those adopted in today's emerging economies in Latin America or Asia (Fernández Pérez and Fernández Moya 2011). However, business-history research stresses that differences tend to prevail across space and time, and it is this diversity in the institutional limitations of aspects which are crucial to determine both the family life and the future of a family business which makes it enormously difficult for business historians to engage in generalisations.

The longitudinal perspective of business history provides an articulated kaleidoscope of cases which are useful in order to interpret many of the features which the present family firms show across the globe, and contribute to a better conceptualisation of what family businesses are in reality, across space and time. Path-dependent environmental factors, particularly attractive for the historian's sensibility, are there to explain cross-national differences in many aspects of country-specific models of family firms across the globe.

Challenging Political Correctness

History is also useful in developing critical approaches. A good example is provided by the debate about the role of family firms in fostering economic growth. Many approaches tend to criticise heavily concentrated family ownership – especially in large companies – as a factor of rigidity which ultimately damages the overall economic welfare. From this perspective, the family control of business groups in many emerging economies is a cause of backwardness, inefficiency and unequal income distribution. The absence of protection for minority-stakeholders, which is characteristic of many family-business groups, as well as their political connections, ultimately determines their backwardness for both the present and the future generations (Morck and Yeung 2004; Morck 2007). Clearly, a large amount of historical evidence – about pre-industrial societies around the world – reinforces these views (Casey 1989; Herr 1989).

Business historians studying industrial societies, capitalist agricultural and commercial societies tend to have a more complex view of the contribution of powerful families and business groups to economic growth. On closer scrutiny, in contexts of economic and institutional backwardness, technological transfer of innovation is costly and family businesses (and concentrated ownership) may play a very significant role in fostering growth and development, at least in some sectors typical of the second industrial revolution (Fernández Pérez and Puig 2007). Most of this literature on the emerging economies and business groups in the world, at least before the Second World War, highlights the complexity of local institutions and historically-determined stages of growth and development, and the different possible contributions that family-controlled business

groups may mean in different historical and geographical environments.

New Wine in Old Bottles

A third relevant advantage of an historical approach lies in its 'scepticism'. As Jones and Khanna (2006) clearly suggest, historical sensibility allows assertions about the 'novelty' of economic phenomena to be avoided. Family firms are clearly evolving, adapting themselves to the evolution in the external environment, but – as shown in the previous sections – many of their features are common to similar organisations in the past, as are the solutions provided for the problems.

History provides a methodologically rigorous 'ex-post' analysis of events at micro-level, thus allowing historians to test theoretical predictions and assumptions. More than other subjects in the field of management studies, family-business studies deal with issues which can only be addressed long term, and in which the time dimension plays a relevant role, as do succession, training, inheritance, longevity, etc. Business history provides rigorous methods for analysing small samples and qualitative data when conventional regression techniques do not apply.

CONCLUSION: FROM NEGLECT TO CO-OPERATION

Takeaways for Business Historians

Business historians who specialise in family-business research have greatly benefited from theoretical contributions coming from family-business research made by management scholars. First, they have progressively become aware of the need to deal with definitions, typologies and analytical interpretative frameworks about the issues which they deal with in their individual case studies. However, even though they do not disdain inductive generalisations, historians are less inclined towards rigid taxonomies and deductive methodologies of analysis. Apart from the rigorous (based upon the investigation of reliable and double-checked data) and critical method in the use of primary (archival) and secondary sources, they generally avoid providing prescriptive models. At a minimum, they make creative use of the instruments available to them in their 'toolbox' in order to re-construct the past events which they consider useful in order to offer evidence and shed light on general issues which are interesting for other social scientists. As stressed in the previous section, in providing longitudinal research, business historians offer evidence which is useful not only for supporting existing theories and analytical frameworks, but also for testing and challenging them (Jones and Khanna 2006). The evidence discussed in the previous sections shows how well historical research can provide useful longitudinal evidence, while simultaneously suggesting new approaches to consolidated research topics, as was the case with performance measurement.

This kind of sensibility may make historians excessively relativist. Even the most interesting narrative written upon the basis of rigorous research methodology needs to confront itself with a strong theoretical framework in order to result in a useful analytical tool. In this respect, there are a number of research areas, as indicated above, in the field of family-business studies which can provide the relevant analytical frameworks with which business historians can fruitfully confront themselves. Elegant and detailed narratives can only draw advantage from solid theoretical background, thereby avoiding ascribing business historians with the frequently used label of 'storytellers'.

A second relevant area in which business historians have benefited and can benefit further from the methodological suggestions of management studies is that concerning quantitative analysis in general. Until now, qualitative analysis based upon single, or a few, case studies has prevailed. Historians have favoured the careful re-construction of single case studies upon the basis of original research. Quantitative research, based upon aggregate data, has, until now, been scarcely practiced, nor have historians oriented their efforts of data collection in the direction of quantitative analysis, even upon a mere descriptive statistical basis. As can be imagined, the main obstacle in this direction is the availability of reliable historical data at aggregate level, starting from those concerning the ownership structures of the largest companies, which could allow further comparative analysis.

Takeaways for Management Scholars

As stressed above, business history has much to offer to improve the analysis undertaken by family-business researchers. First, its emphasis on path-dependency, which always shows how exogenous environmental factors such as geography, institutions, supply and demand, and culture, have a direct interplay with endogenous elements in determining the creation, evolution, end, failure, adaptation, or success, of a variety of family firms in different periods and territories. Second, it provides an identity to the protagonists of family-business histories: management scholars very rarely provide the real names of individuals and families for reasons of privacy, but, for historians, visibility and identification are a requirement, which means that historical analysis can – perhaps – resist the passing of time better, and provide a wealth of real case studies for real families and real economic sectors, which can yield better analysis and better perspectives for applied scholarship. Third, business history emphasises more than other disciplines the difficulties and blunders which it encounters, and thus also provides a more realistic approach to what happens in reality. Fourth, business history usually deals with a variety of multiple sources, of a quantitative and qualitative kind, in order to contrast information and empirical evidence, double-checking the reliability of sources and information, thereby increasing the methodological rigour of the analysis. The only way to be loyal to

Appendix 14.1 History of families in business – selected literature

Author/s	Approach	Area	Period	Keywords	Full reference
Anderson (1980)	Literature overview	Western countries	1500–1914	Theory and Methodology	Anderson, Michael (1980) *Approaches to the History of the Western Family 1500–1914*. London: MacMillan Press.
Arnoldus (2002)	Comparative study	Netherlands	1880–1970	Six family firms in food industry, Netherlands	Arnoldus, Doreen (2002) *Family, Family Firm and Strategy: Six Dutch Family Firms in the Food Industry 1880–1970*. Amsterdam: Free Industry.
Barker (1977)	Case study	United Kingdom	1926–1976	Pilkington	Barker, Thomas (1977) *The Glassmakers. Pilkington: The Rise of an International Company 1926–1976*. London: Weidenfeld and Nicolson.
Berghoff (2006)	Country study	Germany	1949–2000	German family firms; Mittelstand	Berghoff, Hartmut (2006) 'The end of family business? The Mittelstand and German capitalism in transition, 1949–2000', *Business History Review*, 80(2): 263–295.
Burguière (1976)	Comparative study	Western countries	18th–20th centuries	Family dynamics; entrepreneurship in family firms	Burguière, André (1976) 'From Malthus to Max Weber: belated marriage and the spirit of enterprise', in Forster, Robert and Ranum, Orest (eds), *Family and Society: Selections from the Annales*. Baltimore, OH and London, The Johns Hopkins University Press, pp. 237–250.
Casey (1989)	Literature overview	Europe	15th–20th centuries	Social history of the western family	Casey, James (1989) *The History of the Family*. Oxford: Blackwell.

Author/s	Approach	Area	Period	Keywords	Full reference
Church (1982)	Comparative study	20th century	International	Family firms in capital intensive industries	Church, Roy (1982) 'The transition from family firm to managerial enterprise in the motor industry: an international comparison', in Hannah, Leslie (ed.), *From Family Firm to Professional Management: Structure and Performance of Business Enterprise*. Budapest: Akademiai Kiado.
Church (1993)	Comparative study	20th century	International	Family firms in manufacturing	Church, Roy (1993) 'The family firm in industrial capitalism: international perspectives on hypotheses and history', in Jones, Geoffrey and Rose, Mary B., Special Issue 'Family Capitalism', *Business History*, 35(4).
Colli (2003)	Comparative study	1850–2000	International	Family firms around the world and in historical perspective	Colli, Andrea (2003) *The History of Family Business 1850–2000*. Cambridge: Cambridge University Press.
Colli and Rose (1999)	Comparative study	19th–20th centuries	United Kingdom and Italy	Family firms	Colli, Andrea and Rose, Mary B. (1999) 'Families and firms: the culture and evolution of family firms in Britain and Italy in the nineteenth and twentieth centuries', *Scandinavian Economic History Review*, 47(1): 24–47.
Colli and Rose (2002)	Literature overview	20th century	World	Longitudinal analysis of family firms	Colli, A. and Rose, Mary B. (2002) 'Family firms in comparative perspective', in F. Amatori and G. Jones (eds), *Business History Around the World at the Turn of the Century*. Cambridge and New York: Cambridge University Press.
Colli and Rose (2007)	Literature overview	19th–20th centuries	World	Methodological	Colli, Andrea and Rose, Mary B. (2007) 'Family business', in Jones, Geoffrey and Zeitlin, Jonathan (eds), *The Oxford Handbook of Business History*. Oxford: Oxford University Press.

(Continued)

Appendix 14.1 (Continued)

Author/s	Approach	Area	Period	Keywords	Full reference
Colli et al. (2003)	Comparative study	19th–20th centuries	United Kingdom, Italy and Spain	Longitudinal comparison; institutional influence	Colli, Andrea, Fernández Pérez, Paloma and Rose, Mary (2003) 'National determinants of family firm development? Family firms in Britain, Spain and Italy in the nineteenth and twentieth centuries', *Enterprise and Society*, 4(1): 28–64.
Collier and Horowitz (1976)	Case study	19th–20th centuries	USA	Rockefeller family	Collier, Peter and Horowitz, David (1976) *The Rockefellers: An American Dynasty*. Ontario: The New American Library.
Da Silva (2007)	Industry study	19th–20th centuries	World	Family multinationals	Da Silva Lopes, Teresa (2007) *Global Brands: The Evolution of Multinationals in Alcoholic Beverages*. Cambridge: Cambridge University Press.
De Roover (1963)	Case study	15th century	Italy	The Medici Bank	De Roover, Raymond (1963) *The Rise and Decline of the Medici Bank 1297–1494*. Cambridge, MA: Harvard University Press.
Davidoff and Hall (1987)	Country study	1780–1850	United Kingdom	Social history	Davidoff, Eleonore and Hall, Catherine (1987) *Family Fortunes: Men and Women of the English Middle Class, 1780–1850*. Chicago, IL: The University of Chicago Press.
Dritsas (1997)	Country study	20th century	Greece	Family firms in manufacturing; typologies	Dritsas, Margarita (1997) 'Family firms in Greek Industry during the twentieth century', in Dritsas, Margarita and Gourvish, Terry (eds), *European Enterprise: Strategies of Adaptation and Renewal in the Twentieth Century*. Athens: Trochalia.

Author/s	Approach	Area	Period	Keywords	Full reference
Dutta (1996)	Country study	20th century	India	Culture in family firms	Dutta, Sudipt (1996) *Family Business in India*. New Delhi: Sage Publications.
Fear (1997)	Case study	19th–20th centuries	Germany	Thyssen	Fear, Jeffrey (1997) 'August Thyssen and German steel', in McCraw, Thomas (ed.), *Creating Modern Capitalism*. Cambridge, MA: Harvard University Press.
Fernández Pérez and Puig (2007)	Country study	19th–20th centuries	Spain	Longevity of large family firms	Fernández Pérez, Paloma and Puig, Nuria (2007) 'Bonsais in a wild forest? A historical approach to the longevity of large historical family firms in Spain', *Revista de História Económica. Journal of Iberian and Latin American Economic History*, 25(3): 459–497.
Fernández Pérez and Puig (2010)	Country study	20th century	Spain	Internationalization of large family firms	Fernández Pérez, Paloma and Puig, Nuria (2010) 'Silent revolution: the internationalization of large Spanish family firms'. Special Issue on internationalization of firms edited by Peter Buckley and John Wilson, *Business History*, 51(3): 462–483.
Gies and Gies (1987)	Comparative study	12th–15th centuries	Europe	Law and practice	Gies, France and Gies, Joseph (1987) *Marriage and the Family in the Middle Ages*. New York: Harper and Row.
Hannah (2007)	Literature overview	20th century	Western countries	Corporate governance, professionalization	Hannah, Leslie (2007) 'The divorce of ownership from control from 1900 onwards: re-calibrating imagined global trends', *Business History*, 49(4): 404–438.
Hareven (1978)	Comparative study	18th–20th centuries	Western countries	Family change in families in history	Hareven, Tamara K. (1978) *Transitions: The Family and the Life Course in Historical Perspective*. New York: Academic Press.

(Continued)

Appendix 14.1 (Continued)

Author/s	Approach	Area	Period	Keywords	Full reference
Hareven and Plakans (1987)	Literature overview	15th–20th centuries	World	Theory, methodology	Hareven, Tamara K. and Plakans, Andrejs (eds) (1987) *Family History at the Crossroads*. Princeton, NJ: Princeton University Press.
Hedges (1952)	Case study	19th–20th centuries	United States	The Browns of Providence	Hedges, James B. (1952) *The Browns of Providence Plantations*, 2 vols. Cambridge, MA: Harvard University Press.
James (2006)	Comparative study	19th–20th centuries	Germany, France and Italy	Wendels, Haniels, Falcks; family business dynamics	James, Harold (2006) *Family Capitalism in Europe: Wendels, Haniels, Falcks, and the Continental European Model.* Cambridge, MA: Belknap.
Jones and Rose (eds) (1993)	Comparative study	18th–20th centuries	International	Articles on national cases	Jones, G. and Rose, M.B. (eds) (1993) Special Issue Family Capitalism. *Business History*, 35(4).
Kocka (1971)	Case study	1850–1914	Germany	Siemens	Kocka, Jurgen (1971) 'Family and bureaucracy in German industrial management, 1850–1914: Siemens in comparative perspective', *Business History Review* 45(2): 133–156.
Landes (1975)	Comparative study	18th–20th centuries	France and United Kingdom	Dynamics of family firms in different countries	Landes, David S. (1975) 'Bleichröders and Rothschilds', in Rosenberg, Charles E. (ed.), *The Family in History.* Philadelphia, PA: University of Pennsylvania Press.
Landes (2003)	Comparative study	19th–20th centuries	International	Dynamics of family firms in different countries	Landes, David S. (2003) *Dynasties: Fortune and Misfortune in the World's Great Family Business.* New York: Viking.

Author/s	Approach	Area	Period	Keywords	Full reference
Levy-Leboyer (1984)	Country study	19th–20th centuries	France	Large family firms in manufacturing	Levy-Leboyer, M. (1984) 'The large family firm in the French Manufacturing industry', in Ōkōchi, Akio and Yasuoka, Shigeaki (eds), *Family Business in the Era of Industrial Growth: Its Ownership and Management*. Tokyo: University of Tokyo Press, pp. 209–233.
McDonald (2010)	Case study	20th century	India	The Ambanis	McDonald, Hamish (2010) *Mahabaratha in Polyester: The Making of the World's Richest Brothers and their Feud.* Sydney: University of New South Wales Press.
Morikawa (1992)	Country study	19th–20th centuries	Japan	Large firms, Zaibatsu	Morikawa, Hidemasa (1992) *Zaibatsu: The Rise and Fall of Family Enterprise Groups in Japan.* Tokyo: University of Tokyo Press.
Morikawa (2001)	Country study	19th–20th centuries	Japan	Large firms, Zaibatsu	Morikawa, H. (2001) *A History of Top Management in Japan: Managerial Enterprises and Family Enterprises.* Oxford: Oxford University Press.
Müller (1996)	Country study	19th–20th century	Switzerland	Large family firms in manufacturing	Müller, Margrit (1996) 'Good luck or good management? Multigenerational family control in two Swiss enterprises since the 19th century', *Enterprises et Histoire*, 12: 19–47.
Nie et al. (2009)	Country study	20th century	China	Biographies	Nie, W. and Xin K with Zhang, L. (2009) *Made in China: Secrets of China's Dynamic Entrepreneurs.* Singapore: John Wiley and Sons (Asia).
Ōkōchi (1984)	Comparative study	19th–20th centuries	International	Cases of family firms in different countries	Ōkōchi, Akio and Yasuoka, Shigeaki (eds) (1984) *Family Business in the Era of Industrial Growth: Its Ownership and Management.* Tokyo: University of Tokyo Press.

(Continued)

Appendix 14.1   (Continued)

Author/s	Approach	Area	Period	Keywords	Full reference
Payne (1984)	Country study	18th–20th centuries	United Kingdom	Family firms in Britain	Payne, Peter L. (1984) 'Family business in Britain: an historical and analytical survey', in Ōkōchi, Akio and Yasuoka, Shigeaki (eds), *Family Business in the Era of Industrial Growth: Its Ownership and Management*. Tokyo: University of Tokyo Press, pp. 171–206.
Rose (1993)	Country study	18th–20th centuries	United Kingdom	Family firms in Britain	Rose, Mary (1993) 'Beyond Buddenbrooks: the family firm and the management of succession in nineteenth-century Britain', in J. Brown and M.B. Rose (eds), *Entrepreneurship, Networks and Modern Business*. Manchester: Manchester University Press, pp. 127–143.
Rose (1995)	Literature overview	15th–20th centuries	World	Collection of essays about family firms	Rose, Mary B. (ed.) (1995) *Family Business*. Aldershot: Elgar.
Scranton (1993)	Case study	19th century	United States	Small and medium family firms	Scranton, Phil (1993) 'Build a firm, start another: the Bromleys and family firm entrepreneurship in the Philadelphia region', *Business History*, 35(4): 115–141.
Sluyterman (1997)	Case study	18th–20th centuries	Netherlands	De Kuyper	Sluyterman, Keetie E. (1997) 'Three centuries of De Kuyper: the strength and weakness of a family firm', in M. Dritsas and Gourvish, T., *European Enterprise: Strategies of Adaptation and Renewal in the Twentieth Century*. Athens: Trochalia, pp. 105–122.

Author/s	Approach	Area	Period	Keywords	Full reference
Sluyterman (1993)	Country study	1890–1940	Netherlands	Family firms in the Netherlands	Sluyterman, Keetie E. and Winkelman Helene (1993) 'The Dutch family firm confronted with Chandler's Dynamics of Industrial Capitalism 1890–1940', in Jones, G. and Rose, M.B. (eds), Special Issue Family Capitalism, *Business History*, 35(4): 152–183.
Stiefel (1997)	Case study	1872–1931	Austria	Schenker	Stiefel, Dieter (1997) 'The rise and fall of the house of Schenker: the corporate culture of Schenker Forwarding Company in the three generations of family ownership 1872–1931', in Dritsas, Margarita and Gourvish, Terry (eds), *European Enterprise: Strategies of Adaptation and Renewal in the Twentieth Century*. Athens: Trochalia, pp. 161–173.
Socolow (1978)	Case study	1778–1810	Argentina	Merchant families in Buenos Aires	Socolow, Susan M. (1978) *The Merchants of Buenos Aires 1778–1810*. Cambridge: Cambridge University Press.
White (1956)	Case Study	1647–1877	United States	The Beekmans of New York	White, Philip L. (1956) *The Beekmans of New York in Politics and Commerce 1647–1877*. New York: The New York Historical Society.
Wong (1985)	Country study	20th century	China	Corporate governance and family business	Wong, Siu Lun (1985) 'The Chinese family firm: a model', *British Journal of Sociology*, 36(1): 58–72.
Yasuoka (1984)	Comparative study	20th century	Japan	Comparison between Japanese family firms and those in other countries	Yasuoka, Sigeaki (1984) 'Capital ownership in family companies: Japanese firms compared with those in other countries', in Ōkōchi, Akio and Yasuoka, Shigeaki (eds), *Family Business in the Era of Industrial Growth: Its Ownership and Management*. Tokyo: University of Tokyo Press, pp. 1–32.
Yanagisako (2002)	Case studies	20th century	Italy	Study of small family firms and kinship relations	Yanagisako, Sylvia (2002) *Producing Culture and Capital: Family Firms in Italy*. Princeton, NJ: Princeton University Press.

the historical truth when studying business families is often to double-check information coming from families and companies with information coming from other sources (municipal or national registries, census, notarial archives, parish registers, etc.). This is a time-consuming task, but the results tend to be much more solid than those provided by low-redemption-rate questionnaires.

Putting it rather ambitiously, what business historians can give to family-business studies is, possibly, the same that the founders of History, Herodotus and Thucydides, provided: first, an abundance of doubt and scepticism about the truthfulness provided by oral sources of information, and, second, rigorous methods of research based upon the collection and cross-checking of sources from a wide variety of origins. Business historians who specialise in the study of family businesses have used these two basic methodological pillars of work to unveil the history of entrepreneurial individuals and their families, and how they combine their tangible and intangible resources in particular historical contexts to create, expand or destroy a variety of businesses. In this traditional craft, business historians are firmly connected with, and may give solid foundations to, a recent and vast movement that exists in family-business literature, as indicated in this *Handbook*, which argues for the relevance of shifting the unit of analysis from the family firm to the business family.

NOTES

1 *Ironically*, when Chandler wrote about the supposed decline of family ownership of large corporations, in the 1960s, 56 per cent of the USA's largest corporations were possibly or probably controlled by families, some figures he knew and commented on with skepticism, though in a forgotten footnote at the end of *The Visible Hand* (Chandler 1977).

2 The research is based on interviews to contemporary 108 Catalan firms, and published historical biographies of additional 107 entrepreneurial families in the region (see Fernández Pérez 2013).

REFERENCES

Abels, Jules (1965) *The Rockefeller Billions: The Story of the World's Most Stupendous Fortune*. New York: Macmillan.

Amatori, Franco and Colli, Andrea (2011) *Business History: Complexities and Comparisons*. London: Routledge.

Amsden, Alice (1989) *Asia's Next Giant: South Korea and Late Industrialization*. Oxford: Oxford University Press.

Amsden, Alice (2004) *The Rise of the Rest: Challenges to the West from Late-industrializing Economies*. Cambridge: Cambridge University Press.

Anderson, Michael (1980) *Approaches to the History of the Western Family 1500–1914*. London: MacMillan Press.

Anderson, Ronald G. and Reeb, David M. (2003) 'Founding-family ownership and firm performance: evidence from the S&P 500', *Journal of Finance*, 58(3): 1301–1328.

Arnoldus, Doreen (2002) *Family, Family Firm and Strategy. Six Dutch Family Firms in the Food Industry 1880–1970*. Amsterdam: Free University.

Barca, Fabrizio and Becht, Marco (eds) (2001) *The Control of Corporate Europe*. Oxford: Oxford University Press.

Barker, Theodore C. (1960) *Pilkington Brothers and the Glass Industry*. London: Allen.

Barker, Thomas (1977) *The Glassmakers. Pilkington: The Rise of an International Company 1926–1976*. London: Weidenfeld and Nicolson.

Berghoff, Harmut (2006) 'The end of the family business? The Mittelstand and German capitalism in transition, 1949–2000', *Business History Review*, 80(2): 263–295.

Boyce, Gordon (2010) Language and culture in a Liverpool merchant family firm, 1870–1950, *Business History Review*, 84(1): 1–26.

Burguière, André (1976) 'From Malthus to Max Weber: belated marriage and the spirit of enterprise', in Forster, Robert and Ranum, Orest (eds), *Family and Society: Selections from the Annales*. Baltimore, OH and London: The Johns Hopkins University Press, pp. 237–250.

Butel, Paul (1974) *Les négociants bordelaises, l'Europe et les îles au XVIIIe siècle*. Paris: Aubier-Montaigne.

Carr, William H.A. (1965) *The Du Ponts of Delaware*. London: Frederick Muller.

Carney, Michael (2005) 'Corporate governance and competitive advantage in family-controlled firms', *Entrepreneurship: Theory and Practice*, 29(3): 249–265.

Casey, James (1989) *The History of the Family*. London: Blackwell.

Cassis, Youssef (1997) *Big Business: The European Experience in the Twentieth Century*. Oxford: Oxford University Press.

Chadeau, Emmanuel (1993) 'The large family firm in twentieth century France', *Business History*, 35(4): 184–205.

Chandler, Alfred D. (1991) *Scale and Scope: The Dynamics of Industrial Capitalism*. Cambridge, MA: Harvard University Press.

Chandler, Alfred D. (1977) *The Visible Hand: The Managerial Revolution in American Business*. Cambridge, MA: Harvard University Press.

Channon, Derek F. (1974) *The Strategy and Structure of British Enterprise*. London: Macmillan.

Chapman, Stanley D. (1977) *N.M. Rothschild 1777–1836*. London: NMR and Sons.

Church, Roy (1969) *Kenricks in Hardware: A Family Business 1791–1966*. Newton Abbot: David and Charles.

Church, Roy (1982) 'The transition from family firm to managerial enterprise in the motor industry: an international comparison', in Hannah, Leslie (ed.), *From Family Firm to Professional Management: Structure and Performance of Business Enterprise*. Budapest: Akademiai Kiado.

Church, Roy (1993) 'The family firm in industrial capitalism: international perspectives on hypotheses and history', *Business History*, 35(4): 17–43.

Colli, Andrea (2003) *The History of Family Business 1850–2000*. Cambridge: Cambridge University Press.

Colli, Andrea, Fernández Pérez, Paloma and Rose, Mary (2003) 'National determinants of family firm development? Family firms in Britain, Spain and Italy in the nineteenth and twentieth centuries', *Enterprise and Society*, 4(1): 28–64.

Colli, Andrea and Rose, Mary B. (1999) 'Families and firms: the culture and evolution of family firms in Britain and Italy in the nineteenth and twentieth centuries', *Scandinavian Economic History Review*, 47(1): 24–47.

Colli, A. and Rose, Mary B. (2002) 'Family firms in comparative perspective', in F. Amatori and G. Jones (eds), *Business History Around the World at the Turn of the Century*. Cambridge and New York: Cambridge University Press.

Colli, Andrea and Rose, Mary B. (2007) 'Family business', in Jones, Geoffrey and Zeitlin, Jonathan (eds) (2007) *The Oxford Handbook of Business History*. Oxford: Oxford University Press.

Colli, Andrea, De Jong, Abe and Iversen, Martin (2011) 'European business models', *Business History*, 53(1): Special Issue.

Collier, Peter and Horowitz, David (1976) *The Rockefellers: An American Dynasty*. Ontario: The New American Library.

Colpan, Asli, Hikino, Takashi and Lincoln, James R. (eds) (2010) *The Oxford Handbook of Business Groups*. Oxford: Oxford University Press.

Da Silva Lopes, Teresa (2007) *Global Brands: The Evolution of Multinationals in Alcoholic Beverages*. Cambridge: Cambridge University Press.

Davidoff, Eleonore and Hall, Catherine (1987) *Family Fortunes: Men and Women of the English Middle Class, 1780–1850*. Chicago, IL: The University of Chicago Press.

De Roover, Raymond (1963) *The Rise and Decline of the Medici Bank 1297–1494*. Cambridge, MA: Harvard University Press.

Díaz Morlan, Pablo (2002) *Los Ybarra: Una dinastía de empresarios 1801–2001*. Madrid: Marcial Pons.

Dritsas, Margarita (1997) 'Family firms in Greek Industry during the twentieth century', in Dritsas, Margarita and Gourvish, Terry (eds), *European Enterprise: Strategies of Adaptation and Renewal in the Twentieth Century*.

Dutta, Sudipt (1996) *Family Business in India*. New Delhi: Sage Publications.

Dyas, Gareth and Tanheiser, Heinz (1976) *The Emerging European Enterprise*. London: Macmillan.

European Commission (2009) 'Overview of family-business-relevant issues', November, available at: http://ec.europa.eu/enterprise/policies/sme/files/craft/family_business/doc/familybusiness_study_en.pdf (accessed 26 March 2011).

Faccio, Mara and Lang, Larry P. (2002) 'The ultimate ownership of western European corporations', *Journal of Financial Economics*, 65(3): 365–395.

Fellman, Susanna (2001) 'The professionalisation of management in Finland: the case of the manufacturing sector, 1900–1975', *Scandinavian Economic History Review*, 49(3): 257–274.

Fellman, Susanna, and Leino-Kaukiainen, Pirrko (2006) 'Business or culture? Family firms in the Finnish media business in the 20th century', *Scandinavian Economic History Review*, 54(3): 244–272.

Fernández Moya, Maria (2010) 'A family-owned publishing multinational: the Salvat company (1869–1988)', *Business History*, 52(3): 453–470.

Fernández Pérez, Paloma (2003) 'Reinstalando la empresa familiar en la economía y la historia económica', *Cuadernos de Economía y Dirección de la Empresa*, 17: 45–66.

Fernández Pérez, Paloma (2007) 'Small firms and networks in capital intensive industries: the case of

Spanish steel wire manufacturing', *Business History*, 49(5): 647–668.

Fernández Pérez, Paloma (ed.) (2013), *La profesionalizacion de las empresas familiares*. Madrid: LID.

Fernández Pérez, Paloma and Puig, Núria (2007) 'Bonsais in a wild forest? A historical interpretation of the longevity of large Spanish family firms' *Revista de Historia Económica*, 25(3): 459–497.

Fernández Pérez, Paloma and Puig, Nuria (2009) 'Global lobbies for a global economy: the creation of the Spanish Institute of Family Firms in international perspective', *Business History*, 51(5): 712–733.

Fernández Pérez, Paloma and Puig, Nuria (2010) 'Silent revolution: the internationalization of large Spanish family firms'. Special Issue on internationalization of firms edited by Peter Buckley and John Wilson, *Business History*, 51(3): 462–483.

Fernández Pérez, Paloma and Hamilton, Eleanor (2010) 'Making gender visible in family business: past and present', *História Econômica & História de Empresas*, 13(1): 5–30.

Fernández Pérez, Paloma, and Rose, Mary B. (eds) (2010) *Innovation and Entrepreneurial Networks in Europe*. London: Routledge.

Fernández Pérez, Paloma and Fernández Moya, María (2011) 'Making room for emerging economies: a comparative approach of the largest family businesses in China, Mexico and Brazil', *Globalization, Competition and Governability*, 5(1): 76–93.

Forestier, Albane (2010) 'Risk, kinship and personal relationships in late eighteenth-century West Indian trade: the commercial network of Tobin & Pinney', *Business History*, 52(6): 912–931.

Gies, France and Gies, Joseph (1987) *Marriage and the Family in the Middle Ages*. New York: Harper and Row.

Gomez-Mejia, Luis R., Takács Haynes, Katalin, Núñez-Nickel, Manuel, Jacobson, Kathryn J.L. and Moyano-Fuentes, José (2007) 'Socioemotional wealth and business risks in family-controlled firms: evidence from Spanish olive oil mills', *Administrative Science Quarterly*, 52: 106–137.

Goody, Jack, Thirsk, Joan Thompson, Edward P. (eds) (1976) *Family and Inheritance. Rural Society in Western Europe, 1200–1800*. New York: Cambridge University Press.

Goto, Toshio (2006) 'Longevity of Japanese family firms', in Poutzioris, Panikkos, Smyrnios, Kosmas X. and Klein, Sabine B. (eds), *Handbook of Research on Family Business*. London: Elgar, pp. 517–534.

Gutierrez, Miguel (1999) *Full a full. La indústria paperera de l'Anoia (1700–1998): continuïtat I modernitat*. Barcelona: Publicacions de l'Abadia de Montserrat.

Habbershon, Thimoty G. and Williams, Mary L. (1999) 'A resource-based framework for assessing the strategic advantages of family firms', *Family Business Review*, 12: 1–15.

Hannah, Leslie (2007) 'The divorce of ownership from control from 1900 onwards: re-calibrating imagined global trends', *Business History*, 49(4): 404–438.

Hareven, Tamara K. (1977) *Family and Kin in Urban Communities, 1700–1930*. New York: New Viewpoints.

Hareven, Tamara K. (1978) *Transitions: The Family and the Life Course in Historical Perspective*. New York: Academic Press.

Hareven, Tamara K. and Plakans, Andrejs (eds) (1987) *Family History at the Crossroads*. Princeton, NJ: Princeton University Press.

Harlaftis, Gelina and Theotokas, John (2004) 'European family firms in international business: British and Greek tramp-shipping firms', *Business History*, 46(2): 219–255.

Hedges, James B. (1952) *The Browns of Providence Plantations*, 2 vols. Cambridge, MA: Harvard University Press.

Herr, Richard (1989) *Rural Change and Royal Finances in Spain at the End of the Old Regime*. Berkeley, CA: University of California Press.

Howorth, Carole, Rose, Mary and Hamilton, Eleanor (2006) 'Definitions, diversity and development: key debates in family business research' in Casson, Mark, Yeung, Bernard, Basu, Anuradha, Wadeson, Nigel (eds), *The Oxford Handbook of Entrepreneurship*. Oxford: Oxford University Press, pp. 225–247.

James, Harold (2006) *Family Capitalism: Wendels, Haniels, Falcks and the Continental European Model*. Cambridge, MA: Belknap.

James, Harold (2012) *Krupp: A History of the Legendary German Firm*. Princeton, NJ: Princeton University Press.

Jones, Geoffrey and Khanna, Tharun (2006) 'Bringing history (back) into international business', *Journal of International Business Studies*, 37(4): 453–468.

Jones, Geoffrey and Rose, Mary B. (1993) *Family Capitalism*. London: Frank Cass.

Jones, Geoffrey and Zeitlin Jonathan (2007) *Introduction*, in Jones, Geoffrey and Zeitlin Jonathan (eds), *Oxford Handbook of Business History*. Oxford: Oxford University Press.

Knutsen, Sverre, Rose, Mary B. and Sjögren, Hans (1999) 'Introduction to the special issue Institutions and Business', *Scandinavian Economic History Review*, 47(1): 5–9.

Kobrak, Christopher (2009) 'Family finance: value creation and the democratization of cross-border governance', *Enterprise and Society*, 10(1): 38–89.

Kocka, Jurgen (1971) 'Family and bureaucracy in German industrial management, 1850–1914: Siemens in comparataive perspective', *Business History Review*, 45(2): 133–156.

Kowlek–Folland, Angel (2001) 'Gender and business history', *Enterprise and Society*, 2(1): 1–10.

Kowlek Folland, Angel and Walsh Margaret (2007) 'Women in the service industries: national perspectives', *Business History Review*, 81(3): 421–428.

La Porta, Rafael, Lopez De Silanes, Florencio, Shleifer Andrei and Vishny, Robert (1999) 'Corporate ownership around the world', *Journal of Finance*, 54(2): 471–517.

Landes, David S. (1975) 'Bleichröders and Rothschilds', in Rosenberg, Charles E. (ed.), *The Family in History*. Philadelphia, PA: University of Pennsylvania Press.

Landes, David S. (2006) *Dynasties: Fortunes and Misfortunes of the World's Great Family Businesses*. New York: Viking.

Larsson, Mats, Lindgren, Hakan and Nyberg, Daniel (2008) 'Entrepreneurship and ownership: the long-term viability of the Swedish Bonnier and Wallenberg family business groups', in Fellman, Susanna, Iversen, Martin, Sjögren, Hans and Thue, Lars (eds), *Creating Nordic Capitalism. The Business History of a Competitive Periphery*. London: Palgrave Macmillan.

Levy-Leboyer, M. (1984) 'The large family firm in the French manufacturing industry', in Ōkōchi, Akio and Yasuoka, Shigeaki (eds), *Family Business in the Era of Industrial Growth: Its Ownership and Management*. Tokyo: University of Tokyo Press, pp. 209–233.

Lindgren, Hakan (2002) 'Succession strategies in a large family business group: the case of the Swedish Wallenberg family', paper prepared for the 6th European Business History Association Annual Congress in Helsinki, 22–24 August, 2002.

López-Morell, Miguel and O'Kean, José (2008) 'A stable network as a source of entrepreneurial opportunities: the Rothschilds in Spain, 1835–1931' *Business History*, 50(2): 163–184.

Lubinski, Christina (2011) 'Succession in multi-generational family firms: an explorative study into the period of anticipatory socialization', *Electronic Journal of Family Business Studies*, 5(1–2): 4–25.

Mackie, Robin (2001) 'Family ownership and business survival: Kirkcaldy, 1870–1970', *Business History*, 43(3): 1–32.

McDonald, Hamish (2010) *Mahabaratha in Polyester: The Making of the World's Richest Brothers and their Feud*. Sydney: University of New South Wales Press.

Morck, Randall, (ed.) (2007) *A History of Corporate Governance Around the World: Family Business Groups to Professional Managers*. Chicago, IL and London: The University of Chicago Press.

Morck, Randall K. and Yeung, Bernard Yin (2004) 'Special issues relating to corporate governance and family control', *World Bank Policy Research Working Paper* No. 3406. Available at: http://ssrn.com/abstract=625283.

Morikawa, Hidemasa (1992) *Zaibatsu: The Rise and Fall of Family Enterprise Groups in Japan*. Tokyo: University of Tokyo Press.

Müller, Margrit (1996) 'Good luck or good management? Multigenerational family control in two Swiss enterprises since the 19th century', *Enterprises et Histoire*, 12: 19–47.

Nie, W. and Xin K. with Zhang, L. (2009) *Made in China: Secrets of China's Dynamic Entrepreneurs*. Singapore: John Wiley and Sons (Asia).

Ojala, Jari and Lamberg, Juha-Antti (2006) 'Co-evolution of Institutions and Strategies. Finnish Pulp and Paper Industry 1918–1995', *Nordiske Organisasjonsstudier*, 7(3–4): 53–86.

Ojala, Jari, and Luoma-aho, Vilma (2008) 'Stakeholder relations as social capital in early modern international trade', *Business History*, 50(6): 749–764.

Ōkōchi, Akio and Yasuoka, Shigeaki (eds) (1984) *Family Business in the Era of Industrial Growth: Its Ownership and Management*. Tokyo: University of Tokyo Press.

Owens, Alastair (2002) 'Inheritance and the life-cycle of family firms in the early industrial revolution', *Business History*, 44(1): 21–46.

Pavan, Robert J. (1973) 'Strategies and structures of the Italian enterprises', unpub. Diss., Harvard Business School, Allston, MA.

Payne, Peter L. (1984) 'Family business in Britain: an historical and analytical survey', in Ōkōchi, Akio and Yasuoka, Shigeaki (eds), *Family Business in the Era of Industrial Growth: Its Ownership and Management*. Tokyo: University of Tokyo Press, pp. 171–206.

Penrose, Edith T. (1959) *The Theory of the Growth of the Firm*. New York: John Wiley and Sons.

Piore, Michael and Sabel, Charles F. (1984) *The Second Industrial Divide: Possibilities for Prosperity*. New York: Basic Books.

Puig, Nuria and Fernández Perez, Paloma (2009) 'A silent revolution: the internationalization of large Spanish family firms', *Business History*, 51(3): 462–483.

Rose, Mary (1993) 'Beyond Buddenbrooks: the family firm and the management of succession in nineteenth-century Britain', in Brown, Jonathan and Rose, Mary B.

(eds), *Entrepreneurship, Networks and Modern Business*. Manchester: Manchester University Press, pp. 127–143.

Rose, Mary B. (ed.) (1995) *Family Business*. London: Elgar.

Rumelt, Richard P. (1974) *Strategy, Structure and Economic Performance*. Cambridge, MA: Harvard University Graduate School of Business Administration.

Scranton, Philip (1993) 'Build a firm, start another: the Bromleys and family firm entrepreneurship in the Philadelphia region', *Business History*, 35(4): 115–151.

Sluyterman, Keetie E. (1997) 'Three centuries of De Kuyper: the strength and weakness of a family firm', in M. Dritsas and Gourvish, T., *European Enterprise: Strategies of Adaptation and Renewal in the Twentieth Century*. Athens: Trochalia, pp. 105–122.

Sluyterman, Keetie E. and Winkelman, Hélène (1993) 'The Dutch family firm confronted with Chandler's Dynamics of Industrial Capitalism, 1890–1940', *Business History*, 35(4): 152–183.

Smith, Sheila (1993) 'Fortune and failure: the survival of family firms in eighteenth-century India', *Business History*, 35(4): 44–65.

Socolow, Susan M. (1978) *The Merchants of Buenos Aires, 1778–1810*. Cambridge: Cambridge University Press.

Soskice, David and Hall, Peter A. (2001) *Varieties Of Capitalism: The Institutional Foundations of Comparative Advantage*. Oxford: Oxford University Press.

Stiefel, Dieter (1997) 'The rise and fall of the house of Schenker: the corporate culture of Schenker Forwarding Company in the three generations of family ownership 1872–1931', in Dritsas, Margarita and Gourvish, Terry (eds), *European Enterprise: Strategies of Adaptation and Renewal in the Twentieth Century*. Athens: Trochalia, pp. 161–173.

Stone, Lawrence (1977) *The Family, Sex and Marriage in England 1500–1800*. New York: Harper and Row.

Valdaliso, Jesus M. et al. (2010) *Los orígenes históricos del clúster de la industria marítima en el País Vasco y su legado para el presente*. Donostia: Orkestra-Euko Ikaskuntza.

Villalonga, Belen and Amit, Raphael (2006) 'How do family ownership, control and management affect firm value?', *Journal of Financial Economics*, 80: 385–417.

Ward, John L. (1978) *The Arkansas Rockefeller*. Baton Rouge, LA: Louisiana State University Press.

White, Philip L. (1956) *The Beekmans of New York in Politics and Commerce 1647–1877*. New York: The New York Historical Society.

Whitley, Richard (1999) *Divergent Capitalisms: The Social Structuring and Change of Business Systems*. Oxford: Oxford University Press.

Wong, Siu Lun (1985) 'The Chinese family firm: a model', *British Journal of Sociology*, 36(1): 58–72.

Yasuoka, Sigeaki (1984) 'Capital ownership in family companies: Japanese firms compared with those in other countries', in Ōkōchi, Akio and Yasuoka, Shigeaki (eds), *Family Business in the Era of Industrial Growth: Its Ownership and Management*. Tokyo: University of Tokyo Press, pp. 1–32.

Yanagisako, Sylvia (2002) *Producing Culture and Capital: Family Firms in Italy*. Princeton, NJ: Princeton University Press.

PART 3

Entrepreneurial and Managerial Aspects in Family Business Studies

15

Strategic Content and Process in Family Business

Carlo Salvato and Guido Corbetta

INTRODUCTION

Strategic management is different in family firms. In these organizations, a family exercises significant influence over the firm's crucial decision-making processes and choices (Chua et al., 1999). The uniqueness of family business revolves around the important influence of family in terms of determining the firm's vision and control mechanisms, and the creation of unique resources, capabilities and management action patterns (Chrisman et al., 2008; Chua, Chrisman and Sharma, 1999; Sharma, 2004). This family influence makes the family business unique as it creates patterns of goals, strategies and structures that are often formulated, designed, and implemented in ways that can be radically different from nonfamily firms. These differences may result in either positive or negative effects on organizational outcomes such as competitive advantage and financial performance (Miller and Le Breton-Miller, 2006), non-financial performance and the preservation of socioemotional wealth (Gomez-Mejia et al., 2007; Zellweger and Nason, 2008), environmental stewardship (Berrone et al., 2010; Sharma and Sharma, 2011), and diversification decisions (Gomez-Mejia et al., 2010; Miller et al., 2010). Equally importantly, family influence makes the process of strategic management unique. Although the literature on this dimension of strategy is sparse and fragmented, the way decisions are made, solutions implemented and outcomes determined differs significantly in family vs nonfamily firms. In particular, the pervasive presence of the family in both key and everyday activities, the dense web of relationships across strategic decision makers, and the overlap between family and business activities and identities make the distinction between strategic and operational activities difficult to trace (Chrisman et al., 2005; Corbetta and Salvato, 2012; Miller and Le Breton-Miller, 2006; Ward, 1988). Therefore, the traditional separation between strategy content and strategy process tends to evaporate in family firms, in favor of a view in which strategic content, process and outcomes are entwined.

To better capture this uniqueness, this chapter reviews current research on strategy in family business contexts, illustrating the main strategic issues addressed by the existing literature, and potential future extensions. The chapter includes a discussion of the key features of strategy in family businesses, of the potential sources of competitive advantage and disadvantage, and of different aspects of the strategic development process, and it is informed by previous similar efforts at reviewing and conceptualizing the family business strategy literature (Chrisman et al., 2005; De Massis et al., 2012; Dyer and Sanchez, 1998; Sharma, 2004; Sharma et al., 1997). The chapter also includes an illustration of the potential of a set of previously unused frameworks in understanding strategy and a future research agenda.

The chapter is structured along five sections: (1) a description of the *method* that was followed to single out the 77 family business strategy scientific works on which the chapter is grounded; (2) an *overview* of the key issues, theoretical approaches, methods and outcome variables in family business strategy research, as emerging from the selected studies; (3) an illustration of *key business-level strategic contents* as emerging from the extensive literature review, with a focus on *growth in and around the founder's core business*; (4) an illustration of key corporate-level strategic contents, with a focus on *diversification and expansion from the founder's core business*; (5) a concluding section including *directions for future research*, with a focus on gaps in our understanding of strategic processes in family firms.

AN OVERVIEW OF FAMILY BUSINESS STRATEGY LITERATURE

Given the multiple definitions and varying approaches to strategy (Faulkner and Campbell, 2003), it is difficult to clearly trace the boundaries of the family business strategy field. The approach followed in this chapter incorporated this complexity by following two stages: (a) an objective keyword search aimed at capturing contributions squarely focused on family business strategy. This search yielded a selection of 68 peer-reviewed papers; (b) a subjective open search aimed at including contributions systematically cited as referring to strategy in family business, although lacking a specific keyword indexing. This step yielded nine more articles. The 77 family business strategy papers are illustrated in Appendix 15.1, p. 306. The combined approach adopted in exploring existing works offers a relatively encompassing coverage of current knowledge of strategy and strategic management in family firms. Given the chapter's aim to focus on scholarly strategy research, books and book chapters were explicitly excluded from the structured literature search, and are hence not reported in Appendix 15.1, although some of them are used in the text to strengthen emerging insights.

The 77 selected papers (see Appendix 15.1) offer a number of interesting insights into the most recurring: 'focal topic areas'; 'theoretical approach/es' on which the studies are grounded; 'types of study' (i.e., empirical – qualitative and/or qualitative – or conceptual) and 'methods' adopted in empirical papers; 'outcome measure/s' on which the study is focused. Equally important, reflecting on these works directs attention towards a number of overlooked topics and approaches that may offer potential avenues for future research.

Focal topic areas

In reverse order of frequency, the main focal topic areas of the 77 works are: 'resources' (13), 'international strategies' (11), 'planning' (10), 'strategic content' (10), 'strategic orientation' (9), 'turnaround strategies' (4), 'governance and strategy' (3), 'investment strategies' (3), 'innovation' (2), 'strategic process' (2), and 10 other topics covered by just one article each.

A number of interesting insights emerge from reflecting on these outcomes, besides the wide variety of topics addressed by the surveyed literature. First, following the seminal works on family business special attributes (Tagiuri and Davis, 1996) and 'familiness' (Habbershon and Williams, 1999), the most recurring topic is 'family business resources' (see also Rau, 2014). In line with these early contributions, more recent works have either continued the exploration of family-specific resources (e.g., Habbershon et al., 2003), or explored additional resource-related dimensions such as resources accessible through the family's social capital (e.g., Arregle et al., 2007). Second, international strategies are somewhat surprisingly the second most frequent topic, again prompted by early studies by M.A. Gallo (Gallo and Sveen, 1991; Gallo and Garcia Pont, 1996). Third, although formal planning is the third most frequent topic, very limited attention has been paid to subtler processes of strategy formation (two studies) and strategic thinking (one study), despite the frequent observation in the literature about the peculiar approach to management characterizing family firms (e.g., Bertrand and Schoar, 2006; Carney, 2005). The majority of surveyed planning studies focus on formal planning tools, such as the presence or absence of detailed formal plans. Limited attention is paid to the nuanced practice of planning and strategy making, which has recently emerged as key in understanding what planning actually does and how strategy actually unfolds within organizations (Johnson et al., 2007). Fourth, significant attention has been paid to strategic contents and orientations. Coupled with the amount of work devoted to international strategies, this focus highlights a tendency in the literature to see the uniqueness of family business strategy more in the strategic contents than in the underlying processes. Finally, despite focus on contents, surprisingly little attention has been paid to areas that could significantly discriminate strategic activities of family and non-family firms, such as branding, reputation and identity strategies, or social and environmental strategies.

Theoretical Approaches

The vast majority (63) of works were based on a single theory. In reverse order of frequency:

- *Single-theory* (63): design approach (11), resource-based view (RBV) (9), planning approach (8), international management (7), social embeddedness/network (5), agency theory (4), and 12 approaches that were only covered by one or two works.

What we label the design approach – in line with Mintzberg's definition of the Design school, involving strategy formation as a process of rational conception (Mintzberg et al., 1998) – is the most frequently adopted theoretical lens. However, the most striking insight from this overview is that 63 of the papers are based on 18 different theoretical approaches. This fact may signal both lack of a dominant theoretical lens to investigate and to interpret family business strategies, and openness of the field to incorporate and to adopt different standpoints. Not surprisingly, the design approach and planning theories are the most frequently adopted lens to investigating strategy in family firms, although, with few exceptions, planning approach-based articles trace back to the 1980s and 1990s. More recently – and in line with the significant interest in the topic of resources – the relevance of RBV-related frameworks is growing in explaining family business strategic choices and outcomes.

A number of papers (14) are premised on two – complementary or contrasting – theoretical approaches (see Appendix 15.1). Interestingly, agency theory is often used in combination with other theories to explain strategic behaviors and outcomes, as if agency-based behavior were the baseline model against which alternative theoretical explanations must be contrasted to offer novel and potentially interesting results. RBV (see Rau, 2014) is also commonly coupled with other theories such as social capital and threat rigidity (Staw et al., 1981). However, with the exception of socio-emotional wealth (Gomez-Mejia et al.,

2007, 2010) and Sustainable Family Business Theory (Danes et al., 2009), no theory specific to family business strategy has emerged to explain strategic processes, contents and outcomes.

Type of study and methods

The vast majority of studies are empirical (54), with a prevalence of quantitative (37) over qualitative (16) studies. However, a significant number of works are conceptual (23), and only one study adopts mixed methods. The most common quantitative method is traditional multiple regression, while only a small number of studies feature more advanced methodologies such as panel studies, event-history models or structural equation modeling. The vast majority of papers based on qualitative methods adopt a comparative design, while only three are single-case studies. Finally, conceptual studies are mostly aimed at developing theory, rather than at providing insights for practitioners. Interestingly, 'managerial papers' were all published in the 1990s or earlier, while 'theory development' papers were developed over the last decade, with two exceptions (Habbershon and Williams, 1999; Sharma et al., 1997).

Outcome variables

The 77 works – both empirical and conceptual ones – considered a number of different outcome variables:

- *Single outcomes* (67): international expansion (10); strategic orientations (10); financial performance (9); adoption of planning practices (6); innovation (4); strategic flexibility (3); business exit (2); growth (2); social capital (2); capabilities (1); competitive advantage (7); decision making quality (2); diversification (2); and seven other variables explored by just one study each.
- *Multiple outcomes* (9): acquisition activity and diversification (2); family objectives and financial performance (2); and five other outcomes covered by just one article each.

In contrast with strategic management literature in non-family firms – which is focused almost exclusively on explaining competitive advantage and financial performance – there is a striking variety of explained outcomes. However, it is again interesting to see that content-oriented outcomes prevail (e.g., internationalization and strategic orientation), while family-specific outcome variables are overlooked (e.g., socio-emotional wealth, family reputation and identity, other family-specific goals).

The next sections provide a more detailed illustration of the core knowledge emerging from the review of the selected studies. This overview will be focused on content-related strategy issues, which emerge from the review as those that received most attentions, and that may hence allow to take stock of knowledge cumulated so far. In contrast, a separate section will provide directions for future research revolving around topics that have been entirely or relatively neglected so far and, more importantly, theoretical frameworks and process issues that seem to be significantly missing in extant literature. Before delving in this more detailed analysis, the next section offers an overview of the key features of family firms allowing to both interpret current solidified knowledge on family business strategy, and to guide potential future research directions.

BUSINESS-LEVEL STRATEGIC CONTENT IN FAMILY FIRMS: GROWTH IN AND AROUND THE FOUNDER'S CORE BUSINESS

This section provides an illustration of the main competitive strategies pursued by family firms, as emerging from empirical research on strategic content choices – and their outcomes – in family business (see Appendix 15.1). In line with this research, this section is focused on second- and third-generation family firms, where these peculiarities emerge with more clarity. Focus will hence be on the reasons behind choice of specific competitive strategies, on the features of these strategies, and on the average performance outcomes (Miller et al., 2008). While this section will be structured around firm leadership in focused competitive settings – usually around the core business as defined by the founder's strategy – the next section will address the equally important issues of diversification and growth around the core business, and the conditions for profitable growth strategies of family firms.

In examining the competitive strategies of family firms, the dominant mode is niche strategy (Hitt, Ireland and Hoskisson, 2009), which is often the logical outcome of the cultural and historical pattern followed by the family firm across generation (Colli and Fernández Pérez, 2014). As the studies we selected illustrate, the majority of family firms tend to strive to become leaders in a single or a few products or services, market segments, or geographic markets, or by handling internally a single or a few stages in the entire production chain of their product or service.

A niche strategy is not synonymous with a small enterprise. While it is true that this strategy would rarely allow a firm to grow beyond a certain size, depending on the competitive context focused family firms can reach a respectable size. A niche strategy is common in family firms, as it is financially sustainable with family resources alone. What's more, this strategy leverages certain typical resources of these companies (Sirmon and Hitt, 2003): the family history; the technical and commercial competencies accrued over time; the critical business relationships established by members of the family; long lasting bonds with core collaborators; the partnership approach when dealing with customers and suppliers; and the company's roots in its home territory.

Not all family firms are top performers in their specific business fields. As research indicates, there are a number of prerequisites to success with this strategy (Hitt et al., 2009): (a) the competitive arena is bounded by real barriers that make it difficult for other competitors to gain entry, whatever their size; (b) the competitive arena is bounded in such a way that a small to medium-sized company can maintain a leadership position without

having to grow in size, and without running the risk of attracting bigger competitors; (c) continual significant investments (with respect to company size) are made in research, technology, and commercial competencies, to gain and maintain a leadership position; (d) continual significant investments (with respect to company size) are allocated for communicating the firm's story and conveying the uniqueness of its offering in the competitive arena in question; (e) the family makes the conscious choice to avoid growth initiatives which are not consistent with the leadership strategy within the limited competitive arena in question; (f) the family makes the conscious choice to identify at least some areas for growth. As research suggests, without growth strategic inertia may set in, weakening entrepreneurial influence and dampening the interest in the firm of next-generation family members.

Nice strategy is hence a risky strategy that can be jeopardized by a number of changes if the firm fails to respond to them accordingly. First, customers might simply lose interest in the product offering due to a radical shift in consumption models. A second crisis situation for this strategy arises if the market context in question grows significantly, sparking the interest of other larger competitors who might decide to make their entrance by leveraging on their size. In this case, if the incumbent does not have the financial or managerial resources to keep up on the growth path in its competitive arena, and to deter new competitors from entering, the leadership strategy will become a precarious one. Third, a strategy centered on a narrow competitive scope moves onto dangerous ground with the emergence of 'generational drift' (Gersick et al., 1999). This phenomenon, typical of family firms, occurs as the number of family members rises with every new generation. When this happens, the firm may not be able to generate enough resources to support several different family units. Extant research has addressed the options available to remedy this situation by, for instance, selling the firm (Miller, Steier and Le Breton-Miller, 2003).

CORPORATE-LEVEL STRATEGIC CONTENT IN FAMILY FIRMS: DIVERSIFICATION AND EXPANSION FROM THE FOUNDER'S CORE BUSINESS

This section focuses on a specific strategic-content issue that has recently attracted increasing attention, as the literature in Appendix 15.1 suggests: diversified growth in businesses that are less correlated with the original core. To expand this issue, this section contrasts literature on diversification with recent research on 'habitual and portfolio entrepreneurship' in family firms (Heck and Mishra, 2008; Nordqvist and Melin, 2010; Nordqvist and Zellweger, 2010; Rosa, Howorth and Discua Cruz, 2014), and on 'internationalization'.

Besides leadership in the core business discussed in the previous section, a strategy successfully pursued by myriad family firms is diversification from the founder's core business. This is the strategy of choice for companies which, having secured their strongholds within a narrow competitive context, expand into surrounding areas in terms of geography, market segment, product or service, or value chain (Gomez-Mejia et al., 2010).

In some cases, the decision to grow is the outcome of an assessment of comparative convenience. A variety of objectives can drive an entrepreneurial family to pursue a growth path (Casillas and Moreno, 2010; Davis and Stern, 1988; Harris and Reid, 2008): to reinforce the barriers surrounding their core business; to more adeptly diversify risk (as compared to a strategy with an overly narrow scope); to exploit shared resources and competencies (sales networks or brand building competencies); to minimize the risks of succumbing to organizational inertia or being caught off guard strategically when contending with much larger competitors; to make room for a growing number of family members.

However, in some situations growth is reported to be an important determinant of survival. For example, family firms tend to grow in the following situations (Casillas and Moreno, 2010; Harris and Reid, 2008): when

their average size is smaller than key competitors, and when profitability increases with size; when the sectors they compete in become (or will probably become) concentrated, as far as competitors, customers or suppliers; when fixed investments such as R&D or commercial networks increase (Muñoz-Bullon and Sanchez-Bueno, 2011); when opportunities come up to buy out weaker competitors, to prevent them from ending up in the orbit of other contenders who may be new to the playing field.

The strategy of growing around the founder's core is compatible with the innate qualities of family firms. The growth rate is often calibrated to allow the owner family to keep up with the financial resources required. Management is reinforced by gradually integrating professionals from outside the firm with current family and non-family managers. In addition, when expanding into areas related to its current field of business, family businesses tend to continue to exploit their technical and commercial competencies and leverage critical commercial relationships of family members.

As far as managing the process of gradual diversification, research highlights the following dimensions of successful diversified expansion: (a) family firms choose which areas to enter by determining where it would be simplest to replicate the original business idea; (b) the prevailing pattern among family firms entering new areas is incremental, despite the tendency that companies leading in a given strategic territory have to take success for granted in different areas as well; such a step by step approach (in more or less rapid succession) aims at establishing a stronghold in the new strategic territory before entering yet another one; (c) diversified family firms do not overlook their home territory, which often still accounts for substantial revenues and profitability. Essentially, diversified family firms investigated in these studies apply a *duplication* approach, without ever neglecting growth by *scaling* in the original business; (d) even though firms often enter new territories with investments that start small and gradually increase, sometimes breaking into a new area requires a major change (for example, an acquisition). In these more rare cases, transitions of successful family firms seem to be well-planned and clearly thought out; if the company isn't ready for the acquisition, the deal may even be postponed.

A subject related to diversification that is attracting increasing interest in the literature is that of acquisitions. In many of the examples of diversified growth reported in the literature, external growth was an important path that showed the fastest development (e.g., Corbetta, 2005, 2010; Miller, Le Breton-Miller and Lester, 2010). Companies that took the acquisitions approach also attained the biggest size, with few exceptions. To execute these acquisitions as seamlessly as possible, family firms investigated in recent studies employed specialized teams which monitored business opportunities and, once identified, carried out related transactions (Miller et al., 2010). These companies also made conservative calculations of cost effectiveness. Finally, they revamped their organizations, with an eye to learning from past successes or failures.

As regards internationalization – i.e., diversification into new geographical areas – only owner families with an entrepreneurial mission aimed at establishing a solid, stable international position seem to be able to commit to long-term internationalization strategies (Gallo and Sveen, 1991). A mission of this kind is anchored on the international culture of the owner family, which translates into family members' willingness to do the following: travel; take on the hard work associated with breaking into different foreign countries; show openness and curiosity toward different national and corporate cultures; successors' training in different countries by studying and/or working abroad.

A long-range internationalization strategy often also involves foreign direct investments or equity agreements with other companies (Zahra, 2003). This may present a problem for the owner family: the need to present a solid, transparent capital structure. Lacking this, it would be difficult to build or strengthen the indispensable trust of both foreign firms who will act as partners in the new enterprise, and of lenders who will finance the initiative,

at least in part, with debt capital. Without adequate venture capital, the risk inherent to the entrepreneurial initiative intensifies as the level of indebtedness rises.

DIRECTIONS FOR FUTURE RESEARCH

This final section illustrates some possible avenues for future research in family business strategy, which are synthetically reported in Table 15.1.

The analysis of existing research illustrated in previous sections highlighted a number of gaps and controversies both in understanding strategic contents and strategic processes within family businesses. In particular, little attention has been paid to the family-related micro-foundations of *strategic processes* in family firms. The next section will focus on two possible avenues of future research in family business strategic process: *dynamic capabilities* allowing family firms to develop and sustain competitive advantages over extended periods of time; *neuro-cognitive foundations* of strategic thinking in family firms. In addition, limited attention has also been paid to a number of *strategic content*-related issues that may significantly characterize family business strategies: the impact of *ethics* on the content of strategic choices of family firms and possible effects of *cultural variables* on strategic choices and contents. These will be discussed in the subsequent section. Additional related directions for future research on strategic contents are provided in Table 15.1.

Expanding the Understanding of Strategic Processes in Family Firms

Dynamic Capabilities in Family Firms

In the strategic change literature the capability of successful change is increasingly argued to be directly related to the ability of managing different pairs of dualities, and foremost the dualities within stability and change processes (Farjoun, 2010). This approach is evident in the concept of dynamic capabilities. Dynamic capabilities are interpreted as comprising an element of *stability* – the higher-level routines that play the role of components of dynamic capabilities – allowing *change* in the firm's endowment of resources and capabilities (Eisenhardt and Martin, 2000; Zollo and Winter, 2002).

This view of dynamic capabilities raises several conceptual and practical concerns: as routines (including those composing dynamic capabilities) are based on past experience and repetition: How can they provide a full understanding of change requested by dynamic adaptation? How can they incorporate the intentionality requested to break with existing attitudes and action patterns? How can they determine the creativity and new knowledge needed to envision innovative strategic patterns?

Although balancing stability and change is an inherent feature of family firms, surprisingly no efforts have been devoted to either apply the dynamic capabilities literature to family firms, or to understand how strategic processes of family business may illuminate the open questions in the dynamic capability literature. Observing how several family firms balance stability and change may offer rich insights into how these questions can be answered. The role of key family business actors and the actions they perform is central in determining the dynamism of otherwise relatively inertial entities such as organizational routines and capabilities. While family business attitudes and actions patterns are relatively inertial entities, per se, alterations and experiments intentionally decided by key family business actors may gradually, and at times radically, modify pre-determined courses of action. These alterations are relatively commonplace in non-family firms, where radical changes in ownership (for example through mergers and acquisitions) and management teams (for example when the CEO is changed by controlling owners to determine needed course of action) often determine equally radical strategic changes. However, this radical change is rarely observed in non-family firms without such alterations in ownership and top management.

It is hence more difficult in non-family firms to observe how stability and change can be mutually determined and become a duality, while this may become a fruitful research direction in family firms.

On the opposite – as several examples suggest – in family firms elements of stability may determine change. To understand how this is possible, attention can be directed towards the subjectivity, agency and power exerted by key actors, which have the power to leverage and reinterpret deeply rooted values, beliefs and action patterns. Key questions revolving around the dynamic capabilities concept can only be answered through a micro-foundational project aimed at unveiling the detailed practices followed by different types of family firms in performing strategic action. A strategy-as-practice approach, coupled with methodologies aimed at capturing strategy in action (Johnson et al., 2007) may hence allow to fruitfully address dynamic capabilities in family firms and, in turn, to further illuminate the micro-foundations of dynamic capabilities in any type of firm.

Neuro-cognitive Foundations of Strategic Thinking in Family Firms

The psychological and cognitive foundations of strategy have recently received significant attention as an approach that may enable increasingly deep levels of understanding of strategy processes (Hodgkinson and Healey, 2011). This attention is mirrored by growing interest in the family business field in theories drawn from family psychology (Schlippe and Schneewind, 2014). A specific and often overlooked aspect of cognitive processes is their neuro-cognitive dimension. As a second illustration of process research, viewing controlling families and their members from the perspective of cognitive neuro-science may hence draw attention to the different mental processes followed in strategizing activities by family vs non-family members and by family members in different positions (e.g., owners vs non-owners; active vs non-active; first vs next-generations). Recent studies of

Table 15.1 Selected avenues for future research in family business strategy

Focal topic area	Possible theoretical approach	Possible research questions	Methodological issues
PROCESS: Balancing strategic change and stability	Strategic management: dynamic capabilities approach	How do strategic routines performed by family firms provide a full understanding of change requested by dynamic adaptation? How do family members incorporate in strategic routines the intentionality requested to break with existing attitudes and action patterns? How do strategic routines in family firms determine the creativity and new knowledge needed to envision innovative strategic patterns?	Close investigation of micro-practices performed by family and non-family managers sustaining strategic processes, following approaches drawn from the strategy-as-practice (SAP) field (Johnson et al., 2007).
PROCESS: Cognitive roots of strategic thinking	Cognitive neuroscience; neurocognitive studies	How does brain activity of family vs non-family managers differ in similar business circumstances? How does the brain activity of family members from different generations differ in similar business circumstances? To what extent can differential neural activities explain family- and business-related outcomes?	Neuroimaging studies; behavioural, cognitive and functional magnetic resonance imaging (fMRI) data (Dale, 1999).
PROCESS: Genetic roots of strategic thinking	Quantitative genetic theory; behavioral genetics	To what extent are core strategic attitudes heritable? What is the impact of non-shared environmental factors – vs the shared family environment – in determining core strategic attitudes? What are the consequences for the development of effective strategic processes by next-generation members?	Quantitative genetic modeling techniques (Nicolau et al., 2008).
PROCESS: Socio-cultural roots of strategic thinking	Social and cultural anthropology	How do the symbols and rituals embodied in controlling families affect how family and non-family members of the organization participate in and perform strategic processes? How do different family-specific cultural patterns differently affect strategic processes and performance outcomes of the business entity?	Ethnographic approaches, disciplined field research, systematic observation (Gartner and Birley, 2002).
CONTENT: Ethics and strategic choices	Business ethics; entrepreneurial ethics; stakeholder theory	How do controlling families differ as stakeholders from stockholders of a public company and from other interest bearers in a national or local community? To what extent do ethical principles and behavior differ across the controlling family life-cycle stages, and across individuals in each generation? What is the impact on strategic processes, contents and outcomes?	Cross-cultural samples; multi-level, comparative analysis of stakeholder groups; interviews and archival data for comparative case studies (Hannafey, 2003; Sharma and Sharma, 2011).
CONTENT: The impact of international and local culture on strategic choices	Cultural studies; international management	What are the cultural priorities considered by family firms when contemplating a possible international expansion? What is the role of the cultural values drawn from the home territory in affecting strategies of international expansion? What cultural values inform family business expansion strategies: respecting the past and the territory at all costs, or multi-cultural projects as the basis for sustaining long-term growth processes?	Cross-cultural samples; comparative studies of family and non-family firms in different geographical areas; comparative studies of family firms characterized by different extent of geographical and related cultural expansion (Hall and Nordqvist, 2008).

(Continued)

Table 15.1   (Continued)

Focal topic area	Possible theoretical approach	Possible research questions	Methodological issues
CONTENT: Sociological changes in family composition and their impact on strategic choices	Sociology: the influence of societal context and family system characteristics on strategic choices	To what extent are strategic choices and contents affected by long-term changes in family composition? Under what conditions and how do a family's norms, attitudes and values affect the content of family firms' strategic decisions?	Operationalizing 'family' in line with trends in family composition. Developing more longitudinal study designs allowing dynamic inferences about the effects of family system changes on business choices (Aldrich and Cliff, 2003; Colli, 2012).
CONTENT: Governmental action and strategic choices	Public policy; political philosophy, comparative politics	What is the impact of government action targeting family, succession and taxation issues on family firm strategic behavior? To what extent can scholarship, lobbying, and advocacy groups educate public policy makers in the direction of facilitating the strategic action of family firms?	Methodological pluralism suggested by recent trends in Political Science, i.e., formal modeling techniques coupled with field work and behavioral approaches (Schram and Caterino, 2006).

brain-activity of entrepreneurs compared with matched groups of managers show that entrepreneurs tend to rely more than managers on simple decision-making rules when making strategic choices (Laureiro-Martínez et al., 2011). At the neural level entrepreneurs, more than managers, activate brain regions associated with explorative vs exploitative choice. Activity in these regions correlates with their higher level of routinization in decision-making patterns and with overall outcomes of their choices, and may thus represent the specific neural feature of entrepreneurs' superior ability to innovate.

This approach may allow family business scholars to address intriguing research questions such as: How does the brain activity of family vs non-family managers differ in performing similar strategic thinking processes? How do different generations differ in addressing similar strategic situations? To what extent can differential neural activities explain family- and strategy-related outcomes? In terms of suitable methodologies, neuroimaging experimental studies (Dale, 1999) performed in collaboration with neuro-scientists may open up new patterns

of understanding of family business dynamics.

In addition to dynamic capabilities and cognitive neuroscience, Table 15.1 suggests that fruitful avenues of future research may reside in investigating the impact of *genetic* and *socio-cultural roots* on how family firms perform strategic processes over time, and compared to their non-family counterparts (Nicholson, 2014). Together, these streams of possible research may lay the grounds for a micro-foundational theory of family business strategic processes.

Expanding the Understanding of Strategic Contents in Family Firms

Business Ethics

With few exceptions (e.g., Adams et al., 1996) ethics and social responsibilities have only recently been addressed as possible strategic choices (Déniz-Déniz and Cabrera-Suarez, 2005; Dyer and Whetten, 2006; Perrini and Minoja, 2008). An example of this type of study is Sharma and Sharma's (2011) conceptual work on proactive environmental strategies in family firms. These authors argue that family involvement in business does not only influence the contents of competitive strategies, but also the attitudes, subjective norms and perceived behavioral control that direct a family firm's efforts in undertaking proactive environmental strategies.

In line with these preliminary efforts, future research may be directed at addressing a number of interesting research questions on ethical and socially-responsible strategies, such as: Do controlling families differ as stakeholders from stockholders of a public company and from other interest bearers in a national or local community in terms of socially-responsible strategic orientation? If yes, how and in what direction? To what extent do ethical principles and behavior differ across the controlling family life-cycle stages, and across individuals in each generation? What is the impact of proactive socially-responsible strategies on strategic processes, competitive contents and strategic and financial outcomes?

Besides exploring targeted measures of proactive socially-responsible strategies, future studies should try to develop cross-cultural samples of family firms, and to perform multi-level, comparative analysis of stakeholder groups (Hannafey, 2003). As the focus of this line of research is on the attitudes, perceptions, and beliefs of dominant coalitions of the family firm, and how it is affected by family involvement in business and relationships in the controlling family, it would also be important that data collection captures the heterogeneous standpoints of multiple individuals who form the dominant coalition in family and non-family firms. This would require the identification of these members, the involvement of multiple respondents, and the development of a heuristic for aggregation of responses (Sharma and Sharma, 2011). This would probably make comparative case studies and interview-based – or archival-based – data collection the most suitable research design.

Cultural Effects on Strategic Choices and Contents

Another promising stream of literature on strategic contents may address the impact of different cultural variables on strategic contents, such as family culture and cultural attitudes determined by specific religious, ethnic or industry traditions. Among these attitudes, globalization has attracted attention on cultural attitudes determined by the geographical location of the family, which seem promising in expanding knowledge of strategic processes in family firms. Besides examining the key determinants of the extent of international presence, as extant literature has done, future efforts may be directed at understanding how an international culture emerges in family firms, and how it is in turn affected by other contextual cultural variables.

The international culture of the entrepreneurial family may emerge thanks to the inborn vocation of certain family members, or through the cultural maturity the family gains over time. Here, research attention could be directed towards understanding the impact of an increasing awareness and appreciation of the opportunities that other national cultures may have to offer. The speed of this process may depend on the degree of international openness in the industry where family firms do business. Likewise, the contextual conditions of the family – such as socio-cultural or educational aspects – may also play their part. It would be interesting to investigate, for instance, if the unwillingness of the controlling family to accept non-family managers hampers a demanding internationalization process. For a family business to grow within national borders, sooner or later it has to turn to non-family managers, if for no other reason, because there are simply not enough family members to do the job. This need may arise more rapidly when expanding internationally. There may be different reasons for this that are worth being investigated. For example, non-family managers have certain specific knowledge pertaining to the foreign country in question, or greater geographical distance calls for greater delegation of responsibilities, regardless of modern communication systems.

In addition, it could be interesting to explore whether territorial roots lead to any of the following strategic outcomes: (a) the firm may

Appendix 15.1 Sample of 77 studies in family business strategy

Reviewed works	Focal topic area	Theoretical approach/es	Type of study	Methods (empirical papers)	Main results/contributions	Outcome measure/s
Acquaah (2011)	Network strategies	Social embeddedness/ network	Quantitative (multiple regression)	Sample of 54 family firms from Ghana	The benefit of cost-leadership and differentiation strategies is moderated positively by networking with community leaders, but negatively by networking with political leaders.	Financial performance
Acquaah et al. (2011)	Strategic content	Design approach	Quantitative (multiple regression)	Sample of 122 manufacturing firms in Ghana	Family and non-family firms in Ghana use different manufacturing strategies (delivery vs flexibility) to build competitive strategies and resilience to economic recession.	Strategic flexibility
Altindag et al. (2011)	Strategic orientation	Design approach	Quantitative (multiple regression)	Sample of 130 Turkish family firms	Entrepreneurship orientation and innovation orientation (but not customer and learning orientation) have a positive impact on both growth and financial performance.	Growth and financial performance
Aram and Cowen (1990)	Formal planning	Planning approach	Managerial	n.a.	Formal strategic planning must be coupled with team development to implement the 'strategies-in-use' that ensure the successful growth and adaptability of the company.	Growth and strategic flexibility
Arregle et al. (2007)	Resources	RBV and social capital	Conceptual	n.a.	Four drivers contribute to the development of family social capital (stability of family, interactions, interdependence, closure) that in turn influences the development of organizational social capital.	Social capital
Bhalla et al. (2009)	Ethnic influences on strategy	Design approach	Mixed quantitative-qualitative	76 high-growth UK family firms and in-depth fieldwork on 40 of these	The ethnic origin of the controlling family influences the focus of strategic decision making (focus on planning for profit, on survival, on social processes, on culture), but the adopted strategy paradigm has no impact on growth performance.	Growth
Block (2010)	Turnaround strategies	Corporate reputation	Quantitative (multiple regression)	Standard & Poor's 500	Family ownership negatively impacts the likelihood of deep job cuts, whereas family management has no impact on it.	Downsizing (job cuts)
Blumentritt (2006)	Formal planning	Planning approach	Quantitative (multiple regression)	Sample of 133 US firms	The presence of an active board (board of director or advisory board) is positively related to the use of planning activities (both strategic and succession planning) in family businesses.	Planning practices
Carr and Bateman (2009)	International strategies	RBV and threat rigidity	Quantitative (multiple regression)	Sample of the 65 largest Fortune 500 paired with peer non-family firms	Family firms' 'international configurations' were just as worldwide and profitable as those pursued by comparable non-family firms.	International expansion and financial performance

Reviewed works	Focal topic area	Theoretical approach/es	Type of study	Methods (empirical papers)	Main results/contributions	Outcome measure/s
Cater and Schwab (2008)	Turnaround strategies	Social embeddedness/ network	Qualitative (comparative case studies)	Two comparative case studies of US successful turnarounds	Use of standard turnaround strategies (top-management change, infusion of external management expertise, retrenchment) is moderated by strong ties to the family firm, internal orientation, altruistic motives, and long-term goal orientation.	Turnaround
Chen and Hsu (2009)	Governance and strategy	Agency theory	Quantitative (multiple regression)	Sample of 369 Taiwanese firms	The negative impact of 'family ownership' on 'R&D investment' is reduced when the CEO-chair roles are separated and when more independent outsiders are included in the board.	Innovation
Chirico and Salvato (2008)	Resources	Knowledge-based view and dynamic capabilities	Conceptual	n.a.	Knowledge integration (and resulting dynamic strategic adaptation) in family firms is positively affected by internal social capital and affective commitment to change, and negatively by relationship conflicts.	Capabilities
Chirico et al. (2011)	Franchising strategies	RBV	Conceptual	n.a.	When both franchise parties are family firms a competitive advantage is more likely due to their shared 'familiness'.	Competitive advantage
Chrisman et al. (2009)	Resources	RBV	Quantitative (multiple regression)	Sample of 505 small firms from the US Small business Development Center program	Resource stocks (external relationship, internal relationship, functional skills) have a differential impact on performance (sales growth) depending on family priorities (Continuity, Command, Connection, Community; Miller and Le-Breton Miller, 2005).	Growth
Chrisman et al. (2005)	Theory of the family firm	Agency and RBV	Conceptual	n.a.	The three main developments toward a theory of family business are: (1) gradual convergence in the definition of the family firm; (2) empirical evidence that family involvement affects firm performance; (3) emergence of two strategic management oriented explanations for performance differences: agency theory and RBV.	Financial performance
Chrisman et al. (2003)	Resources	RBV	Conceptual	n.a.	Social responsibility and noneconomic goals are important components of resource-based strategies in family firms.	Family objectives and financial performance
Claver et al. (2007)	International strategies	International management	Qualitative (comparative case studies)	Comparative case studies of six Spanish family firms	In line with predictions of the Uppsala School, family firms follow a gradual path in entering foreign markets. In addition, age, size and generation of the family firm significantly influence international strategic alliances.	International expansion

(Continued)

Appendix 15.1 (Continued)

Reviewed works	Focal topic area	Theoretical approach/es	Type of study	Methods (empirical papers)	Main results/contributions	Outcome measure/s
Craig and Moores (2005)	Formal planning	RBV	Conceptual	Action-research (one company)	Family firms benefit from the adoption of the Balanced Scorecard, which includes the additional dimension of 'familiness' captured by the F-PEC variables.	Planning practices
Craig and Moores (2006)	Innovation	Life-cycle theory	Quantitative (multiple regression)	Sample of 278 Australian family-owned businesses	Established family firms appear to place substantial importance on innovation practices and strategy, and they were found to actively manage and adjust their innovation strategies over time.	Innovation
Daily and Thompson (1994)	Strategic orientation	Design approach	Quantitative (multiple regression)	Sample of US family firms	Strategic posture does not differ based on the ownership structure of the firm, and ownership structure has no effect on either strategic posture or firm growth.	Strategic orientation and growth
Danes, Loy and Stafford (2008)	Formal planning	Quality management	Quantitative (multiple regression)	Sample of 572 US SMEs from 1997 National Family Business Study	Different dimensions of quality management planning practices have a positive impact on multiple dimensions of success.	Growth and family-business congruity
Danes et al. (2009)	Resources	RBV – Sustainable Family Business Theory (SFBT)	Quantitative (multiple regression)	331 US family firms from 1997 National Family Business Study (NFBS)	In the short term, family, human, and financial capital contribute more to success than social capital, while in the long terms, family social capital contributes more to success than human and financial capital combined.	Success perception
Davis and Harveston (2000)	International strategies	International management	Quantitative (multiple regression)	1,078 entrepreneur-led US family firms	Internationalization and growth are positively affected by increased use of the Internet and increased investments in IT.	International expansion
Drozdow and Carroll (1997)	Strategic process	Design approach	Prescriptive	n.a.	Given the dynamism of markets and industries, rather than linking planning to life cycle changes, family firms must see strategic development as ongoing, not generational. Simulation to help old family firms accelerate their strategic processes.	Strategic flexibility
Eddleston et al. (2008)	Resources	Agency and RBV	Quantitative (multiple regression)	Sample of 126 family and non-family US firms	The impact of reciprocal altruism (a family-specific resource) and innovative capacity (a firm-specific resource) on financial performance is moderated by strategic planning and technological opportunities.	Financial performance

Reviewed works	Focal topic area	Theoretical approach/es	Type of study	Methods (empirical papers)	Main results/contributions	Outcome measure/s
Fernández and Nieto (2005)	International strategies	International management	Quantitative (panel study)	Panel of approximately 800 small Spanish family firms	There is a negative relationship between family ownership and internationalization, moderated by the role of generational changeovers and stable relationships with other firms through shareholding or agreements aimed to promote international expansion.	International expansion
Fuentes-Lombardo and Fernández-Ortiz (2010)	International strategies	Alliance management	Qualitative (interviews)	Interviews in 19 family firms in the Spanish wine industry	Higher family orientation decreases the likelihood of setting up strategic alliances that may favor entry in foreign markets.	International expansion
Gallo and Garcia Pont (1996)	International strategies	International management	Quantitative (multiple regression)	Sample of 57 Spanish firms	Multigenerational FBs show the highest levels of internationalization. Internationalization is fostered by a number of factors. Among them, managerial attitudes are the strongest predictors.	International expansion
Gallo and Sveen (1991)	International strategies	Design approach	Qualitative (interviews)	Experience, literature review, interviews	Family firms are slower in internationalizing. To improve internationalization processes they should leverage facilitating factors inherent in the company's strategy, organizational structure, culture, and developmental stage.	International expansion
George et al. (2005)	International strategies	International management	Quantitative (multiple regression)	889 Swedish SMEs	CEO and TMT ownership decrease scale and scope of internationalization. Institutional ownership increases scale but not scope.	International expansion
Gomez-Mejia et al. (2010)	Strategic content	Socioemotional wealth	Quantitative (multiple regression)	Sample of 360 firms, 160 of them being family-controlled and the rest (200) non-family-controlled	Family firms diversify less both domestically and internationally than non-family firms, although diversification increases with business risk. Their diversification strategies tend to opt for domestic rather than international diversification, and for regions that are 'culturally close'.	Diversification
Gomez-Mejia et al. (2007)	Strategic content	Socioemotional wealth	Quantitative (panel study)	Population of 1,237 family-owned olive oil mills in Southern Spain	To avoid the loss of their socioemotional wealth, family firms are willing to accept a significant risk to their performance, but they also avoid business decisions that may aggravate such risk.	Socioemotional wealth

(Continued)

Appendix 15.1 (Continued)

Reviewed works	Focal topic area	Theoretical approach/es	Type of study	Methods (empirical papers)	Main results/contributions	Outcome measure/s
Graves and Thomas (2008)	International strategies	International management	Qualitative (comparative case studies)	Comparative study of 8 Australian small family firms	The three key determinants of the internationalization paths taken by investigated family firms are the level of commitment toward internationalization; the financial resources available; the ability to commit and use those financial resources to develop the required capabilities.	International expansion
Gudmunson et al. (1999)	Strategic orientation	Design approach	Quantitative (factor analysis)	Sample of 418 firms in midwestern US state	Family and non-family businesses do not differ in their strategic orientations captured by using Miles and Snow's strategic typology.	Strategic orientations
Habbershon and Williams (1999)	Resources	RBV	Conceptual	n.a.	The bundle of resources that result from family involvement are identified as the distinctive 'familiness' of the family firm. According to RBV, 'familiness' has the potential to provide a sustainable competitive advantage.	Competitive advantage
Habbershon et al. (2003)	Resources	RBV	Conceptual	n.a.	The systemic relationship of resources and capabilities is a source of advantage or constraint to the performance outcomes for family-influenced firms.	Competitive advantage
Harris and Ogbonna (2007)	Strategic control	Agency theory	Qualitative (single case)	UK family firm	Despite closely held ownership, the (family and non-family) management of the firm enjoys strategic control over the firm.	Strategic control
Harris et al. (1994)	Strategic content	Design approach	Prescriptive	n.a.	The strategic management process is similar for both non-family businesses and family businesses. However, the element of family business does affect strategy formulation and implementation.	n.a.
Hoffman et al. (2006)	Resources	Social embeddedness/ network	Conceptual	n.a.	Family capital (a special type of social capital) affects competitive advantage and may hence explain family firms' superior performance.	Competitive advantage
Ibrahim et al. (2008)	Governance and strategy	Design approach and governance	Conceptual	n.a.	Literature review (on planning and strategic management, in particular) reveals that planning is key to FB performance, proposing avenues for future research.	n.a.

Reviewed works	Focal topic area	Theoretical approach/es	Type of study	Methods (empirical papers)	Main results/contributions	Outcome measure/s
Jain and Muthukumar (2010)	Strategic content	International management	Qualitative (single case)	Case study of an Indian family-owned conglomerate	Description of the firm's brand makeover strategy aimed at keeping up with changing customer demographics and increasing focus on international markets.	International expansion
Kashmiri and Mahajan (2010)	Strategic content	Brand identity theory	Quantitative (panel study)	130 publicly listed US family firms over a five-year period (2002–2006)	Compared to non-family-named (NFN) family-named (FN) family firms have: significantly higher levels of corporate citizenship and representation of their customers' voice in the top management team; greater emphasis on value appropriation vs value creation; higher ROA; superior performance partially mediated by their higher corporate citizenship and strategic emphasis.	Financial performance
Kelly et al. (2000)	Governance and strategy	Social embeddedness/ network	Conceptual	n.a.	The family firm's founder has a strong impact on strategic management through influence on top management group and the firm's strategic values, goals and behavior, and the interaction of the firm with the environment.	Family objectives and financial performance
Kim et al. (2004)	Strategic content	Life-cycle theory	Qualitative (archival)	Analysis of secondary data on 19 family conglomerates from different countries	Nine different drivers affect the emergence and evolution of Family Conglomerates (FCs), with different intensity depending on the FC's life-cycle stage.	Diversification
Le Breton-Miller and Miller (2006)	Investment strategies	Design approach and governance	Conceptual	n.a.	Concentrated ownership, lengthy tenures, and profound business expertise prompt some family-controlled businesses (FCBs) to invest deeply in the future of the firm, hence creating capabilities that are sustainable.	Competitive advantage
Lyles et al. (1993)	Formal planning	Planning approach	Quantitative (multiple regression)	188 small independent firms from a midwestern US state	There are significant differences between formal planners and non-formal planners in their emphasis on dimensions of strategic decision-making and in the range of strategic choices made and financial results.	Financial performance
Mazzola et al. (2008)	Formal planning	Planning approach	Qualitative (comparative case studies)	Nine Italian family firms	Involving next-generation family members in the planning process benefits their developmental process by: providing them with crucial tacit business knowledge and skills; facilitating interpersonal work relationships with incumbents; building their credibility and legitimacy.	Succession

(Continued)

Appendix 15.1 (Continued)

Reviewed works	Focal topic area	Theoretical approach/es	Type of study	Methods (empirical papers)	Main results/contributions	Outcome measure/s
McCann et al. (2001)	Competitive strategies	Design approach	Quantitative (analysis of variance)	Sample of 231 Washington State family businesses	Firms categorized as Prospector firms reported more gains in their current market position than all other strategic types and were more likely to develop new quality products and services and career development plans for non-family employees.	Innovation
Micelotta and Raynard (2011)	Branding strategies	Brand identity theory	Qualitative (comparative case studies)	Websites of 92 of the world's oldest family firms	Family firms adopt different branding strategies to communicate the familial component of their businesses: family preservation, family enrichment, and family subordination strategies.	Strategic orientations
Miller and Le Breton-Miller (2006)	Strategic content	Configuration theory	Conceptual	n.a.	The configurational view allows to explain differences between large successful and failing family businesses, by addressing gaps between their priorities and practices.	Financial performance
Miller, Le Breton-Miller and Lester (2010)	Acquisitions and diversification	Agency and family business perspectives	Quantitative (panel study)	Fortune 1000	Family ownership is inversely related to the number and dollar volume of acquisitions. The propensity to make diversifying acquisitions increases with the level of family ownership.	Acquisition activity and diversification
Miller et al. (2011)	Strategic content	Agency and identity theory	Quantitative (panel study)	Fortune 1000	Family owners and CEOs tend to pursue strategies of conservation. Lone founders tend to embrace strategies of growth. Family founders and founder-executives blend both orientations.	Strategic orientations
Moog et al. (2011)	Strategic orientation	Design approach	Qualitative (comparative case studies)	Six comparative case studies	The investigation of familys' entrepreneurial orientation (EO), family orientation (FO), and entrepreneurial family strategic orientation (EFSO) shows that owners highlight autonomy, market strategies, and local community responsibility.	Strategic orientations
Mulholland (1997)	Culture	Cultural management	Quantitative (multiple regression)	Sample of family firms from different ethnicities	The business culture embedded in the shared class background of family entrepreneurs is the best predictor of their strategic approach to the enterprise (entrepreneurial, managerial or preservation strategies). This particular business culture results from the practice of creating, managing and sustaining family capitalism as an expression of middle class social attributes, more than of specific ethnicities.	Strategic orientations

Reviewed works	Focal topic area	Theoretical approach/es	Type of study	Methods (empirical papers)	Main results/contributions	Outcome measure/s
Muñoz-Bullon and Sanchez-Bueno (2011).	Investment strategies	Agency theory	Quantitative (multiple regression)	736 Canadian publicly-listed firms	Publicly-traded family firms in Canada record lower R&D intensity compared with non-family firms.	Innovation
Mustakallio et al. (2002)	Strategic process	Agency and social theories of governance	Quantitative (SEM)	192 family firms in Finland	Different governance mechanisms (i.e., based on formal or social controls) have different impacts on the quality of strategic decision making.	Decision making quality
O'Regan et al. (2010)	Strategic thinking (vs planning)	Strategic thinking theory	Qualitative (comparative case studies)	20 UK family firms	Second and third-generation family firms differ in how they perform strategic thinking activities.	Decision making quality
Pearson et al. (2008)	Resources	RBV and social capital	Conceptual	n.a.	Identification of specific behavioral and social resources that constitute familiness and social capital in family firms.	Social capital
Pistrui et al. (2010)	Strategic orientation	Design approach	Quantitative (panel study)	Random sample of 414 family vs non-family firms	The long-term strategy and culture of family-based entrepreneurial ventures are influenced by a Trans-generational Family Effect (TFE), which enhances vision and wealth creation throughout generation in family businesses.	Strategic orientations
Pittino and Visintin (2009)	Strategic content	Configuration theory	Quantitative (cluster and anova)	141 small Italian family firms	Generation of leadership, succession processes, ownership profile and functional specialization explain family SME's choice among Miles and Snow's strategic configurations.	Strategic orientations
Rue and Ibrahim (1996)	Formal planning	Planning approach	Quantitative (descriptive statistics)	128 small family owned US firms	The study performs a descriptive analysis of the planning practices of a small sample of family SMEs.	Planning practices
Salvato and Melin (2008)	Resources	Social embeddedness/ network	Qualitative (comparative case studies)	4 Italian and Swiss family firms	Family firms create financial value over generations through their ability to renew and to reshape their social interactions within and outside the controlling family.	Financial performance
Salvato et al. (2010)	Turnaround strategies	Commitment escalation and de-commitment	Qualitative (single case)	One large Italian family firm	The paper develops an inductive model describing how inhibitors of exit from the founder's business can be transformed into facilitators of change, through the central role of a 'family champion of continuity'.	Business exit

(Continued)

Appendix 15.1 (Continued)

Reviewed works	Focal topic area	Theoretical approach/es	Type of study	Methods (empirical papers)	Main results/contributions	Outcome measure/s
Scholes et al. (2010)	Investment strategies	Finance	Quantitative (multiple regression)	Sample of 104 MBOs/ MBIs across Europe	There is greater scope for efficiency gains and growth when: the founder was present at time of buyout; no managers with equity stakes or non-executive directors were employed pre-buyout; the private equity investor and management were involved in succession planning. There are efficiency gains in firms with no equity holding of non-family managers pre-buyout.	Financial performance
Sharma and Manikutty (2005)	Turnaround strategies	Commitment escalation and de-commitment	Conceptual	n.a.	A combination of past successes, emotional attachments, and path dependencies can lead to extensive inertia toward divestment in family firms.	Business exit
Sharma et al. (1997)	Formal planning	Planning approach	Conceptual	n.a.	Conceptual model suggesting how different family influences (family interests, goals and culture, succession and intergenerational issues and sibling relationships, inclusion of family and non-family members) affect the different phases of the strategic process.	Planning practices
Sirmon and Hitt (2003)	Resources	RBV	Conceptual	n.a.	Having the appropriate resources is not enough to achieve a competitive advantage: family firms should also manage available resources through resource inventory, resource bundling, and resource leveraging.	Competitive advantage
Sirmon et al. (2008)	Innovation	RBV and threat rigidity	Quantitative (multiple regression)	Multiple regression on a sample of 2,531 French SMEs	Family-influenced firms are less rigid in their response to competitive threats than non-family firms, as they reduce R&D expenditure and internationalization less.	Financial performance
Tagiuri and Davis (1996)	Resources	RBV	Prescriptive	n.a.	Family firms have unique (positive/negative) attributes due to simultaneous roles, shared identity, lifelong common history, emotional involvement, private language, mutual awareness and privacy, unique meaning of family company.	Competitive advantage
Tokarczyk et al. (2007)	Strategic orientation	RBV	Qualitative (comparative case studies)	8 family owned US firms	Familiness dimensions such as strategic focus, customer orientation, family relationships, and operational efficiency, significantly contribute to a propensity for execution of an effective market orientation.	Strategic orientations

Reviewed works	Focal topic area	Theoretical approach/es	Type of study	Methods (empirical papers)	Main results/contributions	Outcome measure/s
Trostel and Nichols (1982)	Strategic orientation	Agency theory	Quantitative (matched pairs)	23 matched pairs US privately- and publicly-held firms	Ownership form (private vs public) has significant implications in strategic content and process.	Strategic orientations
Tsang (2002)	International strategies	International management Organizational learning	Qualitative (comparative case studies)	10 Chinese family firms	Chinese family businesses have distinctly different approaches to dealing with FDIs as compared with non-family businesses.	Internationalization process
Upton et al. (2001)	Formal planning	Planning approach	Quantitative (descriptive statistics)	65 fast-growth family firms	Family firms prepare detailed formal plans, share information with employees, describe their business strategy as 'high-quality producer' and adopt a first-mover or early-follower approach.	Planning practices
Ward (1988)	Formal planning	Planning approach	Prescriptive	n.a.	Overview of the possible roles of planning in facilitating and improving family business strategy.	Planning practices
Zahra (2003)	International strategies	Stewardship theory	Quantitative (multiple regression)	409 US manufacturing firms	Due to the prevalence of stewardship orientation, family ownership and involvement in the firm, as well as the interaction of this ownership with family involvement, are significantly and positively associated with internationalization.	International expansion
Zahra et al. (2008)	Strategic orientation	Stewardship theory	Quantitative (multiple regression)	248 US manufacturing firms	Family firm's culture of stewardship and commitment to the business is positively associated with its strategic flexibility–the ability to pursue new opportunities and respond to threats in the competitive environment.	Strategic flexibility
Zellweger (2007)	Strategic orientation	Finance	Conceptual	n.a.	Family firms display a longer time horizon and, in particular, a longer CEO tenure and the goal of long-term independence and within-family succession.	Strategic orientations

give priority to convenience, instead of focusing on the need to continually take the initiative, which is the key to every success story of growth. When the home territory becomes a safe haven providing refuge for the company, potentially lucrative market opportunities are lost; (b) the firm may give priority to respecting the past and the territory at all costs. This respect impedes any multi-territorial projects, which are essential to sustaining long-term growth processes; (c) the firm may give in to conformism, which precludes any sort of 'contamination' with cultures from other places (Hall, Melin and Nordqvist, 2001). Instead, the key to the success of many family firms is their ability to gradually take on managers from other areas (Hall and Nordqvist, 2008). To complement and contrast these somewhat negative effects of territorial roots on strategy, research may also be directed towards investigating the potentially higher ability some family firms may have in understanding and interpreting foreign cultures when expanding abroad, due to their deeper roots in the local territory of origin.

In terms of methods, research on the cultural roots of strategic choices should adopt cross-cultural samples, performing comparative studies of family and non-family firms in different geographical areas or characterized by different extent of geographical and related cultural expansion (Hall and Nordqvist, 2008).

In addition to business ethics and cultural effects, Table 15.1 suggests that fruitful avenues of future research may reside in investigating sociological changes in family composition and their impact on strategic choices, or the impact of governmental action on strategic choices.

CONCLUSION

This chapter offered an overview of strategic management in family firms from a scholarly perspective. The key aim was to highlight the unique nature of strategic management in family firms, to illustrate dimensions along which such uniqueness can be interpreted, and to offer guidelines for future research efforts. Illustrated topics revolved around the traditional distinction in strategic management

of content, process and outcome dimensions. Yet the pervasive presence of the controlling family in all firm processes and activities tends to blur the boundaries traced by traditional strategic management literature across these dimensions. It is difficult, in family firms, to neatly separate what is strategic from what is operational, what is content from what is process, and what is strategy from what is its outcomes. The centrality of the family and the density of relationships among family members, and between family and non-family members, create a special environment in which a number of traditional assumptions of strategic management do not always neatly hold. As the directions for future research developed in the last section suggest, to avoid getting lost in this complexity, research focus should be on the family itself and on the specific practices of interpersonal action and interaction between and among persons within and across the controlling family. As recent analysis suggests (e.g., Salvato and Aldrich, 2012), developing works in which family factors figure more prominently in driving conceptual models and empirical investigations is the key to achieving interesting family business research.

REFERENCES

Acquaah, M. (2011). Business strategy and competitive advantage in family businesses in Ghana: The role of social networking relationships. *Journal of Developmental Entrepreneurship*, 16(1): 103–126.

Acquaah, M., Amoako-Gyampah, K. and Jayaram, J. (2011). Resilience in family and nonfamily firms: An examination of the relationships between manufacturing strategy, competitive strategy and firm performance. *International Journal of Production Research*, 49(17): 5527–5544.

Adams, J., Taschian, A. and Shore, T. (1996). Ethics in family and nonfamily owned firms: An exploratory study. *Family Business Review*, 9: 157–170.

Aldrich, H.E. and Cliff, J.E. (2003). The pervasive effect of family on entrepreneurship: Toward a family embeddedness perspective. *Journal of Business Venturing*, 18: 573–596.

Altindag, E., Zehir, C. and Acar, A.Z. (2011). Strategic orientations and their effects on firm performance in Turkish family owned firms. *Eurasian Business Review*, 1(1): 18–36.

Aram, J.D. and Cowen, S.S. (1990). Strategic planning for increased profit in the family owned business. *Long Range Planning*, 23: 63–70.

Arregle, J.-L., Hitt, M.A., Sirmon, D. and Very, P. (2007). The development of organizational social capital: Attributes of family firms. *Journal of Management Studies*, 44(1): 73–95.

Bennedsen, M., Meisner, N., Perez-Gonzalez, F. and Wolfenzon, D. (2007). Inside the family firm: The role of families in succession decisions and performance. *Quarterly Journal of Economics*, 20(2), 647–691.

Berrone, P., Cruz, C., Gomez-Mejia, L.R. and Larraza-Kintana, M. (2010). Socioemotional wealth and organizational response to institutional pressures: Do family controlled firms pollute less? *Administrative Science Quarterly*, 55: 82–113.

Bertrand, M. and Schoar, A. (2006). The role of family in family firms. *Journal of Economic Perspectives*, 20(2): 73–96.

Bhalla, A., Lampel, J., Henderson, S. and Watkins, D. (2009). Exploring alternative strategic management paradigms in high-growth ethnic and non-ethnic family firms. *Small Business Economics*, 32(1): 77–94.

Block, J. (2010). Family management, family ownership, and downsizing: Evidence from S&P 500 firms. *Family Business Review*, 23(2): 109–130.

Blumentritt, T. (2006). The relationship between boards and planning in family businesses. *Family Business Review*, 19(1): 65–72.

Carney, M. (2005). Corporate governance and competitive advantage in family-controlled firms. *Entrepreneurship Theory & Practice*, 29(3): 249–265.

Carr, C. and Bateman, S. (2009). International strategy configurations of the world's top family firms. *Management International Review*, 49(6): 733–758.

Casillas, J.C. and Moreno, A.M. (2010). The relationship between entrepreneurial orientation and growth: The moderation role of family involvement. *Entrepreneurship & Regional Development*, 22: 265–291.

Cater, J. and Schwab, A. (2008). Turnaround strategies in established small family firms. *Family Business Review*, 21(1): 31–50.

Chen, H. and Hsu, W. (2009). Family ownership, board independence and R&D investment. *Family Business Review*, 22(5): 347–362.

Chirico, F. and Salvato, C. (2008). Knowledge integration and dynamic organizational adaptation in family firms. *Family Business Review*, 21(12): 169–181.

Chirico, F., Ireland, R.D. and Sirmon, D.G. (2011). Franchising and the family firm: Creating unique sources of advantage through 'familiness'. *Entrepreneurship Theory & Practice*, 35(3): 483–501.

Chrisman, J., Chua, J. and Kellermanns, F. (2009). Priorities, resource stocks, and performance in family and non family firms. *Entrepreneurship: Theory & Practice*, 33(3): 739–760.

Chrisman, J.J., Chua, J.H. and Sharma, P. (2005). Trends and directions in the development of a strategic management theory of the family firm. *Entrepreneurship Theory & Practice*, 29(5): 555–575.

Chrisman, J.J., Chua, J.H. and Zahra, S.A. (2003). Creating wealth in family firms through managing resources: Comments and extensions. *Entrepreneurship: Theory and Practice*, 27(4): 359–365.

Chrisman, J., Steier, L.P. and Chua, J. (2008). Toward a theoretical basis for understanding the dynamics of strategic performance in family firms. *Entrepreneurship: Theory & Practice*, 32(6): 935–947.

Chua, J.H., Chrisman, J.J. and Sharma, P. (1999). Defining the family business by behavior. *Entrepreneurship: Theory and Practice*, 23: 19–39.

Claver, E., Rienda, L. and Quer, D. (2007). The internationalisation process in family firms: Choice of market entry strategies. *Journal of General Management*, 33(1): 1–14.

Colli, A. (2012). Contextualizing performances of family firms: The perspective of business history. *Family Business Review*, 25: 243–257.

Colli, A. and Fernández Pérez, P. (2014). Business history and family firms. In L. Melin, M. Nordqvist and P. Sharma (eds), *The SAGE Handbook of Family Business*. London: Sage.

Corbetta, G. and Salvato, C. (2012). *Strategies for Longevity in Family Firms: A European Perspective*. Basingstoke: Palgrave-Macmillan.

Craig, J. and Moores, K. (2005). Balanced scorecards to drive the strategic planning of family firms. *Family Business Review*, 18(2): 105–122.

Craig, J.B.L. and Moores, K. (2006). A 10-year longitudinal investigation of strategy, systems and environment on innovation in family firms. *Family Business Review*, 19(1): 1–10.

Daily, C. and Thompson, S. (1994). Ownership structure, strategic posture, and firm growth: An empirical examination. *Family Business Review*, 7(3): 237–249.

Dale, A.M. (1999). Optimal experimental design for event-related fMRI. *Human Brain Mapping*, 8: 109–114.

Danes, S.M., Loy, J.T. and Stafford, K. (2008). Business planning practices of family-owned firms within a quality framework. *Journal of Small Business Management*, 46(3): 395–421.

Danes, S.M., Stafford, K., Haynes, G. and Amarapurkar, S.S. (2009). Family capital of family firms: Bridging human, social and financial capital. *Family Business Review*, 22(3): 199–215.

Davis, P. S. and Harveston, P. D. (2000). Internationalization and organizational grow: The impact of internet usage and technology involvement among entrepreneur-led family businesses. *Family Business Review*, 18(1): 107–120.

De Massis, A., Sharma, P., Chua, J.H. and Chrisman, J.J. (2012). *Family business studies. An annotated bibliography*. Cheltenham: Edward Elgar.

Déniz-Déniz, M.C. and Cabrera-Suarez, K. (2005). Corporate Social Responsibility and Family Business in Spain. *Journal of Business Ethics*, 56: 27–41.

Drozdow, N. and Carroll, V.P. (1997). Tools for strategy development in family firms. *Sloan Management Review*, 39(1): 75–88.

Dyer, G.W. and Sanchez, M. (1998). Current state of family business theory and practice as reflected in the Family Business Review 1988–1997. *Family Business Review*, 11(3): 287–295.

Dyer, G.W. and Whetten, D.A. (2006). Family firms and social responsibility: Preliminary evidence from the S&P500. *Entrepreneurship: Theory and Practice*, 30(4): 785–802.

Eddleston, K.A., Kellermanns, F.W. and Sarathy, R. (2008). Resource configuration in family firms: Linking resources, strategic planning and technological opportunities to performance. *Journal of Management Studies*, 45(1): 26–50.

Eisenhardt, K.M. and Martin, J.A. (2000). Dynamic capabilities: What are they? *Strategic Management Journal*, 21: 1105–1121.

Farjoun, M. (2010). Beyond dualism: Stability and change as a duality. *Academy of Management Review*, 35(2): 202–225.

Faulkner, D.O. and Campbell, A. (eds) (2003). *The Oxford Handbook of Strategy*. Oxford: Oxford University Press.

Fernández, Z. and Nieto, M.J. (2005). Internationalization strategy of small and medium-sized family businesses: Some influential factors. *Family Business Review*, 18(1): 77–89.

Fuentes-Lombardo, G. and Fernández-Ortiz, R. (2010). Strategic alliances in the internationalization of family firms: An exploratory study on the Spanish wine Industry. *Advances in Management*, 3(6): 45–54.

Gallo, M.A. and Garcia Pont, C. (1996). Important factors in family business internationalization. *Family Business Review*, 9: 45–59.

Gallo, M.A. and Sveen, J. (1991). Internationalizing the family business: Facilitating and restraining forces. *Family Business Review*, 4(2): 181–190.

Gartner, W.B. and Birley, S. (2002). Introduction to the special issue on qualitative methods in entrepreneurship research. *Journal of Business Venturing*, 17(5): 387–395.

George, G., Wiklund, J. and Zahra, S.A. (2005). Ownership and the internationalization of small firms. *Journal of Management*, 31(2): 210–233.

Gersick, K.E., Davis, J.A., McCollom Hampton, M.E. and Lansberg, I. (1997). *Generation to Generation: Lifecycles of Family Business*. Boston, MA: Harvard Business School Press.

Gomez-Mejia, L.R., Makri, M. and Larraza-Kintana, M. (2010). Diversification decisions in family-controlled firms. *Journal of Management Studies*, 47(2): 223–252.

Gomez-Mejia, L.R., Takacs-Haynes, K., Nuñez-Nickel, M., Jacobson, K.J.L. and Moyano-Fuentes, J. (2007). Socioemotional wealth and business risks in family-controlled firms: Evidence from Spanish olive oil mills. *Administrative Science Quarterly*, 52(1): 106–137.

Graves, C. and Thomas, J. (2008) Determinants of the internationalization pathways of family firms: An examination of family influence, *Family Business Review*, 21(2): 151–167.

Gudmunson, D., Hartman, E.A. and Tower, C.B. (1999). Strategic orientation: Differences between family and nonfamily firms. *Family Business Review*, 12: 27–39.

Habbershon, T. and Williams, M. (1999). A resource-based framework for assessing the strategic advantages of family firms. *Family Business Review*, 12: 1–25.

Habbershon, T.G., Williams, M.L. and McMillan, I.C. (2003). A unified systems perspective of family firm performance. *Journal of Business Venturing*, 18(4): 451–465.

Hall, A. and Nordqvist, M. (2008). Professional management in family businesses: Extending the current understanding. *Family Business Review*, 11(1): 51–69.

Hall, A., Melin L. and Nordqvist, M. (2001). Entrepreneurship as radical change in the family business: The role of cultural patterns. *Family Business Review*, 14(3): 193–208.

Hannafey, F.T. (2003). Entrepreneurship and ethics: A literature review. *Journal of Business Ethics*, 46: 99–110.

Harris, L.C. and Ogbonna, E. (2007). Ownership and control in closely-held family-owned firms: An exploration of strategic and operational control. *British Journal of Management*, 18(1): 5–26.

Harris, R. and Reid, R. (2008). Barriers to growth in family-owned smaller businesses. In Barrett, R. and Mayson (eds), *International Handbook of Entrepreneurship and HRM*. Cheltenham, UK: Edward Elgar. 260–284.

Harris, R., Martinez, J. and Ward, J. (1994). Is strategy different for the family-owned business? *Family Business Review*, 7(2): 159–174.

Heck, R.K.Z. and Mishra, C.S. (2008). Family entrepreneurship. *Journal of Small Business Management*, 46(3): 313–316.

Hitt, M.A., Ireland, D. and Hoskisson, R.E. (2009). *Strategic management concepts*. Mason, OH: Thomson.

Hodgkinson, G.P. and Healey, M.P. (2011). Psychological foundations of dynamic capabilities: Reflexion and reflection in strategic management. *Strategic Management Journal*, 32: 1500–1516.

Hoffman, J., Hoelscher, M. and Sorenson, R. (2006). Achieving sustained competitive advantage: A family capital theory. *Family Business Review*, 19(2): 135–145.

Ibrahim, N., Angelidis, J.P. and Parsa, F. (2008). Strategic management of family businesses: Current findings and directions for future research. *International Journal of Management*, 25(1): 95–110.

Jain, S. and Muthukumar, R. (2010). The Godrej Group: An Indian family-owned business conglomerate's re-branding strategies. *IUP Journal of Entrepreneurship Development*, 7(1/2): 63–76.

Johnson, G., Langley, A., Melin, L. and Whittington, R. (2007). *Strategy as Practice: Research Directions and Resources*. Cambridge: Cambridge University Press.

Kashmiri, S. and Mahajan, V. (2010). What's in a name?: An analysis of the strategic behavior of family firms. *International Journal of Research in Marketing*, 27(3): 271–280.

Kelly, L.M., Athanassiou, N. and Crittenden, W.F. (2000). Founder centrality and strategic behaviour in the family-owned firm. *Entrepreneurship Theory & Practice*, 25(2): 27–42.

Kim, D., Kandemir, D. and Cavusgil, S.T. (2004). 'The role of the family conglomerates in emerging markets: What Western companies should know', *Thunderbird International Business Review*, 46(1): 13–38.

Laureiro-Martínez, D., Canessa, N., Brusoni, S., Zollo, M., Alemanno, F. and Cappa, S.F. (2011). A neural signature of the innovative brain. Unpublished Working Paper.

Le Breton-Miller, I. and Miller, D. (2006). Why do some family businesses out-compete? Governance, long-term orientations, and sustainable capability. *Entrepreneurship Theory & Practice*, 30(6): 731–746.

Lyles, M.A., Baird, I.S., Orris, J.B. and Kuratko, D.F. (1993). Formalized planning in small business: Increasing strategic choices. *Journal of Small Business Management*, 31(2): 38–50.

Mazzola, P., Marchisio, G. and Astrachan, J. (2008). Strategic planning in family business: A powerful developmental tool for the next generation. *Family Business Review*, 21(3): 239–258.

McCann, J.E., Leon-Guerrero, A.Y. and Haley, J.D. (2001). Strategic goals and practices of innovative family businesses. *Journal of Small Business Management*, 39(1): 50–59.

Micelotta, E. and Raynard, M. (2011). Concealing or revealing the family? Corporate brand identity strategies in family firms. *Family Business Review*, 24(3): 197–216.

Miller, D. and Le Breton-Miller, I. (2006). Priorities, practices and strategies in successful and failing family businesses: An elaboration and test of the configuration perspective. *Strategic Organization*, 4(4): 379–407.

Miller, D., Le Breton-Miller, I. and Lester, R.H. (2010). Family ownership and acquisition behavior in publicly-traded companies. *Strategic Management Journal*, 31(2): 121–136.

Miller, D., Le Breton-Miller, I. and Lester, R.H. (2011). Family and lone-founder ownership and strategic behavior: Social context, identity and institutional logics. *Journal of Management Studies*, 48(1): 1–25.

Miller, D., Steier, L. and Le Breton-Miller, I. (2003). Lost in time: Intergenerational succession, change and failure in family business. *Journal of Business Venturing*, 18: 513–531.

Mintzberg, H., Ahlstrand, B. and Lampel, J. (1998). *Strategy Safari: A Guided Tour Through the Wilds of Strategic Management*. New York: The Free Press.

Moog, P., Mirabella, D. and Schlepphorst, S. (2011). Owner orientations and strategies and their impact on family business. *International Journal of Entrepreneurship & Innovation Management*, 13(1): 95–112.

Mulholland, K. (1997). The family enterprise and business strategies. *Work Employment and Society*, 11(4): 685–711.

Muñoz-Bullon, F. and Sanchez-Bueno, M. (2011). The Impact of family involvement on the R&D intensity of publicly traded firms. *Family Business Review*, 24(1): 62–70.

Mustakallio, M., Autio, E. and Zahra, S.A. (2002). Relational and contractual governance in family firms: Effects on strategic decision making. *Family Business Review*, 15(3): 205–222.

Nicholson, N. (2014). Evolutionary theory: A new synthesis for family business thought and research. In L. Melin, M. Nordqvist and P. Sharma (eds), *The SAGE Handbook of Family Business*. London: Sage.

Nicolau, N., Shane, S.A., Hunkin, J., Cherkas, L. and Spector, T. (2008). Is the tendency to engage in entrepreneurship genetic? *Management Science*, 54: 167–179.

Nordqvist, M. and Melin, L. (2010). Entrepreneurial families and family firms. *Entrepreneurship & Regional Development*, 22 (3): 1–29.

Nordqvist, N. and Zellweger, T. (2010). *Transgenerational Entrepreneurship: Exploring Growth and Performance in Family Firms Across Generations*. Cheltenham, UK: Edward Elgar Publishing.

O'Regan, N., Hughes, T., Collins, L. and Tucker, J. (2010). Strategic thinking in family businesses. *Strategic Change*, 19(1/2): 57–76.

Pearson, A.W., Carr, J.C. and Shaw, J.C. (2008). Toward a theory of familiness: A social capital perspective. *Entrepreneurship Theory & Practice*, 32(6): 949–969.

Perrini, F. and Minoja, M. (2008). Strategizing corporate social responsibility: Evidence from an Italian medium-sized, family-owned company. *Business Ethics: A European Review*, 17(1): 47–63.

Pistrui, D., Murphy, P. and Deprez-Sims, A. (2010). The transgenerational family effect on new venture growth strategy. *International Journal of Entrepreneurship & Innovation Management*, 12(1): 3–16.

Pittino, D. and Visintin, F. (2009). Innovation and strategic types of family SMEs: A test and extension of Miles and Snow's configuration model. *Journal of Enterprising Culture*, 17(3): 257–295.

Rau, S.B. (2014). Resource-based view of family firms. In L. Melin, M. Nordqvist and P. Sharma (eds), *The SAGE Handbook of Family Business*. London: Sage.

Rosa, P., Howorth, C. and Discua Cruz, A. (2014). Habitual and portfolio entrepreneurship in the family context: Longitudinal perspectives. In L. Melin, M. Nordqvist and P. Sharma (eds), *The SAGE Handbook of Family Business*. London: Sage.

Rue, L.W. and Ibrahim, N.A. (1996). The status of planning in smaller family-owned business. *Family Business Review*, 9(1): 29–42.

Salvato, C. and Aldrich, H.E. (2012). 'That's interesting!' in family business research. *Family Business Review*, 25(2): 125–135.

Salvato, C. and Melin, L. (2008). Creating value across generations in family-controlled businesses: The role of family social capital. *Family Business Review*, 21(3): 259–276.

Salvato, C., Chirico, F. and Sharma, P. (2010). A farewell to the business: Championing exit and continuity in entrepreneurial family firms. *Entrepreneurship & Regional Development*, 22(3–4): 321–348.

Schlippe, A. von and Schneewind, K.A. (2014). Theories from family psychology and family therapy. In L. Melin, M. Nordqvist and P. Sharma (eds), *The SAGE Handbook of Family Business*. London: Sage.

Scholes, L., Wright, M., Westhead, P. and Bruining, H. (2010). Strategic changes in family firms post management buyout: Ownership and governance issues. *International Small Business Journal*, 28(5): 505–521.

Schram, S.F. and Caterino, B. (eds) (2006). *Making Political Science Matter: Debating Knowledge, Research, and Method*. New York: New York University Press.

Sharma, P. (2004). An overview of the field of family business studies: Current status and directions for the future. *Family Business Review*, 17(1): 1–36.

Sharma, P. and Manikutty, S. (2005). Strategic divestments in family firms: Role of family structure and community culture. *Entrepreneurship Theory & Practice*, 29(3): 293–311.

Sharma, P. and Sharma, S. (2011). Drivers of proactive environmental strategy in family firms. *Business Ethics Quarterly*, 21(2): 309–334.

Sharma, P., Chrisman, J.J. and Chua, J.H. (1997). Strategic management of the family business: Past research and future challenges. *Family Business Review*, 10: 1–35.

Sirmon, D.G. and Hitt, M. (2003). Managing resources: Linking unique resources, management, and wealth creation in family firms. *Entrepreneurship: Theory and Practice*, 27(4): 339–358.

Sirmon, D.G., Arregle, J., Hitt, M. and Webb, J.W. (2008). The role of family influence in firms' strategic responses to threat of imitation, *Entrepreneurship: Theory and Practice*, 32(6): 979–998.

Staw, B.M., Sandelands, L.E. and Dutton, J.E. (1981). Threat-rigidity effects in organizational behavior: A multilevel analysis. *Administrative Science Quarterly*, 26: 501–524.

Tagiuri, R. and Davis, J. (1996). Bivalent attributes of the family firm. *Family Business Review*, 9(2): 199–208.

Tokarczyk, J., Hansen, E. and Green, M. (2007). A resource-based view and market orientation theory examination of the role of 'familiness' in family business success. *Family Business Review*, 20(1): 17–31.

Trostel, A.O. and Nichols, M.L. (1982). Privately-held and publicly-held companies: A comparison of strategic choices and management processes. *Academy of Management Journal*, 25(1): 47–62.

Tsang, E.W.K. (2002). Learning from overseas venturing experience: The case of Chinese family businesses. *Journal of Business Venturing*, 17(1): 21–40.

Upton, N., Teal, E. and Felan, J.T. (2001). Strategic and business planning practices of fast growth family firms. *Journal of Small Business Management*, 39(1): 60–72.

Ward, J. (1988). The special role of strategic planning for family business. *Family Business Review*, 1(2): 105–117.

Zahra, S.A. (2003). International expansion of U.S. manufacturing family businesses: the effect of ownership and involvement. *Journal of Business Venturing*, 18(4): 495–512.

Zahra, S.A., Hayton, J., Neubaum, D.O., Dibrell, C. and Craig, J. (2008). Culture of family commitment and strategic flexibility: The moderating effect of stewardship. *Entrepreneurship Theory & Practice*, 32(6): 1035–1054.

Zellweger, T. (2007). Time horizon, costs of equity capital, and generic investment strategies of firms. *Family Business Review*, 20(1): 1–15.

Zellweger, T. and Nason, R. (2008). A stakeholder perspective on family firm performance. *Family Business Review*, 21(3): 203–216.

Zollo, M. and Winter, S.G. (2002). Deliberate learning and the evolution of dynamic capabilities. *Organization Science*, 13: 339–351.

16

Resource-based View of Family Firms

Sabine B. Rau

INTRODUCTION

The resource-based view is sweeping through the field of family business. The last several years have witnessed a widespread use of the resource-based perspective for research on a variety of topics within the family business field, including entrepreneurship (Aldrich and Cliff, 2003), organizational social capital (Arregle et al., 2007), corporate governance (Carney, 2005), succession (Cabrera-Suárez et al., 2001), internationalization (Graves and Thomas, 2008; Westhead et al., 2001), franchising (Chirico et al., 2011), wealth creation (Sirmon and Hitt, 2003), and organizational culture (Zahra et al., 2004). An emerging resource-based theory of the family firm underlies this research. The perspective considers resources of family businesses at least in parts distinct from those of their non-family counterparts, and its proponents argue that families themselves are sources of valuable, rare, inimitable, and non-substitutable resources which in turn can lead to family-specific competitive advantages and

consequently to superior organizational performance (Habbershon et al., 2003).

What is the impact of this focus on family firm-specific resources on the field of family business? The answer is unclear because agreement on the nature of resources a priori and of family-specific resources in particular has yet to emerge. Furthermore, whether this view constitutes a theory of the family firm, or a theory of family business strategy, or rather an application and potential extension of the resource-based theory is still questionable (see also Chapter 6 in this book; Shukla et al., 2014). Additionally, empirical research based on the resource-based view of the family business is still scarce, and there is no consensus on whether the results add to a family-specific theory or add predictive power to potential outcomes of family firms. On the other hand, as resources in their basic appearance can be traced back to human capital (Campbell et al., 2012; Ployhart and Moliterno, 2011), and family firms are founded by individuals or groups of individuals and thus are fundamentally influenced by human capital resources from the very beginning (Klein, 2007), the family business field might in turn offer a fertile ground to better understand some of the still unsolved questions of resource-based theory (Kraaijenbrink et al., 2010).

Some researchers argue that 'distinctive familiness', defined as an idiosyncratic bundle of resources and capabilities resulting from the interaction of family and business, leads to wealth creating performance (Habbershon et al., 2003). But then, are family-specific resources per definition positive (Sharma, 2008)? Or, in contrary, can we as well think of family-specific resources detrimental to the performance of the family firm (Sirmon and Hitt, 2003)? And, even more complicated, could family-specific resources which at first sight have a positive connotation in turn lead to negative outcomes, as for example, trust, based on family relationships, might lead to decreased alertness and by that to business failure? Or, the other way around, can we think of the lack of resources such as scarcity of financial resources leading to positive outcome as for example innovation? This chapter aims to take stock on what has been done so far in the area of resource-based theory and family firms and by that, laying ground for future research that helps to reconcile at least some of the open questions, both in the family business field as well as giving back to resource-based theory in general.

The chapter is organized as follows. I begin with a theoretical discussion of the resource-based view and its critiques that covers varying views of resources, capabilities, and its potential outcomes such as competitive advantage and superior performance. I then introduce the family firm-specific literature employing an RBV perspective by focusing on two major streams, namely employing the RBV for the development of a general theoretical concept of family firm strategy and performance on one hand, and on employing single resources and/or capabilities as dependent and/or independent variables on the other. The empirical literature on RBV in the family business context is discussed from two different perspectives; first whether and how it adds to an overall theory of the family firm and second whether the family business field offers opportunities to overcome the general critique of the RBV. I close by addressing the questions I asked at the beginning of this chapter and offering some directions for future research.

There are several major conclusions. First, RBV offers a number of useful and empirically grounded insights into the multi-level social processes through which family influence is transferred into and integrated within and across family firms. Second, since the empirical research indicates that family firms in general employ generically similar resources, but do so in a different way, in different amounts, and with different goals (Chrisman et al., 2009), future research instead of looking for the *family business specific resources* rather might concentrate on the family business specific *way to employ* these resources, thus, into resource orchestration (Sirmon et al., 2011). Hence, a theory linking resources and capabilities in family firms to the respective outcome might add a distinct way to acquire/shed, bundle, and leverage resources and capabilities. It is the 'how' more than the 'what' that constitute for the family driven difference.

DEVELOPMENT AND CRITIQUE OF THE RESOURCE-BASED VIEW

The resource-based view, shifting our attention from a market perspective to a firm perspective to explain differences in performance, started in 1959 when Edith Penrose published her book *The Growth of the Firm*. It took another 20–30 years until the initial idea of inter-firm differences explaining success was taken into account by strategy scholars (Prahalad and Hamel, 1990; Wernerfelt, 1984). The resource-based view as we know it today is mainly based on the seminal work of Barney (1991). 'This paper is widely regarded as the first formalization of the then-fragmented resource-based literature into a comprehensive (and thus empirically testable) theoretical framework' (Newbert, 2007: 123). Firms are viewed as having different resources at hand which, if rare, valuable, inimitable, and non-substitutable, will lead to a sustained competitive advantage. As the RBV is simple yet elegant and has immediate face validity, 'the RBV's core message is appealing, easily grasped, and easily taught' (Kraaijenbrink et al., 2010: 350).

The RBV assumes heterogeneity and immobility of resources needed to gain competitive advantage and that firms are able to accrue resources earning rents (Barney, 1991). Hence, as we can assume that any resources stemming from a distinct family are distinct, too, these bundles of resources should display a high level of heterogeneity and immobility. In the RBV 'world' firms are seen as combinations of resources; financial, human, social, and intellectual as well as tangible resources. In family firms, the family itself is seen as a source of valuable, rare, inimitable, and non-substitutable (VRIN) resources that constitute for (potential) competitive advantage (Habbershon and Williams, 1999). These resources are bundled, leveraged, and employed in a way that leads to a competitive advantage (Sirmon et al., 2007, 2011). The RBV approach assumes that firms are managed by boundedly rational managers in already existing distinct markets that are to a certain extent predictable and that tend to move toward equilibrium (Kraaijenbrink et al., 2010; Leiblein, 2003). As the firm has more information about the future value of a specific resource compared to its competitors, the firm is able to accrue resources that will secure its superior position. This observation will even be stronger in firms with a long-term horizon, often ascribed to family firms (Chrisman and Patel, 2012; Le Breton-Miller and Miller, 2006).

Although the RBV is an elegant reduction of the complex system of a firm, the empirical results are miscellaneous. Without being exhaustive, the main papers point to mixed results. While Barney and Arikan (2001) reviewing 166 empirical papers found only

2% of the results contradicting predictions of RBV, Newbert (2007) in his systematic overview of empirical papers comes to not only different, but more importantly, to more differentiated results. From 55 systematically selected empirical papers from academic, double-blind reviewed leading journals he assessed the single analysis run by the respective authors. Only 53% of the analyses from these 55 papers support RBV predictions. Interestingly, the highest level of variance can be found when looking at the independent variable. While single resources were a rather weak predictor of both competitive advantage and performance, single capabilities had a quite high predicting power (Newbert, 2007). In line with Coff (1999) in an additional analysis Newbert (2007) could show that competitive advantage predicts superior performance in 51% of the empirical analysis. While RBV states that superior resource structuring, bundling, and leveraging (Sirmon et al., 2007) will lead to competitive advantage if these resources are valuable, rare, and inimitable (Barney, 2001), the rents generated by this competitive advantage will be appropriated concerning the bargaining power of the involved parties (Coff, 1999). Summing up, the empirical evidence from the so far extensive research on RBV leaves us with still inconclusive results that await further refinements.

The critique of the RBV, thus, has been as extensive as the attempts to validate the concept in order to accept it as a valid theory of the firm (Foss et al., 2008; Kraaijenbrink et al., 2010; Makadok, 2001; Priem and Butler, 2001a). Table 16.1 sums up the critique and its assessment.

Some of the major points of critique do not apply when the RBV is applied with care and its boundaries are respected. For example, Priem and Butler (2001a) assess critically that the RBV lacks managerial implications as it states that valuable, rare, inimitable, and non-substitutable resources lead to a competitive advantage, but that the RBV falls short in showing how these VRIN resources are developed. Because this is a general critique to

Table 16.1 Summary and assessment of critiques to the resource-based view (RBV) following Kraaijenbrink et al. (2010: 360)

Critique	Assessment
1. The RBV has no managerial implications	Not all theories should have direct managerial implications. Through its wide dissemination, the RBV has evident impact.
2. The RBV implies infinite regress	Applies only to abstract mathematical theories. In an applied theory such as the RBV, levels are qualitatively different. It may be fruitful to focus on the interactions between levels rather than to consider higher levels prior as a source of SCA.
3. The RBV's applicability is too limited	Generalizing about uniqueness is not impossible by definition. The RBV applies to small firms and startups as well, as long as they strive for an SCA. Path dependency is not problematic when not taken to the extreme. The RBV applies only to firms in predictable environments.
4. SCA is not achievable	By including dynamic capabilities, the RBV is not purely static, though it only explains *ex post*, not *ex ante*, sources of SCA. Although no SCA can last forever, a focus on SCA remains useful.
5. The RBV is not a theory of the firm	The RBV does not sufficiently explain why firms exist. Rather than requiring it to do so, it should further develop as a theory of SCA and leave additional explanations of firm existence to TCE.
6. VRIN/O is neither necessary nor sufficient for SCA	The VRIN/O criteria are not always necessary and not always sufficient to explain a firm's SCA. The RBV does not sufficiently consider the synergy within resource bundles as a source of SCA. The RBV does not sufficiently recognize the role that judgment and mental models of individuals play in value assessment and creation.
7. The value of a resource is too indeterminate to provide for useful theory	The current conceptualization of value turns the RBV into a trivial heuristic, an incomplete theory, or a tautology. A more subjective and creative notion of value is needed.
8. The definition of resource is unworkable	Definitions of resources are all inclusive. The RBV does not recognize differences between resources as inputs and resources that enable the organization of such inputs. There is no recognition of how different types of resources may contribute to SCA in a different manner.

Note: SCA = sustained competitive advantage; TCE = transaction cost economics; VRIN/O = valuable, rare, inimitable, and non-substitutable resources and capabilities plus organization.

theories in strategy and not specific to RBV (Kraaijenbrink et al., 2010), this criticism does not weaken the evident impact of RBV. A second point mentioned is that the RBV implies infinite regress (Collis, 1994; Priem and Butler, 2001b). As capabilities can be seen as second order constructs enabling a firm to re-combine and bundle resources in a way that allows itself to generate new resources and/or innovate products and processes, the criticism here is that this second order constructs might be overcome by a third order construct and so on. Kraaijenbrink et al. (2010: 352) remark that 'once we appreciate strategic management as a practical engagement with indeterminacy and open-endedness,

the infinite regress critique becomes less useful'. Instead of seeing second order constructs as superior, they might rather be complementary to the first order resources.

The third point stresses that RBV's applicability might be too limited. Taking a closer look, the RBV's applicability to other than corporation is definitely given, as I will show in the following section on RBV and family firms. Taking these thoughts a step further and arguing that families can be assessed as organizations, the RBV might even be applicable to families and help to explain how families develop/shed, bundle and leverage their resources in order to gain a competitive advantage over other families. Hence, we can conclude that the applicability is limited in that it should be applied strictly within the boundaries defined by RBV (Barney, 2002). Another reported weakness, namely that the sustained competitive advantage (SCA) is not achievable, is of theoretic nature. Any SCA is only temporary as there is no such thing as an indefinite SCA. On the other hand, a SCA over a longer period of time can be achieved through constant incremental improvements and dynamic capabilities (Helfat at al., 2007). The fifth point of critique that the RBV is not a theory of the firm can be rejected as it does not aim to explain, for example, boundaries of the firm but rather it can be described as a theory of rents and of sustained competitive advantage (Mahoney, 2001; Priem and Butler, 2001b).

Out of the eight points of critique, Kraaijenbrink et al. (2010, see also Table 16.1) assess the first five to be able to withstand the critique. The last three, namely VRIN resources being neither necessary nor sufficient for SCA, the value of a resource being too indeterminate, and the definition of resource being unworkable, are not so easy to overcome. Applying the RBV to family firms might help to at least weaken some of the critical points brought forward. The discussion whether or not VRIN resources are necessary and sufficient for SCA reveal 'fundamental disagreements about the nature of markets, individuals, and resources and the roles these play in generating SCA' (Kraaijenbrink et al., 2010: 355). SCA then is a result of both VRIN resources and the capabilities to structure, bundle, and leverage them in a way the customer values them (Sirmon et al., 2007), and thus a result of 'resource orchestration' (Sirmon et al., 2011). Family firms do display two types of VRIN resources: those rooted in the firm and those rooted in the family. The VRIN resources of a family business derived from the business sphere can be labeled as 'classical' resources described by RBV. The VRIN resources of a family firm that originate from the family (Habbershon and Williams, 1999; Sharma, 2008; Sirmon and Hitt, 2003) are distinct by

definition as every family is unique and, hence, the resources the family can offer are rare and inimitable. Whether or not these resources are valuable to a great extent depends on how they are seen by the family firm's customers and whether they offer surplus complementarities to the customer's resource portfolio (Adegbesan, 2010).

Another major criticism is that the value as employed in RBV is too indeterminate to provide for a useful theory. The RBV is seen as tautological making value the explanans and the explanandum at the same time (Kraaijenbrink et al., 2010; Priem and Butler, 2001a). As the term 'value' has accounted for several misunderstandings (Rokeach, 1973; Sorenson, 2014), to substantiate this point of critique a more fine grained definition and conceptualization of the terms 'value', 'valuable', and 'uniqueness' will be helpful. Bowman and Ambrosini (2000) advocate to distinguish between value perceived by customers, monetary value in terms of willingness to pay a certain price, and finally the price paid. A resource then can be labeled 'valuable' when it, alone or in combination with other resources, offers a surplus to the customer who in turn is prepared to pay a certain price for the product or service. So while the value of the resource is the explans, the price paid is the explanandum. In family firms specific non-economic goals, driven by the family's values, constitute an important part of the overall goals (Astrachan and Jaskiewicz, 2008; Chrisman and Patel, 2012; Gomez-Mejia et al., 2007). Explaining the influence of non-economic goals derived from the family's values onto the economic outcome of the firm is not only one of the 'hottest' topic of family business research at the moment (Berrone et al., 2014) but will also add to a better understanding of how 'valuable' resources add to sustained competitive advantage.

The last point of critique reported by Kraaijenbrink et al. (2010) is that the definition of resource is unworkable as it is overly inclusive (Priem and Butler, 2001b). Suggesting to distinguish between different types of resources and through this to be more distinct of which resources and/or capabilities lead to SCA under what external circumstances and in which organizational context might further the explanatory power of RBV. Especially in family firms where the distinguishing resources stem from the family (Habbershon and Williams, 1999), the different configurations of resources might be more apt to explain positive/negative influence under different circumstances, both in the firm and in the market. Sirmon et al. (2011) take the RBV discussion a step further by focusing on 'resource orchestration'. By looking at the process *how* resources under different circumstances should be managed they emphasize the impact of the manager onto the resource–competitive advantage relationship. As family firms are reported to be more heterogeneous (Chrisman and Patel, 2012) and at the same time behave more particularistic and personalistic than their non-family counterparts due to the power of the owner-managers (Carney, 2005), they offer a fertile ground for further testing and refining RBV in this specific aspect.

In the following I will present applications of RBV to the family business field put forward so far and evaluate its potential for both the further development of the family business field and its potential to serve as a starting point for a 'theory of the family business' as well as for the further refinement of RBV.

RBV IN THE FAMILY BUSINESS FIELD

Family businesses, although prevalent in most economies, have only recently emerged as a topic of management research (Bird et al., 2002; Yu et al., 2012). In line with the stage of the overall field, a unified perspective on what constitutes a family business as well as a theory of the family business is still missing. 'At the most basic level, what differentiates a family business from other profit seeking organizations is the family's important influence on the decision making and operations of the firm' (Chrisman et al., 2003: 359). Looking at family influence as a continuous variable (Klein, Astrachan, and Smyrnios, 2005), I discuss how this influence 'enters' the business, plays out within the business, and how it affects the output of the respective firm.

Approaches Employing the RBV in family firms

The underlying question throughout the RBV-based work related to family businesses is whether family influence makes a business 'different' from its non-family counterparts. The relevance of this question cannot be assessed high enough. Only if family influence does make a difference, strategy and management of family firms require a distinct theoretical grounding. If, in contrast, family influence does not make a difference, the family business field as it has developed up to now would be lacking legitimacy. While the earlier work on family firms assumes that family influence constitutes for a difference without explicitly arguing why (Beckhard and Dyer, 1983; Lansberg, 1983), recently scholars offer a much clearer rationale for it (Arregle et al., 2007; Carney, 2005; Chrisman et al., 2009).

Familiness – The Bundle of Idiosyncratic Resources Through Family Involvement

Family firms, as any other firm, have to manage their resources effectively in order to gain a competitive advantage (Sirmon and Hitt, 2003). Although already in 1983 Lansberg focuses on the management of human resources as one of the most crucial tasks for family business longevity (Lansberg, 1983), the starting point for RBV in the family business field was the seminal paper of Habbershon and Williams (1999: 1) who suggested that 'the bundle of resources that are distinctive to a firm as a result of family involvement are identified as the "familiness" of the firm'. Familiness as the bundle of idiosyncratic resources of the firm influences in turn the capabilities of the respective firm which leads to a competitive advantage which, finally, is transformed into performance. Beyond other advantages of employing the RBV to explain family business strategy and behavior, it explains 'why intangible assets (like trust and unity) … can induce superior performance' (Habbershon and Williams, 1999: 18).

In a second step, Habbershon et al. (2003) suggested a unified systems perspective to explain family business performance. Built on the notion of distinctive familiness, they proposed that resources and capabilities of the family unit, the individual members, as well as of the business entity interact and add to the overall performance of the family business. The final purpose of the family firm is assumed to be the creation of transgenerational wealth leading to rent generation as a function of resources and capabilities. Although influential, the work of Habbershon and Williams (1999) widely ignored the negative potential of 'familiness' such as nepotism, lack of professionalism, feuding families, as well as the potentially negative outcome of a-priori positive resources such as trust or the potentially positive outcome of a-priori negative familiness such as sibling rivalry or scarcity of financial resources.

Up until today, empirical studies which test the predictions of 'familiness' are scarce. The prediction of the theory is that the bundle of distinct resources of the firm stemming from the family's involvement will lead to competitive advantage and finally to superior performance (Habbershon and Williams, 1999). Although Habbershon and Williams give examples for potential operationalization of familiness, such as cohesion, learning, competency, mid-term efficiency, and long-term wealth outcomes, empirical studies often measure family influence in terms of involvement of the family in either ownership and/or management (for a review see Stewart and Hitt, 2012). A promising future research avenue would be to open the black box 'family' by, e.g., defining the different dimensions on which the 'organization

family' vary and how the resulting different configurations of family impact family business behavior.

A further refinement of the independent variable as a sub-section of familiness was suggested by Craig et al. (2008) who specified 'family-based brand identity' as the independent variable. Employing a data set of 218 Australian SMEs they could show that 'family-based brand identity', although not influencing performance directly, led to higher performance when moderated by a customer-centric orientation. Other family-specific resources stemming from the system interaction between the family, its individual members and the business are innovative capacity and reciprocal altruism. Eddleston and colleagues show that 'family firms that invest in their innovative capacity and foster altruistic family relationships are able to build a competitive advantage' (Eddleston et al., 2008: 41).

Family business studies employing the RBV suffer from the same problems as RBV studies in mainstream research, namely reduced availability of secondary data sources of sufficient distinctiveness and quality. Danes and colleagues (2009) used the National Family Business Survey (NFBS) to find support for the influence of 'family capital' onto firm achievements and firm sustainability. Interviewing the owner-manager of 311 micro family firms (average size 7 employees in 1997, 6 in 2000) that were included in two waves of the NFBS out of 1,100 households, they looked at family capital in terms of family human, family social and family financial capital. 'Gender was the only significant human capital predictor …. Adjustment strategies were the only significant social capital predictor … No other capital variable was statistically significant' (Danes et al., 2009: 208).

Overall, the familiness approach of Habbershon and colleagues still awaits empirical validation in several steps. First, the question of how family-specific resources and capabilities develop from the system interaction between the family, its individual members and the business remains a relevant and interesting research question inviting especially high level qualitative research (e.g., Chenail, 2009; Reay and Zhang, 2014; Tracy, 2010). Second, where these family-specific bundles of resources qualify as valuable, rare, inimitable and non-substitutable, they offer several research opportunities to connect them on one hand directly with competitive (dis)advantage of the respective firms and on the other to show moderating and mediating effects onto these relationships.

Parsimony, Personalism, and Particularism, Long-term Orientation and Social Capital

Inspired by the work of Habbershon and colleagues, scholars asked of whether there are resources and capabilities that are in fact rooted in the family of the family business and that make those firms unique and constitute family-based competitive advantages (Carney, 2005; Chrisman et al., 2005; Sirmon and Hitt, 2003). Carney (2005) established an organizational theory that named factors which lead to family businesses' competitive advantage. Assuming that value-creation of a firm is due to a firm's system of corporate governance, he establishes three dominant propensities; namely parsimony, personalism, and particularism for family firms which are characterized by the unification of ownership and control. Parsimony is defined as 'the alignment of incentives that simultaneously reduces agency costs and motivates efficiency' (Carney, 2005: 254). Personalism allows the family to impel their values and vision onto the business as the authority, as assumed by Carney (2005), is incorporated in the person of the owner-manager. Finally, particularism describes the greater liberty of exercising authority in a way that might even override rational-calculative decisions of, e.g., non-family managers employed in the business. Carney concludes that:

> while the financial and managerial capacity constraints limit value-creating strategies based upon differentiation and broad-market scope, the propensities for parsimony, personalism, and particularism of family-owned and managed firms provide advantages in cost leadership strategies in localized, narrow-scoped markets and facilitate fast and decisive seizure of opportunities that are difficult for professional managers to act upon. (Carney, 2005: 257)

In a nutshell, the 3P model of successful family firms adds to our understanding by explaining how and under which circumstances the unity of ownership and control can lead to rent-generating behavior of the firm.

In line with Carney (2005), Le Breton-Miller and Miller (2006) propose that there are certain drivers of family business longevity, such as the investment in a substantive mission and its required capability, investment in people, especially in knowledge creation and preservation, and investment in enduring, broad-based relationships with external stakeholders. From the long-term orientation of family firms, based on longer CEO tenures, reduced agency costs and surplus resources, and the overlap of family control and ownership, results in superior long-term investment in related capabilities (R&D, brand building, etc.), in a skilled and motivated work-force, and in enduring relationships, and this is enhanced when combined with cumulative capability building and focus. Thus, family firms can build competitive advantage on family-specific resources and capabilities especially when they capitalize on the long-term focus, which is something non-family firms usually cannot do.

A next step in clarifying the role of the family-specific resources in generating a competitive advantage was undertaken by Pearson et al. (2008) employing social capital theory (Adler and Kwon, 2002; Leana and van Buren, 1999; Nahapiet and Goshal, 1998). Distinguishing between the structural dimension (e.g., network ties and appropriable organization), the cognitive dimension (e.g., shared vision and shared language), and the resulting relational dimension (e.g., trust, norms, obligations, and identification) of the family firm's social capital resources, they elaborate on social capital development conditions. Here, the focus is on the systematic interaction and involvement: 'Antecedent conditions to the creation of social capital include (1) time/stability; (2) closure; (3) interdependence; and (4) interaction' (Pearson et al., 2008: 960). Although the model builds on the notion of intermingled family and businesses interactions, and thus on blurred boundaries between the two subsystems of the family business system (Pieper and Klein, 2007), there is still a lack of clarity on whether the resources and capabilities that constitute 'familiness' are developed in the family and transferred to the business (Arregle et al., 2007) or whether they are developed within the family business' business unit in which the family plays a pivotal role.

While empirical testing in the Western countries does not pose any cultural problems, Wu (2008) states that without employing subjective measures empirical testing in the East would be extremely difficult. Wu, in his study of 108 Chinese Hong Kong-based SMEs, employed competitiveness improvement, measured by three items developed and adapted from the work of Choi and Hartley (1996) and Cusumano and Takeishi (1991). Wu (2008) finds support for the idea that the relationships between the dimensions of social capital (trust, network ties, and repeated transactions) and competitive improvement are mediated by information sharing. This study, though thorough and interesting, highlights a problem one finds repeatedly in the family business literature, namely the question of why the study is addressing family firms instead of all firms. Or, put differently, does family influence in this setting make a significant difference?

Resource Management Model for Wealth Creation

The most encompassing theoretical model was presented by Sirmon and Hitt (2003). It can be seen as the starting point of the development of a first family-specific RBV model, leading to a theory of the management of firm resources (Sirmon et al., 2007), which

then was further refined by applying part of it to family firms (Arregle et al., 2007). Only recently, Sirmon and colleagues presented a further refinement in arguing that whether resources and capabilities lead to a competitive advantage is, at least partly, due to the management's ability to appropriately 'orchestrate' the respective resources (Sirmon et al., 2011). Thus, Sirmon, Hitt and colleagues present one of the first fruitful theoretical interactions in which theory development in the family business field inspired theory building in the mainstream and vice versa. Focusing on so-called focal family firms, the 2003 paper presents five distinct different resources, namely human capital, social capital, patient financial capital, survivability capital, and governance structure and costs. To my knowledge, they are the first to explicitly present not only the positive potential these different resources might have for family firms but also some potentially negative consequences, such as the difficulty to attract and retain highly qualified managers in respect to human capital.

Still, the way the resources are presented, some negative consequences are discussed while explicitly negative valence of specific resources such as below market qualification of family members in management positions or the closure of a network through imbalanced strong and weak ties are not yet illustrated. Also, potential positive outcomes of resources with negative valence, for example nepotism, which might result in 'leaders, knowing they are in place as much by birth as by merit, are more likely to be unafraid to (a) have a realistic appraisal of their own weaknesses and (b) appoint as co-leaders people with skills and experience they themselves lack' (Nicholson, 2008: 81), are not yet part of the model presented. Furthermore, Sirmon and Hitt (2003) discuss how these resources might play out in non-family firms. As argued by them, non-family firms usually do not enjoy the advantages of these family-specific resources as they, for example, do not have the commitment of employees and stakeholders to benefit from survivability capital in

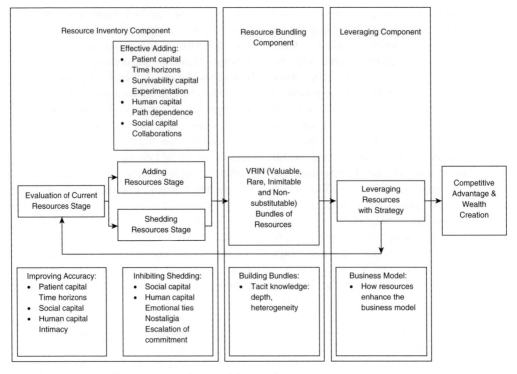

Figure 16.1   Managing resources for wealth creation

Souce: Sirmon and Hitt (2003: 346)

terms of pooled personal resources that family members loan, contribute, and share with the business entity. On the other hand, they are not threatened by the downturns of family-specific resources such as difficulties to attract and retain professional managers. The explicitly negative valence of a resource such as a lack of professionalism in respect to human capital (Bertrand and Schoar, 2006) or nepotism (Jaskiewicz et al., 2013; Padgett and Morris, 2005) is not part of this specific model.

In their model, Sirmon and Hitt (2003) present three stages, the resource inventory component, the resource bundling component, and the leveraging component (Makadok, 2001; Mosakowski, 2002), finally leading to competitive advantage and wealth creation. It is here where they for the first time look into the black box of value creation which they later extend and specify, presenting a 'Dynamic resource management

model of value creation' (Sirmon et al., 2007) not only for family firms but for all types of businesses.

The model (Figure 16.1) depicts how effective management of a family firm's resources can lead to competitive advantage and consequently to value creation. Sirmon and Hitt (2003) point out that finding the optimal time horizon is crucial for correct resource evaluation on one hand, on the other especially in family firms with patient capital managers have the freedom to engage in more creative strategies. Assuming that family firm managers are at least as qualified as non-family managers available on the market, they can develop a more in-depth knowledge of the firm's resources and thus have a higher ability to assess the firm's resources. On the other hand, a family firm's managers may refrain from shedding resources due to emotional ties, nostalgia, and/or escalation of commitment, which is also related to their specific human and social capital (Sharma and Manikutty, 2005). In terms of adding resources, Sirmon and Hitt (2003: 348) propose that 'family firms are likely to absorb new resource stocks more effectively than non-family firms due to higher levels of patient and survivability capital', taking into consideration the moderating (negative) effect of potential deficiencies in the family firm's human capital. With increasing heterogeneity of the family business' management team, the potential short-comings of their human capital is reduced.

A family business' social capital influences its potential to acquire resources from the market (Sirmon and Hitt, 2003). This is partly related to the legitimacy that stems from social capital as the firm and its protagonists are socially accepted and thus have access to resources (Deephouse, 1999). Furthermore, although not explicitly part of the model of Sirmon and Hitt (2003), families with higher levels of social capital will be able to attract higher levels of resources for the next generation, whether this refers to opportunities to learn from other family firms, to have access to better network for the next generation, or even for selecting incoming in-laws with higher human and social capital. As an organization, a family firm with a high level of social capital is more attractive for and better known by potential partners for alliances. As alliances are prime vehicles to gain access to resources (Gulati, 1998), the capability to present one's firm as a worthwhile alliance partner augments the firm's overall resource portfolio. Sirmon and Hitt (2003) argue that family firms do have an advantage in forming alliances as they have a long-term perspective and the ability to develop a higher level of inter-partner trust as well as the ability to transfer tacit knowledge. Taken together, a family firm's social capital influences the acquisition of several resources (Klein, 2007), whether financial, human, or social on the individual level as well as on the group and organizational level. Furthermore, it also influences the firm's ability to gain more value from alliances.

The second phase of the 'Resource Management Model for Wealth Creation' (Sirmon and Hitt, 2003) addresses resource bundling and leveraging. Through bundling of resources capabilities are formed. As capabilities are unique combinations of resources and related services, they are the basis for a family firm to take actions. Sirmon and his colleagues (2007) contend that different types of bundling processes render specific capabilities. For example, they differentiate between processes with the aim to produce incremental changes compared to those that attempt to produce substantial changes. The appropriateness of the different processes is on one hand due to the external environment and its dynamics, and on the other also dependent on the family-specific resources and processes at hand. Leveraging capabilities is at the core of the process through which the family firm makes use of its unique resources. The leverage process involves mobilizing, coordinating, and deploying the firm's capabilities in a way that adds value to the overall seller–buyer–resource combination (Sirmon et al., 2007; Teece et al., 1997). Only capabilities that are leveraged effectively will render value added.

The process of bundling and leveraging is at its core creative and entrepreneurial (Barney and Arikan, 2001) and thus might offer an advantage to family firms over their non-family counterparts. This holds especially true in close relationships with customers in strategic factor markets, defined as markets where 'firms acquire the resources that they use to implement their strategies in product markets' (Maritan and Florence, 2008: 228), as I assume family business-specific criteria like long-term orientation (Arregle et al., 2007; Casson, 1999; Fiss and Zajac, 2004; Miller et al., 2010), risk averseness (Gomez-Mejia et al., 2007; Miller et al., 2008, 2010), and flexibility (Sirmon et al., 2008) to be more important in these markets than in, for example, markets of fast-moving consumer goods. The critical factor, though, is reported to be a deep and heterogeneous tacit knowledge within the family firm (Sirmon and Hitt, 2003). Only if this knowledge is at hand for the family firm, can it develop the ability to better bundle and leverage its resources in order to gain a competitive advantage.

On the other hand, there are authors that explicitly argue that 'even if family and non-family firms invest in resources that are generically similar, they may make their investments in different ways, in different amounts, and for different purposes' (Chrisman et al., 2009: 741). Thus, family influence alters the originally generic resources into at least hard-to-imitate and hard-to-substitute resources. Looking at 505 North-American SMEs (with 10–100 employees), the authors find support for the idea that family influence moderates the relationships of external resource stocks (supplier relations, loyal customers, reputation, banking relations) and functional skills (operations, marketing, developing innovation, products and services) on sales growth. In the same line of thought, Eddleston and colleagues (2008) find that 'family firms that invest in their innovative capacity and foster altruistic family relationships are able to build a competitive advantage …. Thus it seems that both family- and firm-specific resources distinguish successful family firms from their less successful counterparts' (Eddleston et al., 2008: 41).

While the RBV requires the resources to be valuable, rare, inimitable, and non-substitutable (Barney, 1991), only few studies in the family business field explicitly argue why they believe their independent variables to fit the original RBV requirements. Sirmon and colleagues (2008) look explicitly at one of the required pre-conditions, here at inimitability. The question they raise is whether imitability, thus, the lack of a required resource quality for generating a competitive advantage, is more threatening to family than to non-family firms. They can show that family influence mediates the influence of imitability to firm performance, 'we find that family-influenced firms are less rigid in their responses to such

threats, reducing R&D and internationalization significantly less than firms without family influence' (Sirmon et al., 2008: 979). Along that line, although not employing RBV, Chrisman and Patel (2012) demonstrate the heterogeneous responses of family firms regarding R&D investments in the light of performance aspirations and time horizon of goals pursued.

Social Capital as a Specifically Important Resource of Family Firms

Social capital is a specifically important resource when discussing distinct propensities of family firms (Carney, 2005; Pearson et al., 2008). While the studies presented so far employed social capital as one variable among others, in the following section I will look at social capital more specifically. Social capital also in mainstream theory has been identified to make a potentially positive contribution to the firm's success (Nahapiet and Goshal, 1998). Even more surprisingly, only little attention had been paid to its development (Bolino et al., 2002). In order to overcome this gap, Arregle et al. (2007) propose a model of 'family social capital's influence on the development of organizational social capital'. In their work they use 'the context of family firms' (Arregle et al., 2007: 73), because in family firms at least two groups are present, namely family and non-family members (managers as well as employees), which in turn holds potential for conflict: 'These characteristics create a context where inter-group heterogeneity and the intra-group interaction within the family are identifiable and may strongly influence the firm's organizational social capital' (Arregle et al., 2007: 75). In reasoning about the flow from family social capital into the firm and by that creating organizational social capital distinct to this specific family business, Arregle and colleagues offer a first explanation on how organizational social capital might be shaped by a dominant group within an organization.

The mechanisms that link family social capital to the development of organizational social capital are institutional isomorphism of the institution family, organizational identity and rationality, human resource practices, as well as social network overlap. Through coercive, mimetic, and normative pressures (DiMaggio and Powell, 1983) and the responses to institutional pressures (Oliver, 1991), the background institution, here the family, influences the building of the firm's social capital. While isomorphic pressures work mostly through mimetic behavior, organizational identity and rationality is directly influenced by the decisions taken by family members within the organization, while human resource practices have an indirect, yet powerful impact through, for example, selection of employees and managers. Last but not least, the family members active in the business use and make accessible their personal networks, leading to interaction with people they favor and with whom they have a long-standing relationship.

Drivers of family social capital and its effect on organizational social capital are stability, in terms of stability of the nuclear family as well as the ongoing influence of the family onto the firm; interactions, as only through interactions will the flow from one entity to the other take place; interdependence of family and firm; and, finally, closure of the family network, which makes it family specific. Arregle and colleagues show some important contingencies of the family social capital/organizational social capital linkage, such as family involvement and size, as well as self-sufficiency. In conclusion, 'if family firms perform better than most of their non-family competitors, it is in part because they possess strong family social capital' (Arregle et al., 2007: 87).

A study with a slightly different dependent variable is presented by Zahra (2010). He looks at the organizational social capital of 741 US-American SMEs and shows how it impacts the investments that family firms undertake in new ventures, business relationships, and alliances with the new ventures, as

well as how it contributes to the new venture's governance and management. Here, the dependent variables are investments, measured as equity holdings in new ventures, and investment targets differentiated by the individuals/groups who founded the ventures. Second, Zahra (2010) looks at business relationships and alliances with new ventures as dependent variables. Third, he correlates organizational social capital with the contributions (in terms of investor firms' managers' service) to new ventures' governance and management. Because family firms are found to be in a better position to harvest their organizational social capital, he concludes that 'family ownership has subtle effects that can give the organization strategic advantages' (Zahra, 2010: 359).

Zahra et al. (2004), with a sample of 536 US-based manufacturing companies (employee average of 151 for family businesses; 351 for non-family businesses), show that family firms can capitalize on their organizational culture. All dimensions of organizational culture employed, individual vs group cultural orientation, centralized vs decentralized control, and strategic vs financial control orientation, are significantly more impactful on entrepreneurship (measured according to Miller, 1983) than in non-family firms. Only external orientation did not show a significantly different result on entrepreneurship for family versus non-family firms.

Taking Stock: What We Know and What We Don't Know

Family business research is inclined with the question of whether (and how) family influence makes a difference for the family firm. In order to develop the theoretical knowledge in the still young family business field, Chua et al. (2003) recommend discovering relevant dependent variables as they help to establish the boundaries of the field. Other than in more mature fields, in the family business field a multitude of dependent variables can be found (Yu et al., 2012). Out of those dependent variables, RBV-based

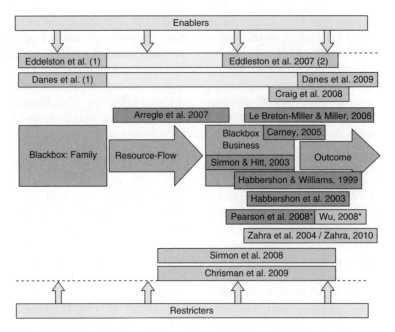

Figure 16.2 Components of theoretical models and studies of RBV in family businesses

Yellow: theoretical/conceptual papers; orange: empirical studies.
Left side of respective quadrant: independent variable; right side: dependent variable.
* Both Pearson et al., 2008 and Wu, 2008 independent variable: business related; dependent: outcome related.

papers in the family business field mainly concentrate on business outcomes, both conceptual and empirical.

I assume that the interaction of two types of organizations, the family and the business, is at the heart of the field (Pieper and Klein, 2007). As far as we know today, there is a resource flow from the family into the business causing family business-specific advantages and disadvantages based on family-specific bundles of resources and capabilities (Habbershon and Williams, 1999). As RBV states a relationship between resources/capabilities and outcomes, we can assume a relationship between the resources and capabilities of the business family and their respective outcome. In a second step we also can predict a relationship of the resources/capabilities inherent in the family firm and the respective outcome. Looking at the papers drawing from RBV in the family

business field so far, Figure 16.2 highlights that attention is focused on the intersection of the business unit and its outcome. Other than Arregle and colleagues (2007), there is no conceptual or theoretical piece of work addressing the family unit as a specific organization which might be better understood by applying RBV. Furthermore, contextualizing RBV-based research in the family business field that looks at the conditions that enable or restrict the development and transfer of resources and capabilities is still missing.

Figure 16.2 shows the two distinct organizations, the family and the related business, as black boxes. I assume a resource flow between the two, as well as, as predicted by RBV, an outcome related to these resources/capabilities. Furthermore, I assume that there are specific conditions which enable or restrict resource development as well as resource flow. Organized by their respective independent and dependent variables, Figure 16.2 sums up the so far presented theoretical and empirical work.

While in the strategy field financial performance is reported to be the most influential dependent variable (Ketchen et al., 1996; Nag et al., 2007; Yu et al., 2012), in the entrepreneurship field opportunity recognition is regarded as one of the most important dependent variables (Short et al., 2010; Yu et al., 2012). In the family business field there is no single most influential variable, instead Yu and colleagues (2012) report 34 dependent variables, grouped into 7 categories. We thus can conclude that RBV-related studies might add to our understanding of family firms but they are too narrow in scope to constitute for a 'theory of the family business'. On the other hand, employing RBV in the family business field might help to extend the boundaries of RBV in two relevant aspects.

Family firms are by far more heterogeneous than other firms (Chrisman and Patel, 2012). Two important dimensions on which they differ to a great extent are the goals they pursue and the time horizon they take on. Not only non-family firms in general stick to financial goals such as performance, there are also family owned and managed firms that follow a commercial logic. Others integrate financial and non-financial goals (Astrachan and Jaskiewicz, 2008; Zellweger and Astrachan, 2008). These family firms in particular protect their non-financial utilities, called 'socio-emotional wealth' (Gomez-Mejia et al., 2007). On a second dimension, family firms differ among each other with respect to the time horizon they take on (Chrisman and Patel, 2012; Stewart and Hitt, 2012). Employing RBV in the family business field requires taking different potential goals, financial and non-financial, into respect as well as accounting for the variance in time horizons applied by those firms. As shown before, transgenerational wealth creation (Habbershon et al., 2003) as a

dependent variable incorporates both long-term time perspective and financial as well as non-financial goals. Devoting work to RBV in family firms thus might open paths to better understanding the conditions under which resources and capabilities can be managed for the long-term success and consequently survival of firms at large. Furthermore, inherent in family business research on RBV is the opportunity to understand the interaction of financial and non-financial goals and how to 'orchestrate' resources to secure a healthy relation between the two types of goals.

In conceptual and theoretical work alike, the dependent variables in RBV studies in the family business field stem from the business entity, namely business outcome. To my knowledge, no empirical work so far has been devoted to the competitive advantage of families stemming from their resource management. Even when we look at the independent variables employed in the studies, only two studies use independent variables from the family system (Danes et al., 2009; Eddleston et al., 2008). As we can see from Figure 16.2, empirical work on RBV in family firms is still scarce and mostly centered on the business–outcome link. There is some evidence that family influence rather moderates the resource–competitive advantage relationship, thus families do the same in a different way. I did not find any studies that look into enablers/restrictors such as political, functional, or normative pressures (Oliver, 1991) or the influence of institutional environments onto organizations and the respective resource/capability work (Suddaby et al., 2010).

Taking stock, we know that family firms can be better understood through research applying RBV. Up until today, many potential paths are still awaiting research. The two biggest blind spots are the family as an organization and how it impacts the business and is affected by the business itself, as well as enablers and restricters to the resource orchestration process in families and businesses. As family firms, even more so than other firms, are confronted with institutional complexity (Greenwood et al., 2011), because they face institutional pressure from the institution 'family' as well as from the institution 'market', they might also offer interesting opportunities to further integrate RBV and institutional theory.

CONCLUSION

From the overview of studies in the family business field employing the RBV there are several learnings. Two basic conclusions have to be made: first, any study attempting to employ the RBV should stay within the boundaries of the theory. Second, a study looking at the resource/competitive advantage link only qualifies as a family business study if the family involvement makes a difference. Just looking at family firms as a sample without giving a rationale why is not enough. Only if resources/capabilities are valuable, rare, inimitable, and non-substitutable does the theory predict a positive effect on competitive advantage.

It is promising that family business research offers a way to further investigate resource orchestration (Sirmon et al., 2011). But, if it is family influence that alters the way resources are employed, the studies need to employ family influence or family-specific behaviors and goals as moderating or mediating variables rather than as independent ones. This comes with the difficulty – which also offers interesting opportunities – of multi-level research (see also McKenny et al., 2014) as the social processes through which family influence is transferred and integrated within and across the firm are inherently multi-level. Third, studies up to now have concentrated mainly on the business–outcome relationship. Family-specific variables such as reciprocal altruism (Eddleston et al., 2008) are mostly ignored. Opening the family black box thus offers future research opportunities. Furthermore, regarding the family as an organization whose competitive advantage over other families in

regard to governing a business is based on its respective resources and capabilities and their management opens a promising avenue for future research, too. Last but not least, I do not know of any studies (nor theoretical concepts) looking into enablers and restricters of the processes underlying the resource acquisition/shedding, bundling, and leveraging in family firms. Contextualizing RBV research in the family business field offers interesting opportunities for generating knowledge that might help on a political level to further assist family firms to develop their strengths, and through that stabilize their country's economies.

REFERENCES

Adegbesan, J.A. 2009. On the origins of competitive advantage: Strategic factor markets and heterogeneous resource complementarity, *Academy of Management Review*, 34(3): 463–475.

Adler, P.S. and Kwon, S.W. 2002. Social capital: Prospects for a new concept. *Academy of Management Review*, 27: 17–40.

Aldrich, H.E. and Cliff, J.E. 2003. The pervasive effects of family on entrepreneurship: Toward a family embeddedness perspective. *Journal of Business Venturing*, 18: 573–596.

Arregle, J.L., Hitt, M.A., Sirmon, D.G., and Very, P. 2007. The development of organizational social capital: Attributes of family firms. *Journal of Management Studies*, 44(1): 73–95.

Astrachan, J.H. and Jaskiewicz, P. 2008. Emotional returns and emotional costs in privately held family businesses: Advancing traditional business valuation. *Family Business Review*, 21(2): 139–149.

Barney, J. 1991. Firm resources and sustained competitive advantage. *Journal of Management*, 17: 99–120.

Barney, J.B. 2002. *Gaining and sustaining competitive advantage*. Upper Saddle River, NJ: Prentice Hall.

Barney, J.B. and Arikan, A.M. 2001. The resource-based view: Origins and implications. In Hitt, M.A., Freeman, R.E., and Harrison, J.S. (eds), *The Blackwell Handbook of Strategic Management*. Oxford: Blackwell, pp. 124–188.

Beckhard, R. and Dyer, G.W. 1983. Managing continuity in the family-owned business. *Organizational Dynamics*, 12: 5–12.

Berrone, P., Cruz, C., and Gomez-Mejia, L.R. 2014. Family-controlled Firms and Stakeholder Management: A Socioemotional Wealth Preservation Perspective. In

Melin, L., Nordqvist, M., and Sharma, P. (eds), *The SAGE Handbook of Family Business*. London: Sage.

Bertrand, M. and Schoar, A. 2006. The role of family in family firms. *Journal of Economic Perspectives*, 20: 73–96.

Bird, B., Welsch, H., Astrachan, J.H., and Pistrui, D. 2002. Family business research: The evolution of an academic field. *Family Business Review*, 15(4): 337–350.

Bolino, M.C., Turnley, W.H., and Bloodgood, J.M. 2002. Citizenship behavior and the creation of social capital in organizations. *Academy of Management Review*, 27: 505–522.

Bowman, C. and Ambrosini, V. 2000. Value creation versus value capture: Towards a coherent definition of value in strategy. *British Journal of Management*, 11: 1–15.

Cabrera-Suárez, K., de Saá-Pérez, P., and García-Almeida, D. 2001. The succession process from a resource- and knowledge-based view of the family firm. *Family Business Review*, 14: 37–48.

Campbell, B.A., Coff, R., and Kryscynski, D. 2012. Rethinking sustained competitive advantage from human capital. *Academy of Management Review*, 37: 376–395.

Carney, M. 2005. Corporate governance and competitive advantage in family-controlled firms. *Entrepreneurship, Theory & Practice*, 29(3): 249–265.

Casson, M. 1999. The economics of the family firm. *Scandinavian Economic History Review*, 47: 10–23.

Chenail, R.J. 2009. Editor's note: Communicating your qualitative research better. *Family Business Review*, 22(2): 105–108.

Chirico, F., Ireland, R.D., and Sirmon, D.G. 2011. Franchising and the family firm: Creating unique resources of advantage through 'Familiness'. *Entrepreneurship, Theory & Practice*, 35: 483–501.

Choi, T.Y., and Hartley, J.L. 1996. An exploration of supplier selection practices across the supply chain. *Journal of Operations Management*, 14: 333–343.

Chrisman, J.J. and Patel, P.C. 2012. Variations in R&D investment of family and non-family firm: Behavioral agency and myopic loss aversion perspectives. *Academy of Management Journal*, 55(4): 976–997.

Chrisman, J.J., Chua, J.H., and Kellermanns, F.W. 2009. Priorities, resource stocks, and performance in family and nonfamiliy firms. *Entrepreneurship, Theory & Practice*, 33: 739–760.

Chrisman, J.J., Chua, J.H., and Sharma, P. 2005. Trends and directions in the development of a strategic management theory of the family firm. *Entrepreneurship, Theory & Practice*, 29: 555–575.

Chrisman, J.J., Chua, J.H., and Zahra, S.A. 2003. Creating wealth in family firms through managing resources: Comments and extensions. *Entrepreneurship, Theory & Practice*, 27: 359–365.

Chua, J.H., Chrisman, J.J., and Steier, L.P. 2003. Extending the theoretical horizons of family business research. *Entrepreneurship, Theory & Practice*, 27: 331–338.

Coff, R.W. 1999. When competitive advantage doesn't lead to performance. *Organization Science*, 10: 119–133.

Collis, D.J. 1994. Research note: How valuable are organizational capabilities? *Strategic Management Journal*, 15 (Winter Special Issue): 143–152.

Craig, J.B., Dibrell, C., and Davis, P.S. 2008. Leveraging family-based brand identity to enhance firm competitiveness and performance in family businesses. *Journal of Small Business Management*, 46(3): 351–371.

Cusumano, M.A. and Takeishi, A. 1991. Supplier relations and management: A survey of Japanese, Japanese transplant, and U.S. auto plants. *Strategic Management Journal*, 12: 563–588.

Danes, S.M., Stafford, K., Haynes, G., and Amarapurkar, S.S. 2009. Family capital of family firms: Bridging human, social, and financial capital. *Family Business Review*, 22: 199–215.

Deephouse, D.L. 1999. To be different, or to be the same? It's a question (and theory) of strategic balance. *Strategic Management Journal*, 20: 147–166.

DiMaggio, P. and Powell, W.W. 1983. The iron cage revisited: Institutional isomorphism and collective rationality in organizational fields. *American Sociological Review*, 48: 147–160.

Donckels, R. and Fröhlich, E. 1991. Are family businesses really different? European experiences from STRATOS. *Family Business Review*, 4(2): 149–160.

Eddleston, K.A., Kellermanns, F.W., and Sarathy, R. 2008. Resource configuration in family firms: Linking resources, strategic planning and technological opportunities to performance. *Journal of Management Studies*, 45: 26–50.

Fiss, P.C. and Zajac, E.J. 2004. The diffusion of ideas over contested terrain: The (non)adoption of a shareholder value orientation among German firms. *Administrative Science Quarterly*, 49: 501–534.

Foss, N.J., Klein, P.G., Kor, Y.Y., and Mahoney, J.T. 2008. Entrepreneurship, subjectivism, and the resource-based view: Toward a new synthesis. *Strategic Entrepreneurship Journal*, 2: 73–94.

Gomez-Mejia, L.R., Haynes, K., Nuñez-Nickel, M.; Jacobson, K., and Moyano-Fuentes, F. 2007. Socioemotional wealth and business risks in family controlled firms. *Administrative Science Quarterly*, 52: 106–137.

Graves, C. and Thomas, J. 2008. Determinants of the internationalization pathways of family firms: An examination of family influence. *Family Business Review*, 21(2): 151–167.

Greenwood, R., Raynard, M., Kodeih, F., Micelotta, E.R., and Lounsbury, M. 2011. Institutional complexity and organizational responses. *The Academy of Management ANNALS*, 5: 317–371.

Gulati, R. 1998. Alliances and networks. *Strategic Management Journal*, 19: 293–317.

Habbershon, T.G. 2006. Commentary: A framework for managing the familiness and agency advantages in family firms. *Entrepreneurship, Theory & Practice*, 30: 879–886.

Habbershon, T.G. and Williams, M. 1999. A resource-based framework for assessing the strategic advantages of family firms. *Family Business Review*, 12(1): 1–25.

Habbershon, T.G., Williams, M., and MacMillan, I.C. 2003. A unified systems perspective of family firm performance. *Journal of Business Venturing*, 18: 451–465.

Helfat, C.E., Finkelstein, S., Mitchell, W., Peteraf, M.A., Singh, H., Teece, D.J., and Winter, S.G. 2007. *Dynamic Capabilities: Understanding Strategic Change in Organizations*. New York: John Wiley.

Jaskiewicz, P., Uhlenbruck, K., Balkin, D., Reay, T. (2013). Is nepotism good or bad? Types of nepotism and implications for knowledge management. *Family Business Review*, 26 (2), 121–139.

Ketchen, D.J., Jr., Thomas, J.B., and McDaniel, R., Jr. 1996. Process, content, and context: Synergistic effects on organizational performance. *Journal of Management*, 22: 231–257.

Klein, S.B. 2007. Family influence on value creation: A resource-based analysis of the value creation process in family firms. *Int. J. Entrepreneurship and Small Business*, 4(2): 110–121.

Klein S.B., Astrachan J.H., and Smyrnios K.X. 2005. The F-PEC scale of family influence: Construction, validation, and further implication for theory. *Entrepreneurship Theory & Practice* 29(3): 321–339.

Kraaijenbrink, J., Spender, J.C., and Groen, A.J. 2010. The resource-based view: A review and assessment of its critiques. *Journal of Management*, 36(1): 349–372.

Lansberg, I.S. 1983. Managing human resources in family firms: The problem of institutional overlap. *Organizational Dynamics*, summer 1983: 39–46.

Le Breton-Miller, I. and Miller, D. 2006. Why do some family businesses out-compete? Governance, long-term orientations, and sustainable capability. *Entrepreneurship, Theory & Practice*, 30: 731–746.

Leana, C.R. and van Buren, H.J. 1999. Organizational social capital and employment practices. *Academy of Management Review*, 24: 538–555.

Leiblein, M.J. 2003. The choice of organizational governance form and performance: Predictions from transaction cost, resource-based and real options theories. *Journal of Management*, 29: 937–961.

Mahoney, J.T. 2001. A resource-based theory of sustainable rents. *Journal of Management*, 27: 651–660.

Makadok, R. 2001. Towards a synthesis of resource-based and dynamic capability views of rent creation. *Strategic Management Journal*, 22: 387–402.

Maritan, C.A. and Florence, R.E. 2008. Investing in capabilities: Bidding in strategic factor markets with costly information. *Managerial and decision economics*, 29: 227–239.

McKenny, A.F., Payne, G.T., Zachary, M.A. and Short, J.C. 2014. Multilevel Analysis in Family Business Studies. In Melin, L., Nordqvist, M., and Sharma, P. (eds), *The SAGE Handbook of Family Business*. London: Sage.

Miller, D. 1983. The correlates of entrepreneurship in three types of firms. *Management Science*, 29: 770–792.

Miller, D., Le Breton-Miller, I., and Scholnick, B. 2008. Stewardship vs. Stagnation: An empirical comparison of small family and non-family businesses. *Journal of Management Studies*, 45(1): 51–78.

Miller, D., Le Breton-Miller, I., and Lester, R.H. 2010. Family ownership and aquisition behavior in publicly-traded companies. *Strategic Management Journal*, 31: 201–223.

Mosakowski, E. 2002. Overcoming resource disadvantages in entrepreneurial firms: When less is more. In M.A. Hitt, R.D. Ireland, S.M. Camp, and D.L. Sexton (eds), *Strategic Entrepreneurship: Creating a New Integrated Mindset*. Oxford: Blackwell Publishing, pp. 106–126.

Nag, R., Hambrick, D.C., and Chen, M.J. 2007. What is strategic management, really? Inductive derivation of a consensus definition of the field. *Strategic Management Journal*, 28: 935–955.

Nahapiet, J. and Goshal, S. 1998. Social capital, intellectual capital, and the organizational advantage. *Academy of Management Review*, 23: 242–266.

Newbert, S.L. 2007. Empirical research on the resource-based view of the firm: An assessment and suggestions for future research. *Strategic Management Journal*, 28: 121–146.

Nicholson, N. 2008. Evolutionary psychology, organizational culture, and the family firm. *Academy of Management Perspectives*, 22: 73–84.

Olivier, C. 1991. Strategic responses to institutional processes. *Academy of Management Review*, 16: 145–179.

Padgett, M.Y. and Morris, K.A. 2005. Keeping it 'All in the Family:' Does nepotism in the hiring process really benefit the beneficiary? *Journal of Leadership and Organizational Studies*, 11(2): 34–45.

Pearson, A.W., Carr, J.C., and Shaw, J.C. 2008. Toward a theory of familiness: A social capital perspective. *Entrepreneurship, Theory & Practice*, 32: 949–969.

Penrose, E. 1959. *The Growth of the Firm*. New York: Wiley.

Pieper, M.T. and Klein, S.B. 2007. The bullseye: A systems approach to modeling family firms. *Family Business Review*, 20: 301–319.

Ployhart, R.E. and Moliterno, T.P. 2011. Emergence of the human capital resource: A multilevel model. *Academy of Management Review*, 36(1): 127–150.

Prahalad, C.K. and Hamel, G. 1990. The core competence of the corporation. *Harvard Business Review*, 68(3): 79–91.

Priem, R.L. and Butler, J.E. 2001a. Tautology in the resource-based view and the implications of externally determined resource value: Further comments. *Academy of Management Review*, 26: 57–66.

Priem, R.L. and Butler, J.E. 2001b. Is the resource-based 'view' a useful perspective for strategic management research? *Academy of Management Review*, 26: 22–40.

Reay, T. and Zhang, Z. 2014. Qualitative Methods in Family Business Research. In Melin, L., Nordqvist, M., and Sharma, P. (eds), *The SAGE Handbook of Family Business*. London: Sage.

Rokeach, M. 1973. *The Nature of Human Values*. New York: The Free Press.

Sharma, P. 2008. Commentary: Familiness: Capital stocks and flows between family and business. *Entrepreneurship, Theory & Practice*, 32: 971–977.

Sharma, P. and Manikutty, S. 2005. Strategic divestments in family firms: Role of family structure and community culture. *Entrepreneurship, Theory & Practice*, 29: 293–311.

Short, J.C., Ketchen, D.J., Jr., Shook, C.L., and Ireland, R.D. 2010. The concept of 'opportunity' in entrepreneurship research: Past accomplishments and future challenges. *Journal of Management*, 36: 40–65.

Shukla, P., Carney, M. and Gedajlovic, E. (2014). Economic theories of family firms. In Melin, L., Nordqvist, M., and Sharma, P. (eds), *The SAGE Handbook of Family Business*. London: Sage.

Sirmon, D.G., and Hitt. M.A. 2003. Managing resources: Linking unique resources, management, and wealth creation in family firms. *Entrepreneurship, Theory & Practice*, 27: 339–358.

Sirmon, D.G., Arregle, J.L., Hitt, M.A., and Webb, J.W. 2008. The role of family influence in firms' strategic responses to threat imitation. *Entrepreneurship, Theory & Practice*, 32: 979–998.

Sirmon, D.G., Hitt, M.A., and Ireland, R.D. 2007. Managing firm resources in dynamic environments to create value: Looking inside the black box. *Academy of Management Review*, 32: 273–292.

Sirmon, D.G., Hitt, M.A., Ireland, R.D., and Gilbert, B.A. 2011. Resource orchestration to create competitive advantage: Breadth, depth, and life cycle effects. *Journal of Management*, 37(5): 1390–1412.

Sorenson, R.L. 2014. Values in Family Businesses. In Melin, L., Nordqvist, M., and Sharma, P. (eds), *The SAGE Handbook of Family Business*. London: Sage.

Stewart, A. and Hitt, M.A. 2012. Why can't a family business be more like a nonfamily business? Modes of professionalization in family firms. *Family Business Review*, 25(1): 58–86.

Suddaby, R., Elsbach, K.D., Greenwood, R., Meyer, J.W., and Zilber, T.B. 2010. Organizations and their institutional environments – bringing meaning, values, and culture back in: Introduction to the special research forum. *Academy of Management Journal*, 53: 1234–1240.

Teece, D.J., Pisano, G., and Shuen, A. 1997. Dynamic capabilities and strategic management. *Strategic Management Journal*, 18: 509–533.

Tracy, S.J. 2010. Qualitative quality: Eight 'big-tent' criteria for excellent qualitative research. *Qualitative Inquiry*, 16: 837–851.

Wernerfelt, B. 1984. A resource-based view of the firm. *Strategic Management Journal*, 5: 171–180.

Westhead, P., Wright, M., and Ucbasaran, D. 2001. The internationalization of new and small firms: A resource-based view. *Journal of Business Venturing*, 16: 333–358.

Wu, W.-P. 2008. Dimensions of social capital and firm competitiveness improvement: The mediating role of information sharing. *Journal of Management Studies*, 45: 122–146.

Yu, A., Lumpkin, G.T., Sorenson, R.L., and Brigham, K.H. 2012. The landscape of family business outcomes: A summary and numerical taxonomy of dependent variables. *Family Business Review*, 25(1): 33–57.

Zahra, S.A. 2010. Harvesting family firms' organizational social capital: A relational perspective. *Journal of Management Studies*, 47: 345–366.

Zahra, S.A., Hayton, J.C., and Salvato, C. 2004. Entrepreneurship in family vs. non-family firms: A resource-based analysis of the effect of organizational culture. *Entrepreneurship, Theory & Practice*, 28: 363–381.

Zellweger, T.M. and Astrachan, J.H. 2008. On the emotional value of owning a firm. *Family Business Review*, 21: 347–363.

17

Corporate Entrepreneurship in Family Businesses: Past Contributions and Future Opportunities

Alexander McKelvie, Aaron F. McKenny,
G.T. Lumpkin and Jeremy C. Short

INTRODUCTION

The study of corporate entrepreneurship (CE) is a growing area of interest in strategic management research. CE centers on the processes by which an established organization creates new organizations, initiates strategic renewal, and innovates within the organization (Sharma and Chrisman, 1999). Corporate entrepreneurship has been shown to influence firm performance (e.g., Rauch et al., 2009), organizational learning (e.g., Dess et al., 2003), and the growth and development of industries (e.g., Ahuja and Lampert, 2001). Thus, it is a potentially important element of a family firm's strategic repertoire. Studies have found that family involvement in the business can also influence diversification (Gómez-Mejía et al., 2010), governance practices and structure (Daily and Dollinger, 1992), and the organization's goals (Tagiuri and Davis, 1992). Given the prominence of family businesses and their influence on the global economy, the role of CE in the performance of family businesses has significant theoretical and practical implications (Gersick et al., 1997).

There are a number of opportunities for the family business and CE literatures to inform each other. Indeed, substantial recent progress has been made in their integration, including special issues related to CE in family business and the publication of several books examining entrepreneurial behavior in family firms (e.g., Hoy and Sharma, 2010; Stewart et al., 2010). This attention reflects the importance of CE to the sustained performance of family firms and also builds upon the strongly-held belief that family businesses may differ in the ways they implement CE strategies.

There are many reasons for the potential differences between family and non-family firms. First, strategic management in family businesses differs from non-family businesses based on their systems of governance and needs for family harmony (e.g., Carney, 2005; Harris et al., 1994). Second, family involvement can result in the development of resources unique to family businesses (i.e., familiness; Habbershon and Williams, 1999). These resources may be leveraged in ways that can influence CE activities (e.g., Borch et al., 1999). Further, agency problems are thought to influence CE, and family businesses experience different agency problems than non-family businesses (Schulze et al., 2001). For these reasons, the intersection of research in family business and CE presents fertile ground for further research.

To facilitate increased research on the CE strategies of family businesses, we assess the current state of the CE literature from a family business perspective (c.f., Dess et al., 2003). As part of our review, we attempted to follow the approach used by Raisch and Birkinshaw (2008) and Short and colleagues (2010) in structuring the review around themes. In the sections that follow, we review and critique existing studies, and pose research questions of interest to both the family business and CE fields. Overall, our review looks at CE as an antecedent, process, and a consequence of family business phenomena. Following trends in the broader family business literature, we note that CE studies in family business have predominantly drawn from agency, resource-based, and organizational identity theories. Empirical research in these areas has used a variety of research methods; however, survey research is becoming increasingly popular. Despite the recent interest in this area, much remains unknown about the role of CE in family businesses, thus creating opportunities for future research.

CORPORATE ENTREPRENEURSHIP IN FAMILY BUSINESSES

Corporate Entrepreneurship

The study of CE began in response to researchers' need to understand how organizational rejuvenation and innovation influence firm performance. As the body of CE research began to grow, a number of differing definitions arose. An early and widely cited attempt

to define CE included two main components: new venture creation within existing organizations (corporate venturing) and organizational transformation via strategic renewal (Guth and Ginsberg, 1990). However, as researchers recognized that venturing could stem from both formal and informal activities, conceptual development of the CE concept expanded (e.g., Zahra, 1991). This expansion often incorporated broader definitions and with a greater focus on the mechanisms through which firms maintain an entrepreneurial spirit. Scholars' inability to agree on a single definition led Sharma and Chrisman (1999) to reconcile the differing views. They suggested a broad conceptualization that included corporate venturing, innovation, and strategic renewal, but also provided distinctions between types of corporate ventures. In our review, we adopt Sharma and Chrisman's (1999) conceptualization of CE; however, it is important to note that the CE literature remains 'fragmented and non-cumulative' (Ireland et al., 2009).

Family Firms and Corporate Entrepreneurship

Despite definitional issues, research in CE has continued to grow (Phan et al., 2009). However, much of this growth has taken place outside of the family business literature, resulting in a gap between what we know about CE in family businesses and CE in general (Chrisman et al., 2005a; Habbershon and Pistrui, 2002). As a consequence, a number of authors have commented on the relatively early developmental state of the understanding of CE in family firms (Hoy, 2006; Lumpkin et al., 2010).

To assess the current state of the CE literature as it relates to family businesses, we identified and analyzed articles where the primary topic of interest was CE or one of its key entrepreneurial processes. We focused on the literature addressing the family firm as the focal unit in which entrepreneurship takes place, rather than entrepreneurial families.

Therefore, we searched a number of databases (EBSCO, JSTOR, Web of Knowledge) for articles that explicitly mentioned *corporate entrepreneurship, corporate venturing, internal ventures, new business venturing, intrapreneurship, strategic renewal, organizational renewal, innovation, strategic entrepreneurship,* or *entrepreneurial orientation* in the title, abstract, or keywords without placing boundaries on time period. We also required that articles contain one of the following: *family business, family firm, family enterprise,* or common derivations (e.g., 'family firms'). This search yielded 86 relevant articles. From this list we eliminated non-academic articles, teaching cases, and those with only weak ties to CE and family business. This resulted in a total of 57 articles from a variety of outlets in management, entrepreneurship, and family business. We complemented this search with other well-known studies that were not captured within these search parameters, such as books (e.g., Hoy and Sharma, 2010; Miller and Le Breton-Miller, 2005), and recent reviews of the family business literature (e.g., Chrisman et al., 2010; Sharma, 2004).

The majority of these studies appear in a few journals. The leader with eleven publications is *Family Business Review,* which is the leading family business journal. A secondary group of journals, including *Entrepreneurship Theory & Practice, Strategic Entrepreneurship Journal, Small Business Economics, Entrepreneurship & Regional Development,* and *Journal of Family Business Strategy,* published the majority of the remaining studies. The remaining articles appear in journals with one or no other publications on the subject. The fact that the majority of studies appear in a relatively small number of outlets is advantageous. The few journals that publish the lion's share of work on CE in family firms are conceivably building expert competencies at the reviewer and editor level. These competencies may improve feedback provided to authors, elevating the overall quality of research looking at CE in family firms.

In our review below, we divide our discussion into three sections: how CE is treated in the family business literature; methodological themes; and the theoretical frameworks used in this literature. Our review focuses on firm-level entrepreneurial phenomena, and thus the choice of search terms was geared towards having the firm as the unit of analysis. However, there is increasing interest in treating the family as the unit of analysis. This includes studies focusing on families who start and run multiple businesses (Habbershon and Pistrui, 2002; Uhlaner et al., 2012), including as part of a distinct family portfolio (Plate et al., 2010; Sieger et al., 2011). We refer those interested in the family level of analysis to Chapter 18 in this *Handbook* (Rosa et al., 2014).

How CE is Treated in the Family Firm Literature

Our review showed that research in CE has been approached in three key ways in the family business literature. The first, and most common treatment of CE, was as an outcome. This included examining CE or related concepts such as risk-taking or innovation as a dependent variable. These studies generally assumed that family-related issues, such as family ownership and culture, would create differences in the level of CE demonstrated by family firms. Many of the studies built upon the premise that family firms employ different strategic processes (Chrisman et al., 2008; Ducassy and Prevot, 2010) and tested if family firms were generally more entrepreneurial or more conservative, risk-averse, and resistant to change (Gersick et al., 1997; Hall et al., 2001).

The second approach looks at how CE affected the performance of family firms. These studies suggested that CE in family businesses might lead to different performance consequences compared to their non-family counterparts. For instance, one study examined moderating factors related to family business characteristics (Casillas et al., 2010). Many of these studies operationalized CE as

Entrepreneurial Orientation (EO), although two studies examined innovation-related predictors (Danes et al., 2007; Zellweger and Sieger, 2012). The relative underrepresentation of family business studies using this approach to CE is noteworthy as this approach is one of the most common in the broader CE literature. For instance, a recent meta-analysis found over 100 empirical studies examining the relationship between EO and performance (Rauch et al., 2009). Three studies fell into both of these streams as they first focused their attention on predicting CE outcomes before examining the impact of CE activities on the performance of the firm (i.e., Kellermanns et al., 2008; Memili et al., 2010; Naldi et al., 2007).

The third stream treated CE as an event or an activity and examined what happens to family firms after engaging in CE. In other words, this approach treats CE as an empirical setting rather than as a variable. For instance, Wong et al. (2010) examined the impact on stock price after corporate venturing. Here, they explained how and why aspects of being a family business might predict how the stock price reacted differently compared to non-family firms.

Methodological Themes

Among the 57 articles looking at CE in family firms, 36 were empirical and directly addressed the role of CE in family firms.[1] We examined study design, the sample used, as well as the specific aspect of CE studied. To code aspects of CE adopted in each article, we employed a set of broad definitional parameters of CE that included innovation, corporate venturing, and strategic renewal, and related concepts such as EO (c.f., Zahra et al., 1999). We outline these studies in Table 17.1.

Of these 36 empirical studies, there was a strong representation of quantitative studies, especially those using surveys. Of the reviewed studies, 22 employed survey methodology. Other quantitative studies employed secondary data from public companies (Wagner, 2010; Ducassy and Prevot, 2010), event analysis

(Chang et al., 2010; Wong et al., 2010) or structured interviews (Pittino and Visintin, 2009). While surveys were the most common, insightful findings have also resulted from longitudinal case studies. In our review, seven studies used case methods using multiple approaches such as matched cases (e.g., Toledano et al., 2010), multiple case studies (e.g., Hall et al., 2001; Zellweger and Sieger, 2012), and singular longitudinal cases (e.g., Salvato et al., 2010). The remaining study employed a method that has been less common in the family business CE literature: Short and colleagues (2009) used content analysis to measure the prominence of language associated with EO in shareholder letters, and used this to compare family and non-family firms' use of EO rhetoric. While the study of CE and family firms has been biased towards the use of surveys, this reflects general trends in the broader entrepreneurship literature (Chandler and Lyon, 2001). Yet, a recent article reviewing methods in entrepreneurship suggests that researchers are developing novel, rigorous, and powerful new approaches to examine entrepreneurship phenomena (Short et al., 2010). These methods may be valuable in family business research as well.

Empirical studies on CE in family firms have tended to use one of two types family firms in their sampling. Twenty-two of the 36 empirical studies specifically examined small family firms, and many of these studies focused on very small firms (i.e. under 50 employees). The alternate approach was to focus on publicly traded family businesses. Among the studies that did this, a common sampling frame was the S&P 500 (e.g., Short et al., 2009; Wagner, 2010). One study (Zahra, 2012) examined both small and large firms. Very few studies examined medium sized firms (e.g., Zellweger and Sieger, 2012) or large, privately held firms (e.g., Bergfeld and Weber, 2011; Sieger et al., 2011). The overall lack of study of larger, public family firms is somewhat surprising as a significant portion of the most successful firms on the Fortune 500 listing are family firms (Anderson and Reeb, 2003; Gómez-Mejía et al., 2003). Yet,

Table 17.1 Main focus of empirical studies of corporate entrepreneurship in family firms

Article	Focus of CE	Type of study	Type of family firms	Country	Aspect of CE
Bergfeld and Weber (2011)	Outcome	Qualitative (interviews)	Large and established firms, multiple industries	Germany	Innovativeness
Casillas and Moreno (2010)	Impact	Quantitative (survey)	Small firms, multiple industries	Spain	EO
Casillas et al. (2010)	Impact	Quantitative (survey)	Small firms, multiple industries	Spain	EO
Casillas et al. (2011)	Outcome	Quantitative (survey)	Small firms, multiple industries	Spain	EO
Chang et al. (2010)	Event	Quantitative (event-study)	Public companies, multiple industries	Taiwan	Innovation
Chirico and Nordqvist (2010)	Outcome	Qualitative (case studies)	Established firms, beverage industry	Switzerland; Italy	EO
Chirico et al. (2011)	Impact	Quantitative (survey)	SMEs, multiple industries	Switzerland	EO
Craig and Dibrell (2006)	Outcome	Quantitative (survey)	SMEs, multiple industries	USA	Innovation
Craig and Moores (2006)	Outcome	Quantitative (survey)	SMEs	Australia	Innovation
Cruz and Nordqvist (2012)	Outcome	Quantitative (survey)	SMEs, multiple industries	Spain	EO
Danes et al. (2007)	Impact	Quantitative (survey)	SMEs, multiple industries	USA	Innovation
Ducassy and Prevot (2010)	Outcome	Quantitative (secondary data)	Publicly traded firms, multiple industries	France	Innovation (diversification)
Eddleston et al. (2008)	Impact	Quantitative (survey)	SMEs	USA	Innovation
Gudmundson et al. (2003)	Outcome	Quantitative (survey)	SMEs, multiple industries	USA	Innovation
Gurrieri (2008)	Outcome	Quantitative (survey)	Small firms, multiple industries (mostly service)	Italy	Innovation
Hall et al. (2001)	Outcome	Qualitative (case studies)		Sweden	Organizational renewal (radical change)
Kellermanns and Eddelston (2006)	Outcome	Quantitative (survey)	Small firms	USA	CE (Miller's 1983 items)
Kellermanns et al. (2008)	Outcome; impact	Quantitative (survey)	Small firms	USA	CE (Miller's 1983 items)
Kellermanns et al. (2012)	Impact	Quantitative (survey)	Small firms	USA	Innovativeness (based on Miller 1983)

Article	Focus of CE	Type of study	Type of family firms	Country	Aspect of CE
Marchisio et al. (2010)	Impact	Qualitative (case studies)	Varying size, chemical manufacturing	Italy	Corporate Venturing
Memili et al. (2010)	Outcome; impact	Quantitative (survey)	Not presented	Switzerland	Risk-taking
Naldi et al. (2007)	Outcome; impact	Quantitative (survey)	SMEs, multiple industries	Sweden	EO, risk-taking
Pistrui et al. (2000)	Context	Quantitative (survey)	Small firms	Germany	Entrepreneurial Intensity
Pittino and Visintin (2009)	Outcome	Quantitative (structured interview)	Small firms	Italy	Innovation (product, process, business model)
Salvato et al. (2010)	Outcome	Qualitative (case study)	Large steel firm	Italy	Organizational renewal (Strategic change via exit)
Scholes et al. (2010)	Outcome	Quantitative (survey)	SMEs, multiple industries	UK	Organizational renewal (Strategic change)
Short et al. (2009)	Outcome	Qualitative (content analysis)	Public companies, multiple industries	USA	EO
Sieger et al. (2011)	Outcome	Qualitative (multiple case studies)	Large firms, multiple industries	Ireland, France, Chile, Guatemala	Family portfolio
Toledano et al. (2010)	Outcome	Qualitative (case studies)	Small firms, metal sector	Spain	Corporate Venturing, Innovation
Wagner (2010)	Outcome	Quantitative (secondary)	Public companies, multiple industries	USA	Innovation
Weismeier-Sammer (2011)	Outcome	Quantitative (survey)	Small firms, food and beverage industry	Austria	CE (Miller's 1983 items)
Wong et al. (2010)	Event	Quantitative (event-study)	Public companies, multiple industries	Taiwan	Corporate Venturing
Zahra (2005)	Outcome	Quantitative (survey)	Small and large firms, manufacturing	USA	Risk-taking
Zahra (2012)	Outcome	Quantitative (survey)	Small and large firms, multiple industries	USA	CE
Zahra et al. (2004)	Outcome	Quantitative (survey)	Small firms, manufacturing	USA	CE (Miller's 1983 items)
Zellweger and Sieger (2012)	Impact	Qualitative (case studies)	Medium sized firms, multiple industries	Switzerland	EO

the focus on small firms may be a reflection of the relative simplicity of effectively capturing family issues or gaining access to executives in smaller firms. It may also be a reflection of the large number of small family firms in the global economy (e.g., Faccio and Lang, 2002). Nevertheless, others have suggested that the focus on small, private firms over larger firms is potentially problematic (Habbershon and Pistrui, 2002) and may provide challenges in drawing robust, generalizable conclusions about CE in family firms.

Our review identified a wide array of industries represented. Many studies included multiple industries in their sampling frame (e.g., Naldi et al., 2007; Scholes et al., 2010). Only a few studies focused on single industries. For example, Chirico and Nordqvist (2010) looked at the beverage industry, Marchisio and colleagues (2010) examined the chemical industry, and Weismeier-Sammer (2011) focused on the food and beverage manufacturing industries. We found it interesting that a number of the multi-industry studies did not control for differences in industry characteristics, which may account for variance in the level and type of CE activities. There are some exceptions, such as those studies that deliberately attempted to capture the 'self-perceived' views of technological opportunities (e.g., Kellermanns and Eddleston, 2006) and those that included moderating variables such as environmental dynamism in their model (e.g., Casillas et al., 2010). The inclusion of increased industry characteristic controls and measurement may be useful for researchers in understanding the effectiveness of entrepreneurial behavior in family firms. For example, one study noted that family firms may have a structural advantage in high-velocity environments as they were able to make quicker decisions (Harris et al., 1994), and thus pursue opportunities in a more expeditious manner. This advantage may stem from family firms' tendency to have more cohesive and homogeneous top management teams (Daily and Dollinger, 1992), reducing conflict or discussions that

may impede decision-making. Understanding environmental characteristics would therefore be vital in capturing these potential advantages.

One potentially interesting observation from our review is the international nature of the studies. This international focus is valuable given the important role of family firms to economies around the world (Gersick et al., 1997). Based on our review, there appear to be a few national clusters of CE-related family business research. This has the advantage of being able to develop some cumulative knowledge within specific national contexts, but also leaves a number of important gaps. For example, of the 36 empirical studies we examine, 12 were from the USA, 10 were from Mediterranean countries (5 from Spain, 4 from Italy, and 1 from France), and 9 were from other Western European countries (3 from Switzerland, 2 from Sweden, 2 from Germany, and 1 each from the UK and Austria). Two other studies examined Taiwanese firms and one studied Australian firms. There were two studies (Chirico and Nordqvist, 2010; Sieger et al., 2011) that examined multiple cases of CE in family firms in more than one country (Italy and Switzerland for Chirico and Nordqvist, 2010; Ireland, France, Chile, and Guatemala for Sieger et al., 2011). There are several important regions where family-related CE research is underrepresented, including Asia,[2] Eastern Europe, Africa, and Latin America (Nordqvist and Melin, 2010). Clearly, much more can still be learned about CE in family firms in many of the regions that currently only have a few studies published. However, recent books, such as that by Au et al. (2011) concerning family business in the Asia Pacific, and by Nordqvist et al. (2011) on Latin America, offer some promise for the future regarding these otherwise underrepresented regions.

Several studies looking at CE in family firms focused on individual components or aspects of CE. Of the 36 empirical studies, 12 examined innovation. While there was variance in the aspect of innovation being explored, the majority of the focus was on new product innovation. Only two studies looked at corporate venturing, an important phenomenon in the CE literature. Strategic renewal was examined in three studies; however, these studies' ties to strategic renewal were weak, focusing more on different aspects of strategic change (e.g., exit: Salvato et al., 2010; radical change: Hall et al., 2001). Nine studies examined EO (e.g., Casillas and Moreno, 2010). Short and colleagues (2009) look at all five dimensions of EO while others examine individual dimensions. For example, the risk-taking dimension was the focus of three studies (Memili et al., 2011; Naldi et al., 2007; Zahra, 2005). Five studies (i.e., Kellermanns et al., 2008; Kellermanns and Eddleston, 2006; Weismeier-Sammer, 2011; Zahra, 2012; Zahra et al., 2004) used a generic CE or entrepreneurship dependent variable, although the actual operationalization was frequently Miller's (1983) items. These items are very similar to items used in EO studies, suggesting that there may be some overlap between these CE studies and those that explicitly address EO.

Only one study looked at multiple components of CE, with innovation and corporate venturing being key variables (Toledano, et al., 2010). The difficulty in capturing multiple aspects of CE may lie in developing a cohesive set of explanatory mechanisms and predictors in one study. The differing components of CE conceivably involve different processes and resources, and decisions on which mode to follow may be a reflection of family preferences for risk and return. As such, each CE activity may have a distinct nomological network. Toledano and colleagues (2010) made a commendable effort and we only identified one other study in the broader CE literature that examined multiple CE activities in one study (i.e., Zahra, 2003).

Theoretical Themes

Chrisman and colleagues (2003) identify a number of useful theoretical frameworks that may guide research related to CE in family

firms. In our review, we found a few studies that did not employ singular and specific theoretical frameworks to guide their inquiries. In some cases, researchers built arguments based on earlier works that had used differing theoretical lenses. However, there were also multiple studies that used theoretical lenses that are applicable to the context of family firms and many of these studies are recent. We believe that studies of CE in family firms are increasing their reliance on theory. The three most salient frameworks employed were the resource-based view (RBV), agency theory, and organizational identity. Not surprisingly, these theories are also commonly used in the broader family business literature (Chrisman et al., 2010; Sharma, 2004). While we treat these theories as content domains for classification purposes, we note that there are overlaps in the logics employed by each. For instance, we used the RBV framework to categorize many issues related to culture (Zahra et al., 2004) and family (Kellermanns and Eddleston, 2006), and therefore also include issues such as time orientation (and generational involvement). However, the time issue also appears to be salient within the organizational identity and agency theories as well.

There appears to be two opposing views of the role of CE in family firms with regards to their ability, willingness, and potential to achieve success in CE activities. Some view the unique nature of family firms as being central in fostering CE (e.g., Aldrich and Cliff, 2003; McCann et al., 2001). Others argue that characteristics of family firms, such as risk aversion or reluctance to change (Cabrera-Suarez et al., 2001), work as inhibitors of CE (Zahra, 2005).

RBV

In a foundational piece, Habbershon and Williams (1999) build upon the resource-based view of the firm (RBV) to explain the intangible behavioral and social phenomena that make family firms distinctive. They coined the term *familiness* to suggest that family firms possess a unique culture that is difficult to imitate, and to provide insight into why family and non-family firms may, in fact, be different. Other family business researchers have extended the argument that attributes of families provide family firms with competitive strengths (Chrisman, et al., 2005a).

For example, arguing that family firm culture is distinct, Zahra and colleagues (2004) identify four salient cultural dimensions that distinguish family from non-family firms: (1) individual vs group orientation; (2) internal vs external cultural orientation; (3) coordination and control; and (4) short vs long-term orientation. They find that a long-term orientation was conducive to entrepreneurship in family firms, as was finding a balance between individual vs group orientation. This balance meant that individual initiatives were supported by the firm, encouraging individuals to take risks. However, the group orientation led to many of these individual efforts being tempered to control and coordinate risk-taking. Roessl and colleagues (2010) present a comprehensive list of culture-related issues to help determine the preparedness of family firms to innovate. Other RBV advantages may be conferred on family firms (Lumpkin et al., 2011), such as increased specific human capital and tacit knowledge stemming from growing up in a family firm (Sirmon and Hitt, 2003), may lead to long-term performance differences.

The temporal theme is a recurring one in the family firm literature. In regards to CE, possessing a long-term orientation is believed to give the family firm a lower willingness to accept risk, and a tendency to be less competitively aggressive compared to short-term orientations (Lumpkin et al., 2010). Specifically, firms with a long-term orientation are expected to evaluate opportunities more thoroughly and equip themselves with the tools to help evaluate and allocate resources in pursuit of opportunities that may have a long-term impact (Miller and Le Breton-Miller, 2005; Zahra et al., 2004). This includes efforts to be more innovative and proactive, even though a long-term orientation is often associated with more conservative behavior (Lumpkin et al., 2010).

There have also been suggestions that short-term orientations are connected to tight financial controls, whereas long-term orientations help promote strategic controls (Zahra et al., 2004). Webb and colleagues (2010) suggest that family firms need to develop a mindset that balances both short- and long-term objectives.

Further work has addressed questions of whether family firms become more or less entrepreneurial over time. Hoy (2006) argued that family firms must contend with organizational life-cycle based fluctuations and therefore must work to maintain their entrepreneurial activities (including renewal) to avoid declines in performance during these fluctuations. As such, family firms' orientations towards risk-taking, innovativeness, and proactiveness should also change over time. To that end, some research has examined the differences between first, second, and multi-generation family businesses (e.g., Aronoff, 1998; Cruz and Nordqvist, 2012; Dyer, 1988; Gersick et al., 1997; Sonfield and Lussier, 2004). In the first generation, many firms are satisfied with continuing to pursue the initial innovation on which the firm was founded. From a cultural perspective, many founders have been shown to retain centralized decision-making, thus having an adverse effect on the exchange of entrepreneurial ideas (Dyer, 1988), sticking to their previously successful strategies (Ward, 1987), or developing emotional attachments to their current strategic positions (Miller et al., 2003). As such, it is common in family firm studies to include variables such as length of CEO tenure and the generation of family ownership of the firm (often called generational involvement) in order to capture issues as to whether founders who were more entrepreneurial early in their careers may become more conservative over time (Zahra et al., 2004; Zahra, 2005), or if there is changing focus as the firm switches generations of family ownership (Cruz and Nordqvist, 2012; Miller, 1983). Chirico and colleagues (2011) find that multigenerational family involvement has a positive effect on financial performance when it is accompanied by high levels of EO and a highly participative strategy, where there is truly 'planned' transgenerational entrepreneurship (see also Nordqvist and Zellweger, 2010).

In later generations, there may be an increased push towards CE activities (Litz and Kleysen, 2001) as a function of changing environmental conditions, customer demand, or the astute identification of opportunities by the new CEO (Salvato, 2004). In some cases, the increase in entrepreneurial activity may also help achieve levels of financial success similar to that experienced by previous generations (Jaffe and Lane, 2004). A preliminary study of the determinants of CE over time found that family-related issues were the main predictors of entrepreneurial behavior in the early stages of the firm and non-family issues such as management and financial resources took precedence later (Cruz and Nordqvist, 2012). Moreover, Casillas et al. (2010) found that EO was only positively related to increased firm performance for second generation family firms, showing that one's willingness to engage in entrepreneurial activity may have varying impacts over time. Brundin et al. (2010) suggest that founder-centric cultures may provide challenges for later entrepreneurial efforts unless these cultures are also tempered with higher levels of autonomy and proactiveness.

A further cultural aspect connected to CE is the willingness to change. An overall willingness to change leads to increased entrepreneurial activity (Kellermanns and Eddleston, 2006). Hall and colleagues (2001) suggested that developing a strong corporate culture that includes a willingness to break away from the traditional family business practices is essential for encouraging radical change. Yet, other researchers have found that some family firms never develop this willingness (e.g., Litz and Kleysen, 2001). This reluctance to change may stem from a fear of creating conflict, related to capital expense outlays, or of 'letting go of the past' (Beckhard and Dyer,

1983; Vago, 2004). As a result, firms that possess these fears or lack this willingness to change have been shown to be associated with the stagnation of performance or a loss of market share (Miller et al., 2003). Nevertheless, investigating why some family firms possess this entrepreneurial spirit where others do not may be an important avenue for future research.

Identity

The notion of identity is important for CE in family firms inasmuch as the goals of family firms may differ from those of their non-family counterparts.[3] An organizational identity represents the central and enduring perceptions of the organization's members with regards to that which makes an organization unique (Albert and Whetten, 1985). Family businesses are thought to have at least two salient identities: a family (normative) identity, and a business (utilitarian) identity (Foreman and Whetten, 2002; Zachary et al., 2011). These multiple identities then drive the economic and non-economic goals of the organization (McKenny et al., 2012; Zellweger et al., 2013). The drive to engage in entrepreneurial activity for financial returns can be thought to be salient to a business (utilitarian) identity. Yet, this does not necessarily appear to be the most salient goal for family firms. Many family firms appear to have as their main goals to ensure the long-term survival of the firm and the ability to offer employment to family members, as opposed to non-family firms who may direct their attention primarily to profit maximization (Athanassiou et al., 2002).[4] These goals are centered on the family (normative) identity of the organization. Indeed, there is some evidence that the key reason family firms are created is to fulfill an underlying purpose of creating a family legacy and offering long-term value creation (Casson, 1999). For existing family firms, the primary focus may be on wealth preservation (Chrisman et al., 2005b), other family interests (Sharma et al., 1997), or maintaining the status quo (Gersick et al., 1997).

From an identity perspective, many of the goals of the family firm are geared towards protecting the family name and legacy of the founders (Dyer and Whetten, 2006; Kelly et al., 2000), including retaining a positive external image. Retaining this positive public identity may explain why family firms tend to exhibit higher levels of corporate social responsibility and care for the environment (Craig and Moores, 2006). This also provides an explanation as to the inclusion of socioemotional wealth into discussions of family business decision-making (Gómez-Mejía et al., 2007). Further, the concern for retaining financial well-being for future generations and maintaining current social status (Naldi et al., 2007; Zellweger et al., 2010) may also explain the observed lower levels of risk-taking long-term orientations.

It is understandable, from an identity perspective, that engaging in potentially risky entrepreneurial activity is not a simple decision, despite the potential benefits to the firm and individual managers. Entrepreneurship has been thought to have the potential to increase performance (Wiklund and Shepherd, 2011), but also may impose major limitations to capital (Carney, 2005) and success is not guaranteed. An empirical example illustrating this was the study examining an Italian steel company, Falck (Salvato et al., 2010). The continuity of the founder's original goal and established identity of the firm offered resistance to strategic renewal. A future-oriented champion collaborating with a group of astute non-family participants was necessary to break through organizational inertia and create a new identity. Memili and colleagues' (2010) study also shows a web of relationships among family firm image, family ownership, family expectations, risk-taking and firm performance.

Whether a family business is 'family-controlled' or merely 'family-owned'[5] may affect the extent to which the family's identity influences the likelihood of engaging in and the goals to be gained from CE. Family-owned firms are argued to have higher dispersion of ownership and be more likely to have a professional (non-family) CEO than family-controlled firms (Schulze et al., 2003a). Thus, in family-controlled firms we would expect

that the more concentrated influence of the family, a sustaining force of the normative (family) identity, would play a larger role in the shaping of the strategy for CE than in family-owned firms, where professional management and diffuse ownership may make the family identity relatively less salient. However, research in this area is needed to determine the validity of this proposition.

Agency

One of the most intriguing aspects about family firms and their governance is the overlap of managers and owners (Daily and Dollinger, 1991). Agency theory was born out of the potential disconnect between the goals and values of ownership and managers (Jensen and Meckling, 1976), and the subsequent inconsistencies of how to maximize the value to shareholders and other stakeholders (Eisenhardt, 1989). However, the goals and values of owners and managers are seemingly aligned in family firms because the roles of manager and owner frequently coincide. This overlap helps to alleviate many of the traditional agency concerns related to opportunistic behavior by agents (Chrisman, Chua and Litz, 2004; Schulze et al., 2001). This suggests that family firms with tight owner-manager relations might exhibit strong levels of CE. As a positive outcome of this phenomena, more centralized decision-making allows for rapid responses and tight ownership controls to promote the usage of resources at the owners' behest (Dyer and Handler, 1994; Shanker and Astrachan, 1996), but also makes the assumption that there will be a greater emphasis on stewardship and the use of resources to increase the value to owner-managers (Steier, 2003). To this end, Zahra (2005) empirically shows that family ownership and involvement help increase entrepreneurial activity with family firms.

However, many of the goals of the owner-managers are not in line with profit maximization. A result of this may be entrepreneurial behaviors with less risk but less potential market impact. This may be one reason for differences in the performance of publicly traded family and non-family firms (Anderson and Reeb, 2003). Further, the governing mechanisms and socioeconomic goals may also encourage altruism, allowing for free riding with other family members, hiring and promotion of employees based on family status, or overcompensating for services with other stakeholders (Lubatkin et al., 2005; Schulze, Lubatkin and Dino, 2003b). Altruism may even result in more lax controls in the monitoring of other family members, thereby either allowing family employees to carry out projects that are not worthwhile and taking up valuable resources. Chang and colleagues (2010) found a negative relationship with the level of family control on the market reaction to innovation announcements, and lesser response to corporate venturing announcements (Wong et al., 2010).

In response to the threat of altruism hurting the CE potential of family firms, Zahra (2003) and Eddleston and Kellermanns (2007) argued that altruism can be a positive force for performance if this comes in the form of stewardship, as family firm members may engage in mutual trust and devotion, as opposed to self-serving agents (Corbetta and Salvato, 2004). Le Breton-Miller and Miller (2009) tried to reconcile the stewardship versus agency issues. However, many of the discussions of agency theory and CE take place in the context of large, publicly traded firms (Le Breton-Miller and Miller, 2009; Morck and Yeung, 2003), whereas the empirical studies have generally focused on small, private firms.

Clearly, each of these three theoretical perspectives – RBV, identity, and agency – have only begun to achieve the promise and potential value they have for understanding the role of corporate entrepreneurship in family firms. We turn next to a discussion of these and other future research opportunities.

OPPORTUNITIES FOR FUTURE RESEARCH

As the discussion and review of the extant literature describes, the work done towards better understanding CE in family firms has been fragmented and focused primarily on specific issues. At this stage in the development of the field of research at the intersection of CE and family firms, a multitude of new potential avenues and opportunities for future research remain.

In this section, we adopt three different approaches for developing new areas for research specifically targeting corporate entrepreneurship in family firms. In our first approach, we adopt a broad view of the family firm CE literature and make a few observations about opportunities for research stemming from our review. Second, we look at other currently espoused family firm frameworks that have not yet been included in discussions of CE. We illustrate how their inclusion in CE discussions may help to initiate novel research questions within the broader CE literature. Third, we discuss some of the current theoretical frameworks and ideas that are employed in CE research, but not yet in family business research. We argue that using the logic from CE-related theories may also initiate potentially important research questions in the family business realm. In keeping with the current treatment of CE and family business literature, we focus primarily on (a) CE as an outcome in family firms and (b) how CE impacts family firms.

Observations From the Review

Our review revealed several current gaps and challenges in the literature. Notably, the overall lack of study of the influences of CE on the performance of family firms is surprising given the focus on performance in the greater field of strategic management. This lack of knowledge is perhaps related to a general dearth of greater knowledge regarding what influences the entrepreneurial behavior of family firms. Yet, given the importance of family firms, developing a better understanding would be highly valuable for both researchers and practitioners. As such, we strongly encourage more research focusing on how CE impacts family firms and how family related issues may moderate or affect how CE activities affect the financial and non-financial performance of family firms.

Of particular interest to the family business literature would be to look at how CE impacts the level of socioemotional wealth of the owning family. Socioemotional wealth reflects the affective benefits that the owning family derives from the ownership and control of the family business (Gómez-Mejía et al., 2007) and is discussed in greater depth in Chapter 10 of this *Handbook* by Berrone et al. (2014). Generally, in situations where CE reallocates resources from the pursuit of non-economic goals to economic goals, one would expect that the relative proportion of wealth generated by the family business would shift from socioemotional to financial. Indeed, a common incentive for engaging in CE is to improve financial performance. However, CE might also be thought to positively influence socioemotional wealth through the revitalization of a family business that had previously had a tarnished image among the firm's stakeholders.

Socioemotional wealth may also be thought to influence the likelihood of engaging in CE or moderate the relationship between CE and economic performance. Prospect theory suggests that individuals that have accumulated wealth will be less likely to take risks with this wealth than those that have lost wealth (Kahneman and Tversky, 1979). Since CE is risky, prospect theory would suggest that families perceiving that CE may diminish their socioemotional wealth would oppose engagement in CE initially. Further, to the extent that CE is pursued, the family members' buy-in and commitment to the venture/project would be diminished, making it less likely to succeed. In sum, integrating socioemotional wealth into the family business CE literature has promise to advance our understanding of CE in family businesses.

Second, there appear to be two types of family firms that are generally studied: small, privately owned firms (SMEs), and larger, publicly traded firms. While we noted a few exceptions in our review, these two categories

of firms seem to represent two extremes of businesses in an economy, and fundamentally reflect differing governing mechanisms and size-based management issues. As such, it is conceivable that entrepreneurial activities are also likely to differ on the basis of their size and governance structures. For instance, in small family firms, close knit family relationships and a lack of resources may have a strong influence on performance. How and with what consequences risk-taking behavior may be enacted in these firms is likely to differ greatly from a publicly traded firm. As such, the potential differences in these types of family firms may provide major challenges to our ability to generate cumulative knowledge in this area, as the combined insights concerning CE in small and private versus large and public may be akin to comparing apples and oranges. To our knowledge, there has yet to be any framework to clearly lay out the differences in these types of firms and how this may impact their entrepreneurial behavior. Efforts along these lines would be welcome additions to helping better categorize and combine our research findings. The division of types of family firms described by Lim et al. (2010) may provide a starting point for understanding such differences. For example, research has found that CEO compensation differs based on the configurations of family involvement evident on the board such as the presence of other family board members beyond the CEO (Combs et al., 2011). Consequently, an examination of how such representation impacts CE in family firms would provide a natural extension of this research stream.

Another area that is ripe for expansion revolves around the international issues and differences that family firms may face as part of carrying out CE activities in varying regions. For instance, we noted that there were many studies carried out in the USA, Western Europe and the Mediterranean region, while many other regions (e.g., Asia, Latin America, Central Europe, Africa) had relatively limited attention in the literature. There may be a number of institutional frameworks that can help shed light on potential differences in CE behaviors across countries. Just as there are differences in number and type of startup entrepreneurial activities across countries, there may also be some heterogeneity across countries in terms of the type and frequency of CE in family firms (Burkart et al., 2003; Steier, 2009). Hofstede's (2001) work that identified important differences across national cultures (e.g., individualism, uncertainty avoidance) may also inform how families from different parts of the world are likely to pursue CE initiatives. Finally, the rich data being generated by the Global STEP project has already begun to shed light on multigenerational CE-related topics in different parts of the world where there was limited work done (e.g., Au et al., 2011; Nordqvist et al., 2011). How issues of renewal, venturing, and innovation are manifest across borders is an important topic for future family business research.

More family business research is also needed into each of the modes of CE – corporate venturing, innovation, and renewal. The vast majority of studies predicting CE have focused on innovation or employed a broad 'entrepreneurship' lens (such as EO) rather than specific CE activities. The processes, including timing, resource needs, and usage, and potential impact may very well differ between innovation, strategic renewal, and corporate venturing. Only one study in our review examined two types of CE outcomes (Toledano et al., 2010). Future research aimed at better understanding why a family firm may choose one mode over another – and with what consequences – would be important to increase understanding of family firm strategy. As a tangential topic, we note that there were no studies that looked at spin-offs – a natural outcome of corporate venturing. Spinning off an internal venture may be a particularly interesting topic as either an avenue of firm growth or as a way to 'remove' an underperforming family venture. In either case, issues such as whether to maintain control of the enterprise

or how to manage family members may reveal important new knowledge about how family firms' operations influence the extent and effectiveness of their entrepreneurial efforts. This issue may however already be addressed in the research examining the family as the unit of analysis.

Another area where future research might advance is to build upon Burgelman's (1983a) conceptualization of induced and autonomous corporate entrepreneurial processes to better understand how CE strategies are implemented in family businesses. Induced CE processes build upon the organization's current strategy and frequently are initiated from the top of the organization whereas autonomous CE processes start outside the current strategy and often are initiated from bottom-up. Many family firm leaders propagate a paternalistic culture where the leader exercises significant control and there is relatively less autonomy for lower-level employees than in alternative cultures (Dyer, 1988). Thus, for family firms with these authoritarian-style leaders, autonomous CE processes are unlikely to provide sufficient control or certainty to create buy-in. Induced CE processes, however, may be more palatable for these leaders as there is a greater sense of control in terms of the direction of the project to ensure that the result does not deviate significantly from their vision for the firm. Thus, researchers might investigate the extent to which family businesses use each type of process. Further, if family businesses do use induced CE more than autonomous CE, identifying whether induced CE outperforms autonomous CE in the family business context would carry significant practical implications for family business managers, consultants, and scholars.

Family Firm Theoretical Perspectives

Increased usage of theoretical frameworks and predictions in the study of CE in family firms is an important step for the further development of the field. We focused on the three most salient theoretical frameworks used in studies of CE in family firms (RBV, identity, and agency). However, there are several theoretical frameworks that are currently in use in other parts of the family business literature that may provide a number of important contributions if applied to a general CE context.

The notion of succession, for instance, is central to studies of family firms and the subject of Chapter 13 in this *Handbook* written by Long and Chrisman (2014). Yet, the theoretical issues surrounding succession have made limited inroads into the realm of CE. A number of important questions develop with using a succession lens, such as whether there are generational influences on opportunity recognition, whether succession planning helps or hurts CE and transition activities, and how organizational knowledge can be sustained through succession. There are a few studies that suggest that later generations were potentially more entrepreneurial than earlier generations. From a succession perspective, one can ask if this increase in entrepreneurial activity is planned, and whether the choice of family member to 'inherit' leadership depends on the propensity of that individual to lead innovative efforts and his/her discretion (Mitchell et al., 2009). Further, a temporal perspective may help to discover the antecedents in the decline of entrepreneurial activity of the founder – at what stage and based on what conditions? There are a number of studies that address the changing need for and nature of entrepreneurial behavior across the lifetime of firms (e.g., Zellweger and Sieger, 2012) and different generations of family leadership (e.g., Cruz and Nordqvist, 2012). Indeed, this issue is one of the pressing issues behind the study of 'transgenerational entrepreneurship' (Nordqvist and Zellweger, 2010). Yet, greater understanding of the mechanisms involved in the need for and choices related to succession, with a particular eye for planned or unplanned entrepreneurial efforts, are desirable. As a whole, Hoy's (2006) and Sharma's (2011) respective calls for more work on the changing nature of family business over time, and in particular the need for entrepreneurship

to change along a lifecycle, seems particularly germane.

This also has a natural overlap to areas relating to the enterprising family (cf. Habbershon et al., 2010). While the unit of analysis in the CE literature has tended to be the firm, greater integration of questions and conclusions from the family unit of analysis may be fruitful moving forward (see also Nordqvist and Melin, 2010; or Chapter 18 in this *Handbook* by Rosa et al., 2014). For instance, questions of why new ventures or portfolio firms are included or excluded from the central family firm, the extent of the overlaps among ideas and innovations in these successive firms, the usage of the central family firms' resources and knowledge in this process, the strategic focus (i.e., exploration, exploitation) of successive firms relative to initial firms, and the enactment of portfolio firms as part of the strategic renewal or rejuvenation of the family's entire wealth seem to have clear opportunities to contribute to both sets of literatures. We do acknowledge the work that distinguishes between strategic diversification and portfolio entrepreneurship as part of a corporate versus family strategy (Sieger et al., 2011) as providing a guiding light in terms of further integration of the CE to the enterprising family literatures.

Further, the family business dynamics between family and non-family members has a strong history of research within the family business realm (Barnett and Kellermanns, 2006; Mitchell et al., 2003). There are a number of potential inroads into the field of CE, such as the role of non-family members within the innovation process, especially on strategic renewal. Salvato and colleagues (2010) show that non-family members can be important in strategic change, but in the case they studied (Falck), there was also a strong family member helping to drive innovation and questioning. A related topic is the role of conflict in family businesses which can involve family versus non-family relationships as well as the tension between the business and the family in understanding family business dynamics.

Research indicates that trust plays an important role as a common governance mechanism in family firms (Eddleston et al., 2010; see also Chapter 25 in this *Handbook* by Steier and Muethel, 2014). Yet, trust in the context of CE may be contingent on the achievement of organizational goals, or in contributing to the long-term orientation of the firm. One area of research that may be important is to understand trust when times are challenging or when some innovative efforts fail, or how trust fits in to long-term orientations. Indeed, being accepting of failure has been shown to be important for encouraging CE activities (Burgelman, 1983b; Hornsby et al., 2002). In the context of a family firm, however, this may be seen in a different light, especially if the person 'charged' with this failure is a family or non-family member. Hence, the effect of trust and/or failure on the CE activities of family firms is a promising area of future research (Lumpkin et al., 2011).

The role of trust is also related to the possible role that differing levels of hierarchy may play in a CE context. Since CE activities are not exclusively carried out in a top-down delegated manner, but rather that employee empowerment and bottom-up initiatives may play vital roles (McGrath and Keil, 2007), the extent to which this is allowed – given some evidence that family firms have centralized decision-making – and in what way, might help to ascertain more about the process by which entrepreneurship 'happens'. In a recent study, Wales et al. (2011) provide guidelines for studying entrepreneurship throughout a hierarchy and across organizational units and departments. This may be useful in guiding future studies of CE-related activities throughout an entire firm.

While the examples above provide some preliminary thoughts as to where existing family business frameworks can be applied in CE research, there is also room for greater examination of other family firm concepts to understanding the extent to which CE activities differ in family firms and how family firms may be impacted differently by CE.

Corporate Entrepreneurship Themes

There are a large number of common themes that have their basis in the CE literature; building off of these theories in a family firm context may prove a promising avenue for future research. In Table 17.2, we attempt to describe a number of potential avenues for future study using various theoretical lenses.[6] In an article in the initial issue of *Strategic Entrepreneurship Journal*, the founding co-editors identified ten themes that might characterize future research (Schendel and Hitt, 2007). Given the similarities between strategic and corporate entrepreneurship, we used the *SEJ* categories they identified to map out not only appropriate theoretical lenses, but also examples of research questions that would be particularly germane for each of these lenses. One example of this is the role of ambidexterity in the management of family firms. Organizational ambidexterity as a concept focuses on the simultaneous balance of being efficient with current business practices while also being adaptive to changes in the environment (Raisch and Birkinshaw, 2008), and sometimes is seen as the simple reconciliation of the tradeoff between exploration and exploitation. Ambidexterity may present an interesting challenge for family firms for a number of reasons. First, the role of socioemotional wealth in family firms (e.g., Gómez-Mejía et al., 2007) might lead to questions such as how the importance of socioemotional wealth influences the processes of exploration and exploitation, and whether one might have priority over the other. Second, the research showing that family firms tend to take fewer risks (e.g., Naldi et al., 2007) may provide a challenge to the extent that being adaptive to the future environmental shifts fundamentally involves taking risks, and having impact on an industry may insinuate engaging in more radical innovation. Finally, the effect of a long-term orientation, generally believed to be

Table 17.2   Family business research opportunities focusing on key CE themes

SEJ theme	Possible research questions	Potential theoretical foundations
Strategy vs entrepreneurship	How might strategy and entrepreneurship processes influence socioemotional wealth in family businesses?	Resource-based view Ambidexterity
	How does socioemotional wealth influence the levels of explore and exploit processes in family businesses?	
Creativity, imagination, and opportunities	To what extent does family ownership influence the propensity to exploit intrapreneurial opportunities?	Agency theory Organizational learning
	Are there generational influences on opportunity recognition in family businesses?	
Risk and uncertainty	Do family businesses pursue strategic renewal differently than non-family businesses?	Real options/prospect theory Transaction cost economics
	Do family businesses restructure their businesses in the face of uncertainty differently than non-family businesses?	
Innovation	How do disruptive innovations impact family businesses differently than non-family businesses?	Disruptive innovation theory Ambidexterity
	Are family businesses more likely to pursue radical or incremental innovations?	
Change	How does the execution of strategic renewal activities affect family members differently than non-family employees?	Organizational justice Transaction cost economics
	Do family and non-family businesses attempt to change different aspects of their businesses?	
Technology	What is the most effective organizational structure for fostering technological innovation in family businesses?	Resource-based view Organizational knowledge
	How can technology be used to maintain organizational knowledge through succession?	
Entrepreneurial actions, innovation, and appropriability	Do family businesses exhibit different patterns of EO than non-family firms?	Entrepreneurial orientation Opportunity creation
	Are family firms more or less innovative than non-family firms?	
Behavioral characteristics of entrepreneurial activity	Do family businesses favor dispersed or focused approaches to CE?	Expected utility theory Agency theory
	How does the process of strategic renewal in family businesses differ from non-family businesses?	
Entrepreneurship and economic growth	What governmental legislations are effective in encouraging internal venturing in family businesses?	Resource-based view Austrian economics
	Do family businesses with CE strategies contribute more to a national economy than those without?	
Social role of entrepreneurship	Are family businesses more or less likely to engage in socially responsible internal corporate ventures?	Stakeholder theory Organizational identity
	Are family businesses more or less likely to engage in lay-offs during strategic renewal?	

common among family firms, may also offer a discerning view of the balance between exploration and exploitation given the timing and long-term impact involved (Webb et al., 2010).

Other theoretical areas that are important for the study of CE, such as organizational learning, knowledge management, and absorptive capacity, may also lead to new insights into how and to what extent these activities take place across time, or vary depending on changes in familiness, or as a function of differing governance structures (agency versus stewardship; types of family clans, etc.). In prior research, these areas have been connected to varying types of environments and knowledge/learning, and are most important in fast moving environments (Wiklund and Shepherd, 2003). Revisiting these issues in family firms may be important, given the argument that the smaller and more cohesive decision-making processes typical of family firms may have a structural advantage in making quick decisions (Harris et al., 1994). Many of these topics have hitherto been ignored in the literature, although Zahra (2012) is a notable exception. We list more such theories and types of questions asked in Table 17.2.

CONCLUSION

The family business literature has begun to look at ways in which the role of the family influences the implementation and success of corporate entrepreneurship strategies. This area of research has increased over the past few years. While there has been much recent progress in understanding CE in family firms, many questions remain unaddressed. These questions relate not only to the fundamental aspects of being in a family firm, such as issues of socioemotional wealth, succession, familiness, and non-family employees, but also to more general questions that stem from applying alternative theories to the context of family firms, such as how the socioemotional wealth influences the propensity to engage in strategic renewal, whether family businesses more or less effective at internal corporate venturing than non-family businesses, and if there are differences among generations in terms of likelihood to engage in corporate entrepreneurship. These offer substantive new avenues that will help guide the future of family business research. The unique characteristics of family firms, such as having multiple identities (e.g., Zachary et al., 2011), unique

resources (Habbershon and Williams, 1999), unique agency issues (e.g., Schulze et al., 2001), and potentially contrarian view of CE (e.g., Do family firms do more of it, or less?) suggest that this is a fertile area of research that has the potential to bring new insights into the broader CE literature. To encourage research in this area, this chapter provided an overview of the corporate entrepreneurship literature looking at family businesses to date and identified areas for future development.

NOTES

1 We eliminated studies that did not directly address CE and family firm issues, such as Hung and Whittington (2011) and Luo and Junkunc (2008), or used case illustrations in order to make a point as opposed to using true empirical methods (e.g., Litz and Kleysen, 2001).
2 Carney and Gedajlovic (2003) are one exception for journal articles. Their article uses a historical perspective on family groups in East Asia in the post-colonial era.
3 We refer interested readers to Chapter 24 on organizational identity in this *Handbook* (Whetten et al., 2014).
4 This may in fact be one reason why much of the family business research has looked at small, private companies, as publicly traded ones may have higher expectation levels of exhibiting profit maximization behavior.
5 These distinctions are covered in greater depth in Chapters 11 and 12 on governance by Gersick and Feliu (2014) and Goel et al. (2014) respectively.
6 Lumpkin et al. (2011) also provide an excellent research agenda regarding the Inputs, Processes, Outputs, and Context of strategic entrepreneurship in family firms. We suggest interested readers to also examine their set of questions and issues.

REFERENCES

Ahuja, G. and Lampert, C.M. (2001) 'Entrepreneurship in the large corporation: A longitudinal study of how established firms create breakthrough innovations', *Strategic Management Journal*, 22: 521–543.

Albert, S. and Whetten, D.A. (1985) 'Organizational identity', in Cummings, L.L. and Staw, B.M. (eds), *Research in Organizational Behavior*. Greenwich, CT: JAI Press, pp. 263–295.

Aldrich, H.E. and Cliff, J.E. (2003) 'The pervasive effects of family on entrepreneurship: Toward a family embeddedness perspective', *Journal of Business Venturing*, 18(5): 573–596.

Anderson, R.C. and Reeb, D.M. (2003) 'Founding-family ownership, corporate diversification, and firm leverage', *Journal of Law and Economics*, 46: 653–684.

Aronoff, C.E. (1998) 'Megatrends in family business', *Family Business Review*, 11(3): 181–186.

Athanassiou, N., Crittenden, W.F., Kelly, L.M., and Marquez, P. (2002) 'Founder centrality effects on the Mexican family firm's top management group: firm culture, strategic vision and goals, and firm performance', *Journal of World Business*, 37(2): 139–150.

Au, K., Craig, J.B., and Ramachandran, K. (2011) *Family Enterprises in the Asia Pacific: Exploring Transgenerational Entrepreneurship in Family Firms*. Cheltenham: Edward Elgar.

Barnett, T. and Kellermanns, F.W. (2006) 'Are we family? Nonfamily employees' perceptions of justice in the family firm', *Entrepreneurship Theory & Practice*, 30(6): 837–854.

Beckhard, R. and Dyer, W.G. (1983) 'Managing continuity in the family-owned business', *Organizational Dynamics*, 12: 5–12.

Bergfeld, M.M.H. and Weber, F.M. (2011) 'Dynasties of innovation: Highly performing German family firms and the owners' role for innovation', *International Journal of Entrepreneurship and Innovation Management*, 13(1): 80–94.

Berrone, P., Cruz, C., and Gomez-Mejia, L.R. (2014) Family-controlled firms and stakeholder management: A socioemotional wealth preservation perspective. In Melin, L., Nordqvist, M., and Sharma, P. (eds), *The SAGE Handbook of Family Business*. London: Sage.

Borch, O.J., Huse, M., and Senneseth, K. (1999) 'Resource configuration, competitive strategies, and corporate entrepreneurship: An empirical examination of small firms', *Entrepreneurship Theory & Practice*, 24: 51–72.

Brundin, E., Nordqvist, M., and Melin, L. (2010) 'Entrepreneurial orientation across generations in family firms: The role of owner-centric culture for proactiveness and autonomy', in Nordqvist, M. and Zellweger, T. (eds), *Transgenerational Entrepreneurship: Exploring Growth and Performance in Family Firms Across Generations*. Cheltenham: Edward Elgar, pp. 123–141.

Burgelman, R.A. (1983a) 'A model of the interaction of strategic behavior, corporate context, and the concept of strategy', *Academy of Management Review*, 8: 61–70.

Burgelman, R.A. (1983b) 'Corporate entrepreneurship and strategic management: Insights from a process study', *Management Science*, 29: 1349–1364.

Burkart, M.C., Panunzi, F., and Shleifer, A. (2003) 'Family firms', *Journal of Finance*, 58(5): 2167–2202.

Cabrera-Suarez, K., Saa-Perez, P., and Garcia-Almeida, D. (2001) 'The succession process from a resource- and knowledge-based view of the family firm', *Family Business Review*, 14: 37–48.

Carney, M. (2005) 'Corporate governance and competitive advantage in family-controlled firms', *Entrepreneurship Theory & Practice*, 29: 249–265.

Carney, M. and Gedajlovic, E. (2003) 'Strategic innovation and the administrative heritage of East Asian family business groups', *Asia Pacific Journal of Management*, 20(1): 5–26.

Casillas, J.C. and Moreno, A.M. (2010) 'The relationship between entrepreneurial orientation and growth: The moderating role of family involvement', *Entrepreneurship & Regional Development*, 22: 265–291.

Casillas, J.C., Moreno, A.M., and Barbero, J.L. (2010) 'A configurational approach of the relationship between entrepreneurial orientation and growth of family firms', *Family Business Review*, 23: 27–44.

Casillas, J.C., Moreno, A.M., and Barbero, J.L. (2011) 'Entrepreneurial orientation of family firms: Family and environmental dimensions', *Journal of Family Business Strategy*, 2: 90–100.

Casson, M. (1999) 'The economics of the family firm', *Scandinavian Economic History Review*, 17(1): 10–23.

Chandler, G.N. and Lyon, D.W. (2001) 'Issues of research design and construct measurement in entrepreneurship research: The past decade', *Entrepreneurship Theory & Practice*, 25: 101–113.

Chang, S., Wu, W., and Wong, Y. (2010) 'Family control and stock market reactions to innovation announcements', *British Journal of Management*, 21: 152–170.

Chirico, F. and Nordqvist, M. (2010) 'Dynamic capabilities and transgenerational value creation in family firms: The role of organizational culture', *International Small Business Journal*, 28: 1–18.

Chirico, F., Sirmon, D.A., Sciascia, S., and Mazzola, P.P. (2011) 'Resource orchestration in family firms: Investigating how entrepreneurial orientation, generational involvement and participative strategy affect performance', *Strategic Entrepreneurship Journal*, 5: 307–326.

Chrisman, J., Chua, J., and Litz, R. (2004) 'Comparing the agency costs of family and non-family firms: Conceptual issues and exploratory evidence', *Entrepreneurship Theory & Practice*, 28: 335–354.

Chrisman, J.J., Chua, J.H., and Sharma, P. (2005a) Trends and directions in the development of a strategic management theory of the family firm, *Entrepreneurship Theory & Practice*, 29: 555–575.

Chrisman, J.J., Chua J.H., and Steier, L.P. (2003) 'An introduction to theories of family business', *Journal of Business Venturing*, 18(4): 441–448.

Chrisman, J.J., Chua, J.H., and Steier, L. (2005b) 'Sources and consequences of distinctive familiness: An introduction', *Entrepreneurship Theory & Practice*, 29: 237–247.

Chrisman, J.J., Kellermanns, F.W., Chan, K.C., and Liano, K. (2010) 'Intellectual foundations of current research in family business: An identification and review of 25 influential articles', *Family Business Review*, 23: 9–26.

Chrisman, J.J., Steier, L.P., and Chua, J.H. (2008) 'Toward a theoretical basis for understanding the dynamics of strategic performance in family firms', *Entrepreneurship Theory & Practice*, 32: 935–947.

Combs, J.G., Penney, C., Crook, R.C., and Short, J.C. (2011) 'The impact of family representation on CEO compensation', *Entrepreneurship Theory & Practice*, 34: 1125–1144.

Corbetta, G. and Salvato, C. (2004) 'The board of directors in family firms: One size fits all?', *Family Business Review*, 17(2): 119–134.

Craig, J.L. and Dibrell, C. (2006) 'The natural environment, innovation, and firm performance: A comparative study', *Family Business Review*, 19: 275–288.

Craig, J.L. and Moores, K. (2006) 'A 10-year longitudinal investigation of strategy, systems, and environment on innovation in family firms', *Family Business Review*, 19: 1–10.

Cruz, C. and Nordqvist, M. (2012) 'Entrepreneurial orientation in family firms: A generational perspective', *Small Business Economics*, 38: 33–49.

Daily, C.M. and Dollinger, M.J. (1991) 'Family firms are different', *Review of Business*, 13(1): 3–5.

Daily, C.M. and Dollinger, M.J. (1992) 'An empirical examination of ownership structure in family and professionally managed firms', *Family Business Review*, 5: 117–136.

Danes, S.M., Stafford, K., and Loy, J.T.C. (2007) 'Family business performance: The effects of gender and management', *Journal of Business Research*, 60: 1058–1069.

Dess, G.G., Ireland, R.D., Zahra, S.A., Floyd, S.W., Janney, J.J., and Lane, P.J. (2003) 'Emerging issues in corporate entrepreneurship', *Journal of Management*, 29: 351–378.

Ducassy, I. and Prevot, F. (2010) 'The effects of family dynamics on diversification strategy: Empirical evidence from French companies', *Journal of Family Business Strategy*, 1: 224–235.

Dyer, W.G. (1988) 'Culture and continuity in family firms', *Family Business Review*, 1(1): 37–50.

Dyer, W.G. and Handler, W. (1994) 'Entrepreneurship and family business: Exploring the connections', *Entrepreneurship Theory & Practice*, 19(1): 71–83.

Dyer, W.G. and Whetten, D.A. (2006) 'Family firms and social responsibility: preliminary evidence from the S&P 500', *Entrepreneurship Theory & Practice*, 30(6): 785–802.

Eddleston, K.A., Chrisman, J., Steier, L., and Chua, J. (2010) 'Governance and trust in family firms: An introduction', *Entrepreneurship Theory & Practice*, 34(6): 1043–1056.

Eddleston, K.A. and Kellermanns, F.W. (2007) 'Destructive and productive family relationships: A stewardship theory perspective', *Journal of Business Venturing*, 22(4): 545–565.

Eddleston, K.A., Kellermanns, F.W., and Sarathy, R. (2008) 'Resource configuration in family firms: Linking resources, strategic planning, and technological opportunities to performance', *Journal of Management Studies*, 45(1): 26–50.

Eisenhardt, K.M. (1989) 'Agency theory: An assessment and review', *Academy of Management Review*, 14(1): 57–74.

Faccio, M. and Lang, L.H.P. (2002) 'The ultimate ownership of western European corporations', *Journal of Financial Economics*, 65: 365–395.

Foreman, P. and Whetten, D. (2002) 'Members' identification with multiple-identity organizations', *Organization Science*, 13(6): 618–635.

Gersick, K.E., Davis, J.A., Hampton, M.M., and Lansberg, I. (1997) *Generation to Generation: Life Cycles in the Family Business*. Boston, MA: Harvard Business School Press.

Gersick, K.E. and Neus, F. (2014) Governing the family enterprise: Practices, performance, and research. In Melin, L., Nordqvist, M., and Sharma, P. (eds), *The SAGE Handbook of Family Business*. London: Sage.

Goel, S., Jussila, I., and Ikäheimonen, T. (2014) Governance in family firms: A review and research agenda. In Melin, L., Nordqvist, M., and Sharma, P. (eds), *The SAGE Handbook of Family Business*. London: Sage.

Gómez-Mejía, L.R., Haynes, K.T., Nuñez-Nickel, M., Jacobson, K.J.L., and Moyano-Fuentes, J. (2007) 'Socioemotional wealth and business risks in family-controlled firms: Evidence from Spanish olive oil mills', *Administrative Science Quarterly*, 52: 106–137.

Gómez-Mejía, L.R., Larraza, M. and Makri, M. (2003) 'The determinants of executive compensation in family controlled public corporations', *Academy of Management Journal*, 46(2): 226–239.

Gómez-Mejía, L.R., Makri, M. and Larraza-Kintana, M. (2010) 'Diversification decisions in family-controlled firms', *Journal of Management Studies*, 47: 223–252.

Gudmundson, D., Tower, C.D., and Hartman, E.A. (2003) 'Innovation in small business: Culture and ownership structure do matter', *Journal of Developmental Entrepreneurship*, 8: 1–18.

Gurrieri, A.R. (2008) 'Knowledge network dissemination in the family-firm sector', *Journal of Socio-Economics*, 37(6): 2380–2389.

Guth, W.D. and Ginsberg, A. (1990) 'Guest editors' introduction: Corporate entrepreneurship', *Strategic Management Journal*, 11: 5–15.

Habbershon, T.G., Nordqvist, M., and Zellweger, T. (2010) 'Transgenerational entrepreneurship', in Nordqvist, M. and Zellweger, T. (eds), *Transgenerational Entrepreneurship: Exploring Growth and Performance in Family Firms Across Generations*. Cheltenham: Edward Elgar, pp. 141–160.

Habbershon, T.G. and Pistrui, J. (2002) 'Enterprising families domain: Family-influenced ownership groups in pursuit of transgenerational wealth', *Family Business Review*, 15(3): 223–237.

Habbershon, T.G. and Williams, M.L. (1999) 'A resource-based framework for assessing the strategic advantages of family firms', *Family Business Review*, 12: 1–25.

Hall, A., Melin, L., and Nordqvist, M. (2001) 'Entrepreneurship as a radical change in family business: Exploring the role of cultural patterns', *Family Business Review*, 14: 193–208.

Harris, D., Martinez, J.L., and Ward, J.L. (1994) 'Is strategy different for the family-owned businesses?', *Family Business Review*, 7: 159–176.

Hofstede, G.H. (2001) *Culture's Consequences: Comparing Values, Behaviors, Institutions and Organizations Across Nations*. Thousand Oaks, CA: Sage Publications.

Hornsby, J.F., Kuratko D.F., and Zahra, S.A. (2002) 'Middle managers' perceptions of the internal environment for corporate entrepreneurship: Assessing a measurement scale', *Journal of Business Venturing*, 17: 253–273.

Hoy, F. (2006) 'The complicating factor of life cycles in corporate venturing', *Entrepreneurship Theory & Practice*, 30: 831–836.

Hoy, F. and Sharma, P. (2010) *Entrepreneurial Family Firms*. Upper Saddle River, NJ: Prentice Hall.

Hung, S.-C. and Whittington, R. (2011) 'Agency in national innovation systems: Institutional entrepreneurship and the professionalization of Taiwanese IT', *Research Policy*, 40(4): 526–538.

Ireland, R.D., Covin, J.G., and Kuratko, D.F. (2009) 'Conceptualizing corporate entrepreneurship strategy', *Entrepreneurship Theory & Practice*, 33: 19–46.

Jaffe, D. and Lane, S. (2004) 'Sustaining a family dynasty: Key issues facing complex multigenerational business- and investment-owning families', *Family Business Review*, 17: 81–98.

Jensen, M.C. and Meckling, W.H. (1976) 'Theory of the firm: Managerial behavior agency costs and ownership structure', *Journal of Financial Economics*, 3(4): 305–360.

Kahneman, D. and Tversky, A. (1979) 'Prospect theory: An analysis of decision under risk', *Economica*, 47: 263–292.

Kellermanns, F.W. and Eddleston, K.A. (2006) 'Corporate entrepreneurship in family firms: A family perspective', *Entrepreneurship Theory & Practice*, 30: 809–830.

Kellermanns, F.W., Eddleston, K.A., Barnett, T., and Pearson, A. (2008) 'An exploratory study of family member characteristics and involvement effects on entrepreneurial behavior in the family firm', *Family Business Review*, 21: 1–14.

Kellermanns, F.W., Eddleston, K.A., Sarathy, R., and Murphy, F. (2012) 'Innovativeness in family firms: A family influence perspective', *Small Business Economics*, 38: 85–101.

Kelly, L.M., Athanassiou, N., and Crittenden, W.F. (2000) 'Founder centrality and strategic behavior in the family-owned firm', *Entrepreneurship Theory & Practice*, 25(2): 27–42.

Le Breton-Miller, I. and Miller, D. (2009) 'Agency vs. stewardship in public family firms: A social embeddedness reconciliation', *Entrepreneurship Theory & Practice*, 33(6): 1169–1191.

Lim, E.N.K., Lubatkin, M.H., and Wiseman, R.M. (2010) 'A family firm variant of the behavioral agency theory', *Strategic Entrepreneurship Journal*, 4(3): 197–211.

Litz, R.A. and Kleysen, R.F. (2001) 'Your old men shall dream dreams, your young men shall see visions: toward a theory of family firm innovation with help from the Brubeck family', *Family Business Review*, 25(4): 335–352.

Long, R.G. and Chrisman, J.J. (2014) Management succession in family business. In Melin, L., Nordqvist, M., and Sharma, P. (eds), *The SAGE Handbook of Family Business*. London: Sage.

Lubatkin, M., Schulze, W., Ling, Y., and Dino, R. (2005) 'The effects of parental altruism on the governance of family-managed firms', *Journal of Organizational Behavior*, 26: 313–330.

Lumpkin, G.T., Brigham, K.H., and Moss, T.W. (2010) 'Long-term orientation: Implications for the entrepreneurial orientation and performance of family businesses', *Entrepreneurship & Regional Development*, 22: 241–264.

Lumpkin, G.T., Steier, L., and Wright, M. (2011) 'Strategic entrepreneurship in family businesses', *Strategic Entrepreneurship Journal*, 5: 285–306.

Luo, Y. and Junkunc, M. (2008) 'How private enterprises respond to government bureaucracy in emerging economies: The effects of entrepreneurial type and governance', *Strategic Entrepreneurship Journal*, 2: 133–153.

Marchisio, G.G., Mazzola, P.P., Sciascia, S.S., Miles, M.M., and Astrachan, J.J. (2010) 'Corporate venturing in family business: The effects on the family and its members', *Entrepreneurship & Regional Development*, 22: 349–377.

McCann, J.E., Leon-Guerrero, A.Y., and Haley, J.D. (2001) 'Strategic goals and practices of innovative family businesses', *Journal of Small Business Management*, 39(1): 50–59.

McGrath, R.G. and Keil, T. (2007) 'The value captor's process: Getting the most out of your new business ventures', *Harvard Business Review*, May: 128–136.

McKenny, A.F., Short, J.C., Zachary, M.A., and Payne, G.T. (2012) 'Assessing espoused goals in private family firms using content analysis', *Family Business Review*, 25(3): 298–317.

Memili, E., Chrisman, J.J., Chua, J.H., Chang, E.P.C., and Kellermanns, F.W. (2011) 'The determinants of family firms' subcontracting: A transaction cost perspective', *Journal of Family Business Strategy*, 2(1): 26–33.

Memili, E., Eddleston, K.A., Kellermanns, F.W., Zellweger, T.M., and Barnett, T. (2010) 'The critical path to family firm success through entrepreneurial risk taking and image', *Journal of Family Business Strategy*, 1: 200–209.

Miller, D. (1983) 'The correlates of entrepreneurship in three types of firms', *Management Science*, 29(7): 770– 791.

Miller, D. and Le Breton-Miller, I. (2005) *Managing for the Long Run: Lesson in competitive advantage from great family businesses*. Boston, MA: Harvard Business School Press.

Miller, D., Steier, L., and Le Breton-Miller, I. (2003) 'Lost in time: Intergenerational succession, change, and failure in family business', *Journal of Business Venturing*, 18: 513–531.

Mitchell, J., Hart, T.A., Valcea, S., and Townsend, D.M. (2009) 'Becoming the boss: Discretion and postsuccession success in family firms', *Entrepreneurship Theory & Practice*, 33(6): 1201–1218.

Mitchell, R.K., Morse, E.A., and Sharma, P. (2003) 'The transaction cognitions of nonfamily employees in the family business setting', *Journal of Business Venturing*, 18(4): 533–551.

Morck, R. and Yeung, B. (2003) 'Agency problems in large family business groups', *Entrepreneurship Theory & Practice*, 27(4): 367.

Naldi, L., Nordqvist, M., Sjöberg, K., and Wiklund, J. (2007) 'Entrepreneurial orientation, risk taking, and performance in family firms', *Family Business Review*, 20: 33–47.

Nordqvist, M., Marzano, G., Brenes, E.R., Jimenez, G., and Fonseca-Paredes, M. (2011) *Understanding Entrepreneurial Family Businesses in Uncertain Environments: Opportunities and Resources in Latin America*. Cheltenham: Edward Elgar.

Nordqvist, M. and Melin, L. (2010) 'Entrepreneurial families and family firms', *Entrepreneurship & Regional Development*, 22(3/4): 211–239.

Nordqvist, M. and Zellweger, T. (2010) *Transgenerational Entrepreneurship: Exploring Growth and Performance in Family Firms Across Generations*. Cheltenham: Edward Elgar.

Phan, P.H., Wright, M., Ucbasaran, D., and Tan, W.L. (2009) 'Corporate entrepreneurship: Current research and future directions', *Journal of Business Venturing*, 24: 197–205.

Pistrui, D., Welsch, H.P., Wintermantel, O., Liao, J., and Pohl, H.J. (2000) 'Entrepreneurial orientation and family forces in the new Germany: Similarities and differences between East and West German entrepreneurs, *Family Business Review*, 13: 251–263.

Pittino, D. and Visintin, F. (2009) 'Innovation and strategic types of family SMEs: A test and extension of Miles and Snow's configurational model', *Journal of Enterprising Culture*, 17(3): 257–295.

Plate, M., Schiede, C., and von Schlippe, A. (2010) 'Portfolio entrepreneurship in the context of family owned businesses', in Nordqvist, M. and Zellweger, T. (eds), *Transgenerational Entrepreneurship: Exploring Growth and Performance in Family Firms Across Generations*. Cheltenham: Edward Elgar, pp. 96–122.

Raisch, S. and Birkinshaw, J.M. (2008) 'Organizational ambidexterity: antecedents, outcomes, and moderators', *Journal of Management*, 34(3): 375–409.

Rauch, A., Wiklund, J., Lumpkin, G.T., and Frese, M. (2009) 'Entrepreneurial orientation and business performance: An assessment of past research and suggestions for the future', *Entrepreneurship Theory & Practice*, 33: 761–787.

Roessl, D., Fink, M., and Kraus, S. (2010) 'Are family firms fit for innovation? Towards an agenda for empirical research', *International Journal of Entrepreneurial Venturing*, 2(3/4): 366–380.

Rosa, P., Howorth, C., and Cruz, A.D. (2014) Habitual and portfolio entrepreneurship in the family context:

longitudinal perspectives. In Melin, L., Nordqvist, M., and Sharma, P. (eds), *The SAGE Handbook of Family Business*. London: Sage.

Salvato, C. (2004) 'Predictors of entrepreneurship in family firms', *Journal of Private Equity*, 7(3): 68–76.

Salvato, C., Chirico, F., and Sharma, P. (2010) 'A farewell to the business: Championing exit and continuity in entrepreneurial family firms', *Entrepreneurship & Regional Development*, 22: 321–348.

Schendel, D. and Hitt, M.A. (2007) 'Introduction to volume 1', *Strategic Entrepreneurship Journal*, 1: 1–6.

Scholes, L., Wright, M., Westhead, P., and Bruining, H. (2010) 'Strategic changes in family firms post-management buyout: Ownership and governance issues', *International Small Business Journal*, 28(5): 505–521.

Schulze, W.S., Lubatkin, M.H., and Dino, R.N. (2003a) 'Exploring the agency consequences of ownership dispersion among the directors of private family firms', *Academy of Management Journal*, 46(2): 179–194.

Schulze, W.S., Lubatkin, M.H., and Dino, R.N. (2003b) 'Toward a theory of agency and altruism in family firms', *Journal of Business Venturing*, 18: 473–490.

Schulze, W.S., Lubatkin, M.H., Dino, R.N., and Buchholtz, A.K. (2001) 'Agency relationships in family firms: Theory and evidence', *Organization Science*, 12: 99–116.

Shanker, M.C., and Astrachan, J.H. (1996) 'Myths and realities: Family businesses contribution to the U.S. economy: A framework for assessing family business statistics', *Family Business Review*, 9: 107–123.

Sharma, P. (2004) 'An overview of the field of family business studies: Current status and directions for the future', *Family Business Review*, 17(1): 1–36.

Sharma, P. (2011) 'Strategic entrepreneurial behaviours in family businesses', *International Journal of Entrepreneurship and Innovation Management*, 13(1): 4–11.

Sharma, P. and Chrisman, J.J. (1999) 'Toward a reconciliation of the definitional issues in the field of corporate entrepreneurship', *Entrepreneurship Theory & Practice*, 23: 11–27.

Sharma, P., Chrisman, J.J., and Chua, J.H. (1997) 'Strategic management of the family business: Past research and future challenges', *Family Business Review*, 10: 1–36.

Short, J.C., Ketchen, D.J., Combs, J.G., and Ireland, R.D. (2010) 'Research methods in Entrepreneurship', *Organizational Research Methods*, 13: 6–15.

Short, J.C., Payne, G.T., Brigham, K.H., Lumpkin, G.T., and Broberg, J.C. (2009) 'Family firms and entrepreneurial orientation in publicly traded firms: A comparative analysis of the S&P 500', *Family Business Review*, 22: 9–24.

Sieger, P., Zellweger, T., Nason, R.A., and Clinton, E. (2011) 'Portfolio entrepreneurship in family firms: A resource-based perspective'. *Strategic Entrepreneurship Journal*, 5(4): 327–351.

Sirmon, D.G. and Hitt, M.A. (2003) 'Managing resources: Linking unique resources, management and wealth creation in family firms', *Entrepreneurship Theory & Practice*, 27(4): 339–358.

Sonfield, M.C. and Lussier, R.N. (2004) 'First-, second-, and third-generation family firms: A comparison', *Family Business Journal*, 17(3): 189–202.

Steier, L. (2003) 'Variants of agency contracts in family financed ventures as a continuum of familial altruistic and market rationalities'. *Journal of Business Venturing* 18: 597–618.

Steier, L. (2009) 'Where do new firms come from? Households, family capital, ethnicity, and the welfare mix'. *Family Business Review*, 22(3): 273–278.

Steier, L. and Muethel, M. (2014) Trust and family businesses. In Melin, L., Nordqvist, M., and Sharma, P. (eds), *The SAGE Handbook of Family Business*. London: Sage.

Stewart, A., Lumpkin, G.T., and Katz, J.A. (2010) *Entrepreneurship and Family Business*. Bingley, UK: Emerald.

Tagiuri, R. and Davis, J.A. (1992) 'On the goals of successful family companies', *Family Business Review*, 5: 43–62.

Toledano, N., Urbano, D., and Bernadich, M. (2010) 'Networks and corporate entrepreneurship: A comparative case study on family business in Catalonia', *Journal of Organizational Change Management*, 23(4): 396–412.

Uhlaner, L.M., Kellermanns, F.W., Eddleston, K.A., and Hoy, F. (2012) 'The entrepreneuring family: A new paradigm for family business research', *Small Business Economics*, 38: 1–11.

Vago, M. (2004) 'Integrated change management: Challenges for family business clients and consultants', *Family Business Review*, 17(1): 71–80.

Wagner, M. (2010) 'Corporate social performance and innovation with high social benefits: A quantitative analysis', *Journal of Business Ethics*, 94(4): 581–594.

Wales, W.J., Monsen, E., and McKelvie, A. (2011) 'The organizational pervasiveness of Entrepreneurial Orientation', *Entrepreneurship Theory & Practice*, 35(5): 895–923.

Ward, J.L. (1987) *Keeping the Family Business Healthy: How to Plan for Continuing Growth, Profitability, and Family Leadership*. San Francisco, CA: Jossey-Bass.

Webb, J.W., Ketchen, D.J., and Ireland, R.D. (2010) 'Strategic entrepreneurship within family-controlled firms', *Journal of Family Business Strategy*, 1: 67–77.

Weismeier-Sammer, D. (2011) 'Entrepreneurial behavior in family firms: A replication study', *Journal of Family Business Strategy*, 2: 128–138.

Whetten, D., Foreman, P., and Dyer, G.W. (2014) Organizational identity and family business. In Melin, L., Nordqvist, M., and Sharma, P. (eds), *The SAGE Handbook of Family Business.* London: Sage.

Wiklund, J. and Shepherd, D.A. (2003) 'Aspiring for, and achieving growth: The moderating role of resources and opportunities', *Journal of Management Studies*, 40(8): 1919–1941.

Wiklund, J. and Shepherd, D.A. (2011) 'Where to from here? EO-as-experimentation, failure, and distribution of outcomes', *Entrepreneurship Theory & Practice*, 35: 925–946.

Wong, Y.-J., Chang, S.-C., and Chen, L.-Y. (2010) 'Does a family-controlled firm perform better in corporate venturing?', *Corporate Governance: An International Review*, 18: 175–192.

Zachary, M.A., McKenny, A., Short, J.C., and Payne, G.T. (2011) 'Family business and market orientation: Construct validation and comparative analysis', *Family Business Review*, 24(3): 233–251.

Zahra, S.A. (1991) 'Predictors and financial outcomes of corporate entrepreneurship: An exploratory study', *Journal of Business Venturing*, 6: 259–285.

Zahra, S.A. (2003) 'International expansion of U.S. manufacturing family businesses: The effect of ownership and involvement', *Journal of Business Venturing*, 18: 495–512.

Zahra, S.A. (2005) 'Entrepreneurial risk taking in family firms', *Family Business Review*, 18: 23–40.

Zahra, S.A. (2012) 'Organizational learning and entrepreneurship in family firms: Exploring the moderation effect of ownership and cohesion', *Small Business Economics*, 38(1): 51–65.

Zahra, S.A., Hayton, J.C., and Salvato, C. (2004) 'Entrepreneurship in family vs. non-family firms: A resource-based analysis of the effect of organizational culture', *Entrepreneurship Theory & Practice*, 28(4): 363–381.

Zahra, S.A., Jennings, D.F., and Kuratko, D. (1999) 'The antecedents and consequences of firm-level entrepreneurship: The state of the field', *Entrepreneurship Theory & Practice,* 24(2): 46–65.

Zellweger, T.M., Nason, R.S., Nordqvist, M., and Brush, C.G. (2013) 'Why do family firms strive for nonfinancial goals? An organizational identity perspective', *Entrepreneurship Theory & Practice*, 37(2): 229–248.

Zellweger, T. and Sieger, P. (2012) 'Entrepreneurial orientation in long-lived family firms', *Small Business Economics*, 38: 67–84.

Zellweger, T., Sieger, P., and Muehlebach, C. (2010) 'How much and what kind of entrepreneurial orientation is needed for family business continuity?', in Nordqvist, M. and Zellweger, T. (eds), *Transgenerational Entrepreneurship: Exploring growth and performance in family firms across generations*. Cheltenham: Edward Elgar, pp. 195–212.

18

Habitual and Portfolio Entrepreneurship and the Family in Business

Peter Rosa, Carole Howorth
and Allan Discua Cruz

INTRODUCTION

It has been observed that the research paths of entrepreneurship and family businesses appear to be fragmented (Anderson et al., 2005). While entrepreneurship is concerned with processes leading to the development of a business venture (either individually or in teams), family business research has been mainly concerned with the sustainability of a family business and its perpetuation through different structures. Despite the parallel evolution of entrepreneurship and family business as separate disciplines, however, an important potential overlap between the two was highlighted early in the 1990s (Brockhaus, 1994; Dyer and Handler, 1994; Hoy and Verser, 1994). From the family business perspective, research agendas were proposed on how risk taking, innovation, new concepts and new forms of organisation and value could arise within the family business to enhance its survivability and growth (Hoy and Verser, 1994). From an entrepreneurship perspective, how the family affected processes of new venture creation and growth was as a key issue (Dyer and Handler, 1994).

Since then the development of research explicitly focusing on entrepreneurship and family business has been slow to materialise compared to other themes, and has not been regarded as an area of research priority until recently. For example, Astrachan (2010) does not include entrepreneurship and the family business as one of the main areas of his suggested family business research agenda. Literature searches for articles where 'family business' and 'entrepreneurship' appear in the same title are surprisingly few. This may be, as Astrachan (2010: 7) explains, because family businesses have been associated by researchers with larger organisations, where planned competitive strategy is the paramount route to success, whereas entrepreneurship has been linked more with small emerging ventures and the opportunity-seeking behaviour of individuals.

The corporate entrepreneurship literature, however, has demonstrated since the 1980s that entrepreneurship in larger businesses is an important component of firm performance (Zahra, 2005a), but there was perhaps an initial reluctance by family business researchers to draw inspiration from this literature as family businesses were regarded as fundamentally different from corporations. More recently, however, there has been an awareness of the need to understand strategic entrepreneurial processes in larger family firms, particularly the role of entrepreneurial orientation in firm performance (Martin and Lumpkin, 2003; Naldi et al., 2007; Short et al., 2009; Dess et al., 2011) and how risk is managed in entrepreneurial family firms (Zahra, 2005b; Gomez-Mejia et al., 2007; Naldi et al., 2007). The importance of an enterprising family culture for change processes in family businesses has been suggested by Hall et al. (2001) and Habbershon in a number of articles (Habbershon and Williams, 1999; Habbershon et al., 2003; Habbershon, 2006). Habbershon has argued that family firms form a unique environment for the development of entrepreneurial value by possessing 'an idiosyncratic bundle of resources and capabilities (termed "familiness") which provide a potential agency advantage in new venture creation' (Habbershon, 2006: 879). Such resources can not only be used to enhance the short-term performance of the family business, but also to produce renewal in the longer term. Habbershon et al. (2003) identified a subset of enterprising family firms who had the capabilities and resources for trans-generational wealth creation.

This recent recognition that entrepreneurship is important for trans-generational renewal of family firms inspired the creation of the Successful Trans-generational Entrepreneurship Practices (STEP) family enterprise research project in 2007. This international project, coordinated by Babson College, involves researchers from all continents conducting exploratory research (mainly case studies) on the nature of long-term entrepreneurial processes in larger family firms. In 2012, it has been ongoing for five years and has a large stock of case studies; academic analysis and outputs are beginning to emerge.

Initially, the STEP project was designed to investigate a model based on entrepreneurial orientation with moderating factors such as familiness. As empirical results have emerged, however, it has become apparent that entrepreneurial processes are much more complex than envisaged by the initial STEP model, especially longer-term processes.

One area that contributes to complexity is habitual entrepreneurship, the creation of multiple businesses by an entrepreneur, either serially (one at a time) or building a group of businesses ('portfolio entrepreneurship'). Researched for some years in mainstream entrepreneurship, it has started to be applied to researching trans-generational entrepreneurship (Rosa et al., 2005). Most research on entrepreneurship in family businesses has taken the 'business' or 'firm' as the unit of analysis. Habitual entrepreneurship research instead focuses on the entrepreneur or entrepreneurial team as the unit of analysis. In a family business context, this switches emphasis from a 'family business' to a 'business family', and permits the research of multiple venture creation by enterprising families, rather than growth of a single business. Trans-generational entrepreneurship is thus not just about renewing a single business, but constantly renewing and growing family wealth through long-term enterprising behaviour, including the creation of new ventures. Research on habitual entrepreneurship in a family business context is growing; recent STEP publications highlight the relevance of family dynamics that lead to the emergence of new ventures (Nordqvist and Zellwegger, 2010; Nordqvist et al., 2011).

This article considers research on habitual and portfolio entrepreneurship and its relevance to the family business context. Following a review of underlying theoretical and methodological issues, it discusses the definitional complexities when habitual entrepreneurship is applied to families. It then examines the entrepreneurial processes of habitual entrepreneurship and its relevance to family business research.

HABITUAL ENTREPRENEURSHIP: AN OVERVIEW

The firm is the main unit for business research and it is usual to conceptualise businesses as single firms with varying degrees of organisational complexity. This is especially the case for the family business, commonly regarded as an organisational entity which has significant family ownership or influence in its organisation and management, and which has a lifecycle that can transcend the generational life span of its owners (Hoy and Sharma, 2010). Closer inspection, however, reveals that many businesses, including family businesses, are actually organised as groups of firms (business groups) which can vary considerably in size and complexity (Iacobucci, 2002), and though the proportion of businesses organised as groups declines as size reduces, a surprising proportion of smaller businesses are still organised as groups (Birley and Westhead, 1993; Scott and Rosa, 1999, Ucbasaran et al., 2008). Moreover, business groups appear to be common in most countries (Ucbasaran et al., 2008).

The reasons for establishing a group rather than a single organisational structure have been debated since the 1970s. Recent meta-analyses of the business group economic and management literature reveal a diversity of theories trying to explain why business groups exist, and why they may confer advantage (Yaprak and Karademir, 2010; Carney et al. (2011). Research, grounded in economic transaction cost theory and the theory of the firm, considered the group as an organisational form to manage diversified or vertically integrated activities (Williamson, 1975; Chandler, 1982; Goto, 1982; Kester, 1992; Shimotani, 1997), and conferring advantages through the alleviation of transaction costs in capital markets as a response to market imperfections (Leff, 1976). Financial portfolio theories have been adopted to explain how diversification into separate firms within the business group spreads and mitigates risk (e.g., Rugman, 1976; Amit and Wernerfelt, 1990). Sociological and political economic

research has examined how business groups help provide common norms and integrative codes of behaviour which can help overcome imperfections in the external institutional environment (Grannovetter, 1994); and can be considered mechanisms for accruing disproportionate wealth in to the hands of a handful of families through rent seeking and interlocking directorships based on kinship (Encarnation, 1989; Gill, 1999; Silva et al., 2006). In recent years there has been increasing interest in why business groups are so prominent in developing countries. It has been suggested that business groups may confer unique advantages when conducting business in the social, economic and political conditions of emerging economies (Ghemawat and Khanna, 1998; Khanna, 2000; Khanna and Palepu, 2000; Khanna and Yafeh, 2005; Yiu et al., 2005; Chang, 2006).

Many large business groups are family owned or managed, but how far these various theories are influenced by family factors had yet to be systematically researched. Interest in family business groups has been slow to develop but is beginning to change. Finance researchers in particular have become to view the family business group as being established by controlling families primarily as a mechanism to manipulate the ownership structures of companies to the advantage of controlling owners (Barca and Becht, 2001; Morck and Yeung, 2006), particularly leveraging and expropriating capital from minority shareholders, whilst retaining control. The advantages of a pyramidal rather than horizontal structure for achieving this are central to the debate, as is the issue of why minority shareholders continue to invest despite their apparent exploitation by family owners (Almeida and Wolfensen, 2006; Khanna and Yafeh, 2007, Masulis et al., 2011). This research, however, has been limited to publically listed family controlled groups, and does not explain the prevalence of business groups in nonlisted family business enterprises.

The fact that many business groups are significantly owned or influenced by individual entrepreneurs or their families, has tended, until recently, to be overlooked (see Carney and Gedajlovic, 2002, for a notable exception). Entrepreneurship introduces an alternative perspective to the formation of business groups. Under traditional management and financial theories, a group structure, involves rationally planned and chosen strategies for optimising the performance of the overall business. From an entrepreneurial perspective, however, the 'business group' can be conceptualised, quite differently, as the end product of an evolving process of entrepreneurial venturing over time, a process which is not necessarily rationally or rigorously planned but is more in tune with an effectuation logic (Sarasvathy, 2001). In developing economies, a network of interrelated family businesses may be the result of a single entrepreneur or an entrepreneurial team pursuing diverse business opportunities based on family interests rather than on planned business objectives (Discua Cruz, 2010). In the entrepreneurial case the business group thus emerges not as a rational process but as the outcome of a series of linked adventures. It is perhaps not a coincidence that where successful entrepreneurs and entrepreneurial families predominate, such as in economically emerging countries, business groups tend to be diversified conglomerates whereas where corporate teams are common, there has been a dismantling of conglomerates, and the emergence of business groups where 'core competencies and focus are the mantras of corporate strategies' (Khanna and Palepu, 1997: 44).

Since the 1980s, entrepreneurs have gained prominence as key players in the emergence of new ventures, corporate entrepreneurship and as drivers of economic performance. Habitual entrepreneurs who start not just one firm, but a succession of firms (in essence who establish and develop business groups) are increasingly recognised as important to the founding, growth and performance of firms (MacMillan, 1986; Westhead and Wright, 1998a; Ucbasaran et al., 2006; Wiklund and Shepherd, 2008). The business group is thus seen as the visible manifestation of entrepreneurial growth processes instigated and led by habitual entrepreneurs (Rosa, 1998), who may possess special qualities, competencies and resources which enable them to successfully start and grow multiple ventures (Ucbasaran et al., 2008).

A 'firm' under this logic is not the source of economic activity, but the organisational consequence when entrepreneurial strategy is implemented successfully. As Sarasvathy and Menon write, 'for the one time entrepreneur, the firm is an end in itself; whereas for the multiple entrepreneur, each firm, whether successful or failed, is an instrument of learning that enables him or her to achieve better performance over time' (Sarasvathy and Menon, 2004: 9). It is the entrepreneur's performance that is being referred to, not that of any specific firm.

The rising interest in habitual entrepreneurs has led to a switch in focus from the firm to the entrepreneur as a unit of analysis (Macmillan, 1986; Scott and Rosa, 1996). Family business as a field of research, however, is only just becoming aware of this change in perspective. Entrepreneurship researchers have observed for some years that ventures, including serial ventures, are commonly started by teams (Gartner et al., 1994; Cooper and Daily, 1997). Many of these teams are family teams (Rosa and Hamilton, 1994; Rosa, 1998; Howorth et al., 2010). The realisation that there is not necessarily just one family business, but a group of family businesses, many of which are the result of entrepreneurial family activities and processes, is one whose implications are fundamental, but yet to be fully conceptualised and investigated. The remainder of this chapter reviews and discusses the complexities and implications of researching habitual entrepreneurship in families rather than individuals.

FAMILY HABITUAL ENTREPRENEURSHIP: CLASSIFICATION AND DEFINITIONS

This section reviews the classification and definitions of habitual entrepreneurs and examines how complexity increases when the unit of analysis is broadened from the individual entrepreneur to the entrepreneurial family.

The definitions surrounding habitual entrepreneurship have evolved since the 1980s. MacMillan (1986: 241) drew a distinction between 'one shot entrepreneurs', who have only one experience of entrepreneurship, and 'habitual entrepreneurs', who are 'business generators', special entrepreneurs starting a succession of new businesses out of 'excitement and challenge', and through boredom moving on to the next one (MacMillan, 1986: 242). Birley and Westhead (1993) and Kolvereid and Bullvåg (1993) developed the typology by highlighting 'novice entrepreneurs', who are starting or have just started a new first business, and divided habitual entrepreneurs into 'serial entrepreneurs' (starting a succession of businesses but only owning one at a time) and 'portfolio entrepreneurs' (starting one or more additional businesses and continuing to own them in parallel as a group). Ucbasaran et al. (2003) further categorised portfolio entrepreneurs into two types, 'habitual starters' (who start more than one business in parallel) and 'habitual acquirers' (individuals who acquire more than one business).

This typology, however, fails to capture the full diversity of entrepreneurial enterprise, especially when enterprises are not formally registered. Plural modes of livelihood or pluriactivity (Fuller, 1990; Gasson, 1992) occur world wide, especially in developing countries where economic activity is constrained severely (Kodithuwakku and Rosa, 2002; Rosa et al., 2006), or in developed countries amongst farmers being 'pushed' into diversification (Carter, 1998; Rønning and Kolvereid, 2006) and self-employed people who pursue more than one form of income (Carter et al., 2004). Pluriactivity could thus be viewed as a form of habitual entrepreneurship, as it involves engaging in more than one enterprise. It is also an embryonic form of habitual entrepreneurship, as enterprises created are not formal organisations. Pluriactivity implies an opposite state (monoactivity) in which a person pursues a single mode of livelihood which is not registered as a business for tax purposes. This is an area that has not been explicitly researched by entrepreneurship investigators.

The Family Dimension

All these different forms of single and habitual entrepreneurship have been proffered with single entrepreneurs as the unit of analysis. If we extend the concept of habitual entrepreneurship to family teams, as shown in Table 18.1, the following forms of habitual family entrepreneurship can be distinguished:

A. *Family entrepreneurship associated with informal enterprises*: Pluriactivity is normally associated with enterprises engaged in by an individual, but in practice people commonly combine with family members to maximise and organise household income and expenditure (Kodithuwakku and Rosa, 2002; Carter et al.; 2004; Rosa et al., 2006). The household family unit is thus, arguably, a more appropriate unit for analysing the nature of pluriactivity. Different forms of family pluriactivity can be differentiated according to whether the economic household unit is the nuclear family, a polygamous family, an extended family where young adults and even children contribute to overall family income; whether the family lives in the same locality or are pursuing different enterprises in different areas of the country. For example, in Uganda it is not uncommon for families to be split between family members residing in a traditional rural small farm, whilst others engage in enterprises in the city some distance away (Rosa et al., 2006). How forms of family pluriactivity differ between developed and developing countries is also an area for future research. There may be hybrid forms of pluriactivity in some contexts, where a registered single business is supplemented by a range of informal unregistered enterprises (such as has been reported in the literature on farm diversification in European countries (Gasson, 1992; Carter, 1998).

B. *One shot family firms*: Businesses that appear to be linked to one entrepreneur or business owner are usually co-owned with a relative of some kind. Introducing a family dimension greatly expands the number of enterprise sub-types:

1 One shot family enterprises vary according to which kinds of relatives co-own it (husband spouse teams; parent children combinations; sibling combinations; combinations of family and outsiders, etc.).

2 Variation occurs in foundation patterns, whether the business is co-founded from the start by different family members, or whether a single entrepreneur starts it and brings in family partners later.

3 One shot businesses that appear to be founded and owned by a single entrepreneur, may in practice involve other family members. Sub-types include (a) the partner is involved informally but not legally in the partnership (for example, in the case of contributing wives or husbands); (b) the entrepreneur founds the business in the name of the spouse but the spouse does not actually manage the business; (c) a business is started separately for the benefit of a family member, such as a spouse wishing to diversify or a son or daughter establishing a separate line. This is particularly common in farming households (Gasson, 1992) and/or to appease incoming generations of family members who decide to break away from the original family firm (Gura, 2011; Discua Cruz et al., 2013). Such businesses might appear to be independent 'one shot' businesses owned by a single entrepreneur, but, in family terms, are multiple family businesses.

C. *Serial entrepreneurship by business families*: The serial entrepreneur creates a succession of businesses by starting one and then closing it, and then starting another. It is theoretically possible for a succession of businesses to be started serially in this way by a family team rather than an individual. The different possible combinations of family members would affect the typology in the same way as described above in points 1 and 2 for 'one shot businesses'. The literature shows that many entrepreneurs do not succeed in their first venture. Some start and close several businesses before they eventually find one that works. The 'one shot' entrepreneur in this scenario is really a serial entrepreneur who settles down to owning and managing a single business. This is arguably different from a serial entrepreneur who starts a business, gets bored or sees a better opportunity, sells it and then starts another, and keeps on doing this throughout his or her working life. We could thus distinguish *occasional serial* from *regular serial* entrepreneurial families. Families can engage in serial entrepreneurship to recreate

previous existing businesses (Kenyon-Rouvinez, 2001; Discua Cruz et al., 2013). In addition, Salvato et al. (2010) illustrate how several family members engage in serial entrepreneurship through generations diverting gradually from their original family business. These family teams rely on their previous experience working together and tend to recreate businesses in the same industry of previously owned businesses. Occasional serial families have a single established business for as long as possible and only change it when forced to by circumstances. Regular serial families change their business regularly when better prospects are identified.

D. *Portfolio entrepreneurship*: A portfolio entrepreneur is a multiple business owner who has founded or acquired two or more companies and continues to manage them as a group. The recognition that many business groups founded and managed by portfolio entrepreneurs are in fact family groups introduces a diversity of possibilities. Different types could be distinguished using a range of factors, including different combinations of family members founding, owning and managing the businesses, social and personal characteristics of these members, the industrial sectors they are operating in, the nature of the companies they start, and the entrepreneurial and managerial strategies they adopt to construct and manage their business groups (Rosa, 1998; Ucbasaran et al., 2008; Iacobucci and Rosa, 2010; Plate et al., 2010).

It may be useful to distinguish generically between loose *uncoordinated* family groups, where there is no overall formal coordination of the businesses created by family members, and *coordinated* groups, where there is a formal structure (such as a holding company). One example of an uncoordinated family group is illustrated in Rosa's (1998) analysis of business group genealogies. The founder established four Sony retail shops and also bought a farm. His daughter developed a horse import export business based on the farm, in which her father had a half share. His son in the meantime developed a business of his own which had no ownership by the father or sister. His father then sold his shops and developed a highly successful roofing business, in partnership with his son.

Table 18.1   Possible types of family single state and habitual entrepreneurship

Type of family entrepreneurship	Definition
A: Informal family enterprise	**No formally registered firm or business.**
Monoactive family	A family with only one unregistered/informal enterprise or economic activity.
Pluriactive family	A family with two or more permanent or seasonal unregistered/ informal enterprises or economic activities.
Hybrid-pluriactive family	A family with a single registered business but supplemented by informal enterprise(s).
B: 'One shot' formal family business	**A family associated with only one formally registered business.**
'One shot' entrepreneur led business family	Founded by a single family member as the only family business, and over time including other family members (formally or informally) in its management and ownership.
'One shot' partner led business family business	Founded by a partnership of non-family members but in time evolving a combination of family members (formally or informally) in its ownership and management.
'One shot' team family business	Founded by a team of family members, commonly husband and wives, fathers and sons, brothers.
'One shot' second-generation family business	A business started by the family for one of their second-generation members but which is not formally linked with the family business.
C: Serial business family	**A family with a serial succession of single businesses.**
Occasional serial business family	Business only changed occasionally when forced to do so by circumstances.
Regular serial business family	Regular changes of business if better opportunities present themselves.
D: Portfolio business family	**A family that has established a group of formally registered businesses.**
Uncoordinated portfolio business family	A family that views itself as a united family but whose members have founded an uncoordinated group of businesses.
Coordinated portfolio business family	A family that has founded a group of businesses formally coordinated through a central managerial mechanism such as a holding company.
E: Branded family businesses	**A business or group of businesses associated with a single family brand name but whose ownership changes over time.**
Corporately owned family business	Once owned by the original family but now no longer in family ownership.
Family owned branded family business	Still in family ownership but not the original founding family.
Complex owned family business	Owned by a mixture of different family or non-family owners over time.
Reverted family business	Reverts back to ownership by the original family.

His son then tried to establish a separate property evaluation business. In this example a significant number of companies were established by the family members, but no single family member had a stake in all the companies. There was no overall control of the family group. There was no coordinated 'family business'.

In the most coordinated groups, it is common for the original company to have been formed by the founding family team (brothers, parent/son, husband/wife), or by a single entrepreneur who is subsequently joined by family members. As individual family members propose new initiatives, the decision to found and establish the new company is a joint one and common ownership is preserved. So family business founders might engage in the development of related businesses with their children, or siblings developing new businesses might team up with their parents to enhance existing firms (Roscoe et al., 2013). This sometimes also requires giving shares to outsiders (Iacobucci and Rosa, 2010), but family ownership remains dominant, and outsider shares only affect the new company, not the whole group.

In large coordinated family business groups it is possible to have complex control and ownership patterns where different family members semi-independently develop their own sub-group of companies, but there still remains overall common ownership and coordination by the family. An interesting example of this is the Sawaris family in Egypt, whose founding father and three sons are listed separately in the Forbes rich list. The founding father of the dynasty, Onsi Sawaris, coordinates a highly successful business group of his own with those of his three sons, Naguib (who founded a group based on telecom industries), Samih (a group based on hotels and property developments) and Nassef (construction). Each son has independently grown his own group within the family, and no other family member has a management role within his group. However, all family members have a minority ownership stake in each other's businesses, and the overall coordination is achieved by the family holding company.

As generations pass it is possible for both coordinated and uncoordinated business groups to emerge in large families. For example, the William Grant family business in Scotland has a main coordinated family business group based on the distillation of whisky. It is one of the few Scottish distilleries remaining in family hands. Many family members have shares in the family business but they have to compete within the family for senior management and board positions. The remaining family members are free to start their own separate family businesses and careers whilst still linked into the main family business group.

This example illustrates that the nature of habitual entrepreneurship does not just get more complicated when a family dimension is added, but that it escalates in complexity over time. The web of business relationships associated with a fourth-, fifth- and sixth-generation business family can become extremely intricate and difficult to map. Entrepreneurship is not just a series of events of new venture creation; it is also a process which evolves over time. To reach a fuller understanding of the nature of family entrepreneurship, particularly habitual entrepreneurship, it is necessary to conceptualise further how it evolves over time, both within a generation and over generations.

Implications for Future Research

There is a growing realisation by family business researchers that family businesses are heterogeneous and that researchers should take this heterogeneity into account when designing and conducting research (Westhead and Howorth, 2007; Howorth et al., 2010). The key question is how best to map this heterogeneity and reduce it into meaningful categories for research purposes. The analysis shows that the habitual entrepreneurship literature provides a useful basis for developing a meaningful typology of entrepreneurial business families. Many of the issues traditionally investigated in family businesses will differ appreciably in how researchers should approach them depending on the type of family entrepreneurial context. For example, the succession processes of a large coordinated family business group will arguably be fundamentally different from those of a one shot nuclear business family.

PROCESSES OF HABITUAL ENTREPRENEURSHIP

Having considered the classification of habitual entrepreneurship and implications for family business research, we now examine the processes and characteristics associated with habitual entrepreneurship. First we examine studies that are concerned with what characterises different types of novice and habitual entrepreneurs and whether the new businesses established by habitual entrepreneurs performed better than those started by novices. Then we consider studies that examine the processes of business group formation by habitual entrepreneurs, in particular how far the addition of new businesses was an entrepreneurial process.

The Characteristics of Habitual Entrepreneurs

Factors which could theoretically differentiate habitual entrepreneurs from novices have been researched empirically in a variety of studies. These factors include motivation, age and experience, parental background, gender, entrepreneurial cognition, human and social capital (Birley and Westhead, 1993; Kolvereid and Bullvåg, 1993; Rosa, 1998; Westhead and Wright, 1998a, 1998b; Scott and Rosa, 1999; Ucbasaran and Westhead, 2002; Ucbasaran et al., 2003; Pasanen, 2003; Westhead et al., 2004; Alsos and Carter, 2006; Baron and Ensley, 2006; Mosey and Wright, 2007; Huovinen and Tihula, 2008; Ucbasaran et al., 2008; Wiklund and Shepherd, 2008; Ucbasaran et al., 2009).

In a detailed review, Ucbasaran et al. (2008) demonstrated that there was empirical support for the contention that habitual entrepreneurs had distinctive characteristics and behaviours when compared to novices. Habitual entrepreneurs (especially portfolio entrepreneurs) tended to start younger than their novice counterparts, have more industry and managerial experience, be better educated, be male rather than female, more likely to have parents already in business (implying socialised knowledge of how to establish new businesses), and be more creative and innovative in identifying opportunities and pursuing resources. They also tended to possess significantly better entrepreneurial abilities and have access to more financial, knowledge and social resources.

These trends, however, were not consistent in all empirical studies, and the superiority of businesses started by habitual entrepreneurs over those started by novices was not always detectable. Moreover, habitual entrepreneurs were found not to be homogeneous.

Significant behavioural differences were detectable between serial and portfolio entrepreneurs. Overall, the overwhelming superior abilities, motivations and qualities of the habitual 'business generators' highlighted in MacMillan's 1986 article have failed to be identified or substantiated conclusively. One reason may be because the most successful habitual entrepreneurs run large businesses and business groups, and were excluded in the entrepreneurship studies, which were almost exclusively focused on the small business sector. Another, perhaps more plausible explanation, however, is that habitual entrepreneurship is a complex phenomenon which is not amenable to simple characterisation.

Implications for Family Business Research

The habitual entrepreneurship research assumes the unit of analysis is the individual entrepreneur, but in reality many of the entrepreneurs sampled in studies were leaders of enterprises that involved family in some way through informal or formal ownership, decision making, management and even employment. There are many unanswered questions on how habitual entrepreneurship (both serial and portfolio) operates in a family context:

1   *Demographics and background*: The literature, as demonstrated earlier, points to habitual entrepreneurs tending to start young, being predominantly male, and many having parents already in business, implying that they already belong to a business family. Earlier we highlighted the wide range of potential types of habitual entrepreneurship when the family context is taken into account. What determines which direction they take? For those habitual entrepreneurs who start as lone entrepreneurs with no family business background, do they continue as lone or non-family operators, or do family get involved as they marry and their children grow up? Does dominant leadership become reinforced as talented family emerges to support their venturing, and a new pool of trusted family managers becomes available? Or does a growing family with their own agendas lead to conflicts and an erosion of

motivation and capability? Gender needs to be examined. Why women are much less likely to be identified as habitual entrepreneurs has not been well researched; the family business context could provide insightful illumination. Studies suggest that women are often central to the family business but not always formally acknowledged (Mulholland, 2003; Hamilton, 2006).

2 *Experience and human capital*: Habitual entrepreneurs may have more management and industry experience and entrepreneurial knowledge. The knowledge and experience of habitually starting new ventures is different from that of growing through the same venture (Wiklund and Shepherd, 2008). Do family members have any advantage in terms of sharing such knowledge? Many of the world's leading entrepreneurs left school or university early (for example, Bill Gates, Steve Jobs, Richard Branson) and did not come from family business backgrounds. Is individual experiential learning more important for entrepreneurship (Cope, 2003)?

3 Many family businesses use family resources to educate their children to become employed professionals rather than entrepreneurs. Birley (2001), for example, indicated that a significant proportion of family business owners did not wish their children to continue in the family business, and many children did not wish to do so either owing to the drudgery and lack of security. Even where there is strong motivation for the business to pass down to the next generation, the typical socialisation process emphasises learning to master the managerial aspects of the existing business and take it over, not to start a new business. Brockhaus (2004) suggested that entrepreneurial training is often overlooked in the succession process. Even when offspring are sent to leading Business Schools, the specialist knowledge of new venture creation is not a priority. However, Discua Cruz et al. (2010) suggest that new generations bring human capital, in terms of specialised education, that can contribute to a collective approach to portfolio entrepreneurship. Family members acting as a team bring complementary entrepreneurial experience and specialised knowledge to pursue new entrepreneurial opportunities.

4 The key question, therefore, is how far knowledge and experience of creating new ventures is being taught to the next generation, and what kinds of family business environments actually produce habitual entrepreneurs? Are such entrepreneurial families common or rare? Are they more common

in some regions of the world than others, and why? Family business research already has insights on many of these issues, but they have failed to look specifically at the specialist human capital requirements of multiple business venturing.

5 Resources: The habitual entrepreneurship research suggests that habitual entrepreneurs may have wider access to financial and social resources. Financial and social capital accumulation makes it easier to establish additional new ventures. The family business literature has recognised for some time that family businesses can access resources that are not available to non-family firms and that these constitute a unique source of competitive advantage (termed 'familiness') (Habbershon and Williams 1999; Cabrera-Suarez at al., 2003; Sirmon and Hitt, 2003; Pearson et al., 2008; Rutherford et al., 2008; Zellweger et al., 2010).

6 Social capital, among other resources, is fundamental to habitual entrepreneurship in developed and developing economies, as shown by Discua Cruz (2010) in his investigation of family business groups in Honduras, Plate et al. (2010), using the RBV perspective and STEP data, within a large multinational family firm in Germany, and Sieger et al.'s (2011) examining data from the STEP project. In comparison to a single portfolio entrepreneur, family entrepreneurial teams can leverage a wider array of contacts, allowing them to access diverse resources when seeking and pursuing opportunities.

7 Further attempts to establish how far and in what ways habitual entrepreneurs with family connections access and leverage these resources or launch additional new ventures and build business groups are warranted. While some advances have been made, this remains an almost totally unexplored field.

Habitual Entrepreneurship and Business Group Formation Processes

The first part of this paper highlighted the fact that non-entrepreneurial theories predominate in the mainstream management literature to explain the formation of business groups, particularly in larger firms. Portfolio entrepreneurs, however, unlike serial entrepreneurs, not only start new ventures, but retain ownership in those they have already started.

Hence, in their case, there appears to be a direct relationship between being a habitual entrepreneur and starting and expanding a business group. The key issue is thus how far the establishment and evolution of a business group is an entrepreneurial process, as is predicted by entrepreneurship theory, or a managerial artifice to render some form of competitive advantage as predicted by various forms of economic and management theory.

Empirical research in the 1990s (Rosa, 1998; Rosa and Scott, 1999; Scott and Rosa, 1999) demonstrated empirically that habitual entrepreneurs have a diversity of motives and strategies for starting a new venture and the motives for adding a new venture may be quite different from those that motivated the start-up of a previous venture. Although some new companies are not directly concerned with business transactions – for example, holding companies; businesses registered to set up family trusts, or non-trading businesses to protect trade marks and names – the majority of new businesses created were trading businesses, mostly associated with some form of entrepreneurial diversification. From these studies it is possible to distinguish different types of entrepreneurial diversification, which may lead to portfolio formation and which, we theorise, may be associated with different patterns of long-term entrepreneurial processes.

1   *Pull opportunistic diversification* occurs when an entrepreneur starts a new diversification (often a new business) motivated by opportunism. Opportunities are not necessarily proactively sought or planned by the entrepreneur, but as time passes opportunities occur or are brought to the entrepreneur's attention by employees, other entrepreneurs, friends or family members (Iacobucci and Rosa, 2010). Often the entrepreneur lets them slip by but every now and again the entrepreneur reacts with enthusiasm and starts a new diversification. This is often a serendipitous process (Roscoe et al., 2013), where the new diversification can be motivated by impulse or even boredom (MacMillan, 1986). Pull diversification is often associated with related diversification; linked to and arising from the entrepreneur's core

business interests. The result is an expansion of the business group through the addition of new firms and new entrepreneurial activities.

2   *Push diversification*, in contrast, is motivated by the need to diversify because the core business is ailing or failing. This is in keeping with Robson et al. (1993) and Sanvig and Coakley (1998), who refer to diversification in SMEs as predominantly a 'defensive' rather than expansionist strategy. Push diversification can arise from sudden traumatic crises. Renewal requires starting businesses in new more promising sectors and is thus likely to be 'unrelated' diversification. In developing economies push diversification may be undertaken by upcoming generations in family businesses, often as a response or means to circumvent the political, economic and social uncertainty in hostile environments (Gonzalez Leon et al., 2011). Push diversification is associated commonly with intensive brainstorming and high levels of planning and when the need is urgent, there is little scope for experimentation or serendipity. As in the case of pull diversification, an additional business or businesses are formed, but for quite different entrepreneurial motives and employing different development procedures. The older ailing businesses are likely to be divested or cease trading in time.

3   *No or little diversification* is characteristic of mature owner managed businesses where conditions are not sufficiently severe to force diversification, but where entrepreneurial energy is low. Rosa (1998) reported that absence of pull or push diversification is often a symptom of barriers preventing the implementation of significant opportunistic diversification, in particular a fear of 'hassle' involved in managing additional businesses, or high debt levels preventing the resourcing of new ventures, or an aversion to risk.

Earlier studies envisaged the act of expanding into new lines of business by starting new additional businesses as the essence of habitual entrepreneurship, but this has had to be modified in the light of more recent research. The entrepreneurial process is the creation of new lines of business (new products, services, markets), but why are some accommodated within a single firm in some cases, and by establishing a separate business in others? Wiklund and Shepherd (2008) observed that habitual entrepreneurs were much more likely to accommodate new diversifications by starting a separate business, whilst one shot or novice entrepreneurs were more likely to manage diversification internally. The diversification is thus the entrepreneurial event, but whether it is managed internally or through establishing a new company is more related to management considerations. The fact that habitual entrepreneurs are more likely to start a new business to accommodate growth implies that habitual entrepreneurship may be a style of management that has to be learnt through experience.

In a study of business groups in Italian manufacturing sectors, Iacobucci and Rosa (2005, 2010) observed that the decision to diversify through a new company was influenced by three main factors:

1 Forced to do so by legal requirements. In some kinds of venture, such as establishing a new export market abroad, it can be a legal requirement to establish a new firm.
2 To accommodate outsiders as partners in the new enterprise. These may be other entrepreneurs with whom a joint deal has been negotiated, or to involve an entrepreneurial employee who has initiated the idea, or to imbed a new manager for the venture. By establishing a new company, the ownership can be shared with these outsiders, without having to share the ownership of the other entrepreneur's businesses. This would not be possible if the new venture is retained in the same firm.
3 To enable the entrepreneur to focus resources on the new venture without risking the main businesses. As a separate unit resources and planning can be more easily obtained and managed, and should it not succeed, it can be divested with minimal damage or contamination to the other businesses.

In none of the studies was a business group strategically formed to spread risk, though the management of risk is a consideration in establishing the new venture. Some habitual entrepreneurs considered an over diversified business group risky, and once a new venture was established, rationalisation and internal mergers could occur (Iacobucci and Rosa, 2010). Hence the management of

business groups over time can be a dynamic process in which they contract as well as expand. Unfortunately little research exists to illuminate these longer-term organic processes.

Implications for Family Business Research

Family business research has concentrated on family factors and dynamics in trying to explore and explain the influence of family on business performance. Strategic management has been particularly prominent in shaping the approaches and agendas of family business research (Chrisman et al., 2005; Astrachan, 2010; Wright and Kellermans, 2011) and the strategic performance of the family has been a primary focus. Families who set clear goals, who share long-term commitment, who have strategic governance mechanisms to regulate family conflicts, disputes and strategies, are much more likely to be successful (Carlock and Ward, 2001). This strategic long-term orientation and commitment to ensure long-term family business continuity and survival is often explained in terms of stewardship behaviour by family leaders (Eddleston and Kellermanns, 2007; Eddleston et al., 2008, Zahra et al., 2008). Astrachan (2010) points to the fact that some low performance organisations can survive for a very long time. This is certainly so for many 'mom and pop' businesses where the same single business is continued for many years, supporting a new generation who may view working in such businesses as drudgery (Birley, 2001). Continuity, from this viewpoint is thus not dependent on entrepreneurship. However, for a family business to perform well consistently over a long period, not only are long-term goals needed, but they must be to be combined with a strong strategic entrepreneurial orientation and strategic flexibility (Nordqvist et al., 2007; Zahra et al., 2008).

Nordqvist and Melin (2010) argue that there has been too much stress on the now mostly discredited 'design school' of strategy, with its relatively simplistic determinism between formal planning processes and outcomes, and not enough on emergent strategy. The habitual entrepreneurship literature provides a basis to explore emergent family behaviour in more realistic empirical detail. How do family firms behave in the longer term in terms of organisational evolution, and how does this link in with dynamic entrepreneurial processes? Is organisational structure and performance determined primarily by well-founded internal family dynamics and strategies (both short and long term) or are strategic goals and strategies aspirations soon superseded by unanticipated and often traumatic events? Are family businesses successful when they plan well, or when they learn to adapt well to unexpected forces? The impact of the external environment on family business management styles and performance appears to be largely missing in current family business research.

The habitual entrepreneurship literature reveals that growth through new venture creation and business group formation is sensitive to external conditions and factors. When the economic and business environment is favourable and the entrepreneur's ventures are profitable, opportunities come to them from a number of sources, pull diversification often occurs resulting in the addition of new ventures to the group. When conditions are unfavourable, new venturing based on pull diversification tends to cease, and where conditions are not threatening, rationalisation and cost cutting tend to be the reaction. When conditions are so unfavourable as to threaten the comfort or even survivability of the business(es) push diversification becomes an option resulting in new ventures being proactively sought to replace the ailing ones.

There is tentative evidence from examining the longer-term history of family businesses that the development, evolutions and distribution of business groups is linked to external factors and events. Roscoe et al. (2013) found that in addition to family dynamics diverse historical, political and environmental factors influence the development of a group of

family businesses. Family businesses which comprise large and successful business groups tend to be more frequent in strong emerging markets. Research into the dynamics of these families is in its infancy, but some research so far by Hatem on high growth Egyptian family businesses (Rosa et al., 2010), Balunywa (2009) on successful Ugandan family businesses and Discua Cruz (2010), seem to illustrate that growth through multiple venturing by family members is the preferred and tested practice. In mature and low growth economies such as Europe, large family businesses have been subjected to low opportunity environments for some years and have learnt to retrench and conserve rather than expand serendipitously. Low rates of new venture creation are observable, with many long established family businesses being single businesses. Where new businesses are formed, these are often motivated by the need to diversify because of adverse circumstances. Rosa (1998) reports, for example, the case of a family of abattoir owners who were forced to diversify suddenly into new ventures following the catastrophic decline of beef consumption during the BSE crisis of the mid 1980s. In Honduras, a radio broadcast entrepreneur was pushed to start a TV broadcasting station, given the amount of competition and the decline in sales of his existing radio stations (Discua Cruz and Howorth, 2008). The desire for renewal in the face of an ailing mature family business appears to be common, and though diversifications in families not used to habitual entrepreneurship is usually planned internally to the firm, many are forced to establish a new venture if external partners are involved in the process.

A closer examination of the long-term trends of business group formation by entrepreneurial families reveals that they tend to exhibit different kinds of portfolio formation according to the circumstances they face. Many large family businesses were founded and expanded to form business groups by entrepreneurial founders, driven by pull diversification as favourable opportunities presented themselves. Catastrophic events (wars, stock market crashes, adverse changes in taxation and regulations), provide traumatic challenges for long established business families often resulting in periods of retrenchment, little new venturing activity and when conditions became very adverse, emergency phases of push diversification. Family crises such as the sudden death of key family members could also provoke similar reactions. Discua Cruz et al. (2010) found that succession crises, ignited by the illness and death of family business leaders, the lack of successors' interest in existing businesses, and diverse family dreams are often a trigger for family entrepreneurial teams to form and engage in portfolio entrepreneurship. Preliminary research appears to show that some families, such as the Madhevanis of Uganda, the Sowaris family of Egypt, have the resilience to bounce back, forming new business groups from the ashes of the old and the continuation of the entrepreneurial spirit into new generations. The formation of business groups and how they relate to changing external and internal conditions is, we believe, a fruitful future area for family business researchers to examine.

CONCLUSION

In reviewing the contentious issue of how economists define a firm, Penrose (2009[1959]: 9) notes confusion in separating out the 'firm' as an independent organisation, registered and legally defined, from an economic transactional unit of 'demand and supply functions', to a unit with wider economic and sociological functions. This confusion presents a challenge for family business researchers confronted with having to conceptualise the nature and implication of habitual entrepreneurship. If a legal perspective on the firm is adopted, a family business group is not strictly a 'firm' at all, but a federation of 'firms' under the differential ownership and control of a diversity of family members. From the orthodox perspective of the theory of the firm, each separate firm has its own

transactions, demand and supply functions. If the resource based view of Penrose is adopted, however, the group itself is part of a wider unit of resource and transaction, which could be viewed as a distinct 'firm', the family business. How far this would be legitimate and desirable would depend on how much interdependence there is between the 'firms' in the business group. A group with strong flows of resources and common transactions between its constituent firms could be functioning as a unified business.

If the family business group is treated as *de facto* a single business, the preoccupations of (a) trying to define what a family business is and (b) researching whether family detracts or enhances firm performance (Astrachan, 2010), would remain important 'firm-focused' agendas. The family provides a focus of additional unity between the firms as an additional pool of extended resources and values to grow and add value to the business. The focus on the 'firm' remains, but is just made more complex by the diversity of transaction and resource streams within it. Conversely, if the unit of analysis is not the 'firm', but the entrepreneur or family, a scenario where the elements are highly diversified and not related would pose some problems of definition. The first part of this review illustrates that habitual entrepreneurship is heterogeneous and could be especially complex in a family context. In particular, pluriactivity and the existence of 'open business groups' with no centralised organisational unity in some families is especially challenging to firm-focused research approaches.

The processes of habitual entrepreneurship when considered in a family context are complex, and much more so than the habitual entrepreneurship literature has been used to, with its focus on the single entrepreneur. The firm-focused strategic management research approaches to date have firstly failed to adequately deal with the practice of many entrepreneurial families of pursuing growth and change through new venturing and the establishment of business groups, rather than grow internally within a single firm. What characterises entrepreneurial families and what makes them successful in multiple venturing compared to their mono-active counterparts, invites future research. Secondly, strategic management approaches by family business researchers have failed to address the challenges thrown out by Mintzberg (1994) that strategic processes are evolutionary and emergent rather than formally planned. This chapter has demonstrated that there may be complex relationships between strategic practices of business group formation and habitual entrepreneurial behaviour, and changing external and internal circumstances. This too provides an exciting area for future research by family business researchers.

To conclude, entrepreneurship and family business has only recently emerged as an important theme in the family business literature. This has been approached to date mostly through firm-focused approaches based on strategic entrepreneurship (particularly entrepreneurial orientation). Habitual entrepreneurship introduces hitherto unforeseen complexities in not only how family businesses are defined, but also in how transgenerational renewal and continuity can be conceptualised and researched.

REFERENCES

Almeida, H. and Wolfenzon, D. (2006) A theory of pyramidal ownership and family business groups, *The Journal of Finance*, 61(6), 2637–2680.

Alsos, G.A. and Carter, S. (2006) Multiple business ownership in the Norwegian farming sector: resource transfer and performance consequences, *Journal of Rural Studies*, 22(3), 313–322.

Amit, R. and Wernefelt, B. (1990) Why do firms reduce risk? *Academy of Management Journal*, 33(3), 520–533.

Anderson, A., Jack, S. and Drakopoulou-Dodd, S. (2005) The role of family members in entrepreneurial networks: beyond the boundaries of the family firm, *Family Business Review*, 18(2), 135–154.

Astrachan, J.H. (2010) Strategy in family business: toward a multidimensional research agenda, *Journal of Family Business Strategy*, 1(1), 6–14.

Balunywa, W. (2009) Portfolio entrepreneurship and economic growth: the case of Uganda. PhD thesis, University of Stirling, Scotland.

Barca, F. and Becht, M. (eds). (2001) *The Control of Corporate Europe*. New York: The European Corporate Governance Network and Oxford University Press.

Baron, R.A. and Ensley, M.D. (2006) Opportunity recognition as the detection of meaningful patterns: evidence from the comparison of novice and experienced entrepreneurs, *Management Science*, 52(9), 1331–1334.

Birley, S. (2001) Attitudes of owner managers' children towards family and business issues: a 16 country study, *Entrepreneurship, Theory & Practice*, 26(2), 5–19.

Birley, S. and Westhead, P. (1993) A Comparison of new businesses established by 'novice' and 'habitual' founders in Great Britain, *International Small Business Journal*, 12(1), 38–60.

Brockhaus, R. (1994) Entrepreneurship and family business research: comparisons, critique and lessons, *Entrepreneurship, Theory & Practice*, 3(2), 125–138.

Brockhaus, R. (2004) Family business succession: suggestions for future research, *Family Business Review*, 17(2), 165–177.

Cabrera-Suarez, K., De Saa-Perez, P. and Garcia-Almeida, D. (2001) The succession process from a resource- and knowledge-based view of the family firm, *Family Business Review*, 14(1), 37–47.

Carlock, R.S. and Ward, J.L. (2001) *Strategic Planning for the Family Business: Parallel Planning to Unite the Family and Business*. New York: Palgrave.

Carney, M. and Gedajlovic E. (2002) The co-evolution of institutional environments and organizational strategies: the rise of family business groups in the ASEAN region, *Organization Studies*, 23(1), 1–29.

Carter, S. (1998) *Portfolio Entrepreneurship* in the farm sector: indigenous growth in rural areas?, *Entrepreneurship & Regional Development*, 10(1), 17–32.

Carter, S., Tagg, S. and Demitritatos, P. (2004) Beyond portfolio entrepreneurship: multiple income sources in small firms, *Entrepreneurship & Regional Development*, 16(6), 481–499.

Chandler, A.D. (1982) The M-Form: Industrial groups, American style,' *European Economic Review*, 19, 3–23.

Chang, S-J. (2006) Business groups in East Asia: Post crisis restructuring and new growth, *Asia Pacific Journal of Management*, 23(2), 407–417.

Chrisman, J.J., Chua, J.H. and Sharma, P. (2005) Trends and directions in the development of a strategic management theory of the family firm, *Entrepreneurship, Theory & Practice*, 29(3), 555–576.

Cooper, A.C. and Daily, C.M. (1997) Entrepreneurial team. In D.L. Sexton and R.W. Smilor (eds), *Entrepreneurship*. Chicago, IL: Upstart Publishing Company, pp. 127–150.

Cope, J. (2003) Entrepreneurial learning and critical reflection: discontinuous events as triggers for 'higher-level' learning, *Management Learning*, 34 (4), 429–450.

Dess, G., Pinkham, B. and Yang, H. (2011) Entrepreneurial orientation: assessing the construct's validity and addressing some of its implications for research in the areas of family business and organizational learning. *Entrepreneurship, Theory & Practice*, 35(5), 1077–1090.

Discua Cruz, A.F. (2010) Collective perspectives in portfolio entrepreneurship: a study of Honduran family business groups. *EDAMBA Journal, 2010 Thesis Competition*, 8, 91–105.

Discua Cruz, A. and Howorth, C. (2008) Family business in Honduras: applicability of agency and stewardship theories. In V. Gupta, N. Levenburg, L. Moore, J. Motwani and T. Schwarz (eds), *Culturally-Sensitive Models of Family Business in Latin America*. Hyderabad: ICFAI University Press, pp. 222–243.

Discua Cruz, A., Howorth, C. and Hamilton, E. (2010) Family entrepreneurial teams: a vehicle for portfolio entrepreneurship. Paper presented at Theories of Family Enterprise Conference. Edmonton: University of Alberta , available from authors.

Discua Cruz, A., Howorth, C. and Hamilton, E. (2013) Intrafamily entrepreneurship: the formation and membership of family entrepreneurial teams, *Entrepreneurship: Theory and Practice*, 37(1), 17–46.

Dyer, W.G. and Handler, W. (1994) Entrepreneurship and family business: Exploring connections, *Entrepreneurship, Theory & Practice*, 19(1), 71–83.

Encarnation, D. (1989) *Dislodging Multinationals: India's Comparative Perspective*. Ithaca, NY: Cornell University Press.

Eddleston, K.A. and Kellermanns, F.W. (2007) Destructive and productive family relationships: a stewardship perspective, *Journal of Business Venturing*, 22(4), 545–565.

Eddleston, K.A., Kellermanns, F.W. and Sarathy, R. (2008) Resource configurations in family firms: linking resources, strategic planning and technological opportunities to performance, *Journal of Management Studies*, 45(1), 26–50.

Fuller, A. (1990) From part-time farming to pluriactivity: a decade of change in rural Europe, *Journal of Rural Studies*, 6, 361–373.

Gartner, W.B., Shaver, K.G., Gatewood, E. and Katz, J.A. (1994) Finding the entrepreneur in entrepreneurship, *Entrepreneurship, Theory & Practice*, 18(3), 5.

Gasson, R. (1992) Farmer's wives: their contribution to the farm business, *Agricultural Economics*, 43(1), 74–87.

Ghemawat, P. and Khanna, T. (1998) The nature of diversified business groups: A research design and two case studies, *The Journal of Industrial Economics*, 46(1), 35–61.

Gill, S. (1999) *The Pathology of Corruption*, New Delhi: Harper/Collins.

Gomez-Mejia, L.R., Haynes, K.T., Nunez-Nickel, M., Jacobson, K.J.L. and Moyano-Fuentes, J. (2007) Socioemotional wealth and business risks in family-controlled firms: evidence from Spanish olive oil mills, *Administrative Science Quarterly*, 52(1), 106–137.

Gonzalez Leon, A.C., Gonzalez Couture, G. and Diaz Matajira, L. (2011) The role of tacit knowledge in the identification of entrepreneurial opportunities: a study of family controlled businesses. In M. Nordqvist, G. Marzano, E.R. Brenes, G. Jimenez and M. Fonseca-Paredes (eds), *Understanding Entrepreneurial Family business in Uncertain Environments: Opportunities and Resources in Latin America*. Cheltenham: Edward Elgar, pp. 203–236.

Goto, A. (1982) Business groups in a market economy, *European Economics Review*, 19(1), 53–70.

Granovetter, M. (1994–2005 edition). Business groups and social organization. In N.J. Smelser & R. Swedberg (eds), *The Handbook of Economic Sociology* (2nd ed.): Princeton, NJ: Princeton University Press, pp. 429–450.

Gura, T.C. (2011) Appeasement Entrepreneurship: family conflict as a source of new business opportunities. In M. Nordqvist, G. Marzano, E.R. Brenes, G. Jimenez and M. Fonseca-Paredes (eds), *Understanding Entrepreneurial Family Businesses in Uncertain Environments: Opportunities and Resources In Latin America*. Cheltenham: Edward Elgar, pp. 125–148.

Habbershon, T.G. (2006) Commentary: A framework for managing the familiness and agency advantages in family firms, *Entrepreneurship: Theory & Practice*, 30(6), 879–886.

Habbershon, T.G. and Williams, M. (1999) A resource-based framework for assessing the strategic advantage of family firms, *Family Business Review*, 12(1), 1–25.

Habbershon, T.G., Williams, M. and MacMillan, I.C. (2003) A unified systems perspective of family firm performance. *Journal of Business Venturing*, 18, 451–465.

Hall, A., Melin, L. and Nordqvist, M. (2001) Entrepreneurship as radical change in the family business: exploring the role of cultural patterns, *Family Business Review*, 14(3), 193–208.

Hamilton, E. (2006) Whose story is it anyway? Narrative accounts of the role of women in founding and establishing family businesses, *International Small Business Journal* 24(3), 253–271.

Howorth, C., Rose, M., Hamilton, E. and Westhead, P. (2010) Family firm diversity and development: an introduction, *International Small Business Journal*, 28(5), 437–451.

Hoy, F. and Sharma, P. (2010) *Entrepreneurial Family Firms*. New York: Prentice Hall.

Huovinen, J. and Tihula, S. (2008) Entrepreneurial learning in the context of portfolio entrepreneurship, *International Journal of Entrepreneurial Behaviour & Research*, 14(3), 152–171.

Iacobucci, D. (2002) Explaining business groups started by habitual entrepreneurs in the Italian manufacturing sector, *Entrepreneurship & Regional Development*, 14(1), 31–48.

Iacobucci, D. and Rosa, P. (2005) Growth, diversification and business group formation in entrepreneurial firms, *Small Business Economics*, 25(1), 65–82.

Iacobucci, D. and Rosa, P. (2010) The growth of business groups by habitual entrepreneurs: the role of entrepreneurial teams, *Entrepreneurship, Theory & Practice*, 34(2), 351–377.

Kenyon-Rouvinez, D. (2001) Patterns in serial business families: theory building through global case study research, *Family Business Review*, 14(3), 175–192.

Kester, W.C. (1992) Industrial Groups in Systems of Contractual Governance, *Oxford Review of Economic Policy*, 8(3), 24–45.

Khanna, T. (2000) Business groups and social welfare in emerging markets: Existing evidence and unanswered questions, *European Economic Review*, 44(4–6), 748–761.

Khanna, T. and Palepu, K. (1997) Why focused strategies may be wrong for emerging markets, *Harvard Business Review*, 75(4), 41–51.

Khanna, T. and Rivkin, J.W. (2001) Estimating the performance effects of business groups in emerging markets, *Strategic Management Journal*, 22(1), 45–74.

Khanna, T. and Yafeh, Y. (2005) Business groups and risk sharing around the world, *Journal of Business*, 78(1), 301–340.

Kodithuwakku, S. and Rosa, P. (2002) The entrepreneurial process and economic success in a constrained environment, *Journal of Business Venturing*, 17(5), 431–465.

Kolvereid, L. and Bullvåg, E. (1993) Novices versus experienced business founders: an exploratory investigation. In S. Birley, I.C. MacMillan and S. Subramony (eds), *Entrepreneurship Research: Global Perspectives*. Amsterdam, Elsevier, pp. 275–285.

Leff, N. (1976) Capital markets in the less developed countries: The group principal. In R. McKinnon (ed.), *Money and finance in economic growth and development*. New York; Dekker, pp. 97–122.

MacMillan, I.C. (1986) To really learn about entrepreneurship, let's study habitual entrepreneurs, *Journal of Business Venturing*, 1, 241–243.

Martin, W.L. and Lumpkin, G.T. (2003) From entrepreneurial orientation to 'family orientation': generational differences in the management of family businesses. In W.D. Bygrave (ed.), *Frontiers of Entrepreneurship Research: Proceedings of the 23rd Annual Entrepreneurship Research Conference*. Babson Park, MA: Babson College, pp. 309–321.

Masulis, R.W., Pham, P.K. and Zein, J. (2011) Family business groups around the world: Financial advantages, control motivations and organizational choices, *Review of Financial Studies*, 24(11), 3556–3600.

Mintzberg, H. (1994) The fall and rise of strategic planning, *Harvard Business Review*, 72(3), 107–114.

Morck, R. and Yeung, B. (2003) Agency problems in large family business groups. *Entrepreneurship: Theory and Practice*, 27(4), 367–382.

Mosey, S. and Wright, M. (2007) From human capital to social capital, a longitudinal study of technology-based academic entrepreneurs, *Entrepreneurship, Theory & Practice*, 31(6), 909–935.

Mullholland, K. (2003) *Class, Gender and the Family Business*. New York, Palgrave MacMillan.

Naldi, L., Nordqvist, M., Sjoberg, K. and Wiklund, J. (2007) Entrepreneurial orientation, risk taking, and performance in family business, *Family Business Review*, 20(1), 33–47.

Nordqvist, M., Habbershorn, T. and Melin, L. (2007) Transgenerational entrepreneurship, exploring entrepreneurial orientation in family firms. In H. Landstrom, H. Crijns and E. Laveran (eds), *Entrepreneurship, Sustainable Growth and Performance*. Cheltenham, Edward Elgar, pp. 93–117.

Nordqvist, M., Marzano, G., Brenes, E.R., Jimenez, G. and Fonseca-Paredes, M. (2011) *Understanding Entrepreneurial Family Businesses in Uncertain Environments: Opportunities and Resources in Latin America*. Cheltenham: Edward Elgar.

Nordqvist, M. and Melin, L. (2010) The promise of the strategy as practice perspective for family business research, *Journal of Family Business Strategy*, 1(1), 15–25.

Nordqvist, M. and Zellweger, T. (2010) *Transgenerational Entrepreneurship: Exploring Growth and Performance in Family Firms across Generations*. Cheltenham: Edward Elgar.

Pearson, A.W., Carr, J.C. and Shaw, J.C. (2008) Toward a theory of familiness: a social capital perspective, *Entrepreneurship Theory & Practice*, 32(6), 949–969.

Penrose, E. (2009[1959]) *The Theory of the Growth of the Firm*, 4th edition. Oxford: Oxford University Press.

Plate, M., Schiede, C. and Schlippe, A. v. (2010) Portfolio entrepreneurship in the context of family owned businesses. In M. Nordqvist and T.M. Zellweger (eds), *Transgenerational Entrepreneurship: Exploring Growth and Performance in Family Firms Across Generations*. Cheltenham: Edward Elgar, pp. 96–122.

Robson, G., Gallagher, C. and Daly, M. (1993) Diversification strategy and practice in small firms, *International Small Business Journal*, 11(2), 37–53.

Rønning, L. and Kolvereid, L. (2006) Income diversification in Norwegian farm households, *International Small Business Journal*, 24(4), 405–420.

Rosa, P. (1998) Entrepreneurial processes of business cluster formation and growth by 'habitual' entrepreneurs, *Entrepreneurship, Theory & Practice*, 22(4), 43–62.

Rosa, P., Balunywa, W. and Iacobucci, D. (2005) Habitual entrepreneurs and the family business: a transgenerational perspective. *Conference of Family Enterprising: Babson Conference, Boston*. Available from the authors.

Rosa, P. and Hamilton, D. (1994) Gender and ownership in UK small firms, *Entrepreneurship, Theory & Practice*, 18(3), 11–27.

Rosa, P., Iacobucci, D. and Hatem, O. (2010) Portfolio entrepreneurship, 'churn' and the family business: a theoretical overview. Paper presented at Theories of Family Enterprise Conference. Edmonton: University of Alberta. Available from the authors.

Rosa, P., Kodithuwakku, S. and Balunywa, W. (2006) Entrepreneurial motivation in developing countries: what does 'necessity' and 'opportunity' really mean?, *Frontiers of Entrepreneurship Research*. Babson Park, MA: Babson College.

Rosa, P. and Scott, M. (1999) The prevalence of multiple owners and directors in the SME sector: implications for our understanding of start-up and growth, *Entrepreneurship and Regional Development*, 11(1), 21–38.

Roscoe, P., Discua Cruz, A. and Howorth, C. (2013) How does an old firm learn new tricks? A material account of entrepreneurial opportunity, *Business History*, 55(1), 53–72.

Rugman, A.M. (1976) Risk reduction by international diversification, *Journal of International Business Studies*, 7(2), 75–80.

Rutherford, M.W., Kuratko, D.F. and Holt, D.T. (2008) Examining the link between 'Familiness' and performance: can the F-Pec untangle the family business theory jungle?, *Entrepreneurship Theory & Practice*, 32(6), 1089–1110.

Salvato, C., Chirico, F. and Sharma, P. (2010) Understanding exit from the founder's business in family firms. In A. Stewart, G.T. Lumpkin and J.A. Katz (eds), *Advances in Entrepeneurship, Firm Emergence and Growth: Entrepreneurship and Family Business, Vol. 12*. Bingley: Emerald Group Publishers, pp. 31–85.

Sandvig, C.J. and Coakley, L. (1998) Best practices in small firm diversification, *Business Horizons*, 41(3), 33–41.

Sarasvathy, S.D. (2001) Causation and effectuation: toward a theoretical shift from economic inevitability to entrepreneurial contingency, *Academy of Management Review* 26(2), 243–263.

Sarasvathy, S.D. and Menon, A. (2004) Failing firms and successful entrepreneurs: serial entrepreneurship as a simple machine, Darden Business School Working Paper 04–05.

Scott, M. and Rosa, P. (1996) Has firm level analysis reached its limits? time for a rethink, *International Small Business Journal*, 14(4), 81–89.

Scott, M. and Rosa, P. (1999) Entrepreneurial diversification, business-cluster formation, and growth, *Environment and Planning C*, 17(5), 527–548.

Shimotani, M. (1997) The History and structure of business groups in Japan. In Shiba, T. & Shimotani, M. (eds), *Beyond the firm: business groups in international and historical perspective* (pp. 5–28). New York: Oxford University Press.

Short, J.C., Payne, G.T., Brigham, K.H., Lumpkin, G.T. and Broberg, J.C. (2009) Family business and entrepreneurial orientation in publicly-traded businesses: A comparative analysis of the S&P 500, *Family Business Review*, 22(1), 9–24.

Sieger, P., Zellweger, T., Nason, R.S. and Clinton, E. (2011) Portfolio entrepreneurship in family firms: a resource-based perspective, *Strategic Entrepreneurship Journal*, 5(4), 327–351.

Silva, F., Majluf, N. and Paredes, R.D. (2006) Family ties, interlocking directors and performance of business groups in emerging countries: the case of Chile, *Journal of Business Research*, 59(3), 315–321.

Sirmon, D.G. and Hitt, M.A. (2003) Managing resources: linking unique resources, management, and wealth creation in family firms, *Entrepreneurship, Theory & Practice*, 27(4), 339–358.

Ucbasaran, D. and Westhead, P. (2002) Does entrepreneurial experience influence opportunity identification?, *Frontiers of Entrepreneurship Research*, Babson College, Babson Park, MA.

Ucbasaran, D., Westhead, P. and Wright, M. (2006) *Habitual Entrepreneurs*. Cheltenham: Edward Elgar.

Ucbasaran, D.P., Westhead, P. and Wright, M. (2009) The extent and nature of opportunity identification by experienced entrepreneurs, *Journal of Business Venturing*, 24(2), 99–113.

Ucbasaran, D., Wright, M. and Westhead, P. (2003) A longitudinal study of habitual entrepreneurs: starters and acquirers, *Entrepreneurship & Regional Development*, 15(3), 207–228.

Ucbasaran, D., Alsos, G.A., Westhead, P. and Wright, M. (2008) *Habitual Entrepreneurs*, Foundations and Trends in Entrepreneurship, 4:4.

Westhead, P. and Howorth, C. (2007) Types of private family firms: an exploratory conceptual and empirical analysis, *Entrepreneurship & Regional Development*, 19(5), 405–431.

Westhead, P., Ucbasaran, D. and Wright, M. (2004) Experience and cognition: do novice, serial and protfolio entrepreneurs differ?, *International Small Business Journal*, 23(1), 72–98.

Westhead, P. and Wright, M. (1998a) Novice, portfolio, and serial founders: are they different?, *Journal of Business Venturing*, 13(3), 173–204.

Westhead, P. and Wright, M. (1998b) Novice, portfolio, and serial founders in rural and urban areas, *Entrepreneurship, Theory & Practice*, 22(4), 63–100.

Wiklund, J. and Shepherd, D.A. (2008) Portfolio entrepreneurship: habitual and novice founders, new entry, and mode of organizing, *Entrepreneurship, Theory & Practice*, 32(4), 701–725.

Williamson, O.E. (1975) *Markets and Hierarchies: Analysis and Antitrust Implications*. New York: Free Press.

Wright, M. and Kellermans, F.W. (2011) Family firms: a research agenda and publications guide, *Journal of Family Business Strategy*, 2(4), 187–196.

Yaprak, A. and Karademir, B. (2010) The internationalisation of emerging market business groups: an integrated literature review, *International Marketing Review*, 27(2), 245–262.

Yiu, D., Bruton, G.D. and Lu, Y. (2005) Understanding business group performance in an emerging economy: acquiring resources and capabilities in order to prosper, *Journal of Management Studies*, 42(1), 183–206.

Zahra, S. (2005a) *Corporate Entrepreneurship and Growth*. The International Library of Entrepreneurship, Elgar Reference Collection. Cheltenham: Edward Elgar.

Zahra, S.A. (2005b) Entrepreneurial risk taking in family firms, *Family Business Review*, 18(1), 23–40.

Zahra, S., Hayton, J., Neubaum, D., Dibrell, C. and Craig, J. (2008) Culture of family commitment and strategic flexibility: the moderating effect of stewardship, *Entrepreneurship, Theory & Practice*, 32(6), 1025–1054.

Zellweger, T.M., Eddleston, K.A. and Kellermans, F.W. (2010) Exploring the concept of familiness: Introducing family firm identity, *Journal of Family Business Strategy*, 1(1), 54–63.

19

Accountability and Stewardship of Family Business Entities

Keith Duncan and Ken Moores

INTRODUCTION

Accounting has been a well-established organisational process for centuries. While over time the specific functions of accounting have evolved in response to prevailing external and internal forces the underlying accounting technology has largely remained intact. The diffusion of this technology to all types of organisations, irrespective of their ownership structures, has been possible because the fundamental purpose of accounting remains that of achieving accountability. Initially operating owners rendered account about their stewardship of enterprise resources to participating families whereas in today's widely held corporations agent-managers report performance to distant principals.

This chapter explores whether current accounting technology fulfils the stewardship and accountability information needs of family business owners. As the influences on contemporary accounting are both *conceptual* and *contextual* we frame our discussion in terms of both the knowledge foundations of

accounting, as informed by various conceptions of the firm, and stakeholder theory. We posit that if prevailing conceptions of the firm impact the knowledge foundations of accounting, and subsequently the nature and form of accounting practice, then it is the conceptions of influential stakeholders that can define the accounting change agenda and affect contemporary accounting practice. We use extant research and practice to identify what conceptions of the firm prevail and whether these are consistent with conceptions of family firms.

We identify two streams of literature relevant to our review. The conceptual stream focuses on conceptions of the firm and the extent to which particular conceptions are encapsulated within accounting regulation and practice. We find that recent international accounting regulation evidences a shift in conceptions of the firm that aligns better with the stewardship orientation of family business owners. The empirical stream largely focuses on financial reporting quality and performance differences between publicly listed family and non-family firms. As the majority of family firms are private, this literature sheds limited light on accountability issues pertinent to family firms. Accordingly we identify opportunities for further empirical research connecting financial reporting quality and performance issues with alternative conceptions of the firm.

The chapter first outlines the internal and external forces behind the evolution of accounting over time. For non-accounting scholars we briefly overview some core accounting constructs. Then we consider various conceptions of the firm and their impact upon accounting. The accounting change agenda is introduced via a discussion of stakeholder theory that identifies if family business advocates influence accounting change in contemporary terms. A review of the empirical literature identifies research gaps that are discussed before we conclude the chapter.

EVOLUTION OF ACCOUNTING 'TECHNOLOGY'

The evolution of accounting has been variously affected by both internal and external *contextual* factors. Internally the objectives of principals, the ownership structures of enterprises, the operational complexities of these enterprises, and prevailing technologies have all affected the nature and form of accounting. In more recent times the external regulatory regime has also been influential in affecting accounting technology.

Accounting is just as much part of technology as the procedures for manufacturing in that technologies relate inputs and outputs using bodies of skills, knowledge and procedures. Accounting technology differs from physical productive technology in that it has both public and private good features. It is largely non-proprietary in nature in that it cannot be controlled and sold but the private benefits that it bestows to decision makers, such as business owners, can be realised through enhanced decision making (Carnegie and Parker 1996). Central to realising these benefits is the notion that decisions are being

made about a focal organisation such as the state, a business, or sub-unit. These focal organisations are referred to as entities and the accounting entity defines the boundaries for accountability. Specifically, owners are seen as separate from the accounting entity they own. Furthermore, reporting on the entity depends on the reference point (i.e., conception of the firm) adopted. Reporting externally to owners and others on the accounting entity is the domain of financial accounting whereas internal reporting to the managers and owner-managers is the domain of management accounting. Auditing is an oversight function as part of the overall accounting technology with the primary purpose of monitoring agents on behalf of principals.

The earliest forms of accounting technology served the needs of the state entity. The Babylonians, Egyptians, Athenians and Romans all had reasonably well-developed systems of accounts using crude recording technologies kept for taxation, storage and disbursement purposes. These records enabled officials to be accountable to their ruling masters. With the development of individual proprietorships, the need for commercial accounting records grew considerably. Not only did owners need to know the state of their holdings but they also needed to monitor the activities of others when they could no longer personally undertake all operational activities. These ownership needs and operational complexities extended the scope and form of accounting by developing various means of monitoring these agents. Ownership changes also prompted evolutionary change. Limited life ventures in the form of entrepreneurial voyages gave rise to captains having to render account to their partners on returning to their home port. Enduring partnerships also posed a host of difficulties concerning agency and the measurement of entitlements. As the size of partnerships grew so did the needs for both ownership accounting and cost accounting. The technology of double entry bookkeeping was a central feature of these systems of accounting from about the thirteenth century and was described in Luca Paciolo's *Summa de Arithmetica, Geometria, Proportioni et Proportionalitia* in 1494. The essential criterion of double entry bookkeeping is commercial proprietorship (Littleton 1927) and unlike earlier bookkeeping, which concentrated on government accounts, these 'modern' accounting technologies facilitated a change in emphasis from agency reporting to proprietorship reporting, especially as partnerships evolved from single voyages/journeys into lengthier commitments. The notion of a 'going concern' (now a core concept underlying periodic accounting and auditing) created even more information needs for business owners interested in long-term performance.

The advent of the public corporation further magnified the accounting problems in the last two centuries. The relatively straightforward needs for bookkeeping as a short-term recording device have been made more complex by the accumulation of large amounts of capital in the corporate enterprise (Shubik 2011). The breakthrough in computational technologies mid last century revolutionised data processing and helped to create bigger firms with far more complex and opaque organisational problems. The warnings of Berle and Means (1932) are now even more important in a world where there is an extra layer and opaqueness between ownership and management. Today's largest corporations not only have passive and ill-informed shareholders but many of them can be second order owners via pooled mutual or pension funds. Recent massive frauds and disastrous bubbles in the economy are in part the creation of highly complex and opaque financial instruments, creative accounting and the lack of a generally accepted good theory of the firm combined with an ad hoc patchwork of laws evolved in a politicised process (Shubik 2011). The inherent adaptability of accounting in being responsive to its social and organisational contexts has been exacerbated by the lack of agreed knowledge foundations and a generally accepted theory of the firm (Zambon and Zan 2000) opening accounting

to change by influence and politicisation (Watts and Zimmerman 1979). This poses the question: have the information needs of family businesses been subjugated?

ENTITIES, THEORIES OF THE FIRM, AND ACCOUNTING THEORY

Historically, accounting has evolved in response to both *contextual* and *conceptual* influences. In this section we focus on the *conceptual* influences. Real enterprises (entities) are managed directly by professional managers, or in the case of many family firms, by owner-managers. These managers often rely upon representations of reality in the form of financial reports to execute their roles as stewards. Accounting provides one such representation of reality that is both enduring and has universal acceptance. However, the accounting representation depends upon an underlying conceptualisation of the firm (Coase 1990) that in turn conditions how income and resources are measured. While accounts provide a financial representation of the firm, it is accounting theory that conceptualises this representation and in so doing introduces elements of a theory of the firm (Zambon and Zan 2000).

Accounting theorists have long argued the need for an orientation postulate to make explicit the reference point to which accounting should relate (Zeff 1978, 2002). The question is whose orientation should dominate and from whose perspective should accounting be performed. Over time the firm has been successively conceived of as (1) a centre of legal relationships, (2) a centre of production factors, (3) a centre of economic operations and (4) a centre of interests in more contemporary times (Ardemani 1968). Furthermore, each conception of the firm, by focusing on a particular aspect of the firm, suggests a specific main economic actor (MEA) from whose perspective accounting could be aligned. The MEA identifies those who should be considered as the bearers of primary interests towards the firm in contrast

Table 19.1   Conceptions of the firm

The firm as a centre of ...	Main economic actor (MEA)	Prevailing perspective	Accounting implications
Legal relationships	Sole trader where firm overlaps with the physical person carrying out the business	Personified view of ownership	Tracked to the theory of 'accounts personification'
Production factors	Proprietor	The owner of the factor assuming risk and therefore owner of the firm's wealth (not of the firm itself)	Proprietors' wealth via balance sheet focus with surplus being the residual after deducting explicit costs, i.e., textbook income
Economic operations	Group in control	Stresses co-ordinating activity performed in the management process	Income focus because of the separation between ownership and control and also majority versus minority shareholders
Interests	Institutional interest bearers	All kinds of actors could be seen as participating in the processes of economic production and long-term risk sharing	Different configurations of surplus according to the definition of constituents and stakeholders

to those that can be defined as external parties. The four conceptions of the firm and their respective MEAs are summarised in Table 19.1.

Accounting theorists have vigorously debated the underlying conceptions of the firm and the implications for the accounting discipline in terms of accounting regulation and policy, the technology used in practice and empirical research. However, the majority of the theoretical debate has focused on two conceptions of the firm – the proprietary view and entity view (Moores and Stedman 1986).[1]

Proprietary theory conceives the enterprise as a vehicle separating the economic resources of the firm from the personal interests of the owners. Accounting reflects the proprietors' objectives and assets and liabilities of the enterprise belong to the proprietors and owners' equity represents the proprietors' interest in the enterprise. Under this view accounting focuses on the change in proprietorship, the net wealth of the proprietors, and the balance sheet is the focus. Accounting regulation and practice will be dominated by balance sheet measurement issues (Kam 1986; Belkaoui and Jones 1996). In contrast, entity theory conceives the enterprise as a body distinct and

separate from owners. Accounting reflects the entity's objective, the assets it controls and the liabilities it owes, and owner's equity is seen as a liability ranking no greater than other obligations of the enterprise. Because the firm is held responsible for meeting the claims of stakeholders (debt and equity holders), entity theory is income focused and the profit and loss statement is dominant (Kam 1986; Belkaoui and Jones 1996). Accountability under the entity theory is focused on performance rather than wealth accretion.

Both the proprietary and entity theoretical perspectives have permeated the accounting literature (Lorig 1964; Gynther 1967; Ricchiute 1979; Moores and Stedman 1986) and have influenced the regulatory debate and subsequent practice of accounting. Gynther (1967) urged the arbitrary adoption of the entity viewpoint as the basis for a general uniform theory of accounting:

if we want a general theory of accounting, together with the higher degree of uniformity and comparability in accounting that it will provide (from small firms to national income accounting), we shall have to make an arbitrary decision as to whether to base it on the proprietary concept or the entity concept. (Gynther, 1967: 289)

While historically accounting practice reflected a proprietary viewpoint (Bartley and Davidson 1982), current practice does not solely follow the implications of either proprietary or entity theory (Kam 1986). For instance, in a multi-entity structure an entity approach is adopted by consolidating the accounts as a group. Nevertheless we treat dividends as distributions of profits but interest as an expense – this is a proprietary theory approach; an entity approach would treat all funding sources equally. Contemporary accounting is thus a mixture of proprietary and entity-based accounting procedures partly because of the historical origins of accounting (proprietorship and partnership forms of business evolving to corporations) and partly because accountants have not adopted a single conception of the firm and revamped regulation and practice accordingly.

CONCEPTION OF THE 'FAMILY' FIRM AND ACCOUNTING

The first two conceptions of the firm, shown in Table 19.1 as *legal relationships* and as *production factors*, are broadly consistent with the proprietary theory of the firm in that the MEA in both conceptions is the proprietor as the owner of the firm or its wealth. While the *economic operations* and *interests* conceptions of the firm are more consistent with entity theory in which the focus shifts from the owner/proprietor to groups in control and interest bearers concerned with co-ordination of the entity.

The four levels of MEA are especially pertinent when considering family businesses. Instead of the traditional dichotomous proprietary vs entity view in which it would be all too easy to conceive family businesses as proprietorships relative to more widely held corporation as entities, the MEA-based conceptions enable a more finely grained categorisation of family enterprises. Family businesses are not homogeneous. Many family business founders see the business as an extension of themselves exemplifying a personified

view of ownership. However, in a multi-generational sense the family becomes the proprietor. The family assumes stewardship for the production factors and becomes responsible for wealth generation across generations. In subsequent generations, or when the firm has grown in operational complexity to the extent that there is a distinct separation between ownership and control, the family owners' conception shifts from an emotion-based one to a more economically oriented relationship. Finally, these broadening conceptions reach maturity for family owners when they see the MEA as multiple generations of the family and other constituents and stakeholders. Accordingly it is possible that families can conceive of their firm in a variety of ways that potentially affects the nature and form of accounting that best meets their needs.

ACCOUNTING REGULATION AND POLICY

A broader range of conceptions of the firm, consistent with the heterogeneity that is evident within family firms, has significant implications for accounting. How the accounting discipline conceives the firm impacts not only accounting technology in practice but also the focus of our regulation and policy debate and the research questions we ask. More importantly for our review this effect can be reinforced through the impact of research on technology. Figure 19.1 captures this interrelationship and suggests that without clarity around the conception of the family firm, the accounting discipline potentially limits its relevance to the family business community.

The choice between technical procedures is not neutral in terms of power and influence, nor is it in terms of knowledge, since choice is typically based on an implicit preference for a given theory of the firm. Prevailing accounting technology is the product of a political process in which conceptions of the firm can dominate through influence exerted by key stakeholders (Watts and Zimmerman

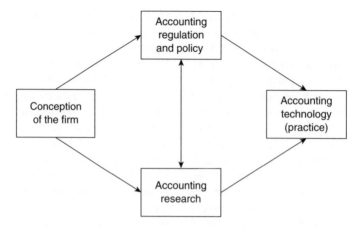

Figure 19.1   Conception of the firm and accounting discipline

1978, 1986). To understand the nature of this influence on policy development we frame our analysis in the context of stakeholder theory (Mitchell et al. 1997).

The fundamental question is: Which group of stakeholders is deserving or requiring the attention of accounting policy makers? A stakeholder in this sense is any group who can affect or is affected by the achievement of the regulatory agency's objectives. In the context of accounting, *power* is the relationship among social actors in which the family business sector can get regulators and researchers to address issues that they would not have otherwise. *Legitimacy* is a generalised perception that the actions of the regulator are desirable, proper, or appropriate. While *urgency* is the impetus for action on family business stakeholder claims due to time sensitivity and criticality. Finally, *salience* is the relative policy making priority of competing stakeholder claims. The parties identified as having all three attributes (power, legitimacy and urgency) are labeled *definitive* stakeholders. Accounting policy decision-makers determine which stakeholders are *definitive*. Their perceptions of the three stakeholder attributes is critical to how they view stakeholder salience. It is the definitive stakeholders with contemporaneous power, urgency and legitimacy, adhering to particular conceptions of the firm, who dominate accounting policy making.

To operationalise this framework we assign 'salience ranks' to the MEA on each of the stakeholder attributes: power, legitimacy and urgency. For each attribute column in Table 19.2 we assign a rank between 1 and 4 from lowest to highest relative rank allowing ties in ranks. These are judgment-based ranks that serve as crude proxies for the relative importance of the attributes rather than absolute measures. Focusing on current regulatory period we argue that *economic operations* conception of the firm dominates due to the power of global capital markets and is assigned a rank of 4 for power. We rate the *production factors* view of the firm, where most family firms are located, second in terms of power. Although one could debate that the wider stakeholder *interests* view has recently gained power. While the sole trader was the definitive stakeholder when Pacioli documented the accounting process this has waned hence we rank the legitimacy for those that hold the *legal relationship* conception of the firm as the lowest. The *economic operations* MEA, due to its role in international capital markets, is ranked as the highest in terms of legitimacy. While the *production factors* and *interests* MEAs we ranked as either 2 or 3 (so 3=) for legitimacy. One might argue that MEAs with wider community *interests* post the global financial crisis (GFC) might warrant a higher legitimacy rating recently.

Table 19.2   Main economic actors and their stakeholder salience: a contemporary ranking

Main economic actor (MEA)	Stakeholder salience			Definitive = highest cumulative rank
	Power	Urgency	Legitimacy	
Sole trader	1	1	1	3
Proprietor	3	2	3 = (2 or 3?)	8
Group in control	4	4	4	12
Institutional interest bearers	2	3	3 = (3 or 2?)	8

Certainly the GFC has heightened the urgency for considering wider interests and stakeholders so we ranked the *production factor* conception of the firm as 2 and *interests* as a 3 in terms of relative importance. The last column is a simple sum of the ranks for each attribute for each conception of the firm and serves as a tool to identify which conception is definitive in that all three attributes are present. Employing this framework the summed ranks suggests that those MEAs with the *economic operations* conception of the firm are highly salient and thus dominate contemporary accounting policy debate.

While our analysis suggests that current accounting technology is being driven by regulators predisposed towards MEAs that are consistent with 'entity inspired' conceptions of the firm, extant regulation evidences the influence of both entity- and proprietary-based conceptions side-by-side (Kam 1986). Because the regulatory agenda and the research approach reflect the influence of the dominant MEA of *economic operations*, both these paths reinforce the impact of the narrow MEA foci. Nevertheless there is some regulatory evidence that family business accounting issues may have gained some traction, highlighting an increased urgency building on the numerical legitimacy. Urgency and power are the key attributes that the family business sector has lacked relative to the highly salient widely held corporations in the past.

We employ this stakeholder salience-firm conception framework as a lens through which to examine contemporary accounting technology. The International Financial Reporting Standards (IFRS) represent the globally dominant embodiment of current accounting technology. Most countries have either adopted IFRS or adapted standards broadly equivalent to IFRS. These standards detail the accounting treatments for general purpose financial statements for profit-oriented entities which are intended to 'meet the common needs of shareholders, creditors, employees, and the public at large for information about an entity's financial position, performance, and cash flows' (International Accounting Standards Board 2010). More importantly, the IFRS standards are developed around the IASB's Conceptual Framework for Financial Reporting 2010. This framework states that the objective of 'general purpose financial reporting is to provide financial information about the reporting entity that is useful to existing and potential investors, lenders and other creditors in making decisions about providing resources to the entity' (International Accounting Standards Board 2010). This fundamental accounting objective, which sits behind the development of all IFRS standards and contemporary practice, clearly adopts an entity focus. Furthermore, this is consistent with the entity-based conceptions of the firm having the highest salience for accounting policy makers as suggested in Table 19.2. However, regulators that emphasise the needs of investors (proprietors) interpose a proprietary focus to regulation. The absence of a clearly agreed conception of the firm contributes to accounting's inability to satisfy the information needs of all entities. For example, the current debate on accounting for revenue highlights the need for clarity and agreement on the conception of the firm (Ohlson et al. 2011).

There is, however, some evidence that the information needs of family firms are finding salience and impacting accounting regulation and policy with explicit recognition in the IASB's constitution, a new reporting standard for SMEs and a renewed focus on stewardship. We will consider each of these developments in turn as they have implications for family firms and accounting research in family business.

Broader IASB Constitution

While the objective of financial reporting under IFRS is primarily investor decision making focused, the objective of the International Accounting Standards Board (IASB) as an organisation implies a broader policy brief. Under the International Accounting Standards Committee Foundation (IASCF) Constitution, the third objective explicitly states that in developing standards the IASB will 'take account of, as appropriate, the special needs of small and medium-sized entities'. Thus the IASB is charged under its constitution with recognising the needs of family firms given many family firms would fall within the definition of small to medium sized entities (SMEs). While there are a significant number of listed family companies captured by the IASB's main financial reporting objective, it is the special needs of the remaining SMEs that have arguably not had the power nor sufficient urgency or legitimacy to dominate the policy agenda. There is some evidence this is changing.

IFRS for SMEs

In 2009 the IASB issued IFRS for SMEs (International Accounting Standards Board 2009). IFRS for SMEs is consistent with the broader focus elucidated in the third objective of the IASB. In 2000 the IASB identified that there was a need for a simplified set of accounting standards for SMEs. This suggests that

while MEA *economic operations* (i.e., listed public) firms may have been definitive, the SME sector, which encompasses a large portion of family firms, had sufficient power, legitimacy and urgency to gain the attention of policy makers. Thus it is arguable that the more heterogeneous MEA of family firms are now formally catered for by either the IFRS for listed financial reporting entities or IFRS for SMEs.

The IFRS for SMEs omits accounting for some more complex issues and generally only allows one accounting treatment and that treatment is simpler than that allowed by the full IFRS. The disclosure requirements are also relaxed relative to the full IFRS making the standards less costly and possibly more relevant to users of SME reports. It is, however, an empirical question whether or not the IFRS for SMEs meets the accounting needs of family firms. Conceivably the IFRS for SMEs may still reflect an entity conception of the firm given the investment decision making focus of IFRS. However, the stated objective is for SME financial statements to provide information that is 'useful for economic decision-making by a broad range of users who are not in a position to demand reports tailored to meet their particular information needs'. While this is a decision making focus it is not an entity-based conception of the firm and is more in line with a broader conception of the firm as *interests*. The IFRS for SMEs also states that financial statements will show the 'results of the stewardship of management' (International Accounting Standards Board 2009). While the objective for SME statements is broader it is not clear that the standard has specifically considered the information needs of family firms.

For example, there is an argument in the literature that family firms tend to develop more internal goodwill than purchased goodwill (Hasso et al., 2012: 146). Larger listed firms tend to purchase intangible assets for expansion. This means that family firm assets, in particular their intangible assets, will be understated relative to other firms. This is only relevant if family owners want to use the balance sheet as a measure of value or as a performance measurement base (i.e., return on assets/ROA). Thus the requirement to expense all R&D and internally generated goodwill and capitalise only purchased goodwill disadvantages SMEs relative to full IFRS reporters who have different reporting options including capitalising cost in some cases. This represents but one issue where empirical research is needed to determine whether the IFRS for SMEs is meeting the needs of family business.

Stewardship Code

The recent Stewardship Code in the UK suggests regulators have a renewed emphasis on stewardship albeit from an *interests* perspective. The GFC highlighted that the second order (via managed funds) ownership of some firms coupled with momentary ownership of high frequency technologically driven trades, created a governance vacuum (Yeoh 2009; Haddrill 2010; Shubik 2011). The Financial Reporting Council (FRC)[2] believed investor monitoring of boards matters and issued the Stewardship Code to encourage good stewardship by institutional shareholders. The objective is to refocus institutional shareholders away from short-term performance and encourage more engagement with companies, to 'build and nurture a critical mass of committed shareholders willing to behave as owners' and hold boards to account (Montagnon 2011). This regulatory response contrasts with the innate stewardship focus of families in business. Stewardship theory suggests that due to their long-term orientation, wealth and reputation risks families in business have an incentive to engage with their management and monitor the firm for the long-term benefit of the family. A potential avenue for future research is to consider the governance implications of a multi-generational family stewardship focus.

In summary, notwithstanding the mixed conceptions of the firm that reflect both entity and proprietary viewpoints that prevail in accounting regulation such as IFRS for SMEs, there is, however, a preoccupation with regulating the measurement of income. This focus tends to emphasise the needs of owners as proprietors for short-term performance measured in the income statement. Regulation therefore reflects an entity view held by distant external investors. In contrast, investing families-in-business with their long-term focus, patient capital and wealth creation across generations will place more emphasis on the balance sheet of the entity. In this way they exemplify a proprietary viewpoint. With this as a backdrop we are now ready to juxtapose the conceptual foundations and regulatory and policy formulation in accounting against the extant family business empirical research.

ACCOUNTING RESEARCH IN FAMILY BUSINESS

We confine ourselves to a macro level review to highlight the fundamental issues facing accounting research in family business. The most important issue is that family business accounting research does not explicitly discuss or consider the conception of the firm despite its importance as identified in the first half of this chapter. The core issue for researchers is that an entity focus is implicit in the research to date and thus limits the nature of questions addressed and the methodology employed. Our message is that more of the same is unlikely to be fruitful.

In our overview of the literature we draw heavily on the detailed reviews of 77 articles by Salvato and Moores (2010) and Hasso and Duncan (2013). Salvato and Moores (2010) review the contributions and challenges of accounting family business research but is restricted to financial accounting (focusing on the financial reporting sub-area), auditing and management accounting topics. Readers should refer to the appendix in Salvato and Moores (2010) for a detailed summary of the 43 empirical articles (plus two conceptual auditing papers) they review. Hasso and Duncan (2013) review 34 financial accounting family business articles relating to the sub-areas of accounting performance, valuation and cost of capital; readers are referred to Hasso and Duncan (2013) for the details on these papers. We classify this entire body of research evidence (i.e., 77 papers) in Table 19.3 in terms of the research domains, sub-areas and foci, the research location, and public/private ownership characteristics. The distribution of research evidence summarised in Table 19.3 provides a useful insight into what we do and do not know about family versus non-family business from an accounting perspective.

The overwhelming majority (48 of 77) of the papers examine the differential impact of family firms on financial reporting outcomes (earnings management/quality, governance, methods and disclosure) and the relative accounting performance (ROA, ROS, income, productivity) versus non-family firms. Much of this research reflects the underlying objective of accounting which is to supply information for economic decision making and the majority of these studies related to publicly owned entities. Accounting quality is operationalised in a number of ways but a common approach is to consider either the earnings response coefficient (relationship between earnings and market value), accounting choices, regulatory environment, level of accruals or discretionary accruals (earnings management) and governance characteristics. The evidence suggests that in markets where ownership is less concentrated, ownership by families positively impacts earnings quality but has a mixed impact on earnings management. Public family firms are less likely to choose income increasing techniques but the evidence is mixed on whether they are more likely to voluntarily disclose financial information. However, the distribution of financial accounting research detailed in Table 19.3 shows that much of this evidence is US public firm centric. While we do have some evidence on European private firms we clearly know very little about private family firms across the world yet this is the dominant form of business.

The performance literature has looked at accounting-based measures of performance, market valuation, as well as key drivers of value, cost of capital. The majority of the accounting performance studies (8 of 15) find family firms exhibit a higher ROA, productivity, efficiency and operating margins than non-family firms. There is some evidence of a U-curve between family ownership and performance, however, others find a negative effect for family involvement, while three studies from the USA, UK and Taiwan find no family effect. There are also generational effects on performance. This limited evidence suggests that public family firms will have a higher earnings response coefficient when regressed on price due to the higher profitability, conditioned on earnings management not undermining the quality of the earnings signal. However, the quantum of research and public firm focus again shows we know precious little about family firm performance.

The valuation literature is even more mixed than the accounting performance literature. While this literature focuses on listed companies, for which there is a market reference price (eleven studies), there is one study of private firms that shows family firms engage in more reputation and customer development that is an important value driver. Market performance, typically measured as Tobin's Q or the related price to book (P/B) ratio, is positively impacted by family involvement especially for the founding generation. Again the research shows that appointing a second generation family CEO lowers performance and control enhancing mechanisms have a negative market performance impact as does corporate opaqueness. However, this research does not capture the full market performance impact from the family's perspective. Astrachan and Jaskiewicz (2008) in their conceptual paper argue that the value of the firm to the family is a function of both financial and emotional value. The research to date has focused on financial value only. This is one area where the accounting entity concept does not provide useful information relevant to the controlling family.

There is also a small body of literature on cost of capital and risk issues that are related to market performance and valuation of family firms. Conceptually, cost of capital is a market-based function of the characteristics of the investment and finance theory suggests that family ownership should be irrelevant (McConaughy 1999). However, the capital asset pricing model's (CAPM) time horizon irrelevance assumption is inconsistent with the long-term investment horizon of family firms (Zellweger 2007). Hence cost of equity capital should be lower for family firms due to their long-term orientation and CEO tenure. The limited evidence summarised in Table 19.3 does not specifically address the issue of cost of capital although the P/B evidence discussed earlier is consistent with family firms having a lower cost of equity. There is some evidence family firms have a lower cost of debt where family ownership is low. There is mixed evidence on risk and leverage preferences and some evidence private family firms have potentially higher agency costs and this is reflected in debt contracts that require greater personal collateral. Finally family firms are more inclined to be entrepreneurial risk takers. A lot more work is needed in this area as our valuation models are dependent on understanding the drivers of cost of capital and pricing of risk.

The last two categories of accounting research relate to the domains of auditing and management accounting, both of which are rather sparsely populated in Table 19.3. The limited empirical audit research suggests agency costs and debt levels drive the demand for audit services. However, auditing assurance services are also integral to reported earnings quality, reducing information asymmetry and there is a growing literature on the governance role of both the audit committee of the board (see Aldamen et al. 2011 for a review and evidence on the role for public companies) and internal auditing functions (Prawitt et al. 2009). As yet these are untapped family business audit research areas.

Management accounting is possibly the area with the greatest potential for family business and family business researchers according to Salvato and Moores (2010), yet this is the least researched area with three papers in Table 19.3. All relate to private family firms and show these firms operate with formal plans, they relied more on formal management accounting systems as the firm matured and were more likely to have strategic and succession plans if they had an advisory board in place. Subsequent to the review by Salvato and Moores (2010), a paper by Giovannoni et al. (2011) found that management accounting affects the transfer of knowledge across generations and between the owner family and management. This recent paper highlights how accounting technology can assist with the nurturing of MEAs to develop consistent conceptions of the firm across multiple generations.

In summary, despite some recent management accounting and auditing family business research, most of the family business accounting research has focused on financial accounting issues. Researchers have tested if family firms are different to non-family firms in terms of a range of accounting phenomena such as performance, accounting quality, market value and cost of capital. This literature does not directly address family business accounting issues but rather it adds 'family' as an explanatory variable to core accounting domain research questions. The implicit assumption in the research is that the firm is an entity and accounting's role is to report on the entity for largely external decision makers in capital markets which is not reflective of the broader MEA of family firms. The vast majority of family firms are privately held hence much of the accounting research today is not directly relevant or transferable. Thus one of the issues moving forward with the accounting research is to better understand the heterogeneity amongst family firms consistent with the broad ranging MEA for family firms discussed earlier. For instance, Dyer's (2006)

Table 19.3 Family business research by accounting research domain/sub-area, location and public/private ownership

Domain	Sub-area	Dominant theory	Secondary theory	Foci	Main findings/issues		USA, Canada	Europe	Asia Pacific	Public/private	Total
Financial accounting	Financial reporting	Agency	Stewardship, governance, behavioural	Earnings management and quality, governance, voluntary disclosure, accounting methods, market relevance	Earnings quality higher for family firms in markets where ownership less concentrated (USA/Canada/UK), lower in markets where ownership more concentrated (e.g. Europe). Mixed evidence on earnings management and voluntary disclosure.	Public	12	8	6.5#	26.5	#
						Private	2	4	0.5	6.5	33
	Accounting performance	Agency	Governance	Return on assets, revenue, income, net profit margin, productivity	Family firms generally exhibit a higher ROA, efficiency and margins. There is some evidence of a U curve, no and negative family effects. Second generation family CEO lower performance than a non-family CEO.	Public	6	3.5	2	11.5	
						Private	1	2.5		3.5	15
	Valuation	Agency	Valuation theory and governance	Tobin's Q, price to book ratio, value enhancing activities	Tobin's Q and P/B positively impacted by family firms especially if founding generation. Second generation family CEO lower performance than a non-family CEO. Control enhancing mechanisms have a negative market performance impact as does low transparency.	Public	6	3	1	10	
						Private	1			1	11
	Cost of capital and risk	Agency	Governance	Cost of equity, cost of debt, risk	Lower cost of debt especially if lower family ownership. Evidence that family firms less diversified, higher and lower debt, more collateral of family and more risk taking.	Public	4	1		4	
						Private	3	1		4	8

Domain	Sub-area	Dominant theory	Secondary theory	Foci	Main findings/issues		USA, Canada	Europe	Asia Pacific	Public/private	Total
Auditing		Agency	Conceptual, resource dependence	Auditing*	Agency costs and debt level drives unregulated demand for voluntary auditing. Public family firms are less likely to demand high quality (i.e. Big X) auditors due to lower agency costs. Curvilinear relation between audit firm size and management ownership.	Public	2			2	
						Private	1	3	1	5	7
Management accounting		Agency	Governance, life cycle	Management accounting	Management accounting systems for control when more mature, strategic and succession plans when advisory board and operational plans for fast growing firms.	Public				0	
						Private	2		1	3	3
Total: Public family firm accounting research							**30**	**14.5**	**9.5**	**54**	
Total: Private family firm accounting research							10	10.5	2.5	23	77

* Two conceptual papers in auditing as discussed by Salvato and Moores (2010) but excluded from the regional and public/private analysis.

Half weights mean that a paper considered both public and private family firms.

four-part typology suggests that there are several different types of family firms and the performance relation is moderated by other family firm characteristics. Dyer (2006) encourages researchers to view family firms through a more complex lens and recognise that the 'family effects' are not uniform. This has implications for the definition of family firm that typically relies on percentages of ownership and management control. A more fine-grained approach is needed in the performance literature going forward. Chrisman et al. (2004) and Anderson et al. (2009) are examples of studies where the authors have tried to unravel the family business and governance situation for the firm.

DISCUSSION AND RESEARCH AGENDA

The adaptability of accounting technology in response to external *contextual* factors is possible due to the absence of an agreed *conception* of the firm. The dominant conception over time has reflected various MEAs that manifest in seeing the firm as centres of *legal relationships*, *production factors*, *economic operations* and *interests*. Evidence of this lack of agreement over the conception of the firm is found both within accounting policy and regulation and extant literature.[3] In particular, this lack of agreement is most often characterised as leading to practices that exemplify a mix of both entity and proprietary conceptions of the firm.

Furthermore, given the politicisation of accounting policy the most recent influence on the conception of the firm has reflected the perspective of widely held corporations. The primary MEAs are their investor owners (proprietors) that are concerned more with short-term income performance. The salience of these stakeholders in the determination of accounting technology (practice) has moved the underlying conception of the firm to be one more aligned with an idiosyncratic interpretation of the proprietary view: a view in which stewardship is narrowly understood to

be predominantly accountable for short-term revenue generation. This is in marked contrast to the longer-term perspective of families in business. They conceive of the firm as an entity in which the bearers of primary interest (MEAs) can and do vary over time with the organisational life cycle but which ultimately reaches a point where the entity is being managed for subsequent generations. Stewardship for these family owners takes on a broader interpretation implying that they are accountable for wealth creation on behalf of their multiple generations: an idiosyncratic interpretation of the entity view.

Our overview of the state of nature for family business accounting regulation, policy development and empirical research suggests a number of key issues and potential future research directions. We will firstly consider the regulation and policy issues then we identify future research directions. The major development in accounting policy is the IFRS for SMEs (International Accounting Standards Board 2009). We argued that this standard reflects that the MEA of a large number of family businesses is not consistent with that of broadly held entities and hence the IASBs IFRS program was not relevant. The adoption/intended adoption of IFRS for SMEs by a large number of countries now begs the question whether the financial reports drafted within the standard meet the information needs of family firms. The stated objective of IFRS for SMEs is to meet the needs of a wider user group and report on stewardship of the firm and this later objective is relevant to family business researchers as stewardship is a core value of many families in business. Research on the applicability, implementation issues and deficiencies in reports based on the IFRS for SME standard, has the potential to scientifically underpin future policy debates and enhance the previously diminished salience for family business in the accounting policy development in recent times.

However, before scholars embark on any empirical work relating to the IFRS for SMEs or any other policy issue it is important that they first consider the conceptual underpinnings of such regulation. A wide range of objectives for accounting have found voice and been debated over the years, however, Gjesdal (1981) argues that there are essentially two different answers to the question what is the objective of financial reporting? Firstly, there is a decision making demand in that financial statements may be of value to investors (in a broad sense) making investment decisions. This definition is in line with the currently espoused IASB objective and is core to the IFRS regulation as it applies to widely held corporations. Secondly, there is a stewardship demand, which as noted earlier is more applicable to regulation such as the IFRS for SMEs. Where investors or proprietors delegate decision making to managers, then there is demand for information about actions that are taken for the purpose of controlling managers. Rosenfield (1974) further defines the stewardship objective of financial statements as 'to report on the control and use of resource by those accountable for their control and use to those to whom they are accountable'. This view of stewardship is potentially a broader view in that it does not focus on a single type of decision and narrow range of decision makers (investors). This theme is picked up in the commentary to the current conceptual framework where it states that the primary decision making objective encompasses providing information that is useful in assessing management's stewardship.

Historically, the concept of stewardship reflected the need for a resource provider to obtain an account of what the stewards (owners or managers) had done with the resources entrusted to them. Under the *production factor* conception of the firm this objective means to provide an account to the proprietor and other resource providers (debt holders) of the steward's actions. For modern corporations stewardship means monitoring the agency actions of managers. So the concept of accountability and stewardship are relevant to family and non-family firms but in different ways. In a family firm the concept of stewardship takes on a much broader

meaning. Families in business often view themselves as the stewards for the family wealth (Miller and Le Breton-Miller 2005; Arregle et al. 2007; Gomez-Mejia et al. 2007). Due to the interdependency of the family with its business, they share a much stronger connection to the firm than non-family owners. This connection between the family and its business leads to managerial practices that differ from non-family businesses. One of the primary manifestations is a more long-term orientation (James 1999). The firm is managed with future generations in mind, and often by CEOs whose job tenure greatly exceeds those of non-family firms (Beckhard and Dyer 1983).

Including stewardship as part of the defined objective of financial reporting potentially captures the long-term steward element of family firms' conception of the firm while remaining consistent with the information needs of atomistic shareholders. Unfortunately this is not the case in the currently espoused conceptual framework. Researchers can help address this discord by researching the impact of conceptual foundations on regulation and applicability to family firms. In particular, what is the impact on regulation if we align our objective statement with the broader conception of the firm and a notion of stewardship that reflects the family firms raison d'être.

The foregoing arguments and state of the literature (see Table 19.3) suggest a range of empirical research options for scholars of accounting in family business; options that range from 'macro' topics through to more 'micro' ones. At the heart of the macro-type topics we would encourage scholars to walk away from the conception of the firm embedded in mainstream accounting literature that largely reflects an idiosyncratic proprietary viewpoint reinforced through agent-theoretic lens. Instead, scholars could explore alternative conceptions of the firm more in accord with 'the family' (a multi-generational concept) as the primary bearer of interest in family firms. This is consistent with a broader understanding of stewardship and how this could manifest in accounting technology (practice) begs development.

Our review of the empirical literature and discussion of future directions is focused on more macro issues.[4] To develop an overall sense of the extant research we summarise the main empirical work by region and public/private organisational form in Table 19.4. We know a lot about North American firms, with 52% of the research coming from this region, whereas a third of the research is focused on European markets and 16% from Asia/Pacific (including South America). This distribution of knowledge is unrepresentative of family business around the world. More importantly, over 70% of this research has focused on publicly traded firms where family ownership, management and control, due to financial and human capital needs, are arguably much lower. Only 29.9% of the research evidence relates to private family firms and yet this is the largest and most prevalent form of business in the world. The research opportunities are therefore huge as are the challenges. Access to data is an equally large barrier to conducting and documenting a verifiable body of research knowledge for private firms. While this challenge is not insurmountable it will take some effort by researchers and co-operation from family businesses willing to release potentially sensitive financial information.

There is also room for further work on the cost of capital implications for family firms including studies from different markets on the cost of equity, costs of debt and leverage as these three factors are key valuation drivers. Also what are the trade-offs in performance measurement and valuation between earning and book value based information signals (Hasso and Duncan, 2013). Do earnings or book value have more information content for family firms relative to non-family firms? Hence where should standard setters focus regulatory development: the measurement of income or resources?

To address these questions researchers should consider the relative foci of family versus non-family proprietors. For example, the requirement to expense all R&D and internally generated goodwill but capitalise and amortise purchased goodwill disadvantages SMEs. Firms employing the full IFRS technology have different reporting options including capitalising cost in some cases. This represents but one issue where empirical research is needed to determine the reporting requirements of family firms and whether regulation, such as the IFRS for SMEs, meets family firm reporting needs. To address this question, though, researchers should first consider the more 'macro' issues of the monitoring value and hence reporting implication of a stewardship orientation. The downplay of stewardship in the full IFRSs vis-a-vis has heightened the role of stewardship both under the recent UK Stewardship Code and more importantly the orientation of family firms as recognised in the objective for the IFRS for SMEs. This highlights that addressing specific reporting issues first requires we address the issue of conceptual foundations otherwise we risk perpetuating the current 'confused' accounting standards (Kam 1986; Ohlson et al. 2011).

At more 'micro' levels the dearth of studies in management accounting and auditing represent a literature gap but here too scholars

Table 19.4   Frequency of research by region and public/private ownership

	USA/Canada	Europe[+]	Asia Pacific	Totals
Public	55.6%	26.9%	17.6%	70.1%
Private	43.5%	45.7%	10.9%	29.9%
Totals	51.9%	32.5%	15.6%	

[+]Includes the UK

should not slavishly follow mainstream accounting research but rather ensure that the underlying conception of the firm is consistent with that held by 'the family' as MEA. The field of management accounting potentially has the most to offer family business by first documenting the management accounting systems (MAS) used by family firms to manage across the generations. This research can then inform the family business community of control system options and demonstrate the design and implementation merits of such systems. In particular, investigating agent theoretic inspired designs may be inappropriate in the context of family owned enterprises. Similarly, research in the related field of auditing, especially internal control systems and governance, could potentially benefit family business.

Another issue is that the research summarised in Table 19.3 has largely relied on agency theory as a core theoretical framework. A few papers have also drawn on governance, resource dependency, stewardship and life cycle theory. It is not sufficient to assume that relaxing the core ownership-management separation assumption of agency theory creates new agency problems or that family owners will engage in entrenchment agency actions. Given the reputational impacts it would seem unlikely that all family firms will behave in the same narrow way. If this were true then all non-family investors would price protect (Jensen and Meckling 1976) and families would bear the full cost of their expected agency actions. As Dyer's (2006) typology suggests there is more than one type of family firm and testing the incentives the respective family firm types have will significantly advance this literature. Again, advancement requires accounting scholars to reflect on the broader MEA and conception of the firm more consistent with reality for family firms.

There are also methodological issues associated with the extant empirical literature to address. While McKenny et al. (2014) and Reay and Zhang (2014) cover methodological issues in family business research in detail in

their chapters in this *Handbook*, there are some issues specific to the accounting domain to note. The methodologies of family business accounting researchers are the same methodologies used in mainstream non-family business research. For example, the standard measures of earnings management are employed with little consideration for what earnings management might look like in family firms. If we overlay the long-term multi-generational orientation of families then earnings management may have less to do with short-term accruals and more to do with real underlying business decisions. Even in the corporate world there is evidence that non-accounting decisions are used to manage earnings (Graham et al. 2005). For example, is it more likely that family firms will use free family labour in tight periods to control costs. One of the authors worked in various family firms under non-commercial reward structures because this was 'family'. Managing real business decisions to change earnings is completely normal and arguably sound business practice yet it impacts discretionary accruals measures necessitating new measures to capture earnings management for family firms.

The issues of accounting research innovation is, however, much broader than family business accounting research. We will end by considering the following quote from Sunder (2011), a leading accounting researcher frustrated with the lack of ingenuity in accounting research:

> Imagine, having our research agendas driven not so much by research methods but by the question or questions we seek to answer. Imagine our academic associations organised by research questions. Imagine our journals organised by research questions instead of methods. Imagine, the sessions of our meetings and doctoral consortia organised by questions, not methods. Will this change our thinking? Will it change what we do, the conclusions we reach, and what we publish. I do not know, but would sure like to try. (Sunder 2011: 8)

Simply doing more of the same and adopting the research frame of reference associated with widely held corporations is unlikely to bear much further fruit. Family business accounting research would benefit greatly from some imaginative non-agency and non-public company research questions to better reflect the MEA of family business.

CONCLUSION

Accounting has evolved over time and this adaptability has largely accommodated the information needs of family businesses. Evolution has been affected by external factors, internal factors and technology. Furthermore, conceptual drivers have also driven some change as various theories of the firm have affected the nature and form of accounting. During most of this process the information needs of family business owners have not been compromised or subjugated to other agendas; at least until relatively recently when the accounting change process has been defined by political dynamics. The accounting policy agenda has largely sought to meet the information needs of remote owner investors separated from management in which a particular conception of the firm dominates. This decision making demand for financial reports has overridden the stewardship demand for reports and has consequently subjugated the information needs of owner-managers in family businesses.

However, there is some evidence that family business owners have recently achieved more definitive stakeholder status in the accounting policy arena with the emergence of IRFS for SMEs. This is perhaps more cosmetic than substantive in that the standard was largely prompted by a desire for simplification of the IFRS requirements for large corporations. There is not yet any fundamental change in terms of the underlying conception of the firm more in line with concepts that coincide with the views of family business owners. Our review suggests that the regulatory and research foci have not matched the needs of the family business stakeholders. The identified research issues

represent a path to enhance the extant scientific evidence which in turn can inform regulatory and policy debates as well as teaching and education agendas. Through knowledge dissemination via policy and education channels accounting may better serve the needs of family business.

Interestingly the notion of stewardship connects accounting and family business. Stewardship reporting has long been recognised as an objective of accounting, and more recently family business scholars are embracing stewardship as potentially capturing families' long-term orientation whereby they manage the business for and on behalf of future generations. However, the interpretation of stewardship by both disciplines is very different. In the case of accounting, stewardship is narrowly interpreted and implies accountability to the major economic actors (MEAs), the investor owners. On the other hand the concept of stewardship for family business scholars is more broadly interpreted in that it is accountability to future family generations as owners. Revisiting the accounting notions of stewardship offers scholars a potential path to link accounting to the implicit conception of the firm held by the MEA of families in business.

Our core message is that more of the same is unlikely to be fruitful. We call on accounting researchers to re-conceptualise not simply re-contextualise accounting for family owned businesses. Concepts consistent with more finely grained MEAs could give rise to the utilisation of multiple theoretical lenses beyond the dominant agent-theoretic paradigm. Linking specific MEA to theoretical lenses such as stewardship theory, transaction cost economics and socio-emotional wealth (Gomez-Mejia et al. 2011) all offer promise.

NOTES

1 It is important to note that the entity view is not synonymous with the accounting entity whereby the business is seen as separate from the owners. That is, the entity theory goes beyond the entity convention regarding

the separation of business and personal affairs (Kam 1986: 305).

2 The FRC is the UK's independent regulator of accounting and actuarial standards and of the audit profession.

3 Note we only reviewed the extant empirical accounting literature within the family business context to establish that it was largely an extension mainstream accounting and as such also reflected the same underlying conception of the firm. The majority of empirical accounting research in this context is financial accounting and reporting using an agency lens which tends to reinforce accountability to investor owners (proprietors).

4 Those readers interested in more detail should see Salvato and Moores (2010) for 17 empirical research questions and suggested methodologies. Also see Hasso and Duncan (2012: 146) for testable propositions in relation to the performance and valuation literature.

REFERENCES

Aldamen, H., K. Duncan, S. Kelly and R. McNamara, 2011, Performance of family firms during the global financial crisis: Does governance matter?, *SSRN eLibrary*, 25 December, available from http://ssrn.com/paper=1976789.

Anderson, R.C., A. Duru and D.M. Reeb, 2009, Founders, heirs, and corporate opacity in the United States, *Journal of Financial Economics* 92, 205–222.

Ardemani, E., 1968, L'evoluzione del concetto di impresa e dei sistemi contabili in Italia [The evolution of firm concept and accounting systems in Italy], *Rivista dei Dottori Commercialisti* 3, 411–430.

Arregle, J., M. Hitt, D. Sirmon and P. Very, 2007, The development of organizational social capital: Attributes of family firms, *Journal of Management Studies* 44, 73–95.

Astrachan, J.H. and P. Jaskiewicz, 2008, Emotional returns and emotional costs in privately held family businesses: Advancing traditional business valuation, *Family Business Review* 21, 139–149.

Bartley, J.W. and L.F. Davidson, 1982, The entity concept and accounting for interest costs, *Accounting and Business Research*, 175–187.

Beckhard, R. and W.G. Dyer, 1983, Managing continuity in the family-owned business, *Organizational Dynamics* 12, 5–12.

Belkaoui, A. and S. Jones, 1996, *Accounting Theory: An Australian Edition* (Harcourt Brace & Company, Sydney).

Berle, A. and G. Means, 1932, *The Modern Corporation and Private Property* (Macmillan, New York).

Carnegie, G.D. and R.H. Parker, 1996, The transfer of accounting technology to the southern hemisphere: The case of William Butler Yaldwyn, *Accounting, Business & Financial History* 6, 23–49.

Chrisman, J.J., J.H. Chua and R.A. Litz, 2004, Comparing the agency costs of family and non-family firms: Conceptual issues and exploratory evidence, *Entrepreneurship: Theory and Practice* 28, 335–354.

Coase, R.H., 1990, Accounting and the theory of the firm, *Journal of Accounting and Economics* 12, 3–13.

Craig, J. and K. Moores, 2010, Strategically aligning family and business systems using the Balanced Scorecard, *Journal of Family Business Strategy* 1, 78–87.

Dyer, W.G., Jr., 2006, Examining the 'family effect' on firm performance, *Family Business Review* 19, 253–273.

Giovannoni, E., M.P. Maraghini and A. Riccaboni, 2011, Transmitting knowledge across generations: The role of management accounting practices, *Family Business Review* 24, 126–150.

Gjesdal, F., 1981, Accounting for stewardship, *Journal of Accounting Research* 19, 208–231.

Gomez-Mejia, L., K. Haynes, M. Nunez-Nickel, K. Jacobson and J. Moyano-Fuentes, 2007, Socioemotional wealth and business risks in family-controlled firms: Evidence from Spanish olive oil mills, *Administrative Science Quarterly* 52, 106–137.

Gomez-Mejia, L.R., C. Cruz, P. Berrone and J. De Castro, 2011, The bind that ties: Socioemotional wealth preservation in family firms, *The Academy of Management Annals* 5, 653–707.

Graham, J.R., C.R. Harvey and S. Rajgopal, 2005, The economic implications of corporate financial reporting, *Journal of Accounting and Economics* 40, 3–73.

Gynther, R.S., 1967, Accounting concepts and behavioral hypotheses, *The Accounting Review* 42, 274–290.

Haddrill, S., 2010, Speech at the Yale Governance Forum, available at http://www.frc.org.uk/images/uploaded/documents/Yale%20Speech%20Stephen%20Haddrill.pdf.

Hasso, T. and K. Duncan, 2013, Valuation of Family Firms: The Limitations of Accounting Information, *Australian Accounting Review* 23, 135–150.

International Accounting Standards Board (IASB), 2009, *The International Financial Reporting Standard for Small and Medium-sized Entities (IFRS for SMEs)* (International Accounting Standards Board, London).

International Accounting Standards Board (IASB), 2010, *Conceptual Framework for Financial Reporting 2010* (International Accounting Standards Board, London).

James, H., 1999, Owner as manager, extended horizons and the family firm, *International Journal of the Economics of Business* 6, 41–55.

Jensen, M.C. and W.H. Meckling, 1976, Theory of the firm: Managerial behavior, agency costs and ownership structure, *Journal of Financial Economics* 3, 305–360.

Kam, V., 1986, *Accounting Theory* (John Wiley & Sons, Inc., New York).

Littleton, A.C., 1927, The antecedents of double-entry, *The Accounting Review* 2, 140–149.

Lorig, A.N., 1964, Some basic concepts of accounting and their implications, *The Accounting Review* 39, 563–573.

McConaughy, D.L., 1999, Is the cost of capital different for family firms?, *Family Business Review* 12, 353–360.

McKenny, A.F., G.T. Payne, M.A. Zachary, and J.C. Short 2014, Multilevel analysis in family business studies. In *The SAGE Handbook of Family Business*. Melin, L., Nordqvist, M. and Sharma, P. (eds) (Sage Publications, London).

Miller, D. and I. Le Breton-Miller, 2005, Managing for the long run: Lessons in competitive advantage from great family businesses, *Family Business Review* 18.

Mitchell, R.K., B.R. Agle and D.J. Wood, 1997, Toward a theory of stakeholder identification and salience: Defining the principle of who or what really counts, *Academy Management Review* 22, 853–886.

Montagnon, P., 2011, Council of Institutional Investors Spring Meeting in Washington DC, available at http://www.frc.org.uk/images/uploaded/documents/P%20Montagnon%20speech%20April%202011.pdf.

Moores, K. and G.T. Stedman, 1986, The comparative viewpoints of groups of accountants: More on the entity-proprietary debate, *Accounting, Organizations and Society* 11, 19–34.

Ohlson, J.A., S.H. Penman, Y. Biondi, R.J. Bloomfield, J.C. Glover, K. Jamal and E. Tsujiyama, 2011, Accounting for revenues: A framework for standard setting, *Accounting Horizons* 25, 577–592.

Prawitt, D.F., J.L. Smith and D.A. Wood, 2009, Internal audit quality and earnings management, *The Accounting Review* 84, 1255–1280.

Reay, T. and Z. Zhang, 2013, Qualitative methods in family business research. In *The SAGE Handbook of Family Business*. Melin, L., Nordqvist, M. and Sharma, P. (eds) (Sage Publications, London).

Ricchiute, D.N., 1979, Standard setting and the entity-proprietary debate, *Accounting, Organizations and Society* 4, 67–76.

Rosenfield, P., 1974, *Stewardship* (AICPA, New York).

Salvato, C. and K. Moores, 2010, Research on accounting in family firms: Past accomplishments and future challenges, *Family Business Review* 23, 193–215.

Shubik, M., 2011, A note on accounting and economic theory: Past, present, and future, *Accounting, Economics, and Law* 1, Article 1, available at: http://www.bepress.com/ael/vol1/iss1/1.

Sunder, S., 2011, Imagined worlds of accounting, *Accounting, Economics, and Law* 1, Article 8, available at: http://www.bepress.com/ael/vol1/iss1/8.

Watts, R.L. and J.L. Zimmerman, 1978, Towards a positive theory of the determination of accounting standards, *The Accounting Review* 53, 112–134.

Watts, R.L. and J.L. Zimmerman, 1979, The demand for and supply of accounting theories: The market for excuses, *The Accounting Review* 54, 273–305.

Watts, R.L. and J.L. Zimmerman, 1986, *Positive Accounting Theory* (Prentice-Hall, EnglewoodCliffs, NJ).

Yeoh, P., 2009, Causes of the global financial crisis: Learning from the competing insights, *International Journal of Disclosure and Governance* 7, 42–69.

Zambon, S. and L. Zan, 2000, Accounting relativism: The unstable relationship between income measurement and theories of the firm, *Accounting, Organizations and Society* 25, 799–822.

Zeff, S., 1978, The rise of economic consequences, *Journal of Accountancy*, 56–63.

Zeff, S., 2002, 'Political' lobbying on proposed standards: A challenge to the IASB, *Accounting Horizons* 16, 43–54.

Zellweger, T., 2007, Time horizon, costs of equity capital, and generic investment strategies of firms, *Family Business Review* 20, 1–15.

20

Internationalization of Family Firms

Zulima Fernández and María Jesús Nieto

INTRODUCTION

Internationalization is a critical strategy for many firms as it allows them to leverage the sustainable competitive advantages that are necessary to compete in a globalized world. Little is known, though, about internationalization in family firms (Astrachan, 2010), with most research seeming to indicate that this is a complex decision that requires much more detailed study. Doing business overseas is a complicated process that requires firms to enter new markets and decentralize decision making, moves which reduce the control of the owner family and increase uncertainty. At the same time, however, internationalization offers growth opportunities and sources of competitive advantages and should be an attractive option for these firms.

Information on how family firms formulate and put this strategy into practice is scarce, as the survey by Kontinen and Ojala (2010) indicates. This survey of relevant work shows that the study of internationalization in family firms is comparatively recent, with the first

articles being published in the 1990s (Gallo and Sveen, 1991; Gallo and García-Pont, 1996). Although interest in the topic has grown since then, relatively little work exists and many questions have yet to be researched. As scholars are currently performing more rigorous studies, however, we should see this topic develop greatly in the future. The rigor of the research and importance of the topic are indicated by the journals in which recent work has been published. In addition to appearing in journals specializing in family firms, we also see articles on the topic in leading journals on management (e.g., *Journal of Management, Journal of Management Studies, Entrepreneurship: Theory and Practice* and *Journal of Business Venturing*). Journals specializing on internationalization (e.g., *Journal of International Business Studies* and *International Business Review*) also show interest in the topic. This clearly reveals its importance for researchers, many of whom were not previously involved in the study of family firms.

Research has moved in parallel with the range of questions analyzed. Early studies focused on the decision to internationalize, typically measured via exports. As studies of internationalization have advanced, though, so have the topics of interest related to family firms. These topics now include most of the decisions linked with internationalization, such as scale and scope, entry modes, the pace of internationalization and international strategies. The development of this line of research will not only make it possible to discover more about the strategies of family firms, but will also help to close the knowledge gap that exists in internationalization business research. As Hitt et al. (2006) point out, the effect of different types of ownership and management on the internationalization of firms has been little analyzed and requires further research.

This chapter reviews the contributions and detects the shortcomings of the main studies in this field, as well as identifying some lines of future research. These studies were selected via the following methodology. First, we performed an extensive search of the relevant existing scholarly works published in peer-reviewed journals listed in ABI/INFORM on ProQuest and the ISI Web of Knowledge databases. It was not necessary to limit the search to any particular time periods because practically all the studies have been published in the last 20 years. We also performed an additional search of journal websites for articles that had not yet been included in databases. Second, after examining the abstracts we carried out an in-depth analysis of those articles that appeared most relevant.

The chapter is organized in the following manner. The next section briefly describes the most relevant international business theoretical frameworks and analyzes the objectives, attitudes and characteristics of family firms that may influence the decision to internationalize. This section also considers the governance of family firms and its relation with internationalization. The following section focuses on how these characteristics affect different aspects of the internationalization strategy and process. The chapter then goes on to reflect on the state of the question – highlighting shortcomings in the existing literature and suggesting potential issues, questions and lines for future research – before ending by presenting its conclusions.

FAMILY FIRMS AND INTERNATIONALIZATION

The field of international business (IB) is grounded in a wide range of theories. A first group comprises theories wholly constructed to understand the phenomenon of the internationalization of firms. A second group includes more general theories that are not specifically dedicated to the study of internationalization, but that have been used to analyze different aspects of it. Agency theory, institutional theory and network theory fall into this category.

The first group of theories wholly constructed for the study of internationalization can in turn be divided into two sub-groups. In the first sub-group we find internalization theory (Buckley and Casson, 1976) and the eclectic paradigm (Dunning, 1980), two theories that explain the existence of multinational enterprises (MNEs) and stress the role of the internalization of intangible assets in international growth. The second sub-group contains approaches that make it possible to explain the internationalization of SMEs; this group includes stage models such as the Uppsala model (Johanson and Vahlne, 1977), which sees internationalization as an incremental learning process, and the international entrepreneurship approach (Oviatt and McDougall, 1994), which explains phenomena such as born-global firms or early internationalization.

Since several approaches highlight the importance of firms' resource endowments in the internationalization process, any study of the decision to internationalize must include them. Analyzing what motivates decision makers may also be worthwhile, as their attitude to growth can influence firms' international activities (Zahra and George, 2002). Although both factors – resource endowments and motivations – can be influenced by type of ownership and management (as is the case in family firms), this line of research has received limited attention. Closing this significant gap in our knowledge is why the study of internationalization in family firms can be so interesting for IB literature.

The Decision to Internationalize

Internationalization is an attractive strategy that allows firms to exploit existing resources and sources of competitive advantage in new international markets; the strategy can also give firms access to different resources that may provide new competitive advantages (Hitt et al., 1997). Internationalization, however, also generates uncertainty because it involves competing in another regulatory and institutional environment, with different clients, competitors and suppliers. This foreign environment obliges firms to decentralize decision making and set up more complex management systems that permit them to coordinate the internationalization process. Although this strategy initially helps to diversify sources of income and thus reduce profit variability, previous research finds that it brings with it an increase in risk (Reeb et al., 1998).

Not surprisingly, then, the decision to internationalize is a difficult one for firms to take. This is especially true for family firms, whose strategies are influenced by family ownership and involvement. Altruism (Schulze et al., 2003), the alignment of interests between owners and managers (Zahra, 2003), patient capital (Sirmon and Hitt, 2003) and the subsequent long-term perspective typical of family firms (James, 1999) will all encourage managers to take strategic decisions like internationalization that strengthen the firm's competitive advantages and improve its chances of survival. In contrast, though, the desire of family firms to maintain control, allied with their conservatism (Sharma et al., 1997) and risk aversion (Naldi et al., 2007), discourages family firms from internationalizing and negatively affects their endowment of fundamental resources for internationalization, such as managerial capabilities and finance.

In fact, some empirical research finds that family firms internationalize less than non-family firms, a finding confirmed with samples of SMEs (Fernández and Nieto, 2005; Thomas and Graves, 2005) and publically traded firms (Gómez-Mejía et al., 2010). Not all authors, however, agree with the premise that family firms are risk averse. Zahra (2003) points out that according to agency theory the alignment of interests of family owners and managers should make family firms more open to risk taking, which in turn should make them more willing to internationalize if this will boost their competitiveness and performance. In accordance with this, the author finds a positive and significant relationship between international sales and family ownership and involvement. For their part, Casillas and Acedo (2005) show that family involvement is negatively related with the perception of risks arising from international expansion.

The assumption that family firms have a single risk attitude may be inadequate and be responsible for these conflicting views. Family owners are concerned not only with financial returns, but also with the socio-emotional wealth they have invested in their firms – in other words, the non-financial aspects of the firm that meet the family's affective needs, such as identity, the ability to exercise family influence, and the perpetuation of family heritage (Gómez-Mejía et al., 2007; see also Berrone et al., 2014, in this *Handbook*). Family firms, then, would have to face two types of risk. The first is business risk, related to the degree of profit variability, and the second is the risk of losing control of the firm (Jones et al., 2008). Family firms are loss averse when their socio-emotional wealth is threatened, because family control is reduced. In this case, family firms would prefer lower levels of internationalization that guarantee them control over the firm. If, however, the survival of the firm is threatened as a consequence of performance decline, family firms will be willing to assume greater risks, which will in turn increase the likelihood of internationalization (Gómez-Mejía et al., 2010).

Resource Endowments of Family Firms and Internationalization

The ability of the firm to grow internationally is dependent on its ability to exploit, acquire and configure its resources to develop globally relevant capabilities. Each family firm has a unique bundle of resources that is the result of the systems of interactions among the family, its individual members, and the business, a concept labeled 'familiness' (Habbershon and Williams, 1999). The long-term perspective typical of family firms favors the accumulation of a series of intangible resources, most notably reputation, general tacit knowledge, human capital, survival capital and social capital (Sirmon and Hitt, 2003; Gedajlovic and Carney, 2010). In contrast, problems of self-control caused by altruism, the family's desire to maintain control and its risk aversion hamper the accumulation of the resources necessary for internationalization. As we shall go on to see, until now research has concentrated on analyzing how the lack of managerial capabilities, financial resources, international knowledge and international alliances helps to explain the low levels of internationalization in family firms.

Human Resources and Managerial Capabilities

Doing business overseas increases the requirements of information processing, as well as the need to coordinate activities in countries with different institutional environments. And firms need qualified managers to deal with these requirements successfully (Sanders and Carpenter, 1998). In line with this, Graves and Thomas (2006) find that the managerial capabilities of family firms lag behind those of non-family firms as they grow internationally, and that this gap is most evident at high degrees of internationalization.

The characteristics of the founder may also have an impact on internationalization. Among entrepreneur-led family businesses, Davis and Harverston (2000) find that internationalization and growth are positively affected when the founder has a higher level of educational attainment. Conversely, aging negatively affects internationalization in family businesses. In general, CEOs of family firms have long tenures (Miller et al., 2008), which is negatively associated with entrepreneurial risk taking (Zahra, 2005). Similarly, Kellermanns et al. (2008) find that the tenure of family firms' CEOs is negatively related to growth. We should point out here that while lack of human resources may be one of the most notable problems of internationalizing family firms, not all family firms are subject to the same limitations. The professionalization or inclusion of new generations is a crucial factor that may mitigate this problem (see the section on new generations for more details).

Financial Resources

Lack of financial resources represents another difficulty for family firms looking to internationalize. Family firms use 'different financial logic', a logic that has to do with the personal preferences of the family decision makers (Gallo et al., 2004). The aversion of family to lose control suggests that family firms adhere to a pecking order when raising additional finance, favoring internally generated equity over debt and outside equity (Graves and Thomas, 2008). This 'different financial logic' may ultimately restrict international growth possibilities of family firms. For this reason, then, the internationalization of family firms may be encouraged by the entry of new investors, such as corporate blockholders, that are able to supply additional financial resources (Fernández and Nieto, 2006). Moreover, the availability of financial resources may also be a determining factor of the degree of international commitment that the firm is willing to assume. Since not all entry modes into international markets require the same level of resources, the choice of one or other may also be determined by the financial resources available (see the section on entry modes for further details).

Alliances

Strategic alliances and networking are highly effective strategies for international expansion.

Contacts with other partners supply international knowledge and access to resources that firms need to grow internationally. Some studies show that the willingness of firms to establish alliances has a significant impact on the level of business due to foreign investment (Gallo and García-Pont, 1996) and that international involvement is encouraged when family firms form alliances with other firms (Fernández and Nieto, 2005). Even the creation of weak ties helps family firms that do not belong to formal networks recognize international opportunities (Kontinen and Ojala, 2011). Despite the importance of alliances, the few studies of family firms show that their desire for independence and inherent conservatism typically prevents them from joining networks (Basly, 2007). Furthermore, when family firms do decide to enter alliances, they prefer to do so with other family firms and to establish social and personal family networks rather than formal economic networks (Basly, 2007; Graves and Thomas, 2008).

International Knowledge

In accordance with the Uppsala model, knowledge of international markets and of the internationalization process itself are critical resources for internationalization (Eriksson et al., 1997). This information makes it possible to detect opportunities in international markets and reduce the level of risk. Thus, Basly (2007) concludes that knowledge of internationalization positively influences the level of internationalization in family SMEs. Similarly, Crick et al. (2006), with a sample composed exclusively of successfully internationalized UK SMEs, stresses how all these firms performed market research before market entry, regardless of whether they were family firms or not.

As Basly (2007) identifies, the problem for family firms is that their conservatism and isolation from other firms negatively affect their knowledge of internationalization. This isolation, along with their shortages of managerial capabilities (Graves and Thomas, 2006), may explain why they also suffer from a lack of information. These are all factors that are likely to reduce their capacity to identify opportunities in international markets.

Governance of Family Firms

Different types of family firms exist, depending on the degree of family ownership and involvement and the current generation of the family. Each of these characteristics exerts an effect on the internationalization decision and process, effects that some studies have begun to explore (though as yet with inconclusive results).

Incorporation of New Generations

Each generation will impose different interests, management styles and objectives on the family firm (Okoroafo, 1999). Its entrepreneurial orientation, background and contacts – both within the family and with third parties – are likely to affect the firm's decisions on internationalization. The relation between entrepreneurship and generation is an important question on which consensus has not been reached (see McKelvie et al., 2014, in this *Handbook*). A first generation family firm is closely linked to its founder and thus is endowed with entrepreneurial verve, which brings with it reduced risk aversion. Thus, Claver et al. (2008) find that first generation family firms perceive less risk related to internationalization. In contrast, Gallo and García-Pont (1996) find that family firms tend to internationalize when the generations that follow the founder have joined the firm. Likewise, Fernández and Nieto (2005) find that the presence of second and succeeding generations moderates the negative relation between family ownership and the propensity and intensity of exports. Conversely, Okoroafo (1999) indicates that family firms that do not internationalize in the first two generations are unlikely to do so in later generations. In summary, the studies performed so far do not provide conclusive results and further research is required.

Family Ownership

Most studies adopt measures of internationalization that do not distinguish the family's ownership stake, its distribution, or the type of non-family shareholders with a stake in the capital. Despite this, there is no doubt that sharing capital with other shareholders may influence the objectives and strategies of a family firm, especially if the firm is publically listed. Once again, the evidence obtained so far is not conclusive. Thus, Zahra (2003) confirms that the percentage of family ownership is positively related to international sales and number of countries involved. Naldi and Nordqvist (2008) reveal that external ownership is not related to international scale and is positively related to international scope. Sciacia et al. (2010) find an inverted 'U' relationship between the proportion of shares owned by the family and internationalization. Fernández and Nieto (2006) show that the presence of corporate blockholders promotes the internationalization of family firms. Sirmon et al. (2008) argue along the same lines and refine the idea that family firms are risk averse. Family firms are risk averse above certain levels of family ownership, but these authors find that when other shareholders participate in the capital these firms are more willing to take risks via internationalization than are non-family firms. All these studies measure internationalization via international sales. For their part, Bhaumik et al. (2010) gauge internationalization via foreign direct investment (FDI) and find that family firms with foreign investors are associated with more outward FDI.

Family Management

Most of the available empirical work uses a definition of family firm that includes the presence of a family CEO. But different types of CEOs exist in family firms. The first question to consider is what happens when the CEO is also the chairman of the board of directors. Studies of non-family firms find CEO duality is negatively related to internationalization (Sanders and Carpenter, 1998). In contrast, studies of family firms reveal that CEO duality brings some advantages. Zahra (2003), for example, finds a positive relation between CEO duality and international sales and number of countries. As firms pass to successive generations,

CEOs may come from outside the family. This will result in an increase in the managerial capabilities of family firms and will also have consequences for their attitudes to risk. In line with this, Naldi and Nordqvist (2008) find that having a non-family CEO positively affects international scale but does not have an impact on scope.

The Board of Directors in Family Firms

The board of directors monitors management and provides resources for the firm. Different types of directors (e.g., internal and external or non-executive) may affect both the propensity to internationalize and the form it takes. The relation between the characteristics of the board of directors (e.g., size, age and experience) and internationalization has been studied in detail in non-family firms (Sanders and Carpenter, 1998). The research performed so far reveals that the presence of heterogeneous directors increases the knowledge and information, points of view, and social capital of firms, and therefore favors and accelerates the international expansion process. This type of analysis is even more necessary in family firms, given that many of the limitations they suffer from are caused by groupthink and a lack of information that amplifies the perceived risks of internationalization. Jones et al. (2008) demonstrate that affiliate directors – external directors that are linked to the family firm by a business relationship – stimulate diversification in publicly traded family firms by sharing their knowledge and experience with family executives. These authors do not consider geographical diversification, but their arguments could be extended to include it. Sundaramurthy and Dean (2008) offer a similar argument; they find that a reduced number of family members on the board and the frequency of board meetings are significantly related to the level of exports. And Calabro et al. (2009) find that family firms with higher levels of non-family directors and board involvement in advising tasks are more likely to be international. Table 20.1

Table 20.1 Internationalization decision and heterogeneity of family firms

Study (authors and year)	Theory	Principles discussed	Sample	Definition of family firm	Measure of internationalization	Key findings
Gallo and García-Pont (1996)	Family business literature	Strategic factors and family issues	57 Spanish firms	Firm self-identified as family firm	Export/total sales International sales/ total sales	Alliances encourage family firms to internationalize.
Davis and Harveston (2000)	Uppsala model	Entrepreneurial characteristics; information availability/access	1,078 US entrepreneur-led family firms	Respondents identify the business as a family business	Percentage of export sales (five-point scale)	Internationalization is positively related to founder's level of educational attainment and negatively with founder's age.
Zahra (2003)	Agency theory; stewardship theory	Risk taking; altruism	537 family and non-family firms in 5 US states	Family ownership and multiple generations in leadership positions	Exports Number of countries in which the firm sold its products	Family ownership and involvement are significantly and positively related with internationalization.
Casillas and Acedo (2005)	Uppsala model	Perception of risk; CEO characteristics	222 Spanish firms	Family involvement (four-point) based on: family share capital; member of the family in top management team; generation	Exports/total sales Interval scale measuring the level of involvement in foreign activities	Family involvement is negative related with the perception of the risks arising from the international expansion.
Fernández and Nieto (2005)	RBV; agency theory	Lack of managerial and financial resources	Panel of 10,579 observations of Spanish SMEs	Family ownership and management	Export propensity; export intensity	Internationalization is negatively related to family ownership and management. Internationalization of family firms is encouraged by the presence of new generations.
Thomas and Graves (2005)	Entrepreneurial framework	Risk aversion; conservatism	9,731 Australian SMEs; 6 case studies of SMEs	Family ownership superior to 50% and family management	Exports	Family firms are less likely to export than non-family firms.
Crick et al. (2006)	RBV	Resources; market knowledge	96 UK SMEs that successfully export	Family ownership	Exports	No difference between bundle of resources of internationally successful family and non-family firms.

(Continued)

Table 20.1 (Continued)

Study (authors and year)	Theory	Principles discussed	Sample	Definition of family firm	Measure of internationalization	Key findings
Fernández and Nieto (2006)	RBV; agency theory	Lack of managerial and financial resources	Panel of 8,497 observations of Spanish SMEs	Family ownership and management	Exports	Internationalization of family firms is positively related to corporate blockholder ownership.
Graves and Thomas (2006)	RBV	Managerial capabilities	891 Australian SMEs	Family ownership greater than 50% and a family member in management	Exports	Family firms' managerial capabilities lag behind those of non-family firms as they internationalize – especially at high levels of internationalization.
Basly (2007)	Uppsala model	International knowledge; alliances; independence orientation	118 French family firms	Family business groups, according to two criteria: family control of capital and involvement in management	Degree of internationalization (Likert scale)	International knowledge positively influences internationalization in family firms. Family firms do not typically belong to networks.
Claver et al. (2008)	Family business literature	Risk perception	92 Spanish family firms	Percentage of family ownership	International commitment (exports, joint ventures and wholly owned subsidiaries)	Risk perception decreases with the presence of the first generation.
Naldi and Nordqvist (2008)	Resource dependence; RBV	Non-family resources	331 Swedish SMEs	Family members own at least 50% of shares and CEO perceives the business as a family firm	Scale: percentage of international sales Scope: number of countries in which firms does business	External ownership in family business is positively related with international scope. Having a non-family CEO affects the scale, not the scope.
Sirmon et al. (2008)	RBV	Resource imitability; family influence as a moderator	2,531 French SMEs	Family influence: a family member is the CEO and the family owns at least 5% of the firm	Entropy measure	Family influences cause firms to internationalize significantly less than firms without family influences.
Sundaramurthy and Dean (2008)	Family business literature	Board characteristics	1,143 US family firms	Family ownership	Exports	Reduced numbers of family members on the board, frequency of board meetings and participation in education programs are related to internationalization.

Study (authors and year)	Theory	Principles discussed	Sample	Definition of family firm	Measure of internationalization	Key findings
Calabro et al. (2009)	RBV	Types of directors	146 Norwegian family SMEs	Family ownership greater than 50% and a family member on the board of directors	Exports	Non-family board members and board involvement in advisory tasks are positively related to export intensity.
Bhaumik et al. (2010)	RBV; institutional theory	Ownership structure. Foreign investors	777 Indian automotive and pharmaceutical family firms	Family is the single largest shareholder in the firm; Herfindahl index is used to capture the overall degree of ownership concentration	Proportion of firm's assets that are held overseas (FDI)	Family firms with foreign investors are associated with more outward FDI. Concentration of ownership in family hands has a detrimental effect on FDI.
Gómez-Mejía et al. (2010)	Behavioral agency model	Two kinds of risk-performance hazard and performance variability; Loss aversion. Socio-emotional wealth	360 US listed firms	Two or more family directors and family ownership equal or greater to 10%	Exports	Family firms: (i) internationalize less than non-family firms; (ii) prefer to internationalize in regions that are culturally close; (iii) are more willing to internationalize when business risk increases.
Sciacia et al. (2010)	Stewardship theory; stagnation theory	International entrepren-eurship; Family characteristics	1,035 US family firms	Percentage of family ownership	Exports	An inverted 'U' relationship exists between family ownership and international entrepreneurship.
Kontinen and Ojala (2011)	Network theory; entrepren-eurship framework	Network ties; opportunity recognition	Case study of Finnish family SMEs operating in France	The family controls the largest block of shares of votes; and has one or more members in key management positions	International opportunities	Family SMEs use weak ties formed at international exhibitions to identify international opportunities.

summarizes the main features of the works reviewed in this section.

INTERNATIONALIZATION PROCESS AND STRATEGY IN FAMILY FIRMS

Entry Modes

The most common modes of entry into foreign markets are exporting (direct and indirect), licensing, joint ventures and wholly owned subsidiaries (see Figure 20.1). Firms will choose the entry mode that offers them the highest risk-adjusted return on investment. Evidence indicates, however, that firms' options may also be determined by resource availability and the need for control (Agarwal and Ramaswami, 1992). Risks, meanwhile, will grow as the firm takes on more decision-making responsibility and commits more resources.

The scarcity of particular resources and the desire to maintain control so typical of family firms will undoubtedly influence the choice of entry mode. This choice raises new paradoxes for family firms as they will be put in a position where they will have to subordinate one of their priorities. In order to gain more control, they will have to commit more resources and that will increase the level of risk. Moreover, the desire to keep control and preserve the independence of the business is likely to make family firms reluctant to adopt entry modes based on collaboration. When considering the twin issues of control and risk, family firms will prefer to opt for entry modes that offer more control (even when this requires the commitment of more resources), as Abdellatif et al. (2010) point out. This paper reveals that family firms establish more wholly owned foreign subsidiaries and turn less to trading companies than do non-family firms. In summary, their findings support the idea that family firms exhibit a stronger inclination to maintain control than do non-family firms.

Entry mode decisions will also largely depend on the degree of family ownership and involvement in the firm. Several works study the choice of entry mode in samples composed solely of family firms with differing degrees of family involvement. Thus, Claver et al. (2009) reveal that the presence of non-family managers is positively related to international commitment. The authors argue

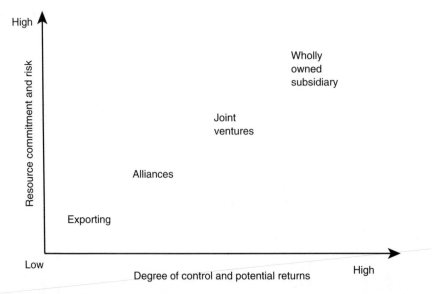

Figure 20.1   Entry modes

that the presence of external managers may mitigate the risk aversion of family members and provide experience and knowledge that is likely to help advance the internationalization process. Interestingly, Claver et al. (2009) also find a negative relation between self-financing and the likelihood of using entry modes that require high levels of resource commitment. Similar results are obtained by Bhaumik et al. (2010), who show that high degrees of family control and concentrated ownership have a detrimental impact on outward foreign direct investment expansion. Family firms, then, will choose entry modes that require less resource commitment when they wish to preserve their financial and managerial independence.

The incorporation of new generations may also influence the choice among entry modes, as shown by three studies that use samples composed solely of family firms. The specific entry modes examined are exporting (Okoroafo and Perryy, 2010), establishing joint ventures (Boyd et al., 2010) and strategic alliances (Claver et al., 2007). In all three cases the results indicate that new generations are more open to considering complex entry modes and are more receptive to new ideas and opportunities in international markets.

Pace of the Process

Another research stream in IB literature examines the dimension of time in international expansion. Specifically, this stream refers to the early start of internationalization activities, the speed of international growth and the pace of international activities over time (Zuchella et al., 2007). Studies in this research stream have largely used theoretical perspectives such as stage models and international entrepreneurship. The first models stress the importance of knowledge and suggest that firms increase their resource commitment gradually by selecting markets that are increasingly psychically distant as they learn more about the internationalization process and markets. For its part, the born global pathway breaks away from the traditional

path put forward by stage models. The internationalization of new venture perspective (Oviatt and McDougall, 1994) is a more recent approach that attempts to explain early internationalization processes or the phenomenon of born-globals (firms that adopt an aggressive international strategy almost from their inception) that are not well handled by the traditional sequential models. This approach stresses the importance of networks in the internationalization process (Madsen and Servais, 1997), in addition to the possession of intangible resources such as knowledge, an international orientation (Knight and Cavusgil, 2004), and entrepreneurial motivations and characteristics such as the need for achievement and a propensity for risk taking (Zahra et al., 2005).

In theory, the characteristics of family firms make them less favorable contexts for a born-global pathway. The same is not true, however, for firms set up by members of an entrepreneurial family, who may be able to take advantage of the knowledge and experience they have accumulated at home to internationalize more quickly (Zuchella et al., 2007). Similarly, succession may trigger a born-again global pathway. If the pace of internationalization for born-globals is rapid, for born-again globals it is rapid but delayed in time (Bell et al., 2001). Born-global firms, then, display a proactive orientation towards internationalization and internationalize from inception, while the internationalization of born-again globals is reactive to critical events such as takeovers and acquisitions (Bell et al., 2003). Succession in family firms can be such a critical event. Graves and Thomas (2008) put forward this idea in a case study research. The authors classify six family firm cases as having followed traditional pathways to internationalization and two as having followed born-again global pathways. The 'critical incident' in both these firms was succession to the next generation. Based on six case studies, Claver et al. (2007) show how the firms under study conform to the model of gradual internationalization put forward by the Uppsala School. This gradual process of internationalization in family firms is also confirmed by the case studied by Boyd et al. (2010).

International Strategies

The choice of strategies and structures in international markets is another highly important issue for internationalization that has not been much studied in family firms. As far as we are aware, Carr and Bateman (2009) is the only work that analyzes the international strategies used; the authors compare the international strategies of the world's 65 largest family firms with those of their non-family peers. Although the paper sets out to prove that family firms pursue less worldwide configurations than non-family firms, it is unable to find empirical evidence to support this expectation. It is not completely surprising that family firms should prefer more worldwide configurations as they may represent options that accord with the desire of multinational family firms to control and centralize important decisions in the value chain. The fact that this refers to the world's largest 65 family firms, however, may introduce a marked sample bias and may explain why these firms do not adopt more inward orientated strategies.

One of the most common methods of monitoring subsidiaries is by using expatriates, a topic that may be of special interest in family firms given their particular endowment of managerial capabilities. Despite this, only two studies address the issue. Abdellatif et al. (2010) compare the number of expatriates sent by family and non-family firms to a specific country, finding no significant differences between the two groups. And Tsang (2002), who finds that family members hold key expatriate positions in family firms, in contrast to expatriate managers in non-family firms who are systematically rotated. This study also finds that non-family firms adopt a more formalized and structured approach to monitoring activities than do family firms. This evidence suggests that in family firms the information and experience

required for international management are concentrated in the family, while in non-family firms the information is more evenly spread among managers. These findings indicate that transnational strategies would cause serious difficulties for family firms. After all, these strategies require the sharing of activities, knowledge and people among different bases – exactly what family firms appear most reluctant to do. Indeed, the desire of family firms for control is likely to lead them to send only family members as expatriates, another factor that may be a limitation as this will depend on the availability of personnel who are qualified for the task and willing to relocate. These expectations have not been tested empirically, however, thus making this a completely unexplored – and highly promising – line of research. Table 20.2 summarizes the features of the works on the international process and strategy in family firms reviewed in this section.

FUTURE RESEARCH

Research into the internationalization of family firms can advance on two fronts. First, scholars need to deepen knowledge of topics that have already received some attention. And second, researchers need to study a range of highly important areas that remains practically unexplored. In the following pages, we will put forward some ideas for future research in both these directions.

Issues for Further Development

This review has enabled us to identify shortcomings and research opportunities in the topics analyzed. Without doubt, more work is required comparing how family and non-family firms deal with the decision to internationalize. Simple comparisons between family and non-family firms are not sufficient as they do not take into account the heterogeneous nature of family firms. Family generation, percentage of family ownership, and family participation at board level and in

Table 20.2 Characteristics of internationalization process and international strategy of family firms

	Study	Theoretical underpinnings	Sample	Definition of family firm	Measure of internationalization	Key findings or conclusions
Entry mode	Claver et al. (2009)	Family business literature; agency theory; stewardship theory	92 Spanish family firms	Most of the ownership and management lies in family hands	Exports; contractual agreements; joint ventures; and wholly owned subsidiaries	The presence of non-family managers is positively related to entry modes involving high levels of international commitment, although self-financing limits this commitment.
	Abdellatif et al. (2010)	Family business literature; multinational literature	759 Japanese listed family and non-family firms	Family members hold management positions or are members of the board of directors	Subsidiaries worldwide	Family firms establish more wholly owned foreign subsidiaries than non-family firms.
	Boyd et al. (2010)	Descriptive study	Case study research of one Danish family firm	Ownership and management by founder's son	Exports; international joint ventures; FDI	This firm's four joint ventures were undertaken by the second generation. The first generation exported and founded wholly owned subsidiaries.
	Okoroafo and Perryy (2010)	Family business literature	187 family firms from Ohio (US)	Family firms identified themselves in the survey	Exports	Second generations use foreign sales representatives more than first generations and are more receptive to many of the typical stimulants of exporting.
Pace of the process	Claver et al. (2007)	Stage model theory (Uppsala model)	Case study research of 6 Spanish family firms	A single family runs and holds a majority of the firm's shareholding	Non-regular exports; experimental exports; exports via agents; joint ventures and wholly owned subsidiaries	The family firms analyzed gradually enter international markets.
	Graves and Thomas (2008)	Stage model theory; born-global framework	Case study research of 8 Australian family firms	Majority family owned and with at least one family member on the management team	First year of internationalization; international growth	Six family firms were classified as having undertaken traditional pathways to internationalization and two as having undertaken born-again global pathways.
International strategy	Tsang (2002)	Organizational knowledge and learning	Case study research of 10 Singaporean firms: 6 family firms and 4 non-family firms	Family owns the majority of stock and exercises full managerial control	FDI	Family members are in charge of key expatriate positions in family firms, compared to systematic rotation of expatriate managers in non-family firms. Family firms adopt a more informal and unstructured approach to the collection and analysis of information than non-family firms.
	Carr and Batema (2009)	Family business literature; Multinational literature	65 of the world's largest family and non-family firms	Family has to own over 50% of the business in a private firm or more than 10% of a public company	International orientation (identified by 9 configurations)	Family firms do not pursue less international configurations than non-family firms.

management may all influence the resource endowments of these firms and their relation to risk. This in turn will have an impact on the scale, scope and process of internationalization, as well as on international strategy. Additionally, the international competitive advantages of family firms cannot be discussed without reference to firms' specific resources and capabilities. More studies are needed that accurately identify the differential resources of family firms and analyze the roles they play in internationalization. While family firms typically lack some resources, they also appear to be well endowed in others.

The review of studies on entry modes reveals that much further research is required. Work also exists that shows how different degrees of family involvement in ownership and management, along with generational factors, influence the choice of entry mode. The evidence remains scarce, though, and more theoretical and empirical studies comparing the choice of entry modes between family and non-family firms are needed. These future studies should consider family firms with differing ownership structures and degrees of family involvement in order to adequately explore the relation of family involvement, investment and control with the resource commitment that the firm is willing to assume.

It should also be noted that exports and direct foreign investments have traditionally been the most analyzed entry modes, while strategic alliances have been neglected. The question remains whether this is because exporting and foreign direct investment are the most common entry modes – or because it is easier to obtain systematic data on international sales and investment, while information on alliances can be much harder to come by. Future studies with richer information on different types of strategic alliances should analyze the determinants of the establishment and success of alliances in the internationalization processes of family firms. Some of the aspects to analyze include the willingness of family firms to form alliances, along with the factors that may favor their formation; the types of agreements; and the comparative

results of each entry mode chosen by family firms. The type of partner may also be a determining factor in deciding to form the alliance and in the results achieved. In line with this, Swinth and Vinton (1993) argue that the likelihood of success of an international joint venture is greater when both parties are family firms. The choice of partner and its consequences for the internationalization of family firms, then, are questions that merit further attention when analyzing the role of strategic alliances in this process.

More work is also needed on the determinants of international pathways undertaken by family firms. Specifically, studies are needed that analyze under what conditions family firms are more likely to internationalize rapidly and in what context succession boosts internationalization. Accordingly, it could be interesting to analyze the phenomenon of born-again global to see how it relates with generational succession. Further theoretical work and more advanced empirical studies on this subject would improve our understanding in the international entrepreneurship literature, which is a relatively young research area in the IB field.

Future research could also look to offer methodological advances that enrich the body of empirical studies. The review of existing work reveals the need for quantitative studies that use wide and representative samples of family firms in different national and sectoral contexts; studies of this kind would also make it possible to offer more generalizable results. Likewise, the measures used to capture the internationalization of family firms need to be improved and extended. The inclusion of measures of direct investment, different types of alliances and the scope of international activity would enrich the empirical analyses greatly.

Quantitative methods offer clear advantages, but other methods may also be required to understand the complexity of the multicultural, multidimensional and dynamic nature of international business topics. Qualitative research methods can play an important role too (see Reay and Zhang,

2014, in this *Handbook*) by providing a deeper understanding of the micro-processes and interplay between culture and context in international activities (Birkinshaw et al., 2011). Qualitative research can enable us to capture the complexity and idiosyncratic nature of the processes of internationalization in family firms. As Birkinshaw et al. (2011) note, however, it is crucial to make sure that the subject matter of a qualitative investigation is truly novel and that the research topics under consideration involve 'cutting-edge research that breaks new ground', as well as being helpful for understanding newly emerging patterns or phenomena in the international business domain.

In addition, regional context may be important in the internationalization of firms (Hitt et al., 2006). For this reason researchers might also analyze their samples for regional and national specificities and perform comparative studies with samples from different locations (as international behavior can vary across countries). Fortunately, the study of family firms covers many countries and institutional contexts, which should make it relatively easy to fill this knowledge gap once the context specificities are identified.

Lastly, it is important to remember that many studies of internationalization do not consider ownership type. Specifically, family ownership and control may exert a moderating effect on the relations studied. The work by Sirmon et al. (2008) provides support for this idea by finding that family influence positively moderates the relation between the imitability of a firm's resources and internationalization. Future studies of internationalization, therefore, could advance our knowledge by including variables for family ownership and management – variables that are not commonly considered – as potential moderators of the relations under study.

Research Gaps

While the previous topics have already received some attention, another whole range of highly important areas remains practically unexplored. The intersection of family business and IB literature has allowed us to identify several important research gaps. One research avenue that merits attention is the relation between the internationalization of family firms and performance. No works exist on this topic, despite the fact that the relation between internationalization and firm performance has received much attention in IB research (Hitt et al., 2006). Future research should analyze the results of internationalization in family firms via different firm outcomes. Internationalization aims to improve performance, but many firms internationalize for other reasons that will indirectly improve their results. Indeed, international expansion makes it possible to enhance resources and thus obtain new competitive advantages. IB research has adopted various measures of performance such as financial results, survival, reputation, innovation and efficiency (Hult et al., 2008). In all likelihood the specific non-financial objectives of family firms (e.g., preserving their socio-emotional wealth) need to be included in studies.

Researchers have devoted significant attention to the exploitation of commercial opportunities in international markets, but we should also remember that other activities in the value chain have assumed an increasingly global perspective over the last 20 years or so. Firms ever more frequently look abroad to gain access to productive inputs or perform value chain activities, constantly searching for new sources of competitive advantages. Many questions can be posed about global sourcing in family firms, because this is a topic that has not been researched in these firms. Some of the motivations for global sourcing can be found in the characteristics of the industry, the economic environment or the product that the firm produces. But some antecedents of these decisions can also be attributed to the characteristics of the firm itself, such as aspects related to management and to the position of the firm in different networks (Quintens et al., 2006). Interesting issues to analyze in family firms include – among other things – the drivers, barriers and facilitators that lie behind the decision to opt for global purchasing. Another crucial point to examine is the decision between sourcing from foreign subsidiaries or from independent suppliers (in this latter case, the selection of suppliers is also of interest). Likewise, the consequences and results that flow from these decisions merit analysis.

International strategies and organizational configurations of multinational family firms is another practically unexplored topic. These studies should consider the extent of local customization or standardization of products, as this may be a determinant of the autonomy of subsidiaries. The desire to centralize control and experience in the hands of family members may make family firms reluctant to opt for strategies that require systematic transfers of knowledge and decentralized decision making by local managers. Future studies need to examine family firms' choice of international strategies depending on their degree of centralization and the coordination tools required to manage interdependence among subsidiaries. Similarly, it would be interesting to analyze the processes of creation and transfer of knowledge from the parent firm and among the subsidiaries, processes that are crucial in the international growth of multinationals. Once again, family firms may be idiosyncratic in their management of knowledge and human resources in subsidiaries. Thus, the management of expatriates is another fundamental area of study, as it brings together two key questions in family firms: their capacity to control the activities of subsidiaries and their ability to find sufficient expatriates.

Lastly, the role of institutional context has not been taken into account in studies of internationalization in family firms. Numerous studies demonstrate the influence of the institutional contexts of home and host country on the international strategy (Henisz and Swaminathan, 2008). Now more research is needed to clarify how regulative, normative or cognitive parameters affect the international strategic choices of family firms: country

selection; entry modes; and international strategies; among others. In accordance with this, institutional perspective may represent a useful theoretical framework. As we have stated, family firms differ from non-family firms in their resource endowments and their desire for control, and we need to connect these characteristics with the institutional parameters. The analysis of entry modes will be greatly improved by including institutional elements. Both legal restrictions and normative and cognitive elements will affect the entry decision, in some cases making it necessary to enter via local partners. The desire of family firms to maintain control may make these options less attractive and thus influence some internationalization decisions.

The importance of institutional context becomes evident in the study of multinational family firms, a fertile area for research (Khanna and Yafeh, 2007). A specialized stream of literature has recently emerged on multinationals from developing countries in general (Gammelhoft et al., 2010), and from Latin America (the multilatinas; Cuervo-Cazurra, 2008) in particular. As many of these are highly established family groups, it is of great interest to analyze how their family nature has affected and continues to affect their international development, along with the role of institutional context in both their birth and internationalization. Some institutional environments are likely to be more favorable than others for the development of international family groups. Given that many family groups arise in emerging countries with limited institutional development, it would be interesting to discover if they look to expand internationally in similar environments, in contexts where they are able to apply their knowledge and experience.

CONCLUSION

The decision to internationalize is an important one for any firm, including of course family firms. Although internationalization may be coherent with family firms' concerns for long-term continuity, it remains a risky and complex decision that runs counter to their traditional desires to maintain control and avoid risk. Knowing more about the internationalization of family firms will have important implications for academics and managers.

The internationalization of family firms has acquired great importance in the last 20 years, proof of which is supplied by the type of journals publishing the research. Initially appearing in journals specialized on family firms, generalist management journals – and even journals specializing on internationalization – are now showing ever-increasing interest in the field. Moreover, not only has the number of papers increased, but their methodological rigor has also improved considerably. More and more rigorous studies are being published. Although some of these studies have been performed with large databases, most continue to work with very small samples or a few case studies.

This chapter allows us to conclude that the internationalization of family firms represents a significant and promising research area for both family business and international business scholars. Advances in this line of research will provide a better knowledge of the behavior of family firms as well as contribute to understanding questions about internationalization where ownership type matters. This research will also fill a knowledge gap in IB research. From a theoretical perspective, progress needs to be made in combining the literature on internationalization and family firms. This will help us understand more thoroughly the relation between family firms and the different decisions linked to internationalization. In many of the works reviewed the theoretical frameworks are poorly developed and make few references to IB literature. From an empirical point of view, more quantitative and qualitative studies are required to enrich the existing body of empirical work on the subject and to answer many other questions where the evidence does not exist or is anecdotal. In summary, research on internationalization in family firms still has a long way to go.

REFERENCES

Abdellatif, M., Amann, B. and Jaussaud, J. (2010). Family versus nonfamily business: A comparison of international strategies. *Journal of Family Business Strategy*, 1, 108–116.

Agarwal, S. and Ramaswami, S.N. (1992). Choice of foreign market entry mode: Impact of ownership, location and internationalization factors. *Journal of International Business Studies*, 23(1), 1–27.

Astrachan, J.H. (2010). Strategy in family business: Toward a multidimensional research agenda. *Journal of Family Business Strategy*, 1, 6–14.

Basly, S. (2007). The internationalization of family SME: An organizational learning and knowledge development perspective. *Baltic Journal of Management*, 2(2), 154–180.

Bell, J., McNaughton, R. and Young, S. (2001). 'Born-again global' firms: An extension to the 'born global' phenomenon. *Journal of International Management*, 7, 173–189.

Bell, J., McNaughton, R., Young, S., and Crick, D. (2003). Towards an integrative model of small firm internationalisation. *Journal of International Entrepreneurship*, 1(4), 339–362.

Berrone, P., Cruz, C. and Gómez-Mejía, L.R. (2014). Family-controlled firms and stakeholder management: A socioemotional wealth preservation perspective, in L. Melin, M. Nordqvist, and P. Sharma (eds), *The SAGE Handbook of Family Business*. London: Sage.

Bhaumik, S.K., Driffield, N. and Pal, S. (2010). Does ownership structure of emerging-market firms affect their outward FDI? The case of the Indian automotive and pharmaceutical sectors. *Journal of International Business Studies*, 41, 437–450.

Birkinshaw, J., Brannen, M.Y. and Tung, R.L. (2011). From a distance and generalizable to up close and grounded: Reclaiming a place for qualitative methods in international business research. *Journal of International Business Studies*, 42, 573–581.

Boyd, B., Goto, T. and Hollensen, S. (2010). Internationalisation of family businesses – evidences from joint venture formations at Danfoss. *International Journal Management Practice*, 4(3), 253–272.

Buckley, J. and Casson, M. (1976). *The Future of the Multinational Enterprise*. London: Macmillan.

Calabro, A., Mussolino, D. and Huse, M. (2009). The role of board of directors in the internationalisation process of small and medium sized family businesses. *International Journal of Globalisation and Small Business*, 3(4), 393–411.

Carr, C. and Bateman, S. (2009). International strategy configurations of the world's top family firms: Another factor affecting performance. *Management International Review*, 49(6), 733–758.

Casillas, J.C. and Acedo, F.J. (2005). Internationalisation of Spanish family SMEs: An analysis of family involvement. *International Journal of Globalisation and Small Business*, 1(2), 134–151.

Claver, E., Rienda, L. and Quer, D. (2007). The internationalisation process in family firms: Choice of market entry strategies. *Journal of General Management*, 33(1), 1–14.

Claver, E., Rienda, L. and Quer, D. (2008). Family firms' risk perception: Empirical evidence on the internationalization process. *Journal of Small Business and Enterprise Development*, 15(3), 457–471.

Claver, E., Rienda, L. and Quer, D. (2009). Family firms' international commitment: The influence of family-related factors. *Family Business Review*, 22(2), 125–135.

Crick, D., Bradshaw, R. and Chaudry, S. (2006). Successful internationalising UK family and non-family-owned firms: A comparative study. *Journal of Small Business and Enterprise Development*, 13(4), 498–512.

Cuervo-Cazurra, A. (2008). The internationalization of developing country MNEs: The case of Multilatinas. *Journal of International Management*, 14 (2), 138–154.

Davis, P. and Harveston, P. (2000). Internationalization and organizational growth: the impact of Internet usage and technology involvement among entrepreneur-led family businesses. *Family Business Review*, 13(2), pp. 107–120.

Dunning, J.H. (1980). Towards an eclectic theory of international production: some empirical tests. *Journal of International Business Studies*, 11(1), 9–31.

Eriksson, K., Johanson, J., Majkgard, A. and Sharma, D. (1997). Experiential knowledge and cost in the internationalization process. *Journal of International Business Studies*, 28(2), 337–360.

Fernández, Z. and Nieto, M.J. (2005). International strategy of small and medium-sized family businesses: Some influential factors. *Family Business Review*, 18(1), 77–89.

Fernández, Z. and Nieto, M.J. (2006). The impact of ownership on the international involvement of SMEs. *Journal of International Business Studies*, 37(3), pp. 340–351.

Gallo, M.A. and García-Pont, C. (1996). Important factors in family business internationalization. *Family Business Review*, 9(1), 45–59.

Gallo, M.A. and Sveen, J. (1991). Internationalizing the family business: Facilitating and restraining factors. *Family Business Review*, 4, 181–190.

Gallo, M.A., Tàpies, J. and Cappuyns, K. (2004). Comparison of family and nonfamily business: Financial logic and personal preferences. *Family Business Review*, 17(4), 303–318.

Gammelhoft, P., Barnard, H. and Madhok, A. (2010). Emerging markets, emerging theory: Macro- and micro-level perspectives. *Journal of International Management*, 16(2), 95–194.

Gedajlovic, E. and Carney, M. (2010). Markets, hierarchies, and families: Toward a transaction cost theory of the family firm. *Entrepreneurship: Theory and Practice*, 34(6), 1145–1172.

Gómez-Mejía, L.R., Makri, M. and Larraza-Kintana, M. (2010). Diversification decisions in family-controlled firms. *Journal of Management Studies*, 47, 223–252.

Gómez-Mejía, L., Takács, K., Núñez-Nickel, M., Jacobson, K. and Moyano-Fuentes, J. (2007). Socioemotional wealth and business risks in family-controlled firms: Evidence from Spanish olive oil mills. *Administrative Science Quarterly*, 52, 106–137.

Graves, C. and Thomas, J. (2006). Internationalization of Australian family businesses: A managerial capabilities perspective. *Family Business Review*, 19(3), 207–224.

Graves, C. and Thomas, J. (2008). Determinants of the internationalization pathways of family firms: An examination of family influence. *Family Business Review*, 21(2), 151–167.

Habbershon, T.G. and Williams, M.L. (1999). A resource-based framework for assessing the strategic advantages of family firms. *Family Business Review*, 12, 1–25.

Henisz, W. and Swaminathan, A. (2008). Institutions and international business. *Journal of International Business Studies*, 39, 537–539.

Hitt, M.A., Hoskisson, R.E. and Kim, H. (1997). International diversification: Effects on innovation and firm performance in product-diversified firms. *Academy of Management Journal*, 40(4), 767–798.

Hitt, M.A., Tihany, L., Miller, T. and Connelly, B. (2006). International diversification: Antecedents, outcomes and moderators. *Journal of Management*, 32(6), 831–867.

Hult, G.T.M., Ketchen, Jr., D.J., Griffith, D.A., Chabowski, B.R., Hamman, M.K., Dykes, B.J., Pollitte, W.A. and Cavusgil, S.T. (2008). An assessment of the measurement of performance in international business research. *Journal of International Business Studies*, 39, 1064–1080.

James, H.S. (1999). What can the family contribute to business? Examining contractual relationship. *Family Business Review*, 12, 61–71.

Johanson, J. and Vahlne, J.E. (1977). The internationalization process of the firm. *Journal of International Business Studies*, 8(2), 12–32.

Jones, C.D., Makri, M. and Gómez-Mejía, L.R. (2008). Affiliate directors and perceived risk bearing in publicly traded, family-controlled firms: The case of diversification. *Entrepreneurship: Theory and Practice*, 32(6), 1007–1026.

Kellermanns, F.W., Eddleston, K.A., Barnett, T. and Pearson, A. (2008). An exploratory study of family member characteristics and involvement: Effects on entrepreneurial behavior in the family firm. *Family Business Review*, 21(1), 1–14.

Khanna, T. and Yafeh, Y. (2007). Business groups in emerging markets: Paragons or parasites? *Journal of Economic Literature*, 45, 331–372.

Knight, G.A. and Cavusgil, S.T. (2004). Innovation, organizational capabilities, and the born-global firm. *Journal of International Business Studies*, 35, 124–141.

Kontinen, T. and Ojala, A. (2010). The internationalization of family businesses: A review of extant research. *Journal of Family Business Strategy*, 1(2), 97–107.

Kontinen, T. and Ojala, A. (2011). Network ties in the international opportunity recognition of family SMEs. *International Business Review*, 20, 440–453.

McKelvie, A., McKenny, A., Lumpkin, G.T. and Short, J.C. (2014). Corporate entrepreneurship in family business: Past contribution and future opportunities, in L. Melin, M. Nordqvist and P. Sharma (eds), *The SAGE Handbook of Family Business*. London: Sage.

Madsen, T.K. and Servais, P. (1997). The internationalization of born global: An evolutionary process? *International Business Review*, 6(6), 561–583.

Miller, D., Le Breton-Miller, I. and Scholnick, B. (2008). Stewardship vs. stagnation: An empirical comparison of small family and non-family businesses. *Journal of Management Studies*, 45(1), 50–78.

Naldi, L., Nordqvist, M. Sjöberg, K. and Wiklund, J. (2007). Entrepreneurial orientation, risk taking, and performance in family firms. *Family Business Review*, 20(1), 33–47.

Naldi, L. and Nordqvist, M. (2008). Family firms venturing into international markets: A resource dependence perspectives. *Frontiers of Entrepreneurship Research*, 28(14), 1–18.

Okoroafo, S.C. (1999). Internationalization of family businesses: Evidence from Northwest Ohio, USA. *Family Business Review*, 12, 147–158.

Okoroafo, S.C. and Perryy, M. (2010). Generational perspectives of the export behavior of family businesses. *International Journal of Economics and Finance*, 2(3), 15–24.

Oviatt, B.M. and McDougall, P.P. (1994). Toward a theory of international new ventures. *Journal of International Business Studies*, 25(1), pp. 45–64.

Quintens, L., Pauwels, P. and Matthyssens, P. (2006). Global purchasing: State of the art and research directions. *Journal of Purchasing and Supply Management*, 12, 170–181.

Reay, T. and Zhang, Z. (2014). Qualitative methods in family business research, in L. Melin, M. Nordqvist and P. Sharma (eds), *The SAGE Handbook of Family Business*. London: Sage.

Reeb, D., Kwok, C. and Baek, Y. (1998). Systematic risk in the multinational corporation. *Journal of International Business Studies*, 29(2), 263–279.

Sanders, G. and Carpenter, M.A. (1998). Internationalization and firm governance: The roles of CEO compensation, top team composition, and board structure. *Academy of Management Journal*, 41(2), 158–178.

Schulze, W.S., Lubatkin, M.H. and Dino, R.N. (2003). Toward a theory of agency and altruism in family firms. *Journal of Business Venturing*, 18, 473–490.

Sciacia, S., Mazzola, P., Astrachan, J.H. and Pieper, T.M. (2010). The role of family ownership in international entrepreneurship: exploring nonlinear effects. *Small Business Economics*, 1–17.

Sharma, P., Chrisman, J.J. and Chua, J.H. (1997). Strategic management of the family business: past research and future challenges. *Family Business Review*, 10, 1–35.

Sirmon, D.G. and Hitt, M.A. (2003). Managing resources: Linking unique resources, management, and wealth creation in family firms. *Entrepreneurship: Theory and Practice*, 27(4), 339–358.

Sirmon, D.G., Arregle, J.L., Hitt, M.A. and Webb, J.W. (2008). The role of family influence in firms' strategic responses to threat of imitation. *Entrepreneurship: Theory and Practice*, 32(6), 979–998.

Sundaramurthy, C. and Dean, M.A. (2008). Family businesses' openness to external influence and international sales: An empirical examination. *Multinational Business Review*, 16(2), 89–106.

Swinth, R. and Vinton, K. (1993). Do family-owned businesses have a strategic advantage in international joint ventures? *Family Business Review*, 6(1), 19–30.

Thomas, J. and Graves, C. (2005). Internationalization of the family firm: The contribution of an entrepreneurial orientation. *Journal of Business and Entrepreneurship*, 17(2), 91–113.

Tsang, E.W.K. (2002). Learning from overseas venturing experience: The case of Chinese family businesses. *Journal of Business Venturing*, 17(1), 21.

Zahra, S.A. (2003). International expansion of U.S. manufacturing family businesses: The effect of ownership and involvement. *Journal of Business Venturing*, 18(4), 495–512.

Zahra, S.A. (2005). Entrepreneurial risk taking in family firms. *Family Business Review*, 18(1), 23–40.

Zahra, S.A. and George, G. (2002). International entrepreneurship: The current status of the field and future research agenda, in M.A., Hitt, R.D., Ireland, S.M. Camp, and D.L. Sexton, (eds), *Strategic Entrepreneurship: Creating a New Mindset*. Oxford: Blackwell Business.

Zahra, S.A., Korri, J.S. and Yu, J. (2005). Cognition and international entrepreneurship: Implications for research on international opportunity recognition and exploitation. *International Business Review*, 14, 129–146.

Zucchella, A. Palamara, G. and Denicolai, S. (2007). The drivers of the early internationalization of the firm. *Journal of World Business*, 42(3), 268–280.

21

Marketing from a Family Business Perspective

Anna Blombäck and Justin Craig

INTRODUCTION

Regardless of the organizational or industry context, marketing essentially centers on the process of delivering customer satisfaction at a profit without damaging current or future generations' ability to maintain social, economic, and environmental sustainability. As a distinct discipline in business and academia, marketing was established only in the first half of the twentieth century. Legitimate positioning as a key subject area was secured with the requisite paradigmatic breadth and depth of understanding and application (Jones and Monieson, 1990; Jones and Shaw, 2002). Following the advent of family business as a distinct research destination, recent developments in the area of marketing have specifically considered the context of family-owned businesses. Although work is still undergoing to identify, understand, and exploit the potential advantages of this vast and vital organizational genre, research focused at the intersection of marketing and family business is limited (Reuber and Fischer, 2011). In this

chapter, therefore, our goal is to add to the discourse aimed to better understand how marketing can leverage the family business character. We review the essence and particularities of family businesses, also taking into account established and emerging marketing discipline doctrine.

Scholars in the family business field regularly emphasize the uniqueness of family businesses in terms of their distinct 'familiness' (Irava and Moores, 2010). Though often labeled as a 'fuzzy' concept, consensus exists that familiness denotes a set of idiosyncratic resources and capabilities that have the potential, when leveraged, to result in competitive advantage, such as more efficient production, greater employee care, higher wages, stronger employee motivation (Habbershon and Williams, 1999), higher levels of organizational trust (Steier, 2001), and financial performance (Miller and Le Breton-Miller, 2005). This so-called familiness factor, it is also argued, can be restrictive and identified as F− rather than F+ (Habbershon et al., 2003). Tagiuro and Davis (1996) similarly outline and analyze what they refer to as 'bivalent attributes,' indicating how distinguishing and inherent family business characteristics can be both an advantage and a disadvantage. Refining these broad approaches, recent contributions to the understanding of family business particularities include the identification and analysis of various forms of capital (Sirmon and Hitt, 2003), including the definition of a special family capital (Hoffman et al., 2006). In addition to the resource-centered notion of familiness, the essence of family business can be captured by identifying key characteristics and behaviors that define the family business, such as a focus on shared visions and a long-term orientation (Chua et al., 1999). Much attention has been paid to the recognition and preservation of socio-emotional wealth, indicating how the pursuit of non-economic goals is fundamental to understanding the essence of family business; such pursuit may shed light on family business behavior related to management process, strategic choice, governance, stakeholder relationships, and business venturing (Gomez-Mejia et al., 2011). In general, researchers suggest that family businesses are companies that encompass both particular resources (e.g., familiness, capital) and raison d'être (e.g., approach, behavior).

The notion of distinguishing characteristics between family businesses and non-family businesses should have an effect on a major and multi-faceted function like marketing. Because a family dimension, including specific individuals' aspirations and capabilities, is present in the business setting, both strategic and operational decisions can be strongly influenced by social considerations (Chrisman et al., 2005). In addition, considering that family businesses are recognized as distinct in the marketplace (Carrigan and Buckley, 2008), particular questions arise whether companies can use the family business classification to position and distinguish their brand in the market. Among family businesses, communicating that they are a family business – for example, by including

the family name in the business's name, presenting generations or family history, and so forth – is quite common. Perhaps the most notable example is the global fifth-generation family business S.C. Johnson, with its accompanying tagline 'A Family Company' on all product advertising.

In this chapter, we provide an overview of the relevant marketing literature, including a review of recent developments in social media, which we couch from a distinctive family business perspective with two fundamental objectives. Our first objective is to capture succinctly the *essence of contemporary marketing*, and our second objective is to identify how the essence of family business *can be exploited with respect to marketing practices and protocols*. The purpose of this dual objective approach is to both clarify the opportunities for further conceptual and empirical research and identify practical and actionable lessons for the family business practitioner and adviser communities.

With regard to our following elaborations, this discussion defines family businesses as companies in which members of the same family represent a dominant coalition that is able, through ownership and presence, to influence the company's strategy and management and that aims to keep the business within the family in the future (Chua et al., 1999).

THE ESSENCE OF MARKETING

Marketing represents a set of processes – including the identification, facilitation, and communication of customer value; value exchange and maintenance of beneficial relationships with customers; and the practice of these processes – to benefit a wide range of stakeholders in society (American Marketing Association, 2007; Grönroos, 2006). From a business perspective, the marketing function centers on the development, promotion, and sale of goods and services for a profit. To offer guidance for marketers, McCarthy (1964) defined the 'marketing mix' as a means to organize and operationalize the complexity of marketing into management practice. This mix comprises four areas: product, price, place, and promotion, commonly referred to as the 4Ps. Essentially, the 4Ps function to schematize decisions in marketing from the perspective of an overall marketing strategy, including aspects such as defining target markets and determining key value propositions. In business practice and education, the 4Ps remain dominant (e.g., Kotler and Armstrong, 2010). The current circumstances of markets, however, necessitate a much broader focus, and the processes involved need to be approached in progressive ways. Parallel to the development of a multi-faceted approach to marketing, the 4Ps approach to explain and direct marketing has been criticized for being production rather than customer oriented (Constantinides, 2006) and for misleadingly offering a rigid set of decision-making areas (Grönroos, 2006).

Stakeholder Interaction and Value Co-Creation

Originally developed with a focus on manufactured goods and private consumers as the customer, marketing theory evolved during the 1970s into separate research streams, with different foci capturing the particularities of industrial or business-to-business marketing (LaPlaca and Katrichis, 2009; Mattsson, 1997) and the marketing of services (Brown et al., 1994). As a consequence, scholars also questioned the dominant marketing logic, which had been principally characterized by (1) a transactional focus, (2) manufacturing contexts, (3) mass-marketing, and (4) a view on consumers as passive receivers (Grönroos, 1994a; Gummesson, 1987). In line with the path of any emerging discipline (Dubin, 1969; Kuhn, 1996), new ideas about how to approach the topic of marketing gained traction and instigated a fundamental change in the way marketing was researched and, to some extent, taught.

An important change, by some referred to as a marketing paradigm shift, was the introduction of a relationship marketing approach

(Grönroos, 1994a, 1994b; Gummesson, 2008; Sheth and Parvatiyar, 1995). The new focus resulted from the realization that maintenance of customer relationships can save costs and create competitive advantage over time. In marketing practice, relationship marketing implies a change from a tactical and short-term focus to a strategic and long-term focus. Closely related to this notion is the network approach, which describes how the performance of each firm relates to its position in a larger network of shared resources, activities, and actors (Håkansson and Snehota, 1989; Mattsson, 1997).

This development, emphasizing relationships and networks to understand and better manage the marketing process, made the view of value-added relationships salient in marketing literature. The underlying rationale was that the focal company could only realize long-term value when value was also realized for customers and other constituent stakeholders (Grönroos, 1997; Normann and Ramirez, 1993). The contemporary *essence* of marketing, therefore, boils down to value exchange. In this exchange, there is a reciprocal need for companies to understand and manage that which, beyond the actual product offer, constitutes value for customers. Consequently, in stark contrast with the original focus on exchange, customer orientation and interaction have gained a strong foothold in marketing research discourses (Grönroos, 2006; Woodruff, 1997).

Strongly related to this, contemporary marketing thought was further fueled by a shift in logic from the so-called goods-dominant logic of marketing to the service-dominant logic (Vargo and Lusch, 2004, 2008). The service-dominant logic describes service as the 'common denominator for exchange' (Payne et al., 2008: 83) and the general activity of 'doing something for and with another party' (Vargo and Lusch, 2010: 222). It emphasizes that the basis for value creation, for all marketers, lies in the company's service base (knowledge and skills) rather than the goods or services ultimately marketed and provided (Vargo and Lusch, 2010). Significant for the service-dominant logic is also the view that customers are active participants in the exchange process, increasingly enabled by technology development, which empowers consumers with regard to information, dialogue, and reach (Prahalad and Ramaswamy, 2004a). Lusch et al. (2007) conclude that the move toward the service-dominant logic implies an internalization of the customer in marketing, promoting marketing as a collaborative process (i.e., marketing *with* rather than marketing *to*). In summary, the service-dominant logic connects strongly with the ideas in relationship marketing and network theory, further clarifying that firm performance hinges on interaction and the co-creation of value (Normann and Ramirez, 1993, Payne et al., 2008; Prahalad and Ramaswamy, 2004a, 2004b). As such, the essence of the contemporary marketing discourse firmly situates marketing as a strategic function.

Brand Management

The contemporary commercial landscape is typified by an excess supply and overwhelming amount of information. It requires firms not only to develop product offerings attuned to ever-changing customer needs and wants but also to communicate and interact with the market in ways that distinguish their offering from similar others and persuade customers to buy. Relatedly, since the 1980s, the focus has increasingly been on intangible assets to explain corporate value (Aaker, 1991; Madden et al., 2006). Within the marketing context, this is mirrored in the vast literature and research on brand management (Balmer, 2010; Keller et al., 2008) and corporate reputation (Fombrun, 1996; Fombrun and Shanley, 1990; Gotsi and Wilson, 2001). This development is partly driven by increasing market competition and a need to be noticed and remembered, but it also includes a focus on customers' perceptions and the co-creation of value, which drives the service-dominant logic (Hatch and Schultz, 2010; Merz et al., 2009). This focus has become increasingly

challenging in a global market made smaller by technology advances, which have also significantly accelerated market changes and product developments. With rapid changes in product offerings on the market, the realization of brand knowledge and loyalty among customers is increasingly valuable.

Furthermore, contemporary markets include discerning and conscious consumers, who make purchasing decisions that are informed in real time by blogs and web-based social network conversations. These decisions are increasingly related, but not limited, to the sustainable and ethical business practices of market players. Thus, as a result, some scholars have suggested that though the essence of marketing will remain constant, the ability of marketing to account for a socially responsible approach to business will be scrutinized more closely (Maignan et al., 2005), and the service-dominant logic will require more attention than ever before (Ballantyne and Varey, 2008).

The Social Media Revolution

Recent technology developments and ideological changes in the function of the Internet have spurred the move toward Web 2.0 and, subsequently, what could be referred to as the social media revolution. In an attempt to explain social media, Kaplan and Haenlein (2010) categorize social media into collaborative projects, blogs, content communities, social networking sites, virtual game worlds, and virtual social worlds. Internet-based applications for social interaction and user-generated content (e.g., Wikipedia, YouTube, Twitter, Facebook, LinkedIn, Second Life) are now common practice for a considerable, and growing, population (Kaplan and Haenlein, 2010). Research indicates that contemporary consumer behavior related to marketing communications has indeed changed as an outcome of social media development. Summarizing the important aspects of this development, Mangold and Faulds (2009) suggest that consumers' demand for control and quick access has increased, that they ignore the traditional sources of advertising for information and purchase decisions in favor of different types of social media, and that they perceive social media as more trustworthy than company-managed information in traditional advertising. Provided that younger generations are accustomed to social media as part of their communication patterns, any marketing strategy will also need to consider these media to reach and capture the attention of new customers.

From a marketers' perspective, we suggest that social media represents a dual outcome. Not only does it provide companies with the means to interact with, entice, and engage customers, but it also simplifies peer communication among consumers (Mangold and Faulds, 2009). Understanding this duality also means further recognizing social networking sites as a mechanism for people to interact and build relationships with one another. A key feature of such media, compared with most traditional forms of marketing communications, is that they enable and promote a continuous dialogue among parties. As such, social media represents an opportunity for companies not only to manage their brand equity and public relations in general but also to reach their target markets with promotional messages and product introductions (Mangold and Faulds, 2009). For example, company-sponsored platforms work to connect like-minded consumers in communities that enhance consumer brand experiences and increase loyalty. In addition, this direct link between consumer and company is a source of value add. For consumers, the feeling of being involved can further support brand commitment; for companies, both the value of immediate access to market information and the opportunity to respond promptly to any consumer requests or misunderstanding enable them to maintain a competitive market presence and beneficial relationships.

An important part of the social media discourse is the concept of 'word-of-mouth marketing' (WOMM). WOMM is 'the intentional influencing of consumer-to-consumer communication by professional marketing techniques' (Kozinets et al., 2010: 71). It comprises a range of related concepts, such as viral, buzz, and guerilla marketing (Ahuja et al., 2007; Ferguson, 2008; Helm, 2000; Palka et al., 2009). Although the power of WOM, in terms of influencing consumer purchase decisions, has long been known, the development of Internet-based social media has fundamentally altered marketers' ability to influence and control it (Kozinets et al., 2010). Because this dialogue among a wide range of actors results in narratives related to a firm and its offerings co-produced by consumers (Kozinets et al., 2010), companies that employ WOM methods (e.g., sampling to bloggers) have only partial control of their messages (Mangold and Faulds, 2009). Moreover, Kozinets et al. (2010) show that depending on the WOM forum's character and norms, company-led campaigns can create frustration and critique. The integrity and motive of bloggers who showcase a particular item provided to them for free by a company have been frequently questioned by blog readers. Consequently, not only might the blogger's brand be affected by such events, but the brand of the item might be as well. However, companies often monitor their WOMM campaigns, which give them the chance to observe and influence the development of narratives, something that previously took place in closed or anonymous consumer forums or offline.

Does the significant influence of social media demand that the essence of marketing be reconsidered? Given the newness of social media, contemporary marketers have yet to master them as an efficient component in their marketing management. The importance of social media is growing rapidly though, as indicated by widespread use in business practice and the focus in research on how these media can be employed effectively. For a state-of-the-art marketing management process, companies need to take the inherent opportunities of and challenges associated with various social media into account.

Conclusion

The paradigmatic changes in marketing, which are primarily defined by the service-dominant logic, are echoed in the access to and practice of social media. Likewise, the modern brand management discourse, which today is central to any marketing function, centers on the maintenance of relationships and dialogue with stakeholders. All in all, we conclude that the essence of marketing at this point refers to continuous attention to, dialogue with, and inclusion of various stakeholders with the aim to understand and reach value exchanges. In view of this, we turn to consider how this contemporary essence of marketing corresponds with the idiosyncratic essence of family businesses.

MARKETING IN AND OF THE FAMILY BUSINESS

Fundamentally, family businesses are distinct because of the overlap of the family system and the ownership and management systems. Scholars focusing on firm-level analyses have recognized that the integration of systems results in unique firm features, resources, and capabilities, which in turn influence the business's operations and performance. The notion of familiness is regularly used to indicate this relationship and its outcome, which can be positive and negative (Chrisman et al., 2003; Habbershon and Williams, 1999).

Features such as having extensive social capital (Arregle et al., 2007), being long-term oriented (Chua et al., 1999), and being guided by stewardship, as opposed to principal-agency relationships (Miller and Le Breton-Miller, 2005), are commonly identified as constituting the family business character. In the following sections we reconsider these family business particularities in view of the above elaborated marketing essence. We outline three perspectives, which combine main points of the marketing and family essences, namely: *Family Business Reputation and Branding*, *Capital and Market Orientation*, and *Stewardship and Longevity*.

Family Business Reputation and Branding

A general assumption related to the family essence in family business is that it denotes something positive; for example, being a family connotes affirmative and close ties and a friendly atmosphere. Thus, from a marketing perspective, an important question is how this seemingly common image of family can be used effectively to market family businesses. More specifically, does the notion that they are indeed family businesses and can communicate as such influence their intangible assets; like corporate reputation, trust, brands, customer relationships, employee commitment, and other human resources? To address this quandary, Sundaramurthy and Kreiner (2008) employ a boundary discussion to suggest that family businesses can choose either an integrated or a segmented identity pattern. They identify image as one dimension, which reflects whether the business shows a family connection in its marketing communications. Furthermore, scholars have taken an interest in the perceptions and expectations of the family business as an organizational category (e.g., Krappe et al., 2011) and, as such, the potential value of communicating that a particular company is indeed a family business (e.g., Blombäck and Botero, 2013; Craig et al., 2008; Dyer, 2006; Zellweger et al., 2010).

Overall, topics related to positioning have gained increasing attention, and scholars have approached it with varying foci. For example, research has focused on communication of the family business status (Blombäck and Ramirez-Pasillas, 2012; Botero, 2010; Memili et al., 2010; Micelotta and Raynard, 2011), perceptions of family businesses among consumers (Carrigan and Buckley, 2008; Okoroafo and Koh, 2009) and potential employees (Covin, 1994), and the positive correlation between communicating family business and financial performance (Craig et al., 2008). A common denominator for research in this area has been relating family businesses to corporate marketing literature, including corporate identity, corporate reputation, corporate communications, and corporate brand management. Craig et al. (2008) specifically coin the expression 'family-based brand identity.' Further indication of the salience of the evolving brand- and marketing-related discussion in family business research comes from the first special issue on marketing in *Family Business Review*. Significantly, two of the four articles published in this issue connect family (business) with branding (see Micelotta and Raynard, 2011; Parmentier, 2011). This increase of researcher interest in family business as it relates to brand management is an important development toward establishing marketing-related thought in the field but also points to an important opportunity for family businesses in meeting the current demand for strong brands in the market. Research based on brand management theory allows for the exploration of marketing matters within the family business and with stakeholders external to the firm.

A salient part of this research stream constitutes studies that explore consumers' expectations regarding family businesses. In their study of Irish convenience stores, Carrigan and Buckley (2008) conclude that the respondents had positive and high expectations of family businesses. Their results also highlight consumers' tendency to equate smallness with family businesses. In grocery retailing, Orth and Green (2009) report that compared with non-family businesses, consumers believe that family businesses are more effective in service, staff kindness, and problem-solving orientation. However, their findings also indicate that consumers believe that family businesses in general perform worse in in-store assortment and price/value. In addition, Okoroafo and Koh (2009) find that consumers' purchasing intentions are positively related to the recognition of family business and therefore suggest that companies should communicate their status as a family business.

Closely connected with studies on consumer perceptions is whether a family business dimension has a function in branding. Litz and Rajaguru (2011) investigate whether consumers perceive family involvement in the business as an important element for positive hardware store transaction experiences; they find that consumers think highly of the family dimension. However, they also find that the notion of family for success is positively related to the size of the business (e.g., small equals familiar, friendly, and locally responsible). These findings suggest important questions regarding whether family businesses can indeed leverage the family dimension in marketing communications. They also imply that the family business is primarily a complement to the core offer, not the key itself to consumer choice. In addition, Blombäck (2011) suggests that the family business dimension in branding should be considered a secondary element, that is, one that is complementary but also capable of enhancing the focal offer or brand.

One assumption in research is that consumers tend to value the connection with a prominent family, especially in certain types of industries. Dyer (2006) maintains that family-based brand identity should be especially important in the sales of services and reputation- (or brand-) sensitive products. The financial markets represent a case in point; here, Donnelly (1988) finds that trust is important and that family ties can create a competitive advantage for both customers and business networks. Although the service offer of a family is intangible, this component might help customers connect with the brand. Similarly, for brand-sensitive products, the ability to differentiate and add customer perceived value to the marketed offer is important. The inclusion of a family component in branding to represent trustworthiness and commitment over time indeed becomes an example of an idiosyncratic opportunity for family businesses (Donnelly, 1988). Related to the use of family references in marketing communications is also the question whether the family concept is static and whether the connotations can be controlled. Byrom and Lehman (2009) show that companies can influence the perceptions of 'family' among other stakeholders (i.e., staff and consumers) so that they, too, can perceive themselves as part of the family. Blombäck and Botero (2013) also argue that the existence of a family business reputation represents a source of value. A generic family business reputation, however, is largely beyond a single company's control; this implies that businesses should further consider how and toward whom they should employ the family business reference.

A distinct area of research related to positioning and branding considers the family business the focal player (as opposed to consumers). Micelotta and Raynard (2011) investigate branding strategies of old family businesses and find variations in terms of both how much companies exhibit the family angle and the meanings they associate with family involvement. The first strategy, which emphasizes family traditions and the importance of family to ensure continuity, pertains primarily to small and locally oriented firms (e.g., the hospitality sector). The second strategy, which emphasizes the importance of the family to ensure quality, pertains primarily to firms that refer to craftsmanship and innovation to differentiate themselves (e.g., luxury goods). Micelotta and Raynard also identify a third strategy, which does not focus on the family, but rather emphasizes growth and innovation. This strategy primarily pertains to firms with high geographical spread and dispersed ownership.

In her study on 'the Beckhams,' Parmentier (2011) examines the actual development of a family into a business brand. The study reveals the importance of familiarizing the market with the family (visibility), providing 'family persona cues,' and presenting a convincing family biography (distinctiveness). In view of this research, consider the heterogeneity among family businesses. While one firm archetype might emphasize a family-oriented branding, another firm might not. Thus, in excavating research in this area,

scholars should pay careful attention to the difference between a business having a family business identity (essentially operating the business as a family business) and a business relying on the family business reputation for brand management. Anecdotal evidence suggests that all firms do not aspire to be known as family businesses even if the family dimension is important for how the company is managed. Parmentier's research further recognizes that family businesses are made up of individuals who themselves might also be identifiable brands. Thus, branding research in family businesses should also consider what should be or is branded. Is it the family, the family business, or both? Although an inherent overlap exists between the family and business identities, the implications of focusing on one or the other in reputation and brand management – for family members and the company, respectively – should also be explored.

All in all, research on the relationship among family business, reputation, and brand management helps position marketing in the family business research area. Relevant findings already at hand suggest that family businesses can have idiosyncratic values, but additional questions to study are also necessary. Researchers should try to answer when, how, and toward whom a family business dimension should be employed in marketing communications. Further research should also explore the various strategies and brand management practices identified in family businesses to learn (1) which strategies can be more successful and (2) whether companies that do not overtly present a family dimension can still leverage this identity in related areas (e.g., internal and external branding).

Family Business Capital and Market Orientation

A way to position the essence of a family business is to use various sources of capital (e.g., social, human, financial). Social capital represents resources that exist in individuals' and organizations' relationships and networks

(Burt, 1997) and renders a variety of approaches (i.e., structural, relational, and cognitive) to understand family business uniqueness (Pearson et al., 2008). The structural dimension of social capital explains patterns of social and professional networks, which are built around family members and the family business, as well as the implication of these networks for generating resource access for the business. The relational dimension refers to aspects such as norms, obligations, and identity that clarify how expectations on certain behaviors foster a pattern of trust between family members and related stakeholders (Arregle et al., 2007; Coleman, 1988; Pearson et al., 2008). Last, the cognitive dimension explains how family members' sharing of representations, interpretations, and systems of meaning can lead to a common focus to continue the company. When specifically limited to the relationships existing among family members, social capital is also referred to the 'family capital' or 'family social capital' (Hoffman et al., 2006). In addition to social capital, Sirmon and Hitt (2003) introduce *human capital* (Lane and Lubatkin, 1998), *patient financial capital*, and s*urvivability capital* (Haynes et al., 1999) to understand the particularities of family businesses.

Broadly speaking, all four types of capital can be tied to family business opportunities in the marketing area. Primarily, though, for the contemporary customer-oriented view on marketing strong, trustful, and loyal relationships are important and, thus, the notion of family social capital should be specifically considered. Previous research also has investigated how family businesses deal with customer relationships (Cooper et al., 2005; Lyman, 1991). A recurring assumption is that family businesses are particularly conscious about providing excellent customer service and expert at maintaining strong customer relationships (Hoover and Hoover, 1999; Ward, 1997) – again, factors that require shared norms and behavior to fully succeed. Biberman (2001) presents a case of a small family-run bookstore that managed to compete with a neighboring industry giant, concluding that the outcome was due to the family business's ability to present superior customer service and subsequently gain consumer loyalty.

In general, researchers have essentially focused on theorizing or studying consumer services. Scarce attention has been paid to other dimensions of the relationship and network area, such as the value of family social capital for managing industrial networks, supply chains, and a range of stakeholder relationships in the value chain. The shift towards a service dominant logic suggests that excellent ties in these areas will be increasingly important and, thus, implies an important competitive opportunity in the strength of social capital among family businesses. Opportunities for further research exist.

Market Orientation

Market orientation is the underlying concept for a company-wide approach to understand and deliver customer value while also monitoring the competition to maintain competitive advantage (Tokarczyk et al., 2007). In view of the competitive nature of most markets and consequent focus to understand and internalize customers in the delivery of value, the importance of market orientation is evident, also in the area of family business. To become market oriented, family businesses should ensure shared values throughout the company and foster relational and cognitive social capital, an area in which they have an advantage. Research on market orientation in family businesses is not consistent though and more research is warranted to clarify if and how the family business essence generates or necessitates a certain approach to foster market orientation. While Tokarczyk et al. (2007) find a positive relationship among familiness and market orientation, and firm performance, in their recent analysis of publicly traded firms on the S&P 500, Zachary et al. (2011) reveal that family-controlled companies exhibit less market orientation than non-family firms. Furthermore, Cooper et al. (2005) find evidence indicating that family businesses employ particular customer relationship management initiatives to a lesser extent than non-family businesses, while Beck et al. (2011) find that generation has an impact on market orientation and innovation in small family businesses. Firms controlled by the founding generation show greater market orientation than firms controlled by subsequent generations. In light of this, researchers involved in the Successful Transgenerational Entrepreneurship Practices (STEP) global research initiative, in which the researcher/family relationship has been developed and is strong, could consider investigating how successful family businesses have transitioned or are transitioning their marketing focus during generational transfer.

Product Development and Service Flows

Regarding the centrality of product development in marketing and for maintaining competitive strength on markets with fast-changing product life-cycles and technology, the patient capital ascribed to family business is especially noteworthy. Access to capital without immediate demands of return can favor product development and innovation – that is, the ability to adapt continually to current demands and opportunities in the market. Product innovation can be continuous, dynamically continuous, or discontinuous, depending on the extent to which companies are either reactive or proactive in responding to consumer demands and behavior (Robertson, 1967). Depending on which innovation approach a company employs, different marketing approaches are needed for success. The long-term focus and patient capital primarily ascribed to family businesses indicate that opportunities exist for a dynamically continuous product innovation strategy; this type of strategy is proactive and ultimately can lead to first-mover advantages in the market (Lumpkin et al., 2010). Finally, in view of companies' current focus on co-creation, social capital can potentially strengthen family businesses' abilities to maintain dialogue with relevant actors to develop products (or service flows) that provide beneficial value exchanges.

Family Business Stewardship and Longevity

Founding families and their successor generations plan more for the long term than atomistic shareholders (Le Breton-Miller and Miller, 2006; Stein, 1988, 1989). This long-term steward-like orientation most likely influences the business's marketing practices and/or provides additional opportunities. Specifically, a long-term focus has the potential to contribute to a substantive business culture and to maintain long-standing relationships with other business actors both up and down the value chain, including suppliers, wholesalers, retailers, and employees. Family firms also tend to develop more long-term relationships with customers, as Miller and Le Breton-Miller (2005) demonstrate in their study on long-lived family business. In parallel, a long-term orientation towards customers is likely to generate an understanding for the customers' needs and value creation, currently described as the cornerstone of marketing.

Stewardship theory, which explains how owners' and managers' shared visions and objectives can influence organizational control and motivation mechanisms, is commonplace in family business research (Miller and Le Breton Miller, 2005; Zahra et al., 2008). Managers' recognition of non-financial and collective rewards, as well as a long-term orientation, is central to the theory, as is owners' focus on empowerment rather than strict (financial) monitoring (Davis et al., 1997). In short, 'stewards' are loyal to their business organization and strive to make it succeed. Stewardship is particularly salient in family businesses, in which family members are both owners and managers and business aims are guided by both financial and family considerations (Corbetta and Salvato, 2004; Craig, Dibrell, Neubaum, and Thomas, 2011; Thompson, 1960). From a marketing perspective, the existence of a 'stewardship culture' (Zahra et al., 2008) can determine how decisions are made in terms of stakeholder relationships, market offers, and communications. The assumed focus on non-financial and long-term objectives increases the likelihood that decisions are made to reduce risk in both business reputation and survivability by focusing on short-term financial outcomes. The visibility of the family, especially in companies that make use of the family name in marketing, further supports the desire to preserve a good corporate reputation. Arguably, such visibility fosters not only a responsible business behavior overall but also, from a marketing perspective, the offering of quality products and honest messages (Donnelly, 1988, Dyer and Whetten, 2006). Miller et al. (2008) find the existence of such stewardship in smaller family businesses, which focus on longevity through the intentional development of market share and reputation, employee retention, and customer relationships. The recurrent long-term orientation among family businesses also suggests an opportunity to foster an image of reliability and trustworthiness among relevant stakeholders, which could be valuable for the family business's competitive position in terms of pricing, delivery options and contracting, and new product introduction.

In summary, relevant aims for further research include exploring how stewardship cultures and long-term orientations influence the approach to market offer developments and, relatedly, investments in infrastructures for co-creation. In addition, further research should examine the effects of such cultures and orientations on existing and potential exchange partners and consumers.

Balancing Tradition and Progress

An inherent part of longevity is tradition, which is recurrent in family businesses' marketing communications (Micelotta and Raynard, 2011). Byrom and Lehman (2009) show how references to family in combination with the business's traditions and heritage can work to create competitive advantage. Primarily, this indicates a marketing strategy that employs longevity to convey trustworthiness and a competitive edge. Strong heritage and traditions can also become drawbacks however, for example, by hampering necessary product development and market orientation processes (Donnelly, 1988). Currently, the new generations of family businesses are challenged with combining traditional ways of doing business with the influence of new technology and contemporary markets (e.g., the social media revolution). Because family businesses are often viewed as conservative and slow to adapt to environmental changes, the notion of not projecting a tradition image without being old-fashioned is worth attention.

In a study of high-growth firms in the United States, Teal et al. (2003) find that firms that have a majority-owner family and a family member as CEO typically allocate more of their marketing budget to mass-marketing campaigns. This finding is positive and clarifies the importance of marketing in these firms. A more critical interpretation is that family businesses are conservative in their marketing strategies and do not adopt to paradigmatic changes as well as other companies, which would imply more spending on alternative communication measures. Thus, we suggest that studies on family businesses should combine the inherent potential of leveraging longevity and sincerity with modernity and flexibility.

Family businesses that rely on traditional ways and thus are more rigid than other firms might confront challenges in meeting consumer demands and gaining market presence unless they comply with relevant ways to communicate to their target audiences. An illustration is that of Leanne de Bortoli, manager and third-generation family member at De Bortoli Winery & Restaurant Yarra Valley in Australia, who has embraced social media. The company's webpage (http://www.debortoli.com.au/) provides access to the company's Facebook, twitter, and blog pages, which Leanne actively monitors in real time. She personally responds to both positive and negative comments and, by doing so, is able to control the discourse with users (i.e., current and future customers). That is, by engaging with customers, she can immediately address misconceptions about products. In addition, the company has used technology to pilot 'virtual wine tastings' with wine critics around the world to introduce new products to the market, which has proved both efficient and cost effective.

As this example illustrates, family businesses can benefit from the family dimension in social media, provided that consumers perceive the family's interaction and conversations with its members as authentic and natural. Conversely, if the family dimension implies features such as genuine honesty, strong values, ethical, and responsible, the use of WOMM should be carefully considered. This is because the active promotion of spokespeople and other forms of concealed buzz run the risk of being perceived as attempts to deceive. Possibly, if consumers actually do imagine family businesses as having a higher integrity, the brand damage to a corporation with widespread ownership could be less severe in such circumstances.

In general, implementing different types of social media is easy and cheap. However, leveraging these media to their fullest potential (e.g., proactively observing consumer interactions and fostering relationships, which implies continuous presence and monitoring) can be expensive. Active engagement in the social media sphere exerts pressure on continuously delivering what has been promised. Many family businesses are small to medium-sized enterprises, and thus such an initial lucrative opportunity runs the risk of failure when the actual costs are realized because of the extra strain on an already potentially tight resource base and marketing budget. Companies today have no choice but to take part in the social media revolution, but they can decide how and to what extent they need to or should get involved themselves. Further research on consumers' associations with social media and the implications of firms having versus not having an active

social media approach is necessary to guide practice and advance theory in the area.

SYNTHESIS AND FURTHER RESEARCH

Considering that research has yet to comprehensively explore the intersection of family business and marketing, a potential risk is that researchers will begin by reproducing previous mainstream research to gain momentum and findings relevant to the broader academic community. To be relevant, however, research must account for and monitor the current waves of change related to marketing management. Researchers in marketing need to consider whether previous discussions are redundant in light of the changing powers of consumers and nature of communications. Guided by our initial outline of contemporary marketing essence, we have elaborated on how the essence and particularities of family businesses can generate particular benefits in marketing management. Thus, we have attempted to identify the familiness of marketing – that is, how the inclusion of family in business can lead to competitive advantage and performance related specifically to marketing. As a way to synthesize our discussion and suggestions for further research, we combined the familiar 4Ps framework with the rising discourse of the service-dominant logic (see Table 21.1). Although the 4Ps are important for the goods-dominant and transaction-oriented approach to marketing, we suggest that this approach provides merely a basis for discussion, which can be reinterpreted to indicate the presence and essence of relationships (Zineldin and Philipson, 2007). In a similar vein, Lusch, Vargo and O'Brien (2007) suggest that the service-dominant logic, originating from a focus on interaction and collaboration with customers and partners, facilitates a more comprehensive and strategic approach to the 4Ps, translating these into service flows, value propositions, networks, and conversation. This combination allows for a discussion about marketing in the family business context that

Table 21.1 Synthesizing the essence of marketing and family business: research avenues

Contemporary marketing essence
Stakeholder interaction and value co-creation; brand management; the social media revolution

Marketing mix	Service-dominant logic	Family business dimension for potential marketing leverage	Application/research questions
Product →	Service flows	Patient capital, social capital, stewardship, longevity	Does family social capital have a positive or hampering influence on family business market orientation?
			Does longevity have a positive or hampering influence on market orientation?
			Does patient capital influence the market orientation of family businesses?
			Is stewardship culture important for the development of market offers and for planning exchange processes?
Place →	Value networks and processes	Social capital, stewardship, reputation	What is the influence of stewardship and family social capital on family business approaches to value co-creation? Does family social capital infer advantages for family businesses in network creation?
			Can family businesses leverage their reputation in value exchanges and processes?
Promotion →	Conversation and dialog	Reputation, social capital, longevity	What is the value of using the family business as an element in brand management and marketing communications?
			How do family businesses relate to the social media revolution, and are there particular challenges and benefits related to these channels for family businesses? How can/should the family and business heritages be combined to generate value?
			Does longevity present family businesses with an advantage in new product launch.
Price →	Value proposition	Stewardship, longevity, reputation	Does a stewardship culture influence family businesses to refrain from opportunistic pricing?
			Does longevity influence family businesses opportunity to price their market offer?
			Can family businesses leverage a general family business reputation to charge more for their market offer?

incorporates particularities related to both tactical and internal management processes and long-term and externally oriented relationship processes.

Importantly, the extent to which marketing can leverage family business characteristics needs to be considered in view of these businesses' heterogeneity. Such differences pertain to but are not limited to firm size, industry, generation involvement, commitment, and ownership concentration. As an illustration, research in the tourism industry typically focuses on familiness as an indication of hospitality (e.g., Presas et al., 2011). Getz and Carlsen (2005: 237) observe that direct interactions with the family 'are often vital to customer experience and satisfaction.' Such leverage of family capital (social

Table 21.2   Family business archetypes and marketing priorities

Family business archetype	Strategies[1]	Family business driving priorities (4Cs)	Marketing priorities (4Ps)
Brand builder	'Brand builder strategies aim at building a differentiated brand and brand reputation that customers are willing to pay extra for.'	Continuity and community	Promotion and place
Craftsmen	'Craftsman strategies focus on making the best-quality products on the market, those that deliver extra functionality or exceed on important dimensions the offerings of the competition.'	Continuity and community	Product and promotion
Superior operator	'Superior operations strategies provide the most economical offerings through hyper-efficient operations.'	Continuity and connection	Place and price
Innovator	'Innovation strategies create state-of-the-art products that are beyond what rivals can offer.'	Community and command	Product and promotion
Deal maker	'The deal making strategy grows the business through entrepreneurial business getting and related diversification efforts.'	Connection and command	Place and promotion

[1]Miller and Le Breton-Miller (2006: 384)

and human) is not possible for all industries, and thus research is necessary to clarify which dimensions of the family business essence can best be leveraged and in which industries. Likewise, although continuous market changes have blurred the lines between business-to-business and business-to-consumer marketing practice (Wind, 2006), this difference is still relevant. The significance for marketing of the identified particularities of family likely varies depending on the type of customer examined.

To further capture the heterogeneity of family businesses, we suggest that research build on Miller and Le Breton-Miller's (2005, 2006) five archetypes, based on long-lived family businesses. Each archetype (brand builder, craftsmen, deal makers, innovators, and superior operators) represents a strategy aimed at a different source of competitive advantage and is sketched according to configurations of four priorities (continuity, community, connection, and command [the 4Cs]), which can be particularly salient in family businesses. For each archetype, two priorities are considered more prominent than the other two. In a similar

vein, perhaps research should examine a configuration approach for the 4Ps in marketing to help address family business heterogeneity in terms of whether (where) familiness is present in marketing.

Specifically, the 'Millerian' 4Cs signify aspects that are reinforced by the presence of a dominant-owner family over generations. As we noted previously, such presence also has repercussions on the opportunities for marketing management. In Table 21.2, we present a configuration that we hope will be the catalyst for further discussion and investigation. Basically, the configuration implies that family businesses, depending on their market strategy, will focus on different facets of marketing. By analysing firms in the light of these market strategies and how, in pursuing these, they leverage the family business essence it should be further possible to reveal the influence of the family business essence on competitive positioning and marketing success. Studies drawing on these configurations could thereby explore how the idiosyncratic benefits of family business can be leveraged, through variations in marketing practice, and possibly reveal whether equi-final conditions lie behind some family businesses' competitive advantages.

CONCLUSION

Thus far, the family business research agenda has not included an extensive application of marketing theory. By itself, filling a research gap is not a good enough argument for further research. In this chapter, we provide a discussion to support why research should further consider the integration of family business and marketing. Our review and discussion suggest that being a family business offers advantages in terms of marketing *in* and *of* family businesses. More specifically, we explore how the family business essence, or its idiosyncratic resources, approaches, and behavior, can be leveraged in the marketing process.

Our basic question centers on interpreting the vast marketing literature through the family business lens. In doing so, we find that the essence of marketing as it currently stands with the development of a service-dominant logic is consistent with the basic assumptions and particularities of family businesses. Primarily, we note that family social capital and long-term orientation, with its subsequent influence on stakeholder relationships, are both prominent features of family business characteristics that increasingly are posited as the keys to successful marketing. Thus, we conclude that family businesses have several distinct opportunities in terms of marketing management as it moves toward a service-dominant logic.

We also recognize idiosyncratic opportunities related to reputation and brand management based on the combination of a family and business identity. In markets of increasingly choosy consumers, financial turmoil, and information overload, the addition of a family dimension in branding could provide recognition, trust, and a competitive edge. That is, the positioning and profiling of family businesses *as* family businesses will be an increasingly important aspect to monitor. However, with the current flux associated

with the paradigm shift caused by social media and technology, it is difficult to predict how families will leverage their distinct advantage. Currently, the full effects of social media are neither known nor understood. Unless a (unlikely) complete eradication of current developments in social media occurs, these changes markedly move the original modes of marketing toward obsolescence and also indicate that the shift toward value co-creation and service orientation is not a momentary fad but rather a starting point of revolutionary change in the marketing paradigm. Thus, although it is too early to predict the most beneficial practices in the area, family businesses still need to make informed decisions regarding social media in marketing. Therefore, we recommend that researchers and practitioners work together to monitor the opportunities and threats that these rapidly changing events present.

REFERENCES

Aaker, D.A. (1991) *Managing Brand Equity: Capitalizing on the Value of a Brand Name.* New York: Free Press.

Ahuja, R.D., Michels, T.A., Walker, M.M., and Weissbuch, M. (2007) 'Teen perceptions of disclosure in buzz marketing', *Journal of Consumer Marketing*, 24(3): 151–159.

American Marketing Association (2007) Definition of marketing, http://www.marketingpower.com/AboutAMA/Pages/DefinitionofMarketing.aspx (accessed 18 October, 2011).

Arregle, J., Hitt, M.A., Sirmon, D.G., and Very, P. (2007) 'The development of organizational social capital: Attributes of family firms', *Journal of Management Studies*, 44(1): 73–95.

Ballantyne, D. and Varey, R.J. (2008) 'The service-dominant logic and the future of marketing', *Journal of the Academy of Marketing Science*, 36(1): 11–14.

Balmer, J.M.T. (2010) 'Explicating corporate brands and their management: Reflections and directions from 1995', *Journal of Brand Management*, 18: 180–196.

Beck, L., Janssens, W., Debruyne, M., and Lommelen, T. (2011) 'A study of the relationships between generation, market orientation, and innovation in family firms', *Family Business Review*, 24(3): 252–272.

Biberman, J. (2001) 'The little shop that could', *Family Business Magazine*, 12(1): 23.

Blombäck, A. and Botero, I. (2013) 'Reputational capital in family firms: Understanding uniqueness from the stakeholder point of view', in Poutziouris, P. Smyrnios, K. Goel, S. (eds), *Handbook of Research on Family Business*, 2 edn. Cheltenham: Edward Elgar.

Blombäck, A. and Ramirez-Pasillas, M. (2012) 'Exploring the logics of corporate brand identity formation', *Corporate Communications – An International Journal*, 17(1): 7–28.

Blombäck, A. (2011) 'Realizing the value of family business identity as corporate brand element – A research model'. JIBS Working Paper Series No. 2011-17, Jönköping International Business School.

Botero, I. (2010) 'Are family-owned businesses taking advantage of their websites as strategic communication tools?'. White paper series, Family Enterprise USA.

Brown, S.W., Fisk, R.P., and Bitner, M.J. (1994) 'The development and emergence of services marketing thought', *International Journal of Service Industry Management*, 5(1): 21–48.

Burt, R.S. (1997) 'The contingent value of social capital', *Administrative Science Quarterly*, 42: 339–365.

Byrom, J. and Lehman, K. (2009) 'Coopers Brewery: heritage and innovation within a family firm', *Marketing Intelligence & Planning*, 27(4): 516–523.

Carrigan, M. and Buckley, J. (2008) 'What's so special about family business? An exploratory study of UK and Irish consumer experiences of family businesses', *International Journal of Consumer Studies*, 32(6): 656–666.

Chrisman, J.J., Chua, J.H., and Steier, L. (2005) 'Sources and consequences of distinctive familiness: An introduction', *Entrepreneurship: Theory and Practice*, 29: 237–247.

Chrisman, J.J., Chua, J.H., and Litz, R. (2003) 'A unified systems perspective of family firm performance: An extension and integration', *Journal of Business Venturing*, 18: 467–472.

Chua, J., Chrisman, J.J., and Sharma, P. (1999) 'Defining the family business by behavior', *Entrepreneurship: Theory and Practice*, 23(4): 19–39.

Coleman, J.S. (1988) 'Social capital in the creation of human capital', *The American Journal of Sociology*, 94: S95–S120.

Constantinides, E. (2006) 'the marketing mix revisited: Towards the 21st century marketing', *Journal of Marketing Management*, 22(3–4): 407–438.

Cooper, M. J., Upton, N., and Seaman, S. (2005) 'Customer relationship management: a comparative analysis of family and nonfamily business practices', *Journal of Small Business Management*, 43(3): 242–256.

Corbetta, G. and Salvato, C. (2004) 'Self-serving or self-actualizing? models of man and agency costs in different types of family firms: A commentary on "Comparing the agency costs of family and non-family firms: conceptual issues and exploratory evidence"', *Entrepreneurship: Theory and Practice*, 28: 355–362.

Covin, T.J. (1994) 'Profiling preference for employment in family-owned firms', *Family Business Review*, 7(3): 287–296.

Craig, J.B., Dibrell, C., and Davis, P.S. (2008) 'Leveraging family-based brand identity to enhance firm competitiveness and performance in family businesses', *Journal of Small Business Management*, 46(3): 351–371.

Craig, J.B., Dibrell, C., Neubaum, D., and Thomas, C. (2011) 'Stewardship climate scale: Measurement and an assessment of reliability and validity', *Academy of Management Conference Best Paper Proceedings*, San Antonio, Texas.

Davis, J.H., Schoorman, F.D., and Donaldson, L. (1997) 'Toward a stewardship theory of management', *Academy of Management Review*, 22(1): 20–47.

Donnelly, R.G. (1988) 'The family business', *Family Business Review*, 1(4): 427–445.

Dubin, R. (1969) *Theory Building*. New York: Free Press.

Dyer, W.G. (2006) 'Examining the "family effect" on firm performance', *Family Business Review*, 19: 253–273.

Dyer, W.G. and Whetten, D.A. (2006) 'Family firms and social responsibility: Preliminary evidence from the S&P 500', *Entrepreneurship: Theory and Practice*, 30: 785–802.

Ferguson, R. (2008) 'Word of mouth and viral marketing: taking the temperature of the hottest trends in marketing', *Journal of Consumer Marketing*, 25(3): 179–182.

Fombrun, C.J. and Shanley, M. (1990) 'What's in a name? Reputation building and corporate strategy', *Academy of Management Journal*, 33(2): 233–258.

Fombrun, C.J. (1996) *Reputation: Realizing Value From the Corporate Image*. Cambridge, MA: Harvard Business School Press.

Getz, D. and Carlsen, J. (2005) 'Family business in tourism: State of the art', *Annals of Tourism Research*, 32(1): 237–258.

Gomez-Mejia, L.R., Cruz, C. Berrone, P., and De Castro, J. (2011) 'The bind that ties: Socioemotional wealth preservation in family firms', *The Academy of Management Annals*, 5(1): 653–707.

Gotsi, M. and Wilson, A.M. (2001) 'Corporate reputation: seeking a definition', *Corporate Communications: An International Journal*, 6(1): 24–30.

Grönroos, C. (1994a) 'From marketing mix to relationship marketing: Toward a paradigm shift in marketing', *Management Decision*, 32(2): 4–32.

Grönroos, C. (1994b) 'Qua vadis, marketing? Toward a relationship marketing paradigm', *Journal of Marketing Management*, 10(5): 347–360.

Grönroos, C. (1997) 'Value-driven relational marketing: From products to resources and competencies', *Journal of Marketing Management*, 13(5): 407–419.

Grönroos, C. (2006) 'On defining marketing: Finding a new road map for marketing', *Marketing Theory*, 6(4): 395–417.

Gummesson, E. (1987) 'The new marketing – Developing long-term interactive relationships', *Long Range Planning*, 20(4): 10–20.

Gummesson, E. (2008) *Total Relationship Marketing*, 3rd edn. Oxford: Butterworth-Heinemann.

Habbershon, T.G. and Williams, M.L. (1999) 'A resource-based framework for assessing the strategic advantages of family firms', *Family Business Review*, 12(1): 1–26.

Habbershon, T.G., Williams, M., and MacMillan, I.C. (2003) 'A unified systems perspective of family firm performance', *Journal of Business Venturing*, 18(4): 451–465.

Håkansson, H. and Snehota, I. (1989) 'No business is an island: The network approach concept of business strategy', *Scandinavian Journal of Management*, 5(3): 187–200.

Hatch, M.-J. and Schultz, M. (2010) 'Toward a theory of brand co-creation with implications for brand governance', *Journal of Brand Management*, 17: 590–604.

Haynes, G.W., Walker, R., Rowe, B.R., and Hong, G. (1999) 'The intermingling of business and family finances in family-owned businesses', *Family Business Review*, 12(3): 225–239.

Helm, S. (2000) 'Viral marketing – Establishing customer relationships by "word-of-mouse"', *Electronic Markets*, 10(3): 158–161.

Hoffman, J., Hoelscher, M., and Sorenson, R. (2006) 'Achieving sustained competitive advantage: A family capital theory', *Family Business Review*, 19: 135–145.

Hoover, E.A. and Hoover, C.L. (1999) 'What you see ahead', *Family Business Magazine*, 11(4): 31–34.

Irava, W.J. and Moores, K. (2010) 'Clarifying the strategic advantage of familiness: Unbundling its dimensions and highlighting its paradoxes', *Journal of Family Business Strategy*, 131–144.

Jones, D.G.B. and Monieson, D.D. (1990) 'Early development of the philosophy of marketing thought', *Journal of Marketing*, 54(1): 102–113.

Jones, D.G.B. and Shaw, E. (2002) 'History of marketing thought', in Weitz, B. and Wensley, R. (eds), *Handbook of Marketing*. London: Sage, pp. 39–65.

Kaplan, A.M. and Haenlein, M. (2010) 'Users of the world, unite! The challenges and opportunities of Social Media', *Business Horizons*, 53(1): 59–68.

Keller, K.L., Apéria, T., and Georgson, M. (2008) *Strategic Brand Management: A European Perspective*. Harlow, England: Pearson Education.

Kotler, P. and Armstrong, G. (2010) *Principles of Marketing*, 13th edn. Englewood Cliffs, NJ: Pearson Prentice Hall.

Kozinets, R.V., de Valck, K., Wojnicki, A.C., and Wilner, S.J.S. (2010) 'Networked narratives: Understanding word-of-mouth marketing in online communities', *Journal of Marketing*, 74(2): 71–89.

Krappe, A., Goutas, L., and von Schlippe, A. (2011) 'The "family business brand": an enquiry into the construction of the image of family businesses', *Journal of Family Business Management*, 1(1): 37–46.

Kuhn, T. S. (1996) *The Structure of Scientific Revolutions*, 3rd edn. Chicago, IL: Chicago University Press.

Lane, P.J. & Lubatkin, M. (1998) Relative absorptive capacity and interorganizational learning. *Strategic Management Journal*, 19: 461–477.

LaPlaca, P.J. and Katrichis, J.M. (2009) 'Relative presence of business-to-business research in the marketing literature', *Journal of Business-to-Business Marketing*, 16(1): 1–22.

Le Breton-Miller, I. and Miller, D. (2006) 'Why do some family businesses out-compete? Governance, long-term orientations, and sustainable capability', *Entrepreneurship: Theory and Practice*, 30: 731–746.

Litz, R.A. and Rajaguru, G. (2011) 'When customers see "family" as adding value to the transaction: insights from the retail hardware industry'. Paper presented at the 7th Workshop on Family Firms Management, Witten, Germany.

Lumpkin, G.T., Brigham, K.H., and Moss, T.W. (2010) 'Long-term orientation: Implications for the entrepreneurial orientation and performance of family businesses', *Entrepreneurship & Regional Development*, 22(3–4): 241–264.

Lusch, R.F., Vargo, S.L., and O'Brien, M. (2007) 'Competing through service: Insights from service-dominant logic', *Journal of Retailing*, 83(1): 5–18.

Lyman, A. (1991) 'Customer service: Does family ownership make a difference?', *Family Business Review*, 4(3): 303–324.

Madden, T.J., Fehle, F., and Fournier, S. (2006) 'Brands matter: An empirical demonstration of the creation of shareholder value through branding', *Journal of the Academy of Marketing Science*, 34(2): 224–235.

Maignan, I., Ferrell, O.C., and Ferrell, L. (2005) 'A stakeholder model for implementing social responsibility in marketing', *European Journal of Marketing*, 39(9/10): 956–977.

Mangold, W.G. and Faulds, D.J. (2009) 'Social media: The new hybrid element of the promotion mix', *Business Horizons*, 52(4): 357–365.

Mattsson, L.-G. (1997) '"Relationship marketing" and the "markets-as-networks approach" – a comparative analysis of two evolving streams of research', *Journal of Marketing Management*, 13(5): 447–461.

McCarthy, E.J. (1964) *Basic Marketing: A Managerial Approach*. Homewood, IL: Richard D. Irwin.

Memili, E., Eddleston, K.A., Kellermanns, F.W., Zellweger, T.M., and Barnett, T. (2010) 'The critical path to family firm success through entrepreneurial risk taking and image', *Journal of Family Business Strategy*, 1(4): 200–209.

Merz, M., He, Y., and Vargo, S.L. (2009) 'The evolving brand logic: A service dominant logic perspective', *Journal of the Academy of Marketing Science*, 37(3): 338–344.

Micelotta, E.R. and Raynard, M. (2011) 'Concealing or revealing the family? Corporate brand identity strategies in family firms', *Family Business Review*, 24(3): 197–216.

Miller, D. and Le Breton-Miller, I. (2005) *Managing for the Long Run: Lessons in Competitive Advantage from Great Family Businesses*. Boston, MA: Harvard Business School Press.

Miller, D. and Le Breton-Miller, I. (2006) 'Priorities, practices and strategies in successful and failing family businesses: an elaboration and test of the configuration perspective', *Strategic Organization*, 4(4): 379–407.

Miller, D., Le Breton-Miller, I. and Scholnick, B. (2008) 'Stewardship vs. stagnation: an empirical comparison of small family and non-family businesses', *Journal of Management Studies*, 45(1): 50–78.

Normann, R. and Ramirez, R. (1993) 'From value chain to value constellation: Designing interactive strategy', *Harvard Business Review*, 71: 65–77.

Okoroafo, S.C. and Koh, A. (2009) 'The impact of the marketing activities of family owned businesses on consumer purchase intentions', *International Journal of Business and Management*, 4(10): 3–13.

Orth, U. and Green, M. (2009) 'Consumer loyalty to family versus non-family business: The role of trust, store image, trust and satisfaction', *Journal of Retailing & Consumer Services*, 16(4): 248–259.

Palka, W., Pousttchi, K., and Wiedemann, D.G. (2009) 'Mobile word-of-mouth: A grounded theory of mobile viral marketing', *Journal of Information Technology*, 24(2): 172–185.

Parmentier, M.-A. (2011) 'When David Met Victoria: Forging a strong family brand', *Family Business Review*, 24(3): 217–232.

Payne, A.F., Storbacka, K., and Frow, P. (2008) 'Managing the co-creation of value', *Journal of the Academy of Marketing Science*, 36(1): 83–96.

Pearson, A.W., Carr, J.C., and Shaw, J.C. (2008) 'Toward a theory of familiness: A social capital perspective', *Entrepreneurship: Theory and Practice*, 32: 949–969.

Prahalad, C.K. and Ramaswamy, V. (2004a) 'Co-creation experiences: The next practice in value creation', *Journal of Interactive Marketing*, 18: 5–14.

Prahalad, C.K. and Ramaswamy, V. (2004b) *The Future of Competition: Co-Creating Unique Value with Customers*. Boston, MA: Harvard Business School Press.

Presas, P., Muñoz, D., and Guia, J. (2011) 'Branding familiness in tourism family firms', *Journal of Brand Management*, 18(4/5): 274–284.

Reueber, R. and Fischer, E. (2011) 'Marketing (in) the family firm', *Family Business Review*, 24(3): 193–196.

Robertson, R.S. (1967) 'The process of innovation and the diffusion of innovation', *Journal of Marketing*, 31(1): 14–19.

Sheth, J.N. and Parvatiyar, A. (1995) 'The evolution of relationship marketing', *International Business Review*, 4: 397–418.

Sirmon, D.G. and Hitt, M.A. (2003) 'Managing resources: Linking unique resources, management, and wealth creation in family firms', *Entrepreneurship: Theory and Practice*, 27: 339–358.

Steier, L. (2001) 'Family firms, plural forms of governance, and the evolving role of trust', *Family Business Review*, 14(4): 353–368.

Stein, J. (1988) 'Takeover threats and managerial myopia', *Journal of Political Economy*, 96: 61–80.

Stein, J. (1989) 'Efficient capital markets, inefficient firms: A model of myopic corporate behavior', *Quarterly Journal of Economics*, 103: 655–669.

Sundaramurthy, C. and Kreiner, G.E. (2008) 'Governing by managing identity boundaries: The case of family businesses', *Entrepreneurship: Theory and Practice*, 32(3): 415–436.

Tagiuri, R. and Davis, J.A. (1996) 'Bivalent attributes of the family firm', *Family Business Review*, 9(2): 199–208.

Teal, E.J., Upton, N., and Seaman, S.L. (2003) 'A comparative analysis of strategic marketing practices of high-growth U.S. family and non-family firms',

Journal of Developmental Entrepreneurship, 8(2): 177–195.

Thompson, T. (1960) *Stewardship in Contemporary Theology*. New York: Association Press.

Tokarczyk, J., Hansen, E., Green, M., and Down, J. (2007) 'A resource-based view and market orientation theory examination of the role of "familiness" in family business success', *Family Business Review*, 20(1): 17–31.

Vargo, S.L. and Lusch, R.F. (2004) 'Evolving to a new dominant logic for marketing', *The Journal of Marketing*, 68(1): 1–17.

Vargo, S.L. and Lusch, R.F. (2008) 'Service-dominant logic: Continuing the evolution', *Journal of the Academy of Marketing Science*, 36(1): 1–10.

Vargo, S. and Lusch, R. (2010) 'A service dominant logic for marketing', in MacLaran, P., Saren, M., Stern, B., and Tadajewski, M. (eds), *The Sage Handbook of Marketing Theory*. London: Sage Publications.

Ward, J.L. (1997) 'Growing the family business: Special challenges and best practices', *Family Business Review*, 10(4): 323–337.

Wind, Y. (2006) 'Blurring the lines: Is there a need to rethink industrial marketing?', *Journal of Business & Industrial Marketing*, 21(7): 474–481.

Woodruff, R. (1997) 'Customer value: The next source for competitive advantage', *Journal of the Academy of Marketing Science*, 25(2): 139–153.

Zachary, M.A., McKenny, A., Short, J., and Payne, G.T. (2011) 'Family business and market orientation: Construct validation and comparative analysis', *Family Business Review*, 24(3): 233–251.

Zahra, S.A., Hayton, J.C., Neubaum, D.O., Dibrell, C., and Craig, J. (2008) 'Culture of family commitment and strategic flexibility: The moderating effect of stewardship', *Entrepreneurship: Theory and Practice*, 32: 1035–1054.

Zellweger, T., Eddleston, K.H., and Kellermanns, F.W. (2010) 'Exploring the concept of familiness: Introducing family firm identity', *Journal of Family Business Strategy*, 1(1): 1–10.

Zineldin, M. and Philipson, S. (2007) 'Kotler and Borden are not dead: myth of relationship marketing and truth of the 4Ps', *Journal of Consumer Marketing*, 24(4): 229–241.

22

Family Firms and Social Innovation: Cultivating Organizational Embeddedness

Shaker A. Zahra, Rania Labaki, Sondos G. Abdel Gawad and Salvatore Sciascia

INTRODUCTION

Mounting evidence highlights family firms' contributions to their communities and societies (Bingham et al., 2011; De la Cruz Deniz Deniz and Suarez, 2005; Uhlaner et al., 2004). Family firms create jobs and introduce innovative technologies that improve their communities' quality of life. They also enrich their communities' cultural, artistic, and social life (Dyer and Whetten, 2006). These firms' embeddedness in their communities also creates an expectation that they will contribute to the common good (Perrini and Minoja, 2008; Zahra, 2010). Family firms are usually interwoven with their communities and derive considerable value from their identification with them.

Despite these crucial contributions, the social role of family forms has fuelled debate. Some believe that family businesses enrich the financial (Amit and Villalonga, 2014, in this Handbook; Anderson and Reeb, 2003) and social performance (Allouche and Amann, 1995) of a country. They also note

that family firms engage in socially responsible practices on their own (Capron and Quairel Lanoizelée, 2007), while pursuing financial and socioemotional wealth creation (Astrachan and Jaskiewicz, 2008; Berrone et al., 2014, in this Handbook; Gomez-Mejia et al., 2007). Yet, others have noted that some family firms gain considerable powers which they use to stifle competition and innovation (e.g., Banfield, 1958; Morck and Yeung, 2004; Putnam et al., 1993).

These conflicting views on family firms' social role stems, in part, from researchers' broad and often abstract focus on 'social performance' (e.g., Barnea and Rubin, 2010) and 'corporate social responsibility' (e.g., Perrini and Minoja, 2008). We believe that a more focused approach that examines these contributions to particular facets of this role might yield deeper insights. One area where these contributions become evident is social innovation, defined as 'new concepts and measures that are accepted by impacted social groups and are applied to overcome social challenges' (Hochgerner in Howaldt and Schwarz, 2010: 23). These innovations address society's most perplexing problems. Given family firms' embeddedness in their communities and the symbiotic relationships that exist between them and their society (Zahra, 2010), the contributions of family firms to social innovation is the focus of this chapter.

OBJECTIVE AND CONTRIBUTIONS

Specifically, we examine the potential contributions of family firms to social innovations, highlight the key factors that enhance (or limit) these contributions, and outline key areas worthy of future research. While definitions of family firms abound in the literature, we define them as those companies that benefit from the strong presence of an owner family that controls a large percentage of their equity (Anderson et al., 2009; Zahra, 2005, 2010). To understand these firms' role in social innovations, we will first define these innovations and how they relate to social entrepreneurship. Next, we will discuss the role of family firms in promoting social innovations. We will then highlight key inducements and barriers to family firms' involvement in social innovations. We conclude by outlining key areas that require research attention and the theories that could be useful in this regard.

Our focus on social innovation is timely because of the growing recognition of the multiplicity and complexity of the social issues left unaddressed by governments and states. Family firms have the credibility, resources, and capabilities that could be combined with those of other groups to ameliorate these problems. As a result, communities and societies have come to expect private and public organizations to join forces to address these persistent problems through collective action. Private companies and public organizations often have different but complementary resources, skills, and capabilities that could be deployed to introduce innovative solutions to these problems, without regard for profit.

Studying social innovations also allows us to examine how family firms add to the creation of social *and* financial wealth. Social wealth refers to the social value created minus social costs (Zahra et. al., 2009). By focusing on social innovations and social wealth creation, we can better appreciate what the consequences of family firms' embeddedness in their communities are and how they use non-market strategies to adapt, gain and retain legitimacy, and amass social capital (Zahra, 2010). Yet, embeddedness challenges the autonomy of family firms and sometimes constrains their ability to gain access to resources or even revise their missions.

Social innovations also enable family firms to gain greater discretion when navigating their competitive landscape. Moreover, by connecting with other companies, non-governmental organizations (NGOs) and governmental agencies, family firms become better linked to key players in their broader ecosystems where they can influence and shape events, learn and gain new knowledge, ensure the supply of resources needed for their operations, and use as well as apply their unique capabilities in creating wealth for the common good. Social innovations further bond family firms with their external environments, enabling these firms' executives to manage critical interdependencies that could influence their long-term performance and even survival. Focusing on social innovation, therefore, gives researchers an opportunity to understand how family firms' embeddedness can influence their strategic choices and actions, potentially improving their entrepreneurial activities.

Studying social innovations can also contribute to improving our understanding of how these companies create socioemotional wealth. Family members have their own social causes which they would like to support through active engagement. This can contribute to creating business opportunities that support family firms' growth. Participation in social innovations could also fulfill the social and relatedness needs of family members, creating greater satisfaction. This, in turn, can promote these family members' willingness to explore additional areas for social innovation, generating positive social capital that can enhance the exploration of new opportunities (Zahra, 2010), promoting entrepreneurship and market responsiveness.

SOCIAL INNOVATIONS AND ENTREPRENEURIAL CAPABILITY AMONG FAMILY FIRMS

Social innovations mean different things to different people. As Brooks (1982) notes, they typically embody such a different set of activities as market innovations (e.g., introducing new forms of transacting), management innovations (e.g., developing and institutionalizing new forms of organizing), political innovations (e.g., building new forms of coalitions), and institutional innovations (e.g., creating new organizational models and forms). These innovations target social issues and needs that have not been satisfactorily addressed because of their complexity and costliness, market failure, institutional voids or gaps (e.g., the collapse of central governments, the lack of social regulations and systems), and the aggressive pursuit of privatization and austerity programs around the globe. Privatization programs have often been accompanied by efforts to reform the content of state social networks (e.g., types of help offered) or how these efforts are supported (i.e., who pays for which services and how much the pay is).

Social Innovations vs Reform Programs

Social innovations typically go well beyond the familiar 'reform' programs enacted by states or countries. In Table 22.1, we differentiate between these reforms and social innovations. Reform programs are issue-driven and cost-oriented with quantitative performance criteria. These reforms might change the way these programs are organized and managed. In contrast, social innovations typically focus on bringing about fundamental social changes by altering (or improving) the way things are done (processes), who is involved (e.g., key actors), and the goals emphasized (e.g., improving quality of life). As we note in Table 22.1, these innovations often require the effective partnership of private and public institutions (corporations, government, not-for-profit organizations and NGOs) along with traditional institutions (family, religious, and tribal institutions) to address social issues. These partnerships focus on developing and implementing innovative solutions, not only reducing costs.

Social Innovation vs Social Entrepreneurship

Social entrepreneurship 'encompasses the activities and processes undertaken to discover, define, and exploit opportunities in order to enhance social wealth by creating new ventures or managing existing organizations in an innovative manner' (Zahra et al., 2009: 522). Social entrepreneurs locate needs that require attention, setting the stage for

Table 22.1 Reform programs vs social innovations

Variables	Reform programs	Social innovations
Focus	Public services	Social issues, problems and needs
Objective	Usually cost reduction by streamlining operations and processes	Usually effective social change by reframing issues, building momentum for collective action
Agents of change	Public bureaucrats and politicians	Coalitions of different companies
Performance metrics	Cost, timeliness, efficiency, number of services, and number of recipients	Same as reform programs, plus empowerment, improving quality of life, and promoting civic engagement

Table 22.2 Social entrepreneurship vs social innovations

Variables	Social entrepreneurship	Social innovations
Focus	Social venture creation and growth	Using multiple organizational forms (including social ventures) to address social issues, needs and aspirations
Priorities	Addressing social issue while making a profit	Addressing social issues without regard for profit
Locus of activities	Independent entrepreneurs	Collective action

social innovations of different types and then diffusing them locally or even internationally (Zahra et al., 2008). Conversely, social innovations generate momentum for new forms of organizations, processes and practices that provide the services necessary to respond to social needs and create social wealth. Only some social innovations lead to the creation of social ventures. Many of these social innovations take the form of collaborative ventures that address local issues and concerns, without regard to scaling up their operations or pursuing a profit – as commonly done in many social ventures (Zahra et al., 2009).

Overall, three qualities distinguish social innovations from social entrepreneurship. First, these innovations are broader than social entrepreneurship which frequently focuses primarily on new venture creation and growth. Second, social innovations emphasize addressing social issues and improving the social and economic wealth of their communities. These innovations focus on enhancing and enriching the quality of life in a community, region, or society. Social entrepreneurs typically pursue the dual goal of addressing social issues *and* making a profit (Zahra et al., 2008, 2009). Third, social innovators rely on collective action in pursuing their goals. Social entrepreneurs most often work independently or in very small teams as they create their ventures and devise solutions to chosen causes. Social ventures' founding teams are usually brought together by common interests, complementary skills, or the desire to make a profit. The differences between social innovations and social entrepreneurship are summarized in Table 22.2.

The differences noted in Table 22.2 between social innovations and social entrepreneurship

suggests that social innovations can have powerful effects on family firms' entrepreneurial capability. Entrepreneurial capability refers to a firm's capacity to conceive, identify, and pursue opportunities associated with social issues. This capability is at the core of what family firms' strategic renewal activities promote risk-taking in their operations as well as revitalize how they position themselves and compete. These capabilities can be an important means of successful learning that revises family firms' knowledge bases and enables them to chart new strategic directions. To understand these important contributions, we need to reflect on the role of innovation in family firms' strategic moves, especially their innovativeness.

Family Firms' Innovativeness

Innovativeness refers to a firm's ability to introduce discoveries and novel solutions through experimentation and creative problem solving (Lumpkin and Dess, 1996). As such, it can occur in the firm's products (goods and services), operations, decision making processes, internal organizations, resource allocations, and strategies. Innovativeness enhances a company's competitiveness.

The literature on family firms' innovativeness and entrepreneurship is growing (see McKelvie et al., 2014, in this *Handbook*). Evidence indicates that family firms are innovative, though they spend less on R&D activities than other companies (Zahra, 2005). One reason is the 'long-term nature of family firms' ownership [that] allows them to dedicate required resources for innovation' (Zahra et al., 2004: 363). Family firms have several other qualities that can promote innovativeness, including their external orientation, decentralized structures, and focus on long-term investment horizons (Zahra et al., 2004). Research suggests that the stronger the long-term orientation, the higher the firm's innovativeness because longer time horizons stimulate experimentation and unleashes creativity (Lumpkin et al., 2010). Family ownership is also conducive to venturing into new markets to develop new revenue streams that can enrich family members while creating growth options. When the family is also involved in the management of the company, firms are more likely to develop more radical innovation than non-family firms, except when the CEO enjoys a long tenure (Zahra, 2005). Innovativeness also increases with generational changes in family firms' leadership.

What makes these research results intriguing is the growing recognition that some family firms are reluctant to support R&D. Morck et al. (2000) reached this conclusion using Canadian data. Recently, their results have been further validated by Munari et al. (2010) in Europe, by Block (2010a) in the USA and by Muñoz-Bullòn and Sanchez-Bueno (2011) again in Canada. According to Munari et al. (2010), higher shareholdings by families are negatively associated with R&D investments because controlling families tend to be risk-averse and need to stabilize cash flow. Also, family owners are less able to monitor managers because of family conflicts and may seek private control-oriented benefits, i.e., dividends over firm growth (Block, 2010b). Furthermore, Muñoz-Bullòn and Sanchez-Bueno (2011) note that family firms are limited in resource availability, which may reduce their capability to invest in R&D.

Research on family firms' innovativeness has long viewed R&D spending as well as product and process innovation-related activities through a competitive lens. Accordingly, innovative activities help the firm to serve the customer better or cheaper than rivals and thus to increase a firm's wealth. However, there are limits to the competitive and economic gains family firms are able to

achieve through innovation. Products and processes become obsolete quickly and knowledge about them diffuses, encouraging imitation. Competitors can also invent around rivals' innovations. Gains from family firms' innovations could be sustained or even enhanced if family firms also engage in social innovations. Social innovations help family firms make significant inroads into market arenas, even though this is not always the primary motivation for family firms to pursue these innovations. Yet, researchers have not examined family firms' social innovativeness and their implications for companies or communities. This research gap is puzzling, given the growing attention to family firms' social role.

Family firms' innovativeness can improve social conditions and enhance the quality of human existence. The rapid pace of social changes around the globe means that social issues change constantly, becoming global in their scale and effects. These issues, in turn, demand innovative solutions. Further, several governments have dramatically cut their spending on social services, such as community development and education, emphasizing the necessity of addressing rising social challenges, albeit with fewer resources – a classic challenge for innovators.

Globalization has also increased awareness of opportunities for social improvement. Innovativeness offers entrepreneurs the tools to spot promising opportunities to increase social wealth. Poverty, malnutrition, disease, illiteracy, and unemployment have been common problems in developing and emerging economies. Many of these problems are now afflicting developed economies as well. Therefore, innovations that tackle these problems could be adapted and introduced across the globe. This makes it possible to reduce costs, share expertise, and build momentum for developing and implementing social innovations. As family firms join other groups seeking to address these issues, they are also likely to learn about the dynamics of innovations and how to cultivate their embeddedness in their communities. As a result, researchers need to examine the intimate links between the characteristics of family firms and the social innovations they can develop alone or in collaboration with other groups.

FAMILY FIRMS' CONTRIBUTIONS TO SOCIAL INNOVATIONS

Over a decade ago, Litz and Kleysen (2001: 335) inspired research by asking the question, 'What is the relationship between the presence of family within a business enterprise and its capacity for innovation?' While scholars have studied the social orientation of these firms (e.g., Dyer and Whetten, 2006) and their entrepreneurial activities, only a few have examined innovations from a social perspective (e.g., Wagner, 2008). The few studies that have been published to date suggest that family businesses are more socially oriented and innovative than other businesses. Still, some have observed that families may take ethical risks as part of their entrepreneurial activities (Fisscher et al., 2005), caring more about their own needs to the detriment of their societies, engage in different forms of corruption, and even usurping minority stakeholders' wealth (Anderson et al., 2009; Morck and Yeung, 2004).

Currently, there is limited empirical research on family firm's social role. Yet, it is worth reflecting on the key findings to better understand what family firms can do to promote social innovations. Researchers have studied the social orientation of family businesses – applying different theoretical perspectives that include stewardship, corporate social responsibility, corporate citizenship, social entrepreneurship, philanthropy, sustainable development, and socioemotional wealth, among others. While these studies have oftentimes relied on common theories (e.g., stewardship and stakeholders theories), confusion persists on the definition and content of the constructs used to gauge the social orientation of family firms. Researchers also appear to define social orientation in broad

terms to denote their commitments to external stakeholders as well as their adherence to ethical codes of conduct. Applying this perspective, some researchers propose that family firms are more socially oriented than other businesses. This research suggests that family businesses contribute the most to the economy from financial (Anderson and Reeb, 2003) and social perspectives (Allouche and Amann, 1995). Other researchers suggest that families may consider ethical issues as integral parts of entrepreneurial activities (Fisscher et al., 2005) and justify their active involvement in corrupt business practices (Morck and Yeung, 2004). To better appreciate the diversity of existing views on the social role of family firms, in Table 22.3 we present a summary of prior research. Though our review is not exhaustive, it clearly shows that there is no agreement on the nature and effect of this social role.

As the research cited in Table 22.3 makes clear, family businesses are not homogeneous in terms of their social orientations and behaviors (De la Cruz Deniz Deniz and Suarez, 2005). Innovations are also likely to change over the course of family firms' life cycles (Bergfeld, 2011), reinforcing the need to specifically examine family firms' contributions to social innovation over time. The portfolio of these innovations is likely to change as family firms undergo their life cycle transitions.

One important factor that can explain this heterogeneity is these firms' geographical locations and the associated cultural context. Cultural and competitive differences across regions are expected to create pronounced differences in these firms' perceived incentives to pursue social activities (Table 22.3) and innovation. For example, family firms in developing countries may view social innovation as a means to address institutional failure, gain acceptance among the political elite and build relational contacts with special stakeholders (Bruton et al., 2008). As a result, social innovations become an important driver of these firms' business practices to improve access to state aid and debt

Table 22.3   Overview of empirical research on the social role of family firms

Study	Focus	Key findings
Allouche and Amann (1995)	Differences in social performance between French listed and non-listed family and non-family firms.	Higher levels of performance referring to less employee turnover, higher employment flexibility, longer tenure, higher compensation, and higher levels of employee training and skill development.
Dyer and Whetten (2006)	Social responsibility activities in 500 largest US companies using data from S&P 500.	Family businesses are more concerned about CSR and exhibit a more positive CSR behaviour than non-family businesses.
Uhlaner et al. (2004)	Survey of CSR in Dutch firms.	Higher awareness and corporate sustainability activity of family firms. Perceived social responsibility is higher in firms where the family surname is included.
Graafland (2002)	Survey of CSR in Dutch firms.	Family firms are more concerned about CSR and exhibit a positive relationship between long-term added value CSR activities.
Mignon (2000)	Qualitative survey of French family firms' longevity antecedents.	Social responsibility and values are key in explaining the family firms longevity.
De la Cruz Deniz Deniz and Suarez (2005)	Survey of Spanish family firms' determinants of different corporate social orientations and behaviours.	Family firms are not homogeneous regarding their social involvement and vision of social responsibility.
Gnan and Montemerlo (2002)	Survey of Italian SMEs.	Family firms are unlikely to uproot their employees; they usually maintain their installations in the original places; and the owner families generally sit on the boards of hospitals, churches, schools, and charities that contribute to the welfare of the local community.
Block (2010b)	Relationship between family firms and downsizing in S&P 500.	Family owners care more about their reputation for social responsibility than do other owners, motivating them to pursue less severe job cuts.
Craig and Dibrell (2006)	US small and medium-sized firms.	Family firms are better able to facilitate environmentally friendly firm policies associated with improved firm innovation and greater financial performance more effectively than their non-family competitors.
Niehm et al. (2008)	Antecedents and consequences of community social responsibility (CSR) for family firms operating in US small and rural markets.	Commitment to the community, community support, and sense of community, account significantly for the variation in family business operators' CSR.
Miller et al. (2008)	Small Canadian family and non-family businesses.	Stewardship is manifested by unusual devotion to the *continuity* of the company, by more assiduous nurturing of a *community* of employees, and by seeking out closer *connections* with customers to sustain the business.
Wagner (2008)	Panel data for a set of US firms.	Moderating role of family firms on the link of sustainability innovation and performance. Being a family firm does not have a positive effect on actions that are beneficial for sustainability.
Anderson et al. (2009)	US publicly listed family and non-family firms.	Family firms exploit opacity to extract private benefits at the expense of minority investors.
Morck and Yeung (2004)	Dimensions of societal progress (economic development, physical infrastructure, health care, education, quality of government, and social development) of family-controlled firms in 27 of the larger industrialized countries in the world.	Countries controlled by family businesses are more backward in a number of dimensions (worse public goods including worse infrastructure, worse healthcare, worse education, and more irresponsible macroeconomic policies) because family businesses seek to protect their own parochial interests at the detriment of the broader societies in which they are embedded by fostering corruption.

financing. Similarly, using social innovations to establish strong ties with powerful stakeholders may counterbalance the obligations that strong extended family ties may create in some world regions (Khavul et al., 2009). Thus, the type and frequency of the social innovations family firms implement are expected to be an outcome of their cultural, competitive and institutional factors.

Social innovations can make a major, positive difference in the case of family firms. These innovations provide the opportunity and the formalized means to focus family firms' corporate social responsibility (CSR) activities. Social innovations help family firms identify and target those issues and causes that can have significant social impact while enhancing these companies' market positions. Family firms often focus on innovations in the vicinity of their immediate customers and markets. This focus would reflect these companies' interest in remaining close to their businesses' center of gravity while rationing the use of their limited resources. As they gain experience in collaborating with other organizations and groups, family firms might pursue bigger projects by leveraging their expertise and resources. Family firms might also join other groups in drawing attention to the more complex issues facing their community, industry, and society. With their commitment to social innovation proven, family firms become an integral part of a growing movement that brings about desirable social change – without damaging their own reputation or market standing.

Family firms can also contribute to the success of social innovations by providing the technical and other types of expertise that not-for-profit organizations lack. Because some social issues are complex, solving them may require significant resources and 'patient' capital over multiple years. These resources are not charitable contributions. Rather, they are important investments in building and cementing family firms' ongoing relationships with their external environments and stakeholders. The amounts and types of resources that family firms devote to social innovations is likely to vary based on their interests, the congruence of these innovations with their missions, and the magnitude of expected social outcomes. Paybacks and gains from social innovations cannot be measured solely using traditional financial models or economic criteria; these innovations contribute to social wealth.

Family firms can also contribute to social innovations by serving as a bridge that connects different actors who have an interest in promoting these innovations. This bridging role enables different parties with different cultures, goals, and agendas to negotiate their differences and participate in these innovations. This role is conducive to family firms recognizing valuable business opportunities that they can successfully exploit. Given these potential contributions by family firms to social innovation, we should ask: What motivates these firms to engage in social innovation in the first place? Understanding these motives can provide rich insights into these families' extent and durability of the commitments to social innovation, as discussed next.

INDUCEMENTS TO FAMILY FIRMS' CONTRIBUTION TO SOCIAL INNOVATION

Whereas some of the factors that encourage family firms to pursue social innovation are common to all organizations, others are unique to family firms. Below, we discuss key factors that can promote social innovations and highlight what distinguishes family firms in terms of the inducements to their contribution to these innovations.

Financial vs Socioemotional Wealth Considerations

Social innovations provide a forum where family firms can connect to their stakeholders in their community, acquire valuable social capital, enhance their legitimacy, and improve their reputations and standing in their markets. Social innovations can also enrich a community's quality of life and may increase demand on family firms' products, thereby enhancing their financial performance. Improved quality of life could also help attract civic-minded employees who can work with these companies and thus contribute to improving the quality of the family firms' intellectual capital. These gains could improve family firms' performance.

Besides financial wealth considerations, connecting to external stakeholders is a good reason for family firms to champion and pursue social innovation. According to social exchange theory, parties will engage in mutually beneficial relational exchanges in pursuit of both tangible and intangible outcomes (Emerson, 1976). Social innovations are oftentimes intangible and their value lies in the satisfaction of transacting parties, a key determinant of future repeated exchanges (Makoba, 1993). Pursuing social innovation, therefore, generates benefits through exposure to various external stakeholders, co-developing these innovations with partners and creating inter-partner synergy. Family firms are best positioned to harness these effects because of the prevalence of altruism and long-term orientation.

Altruism in family firms enables generalized reciprocity as a rule of social exchange theory. Generalized reciprocity refers to indefinite reimbursement period that lacks immediacy of returns. As a result, family firms will be best positioned to leverage their altruistic behavior to connect to external stakeholders through social innovation. However, sustaining these connections is time consuming and requires perseverance on the part of all parties. Family firms have the necessary extended time horizon to nurture their complex relationships and harvest their long-term implications (Lumpkin and Brigham, 2011).

Participating in social innovations also provides an opportunity to maintain or increase the socioemotional wealth of the family. Engaging the next generations of family firms in the dynamics and challenges of social innovation can help the regeneration of their social capital by continuously

building alliances and partnerships within and across industry lines with community organizations and NGOs. This training also prepares the next generations of family members to independently lead their own organizations, pursue their own civic interests, and develop their own networks. Members of the next generations can also learn new skills and different ways of managing which they can then transfer to their own family firms, contributing to the well-being of their family and other employees. Exposure to different knowledge sources can further improve the ability of members of a family's next generation to spot important opportunities for profitability and growth.

Sometimes, the pursuit of social innovations that increase socioemotional wealth can be detrimental to a family's financial wealth. This problem arises because family and the non-family stakeholders, in particular the minority stakeholders, differ in the value they attach to socioemotional wealth and their preferences of the best approaches to achieve it. Some have noted that family firms expropriate wealth at the detriment of the society (Anderson et al., 2009; Fisscher et al., 2005; Morck and Yeung, 2004). The legal and cultural characteristics and/or gaps in a country play a big role in explaining potential discrepancies. These existing gaps may lead family firms to 'take charge' of the development of the community through social innovation while amassing their own financial wealth. This is especially true in countries with major economic problems, where corruption is widespread. Although sometimes non-family stakeholders are aware of potential financial expropriation done by family firms, they may believe that the social benefits provided by the family business outweigh the financial expropriation (Goel and Labaki, 2010). These social benefits ('social dividends') could relate to the goodwill resulting from privileged relationships that the family employs 'illegally' but benefit the business (Sachs et al., 2008).

To summarize, social innovations serve multiple important purposes with regard to the next generations of family firm owners. They help connect family firms with external stakeholders. They also help empower and train members of the next generation(s), enhancing their leadership potential. These innovations allow members of a family's different generations to collaborate and make use of their respective resources, abilities and skills, creating a sense of commonality and growing cohesion across these generations. This cohesion facilitates the accomplishment of family firms' financial and non-financial goals. It is also useful in resolving potential conflicts that could arise from these companies' missions and strategies.

Family vs Non-Family Business Characteristics

Clearly, family firms are well positioned and have good reasons to contribute to social innovations which, in turn, can hone their entrepreneurial capabilities that improve their competitive advantages. However, as we indicate in Table 22.4, these advantages arise from these firms' flexibility in resource mobilization for social innovations, selectivity in pursuit of particular types of innovations,

timing, speedy decision-making processes related to initiating social innovations, and the continuous commitment to social causes. A source of advantage for family firms lies in the ideologies and priorities that guide their decision-making and resource allocations as well as commitment to particular social causes.

The differences we highlight in Table 22.4 suggest that family firms are likely to use their entrepreneurial capabilities to target different types of opportunities, benefiting from different network-based relationships that reinforce their commitment to select social issues. These relationships renew and create social capital (Zahra, 2010), a key ingredient in transferring knowledge and other resources from other organizations engaged with family firms in developing social innovations. Family firms' deep involvement in these innovations also facilitates their learning, allowing them to become more proficient in selecting and pursuing particular opportunities. As these entrepreneurial capabilities become better developed and deployed, family firms can also identify a wider array of social issues in which they can participate. Having such entrepreneurial capabilities and honing them

Table 22.4   A comparison of family and non-family firms' social innovations

| Variable | Type of firm | |
	Family	Non-family
Speed of the decision-making process related to social innovation	Fast	Slow
Timing of decisions related to social innovation across the business life cycle	Early, middle, and late life cycle stages.	Mainly late life cycle stages.
Strength and structure of social networks and partners	Predominantly closely-knit family and local / regional communities.	Predominantly weak but dispersed national and international partners.
Focus of involvement	Causes related to the sphere of family firms' operations and networks and to the family background.	More akin to standard corporate social responsibility practices.
Investment ideology	Social-business portfolio.	Primarily business portfolio.
Social innovation elicitors	Mainly guided by the family business continuity across generations as a means to transfer values to and involve the next generation, and to strengthen family cohesion.	Mainly guided by competitive, ideological and regulatory considerations as a means to survive and increase performance.

over time enables family firms to successfully pursue promising opportunities for social innovation.

BARRIERS TO FAMILY FIRMS' CONTRIBUTION TO SOCIAL INNOVATIONS

Despite the importance of social innovations for family firms, several factors might inhibit their participation in developing, diffusing and implementing these innovations. For example, social innovations have several features that distinguish them from commercial innovation. According to Austin et al. (2006), there are three key differences between social and commercial innovation. First, while commercial innovations are primarily oriented to generate private gains, social innovations are more concerned with creating social value. Second, while the effects of commercial innovation may be easily measured by well-known indicators of profitability and/or sales growth, the performance measures for social innovation are less standardized. Third, financial and human resources are more difficult to be mobilized for social innovation than commercial innovation, because of the limited allure of potential financial return for investors and employees.

Other differences exist between social and commercial innovations, reflecting the nature of the opportunities addressed. Zahra et al. (2008) note that there are four main features that distinguish social opportunities. First, compared to commercial opportunities, social opportunities are characterized by higher prevalence, i.e., the social needs to be satisfied pervade a larger global population. Second, social opportunities are more urgent and require quick, immediate responses. Third, social opportunities are less accessible, i.e., they call for innovative solutions to problems that are unlikely to be met through traditional means in arenas less accessible to traditional providers. Last, social opportunities are characterized by radicalness, and radical innovation is needed to solve problems of lower accessibility and higher prevalence and urgency.

The above-mentioned variables may limit the potential contributions of family firms to social innovations. Together, these features make some social issues difficult to comprehend. Moreover, several factors related to family firms create additional difficulties in this regard. These include: the relational conflicts, the misunderstandings and misuse of altruism, the perceived riskiness of social innovations and their implications for the family firm, and the transient versus sustainable nature of these innovations, as discussed next.

Relational Conflicts

Family firms are 'fertile fields for conflict' (Harvey and Evans, 1994: 331). They are often plagued by relational conflicts that include tension, animosity, and annoyance among group members (Kellermanns and Eddleston, 2004). Jehn (1995) posits that relational conflicts usually have greater negative effects in highly closed and interdependent communities, such as family firms, than in other social groups. Further, relational conflicts often overshadow task conflicts, or the disagreements that refine the firms' goals and strategies by considering options more comprehensively (Jehn, 1995; Kellermanns and Eddleston, 2004). Resolved satisfactorily, task-related conflicts could improve and enrich organizational performance. As relational conflicts surface, members of the organization may confuse them for task-related conflicts and vice versa. This can delay effective interventions intended to address task-related conflicts.

Relational conflicts usually arise from different perceptions regarding values, priorities, status, and other factors that determine interaction among the owner family members. Sibling rivalry might also intensify and perpetuate these conflicts. Relational conflicts often have negative effects on innovative activities. In fact, some research shows a negative association between relational conflicts and innovation behavior and group performance (Pelled, 1996). These results may reflect the fact that relational conflicts reduce employees' ability to recognize innovation opportunities and exploit them by integrating heterogeneous knowledge sources (Jehn and Bendersky, 2003). Relational conflicts that afflict family members could become a barrier to social than commercial innovation. On the one hand, the greater difficulties encountered in measuring potential and actual results of social innovation may hamper the possibilities of agreement among family members on the actions to be taken. On the other hand, the fact that social innovations are more concerned with creating social value than private gains could raise the inertia of those family members that are just interested in dividends because it will be non-active in the management of the firm.

Altruism as an Impediment to Social Innovation

In family firms, altruism sometimes colors managers' perceptions of the quality of skills and abilities of other family members. As a result, altruism might reduce family members' monitoring and honest assessment of each other's contributions (Schulze et al., 2001). Parents in particular may also act generously toward their children, compensating them well above their real contributions to the business. However, asymmetric family altruism may lead to distributive injustice, where less competent family members receive more support than the better performing members or non-family members. Misguided altruism might lead some family members to engage in self-indulging activities, instead of building the firm's social or market position. Thus, the company's resources are consumed for self-gratification, instead of building effective relationships with the external stakeholders.

Over time, a focus on self-gratification might lead to diverting a firm's resources away from social innovation, whose value is uncertain. This situation is more problematic for social than for commercial innovation

because of the pre-existing difficulties in mobilizing resources. In other cases, family members may adopt questionable social causes and divert important firm resources to support social innovations that might have little redeeming social or organizational value. These behaviors may impede the pursuit of other compelling social opportunities that require urgent interventions and massive resource mobilization for radical innovation.

Riskiness of Social Innovations

Despite the excitement surrounding social innovations, compelling empirical evidence about their implications does not exist. The bulk of existing evidence is anecdotal in nature. However, social innovations are risky and in most cases it is hard to find a partner to share the risks involved. Given the low accessibility of social opportunities, family firms might have to face the risk of opportunity exploitation unilaterally. In the best case of having a partnership, the diversity of partners can fuel opportunism and free riding problems. Given the social capital to be gained from social innovations, some companies might pledge their support and involvement but fail to deliver. Partners may also have incongruent goals and decision making styles.

Other problems could exacerbate the risks associated with social innovations. For instance, partners often work under internal organizational constraints that could slow down the flow of resources and other types of commitments. Poor partner selection and the complexity of coordination can undermine the success of social innovations because participating companies often have limited controls on social innovations. The failure of these innovations can damage the family firm's reputation, weakening its market position and performance. Together, these factors might limit family firms' interest and participation in social innovations, creating risk-adverse organizations (Naldi et al., 2007). This risk is likely to be higher for social than for commercial innovation because of its higher radicalness.

Sustainability of Social Innovations

Involvement in social innovations also serves as a means of ensuring a family firm's continuity for future generations. However, by definition, most social innovations are not sustainable because they spot urgent opportunities and have their own short life cycles. In the case of longer life cycles, benefits from social innovations vary across the stages of these cycles. Further, as social innovations become successful, they may attract more groups of stakeholders to participate, diffusing the family firms' gains. The success of social innovations also invites imitation, which increases social wealth but reduces family firms' ability to appropriate any idiosyncratic reputational or financial gains that might result. This risk is higher for social than commercial innovation, given the global prevalence of social opportunities. These factors might limit family firms' willingness and ability to participate in social innovations.

PROMISING RESEARCH DIRECTIONS

The important role that family firms play in promoting social innovations offers researchers an opportunity to explore several issues. In particular, several issues deserve systematic research attention. These issues center on family firms' social orientation, variety of social innovations, level of family firms' social engagement, the relationship between financial and social wealth, and the link between internationalization and social innovations.

Family Firms' Social Orientation

Earlier, we noted the paucity of empirical research into the social orientation and responsibility of family firms. We have also highlighted some key studies that examined family firms' social responsibility in Table 22.3. Given the social focus of family firms, it is essential to examine these issues closely

in future research. There is a considerable body of research on both CSR and socioemotional wealth. Future researchers could build on the progress made in this research when mapping their research agenda.

Future studies need to give special attention to the dimensions of social orientation that might be especially unique to family firms. Once these dimensions are identified and measured, they could be empirically related to other facets of a family firm's social orientation. Researchers could then proceed to establish how these unique dimensions relate to family firms' strategic moves, financial performance, growth, and survival. Researchers can also identify the contingencies that determine the gains that family firms might achieve by participating in social innovation. These contingencies might vary across industries, stages of firm growth, and different family firm ownership structures. It would be possible also to link these dimensions of family firms' social orientation to the various types of social innovations in which these firms participate or undertake. While it is reasonable and logical to assume a significant relationship between social orientation and social innovation, empirical research would help to clarify how this orientation might influence social innovation and vice versa.

Variations in Social Innovations

Social innovations differ significantly in their purpose, time span, resource and skill requirements, affected stakeholders, and potential social and financial results. Currently, there is no widely accepted typology of these innovations, making it essential to examine and document the types of social innovations garner family firms' participation. This raises several questions. What role do the nature, scope, timeliness, and potential effect of these innovations have in determining this involvement? Do these firms favor social innovations that are likely to have immediate and mostly local impact? Further, what role does the identity of participants have in this regard? The composition of participants can significantly affect the potential social capital family firms can amass from their involvement; this might give some family firms an incentive to become more actively engaged in particular social innovations. Likewise, how do the potential gains from this involvement influence family firms' choices of social innovations?

Another important avenue for research is to explore the various mechanisms by which social innovations enrich family firms' entrepreneurial capabilities. We have highlighted the importance of these firms' learning from and through social innovations. Other mechanisms might be relevant and need documentation. Toward this end, it would be useful to validate the potential differences between family and non-family firms that we have presented in Table 22.4 and understand how they might influence the types and evolution of their entrepreneurial capabilities. Perhaps different types of family firms emphasize different constellations of capabilities that, collectively, lead to variations in pursuit of social innovations, profitability and growth.

Variations in Family Firms' Scale (Level) of Engagement

Family firms will typically have multiple opportunities to pursue social innovations. Some may focus a specific social innovation. Others might pursue multiple innovations. This raises a question: How do family firms make these choices? If they pursue multiple social innovations, how do they sequence their participation in these activities? Being active in multiple innovation domains can tax both the resources of the organization and the attention of senior executives. Consequently, we need to pay greater attention to understanding how managers sequence their involvement.

Another area that deserves research attention is how family firm managers learn from one innovation and subsequently use this learning when they undertake other social innovations. Innovation is

rarely a straightforward process, and family firm managers learn from not only their efforts but also their mistakes. Also, there might be vicarious learning. These different types of learning can add to the knowledge base of the family firm, especially about social innovations. To understand this effect, researchers need to document family firms' different learning outcomes, and how firms capture this learning, and use it in their own operations. Fortunately, the organizational learning theory (Argote, 1999; Huber, 1991) and knowledge-based view of the firm (Grant, 1996) offer a great deal of insight into these issues. Applying these theories to family firms could enrich the literature (Cabrera-Suarez et al., 2001). Similarly, regional and national institutions might influence collaborative activities such as social innovations. It would be instructive to extend the application of neo-institutional theory to examining family firms' decisions about these innovations.

Different members of the owner family might also support different innovations and resist coordination, hoping to retain their flexibility and responsiveness as conditions change. This approach can lead to the fragmentation of focus and effort, raise costs, and even deprive family firms from achieving the benefits that could accrue from social innovations. Empirical research would help us better understand how family firms coordinate the various activities associated with social innovation. Some firms might keep these activities independent while others may follow a portfolio approach to developing and managing these innovations, thus capitalizing on their interdependence. Research into these issues can clarify why family firms may benefit differentially from their involvement with different types of social innovations. Future research should also document how a family firm's culture might promote or discourage this coordination. As with other innovations, social innovation can be encouraged at the family and business levels through the organizational culture of the family business (Zahra et al., 2004). Since organizational culture often influences a firm's most important decisions, this influence also pertains to social innovation-related decisions. In organizational cultures that focus on the group rather than the individual (Hofstede, 2001), one can expect greater interest in social innovation.

The Relationship between Financial and Social Wealth

Some social innovations ameliorate particular social problems but may not result in financial wealth creation. Other innovations simply promote social wealth. This raises the question: How do family firms transform this social wealth to competitive or financial gains? What are the key mechanisms that effect this transformation? We have addressed this issue partially by underscoring the critical importance of social entrepreneurship. However, other mechanisms might exist and our earlier discussion highlights some of these, including the creation and maintenance of social capital (Zahra, 2010), building connections to existing networks, solidifying and improving the firm's reputation, enhancing the legitimacy of the company and its operations, attracting new customer groups, accumulating slack resources, and promoting learning as well as increasing knowledge production and use. Researchers need to identify the approaches that family firms employ to capture value from participating in social innovations. They also need to explore key conditions under which these benefits materialize and, in turn, how they relate to financial wealth which is essential in building the slack resources that enable family firms to support social innovations and CSR activities that generate social wealth.

Internationalization and Social Innovations

With family firms rapidly increasing their international operations (Fernández and Nieto,

2014, in this *Handbook*), it becomes important to explore how their growing global presence might influence their support for social innovations. Opportunities for social innovations frequently transcend national borders because of the growing connectedness of countries, industries, and businesses. Indeed, some of the same social issues appear to afflict different parts of the globe, sometimes for different reasons but with the same devastating effects. Solutions devised in one country could be diffused to other countries.

The prevalence, scope and adverse effect of social problems often influence family firms' attention to them (Zahra et al., 2008). This is why we need to probe how family firms decide which social issues to tackle domestically and which ones globally. What are the variables that determine such differential attention? Do these firms allocate different resources to these causes? How do they coordinate the various activities related to domestic and internationally focused social innovations? Given that family firms make decisions based on financial and non-financial considerations (Hirigoyen and Labaki, 2012), how do these variables influence the mix of global opportunities pursued and types of social innovations introduced? Given that internationalization provides a setting in which organizations learn, we should ask: What do family firms learn from their engagement in such innovations that are global in scope and scale? Is this learning different from what family firms experience domestically? How do these companies capture and then use that learning from social innovations in their domestic and international operations? Does engagement in global social issues open business opportunities for family firms? If so, how and when does it happen?

CONCLUSION

The important role of family firms has drawn attention to their potential contributions to social innovations. These innovations are usually complex, expensive and time consuming.

They also require collective action, prompting family firms to join forces with other private companies, public organizations, non-government entities, and traditional institutions (e.g., religious, tribal etc.). Social innovations, however, focus on improving the common good, transcending the reforms enacted by the state *and* exceeding familiar social entrepreneurial activities. Yet, these innovations are also risky and their failure can undermine the reputation and market standing of family firms. Conversely, social innovations can enrich the family firms' knowledge base through learning, enhance firms' innovativeness and social capital, and provide opportunities to engage and develop members of the family's next generations. By pursuing these innovations, family firms stand to profit and grow while enriching their community or nation's social wealth. Clearly, social innovations and the role family firms play in promoting them are an area that demands thoughtful analysis and study. We hope our work encourages future researchers to systematically examine the contributions of family firms to social innovations and how their participation in these innovations might transform their businesses and operations.

REFERENCES

Allouche, J. and Amann, B. (1995). Le retour triomphant du capitalisme familial. *De Jacques Coeur à Renault: gestionnaires et organisations.* Toulouse: Presses de l'Université des Sciences Sociales de Toulouse.

Amit, R. and Villalonga, B. (2014). Financial performance of family firms. In L. Melin, M. Nordqvist, and P. Sharma (eds), *The SAGE Handbook of Family Business:* London: Sage.

Anderson, R.C., Duru, A., and Reeb, D.M. (2009). Founders, heirs, and corporate opacity in the United States. *Journal of Financial Economics*, 92(2), 205–222.

Anderson, R.C. and Reeb, D.M. (2003). Founding family ownership and firm performance: Evidence from the S&P 500. *The Journal of Finance*, 58(3), 1301–1328.

Argote, L. (1999). *Organizational Learning: Creating, Retaining and Transferring Knowledge.* Boston, MA: Kluwer.

Astrachan, J.H. and Jaskiewicz, P. (2008). Emotional returns and emotional costs in privately held family businesses: Advancing traditional business valuation. *Family Business Review*, 21(2), 139–149.

Austin, J., Stevenson, H., and Wei-Skillern, J. (2006). Social and commercial entrepreneurship: same, different, or both? *Entrepreneurship: Theory and Practice*, 30(1), 1–22.

Banfield, E.C. (1958). *The Moral Basis of a Backward Society.* Glencoe, IL: Free Press.

Barnea, A. and Rubin, A. (2010). Corporate social responsibility as a conflict between shareholders. *Journal of Business Ethics*, 97(1), 71–86.

Bergfeld, M.-M. (2011). Germany's high performance family firms pursue pan-generational entrepreneurship along technology lifecycles. Paper presented at the FERC, Grand Rapids.

Berrone, P., Cruz, C., and Gomez-Mejia, L.R. (2014). Family controlled firms and stakeholder management: A socioemotional wealth preservation perspective. In L. Melin, M. Nordqvist, and P. Sharma (eds), *The SAGE Handbook of Family Business*: London: Sage.

Bingham, J.B., Gibb Dyer, W., Smith, I., and Adams, G.L. (2011). A stakeholder identity orientation approach to corporate social performance in family firms. *Journal of Business Ethics*, 99(4), 565–585.

Block, J.H. (2010a). R&D investments in family and founder firms: An agency perspective. *Journal of Business Venturing*, 27(2), 248–265.

Block, J. (2010b). Family management, family ownership, and downsizing: evidence from S&P 500 firms. *Family Business Review*, 23(2), 109.

Brooks, H. (1982). Social and technological innovation. In S.B. Lundstedt and E.W. Colglazier Jr. (eds), *Managing Innovation. The Social Dimensions of Creativity, Invention and Technology* (pp. 1–30). New York: Pergamon Press.

Bruton, G.D., Ahlstrom, D., and Obloj, K. (2008). Entrepreneurship in emerging economies: Where are we today and where should the research go in the future. *Entrepreneurship: Theory and Practice*, 32(1), 1–14.

Cabrera-Suarez, K., De Saa-Perez, P., and Garcia-Almeida, D. (2001). The succession process from a resource- and knowledge-based view of the family firm. *Family Business Review*, 14(1), 37–46.

Capron, M. and Quairel Lanoizelée, F. (2007). *La responsabilité sociale d'entreprise*. Paris: La Découverte.

Craig, J. and Dibrell, C. (2006). The natural environment, innovation, and firm performance: A comparative study. *Family Business Review*, 19(4), 275–288.

De la Cruz Déniz Déniz, M. and Suarez, M.K.C. (2005). Corporate social responsibility and family business in Spain. *Journal of Business Ethics*, 56(1), 27–41.

Dyer, W.G. and Whetten, D.A. (2006). Family firms and social responsibility: Preliminary evidence from the S&P 500. *Entrepreneurship: Theory and Practice*, 30, 785–802.

Emerson, R.M. (1976). Social exchange theory. *Annual Review of Sociology*, 2, 335–362.

Fernández, Z. and Nieto, M.J. (2014). Internationalization of family firms. In L. Melin, M. Nordqvist, and P. Sharma (eds), *The SAGE Handbook of Family Business*. London: Sage.

Fisscher, O., Frenkel, D., Lurie, Y., and Nijhof, A. (2005). Stretching the frontiers: Exploring the relationships between entrepreneurship and ethics. *Journal of Business Ethics*, 60(3), 207–209.

Gnan, L. and Montemerlo, D. (2002). The multiple facets of family firms' social role: Empirical Evidence from Italian SMEs. Paper presented at the Family Business Network 13th Annual Conference, Helsinki, Finland.

Goel, S. and Labaki, R. (2010). Wealth appropriation from minority investors – A nuanced, multi-objective comparison between family and non-family governance modes. Paper presented at the Family Enterprise Research Conference (FERC).

Gomez-Mejia, L.R., Haynes, K.T., Nunez-Nickel, M., Jacobson, K.J.L., and Moyano-Fuentes, J. (2007). Socioemotional wealth and business risks in family-controlled firms: Evidence from Spanish olive oil mills. *Administrative Science Quarterly*, 52(1), 106–137.

Graafland, J.J. (2002). Corporate social responsibility and family business. Paper presented at the Research Forum of the13th Annual Family Business Network Conference, Helsinki, Finland.

Grant, R.M. (1996). Toward a knowledge-based theory of the firm. *Strategic Management Journal*, 17, 109–122.

Harvey, M. and Evans, R.E. (1994). Family business and multiple levels of conflict. *Family Business Review*, 7(4), 331–348.

Hirigoyen, G. and Labaki, R. (2012). The role of regret in the owner-manager decision-making in the family business: A conceptual approach. *Journal of Family Business Strategy*, 3(2), 118–126.

Hofstede, G. (2001). *Culture's Consequences* (2nd edn). Beverley Hills, CA: Sage Publications.

Howaldt, J. and Schwarz, M. (2010). Social innovation: Concepts, research fields and international trends. Available at: http://www.sfs-dortmund.de/odb/Repository/Publication/Doc%5C1289%5CIMO_Trendstudie_ Howaldt_Schwarz_englische_Version.pdf (accessed August 20, 2011).

Huber, G.P. (1991). Organizational learning: The contributing processes and the literatures. *Organization Science*, 2(1), 88–115.

Jehn, K.A. (1995). A multimethod examination of the benefits and detriments of intragroup conflict. *Administrative Science Quarterly*, 256–282.

Jehn, K.A. and Bendersky, C. (2003). Intragroup conflict in organizations: A contingency perspective on the conflict-outcome relationship. *Research in Organizational Behavior*, 25, 187–242.

Kellermanns, F.W. and Eddleston, K.A. (2004). Feuding families: When conflict does a family firm good. *Entrepreneurship: Theory and Practice*, 28(3), 209–228.

Khavul, S., Bruton, G.D., and Wood, E. (2009). Informal family business in Africa. *Entrepreneurship: Theory and Practice*, 33(6), 1219–1238.

Litz, R.A. and Kleysen, R.F. (2001). Your old men shall dream dreams, your young men shall see visions: Toward a theory of family firm innovation with help from the Brubeck family. *Family Business Review*, 14(4), 335.

Lumpkin, G.T. and Brigham, K.H. (2011). Long-term orientation and intertemporal choice in family firms. *Entrepreneurship: Theory and Practice*, 35(6), 1149–1169.

Lumpkin, G.T., Brigham, K.H., and Moss, T.W. (2010). Long-term orientation: Implications for the entrepreneurial orientation and performance of family businesses. *Entrepreneurship and Regional Development*, 22(3–4), 241–264.

Lumpkin, G.T. and Dess, G.G. (1996). Clarifying the entrepreneurial orientation construct and linking it to performance. *Academy of Management Review*, 21, 135–172.

McKelvie, A., McKenny, A., Lumpkin, G.T. and Short, J.C. (2014). Corporate entrepreneurship in family business: Past contribution and future opportunities. In L. Melin, M. Nordqvist, and P. Sharma (eds), *The SAGE Handbook of Family Business*. London: Sage.

Makoba, J.W. (1993). Toward a general theory of social exchange. *Social Behavior and Personality: An International Journal*, 21(3), 227–239.

Mignon, S. (2000). La pérennité des entreprises familiales: un modèle alternatif à la création de valeur pour l'actionnaire. *Finance, Contrôle, Stratégie*, 3(1), 169–196.

Miller, D., Le Breton-Miller, I., and Scholnick, B. (2008). Stewardship vs. stagnation: An empirical comparison of small family and non-family businesses. *Journal of Management Studies*, 45(1), 51–78.

Morck, R., Stangeland, D.A., and Yeung, B. (2000). Inherited wealth, corporate control, and economic growth: The Canadian disease. In R. Morck (ed.),

Concentrated Corporate Ownership (pp. 319–369). Chicago, IL: University of Chicago Press.

Morck, R. and Yeung, B. (2004). Family control and the rent-seeking society. *Entrepreneurship: Theory & Practice*, 28(4), 391–409.

Munari, F., Oriani, R., and Sobrero, M. (2010). The effects of owner identity and external governance systems on R&D investments: A study of Western European firms. *Research Policy*, 39(8), 1093–1104.

Muñoz-Bullón, F. and Sanchez-Bueno, M.J. (2011). The Impact of family involvement on the R&D intensity of publicly traded firms. *Family Business Review*, 24(1), 62–70.

Naldi, L., Nordqvist, M., Sjöberg, K., and Wiklund, J. (2007). Entrepreneurial orientation, risk taking, and performance in family firms. *Family Business Review*, 20(1), 33–47.

Niehm, L.S., Swinney, J., and Miller, N.J. (2008). Community social responsibility and its consequences for family business performance. *Journal of Small Business Management*, (3), 331–350.

Pelled, L.H. (1996). Demographic diversity, conflict, and work group outcomes: An intervening process theory. *Organization Science*, (6), 615–631.

Perrini, F. and Minoja, M. (2008). Strategizing corporate social responsibility: Evidence from an Italian medium-sized, family-owned company. *Business Ethics: A European Review*, 17(1), 47–63.

Putnam, R.D., Leonardi, R., and Nanetti, R. (1993). *Making Democracy Work: Civic Traditions in Modern Italy*. Princeton, NY: Princeton Univ Press.

Sachs, W.M., Dieleman, M., and Suder, G.G.S. (2008). Expropriation of minority shareholders or social dividend? Beware of good corporate citizens. *International Business under Adversity: A Role in Corporate Responsibility, Conflict Prevention and Peace* (pp. 57–72). Cheltenham, UK and Northampton, MA: Edward Elgar.

Schulze, W.S., Lubatkin, M.H., Dino, R.N., and Buchholtz, A.K. (2001). Agency relationships in family firms: Theory and evidence. *Organization Science*, 99–116.

Uhlaner, L.M., Goor-Balk, H.J.M.V., and Masurel, E. (2004). Family business and corporate social responsibility in a sample of Dutch firms. *Journal of Small Business and Enterprise Development*, 11(2), 186–194.

Wagner, M. (2008). *Links Between Sustainability-Related Innovation and Sustainability Management* (Discussion Paper 2008–046). Berlin: Technische Universität München.

Zahra, S.A. (2005). Entrepreneurial risk taking in family firms. *Family Business Review*, 18(1), 23–40.

Zahra, S.A. (2010). Harvesting family firms' organizational social capital: A relational perspective. *Journal of Management Studies*, 47(2), 345–366.

Zahra, S.A., Gedajlovic, E., Neubaum, D.O., and Shulman, J.M. (2009). A typology of social entrepreneurs: Motives, search processes and ethical challenges. *Journal of Business Venturing*, 24(5), 519–532.

Zahra, S.A., Hayton, J.C., and Salvato, C. (2004). Entrepreneurship in family vs. non-family firms: A resource-based analysis of the effect of organizational culture. *Entrepreneurship: Theory & Practice*, 28(4), 363–381.

Zahra, S.A., Rawhouser, H.N., Bhawe, N., Neubaum, D.O., and Hayton, J.C. (2008). Globalization of social entrepreneurship opportunities. *Strategic Entrepreneurship Journal*, 2(2), 117–131.

PART IV

Behavioral and Organizational Aspects in Family Business Studies

23

Values in Family Business

Ritch L. Sorenson

INTRODUCTION

Why should we focus research attention on values in family businesses? Like other kinds of businesses, family businesses are social systems. However, unlike other businesses, in family businesses the family is part of the overall business enterprise's social system. Values help participants of social systems agree on what is important. Values are the 'implicit or explicit conceptions of the desirable' (Koiranen, 2002). We can better understand family businesses by understanding the values that are important in the family and in the business, the relationship between family and business values, antecedents to values, and how values relate to family and business outcomes. Assessing values in the business and the family provides one way to determine the extent to which the family and the business are aligned, or in other words, the extent to which the business is a *family* business.

Values provide a basis for policies and practices. For example, a pivotal value in family firms is the priority given to family or to business. Families that prefer business stability and performance over family outcomes may adopt policies and practices that minimize family involvement or that require family members to meet strict business qualifications and performance standards to work in the business. Business families that give priority to the family may develop policies and practices that enable family members to gain management experience in their businesses or to start businesses, providing opportunities that family members might not otherwise have.

Culture defines how individuals in the family and the business are expected to behave socially. Values, combined with common beliefs, meanings, norms, and symbols, make up the culture in the family and the business. Values are the core element of culture. Thus, the purpose of this chapter is to provide an overview of foundational and family business research about values and culture in an effort to summarize how family values and culture become a part of the business and suggest further opportunities for values and culture research in family business.

RESEARCH ABOUT VALUES AND CULTURE

The literature on values extends back to the writings of Plato and other early philosophers. Reviewing this extensive literature is not possible within this chapter. Therefore, I briefly summarize selections of recent foundational research on values and culture written by well-recognized scholars within a broad context that may be applicable to family business research. Then, I provide further examples of values and culture research that specifically focus on family business.

The values and culture research were conducted using questionnaire survey and qualitative research methodologies. First, I summarize examples of research that use a questionnaire survey approach. Questionnaire surveys allow researchers to quickly gather information from large samples and obtain comparisons, contrasts, and correlations among values, culture, and other variables. Then, I provide an overview of qualitative research. Qualitative research uses several research methods to identify how values and culture come about and to what effect. Because of its in-depth nature that includes interviews, field notes, and archival data, qualitative research typically has a low sample size.

The following overview includes research approaches, definitions, and findings relevant to family business.

Foundational Values and Culture Questionnaire Survey Research

Milton Rokeach (1973) developed a survey questionnaire called the Rokeach Values Survey. He found that people have similar values but rank them differently. Rokeach indicated that 'values are generalized, enduring beliefs about the personal and social desirability of certain modes of conduct or end-states of existence' (1973: 5). The strength of the Rokeach Values Survey is that it can be used individually or across groups to assess values similarities and differences.

Rokeach (1973) categorized values into two major types. He referred to values that related to preferred modes of conduct as *instrumental values* and to values that related to preferred end states of existence as *terminal values*.

Rokeach (1973) subcategorized instrumental values into two types. *Moral values* refer to maintaining interpersonal relationships; when moral values are violated, they result in 'pangs of conscience or feelings of guilt for wrongdoing ... Thus behaving honestly and responsibly leads one to believe he is behaving morally' (Rokeach, 1973: 8). *Moral values* include qualities of being 'courageous,' 'forgiving,' 'helpful,' 'honest,' 'loving,' 'obedient,' 'polite,' 'responsible,' and 'self controlled.' *Competence values* refer to personal characteristics and include attributes of being 'ambitious,' 'capable,' 'imaginative,' 'independent,' 'intellectual,' and 'logical.'

Terminal values refer to desirable 'end-states of existence' or outcomes, and Rokeach (1973) indicates that there are two kinds of terminal values. *Personal values* include preferred personal outcomes such as 'a comfortable life,' 'an exciting life,' 'a sense of accomplishment,' 'happiness,' 'inner harmony,' 'pleasure,' 'salvation,' and 'wisdom.' *Social values* include preferred group or societal outcomes such as 'a world at peace,' 'a world of beauty,' 'equality,' 'family security,' 'national security,' 'and 'social recognition.'

Rokeach conducted extensive survey research, and his work continues to influence family business researchers. This chapter frequently refers to Rokeach's work and values terminology, primarily to moral and competence values.

Shalom Schwartz (1992), who based his work in part on Rokeach (1973), developed a Theory of Human Values, which has received considerable empirical support. Schwartz indicated that values are motivational beliefs that transcend specific situations; they serve as criteria for the selection and evaluation of actions and they are ordered in importance in relation to one another (Schwartz, 2006). Using survey questionnaires he found ten values that are common across cultures: 'self-direction,' 'stimulation,' 'hedonism,' 'achievement,' 'power,' 'security,' 'conformity,' 'tradition,' 'benevolence,' and 'universalism.' He examined relationships among these ten values and found that values are related to one another (Schwartz, 1992). For example, the values of self-direction, hedonism, and stimulation are positively related to one another; furthermore the values of security, conformity and tradition are also positively related to one another. But in these two examples, the first set of values is somewhat negatively related to the second set of values.

Geert Hofstede (1980, 1997, 2001) studied values as a part of organizational and national cultures. In his book *Cultures and Organizations: Software of the Mind,* Hoftstede provides the following definition:

> Values are broad tendencies to prefer certain states of affairs over others. Values are feelings with an arrow to them: they have a plus and a minus side. They deal with evil vs good, dirty vs clean, ugly vs beautiful … . (1997: 5–6)

Hofstede indicates that emotions associated with values differ in degrees of intensity – some outcomes may feel good or very good and others feel bad or very bad. Hofstede studied cultures within organizations around the world. Based on his research, he suggested that all cultures have similar values; however, 'standards for values that exist within a group or category of people' make each culture unique (Hofstede, 2001: 9).

Hofstede used survey questionnaires to gather and aggregate data to develop national cultural dimensions. The national culture dimensions are 'power distance,' 'individualism vs collectivism,' 'uncertainty avoidance,' 'masculinity vs femininity,' 'long-term orientation,' and 'indulgence vs restraint.'

House et al. (2004) in *Culture, Leadership, and Organizations: The GLOBE Study of 62 Societies,* examine the interface of culture, leadership, and organization using both quantitative and qualitative data. The GLOBE research project examined culture as practices of 'the way things are done,' and values

as 'the way things should be done.' This research expanded Hofstede's culture dimensions from six to nine dimensions: 'future orientation,' 'gender egalitarianism,' 'assertiveness,' 'humane orientation,' 'in-group collectivism,' 'institutional collectivism,' 'performance orientation,' 'power distance,' and 'uncertainty avoidance.' Based on their data, House et al. (2004) demonstrate that societal systems and worldviews have major effects on organizational cultures. Using their data, they identified ten culture clusters across the globe. This research is especially relevant to family business because it explores the influence of family on cultural, leadership, and organizational practices.

Family Business Values and Culture Questionnaire Survey Research

Below, I summarize survey research about values and culture that has been conducted in family businesses. Where relevant, I show relationships between family business research and the foundational research described above.

Donckels and Fröhlich (1991) used survey data from the STRATOS (strategic orientations of small- and medium-sized enterprises) project to examine the differences between family and non-family firms across eight European countries. From the values and attitudes portion of their survey, Donckels and Fröhlich found that compared with other owners, owners of family businesses agreed that 'satisfied employees were always good employees,' and that 'innovation involves too much risk.' Donckels and Fröhlich also found that in comparison to non-family firms, owners of family firms disagreed more frequently that 'employees should share in ownership,' 'clear hierarchical relationships should be established,' 'managers should encourage even risky innovation,' '[the business owner] should inform its employees regularly about its policy,' and 'firms should cooperate with other firms … even at the expense of some independence.'

Matti Koiranen (2002) asked family executives of Finnish family firms to assess how a list of values, presented as adjectives, had fundamentally influenced family firms to last more than 100 years. Three of the top values might be classified as moral values – 'honesty,' 'credibility,' and 'obeying the law.' Two of the values might be considered under Rokeach's definition competence values – 'quality' and 'industrious/hardworking.' Surprisingly, economic return to owners was rated low.

Koiranen (2002) asked respondents which values described the family and the present generation controlling the firm. Moral values listed were 'responsible' and 'fair,' and competence values were 'committed' and 'hardworking.' In general, the families in this study tended to place much higher emphasis on the means (instrumental values) rather than on the ends (terminal values).

Garcia-Alvarez and López-Sintas (2001) studied the values of family business founders. They defined values as, 'standards that guide our behavior and lead us to take a particular position on social issues and influence others.' They also indicated that values guide daily activities and reflect human needs. A contribution of this study is that the field interviews were used to develop a list of values specific to family businesses, which more tightly align with family firms than those coming from more general frameworks (e.g., Rokeach, 1973; Hoftstede, 2001; Schwartz, 2006).

Garcia-Alvarez and López-Sintas (2001) used a multidimensional scaling technique to reveal two dimensions underlying owners' values, which they labeled 'business' and 'psychosocial dimensions.' The authors labeled one end of the business dimension, 'family business as an end.' Values at the extreme of this dimension included 'business orientation,' 'ambition,' 'entrepreneurship,' and 'firm growth.' The other end of the business dimension was labeled 'business as a means.' Values at the extreme of this dimension included 'innovation,' 'family orientation,' and 'cosmopolitan orientation.'

The psychosocial dimension was anchored at one end by 'self-fulfillment.' Values at the extreme of this dimension included 'determination,' 'hard work,' and 'sense of achievement.'

The other anchor for the psychosocial dimension was 'group orientation.' The values at the extreme of this dimension included 'risk aversion,' 'stability,' 'sense of family,' 'constancy,' and 'satisfaction.'

Founders fell into one of four quadrants based on their combined set of values. About one-fourth of the founders emphasized moral values and strong personal relationships. About one-half viewed the business as a means to support the family; otherwise, they emphasized values associated with entrepreneurship or technical business performance. About one-quarter of the founders valued business growth and self-fulfillment, but not interpersonal relationships. Overall, the founders with a group orientation were risk averse and desired to maintain family satisfaction. For those who saw the business as a means, wealth and social status seemed somewhat of a high priority.

Astrachan et al. (2002) developed a survey designed to assess family influence on the business (see also Klein et al., 2005). The questionnaire, called the F-PEC Scale, assessed power, experience, and culture. Three of the culture items in the F-PEC assess the extent to which family members share values with one another and with the business. Other culture items measure the extent to which family members are committed to and invest themselves in the business's goals and vision.

Zahra et al. (2008) indicate that family businesses may have what they refer to as 'cultures of commitment' (measured by some of the culture items from F-PEC; Astrachan et al., 2002) and 'cultures of stewardship.' From their survey, they found that stewardship-oriented organizational cultures positively moderate the relationship between family commitment and strategic flexibility in family firms.

Zahra et al. (2004) used survey data to examine relationships between family business cultures and entrepreneurship. Culture was defined as coherent patterns of values and beliefs. Significant findings in this study were that the following family business cultural orientations were positively related to entrepreneurship: (1) moderate individualistic orientation; (2) external orientation; (3) emphasis on decentralization and entrepreneurship; (4) emphasis on strategic rather than financial controls; and (5) a long-term orientation. This study defined dimensions that seemed similar to the cultural dimensions developed by Hofstede (1997, 2001).

Denison et al. (2004) used the Denison Organizational Culture Survey – a measure of cultural beliefs and assumptions in business organizations – to compare family and non-family firms. Although the sample of family firms was relatively small (20) compared to non-family firms (389), they found that the cultures of family firms were more 'positive' than non-family firms. Family firms scored higher on all 12 dimensions. Only 'capability development' was significantly different ($p = 0.05$), however. Measures of 'core values' and 'agreement' were marginally significantly different ($p = 0.20$).

Foundational Values and Culture Qualitative Research

Florence Kluckhohn and Fred Strodtbeck (1961) introduced Value Orientation Theory. They examined cross-cultural and intergenerational values within small communities. Their approach was heavily influenced by Clyde Kluckhohn, who defined a value as, 'A conception, explicit or implicit, distinctive of an individual or characteristic of a group, of the desirable which influences the selection from available modes, means and ends of action' (Kluckhohn, 1951: 395). To gather information about values, Kluckhohn and Strodtbeck used intensive interviews, often asking interviewees for responses to moral dilemmas.

Organizational Culture studies emerged in the 1980s designed to uncover and explain 'how things are done around here.' Researchers used interviews, archival data, and summary observations of symbolic artifacts, sayings, stories, and the like to reveal and identify organizational culture. Below, I provide representative comments from leading scholars about organizational culture:

Social action is considered possible because of consensually determined meanings for experience that, to an external observer, may have the appearance of an independent rule-like existence. (Linda Smircich, 1983: 352)

To analyze *why* members behave the way they do, we often look for the values that govern behavior ... [and] the *underlying assumptions,* which are typically unconscious but which actually determine how group members perceive, think, and feel. (Edgar Schein, 1985: 3)

[E]xamined from a cultural viewpoint, ... organizational life ... such as the stories people tell newcomers ... the ways in which offices are arranged ... jokes people tell, the working atmosphere ... and the relations among people ... [reveals] patterns of meaning that link these manifestations together ... . (Joanne Martin, 2002: 1)

[O]rganizational culture ... include[s] values and assumptions about social reality, but for me values are less central and less useful than meanings and symbolism in cultural analysis. (Mats Alvesson, 2002: 3)

Together, these comments illustrate that culture encompasses values, beliefs, and assumptions, which are not directly observable but can be revealed through rituals, symbols, stories, behavior, and artifacts.

Because a complete review is beyond the scope of this chapter, researchers examining family business culture should review the organizational culture/symbolism and other relevant organizational literature to enrich family business studies (e.g., see Alvesson, 1993; Barney, 1986; Martin, 2002: Schoenenberger, 1997).

Family Business Value and Culture Qualitative Research

Dyer (1986), in *Cultural Change in Family Firms*, reports an in-depth study of culture in family firms using multiple methods for gathering information. Dyer defined culture as the values and assumptions that pervade a family firm, and he defined values as 'broader transituational principles that serve as a guide for overall behavior' (Dyer, 1986: 8).

Dyer suggests that different cultures may be found in each part of the family business system – the business, the family and the board. These cultures change over a family firm's lifecycle. Based on in-depth studies of 40 family firms, Dyer identified four common cultural patterns of leadership: 'paternalistic,' 'laissez-faire,' 'participative,' and 'professional.' He illustrates how underlying values and assumptions are revealed in organizational practices. Dyer summarized elements of culture in a 'culture map,' which will be discussed later in this chapter.

Payne et al. (2011) used content analyses to examine the presence of organizational virtues in letters written to shareholders in firms listed in the S&P 500 Index from 2001 through 2005. They operationalized organizational virtues as an orientation towards ethical beliefs and values. Payne et al. (2011) found that compared with non-family businesses, family firms made significantly more references to the virtues of 'empathy,' 'warmth,' and 'zeal,' and significantly less reference to 'courage.' Payne et al. (2011) noted that empathy and warmth demonstrate the importance of 'concern,' 'reassurance,' 'supportiveness,' 'sympathy,' 'friendliness,' 'openness,' 'pleasantness,' and 'straight-forwardness,' which are consistent with a 'harmonious culture.' These virtues seem consistent with Rokeach's (1973) moral values that promote interpersonal relationships. Zeal was associated with 'excitement,' 'imagination,' 'innovation,' and 'spirit,' which may be associated with the family's identity with the ideology and legacy of the founder.

The one virtue that family firms mentioned much less frequently than non-family firms was 'courage.' Courage included the ideals of 'achievement,' 'ambition,' 'competency,' and 'leadership,' similar to Rokeach's (1973) competency values.

Hall et al. (2001) examined the impact of family business culture on entrepreneurial change in family firms. Based on the organizational literature, they developed a conceptual framework that showed how family business cultures can (1) emanate from one person or a family; (2) be open or closed to external influence; and (3) be implicit (unrecognized), or explicit (recognized). They used interviews and observations to study in-depth the cultures of two family firms and found that family firms enable change when cultures become open and explicit.

Ceja et al. (2010) examined and compared the value statements of the world's largest non-family (150) and family firms (100). The top three values mentioned for both types of firms were 'integrity,' 'respect,' and 'customers.' Most of the remaining values were similar for both types of firms. Values unique to family-owned firms were 'generosity,' 'humility,' 'communication,' 'service,' 'quality,' 'excellence,' 'creativity' and 'entrepreneurship.'

Sorenson (2011) convened a conference among family business owners, advisors, and researchers which structured dialogue among the participants to enable a better understanding of social capital in family firms. Conference presentations, dialogue, and papers provided insights about how values and cultures are developed in family firms. The conference process occurred in the following manner: (1) participants were prepared for dialogue by papers and presentations that summarized social capital research, language, and concepts; (2) following the presentations, participants engaged in a dialogue that enabled them to explore the concepts from their own experiences and perspectives; (3) participants developed an accumulated body of knowledge through attending three two-hour dialogue sessions; (4) researchers, advisors, and owners met in peer groups to discuss possible applications of the knowledge; and (5) researchers revised their papers and advisors and owners wrote papers that discussed how social capital concepts applied in their professions or families. Published proceedings of the conference included participant papers and summaries of dialogue (Sorenson, 2011).

The structured dialogue revealed the following about developing social capital in families: Open communication guided by rules and patterns provide the foundation for family social capital. Family, business, and family-business identities shape how family members relate to one another, to the business, and to the larger community (see Whetten et al., 2014, in this *Handbook*, for a discussion of organizational identity). Communication that promotes a common identity and a strong emotional bond promotes common trust.

Summary and Research Implications

While this overview of values and culture research is not comprehensive, it provides insight into how questionnaire survey and qualitative research have been used to understand values and culture. Below, based on the preceding summary, I provide a selective review of opportunities for research about family business values and culture:

- Rokeach's (1973) moral and competence values reappeared in much of the research summarized in this chapter. Moral values emerged most when referring to family or group relationships. Competence values related primarily to business performance (see also Tapies and Ward, 2008). Researchers might examine the antecedents and outcomes of moral and competence values in both the family and the business.
- Schwartz's (1992) research revealed how values cluster together. Similar to Schwartz, family business researchers might fruitfully examine values clusters within and across family firms.
- Garcia-Alvarez and López-Sintas (2001) provide an exemplar study for examining clusters of values in family firms. Future research might build upon this type of study to explore values clusters and their relationships to family and business outcomes.
- Hofstede's (1997, 2001) and House et al.'s (2005) GLOBE research might be used to examine the effect of national cultures and culture clusters on family business cultures and practices. For example, do long-term orientation cultures produce family firms that endure across generations? Do family businesses in cultures high in power distance have more or less difficulty with succession? Do family businesses in high uncertainty avoidance cultures have less entrepreneurship?
- The F-PEC scale (Astrachan et al., 2002) reveals values consistency within families, and between families and businesses. Researchers might use qualitative methods to determine the practices that produce common values. In addition, the F-PEC measure includes survey questions about family commitment to business values and goals. As Zahra et al. (2004) have done, researchers might examine the impact of cultures on organizational activity and outcomes. In addition, they might use qualitative research to determine what produces cultures of family commitment to business vision and goals.
- Several qualitative approaches to understanding values and culture were summarized. In addition, a chapter summarizing an anthropological approach to qualitative research is provided by Stewart, 2014, in this *Handbook*. As was indicated previously, qualitative research might be used to identify norms and practices that are associated with values within a few businesses. Then, based on qualitative researcher findings, researchers might develop questionnaires to survey many families and businesses to compare values and cultures. For example, Sorenson (2000) developed a questionnaire based on Dyer's (1986) leadership cultures to examine leadership across family businesses.

Much of the research provided above was based on the assumption that in family firms, family values and culture influence business values and culture. Below, based partially on the research referred to above, but primarily quantitative research, I suggest *how* values are developed in families and then how family values become a part of the business. The intent of this summary is to stimulate research about values and culture in family business.

HOW DO FAMILIES ESTABLISH COMMON VALUES?

The social capital literature provides insights into how owning families and business social systems develop common values and culture (e.g., Coleman, 1988; Hoffman et al., 2006; Nahapiet and Ghoshal, 1998; Pearson et al., 2008). This literature suggests that for individuals to work together, they must communicate in a manner that helps them develop common values and culture (e.g., Hoffman et al., 2006). The concept of social capital emerged when organizers gathered leaders in communities to work together on projects. Developing communication among community leaders enabled them to identify common values and goals so they could work together for their common good.

The fundamental organizing element of social capital is communication. Communication is a conduit for sharing information. Communication provides the basis for finding common values, goals, norms, and expectations. Sorenson and an anonymous daughter and granddaughter (2011) of 'George and Sandra' (fictitious names to keep their identities private) describe how common family values and culture were developed within their business family. George and Sandra lived in separate communities in the 1950s, and they wrote and saved over 400 letters that revealed how their values, norms, and goals were developed while they courted.

In letters, their pattern was that one person introduced issues and responded to comments made by the other in a previous letter. In their comments, each person revealed what was important. For example, both were Catholic, and they discussed how their marriage would be a reflection of their faith and family values:

> [Sandra describing an acquaintance] 'He is the best family man and so patient with the children – oh, what an ideal husband … just like I think you'll be, if you have the chance.' George echoes her enthusiasm for raising a family and fulfilling the norms of their life together, summing it up by saying, 'Darling, it's going to be so wonderful … living together, planning together, working together (you do the dishes, I'll mow the lawn) ha-ha – and having a whole bunch of kids – blondes, brown haired, red haired, large, small, all sizes and shapes.' (Sorenson et al., 2011: 139)

Through many personal communications, George and Sandra developed common values, norms, and goals that formed a social foundation for their family. Much of their communication focused on moral (e.g., loving, helpful, and responsible) and personal values

(e.g., family security, happiness, and eternal marriage). However, they also addressed competence values associated with their work and home lives (e.g., ambitious, capable, and intelligent).

They visualized personal aspirations and described how their values would be realized. When one person mentioned an aspiration, the other often embellished it, offered a variation, suggested how he/she might contribute, or simply validated the other. They also sometimes 'owned' the other's aspirations, and encouraged the other's achievement of that aspiration.

After they were married, children were added to the family. The patterns of home and business life they had discussed and dreamed about became a reality. The values and patterns established by George and Sandra became the social environment for their children. Hofstede (2001) suggests that values are among the first thing children learn, not consciously, but implicitly through the patterns of interaction around them.

Bruess describes communication patterns at home as rituals. She describes how rituals instill and reinforce values in children:

> Rituals are frequently an invisible aspect of family dynamics; as part of the fabric of daily and sometimes mundane interaction, we often take them for granted and/or minimize their value. Yet intentionally creating and protecting family rituals can increase positive family functioning, satisfaction, help families create and maintain a shared belief structure, and encourage the intergenerational transmission of family values and attitudes. (Bruess, 2009: 1)

A daily family dinner was one of George and Sandra's rituals. While their children set the table, George and Sandra relaxed with a 'gin and tonic' and talked. Sandra had worked in their family business early on and stayed actively involved in business social functions. So the pre-dinner discussion addressed the business and the family, which allowed George and Sandra to reflect on the extent to which business and family values were aligned.

Then the family gathered around the table, said a prayer, and each family member described the events of his or her day. This daily ritual enabled the family to get caught up on individual events and subtly reinforce common values and culture.

Apparently, a ritual of dinnertime conversation is common in many business families. Angela Pritchard works in her family's business and described the dinnertime ritual in her family before she joined the business:

> One of the most important rituals our CEmO [chief emotional officer] sustained in order to protect the importance of family was dinnertime. Regardless of the situation, dinner was a priority at the Pritchard house. It was a time when business was shut off and we could simply be a family ... Our CEmO would spend her mornings before leaving for the office, or the evenings after coming home to cook and bake a beautiful meal. The dinner was always a reflection of our family's current dynamic; pasta for the older girls because they had a track meet the next evening, but with asparagus because that was my dad's favorite, some carrots for our littlest sister and a side salad in case my brother was cutting weight for wrestling ... It was a ritual, a symbolic act that we unquestionably maintained because of the value it added to our lives ... After sitting down together, praying, and dishing up our food, we would go around the table and ask one another about the best part of our day ... That one small ritual was like a green light, giving our family the go-ahead to communicate with one another about our lives. It would lead into discussions about school, sports, friends, and everything else we felt like sharing. As the years have progressed, our average dinner times have evolved into two and three hour long conversations of telling stories, reflecting on life, sharing goals, and making memories. (Pritchard, 2011: 181)

The informal communication in this family reinforces important family values. The event itself emphasizes values – each family member is important, as is gathering together as a family. What the family chose to talk about and how they talked with one another all contributed to values and culture. Much of the interplay of values in these interactions may occur at a very deep level, inter-subjectively.

Bruess suggests that what seems like normal and mundane events in families' lives, such as the dinnertimes described above, are a rich source for symbolically expressing, reinforcing, and developing values in families:

> As 'symbolically significant' interactions, rituals become important places where family 'business' is indeed accomplished, including the work of keeping in touch, updating each other on daily events, sharing fleeting (or ongoing) emotions, creating and perpetuating family identity, expressing positive or negative regard, touching base, planning, organizing, coordinating schedules, and transmitting family values between generations, among multiple other functions ... Family identity – those beliefs, values, norms, rules and expectations shared among and between members – is also sustained by family rituals. (Bruess, 2011: 115)

Values may be either explicit or implicit. *Explicit values* are verbalized. *Implicit values* are practiced but may not be recognized or verbalized. Families may be unaware of the values and culture expressed in their patterns and rituals. But together they build and reinforce family values and culture.

This brief summary is meant to provide some insights about how family values and culture are established. From a social capital perspective, families must have sufficient communication to establish common beliefs, values, norm, and expectations. From a culture perspective, when frequent communication results in common rituals, symbols, stories, and heroes, families are more likely to have common values and culture.

HOW DO FAMILY VALUES BECOME BUSINESS VALUES?

> [W]hat makes a family business unique is that the pattern of ownership, governance, management, and succession materially influences the firm's goals, strategies, structure and the manner in which each is formulated, designed and implemented. In other words, we study family businesses because researchers believe that the family component shapes the business in a way that the family members of executives in non-family firms do not and cannot. (Chua et al., 1999: 22)

Families and businesses are both social institutions. However, families are institutions that fundamentally nurture and sustain relationships, and businesses are institutions that fundamentally nurture and sustain economies. They both use values and culture to guide social behavior. However, because they have fundamentally different purposes, the values and culture of family and non-family firms may differ based on the level of family social influence in the business. For example, research summarized earlier indicates that family firms may emphasize moral values more than non-family firms. And non-family firms may emphasize competence values more than family firms.

Below, I suggest several means by which family values may become incorporated into the social fabric of the business: (1) multiple family members own and work in the business and use family values and culture to guide business interaction; (2) founders incorporate his or her own family's values and culture into the business; (3) common family values and culture are emphasized in succeeding generations; (4) values and culture become institutionalized in common symbols, rituals, stories, and heroes; (5) families formalize values in collaborative documents; and (6) active involvement of family members in business governance

maintains family values and culture within the business (see Figure 23.1). Consistent with social capital theory, my assumption is that the greater the interaction and communication between the family and the business, the greater the likelihood that family values will become a part of the business.

Multiple Family Members Work in the Business

The greatest amount of social contact between family and business exists when multiple family members own and work in the business. When this occurs, there is high likelihood that values emphasized by the family will be integrated within the business. When multiple family members work in the business, family values and patterns of interaction likely become the basis for business values and culture.

When the owning family engages in values-based rituals or patterns, employees likely feel obliged to emphasize similar values and, to an extent, adopt family patterns and rituals for business purposes. Often, for example, non-family employees comment that a family business feels more like a family than a business.

These kinds of firms tend to rely on an informal structure tied to values rather than

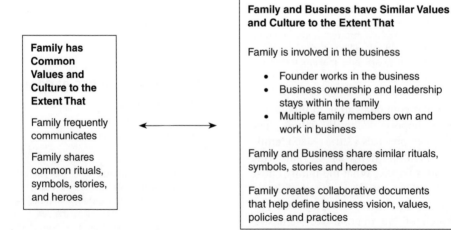

Family has Common Values and Culture to the Extent That

Family frequently communicates

Family shares common rituals, symbols, stories, and heroes

←——————→

Family and Business have Similar Values and Culture to the Extent That

Family is involved in the business

- Founder works in the business
- Business ownership and leadership stays within the family
- Multiple family members own and work in business

Family and Business share similar rituals, symbols, stories and heroes

Family creates collaborative documents that help define business vision, values, policies and practices

Figure 23.1   Social Processes that Develop Similar Values and Culture in Family and Business

the more formal bureaucratic and hierarchical structures used in some businesses (see Donckels and Fröhlich, 1991). This structure works because there is sufficient communication among family members and employees to obtain closure. Closure means that sufficient connections and communication guarantee observance of values-based norms (e.g., Coleman, 1988; Hoffman et al., 2006). Over time and through experience, non-family employees adapt to a family values- and culture-based social system.

Because some values are implicit, both family and non-family employees may not fully understand them. Over time, it might be in the best interest of the family firm to attempt to make implicit values explicit, especially when a family business desires change. For example, Hall et al. (2001) found entrepreneurial change was facilitated by making cultures open and explicit.

Dyer (1986) suggests one way to make values explicit is by creating a culture map. The map makes the implicit values, norms, and assumptions explicit so that the family can see its own values-based culture. A culture map may help the family assess its values and culture, which may stimulate a desire to change. Dyer provides an example of how he created a culture map for the Brown Corporation. The firm had the competency values of 'innovation' and 'creativity,' and the moral values of a 'work ethic,' 'security,' 'loyalty,' and 'obedience.' However, other less positive values were 'authority-based decision-making,' 'secrecy,' and 'low trust of non-family employees.'

Changing cultural norms is difficult but may be incrementally accomplished with purposeful effort, perhaps with the aid of external advisors. Cultural change may also come when the firm transitions to the next generation, hires a higher percentage of non-family employees, or adopts more professional and bureaucratic norms.

Founders

Another means for embedding family values and culture into the business is through the founder/owner. Business founders have the opportunity to build an organizational culture around their own values and beliefs.

Schein (1983; 1985) described how business founders embed their values into their businesses. The founder is often a charismatic individual who surrounds himself or herself with supportive followers (Dyer, 1986). The leader articulates his/her beliefs, values, and assumptions, which provide social guidance for the group. Together, the leader and his/her followers apply founder beliefs, learn through experience, and adapt beliefs to accomplish the owner's objectives. Followers learn leader values by observing what the founder pays attention to, how the leader reacts to important incidents, and who the leader includes or excludes from his/her group of insiders (Schein, 1983, 1985). The leader also coaches employees in his/her beliefs and values, and likely hires individuals with beliefs and values compatible with his/her own.

In the first generation, the founder may be the only member of the family who works in the 'family firm.' Thus, one might question the extent to which the foundational values for the firm's culture represent family values. The values that ultimately emerge from the founder's interaction with followers may differ from family values because the focus of a business is economic success.

In addition, the founder's personal preferences may either severely limit or promote family involvement in the business. For example, in a study of family businesses in Spain, about one-third of the participating family businesses separated family from business (Basco and Rodriquez, 2009). Family values may not be prominent in such businesses. Perhaps, similar to some of the Spanish businesses described by Garcia-Alvarez and López-Sintas (2001), these businesses emphasized growth and technical competence and limited emphasis of moral values that would be more prevalent in families.

Whether or not the founder chooses to involve the family, values are relatively stable and transitional across situations (Dyer, 1986). The founder can respond to social issues in similar ways at work as he/she does in the family. Nevertheless, if he/she chooses to keep the family and business separate, there may be very little social contact between family and business. There may be little discussion of the business in the family or of the family in the business. On the other hand, if the founder values family involvement, he or she may coach family members and employees in similar values at home and at the business. In the family, the founder may tell stories about work and describe business experiences (Parada and Viladás, 2010), which may influence family values. Family members may be invited to attend business meetings and social gatherings. And owners may invite young family members to gain work experience through employment in the business.

Moreover, a founder may actively seek the input of key family members as he or she makes decisions about the business. In the case study about George and Sandra (Sorenson et al., 2011), for many years George was the only family member who worked in the business. Nevertheless, he sought Sandra's opinion on a variety of issues, and there was evidence that family values influenced business values.

For example, George did not like the moral values he saw in the businesses he worked in after graduating from college. He and Sandra discussed starting a business that was consistent with their moral beliefs. After starting the business, George continued to value Sandra's opinion about the business, and Sandra sought to learn more about the business and express her feelings about it. She developed relationships with many firm employees and all of the board members. Thus, Sandra had much opportunity to be involved, voice her views, and reinforce family moral values in the business.

Succession

Often, when we think of succession in family firms, we think of succession of the CEO. There is also an ownership succession. One major difference between family and non-family firms is the potential for continuity of values across generations. One generation can prepare the next generation to sustain founding owner and family values. Much of the preparation comes through personal socialization, allowing both the founder and the family to emphasize common values.

García-Álvarez et al. (2002) studied the succession processes in several Spanish family firms and indicated that values are the social bedrock for next generation socialization. For example, they found that values that were important for next generation owners were 'a business orientation,' 'hard work,' 'a family orientation,' 'autonomy,' and 'entrepreneurship.'

In a large survey of Canadian family managers in family firms, Chrisman et al. (1998) found that the top-rated characteristic for a potential successor was 'moral integrity.' Integrity refers to strict adherence to a moral code, and transparency and harmony between what one says and does. High on the list of characteristics is that the potential successor be trusted by both the family and non-family employees, and be respected by actively participating family members. Sharma and Roa (2000) repeated this survey with Indian family firms and again found that integrity was rated as the most important moral value.

Common Rituals, Symbols, Stories, and Heroes

Symbols, rituals, and heroes reveal values and culture (e.g., Hofstede, 2001) in the family and the family business. They can be purposefully designed to call attention to desired values (e.g., Schein, 1985).

Previously, I discussed dinnertime rituals that reinforce common values in the family. Family firms also create rituals within their businesses. Some family firms, for example, develop a sense of family in the business by sponsoring family picnics and other social gatherings for the families of employees. For example, one founder and his family attended the marriages of all children of employees. Such rituals reinforce the sense of 'family' in the firm. From the case described earlier (Sorenson et al., 2011), George wanted to establish a sense of family in his business. So in the early days of the business, all managers and employees gathered in one room, took turns making lunch, and participated in cleaning up, much like a family.

Heroes are those individuals who are the embodiment of important values. For example, a family firm may create cultural heroes by rewarding employees for 'extra-care' service or for taking on additional responsibilities so that other employees can attend special events for members of their families.

Stories help to define family values (Parada and Viladás, 2010). For example, in the George and Sandra family business case (Sorenson et al., 2011), board members retell the story about how Sandra often took them aside and reminded them that the family's reputation depended on their decisions. Another story retold in their family and their business relates to the importance of business presentations; George often worked through the night to make sure they were accurate and professional.

Symbols can provide a constant reminder of values common to family and business. Angela Pritchard describes a symbol created in her business that united the family, employees, and even community members:

> Rather than allowing the business-first mentality to progress, our CEO and CEmO brainstormed and developed a way to tie all of the businesses together. They gave the foundation of the dealerships an identity, a name that reflected what truly made the company what it was. Pritchard Family Auto Stores became the organization that each individual dealership was linked to. Not only did that name put the family part back in the business, our CEmO designed a logo to reinforce the family aspect and pay tribute to the foundation on which the business was built. (Pritchard, 2011: 182)

Collaboration and Collaborative Documents

Collaboration can help families formalize a common family point of view about values (Sorenson, 1999; Sorenson et al., 2009).

Often, these values are incorporated into collaborative documents such as vision, mission, goals, policies, practices, and the like, often compiled as a constitution or charter.

Families vary in the extent to which they collaborate. Those that collaborate are willing to identify issues and openly discuss them (e.g., Hall et al., 2001). Families with autocratic and paternalistic leaders often create cultures that limit open dicussions which also limit family and business outcomes (Dyer, 1986; Sorenson, 2000). Families that create a culture of collaboration and engage in transparent dialogue enable the family to agree on important common values (Sorenson, et al., 2009) and to generate a culture of family commitment (Astrachan et al., 2002; Zahra et al., 2008).

Collaboration can extend beyond the family to the business and to stakeholders outside the business. Over time, collaboration can result in a collaborative network that promotes common values, or at least a clear understanding of family values (Sorenson et al., 2008). Collaborative dialogue can occur both informally and formally in regular, formal meetings (Sorenson, 1999). For firms with multiple family owners, formal processes may be required for creating collaborative agreements and common values that are reflected in a vision statement, for example, are positively related to decision quality and decision commitment in the business (e.g., Mustakallio et al., 2002). Thus, formal collaborative processes within families and between families and businesses promote common values that unite the family and the business (Distelberg and Blow, 2010). Aronoff and Ward describe the need for common values:

> Family and business are so fundamentally different they naturally pull apart over time ... There must be common ground that is stronger than the forces that pull family and business apart. Many families in search of this third dimension turn to shared values. Values are often the only glue strong enough. (2007: 17)

Cultures of collaboration and commitment can be reinforced in each generation by maintaining formal collaborative processes that visit and update collaborative documents so as to be consistent with the values of each generation.

Active Family Owners

> The family business is a business governed and/or managed with the intention to shape and pursue the vision of the business held by a dominant coalition controlled by members of the same family or a small number of families in a manner that is potentially sustainable across … . (Chua et al., 1999: 25)

Schein (1983; 1985) suggests that the business founder builds relationships with key employees and helps them integrate his or her beliefs and values into the business. Over time, these values become institutionalized into the business structure, systems, procedures, and physical spaces (see also Bjerke, 1999). Stories, myths, legends, and a variety of symbols also reinforce values. Formal family statements of values, charters, and constitutions make the policies and practices associated with values explicit. All of these institutional forces tend to be self-reinforcing and have remarkable ability to sustain the values and culture.

However, the culture is more likely to stay on its values-based course when the owning family retains its influence in governing the business. To do this effectively, families can engage in frequent communication with the business in board meetings and in rituals that bring family and business members together (Astrachan et al., 2002; Zahra et al., 2008). If the owning family can create repetitive rituals and communication processes, values can be reinforced across generations.

Over time, some large owning families, such as the Bancroft family that owned Dow Jones, lose a connection with the business and, perhaps, with one another. Having become disengaged, they may not maintain active governing oversight, which may result in a weak common culture.

Compared to shareholders of publically traded firms whose only common interest is often short-term profits, family shareholders have a common heritage which has the potential for emphasis on a common set of values. They can reinforce their common cultural heritage by vigilantly maintaining family rituals, focusing attention on common symbols, and revisiting family stories. In addition, maintaining collaborative processes among family shareholders for governance purposes will enable the family to develop and reinforce business policies and practices that are consistent with family values and culture.

Shepard (2011) describes how her family had lost a connection to the business and to one another in the fifth generation of her family business. Then she describes how owners united and reconnected with the business:

> The process of reviving our family firm identity had actually begun 10 years earlier with an effort by a fifth generation family board member who began a process to reunite and reengage the family. She started an annual family picnic... arranged for printing and distributing a family tree … [and sent] out company-related birthday gifts to the young children … This included a children's book about the company. [The] chairman of the board … [hired] someone to write a family history … .

> … our non-family CEO … suggested that we needed a family council … A few family members took on the task of creating a proposal for the council and planning the first family meeting … One family member, who was a documentary film maker, created a film about the family's history, which was shown at the inaugural family gathering. The release of the family history book, the showing of the family documentary, and the gathering of the family to celebrate their legacy energized everyone. It made them feel they were not only a part of the family, but also a legacy that involved owning a business together for 150 years. At the end of the film there were tears and hugs. We had arrested the forces pushing the family apart and there was a palpable feeling of longing for reunification and family identification. (Shepard, 2011: 205)

Shepard further describes how the family formed a family council, reclaimed leadership on the board, established communication among family shareholders, and arranged for family owners to meet regularly with board members and firm managers. Their annual report summarizes the importance of values to the owning family:

> As the third-oldest privately held manufacturing company in the US, our company holds a unique position in business history. We've been a good employer and a responsible, active corporate citizen for 160 years, holding firm to the values on which the company was founded. It is clear that the same values that have served the company so well in its first 160 years will sustain us far into the future. (Shepard, 2011: 208)

Summary and Research Questions Regarding Common Values and Culture

The preceding portion of the paper provided an overview of social processes that may enable the family to develop common values and culture, as summarized in Figure 23.1. While Figure 23.1 has some support, more research is needed to better understand values and culture, how they are developed, and their effect.

For example, while the figure shows a positive relationship between communication frequency and common values in family firms, additional questions remain. Do communication frequency and common rituals produce common values and culture? What kind of communication and rituals are effective and what kind are ineffective?

The second example in figure 23.1 shows that family involvement in the business creates similar values and culture in the family and the business. But, what kind of family involvement in the business helps to create common values and culture? To what extent is common values and culture necessary and helpful? How do business families retain core values and culture, but enable each generation to adapt values to their generation and circumstances?

A third example indicates that family and business cultures are similar to the extent that they share common rituals, stories, symbols, and heroes. But, to what extent can both family and business usefully share and profitably focus on common symbols? When is a focus on common symbols meaningful and helpful to both the business and the family?

A final example indicates that family and business values and cultures are more similar when in each generation family members engage in collaboration to create documents that express family values in business vision, goals, policies, and practices. But, to what extent, in what form, and with what effect does family involvement influence business goals and policies?

Ultimately, researchers could examine the extent to which the practices outlined in Figure 23.1 lead to more open and explicit values and culture (Dyer, 1986; Hall et al., 2001). Thus, exploring the overarching questions. Does an open and explicit culture produce positive change or merely conflict? And, what processes help to promote positive change?

CONCLUSION

Values and culture research provide insights into how families can influence family business. Such research can help scholars to better understand how family and business social systems influence one another. Both qualitative and quantitative research methods contribute to our understanding of values and culture in family firms. Qualitative methods typically provide insights about individual or small numbers of family businesses. Quantitative methods typically obtain information that can be aggregated to compare and contrast values, clusters of values, and cultures among many family businesses. Either type of research can help scholars understand how values and cultures are created and maintained, and how they are related to family and business outcomes. Researchers have conducted relatively little research about values and culture in family business. This chapter suggests many research opportunities.

REFERENCES

Alvesson, M. (1993) *Cultural Perspectives in Organizations*. Cambridge: Cambridge University Press.

Alvesson, M. (2002) *Understanding Organizational Culture*. Thousand Oaks, CA: Sage.

Aronoff, C.E. and Ward, J.L. (2007) *From Siblings to Cousins: Prospering in the Third Generation*. Marietta, GA: Family Enterprise Publishers.

Astrachan, J.H., Klein, S.B., and Smyrnios, K.H. (2002) The F-PEC Scale of Family Influence: A proposal for solving the family business definition problem. *Family Business Review*, 15(1), 45–58.

Barney, J.B. (1986) Organizational culture: Can it be a source of sustained competitive advantage? *Academy of Management Review*, 11(3), 656–665.

Basco, R. and Rodriquez, M.J.P. (2009) Studying the family enterprise holistically: Evidence for integrated family and business systems. *Family Business Review*, 22(1), 82–95.

Bjerke, B. (1999) *Business Leadership and Culture: National Management Styles in a Global Economy*. Northampton, MA: Edward Elgar.

Bruess, C.J. (2009) Family rituals, communication, and family social capital: An exploration of meaning-making. Paper presented at Family Capital, Family Business and Free Enterprise Conference, Minneapolis, September.

Bruess, C.J. (2011) Family rituals, communication, and family social capital: An exploration of meaning-making. In R.L. Sorenson (ed.), *Family Business and Social Capital*, pp. 115–128. Cheltenham: Edward Elgar.

Ceja, L., Agulles, R., and Tàpies, J. (2010) *The importance of values in family owned firms*. IESE Business School Working Paper WP-875.

Chrisman, J.J., Chua, J.H., and Sharma, P. (1998) Important attributes of successors in family business: An exploratory study. *Family Business Review*, 11(1), 19–34.

Chua, J.H., Chrisman, J.J., and Sharma, P. (1999) Defining the family business by behavior. *Entrepreneurship: Theory and Practice*, Summer, 19–39.

Coleman, J.S. (1988) Social capital in the creation of human capital. *American Journal of Sociology*, 93, 291–321.

Denison, D., Lief, C., and Ward, J.L. (2004) Culture in family-owned enterprises: Recognizing and leveraging unique strengths. *Family Business Review*, 17(1), 61–70. doi:10.1111/j.1741–6248.2004.00004.x.

Distelberg, B. and Blow, A. (2010) The role of values and unity in the family business. *Journal of Family and Economic Issues*, 31(4), 427–441.

Donckels, R. and Fröhlich, E. (1991) Are family businesses really different? European experiences from STRATOS. *Family Business Review*, 2(4), 149–160.

Dyer Jr, W.G. (1986) *Cultural Change in Family Firms: Anticipating and Managing Business and Family Transitions*. San Francisco, CA: Jossey-Bass.

García-Álvarez, E. and López-Sintas, J. (2001) A taxonomy of founders based on values: The root of family business heterogeneity. *Family Business Review*, 14(3), 209–230.

García-Álvarez, E., López-Sintas, J., and Saldaña-Gonzalvo, P. (2002) Socialization patterns of successors in first- to second-generation family businesses. *Family Business Review*, 15(3), 189–203. doi:10.1111/j.1741–6248.2002.00189.x.

Hall, A., Melin, L., and Nordqvist, M. (2001) Entrepreneurship as radical change in the family business: Exploring the role of cultural patterns. *Family Business Review*, 24(3), 193–208.

Hoffman, J., Hoelscher, M., and Sorenson, R. (2006) Achieving sustained competitive advantage: A family capital theory. *Family Business Review*, 24(2), 137–146.

Hofstede, G. (1980) *Culture's Consequences: International Differences in Work-related Values*. Beverly Hills, CA and London: Sage.

Hofstede, G. (1997) *Cultures and Organizations: Software of the Mind*. New York, NY: McGraw-Hill.

Hofstede, G. (2001) *Cultures Consequences: Comparing Values, Behaviors, Institutions, and Organizations Across Nations*. Thousand Oaks, CA. Sage Publications.

House, R.J., Hanges, P.J., Javidan, M., Dorfman, P.W., and Gupta, V. (eds) (2004) *Culture, Leadership, and Organizations: The GLOBE Study of 62 Societies*. Thousand Oaks, CA: Sage.

Klein, S.B., Astrachan, J.H., and Smyrnios, K.X. (2005) The F-PEC scale of family influence: Validation, and further implication for theory. *Entrepreneurship: Theory and Practice*, 29(3) 321–339.

Kluckhohn, C.K. (1951) Values and value orientations in the theory of action. In T. Parsons and E.A. Shils (eds), *Toward a General Theory of Action*. Cambridge, MA: Harvard University Press.

Kluckhohn, F.R. and Strodtbeck, F.L. (1961) *Variations in Value Orientations*. Evanston, IL: Row, Peterson.

Koiranen, M. (2002) Over 100 years of age but still entrepreneurially active in business: Exploring the values and family characteristics of old Finnish family firms. *Family Business Review*, 15(3), 175–187.

Martin, J. (2002) *Organizational culture: Mapping the terrain*. Thousand Oaks, CA: Sage.

Mustakallio, M., Autio, E. and Zahra, S.A. (2002) Relational and contractual governance in family firms: Effects on strategic decision making. *Family Business Review*, 15(3), 205–222.

Nahapiet, J. and Ghoshal, S. (1998) Social capital, intellectual capital, and the organizational advantage. *Academy of Management Review*, 23, 242–266.

Parada, M.J. and Viladás, H. (2010) Narratives: A powerful device for values transmission in family businesses. *Journal of Organizational Change Management*, 23(2), 166–172.

Payne, G.T., Brigham, K.H., Brober, J.C., Moss, T.W., and Short, J.C. (2011) Organizational virtue orientation and family firms. *Business Ethics Quarterly*, 21(2), 257–285.

Pearson, A.W., Carr, J.C., and Shaw, J.C. (2008) Toward a theory of familiness: A social capital perspective. *Entrepreneurship Theory & Practice*, 32(6), 949–969.

Pritchard, A. (2011) Putting family in family business: The role of the chief emotional officer. In R.L. Sorenson (ed.), *Family Business and Social Capital*, pp. 178–185. Cheltenham: Edward Elgar.

Rokeach, M. (1973) *The Nature of Human Values*. New York, NY: The Free Press.

Schein, E.H. (1983) The role of the founder in creating organizational culture. *Organizational Dynamics*, Summer.

Schein, E.H. (1985) *Organizational Culture and Leadership*. San Francisco, CA: John Wiley & Sons.

Schoenenberger, E. (1997) *The Cultural Crisis of the Firm*. Oxford: Blackwell.

Schwartz, S.H. (1992) 'Universals in the content and structure of values: Theoretical advances and empirical tests in 20 countries.' *Advances in Experimental Social Psychology*, 25, 1–65.

Schwartz, S.H. (2006) *Basic Human Values: An Overview*. The Hebrew University of Jerusalem.

Sharma, P. and Rao, A.S. (2000) Successor attributes in Indian and Canadian family firms: A comparative study. *Family Business Review*, 13(4), 313–330.

Shepard, S. (2011) Reclaiming our identity as a business-owning family. In R.L. Sorenson (ed.), *Family Business and Social Capital*, pp. 198–208. Cheltenham: Edward Elgar.

Smircich, L. (1983) Concepts of culture and organizational analysis. *Administrative Science Quarterly*, 28(3), 339–358.

Sorenson, R.L. (1999) Conflict strategies used by successful family businesses. *Family Business Review*, 12(4), 325–339.

Sorenson, R.L. (2000) The contribution of leadership styles and practices to family and business success. *Family Business Review*, 13(3), 183–200.

Sorenson, R.L. (ed.) (2011) *Family Business and Social Capital*. Cheltenham: Edward Elgar.

Sorenson, R.L., with anonymous daughter and anonymous granddaughter (2011) Creating family and business social capital: A co-investigation with a daughter and granddaughter. In R.L. Sorenson (ed.), *Family Business and Social Capital*, pp. 129–145. Cheltenham: Edward Elgar.

Sorenson, R.L., Folker, C.A., and Brigham, K.H. (2008) The collaborative network orientation: Achieving business success through collaborative relationships. *Entrepreneurship: Theory and Practice*, 32(4), 615–634.

Sorenson, R.L., Goodpaster, K.E., Hedberg, P.R., and Yu, A. (2009) The family point of view, family social capital, and firm performance: An exploratory test. *Family Business Review*, 22(3), 239–253.

Stewart, A. (2014) The anthropology of family business: An imagined ideal. In L. Melin, M. Nordqvist, and P. Sharma (eds), *The SAGE Handbook of Family Business*. London: Sage.

Tapies, J. and Ward, J.L. (eds) (2008) *Family Values and Value Creation: The Fostering of Enduring Values Within Family-owned Businesses*. New York, NY: Palgrave, Macmillan.

Whetten, D., Foreman, P. and Dyer Jr, G.W. (2014) Organizational identity and family business. In L. Melin, M. Nordqvist, and P. Sharma (eds), *The SAGE Handbook of Family Business*. London: Sage.

Zahra, S.A., Hayton, J.C., Neubaum, D.O., Dibrell, C., and Craig, J. (2008) Culture of family commitment and strategic flexibility: The moderating effect of stewardship. *Entrepreneurship: Theory and Practice*, 32(6) 1035–1053.

Zahra, S.A., Hayton, J.C., and Salvato, C. (2004) Entrepreneurship in family vs. non-family firms: A resource-based analysis of the effect of organizational culture. *Entrepreneurship: Theory and Practice*, 28(4), 363–381.

24

Organizational Identity and Family Business

David Whetten, Peter Foreman and W. Gibb Dyer

INTRODUCTION

In the English language compounds are used to combine ordinarily separate words into a single expression. In sociological terms, compound nouns in particular often signify an emergent social category, combining two otherwise separate categories, e.g., church school, cooperative bank, or social enterprise. This is the case with family business, which denotes a type of organization that is intentionally constructed as a combination of two otherwise separate social categories. The terms 'family' and 'business' conjure up well-known social forms: each heavily laden with beliefs, emotions, values, understandings, and expectations. The identity construct – taken as how individuals and social entities define 'who' or 'what' they are (Albert and Whetten, 1985) – offers a way of examining and better understanding the meaning structures of the family and business components of a 'family business'.

In identity terms, a family business is referred to as a type of hybrid-identity-organization (HIO) (Albert and Whetten, 1985: 95), in the sense that it is the intentional amalgamation of two organizational forms or types which would normally be considered mutually exclusive. In these cases, the compound noun denotes an inherent tension between two different sets of organizing rules or scripts, including culture-specific social expectations for how certain kinds of organizations are expected to operate (Kraatz and Block, 2008). Within the study of organizational identity, hybrids constitute an 'extreme case'. Metaphorically, these organizations have chosen to organize their activities astraddle a known 'institutional fault line' – demarcating distinctly different identity categories. Operating in this precarious zone, members are constantly reminded by their surroundings that they're both a Type A and a Type B organization. Logically, hybrids challenge the 'coherence premise' of identity theory – i.e., that an actor's identity provides a strong foundation upon which a coherent (temporally and spatially consistent) set of beliefs, attitudes, and actions can be built (Stets and Burke, 2000). Practically, hybrids are difficult to operate because the organization operates under the constant worrisome possibility that the next major decision could alienate certain stakeholders, or in the extreme case provoke an internal civil war or threaten the organization's external legitimacy.

Family businesses are, of course, one such type of HIO, combining identity elements of the 'family' and 'business' social forms or categories. It is logically possible to think of this combination in one of three ways. First, the 'family' component can be seen as a modifier of the 'business' social category (f-B), signifying a particular type of business, in which family members are primarily employed (Hilburt-Davis and Dyer, 2003). Second, the 'business' component can be seen as an extension of the 'family' social category (F-b), expressing a particular way in which families engage in a business activity to support family goals (e.g., the continued immigration of family members into the business). Finally, the compound noun of 'family business' can denote a more-or-less equal or balanced integration of these mutually exclusive social categories (F-B).

The concepts of organizational identity and hybrid identity organizations described in this chapter are highly relevant for family business scholarship. They constitute a coherent framework for understanding this type of organization as an amalgam of equally important social forms. They also allow family business scholars to span multiple levels of analysis in their theorizing and empirical investigations, examining the interplay between institutional, organizational, and individual dynamics. In addition, by treating family businesses as HIOs family business scholarship can inform and be informed by a growing body of research on related organizations, such as orchestras, hospitals, cooperatives, and universities.

In this chapter, we first provide a review of the organizational identity construct, beginning with its roots in psychology and sociology, and the associated concept of organizational identification. This provides a conceptual foundation for us to discuss the hybrid identity

organization and explore the challenges and opportunities inherent in the hybrid form. We begin this task by first distinguishing HIOs from the broader case of organizational identity, in the sense that whereas all organizations have multiple identities, a small percentage of organizations satisfy the '3Is' definition of HIOs. We next introduce a simple framework for classifying different kinds of HIOs and examine its ramifications for the study of identity conflict within such hybrids. We conclude with a discussion of the implications for family business research.

IDENTITY THEORY

Organizational identity has its roots in individual-level theories of identity, borrowing from both sociological and psychological conceptualizations of the self and identity. Identity theory offers a distinctive explanatory focus, briefly characterized as an individual's subjective understanding of his or her unique social space and associated expectations – sometimes referred to as the socialized self-view (Hogg et al., 1995; Stets and Burke, 2000). In comparison with behaviorism, identity theory operates from a more agentic perspective, in the sense that actors actively shape their identity via the adoption of new roles and group memberships. According to identity theory, individuals also have some latitude in interpreting how they enact their identity referents, e.g., how they play the role of professor or parent. The agentic flavor of this perspective is also reflected in terms inspired by identity theory, like self-management and self-actualization. Furthermore, identity theory posits that a person's self-view is a relatively stable conception, both temporally and spatially, that provides coherence to each person's attitudes, beliefs, and actions. In the context of a family business, the firm's identity is often initially seen as the extension of the individual founder who creates the enterprise (Dyer and Whetten, 2006; Haveman and Khaire, 2004; Schein, 1983), and this identity transitions to a family identity over time if and when other family members begin to own and manage the enterprise along with the founder (Dyer, 1986). Given the individual-level theoretical roots of organizational identity, along with the central influence of the founder in establishing the self-definitions of the typical new venture, we begin our conceptual overview with a brief discussion of individual identity theory.

Individual Identity Scholarship

As several scholars have explained (e.g., Hogg et al., 1995; Pratt, 1998; Stets and Burke, 2000), current theories of the self and identity draw primarily on two conceptual foundations: role-identity theory (RIT) and social identity theory (SIT). We discuss each of these in brief. There is a line of work in sociology that argues for an 'interactionist' view of the self, leading to the development of the role-identity construct (McCall and Simmons, 1978; Stryker, 1980). According to RIT, an individual's self-view is defined by their roles – structurally determined patterns of behavior associated with a given social setting. An individual embodies multiple identities that match the various roles that they play, and the demands of the social context evoke the relative salience of a given role. Such role-identity plurality is particularly evident in a family business, where individuals typically have a plethora of roles: owner, founder, parent, manager, board member, and so forth (Hilburt-Davis and Dyer, 2003). The challenge is dealing with the inevitable identity conflict that results when multiple roles are evoked with competing demands (Golden-Biddle and Rao, 1997; Shepherd and Haynie, 2009).

A parallel line of thinking, influenced by social psychology, focuses on the ways in which external social affiliations or categorizations define the self and shape one's identity. This interpersonal focus is the basis of SIT (Tajfel, 1978; Turner, 1982), where 'who I am' is reflected in what it means to be a member of particular demographic categories or social groups – what is known as the extended self-concept. From this perspective, individuals internalize the definitional characteristics and expectations associated with these categories or groups, referred to as collective or social identities; and the composite of a person's particular memberships in salient groups constitutes a unique social identity profile (Pratt, 1998). With respect to family businesses, an owner-operator's identity would be shaped by the social groups that follow from their business (e.g., being a farmer or chef or insurance agent), as well as their personal life (e.g., being a Habitat volunteer, marathon runner, or church member); and they must then meet the various stakeholder expectations associated with those groups (Bingham et al., 2011; Zellweger and Nason, 2008).

Organizational Identity

Originating in Albert and Whetten's (1985) essay, the concept of organizational identity (OI) consists of members' self-definitions of their organization – i.e., their consensual answers to the question 'Who are we?' (Ashforth and Mael, 1989; Pratt and Foreman, 2000). Identity constitutes not only social claims about an organization, but to a certain degree also social facts – i.e., generally recognized notions of what the organization is and is about (Gioia et al., 2010; Whetten, 2006). According to Albert and Whetten (1985), an organization's identity is that which is *central, enduring*, and *distinct* (CED). By central, we mean that identity is concerned with those things that are core rather than peripheral. By enduring, we mean that identity is focused on those core elements that endure over time, rather than those that are ephemeral. By distinctive, we mean that identity consists of a set of core features and characteristics which stake out how the organization is both similar to and different from others.

Over the past two decades, two versions of the OI concept have taken root (Gioia et al., 2010; Ravasi and Schultz, 2006; Whetten, 2006): a realist/essentialist approach (or the social actor [SA] view) and an interpretivist perspective (or the social constructionist [SC] view). While the SA view of organizational identity focuses on the sense-giving role of organizational identity (taken-for-granted CED attributes), the SC view treats OI as a form of sense-making, a more or less shared conception of 'who we are' as members of an organization that is relatively malleable. Scholars employing the SC view tend to focus on how individuals make sense of their experience as members of a particular organization (e.g., Gioia et al., 2000). From this perspective, organizational identity operates much like collective identity in SIT (Ashforth and Mael, 1989) – i.e., as the aggregate of individuals' self-views. The SC view has been shown to be particularly relevant when seeking to understand different conceptions of a single organization's identity. Scholars using this approach have tended to be focused on the process of organizational identity creation or change, especially in the face of major organizational crises (e.g., Gioia et al., 2010; Ravasi and Shultz, 2006).

The SA view of OI also begins from the perspective of individual identity, but then argues that organizations, like individuals, are social actors with similar identity requirements (Whetten, 2006). Hence, OI is viewed as a global property of organizational actors, operating as a sense-giving component of members' shared experience (Whetten and Mackey, 2002). From this perspective, OI is a social fact, in contrast to the SC view of OI as a shared emergent property of organizations. The objective, essentialist nature of the SA approach makes it particularly useful for scholars categorizing or comparing different types of organizations on the basis of their identity (e.g., Battilana and Dorado, 2010; Hsu and Hannan, 2005; Moss et al., 2011), or studying the impact of an organization's identity on various individual and organizational outcomes, such as commitment, legitimacy, reputation, or economic performance (e.g., Foreman and Whetten, 2002; Foreman et al., 2012; Smith, 2011; Zuckerman, 1999).

This distinction between a SA and SC perspective has particularly significant implications for family business scholarship, in that it directs attention to the question of distinguishing hybrid identity organizations from non-hybrids. From a social construction perspective, hybridity is not a categorical distinction. In fact, given the SC focus on collective perceptions, such a distinction might not even be an important one to make. As a result, companies with no ties to a particular family but that foster a 'family culture' might be viewed the same as companies that are owned and operated by members of a single family. In contrast, the social actor view of organizational identity posits that there is a qualitative difference between mono-identity and hybrid-identity organizations – one that is rooted in structural, not merely perceptual, differences. From this SA view, a clear categorical distinction can be made between a family-owned-and-controlled entity (e.g., Cargill or Chik-Fil-A) and 'pseudo family businesses' – those who profess to operate according to family values (e.g., Disney or Reader's Digest).

Furthermore, this realist, social actor view of OI adopts an institutionalist approach to what are referred to in the literature as organizational identity claims (Ravasi and Schultz, 2006; Gioia et al., 2011). Given that organizations are socially constructed entities, possessing no identifying properties equivalent to individual traits like gender or ethnicity, it is argued that organizations are literally what/who they claim to be. An institutional perspective draws attention to the ways in which these identity claims follow from the social 'type' or form that the organization belongs to or represents, and as such highlights the legitimacy requirements associated with these adopted social forms (Hsu and Hannan, 2005; Smith, 2011). These identity-related requirements are akin to the functional obligations accompanying roles in RIT and the group-related norms of social categories in SIT. That is, like an individual who embodies a given role (mother, doctor, school board member, etc.) or is defined by a particular group or category (university professor, expert skier, NRA member, etc.), an organization must analogously meet certain expectations that follow from its adopted type or form (King and Whetten, 2008). A commercial bank is expected to lend money (its role), and a church is expected to follow certain doctrines (its category); failure to do so calls into question that organization's very right to exist.

Recent work in organizational sociology has examined the difficulties organizations face when asked to fulfill multiple roles (Zuckerman, 1999) or when attempting to span multiple social categories (Kraatz and Block, 2008; Pache and Santos, 2010). These identity-based tensions are particularly endemic to family businesses as a hybrid organizational form. Family businesses face two sets of form-related expectations and requirements, stemming from their dual identities. Early work by Taguiri and Davis (1992) demonstrated that family business leaders were committed to achieving both business-related (e.g., profits, quality products, etc.) and family-related goals (e.g., financial security, stability). Other studies have noted that role conflict is common in family firms as members try to determine which rules to use – business or family – when managing relationships, evaluating performance, or promoting people (Hilburt-Davis and Dyer, 2003; Shepherd and Haynie, 2009). Thus, family businesses that fail to satisfy either set of expectations risk losing the crucial support of vital constituents – the family and/or the market (Bingham et al., 2011; Habbershon et al., 2003). Among the many ways that these identity tensions are manifested is in the very critical issue of member identification and commitment, which we address in the next section.

Organizational Identification

While having shared etymology, organizational identity and identification have not necessarily been conceptually related in the literature. Historically, the construct of organizational identification (OID) has been bound up with a range of similar and related notions of attachment, internalization, affiliation, and loyalty (Ashforth et al., 2008).

More recent research on OID has been more specifically guided by social identity theory, along with self-categorization theory (Pratt, 1998). As noted above SIT begins with the premise that people classify themselves and others according to their relationships with various social or demographic groups. This social classification scheme provides an individual with a means of defining themselves through a sense of oneness, or identification, with various particular groups. Organizational identification is essentially a subtype of the broader concept of social identification (Ashforth and Mael, 1989). That is, organizational identification captures a member's 'perceived oneness' or 'sense of connectedness' with an organization as a social group (Ashforth et al., 2008). Members are making cognitive assessments of their relative 'fit' with the organization – i.e., the degree to which they would use the organization as a social group or category that defines their own selves (Dutton et al., 1994).

From a social actor perspective, OID can thus be seen as the relative congruence between the identities of two social actors – the individual and the organization (Brickson, 2013; Foreman and Whetten, 2002; Pratt, 1998). That is to say, to the degree that an individual feels that their organization embodies and displays identity attributes consistent with their personal identity and in ways that are important to them, they will have a greater sense of identification with that organization, leading to stronger bonds of attachment. The Foreman and Whetten study empirically demonstrated that this identity congruence approach to identification significantly affected commitment. In a family business context, when your family name is, in fact, 'on the building', like the Marriott family name, your identification with and commitment to the organization may be significantly enhanced.

Interestingly, Foreman and Whetten developed and tested their model in a context genetically similar to family businesses. Agricultural cooperatives are an organizational form fundamentally comprised of multiple identities (see Foreman, 1998, for a concise review). In addition to their role as bargaining associations for addressing economic issues of farmers, co-ops also are imbued with tremendous social capital, expected to foster a sense of rural community and farmer solidarity through shared governance, educational programs, and political action, among other things. As Foreman and Whetten (2002) showed, different members of cooperatives identified to varying degrees with the dual identities of this HIO: some placing much greater importance on the business aspect, others highly emphasizing the community element, and many valuing both equally. Cooperatives face the delicate balancing act of 'living out' their economic and social identities, recognizing that moving too far in either direction risks alienating a significant portion of their constituency.

This view of OID helps observers of family businesses better understand why conflicts within them are often so problematic. Inasmuch as OID refers to the perceived overlap between a member's identity and the identity of the organization, organizational changes that appear to diminish the importance of either element of a family business compromise the identity integrity of the entire organization, risking an identification backlash. Such fissures potentially threaten not just the social or financial interests of members, but their very identity – i.e., the 'core' of their being. However, we must also recognize that such tension between competing identities can also be the foundation for creativity and high organizational performance as family business leaders attempt to reconcile different logics and meet a variety of stakeholder needs.

HYBRID IDENTITY ORGANIZATIONS

As we have noted, Albert and Whetten (1985) introduced the notion of a hybrid identity organization. A hybrid denotes mixed ancestry or origin. Biologically, it is the offspring of different species. More broadly, a hybrid is anything that 'derives from heterogeneous [elements] or [is] composed of different or incongruous elements' (Oxford English Dictionary, 1994). Organizations, by their very nature, are composed of multiple elements, including different technologies, operating routines, strategies, etc. However, hybrid identity organizations are those in which hybridization occurs at the level of identity; that is to say, what is core, enduring, and distinctive about the organization is the combination of 'different or incongruous elements'. Following from our discussion of organizational identity above, an HIO equally embodies two distinct social forms, often evident in their very names: a research university, a grain marketing cooperative, a development bank, a teaching hospital, or a credit union. We posit that when asked 'What's CED about your organization?' informed members of hybrids would respond, 'We're both a Type A and a Type B organization'. In their brief discussion of HIOs, Albert and Whetten (1985) suggested a generic type, combining normative and utilitarian values, as exemplified by the family business hybrid (Boers and Nordqvist, 2012).

A growing body of scholarship has examined various types of HIOs, including symphony orchestras (Glynn, 2000), professional theaters (Voss et al., 2006), community service organizations (Golden-Biddle and Rao, 1997), social enterprises (Moss et al., 2011), microfinance development associations (Battilana and Dorado, 2010), sport event organizations (Foreman and Parent, 2008), and healthcare delivery systems (Pratt and Rafaeli, 1997), among others. The primary subject of these studies is the challenges HIOs face satisfying inconsistent social expectations (Fiol et al., 2009; Kraatz and Block, 2008). Scholars have begun to see family businesses as embodying multiple identities (Shepherd and Haynie, 2009; Sundaramurthy and Kreiner, 2008) – in some cases clearly framing them as HIOs (Boers and Nordqvist, 2012; Dyer and Whetten, 2006) – and have similarly explored how identity-related conflicts can be addressed. In the following sections, we draw on the broader body of OI literature, as well as the nascent stream of work on identities in family businesses, to define and classify HIOs and discuss how they are managed.

Characterizing Hybrid Identity Organizations

The question of what is and isn't a hybrid identity organization requires some careful discussion. As a means of distinguishing HIOs from the more common case of organizations possessing multiple identities, an ideal type has been proposed by Albert and colleagues (Albert et al., 1998; Albert and Adams, 2002), which we draw on here. Summarized as the '3I's' of the HIO form, the authors posit a set of distinguishing dimensions for hybrids. While we recognize that collectively these depict an 'extreme case' – one which may not characterize many/most hybrids found in society, an understanding of the ideal allows us to make clearer conceptual arguments about hybrids in general and family businesses in particular.

The first 'I' is the truly distinctive feature of hybrid-identity organizations: the degree to which two or more of their identities are generally considered to be *incompatible*. One way of visualizing this characteristic is that hybrid identities are selected from disparate categories within a typology of social forms: e.g., the Salvation Army – a church/mission that is structured like an army, with 'sergeants' and 'captains' and 'generals'. In the case of family businesses, firms have elected to organize themselves according to the very different and competing expectations of being both a family and a business (Boers and Nordqvist, 2012). The 'incompatible identities' attribute of hybrids distinguishes this organizational form from the existence of multiple but highly related identities within organizations. Such instances, like the church relief agency, bring together two social forms that have very similar 'genetic codes': as the Catholic Church seeks to 'feed the poor' and 'care for the sick', maintaining an ongoing Third World relief organization – Catholic Relief Services – serves as a direct extension of its core (spiritual) mission. In contrast, the incompatible attribute suggests that HIOs embody identity elements that seem incongruous or inconsistent. For hybrids, their central and enduring feature is that 'we are committed to doing what others might consider impossible'.

The second 'I' stipulates that each and every identifying feature plays an *indispensible* role in guiding coherent collective action and effective social intercourse. For hybrids this means that in cases where multiple identities are in conflict, simply jettisoning one of the identities is not a viable option. At the individual level of analysis, the study and practice of work–family balance is predicated on the notion that in cases when being a parent/spouse and being a professor are in conflict, few individuals are willing to simply abandon either of these central, enduring, and distinguishing features of who they are. Similarly, for most family businesses, the owners cannot cease treating one another like family, and neither can they afford to cease operating like a business. This 'indispensible identities' characteristic of HIOs distinguishes them from organizations where multiple identities might come into conflict (e.g., low cost producer and employee focused) and pressures of the marketplace force the organization to remove one, or when a new identity has been assimilated via a merger or acquisition (e.g., GE becoming a 'media' company through acquiring NBC) and is later eliminated through divestiture (Pratt and Foreman, 2000). In contrast, because each identity element of an HIO is central to "who we are", removing or minimizing any aspect is paramount to the death of the organization as its members know it.

Third, hybrid identities are *inviolate*, in the sense that they reflect established social expectations for how certain kinds of organizations should look like and how they should behave (King and Whetten, 2008). Claiming to be a certain kind of organization but failing to adopt the values, norms, routines, and practices that are typical of members of that group/social category risks identity confusion – a potentially fatal condition for organizations. Organizations with hybrid identities must fulfill the expectations associated with each adopted social form/identity in its entirety – anything less will be viewed as compromising the integrity of the organization and potentially making it unrecognizable. As previously noted, research on agricultural cooperatives (Foreman and Whetten, 2002) demonstrated that farmer-members had strong normative and utilitarian expectations of their local co-op – and any perceptions of failure to meet either set of requirements resulted in decreased commitment to the organization. The 'inviolate identities' attribute of HIOs distinguishes them from the common phenomenon of organizations having competing expectations associated with multiple stakeholders. While such instances present a given organization with competing demands, the question of its identity and the related issue of legitimacy do not hinge on successfully meeting all these demands (Pache and Santos, 2010). If Exxon-Mobil does not effectively manage the expectations of the Environmental Protection Agency or the Sierra Club, it may face lengthy court battles and a damaged reputation – but nobody will question its identity as an energy company. In contrast, if the Olympics are no longer viewed as exhibiting the most elite level of athletic competition, or if they are seen as wavering in their pursuit of advancing human ideals such as equality, integrity, and inclusiveness, they will no longer be recognizable as the iconic organization that they are (Foreman and Parent, 2008).

As foreshadowed in our introduction to organizational identity scholarship, the 3Is conception of HIOs is consistent with an institutional theory view of organizations, especially its emphasis on legitimacy. An organization's legitimacy is derived from its being readily recognized as a certain kind of organization, a member of a particular social category – a community college, a fast-food restaurant, a credit union (Hsu and Hannan,

2005; Zuckerman, 1999). Using identity terminology, organizations whose identifying features are congruent with the prototypic identity of a self-defining social category are deemed to be recognizable, appropriate members of that category (King and Whetten, 2008). The universal need for social legitimacy dictates that organizations must treat their self-defining group memberships as inviolate and indispensable. The observation that, whereas all organizations have multiple identities, HIOs claim membership in seemingly mutually exclusive social categories implies that this organizational form is particularly prone to legitimacy challenges (Kraatz and Block, 2008; Pache and Santos, 2010). Today's managed-care organizations are but one example of this conundrum. Such health-care systems face the nearly irreconcilable conflict of containing costs and maintaining a profit while providing the highest quality care for all patients who need it. Failure to fulfill either set of these expectations would risk the very survival of the organization.

Thus, a fundamental challenge for the hybrid is to organize its activities around core, identifying elements that 'hang together' internally, and to garner external legitimacy by acting in harmony with the institutionalized attributes of the two 'donor' types or forms. Each social form comprising the HIO possesses a clear and distinctive set of values, norms, practices, routines, etc. Because a non-hybrid links to a single social form (e.g., a school, church, army, firm, etc.), the organization need only conform to this particular set of institutional identity requirements. The HIO, conversely, contains multiple legitimacy-granting 'organizing recipes' (Rao, 1994), which must somehow hang together (cohere) if the hybrid is to survive (Kraatz and Block, 2008).

At this point, readers who have spent years studying family businesses are justified in asking, 'If the survival risks for HIOs are so high, why do we observe so many successful hybrids, including family businesses?' The concept of reputation offers a clue for resolving this conundrum. Whereas legitimacy refers to the perceived congruence between an organization's identity claims and the prototypical attributes of a particular kind of organization, reputation is linked to the positively distinguishing attributes of the 'ideal' group member – that which makes a group member stand out as particularly 'distinctive' (King and Whetten, 2008; Rao, 1994; Smith, 2011). Hence, legitimacy can be seen as primarily related to the similarity aspect of identity, with reputation being more closely linked to uniqueness. Said another way, legitimacy highlights those self-definitional features that are identity requirements, while reputation draws attention to those defining characteristics that are identity ideals (Foreman et al., 2012).

From a reputational perspective it is possible to see how HIOs might enjoy an inherent advantage over their mono-identity counterparts (Dyer and Whetten, 2006). Framed in terms of a generic normative-utilitarian hybrid, it is not difficult to imagine the normative element enhancing the credibility, attractiveness and reputability of the utilitarian aspect, and vice-versa. In general, the reason why utilitarian organizations, such as businesses, suffer from a poor reputation is that they are perceived as being 'too utilitarian' – the ends too often justify the means. Hence, the ideal utilitarian organization is one which is guided by a higher set of values and principles – a normative identity. The requirements of being a family are coincidentally the ideals of being a business. This is perhaps why so many companies engage in social practices and invoke values and principles reminiscent of family norms (Moss et al., 2011). In the case of the cooperative organizational form, the normative identity elements of education and support for farmer-members enhances the value created through the utilitarian functions of marketing grain or purchasing supply inputs – thereby giving cooperatives a distinctive competitive position against their mono-identity rivals (Foreman, 1998; Foreman and Whetten, 2002).

On the other hand, highly normative organizations, like churches or religious associations, often suffer from outsiders' prejudicial attributions of dogmatism and anti-intellectualism – they are deemed 'too normative'. In response, many have started colleges or universities, whereby the utilitarian identity of academic rigor and scientific advancement adds credibility to the church. Some of the key requirements of being a university are in many ways the ideals of being a church. In another example, microfinance organizations, as a form of social enterprise, typically have a greater ability to attract investors and raise the necessary capital to advance their social mission when they are established on a strong 'banking' identity foundation – a recognition of fiduciary responsibility enhances the credibility of the altruistic aims of the enterprise (Battilana and Dorado, 2010). In sum, hybrids thus may accrue a reputation advantage over their mono-identity counterparts.

Classifying Hybrid Identity Organizations

Having explored what it means to be a hybrid identity organization – how HIOs are fundamentally different from the mere presence of multiple identities in organizations – we now turn our attention to within-population distinctions – how some hybrids might vary from others. Among the various dimensions upon which HIOs may be classified we focus on two attributes: the degree to which their incompatible identities are structurally integrated, and the extent to which decision-makers establish priorities for resolving identity conflicts.

Degree of Identity Integration – The Locus of Duality

The first dimension of integration is characterized as 'A + B' and 'A x B', signifying in Albert and Whetten's (1985) terminology *ideographic* and *holographic* identities.

The level of integration within hybrids is a function of the relationship between the organization's hybrid identities and group- and individual-level activities. In the case of ideographic HIOs, particular work units and individuals are likely to operate as Type A or Type B organizations, but not both – e.g., in a healthcare organization where some members act as physicians or nurses while others act as accountants or office managers. In contrast, within a holographic hybrid, the work of every element, at every level, bears the stamp of the organization's distinctive commitment to be a Type A and a Type B organization – e.g., doctors weighing both the therapeutic value and the cost implications of their medical treatments or the family business CEO weighing trade-offs between family financial security and the growth of the business.

One indication of whether a hybrid is best classified as an ideographic or holographic hybrid is the expressed focus of member identification. As noted earlier, members tend to identify most with specific components of an organization's identity, which for them constitutes their core belief of 'who we are' as an organization (Ashforth and Mael, 1989; Pratt, 1998). In ideographic hybrids, members' level of identification with the organization's Type A and Type B identity claims would be highly correlated with their work assignments – their functional or geographic units (e.g., Pratt and Rafaeli, 1997; Voss et al., 2006). In contrast, in a holographic hybrid, there would be relatively high levels of identification for both sets of identity claims among all or most members (e.g., Foreman and Whetten, 2002).

In general, we would expect to see relatively few holographic HIOs, for several reasons. First of all, it is difficult to hire individuals who equally identify with, and are capable of implementing, multiple sets of distinctly different identity claims (Batillana and Dorado, 2010). This challenge becomes even more difficult as the organization grows in size and scope. It is also difficult

to organize internal operations in such a manner that conflicting identity claims are equally represented or manifested (Voss et al., 2006). Recalling Albert and Whetten's (1985) generic normative-utilitarian hybrid, it is often the case that organizers combine a normative organizational mission with a utilitarian organizational form – as in the case of healthcare systems (Pratt and Rafaeli, 1997), development banks (Battilana and Dorado, 2010), or professional orchestras (Glynn, 2000). This way of organizing naturally lends itself to an ideographic structure and culture, wherein traditional utilitarian operations are employed to accomplish seemingly incompatible normative outcomes (e.g., advancement of the arts or rural development).

Within the population of family businesses we suspect this general observation holds true. As noted by family business scholars, there are two major structural issues within family businesses: the degree of family ownership and/or control, and the proportion of family versus non-family members (Dyer, 2006; Lambrecht and Lievens, 2008). Major fault lines in these aspects are most likely observed in large, successful, especially technical, family firms, where the needs for professional management staff and other specialized skills, as well as overall manpower requirements, outstrip available family human resources. These types of family businesses are similar to what Dyer (2006) has called 'professional' family firms, and are most likely to be configured as ideographic hybrids, where the family maintains significant ownership and control, and also acts as guardians of the company culture, but depends on professional managers to run the day-to-day operation (e.g., Wal-Mart or Marriott). In contrast, the holographic hybrid form is more likely observed in smaller, first-generation family businesses with limited human resource requirements, both in terms of total number and specialized skills. Here the family fully owns and operates the enterprise themselves and is committed to the goals and values of both business and

		Degree of Identity Integration (Locus of Duality)	
		Low: A + B Ideographic Hybrid	High: A x B Holographic Hybrid
Degree of Identity Priority (Order of Duality)	**High: Ab / aB** Default 'trumping-rights'	1. *Segregated and Unequal Identities*	2. *Integrated and Unequal Identities*
	Low: AB Situational 'trumping-rights'	3. *Segregated and Equal Identities*	4. *Integrated and Equal Identities*

Figure 24.1   Classifying Hybrid Identity Organizations

family – what Dyer (2006) refers to as 'clan' family firms. In brief, we suspect that some of the key indicators of whether family firms are organized as ideographic or holographic hybrids are their size and specialized human resource requirements. Sundaramurthy and Kreiner (2008) have proposed a similar relationship between the degree of identity integration and several structural elements, including family/non-family personnel and ownership and governance arrangements.

Degree of Identity Priority – The Order of Duality

The second classifying dimension we propose focuses on the importance assigned to the HIO's multiple identities. Specifically, it centers on whether or not an organization has established an a priori ordering of their identity claims, what we refer to as the presence or absence of 'trumping rights', signified as 'High: Ab/aB' vs 'Low: AB'. In other words, in the rare cases in which an operational or strategic decision requires organizational leaders to choose between their Type A and Type B identities, can decision-makers invoke a widely accepted organizational rule specifying which identity claim should be given priority? In the absence of a predetermined ordering of identity claims, the default is for decision makers to give preferential treatment to one of the organization's identities on the basis of situation-specific

factors. This distinction can be broadly depicted as rule-based (permanent trumping rights) vs situation-based (temporary trumping rights) identity conflict resolution.

Using the terminology of this chapter, this dimension of Figure 24.1 addresses the question: Have the individuals with the ultimate decision making authority ('owners') prioritized the organization's incompatible identity claims? Few decisions are justified using an organization's identity claims. ('Because this is who we are, we must choose this alternative.' 'If we choose that alternative, we would cease being the kind of organization we've historically claimed to be.'). Most decisions do not require decision makers to invoke their organization's identity. For example, universities are likely to decide how much tuition to charge on the basis of a competitive analysis. In cases where invoking the organization's identity claims is optional, we would expect to see less use of this criteria in HIOs – due to the internal threat of a civil war or the external threat of loss of legitimacy.

Given the inherent risks of an identity crisis or conflict, we might expect to see 'owners' of HIOs making it clear that if a decision requires us to prioritize our incompatible, indispensable, inviolate identity claims, we will honor 'A' above all others. The likelihood of such a written or unwritten policy seems greatest in HIOs that have experienced a decision-induced identity crisis. Inasmuch as such conflicts are more likely in ideographic hybrids, we would expect to see mature, large, diversified family firms, for example, formulating rule-based decision criteria.

Family business scholars interested in governance processes have consistently noted the benefits of deliberate, long-term planning. Specific instances include the use of 'family constitutions' (Lambrecht and Lievens, 2008) and succession plans (Brockhaus, 2004). The prescriptive tone of this scholarship suggests that rule-based decision making is the exception, not the norm, in family firms. Family business lore is replete with tales of brother-turned-against-brother as well as inter-generational alienation and disaffection (Dyer, 1986). Surely this is not what family firm founders intend.

Within the category of rule-based decision making, it is tempting to speculate about the conditions surrounding an Fb vs fB focus at a particular point in an organization's life cycle. Especially during the early history of a family business, the intent of the founder is obviously consequential – that is, whether the initial goal was to use available family resources to support an emerging business opportunity (fB), or to use the assets from a sustainable business to support a family's (nuclear or extended) financial needs (Fb). Over time, the size/ success and age of a family firm will likely play into the trumping-rights equation. In particular, it is likely that a combination of high firm size/success and a high number of generations of family members with a 'stake' in the firm will produce an fB focus. In the extreme fB case, family owners end up focusing more on wealth generation and preservation than on what kind of business activities are the source of their financial gain.

Conflict in Different Kinds of Hybrid Identity Organizations

Inasmuch as the subject of identity-related conflict is central to the literature on hybrid identity organizations (Glynn, 2002;

Golden-Biddle and Rao, 1997; Kraatz and Block, 2008; Pratt and Rafaeli, 1997), we will use it to explore how Figure 24.1 might be used to make systematic comparisons between different kinds of HIOs. While it is axiomatic that HIOs are more prone to identity-related conflicts, little scholarship has examined the incidence and consequences of these conflicts among different kinds of hybrids. Thus, to illustrate the merits of incorporating the HIO-type into this body of research, we briefly explore how the dimensions in Figure 24.1 might affect the nature of identity conflict in HIOs.

It is expected that the two dimensions used to construct Figure 24.1 are both correlated with the likelihood of identity-related conflicts (identity crises). Starting with the degree of identity integration dimension, scholars have argued that when hybrid identities are pervasive and embedded in all facets of the organization (i.e., a holographic HIO), as opposed to isolated in select units (i.e., an ideographic HIO), identity conflicts will be more substantial, consequential, and intractable (Fiol et al., 2009; Pache and Santos, 2010; Pratt and Foreman, 2000). Furthermore, such conflict is exacerbated when those hybrid identities are associated with powerful stakeholders (Pratt and Foreman, 2000), have significant financial implications (Reger et al., 1998), and/or reflect deeply-held, historically rooted organizational values, goals, purposes, etc. (Albert et al., 1998; Kraatz and Block, 2008).

The 'locus' of identity conflicts within HIOs can be predicted based on the type and/ or degree of hybrid identity integration. In an ideographic HIO such tensions are likely to occur *between* positions, units and programs. This form of identity crisis risks being escalated into an organizational civil war, where deeply entrenched positions battle over 'Who are we, as an organization … really!?' In contrast, identity conflicts within holographic hybrids are more likely to be manifested *within* positions, units and programs. In cases where all/most individuals identify strongly with both identities (e.g., family members in a rapidly growing family-owned-and-operated business), this conflict occurs internally as an existential struggle over 'Who am I … really!?' The comparison between 'organizational multiple-personality-disorder' and 'individual multiple-personality-disorder' (suggested by a psychiatrist whose patient list included several medical doctors practicing in an evolving health care system) vividly contrasts the locus of identity crises in these two kinds of HIOs.

Switching to the second dimension, degree of identity prioritization, it has been posited that conflicts between competing identities may be minimized by an unambiguous prioritization of identities (Albert et al., 1998), as in a clear identity hierarchy (Pratt and Foreman, 2000). Such mitigation may be the result of singular demands from the institutional environment (Kraatz and Block, 2008; Pache and Santos, 2010), a compelling signal from the market (Reger et al., 1998), functional requirements for legitimacy (Moss et al., 2011; Zuckerman, 1999), or the strength of the founding mission (Albert et al., 1998). In any case, such clear prioritization, especially if understood and accepted by most stakeholders, removes many issues from being potential sources of conflict. While fork-in-the-road decisions are relatively uncommon in organizations, including HIOs, the challenge facing low-identity-prioritization HIOs is the ever-present uncertainty about which identity will prevail if and when such a situation arises, possibly reflecting the identity preferences of the particular leader(s) making the decision. In contrast, in high-prioritization HIOs it is widely understood that when faced with an identity dilemma (a choice requiring the organization to express a preference for one of its incompatible identities) decision makers should consistently favor the highest priority identity.

The identity prioritization dimension suggests insights into the possible negative consequences of identity conflicts in different kinds of HIOs. At the onset of an identity crisis in low-prioritization organizations (AB), we would expect to observe a very high level of anticipatory stress, due to the uncertainty over which fork in the road will be chosen. Following the resolution of the crisis in low-prioritization HIOs, key stakeholders who identify with one of the organization's identities are likely to draw conclusions about the degree of future support for 'their side' – possibly leading some to feel disenfranchised. If enough members who identify primarily with one element of a hybrid's identity leave the organization over a long enough period of time, the organization's identity is likely to change. More specifically, an un-prioritized (AB) hybrid organization is likely to drift into a highly-prioritized (Ab/aB) one.

IMPLICATIONS FOR FAMILY BUSINESS SCHOLARSHIP

The concept of organizational identity and its derivative, hybrid identity, are well suited for family business scholarship. Although these terms are not commonly used among family business researchers, it is likely that, within the hybrid-identity-organizational population, family businesses are the most widely studied example. Recent research on family businesses would seem to confirm this assertion (e.g., Boers and Nordqvist, 2012; Dyer and Whetten, 2006; Shepherd and Haynie, 2009; Sundaramurthy and Kreiner, 2008). What the identity perspective offers is a coherent theoretical framework and associated vocabulary for the raison d'être of family business research – understanding the unique properties of family-owned business enterprises. In this final section, we suggest a few potentially interesting lines of inquiry whereby the material outlined in this chapter might inform family business scholarship, which in turn may advance the broader understanding of organizational identity.

At the core of this chapter we presented a conceptualization of the hybrid-identity-organization as an ideal type, and then provided a two-dimensional framework as a means of distinguishing among various kinds of HIOs. Recognizing the almost prototypical nature of family businesses as HIOs, future research in this domain might employ the classification scheme as a means of better explicating readily-observed differences in family businesses. Given the size and diversity of this organizational population, family business scholars are in a unique position to systematically make comparisons between the different kinds of HIOs depicted in Figure 24.1. Are some cells more common than others, and if so, how or why? Under what set of circumstances or conditions might one expect to find a given form of HIO rather than others? Are some types more stable than others? It may be that some cells are more like transitional forms or states. Comparing how samples of family businesses representing each dimension or cell respond to the same business challenges and understanding the developmental, evolutionary pathways from one type to another would greatly deepen our understanding of hybrid-identity organizations. Furthermore, changes in identity prioritization over time, due in part to increased organizational size and maturity, have been implied in prior research (e.g., Albert and Whetten, 1981; Pratt and Foreman, 2000; Foreman and Parent, 2008), but there has been virtually no empirical examination of this issue to date.

In addition to enhancing the understanding of differences in types of family businesses, the HIO concept offers the opportunity for greater insight into perhaps the most compelling issue in family businesses – conflict. To date, studies have shown that conflicts in family firms are most often precipitated by decisions pertaining to such things as priorities and goals, working relationships, decision-making and control, monitoring and rewards, hiring criteria, and succession (e.g., Brockhaus, 2004; Chrisman et al., 2004; Daily and Dollinger, 1992; Eddleston and Kellermanns, 2007; Lambrecht and Lievens, 2004; Tagiuri and Davis, 1992). Most, if not all of these issues can be seen as related to and following from the organization's identity. Moving forward, research might examine whether this pattern of identity-related 'trigger decisions' is consistent across the dimensions and cells in Figure 24.1. Are certain kinds of events, circumstances, structures, relationships, decisions, etc. more significant in precipitating conflict in certain quadrants? Moreover, it is logical that the nature of conflict (frequency, intensity, pervasiveness, duration, etc.) varies across the different types of HIOs, and family businesses would likely demonstrate that. While there are numerous examples of how business decisions have destroyed family ties, research might explore the moderating effects of identity integration and prioritization. For example, perhaps significant conflict in large, mature family businesses, where family owners have clearly delegated operational authority to professional managers (cell #1), is limited to a few pivotal 'identity-defining' inflection points, such as selling the business.

Shifting our focus to how future research in family business might contribute to identity theory, the HIO ideal type – and the family firm as an exemplar of that type – provides a reference point for examining the all-too-common phenomenon of multiple or multifaceted identities in organizations. Recognizing that not all family-owned-and-operated enterprises are created equal – and that there are deviations from the HIO ideal type, we can use the framework developed here to more clearly explicate the overlap and distinctions between the presence of multiple organizational identities and the existence of a true hybrid-identity-organization.

Earlier we discussed the distinction between the social actor and social constructionist view of organizational identity, and noted its relevance for family business research, helping clearly distinguish between family-owned and operated businesses and firms that profess to operate according to family values. An SC view of an organization often captures the multifaceted nature of its identity, as a reflection of different stakeholder perceptions. As such, the organization may certainly be said to have multiple identities; however, it may not necessarily be a structural hybrid. That is to say, the HIO concept, specifically when applied in the context of family businesses, helps make a distinction in cases where the presence of hybrid values, logics, or objectives does not necessarily infer a HIO – particularly if the multiple identities are not incompatible, indispensible, and inviolate. As Pratt and Foreman (2000) noted, in the case of an organization where one of its plural identities is located in a particular 'added-on' unit, which came about as the result of a merger or acquisition, that identity may not be 'indispensible' or 'inviolate', and therefore conflict can be mitigated by isolating or even removing that unit. But in the typical family firm, where family members founded the enterprise and still have ownership if not decision-making authority, such 'segregation' or 'pruning' inexorably alters the hybrid identity of the organization.

As we also discussed above, the concept of organizational identification seems particularly pertinent to family business scholarship, and in turn offers opportunities to expand our understanding of the identification process. While it is often difficult to understand what it is about most organizations that members identify with, this point of reference tends to be much clearer in a family business – and yet much more complicated. As a result of having multiple bases of identification – both the family and the firm – and the overlap between them, a family member who is an owner-operator of the firm would likely have stronger OID than the non-family employee, leading to greater loyalty, satisfaction, commitment, etc. By way of contrast, in large, mature family businesses that are more ideographic, where there is a clear separation between family ownership and managerial control, one would expect to find that OID differs significantly among individuals, based on their group/category membership. Moreover, these different forms of family businesses would logically display dissimilar antecedents and consequences of identification. In sum, the clarity of the targets of identification in family businesses, coupled with the variation in the structure and types of family businesses as HIOs, provide opportunities for expanding our understanding of organizational identification.

Finally, two concepts closely related to organizational identity – legitimacy and reputation – shed light on the broader question of whether family involvement is an asset or liability for family businesses. The liability most often noted stems from the challenge of satisfying incompatible legitimacy requirements, typically stemming from multiple stakeholder expectations (Zellweger and Nason, 2008). In contrast, family businesses often enjoy reputation benefits, especially in arenas like social enterprise where the ideal business is expected to operate like a family, or with highly normative principles (Bingham et al., 2011; Moss et al., 2011). However, we also described a means-ends inversion wherein family members become so focused on wealth accumulation that they engage in family-identity-destroying activities. In these instances the reputations of both the firm and the family are likely to be damaged. Moving forward, we see several promising research questions. Compared with other HIOs exhibiting a similar combination of normative and utilitarian values (e.g., professional orchestras, marketing cooperatives, development banks), do family businesses experience similar legitimacy-reputation trade-offs? What are the contextual conditions (e.g., cultural norms, economic and political structures, type of industry) that moderate the potential reputational benefits of family ownership? How do different levels of family ownership and operational involvement impact either the legitimacy threats or the reputational benefits experienced by this type of HIO? And, in line with Figure 24.1, how might the interplay between identity, legitimacy, and reputation vary among family businesses with different levels of identity integration and prioritization?

REFERENCES

Albert, S.A. and Whetten, D.A. (1985). Organizational identity. In L.L Cummings and B.M. Staw (eds), *Research in Organizational Behavior* (Vol. 7, pp. 263–295). Greenwich, CT: JAI.

Albert, S.A., Godfrey, P.C., and Whetten, D.A. (1998). Hybrid identity organizations. Working paper, Marriott School of Management, Brigham Young University, Provo, Utah.

Albert, S.A. and Adams, E. (2002). The hybrid identity of law firms. In B. Moingeon and G. Soenen (eds), *Corporate and Organizational Identities: Integrating Strategy, Marketing, Communication and Organizational Perspectives* (pp. 35–50). London: Routledge.

Ashforth, B.E. and Mael, F. (1989). Social identity theory and the organization. *Academy of Management Review*, 14, 20–39.

Ashforth, B.E., Harrison, S., and Corley, K. (2008). Identification in organizations: An examination of four fundamental questions. *Journal of Management*, 34(3), 325–374.

Battilana, J. and Dorado, S. (2010). Building sustainable hybrid organizations: the case of commercial microfinance organizations. *Academy of Management Journal*, 53, 1419–1440.

Bingham, J.B., Dyer, W.G., Smith, I., and Adams, G.L. (2011). A stakeholder identity orientation approach to corporate social performance in family firms. *Journal of Business Ethics*, 99(4), 565–585.

Boers, B. and Nordqvist, M. (2012). Understanding hybrid-identity organizations: The case of publicly listed family businesses. In A.L. Carsrud and M. Brannback (eds), *Understanding Family Businesses* (pp. 251–269). Springer.

Brickson, S.L. (2013). Athletes, best friends, and social activists: An integrative model accounting for the role of identity in organizational identification. *Organization Science*, 24(1), 226–245.

Brockhaus, R.H. (2004). Family business succession: Suggestions for future research. *Family Business Review*, 17, 165–177.

Chrisman, J.J., Chua J.H., and Litz, R.A. (2004). Comparing the agency cost of family and non-family firms. *Entrepreneurship Theory & Practice*, 28(4), 335–354.

Daily, C.M. and Dollinger, M.J. (1992). An empirical examination of ownership structure in family and professionally managed firms. *Family Business Review*, 5(2), 117–136.

Dutton, J.E., Dukerich, J.M., and Harquail, C.V. (1994). Organizational images and member identification. *Administrative Science Quarterly*, 39(2), 239–263.

Dyer, W.G. (1986). *Cultural Change in Family Firms: Anticipating and Managing Business and Family Transitions*. San Francisco, CA: Jossey-Bass.

Dyer, W.G. (2006). Examining the 'family effect' on firm performance. *Family Business Review*, 19(4), 253–273.

Dyer, W.G. and Whetten, D.A. (2006). Family firms and social responsibility: Preliminary results from the S&P 500. *Entrepreneurship Theory & Practice*, 30, 785–802.

Eddleston, K. and Kellermanns, F.W. (2007). Destructive and productive family relationships: A stewardship theory perspective. *Journal of Business Venturing*, 22 (4), 545–565.

Fiol, C.M., Pratt, M.G., and O'Connor, E.J. (2009). Managing intractable identity conflict. *Academy of Management Review*, 34(1), 32–55.

Foreman, P.O. (1998). Slaying the chimera? Threats to the survival of agricultural cooperatives as multiple identity organization. In D.A. Whetten and P. Godfrey (eds), *Identity in Organizations: Building Theory Through Conversations*. Thousand Oaks, CA: Sage.

Foreman, P.O., Parent, M.M. (2008). The process of organizational identity construction in iterative organizations. *Corporate Reputation Review*, 11(3), 222–245.

Foreman, P.O., Whetten, D.A. (2002). Members' identification with multiple-identity organizations. *Organizational Science*, 13(6), 618–635.

Foreman, P.O., Whetten, D.A., and Mackey, A. (2012). An identity-based view of reputation, image, and legitimacy: Classifications and distinctions among related constructs. In M. Barnett and T. Pollock (eds), *Oxford Handbook of Organizational Reputation* (pp. 179–200). Oxford: Oxford University Press.

Gioia, D.A., Schultz, M.J., and Corley, K.G. (2000). Organizational identity, image, and adaptive instability. *Academy of Management Review*, 25(1), 63–81.

Gioia, D.A., Price, K.N., Hamilton, A.L., and Thomas, J.B. (2010). Forging an identity: An insider-outsider study of processes involved in the formation of organizational identity. *Administrative Science Quarterly*, 55(1), 1–46.

Glynn, M.A. (2000). When cymbals become symbols: Conflict over organizational identity within a symphony orchestra. *Organization Science*, 11(3), 285–298.

Golden-Biddle, K. and Rao, H. (1997). Breaches in the boardroom: Organizational identity and conflicts of commitment in a non-profit organization. *Organization Science*, 8(6), 593–611.

Habbershon, T.G., Williams, M., and MacMillan, I.C. (2003). A unified systems perspective of family firm performance. *Journal of Business Venturing*, 18(4), 451–465.

Haveman, H.A. and Khaire, M.V. (2004). Survival beyond succession? The contingent impact of founder succession on organizational failure. *Journal of Business Venturing*, 19(3), 437–463.

Hilburt-Davis, J. and Dyer, W.G. (2003). *Consulting to Family Businesses*. San Francisco, CA: Jossey-Bass.

Hogg, M.A., Terry, D.J., and White, K.M. (1995). A tale of two theories: A critical comparison of identity theory with social identity theory. *Social Psychology Quarterly*, 58, 225–269.

Hsu, G. and Hannan, M.T. (2005). Identities, genres, and organizational forms. *Organization Science*, 16, 474–490.

King, B.G. and Whetten, D.A. (2008). Rethinking the relationship between reputation and legitimacy: A social actor conceptualization. *Corporate Reputation Review*, 11, 192–207.

Kraatz, M.S. and Block, E.S. (2008). Organizational implications of institutional pluralism. In R. Greenwood, C. Oliver, R. Suddaby and K. Sahlin-Andersson (eds), *Handbook of Organizational Institutionalism* (pp. 243–274). London: Sage.

Lambrecht, J. and Lievens, J. (2008). Pruning the family tree: An unexplored path to business continuity and family harmony. *Family Business Review*, 21, 295–313.

McCall, G.J. and Simmons, J.L. (1978). *Identities and Interactions: An Examination of Associations in Everyday Life* (revised edition). New York: The Free Press.

Moss, T.W., Short, J.C., Payne, G.T., and Lumpkin, G.T. (2011). Dual identities in social ventures: An exploratory study. *Entrepreneurship Theory & Practice*, 35(4), 805–830.

Pache, A.C. and Santos, F. (2010). When worlds collide: The internal dynamics of organizational responses to conflicting institutional demands. *Academy of Management Review*, 35(3), 455–476.

Pratt, M.G. and Rafaeli, A. (1997). Organizational dress as a symbol of multilayered social identities. *Academy of Management Journal*, 40(4), 862–898.

Pratt, M.G. (1998). To be or not to be? Central questions in organizational identification. In D.A. Whetten and P.C. Godfrey (eds), *Identity in Organizations:* *Building theory Through Conversations* (pp. 171–207). Thousand Oaks, CA: Sage.

Pratt, M.G. and Foreman, P.O. (2000). Classifying managerial responses to multiple organizational identities. *Academy of Management Review*, 25, 18–42.

Rao, H. (1994). The social construction of reputation: Certification contests, legitimation, and the survival of organizations in the American automobile industry: 1895–1912. *Strategic Management Journal*, 14, 29–44.

Ravasi, D. and Schultz, M.J. (2006). Responding to organizational identity threats: Exploring the role of organizational culture. *Academy of Management Journal*, 49, 433–458.

Reger, R.K., Barney, J., Bunderson, S., Foreman, P., Gustafson, L.T., Huff, A.S., Martens, L., Sarason, Y., and Stimpert, L. (1998). A strategy conversation on the topic of organizational identity. In D.A. Whetten and P. Godfrey (eds), *Identity in Organizations: Developing Theory Through Conversations* (pp. 99–168). Thousand Oaks, CA: Sage.

Schein, E.H. (1983). The role of the founder in creating organization cultures. *Organizational Dynamics*, Summer, 13–28.

Shepherd, D. and Haynie, J.M. (2009). Family business, identity conflict, and an expedited entrepreneurial process: A process of resolving identity conflict. *Entrepreneurship Theory & Practice*, 33(6): 1245–1264.

Smith, E.B. (2011). Identities as lenses: How organizational identity affects audiences' evaluation of organizational performance. *Administrative Science Quarterly*, 56, 61–94.

Stets, J.E. and Burke, P.J. (2000). Identity theory and social identity theory. *Social Psychology Quarterly*, 63, 224–237.

Stryker, S. (1980). *Symbolic Interactionism: A Social Structural Version*. Menlo Park, CA: Benjamin/Cummings.

Sundaramurthy, C. and Kreiner, G.E. (2008). Governing by managing identity boundaries: The case of family businesses. *Entrepreneurship Theory & Practice*, 32(3), 415–436.

Tagiuri, R. and Davis, J.A. (1992). On the goals of successful family companies. *Family Business Review*, 5(1), 43–62.

Tajfel, H. (1978). Social categorization, social identity, and social comparison. In H. Tajfel (ed.), *Differentiation Between Social Groups: Studies in the Social Psychology of Intergroup Relations* (pp. 61–76). London: Academic Press.

Turner, J.C. (1982). Towards a cognitive redefinition of the social group. In Tajfel, H. (ed.), *Social Identity and*

Intergroup Relations (pp. 15–40). Cambridge: Cambridge University Press.

Voss, Z.G., Cable, D.M., and Voss, G.B. (2006). Organizational identity and firm performance: What happens when leaders disagree about 'who we are?'. *Organization Science*, 17(6), 741–755.

Whetten, D.A. and Mackey, A. (2002). A social actor conception of organizational identity and its implications for the study of organizational reputation. *Business and Society*, 41(4), 393–414.

Whetten, D.A. (2006). Albert and Whetten revisited: Strengthening the concept of organizational identity. *Journal of Management Inquiry*, 15(3), 219–234.

Zellweger, T.M. and Nason, R.S. (2008). A stakeholder perspective on family firm performance. *Family Business Review*, 21(3), 203–216.

Zuckerman, E.W. (1999). The categorical imperative: Securities analysts and the illegitimacy discount. *American Journal of Sociology*, 104(5), 1398–1438.

25

Trust and Family Businesses

Lloyd Steier and Miriam Muethel

INTRODUCTION

Trust constitutes an essential ingredient of economic exchange and is manifest in organizing activities throughout the world. This chapter examines trust and the ancillary concept of social capital within the context of family enterprise. As a starting point, we subscribe to two of the most commonly used working definitions of trust: Individual trust: 'the willingness of a party to be vulnerable to the actions of another party based on the expectation that the other will perform a particular action important to the trustor, irrespective of the ability to monitor or control that other party' (Mayer et al., 1995: 712). Collective trust: 'the ability to rely on the group, the family, and/or the business' (Sorenson, 2011: 15). Trust has been shown to nurture private (Larzelere and Huston, 1980) as well as economic partnerships (Kramer, 1999). In family businesses, private and economic partnerships meet each other and create a unique context for trust.

Conceptually, categories such as the nuclear family and extended family are common-sense, indispensable designations for 'describing and circumscribing the organizational field' (Caplow, 1964: 49). Families are often naturally occurring 'high trust' organizations and this trust typically extends to family-based business relationships. Indeed familial trust provides an essential 'lubricant' that facilitates exchange relationships at a variety of levels ranging from the creation of new firms to the governance of nations and international trade.

Theories relative to trust highlight two disparate approaches to economic exchange: on the one hand, there are certain social institutions such as the family that facilitate trust; on the other hand, rational actors have incentives to act in their own self-interest and not necessarily in the best interests of the group. Trust is also embedded in a larger debate on agency relations and opportunism (Cruz et al., 2010). At the heart of this debate (Cruz et al., 2010: 70) is 'the prescription of agency theorists that it is prudent for principals to assume that agents may act opportunistically' versus the claim that certain actors 'intrinsically value co-operative behaviour' and will make decisions that are in the best interests of the group. Importantly, trust facilitated cooperation exhibited in familial groupings often yields greater benefits to the collective – as well as individuals within the collective – then to individuals acting alone. We suggest that further interesting aspects of trust relative to family firms include the changing nature of governance, temporality, and permutations of optimal trust.

It is also possible to make a broad distinction between family firms and their non-family counterparts relative to firm creation, growth, and the evolution of trust (Steier, 2001a; Sundarmurthy, 2008). A notable feature of family firms is they are often founded as 'high trust' organizations that benefit greatly from reduced agency costs. However, this trust is often replaced by conflict and strife as firms – and families – naturally evolve and grow. On the other hand, in non-family businesses 'formal contracts and controls are initially used to start business relationships, which are gradually complemented with relationship-based (identification) trust …' (Sundarmurthy, 2008: 98). In these two scenarios, the role of trust in firm governance has distinctly different evolutionary paths.

The remainder of this chapter further explores the concept of trust relative to family business and is divided into six sections. The next section provides an overview of manifestations of familial trust in various economic exchange contexts. We then introduce social capital and discuss its general relationship to trust in familial contexts. In the third section, we rely on metaphor to further illustrate key aspects of trust and social capital that have useful applications to family business. The fourth section further explores theoretical framings of trust, including a discussion of distrust. The fifth section discusses future research directions. The final section offers conclusions.

MANIFESTATIONS OF FAMILIAL TRUST IN VARIED ECONOMIC EXCHANGE CONTEXTS

As a 'lubricant' of economic exchange, trust is an elusive multidimensional concept with many manifestations. While exploring the more general relationship between trust and entrepreneurship, Welter (2012: 4) offers some useful distinctions related to the forms, levels, and objects of trust: At the micro level, trust is manifest at the personal level with the object of trust being personal relationship. At the meso level, trust is manifest at the level of the collective with object being the community and/or the organization. At a more macro level, trust is manifest in various institutions with the object being cultural rules, formal regulations, business infrastructure, or government. In addition to being a multidimensional concept, trust (Welter, 2012: 4) has 'recursive links between different levels, forms and sources'. Below, we further elaborate some of these dimensions in family contexts.

At the micro level we see many examples of familial trust – particularly in the realm of altruistic-based family financing of new ventures (Steier, 2003). Additionally, new ventures often experience a substantial liability of newness (Stinchcombe, 1965) and one of the primary reasons for their high mortality rate is the challenge of establishing relationships with strangers. Stinchcombe (1965) stressed that it was much easier to rely on existing relationships – wherein that all-important trust already exists – than it is to establish relations with strangers. When families become involved in business there are at least two bases for trust: 'emotional bonds and commitment to a family-business identity' (Sorenson, 2011: 16). This trust translates into certain advantages. For example, family members potentially offer a rich repository of resources for the venture creation process (Steier, 2003, 2007). Similarly, households (Steier, 2009a) represent important business incubators wherein entrepreneurs find it helpful to rely on family members either because it is expedient or they are resources of last resort. For instance, family members will commonly lend money for business ventures (Steier, 2003) simply because they trust their kin and not so much because they support a particular idea. Similarly, Karra et al. (2006) studied an entrepreneurial firm that began international operations very soon after founding. As this venture grew, they noted it was built on trust relationships beginning with family and close kin and then extending to distant kin and ethnic ties. However, as this firm grew further and eventually became both international and of a significantly large size, a trust-based system based on kin and community ties became problematic.

Steier (2001a) also explores temporal aspects as well as the changing nature of trust in family firms. He notes that 'in the early stages of firm development, the trust indigenous in most family relationships allows firms to reduce transaction costs substantially. As family firms evolve, so does the optimal role of trust as a governance mechanism' (2001a: 353). He further notes that, for some family firms, what was once a resilient trust can sometimes evolve into an atmosphere of fragile trust or even distrust. He then suggests that various stages of family firm evolution (for example, owner-founder, sibling partnership, cousin consortium) each have their own governance imperatives and different permutations of trust.

At a more meso level, the organizational theory and economics literatures portray trust as a key mechanism in organizational governance. Along with market and hierarchy, it is sometimes represented as a third generic form of economic organization (Bradach and Eccles, 1989; Williamson, 1991). Bradach and Eccles (1989: 116) further note that the three major models of governance (market, hierarchy, and relational contracting based on trust) are often 'combined with each other in assorted ways in the empirical world...' Overall, trust remains the least understood (Bradach and Eccles, 1989) mechanism of governance. Family businesses offer particularly unique sites within which to study trust as a governance mechanism. In addition to being organizations that

rely on trust-based governance, they often have a natural capacity to create a 'resilient' or enduring trust (Pearson and Carr, 2011).

Similarly – at a more macro national and societal levels – trust is viewed as an essential element of economic progress (Fukuyama, 1995; Putnam, 1993). Studies on the global history of corporate governance (Morck and Steier, 2005) suggest an overarching question: 'To Whom Dare We Entrust Corporate Governance?' Modern day capitalism represents a diversified collection of economic systems with different manifestations of market, hierarchy, and relational contracting based on trust. For Fukuyama (1995), essential questions include whether a nation's history enables it to facilitate the maintenance of enduring family businesses and/or enables it to create economic institutions that transcend kin-based organizations. Using Sweden as an example, Hogfeldt (2005) illustrates how one nation has chosen to entrust family-controlled business groups as the primary links to the private sector. Other nations (Morck, 2005) either by choice – or accidents of history – illustrate different permutations of familial trust, market, and hierarchical forms of governance.

Thus, trust, often naturally occurring in familial contexts, can be observed in a variety of organizing contexts ranging from start-ups to larger mature organizations. It has also been attributed to playing a role in the competitive advantage of nations. Albeit important in conferring certain advantages, trust is also recognized as being accompanied by certain 'fragility' that can rapidly evolve to distrust with implications for firm and family well-being. Importantly, for many firms, optimal trust has an evolutionary aspect that must also be recognized and managed. Trust has also further been portrayed as representing an essential element in the broader notion of social capital; below we briefly explore these linkages.

TRUST AND SOCIAL CAPITAL

Social capital – alongside physical capital and human capital – is typically represented as one of the three basic types of capital that confer business advantage. Eddleston et al. (2010) note that trust is closely linked to social capital theory. Similarly Hubler (2011: 45) describes trust as a 'central component in the development of a family firm's social capital'. Recently, a 'considerable amount' of attention (De Massis et al., 2012) has been devoted to the social capital of family firms – particularly its relationship to competitive advantage.

Adler and Kwon (2002: 18) describe the 'core intuition' of social capital theory as: 'the goodwill that others have towards us is a valuable resource' and further argue (2002: 22) that trust is a key source of social capital. Steier (2001b: 259) notes that social capital includes 'those assets embedded in relationships with other players and organizations' and further adds (2001b: 260) that it can also be observed from utilizing levels of analysis, including 'individual, organizational, interorganizational, and societal'. Many definitions of social capital include trust as a key dimension. For example, Adler and Kwon (2002: 18) include trust as an essential element of the goodwill that constitutes social capital: 'sympathy, trust, and forgiveness offered us by friends and acquaintances.' Arregle et al. (2007: 73) define social capital as 'the goodwill and resources made available to an actor via reciprocal, trusting relationships … .' Leana and Van Buren (1999: 540) portray social capital as 'the character of social relationships within the organization, realized through members' levels of collective goal orientation and shared trust'.

Putnam (1993) also identifies various dimensions of organizational and societal social capital including network structure, norms of reciprocity, and trust. Adler and Kwon (2002: 26) note that the relationship between trust and social capital generates a certain amount of confusion and cite some of the major works on trust to illustrate this observation:

> Some authors equate trust with social capital (Fukuyama, 1995, 1997), some see trust as a source of social capital (Putnam, 1993), some see it as a form of social capital (Coleman, 1988), and some see it as a collective asset resulting from social capital construed as a relational asset (Lin, 1999). In the opportunity-motivation ability schema, trust presents itself as a key motivational source of social capital …

Akin to the concept of trust, social capital strongly supports resource-based views (RBV) of the firm. Subscribing to an RBV view, Arregle et al. (2007: 74) observe that family members – particularly through their propensity to model trust – offer ideal conditions to build repositories of social capital that might be utilized for competitive advantage. They further note that, for family firms, at least two types of social capital coexist, 'the family's and the firm's'. A family's social capital (FSC) may be utilized in the development (or destruction) of organizational social capital (OSC). They also observe (2007: 76) that family can be a source, builder, and user of social capital; families by modeling trust provide a foundation for cooperation and coordination. Similarly, Pearson et al. (2008: 949) present 'familiness' as 'resources and capabilities that are unique to the family's involvement and interactions in the business' and suggest that social capital is a resource that uniquely resides in family firms.

Subscribing to a broader societal context, Fukuyama (1995: 7) offers a further illustration of the importance of trust and social capital: 'one of the most important lessons we can learn from an examination of economic life is that a nation's well-being, as well as its ability to compete, is conditioned by a single, pervasive characteristic: the level of *trust* inherent in the society.' He (1995: 62) further describes the capacity to build new bonds of trust as 'sociability' and notes that bonds 'based on family and kinship' represent an important repository of social capital that characterizes a pathway to prosperity.

The benefits and risks of exchange systems that rely on familial trust and social capital can be conceptualized and illustrated in many ways. Below, we briefly introduce metaphor to further illustrate and explore the benefits and risks of trust-based exchange systems.

COMMON METAPHORS RELEVANT TO FAMILIAL TRUST, SOCIAL CAPITAL, AND FAMILY ADVANTAGE

A Metaphor is commonly regarded as a powerful tool for understanding organizations and management. According to Morgan (1996: 5) 'all theory is metaphor' and the use of metaphor provides useful – albeit partial – insights into organizational life. There are certain social trust mechanisms that play an important role in cooperative behaviour (Tyler and Kramer, 1996: 5). Although families are social organizations that offer a unique dynamic wherein cooperative behaviour is most likely to occur, there are also times when family dynamics foster distrust. Below, we briefly introduce five metaphors commonly used to illustrate the nature and benefits of trust – as well as implications of distrust – in family and societal contexts.

Biological Metaphors

Nicholson (2008), referring to research in biology and evolutionary psychology, suggests that humans are 'hard-wired' to cooperate and this tendency is manifest in economic activity. Of course, the animal kingdom also offers many examples wherein the tendency to organize as family units is profound. In essence, family-based groups and their general tendency to take care of one another is biologically innate fact (Axelrod and Hamilton, 1981) and humans tend to continue to organize along patterns of kinship long after the biological necessity is removed.

Aesop's Bundle of Sticks

Aesop's fable portrays a family situation, where a father frustrated by his three sons constant quarrelling, offers a poignant example of the consequences of discord whilst extolling the benefits of cooperation:

> A certain Father had a family of Sons, who were forever quarreling among themselves. No words he could say did the least good, so he cast

about in his mind for some very striking example that should make them see that discord would lead them to misfortune. One day when the quarreling had been much more violent than usual and each of the Sons was moping in a surly manner, he asked one of them to bring him a bundle of sticks. Then handing the bundle to each of his Sons in turn he told them to try to break it. But although each one tried his best, none was able to do so. The Father then untied the bundle and gave the sticks to his Sons to break one by one. This they did very easily. 'My Sons,' said the Father, 'do you not see how certain it is that if you agree with each other and help each other, it will be impossible for your enemies to injure you? But if you are divided among yourselves, you will be no stronger than a single stick in that bundle.' (Encyclopedia.com – Aesop, 2005)

The Tragedy of the Commons

The 'Tragedy of the Commons' illustrates the damage created when multiple individuals, acting in their own self-interest, destroy a fundamentally sustainable resource. In this case, European herdsmen (Hardin, 1968) have joint access to common grazing land. If they simply cooperate – each grazing the number of cows within their allotment – the resource is sustainable indefinitely. However, if even just a few act in their own self-interest and graze beyond their allotment in order to receive additional benefits, the resource will soon be depleted – eventually destroyed for all.

The Stag Hunt

The 'Stag Hunt' is generally attributed to the philosopher Jean-Jacques Rousseau (1755) and is often used to explore dimensions of trust through games and simulations (Fang et al., 2002; Skyrms, 2004). In Fang et al. (2002),

> According to Rousseau: When it came to tracking down a deer, everyone realized that he should remain dependably at his post, but if a hare happened to pass within the reach of one of them, he undoubtedly would not have hesitated to run off after it and after catching his prey, he would have troubled himself little about causing his companions to lose theirs.

Everyone typically prefers to share a stag over a hare; however, this benefit is only realized when individuals sacrifice their own self-interest for the good of the collective.

The Social Trap

The 'Social Trap' (Platt, 1973) is often presented as an extension of the stag hunt metaphor; it usefully illustrates situations where social actors' behaviour is determined by their assessments of what others will do in the future.

Rothstein (2005: 12) describes the essential logic of this trust dynamic:

- The situation is such that 'everyone' wins if 'everyone' *chooses to cooperate.*
- But, if people cannot trust that 'almost everyone else will cooperate, it is meaningless to choose to cooperate, because the end is contingent on *cooperation by almost everyone else.'*
- Thus, non-cooperation may be rational when people *do not trust that others will also cooperate.*
- Conclusion: efficient cooperation for common purposes can come about only if people trust that most other people will choose to cooperate.
- Lacking that trust, the social trap will slam inexorably shut. That is, we end up in a state of affairs that is worse for everyone, even though everyone realizes they would profit by *choosing to cooperate.*

The preceding metaphors enable us to reflect on the nature of familial trust, social capital, and family advantage. First, in some circumstances certain elements of trust may be biologically innate. Second, trust behaviour will also emerge as a result of learning. Third, trusting relationships create a powerful synergy and a resultant 'social capital' that is greater than what individuals could normally create alone – in other words trust represents a key element of social capital. Fourth, social groups or institutions that generate social capital through trust endowments can be conceived in many ways; families represent unique social systems wherein cooperative behaviour, based on trust, is nurtured. Fifth, trust-based systems

have a certain fragility wherein trust can rapidly become distrust. Sixth, benevolence-based trust is 'a subjective perception based on a trustor's interpretation of the behaviour of a trustee' (Cruz et al., 2010: 69). Finally, familial trust-based systems and resultant social capital may be operationalized at individual, organizational, and societal levels.

FURTHER THEORETICAL FRAMINGS OF TRUST

As discussed above, trust has both an interpersonal dimension as well as a broader institutional dimension. In this vein, we can distinguish interpersonal trust between the family (and non-family) members of a family firm and a broader institutional trust. Within these contexts we now introduce some of the more general theoretical framings of trust and comment on their relevance to family business.

Interpersonal Trust and Relationships Among Members of the Family Firm

As illustrated in the previous metaphors – particularly the stag hunt and social trap – the notion of vulnerability captures the very essence of trust (Bigley and Pierce, 1998).

Vulnerability refers to the willingness to make one's self vulnerable largely depends on the perceived trustworthiness of the other party. As perceived vulnerability is highly contextual (Tsui-auch and Möllering, 2010), trusting behaviours in family firms are likely to vary from those of other firms. For example, the perceived continuity of the family as a social unit enables family stakeholders to engage in more trusting behaviour than they normally would with strangers with whom they have a more tenuous relationship. Furthermore, repeated relations – such as those found within family contexts – often increase trust (Ensminger, 2003).

Mayer et al. (1995) also suggest that integrity, benevolence and ability to be the most important factors of trustworthiness. Additionally, consistency (Bhattacharya and Devinney, 1998; Hosmer, 1995; Whitener et al., 1998) and openness (Adler, 2001; Mishra, 1996) are often mentioned as additional factors of trustworthiness. Below we expand on these five dimensions of interpersonal trust.

Integrity

Integrity targets 'the reputation for honesty and truthfulness in the part of the trusted individual' (Hosmer, 1995: 384). It is closely related to honesty, which is described as 'refusal to pretend that facts are other than what they are' (Becker, 1998: 158). Mirroring the 'expectancy held by an individual that the partner's word or written statement can be relied on' (Ganesan, 1994: 3), integrity also reflects high levels of credibility. Even further, integrity is linked to morality, describing integrity as 'honest and moral character' (Butler Jr, 1991). In this vein, Mayer et al. refers to integrity as 'the trustor's perception that the trustee adheres to a set of principles that the trustor finds acceptable' (1995: 719). In consequence, integrity limits the possible behaviours of the other party to those that are driven by general principles. Most societies and religions place a strong emphasis on familial responsibilities and clearly articulate what it means to be a good mother, father, son or daughter.

Consistency

Consistency, like integrity, also hints to the reduction of risk (Brockner et al., 1997). Here, the range of possible behaviours is not bound to universal principles or moral standards, but to predictability. Hence, the behavioural limitation is based on the expected behaviour regardless of their moral impact and the concordance of planned, i.e., actively communicated, and actual behaviour becomes the basis for the evaluation of trustworthiness. As such, consistency is defined as 'the reliability, predictability and good judgment in handling situations' (Hosmer, 1995: 384). While dependability (Giffin, 1967) and

reliability are associated with making 'good-faith efforts to behave in accordance with prior commitments' (Dyer and Wujin, 2003: 58), predictability encompasses 'acting and making decisions consistently, in such ways as to prevent others' anxiety caused by the unexpected' (Butler Jr, 1991: 646). According to Friedman (1993), predictability allows the individual to assume how others will act, and that only then it is possible for an individual to choose reasonable courses of action in any given situation.

Ability

Ability points to another aspect of reducing risk. Whereas, integrity and consistency focus on the choice of a specific behaviour (which is expected by the trustor), ability points to the successful execution of that behaviour. As such, ability comprises skills, competencies, and characteristics that 'enable a party to have influence within some specific domain' (Mayer et al., 1995: 717). More specific, ability is associated with the 'technically competent performance' (Barber, 1983) or 'technical knowledge and interpersonal skill needed to perform the job' (Hosmer, 1995: 384). Ability is thus related to a specific task as the trustee might be highly competent in one area but not in another. Thus, only necessary skills and knowledge with regard to completing some specific task successfully are considered when determining trustworthiness (Zand, 1972). Rosen and Jardee (1977) follow this rationale, using the term 'competence', while Giffin (1967), on the other hand, uses expertness as synonym of ability.

Benevolence

Benevolence is the 'extent to which A believes that B has intentions and motives beneficial to A when new conditions arise, conditions for which a commitment was not made' (Ganesan, 1994: 3). It suggests that the trustee has some specific attachment to the trustor, and 'is believed to want to do good to the trustor, aside from an egocentric profit motive' (Mayer et al., 1995: 718). The egocentric motive, also mirrored in not taking 'advantage of an exchange partner even when the opportunity is available' (Dyer and Wujin, 2003: 58) furthermore points to the interrelation of benevolence and goodwill (Ring and Van de Ven, 1992: 488), which is defined as the 'feeling that others will act in a way that does not hurt one's interest' (Friedman, 1993: 440). Similarly, carefulness hints to 'taking care to avoid mishap or harm' (Oxford Dictionaries, 2013) and is also used as synonym for benevolence (Giffin, 1967). Families are social systems that encourage benevolent behaviour and, as the stag hunt and social trap metaphors illustrate, what people do depends on what they believe others will do.

Openness

Openness refers to being 'mentally open and receptive to the giving and accepting of ideas' (Butler Jr, 1991: 647), thus being willing to 'share ideas and information freely with others' (Hosmer, 1995: 384). Information sharing thus depends on the availability of being physically present when needed (Butler Jr, 1991) and on responsiveness as 'responding readily and positively' (Oxford Dictionaries, 2013).

Institutional Trust – Trust in the Family Firm as a Social Institution

Family firms are sometimes represented as benevolent organizations. For example, family members often feel responsible for the long-term development of the firm and for continuous, long-term employment of employees. Therefore, profit estimations are more conservative as compared to non-family firms. Often family firms are engaged in business for the 'long-run' (Miller and Le Breton-Miller, 2005) thus offering economic as well as non-economic benefits to their employees, subsequently creating an organizational culture that is driven by respect and value of their employees.

In addition, the relationship between the family firm and other stakeholders, such as suppliers, are likely to differ from those of other firms. For example, Miller and Le Breton-Miller (2005) note that family firms tend to build strong and enduring relationships that are not driven simply by profit motives. Rather, family firms are willing to compromise on economic profit in order to maintain their business relationship in times of crises. This engagement may be reciprocated by the business partners (Bishop et al., 2005). Of course the heterogeneity of family firms introduces various permutations regarding the governance of these relationships – the result being complex 'hybrid' types of organization that subscribe to both market and trust forms of governance.

As described earlier, institutional trust in family firms mirrors benevolence-based trust. Moreover, trust in family firms as a social institution is also driven by integrity and consistency-based trust. In this vein, family firms (Adams et al., 1996) have been shown to be particularly high in ethical decision making, as positive role modeling behaviour by the founder and the members of the family are translated into ethical management processes. Ethical behaviour also influences the long-term commitment of family firms to their partner companies. Family firms and their business partners hold an open attitude towards the initiatives of the other party and are willing to collaborate in order to solve joint challenges, such as new product development. In this vein, family firms have been shown to be particularly successful in the field of open innovation (Lichtenthaler and Muethel, 2011). Consequently, family firms do not only gain benevolence, integrity, and consistency-based trust, but also competence-based trust as they are able to use their business relationships in order to create sustained competitive advantage.

While institutional trust in family firms appears to be high on all levels, they are at the same time, particularly affected by institutional distrust in cases of organizational failure. It is thus not only the role of trust, which is likely to differ in the context of family firms as compared to other companies, but also the role of distrust.

Trust, Distrust, and Overembeddedness in Family Firms

As Muethel and Bond 2013 note: "trust fosters cooperative, altruistic and extra-role behavior (Fukuyama, 1995), voluntary deference (Gulati & Westphal, 1999; Kramer, 1999), and a high level of information exchange (Li, Poppo, & Zhou, 2010; Malhotra & Murnighan, 2002)" (p. 312). However, it has been argued that trust is not a panacea (Kramer, 2002), but that there are contingencies under which high trust can even be harmful (Langfred, 2004). Hence, high levels of trust are not per se beneficial, instead, there is an optimal level of trust to be considered (Wicks et al., 1999). The optimal level of trust, however, can be regarded from two perspectives representing two competing assumptions of the character of interpersonal trust, i.e., trust being a one-dimensional versus trust being a multidimensional construct.

First, when interpersonal trust is seen as a one-dimensional construct, then trust and distrust are considered to be opposite sides of a single trust continuum (Rotter, 1971). The optimum lies somewhere within this dimension, and low trust is equal to high distrust. Processes influencing the level of trust (or distrust) encompass trust violence (Kim et al., 2004) and trust repair (Ferrin et al., 2007). With trust and distrust being parameters of the same construct, the antecedents of distrust are considered to be the negative parameters of the constructs known to influence trust. Outcomes of distrust are considered to function in the same way.

While trust among family members is a crucial driver of performance in family firms, distrust between the family members can become a severe problem. Pearson and Carr (2011: 33) note that within family firms 'it is almost inevitable that a family member at some point will violate the trust and integrity of the family'. Private relationships in families are characterized by a high level of emotional intensity. Thus, in families,

affect-based trust appears to be much stronger than cognition-based trust. However, the setup of the emotional relationships between members of a family firm can change (e.g., in cases of a marriage, divorce, birth of a child) or emotions (due to prior experience in the family) can induce emotional distrust between the parties. Spill over effects from the private, emotionally laden relationships are very likely to affect business relationship within the family firm and might translate into cognition-based distrust. Although it appears as if cognition-based trust expectations are not met, in fact it is affect-based trust expectations outside the family business which are distorting the business relationships.

Conflict, often naturally occurring in family-based systems, can diminish or destroy trust. McKee et al. (2014) in this *Handbook* note that conflict has a 'myriad' of sources relative to family firms including: reluctance of family members to leave the business, sibling rivalry, marital problems, ownership dispersion, trans-generational differences, lack of liquidity, and the feeling of being 'locked in' to the family business.

In some family systems, conflict can spawn an atmosphere that lacks trust. Distrust refers to suspicion of the family member and a general expectation of negative outcomes arising from a relationship (Gelade et al., 2006). Distrust generates fear, vigilance and suspicion (Vlaar et al., 2007). When distrust arises family members lack confidence in each other, assuming that other family members are indifferent to their welfare and intend hostile or harmful acts (Kramer, 1999), or if other family members appear to hold malevolent intentions (Bigley and Pearce, 1998). The individual probably demonstrates little willingness to depend on other family members, and tries to buffer themselves from the effects of another's conduct (Lewicki et al., 1998), leading the individual to avoid or limit any interaction with these family members (McKnight et al., 1998). Having negative expectations concerning other family members' trustworthiness, individuals demonstrate wariness and watchfulness. Also, when assuming harmful motives, individuals may engage in pre-emptive strikes, offending the other party in order to defend themselves (Lewicki et al., 1998). A vicious cycle can thus be initiated. Similar to the dynamics introduced earlier in the stag hunt and social trap metaphors, the system breaks down to the detriment of all.

Too much trust can also be problematic. Adler and Kwon (2002: 31) describe this as the problem of 'overembeddedness' suggesting that: 'Strong norms in a community may dictate the sharing of resources among extended family members, which may in turn, reduce the incentives for entrepreneurial activity and, thus, slow the accumulation of capital.' Strong solidarity within a group – whilst conferring certain benefits – may also introduce a myriad of problems such as free-riding, resistance to outsiders and/or new ideas. For example, certain family members may exploit their privileged position with the group for individual benefit at group expense; inter-firm level supply chains that are less competitive than their more open counterparts; certain ethnic groups that, although demonstrating a high level of trust within the group, create insular systems that can be uncompetitive and in-efficient. Finally, similar to too much family social capital (Arregle et al., 2007), too much trust among an exclusive group of family members can serve to alienate outsiders (such as employees) to the detriment of the firm.

FUTURE RESEARCH DIRECTIONS

Family firms are ubiquitous. Their sheer numbers present a myriad of empirical sites throughout the world. Within the realm of trust, their unique governance structures and evolutionary patterns offer a wide array of research topics. This ubiquity and variation dictates that the field would benefit from a variety of methodological approaches ranging from qualitative to quantitative, as well as mixed methods. Below we suggest a number of topics for further research.

General Factors of Trustworthiness and their Relationship to Family Business

In the previous section we discussed five factors generally associated with trust: integrity, consistency, ability, benevolence, and openness. We believe there is much merit in further exploring these factors in relationship to family firms – particularly their relative importance and configurations. For example, integrity is a universal factor of trustworthiness, important in various contexts (House et al., 2004). However, as Muethel and Hoegl (2012) note, the context is likely to influence how we understand what integrity is supposed to capture. What, for example, is the role of honesty and openness in family firms? As the roles of a member of the family firm cannot be completely delineated from the roles of a family member (i.e., each person is always both: business partner and a husband, mother, brother, etc.) it might be questioned how trust expectations within the family influence trust expectations within the family firm. Within the family, justice is often understood as equal sharing. Does this interpretation of integrity translate into trust expectations within the family firm? For example, do members of the family expected equal share of the family firm? Or, on the other hand, do firm inequalities (for example, due to different levels of expertise between the family members) induce the perception of inequality in the private relationships between the members of the family firm? Factors of trustworthiness might thus be interpreted dependent on whether members of the family firm consider their private or their business relationships. Also, the relative importance of the different factors might vary. In other words, there is much to be learned regarding the social mechanisms within family firms – particularly research that offers a finer-grained picture of the role of interpersonal trust in the family firm.

Organizational Evolution and Trust

A distinguishing feature of family firms is that they typically have a long-term orientation and often experience a natural evolution in management, ownership and control as they grow over time. For example, commonly depicted trajectories such as owner-founder, sibling partnership and cousin consortiums all suggest that there are certain optimal permutations of trust as firms evolve and grow (Steier, 2001a). We would greatly benefit from additional typologies that classify these permutations.

Implications of Relying on Trust in the Governance of Family Versus Non-Family Firms

Much of our discussion has suggested that trust has a distinctly different role in the governance of family firms versus non-family firms. This observation suggests the following questions: To what extent do family firms rely on trust as a governance mechanism relative to their non-family counterparts? For family firms, to what extent does familial trust – naturally occurring within the family – enable an organization to reduce transaction costs relative to their non-family counterparts?

Family Firms and Temporal Aspects of Trust and Governance

Trust appears to be a prominent feature in the governance of family firms relatively early in their development. For example, in the start-up phase, family members often provide critical resources necessary for firm survival and success with these benefactors relying on previously established trust relationships instead of commonly used criteria such as business plans or experience of the management team. However, as firms grow, strategic imperatives often dictate new skill sets and modes of governance; firing a family member has much different consequences than firing an employee whom one never has to meet again. Conversely, some of the world's oldest and largest firms (Morck and Steier, 2005) continue to be high trust, family dominated organizations, and we know very little about the mechanisms that contribute to the longevity of these firms.

Trust Metaphors in Family Business

Morgan (1996) sensitizes us to the important contributions of metaphor relative to theorizing about organizations. In this paper we have provided several examples illustrative of the role of trust in family business. We believe there is merit in further exploring this line of inquiry in a fashion similar to that adopted by Morgan (1996).

The Evolution of Trust and Governance in Family Versus Non-Family Firms

As noted earlier, a distinguishing feature of family firms versus non-family firms may be the evolution of trust and governance. Family firms are often founded as 'high trust' organizations relative to their non-family counterparts. However, over time these organizations often experience agency related problems and find it necessary to introduce more formalization. In contrast, their non-family firms often rely on contracts and more relationship specificity early in their creation in order to overcome the liabilities of doing business with strangers. Within these relationships, trust often grows with repeated interaction, sometimes replacing formal contract as the primary governance mechanism. These characteristics and differences suggest a need for further research on founding conditions, manifestations and evolution of trust in family versus non-family firms.

The Study of Family Firms as a Bridge Between Trust and Agency Literatures

Agency theory (Cruz et al., 2010: 69) has long provided: 'the dominant paradigm' in corporate governance. Until recently, trust has been largely ignored by agency theorists. Trust scholars have argued that relationships within and among firms are much more than a nexus of agency contracts. Family firms offer excellent empirical sites for the further examination of the complex interaction between opportunistic and benevolence-based behaviour.

Trust-based Relationships with Family Versus Non-Family Firms and Perceptions of Outsiders

Another interesting area of research is comparing perceptions of trust in family firms relative to non-family firms. For example, a distinguishing feature of family firms is that they take a long-term view of business (Miller and Le Breton-Miller, 2005) and subsequently emphasize certain attributes such as reputation and stewardship. What are the attributes of family firms that make them perceived by outsiders to be more – or less – trustworthy than their non-family counterparts?

The Disintegration of Trust

The experience of many family firms – well-documented in books and the popular media – often reflects the story of firm founded as a high-trust organization that disintegrates to an atmosphere of distrust. Although there are many reasons for the disintegration of trust (for example, sibling rivalry, succession, estate squabbles, divorce) we could benefit further from a more comprehensive typology of the disintegration of trust.

Stakeholder Trust

Relatively little of the existing trust research has distinguished 'between the varying dimensions on which stakeholders base their trust' (Pirson and Malhotra, 2011: 1098). Family firms represent organizations that have multiple stakeholders

who occupy different – and sometimes overlapping – roles within the organization. For example: grandparent, parent, sibling, child, manager, owner, shareholder, etc. Family firms offer rich empirical sites within which to examine the dimensions of stakeholder trust.

Trust, Family Business, and the Architecture of Capitalism

Capitalist economies throughout the world exhibit considerable variation (Hall and Soskice, 2001). Although firms having a familial dimension can be found everywhere (La Porta et al., 1999; Morck and Steier, 2005) the varieties of capitalism literature suggests that family firms and their 'trust-based systems' are particularly suited in environments where there is a lack of trust in broader institutions such as reliable governments, banks, or stock markets. Further inquiry related to the varying roles of familial-based trust systems in the architecture of governance would greatly inform us about economic organization throughout the world.

The Role of Family Firms in Building Societal Trust

Fukuyama (1995) links the level of societal trust to a nation's well-being. He notes that family and kinship provide an important mechanism for building societal trust. We would benefit greatly from further study of institutional contexts and the environments where familial-based systems contribute to societal trust and, consequently, foster productive governance systems.

Trust and Social Capital in Family Firms

We noted that trust is closely linked to social capital. An enduring question is how does trust assist in the creation of social capital? We further noted that social capital has many facets and dimensions. The role of trust in the creation and maintenance of social capital in familial contexts remains relatively unexplored – particularly the interaction between various dimensions of social capital.

Trust in Family Business as a Mechanism of Economic Development

A global history of corporate governance (Morck and Steier, 2005) suggests an overarching question: 'To Whom Dare We Entrust Corporate Governance?' Modern day capitalism represents a diversified collection of economic systems. For example, Sweden offers an illustration of an economy that places a great deal of trust in family-controlled business groups whereas other nations have chosen different paths. How nations come to embrace different governance paths remains an interesting question.

Distrust in Family Business as an Organizing Template and their Resilience as an Organizational Form

Anglo-American capitalism has sometimes been described as providing the dominant template for what a modern firm should be. This template prescribes a clear separation between ownership and control (Berle and Means, 1932) wherein, ideally, firms are to be run by professional managers and there is little latitude for family involvement (Steier, 2009b). In other words, one could argue that Anglo-American capitalism illustrates a fundamental distrust in family business as an organizing template. However, family businesses – albeit often underappreciated – can still be seen to powerfully exist within the Anglo-American model (Anderson and Reeb, 2003; La Porta et al., 1999). Within this context two broad research questions emerge: What accounts for the distrust of family firms? What accounts for their resilience as an organizational form in the midst of distrust?

CONCLUSION

In summary, trust is a most important aspect of economic exchange and it is particularly relevant for family firms. In this chapter we explored manifestations of familial trust in various economic exchange contexts and also linked it to the broader notion of social capital. We further introduced trust and social capital metaphors to illustrate that, within familial contexts, cooperative behaviour and trust are fundamental organizing principles. We then offered a further theoretical framing of key concepts relative to trust followed by suggestions for further research. Contexts such as time, place, age, and interpersonal dynamics have important consequences for trust and governance in family business. Although the concept of trust has previously been the focus of much attention in both theory and application, it remains a most intriguing topic relative to family firms.

REFERENCES

Adams, J.S., Taschian, A., and Shore, T.H. (1996). Ethics in family and non-family owned firms: An exploratory study. *Family Business Review*, 9, 157–170.

Adler, Paul S. and Kwon, Seok-Woo (2002). Social capital: Prospects for a new concept. *The Academy of Management Review*, 27, 17–40.

Adler, S. (2001). Market, hierarchy, and trust: The knowledge economy and the future of capitalism. *Organization Science*, 12, 215–234.

Aesop (2005). In *Encyclopedia of World Biography*. Retrieved from http://mythfolklore.net/aesopica/milowinter/13.htm

Anderson, R. and Reeb, D. (2003). Founding-family ownership and firm performance: Evidence from S and P 500. *Journal of Finance*, 58, 1301–1328.

Arregle, J., Hitt, M., Sirmon, D., and Very, P. (2007). The development of organizational social capital: Attributes of family firms. *Journal of Management Studies*, 44, 73–95.

Axelrod, R. and Hamilton, W. (1981). The evolution of cooperation in biological systems. *Science*, 211, 1390–1396.

Barber, B. (1983). *The Logic and Limits of Trust*. New Brunswick, NJ: Rutgers University Press.

Becker, T.E. (1998). Integrity in organizations: Beyond honesty and conscientiousness. *Academy of Management Review*, 23, 154–161.

Berle, A. and Means, G. (1932). *The Modern Corporation and Private Property*. New York: Macmillan.

Bhattacharya, R. and Devinney, T.M. (1998). A formal model of trust based on outcomes. *Academy of Management Review*, 23, 459.

Bigley, G.A. and Pearce, J.L. (1998). Straining for shared meaning in organization science: Problems of trust and distrust. *Academy of Management Review*, 23, 405.

Bishop, J.W., Scott, K.D., Goldsby, M.G., and Cropanzano, R. (2005). A construct validity study of commitment and perceived support variables: A multifoci approach across different team environments. *Group Organization Management*, 30, 153–180.

Bradach, J.L. and Eccles, R.G. (1989). Price, authority, and trust: From ideal types to plural forms. *Annual Review of Sociology*, 15, 97–118.

Brockner, J., Siegel, A., Daly, J.P., Tyler, T., and Martin, C. (1997). When trust matters: The moderating effect of outcome favorability. *Administrative Science Quarterly*, 42, 558–583.

Butler Jr, J.K. (1991). Toward understanding and measuring conditions of trust: Evolution of a conditions of trust inventory. *Journal of Management*, 17, 643–664.

Caplow, T. (1964). *Principles of Organization*. New York: Harcourt, Brace & World Inc.

Coleman, J.S. (1988). Social capital in the creation of human capital. *American Journal of Sociology*, 94(Supplement), S95–S120.

Costa, A.C., Roe, R.A., and Taillieu, T. (2001). Trust within teams: the relation with performance effectiveness. *European Journal of Work and Organizational Psychology*, 10, 225–244.

Cruz, C., Gomez-Mejia, L.R., and Becerra, M. (2010). Perceptions of benevolence and the design of agency contracts: CEO-TMT relationships in family firms. *Academy of Management Journal*, 53, 69–89.

De Massis, A., Sharma, P., Chua, J. and Chrisman, J. (2012). *Family Business Studies: An Annotated Bibliography*. Northampton, MA: Edward Elgar.

Dyer, J.H. and Wujin, C. (2003). The role of trustworthiness in reducing transaction costs and improving performance: Empirical evidence from the United States, Japan, and Korea. *Organization Science*, 14, 57.

Eddleston, K.A., Chrisman, J.J., Steier, L.P., and Chua, J.H. (2010). Governance and trust in family firms: An introduction. *Entrepreneurship: Theory and Practice*, 34, 1043–1056.

Ensminger, J. (2003). Reputations, trust, and the principal-agent problem. In K.S. Cook (ed.), *Trust in Society*. New York: Russell Sage Foundation, pp. 185–201.

Fang, C., Kimbrough, S.O., Valluri, A., and Zheng, Z. (2002). On adaptive emergence of trust behavior in the game of stag hunt. *Group Decision and Negotiation*, 11, 449–467.

Ferrin, D.L., Kim, H., Cooper, C.D., and Dirks, K.T. (2007). Silence speaks volumes: The effectiveness of reticence in comparison to apology and denial for responding to integrity- and competence-based trust violations. *Journal of Applied Psychology*, 92, 893–908.

Friedman, R.A. (1993). Bringing mutual gains bargaining to labor negotiations: The role of trust, understanding, and control. *Human Resource Management*, 32, 435.

Fukuyama, F. (1995). *Trust: The Social Virtues and the Creation of Prosperity*. New York: Free Press.

Fukuyama, F. (1997). Social capital and the modern capitalist economy: Creating a high trust workplace. *Stern Business Magazine*, 4(1).

Ganesan, S. (1994). Determinants of long-term orientation in buyer-seller relationships. *Journal of Marketing*, 58, 1–20.

Gelade, G.A., Dobson, P., and Gilbert, P. (2006). National differences in organizational commitment: Effect of economy, product of personality, or consequence of culture? *Journal of Cross-Cultural Psychology*, 37, 542–556.

Giffin, K. (1967). The contribution of studies of source credibility to a theory of interpersonal trust in the communication department. *Psychological Bulletin*, 68, 104–120.

Gulati, R. and Westphal, J.D. (1999). Cooperative or controlling? The effects of ceo-board relations and the content of interlocks on the formation of joint ventures. *Administrative Science Quarterly*, 44, 473–506.

Hall, A. and Soskice, D. (2001). An introduction to varieties of capitalism. In P.A. Hall and D. Soskice (eds), *Varieties of Capitalism: Institutional Foundations of Comparative Advantage*. Oxford: Oxford University Press, pp. 1–68.

Hardin, G. (1968). The tragedy of the commons. *Science*, 162, 1243–1248.

Hogfeldt, P. (2005). The history and politics of corporate ownership in Sweden. In R. Morck (ed.), *The History of Corporate Governance Around the World: Family Business Groups to Professional Managers*. Chicago, IL: University of Chicago Press.

Hosmer, L.T. (1995). Trust: The connecting link between organizational theory and philosophical ethics. *Academy of Management Review*, 20, 379.

House, R., Hanges, P., Javidan, M., Dorfman, P., and Gupta, A. (2004). *Culture, Leadership, and Organizations: The GLOBE Study of 62 Societies.* Thousand Oaks, CA: Sage.

Hubler, T. (2011). The trust paradox of family businesses. In R.L. Sorenson (ed.), *Family Business and Social Capital.* Cheltenham: Edward Elgar, pp. 45–50.

Karra, N., Tracey, P., and Phillips, N. (2006). Altruism and agency in the family firm: Exploring the role of family, kinship and ethnicity. *Entrepreneurship Theory & Practice*, 30, 861–877.

Kim, H., Ferrin, D.L., Cooper, C.D., and Dirks, K.T. (2004). Removing the shadow of suspicion: The effects of apology versus denial for repairing competence-versus integrity-based trust violations. *Journal of Applied Psychology*, 89, 104.

Kramer, R.M. (1999). Trust and distrust in organizations: Emerging perspectives, enduring questions. *Annual Review of Psychology*, 50, 569–598.

Kramer, R.M. (2002). When paranoia makes sense. *Harvard Business Review*, 80, 62–69.

La Porta, R., López-de-Silanes, L., Shleifer, A., and Vishny, R. (1999). Corporate ownership around the world. *Journal of Finance*, 54, 471–520.

Langfred, C.W. (2004). Too much of a good thing? Negative effects of high trust and individual autonomy in self-managing teams. *Academy of Management Journal*, 47, 385–399.

Larzelere, R.E. and Huston, T.L. (1980). The dyadic trust scale: Toward understanding interpersonal trust in close relationships. *Journal of Marriage and Family*, 42, 595–604.

Leana, C.R. and Van Buren, H.J. (1999). Organizational social capital and employment practices. *Academy of Management Review*, 24, 538–555.

Lewicki, R.J., McAllister, D.J., and Bies, R.J. (1998). Trust and distrust: New relationships and realities. *Academy of Management Review*, 23, 438–458.

Lichtenthaler, U. and Muethel, M. (2011). Family firms and the field of open innovation. Working Paper.

Lin, N. (1999). Social networks and status attainment. *Annual Review of Sociology*, 25, 467–487.

Malhotra, D. and Murnighan, J.K. (2002). The Effects of contracts on interpersonal trust. *Administrative Science Quarterly*, 47, 534.

Mayer, R.C., Davis, J.H., and Schoorman, F.D. (1995). An integrative model of organizational trust. *Academy of Management Review*, 20, 709–734.

McKee, D.N., Madden, T.M., Kellermanns, F.W., and Eddleston, K.A. (2014). Conflict in family firms: The good and the bad. In M. Nordqvist, L. Melin, P. Sharma (eds), *The SAGE Handbook of Family Business.* London: Sage.

McKnight, D.H., Cummings, L.L., and Chervany, N.L. (1998). Initial trust formation in new organizational relationships. *Academy of Management Review*, 23, 473–490.

Miller, D. and Le Breton-Miller, I. (2005). *Managing for the Long Run.* Boston, MA: Harvard Business School Press.

Mishra, A.K. (1996). Organizational responses to crisis: the centrality of trust. In R.M. Kramer and T. Tyler (eds), *Trust in Organizations.* Newbury Park, CA: Sage, pp. 261–287.

Morck, R. (2005). *The History of Corporate Governance Around the World: Family Business Groups to Professional Managers.* Chicago, IL: University of Chicago Press.

Morck, R. and Steier, L. (2005). The global history of corporate governance: An introduction. In R. Morck (ed.), *The History of Corporate Governance Around the World: Family Business Groups to Professional Managers.* Chicago, IL: University of Chicago Press, pp. 1–64.

Morgan, G. (1996). *Images of Organization.* London: Sage.

Muethel, M., and Bond, M.H. (2013). National context and individual employees' trust of the out-group: The role of societal trust. *Journal of International Business Studies*, 44, 312–333.

Muethel, M., and Hoegl, M. (2007). Initial Distrust - On the Role of Perceived Dishonesty in International Innovation Teams. *Zeitschrift für Betriebwirtschaft (ZfB) Special Issue*, 4, 103–124.

Muethel, M. and Hoegl, M. (2012). The influence of social institutions on managers' concept of trust: Implications for trust-building in Sino-German relationships. *Journal of World Business*, 43(3), 420–434.

Nicholson, N. (2008). Evolutionary psychology and family business: A new synthesis for theory, research and practice. *Family Business Review*, 21, 103–118.

Oxford Dictionaries (2013). Compact Oxford English Dictionary. Online: http://oxforddictionaries.com/

Pearson, A.W. and Carr, J.C. (2011). The central role of trust in family firm social capital. In R.L. Sorenson (ed.), *Family Business and Social Capital.* Cheltenham: Edward Elgar, pp. 33–44.

Pearson, A.W., Carr, J.C., and Shaw, J.C. (2008). Toward a theory of familiness: A social capital perspective. *Entrepreneurship: Theory and Practice*, 32, 949–969.

Pirson, M. and Malhotra, D. (2011). Foundations of organizational trust: What matters to different stakeholders? *Organization Science*, 22, 1087–1104.

Platt, J. (1973). Social traps. *American Psychologist*, 28, 641–651.

Putnam, R. (1993). *Making Democracy Work: Civic Tradition in Modern Italy*. Princeton, NJ: Princeton University Press.

Ring, S. and Van de Ven, A.H. (1992). Structuring cooperative relationships between organizations. *Strategic Management Journal*, 13, 483.

Rosen, B. and Jardee, T.H. (1977). Influence of subordinate characteristics in trust and use of participative decision making strategies in a management simulation. *Journal of Applied Psychology*, 628–631.

Rothstein, B. (2005). *Social Traps and the Problem of Trust: Theories of Institutional Design*. Cambridge: Cambridge University Press.

Rotter, J.B. (1971). Generalized expectancies for interpersonal trust. *American Psychologist*, 26, 433–452.

Rousseau, J.J. (1755). *Discours sur l'origine et les fondemens de l'inegalité parmi les hommes*. Amsterdam.

Skyrms, B. (2004). *The Stag Hunt and Evolution of Social Structure*. Cambridge: Cambridge University Press.

Sorenson, R.L. (2011). *Family Business and Social Capital*. Cheltenham: Edward Elgar.

Steier, L. (2001a). Family firms, plural forms of governance and the evolving role of trust. *Family Business Review*, 14, 353–367.

Steier, L. (2001b). Next-generation entrepreneurs and succession: An exploratory study of modes and means of managing social capital. *Family Business Review*, 14, 259–276.

Steier, L. (2003). Variants of agency contracts in family-financed ventures as a continuum of familial altruistic and market rationalities. *Journal of Business Venturing*, 18, 597–618.

Steier, L. (2007). New venture creation and organization: A familial sub-narrative. *Journal of Business Research*, 60, 1099–1107.

Steier, L. (2009a). Where do new firms come from? Households, family capital, ethnicity, and the welfare mix. *Family Business Review*, 22, 273–278.

Steier, L. (2009b). Familial capitalism in global institutional contexts: Implications for corporate governance and entrepreneurship in East Asia. *Asia Pacific Journal of Management*, 26, 513–535.

Stinchcombe, A. (1965). Organizations and social structure. In J. March (ed.), *Handbook of Organizations* (153–193). Chicago, IL: Rand McNally.

Sundaramurthy, C. (2008). Sustaining trust within family businesses. *Family Business Review*, 21, 89–102.

Tsui-auch, L. and Möllering, G. (2010). Wary managers: Unfavorable environments, perceived vulnerability, and the development of trust in foreign enterprises in China. *Journal of International Business Studies*, 41, 1016.

Tyler, T.R. and Kramer, R.M. (1996). Whither trust? In R.M. Kramer and T. Tyler (eds), *Trust In Organizations*. Newbury Park, CA: Sage, pp. 261–287.

Vlaar, P.W.L., Van den Bosch, F.A.J., and Volberda, H.W. (2007). On the evolution of trust, distrust, and formal coordination and control in interorganizational relationships: Toward an integrative framework. *Group Organization Management*, 32, 407–428.

Welter, F. (2012). All you need is trust? A critical review of the trust and entrepreneurship literature. *International Small Business Journal*, 30,193–212.

Whitener, E.M., Brodt, S.E., Korsgaard, M.A., and Werner, J.M. (1998). Managers as initiators of trust: An exchange relationship framework for understanding managerial trustworthy behavior. *Academy of Management Review*, 23, 513.

Wicks, A.C., Berman, S.L., and Jones, T.M. (1999). The structure of optimal trust: Moral and strategic implications. *Academy of Management Review*, 24, 99.

Williamson, O.E. (1991). Comparative economic organization: The analysis of discrete structural alternatives. *Administrative Science Quarterly*, 36, 269–296.

Zaheer, A., McEvily, B., and Perrone, V. (1998). Does trust matter? Exploring the effects of interorganizational and interpersonal trust on performance. *Organization Science*, 9, 141–159.

Zand, D.E. (1972). Trust and managerial problem solving. *Administrative Science Quarterly*, 17, 229.

26

Conflicts in Family Firms: The Good and the Bad

D'Lisa McKee, Timothy M. Madden, Franz W. Kellermanns and Kimberly A. Eddleston

INTRODUCTION

Conflict has the potential for disastrous consequences and the demise of family firms (Gordon and Nicholson, 2008), making it one of the most important areas for family firm research. Conflict can be particularly taxing as family entanglements worsen stressful situations, which results in the assumption that conflict is damaging to family firms (Levinson, 1971). Overlapping family and business relationships may complicate how firms are managed (Daily and Dollinger, 1992) and potentially increase the intensity and frequency of conflicts (Harvey and Evans, 1994; Lee and Rogoff, 1996). Managing the multitude of family relationships makes conflict particularly pervasive in family firms (Kellermanns and Eddleston, 2004).

Sibling rivalry, marital problems, ownership dispersion, transgenerational involvement, altruistic inclinations, and succession issues all present opportunities for family firm conflict (Kellermanns and Eddleston, 2004). Additionally, family members can become

tied to the business through an inability to sell their shares or a desire to retain perquisites associated with the business (Gersick et al., 1997; Schulze et al., 2003a, 2003b). This feeling of being 'locked in' (Kellermanns and Eddleston, 2006) may further contribute to the potential for conflict in family firms (Lee and Rogoff, 1996). Trans-generational involvement, as well as altruistic inclinations, can also play an important role in how conflict influences family businesses (Kellermanns and Eddleston, 2004). Therefore, understanding conflict between family business members requires an examination of the forms of conflict that occur within family firms as well as the unique dynamics that influence relationships within family firms (Kellermanns and Eddleston, 2004).

Initially, it would seem that mitigating any and all types of conflict would be in the firm's best interest, as conflict has the potential to hinder performance; however, not all types of conflict are inherently detrimental (Jehn, 1992, 1997a, 1997b). Conflict can, at times, improve family firm performance (e.g., Kellermanns and Eddleston, 2007) since it is the *type* of conflict, rather than the presence or absence of conflict, that influences performance. Indeed, generally three types of conflict are discussed (relationship conflict, cognitive conflict, process conflict), which can be either desirable (Tjosvold, 1991) or undesirable (Wall Jr and Callister, 1995), based on the type of conflict, its frequency, its intensity (De Dreu and Van Vianen, 2001; Jehn, 1995), and what outcomes are expected to result from the conflict (Jehn and Bendersky, 2003). It is important to note that the three types of conflict can occur independently of each other, yet, on occasion, one type of conflict can turn into another or they can occur simultaneously. Accordingly, it is not only important to understand the individual types of conflict, but also the interrelationships amongst them.

This chapter provides an overview of the different types of conflict found within family firms, mechanisms for coping with interpersonal conflict, and common outcomes of conflict within family firms. Despite the importance of this topic to family firms, the number of empirical studies are very limited (for recent overview see also Frank et al., 2011). The chapter concludes with a discussion of managerial implications and future research directions needed to better understanding the dynamics of interpersonal conflict within family firms.

TYPES OF CONFLICT

Although conflict may be a source of decreased performance and a precursor to group destruction (Wall Jr and Callister, 1995), conflict among family firm members can have both positive and negative effects on firm performance, largely due to the type of conflict experienced. Relationship conflict does not directly relate to business operations, involves negative affect and emotions. (Eddleston and Kellermanns, 2008), and is most commonly associated with decreased performance. Other types of conflict, such as cognitive and process conflict, revolve around work issues and may actually improve

organizational performance by improving decision-making and focusing attention on alternatives about what the organization should do and how to do it. (Jehn, 1995, 1997b). Cognitive conflict focuses on disagreements about the pursuit of particular strategies and goals and process conflict focuses on the assignment of tasks within the business. These types of conflict can be useful tools to increase the number of alternatives the firm has. From these types of conflict, disagreement can lead to discussion and the discovery of new and better ideas (Tjosvold, 1991). Unlike relationship conflict, cognitive and process conflict are desirable and many even improve performance. Discriminating between these three types of conflict reveals that when conflict is properly managed, family firms may actually benefit from conflict (Kellermanns and Eddleston, 2004; Kellermanns and Eddleston, 2007).

RELATIONSHIP CONFLICT

Although conflict is assumed to negatively influence performance (Beckhard and Dyer Jr, 1983; Danes et al., 1999; Gersick et al., 1997; Gordon and Nicholson, 2008; Levinson, 1971), these negative consequences likely result from the effects of relationship conflict (Jehn, 1995, 1997b). Relationship conflict centers on negative emotions and affect such as anger, annoyance, frustration, and dislike (Jehn and Mannix, 2001; Simons and Peterson, 2000). This dysfunctional type of conflict breeds distrust, animosity, and intense rivalry among family members (Eddleston and Kellermanns, 2007). If harmonious and close family relationships are a source of competitive advantage for family firms (Habbershon et al., 2003; Sirmon and Hitt, 2003), relationship conflict has the potential to undercut stewardship and altruism (Eddleston and Kellermanns, 2007), hamper a family firm's ability to compete and thrive, and ultimately decrease firm performance. Thus, although relationship conflict often has an immediate effect on interpersonal interactions, the long-term effects of relationship conflict can also compromise family cohesion, effectiveness, and firm performance (Kellermanns and Eddleston, 2004, 2007).

POTENTIALLY BENEFICIAL FORMS OF CONFLICT

Cognitive and process conflict are devoid of affect and emotions and are therefore distinct from relationship conflict. These types of conflict result from discussions about the organizational strategies and activities that the family firm should engage in. Cognitive and process conflict focus on solving a problem, rather than attacking an individual, and may benefit the organization (Jehn, 1992, 1997a, b; Jehn and Mannix, 2001; Putman, 1994).

Cognitive Conflict

Unlike relationship conflict, cognitive conflict is task-related (Jehn and Bendersky, 2003), free of negative emotions, and develops from the discussion of opposing ideas and opinions about which tasks the organization should pursue (Kellermanns and Eddleston, 2007). This process encourages closer examination of diverse courses of action, and allows for innovative alternatives to emerge (Jehn, 1995). Opposing ideas bring to light new options, and through this, decision quality improves (Kellermanns and Eddleston, 2007). Indeed, information diversity and communication within the top management team are necessary for family firm performance (Ling and Kellermans, 2010) and cognitive conflict allows the organization to evaluate its goals and strategies and more clearly recognize the issues that influence the business (Putman, 1994). The discussion of different viewpoints increases the number of choices available and can reduce the risk of groupthink or premature consensus (Kellermanns et al., 2008; Kellermanns et al., 2005). Cognitive

conflict also encourages creativity and can reduce or eliminate opportunistic behavior in individual organization members (Jehn and Bendersky, 2003). As such, cognitive conflict can benefit the organization, and consequently, its performance, by providing more opportunities for creativity, a greater number of strategic options (Jehn and Bendersky, 2003), and better decisions (Kellermanns and Eddleston, 2007).

Family firms may especially benefit from cognitive conflict as they are often slow to react to changes in the environment and risk stagnation (Ward, 1987). Additionally, decisions in family firms tend to be made by a highly-centralized CEO with little discussion of alternatives (Kelly, Athanassiou and Crittenden, 2000). Cognitive conflict exposes family firm members to alternatives that may lead to new strategies for adaptation, performance, and survival; however, researchers acknowledge the complexity of the relationship between cognitive conflict and performance. Research on non-family firms (De Dreu, 2006), suggests that the relationship between cognitive conflict and performance is likely also non-linear (Kellermanns and Eddleston, 2004); thus, a moderate degree of cognitive conflict is likely advantageous because the discovery and debate of ideas increases the number of alternatives a firm has to choose from, thereby improving the decision-making process; however, there is likely an upper limit to the performance benefits from cognitive conflict. High levels of cognitive conflict may result in diminishing returns as immobility, indecisiveness, and difficulties resolving problems (Kellermanns and Eddleston, 2004) set in. For example, excessive cognitive conflict may limit performance through the discovery of too many alternatives. Worse, organizations risk stagnation or immobility when managers are overwhelmed by possibilities and are unable to reach consensus. Excessive levels of cognitive conflict can also be misinterpreted as personal attacks, leading to relationship conflict if individuals invest emotion into the conflict

(Kellermanns and Eddleston, 2007). This expected curvilinear relationship between cognitive conflict and performance suggests that the benefits of cognitive conflict are not consistent and the benefits of cognitive conflict are most apparent at low to medium levels. This curvilinear relationship has never been empirically tested for family firms, although it has been described in a non-family firm setting (De Dreu, 2006).

Process Conflict

Like cognitive conflict, process conflict is work-focused and free of negative emotions; however, although cognitive conflict focuses on *which* goals and strategies the organization should pursue, process conflict focuses on *how* these goals and strategies should be achieved (Jehn and Bendersky, 2003). This conflict arises from decisions regarding how a course of action should be pursued and how individual capabilities should be matched to organizational needs (Jehn and Mannix, 2001). Through disagreements about how tasks should be performed and which employees should be assigned to these tasks, organizations uncover new possibilities for matching the right employee to the right job (Jehn, 1997b), which may contribute to improvements in task completion and firm performance (Jehn, 1997b). Additionally, process conflict encourages the discussion of how resources should be utilized and how performance standards can be set for individual tasks. Although process conflict does not ensure increased performance (Jehn and Mannix, 2001), it does provide the opportunity for the organization to discover better ways to achieve its goals and strategies.

Process conflict can be particularly important in family firms (Kellermanns and Eddleston, 2004), as employees are often employed by virtue of their family status rather than their abilities and skill sets; consequently, family members can feel entitled to a particular job and perform tasks for which they are not the best suited (Lansberg,

1983). Process conflict can provide the opportunity for the family to discuss qualifications for a job (e.g., Jehn, 1997b) and can ensure that they align employee capabilities with organizational needs. This may be of particular importance at higher levels in the organization because family firms often offer executive-level positions to under-qualified family members in an effort to maintain family control (Kellermanns and Eddleston, 2004). As such, process conflict can prevent problems related to nepotism and improve the effectiveness of family firms.

Like cognitive conflict, too much process conflict may also be harmful to family firms. When family members cannot agree on how a course of action should be pursued or who should be assigned to particular jobs, stagnation may result. Further, family firms that are constantly changing processes, methods, and job assignments will have difficulties reaching goals and creating a sense of continuity. Process conflict should enhance the performance of family businesses but its limitations suggest that low to moderate levels of process conflict would be most beneficial to family firm performance.

CONFLICT MANAGEMENT STRATEGIES

Relationship, cognitive, and process conflict do not always exist independently of each other; rather, they can interact and influence each other (Kellermanns and Eddleston, 2004; Mooney et al., 2007). Conflict management strategies should be employed to manage general interpersonal conflicts as well as specific types of conflict. The five main strategies for managing conflict: *avoiding, contending, compromising, collaboration*, and *third party intervention* (De Dreu, 1997; De Dreu et al., 2001; Sorenson, 1999; Wall Jr and Callister, 1995) are often related to a specific type of conflict, but due to the complexities of conflict within a family business context, these strategies may also apply to combined forms of conflict (Kellermanns and Eddleston, 2006).

Although conflict can occur amongst family and non-family members, and cognitive conflict amongst both family and family and non-family members should be encouraged, the discussion of conflict management in family firms centers almost exclusively on conflict among family members. Indeed, particular emphasis is placed on managing relationship conflict among family members. In our comments below, we follow this tradition by focusing on conflict among family members. However, when we draw on broader management research, we sometimes refer to *teams* to highlight that these conclusions were not derived from family firm settings or informed by family firm research.

Avoiding

Avoiding means that the source of conflict is ignored, i.e., not addressed. Avoiding helps alleviate conflict because individuals recognize potential sources of conflict and attempt to delay dealing with the conflict and its consequences. Avoiding can be, to an extent, beneficial to team performance (De Dreu and Van Vianen, 2001; Jehn, 1997b) because team members choose to avoid addressing minor or inconsequential disagreements that, if discussed, could detract from the task at hand or escalate into a more serious form or level of conflict. At the team level, avoiding can improve perceptions of performance (De Dreu et al., 2001), but this research does not accurately reflect a family business setting. Non-family business teams often dissolve after a period of time, and thus conflict can be forestalled into an indefinite, but short, future. Family business, members experience conflict differently due to the unique mix of family relationships and business demands. An avoiding strategy is more difficult to achieve (Kellermanns and Eddleston, 2006) as family business members are likely to be in contact with each other throughout their business and personal lives. In this context, an avoiding strategy may result in discontent and grudges among family members that eventually escalate to a more serious level of conflict. Avoidance in family firms is associated with low family satisfaction, high sibling rivalry, and low mutual trust (Kaye and McCarthy, 1996). Thus, although avoiding may have some utility for teams, it is not an ideal conflict management strategy for family businesses.

Contending

Contending, also referred to as competing, is the form of conflict management that results when an individual forces their initiatives and ideas into action (De Dreu and Van Vianen, 2001) without concern for others. As a response to relationship conflict, this individualistic strategy (Kellermanns and Eddleston, 2006) causes tension and can induce negative affect and damage family relationships (Sorenson, 1999).

Similarly, contending can have undesired outcomes in situations of cognitive and process conflict (Alper et al., 2000; De Dreu and Van Vianen, 2001). Contending may involve threats or forced compliance, and can be used to promote personal agendas (Sorenson, 1999) which may decrease the diversity of ideas, potential strategic choices, and decision quality (Kellermanns and Eddleston, 2006). Contending escalates relationship conflicts and lowers decision quality, both of which can impede firm performance, and also leads to anger and mistrust, making it a suboptimal strategy for resolving family firm conflicts (Kellermanns and Eddleston, 2006).

Compromising

Compromising results from trying to find a resolution that at least partially appeases all parties involved. Compromising may create a temporary solution, but does not create a long-term solution to the conflict (Kellermanns and Eddleston, 2006; Murninghan and Conlon, 1991). Some amount of give-and-take can be beneficial to the interaction and operations of the family firm (Sorenson, 1999), but compromising can also limit the discussion of new ideas, and decrease the likelihood of finding the best possible solution. In response to relationship conflict, compromising can be a useful way to maintain family relationships, as there can be performance benefits to compromising in relationship conflicts; however, using a compromising strategy to manage cognitive and process conflict may lead to performance decreases for family firms (Sorenson, 1999) because the goal is satisfying rather than selecting the optimal outcome. As such, compromising may preserve family relationships in the short run, but is unlikely to improve firm performance in the long run.

Collaborating

Collaborating involves individuals working together and sharing ideas to come up with a mutually-agreed-upon solution that addresses the concerns of all involved parties (De Dreu et al., 2001). Collaborating can lead to mutually-acceptable solutions in the short term and may also reduce the occurrence of conflicts in the future (Pruitt and Rubin, 1986; Tjosvold, 1997). Collaborating creates a cooperative environment that can meet the interests of all parties involved. Collaborating in situations of relationship conflict can increase cooperation and commitment (Kellermanns and Eddleston, 2006). In instances of cognitive and process conflict, collaborating encourages teamwork and organizational learning (Sorenson, 1999), and improves decision quality and overall performance for the firm (De Dreu et al., 2001). Of the conflict management strategies presented, collaborating has the potential to create the best outcomes for family businesses (Sorenson, 1999) by focusing on the common short and long-term goals and the ability to achieve transgenerational sustainability of the business.

Third Party Intervention

Third party intervention differs from the prior four conflict management strategies in that avoiding, contending, compromising, and collaborating all involve the direct participation of those involved in the conflict. With third party intervention, parties outside the conflict are introduced in an effort to mediate or resolve the conflict when those involved are unable or unwilling to do so themselves (Wall Jr and Callister, 1995). In a family firm, third party interventions maybe particularly useful since they provide an opportunity to introduce a neutral 'outsider' who can offer a fresh perspective from outside of the family (Kaye, 1991). The benefit of third party intervention is that through mediation or arbitration, the intent is to resolve the conflict, rather than find a temporary fix for it. Furthermore, bringing in another party to intervene can, through the course of resolving the conflict, improve family member communication and interactions (Kaye, 1991; Kellermanns and Eddleston, 2007). As a conflict management strategy, third party intervention can also positively influence family business performance through the resolution of conflicts and improved communication of family and business members.

ACHIEVING CONSTRUCTIVE CONFRONTATION

An important consideration for addressing and resolving conflict in family businesses is the awareness that family relationships are deeply intertwined with the business. As such, problems affecting the business also have the potential to affect the family and vice versa. Family firm members have a number of alternatives for managing and resolving their conflicts and the type of conflict-management strategy employed can influence the outcome of the conflict, subsequent family relationships, and firm performance. Efforts to resolve conflict must recognize these overlapping relationships. Before choosing a conflict management strategy, it is imperative that family firm members understand how conflicts can be resolved and the possible consequences associated with each conflict management strategy. As each conflict is unique, it is important that the firm understand both the type of conflict it is facing and the potential desired outcomes of each conflict resolution strategy the firm may employ; hence, although one strategy may be effective for resolving relationship conflict, the same strategy may not produce the same results when resolving cognitive or process conflict.

Due to the temporal aspect of family firms (Kellermanns and Eddleston, 2006), avoidance may not be a realistic alternative for family firms that persist across generations, as avoidance will not address the conflict. Instead, conflict will likely escalate and may even destroy the firm. Similarly, a contending strategy may alleviate some process or cognitive conflict, but can result in further relationship conflict and animosity among family firm members. Rather, a preferred method of conflict resolution for the family firm may lie in collaboration or third party intervention. For particularly destructive relationship conflict, it may be possible to reduce conflicts and resolve family business disagreements through the use of an impartial third party. Ideally, outsiders are not invested in either side of the conflict and can provide unbiased perspectives as they facilitate the resolution of conflict (Kellermanns and Eddleston, 2006).

Ultimately, the goal of the family firm, like any other organization, is likely to be the achievement of constructive confrontation (Kellermanns et al., 2008). Here, relationship conflict or the potential for relationship conflict is minimized, but cognitive and process conflicts are encouraged to develop at healthy levels. This will minimize negative effects and enhance decision making efforts and, ultimately, performance.

DISCUSSION

Family relationships bridge firm members' work and personal lives, necessitating that conflict be better understood within this unique organizational context. Despite the early interest in family firm conflict (Donnelley, 1964; Levinson, 1971) and the strong presence of this topic in practitioner-oriented books (Gersick et al., 1997; Gordon and Nicholson, 2008), the number of empirical studies is extremely limited. For example, only one study empirically demonstrates a positive relationship between process conflict in family firms and performance (Kellermanns and Eddleston, 2007). Table 26.1 provides a summary of the key findings from all empirical research on conflict in family firms. For another recent overview article see also Frank et al., 2011.

Drawing on these studies and related theoretical research, this review of the current family business conflict literature discusses the different forms of conflict and the common strategies individuals employ to attempt to reconcile conflict. As suggested above, the majority of the research was focused on conflict amongst family members only and centered on relationship conflict. Thereby, much of the research on conflict in family firms is informed by the broader interpersonal conflict literature (Jehn and Bendersky, 2003). As family firms comprise groups of individuals that work and stay together for extended periods of time, they can provide an ideal research setting for understanding how potentially very cohesive and stable groups can both benefit and be harmed by the three types of conflict. As such, we believe that findings from family firm research have the ability to contribute back to the broader management literature.

This chapter concludes with recommendations for future research focusing on moderators and outcomes of family firm conflict, new methodological avenues for advancing these research streams, and best-practice recommendations for managers.

Family Firm Conflict Antecedents

The empirical research on antecedents of conflict in family firms is sparse and although

Table 26.1 Review of empirical interpersonal conflict studies focusing on family firm contexts

Davis and Harveston (1999)	535 US family businesses	This study examined the presence of conflict in subsequent generations of family businesses. Findings revealed that family firms led by third or later generations have higher levels of conflict than founder or second generation led firms. Thus, conflict appears to increase with each generation. Additionally, after the generational transition, the presence or 'shadow' of the founder in the firm is associated with higher levels of conflict within the family business.
Sorenson (1999)	59 Texas family businesses	This study found partial support for hypotheses that family firms with relatively positive business and family outcomes will rely more on collaboration, compromise, and accommodation than family firms with relatively negative outcomes. Support, however, was not found for businesses with negative outcomes utilizing more competition and avoidance to manage conflicts. The results of this study suggest that compromise and accommodation may be able to enhance firm performance over competition and avoidance.
Davis and Harveston (2001)	457 US family businesses	This study examined the number of family members working in a family business, and how this influences conflict. The results of the study suggest that when there are more numbers of family members in high organizational roles, the frequency of conflict increases. The influence of non-involved family members also increased the extent of conflict in first generation family firms, but significantly reduced both the extent and frequency of conflict in third or later generation firms. Lastly, increasing social interaction among family members was found to increase the extent of conflict in family firms.
Ensley and Pearson (2005)	224 top management teams	As part of a study on family business top management teams, the researchers examined the prevalence of idea and relationship conflict in family versus non-family top management teams. Results from the study suggest that non-family top management teams have more idea conflict, whereas parental top management teams had the least relationship conflict.
Eddleston and Kellermanns (2007)	60 family firms	This study examined the relationship of altruism and the level of ownership control concentration on participative strategy process and relationship conflict. Using structural equation modeling to test the hypothesized model, the findings suggest that altruism can reduce relationship conflict, as well as enhance participative strategy process. Furthermore, the study found that relationship conflict can negatively impact firm performance. Control concentration was not found to influence relationship conflict.
Ensley et al. (2007)	200 executive teams	This study examined the effect of pay dispersion in top management teams on affective conflict, cognitive conflict, and cohesion. The study also compares family versus non-family firms. Utilizing structural equation modeling, the study determines that pay dispersion negatively impacts affective conflict, cognitive conflict, and cohesion in family firms, and that this is magnified as compared to non-family firms.
Kellermanns and Eddleston (2007)	51 family firms	This study examined the effect of cognitive and process conflict on firm performance, with family-member exchange and generational ownership dispersion as moderators. The study found that cognitive conflict is negatively related to the performance and that this relationship is further moderated by both family-member exchange and generational ownership dispersion. Family-member exchange also moderated the relationship between process conflict and performance. Together, the results indicate, contrary to expectations, that the highest performance for family firms occurs with higher family-member exchange and low levels of cognitive conflict. Furthermore, in situations of low family-member exchange, process conflict hinders performance.

(Continued)

Table 26.1   (Continued)

Eddleston et al. (2008)	86 individual family members; 37 family firms; US privately held family firms via HLM	This study examined the relationship between participative decision making among family members and both cognitive and relationship conflict, finding that these relationships are moderated by multi-generational ownership dispersion. For multiple generations, participative decision-making is positively related to cognitive and relationship conflict, but for firms with only one or two generations, participative decision-making is negatively related to the two types of conflict. The authors suggest that for multi-generational firms, although benefits can be reaped from cognitive conflict, the likelihood of accompanying relationship conflict may hinder the overall benefits of cognitive conflict. They further conclude that, due to the difference in generations, the effects of conflict can vary due to the context in which they occur.
Amarapurkar and Danes (2005)	206 married couples owning family farm	This study examines business tensions in husband–wife pairs owning family farms. The researchers hypothesized that higher levels of business tension would be related to less constructive relationship conflict. Results of the study found that husbands reported higher level business tension than wives, and furthermore, reported less constructive relationship conflict.

some studies have investigated process-related issues such as participation in decision making (e.g., Eddleston et al., 2008; Kellermanns and Eddleston, 2007), few have investigated ownership (e.g., Eddleston et al., 2008) or family structure as potential antecedents of conflict (e.g., Danes, 2006). Family firms are heterogeneous (Gersick et al., 1997; Westhead and Howorth, 2007) in terms of ownership, managerial involvement, the number of family members involved in the firm, and generational differences, and future research should investigate these types of family firm specific antecedents of conflict and the process issues that arise from family member involvement.

As already suggested above, the majority of conflict research on family firms is focused on conflict among family members, yet family members often only constitute a minor percentage of employees in family firms. Future research may want to investigate how the make-up of decision-making teams affects the occurrence and management of conflict in family firms. In addition to exploring family-induced diversity as antecedents of conflict, the demographical diversity of the decision making teams and the composition of this diversity along family and non-family member faultlines might be very fruitful.

Family Firm Conflict Moderators

Outcomes of interpersonal conflict are often contingent on which goals managers are hoping to achieve (Jehn and Bendersky, 2003). A recent meta-analysis on cognitive conflict and group performance (De Dreu and Weingart, 2003) found little support for a direct effect, suggesting that a number of moderating variables may influence this relationship. Moderated models of interpersonal conflict describe a constellation of possible moderators in terms of their ability to amplify, suppress, ameliorate, or exacerbate the relationship between different conflict types and outcomes (Jehn and Bendersky, 2003). Altruism has been tested as an antecedent of family firm performance (Eddleston and Kellermanns, 2007), but may also moderate the relationship between other variables of interest. Generational ownership dispersion moderates the relationship between decision-making styles and interpersonal conflicts (Eddleston et al., 2008) and family member exchange (FMX) (Kellermanns and Eddleston, 2007) has also been shown to moderate the relationship between conflict and firm performance. These studies provide a springboard for testing new moderators from the broader interpersonal conflict literature such as group diversity, individual emotions, norms, and task interdependence (Jehn and Bendersky, 2003) and their inclusion allows family firm researchers the opportunity to more fully describe the process of conflict development and resolution.

Family Firm Conflict Outcomes

The eight studies summarized in Table 26.1 all report relationships between levels of conflict and a measure of family firm performance. Although organizational performance is the primary outcome of interest to strategy researchers (Hoskisson et al., 1999), the broader field of interpersonal conflict examines linkages between conflict and other outcomes beyond performance. For example, miscommunicating firm performance outcomes can become a source of conflict as some family members focus on growing the business while others focus on maintaining good relationships with family members at all costs (Astrachan and McMillan, 2003). For this reason, family firm scholars must recognize that non-financial outcomes are important to family business members and should endeavor to examine outcomes from the broader conflict literature within the family firm context. Indeed, economic and non-economic (i.e., socio-emotional) goals play important parts in the decision-making process of family firms (e.g., Chrisman et al., 2012; Gómez-Mejía et al., 2007; Zellweger et al., 2012). Understanding the individual drivers of socio-emotional considerations may be instrumental in preventing negative conflict and encouraging its positive forms.

In addition to their impacts on financial performance, relationship, cognitive, and process conflict have been theoretically linked to three non-performance-based outcomes: creativity, satisfaction, and consensus (Jehn and Bendersky, 2003). Creative output often results from conflicting ideas (Chen, 2006), and although stifling the ability to air conflicting viewpoints may streamline efficiencies in the short-term, it may also ultimately limit creative outcomes

(Thompson, 1965). Satisfaction impacts morale at the individual level, with excessive levels of non-productive relationship conflict leading to increased absenteeism and turnover (Giebels and Janssen, 2005). Job satisfaction models such as the exit, voice, loyalty, or neglect (EVLN) model of employee responses to job dissatisfaction (Farrell, 1983; Withey and Cooper, 1989) have long been used to link job satisfaction with turnover and absenteeism outcomes, although it may not adequately predict family member responses to job dissatisfaction, given that family employees are often less able to move freely between employers (Schulze et al., 2003a). Additional research on the ways that conflict impacts member satisfaction would contribute to our understanding of the coping mechanisms employed in stressful family firm workplaces where quitting is not a viable option and may also speak to the overall succession process in family firms (see also De Massis et al., 2008). Finally, consensus as a conflict-related outcome contributes to our understanding of family harmony as a beneficial product of family business member interactions (Sharma, 2004). Despite the inherent difficulty in measuring these non-performance outcomes, scholars can begin to assess the impact of different types of conflict, the various coping strategies employed by family firm members, and their collective impact on organizationally relevant outcomes.

Methodological Frontiers of Family Firm Research

Scholars have adapted measures of conflict from prior management studies for use in family firm research (e.g., Amason, 1996; Jehn, 1995, 1997a, 1997b) and Table 26.2 provides an overview of these items (i.e., Eddleston and Kellermanns, 2007; Kellermanns and Eddleston, 2007). We encourage future research to use these items and further refine them for the realm of family business.

Table 26.2   Recommended measurement of the three types of conflict in family firms

Type of conflict	Items
Process conflict	We often have disagreements about who should do what in our family firm.
	There is much conflict in our family firm about task responsibilities.
	We often disagree about resource allocation in our family firm.
Cognitive conflict	There is much conflict of ideas in our family firm.
	We often have disagreements within our family firm about the tasks we are working on.
	We often have disagreements within our family firm about the future strategy.
Relationship conflict	There is much relationship conflict in our family firm.
	People often get angry while working in our family firm.
	There is much emotional conflict in our family firm.

Source: Kellermanns and Eddleston (2007) and Eddleston and Kellermanns (2007)

Each of the empirical studies presented in Table 26.1 has employed questionnaires as the primary method for data collection, but a variety of methodological approaches have been used for data analysis, including structural equation modeling (Eddleston and Kellermanns, 2007), hierarchical linear modeling (Eddleston et al., 2008), and means tests (Sorenson, 1999). Surveys are appropriate and widely used for the study of family firm conflict (Davis and Harveston, 2001), but only permit answers to particular questions. These quantitative studies offer valuable answers to 'what' questions that describe the relationships between conflict types and performance outcomes, but lack the ability to answer the 'how' and 'why' questions that necessitate qualitative research tools and methods. Current research in this area clearly illustrates the assertion that 'performance of family firms cannot be fully understood without taking into account the psychodynamic effects of family relationships' (Eddleston and Kellermanns, 2007: 560). To better understand the underlying interpersonal processes that occur during family firm conflict resolution, future research on different types of family firm conflict (Kellermanns and Eddleston, 2007), and conflicts that arise from intergenerational differences (Davis and Harveston, 1999)

would likely benefit from mixed-methods techniques such as interviews, focus groups, or site visits to more fully experience and describe when and how family firm members employ different conflict management strategies to cope with different types of conflict. The use of qualitative methodological approaches to study family firm conflict may also uncover new moderators that further influence the relationship between conflict and firm performance.

Practitioner Recommendations

Conflict needs to be viewed as part of the overall governance of the organization (Baus, 2007; Fabis, 2009; Kellermanns and Schlippe, 2011) and governance contracts among family members should include conflict-related clauses to heighten the awareness of the involved family members and family branches. Any immediate and open negative conflict should be addressed within 48 hours of the occurrence (Kellermanns and Schlippe, 2011). In addition, a board or regular shareholder meeting with conflict-related authority can be beneficial. Practice also shows that it is beneficial to elect a 'go to' person, on a yearly basis, who is in charge of addressing critical issues among family members and serves as a first regulating authority. and even the establishment of 'family days,' i.e., meetings scheduled at regular intervals, can be a useful tool in regulating conflict.

The aforementioned governance mechanisms need to anticipate future changes in the family structure so that mechanisms can address the complexity of the family and its future structures and have provisions to deal with these changes. Without such anticipatory governance, processes may not be put into place once conflict has begun to escalate. For example, conflict that has been brewing under the surface for years or is of 'murky' origin, may benefit from the use of an independent third party. If this resolution strategy is desired by one part of the family, it is important that the party is not opposed and that decisions are binding for everyone involved.

Related Research on Conflict and Family Business

Although the majority of the research discussed above has focused on the three types of conflict, their management strategies, and performance outcomes, other related research streams can also provide fruitful extensions to the current literature. For example, research within the area of family business conflict examines work-family conflict and household conflict. Tensions in entrepreneurial ventures can impact work-family conflict, and consequently influence firm performance (Danes, 2006; Danes and Lee, 2004; Shelton et al., 2008; Werbel and Danes, 2010). As these studies indicate, conflict is not only limited to business matters that occur within the confines of the business, but also occurs at home, influencing the family business owner and the business. Studies that consider household and spousal conflict take a unique approach to relationship conflict and improve our understanding of how familial relationships can impact family businesses (Danes et al., 2000; Danes and Olson, 2003). This stream of literature considers both the performance of the firm and the performance of the household, both of which can impact goal achievement in the firm and the family (Danes et al., 1999). Although the nature of studies on spousal or household relations tend to focus on the conflict between a few individuals, these studies also contribute to the general conflict literature by considering the greater performance impact of familial conflict on the family firm. Accordingly, the examination of marital and household tensions and conflict within the context of the family further enriches the study of family business conflict.

CONCLUSION

Conflict management in family firms influences relationships in families and family firm performance. However, as this review reveals, family firm research is in its infancy in terms of empirically exploring how different types of conflict affect firm performance and other outcomes such as socio-emotional wealth. In addition to confirming the established main effects of conflict on performance, more research on intermediate outcomes and potential moderators of the conflict–performance relationship is warranted. Furthermore, research on the effectiveness of conflict management strategies in family firms is needed. Thus, we hope that future studies use this review as a starting point to conduct more family firm conflict research that will inform research, practice and teaching.

REFERENCES

Alper, S., Tjosvold, D., and Law, K.S. 2000. Conflict management, efficacy, and performance in organizational teams. *Personnel Psychology*, 53(3): 625–642.

Amarapurkar, S.S. and Danes, S.M. 2005. Farm business-owning couples: Interrelationships among business tensions, relationship conflict quality, and satisfaction with spouse. *Journal of Family and Economic Issues*, 26(3): 419–441.

Amason, A.C. 1996. Distinguishing the effects of functional and dysfunctional conflict on strategic decision making: Resolving a paradox for top management teams. *Academy of Management Journal*, 39(1): 123–148.

Astrachan, J. and McMillan, K. 2003. *Conflict and Communication in the Family Business*. Marietta: Family Enterprise Publishers.

Baus, K. 2007. *Die Familienstrategie: Wie Familien ihr Unternehmen über Generationen sichern*. Wiesbaden: Gabler.

Beckhard, R. and Dyer Jr, W.G. 1983. SMR Forum: Managing change in the family firm – issues and strategies. *Sloan Management Review*, 24: 59–65.

Chen, M.-H. 2006. Understanding the benefits and detriments of conflict on team creativity process. *Creativity and Innovation Management*, 15(1): 105–116.

Chrisman, J.J., Chua, J.H., Pearson, A.W., and Barnett, T. 2012. Family involvement, family influence, and family-centered non-economic goals in small firms. *Entrepreneurship: Theory and Practice*, 36(2): 267–293.

Daily, C.M. and Dollinger, M.J. 1992. An empirical examination of ownership structure in family and professionally managed firms. *Family Business Review*, 5(2): 117–136.

Danes, S.M. 2006. Tensions within family business-owning couples over time. *Stress, Trauma and Crisis*, 9(3–4): 227–246.

Danes, S.M. and Lee, Y.G. 2004. Tensions generated by business issues in farm business-owning couples. *Family Relations*, 53: 357–366.

Danes, S.M., Leichtentritt, R., and Metz, M. 2000. Effects of conflict severity on quality of life of men and women in family businesses. *Journal of Family and Economic Issues*, 21(3): 259–286.

Danes, S.M. and Olson, P.D. 2003. Women's role involvement in family businesses, business tensions, and business success. *Family Business Review*, 16(1): 53–68.

Danes, S.M., Zuiker, V., Kean, R., and Arbuthnot, J. 1999. Predictors of family business tension and goal achievement. *Family Business Review*, 12(3): 241–252.

Davis, P.S. and Harveston, P.D. 1999. In the founder's shadow: Conflict in the family firm. *Family Business Review*, 12(4): 311–323.

Davis, P.S. and Harveston, P.D. 2001. The phenomenon of substantive conflict in the family firm: A cross-generational study. *Journal of Small Business Management*, 39(1): 14–30.

De Dreu, C.K.W. 1997. Productive conflict: The importance of conflict management and conflict issue. In C.K.W. De Dreu and E. Van de Vliert (eds), *Using conflict in Organizations*: 9–22. London: Sage.

De Dreu, C.K.W. 2006. When too little or too much hurts: Evidence for a curvilinear relationship between task conflict and innovation in teams. *Journal of Management*, 32(1): 83–107.

De Dreu, C.K.W., Evers, A., Beersma, B., Kluwer, E.S., and Nauta, A. 2001. A theory-based measure of conflict management strategies in the workplace. *Journal of Organizational Behavior*, 22: 645–668.

De Dreu, C.K.W. and Van Vianen, A.E.M. 2001. Managing relationship conflict and the effectiveness of organizational teams. *Journal of Organizational Behavior*, 22: 309–328.

De Dreu, C.K.W. and Weingart, L.R. 2003. Task versus relationship conflict and team effectiveness: A meta-analysis. *Journal of Applied Psychology*, 88: 741–749.

De Massis, A., Chua, J.H., and Chrisman, J.J. 2008. Factors preventing intra-family succession. *Family Business Review*, 21(2): 183–199.

Donnelley, R.G. 1964. The family business. *Harvard Business Review*, 42: 93–105.

Eddleston, K. and Kellermanns, F.W. 2007. Destructive and productive family relationships: A stewardship theory perspective. *Journal of Business Venturing*, 22(4): 545–565.

Eddleston, K., Otondo, R., and Kellermanns, F.W. 2008. Conflict, participative decision making, and multi-generational ownership: A multi-level analysis. *Journal of Small Business Management*, 47(1): 456–484.

Ensley, M.D. and Pearson, A.W. 2005. A comparison of the behavioral processes of top management teams in family and non-family firms: Cohesion, conflict, potency, and consensus. *Entrepreneurship: Theory and Practice*, 29(3): 267–284.

Ensley, M.D., Pearson, A.W., and Sardesmukh, S.R. 2007. The negative consequences of pay dispersion in family and non-family top management teams: an exploratory analysis of new venture, high-growth firms. *Journal of Business Research*, 60(10): 1039–1047.

Fabis, F. 2009. Instrumentarien zur Vermeidung und Lösung von Gesellschafterkonflikten in Familienunternehmen. In A. v. Schlippe, T. Rüsen, and T. Groth (eds), *Beiträge zur Theorie des Familienunternehmens*: 269–290. Lohmar: Eul.

Farrell, D. 1983. Exit, voice, loyalty, and neglect as responses to job dissatisfaction: A multidimensional scaling study. *Academy of Management Journal*, 26(4): 596–607.

Frank, H., Kessler, A., Nosé, L., and Suchy, D. 2011. Conflicts in family firms: State of the art and perspectives for future research. *Journal of Family Business Management*, 1(2): 130–153.

Gersick, K.E., Davis, J.A., Hampton, M.M., and Lansberg, I. 1997. *Generation to Generation: Life Cycles of the Family Business*. Boston, MA: Harvard Business School Press.

Giebels, E. and Janssen, O. 2005. Conflict stress and reduced well-being at work: The buffering effect of third-party help. *European Journal of Work and Organizational Psychology*, 14(2): 137–155.

Gómez-Mejía, L.R., Haynes, K.T., Núñez-Nickel, M., Jacobson, K.J.L., and Moyano-Fuentes, H. 2007. Socioemotional wealth and business risk in family-controlled firms: Evidence from Spanish olive oil mills. *Administrative Science Quarterly*, 52(1): 106–137.

Gordon, G. and Nicholson, N. 2008. *Family Wars: Classic Conflicts in Family Business and How to Deal With Them*. London/Philadelphia: Kogan Page.

Habbershon, T.G., Williams, M., and MacMillan, I.C. 2003. A unified systems perspective of family firm performance. *Journal of Business Venturing*, 18: 451–465.

Harvey, M. and Evans, R.E. 1994. Family business and multiple levels of conflict. *Family Business Review*, 7(4): 331–348.

Hoskisson, R.E., Hitt, M.A., Wan, W.P., and Yiu, D. 1999. Theory and research in strategic management: Swings of a pendulum. *Journal of Management*, 25(3): 417–456.

Jehn, K.A. 1992. *The Impact of Intragroup Conflict on Effectiveness: A Multimethod Examination of the Benefits and Detriments of Conflict*. Unpublished doctoral dissertation, Northwestern University Graduate School of Management, Evanston, IL.

Jehn, K.A. 1995. A multimethod examination of the benefits and detriments of intragroup conflict. *Administrative Science Quarterly*, 40: 256–282.

Jehn, K.A. 1997a. Affective and cognitive conflict in work groups: Increasing performance through value-based intragroup conflict. In D. Dreu, and E. Van de Vliert (eds), *Using Conflict in Organizations*: 87–100. London: Sage.

Jehn, K.A. 1997b. A quantitative analysis of conflict types and dimensions in organizational groups. *Administrative Science Quarterly*, 42(3): 530–558.

Jehn, K.A. and Bendersky, C. 2003. Intragroup conflict in organizations: A contingency perspective on the conflict-outcome relationship. *Research in Organizational Behavior*, 25: 187–241.

Jehn, K.A. and Mannix, E.A. 2001. The dynamic nature of conflict: A longitudinal study of intragroup conflict and group performance. *Academy of Management Journal*, 44(2): 238–251.

Kaye, K. 1991. Penetrating the cycle of sustained conflict. *Family Business Review*, 4(1): 21–44.

Kaye, K. and McCarthy, C. 1996. Healthy disagreements. *Family Business*, Autumn: 71–72.

Kellermanns, F.W. and Eddleston, K. 2004. Feuding families: When conflict does a family firm good. *Entrepreneurship: Theory and Practice*, 28(3): 209–228.

Kellermanns, F.W. and Eddleston, K. 2006. Feuding families: The management of conflict in family firms. In P. Poutziouris, K. Smyrnios, and B. Klein (eds), *Family Business Research Handbook*: 358–368. Northampton, MA: Edward Elgar Publishing.

Kellermanns, F.W. and Eddleston, K. 2007. Family perspective on when conflict benefits family firm performance. *Journal of Business Research: Special Issue on Family Firms*, 60: 1048–1057.

Kellermanns, F.W., Floyd, S., Pearson, A., and Spencer, B. 2008. The interactive effects of shared mental models and constructive confrontation on decision quality. *Journal of Organizational Behavior*, 29: 119–137.

Kellermanns, F.W. and Schlippe, A. v. 2011. Beziehungskonflikte in Familienunternehmen und ihre Bedeutung für die Unternehmensführung (slightly modified and updated). In A. Koeberele-Schmid (ed.), *Governance in Familienunternehmen*, 2nd edn. Berlin: Erich Schmidt Verlag.

Kellermanns, F.W., Walter, J., Lechner, C., and Floyd, S.W. 2005. The lack of consensus about strategic consensus: Advancing theory and research. *Journal of Management*, 31(5): 719–737.

Kelly, L.M., Athanassiou, N., and Crittenden, W.F. 2000. Founder centrality and strategic behavior in the family-owned firm. *Enterpreneurship: Theory and Practice*, 25(2): 27–42.

Lansberg, I.S. 1983. Managing human resources in family firms: The problem of institutional overlap. *Organizational Dynamics*, 12: 39–46.

Lee, M.-S. and Rogoff, E.G. 1996. Research note: Comparison of small businesses with family participation versus small businesses without family participation: An investigation of differences in goals, attitudes, and family/business conflict. *Family Business Review*, 9(4): 423–437.

Levinson, H. 1971. Conflicts that plague family businesses. *Harvard Business Review*, 49: 90–98.

Ling, Y. and Kellermans, F. 2010. The effects of family firm specific sources of TMT diversity: The moderating role of information exchange frequency. *Journal of Management Studies*, 47(2): 322–344.

Mooney, A.C., Holahan, P.J., and Amason, A.C. 2007. Don't take it personally: Exploring cognitive conflict as a mediator of affective conflict. *Journal of Management Studies*, 44(5): 733–758.

Murninghan, J.K. and Conlon, D.E. 1991. The dynamics of intense work groups: A study of British string quartets. *Administrative Science Quarterly*, 36: 165–186.

Pruitt, D.G. and Rubin, J.Z. 1986. *Social Conflict: Escalation, Stalemate, Settlement*. New York: Random House.

Putman, L.L. 1994. Productive conflict: Negotiation as implicit coordination. *International Journal of Conflict Management*, 9: 285–299.

Schulze, W.S., Lubatkin, M.H., and Dino, R.N. 2003a. Exploring the agency consequences of ownership dispersion among the directors of private family firms. *Academy of Management Journal*, 46(2): 179–194.

Schulze, W.S., Lubatkin, M.H., and Dino, R.N. 2003b. Toward a theory of agency and altruism in family firms. *Journal of Business Venturing*, 18(4): 473–490.

Sharma, P. 2004. On overview of the field of family business studies: Current status and directions for future. *Family Business Review*, 17(1): 1–36.

Shelton, L.M., Danes, S.M., and Eisenman, M. 2008. Role demands, difficulty in managing work-family conflict, and minority entrepreneurs. *Journal of Developmental Entrepreneurship*, 13(3): 315–342.

Simons, T.L. and Peterson, R.S. 2000. Task conflict and relationship conflict in top management teams: The pivotal role of intragroup trust. *Journal of Applied Psychology*, 85(1): 102–111.

Sirmon, D.G. and Hitt, M.A. 2003. Managing resources: Linking unique resources, management and wealth creation in family firms. *Entrepreneurship: Theory and Practice*, 27(4): 339–358.

Sorenson, R.L. 1999. Conflict management strategies used in successful family businesses. *Family Business Review*, 12(4): 325–339.

Thompson, V.A. 1965. Bureaucracy and innovation. *Administrative Science Quarterly*, 10(1): 1–20.

Tjosvold, D. 1991. Rights and responsibilities of dissent: Cooperative conflict. *Employee Responsibilities and Rights Journal*, 4(1): 13–23.

Tjosvold, D. 1997. Conflict within interdependence: Its value for productivity and individuality. In C.K.W. De Dreu and E. Van de Vliert (eds), *Using Conflict in Organizations*: 23–37. Thousand Oaks, CA: Sage.

Wall Jr, J.A. and Callister, R.R. 1995. Conflict and its management. *Journal of Management*, 21(3): 515–558.

Ward, J.L. 1987. *Keeping the Family Business Healthy: How to Plan for Continuing Growth*. San Francisco, CA: Jossey-Bass.

Werbel, J.D. and Danes, S.M. 2010. Work family conflict in new business ventures: The moderating effect of spousal commitment to the new business venture. *Journal of Small Business Management*, 48(3): 421–440.

Westhead, P. and Howorth, C. 2007. 'Types' of private family firm: An exploratory conceptual and empirical analysis. *Entrepreneurship & Regional Development*, 19: 405–431.

Withey, M.J. and Cooper, W.H. 1989. Predicting exit, voice, loyalty, and neglect. *Administrative Science Quarterly*, 34(4): 521–539.

Zellweger, T.M., Kellermanns, F.W., Chrisman, J.J., and Chua, J.H. 2012. Family control and family firm valuation by family CEOs: The importance of intentions for transgenerational control. *Organization Science*, 23: 851–868.

27

Emotions in Family Firms

Ethel Brundin and Charmine E.J. Härtel

INTRODUCTION

Emotion dimensions pervade the full spectrum of human behavior and interaction, and the organizational arena is no exception. In recognition of this, research on emotions in organizational settings has been developing fast with an upsurge of academic interest in the subject (Härtel et al., 2011). Despite the increase over the last decade in the knowledge base about the role of emotions in work settings, little attention has been given to the family business context. This is especially surprising given the family business' specific characteristics and intertwinement of the two systems of the family and the firm (Astrachan and Jaskiewicz, 2008) giving room for a lot of emotions. Or, as Fletcher (2000: 164) argues, 'the interpersonal linkages, emotional bondings and affectionate ties that characterize all firms are possibly more complex and embedded in family firms'. In this chapter, we introduce the emotional organization view of family business, providing deeper insight into the role of emotions in family firms and pointing to an increasing number of studies that show that emotions play an important role in the running of a business.

However, to recognize the importance of emotions also means to confess to its complex nature in the family business setting, which is often characterized by a strong culture, long traditions and genuine relations among family members who find much of their identity in their firm (Härtel et al., 2009). This complexity may lead to unwanted outcomes such as conflicts and even family feuds, but it can also constitute a strong glue between family members, which has the potential to provide competitive advantage.

The purpose of this chapter is to portray the emotional landscape of family business and link it to the quality of the family and business outcomes and to highlight the conditions under which emotions can lead to better or worse outcomes in this unique context. In order to meet our purpose, the chapter seeks to address the following four questions:

1 What are emotions and how have emotions been studied?
2 What is the nature of emotions in the family business?

3   What emotion constructs can inform emotionally charged practices in the family business?
4   What future research agenda on emotions can contribute to knowledge and practice in family businesses?

By addressing these four questions the chapter provides a framework to theoretically and empirically grounded emotion theories and constructs in the family business setting and portrays the emotional landscape of family firms.

The remainder of the chapter is structured around the four questions above, beginning with an overview of what we know today about emotion in organizations. Next, we review the existing literature on emotions in family firms. Thereafter, we identify two emotion challenges that are especially pertinent to family firms: emotional dissonance and emotional ambivalence. We conclude with suggestions for a future research agenda including methodological suggestions.

EMOTIONS IN ORGANIZATIONS

What are Emotions?

Emotions are affective reactions to a specific event (Keltner and Haidt, 1999) and the interpretation an individual makes of an emotionally charged event signals how he or she will feel and behave (Fineman, 2003). In this chapter, we are concerned with both so-called primary and secondary emotions. Examples of the former are joy, sadness, anger, fear and surprise; also called basic emotions (Ekman, 1992). Examples of secondary emotions are affection, pride, nostalgia, remorse and envy, and these are the result of how a specific event is interpreted in a social interaction (Kemper, 1987). The way in which an event is interpreted is not only a function of an individual's psychological make-up including important goals, but the interaction of that make-up with characteristics of the setting associated with the event (Wrzesniewski et al., 2003). Thus, other actors, norms, past experiences and physical characteristics (e.g., noise, light, space) associated with a setting all come

into play when interpreting the significance of an event to the self. As such, secondary emotions provide important clues into the goals and relationships that are important to individuals and groups (Keltner and Haidt, 1999).

The sense-making perspective of emotions may help individuals to coordinate behavior and anticipate and negotiate outcomes. Positive emotions serve to indicate when goals are being achieved whereas negative emotions signal the need to prepare to deal with threat and change (Fong, 2006). The more quickly affective information is recognized and considered by individuals, the more opportunity there is to achieve desirable outcomes (Gross, 2001). Attempts at emotional regulation and control, however, are not always effective, with some strategies shown to be more useful than others in various circumstances. For example, Gross (2001) showed that taking a different perspective of an event outside one's control leads to more productive and beneficial outcomes then continuing to view it as first appraised. When events are in one's control, however, acting to change the trajectory of the event to achieve a more favorable outcome is preferable to reframing the situation.

Emotion Studies in Organizations

The study of emotions started in the 1940s with a managerial interest in emotions as part of job satisfaction. Forty years later, Hochschild (1983) made a path-breaking entrance into the emotion field with her book *The Managed Heart*, where she gave an account of flight attendants' emotional labor. In doing so, she theorized the production and fabrication of emotions (emotional labor); the communication of emotions (display of emotions); and the suppression of emotions (emotional dissonance or surface acting). The book thus sets the terminology for a set of emotion concepts that have been taken as common knowledge within the field.

Ten years later, when Fineman (1993) introduced the organization as an emotional arena, the starting signal was given to increase exploration of the role of emotions in organizations.

Emotions have since been studied from a variety of perspectives and on different levels. A so-called cultural turn was taken by Van Maanen and Kunda (1989) when they used Disney Land as the empirical foundation for their theorizing of management of emotions as part of organizational culture. A set of studies about emotions in the service sector followed, whereas the studies of Rafaeli and Sutton have been widely acknowledged. In their work, the authors address the emotional display among service employees and find that during busy times they are less likely to display positive emotions whereas they do during slow times and towards demanding customers (Sutton and Rafaeli, 1988; Rafaeli and Sutton, 1990). Sales were thus rather related to store pace and were the cause of the display of emotions, and not vice versa. Neither did customers expect positive emotions to be displayed during rush hours.

As a resistance to the commercialization of emotions, a critical turn took place in the late 1990s and early twenty-first century when scholars brought up norms and structures of emotions and the questions of in who's interest emotions were managed and where the dark side of emotions was made visible (Mastenbroek, 2000). During the late 1990s, the concept of emotional intelligence (EI) made its entrance with Goleman's (1995, 1998) search for the emotionally intelligent workplace, followed by a bloom of interest in the issue around the world during the first decade of the twentieth century. Contemporary research shows an emerging interest in the positive virtue of emotions and emotional resilience in crises (e.g., Härtel, 2008).

In recent years, management scholars and practitioners have become aware of emotions in context, that is, the impact of shared emotions on employee performance and satisfaction. Through sharing emotions, whether verbally or non-verbally, groups and organizations develop a typical emotional state, referred to as emotional climate. Emotional climates characterized by more positive than negative emotions have been linked with greater workgroup satisfaction, customer service (Härtel

et al., 2006), adaptability, creativity and organizational functioning (Fredrickson, 2001, 2003; Fredrickson and Losada, 2005). Organizations can also develop an unhealthy or toxic emotional culture, which undermines creativity, resilience, collaboration and performance potential (Härtel, 2008). For these reasons, organizational leaders are advised to engage in positive leadership to foster a positive work environment where the emotional health and welfare of employees is prioritized (Härtel, 2008).

Recognizing the operation of emotions at multiple levels within the organization is essential for understanding how emotions influence organizational outcomes and the necessity for effective emotion management. For example, the emotions an individual is experiencing will moderate his/her thinking and problem-solving processes (Isen, 2004), learning (Shepherd, 2003; Vince and Saleem, 2004; Zhao and Olivera, 2006), motivation (Ilies and Judge, 2005) and discretionary behavior (Spector and Fox, 2002). Emotions experienced during interpersonal interactions influence cooperation levels, trustworthiness and conflict (Barsade, 2002; Miller, 2001; Morrow et al., 2004; Stecher and Rosse, 2005). Emotions at the group/organizational level influence the quality of learning climate (Domagalski, 1999) and coordination (Sy et al., 2005) and counterproductive work behaviors (Fox et al., 2001).

Since family businesses are one of the major organizational forms, we now turn specifically to see how emotions are portrayed in this context.

THE EMOTIONAL LANDSCAPE OF FAMILY BUSINESS

Emotions in the Family Business Literature

Only an emerging stream of literature focuses explicitly on emotions in family firms. The emotion perspective is, however, both relevant and present indirectly in the family business literature (Berrone et al., 2012). Adopting the perspective that family business comprises the family, the business and the dimension of ownership (Gersick et al., 1997), all having their own aims and tasks (Taguiri and Davis, 1996), it is appropriate to review emotions in family firms with these three dimensions as a point of departure. Acknowledging that the three dimensions overlap, we take both intra-individual and inter-individual emotions into account (see Table 27.1). Following this approach, our review[1] led us to group emotions into five categories: (a) business-focused emotions such as emotional returns and costs; (b) business- and self-focused emotions such as envy, grief, pride; (c) relations- and other-focused emotions such as love, grief, shame, guilt; (d) affective based emotions (attitudes) such as trust, loyalty, commitment, fairness; and (e) ownership related emotions such as pride, joy and feelings of wanting to be in control.

Results from the Review

Following our categorization of emotions, we will highlight some of the trends and contributions made within each category.

Business-focused emotions (the business system)

In this category we find an emerging interest in the concept of socio-emotional wealth and emotional costs and returns. The notion of socio-emotional wealth builds on the individual's self-concept of belonging to a social category (Tajfel, 1982) and includes, among other things, authority, satisfaction, need for belonging, preservation of the family dynasty and the fulfillment of family obligations (Gómez-Mejía et al., 2007). Even if emotions are not explicit in the first entries on socio-emotional wealth, the literature indicates that emotional ownership provides the

Table 27.1   A review of emotions in the family business literature

Category	Author and journal	Key emotion/emotion concept
Business focused emotions (the business system)	Gómez-Mejía, L.R. et al. (2007). Socioemotional wealth and business risks in family-controlled firms: evidence from Spanish olive oil mills. *Administrative Science Quarterly*, 52, 106–137.	A socio-emotional wealth model.
	Astrachan, J.H. and Jaskiewicz, P. (2008). Emotional returns and emotional costs in privately held family businesses: advancing traditional business valuation. *Family Business Review* 21(2), 139–149.	Emotional returns and emotional costs.
	Zellweger, T.M. and Astrachan, J.H. (2008). On the emotional value of owning a firm. *Family Business Review*, 4, 347–363.	Emotional value, emotional costs and emotional benefits.
	Berrone, P., Cruz, C. and Gómez-Mejía, L.R. (2012). Socioemotional wealth in family firms: theoretical dimensions assessment approaches, and agenda for future research. *Family Business Review*, 25, 258–279.	Five dimensions of socio-emotional wealth: family control and influence; family members' identification with the firm; binding social ties; renewal of family bonds to the firm through dynastic succession; and emotional attachment (tenacity, aggression and blame).
Business and self-focused emotions/ (the family member and business system)	Levinson, H. (1971). Conflicts that plague family businesses. *Harvard Business Review*, 90–95.	Guilt and frustration from rivalry.

Category	Author and journal	Key emotion/emotion concept
	Brundin, E. and Nordqvist, M. (2008). Beyond facts and figures: the role of emotions in boardroom dynamics. *Corporate Governance: An International Review*, 16(4), 326–341.	Emotional energy leading to power and status positions in and outside the boardroom.
	Stanley, L. (2010). Emotions and family business creation: an extension and implications. *Entrepreneurship: Theory and Practice*, 34(6), 1085–1092.	Experienced positive and negative emotions and their relation to risk taking behavior.
	Brundin, E. and Sharma, P. (2011). Love, hate and desire. The role of emotional messiness. In Carsrud A. and Brannback M. (eds), *International Perspectives on Future Research in Family Business: Neglected Topics and Under-utilized Theories*. New York: Springer.	Mix of felt emotions that can lead to positive or negative consequences for the individual, the family or the business.
	Brundin, E. and Languilaire, J.C. (2012). Känslomässig harmoni eller disharmoni. Känsloregler och gränsdragningar avseende tid, plats och relationer. (Emotional harmony or disharmony: feeling and boundary rules in time, space and relations.) In Brundin, E. et al. (eds) *Familjeföretagandets väsen. (Characteristics of the Family Firm.)* Stockholm: SNS Förlag.	Emotional boundary-making in relation to time, space and relations between and across the two spheres of family and the business.
	Hirigoyen, G. and Labaki, R. (2012). The role of regret in the owner-manager decision-making in the family business: a conceptual approach. *Journal of Family Business Strategy*, 3, 118–126.	Owner manager regret in decision-making including family-based regret and business-based regret as well as the expected and the experienced regret.
Relations- and other-focused emotions (the family system)	Hubler, T.M. (2005). Forgiveness as an intervention in family-owned business: a new beginning. *Family Business Review*, 18(2), 95–103.	The ritual of forgiveness, building on the family's history and use of religious traditions, is a way to heal family business relations and to start anew.
	Sund, L-G. and Smyrnios, K.X. (2005). Striving for happiness and its impact on family stability: an exploration of the Aristotelian conception of happiness. *Family Business Review*, 18(2), 155–170.	An exploration of the Aristotelian conception of happiness (wisdom, virtue and pleasures) and how it relates to family stability. The relative willingness to support and share the interest of a partner is important to reach happiness.
	Trevinyo-Rodríguez, R.N. (2010). Family ties and emotions: a missing piece in the knowledge transfer puzzle. *Journal of Small Business and Enterprise Development*, 17(3), 418–436.	Positive and negative emotions' impact on intergenerational learning.
	Mehrotra, V., Morck, R., Shim, J. and Wiwattanakantang, Y. (2011). Must love kill the family firm? Some exploratory evidence. *Entrepreneurship: Theory and Practice*, 35(6), 1121–1148.	Love (arranged marriages).
Affective based emotions/attitudes (the family and business systems)	Steier, L. (2001). Family firms, plural forms of governance, and the evolving role of trust. *Family Business Review*, 14, 353–367.	Trust in governance.

(Continued)

Table 27.1   (Continued)

Category	Author and journal	Key emotion/emotion concept
	Koiranen, M. (2002). Over 100 years of age but still entrepreneurially active in business, exploring the values and family characteristics of old Finnish family firms. *Family Business Review*, 15(3), 175–187.	Honesty and credibility – for long-term survival. Commitment, responsibility and fairness. (Self assessment of century-old characteristics).
	Kellermans, F.W. and Eddleston, K.A. (2004). Feuding families: when conflict does a family firm good. *Entrepreneurship: Theory and Practice*, 28(3), 209–228.	Altruism; effects of task, process and relationship conflict.
	Sharma, P. (2004). An overview of the field of family business studies: current status and directions for the future. *Family Business Review*, 17(1), 1–36.	Emotional capital: low/high emotional capital (and low/high financial capital).
	Sharma, P. and Irving, P.G. (2005). Four bases of family business successor commitment: antecedents and consequences. *Entrepreneurship: Theory and Practice*, 29(1), 13–33.	Four types of successor commitment: affective, normative, calculative and/or imperative commitment.
	Brundin, E. and Melin, L. (2006). Beyond facts and figures: the role of emotions in boardroom dynamics. *Corporate Governance: An International Review*, 16(4), 326–341.	Confidence and frustration as driving or counteracting strategic change.
	Davis, J.H., Allen, M.R. and Hayes, D.H. (2010). Is blood thicker than water? A study of stewardship perceptions in family business. *Entrepreneurship: Theory and Practice*, 34(6), 1093–1115.	Trust and commitment as explanation for stewardship variance in family and non-family firms.
	Eddleston, K.A., Chrisman, J.J., Steier, L.P. and Chua, J.H. (2010). Governance and trust in family firms: an introduction. *Entrepreneurship: Theory and Practice*, 34(6), 1043–1056.	Trust As an organizing principle Founder's imprint Interpersonal trust Intra-organizational trust Transaction-based trust.
	Kidwell, R.E., Kellermanns, F.W. and Eddleston, K.A. (2012). Harmony, justice, confusion, and conflict in family firms: implications for ethical climate and the 'Fredo effect'. *Journal of Business Ethics*, 106, 503–517.	Harmony norms, distributive fairness, role ambiguity and relations conflict leading to harmful behavior that leads to impediment for the firm.
Ownership	Björnberg, Å. and Nicholson, N. (2008). *Emotional Ownership: The Critical Pathway Between the Next Generation and the Family Firm*. London: The Institute for Family Business.	Emotional ownership which is gender and culturally influenced.
	Brundin, E., Melin, L. and Florin-Samuelsson, E. (2008) *The Family Ownership Logic: Chore Characteristics of Family Controlled Businesses*. Jönköping: Jönköping International Business School, Working Paper.	Psychological/emotional ownership as part of identification with the family firm.
	Björnberg, Å, and Nicholson, N. (2012) Emotional ownership: the next generation's relationship with the family firm. *Family Business Review*, 25, 374–390.	An analysis of key questions about the nature of emotional ownership.

driving force to protect the sustainability and the trans-generational potential of the firm (Gómez-Mejía et al., 2007; Zellweger and Astrachan, 2008). In Berrone et al. (2012), emotional attachment is explicitly added as a dimension of the socio-emotional wealth model. Nonetheless, the authors claim that there is a need to investigate what types of emotions have a positive or negative impact on socio-emotional wealth formation and what effect emotions have on relationship conflicts and role conflicts.

Business- and self-focused emotions (the family member in the business system)

An early entry within this category is Levinson (1971), who brings up conflict in the form of father–son rivalry,[2] claiming that such rivalry includes feelings of guilt. The conflict is explained as a dilemma between strong feelings of viewing the business as an extension of oneself where the firm is regarded as one's baby, mistress and instrument of power – something the father wants to share and pass on to his son. However, in doing so the father loses both control and his baby. The father's behavior therefore becomes contradictory with feelings of guilt. The son, on the other hand, wants to show his maturity; however, when thwarted in his attempts, he will start acting as a rebellious teenager filled with frustration as well as guilt for his behavior. The same phenomenon can occur between rivaling brothers, often supported by their father.

Brundin and Sharma (2011) show that the mix of positive and negative emotions in family firms may lead to emotional messiness, which has clear connections to emotional ambivalence (Fong, 2006) where a mix of positive and negative emotions are simultaneously at play, pointing at the emotional complexity of organizational life (Stratton, 2010). Such emotional messiness may lead to positive and/or negative consequences, mainly depending on the level of emotional intelligence among the family members.

In a Swedish setting, Brundin and Nordqvist (2008) draw on the concept of emotional energy in the context of the boardroom where low emotional energy diminishes the influence of the family business CEO. Stanley (2010) couples emotional experiences of the owner to risk-taking and Brundin and Melin (2006) show in a longitudinal study how the display of a CEO's emotions in family firms impacts the strategic process in the firm insofar that the display drives or restrains the process. The individual family members' way of relating their emotion rules to time, space and relations in the interaction of the spheres of the family and the business may lead to either family harmony or family disharmony (Brundin and Languilaire, 2012).

Relations- and other-focused emotions (the family in the family system)

Only a couple of studies were found in this category, indicating a gap where we know little about the impact of the family members that do not actively work in the business. They may play an important role when it comes to the emotional climate in the business family. Labaki et al. (2012) draw a similar conclusion when they claim that the field is still dismissive of the family in the family business and especially the role of emotions. According to the authors, contemporary literature points to the importance of emotions by integrating the two systems of family and business into a more holistic view that recognizes their mutual existence and a recognition of the family influence on the business. Even so, the authors claim that the existing literature mainly focuses on the overlap of the family system and the business system and that the family per se is still put at a disadvantage and thereby so too the role of emotions. Further, the term 'emotional is used to capture all possible components of psychological, behavioral, social and cognitive aspects' (Labaki et al., 2012: 13), leading to either a misuse of the meaning of emotions or an overall labeling of all 'soft issues' into one sole category of emotions.

Affective based emotions/attitude (the family and the business system)

Within this category, the most salient emotions are trust and commitment and the theme is comparatively well covered in the literature. As an example, Sharma and Irving (2005) argue that reasons to take over a family firm may be emotional where commitment is a strong driving force to do so. Genuine relations (Hall, 2003) and family ties, where family members are bonded by strong emotional ties (Davis, 1983), are often referred to as the foundation for the affective based attitudes in the family firm.

Family business oriented emotions (ownership system)

The role of ownership in relation to emotion is little developed. An example from this category is Björnberg and Nicholson (2008, 2012), who extend financial/formal ownership by using the concept of emotional ownership and find that it is strong among family business members, especially in the Latin countries. Their results underline that emotions are an influential factor for experiences across cultures (Markus and Kitayama, 1991) or that culture influences emotion (Matsumoto, 1993). Emotional ownership is also one of the characteristics that is part of the family ownership logic as suggested by Brundin et al. (2008).

Explanations for the Family Firm as an Emotional Arena

A review of emotions in family firms indicate why family firms are an organizational type that is more emotional compared to other organizational forms. Stewart and Hitt (2012) summarize a set of prevailing dichotomies that would distinguish family firms from non-family firms where the management of family firms is regarded as emotional and intuitive in contrast to the view of non-family firms' management as rational and analytical (cf. Zellweger and Astrachan, 2008). Definitions of family businesses exist that underline such a view:

'a family business is a unique organization since it encompasses the overlap of a system based on rational, economic principles and a system organized and based on emotions' (Kets de Vries et al., 2007: 26). The family business literature in its early days tended to portray the family system as interfering negatively with the business system due to its emotive side. This has led to assumptions that the two systems of family and business should be separated to avoid mixing the emotional and rational arenas so that emotions do not 'interfere' with the business (e.g., Kepner, 1983; Hollander and Elman, 1988; Whiteside and Brown, 1991). A more 'modern' view, to which we subscribe, is that the boundaries between the two systems of family and business are permeable (McCollom, 1988; Whiteside and Brown, 1991) and the systems – or rather spheres – intertwine with each other in a natural way. The main point then is that individuals need to make clear to themselves how their expectations and their own emotion rules affect and are affected by the firm (Brundin and Sharma, 2011; Brundin and Languilaire, 2012).

In the literature we find two main reasons for regarding family firms as emotional arenas:

1   *Hybrid identities.* A major explanation in the literature is that family firms are hybrid identity organizations (Albert and Whetten, 1985). The hybrid identity concept builds on the notion that the family business is built on two different types of organizations, that of the family and that of the business and these are seemingly incompatible. The family is a normative system building on norms, values and altruism where emotions are a natural part, whereas the business system is utilitarian in which emotions are regarded as irrational and having no place (Whiteside and Brown, 1991), building on profit maximization (Foreman and Whetten, 2002). To view a family business as an integrated part of the family as well as the business has led to recognition that issues belonging to the family system may be dealt with as a business issue, and issues belonging to the business system may be dealt with as a family matter (Davis and Stern, 1980). A common example is to

bring up business issues during the family dinner and other family celebrations and to discuss family members' future at board and management team meetings. No matter how hard the individuals in a family firm try to draw a line between the two systems, it is unachievable as the family and business have become one. The enmeshing of the family and the business creates a context of hybrid identities where family members may have difficulties solely identifying with either the business logic or the family logic, and where identity clashes and role conflicts may occur (Albert and Whetten, 1985; Tompkins, 2010). For example, a family business CEO may come into a situation where her son is not performing according to the standards of the business. Following the business logic, she would have to let him go, but following the family logic, she doesn't want to see him made redundant. Further, family members often feel that the business is part of their identity and a place where they belong (Pierce et al., 2001; Brundin et al., 2008). This makes them vulnerable to threats of losing the business, either in a succession process (Sharma and Irving, 2005) or in turbulent times. In such a context it is not surprising that emotions play an important role. That the family business is a source of ample opportunities to study emotional processes is also acknowledged by researchers such as Van-den-Heuval et al., (2007) and Klein (2008).

2   *Emotional ownership.* Another reason for family firms to be an emotional context is that the informal ownership makes a difference, in the family firm literature labeled emotional ownership (Björnberg and Nicholson, 2008; 2012). Björnberg and Nicholson (2012: 8) refer to emotional ownership as a 'cognitive and affective state of association that describes a (young) family member's attachment to and identification with his or her family business'. The emotional attachment to the family firm gives rise to emotions of pride and joy, as well as emotions of wanting to be in control and in power (Brundin and Sharma, 2011). The ownership dimension plays a special role in emotions in family firms. Traditionally, ownership has been referred to as merely legal and formal, for example, in the percentage of financial ownership. However, there are also other forms of ownership, such as psychological ownership (Pierce, Kostova & Dirks, 2001; Brundin et al., 2008; Brundin and Sharma, 2011) and socio-symbolic ownership (Nordqvist, 2005), that are of special interest in family firms where the focus is on emotions and emotional states. More specifically, the concept of psychological ownership refers to the feelings of 'oneness' with the family firm and where the possessiveness is a prominent feature. The oneness and possessiveness may lead to a full identification with the firm in the sense that it becomes necessary for one's well-being and feelings of emptiness if lost. Psychological ownership is the result of an individual's investment in, and intimate knowledge about, the target of 'owning', and the need to be in control. At the same time it creates positive emotions of joy, pride, satisfaction, loyalty and so on (Avey et al., 2009). However, some family members may feel the burden of ownership, which may lead to emotions of grief (the emotion of extreme sadness when something unpleasant happens) (Collin's Cobuild, 1987) and emotions of being shut-in or trapped when being 'forced to take over the business'. The loss of a family firm, that is, a dear and valuable heirloom, may also lead to grief (cf. Shepherd, 2003). Among siblings, the psychological ownership may lead to envy (the emotion when one wants something that someone or something else has) and jealousy (the emotion when you fear something or someone might be taken away from you).

Collective psychological ownership

Recent literature has shifted its focus to collective psychological ownership, which results from the interactive dynamics of a group of people such as a family and how they collectively build up emotions of ownership for a specific object, for example, the family firm (Pierce and Jussila, 2009). Viewed this way, the 'oneness' becomes the 'our-ness'. Building on notions of psychological ownership, Pierce and Jussila (2009) argue that the feeling of 'it's MINE' is extended to a recognition that more people are tied to the object, such as the family firm, and include them into the feeling of 'it's OURS'. The interactive dynamics of verbal and non-verbal language in the group form a collective as well as cognitive/affective state from the 'mine' to the 'ours' in regard to this object, that is, the family firm. Viewed this way, such a joint process is part of the emotional climate in the firm with its good points and its bad points and for better or for worse (cf. Härtel, 2008).

The socio-symbolic ownership

The socio-symbolic ownership takes place in the context of social interaction and may include negotiations regarding ownership. It stems from the symbolic interactionist perspective and includes the meaning and sense-making of ownership (Nordqvist, 2005). It takes into account the specific context where ownership is linked to certain values and interests (Grunebaum, 1987). Such ownership is likely to lead to a need to be identified with the business – the business becomes an extension of one's 'self' (Belk, 1988) – and therefore a bankruptcy or a selling of a family business can result in the loss of a major social arena where the family members have spent most of their time, creating an emotionally charged experience comprising 'mourning, anger, depression, sorrow and fear of the unknown, the future and the ambiguous present' (Harris and Sutton, 1986: 11). It is similar to a situation when a close relationship is ended.

DISPLAY OF EMOTIONS: EMOTIONAL DISSONANCE

Labaki et al. (2012) point out emotional dissonance as an important and neglected concept to understanding the family business phenomenon. Next we therefore provide more detail on the display of emotions and the construct of emotional dissonance that we argue is of particular relevance to the family business context.

The family business constitutes a context where specific so-called framing rules of emotions more or less dictate how a family member should interpret the meaning of a situation (cf. Hochschild, 1983). Within these framing rules, family members follow certain display and feeling rules, built up over the years as a consequence of the family firm's specific norms and values.[3] The family members thus learn what emotions are accepted to display or express and what emotions they ought to feel in different situations. So, for example, siblings may be expected to

show and feel love towards each other also in situations when they may not feel such love.

Individuals do not necessarily display emotions that are consistent with their authentic feelings (Ekman and Oster, 1979; Hochschild, 1983) since emotions can be masked, hidden, controlled or displayed without being experienced. Different frameworks and professions apply to different emotion rules that guide what emotions are appropriate to display – and to even feel (Hochschild, 1983). So, for instance, Hochschild (1983) showed in her classical study of flight attendants that it is important for them to display positive emotions, even if they basically do not experience these emotions. The emotion rules for flight attendants require them to put on a smile for the customer as part of an intentional act even if he or she is stressed or irritated. When someone displays an emotion that is not actually experienced this is called emotional dissonance (or surface acting).

On the other hand, if a flight attendant displays his/her felt irritation, that is, his or her authentic emotions, this is called deep acting. Deep acting is most often unproblematic for the individual. What may be problematic for the individual is if he or she is never allowed to display authentic emotions. Continuous emotional dissonance, that is, the gap between what the individual feels and displays, may lead to stress and even severe illnesses such as burn-out (Hochschild, 1983; Härtel et al., 2002; Grandey, 2003).

In some cases, an individual may be so 'indoctrinated' into the emotion rules that she or he feels the emotion they display even when they don't actually experience it. For instance, being put in the situation in their work outfit, the flight attendants may quasi-believe they feel the emotion they display. This means that they may identify so much with the role that they feel joy in relation to the passengers, even if they are dead tired and stressed and in the same situation in another context would not feel this joy. However, dressed in their uniform and entering the airplane, the emotion rules automatically come through.

Emotional Dissonance in Family Firms

In the family business setting, emotion rules may stipulate that a son or daughter is not supposed to display anger or disappointment with their parents or that negative emotions are to be kept within the family and not displayed for non-family members. The family business culture and the emotional climate may thus play an important role for the display of emotions. In some family businesses it is *comme-il-faut* to display authentic emotions even if it leads to emotional outbursts and conflicts whereas, in another family business setting, it is inappropriate, or even taboo, to show emotions at all if this creates a risk for conflicts and/or a bad rumor. Further, it is inbuilt in most people that there are different emotion rules at work and at home (cf. Ashforth et al., 2000). So, for example, it may be acceptable to cry and be angry at home, while it would be inappropriate to show the same feelings at work. Displayed emotions in family firms become a function of values and norms in the family firm in addition to those associated with age, sex and societal norms and values (Kemper, 1987).

Many family firms are characterized by having a strong founder centric or owner centric culture (Schein, 1983; Kets de Vries, 1993; Kelly et al., 2000; Brundin et al., 2010). Such a culture is often characterized by strong norms and values, often pointing to a closely united family where the family business represents continuity, long-term orientation and stability (Miller and Le Breton Miller, 2005; Brundin et al., 2008). In such a context, many positive as well as negative emotions are likely to be displayed. However, the family and the business may have incompatible goals (Lansberg, 1983) and it may be difficult to display authentic emotions. This is also mentioned in some family business research although not explicitly. For

example, Tagiuri and Davis (1996) observe that family members may avoid expressing emotions in order not to cause embarrassment and Kepner (1983) depicts the expression of emotions as resigned, inhibited or ritualized (cf. dissonance, masked or deep acting).

In a context that is characterized by genuine relations, the authentic display of emotions may be difficult. Genuine relations in a family business refer to relations that are not exchangeable (Hall, 2003). For instance, it is not possible to give notice to a sister or daughter with the belief that the relationship will come to an end. The relationship continues to exist, whether it be more or less dense and intimate. This may lead to situations where a family member is reluctant to display authentic emotions out of consideration for the sibling or the firm or because of restrictions in the cultural display rules. If the authentic emotions are displayed, the genuine relationship may lead to a destruction of the kinship, at the same time, however, the emotional dissonance may result in damage to the business. For a family member to experience emotional dissonance over time may in the end lead to sudden emotional outbursts that are hard for the environment to understand, or to stress and other dysfunctional behavior (Schaubroeck and Jones, 2000).

A closely related construct to emotional dissonance is ambivalence of emotions. Whereas the former construct implies the display of non-authentic emotions, emotional ambivalence is the experience of multiple emotions. Next, we turn our attention to the role emotional ambivalence might play in the family business context.

EMOTIONAL AMBIVALENCE

Within organizational settings, we are presented with opportunities, challenges, decisions, processes and interactions that are likely to evoke mixed emotions. Emotional ambivalence is the term used to describe the simultaneous experience of multiple and mixed emotions about the same event or situation, and it is a common workplace phenomenon. For example, going for a promotion, getting a new boss or receiving a performance review is likely to evoke feelings of both anxiety and excitement (Fong, 2006). Similarly, research has shown that women in high status positions face competing goals leading to feelings of happiness and sadness (Fong and Tiedens, 2002), and that personal web use at work may lead to 'guilty pleasure' (Stratton, 2010).

Emotional ambivalence, when managed well, is functionally useful in that it is linked to increased creativity (Fong, 2006). One explanation for this finding is that mixed emotions signal an unusual environment, prompting re-examination of assumptions and perspective taking. Of special interest are situations where both negative and positive emotions co-exist and where one side overtakes the other, since this may inform the individual about his or her preference for different types of approach or avoidance behaviors in specific situations (Stratton, 2010).

Emotional Ambivalence in the Family Firm

As pointed out earlier, the family business constitutes a special framing with its intertwinement of the family and the business. With its hybrid identity characteristics, and the overlap of a normative and utilitarian system (Albert and Whetten, 1985), conflicting goals are a common phenomenon in this setting, leading to possible emotional ambivalence. Genuine relations (Hall, 2003) between siblings are another example. A sister and brother may love each other because they share their upbringing and a lot of memories, at the same time that they hate each other because they feel that one of them has more benefits or they feel rivalry about a management position. The situation can also occur where a family member has a love–hate relationship towards the business, desiring the business at the same time

as desiring to leave it and try out opportunities elsewhere (Brundin and Sharma, 2011).

The consequences of emotional ambivalence have been addressed indirectly in a couple of studies, such as Sharma and Manikutty (2005), who claim that conflict avoidance may be the norm and therefore it is not *comme-il-faut* to display conflicting emotions. In another study, Sharma and Irving (2005) claim that conflicting emotions may affect the succession commitment in the business so that the successor may take over for the normative (ought-to) reason, calculative (have too much to lose if I don't take over) reason and the imperative (I wouldn't make it in any other business) reason instead of for the affective (want-to) reason. Brundin and Sharma (2011) address emotional ambivalence explicitly when they refer to emotional messiness as a consequence of emotional bonding to the firm and expectations between the individual and the family firm she or he works in. When the emotional bonding becomes strong and/or a taken-for-granted agreement is not fulfilled, or violated, emotional messiness may occur, defined as the simultaneous experience of positive and negative emotions. An example from their study is the daughter who has worked in the firm for many years, educated herself in the business trade, and also prepared for a future management position, with the expectations that she would take over the firm after her father. However, her father, who in turn has encouraged his daughter to educate herself for the benefit of the firm, eventually tells her that he wants her husband to take over, leading to a lot of mixed positive and negative emotions for the daughter. Emotional messiness is thus equivalent to emotional ambivalence and according to the authors, emotional messiness is natural and as such neither a negative or positive emotional state, rather with a possible positive or negative outcome. Such an outcome may affect the next generation succession commitment, the extent of family harmony and result in a possible loss of resources in the family firm, for example, human and social capital. Building on previous work by Härtel et al., (2006) and Härtel (2008) there is reason to believe that the way in which emotional ambivalence is managed shapes the family business emotional climate such that there may be either a healthy or unhealthy impact on family

well-being and, in turn, the performance potential of the firm. The same holds for emotional dissonance.

The following illustration exemplifies the two concepts of emotional dissonance and emotional ambivalence.

Illustration: Emotional dissonance and emotional ambivalence

Charlene is third generation in Searles and Sons. Her older brother Andrew works as marketing director and has been a member of the board for two years. Other permanent members of the board are her father and four external members. One of these is also a friend of the family. Charlene was appointed a deputy member of the board a year ago as a first step to become a permanent member after yet another year. However, Charlene decided to step down from the board after her first period as deputy member. She tells why:

> In one of my first board meetings, all board members were encouraged to bring forward ideas about a marketing campaign with some new overseas partners. I worked very hard to come up with a presentation for the board – my degree is after all in marketing. In my presentation I suggested that in the long run we should establish a sales office in the Middle East and get rid of all other sales representatives in the USA and South Europe and only keep these in Northern Europe. Once I had presented my father was first dead silent and then he says:

> 'Dear Charlene, this is something out of your reach. This is not how we do things here and you should know that our policy as a family firm doesn't allow us to start a sales office abroad, neither to just let competent people be made redundant'. My brother, whom I know actually agrees with me, did not say a word.

> And this was not the first time, and my father, who is the chairperson, has repeatedly treated me as a child and not in my role as a board member. The first time I really got surprised and angry but didn't want to argue with my father in the boardroom. Other times, I got humiliated but tried not to show my hurt feeling in front of the board. I tried hard to show professionalism. I love my father but at times like this, I almost hate him. So, for the sake of our relationship, it's better that I resign. The odd thing is that my father treats Andrew differently. I have been very jealous of my brother over the years since he has been treated as the heir of the business – a business I love and desire as much as he does. Of course I have tried to disguise that jealousy from my parents since I want to take my responsibility within the firm and help my brother to develop it.

> When my mother asked me why I didn't want to continue in the board, I lied and said that to sit in the board was probably not my cup of tea. Now my mother and the rest of the family believe that I'm not interested in the family business – and they couldn't be more wrong. But how can I tell them what I really want, now that I have more or less refused to take responsibility for the firm.

In the illustration above, emotional dissonance occurs when Charlene chooses not to display her authentic emotions in the boardroom as she finds this unprofessional. This was the case when she felt anger and frustration but also when she felt humiliated and hurt. It can be argued that it was a suitable solution in the boardroom where the display rules indicate

professionalism (which, by the way, Charlene's father did not always conform to). However, Charlene continues to suppress her authentic emotions to her parents and brother after she has resigned from the board. She doesn't tell them how much she desires the firm and wants to be involved. Neither does she express her feelings of jealousy to her parents. This leads to emotional ambivalence for Charlene who expresses that she simultaneously both loves and hates her father. Her emotional behavior also leads to feelings of guilt, both towards the business and the family. In the long run this may lead to future conflicts and other emotional implications and in the end an unhealthy emotion orientation pattern, where she is caught in not being able to display or express her authentic emotions and an inability to deal with her emotional ambivalence.

The family firm with its melding of family and business systems is a particularly emotionally complex organizational form. Family businesses thus require leaders equipped with emotional competencies, to foster a positive work environment and to help individuals within the firm to constructively traverse the complex emotional terrain that is the family firm.

The high levels of psychological/emotional and collective ownership characteristic of family firms means that there are likely to be times where coaching from independent experts is needed to accurately map a family business' dual system characteristics such as family values and business goals (Härtel et al., 2009). Critical points in a family firm's lifecycle where such assistance is especially likely include the succession period where the transitioning from founder to successor may take years; the role transitions that follow such processes; and the development of policies for managing family and non-family employees.

Effective management of emotional ambivalence requires identifying in what situations such ambivalence occurs and what meaning is attached to the ambivalence (Fong and Tiedens, 2002; Weiss et al., 1999).

CONCLUSION: A FUTURE RESEARCH AGENDA AND METHODOLOGICAL SUGGESTIONS

In this chapter, we described the growing body of evidence on emotions in organizations, showing that this field of study has much to offer the family business literature, which to date has largely ignored this line of inquiry. We portrayed the emotional landscape of family firms in which the extant literature on emotions in organizations can inform our understanding and research agenda in the family business field.

Emotions serve as strong social signals of what is threatening or fulfilling to one's goals as well as of how others are perceiving events around them. Emotions thus provide a key impetus for propelling individuals forward or repelling them away from specific activities. We present convincing evidence that family firms can only be fully understood by taking into account the complexity of the emotion setting created by the intertwinement of the family and business systems.

Our review on emotions in family firms uncovered two primary emotion management challenges for family firms: emotional dissonance and emotional ambivalence. Emotional dissonance and emotional ambivalence are common phenomena in all organizations, however, and as we showed in our illustration, put in the family business context, they can lead to consequences that affect not only the business but also the individual as well as the family's well-being. If people within the business lack the skills or do not apply healthy emotion orientation patterns such as reframing the situation to create emotional harmony, they fall into the trap of unhealthy emotion orientation patterns such as avoiding dealing with issues that are causing psychological or physical harm for themselves or refusing to acknowledge the emotions and consequences that others share, fuelling an unhealthy or toxic work/family environment.

We argue that the increased emotional costs and benefits associated with family firms can inhibit authentic emotional expression and increase the likelihood of ineffective management of emotional ambivalence. The increase in ineffective management of emotional ambivalence, in turn, increases the likelihood of responding in ways that undermine individuals the goals of the firm and its human and social capital. For example, highly educated and competent family members may leave the firm and valuable social ties may get lost as may the commitment to take over the firm (cf. Sharma and Irving, 2005). Further, the family business loses the potential creativity gains offered by effective management of emotional ambivalence. A deeper understanding of the types of mixed emotions occurring in family firms and their antecedents along with examination of the consequences of different strategies for managing emotional ambivalence is accordingly important to advance theory and practice in family business.

Not all situations where members of a family business experience emotional dissonance are likely to be problematic. Thus, research is needed to identify the types of situations in family firms that are more likely to produce emotional dissonance that undermine the welfare of the family and the firm. Additionally, some family businesses may be better able to deal with emotional dissonance than others and, thus there is a need to examine what explains this. For example, is it a function of family and business culture features, quality of ties, the pattern of individual traits and skills, or some combination thereof?

Future intensive fieldwork is also called for to map in more detail the precursors to various mixed emotions patterns along with how emotion management strategies alter the course and consequence of such emotional experiences on the welfare of the family and the firm.

In order to create such an understanding there is a need to consider methodological alternatives that can help the researcher to come close to the study of emotions. In order to get more in-depth knowledge and deeper insights there is a need to find ways to understand the complexity of emotions and their implications. In line with this reasoning, a call for more qualitative, interpretive research has been made by Nordqvist et al. (2009). The authors argue that the complexity of family firms require more in-depth studies with an interpretive approach. Such an approach is aimed at answering questions of *how* and *why*, which are important if we want to get to the meaning that family business members assign to emotional processes and their implications. This opens up for different research designs such as inductive and ethnographic studies (cf. Van Maanen, 1998, and the chapter on the anthropology of family business in this *Handbook*: Stewart, 2014) where the researcher is willing to spend considerable time in the field. Longitudinal studies also provide the opportunity for studying emotional processes in real-time so that they can be captured as they happen (Brundin, 2007). To actively engage with the different actors in the family business is a way to jointly study emotions with the family business members. Engaged scholarship (Van de Ven, 2007) is a highly relevant way to meet demands of being trustworthy and to capture the elusiveness of emotions where not even the family business member her-/himself is aware at times of what is going on.

Our suggestions above for alternative research methods on emotions demand a creative and challenging design of the methodology. Such a design can involve observations, intimate conversations, diary notes from family members, video filming of encounters, drawing of pictures, discourse analysis on the talk about emotions, or suitable combinations to capture the meaning of emotions. To be able to advance methodological issues requires sensitiveness from the researcher and we argue that it needs an experienced researcher who is able to be both flexible and responsive to what may evolve in such a process.

NOTES

1 For the review we used search words such as emotion, feeling, emotional attitude, emotional expression/display in combination with 'family firm' or 'family business' or 'business family'. We limited the research from year 2000 to date with the exception of the article by Levinsohn, which we regard as one of the starting points for the perspective of emotions in family firms. The search was made through Scopus and we did not exclude any academic journals. In addition we searched

for articles in press in *Family Business Review, ET&P, Journal of Family Business Management* and *Journal of Family Business Strategy*.

2   The question of gender is not an issue at the time of the publication of this chapter, and the male norm was prevalent.

3   The display of emotion is understood as observable changes in face, voice, body and activity level that are accompanied by emotional states (Lewis, 1998).

REFERENCES

Albert, S.D. and Whetten, D.A. (1985). Organizational identity. In Staw, B. and Cummings, L.L. (eds), *Research in Organizational Behavior*, Vol. 7, pp. 263–295. Greenwich, CT: JAI Press.

Ashforth, B.E., Kreiner, G.E. and Fugate, M. (2000). All in a day's work: boundaries and micro role transitions. *Academy of Management Review*, 25(3), 472–491.

Astrachan, J.H. and Jaskiewicz, P. (2008). Emotional returns and emotional costs in privately held family businesses: advancing traditional business valuation. *Family Business Review* 21(2), 139–149.

Avey, J.B., Avolio, B.J., Crossley, C.D. and Luthans, F. (2009). Psychological ownership: theoretical extensions, measurement and relation to work outcomes. *Journal of Organizational Behavior*, 30, 173–191.

Barsade, S.G. (2002). The ripple effect: Emotional contagion and its influence on group behavior. *Administrative Science Quarterly*, 47, 644–675.

Belk, R.W. (1988). Possessions and the extended self. *Journal of Consumer Research*, 15(2), 139–168.

Berrone, P., Cruz, C. and Gomez-Mejia, L.R. (2012). Socioemotional wealth in family firms: theoretical dimensions, assessment approaches, and agenda for future research. *Family Business Review*, 25, 258–279.

Björnberg, A. and Nicholson, N. (2008). *Emotional Ownership: The Critical Pathway Between the Next Generation and the Family Firm*. London: The Institute for Family Business.

Björnberg, Å. and Nicholson, N. (2012). Emotional ownership: the next generation's relationship with the family firm. *Family Business Review*, 25, 374–390.

Brundin, E. (2007). Catching it as it happens. In Nergaard, H. and Ulhoj, J.P. (eds), *Handbook for Qualitative Methods in Entrepreneurship Research*. Camberley: Edward Elgar.

Brundin, E. and Languilaire, J.C. (2012). Känslomässig harmoni eller disharmoni. Känsloregler och gränsdragningar avseende tid, plats och relationer. (Emotional harmony or disharmony: feeling and boundary rules in time, space and relations.) In Brundin, E. et al. (eds), *Familjeföretagandets väsen.* (*Characteristics of the Family Firm*) Stockholm: SNS Förlag.

Brundin, E. and Melin, L. (2006). Unfolding the dynamics of emotions: how emotion drives or counteracts strategizing. *International Journal Work Organisation and Emotion*, 1(3), 277–302.

Brundin, E. and Nordqvist, M. (2008). Beyond facts and figures: the role of emotions in boardroom dynamics. *Corporate Governance: An International Review*, 16(4), 326–341.

Brundin, E. and Sharma, P. (2011). Love, hate and desire. In Carsrud, A. and Brannback, M. (eds), *International Perspectives on Future Research in Family Business: Neglected Topics and Under-utilized Theories*. New York: Springer.

Brundin, E., Melin, L. and Florin-Samuelsson, E. (2008). *The Family Ownership Logic: Chore Characteristics of Family Controlled Businesses*. Jönköping: Jönköping International Business School, Working Paper.

Brundin, E., Nordqvist, M. and Melin, L. (2010). Owner centric cultures: transforming entrepreneurial orientation in transgenerational processes. In: Nordqvist, M. and Zellweger, T. (eds), *Transgenerational Entrepreneurship: Exploring Growth and Performance of Family Firms across Generations*, Cheltenham: Edward Elgar.

Collin's Cobuild (1987). *English Language Dictionary*. Editorial team: Sinclair, J., Hanks, P., Fox, G., Moon, R. and Stock, P. London: Harper Collins Publishers.

Davis, M.H. (1983). The effects of dispositional empathy on emotional reactions and helping. A multidimensional approach. *Journal of Personality*, 51(2), 167–184.

Davis, J.H., Allen, M.R. and Hayes, D.H. (2010). Is blood thicker than water? A study of stewardship perceptions in family business. *Entrepreneurship: Theory and Practice*, 34(6), 1093–1115.

Davis, P. and Stern, D. (1980). Adaptation, survival, and growth of the family business: an integrated systems perspective. *Human Relations*, 34(4), 207–224.

Domagalski, T.A. (1999). Emotion in organizations: main currents. *Human Relations*, 52(6), 833–853.

Eddleston, K.A., Chrisman, J.J., Steier, L.P. and Chua, J.H. (2010). Governance and trust in family firms: an introduction. *Entrepreneurship: Theory and Practice*, 34(6), 1043–1056.

Ekman, P. (1992). Are there basic emotions? *Psychological Review*, 99(3), 550–553.

Ekman, P. and Oster, H. (1979). Facial expressions of emotion. *Annual Review of Psychology*, 30, 527–554.

Fineman, S. (1993). Organizations as emotional arenas. In Fineman, S. (ed), *Emotion in Organizations*. Thousand Oaks, CA: Sage Publications.

Fineman, S. (2003). *Understanding Emotion at Work*. London: Sage.

Fletcher, D. (2000). Family and enterprise. In Carter, S. and Jones-Evans, D. (eds), *Enterprise and Small Business: Principle, Practice and Policy*, pp. 155–165. Harlow, Essex: Pearson Education.

Fong, C. (2006). The effects of emotional ambivalence on creativity. *Academy of Management Journal*, 49(5), 1016–1030.

Fong, C.T. and Tiedens, L.Z. (2002). Dueling experiences and dual ambivalences: emotional and motivational ambivalence of women in high status positions. *Motivation and Emotion*, 26(1), 105–121.

Foreman, P. and Whetten, D.A. (2002). Members' identification with multiple-identity organizations. *Organization Science*, 13(6), 618–635.

Fox, S., Spector, P.E. and Miles, D. (2001). Counterproductive work behavior (CWB) in response to job stressors and organizational justice: some mediator and moderator tests for autonomy and emotions. *Journal of Vocational Behavior*, 59, 291–309.

Fredrickson, B.L. (2001). The role of positive emotions in positive psychology: the broaden-and-build theory of positive emotions. *American Psychologist*, 56, 218–226.

Fredrickson, B.L. (2003). Positive emotions and upward spirals in organizational settings. In Cameron, K., Dutton, J. and Quinn, R. (eds) *Positive Organizational Scholarship: Foundations of a New Discipline*, pp. 163–175. San Francisco, CA: Berrett-Koehler Publishers Inc.

Fredrickson, B.L. and Losada, M.F. (2005). Positive affect and the complex dynamics of human flourishing. *American Psychologist*, 60, 678–686.

Gersick, K., Davis, J., Hampton, M. and Lansberg, I. (1997). *Generation to Generation: Life Cycles of the Family Business*. Boston, MA: Harvard Business School Press.

Goleman, D. (1995). *Emotional Intelligence*. New York: Bantam Books.

Goleman, D. (1998). *Working with Emotional Intelligence*. New York: Bantam Books.

Gómez-Mejía, L.R., Takács Haynes, K., Nunez-Nickel, M., Jacobson, K.J.L. and Moyano-Fuentes, J. (2007). Socioemotional wealth and business risks in family-controlled firms: evidence from Spanish olive oil mills. *Administrative Science Quarterly*, 52, 106–137.

Grandey, A.A. (2003). When 'the show must go on': surface acting and deep acting as determinants of emotional exhaustion and peer-rated service delivery. *Academy of Management Journal*, 46(1), 86–96.

Gross, J. (2001). Emotion regulation in adulthood: timing is everything. Current Directions in Psychological Science, 10, 214–219.

Grunebaum, J.O. (1987). *Private Ownership*. London and New York: Routledge & Kegan Paul.

Hall, A. (2003). Strategising in the context of genuine relations. An interpretative study of strategic renewal through family interaction. Doctoral dissertation No. 018, Jönköping, Sweden: Jönköping International Business School.

Harris, S. and Sutton, R. (1986). Functions of parting ceremonies in dying organizations. *Academy of Management Journal*, 29, 5–30.

Härtel, C.E.J. (2008). How to build a healthy emotional culture and avoid a toxic culture. In Cooper, C.L. and Ashkanasy, N.M. (eds), *Research Companion to Emotion in Organization*, pp. 575–588. Cheltenham: Edward Elgar Publishing.

Härtel, C.E.J., Ashkanasy, N.M. and Zerbe, W.J. (2011). Overview: what have we learned? Ten years on. In Härtel, C.E.J., Ashkanasy, N.M. and Zerbe, W.J. (eds), *Research on Emotion in Organizations: What Have We Learned? Ten Years On*, pp. 1–12. Bingley, UK: Emerald Group Publishing.

Härtel, C.E.J., Bozer, G. and Levin, L. (2009). Family business leadership transition: how an adaptation of executive coaching may help. *Journal of Management & Organization*, 15(3), 378–391.

Härtel, C.E.J., Gough, H. and Härtel, G.F. (2006). Service providers' use of emotional competencies and perceived workgroup emotional climate to predict customer and provider satisfaction with service encounters. *International Journal of Work, Organisation and Emotion*, 1(3), 232–254.

Härtel, C.E.J., Hsu, A.C.F. and Boyle, M.V. (2002). A conceptual examination of the causal sequences of emotional labor, emotional dissonance and emotional exhaustion: the argument for the role of contextual and provider characteristics. In Ashkanasy, N.M., Zerbe, W. and Härtel, C.E.J. (eds), *Managing Emotions in the Workplace*. Armonk, NY: M.E. Sharpe.

Hirigoyen, G. and Labaki, R. (2012). The role of regret in the owner-manager decision-making in the family business: a conceptual approach. *Journal of Family Business Strategy*, 3, 118–126.

Hochschild, A.R. (1983). *The Managed Heart: Commercialization of Human Feeling*. Berkeley, CA: University of California Press.

Hollander, B.S. and Elman, N.S. (1988). Family-owned businesses: an emerging field of inquiry. *Family Business Review*, 1(2), 145–164.

Hubler, T. (2005). Forgiveness as an intervention in family-owned business: a new beginning. *Family Business Review*, 18(2), 95–103.

Ilies, R. and Judge, T.A. (2005). Goal Regulation across time: the effects of feedback and affect. *Journal of Applied Psychology*, 90, 453–467.

Isen, A.M. (2004). Some perspectives on positive feelings and emotions: positive affect facilitates thinking and problem solving. In Manstead, A.S.R., Frijda, N. and Fischer, A. (eds), *Feelings and Emotions: The Amsterdam Symposium*, pp. 263–281. New York: Cambridge.

Kellermans, F.W. and Eddleston, K.A. (2004). Feuding families: when conflict does a family firm good. *Entrepreneurship: Theory and Practice*, 28(3), 209–228.

Kelly, L.M., Athanassiou, N. and Crittenden, W.F. (2000). Founder centrality and strategic behavior in the family-owned firm. *Entrepreneurship: Theory and Practice*, 25(2), 27–42.

Keltner, D. and Haidt, J. (1999). Social function of emotions at four levels of analysis. *Cognition & Emotion*, 13(5), 505–521.

Kemper, T. (1987). How many emotions are there? Wedding the social and the autonomic components. *The American Journal of Sociology*, 93(2), 263–289.

Kepner, E. (1983). The family and the firm: a co-evolutionary perspective. *Organizational Dynamics*, 12(1), 57–70.

Kets de Vries, M.F.R. (1993). The dynamics of family controlled firms: the good and the bad news. *Organizational Dynamics*, 21, 59–71.

Kets de Vries, M.F.R., Carlock, R.S. and Florent-Treacy, E. (2007). *Family Business on the Couch: A Psychological Perspective*. Chichester: John Wiley & Sons.

Kidwell, R.E., Kellermanns, F.W. and Eddleston, K.A. (2012). Harmony, justice, confusion, and conflict in family firms: implications for ethical climate and the 'Fredo effect'. *Journal of Business Ethics*, 106, 503–517.

Klein, S.B. (2008). Commentary and extension: moderating the outcome of identity confirmation in family firms. *Entrepreneurship: Theory and Practice*, 1083–1088.

Koiranen, M. (2002). Over 100 years of age but still entrepreneurially active in business exploring the values and family characteristics of old Finnish family firms. *Family Business Review*, 15(3), 175–187.

Labaki, R., Michael-Tsabari, N. and Zachary, R.K. (2012). Emotional dimensions within the family business: toward a conceptualization. In Smyrnios,

K., Poutziouris, P.Z. and Goel, S. (eds), *Handbook of Research on Family Business*, 2nd edn. Cheltenham: Edward Elgar Publishing in association with International Family Enterprise Research Academy.

Lansberg, I. (1983). Managing human resources in family firms. *Organizational Dynamics*, 39–46.

Levinson, H. (1971). Conflicts that plague family businesses. *Harvard Business Review*, 90–95.

Lewis, M. (1998). The development and structure of emotions. In Mascolo, M.F. and Griffin, S. (eds), *What Develops in Emotional Development?* New York and London: Plenum Press.

Markus, H.R. and Kitayama, S. (1991). Culture and self: implications for cognition, emotion and motivation. *Psychological Review*, 98(2), 224–253.

Mastenbroek, W. (2000). Organizational behaviour as emotion management. In Ashkanasy, N.M., Härtel, C.E.J. and Zerbe, W. (eds), *Emotions in the Workplace: Research, Theory, and Practice*, pp. 19–35. Westport, CT: Quorum Books.

Matsumoto, D. (1993). Ethnic differences in affect intensity, emotion judgments, display rules attitudes and self-reported emotional expression in an American sample. *Motivation and Emotion*, 17(2), 107–123.

McCollom, M.E. (1988). Integration in the family firm: when the family system replaces controls and culture, *Family Business Review*, 1, 399–417.

Mehrotra, V., Morck, R. Shim, J. and Wiwattanakantang, Y. (2011). Must love kill the family firm? Some exploratory evidence. *Entrepreneurship: Theory and Practice*, 35(6), 1121–1148.

Miller, D.T. (2001). Disrespect and the experience of injustice. *Annual Review of Pscyhology*, 52: 527–553.

Miller, D. and Le Breton-Miller, I. (2005). *Managing for the Long Run: Lessons in Competitive Advantage from Great Family Businesses*. Boston, MA, Harvard Business School Press.

Morrow, J.L., Hansen, M.H. and Pearson, A.W. (2004). The cognitive and affective antecedents of general trust within cooperative organizations. *Journal of Managerial Issues*, 16, 48–64.

Nordqvist, M. (2005). Understanding the role of ownership in strategizing: a study of family firms. JIBS Dissertation Series No. 029, Jönköping, Sweden: Jönköping International Business School.

Nordqvist, M., Hall, A. and Melin, L. (2009). Qualitative research on family businesses: the relevance and usefulness of the interpretative approach. *Journal of Management & Organization*, 15, 294–308.

Pierce, J.L., Kostova, T. and Dirks, K.T. (2001). Toward a theory of psychological ownership in organizations. *Academy of Management Review*, 26(2), 298–310.

Pierce, J.L. and Jussila, I. (2009). Collective psychological ownership within the work and organizational context: construct introduction and elaboration. *Journal of Organizational Behavior*, 31, 810–834.

Rafaeli, A. and Sutton, R.I. (1990). Busy stores and demanding customers: how do they affect the display of positive emotion? *Academy of Management Journal*, 33(3), 623–637.

Schaubroeck, J. and Jones, J.R. (2000). Antecedents of workplace emotional labor dimensions and moderators of their effects on physical symptoms. *Journal of Organizational Behavior*, 21, 163–183.

Schein, E.H. (1983). The role of the founder in creating organizational culture. *Organizational Dynamics*, 12(1), 13–28.

Sharma, P. (2004). An overview of the field of family business studies: current status and directions for the future. *Family Business Review*, 17(1), 1–36.

Sharma, P. and Irving, G. (2005). Four bases of family business successor commitment: antecedents and consequences. *Entrepreneurship: Theory and Practice*, 29(1), 13–33.

Sharma, P. and Manikutty, S. (2005). Strategic divestments in family firms: role of family structure and community culture. *Entrepreneurship: Theory and Practice*, 29(3), 293–312.

Shepherd, D.A. (2003). Learning from business failure: propositions about the grief recovery process for the self-employed. *Academy of Management Review*, 28(2), 318–329.

Spector, P.E. and Fox, S. (2002). An emotion-centered model of voluntary work behavior: some parallels between counterproductive work behavior (CWB) and organizational citizenship behavior (OCB). *Human Resource Management Review*, 12(2), 269–292.

Stanley, L. (2010). Emotions and family business creation: an extension and implications. *Entrepreneurship: Theory and Practice*, 34(6), 1085–1092.

Stecher, M.D. and Rosse, J.G. (2005). The distributive side of interactional justice: the effects of interpersonal treatment on emotional arousal. *Journal of Managerial Issues*, 17, 229–246.

Steier, L. (2001). Family firms, plural forms of governance, and the evolving role of trust. *Family Business Review*, 14, 353–367.

Stewart, A. (2014). The anthropology of family business: An imagined ideal. In Melin, L., Nordqvist, M., and Sharma, P. (eds), *The SAGE Handbook of Family Business*. London: Sage.

Stewart, A. and Hitt, M.A. (2012). Why can't a family business be more like a nonfamily business? Modes of professionalization. *Family Business Review*, 25(1), 58–86.

Stratton, M.T. (2010). Uncovering a new guilty pleasure: a qualitative study of the emotions of personal web usage at work. *Journal of Leadership & Organizational Studies*, 17, 392–410.

Sund, L.-G. and Smyrnios, K.X. (2005). Striving for happiness and its impact on family stability: an exploration of the Aristotelian conception of happiness. *Family Business Review*, 18(2), 155–170.

Sutton, R.I. and Rafaeli, A. (1988). Untangling the relationship between displayed emotions and organizational sales: the case of convenience stores. *Academy of Management Journal*, 31(3), 461–487.

Sy, T., Cote, S. and Saavedra, R. (2005). The contagious leader: impact of the leader's mood on the mood of group members, group affective tone, and group processes. *Journal of Applied Psychology*, 90(2), 295–305.

Tagiuri, R. and Davis, J. (1996). Bivalent attributes of the family firm. *Family Business Review*, 9(2), 199–208.

Tajfel, H. (1982). Social psychology of intergroup relations. *Annual Review of Psychology*, 33, 1–39.

Tompkins, R. (2010). The organizational identity of a family business: the role of hybrid identity in organizational events. Doctoral dissertation, The George Washington University.

Trevinyo-Rodríguez, R.N. (2010). Family ties and emotions: a missing piece in the knowledge transfer puzzle. *Journal of Small Business and Enterprise Development*, 17(3), 418–436.

Van-den-Heuval, J., Goel, S., Van Gils, A. and Voordeckers, W. (2007). *Family Businesses as Emotional Arenas: The Influence of Family CEOs' Empathy and External Monitoring on the Importance of Family Goals*. Research Center for Innovation and Entrepreneurship (KIZOK), University of Hasselt, the Netherlands.

Van de Ven, A.H. (2007). *Engaged Scholarship: Creating Knowledge for Science and Practice*. Oxford: Oxford University Press.

Van Maanen, J. (1998). *On Tales of the Field: On Writing Ethnography*. Chicago, IL: University of Chicago Press.

Van Maanen, J. and Kunda, G. (1989). Real feelings: emotional expressions and organization culture. In Staw, B. and Cummings, L.L. (eds), *Research in Organization Behavior*, Vol. 11, pp. 43–103. Greenwich, CT: JAI Press.

Vince, R. and Saleem, T. (2004). The impact of caution and blame on organizational learning. *Management Learning*, 35(2), 133–154.

Weiss, H.M., Suckow, K. and Cropanzano, R. (1999). Effects of justice conditions on discrete emotions. *Journal of Applied Psychology*, 84(5), 786–794.

Whiteside, M.F. and Brown, F.H. (1991). Drawbacks of a dual systems approach to family firms: can we expand our thinking. *Family Business Review*, 4(4), 383–395.

Wrzesniewski, A., Dutton, J. and Debebe, G. (2003). Interpersonal sensemaking and the meaning of work. *Research in Organizational Behavior*, 25, 93–135.

Zellweger, T.M. and Astrachan, J.H. (2008). On the emotional value of owning a firm. *Family Business Review*, 4, 347–363.

Zhao, B. and Olivera, F. (2006). Error reporting in organizations. *Academy of Management Review*, 31(4), 1012–1030.

PART V

Methods in Use in Family Business Studies

28

Scales in Family Business Studies

Allison W. Pearson, Daniel T. Holt and Jon C. Carr

The point is not that accurate measurement is 'nice'. It is necessary, crucial. Without it we have nothing.

Korman (1974: 194)

INTRODUCTION

As family business research has matured, researchers have reflected on its progression as a field of study (e.g., Bird et al., 2002; Casillas and Acedo, 2007). These reflections offer similar conclusions about the positive contributions that have been made and the field's bright future (Litz et al., 2012). Moores (2009), drawing on Kuhn's (1970) comments regarding the evolution of a scientific discipline, concluded that 'paradigm consensus has occurred in the family business discipline and that the paradigm now needs to be further articulated using the integration of accepted theories to better explain the subject body of the phenomena' (1970: 170). As the field of family business is further articulated, increasing the rigor of research methods and measurement has been emphasized and researchers have been challenged to develop appropriate measurement scales such that better explanations of the phenomena can be proffered (Litz et al., 2012). In short, for the field of family business to advance, proper measurement of constructs relevant to family business research is essential.

A construct is defined as 'a broad mental configuration of a given phenomenon' (Bacharach, 1989: 500), alternatively as 'terms which though not observational either directly or indirectly, may be applied or even defined on the basis of observables' (Kaplan, 1964: 55). Constructs – those mental configurations of a concept requiring the development of observable indicators – should be sufficient and parsimonious in their representation of the domain of interest (Bacharach, 1989). If the construct is intended for scientific study, it is necessary to identify possible linkages between the construct and other related constructs, which is referred to as a nomological net (Cronbach and Meehl, 1955). The nomological net is used to draw inferences about constructs and validity, and their associated relationships (Schwab, 1980). The development of a nomological net represents the essence of theory-building, allowing for more theoretically driven interpretation, measurement, analysis, and ultimately generalizations to a given field.

In primary data collection for studies like those examining family businesses, researchers commonly rely on questionnaires. These questionnaires can include multiple items which are thought to reflect a particular construct, and are deemed to be a measurement scale (also referred to as a measure). When the scale items are used in theory testing prior to adequate evidence of validity and reliability, researchers run the risk of drawing theoretical conclusions that are incorrect or would likely contradict future research findings (Schwab, 1980). Psychometric theory helps us mitigate this risk by providing guidelines needed to design the items and measures that are used to assess constructs, such as general attitudes or those specific to family firms, to include constructs such as familiness or socioemotional wealth. The tools and techniques from psychometric theory allow researchers to assess how well a measure reflects a specific construct, allowing us to understand the precision of that measure and reduce the inappropriate inferences that might be drawn from measurement that is *not* psychometrically grounded and tested.

Chandler and Lyon (2001) suggested that this measurement challenge may have plagued the field of entrepreneurship in its early growth. Although Crook et al. (2010) demonstrated that practices have improved regarding entrepreneurship measurement. Crook et al. argued that the field of entrepreneurship still needed to advance its construct measurement practices, recommending domain-specific training for entrepreneurship researchers. While we do not believe that family business is a subfield of entrepreneurship, we feel, along with others (Bird et al., 2002), that family business research has followed a trajectory that is similar to other fields regarding construct development. Accordingly, similar conclusions regarding measurement can likely be applied to constructs measured in

family business research. This reasoning has been supported as family business scholars have indicated that measurement issues were one of the field's greatest challenges (Litz et al., 2012).

With this in mind, we examine constructs central to family business research and evaluate the measurement scales used to gauge them. Doing this, we provide a critical assessment of family business measures and scales, offering researchers an example-list of scales and the psychometric evidence associated with each. This assessment is crucial because it would generally be a poor decision for researchers to use a scale if it failed to meet basic criteria of validity and reliability. Moreover, we provide family business researchers with a heuristic that can guide them as measures of family business are further developed, refined, and empirically tested. Finally, we identify several theoretical areas for which there are few measures such as familiness, socioemotional wealth, and family firm value, and encourage future research to incorporate the necessary validity and reliability requirements needed for these scales.

Measurement within Family Business Research

Generally, there are two types of measures used in family business research: single-item, observed variables (e.g., profit, return on investment) and latent constructs, operationalized by multi-item scales (e.g., conflict, family harmony). Because family business research is largely grounded in agency theory and the resource based view of the firm (Chrisman et al., 2010), much of family business research measurement is based on financial indicators, including many single-item observed variables to represent constructs like performance (e.g., profit) or categorically coded variables to represent constructs like industry. These studies have contributed valuable knowledge to our understanding of the theoretical and practical issues of family business, such as the importance of noneconomic goals, vision, and the family culture in determining family firm behavior. The focus of this chapter is on the second form of measurement in family firm research – measurement involving latent constructs. Latent constructs are measured through multi-item scales that can be developed, refined, and evaluated using the tools provided by psychometric theory.

Criteria for the Evaluation of Measurement Scales

We adopted a framework to evaluate scales based on the classical ideas that have been presented in the psychometric theory literature (American Psychological Association [APA], 1985; Messick, 1989; Nunnally and Bernstein, 1994). These include (a) content validity (i.e., evidence of systematic scale development and item screening), (b) construct validity (i.e., evidence of a scale's structure and dimensionality along with evidence of the nomological net [convergent and discriminant validity]), (c) predictive validity (i.e., evidence of postdictive, concurrent, and predictive validity), and (d) reliability (i.e., evidence of test-retest reliability and internal consistency).

Each form of validity and reliability along with the appropriate supporting evidence used is summarized in Table 28.1. An ideal instrument has several types of evidence which span all forms of validity and reliability. Other things being equal, more sources of evidence are better than fewer. Still, the quality of evidence is critical, with a single line of solid evidence being preferred over several lines of evidence of questionable quality (APA, 1985). Table 28.1 also provides references that illustrate empirical tests that researchers should conduct as measures are developed and refined.

Measurement Validity

Content validity

Generally, validity refers to the evidence that has accumulated to demonstrate that a

Table 28.1 Framework to evaluate validity and reliability of instruments

Validity types	Description	Evidence	Citations for Validity and Reliability Evidence
1. Content validity: construct development process	Systematic approach used to develop the construct definition and the instrument's items.	Deductive Inductive	Hinkin (1998)
2. Content validity: item evaluation process	Extent to which an instrument's items are a proper representation of the domain they are designed to assess.	Review by expert judges Q-sort Substantive validity test	Anderson and Gerbing (1991) Hinkin and Tracey (1999) Schriesheim et al. (1993)
3. Construct validity	Extent to which an instrument's items measure distinguishable constructs and these constructs are systematically related (and unrelated) to other known concepts and constructs.	Exploratory factor analysis (EFA) Confirmatory factor analysis (CFA) Convergent validity Discriminant validity Known-groups analysis	Ford et al. (2002) Anderson and Gerbing (1988) Bagozzi et al. (1991)
4. Predictive validity	Extent to which an instrument's constructs are systematically related to relevant outcome variables.	Postdictive measure of criterion Concurrent measure of criterion Predictive measure of criterion	APA (1985) Nunnally and Bernstein (1994)
5. Reliability estimates	Extent to which an instrument's items and constructs are stable over time and dependable.	Coefficient alpha Parallel forms Split-half correlations Test-retest	Nunnally and Bernstein (1994)

measure represents the intended construct. Content validity refers to the extent to which a measurement instrument adequately represents the defined universe or domain of the given construct (Messick, 1989). As such, content validity provides judgmental evidence in support of a scale's (and its respective item's) relevance to the domains or constructs of interest. Content validity is established through the process of defining the construct and testing the extent to which the items reflect that definition (and not those of other dimensions). The first task, accordingly, is to theoretically specify the construct such that the universe of content that a construct represents is defined.

The process used to develop this content and identify the relevant constructs (and instrument's items) follows a deductive or inductive approach (Hinkin, 1998). Deductive approaches rely on existing theoretical frameworks to develop the construct definitions and the scale items designed to measure that construct. Alternatively, a construct may be developed inductively by relying on the qualitative analysis of subject matter experts' input, or based on practitioner experiences related to that construct. Once the construct is defined and its relevant dimensions are identified, items are written to reflect the defined content. Several methods have been described to assess the content validity of items (e.g., Anderson and Gerbing, 1991; Hinkin and Tracey, 1999; Schriesheim et al., 1993).

Construct validity

There are several different types of validity that can be considered as demonstrations of construct validity. Structural validity is one type and refers to whether or not the structure (e.g., unidimensional or multidimensional) of the measured construct matches the structure of the theoretical construct. This is tested with reduction approaches that explicitly assess the degree to which multiple items represent a construct and the error associated with the measure. Factor analytic techniques, namely, exploratory and confirmatory factor analysis, are applied in such circumstances.

Another aspect of construct validation is to specify the nomological network (Cronbach and Meehl, 1955), wherein the relationship of the focal construct with other known constructs is hypothesized and investigated with respect to convergent and discriminant validity. Convergent validity concerns the extent to which alternative measures of the construct share statistical variance (Schwab, 1980). Campbell notes that discriminant validity 'is the requirement that a test not correlate too highly with measures from which it is supposed to differ' (1960: 548). For example, as Davis and his colleagues (2010) developed a measure of stewardship, they investigated the extent to which it was distinct yet related to altruism which other family business researchers have used as a proxy for stewardship (Eddleston and Kellermanns, 2007). Davis et al. provided evidence of convergent validity finding that stewardship and altruism were significantly correlated but were distinct, as shown by the factor structure that emerged from the exploratory factor analysis.

Predictive validity

Finally, it is important to investigate the predictive validity which is the extent to which a measurement scale is systematically related to relevant outcome variables. Nunnally and Bernstein (1994) outlined three study designs for obtaining predictive validity evidence based on the time that the outcome or criterion variable is measured. Predictive designs obtain outcome information after the instrument being assessed is administered. A concurrent design serves the same purpose, where the measure of interest is assessed against a meaningful outcome variable that is measured at the same time. Finally, a postdictive design measures the outcome variable prior to the instrument being assessed. For instance, Smilkstein et al.'s (1982) 5-item measure of family functioning which has been used in family business research (e.g., Danes et al., 1999) predicted, as expected, a patient's psychological distress over an 18-month period using a predictive study design. Regardless of the design, the choice of an outcome and the procedures used to measure the outcome are critical, and the value of predictive validity evidence depends on the relevance, validity, and reliability of the outcome variable.

Reliability

While validity is the most important consideration as measures are developed (APA, 1995), reliability is a necessary condition for validity. Nunnally and Bernstein (1994) state that reliability refers to how repeatable observations are (a) when different persons make measurements, (b) when alternative instruments that are known to measure the same construct are used, and (c) when incidental variation exists in the conditions of measurement. Reliability can be demonstrated by assessing the extent to which the scores that are derived from a multi-item scale are consistent across all items.

Nunnally and Bernstein (1994) suggest that the desired level of consistency can be demonstrated with multiple measures of the same item. This is termed as internal consistency reliability and is often demonstrated with computations like coefficient alpha or split half correlations. Other methods of demonstrating consistency include different respondents making the same assessments (i.e., inter-rater or inter-observer reliability) and different measures of the same construct being compared (i.e., parallel forms reliability). Another aspect of scale consistency comes with stability of the scale across time (Nunnally and Bernstein, 1994). Accordingly, another way of demonstrating reliability comes with some correlation between scores on the same test that are administered at two points in time (i.e., test–retest reliability).

In summary, we use these criteria to develop a methodology and examine extant literature within the family business field. Based upon this examination, we provide recommendations regarding scale development and measurement within family business research.

METHOD

Population of Manuscripts and Scales

To identify scales in the family business literature, four journals were manually searched (*Family Business Review*, *Journal of Business Venturing*, *Entrepreneurship: Theory and Practice*, and *Journal of Small Business Management*). We started with the year 1988 when the first issue of *Family Business Review* was published, as this marked a milestone wherein a dedicated academically oriented outlet for family business-related research was established. Next, we conducted an automated search of Business Source Complete, Web of Science, Psych Info, and ScienceDirect electronic databases. Key words guiding these searches included: family business, family firms, family involvement, family ownership, and familiness. Additionally, we reviewed special issues of journals dedicated to family business research (e.g., *Journal of Management Studies*, *Journal of Business Research*, *Business Ethics Quarterly*, and *Strategic Entrepreneurship Journal*).

These procedures yielded 12,713 journal articles. For a manuscript to be included, it had to focus on family business as the topic of interest. This criterion eliminated several thousand manuscripts which were unrelated to family firms (e.g., 'family involvement' in health care). Manuscripts had to appear in peer-reviewed, English language journals. Finally, the manuscript had to report an empirical study. We broadly defined empirical studies as those that included some kind of data or data analysis, including statistical or qualitative analyses. Those manuscripts that reviewed or synthesized the literature, presented theoretically grounded untested models (and propositions), reviewed books, reported the transcripts from interviews with practitioners, or offered mathematical models were not evaluated. Using these criteria, we were able to eliminate over 10,000 manuscripts.

The remaining manuscripts were reviewed to identify multi-item, subjective scales. Scales were identified and grouped into meaningful categories. We did not include single-item measures. Nunnally and Bernstein (1994) argue that single-item scales are acceptable when they relate to simple *unidimensional* constructs that can be measured with minimal measurement error. Several have suggested that these assumptions do not likely hold for constructs like those measured in family business studies, claiming multi-item scales are better alternatives (Venkatraman and Grant, 1986). Additionally, we did not consider objective measures or measures from secondary data, where original sources and items could not be ascertained.

Coding

Consistent with psychometric theory literature (American Psychological Association [APA], 1985; Messick, 1989; Nunnally and Bernstein, 1994), each measure was coded and evaluated to assess its (a) content validity (i.e., evidence of systematic scale development), (b) construct validity (i.e., evidence of convergent and discriminant validity), (c) predictive validity (i.e., evidence of theoretical relationships between the focal measure and outcomes), and (d) reliability (i.e., evidence of test-retest reliability and internal consistency). In addition, we highlight (a) measures developed specifically for family firm research, (b) instances where variables were operationalized with borrowed or adapted measures, and (c) opportunities that are available for further measurement development.

ANALYSIS OF SCALES

Measurement of Family Business

Arguably, the most important measures in this field would be measures which capture the extent to which any firm is a family business. Reay and Whetten (2011) stress that an accurate description of a phenomenon, such as family business, is an essential precursor to the development of theory. Despite this, it was surprisingly difficult to identify such measures as there is considerable variation in the definition of a family business. Chua et al. (1999), for instance, discovered no fewer than 21 definitions of family business with Litz (2008), more recently, identifying 30 definitions of family business.

While it is beyond our scope to resolve this discussion, theoretical definitions are needed to assess the content validity of an instrument and to provide a starting point for the generation of items. With this in mind, Chrisman et al. (2005) highlighted two basic elements that shed light on the theoretical dimensions that define a family firm. The first, termed the *components of involvement*, assumes that family involvement is all that is necessary to make a firm a family business. This involvement can be manifested in different ways that can include ownership, governance, and/or management. Chrisman et al. (2012) stated that the most frequently used measures of involvement include: (a) percentage of ownership among family members, (b) number of family members involved as managers, and (c) number of generations of family members involved in management and ownership. Klein et al. (2005) presented a three-item, objective measure of involvement. It combined some of these concepts and included items asking (a) the proportion of family members that share ownership; (b) the percentage of family members on the firm's board; and (c) the percentage of family members on the management team. Although there may be issues with the measure's validity,[1] Klein et al. (2005) found through factor analyis that these objective observations were closely related and reported a high internal consistency (alpha = .75).

The second element, termed *essence*, assumes that involvement is a necessary but insufficient condition for a firm to be a family business. Thus, the family must actively transform its involvement into distinctive attributes that are important to the firm (Craig and Moores, 2005; Rutherford et al., 2008). As a surrogate of essence, Chrisman and his colleagues (2005) have suggested that the extent to which a firm can be characterized as a family business is reflected in the intentions of the family to preserve the firm as a distinct entity. There are several single-item measures that classify firms as family businesses based on succession plans (e.g., Chrisman et al., 2005). One example asks whether owners or CEOs 'intend the future successor as president of the business to be a family member' (coded as 1 = transgenerational succession within the family; 0 = no intention; Chua et al., 2011: 478). Like single-item measures of involvement, the extent to which the construct validity and reliability of these measures can be assessed is limited. Moreover, the dichotomous classification of firms based on these types of measures discounts the premise that firms vary along a continuum with regards to the extent to which they are or are not a family firm.

One multi-item subjective measure of the essence dimension was the culture scale presented as part of Klein et al.'s (2005) F-PEC measure. In this measure, the family business culture reflects the extent to which (a) the family's goals and values align with the firm's and (b) the family members are affectively committed to the firm. Klein et al. measured culture with 13 items based on Carlock and Ward's (2001) measure of family business commitment, which was adapted from Mowday et al.'s (1979) organizational commitment questionnaire.[2] Holt et al. (2010) extended Klein et al.'s (2005) findings with additional tests of validity and reliability, identifying three items that did not reflect the construct. Table 28.2 provides a summary of how the culture scale's items evolved from the original commitment scale presented by Mowday et al. (1979) and the validity and reliability evidence that has been accumulated, suggesting that this instrument may have considerable promise as future measures of essence are developed. Recent

research oriented around the internal social capital within family firms has continued this trend (Carr et al., 2011).

Measurement Scales in Family Business Research

While the measurement of family business is a complex and challenging issue, other measures of family business constructs have been developed. Table 28.3 summarizes these constructs. These measures can be categorized to reflect the following constructs: (1) family goals; (2) family and business interface; (3) family cohesion and harmony; (4) transgenerational succession intentions; (5) transgenerational succession processes; (6) successor preparation; and (7) owner–successor relationship.

Not suprising, succession-related measures appeared to be the most commonly developed measures. Likewise, family issues (goals and cohesion), as well as the family and business interface, provided the remainder of scales that had been developed specifically for family firm research. These align with the findings of Yu et al. (2012) who identified dependent variables used in family business research (between 1998 and 2009).

Looking across these measures with regard to psychometric criteria, we found the majority of studies provided some evidence of construct validity, often in the form of exploratory factor analysis. While exploratory factor analysis is useful for initially identifying factor structures, confirmatory factor analysis (CFA) is a useful technique for verifying factor structures derived from theory. Most studies also reported reliability evidence in the form of coefficient alpha, which provides researchers information critical in evaluating whether a scale should be adopted. Further, most of the scales developed specifically for family business studies yielded alpha values in excess of .70, which has been suggested as a cut-off to consider a newly developed measure as reliable (Nunnally, 1978).[3]

Table 28.2 The evolution of the F-PEC culture scale items

	Mowday et al.'s (1979) Organizational Commitment Questionnaire	Carlock and Ward's (2001) Family Business Commitment Questionnaire	Vilaseca's (2002) Organizational Commitment Questionnaire	Astrachan et al.'s (2002) and Klein et al.'s (2005) Family-Culture Scale	Holt et al.'s (2010) Family-Culture Scale	Chrisman et al.'s (2012) Family Commitment Scale
Items	I am proud to tell others that I am part of this organization.	I am proud to tell others that I am part of the family business.	I am proud to tell others that I am a shareholder of this organization.	We are proud to tell others that we are part of the family business.[a]	As family, we are proud to tell others that we are part of the family business.	Family members are proud to be part of my business.
	I feel very little loyalty to this organization.	I feel loyalty to the family business.	I feel very little loyalty to this organization.	We feel loyalty to the family business.[a]	As family, we feel loyalty to the family business.	Family members feel loyal to the family business.
	Often, I find it difficult to agree with this organization on important matters relating to its employees.	I agree with the family business' goals, plans, and policies.	Often, I find it difficult to agree with this organization's objectives.	We agree with the family business goals, plans, and policies.[a]	As family, we agree with the family business goals, plans, and policies.	Family members agree with the goals, plans, and policies of my business.
	Deciding to work for this organization was a definite mistake on my part.	Deciding to be involved with the family business has had a positive influence on my life.	Being a shareholder in this organization was a definite mistake on my part.	Deciding to be involved with the family business has a positive influence on my life.	As a single member of the family, deciding to be involved with the family business has had a positive influence on my life.	
	I am willing to put a great deal of effort beyond what is expected to help this organization be successful.	I am willing to put a great deal of effort beyond what is expected to help the family business be successful.	I am willing to put a great deal of effort beyond what is expected to help this organization be successful.	Family members are willing to put in a great deal of effort beyond that normally expected to help the family business be successful.	Our family members are willing to put in a great deal of effort beyond that normally expected of non-family employees in order to help the family business be successful.	Family members are willing to put in extra effort to help my business be successful.
	I find my values and the organization's values are very similar.	I find my values are compatible with the business' values.	I find my values and the organization's values are very similar.	Your family and business share similar values.	Your family and business share the same values.[c]	My family and my business have similar values.

Mowday et al.'s (1979) Organizational Commitment Questionnaire	Carlock and Ward's (2001) Family Business Commitment Questionnaire	Vilaseca's (2002) Organizational Commitment Questionnaire	Astrachan et al.'s (2002) and Klein et al.'s (2005) Family-Culture Scale	Holt et al.'s (2010) Family-Culture Scale	Chrisman et al.'s (2012) Family Commitment Scale
I tell my friends this is a great organization to work for.	I support the family business in discussions with friends, employees, and other family members.	I tell my friends this is a great organization to invest in.	We support the family business in discussions with friends, employees, and other family members.[a]	As family, we support the family business in discussions with friends, employees, and other family members.	Family members publicly support my business.
There is not much to be gained by sticking with this organization indefinitely.	There is much to be gained by participating with the family business on a long term basis.	There is not much to be gained by sticking with this organization as a shareholder indefinitely.	There is so much to be gained by participating with the family business on a long term basis.		
I really care about the fate of this organization.	I really care about the fate of the family business.	I really care about the fate of this organization.	We really care about the fate of the family business.[a]		Family members really care about the fate of my business.
I would accept almost any type of job assignment in order to keep working for this organization.		I will keep my investment in this organization, even during periods of loss.			
I could just as well be working for a different type of organization as long as the type of work were similar.		I could just as well be a shareholder of a different organization as long as the return were similar.			
This organization really inspires the very best in me in the way of job performance.		This organization really inspires the very best in me in the role I must undertake as shareholder.			

(Continued)

Table 28.2 (Continued)

	Mowday et al.'s (1979) Organizational Commitment Questionnaire	Carlock and Ward's (2001) Family Business Commitment Questionnaire	Vilaseca's (2002) Organizational Commitment Questionnaire	Astrachan et al.'s (2002) and Klein et al.'s (2005) Family-Culture Scale	Holt et al.'s (2010) Family-Culture Scale	Chrisman et al.'s (2012) Family Commitment Scale
	It would take very little change in my present circumstances to cause me to leave this organization.		It would take very little change in my present circumstances to cause me to step out as a shareholder.			
	I am extremely glad that I chose this organization to work for over others I was considering at the time I joined.		I am extremely glad that I chose this organization to be a shareholder over others I was considering at the time I joined.			
	For me, this is the best of all possible organizations to work for.		For me, this is the best of all possible organizations to invest in.			
		I understand and support my family's decisions regarding the future of the family business.		I understand and support my family's decisions regarding the future of the family business.	I understand and support my family's decisions regarding the future of the family business.	
				Your family members share similar values.	Your family members share similar values.[c]	
				Your family has influence on your business.	Your family has influence on your business.[c]	
				We find that our values are compatible with those of the business.[b]		
Content validity evidence	Relied on Mowday et al., 1979			Relied on Carlock and Ward (2001)		

	Mowday et al.'s (1979) Organizational Commitment Questionnaire	Carlock and Ward's (2001) Family Business Commitment Questionnaire	Vilaseca's (2002) Organizational Commitment Questionnaire	Astrachan et al.'s (2002) and Klein et al.'s (2005) Family-Culture Scale	Holt et al.'s (2010) Family-Culture Scale	Chrisman et al.'s (2012) Family Commitment Scale
Construct validity evidence	EFA (across 9 samples) Convergent validity test (with organizational attachment) Discriminant validity (with job involvement)			EFA and CFA (using same sample)	EFA and CFA (two samples) Convergent validity test (with succession)	CFA
Predictive validity evidence	Predictive validity (with turnover)					
Reliability estimates	Alpha .88–.90 Test–retest (tested over two samples)			Alpha .75	Alpha .87	Alpha .96

[a]'We' is replaced by 'family members' in Klein et al. (2005)

[b]Item included in Astrachan et al. (2002) but excluded from in Klein et al. (2005)

[c]Items were removed after their initial factor analysis as the items loadings did not meet the retention criteria.

There are opportunities for improvements, however, based on the results presented in Table 28.3. Few studies provided content validity information. Content valid scales should be grounded in a well-defined domain of interest that is theoretically derived. Further, a clear, concise construct definition is needed to guide item development. As the field of family business continues to grow and mature, and develop unique family business theories, construct definition and content validity of measures should improve.

Also, no family business scales were examined for predictive validity. This, however, was not completely surprising given the field's early stage of development. Without unique theory that clearly establishes substantive relationships among family business constructs, it is difficult to test predictive validity. As the field continues to evolve and unique theories emerge, we recommend that the predictive validity of scales should be examined.

General Measures and Adapted Scales for Family Business Research

In addition to scales developed specifically for family firms, researchers have borrowed or adapted a variety of measures from prior research. Hinsz and Nelson (1990) were some of the first family business researchers to do so, borrowing the job diagnostic survey (JDS). The JDS was designed to measure (a) objective job characteristics; (b) affective job reactions; and (c) receptivity to motivating jobs. They used it to assess the rewards family members garnered from their jobs. To make our review meaningful to family firm researchers, we do not summarize all of these instruments, focusing instead on those scales that measured common themes in family firm research such as altruism, agency, stewardship, and strategic planning (see Steier and Ward, 2006, for a complete review of common family firm topics and Yu et al.'s, 2012 review of dependent

variables). Table 28.4 provides a summary of measures that have been adapted or borrowed from other fields.

When researchers borrow or adapt existing measures, they can rely on the previously published psychometric evidence of the scale or reevaluate the scale attributes. Davis et al. (2010), for instance, adapted an altruism scale originally developed by Becker and Vance (1993) and later utilized by Eddleston and Kellermans (2007). The scale developers provided original validity evidence, and Davis and colleagues (2010) also provided additional validity evidence with an exploratory factor analysis and reliability estimates. This process of borrowing and adapting scales can help refine construct measurement as long as the researchers provide validity and reliability evidence for others to review and evaluate.

One notable result in comparing Tables 28.3 and 28.4 is that measures of performance are included in Table 28.4, which summarizes adapted measures. While performance is measured with single item observed variables (e.g., return on investment), several researchers have used perceptual measures of performance using multi-item scales. While these measures resulted in high reliability estimates, we were unable to find perceptual measures of performance (single-item, observed or multi-item perceptual) that were uniquely relevant to family firms. For example, the concept of socio-emotional wealth has received much recent attention in the literature (e.g., Berrone et al., 2010) and may be unique to family firms; despite this, no multi-item measure of this construct could be found. Alternatively, with agency theory dominating family firm research, we did identify multi-item measures of agency with sufficient evidence of validity and reliability. Likewise, measures of stewardship were identified that provided excellent psychometric evidence.

Regardless of whether scholars choose to develop a scale or adapt an existing scale, good measurement is essential to establish that we have indeed measured what we think

Table 28.3 Summary of family business scales and validity and reliability evidence

Theoretical construct	Measured variable (number of items)	Source and adapted from	Content	Construct	Reliability evidence (alpha values unless noted)
Family goals	Family goals (13)	Habbershon and Astrachan (1997)	Deductive	EFA	.76
	Attitude toward family control (3)	Romano et al. (2001)		EFA	.45
	Owner's financial security and benefits (6)	Tagiuri and Davis (1992)	Inductive	EFA	
Family and business interface	Family disruption (2)	Owen and Winter (1991)		EFA	
	Interrole conflict (4)	Smyrnios et al. (2003) from Australian Leaving Standards Study		EFA	.79
	Work-to-household conflict (2)	Smyrnios et al. (2003) from Frone et al. (1992)		EFA	.78
	Work-family conflict (7)	Boles (1996)		None reported	.90
	Emotional ownership (8)	Bjornberg and Nicholson (2012)	Deductive	EFA	.85
Family cohesion and harmony	Social interaction (3)	Mustakallio et al. (2002)		CFA	.73
	Perceived sense of belonging (3)	Ensley et al. (2007) from Bollen and Hoyle (1990)		CFA	.86
	Perceived feelings of morale (3)	Ensley et al. (2007) from Bollen and Hoyle (1990)		CFA	.89
	Family cohesion (12)	Lansberg and Astrachan (1994) from Olson (1988, 1986)		CFA	.89
	Family cohesion (5)	Smyrnios et al. (2003)		EFA	.89
	Family adaptability (12)	Lansberg and Astrachan (1994) from Olson (1988, 1986)			.77
	Family tensions	Olson et al. (2003)			
	Collaborative dialog (5)	Sorenson et al. (2009)		CFA	.76
				Discriminant validity	
	Acceptance of individual roles (8)	Sharma et al. (2003)			.88
	Family-member exchange (3)	Kellermanns and Eddleston (2007) from Seers (1989)			.93
	Open communication (8)	Bjornberg and Nicholson (2007)	Q sort	EFA and CFA (same sample)	.85
	Intergenerational authority (8)	Bjornberg and Nicholson (2007)	Q sort	EFA and CFA (same sample)	.75
	Intergenerational attention (8)	Bjornberg and Nicholson (2007)	Q sort	EFA and CFA (same sample)	.81

(Continued)

Table 28.3 (Continued)

Theoretical construct	Measured variable (number of items)	Source and adapted from	Content	Construct	Reliability evidence (alpha values unless noted)
	Cognitive cohesion (8)	Bjornberg and Nicholson (2007)	Q sort	EFA and CFA (same sample)	.89
	Emotional cohesion (8)	Bjornberg and Nicholson (2007)	Q sort	EFA and CFA (same sample)	.89
	Adaptability (8)	Bjornberg and Nicholson (2007)	Q sort	EFA and CFA (same sample)	.86
Transgenerational succession intentions	Desirability (3)	Sharma et al. (2003)			.62
	Conformance with social norms (2)	Sharma et al. (2003)			.68
	Agreement to maintain family involvement (2)	Sharma et al. (2003)			.70
	Family commitment (3)	Lansberg and Astrachan (1994)			.70
	Family commitment (2)	Mahto et al. (2010)		CFA	.81, .80
	Propensity of the incumbent to step aside (2)	Sharma et al. (2003)			.68
Transgenerational succession process	Satisfaction with succession process (12)	Sharma et al. (2003)	Deductive	EFA and CFA	.93
	Satisfaction with succession process (4)	Venter et al. (2005)		EFA	.67
	Succession planning (2)	Lansberg and Astrachan (1994)			.70
	Extent of succession planning (15)	Sharma et al. (2003)			.85
	Continuity planning (5)	Malone (1989)			.78
	CEO succession planning (3)	Poza et al. (1997)			.70
Successor preparation	Preparation level of successor (4)	Venter et al. (2005)	Inductive	EFA and CFA	.78
	Early involvement of children (2)	Birley (2001)		EFA	.70
	Willingness of successor to take over (2)	Sharma et al. (2003)		EFA and CFA	.91
	Willingness of successor to take over (5)	Venter et al. (2005)			.60
	Successor training (3)	Lansberg and Astrachan (1994)			.81
	Successor selection and training (5)	Sharma et al. (2003)			.68
	Importance of succession planning (3)	Marshall et al. (2006)			
Owner-Successor relationship	Owner-manager and successor relationship (6)	Lansberg and Astrachan (1994)		EFA and CFA	.78
	Owner-manager and successor relationship (3)	Venter et al. (2005)			.82

Note: Blanks indicate that no information was reported. EFA= exploratory factor analysis; CFA = confirmatory factor analysis.

Table 28.4 Summary of adapted scales and validity and reliability evidence

Theoretical construct	Measured variable (number of items)	Source and adapted from	Content	Construct	Reliability evidence (alpha values unless noted)
Performance	Performance (8)	Kellermanns and Eddleston (2006) and Eddleston and Kellermanns (2007)			.90, .88
	Perceived financial performance (7)	Rutherford et al. (2008)		EFA	.92
	Weighted average of performance (6)	Westhead and Howorth (2006)			.85
	Performance satisfaction (5)	Mahto et al. (2010)		CFA	.83, .83
Agency	Agency (3)	Davis et al. (2010) from Frankforter et al. (2007)		EFA	.90
	Overall monitoring (5)	Chrisman et al. (2007)		EFA	.88
	Board monitoring (5)	Mustakallio (2002) from Hitt et al. (1996)	Deductive	CFA	.87
Altruism	Altruism (5)	Davis et al. (2010) from Becker and Vance (1993)	Inductive	EFA	.90
	Family altruism (7)	Eddleston and Kellermanns (2007) from Becker and Vance (1993)		EFA	
Stewardship	Stewardship (3 items)	Davis et al. (2010)	Inductive	EFA Convergent validity (altruism)	.70
	Stewardship culture (4)	Zahra et al. (2008)	Deductive	EFA	.76
	Stewardship motivation (5)	Zahra et al. (2008)	Deductive	EFA	.87
Family social support and functioning	APGAR measure of family functioning (5)	Danes et al. (1999) from Smilkstein et al. (1982)		EFA Convergent	.82 Split half
Opportunity recognition	Perceived technological opportunities (4)	Kellermanns and Eddleston (2006)			.84
Strategic planning	Strategic planning (4)	Kellermanns and Eddleston (2006)			.86
	Strategic controls (5)	Zahra et al. (2008)	Deductive		.68
	Strategic flexibility (6)	Zahra et al. (2008)	Deductive	EFA	.88
	Participative strategy process (5)	Eddleston and Kellermanns (2007)			.79
	Family involvement (5)	Zahra (2003)			.64

(Continued)

Table 28.4 (Continued)

Theoretical construct	Measured variable (number of items)	Source and adapted from	Content	Construct	Reliability evidence (alpha values unless noted)
Entrepreneurial orientation	Innovation (3)	Craig and Moores (2006)		EFA	.75
Identity	Value commitment (9)	Davis et al. (2010) from Schechter (1985)			.90
Trust	Trust	Davis et al. (2010) from Davis et al. (2000)			.79
Values	Individual vs group cultural orientation (4)	Zahra et al. (2004)	Deductive		.67
	External vs internal cultural orientation (5)	Zahra et al. (2004)	Deductive		.78
Corporate social performance	Corporate citizenship (6)	Tagiuri and Davis (1992)	Inductive	EFA	
Conflict	Task conflict (3)	Ensley (2006) from Jehn (1995)			
	Process conflict	Kellermanns and Eddleston (2007)			.90
	Relationship conflict (3)	Eddleston and Kellermanns (2007) from Jehn (1995)			.92

Note: Blanks indicate that no information was reported. EFA= exploratory factor analysis; CFA = confirmatory factor analysis.

we measured. As the field of family business continues to develop, researchers can enhance theory development by following best practices in scale development.

BEST PRACTICES FOR SCALE DEVELOPMENT

We would recommend that researchers turn to the many resources that are available to assist them (i.e., Robinson et al., 1991 provide a compendium of existing measures along with reviews). These resources include *Organizational Research Methods*, a journal devoted to measurement and statistical techniques, as well as articles and books focused on scale development (e.g., Nunnally, 1978). Hinkin (1998) lays out six general steps that should be followed. These steps included: (a) item generation; (b) questionnaire development and administration; (c) initial item reduction; (d) confirmatory factor analysis; (e) testing for convergent and discriminant validity; and (f) study replication.

Hinkin (1998) provides a rich resource that details how one would go about accomplishing each general step and the tests that should be conducted. After examing the content validity of items, for instance, scales should be tested in a field setting. As this questionnaire is developed, researchers should consider related scales, as well as antecedent or outcome constructs that reflect the nomological net that is theorized around the new scale. These additional scales allow tests of convergent and discriminant validity after the factor structure of the instrument is tested. Further, the data from this first administration should be subjected to an exploratory factor analysis (EFA). Conway and Huffcutt (2003) and Ford et al. (1986) have done comprehensive reviews of how EFA has been used in the literature, offering clear guidance as to how the data should be analyzed, evaluated, and reported.

As we have noted, sound instruments would have evidence that spans all forms of validity and reliability. Other things being equal, more sources of evidence are better than fewer while quality of evidence is always an important consideration. This is particularly important when one considers that the different indicators of validity and reliability address different components that collectively represent the instrument's effectiveness. It would be possible, for instance, to develop a relatively short list of items that have a consistent factor structure and an acceptable alpha (i.e., estimate of internal consistency) that no longer measure the construct's domain.

FUTURE OPPORTUNITIES REGARDING MEASUREMENT IN FAMILY BUSINESS

Empirical testing of family firm theories requires valid, reliable measures. This review revealed that (a) many measures are often reported with basic evidence of construct validity and reliability, and (b) a limited number of measures have been developed for specific use in family firm studies. While many measures offered limited evidence, some areas showed promise. As we noted, the area of succession appears to have matured with several measures available (e.g., Sharma et al., 2003; Venter et al., 2005) which have demonstrated evidence of structural validity and reliability. Still, no instrument has been accepted as the standard nor has the research converged around the most important theoretical facets involved with succession.

Hence, even with this promise, we would recommend measures be subjected to further validity and reliability testing. Specifically, little attention has been given to content validity. Several offered relatively brief definitions and identified items from existing scales stating that the items 'best represented each construct' (e.g., Sorenson et al., 2009: 243). There are exemplars, however, of succinct descriptions of how constructs were derived (Astrachan et al., 2002) and the associated items were developed (e.g., Carr et al., 2011; Lansberg and Astrachan, 1994). Taguiri and Davis

(1992), as an example, explained the inductive process used to develop a list of goals and purposes of family firms. Following a deductive approach, Daily and Thompson (1994) cited the theoretical literature on which their measure of strategic posture was based.

With that said, the limited number of measures present opportunities. Family firm concepts like socio-emotional wealth were noticeably absent or scant in the measures identified for this chapter. Berrone et al. (2012) have acknowledged this, proposing that the construct is represented by several dimensions (i.e., family control and influence; identification of family members with the firm; binding social ties; emotional attachment of family members; renewal of family bonds to the firm through dynastic succession). Further, they propose a set of items that might be used to measure these dimensions which require psychometric testing.

In sum, this suggests that typical measures of performance (e.g., Tobin's q, return on assets) may not fully capture the impact of family on firm performance, and led Dyer to more specifically conclude 'family has been a neglected variable in organizational research' (2003: 402). Along these lines, we did not find an abundance of measures on the 'family effect' (Dyer, 2006) or familiness. Perhaps one of the reasons family is not included is that we do not have an appropriate measure of the family. Other family firm topics that were noticeably absent from our review of measures and suggested by Yu et al. (2012) included family values, familiness, communication, as well as topics from 'the dark side' of family dynamics, including favoritism and jealousy. We did not find a measure of family firm cultures that could potentially differentiate between myriad types of families in business.

In closing, better measures of relevant constructs are needed as the field of family business continues to mature. We hope readers can use this review as a springboard to begin refining instruments, reviewing scales against the most rigorous development practices. In addition, we would hope these practices are used to begin developing measures of the family firm ideas or topics do not have sound measures. When the construct can not be measured, the theory can not be tested. As such, the advancement of our rich and vibrant field may be stymied by limited measurement development.

ACKNOWLEDGEMENTS

This research was supported, in part, with a Family Owned Business Institute (FOBI) scholarship of $5,000. We would like to express our appreciation to Grand Valley State University for sponsoring this award.

NOTES

1   One could argue the scale does not represent the construct (i.e., it lacks content validity) because an element like generational involvement, which is one of the most frequently used measures, is not incorporated (Chrisman et al., 2012). With that said, Klein et al. (2005) have incorporated involvement in another scale that is part of their F-PEC measure.
2   Several family business researchers have used modifications of Mowday et al.'s (1979) instrument to measure commitment. They include: Chrisman et al. (2012); Jaskiewicz and Klein (2007); and Zahra et al. (2008).
3   Many interpret the .70 alpha as an absolute standard. Nunnally (1978) did not advocate for a single reliability standard, suggesting that reliability standards become more rigorous as fields advance. Thus, we recommend the field improve measures to exceed alpha values of .70.

REFERENCES

American Psychological Association (APA) (1985). *Standards for Educational and Psychological Testing.* Washington, DC: American Psychological Association.

Anderson, J.C. and Gerbing, D.W. (1991). Predicting the performance measures in a confirmatory factor analysis with a pretest assessment to their substantive validity. *Journal of Applied Psychology*, 76, 732–740.

Anderson, J.C. and Gerbing, D.W. (1988). Structural equation modeling in practice: A review and recommended two-step approach. *Psychological Bulletin*, 103, 411–423.

Astrachan, J.H., Klein, S.B., and Smyrnios, K.X. (2002). The F-PEC Scale of family influence: A proposal for solving the family business definition problem. *Family Business Review*, 15(1), 45–58.

Bacharach, S.B. (1989). Organizational theories: Some criteria for evaluation. *Academy of Management Review*, 14(4), 496–515.

Bagozzi, R.P., Yi, Y., and Phillips, L.W. (1991). Assessing construct validity in organizational research. *Administrative Science Quarterly*, 36, 421–458.

Becker, T.E. and Vance, R.J. (1993). Construct validity of three types of organizational citizenship behavior: An illustration of the direct product model with refinements. *Journal of Management*, 19(3), 663–682.

Berrone, P., Cruz, C., and Gomez-Mejia, L.R. (2012). Socioemotional wealth in family firms: Theoretical dimensions, assessment approaches, and agenda for future research. *Family Business Review*, 25(3), 258–279.

Berrone, P., Cruz, C., Gomez-Mejia, L.R., and Larraza-Kintana, M. (2010). Socioemotional wealth and corporate responses to institutional pressures: Do family-controlled firms pollute less? *Administrative Science Quarterly*, 55(1), 82–113.

Bird, B., Welsch, H., Astrachan, J.H., and Pistrui, D. (2002). Family business research: The evolution of an academic field. *Family Business Review*, 4, 337–350.

Birley, S. (2001). Owner-manager attitudes to family and business issues: A 16 country study. *Entrepreneurship: Theory and Practice*, 25, 63–76.

Bjornberg, A. and Nicholson, N. (2007). The family climate scales: Development of a new measure for use in family business research. *Family Business Review*, 20, 229–246.

Bjornberg, A. and Nicholson, N. (2012). Emotional ownership: The next generation's relationship with the family firm. *Family Business Review*, doi:10.1177/0894486511432471.

Boles, J.S. (1996). Influences of work-family conflict on job satisfaction, life satisfaction and quitting intentions among business owners: The case of family-operated businesses. *Family Business Review*, 9(1), 61–74.

Bollen, K.A. and Hoyle, R.H. (1990). Perceived cohesion a conceptual and empirical examination. *Social Forces*, 69, 479–504.

Campbell, D.T. (1960). Recommendations for APA test standards regarding construct, trait, or discriminant validity. *American Psychologist*, 15, 546–553.

Carlock, R.S. and Ward, J.L. (2001). *Strategic Planning for the Family Business: Parallel Planning to Unify the Family and Business*. Houndsmill, NY: Palgrave.

Carr, J.C., Cole, M.S., Ring, J.K., and Blettner, D.P. (2011). A measure of variations in internal social capital among family firms. *Entrepreneurship: Theory and Practice*, 35, 1207–1227.

Casillas, J. and Acedo, F. (2007). Evolution of the intellectual structure of family business literature: A bibliometric study of FBR. *Family Business Review*, 20(2), 141–162.

Chandler, G.N. and Lyon, D.W. (2001). Issues of research design and construct measurement in entrepreneurship research: The past decade. *Entrepreneurship: Theory and Practice*, 25, 101–113.

Chrisman, J.J., Chua, J.H., and Sharma, P. (2005). Trends and directions in the development of a strategic management theory of the family firm. *Entrepreneurship: Theory and Practice*, 29(5), 555–575.

Chrisman, J.J., Chua, J.H., Kellermanns, F.W., and Chang, E.P.C. (2007). Are family managers agents or stewards? An exploratory study in privately held family firms. *Journal of Business Research*, 60(10), 1030–1038.

Chrisman, J.J., Chua, J.H., Pearson, A.W., and Barnett, T. (2012). Family involvement, family influence, and family-centered non-economic goals in small firms. *Entrepreneurship: Theory and Practice*, 36(2), 267–293.

Chrisman, J.J., Kellermanns, F.W., Chan, K.C., and Liano, K. (2010). Intellectual foundations of current research in family business: An identification and review of 25 influential articles. *Family Business Review*, 23(1), 9–26.

Chua, J.H., Chrisman, J.J., and Sharma, P. (1999). Defining the family business by behavior. *Entrepreneurship: Theory and Practice*, 23(4), 19–39.

Chua, J.H., Chrisman, J.J., Kellermanns, F., and Wu, Z. (2011). Family involvement and new venture debt financing. *Journal of Business Venturing*, 26(4), 472–488.

Conway, J.M. and Huffcutt, A.I. (2003). A review and evaluation of exploratory factor analysis practices in organizational research. *Organizational Research Methods*, 6(2), 147–168.

Craig, J. and Moores, K. (2005). Balanced scorecards to drive the strategic planning of family firms. *Family Business Review*, 18(2), 105–122.

Craig, J. and Moores, K. (2006). A 10-year longitudinal investigation of strategy, systems, and environment on innovation in family firms. *Family Business Review*, 18(2), 105–122.

Cronbach, L.J. and Meehl, P.E. (1955). Construct validity in psychological tests. *Psychological Bulletin*, 52, 281–302.

Crook, T.R., Shook, C.L., Morris, M.L., and Madden, T.M. (2010). Are we there yet? An assessment of research design and construct measurement practices in entrepreneurship research. *Organizational Research Methods*, 13, 192–206.

Daily, C.M. and Thompson, S.S. (1994). Ownership structure, strategic posture, and firm growth: An empirical examination. *Family Business Review*, 7(3), 237–249.

Danes, S.M., Zuiker, V., Kean, R., and Arbuthnot, J. (1999). Predictors of family business tensions and goal achievement. *Family Business Review*, 12, 241–252.

Davis, J.H., Allen, M.R., and Hayes, H.D. (2010). Is blood thicker than water? A study of stewardship perceptions in family business. *Entrepreneurship: Theory and Practice*, 34(6), 1093–1116.

Davis, J.H., Mayer, R., Schoorman, D., and Hoon, T.H. (2000). The trusted general manager and business unit performance: Empirical evidence of a competitive advantage. *Strategic Management Journal*, 21(5), 563–576.

Dyer, G. (2003). The family: The missing variable in organizational research. *Entrepreneurship: Theory and Practice*, 27(4), 401–415.

Dyer, G. (2006). Examining the 'family effect' on firm performance. *Family Business Review*, 14(4), 253–273.

Eddleston, K.A. and Kellermanns, F.W. (2007). Destructive and productive family relationships: A stewardship theory perspective. *Journal of Business Venturing*, 22(4), 545–565.

Ensley, M. (2006). Family businesses can out-compete: As long as they are willing to question the chosen path. *Entrepreneurship: Theory and Practice*, 30(6), 747–754.

Ensley, M.D., Pearson, A.W., and Sardeshmukh, S.R. (2007). The negative consequences of pay dispersion in family and non-family top management teams: An exploratory analysis of new venture, high-growth firms. *Journal of Business Research*, 60(10), 1039–1047.

Ford, J.K., MacCallum, R.C., and Tait, M. (1986). The application of exploratory factor analysis in applied psychology: A critical review and analysis. *Personnel Psychology*, 39, 291–314.

Frankforter, S., Davis, J.H., Vollrath, D.A., and Hill, V. (2007). Determinants of governance structure among companies: A test of agency predictions. *International Journal of Management*, 24(3), 454–462.

Frone, M.R., Russell, M., and Cooper, M.L. (1992). Antecedents and outcomes of work-family conflict: Testing a model of the work family interface. *Journal of Applied Psychology*, 1992(1), 65–78.

Habbershon, T.G. and Astrachan, J.H. (1997). Research note: Perceptions are reality: How family meetings lead to collective action. *Family Business Review*, 10(1), 37–52.

Hinkin, T.R. (1998). A brief tutorial on the development of measures for use in survey questionnaires. *Organizational Research Methods*, 1, 104–121.

Hinkin, T.R. and Tracey, J.B. (1999). An analysis of variance approach to content validation. *Organizational Research Methods*, 2(2), 175–186.

Hinsz, V.B. and Nelson, L.C. (1990). Family farmers' reactions to their work: A job diagnostic survey. *Family Business Review*, 3(1), 35–44.

Hitt, M.A., Hoskisson, R.E., Johnson, R.A., and Moesel, D.D. (1996). The market for corporate control and firm innovation. *Academy of Management Journal*, 39(5), 1084–1119.

Holt, D.T., Rutherford, M.W., and Kuratko, D.F. (2010). Advancing the field of family business research: Further testing the measurement properties of the F-PEC. *Family Business Review*, 23(1), 76–88.

Jaskiewicz, P. and Klein, S. (2007). The impact of goal alignment on board composition and board size in family businesses. *Journal of Business Research*, 60(10), 1080–1089.

Jehn, K.A. (1995). A multimethod examination of the benefits and detriments of intra-group conflict. *Administrative Science Quarterly*, 40, 256–282.

Kaplan, A. (1964). *The Conduct of Inquiry*. San Francisco, CA: Chandler.

Kellermanns, F.W. and Eddleston, K.A. (2006). Corporate entrepreneurship in family firms: A family perspective. *Entrepreneurship: Theory and Practice*, 30(6), 809–830.

Kellermanns, F.W. and Eddleston, K.A. (2007). A family perspective on when conflict benefits family firm performance. *Journal of Business Research*, 60(10), 1048–1057.

Klein, S.B., Astrachan, J.H., and Smyrnios, K.X. (2005). The F-PEC scale of family influence: Construction, validation, and further implication for theory. *Entrepreneurship: Theory and Practice*, 29(3), 321–339.

Korman, A.K. (1974). Contingency approaches to leadership: An overview. In J.G. Hunt and L.L. Larson (eds), *Contingency Approaches to Leadership*. Carbondale, IL: Southern Illinois University Press.

Kuhn, T.S. (1970). *The Structure of Scientific Revolutions*. Chicago, IL: Chicago University Press.

Lansberg, I. and Astrachan, J.H. (1994). Influence of family relationships on succession planning and training: The importance of mediating factors. *Family Business Review*, 7(1), 39–59.

Litz, R.A. (2008). Two sides of a one-sided phenomenon: Conceptualizing the family business and business family as a Mobius strip. *Family Business Review*, 21(3), 217–236.

Litz, R.A., Pearson, A.W., and Litchfield, S. (2012). Charting the future of family business research: Perspectives from the field. *Family Business Review*, 25, 16–32.

Mahto, R.V., Davis, P.S., Pearce II, J.A., and Robinson Jr., R.B. (2010). Satisfaction with firm performance in family businesses. *Entrepreneurship Theory and Practice*, 34(5), 985–1001.

Malone, S.C. (1989). Selected correlates of business continuity planning in the family business. *Family Business Review*, 2(4), 341–353.

Marshall, J.P., Sorenson, R., Brigham, K., Wieling, E., Reifman, A., and Wampler, R.S. (2006). The paradox for the family firm CEO: Owner age relationship to succession-related processes and plans. *Journal of Business Venturing*, 21(3), 348–368.

Messick, S. (1989). Validity. In R.L. Linn (ed.), *Educational Measurement* (3rd edn, pp. 13–103). New York: MacMillan Publishing Company.

Moores, K. (2009). Paradigms and theory building in the domain of business families. *Family Business Review*, 22, 167–180.

Mowday, R.T., Steers, R.M., and Porter, L.W. (1979). The measurement of organizational commitment. *Journal of Vocational Behavior*, 14, 224–247.

Mustakallio, M., Autio, E., and Zahra, S.A. (2002). Relational and contractual governance in family firms: Effects on strategic decision making. *Family Business Review*, 15(3), 205–222.

Nunnally, J.C. (1978). *Psychometric Theory* (2nd edn). New York: McGraw-Hill.

Nunnally, J.C. and Bernstein, I.H. (1994). *Psychometric Theory* (3rd edn). New York: McGraw-Hill.

Olson, D.H. (1986). Circumplex model: Validation studies and FACES III. *Family Process*, 25, 337–351.

Olson, D.H. (1988). The circumplex model of family systems VIII: Family assessment and intervention. In D.H. Olson, C.S. Russell, and D.H. Sprenkle (eds), *The Circumplex Model: Systemic Assessment and Treatment of Families*. New York: Haworth.

Olson, P.D., Zuiker, V.S., Danes, S.M., Stafford, K., Heck, R.K.Z., and Duncan, K.A. (2003). The impact of the family and the business on family business sustainability. *Journal of Business Venturing*, 18(5), 639–666.

Owen, A.J. and Winter, M. (1991). Research note: The impact of home-based business on family life. *Family Business Review*, 4(4), 425–432.

Poza, E.J., Alfred, T., and Maheshwari, A. (1997). Stakeholder perceptions of culture and management practices in family and family firms – a preliminary report. *Family Business Review*, 10(2), 135–155.

Reay, T. and Whetten, D.A. (2011). What constitutes a theoretical contribution? *Family Business Review*, 24, 105–110.

Robinson, J.P., Shaver, P.R., and Wrightsman, L.S. (eds) (1991). *Measures of Personality and Social Psychology Attitudes*. Oxford: Elsevier.

Romano, C.A., Tanewski, G.A., and Smyrnios, K.X. (2001). Capital structure decision making: A model for family business. *Journal of Business Venturing*, 16(3), 285–310.

Rutherford, M.W., Kuratko, D.F., and Holt, D.T. (2008). Examining the link between 'familiness' and performance: Can the F-PEC untangle the family business theory jungle? *Entrepreneurship: Theory and Practice*, 32(6), 1089–1109.

Schechter, D.S. (1985). Value and continuance commitment: A field test of dual conceptualization of organizational commitment. Unpublished doctoral dissertation. University of Maryland, College Park.

Schriesheim, C.A., Powers, K.J., Scandura, T.A., Gardiner, C.C., and Lankau, M.J. (1993). Improving construct measurement in management research: Comments and a quantitative approach for assessing the theoretical content adequacy of paper-and-pencil survey-type instruments. *Journal of Management*, 19, 385–417.

Schwab, D. (1980). Construct validity in organizational behavior. In B.M. Staw and L.L. Cummings (eds), *Research in Organizational Behavior*, Vol. 2, pp. 3–43. Greenwich, CT: JAI Press.

Seers, A. (1989). Team-member exchange quality: A new construct for role-making research. *Organizational Behavior and Human Decision Processes*, 43, 118–135.

Sharma, P., Chrisman, J.J., and Chua, J.H. (2003). Predictors of satisfaction with the succession process in family firms. *Journal of Business Venturing*, 18(5), 667–687.

Sharma, P., Chrisman, J.J., and Chua, J.H. (2003). Succession planning as planned behavior: Some empirical results. *Family Business Review*, 16(1), 1–15.

Smilkstein, G., Ashworth, C., and Montano, D. (1982). Validity and reliability of the family APGAR as a test of family function. *The Journal of Family Practice*, 15, 303–311.

Smyrnios, K.X., Romano, C.A., Tanewski, G.A., Karofsky, P.I., Millen, R., and Yilmaz, M.R. (2003). Work-family conflict: A study of American and Australian family businesses. *Family Business Review*, 16(1), 35–51.

Sorenson, R.L., Goodpaster, K.E., Hedberg, P.R., and Yu, A. (2009). The family point of view, family social capital, and firm performance: An exploratory test. *Family Business Review*, 22(3), 239–253.

Steier, L.P. and Ward, J.L. (2006). If theories of family enterprise really do matter, so does change in management education. *Entrepreneurship: Theory and Practice*, 30(6), 887–895.

Tagiuri, R. and Davis, J.A. (1992). On the goals of successful family companies. *Family Business Review*, 5(1), 43–62.

Venkatraman, N. and Grant, J.H. (1986). Construct measurement in organizational research: A critique and proposal. *Academy of Management Review*, 11, 71–87.

Venter, E., Boshoff, C., and Maas, G. (2005). The influence of successor-related factors on the succession process in small and medium-sized family businesses. *Family Business Review*, 18(4), 283–303.

Vilaseca, A. (2002). The shareholder role in the family business: Conflict of interests and objectives between nonemployed shareholders and top management team. *Family Business Review*, 15(4), 299–320.

Westhead, P. and Howorth, C. (2006). Ownership and management issues associated with family firm performance and company objectives. *Family Business Review*, 19(4), 301–316.

Yu, A., Lumpkin, G.T., Sorenson, R.L., and Bingham, K.H. (2012). The landscape of family business outcomes: a summary and numerical taxonomy of dependent variables. *Family Business Review*, 25, 33–57.

Zahra, S.A. (2003). International expansion of US manufacturing family businesses: the effect of ownership and involvement. *Journal of Business Venturing*, 18(4), 495–512.

Zahra, S.A., Hayton, J.C., and Salvato, C. (2004). Entrepreneurship in family vs. non-family firms: A resource-based analysis of the effect of organizational culture. *Entrepreneurship: Theory and Practice*, 28(4), 363–381.

Zahra, S.A., Hayton, J.C., Neubaum, D.O., Dibrell, C., and Craig, J. (2008). Culture of family commitment and strategic flexibility: The moderating effect of stewardship. *Entrepreneurship: Theory and Practice*, 32(6), 1035–1054.

Qualitative Methods in Family Business Research

Trish Reay and Zhen Zhang

INTRODUCTION

Qualitative research methods are becoming increasingly well established and well respected in organizational studies. In family business research, there is ongoing interest in qualitative research and the field is well positioned for future growth. This is important, since many critical (but so far unanswered) questions in family business could best be approached through qualitative methods. For example, we know that successful family businesses are reliant on supportive interpersonal dynamics, the engagement of family and employees in effective business processes, and overall integration of family and business values – however, we know relatively little about how these processes can be developed. These are all topics that are well suited to fine-grained, qualitatively based investigations.

In attempting to get the 'lay of the land' and understand what types of qualitative research in family business have been published, and where, we engaged in a systematic review of the literature to identify and categorize empirical family business articles based on qualitative methodology. Here, we provide a brief description of qualitative methods used and show examples of studies that are leading the way. We also identify areas where we see particular opportunities for the use of qualitative methods. We hope that this chapter will be helpful to new or experienced family business researchers, and we encourage more scholars to engage in qualitative methods in family business research.

QUALITATIVE METHODOLOGY

All research is designed to understand phenomena of interest, but a researcher's worldview may lead to different research methodologies of exploring reality. Quantitative research is normally based on a positivist view that an objective world exists independent of the mind, and it can be uncovered by scientific data and theories.

Scholars who take this view believe that the way to understand the socially complex nature of phenomena is to 'detect, decipher, or translate' the facts and then compare these facts through hypothesis testing of prior findings (Nordqvist et al., 2009). Most qualitative researchers, however, take an interpretive or social constructivist standpoint. From this perspective, there is no objective reality that can be discovered or replicated; the knowledge of meaning is a production of social construction (Berger and Luckmann, 1966). Therefore, understanding social process cannot occur through hypothetical deduction. Instead it must occur by getting inside the world of those generating social process, understanding the meanings used by societal members, and employing 'words, talk and texts as meaningful representations of concepts' (Gephart, 2004).

The procedures used to conduct rigorous qualitative research must meet the overall requirement of trustworthiness (Lincoln and Guba, 1985). Trustworthiness in qualitative research is comparable to issues of reliability and validity in quantitative approaches; the qualitative concepts of credibility, transferability, dependability and confirmability are aligned with internal validity, external validity, reliability and objectivity in quantitative work (Krefting, 1991). There are many textbooks or handbooks that provide valuable reference information about how to conduct qualitative research. The following books on qualitative methods are ones that we have found particularly helpful: Denzin and Lincoln, 2000; Miles and Huberman, 1994; Patton, 2002. We also recommend two books focused on qualitative methods in organization studies: Lee, 1999; Myers, 2009.

WHY ENCOURAGE QUALITATIVE RESEARCH IN FAMILY BUSINESS?

We believe that family business researchers should develop the required skill sets to design and carry out research based on qualitative methods for several reasons. First, qualitative research can answer important questions about family business. For example, Chrisman et al. (2010) identified several underdeveloped themes in family business literature. They say that we need to know more about how family governance systems actually work, and how the pursuit of noneconomic goals impacts the strategic direction of a family firm – these are questions of 'how', and quantitative studies are ill equipped to answer them.

In contrast, qualitative studies are designed to answer questions that begin with 'how' or 'why'. Examples are: how do people encourage family and non-family to work together in family firms, or why do family firm managers devote time and resources to facilitating positive relationships among family members? By answering these 'how' or 'why' questions, researchers can gain new insights about successful management strategies. But in order to do this, researchers must learn from the people themselves – those who make decisions within family firms. If we want to know how or why people do the things they do, we really need to ask them (Myers, 2009). This can be done by analyzing secondary texts of what people said in printed documents or recorded statements. More often, researchers gather data by directly questioning people who are (or have been) engaged in the phenomenon of interest.

The second reason for using qualitative methods is that they are well suited to developing theory. As a relatively new area of study, family business is continuously building its theory base. Qualitative data (when appropriately gathered and analyzed) provides a strong foundation for understanding dynamic processes within organizations. In addition, studies based on qualitative data can help improve our understanding of relationships among different organizations. As such, they are powerful tools for theory-building that can move the field of family business forward.

In addition, qualitative methods can be the first step in a research process – to gather preliminary information for a future large scale quantitative study; a qualitative study can be exploratory. It can also be a follow-up to quantitative studies – helping researchers to understand the results of large scale studies that identify correlations but do not explain why those correlations exist. A qualitative study can also 'stand alone' to understand unusual situations – such as outliers, or minority views. For example, if only a few family firms are able to successfully transition across generations, seeking out and studying these positive outliers may provide insights that help build theory about successful generational transfer.

SEARCHING THE LITERATURE FOR QUALITATIVE FAMILY BUSINESS STUDIES

We systematically searched the literature for peer-reviewed journal articles on the topic of family business. We followed the methodology of Debicki et al. (2009), deriving an initial list of 30 management journals appropriate for family business research articles. We also included two journals with a focus on family business research that were recently launched – *Strategic Entrepreneurship Journal* and the *Journal of Family Business Strategy*. The range of publication dates included was from 1999 to 2010. The start date was determined by electronic access to *Family Business Review* beginning in 1999, and the end date of 2010 included the most recent full year.

We searched for the terms 'Family Business', 'Family Enterprise', 'Family Firm' as well as their common derivations (for example, 'Family Businesses'). In this sense, all *Family Business Review* and *Journal of Family Business Strategy* articles were included as those two outlets focus exclusively on family business research. Furthermore, we conducted a hand search (following up on reference lists in other articles and book chapters) in an attempt to locate all studies of family business in the 32 selected journals. This resulted in a list of 656 relevant articles.

Next, we restricted our search to empirical studies based on qualitative methodology. To do so, we eliminated all articles without empirical contents (that is, editorials, book reviews, commentaries, and conceptual articles) or articles based on quantitative methods. The final result was a set of 78 articles – most of them published in *Family Business Review* (41 articles). Ten were published in the *International Small Business Journal*, 5 in the relatively new *Journal of Family Business Strategy*, 4 articles in the *Journal of Business Venturing*, 3 articles in *Entrepreneurship and Regional Development*, and 2 articles were in *Entrepreneurship: Theory and Practice*. Other articles were published in a variety of other journals. See Table 29.1 for a full listing of the articles considered here. The numbers of articles published per year are graphically displayed in Figure 29.1.

We drew on Myers (2009) to categorize the types of qualitative research published and the specific methods used to gather data and analyze findings. This textbook is consistent with most explanations of qualitative methodology, and provides a relatively straightforward approach that we found helpful. Myers' organizing framework first considers the research design (case study, ethnographic, interpretive or grounded theory, or action research design) as the overarching and guiding approach to the research. The next consideration is how data is collected (interviews, participant observation, documents, or narratives). In all cases there may be overlap and addition. That is, research designs can have more than one component, and data collection can include multiple sources. We categorized family business studies based on the primary research design and included all data collection methods described. In the next sections of this chapter, we provide a short explanation of the research design and data collection categories, describe the patterns identified in our identified set of articles, explain how exemplary articles in each category contribute to the literature, and provide suggestions for future research.

Table 29.1   Research articles based on qualitative methodology (1999–2010)

	Interviews	Narratives	Observations	Documents
Single case study design				
Bhalla et al. (ISBJ, 2006)	Yes		Yes	Yes
Dielemjan and Sachs (JMS, 2008)	Yes			Yes
Dyck et al. (JBV, 2002)	Yes			
Ibrahim et al. (FBR, 2001)				Yes
Karra et al. (ETP, 2006)	Yes			Yes
Litz (JFBS, 2010)	Yes		Yes	Yes
Mickelson and Worley (FBR, 2003)	Yes			
Ng and Keasey (ISBJ, 2010)	Yes			Yes
Perricone et al. (FBR, 2001)	Yes			
Ram (HR, 2001)	Yes		Yes	Yes
Salvato et al. (ERD, 2010)	Yes			Yes
Steen and Welch (FBR, 2006)	Yes			Yes
Steier (JBR, 2007)	Yes			
Tsang (JSBM, 2001)	Yes		Yes	Yes
Watson (ISBJ, 2009)	Yes	Yes		
Multiple case study design				
Ainsworth and Cox (Org Studies, 2003)	Yes			
Andersson et al. (FBR, 2002)	Yes			
Bachkaniwala et al. (ISBJ, 2001)	Yes		Yes	
Boutilier (JBE, 2009)	Yes			
Cabrera-Suarez (LQ, 2005)	Yes			Yes
Cadieux et al. (FBR, 2002)	Yes			
Cadieux (FBR, 2007)	Yes			
Cater and Justis (FBR, 2009)	Yes		Yes	Yes
Cater and Schwab (FBR, 2008)	Yes		Yes	Yes
Chirico (ISBJ, 2008)	Yes		Yes	Yes
Chirico and Nordqvist (ISBJ, 2010)	Yes		Yes	Yes
Dunn (FBR, 1999)	Yes			Yes
Dyer and Mortensen (FBR, 2005)	Yes			
Farias et al. (JBR, 2009)	Yes			
Garcia-Alvarez and López-Sintas (FBR, 2001)	Yes		Yes	Yes
Gilding (FBR, 2000)	Yes			
Graves and Thomas (FBR, 2008)	Yes		Yes	Yes
Haberman and Danes (FBR, 2007)	Yes			
Hall et al. (FBR, 2001)	Yes		Yes	Yes
Hall and Nordqvist (FBR, 2008)	Yes		Yes	
Hamilton (ISBJ, 2006)	Yes	Yes		
Howorth et al. (JBV, 2004)	Yes			
Howorth and Ali (FBR, 2001)	Yes		Yes	
Irava and Moores (JFBS, 2010)	Yes		Yes	Yes
Janjuha-Jivraj and Woods (ISBJ, 2002)	Yes			
Johannisson and Huse (ERD, 2000)	Yes			
Kenyon-Rouvinez (FBR, 2001)	Yes			Yes
Khavul et al. (ETP, 2009)	Yes			
Lambrecht (FBR, 2005)	Yes			Yes
Lambrecht and Lievens (FBR, 2008)	Yes			

	Interviews	Narratives	Observations	Documents
Lee and Tran (FBR, 2001)	Yes			Yes
Manikutty (FBR, 2000)	Yes			Yes
Marchisio et al. (ERD, 2010)	Yes			
Miller et al. (JBV, 2003)			Yes	Yes
Murray (FBR, 2003)	Yes			
Ng and Roberts (HR, 2007)	Yes			
Niemelä (FBR, 2004)	Yes			
Nordqvist and Melin (LRP, 2008)	Yes		Yes	Yes
Nordqvist and Melin (JFBS, 2010)	Yes		Yes	Yes
Parada et al. (FBR, 2010)	Yes			Yes
Salvato and Melin (FBR, 2008)	Yes			Yes
Steier (FBR, 2001)	Yes		Yes	Yes
Steier and Miller (JFBS, 2010)	Yes			Yes
Tan and Fock (FBR, 2001)	Yes			Yes
Thomas (FBR, 2002)	Yes		Yes	Yes
Tokarczyk et al. (FBR, 2007)	Yes			
Tsang (JBV, 2002)	Yes			
Tsui-Auch (JMS, 2004)	Yes	Yes		Yes
Tsui-Auch (Org Studies, 2005)	Yes	Yes		Yes
Van der Heyden et al. (FBR, 2005)	Yes			
Vera and Dean (FBR, 2005)	Yes			
Yeung (FBR, 2000)	Yes			Yes
Ethnographic design				
Jones and Craven (ISBJ, 2001)			Yes	
Interpretive *or* grounded theory design				
Blumentritt, Keyt, and Astrachan (FBR, 2007)	Yes			
Cole and Johnson (FBR, 2007)	Yes			
Curimbaba (FBR, 2002)	Yes			
DeNoble et al. (FBR, 2007)	Yes			
Fletcher (2010, ISBJ)	Yes			
Mazzola et al. (FBR, 2008)	Yes		Yes	Yes
Parada and Viladas (JOCM, 2010)	Yes	Yes		
Action research design				
Craig and Moores (FBR, 2005)	Yes		Yes	
Craig and Moores (JFBS, 2010)	Yes		Yes	
Poza and Messer (FBR, 2001)	Yes			

Key:
ETP = *Entrepreneurship: Theory and Practice*
ERD= *Entrepreneurship & Regional Development*
FBR = *Family Business Review*
HR = *Human Relations*
ISBJ = *International Small Business Journal*
JBE = *Journal of Business Ethics*
JBR = *Journal of Business Research*
JBV = *Journal of Business Venturing*
JFBS = *Journal of Family Business Strategy*
JMS = *Journal of Management Studies*
JOCM = *Journal of Organizational Change Management*
LQ = *The Leadership Quarterly*

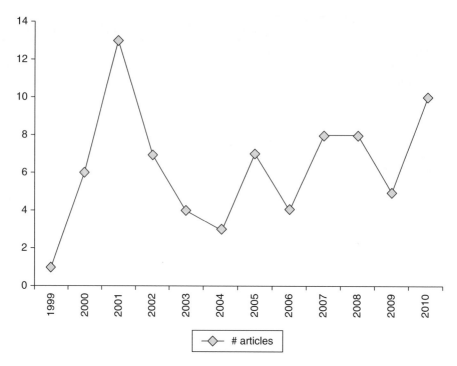

Figure 29.1   Numbers of family business qualitative research articles published by year

DESIGNING QUALITATIVE RESEARCH

Although we sometimes talk as if qualitative research is all the same, there are significant differences in research design. As is the case with all research, researchers must use a methodology that is appropriate for the research question (Creswell, 1998; Lee, 1999). Within a qualitative approach there are four broad research designs that we discuss below: case study, ethnographic, interpretive or grounded theory, and action research.

Case Study Design

'A case study is a research strategy that focuses on understanding the dynamics present within single settings' (Eisenhardt, 1989: 533). Researchers can also choose to study a number of case studies that are theoretically interesting to compare and contrast – leading to a multiple case study (Eisenhardt, 1989). Single and multiple case studies are attractive designs for

family business research because they can be focused on the organizational unit of a family firm, or a small number of family firms. Case studies are important and particularly relevant to organizational studies because they provide the opportunity to study a contemporary phenomenon within its real-life context (Yin, 1993; 2003; Stake, 1995, 2006). Single case studies allow for in-depth understanding of one family firm. A comparative case study allows consideration of similarities and differences across family firms. In our article set case studies were very popular. Of the 78 studies identified, 67 used either single or multiple case study design.

A single case study is a common design for organizational studies using qualitative methods. In the set of studies identified here, there were 15 single case studies. These studies delved deeply into understanding processes or dynamics within one family business. We identified two exemplary articles based on qualitative methods with a single case design. (See Table 29.2 for exemplary articles associated with research designs and data collection strategy.) Dyck et al. (2002) focused on the process of succession over time and identified critical success factors of sequence, timing, technique and communication. Similarly, the single case design of Steen and Welch (2006) allowed an in-depth investigation of how the family perspective influenced responses to a prospective merger. A single case study can be ideal for gaining a deep understanding of dynamic processes or other phenomena. Flyvbjerg (2006) and Yin (2003) argue that findings from a single case study can be generalized to a larger population, however, many researchers believe that it is critical to employ a multiple case study design when generalizability is desired (Eisenhardt and Graebner, 2007). We see that there is a trade-off between depth and breadth. Single case studies allow researchers to develop in-depth perspectives on a phenomenon such as succession, but the extent to which the findings will apply in other family firms may not be clear. On the other hand, comparative case studies facilitate research breadth but cannot provide the same level of depth that is possible in single case studies.

Many family business researchers have chosen breadth over depth. In the set of qualitative articles we identified, 52 of the 78 articles were designed as comparative case studies. Data gathered from multiple sites helps to reduce concerns associated with a single case – that any one case may be somehow unique and therefore of little value in terms of contribution to the literature. Such concerns are particularly worrisome to those who take a more positivist ontological stance. By carefully setting up case comparisons with structurally equivalent analysis of each site, researchers can explain more about the phenomenon of interest as it occurs in multiple locations. For example, Kenyon-Rouvinez (2001) wanted to understand how (and why) serial business families recreated a series of operating businesses. She therefore sought out appropriate cases, following Eisenhardt's (1989) advice to be clear on initial definitions

and required characteristics of cases to be included in the study. Effective comparative case studies, such as this one, can enable meaningful comparisons across sites, convince readers that theory generated is more than a 'one-off phenomenon', and facilitate the development of new theory in areas that had previously been over-looked or black-boxed.

Overall, this set of studies shows that case studies can effectively investigate family business while maintaining an integrated consideration of context. Multiple case studies allow comparison across firms and their contexts; they can help to convince readers that findings and theories are more broadly generalizable. We see that both single and multiple case studies are important. Single case studies can provide rich data that leads to increased understanding of, for example, internal firm process or family business dynamics that are at the heart of family firm studies. More single case studies could provide the field with important insights and contribute to the development of new theory in this regard. Multiple case studies can also be effective in developing theory, but as illustrated in the exemplary articles (Table 29.2), cases must be carefully selected so that cross-case comparisons are meaningful and highlight the phenomena of interest.

Ethnographic Design

An ethnographic research design requires that researchers spend time observing and experiencing organizational life in a particular firm (or possibly firms). Ethnography is designed to provide a wealth of in-depth data that is ideal for developing 'rich insights into the human, social and organizational aspects of business organizations' (Myers, 2009: 92). This research approach is particularly suited to studying aspects of organizational culture, since it is only by experiencing organizational life, that the underlying values and beliefs commonly held by organizational members can even begin to be understood. Researchers must spend lengthy periods of time immersed in the

Table 29.2 Selected exemplars of qualitative family business studies

Research design	Data collection strategy	Author (journal, year)	Topic	Theory/concepts	Main findings and contribution
Single case study	Interviews	Dyck et al. (JBV, 2002)	The actual process of a failed executive succession in a small family firm	Executive succession, Relay race theory	The four factors of sequence, timing, baton-passing technique and communication influences succession success.
	Interviews, document review	Steen and Welch (FBR, 2006)	The responses of family firms to the emerging environment of mergers and acquisitions	Family embeddedness, network theory, international business	Family concerns are central to the responses by a family company faced with takeover. Acceding to acquisition can be a legitimate response rather than an endpoint for family firms.
Multiple case study	Interviews (group and individual interviews)	Haberman and Danes (FBR, 2007)	Comparison of father–daughter and father–son management transfer	Family dynamics based on FIRO theory (fundamental interpersonal relationship orientation theory)	Females in the father–son transfer experienced feelings of exclusion, and greater conflict among family members; females in the father–daughter transfer experienced feelings of inclusion and lower levels of conflict.
	Interviews, document review	Kenyon-Rouvinez (FBR, 2001)	Patterns in serial business families	Family business three-circle model, governance	Serial business families follow a three-stage process. The original business, in terms of family, ownership, business, and governance, has a strong influence on the next businesses created.
	Narrative (oral history data), interviews, document review	Tsui-Auch (Org Studies, 2005)	A comparative study of Indian and Chinese entrepreneurs and their subgroups in Singapore	Ethnic entrepreneurship	Chinese entrepreneurs were more likely to incorporate outsiders into their operational management and more likely to pursue unrelated diversification than their Indian counterparts. There is an intra-ethnic division in business structure among the ethnic Indians. Intra-ethnic structural differences are attributed to the subgroups' strength of ties to their region/dialect-based networks.
	Structured interviews	Vera and Dean (FBR, 2005)	An examination of the challenges daughters face in family business succession	Gender and succession	Daughter successors encountered employee rivalry, experienced work-life balance difficulties, and did not assume they would be the successor. Although successors reported few problems with their fathers upon succession, many experienced difficulties succeeding their mothers.
Ethnography	Observations	Jones and Craven (ISBJ, 2001)	The process of new knowledge acquisition in a mature manufacturing firm	Innovation networks, absorptive capacity	The absorptive capacity of any organization depends on the role of key boundary spanner who links the organization to its environment. Effective innovation is reliant on managers instituting appropriate mechanisms for the capture and sharing of information.

Research design	Data collection strategy	Author (journal, year)	Topic	Theory/concepts	Main findings and contribution
Interpretive approach/ grounded theory	Interviews, narratives	Parada and Viladas (JOCM, 2010)	How are core values successfully transmitted in family businesses via narratives?	Narrative, sense making, and the transmission of values	Narratives are a powerful device for transmitting values through generations. By telling stories, family businesses were able to build identity and shared meanings leading to successful performance in terms of revenues, reputation, shared identity, and continuity of the family business history.
	Semi-structured interviews, observations, document review	Mazzola et al. (FBR, 2008)	The issue of training next generation family members	Succession, strategic planning	Involving next generation family members in the strategic planning process provides the next generation with crucial tacit business knowledge and skills, facilitating interpersonal work relationships between incumbents and next-generation leaders and building credibility and legitimacy for the next generation.
	Group interviews	Blumentritt et al. (FBR, 2007)	How can a family firm create an environment that gives a non-family CEO the best opportunity to succeed?	Agency theory, stewardship theory	Successful non-family CEO engagements are characterized by the selection of an individual with both business and interpersonal competencies, and the support of both family business boards and councils.
Action research	Interviews, observations	Craig and Moores (JFBS, 2005)	Strategically aligning family and business systems using the balanced scorecard	Family business strategy, balanced scorecard (BSC)	In the family domain, the BSC assists in the education of, and communication among, family members. From a business system perspective, the BSC is a useful tool to link and align the family with the business.
	Interviews	Poza and Messer (FBR, 2001)	Spousal leadership and continuity in the family firm	Role of spouses	A typology of spouse styles and their possible influence on succession and continuity are presented.

Key:
ETP = Entrepreneurship: Theory and Practice
ERD= Entrepreneurship & Regional Development
FBR = Family Business Review
HR = Human Relations
ISBJ = International Small Business Journal
JBE = Journal of Business Ethics
JBR = Journal of Business Research
JBV = Journal of Business Venturing
JFBS = Journal of Family Business Strategy
JMS = Journal of Management Studies
JOCM = Journal of Organizational Change Management
LQ = The Leadership Quarterly
Org Studies = Organization Studies

organization, and typically generate very large volumes of data. As a result, it can be challenging for researchers to condense their data in ways that are appropriate for publication in organizational journals. However, it is certainly possible. Outside the field of family business, there are many examples of well-cited and even award winning articles. For example, Kellogg (2009) reported on an ethnographic study conducted in two hospital units. This article develops new theory about how institutionalized practices can be changed. Books are also an effective way to present such research, giving authors more space to show the volume and richness of the data.

So far there is only a small number of family business research articles published that are based on an ethnographic design. We identified only one such study (Jones and Craven, 2001) where the two authors were participant observers for two years in a family-owned manufacturing business to examine how absorptive capacity contributed to the firm's ability of innovation. They drew on their rich data to develop interesting new insights into how key boundary spanners encourage innovation in a firm. In addition, other studies in our dataset used participant observation as a component of case study or interpretive research. They are not categorized here since they primarily followed a different design, but it is important to note that ethnographic methods can be a component of other research designs, and can be very effective in generating additional contextual information that contributes to a more full understanding of the organization and its context.

We hope that more ethnographic research on family firms will be conducted and published. There are many unanswered questions about family firms that relate to organizational culture – for example, how family values become entwined with those of the business, or how values of the founding generation are passed on to those that follow. Graduate students, in particular, should be encouraged to include at least some ethnographic component of their dissertation work. By taking the time and energy required to engage in ethnographic work, researchers can gain valuable information about context, how things really work inside a firm, and therefore have the groundwork in place to push forward with developing new and important theoretical contributions to the field of family business and perhaps the organizational literature more broadly.

Interpretive or Grounded Theory Design

Although there are differences between grounded theory and an interpretive research approach, we consider them together here since both are based on an underlying principle that new theory emerges from the data as researchers engage in intensive data analysis. Researchers themselves are integral components of the research process, and it is the engagement of researchers with their data that leads to important new insights. To illustrate some of the differences: an interpretive research design is one where researchers seek to understand a phenomenon through the interpretation of meanings (Nordqvist et al., 2009), while grounded theory (in its original presentation) begins with a blank slate and researchers gather data following a constant comparative process to identify important themes for further analysis (Glaser and Strauss, 1967; Locke, 2001). More recent versions of grounded theory do not suggest that researchers start without any preconceived ideas of what they are looking for or what they will find. In organization studies that is simply not reasonable or feasible (Suddaby, 2006). Instead, grounded theory is best described as 'a qualitative research method that seeks to develop theory that is grounded in data systematically gathered and analyzed'. Furthermore, 'there should be a continuous interplay between data collection and analysis' (Myers, 2009: 106). These same principles are now commonly used to describe interpretivist research (Nordqvist et al., 2009).

Whether the research design is labeled interpretive or grounded study, this type of research is one where researchers are primarily interested in gaining an in-depth understanding of 'something' (for example, succession, father–daughter relationships, firm failure). In order to gain this knowledge, researchers gather the best data to answer their research questions. Although there is certainly overlap between a multiple case study design, for example, and an interpretive design, for the purposes of this classification, we considered whether researchers set up their study primarily to understand 'something' or to compare a number of family firms with regard to 'something'.

We identified seven articles where an interpretive research design (including a grounded theory design) was used. In these articles, the researchers wanted to understand questions such as maintaining successful business relationships (Cole and Johnson, 2007), how women succeed in family business (Curimbaba, 2002), how new leaders succeed in family firms (DeNoble et al., 2007), how next-generation family members are trained (Mazzola et al., 2008) and how core values can be transmitted across generations (Parada and Viladas, 2010). In conducting these studies, the researchers drew on the rich qualitative data to develop new theory about, for example, the importance of story-telling as a way to transmit family values (Parada and Viladas, 2010), or new conceptual models of role dynamics within family firms (Curimbaba, 2002). It is this type of study that is highly likely to provide insights into micro-processes of interpersonal dynamics that helps to improve the theory base of family business research, and potentially organization theory more broadly.

Action Research Design

Action research is designed to solve particular organizational problems and allow researchers to study the process of change as it unfolds (Myers, 2009; Patton, 2002). It requires a very high degree of cooperation between the research team and the research subjects because each relies on the other for success. Unlike other types of research, action research is based on deliberative intervention by researchers and continued engagement in the intervention. The tight connection between researchers and subjects is sometimes criticized for leading to a lack of objectivity; however, it is this very closeness to the subject of study that can lead to otherwise unrealized new insights that make significant contributions to our knowledge about organizational issues.

In the set of articles considered here, we identified three that are based on action research. Each of them report on findings generated through engaged interactions with a single family firm (Craig and Moores, 2005, 2010) or with a group of workshop participants (Poza and Messer, 2001). In particular, and as set out in Table 29.2, Craig and Moores (2005) worked with a family firm implementing a balanced scorecard (BSC) approach to strategic decision-making. As a result of their close working relationship with the firm, they were able to gain in-depth and interesting information about how processes of education and communication were integrated with the BSC. Through these insights, the researchers further developed theories concerning the role of a BSC in aligning the family with the business.

Action research remains relatively rare but offers a number of advantages for family business researchers who often have excellent working relationships with particular family firms. Of course, these cannot be consulting arrangements where the only objective is to improve firm performance. Instead, the goals of research (contribution to knowledge) must be primary. But when the appropriate conditions of action research are met, the result can be actionable knowledge for the participating family firm(s) or family members in the short run, and more broadly usable knowledge in the longer run through publications and theory development. More research of this type seems highly desirable.

DATA COLLECTION TECHNIQUES

After choosing a research design, researchers decide on the type of data to collect. We discuss each of the following data types and report our findings in terms of family business studies – whether we see the use of all data types or combinations.

Interviews

Overall, qualitative researchers tend to rely heavily on data collected through interviews. That was certainly the case in the articles analyzed here. Seventy-five of the 78 studies used interview data – either alone or in combination with other data sources. The extent to which interview data was used is somewhat surprising; however, since an inherent interest in family businesses is the people who own, manage or work in them, the focus on interview data makes good sense. For researchers to understand what is going on in family businesses, it is important to ask knowledgeable people for their views, observations and opinions. As Myers (2009: 121) puts it, 'A good interview helps us to focus on the subject's world'. It provides an opportunity for researchers to gather rich data that helps them understand issues from different perspectives and to see more deeply into the dynamics of organizational life than would otherwise be possible (Fontana and Frey, 2000).

Interviews can be categorized into three basic types – structured, unstructured and semi-structured. The choice should match with the research question. Structured interviews use a series of pre-developed questions that the interviewer usually asks in a specified order. These interviews come close to survey design because there is little (if any) room to deviate from the script. The disadvantage of structured interviews is that there is little room for improvisation or consideration of new unexpected ideas. They are used when consistency across interviews is paramount, for example when comparing across family firms is a prime research objective. Unstructured interviews, at the other end of

the spectrum, are designed to maximize the interviewee's freedom to respond. They are appropriate when researchers want to gain a broad understanding of what interviewees consider important, or when probing deeply held beliefs or values where lengthy (and potentially rambling) responses may be required to evoke thoughtful responses. The downside of unstructured interviews is the potential for such unstructured responses that they are of minimal value for research purposes. Interviewers must be particularly skilled to keep interviewees on point and to encourage non-talkative individuals to expand on short answers. The third type of interview – semi-structured – is in the middle of the other two. Interviews are set up with a list of questions to be asked; however, interviewers try to encourage a variety of open-ended responses and have flexibility to deviate from the order. In many ways semi-structured interviews offer the best of both worlds and tend to minimize the disadvantages of each. They can facilitate comparison across family firms through a structured interview guide and they allow room (within the structure) to elicit broad, and potentially unexpected, responses from interviewees.

In the articles analyzed here, authors did not always indicate the type of interviews they conducted; however, semi-structured interviews were the most commonly reported. Only two studies (Dyer and Mortensen, 2005; Vera and Dean, 2005) indicated the use of structured interviews and eight studies reported using unstructured interviews. All others (65 studies) did not state the type or reported semi-structured interviews. This 'middle of the road' approach (semi-structured) is not particularly surprising given the obvious appeal of minimizing the downsides of structured or unstructured interviews while still allowing for thoughtful responses. This approach also matches with the high prevalence of multiple case studies where cross-comparisons are desired. (Although as the number of cases increases, we would expect more structured interviews to be used to allow comparison.) There is a large degree of variation in the open-endedness of semi-structured interviews conducted. However, our review suggests that more open-ended and unstructured interviews could facilitate the investigation of deeply held values and complex dynamics of family and business that underlie many currently unanswered questions.

Participant Observation

Many qualitative research studies incorporate fieldwork or participant observation (we use these terms synonymously) into the data collection strategy. The goal of participant observation is 'to gather qualitative data about the social world by interacting with people and observing them in their own 'natural' setting (Myers, 2009). This data collection strategy thus requires the researcher to spend time in the organization to experience how people go about their everyday work. Unlike interviews that occur at designated times and in at least partial isolation from the workplace, participant observation occurs in real time. Thus researchers have an opportunity to observe activities and interactions (not only hear about them in interviews). Researchers may also be able to engage in informal conversations and hear 'unofficial' in addition to 'official' stories. All of this informal data can help the researcher to understand issues from multiple perspectives.

An ethnographic study might be based only on participant observations, but more commonly in organizational studies, observation is used to supplement (or contrast with) data collected through interviews or document analysis. We indentified 22 family business articles where authors reported the use of participant observation data in addition to that collected through interviews and document review. These studies incorporated observations where researchers watched people interact as part of organizational life. The following excerpt from Mazzola et al. (2008: 245) illustrates this data collection strategy:

> Second, we obtained our data from the direct field observations. In 13 out of the 18 companies

the researchers had the opportunity to assist at one or two meetings and working sessions where the next generation received information for preparing the strategic plan and their presentations and/or where the family had to make decisions.

In addition to observing, researchers must make field notes to record their observations. Sometimes this can be done while observations are taking place. For example, researchers can take notes while they are sitting in on a meeting. However, this is sometimes too distracting for the meeting participants, in which case researchers might find that they must write notes immediately following the meeting. This is, of course, quite difficult to do. In either case, the important point is that observations are recorded and can then be analyzed alongside other types of data (Patton, 2002). In the studies analyzed here, note-taking was not well explained and it was rare to see any actual traces of data from observations in the data analysis section. Instead, researchers seemed to be using the observational data as background material rather than data to be analyzed. We note that by giving more attention to field notes (especially in terms of reporting observations) researchers can present their work in ways that show the importance of context. Participant observation is one of the few opportunities where researchers can come close to 'seeing things as they really are'. However, in order to take advantage of such opportunities, researchers must take notes that can then be systematically used as data. More attention to this aspect of data collection could improve our knowledge of organizational life in family firms.

Documents and Other Recordings

Almost every organization records a substantial amount of information about itself. This is done through written documents (paper or electronic), pictures and sound or video recordings. In addition, there is often a large amount of information about an organization that is recorded by others. All of this can be excellent data for qualitative researchers, but it is sometimes difficult to access such materials. It can also be a time-consuming task to organize and systematically analyze the data. However, qualitative research based wholly or partly on this type of data can provide rich insights into processes that individuals within the organization do not understand because of their limited perspective. Documents allow researchers to consider time horizons that are longer than a typical research study, and even longer than a particular individual's lifespan. As such, they are highly suited for family business researchers who are interested in long term trends or multiple generation of ownership.

In the set of articles analyzed here, we found only one that drew exclusively on document analysis (Ibrahim et al., 2001). In this study the authors collected public documents about a single family firm and analyzed the text chronologically to understand how succession occurred through multiple generations. Other studies in our set of articles also used document data, but they did so as a supplement to interview or observational data. However, similar to our comments about observation data above, when authors added document data to interview data, they tended to report relatively little in terms of how they systematically identified, organized (and ultimately analyzed) the data. This is somewhat of a missed opportunity, since it is the systematic analysis of documents that can bring new concepts to the fore.

Narrative

Although some consider narrative analysis as a special category of qualitative research, we categorize it here as a data collection strategy because research of this type relies on the collection and analysis of narratives (stories). Narrative data could be collected as part of a research design described above (case study, ethnographic, interpretive/grounded theory, or action research). The critical component of narrative analysis is the unit of analysis – the narrative. Researchers must be focused on narratives as they gather data, but narratives can be collected in different ways. First,

and perhaps most commonly, researchers can ask people to tell stories in an interview format. This strategy should be pre-planned. That is, interviews should be designed to elicit narratives rather than the accidental occurrence of story-telling (Gabriel, 2000; Czarniawaska, 2004). Sometimes the entire interview, or several interviews, is considered a narrative (for instance, life stories). In other cases, a portion of the interview is designed so that respondents tell a short story about a particular issue (such as, examples of overcoming financial adversity). These short stories are sometimes called vignettes (Miles and Huberman, 1994). The second way of collecting narratives is through the analysis of documents or other archival data. Primary sources such as diaries or autobiographies can be used. Less commonly, researchers use secondary sources such as biographies, magazine articles or historical texts.

Narrative analysis is of increasing interest in organization studies generally and entrepreneurship in particular (Larty and Hamilton, 2011). Researchers have collected and analyzed narratives to provide important new insights into the motivations and activities of entrepreneurs (for example, Dodd, 2002; Martens et al., 2007). This interest in narrative studies is only beginning to appear in family business research. In the set of articles analyzed here, we identified five empirical studies based on narrative analysis (Hamilton, 2006; Parada and Viladas, 2010; Tsui-Auch, 2004, 2005; Watson, 2009). Each of these studies brings a new understanding of family dynamics to light – such as deeply held feelings regarding generational transfer and identity concerns within family relationships. Clearly, narrative analysis holds excellent promise for future work.

ANALYZING DATA

In addition to collecting data systematically, qualitative researchers must also explain how they have systematically analyzed their data. There are a multitude of reference books on qualitative analysis. All of them provide helpful guidance, and following any of them (and referencing those sources in the manuscript) will help to convince readers that the author has engaged in scholarly work rather than anecdotal reporting. Commonly used references for family business case studies are Eisenhardt (1989), and Yin (2003). Less commonly used, but more appropriate for in-depth interpretive analyses of single cases (in our view) is Stake (1995, 2006). In the interpretive/grounded theory studies, authors referred to Creswell (1998), Glaser and Strauss (1967) and Lincoln and Guba (1985) to justify the analytic techniques employed. Although there are exceptions (see Cole and Johnson, 2007, for a positive example), analysis procedures tended to be under-reported in that the methodology or data analysis section did not give the reader a clear picture of how researchers analyzed their data. This is particularly evident when researchers report that they gathered multiple sources of data, but neglect to explain how they analyzed anything other than the interview data. Part of the reason for this under-reporting is the constraining limit on number of pages, but we believe that qualitative researchers are wise to improve the information provided about data analysis. With more full explanations, reviewers can better evaluate the strengths of a qualitative methodological choice.

We rarely found that authors reported the use of qualitative analysis software (for example, AtlasTI or NVivo). (A notable exception is Salvato et al., 2010, where their use of analysis software is well explained.) With the growing use of qualitative analysis software, we see that using it and reporting on how it was used is increasingly important. Although using qualitative software is certainly not a requirement, it does help researchers to manage the analysis work of developing categories and understanding relationships among the different categories. It also helps researchers show readers (and reviewers) that they have engaged in systematic analysis of their data.

Our final point regarding data analysis is a more general one. Qualitative research can appear mysterious and thus become targeted as unscientific. That is simply not the case. There is now a strong foundation supporting qualitative methods, including articles that provide helpful guidance about how to generate new insights 'abductively' from systematically gathered qualitative data (for example, Alvesson and Skoldberg, 2000; Locke et al., 2008; Nordqvist et al., 2009). Van de Ven (2007) described abduction as the conjecture or hypothesis researchers use to explain anomaly or surprises encountered. Locke et al. (2008) pointed out that doubt acts as the engine of abduction, providing advice for researchers to purposefully foster doubts in the research process. Data analysis is typically a sticking point for qualitative researchers – it is difficult to think abductively (move from data to theory), and difficult to describe the process in a journal article. We believe that the more clearly researchers are able to carry out this component of qualitative research, the more successful they will be in developing high quality articles.

WRITING UP FINDINGS AND PUBLISHING THE RESEARCH

Qualitative research commonly results in large volumes of data and potentially book-length (rather than the required article-length) findings. Crafting an article for a peer-reviewed journal can be a daunting task. Similar to all research, it must tell a succinct and interesting story while also making a contribution to theory (Reay and Whetten, 2011). The articles analyzed here have successfully gone through the peer-review process (and likely been improved as a result). To varying degrees, they all make a contribution to theory about family business. That is, they change the way we think about family firms. For example, Parada et al. (2010) extend existing theory about how the institutional environment affects family firms – showing the (previously unrecognized) strong role that professional associations can play in the transformation of family firm values. Cole and Johnson (2007) provide another example of contribution to theory. These authors showed that (contrary to previous theoretical models) successful post-divorce copreneur relationships required more than tangible, practical resources such as financial capital, they particularly required multiple intangible emotional factors such as trust. In terms of books or articles that can help other researchers develop publishable articles based on qualitative data, Chenail (2009) provides suggestions specifically focused on family business studies. Golden-Biddle and Locke (2007) is another resource we highly recommend. This book is based on the authors' and other researchers' experiences with the process of publishing qualitative research. It provides pragmatic and insightful advice for researchers – focusing on the importance of telling a story and developing organizational theory from that empirical story.

LOOKING FORWARD

In summary, we believe that the future looks bright for family business scholars interested in developing and using qualitative research methods. The groundwork is set. As we have shown here, there are examples of all types of qualitative research published in family business or entrepreneurship journals. There are also a few studies published in broader organizational journals. The appropriate standards for qualitative approaches are becoming more widely understood and appreciated by journal editors and reviewers. In fact, most journals have identified particular associate editors and reviewers with interest and experience in qualitative methodology, ensuring that qualitative research studies are reviewed by knowledgeable individuals. We see all of these advancements as a promising foundation that family business scholars can build upon.

More specifically, we see significant opportunities for advancement in terms of process research – how things happen over time (Langley, 1999; Van de Ven and Poole, 1995). As we have shown in our review of the literature, qualitative methods are particularly helpful in addressing the 'how' questions that are fundamental to process research. This type of research stands in contrast to a variation approach where specific variables are identified and measured to determine, for example, conditions under which successful generational transfer is most likely to occur. In contrast, process studies of generational transfer might focus on how founders establish a culture that supports transfer of the business, or how family business advisors work with family members to develop trusting relationships leading to generational transfer. In addition to succession, qualitative methodology can help to answer many important but so far insufficiently answered questions about family firm processes. For example, we still know little about how dynamics among family members impact strategic decision-making, or how some family leaders work very effectively with non-family managers over lengthy periods of time.

We encourage future researchers to engage in in-depth qualitative studies based on various combinations of interview, ethnographic, narrative or documentary data analysis because we see this as vital to the future of family business studies. Well-designed and appropriately implemented qualitative studies will help in developing a much stronger understanding of critical family firm processes that will in turn contribute to the literature by filling significant gaps in our knowledge about the behavior of family firms.

As the field of family business studies continues to mature, we see increasing opportunities for family business research to contribute to the larger organizational literature. Research based on qualitative methodology is particularly well placed for this next important step because family firms provide an excellent setting to address many of the current puzzles in organization theory. For example, institutional theorists are currently engaged in questions about how multiple (and potentially conflicting) societal logics are effectively managed at the organizational level (see Greenwood et al., 2011, for further discussion). Family firms must consistently manage the interface between family and business logics. In addition, they may also be influenced by logics associated with the state or religion. Further research in this regard based on qualitative data could contribute to the development of important new theory about the role of multiple logics in institutional change.

In addition, the long duration of many family firms makes them excellent settings for longitudinal studies that contribute to organizational theory development. For example, theory based on the resource based view of the firm could be advanced by qualitative studies of family firms examining how unusual resources (for example, family relationships) can be drawn on to advance firm competitiveness. Similarly, studies of family firms that have survived over many generations may provide opportunities for researchers to build new theory about how tacit knowledge held by people within a firm can be used as a long term resource to maintain competitive advantage over lengthy periods of time. These examples show how studies of family business can be used to develop theory more broadly. We hope that more researchers will take advantage of such opportunities, increasing the number of family business studies appearing in mainstream organizational journals.

CONCLUSIONS

We note that many of the important questions about family business concern processes or dynamics within the firm or those that connect the family firm with its environment. These are largely questions of 'how?' and 'why?' that can best be answered with qualitative methodology. The 78 articles identified and analyzed here show that excellent work has been done, but we still need more – more in terms of volume and in journal placement. We hope that this review provides encouragement for qualitative research and helps researchers identify opportunities for further research.

REFERENCES

Ainsworth, S. and Cox, J. (2003) 'Families divided: Culture and control in small family business', *Organization Studies*, 24(9): 1463–1485.

Alvesson, M. and Sköldberg, K. (2000) *Reflexive Methodology: New Vistas for Qualitative Research*. London: Sage.

Andersson, T., Carlsen, J. and Getz, D. (2002) 'Family business goals in the tourism and hospitality sector: Case studies and cross-case analysis from Australia, Canada, and Sweden', *Family Business Review*, 15(2): 89–106.

Bachkaniwala, D., Wright, M. and Ram, M. (2001) 'Succession in south Asian family businesses in the UK', *International Small Business Journal*, 19(4): 15–27.

Berger, P.L. and Luckmann, T. (1966) *The Social Construction of Reality*. New York: Doubleday.

Bhalla, A., Henderson, S. and Watkins, D. (2006) 'A multiparadigmatic perspective of strategy: A case study of an ethnic family firm', *International Small Business Journal*, 24(5): 515–537.

Blumentritt, T., Keyt, A. and Astrachan, J. (2007) 'Creating an environment for successful nonfamily CEOs: An exploratory study of good principals', *Family Business Review*, 20(4): 321–335.

Boutilier, R. (2009) 'Globalization and the careers of Mexican knowledge workers: An exploratory study of employer and worker adaptations', *Journal of Business Ethics*, 88(2): 319–333.

Cabrera-Suarez, K. (2005) 'Leadership transfer and the successor's development in the family firm', *The Leadership Quarterly*, 16(1): 71–96.

Cadieux, L. (2007) 'Succession in small and medium-sized family businesses: Toward a typology of predecessor roles during and after instatement of the successor', *Family Business Review*, 20(2): 95–109.

Cadieux, L., Lorrain, J. and Hugron, P. (2002) 'Succession in women-owned family businesses: A case study', *Family Business Review*, 15(1): 17–30.

Cater, J. and Justis, R. (2009) 'The development of successors from followers to leaders in small family firms: An exploratory study', *Family Business Review*, 22(2): 109–124.

Cater, J. and Schwab, A. (2008) 'Turnaround strategies in established small family firms', *Family Business Review*, 21(1): 31–50.

Chenail, R. (2009) 'Communicating your qualitative research better', *Family Business Review*, 22(2): 105–108.

Chirico, F. (2008) 'Knowledge accumulation in family firms', *International Small Business Journal*, 26(4): 433–462.

Chirico, F. and Nordqvist, M. (2010) 'Dynamic capabilities and trans-generational value creation in family firms: The role of organizational culture', *International Small Business Journal*, 28(5): 487–504.

Chrisman, J., Kellermanns, F., Chan, K. and Liano, K. (2010) 'Intellectual foundations of current research in family business: An identification and review of 25 influential articles', *Family Business Review*, 23(1): 9–26.

Cole, P. and Johnson, K. (2007) 'An explanation of successful copreneurial relationships postdivorce', *Family Business Review*, 20(3): 185–198.

Craig, J. and Moores, K. (2005) 'Balanced scorecards to drive the strategic planning of family firms', *Family Business Review*, 18(2): 105–122.

Craig, J. and Moores, K. (2010) 'Strategically aligning family and business systems using the balanced scorecard', *Journal of Family Business Strategy*, 1(2): 78–87.

Creswell, J.W. (1998) *Qualitative Inquiry and Research Design: Choosing among Five Traditions*. Thousand Oaks, CA: Sage.

Curimbaba, F. (2002) 'The dynamics of women's roles as family business managers', *Family Business Review*, 15(3): 239–252.

Czarniawaska, B. (2004) *Narratives in Social Science Research*. London: Sage.

Debicki, B., Matherne, C., Kellermanns, F. and Chrisman, J. (2009) 'Family business research in the new millennium', *Family Business Review*, 22(2): 151–166.

DeNoble, A., Ehrlich, S. and Singh, G. (2007) 'Toward the development of a family business self-efficacy scale: A resource-based perspective', *Family Business Review*, 20(2): 127–140.

Denzin, N.K. and Lincoln, Y.S. (eds) (2000) *Handbook of Qualitative Research*, 2nd edn. London: Sage. (1st edn, 1994.)

Dielemjan, M. and Sachs, W. (2008) 'Coevolution of institutions and corporations in emerging economies: How the salim group morphed into an institution of suharto's crony regime', *Journal of Management Studies*, 45(7): 1274–1300.

Dodd, D. (2002) 'Metaphors and meaning: A grounded cultural model of us entrepreneurship', *Journal of Business Venturing*, 17 (5): 519–535.

Dunn, B. (1999) 'The family factor: The impact of family relationship dynamics on business-owning families during transitions', *Family Business Review*, 12(1): 41–60.

Dyck, B., Mauws, M., Starke, F. and Mischke, G. (2002) 'Passing the baton: The importance of sequence, timing, technique and communication in executive succession', *Journal of Business Venturing*, 17(2): 143–162.

Dyer, W.G. and Mortensen, S. (2005) 'Entrepreneurship and family business in a hostile environment: The case of Lithuania', *Family Business Review*, 18(3): 247–258.

Eisenhardt, K. (1989) 'Building theories from case study research', *Academy of Management Review*, 14(4): 532–550.

Eisenhardt, K.M. and Graebner, M.E. (2007) 'Theory building from cases: Opportunities and Challenges', *Academy of Management Journal*, 50(1): 25–32.

Farias, S., Nataraajan, R. and Kovacs, E. (2009) 'Global business partnering among family-owned enterprises', *Journal of Business Research*, 62(6): 667–672.

Fletcher, D. (2010) 'Life-making or risk taking? Co-preneurship and family business start-ups', *International Small Business Journal*, 28(5): 452–469.

Flyvbjerg, B. (2006) 'Five misunderstandings about case-study research', *Qualitative Inquiry*, 12(2): 219–245.

Fontana, A. and Frey, J.H. (2000) 'The interview: From structured questions to negotiated text', in K. Norman Denzin and S. Yvnna Lincoln (eds), *Handbook of Qualitative Research*, 2nd edn. Thousand Oaks, CA: Sage, pp. 645–672. (1st edn, 1994.)

Gabriel, Y. (2000) *Storytelling in Organizations: Facts, Fictions, and Fantasies*. London: Oxford.

García-Álvarez, E. and López-Sintas, J. (2001) 'A taxonomy of founders based on values: The root of family business heterogeneity', *Family Business Review*, 14(3): 209–230.

Gephart, R. (2004) 'From the editors: Qualitative research and the Academy of Management Journal', *Academy of Management Journal*, 47(4): 454–462.

Gilding, M. (2000) 'Family business and family change: Individual autonomy, democratization, and the new family business institutions', *Family Business Review*, 13(3): 239–250.

Glaser, B.G. and Strauss, A.L. (1967) *The Discovery of Grounded Theory: Strategies for Qualitative Research*. Chicago, IL: Aldine.

Golden-Biddle, K. and Locke, K. (2007) *Composing Qualitative Research*. Thousand Oaks, CA: Sage.

Graves, C. and Thomas, J. (2008) 'Determinants of the internationalization pathways of family firms: An examination of family influence', *Family Business Review*, 21(2): 151–167.

Greenwood, R., Raynard, M., Farah, K., Micelotta, E. and Lounsbury, M. (2011) 'Institutional complexity and organizational responses', *Academy of Management Annals*, 5(1): 317–371.

Haberman, H. and Danes, S. (2007) 'Father-daughter and father-son family business management transfer comparison: Family FIRO model application', *Family Business Review*, 20(2): 163–184.

Hall, A., Melin, L. and Nordqvist, M. (2001) 'Entrepreneurship as radical change in the family business: Exploring the role of cultural patterns', *Family Business Review*, 14(3): 193–208.

Hall, A. and Nordqvist, M. (2008) 'Professional management in family business: Toward an extended understanding', *Family Business Review*, 21(1): 51–69.

Hamilton, E. (2006) 'Whose story is it anyway? Narrative accounts of the role of women in founding and establishing family businesses', *International Small Business Journal*, 24(3): 253–271.

Howorth, C., and Ali, Z. (2001) 'Family business succession in Portugal: An examination of case studies in the furniture industry', *Family Business Review*, 14(3): 231–244.

Howorth, C., Westhead, P. and Wright, M. (2004) 'Buyouts, information asymmetry and the family management dyad', *Journal of Business Venturing*, 19(4): 509–234.

Ibrahim, A., Soufani, K. and Lam, J. (2001) 'A study of succession in a family firm', *Family Business Review*, 14(3): 245–258.

Irava, W. and Moores, K. (2010) 'Clarifying the strategic advantage of familiness: Unbundling its dimensions and highlighting its paradoxes', *Journal of Family Business Strategy*, 1(3): 131–144.

Janjuha-Jivraj, S. and Woods, A. (2002) 'Successional issues within Asian family firms: Learning from the Kenyan experience', *International Small Business Journal*, 20(1): 77–94.

Johannisson, B. and Huse, M. (2000) 'Recruiting outside board members in the small family business: an ideological challenge', *Entrepreneurship and Regional Development*, 12(4): 353–378.

Jones, O. and Craven, M. (2001) 'Expanding capabilities in a mature manufacturing firm: Absorptive capacity and the TCS', *International Small Business Journal*, 19(4): 39–55.

Karra, N., Tracey, P. and Philips, N. (2006) 'Altruism and agency in the family firm: Exploring the role of family kinship, and ethnicity', *Entrepreneurship: Theory and Practice*, 30(6): 861–877.

Kellogg, K. (2009) 'Operating room: Relational spaces and microinstitutional change in surgery', *American Sociological Review*, 115(3): 657–711.

Kenyon-Rouvinez, D. (2001) 'Patterns in serial business families: Theory building through global case study research', *Family Business Review*, 14(3): 175–192.

Khavul, S., Bruton, G. and Wood, E. (2009) 'Informal family business in Africa', *Entrepreneurship: Theory and Practice*, 33(6): 1219–1238.

Krefting, L. (1991) 'Rigour in Qualitative Research: The assessment of trustworthiness', *The American Journal of Occupational Therapy*, 45(3): 214–222.

Lambrecht, J. (2005) 'Multigenerational transition in family businesses: A new explanatory model', *Family Business Review*, 18(4): 267–282.

Lambrecht, J. and Lievens, J. (2008) 'Pruning the family tree: An unexplored path to family business continuity and family harmony', *Family Business Review*, 21(4): 295–313.

Langley, A. (1999) 'Strategies for theorizing from process data', *Academy of Management Review*, 24(4): 691–710.

Larty, J. and Hamilton, E. (2011) 'Structural approaches to narrative analysis in entrepreneurship research: Exemplars from two researchers', *International Small Business Journal*, 29(3): 220–237.

Lee, J. and Tan, F. (2001) 'Growth of Chinese family enterprises in Singapore', *Family Business Review*, 14(1): 49–74.

Lee, T.W. (1999) *Using Qualitative Methods in Organizational Research*. Thousand Oaks, CA: Sage.

Lincoln, Y.S. and Guba, E.G. (1985) *Naturalistic Inquiry*. Beverly Hills, CA: Sage.

Litz, R. (2010) 'Jamming across the generations: Creative intergenerational collaboration in the Marsalis family', *Journal of Family Business Strategy*, 1(4): 185–199.

Locke, K. (2001) *Grounded Theory in Management Research*. London: Sage.

Locke, K., Golden-Biddle, K. and Feldman, M. (2008) 'Making doubt generative: Rethinking the role of doubt in the research process', *Organization Science*, 19(6): 907–918.

Manikutty, S. (2000) 'Family business groups in India: A resource-based view of the emerging trends', *Family Business Review*, 13(4): 279–292.

Marchisio, G., Mazzola, P., Sciascia, S., Miles, M. and Astrachan, J. (2010) 'Corporate venturing in family business: The effects on the family and its members', *Entrepreneurship and Regional Development*, 22(3–4): 349–377.

Martens, M., Jennings, J. and Jennings, P. (2007) 'Do the stories they tell get them the money they need? The role of entrepreneurial narratives in resource acquisition', *Academy of Management Journal*, 50(5): 1107–1132.

Mazzola, P., Marchisio, G. and Astrachan, J. (2008) 'Strategic planning in family business: A powerful developmental tool for the next generation', *Family Business Review*, 21(3): 239–258.

Mickelson, R. and Worley, C. (2003) 'Acquiring a family firm: A case study', *Family Business Review*, 16(4): 251–268.

Miles, M.B. and Huberman, M.A. (1994) *Qualitative Data Analysis*, 2nd edn. Thousand Oaks, CA: Sage. (1st edn, 1984.)

Miller, D., Steier, L. and Breton-Miller, I. (2003) 'Lost in time: Intergenerational succession, change, and failure in family business', *Journal of Business Venturing*, 18(4): 513–531.

Murray, B. (2003) 'The succession transition process: A longitudinal perspective', *Family Business Review*, 16(1): 17–34.

Myers, M.D. (2009) *Qualitative Research in Business and Management*. London: Sage Publications.

Ng, W. and Keasy, K. (2010) 'Growing beyond smallness: How do small, closely controlled firms survive?', *International Small Business Journal*, 28(6): 620–630.

Ng, W. and Roberts, J. (2007) 'Helping the family: The mediating role of outside directors in ethnic Chinese family firms', *Human Relations*, 60(2): 285–314.

Niemelä, T. (2004) 'Interfirm cooperation capability in the context of networking family firms: The role of power', *Family Business Review*, 17(4): 319–330.

Nordqvist, M., Hall, A. and Melin, L. (2009) 'Qualitative research on family businesses: The relevance and usefulness of the interpretive approach', *Journal of Management & Organization*, 15(3): 294–308.

Nordqvist, M. and Melin, L. (2008) 'Strategic planning champions: Social craftspersons, artful interpreters and known strangers', *Long Range Planning*, 43(3): 326–344.

Nordqvist, M. and Melin, L. (2010) 'The promise of the strategy as practice perspective for family business strategy research', *Journal of Family Business Strategy*, 1(1): 15–25.

Parada, M., Nordqvist, M. and Gimeno, A. (2010) 'Institutionalizing the family business: The role of professional associations in fostering a change of values', *Family Business Review*, 23(4): 355–372.

Parada, M. and Viladas, H. (2010) 'Narratives: A powerful device for values transmission in family businesses', *Journal of Organizational Change Management*, 23(2): 166–172.

Patton, M.Q. (2002) *Qualitative Research and Evaluation Methods*. Thousand Oaks, CA: Sage.

Perricone, P., Earle, J. and Taplin, I. (2001) 'Patterns of succession and continuity in family-owned businesses: Study of an ethnic community', *Family Business Review*, 14(2): 105–122.

Poza, E. and Messer, T. (2001) 'Spousal leadership and continuity in the family firm', *Family Business Review*, 14(1): 25–36.

Ram, M. (2001) 'Family dynamics in a small consultancy firm: A case study', *Human Relations*, 54(4): 395–418.

Reay, T. and Whetten, D. (2011) 'What constitutes a theoretical contribution in family business?', *Family Business Review*, 24(2): 105–110.

Salvato, C., Chirico, F. and Sharma, P. (2010) 'A farewell to the business: Championing exit and continuity in entrepreneurial family firms', *Entrepreneurship & Regional Development*, 22(3–4): 321–348.

Salvato, C. and Melin, L. (2008) 'Creating value across generations in family-controlled businesses: The role of family social capital', *Family Business Review*, 21(3): 259–276.

Stake, R.E. (1995) *The Art of Case Study Research*. Thousand Oaks, CA: Sage.

Stake, R.E. (2006) *Multiple Case Study Analysis*. New York: Guilford.

Steen, A. and Welch, L. (2006) 'Dancing with giants: Acquisition and survival of the family firm', *Family Business Review*, 19(4): 289–300.

Steier, L. (2001) 'Next-generation entrepreneurs and succession: An exploratory study of modes and means of managing social capital', *Family Business Review*, 14(3): 259–276.

Steier, L. (2007) 'New venture creation and organization: A familial sub-narrative', *Journal of Business Research*, 60(10): 1099–1107.

Steier, L. and Miller, D. (2010) 'Pre-and post-succession governance philosophies in entrepreneurial family firms', *Journal of Family Business Strategy*, 1(3): 145–154.

Suddaby, R. (2006) 'What grounded theory is not', *Academy of Management Journal*, 49(4): 633–642.

Tan, W. and Fock, S. (2001) 'Coping with growth transitions: The case of Chinese family businesses in Singapore', *Family Business Review*, 14(2): 123–140.

Thomas, J. (2002) 'Freeing the shackles of family business ownership', *Family Business Review*, 15(4): 321–336.

Tokarczyk, J., Hansen, E., Green, M. and Down, J. (2007) 'A resource-based view and market orientation theory examination of the role of "familiness" in family business success', *Family Business Review*, 20(1): 17–31.

Tsang, E. (2001) 'Internationalizing the family firm: A case study of a Chinese family business', *Journal of Small Business Management*, 39(1): 88–94.

Tsang, E. (2002) 'Learning from overseas venturing experience: The case of Chinese family businesses', *Journal of Business Venturing*, 17(1): 21–40.

Tsui-Auch, L. (2004) 'The professionally managed family-ruled enterprise: Ethnic Chinese business in Singapore', *Journal of Management Studies*, 41(4): 693–723.

Tsui-Auch, L. (2005) 'Unpacking regional ethnicity and the strength of ties in shaping ethnic entrepreneurship', *Organization Studies*, 26(8):1189–1216.

Van der Heyden, L., Blondel, C. and Carlock, R. (2005) 'Fair process: Striving for justice in family business', *Family Business Review*, 18(1): 1–21.

Van de Ven, A.H. (2007) *Engaged Scholarship*. New York: Oxford University Press.

Van de Ven, A.H. and Poole, M.S. (1995) 'Explaining development and change in organizations', *Academy of Management Review*, 20(3): 510–540.

Vera, C. and Dean, M. (2005) 'An examination of the challenges daughters face in family business succession', *Family Business Review*, 18(4): 321–345.

Watson, T. (2009) 'Entrepreneurial action, identity work and the use of multiple discursive resources', *International Small Business Journal*, 27(1): 251–274.

Yeung, H. (2000) 'Limits to the growth of family-owned business? The case of Chinese transnational corporations from Hong Kong', *Family Business Review*, 13(1): 55–70.

Yin, R.K. (1993) *Applications of Case Study Research*. Beverly Hills, CA: Sage.

Yin, R.K. (2003) *Case Study Research: Design and Methods*, 3rd edn. Thousand Oaks, CA: Sage. (1st edn, 1989.)

30

Multilevel Analysis in Family Business Studies

Aaron F. McKenny, G. Tyge Payne, Miles A. Zachary and Jeremy C. Short

INTRODUCTION

Organizational data are inherently nested – individuals within a group, groups within a subunit, subunits within an organization, organizations within a network, and networks within an environment (Aguinis et al., 2011; Hitt et al., 2007). In the family business literature, the influence of the family can be found at each of these levels (Sharma, 2004). For example, at the individual level, family founders are thought to have different affective responses to founding a family business than do non-family managers (Morris et al., 2010). At the environmental level, family businesses have been shown to be major contributors to the global economy (International Family Enterprise Research Academy, 2003). Nevertheless, organizational and family business scholars have primarily focused on single-level analyses in empirical tests of family firms (Chrisman et al., 2007; Kozlowski and Klein, 2000). As a result, many important relationships within the family business field of study have yet to be fully explored. Recognizing this, scholars have called for more multilevel theory development and testing both in family business research and in the broader organizational studies literature (Chrisman et al., 2007; Hitt et al., 2007; Klein et al., 1999; Payne et al., 2011).

Despite the call for more multilevel organizational research, scholars have been reluctant to engage in such research. There are two prominent reasons scholars are hesitant to conduct multilevel research. First, multilevel theory is difficult to develop well and faces complexities not common to single-level research (Hitt et al., 2007). Second, and perhaps the more common reason, is that scholars are uncomfortable with the additional analytical complexity introduced by nested data (Kozlowski and Klein, 2000). For instance, many of the analytical methods common in the family business literature (e.g., t-tests, ANOVA, OLS linear regression) are ill-equipped to handle complex multilevel models. T-tests and ANOVAs have been used extensively to show that family businesses differ from non-family businesses in their strategic orientations (e.g., Short et al., 2009; Zachary et al., 2011), governance models (e.g., Gubitta and Gianecchini, 2002), and financial logics (e.g., Gallo et al., 2004). However, while *t*-tests and ANOVAs can identify that differences exist between family and non-family firms, they cannot identify what aspect of the family business drives these differences (Kozlowski and Klein, 2000). Further, many of these analytical techniques have assumptions about the independence of observations that can be difficult to manage with nested data (Glick and Roberts, 1984). Thus, the complexity of data and limited range of analytical techniques commonly used in the family business literature may be stifling multilevel research in this field, even if multilevel theory is appropriately developed.

Echoing the call for more multilevel research in the family business literature made by Chrisman and colleagues (2007), this chapter's purpose is to facilitate such research by (1) reviewing the levels of analysis and analytical techniques commonly used over the past ten years of family business research, and (2) profiling several analytical techniques common in multilevel studies and providing examples of how each technique might inform the family business literature. Although many family business articles contain cross-level or multilevel assumptions, most do not use analytical techniques that facilitate the testing of multilevel theory. Overall, we argue that embracing multilevel research through the use of advanced analytical techniques may increase our understanding of how the family influences, and is influenced by, individuals, organizations, environments, and other levels of analysis.

THE STATE OF MULTILEVEL FAMILY BUSINESS RESEARCH

To identify the ways and extent to which multilevel research is being utilized in the family business literature we drew articles from 32 management, entrepreneurship, and family business journals over the 2001–10 period. We started with the list of 30 journals used by Debicki et al. (2009) to review the publication patterns of scholars doing family business research. We then added two journals that have been launched recently and have published family business research (*Strategic Entrepreneurship Journal* and *Journal of Family Business Strategy*).

To isolate those articles looking at family business-related phenomena we conducted a search of multiple databases indexing these journals (e.g., EBSCO, JSTOR, Web of Knowledge, etc). In this search we used the keywords 'Family Business', 'Family Enterprise', 'Family Firm' as well as their common derivations (e.g., 'Family Businesses'). All *Family Business Review* and *Journal of Family Business Strategy* articles were included as those two outlets focus exclusively on family business research. This initial search resulted in a list of 613 articles. Two of these articles were eliminated because the authors determined that they did not pertain to family business, resulting in a list of 611 articles relevant to the family business literature. From this list we eliminated all articles without empirical content (i.e., editorials, book reviews, commentaries, and conceptual articles) or where variables were not clearly specified. This process resulted in a list of 283 empirical articles. Finally, we eliminated all studies using qualitative research methods, resulting in a final list of 223 articles to be reviewed. Qualitative methods are a valuable tool for conducting multilevel family business research; however, issues related to qualitative research are thoroughly addressed by Reay and Zhang (2014) in Chapter 29 of this *Handbook*. Table 30.1 outlines the distribution of family business articles across the journals selected over the 2001–10 sampling frame. Also, Figure 30.1 shows the overall number of relevant articles published between 2001 through 2010.

Table 30.1   Family business articles 2001–10 by journal

Journal	Total articles	Quantitative articles
Academy of Management Journal	4 (0.65%)	4 (1.79%)
Academy of Management Review	1 (0.16%)	0 (0.00%)
Administrative Science Quarterly	4 (0.65%)	4 (1.79%)
Business Ethics Quarterly	2 (0.33%)	1 (0.45%)
California Management Review	0 (0.00%)	0 (0.00%)
Corporate Governance: An International Review	22 (3.60%)	16 (7.17%)
Entrepreneurship and Regional Development	8 (1.31%)	3 (1.35%)
Entrepreneurship: Theory and Practice	91 (14.89%)	22 (9.87%)
Family Business Review	304 (49.75%)	94 (42.15%)
Harvard Business Review	2 (0.33%)	0 (0.00%)
Human Relations	2 (0.33%)	0 (0.00%)
International Small Business Journal	19 (1.47%)	4 (1.79%)
Journal of Applied Psychology	0 (0.00%)	0 (0.00%)
Journal of Business Ethics	9 (1.47%)	6 (2.69%)
Journal of Business Research	16 (2.62%)	8 (3.59%)
Journal of Business Venturing	23 (3.76%)	8 (3.59%)
Journal of Family Business Strategy†	25 (4.09%)	8 (3.59%)
Journal of Management Studies	18 (2.95%)	11 (4.93%)
Journal of Organizational Behavior	1 (0.16%)	0 (0.00%)
Journal of Management	0 (0.00%)	0 (0.00%)
Journal of Small Business Management	27 (4.42%)	18 (8.07%)
The Leadership Quarterly	1 (0.16%)	0 (0.00%)
Long Range Planning	1 (0.16%)	0 (0.00%)
Management Science	0 (0.00%)	0 (0.00%)
MIT Sloan Management Review	1 (0.16%)	0 (0.00%)
Organizational Dynamics	1 (0.16%)	0 (0.00%)
Organization Science	6 (0.98%)	5 (2.24%)
Organization Studies	5 (0.82%)	0 (0.00%)
Small Business Economics	12 (1.96%)	8 (3.59%)
Strategic Entrepreneurship Journal†	2 (0.33%)	1 (0.45%)
Strategic Management Journal	1 (0.16%)	1 (0.45%)
Strategic Organization	3 (0.49%)	1 (0.45%)

†: Journal launched during sampling frame

Each article was coded to identify the variables and analytical techniques incorporated by family business scholars. After identifying each variable used in the study, the authors identified the levels of analysis used in the article. Because we are concerned with the use of levels of analysis in family business articles, rather than the number of variables at each level in each article, we created dummy variables for the presence of variables at each level. In identifying the levels of analysis relevant for this study, we drew from Hitt and colleagues' (2007: 1387) 'multilevel nesting arrangement', which includes environments, interorganizational networks, organizations, subunits, groups, and individuals.

We found family-related variables associated with several of the six levels of analysis coded. The majority of studies reviewed looked at the family as an organizational-level characteristic (e.g., Anderson and Reeb,

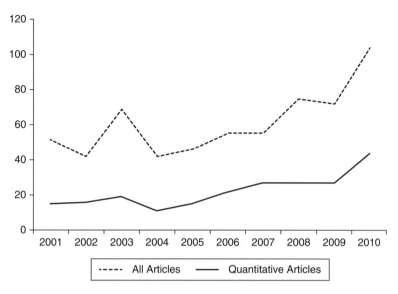

Figure 30.1   Number of family business articles published annually 2001–10

2004; Gómez-Mejía et al., 2007). Several studies also examined individual-level characteristics based on that person's (e.g., CEO, top management team member) connection to the founding family (e.g., Berrone et al., 2010; Cruz et al., 2010). However, families can also exert their influence at other levels. For instance, families are of central importance within diversified interorganizational networks known as family conglomerates or chaebols (e.g., Moskalev and Park, 2010; Poza, 1995). Also, the family might be considered a group or subunit within the organization or even a separate entity altogether. One recent example of this is in Brewton and colleagues' (2010) study looking at how family-level and organizational-level resources, structures, and constraints influence resilience in the face of disruption.

In our review, we found that 160 (72%) quantitative articles from 2001 through 2010 contained variables at two or more levels of analysis. For example, one early study included variables at four levels (individual, organizational, interorganizational network, and environmental) to look at the success factors of young family and non-family businesses in Finland (Littunen, 2003). An article later in our sample looked at

organizational-level (e.g., being a family firm) and environmental-level (e.g., being in a common law country) variables in a study of how shareholders influence firm value (Jara-Bertin et al., 2008). Table 30.2 presents the breakdown of articles by the number of levels included in the study. Over the ten-year sampling frame, there was a negative relationship between publication year and the number of levels used in the study ($\rho = -0.18$, $p < 0.01$). This trend, as illustrated in Figure 30.2, suggests that family business research is declining in the incorporation of multiple levels of analysis. The negative relationship we observed may be a function of the evolution of the family

Table 30.2   Number of levels represented in each study

Number of levels	Number of articles	Percent of sample
1	63	28%
2	124	56%
3	34	15%
4	2	1%
5	0	0%
6	0	0%

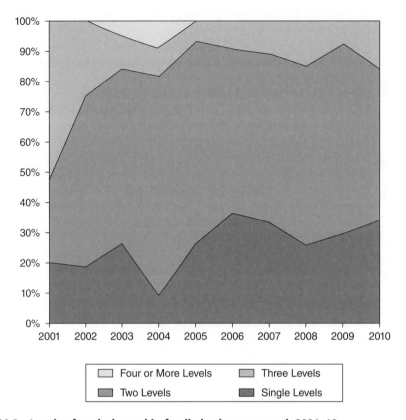

Figure 30.2   Levels of analysis used in family business research 2001–10

business literature. The family business literature may be transitioning from an exploratory phase wherein scholars broadly investigate phenomena to create broad knowledge of the idiosyncrasies of family businesses to more narrow and targeted studies. Despite the decline, the large number of studies incorporating variables at multiple levels in the family business literature reinforces our and others' (e.g., Chrisman et al., 2007) suggestion that family business presents a valuable context in which to conduct multilevel research.

Although we found that family business articles frequently include variables at multiple levels of analysis, only one article, over the entire ten-year time frame, used a technique specifically designed to test multilevel hypotheses. In the only study with a multilevel analytical technique, Eddleston and colleagues (2008) used Hierarchical Linear

Modeling (Bryk and Raudenbush, 1992) to examine how organizational-level variables, such as ownership and dispersion, and individual-level decision-making influence cognitive and relationship conflict in family firms. Based on the limited number of exemplars, we conducted a second, less-systematic search of the family business literature looking specifically for studies using multilevel methods, regardless of the publication date. This search revealed only two additional studies (i.e., Dawson, 2011; Distelberg and Blow, 2011).

Although there are very few family business studies that explicitly use multilevel methods, this does not mean that the existing studies only examine a single level or use inappropriate statistical analyses. Rather, the *t*-tests, ANOVAS and regression techniques commonly seen in the family business literature can be used effectively to test multilevel models; these techniques can be used effectively to test for differences between family and non-family firms (e.g., Littunen, 2003) or between generations (e.g., Sonfield and Lussier, 2004). Variables at multiple levels can also be specified as covariates/control variables to control for influences from other levels of analysis (e.g., Anderson and Reeb, 2004; Braun and Sharma, 2007). Nevertheless, as the family business literature continues to expand, more sophisticated techniques will be needed. For instance, ANOVA and regression are sufficient to identify that family businesses differ from non-family businesses along certain dimensions; however, to identify what aspects of the family business drive these differences, multilevel analysis techniques become more useful because they do not have the same independence of observation assumptions.

Having coded for the levels of the variables used in each study, we then assessed the predominance of each level in the family business literature. Our review found that family business research has used variables at each level of analysis. However, upon closer investigation, there are some levels that are clearly more common than others. By far, family business research has concentrated on the organizational level, with variables at the organizational level being observed in 93% of the studies we reviewed. Table 30.3 presents an overview of the number of studies in our sample using variables at each level of analysis. This table shows that the individual, environmental, and organizational levels are each at least thirteen times more prevalent than the next most common level (groups). Further, if we eliminate those variables used purely as control variables, the environment level would drop from 121 studies (54.3%) to 36 studies (16.1%), leaving the organizational and individual levels as the dominant levels in family business research.

DISCUSSION

Family business scholars have long recognized the importance of multilevel theory and empirics (e.g., Bird et al., 2002; Handler and Kram, 1988; Harvey and Evans, 1994; Sharma, 2004). Indeed, as an organizational science, the family business domain investigates phenomena that are naturally hierarchically interrelated (Hitt et al., 2007). Nevertheless, our findings are consistent with other scholars' observations that the family business domain is just scratching the surface of what is possible with multilevel methods (Chrisman et al., 2007).

Implications and Directions for Empirical Research

In the past ten years of empirical family business research, over 70% of studies incorporated variables at multiple levels, but only one

Table 30.3   Use of levels in family business articles

Level	Number of articles	Example variable
Individual	81 (36%)	Interest in pursuing a career in family business (e.g., DeMoss, 2002) Propensity to step down (e.g., Sharma et al., 2003)
Group	6 (3%)	Group cohesion (e.g., Ensley and Pearson, 2005) Task conflict (e.g., Ensley, 2006)
Subunit	1 (< 1%)	Finance department characteristics (e.g., Gallo et al., 2004)
Organization	208 (93%)	Family business status (e.g., Gómez-Mejía et al., 2007) Owning family resilience (e.g., Brewton et al., 2010)
Interorganizational network	4 (2%)	Changes in network (e.g., Littunen, 2003) Diversification in business group (e.g., Chung and Luo, 2008)
Environment	121 (54%)	Industry sales growth (e.g., Schulze et al., 2003) Environmental hostility (e.g., Casillas et al., 2010)

took advantage of multilevel techniques that were created to analyze such data (i.e., Eddleston et al., 2008). One reason for the slow incorporation of multilevel techniques may have to do with the natural progression of the family business literature. The family business literature is in a similar position as the broader entrepreneurship literature where single-level research also dominates (Davidsson and Wiklund, 2001; Dean et al., 2007); however, both of these domains lag behind older areas of research such as organizational behavior where multilevel research is more common. Over the past 30 years there has been considerable emphasis on identifying meaningful ways in which family businesses differ from non-family businesses (e.g., Gubitta and Gianecchini, 2002; Tagiuri and Davis, 1992; Payne et al., 2011; Zachary et al., 2011). For studies looking at differences between family businesses and non-family businesses, the techniques commonly found in the family business research (e.g., ANOVA, regression, etc.) may be appropriate. However, since a salient goal of family business research is to improve the performance and goal accomplishment of family businesses (Chua et al., 1999), the next logical stage in family business research is to identify what aspects of the family business drive these differences and why. Indeed, a number of studies have begun to explore these areas and have suggested that the pursuit of socioemotional wealth (Gómez-Mejía et al., 2007) and unique family resources (Habbershon and Williams, 1999) may influence a number of organizational phenomena. Unfortunately, reliance on single-level methods will hamper the progress of this stream of research because many of these methods are ill-equipped to handle nested data (Kozlowski and Klein, 2000).

For an illustration of a next-generation research question that would be difficult to test using a single-level method, consider a study looking at the characteristics of family businesses that may influence the job satisfaction of non-family employees. At the individual level, the researcher might measure job satisfaction and control variables from a number of non-family employees across a sample of family businesses. At the organizational level, the researcher would gather the characteristics of family businesses hypothesized to influence job satisfaction as well as other organizational-level controls. It may be tempting to use linear regression to identify the extent to which family business characteristics influence the job satisfaction of non-family employees; however, to do so would violate the independence in error terms assumption of general linear models (Hair et al., 2010). Specifically, the researcher will have gathered data about individuals and their associated firms. However, since data was collected from multiple individuals within multiple firms, the individual-level data in each record is not independent from one observation to the next.

Fortunately, advances in multilevel research methods have produced a number of techniques that facilitate research using nested data (Snijders and Bosker, 1999). Specifically, this research question might use random coefficients modeling (RCM), also referred to by the name of a popular implementation of the method: Hierarchical Linear Modeling (Bryk and Raudenbush, 1992), to identify the characteristics of family businesses that influence non-family employee job satisfaction. RCM was created specifically to test theoretical models that cross hierarchical levels (Bliese, 2002; Hofmann, 1997). RCM works by allowing the researcher to model the regression coefficients of lower-level variables and the lower-level regression intercept as dependent variables in a simultaneous regression at higher levels of analysis (Bryk and Raudenbush, 1992). This allows the coefficients at the lowest level of analysis to vary depending on the group being modeled, thus accounting for collective-level effects on the individual-level outcomes. For instance, RCM can test whether the pursuit of socioemotional wealth directly influences the job satisfaction of non-family employees or whether it influences the job satisfaction of non-family employees indirectly through moderating lower-level relationships (e.g., between person-job fit and job satisfaction).

While random coefficient modeling is the only explicitly multilevel method we found in the family business literature to-date (e.g., Dawson, 2011; Distelberg and Blow, 2011; Eddleston et al., 2008), there are several multilevel methods in use in the organizational studies literature (Kozlowski and Klein, 2000: 48; Snijders and Bosker, 1999). For instance, multilevel logistic regression also seeks to explain variance of dependent variables at the lowest level of analysis using data from higher levels. As with simple logistic regression, multilevel logistic regression is appropriate when the dependent variable is dichotomous (Reise, 2000). A recent study by LaHuis and Copeland (2009), which investigated how survey item difficulty and individual traits influence the likelihood of faking responses to a personality assessment, serves as a good example of how multilevel logistic regression might be utilized. In this case, the binary dependent variable of faking on a particular item is a function of the characteristics of the item and the characteristics of the individual, which is a higher level of analysis. In the family business literature, there are numerous opportunities for analyzing similarly nested data using multilevel logistic regression. Binary dependent variables of interest might include CEO as family member, decision for a family firm to go public, and the traditional dichotomous family firm variable.

Within-and-between-entity analysis (WABA; Dansereau et al., 1984) is also a potentially useful technique for family business scholars. In contrast to RCM, WABA does not require researchers to specify levels of analysis a priori, but allows researchers to determine appropriate levels of analysis for both variables and relationships (Gooty and Yammarino, 2011). Therefore, WABA can help to identify whether a relationship should be considered as one among collective-level constructs (wholes), one between individuals within the collective (parts), or one of individuals independent of collective-level factors (Markham and Halverson, 2002; Yammarino et al., 1997). As family business

research continues to develop organizational-level constructs that are influenced by the cognitions of individuals (e.g., socioemotional wealth) and group membership (e.g., the family), WABA can be applied to measure the extent to which the variance in the construct is driven by the individual, group, or the organization.

Finally, multilevel covariance structure analysis (MCSA) and multilevel confirmatory factor analysis (MCFA) can be used to test multilevel structural models where one might otherwise use single-level structural equation modeling and confirmatory factor analysis techniques (Dyer et al., 2005; Muthén, 1994). While these techniques are still new to the organizational studies literature, some scholars have begun using these techniques to validate constructs (e.g., Hanges and Dickson, 2006) and could be used similarly for constructs unique to family business research. For instance, if items of an instrument are developed to refer to the 'family' (e.g., the Family influence on Power, Experience, and Culture scale, F-PEC), we must assume that the factor structure would be in accordance with the family level of analysis. However, regarding the individual level, it is unclear how individual differences contribute to the factor structure.

Table 30.4 outlines a number of opportunities for future research, showing how multilevel techniques can improve our understanding of the family business. For example, since interorganizational networks influence post-IPO financial success (Gulati and Higgins, 2003) and families derive both financial and socioemotional wealth from their family business (Gómez-Mejía et al., 2007), family businesses might evaluate the value of their network differently than non-family businesses. To examine this, one study could look at characteristics of family and non-family firms' interorganizational networks and use multilevel logistic regression to evaluate their influence on the firm's decision to go public. Such a study would not only contribute to the family business literature by advancing what we know about

Table 30.4   Possible future family business studies using multilevel methods

Research question	Levels	Method
Are the functional subunits of family businesses structured differently than those of non-family businesses?	Organization, subunit	ANOVA/ANCOVA
How do goal orientation differences between family and non-family team members affect team performance?	Group, individual	OLS Regression
How do characteristics of family businesses influence the job satisfaction of non-family employees?	Organization, individual	Random coefficients modeling
Within different industries, how do entire family businesses differ in socioemotional wealth, leadership climate, and entrepreneurial orientation, collectively?	Environment, organization, family	Multilevel covariance structure analysis
Do family business' network position and network ties influence the decision to go public?	Interorganizational network, organization	Multilevel logistic regression
How do the political institutional context, national culture, and industry factors influence the decision to launch a venture as a family versus non-family business?	Environment, individual	Random coefficients modeling
How does the temporal orientation of the founding family members relate to the espousal of a long-term orientation by the family business?	Individual, family, organization	Within-and-between-entity analysis

the way family businesses view their networks, it would also make a methodological contribution by introducing the multilevel logistic regression technique to the literature.

Scholars looking at multilevel issues in family business might consider three different models for their research. The first model is a single-level model where constructs at a lower level emerge at a higher level (Kozlowski and Klein, 2000). For instance, research has argued that team efficacy represents the collective beliefs of the individual team members regarding the team's ability to achieve specific tasks (Bandura, 1997). Thus, a model looking at the relationship between team efficacy and team performance in family firms would exemplify the single-level model. The second model is a cross-level model where independent constructs and dependent constructs may be at different levels (Kozlowski and Klein, 2000). Cross-level models are where methods such as hierarchical linear modeling and multilevel covariance structure analysis become useful tools for researchers. A study looking at how

characteristics of family businesses influence the job satisfaction of non-family employees illustrates the cross-level model. Finally, homologous or isomorphic models suggest that the constructs and relationships hypothesized at one level also occur at other levels (Kozlowski and Klein, 2000; Rousseau, 1985). Staw and colleagues (1981) provide an often-cited example of a homologous model in their study looking at threat rigidity at the individual, group, and organizational levels. Likewise, Payne and colleagues (2011) recently suggested that social capital, an increasingly important theoretical perspective for family business research (e.g., Lester and Cannella, 2006; Chang et al., 2009), may be homologous. Specifically applied to the family business literature, one could test if differences exist for social capital relationships applied to individual family members, the family, and the family business. Understanding if and how these differences might influence various family business outcomes could contribute to both the family business literature as well as the social capital literature as a whole.

Treating the 'family' as its own level of analysis is also fertile ground for multilevel family business research. Presently, most studies look at family-related variables at the organizational (e.g., percentage ownership by the family) or individual (e.g., the CEO is a family member) levels. However, such variables miss aspects of the family itself that may influence phenomena in the family business. Family functional integrity and family structural integrity have both been shown to be important predictors of family firm resilience in both urban and rural firms (Brewton et al., 2010). Socioemotional wealth, in particular, has been quickly garnering interest in family business research and can be conceptualized at the family level. Socioemotional wealth can be defined as the affective benefits accruing to the family from family business ownership (Gómez-Mejía et al., 2007). According to this definition, one needs only be a member of the owning family to gain socioemotional wealth from the family business. For example, Berrone and colleagues (2010) argue that family members value the legitimacy afforded to them by owning an environmentally responsible company, and that they act to preserve this source of socioemotional wealth by having better environmental performance than their non-family counterparts (see Chapter 10 by Berrone et al., 2014, in this *Handbook* for a more complete account of the socioemotional wealth construct and its promise for the family business literature). Future studies might also look at how other family-level variables such as family commitment to the business (c.f., Lansberg and Astrachan, 1994) or family climate (c.f., Björnberg and Nicholson, 2007) influence the relative salience of noneconomic (family-related) goals in the family business.

While multilevel research creates significant opportunities for empirical studies, it also requires special consideration in sampling design. Conducting multilevel analyses often requires significantly more data than single level studies to provide sufficient explanatory power both at the between-individual and between-organization level (Cohen, 1998). Further, in family business research it is important to gather sufficient data from both family and non-family firms to answer questions about how and why family firms differ from non-family firms. As a result, simple random sampling may not be practical in multilevel studies, rendering a multi-stage sampling method more useful in these studies (Snijders and Bosker, 1999). Unfortunately, the difficulty of gathering sufficient data at multiple levels of analysis and selecting non-random sampling methods also increase the risk of selection bias (Heckman, 1979). Thus, scholars must be careful in developing a sampling strategy in multilevel studies and use statistical techniques to test for bias (c.f., Bellio and Gori, 2003).

Implications and Directions for Conceptual Research

Despite the promise of multilevel research techniques in the development of the family business literature, the opportunities for multilevel research are not limited to these methodological opportunities. Although a secondary topic of interest in this chapter, our analysis of the last decade of family business research indicated a strong bias toward the individual and organizational levels (as shown in Table 30.3). Relative to these levels, we understand less about group, subunit and interorganizational network phenomena in family businesses. Further, we found that only 30% of studies looking at environmental variables used them as more than control variables (e.g., Chrisman et al., 2002). While incorporating environmental controls is valuable in isolating the variance explained by variables at other levels of analysis, the lack of theory development and testing of hypotheses about family businesses' interactions with their environments hampers our understanding of family business. For instance, the family business literature has found that family businesses tend to be underrepresented in some industries (c.f., Astrachan and Kolenko, 1994). We also find that family businesses are ubiquitous in some countries, and less so in others (c.f., Mishra and McConaughy, 1997). However, less research has been done to identify why these and other environmental factors influence family businesses or how family businesses influence their environments. Thus, there are significant opportunities to advance the family business literature by examining phenomena at these underrepresented levels in the family business context.

Despite the lack of emphasis in the last ten years, the two studies looking at the subunit level of analysis present convincing arguments for examining subunits in the family business literature. Gallo and colleagues (2004) included characteristics of the finance department in their study looking at how the financial logics of family businesses differ from those of non-family businesses. Taking a different approach, Salvato and colleagues (2010) look at entire lines of business rather than functional subunits in their study exploring business exit in the family business. Some research exists looking at the organizational structure of family businesses (e.g., Barry, 1975; Kahn and Henderson, 1992); nevertheless, further bridging the organizational structure and family business literatures may surface new insights into the inner operations of family firms. For instance, a future study might investigate how the organizational structure of family businesses might influence the pursuit and attainment of noneconomic goals. Subunit-level research might also draw from the diversification, mergers, and acquisitions literatures to better understand the process by which family businesses socialize the employees of newly acquired non-family businesses into their culture. Specifically, if the acquired firm becomes a new business unit in the family business, does that business unit continue to operate using a non-family, economically focused logic?

While a full review of best practices for multilevel theory building was outside the scope of this chapter, there is a body of literature advocating and offering best practices for multilevel theory building. Denise Rousseau, in her well-known (1985) chapter on multi- and cross-level research provides an in-depth review of the hazards of multilevel research and provides a set of guidelines for researchers to follow, facilitating rigor in both conceptual and empirical studies. Klein and colleagues (1994) emphasize the importance of understanding variance in multilevel theory development. Specifically, they identify three ways in which individual-level constructs may vary within groups: homogeneity, heterogeneity, and independence. They then provide a number of suggestions for how understanding this variance should influence theoretical development and empirical testing considerations. Morgeson and Hofmann (1999) take a more focused approach, addressing the role of collective constructs in multilevel theory development. They highlight the importance of understanding the emergence of the collective construct and offer eleven guidelines for researchers using collective constructs in their research. Finally, Kozlowski and Klein (2000) provide a very comprehensive guide to multilevel theory development, breaking up their guidelines into categories addressing the 'what', 'how', 'where', 'when', and 'why' aspects of multilevel theory building. In addition to the general literature on multilevel research, many of the organizational studies subdisciplines have articles that may inform family business multilevel research (e.g., Bliese et al., 2002; Ostroff and Bowen, 2000; Payne et al., 2011).

Limitations of the Study

The scope of this review necessarily presents limitations to its generalizability. First, we reviewed family business research in the ten-year period (2001–10); however, other studies not limited to this time frame have also come to the same conclusion regarding the state of multilevel research in the family business domain (e.g., Chrisman et al., 2007). Second, we limited the scope of our review to 32 top outlets for family business research. These journals are consistent with other reviews of the family business and entrepreneurship literatures (e.g., Debicki et al., 2009). Third, we limited our studies to quantitative research methods. However, we refer the reader to Chapter 29 by Reay and Zhang (2014), which provides a comprehensive review of qualitative work (single and multilevel) in the family business literature. Finally, in coding each article we looked only at the levels of the variables and the analytical techniques used. We did not code for whether traditional single-level techniques (e.g., ANOVA or OLS Regression) were being correctly used to test simple multilevel models, nor if other multilevel modeling techniques (e.g., aggregating individual level data) were being utilized and utilized appropriately. This limitation presents an opportunity for future research to investigate the accuracy with which the family business literature has specified and tested empirical models.

CONCLUSION

The results of our study, which suggest limited utilization of multilevel analytical techniques in the family business literature, should not be viewed as a limitation of past research, but rather an opportunity for future studies. Indeed, we feel that the uniqueness and complexity of the family business creates incredible opportunities for multilevel research that may inform not only family business scholars but also scholars studying more general phenomena. In this chapter, we have discussed several opportunities for future research, but recognize that many more exist due to availability of more sophisticated statistical techniques that can easily analyze nested data. We encourage scholars to utilize these techniques to specify and investigate the more complex relationships that reside within, between, and around the family business. Without doubt, investigating these important complexities is no longer the goal of future research, it is the challenge of today.

REFERENCES

Aguinis, H., Boyd, B., Pierce, C.A., and Short, J.C. (2011). Walking new avenues in management research methods and theories: Bridging macro and micro domains. *Journal of Management*, 37(2), 395–403.

Anderson, R.C. and Reeb, D.M. (2004). Board composition: Balancing family influence in S&P 500 firms. *Administrative Science Quarterly*, 49, 209–237.

Astrachan, J.H. and Kolenko, T.A. (1994). A neglected factor in explaining family business success: Human resource practices. *Family Business Review*, 7, 251–262.

Bandura, A. (1997). *Self-efficacy: The Exercise of Control*. New York: Freeman.

Barry, B. (1975). The development of organization structure in the family firm. *Journal of General Management*, 3, 42–60.

Bellio, R. and Gori, E. (2003). Impact evaluation of job training programmes: Selection bias in multilevel models. *Journal of Applied Statistics*, 30, 893–907.

Berrone, P., Cruz, C., and Gómez-Mejía, L.R. (2014). Family-controlled firms and stakeholder management: A socioemotional wealth preservation perspective. In Melin, L., Nordqvist, M. Sharma, P. (eds), *The SAGE Family Business Handbook*. London: Sage.

Berrone, P., Cruz, C., Gómez-Mejía, L.R., and Larraza-Kintana, M. (2010). Socioemotional wealth and corporate responses to institutional pressures: Do family-controlled firms pollute less? *Administrative Science Quarterly*, 55, 82–113.

Bird, B., Welsch, H., Astrachan, J.H., and Pistrui, D. (2002). Family business research: The evolution of an academic field. *Family Business Review*, 15, 337–350.

Björnberg, Å. and Nicholson, N. (2007). The family climate scales – Development of a new measure for use in family business research. *Family Business Review*, 20, 229–246.

Bliese, P.D. (2002). Using multilevel random coefficient modeling in organizational research. In Drasgow, F. and Schmitt, N. (eds), *Advances in Measurement and Data Analysis* (pp. 401–445). San Francisco, CA: Jossey-Bass.

Bliese, P.D., Halverson, R.R., and Schriesheim, C.A. (2002). Benchmarking multilevel methods in leadership: The articles, the model and the data set. *The Leadership Quarterly*, 13, 3–14.

Braun, M. and Sharma, P. (2007). Should the CEO also be chair of the board? An empirical examination of family-controlled public firms. *Family Business Review*, 20, 111–126.

Brewton, K.E., Danes, S.M., Stafford, K., and Haynes, G.W. (2010). Determinants of rural and urban family firm resilience. *Journal of Family Business Strategy*, 1, 155–166.

Bryk, A.S. and Raudenbush, S.W. (1992). *Hierarchical Linear Models: Applications and Data Analysis Methods*. Newbury Park, CA: Sage.

Casillas, J.C., Moreno, A.M., and Barbero, J.L. (2010). A configurational approach of the relationship between entrepreneurial orientation and growth of family firms. *Family Business Review*, 23, 27–44.

Chang, E.P.C., Memili, E., Chrisman, J.J., Kellermanns, F.W., and Chua, J.H. (2009). Family social capital, venture preparedness, and start-up decisions: A study of Hispanic entrepreneurs in New England. *Family Business Review*, 22(3), 279–292.

Chrisman, J.J., Chua, J.H., and Steier, L.P. (2002). The influence of national culture and family involvement on entrepreneurial perceptions and performance at the state level. *Entrepreneurship: Theory & Practice*, 26, 113–130.

Chrisman, J.J., Sharma, P., and Taggar, S. (2007). Family influences on firms: An introduction. *Journal of Business Research*, 60, 1005–1011.

Chua, J.H., Chrisman, J.J., and Sharma, P. (1999). Defining the family business by behavior. *Entrepreneurship: Theory & Practice*, 23, 19–39.

Chung, C.-N. and Luo, X. (2008). Institutional logics or agency costs: The influence of corporate governance models on business group restructuring in emerging economies. *Organization Science*, 19, 766–784.

Cohen, M. (1998). Determining sample sizes for surveys with data analyzed by hierarchical linear models. *Journal of Official Statistics*, 14, 267–275.

Cruz, C.C., Gómez-Mejía, L.R., and Becerra, M. (2010). Perceptions of benevolence and the design of agency contracts: CEO-TMT relationships in family firms. *Academy of Management Journal*, 53, 69–89.

Dansereau, F., Alutto, J.A., and Yammarino, F.J. (1984). *Theory Testing in Organizational Behavior: The Variant Approach*. Englewood Cliffs, NJ: Prentice-Hall.

Davidsson, P. and Wiklund, J. (2001). Levels of analysis in entrepreneurship research: Current research practice and suggestions for the future. *Entrepreneurship: Theory & Practice*, 25, 81–100.

Dawson, A. (2011). Private equity investment decisions in family firms: The role of human resources and agency costs. *Journal of Business Venturing*, 26, 189–199.

Dean, M.A., Shook, C.L., and Payne, G.T. (2007). The past, present, and future of entrepreneurship research: Data analytic trends and training. *Entrepreneurship: Theory & Practice*, 31(4): 601–618.

Debicki, B.J., Matherne, C.F., Kellermanns, F.W., and Chrisman, J.J. (2009). Family business research in the new millennium: An overview of the who, the where, the what, and the why. *Family Business Review*, 22, 151–166.

DeMoss, M. (2002). Developing consumer-driven services in university-based family business programs. *Family Business Review*, 15, 119–129.

Distelberg, B.J. and Blow, A. (2011). Variations in family system boundaries. *Family Business Review*, 24, 28–46.

Dyer, N.G., Hanges, P.J., and Hall, R.J. (2005). Applying multilevel confirmatory factor analysis techniques to the study of leadership. *The Leadership Quarterly*, 16, 149–167.

Eddleston, K.A., Otondo, R.F., and Kellermanns, F.W. (2008). Conflict, participative decision-making, and generational ownership dispersion: A multilevel analysis. *Journal of Small Business Management*, 46, 456–484.

Ensley, M.D. (2006). Family businesses can out-compete: As long as they are willing to question the chosen path. *Entrepreneurship: Theory & Practice*, 30, 747–754.

Ensley, M.D. and Pearson, A.W. (2005). An exploratory comparison of the behavioral dynamics of top management teams in family and nonfamily new ventures: Cohesion, conflict, potency, and consensus. *Entrepreneurship: Theory & Practice*, 29, 267–284.

Gallo, M.Á., Tápies, J., and Cappuyns, K. (2004). Comparison of family and nonfamily business: Financial logic and personal preferences. *Family Business Review*, 17, 303–318.

Glick, W.H. and Roberts, K.H. (1984). Hypothesized interdependence, assumed independence. *Academy of Management Review*, 9, 722–735.

Gómez-Mejía, L.R., Haynes, K.T., Núñez-Nickel, M., Jacobson, K.J.L., and Moyano-Fuentes, J. (2007). Socioemotional wealth and business risks in family-controlled firms: Evidence from Spanish olive oil mills. *Administrative Science Quarterly*, 52, 106–137.

Gooty, J. and Yammarino, F.J. (2011). Dyads in organizational research: Conceptual issues and multilevel analyses. *Organizational Research Methods*, 14(3), 456–483.

Gubitta, P. and Gianecchini, M. (2002). Governance and flexibility in family-owned SMEs. *Family Business Review*, 15, 277–297.

Gulati, R. and Higgins, M.C. (2003). Which ties matter when? The contingent effects of interorganizational partnerships on IPO success. *Strategic Management Journal*, 24, 127–144.

Habbershon, T.G. and Williams, M.L. (1999). A resource-based framework for assessing the strategic advantages of family firms. *Family Business Review*, 12, 1–25.

Hair, J.F., Black, W.C., Babin, B.J., and Anderson, R.E. (2010). *Multivariate Data Analysis* (7th edn). Upper Saddle River, NJ: Pearson Hall.

Handler, W.C. and Kram, K.E. (1988). Succession in family firms: The problem of resistance. *Family Business Review*, 1, 361–381.

Hanges, P.J. and Dickson, M.W. (2006). Agitation over aggregation: Clarifying the development of and the nature of the GLOBE scales. *The Leadership Quarterly*, 17, 522–536.

Harvey, M. and Evans, R.E. (1994). Family business and multiple levels of conflict. *Family Business Review*, 7, 331–348.

Heckman, J.J. (1979). Sample selection bias as a specification error. *Econometrica*, 47, 153–161.

Hitt, M.A., Beamish, P.W., Jackson, S.E., and Mathieu, J.E. (2007). Building theoretical and empirical bridges across levels: Multilevel research in management. *Academy of Management Journal*, 50, 1385–1399.

Hofmann, D.A. (1997). An overview of the logic and rationale of hierarchical linear models. *Journal of Management*, 23, 723–744.

International Family Enterprise Research Academy (2003). Family businesses dominate: International Family Enterprise Research Academy (IFERA). *Family Business Review*, 16, 235–240.

Jara-Bertin, M., López-Iturriaga, F.J., and López-de-Foronda, Ó. (2008). The contest to the control in European family firms: How other shareholders affect firm value. *Corporate Governance*, 16, 146–159.

Kahn, J.A. and Henderson, D.A. (1992). Location preferences of family firms: Strategic decision making or 'Home Sweet Home'? *Family Business Review*, 5, 271–282.

Klein, K.J., Dansereau, F., and Hall, R.J. (1994). Levels issues in theory development, data collection, and analysis. *Academy of Management Review*, 19, 195–229.

Klein, K.J., Tosi, H., and Cannella, A.A. (1999). Multilevel theory building: Benefits, barriers, and new developments. *Academy of Management Review*, 24, 243–248.

Kozlowski, S.W.J. and Klein, K.J. (2000). A multi-level approach to theory and research in organizations: Contextual, temporal, and emergent processes. In Klein, K.J. and Kozlowski, S.W.J. (eds), *Multilevel Theory, Research, and Methods in Organizations: Foundations, Extensions, and New Directions* (pp. 3–90). San Francisco, CA: Jossey-Bass.

LaHuis, D.M. and Copeland, D. (2009). Investigating faking using a multilevel logistic regression approach to measuring person fit. *Organizational Research Methods*, 12, 296–319.

Lansberg, I. and Astrachan, J.H. (1994). Influence of family relationships on succession planning and training: The importance of mediating factors. *Family Business Review*, 7, 39–59.

Lester, R.H. and Cannella, A.A., Jr. (2006). Interorganizational familiness: How family firms use interlocking directorates to build community-level social capital. *Entrepreneurship: Theory & Practice*, 30(6), 755–775.

Littunen, H. (2003). Management capabilities and environmental characteristics in the critical operational phase of entrepreneurship: A comparison of Finnish family and nonfamily firms. *Family Business Review*, 16, 183–197.

Markham, S.E. and Halverson, R.R. (2002). Within- and between-entity analyses in multilevel research: A leadership example using single level analyses and boundary conditions (MRA). *The Leadership Quarterly*, 13, 35–52.

Mishra, C.S. and McConaughy, D.L. (1999). Founding family control and capital structure: The risk of loss of control and the aversion to debt. *Entrepreneurship: Theory & Practice*, 23, 53–64.

Morgeson, F.P. and Hofmann, D.A. (1999). The structure and function of collective constructs: Implications for multilevel research and theory development. *Academy of Management Review*, 24, 249–265.

Morris, M.H., Allen, J.A., Kuratko, D.F., and Brannon, D. (2010). Experiencing family business creation: Differences between founders, nonfamily managers, and founders of nonfamily firms. *Entrepreneurship: Theory & Practice*, 34, 1057–1084.

Moskalev, S. and Park, S. (2010). South Korean chaebols and value-based management. *Journal of Business Ethics*, 92, 49–62.

Muthén, B. (1994). Multilevel covariance structure analysis. *Sociological Methods, and Research*, 22, 376–398.

Ostroff, C. and Bowen, D.E. (2000). Moving HR to a higher level: Human resource practices and organizational effectiveness. In K.J. Klein and S.W.J. Kozlowski (eds), *Multilevel Theory, Research, and Methods in Organizations* (pp. 211–266). San Francisco, CA: Jossey-Bass.

Payne, G.T., Brigham, K.H., Broberg, J.C., Moss, T.W., and Short, J.C. (2011). Organizational virtue orientation and family firms. *Business Ethics Quarterly*, 21(2): 257–285.

Payne, G.T., Moore, C.B., Griffis, S., and Autry, C. (2011). Multilevel challenges and opportunities in social capital research. *Journal of Management*, 37, 395–403.

Poza, E.J. (1995). Global competition and the family-owned business in Latin America. *Family Business Review*, 8, 301–311.

Reay, T. and Zhang, Z. (2014). Qualitative methods in family business research. In L. Melin, M. Nordqvist, P. Sharma (eds), *The SAGE Handbook of Family Business*. London: Sage.

Reise, S.P. (2000). Using multilevel regression to evaluate person-fit in IRT models. *Multivariate Behavioral Research*, 35, 543–568.

Rousseau, D.M. (1985). Issues of level in organizational research: Multi-level and cross-level perspectives. In Cummings. L.L. and Staw, B.M. (eds), *Research in Organizational Behavior* (Vol. 7, pp. 1–37). Greenwich, CT: JAI Press.

Salvato, C., Chirico, F., and Sharma, P. (2010). A farewell to the business: Championing exit and continuity in entrepreneurial family firms. *Entrepreneurship and Regional Development*, 22, 321–348.

Schulze, W.S., Lubatkin, M.H., and Dino, R.N. (2003). Exploring the agency consequences of ownership dispersion among the directors of private family firms. *Academy of Management Journal*, 46, 179–194.

Sharma, P. (2004). An overview of the field of family business studies: Current status and directions for the future. *Family Business Review*, 17, 1–36.

Sharma, P., Chrisman, J.J., and Chua, J. (2003). Succession planning as planned behavior: Some empirical results. *Family Business Review*, 16, 1–16.

Short, J.C., Payne, G.T., Brigham, K.H., Lumpkin, G.T., and Broberg, J.C. (2009). Family businesss and entrepreneurial orientation in publicly traded firms: A comparative analysis of the S&P 500. *Family Business Review*, 22, 9–24.

Snijders, T. and Bosker, R. (1999). *Multilevel Analysis: An Introduction to Basic and Advanced Multilevel Modeling*. London: Sage Publications.

Sonfield, M.C. and Lussier, R.N. (2004). First-, second-, and third-generation family firms: A comparison. *Family Business Review*, 17, 189–202.

Staw, B.M., Sandelands, L.E., and Dutton, J.E. (1981). Threat rigidity effects in organizational behavior: A multilevel analysis. *Administrative Science Quarterly*, 26, 501–524.

Tagiuri, R. and Davis, J.A. (1992). On the goals of successful family companies. *Family Business Review*, 5, 43–62.

Yammarino, F.J., Dubinsky, A.J., Comer, L.B., and Jolson, M.A. (1997). Women and transformational and contingent reward leadership: A multiple-levels-of-analysis perspective. *Academy of Management Journal*, 40, 205–222.

Zachary, M.A., McKenny, A.F., Short, J.C., and Payne, G.T. (2011). Family business and market orientation: Construct validation and comparative analysis. *Family Business Review*, 24, 233–251.

PART VI

The Future of the Field of Family Business Studies

The Future of the Field of Family
Business Studies

31

The Future of Family Business Research Through the Family Scientist's Lens

Sharon M. Danes

INTRODUCTION

Families are very heterogeneous organizations, and there is a very basic conceptual difference distinguishing families from most other groups. In the words of Cook and Kenny (2006: 215), 'It has been said that the difference between a group of individuals and a family system is like the difference between a pile of bricks and a house.' Investigating owning family functioning within family business research has been treated more like a pile of bricks than a house. As we move forward, we need to emphasize processes owning families use to fit together and fit with their businesses. Processes are the cement that transform individual bricks into strong, sturdy houses. It is these processes that are this essay's focus. We start by identifying the knowledge state within the field from theoretical and family capital perspectives. Future directions to accelerate the field's development are recommended. Table 31.1 outlines the major essay points. Methodological implications are embedded within the discussion to clarify the house's blueprint.

Table 31.1 Current State Of and Future Directions For Family Business Discipline

Current state	Future direction
Theoretical perspective	
Structural focus	Process focus; longitudinal
Single discipline	Multidisciplinary
Firm financial performance	Multi-dimensional sustainability
Family capital perspective	
Stocks (types and levels)	Flows (processes)
Human and financial capital	Bridging human, financial and social capital
Resource endowments	Family firm resiliency

THEORETICAL PERSPECTIVE

When family business research began about 25 years ago, there were few conceptual frameworks in which to ground family business studies. Researchers can now choose from a number of family firm conceptualizations and theories. But with this richness comes questions of how to determine which conceptual grounding to use in any particular research study. In laying the foundation from which to address this question, we first will lay out Sztompka's (1974) clear criteria for what constitutes a conceptual framework and a theory.

Conceptual frameworks generate a language for theory construction. Conceptual frameworks include a set of general assumptions/propositions that define relationships between and among framework constructs. That framework, according to Sztompka, defines the dimensions of variability and/or the polar opposites in measurement within the individual constructs. Conceptual frameworks, then, are precursors to theory development.

Sztompka (1974) further identifies seven requirements for a theory: (1) specification of the properties and scope of the problem or outcome of the theory; (2) general assumptions designating relationships between and among constructs; (3) testable propositions; (4) propositions must be justified in that, when tested, the results must be positive; (5) pragmatic completeness of propositions in that they must not create new problems of an explanatory nature in place of solved ones; (6) semantic consistency in that there are a definitive number of concepts coming from the same conceptual realm with consistent conceptual language being used; and (7) unification of theory, either downward unification in that theories can be linked by a common problem or outcome or upward unification where theories can be linked by common explanatory constructs.

Current conceptual frameworks and theories within the family business literature include, alphabetically: (a) the Bulleye model of an open-system approach (Pieper and Klein, 2007); (b) Family Embeddedness Perspective (FEP) (Aldrich and Cliff, 2003); (c) Resource-Based Framework (RBV) (Habbershon and Williams, 1999); (d) Sustainable Family Business Theory (SFBT)

(Danes et al., 2008a; Stafford et al., 1999; Danes and Brewton, 2012); (e) Theory of Agency and Altruism in Family Firms (TAA) (Schulze et al., 2003); and (f) Unified Systems Perspective of Family Firm Performance (USP) (Habbershon et al., 2003). An in-depth comparative analysis of these works is beyond this essay's scope, but their development has implications for the field's future directions.

These conceptual frameworks and theories have primarily developed via two paths reflecting the two systems – business and family. Some have emanated primarily from business such as RBV and TAA. They emerged as leading strategic management frameworks but do not address the influence between family and business (Chrisman et al., 2005). Other models such as the Bulleye and USP models address those reciprocal influences (Sharma, 2004). The USP framework does so by analyzing resources and capabilities of only the business in a manner consistent with RBV (Habbershon et al., 2003). The Bulleye model addresses reciprocity by analyzing heterogeneity among business structures and integrating individual members of a family within multi-level analyses of firms (Pieper and Klein, 2007). Frameworks and theories from business do not address heterogeneity among families, and only partially or indirectly address reciprocity between firms and owning families through analyses of businesses.

Another path in family business conceptual theory development evolved from within sociology and family science. These emphasize processes within family systems to a greater degree. Cramton (1993), in her in-depth qualitative study, first documented the value of analyzing owning families. FEP and SFBT exemplify this path of theoretical development. FEP has its roots in sociology and focuses on interaction between families and their businesses, but does so by tracing changes in family structure, roles, and rules (Aldrich and Cliff, 2003). SFBT has its roots in family science and focuses on family processes as well as family-business interaction processes rather than emphasizing structure, roles, and rules. It stipulates that long-term business sustainability is a function of both firm success and family functionality and recognizes that family capital effects can be simultaneously positive and negative. An SFBT advantage is its downward and upward unification with other theories, primarily because of its systems approach.

Frameworks (theories) developed in sociology and family science address the heterogeneity of both families and firms. However, FEP and SFBT address heterogeneity of families using different approaches. Aldrich and Cliff (2003) address the relevance of heterogeneity among families to the family business field and document that diversity via demographic changes in families. They then link family demographic characteristics to firm characteristics. Scholars using SFBT control for family and business structures, but they place more emphasis on the heterogeneity of family processes and link those processes to family business processes and outcomes (Danes et al., 2007, 2009a). Family business owners can change their processes more easily than they can change their family structures, roles, and rules.

Understanding differences among theories assists in assessing the developmental stage of the discipline. Further understanding nuances of theory development assists a multidisciplinary field in adopting research strategies to facilitate synthesis of results about the multiple dimensions of our focus entity – family businesses. For example, with unification of theory as a requirement for theory development, perhaps the disciplinary goal should not be a sole theory, but rather a number of well-developed theories that are linked by upward or downward unification.

Which one is chosen for a particular family firm study would then depend on the nature of the research question (e.g., one solely business system focused or one that focuses on a problem that entails resources or processes at the family/business intersection). Such a multi-disciplinary approach in continued theory development would create greater synthesis across researchers

in the future. At the same time, the complexities of the family business system and the heterogeneity of the owning family system would be addressed by multiple disciplines under varied conditions. Where we go from here necessitates greater conceptual and theoretical precision. At the same time, we need to use a theoretical approach that considers heterogeneity of the businesses and the owning families as they start, maintain, and transfer these vital global economic organizations.

The need for more investigation of the multidimensionality of family firm success focuses on Sztompka's requirement of specification of the properties and scope of the outcome construct within family firm research (Danes et al., 2008b). Although most business studies use financial performance as the firm success indicator, a growing number of studies are beginning to use non-financial measures to address issues associated with using solely financial data (Oughton and Wheelock, 2003). The financial bottom line is essential for continued firm viability, but when financial performance is the sole measure of firm success, understanding firm sustainability is compromised. Subjective, non-pecuniary firm success measures provide more insight into owner commitment to or passion for the firm (Gimeno, 2005; Stanforth and Muske, 2001). With certain research questions or under certain circumstances, family firm success would be more valid if it were inclusive of firm success and family functionality. Furthermore, facing continuingly rapid changes, family firms will need more emphasis on developing exception routines for times of change to remain competitive (Stallings, 1998).

Much work yet remains to be done to reach pragmatic completeness of our propositions. There are three stages of development in doing so; the first stage focuses on structure, the second stage focuses more on processes, and the third focuses on processes over time. Thus far, researchers in the field have focused primarily on static structures, the natural place to start in a new field. It has been only recently that research has begun to analyze the more dynamic processes. However, further research on processes is needed.

We need to continually build on social systems theory and analyses based on such. Statistical procedures such as structural equation and hierarchical linear modeling now allow us to investigate dynamic processes while taking into account complex structures. A system's theory assumption critical to incorporate is parallel firm and family concepts. Greater emphasis on dynamic processes will not only contribute to upward and downward theory unification but yield more fertile results that can be applied to practice. Furthermore, although there have been some notable recent longitudinal studies (Danes et al., 2009a, 2009b; Gomez-Mejia et al., 2003; Salvato et al., 2010), more longitudinal research is needed to capture patterns and process trajectories and outcomes over time.

One cannot discuss family business research without saying something about the importance of levels of analyses. Family firm research concerns itself with organizational levels of analysis. For instance, Pearson et al. (2008) described family, organization, dominant coalition, or groups within family firms as levels of analysis in assessing familiness. Pieper and Klein (2007) specifically discussed the usefulness of the Bulleye Model for multi-level analysis of firms. More attention needs to be placed on levels of analysis with respect to measuring family functioning – family as a whole, any number of dyadic subsystems, and cross-generational families (Cook and Kenny, 2006). The systems theory assumption that the whole is greater than the sum of its parts implies that subsystems are embedded within one another; thus assessment is appropriate at each potential level (Grotevant and Carlson, 1989). In the future, researchers need to be cognizant of appropriate levels of analysis for their research question. Grotevant and Carlson (1989) further indicate that it is important to remember that self-report measures are measures of one

individual's perception of system reality. To address this constraint, future sampling procedures need to include more voices than the business owner.

FAMILY CAPITAL PERSPECTIVE

We know most about family human and financial capital. In the future, higher priority needs to be placed on family social capital. Social capital is typically consumed only when it is needed (Bengston et al., 2005). It can be relied upon to uphold social norms and reciprocate favors (Zuiker et al., 2003) for the firm's benefit. Wright et al. (2001) identify family as the key institution through which social capital is transmitted via investment in time and effort, development of affective ties, and establishment of guidelines about acceptable and unacceptable behaviors. These relational behaviors are based on contextual values, beliefs, and norms that emanate out of family structure (Arregle et al., 2007).

In 2009, Danes et al. (2009a) defined family capital as the total bundle of human, social, and financial capital. This definition bridges financial, social, and human capital and differs from other research. Other research conceptualized family capital solely as current social capital rooted in close family ties (Danes et al., 2008a; Hoffman et al., 2006), or emphasized either family members' human capital investments in firms or their firm financial capital investment (Sirmon and Hitt, 2003). While Danes et al.'s family capital definition implies a simple resource sum, future research should allow for the systems proposition application that the whole is greater than the sum of its parts to family capital because resources can be combined in different ways in varying circumstances and have a snowball effect over time.

Family capital is inherently a stock concept, but it can be operationally defined through both stock and flow measures (Arregle et al., 2007; Danes et al., 2009a).

Family capital is amounts of family resources available for use; actual use of family capital stocks occurs in the form of processes. Interpersonal and resource processes in the family and business create, maintain, deplete, or develop future family capital stocks. Research has assumed that if there is a stock, it will be used by the family firm. However, emphasizing only family capital stocks and then only stocks of owning family members employed formally within the firm has deterred the advancement of the field. When the family business field has more longitudinal studies, researchers will be able to capture long-run effects of the use of family capital stocks.

Measuring stocks at only one time point has affected our thinking, and thus, our interpretations of findings. For example, there is a thread of research about family conflict that refers to the tension paradox, meaning that some conflict can be beneficial while other conflict can be deleterious. This view results from time snapshots. When we think of tension dynamics as a process and analyze it as such over time, we begin to view tension as the result of processes that form a continuum from constructive to destructive with a threshold at which productivity is affected rather than a paradox or set of conflicting research results.

Operationalizing family capital is best illustrated through an input/output model. In present time (T_1), owning families access and use capital stocks that currently exist but were developed in the past (T_0). Processes of drawing upon this stock create changes in that stock (either enhancement or reduction), that when added to the original level, is the current period's output (T_1) that becomes input for the next time period (T_2). Understanding capital flows as well as stocks is critical to understanding long-term sustainability because Danes et al. (2009a) found when studying family capital's contribution to firm performance, access to and utilization of family social capital over time was more important for sustainability than capital levels.

In the future, greater conceptual precision is needed (Danes et al., 2009a; Sharma, 2008). For example, business studies have found that a structural measure of married/not married has been significant in predicting new venture success (Chrisman et al., 2002). However, if we are to build upon this knowledge to help business founders, we need to progress beyond using dichotomous variables. Spousal process measures such as spousal commitment, emotional support, and work/family conflict are what's critical in new venture sustainability, not the state of being married (Danes et al., 2010).

Three family capital characteristics facilitate bridging human, financial and social capital into one construct: storability, transformability, and interaction. Storability refers to the stock characteristic of family capital. Owners can *store* human and social capital just like financial capital (Light, 2001). For instance, family social capital can be thought of as resilience capital of the family firm. It is important to recognize capital of all family members, whether or not employed in the firm; family members not working in the firm can have a substantial influence not only monetarily, but also through injection of family values into firm goals, decision systems, and ways of interacting at the family/firm interface (Van Auken and Werbel, 2006).

Transformability and interaction characteristics refer to the process component of family capital. Just as financial capital can be *transformed* into physical assets or vice versa, social and human capital can be transformed into financial capital. For example, when family members commit to firm success by volunteering to work in the firm during high demand times, that family social capital has been transformed into firm human and financial capital. These are processes performed by family members that may or may not be formally employed within the family business, but whose actions and behavior affect firm sustainability.

Interaction of various capitals is a significant aspect of the owning family capital bundle. For instance, consider family financial capital use to purchase firm inventory. Firm decisions to use money supplied by family requires expenditure of social and human capital. Social relationships between family and firm determine a family's willingness to offer financial capital. Therefore, all three capital forms interact whenever transfers take place between family and firm; they create a family resilience capacity to address normative and non-normative changes.

FAMILY RESILIENCE CAPACITY

Family is the repository of resilience capacity for family firms (Danes et al., 2009b). Resilience capacity is a construct that focuses on family structural and functional integrity rather than on personal qualities of individuals. If owning families have built a stored capacity for resilience, when a planned change or an unplanned disruption is encountered, the store of trust and creativity in problem solving can be more easily and quickly tapped and adapted to new situations (Danes et al., 2002). Family functional and structural integrity are two dimensions of family resilience capacity within family firms (Danes and Stafford, 2011).

Family functional integrity (family stability) is measured by Family APGAR with five components: **a**daptation, **p**artnership, **g**rowth, **a**ffection, and **r**esolve (Smilkstein et al., 1982). Components represent important family science constructs; each component has a unique family function, yet is related to the whole (Danes and Morgan, 2004). Family structural integrity represents congruity about decision making and activity coordination between family and firm. It establishes the extent to which different aspects of families and firms, both individually and collectively, fit together harmoniously at the family/firm interface into family knowledge and action (Avery and Stafford, 1991). At any point in time, lack of congruity undermines efficiency, reduces cooperation and decreases resilience (Stafford and Avery, 1993).

EXCEPTION ROUTINES IN TIMES OF CHANGE

Family and firm are affected by environmental and structural change. Owners constantly monitor internal firm and external environmental problems and changes to maintain competitive advantage (Olson et al., 2003). Firm owners perceive, process, and respond to changing environments and reconstruct processes to ensure sustainability over time, whether disruptions come from the community, such as public policy changes, or from inside the family business (Danes et al., 2005). During stable periods, family and firm are managed within their boundaries, but during change, resources are exchanged across family/firm boundaries (Danes et al., 2008b).

Processes such as family and firm management are foci of family firm research. These processes can be thought of as routine or standard operating procedures. How families use resources and processes during change, however, facilitates or inhibits firm sustainability even more than the nature of standard operating procedures (Danes et al., 2002). During change, routine procedures may not be as effective as they are in stable times, so exception routines must be used (Stallings, 1998). Exception routines are mechanisms for addressing restoration of social order and reestablishment of routines that were disrupted. Exception routines draw on owning family resilience capacity and occur at the family/firm boundary where resources are shared.

Although family firm sustainability depends, in part, upon how it adapts to change, it is important to understand resource and interpersonal transactions that increase the probability of successful change. Family adjustment strategies occur at the family/firm interface and they build resilience capacity. There are six potential strategies: (1) personal time reallocation; (2) obtaining additional help; (3) adjusting family resources; (4) adjusting firm resources; (5) intertwining tasks; and (6) intermingling of family and firm finances (Fitzgerald et al., 2001). Family adjustment strategy patterns automatically kick in when planning a change.

Family capital stock availability is a prerequisite to management. Family capital supports family firm managerial functions directly through use of family money and labor or indirectly by creating relationship and activity patterns to be drawn upon. This difference in impact of capital stock versus flow on firm achievements and sustainability means that researchers in the future should pay careful attention to whether stock or process measures of family capital are used when reviewing research or when conducting their own research. They should also ascertain both stocks available and stock used rather than assuming family capital stock available is used. For researchers and consultants, this distinction is particularly important. Prior to recommending family capital use, one should ascertain the stock available. It is also important to note that non-use of family capital does not necessarily indicate absence of family capital.

CONCLUSION

We started out this essay quoting Cook and Kenny, who said that the difference between a group of individuals and a family is like the difference between a pile of bricks and a house. In the early stages of our field development, researchers focused on structure (the bricks), but our field has now developed to the point where we have entered stage two of development where we investigate processes (the cement). The third stage of investigating the richness and dynamics of longitudinal process patterns and trajectories is the future direction of the family business field.

Future family firm research needs theories that recognize the heterogeneity of families and businesses and that address process as well as structure. Future research needs theories that facilitate synthesis of results from various disciplines and foci. In other words, the field would benefit from the use of theories that acknowledge family resilience capacity comprised of family social capital stocks and flows that interconnect family and business systems, that recognize that processes differ in times of stability and change, and that identify processes affecting not only the short term but also the long term. Understanding dynamics of processes over time will contribute greatly to the application of research results to practice. Researchers need to build on social systems theory concepts and in so doing Sztompka's theoretical requirement for upward and downward unification of theory could be met. Attention needs to be given to greater conceptual precision when measuring family processes. Furthermore, family business research needs to incorporate multi-dimensional definitions of major family and business outcomes.

Sampling procedures need to include more than the business owner's voice. Questions need to be inclusive of family and business system management. Data needs to be longitudinal to capture resource flows as well as resource stocks, and to understand standard operating procedures as well as exception routines. Measures need to reflect not only resource stocks and flows but also resource and interpersonal transactions. For example, 'family' measures should be more than dummy variables such as married/non-married.

Just as businesses need to grasp effects of the global market, we, as a family business field need to capture effects of bonding and bridging characteristics of family social capital. But it is not just the level of family social capital that we need to more fully understand. We need to more fully grasp the intricate processes that construct family social capital development and maintenance over time if we are to capture the competitive advantage those processes have to offer family businesses.

ACKNOWLEDGEMENT

The author thanks Kathryn Stafford, Associate Professor, Ohio State University for her insightful review of this essay.

REFERENCES

Aldrich, H.E. and Cliff, J.E. (2003). The pervasive effects of family on entrepreneurship: Toward a family embeddedness perspective. *Journal of Business Venturing*, 18, 573–596.

Arregle, J., Hitt, M.A., Sirmon, D.G., and Very, P. (2007). The development of organizational social capital: Attributes of family firms. *Journal of Management Studies*, 44(1), 73–95.

Avery, R.J. and Stafford, K. (1991). Toward a scheduling congruity theory of family resource management. *Lifestyles: Family Economic Issues*, 12(4), 325–344.

Bengston, V.L., Acock, A.C., Allen, K.R., Dilworth-Anderson, P., and Klein, D.M. (2005). *Sourcebook of Family Theory and Research*. Thousand Oaks, CA: Sage Publications.

Chrisman, J.J., Chua, J.H., and Sharma, P. (2005). Trends and directions in the development of a strategic management theory of the family firm. *Entrepreneurship: Theory and Practice*, 29(5), 555–575.

Chrisman, J.J., Chua, J.H., and Steier, L.P. (2002). The influence of national culture and family involvement on entrepreneurial perceptions and performance at the state level. *Entrepreneurship: Theory and Practice*, 126(4), 113–129.

Cook, W.L. and Kenny, D.A. (2006). Examining the validity of self-report assessments of family functioning. *Journal of Family Psychology*, 20(2), 209–216.

Cramton, C.D. (1993). Is rugged individualism the whole story? Public and private accounts of a firm's founding. *Family Business Review*, 6, 233–261.

Danes, S.M. and Brewton, K.E. (2012). Follow the capital: Benefits of tracking family capital across family and business systems. In A. Carsrud and M. Brannback (eds), *Understanding Family Businesses: Undiscovered Approaches, Unique Perspective, and Neglected Topics*. New York: Springer.

Danes, S.M., Haberman, H.R., and McTavish, D. (2005). Gendered discourse about family business. *Family Relations*, 54, 116–130.

Danes, S.M., Lee, J., Amarapurkar, S., Stafford, K., and Haynes, G.W. (2009b). Determinants of family business resilience after a natural disaster by gender of business owner. *Journal of Developmental Entrepreneurship*, 14(4), 333–354.

Danes, S.M., Lee, J., Stafford, K., and Heck, R.K.Z. (2008a). The effects of ethnicity, families and culture on entrepreneurial experience: An extension of sustainable family business theory. Invited Paper for *Journal of Developmental Entrepreneurship*, 13(3) 2229–2268.

Danes, S.M., Loy, J.T., and Stafford, K. (2008b). Management practices of small private firms within a quality framework. *Journal of Small Business Management*, 46(3), 395–421.

Danes, S.M., Matzek, A.E., and Werbel, J.D. (2010). Spousal context during the venture creation process. In J.A. Katz and G.T. Lumpkin (series eds) and A. Stewart, G.T. Lumpkin, and J.A. Katz (vol. eds), *Advances in Entrepreneurship, Firm Emergence and Growth* (pp. 113–162). New Milford, CT: Emerald.

Danes, S.M. and Morgan, E.A. (2004). Family business-owning couples: An EFT view into their unique conflict culture. *Contemporary Family Therapy*, 26(3), 241–260.

Danes, S.M., Rueter, M.A., Kwon, H.K., and Doherty, W. (2002). Family FIRO model: An application to family business. *Family Business Review*, 15(1), 31–43.

Danes, S.M. and Stafford, K. (2011). Family social capital as family business resilience capacity. In R. Sorenson (ed.), *Family Business and Social Capital* (pp. 79–105). Cheltenham: Edward Elgar.

Danes, S.M., Stafford, K., and Loy, J.T. (2007). Family business performance: The effects of gender and management. *Journal of Business Research*, 60(10), 1058–1069.

Danes, S.M., Stafford, K., Haynes, G., and Amarapurkar, S. (2009a). Family capital of family firms: Bridging human, Social, and financial capital. *Family Business Review*, 22(3), 199–215.

Fitzgerald, M.A., Winter, M., Miller, N.J., and Paul, J.J. (2001). Adjustment strategies in the family business: Implications of gender and management role. *Journal of Family and Economic Issues*, 22, 265–291.

Gimeno, A. (2005). Performance in the family business: A causal study of internal factors and variables, PhD dissertation, ESADE Universitat Ramon Llull, Spain.

Gomez-Mejia, L.R., Larraza-Kintana, M., and Makri, M. (2003). The determinants of executive compensation in family controlled public corporations. *American Management Journal*, 46(2), 226–239.

Grotevant, H.D. and Carlson, C.I. (1989). *Family Assessment: A Guide to Methods and Measures*. New York: Guilford.

Habbershon, T.G. and Williams, M.L., (1999). A resource-based framework for assessing the strategic advantages of family firms. *Family Business Review*, 12, 1–25.

Habbershon, T.G., Williams, M.L., and MacMillan, I.C. (2003). A unified systems perspective of family firm performance. *Journal of Business Venturing*, 18(4).

Hoffman, J., Hoelscher, M., and Sorenson, R. (2006). Achieving sustained competitive advantage: A family capital theory, *Family Business Review*, 19(2), 135–145.

Light, I. (2001). Social capital's unique accessibility. Paper presented at the Danish Building and Urban Research/EURA Conference, May 2001, Copenhagen.

Olson, P.D., Zuiker, V.S., Danes, S.M., Stafford, K., Heck, R.K., and Duncan, K.A. (2003). The impact of the family and business on family business sustainability. *Journal of Business Venturing*, 18, 639–666.

Oughton, E. and Wheelock, J. (2003). A capabilities approach to sustainable household livelihoods. *Review of Social Economy*, 61(1), 1–22.

Pearson, A.W., Carr, J.C., and Shaw, J.C. (2008). Toward a theory of familiness: A social capital perspective. *Entrepreneurship: Theory and Practice*, 32(6), 949–969.

Pieper, T.M. and Klein, S.B. (2007). The Bulleye: A systems approach to modeling family firms. *Family Business Review*, 20(4), 301–319.

Salvato, C., Chirico, F., and Sharma, P. (2010). A farewell to the business: Championing exit and continuity in entrepreneurial family firms. *Entrepreneurship and Regional Development*, 22(3–4), 321–348.

Schulze, W.S., Lubatkin, M.H., and Dino, R.N. (2003). Toward a theory of agency and altruism in family firms. *Journal of Business Venturing*, 18(4), 473–490.

Sharma, P. (2004). An overview of the field of family business studies: Current status and directions for future. *Family Business Review*, 17(1), 1–36.

Sharma, P. (2008). Commentary: Familiness: Capital stocks and flows between family and business. *Entrepreneurship: Theory and Practice*, 32(6), 971–977.

Sirmon, D.G. and Hitt, M.A. (2003). Managing resources: Linking unique resources, management, and wealth creation in family firms. *Entrepreneurship: Theory and Practice*, Summer, 339–358.

Smilkstein, G., Ashworth, C., and Montano, D. (1982). Validity and reliability of the family APGAR as a test of family function. *The Journal of Family Practice*, 15(2), 303–311.

Stafford, K. and Avery, R.J. (1993). Scheduling congruity theory of family resource management. In R. von Schweitzer (ed.), *Cross Cultural Approaches to Home Management* (pp. 17–41). Boulder, CO: Westview Press.

Stafford, K., Duncan, K.A., Danes, S.M., and Winter, M. (1999). A research model of sustainable family businesses. *Family Business Review*, 12(3), 197–208.

Stallings, R. (1998). Disaster and the theory of social order. In E.L. Quarantelli (ed.), *What is a Disaster? Perspectives on the Question* (pp. 127–145). New York: Routledge.

Stanforth, N. and Muske, G. (2001). *An Exploration of Entrepreneurship*. Stillwater, OK: Department of Design, Housing & Merchandising, Oklahoma State University.

Sztompka, P. (1974). *System and Function: Toward a Theory of Society*. New York: Academic Press.

Van Auken, H. and Werbel, J. (2006). Family dynamic and family business financial performance: Spousal commitment. *Family Business Review*, 19(1), 49–64.

Wright, J.P., Cullen, F.T., and Miller, J.T. (2001). Family social capital and delinquent involvement. *Journal of Criminal Justice*, 29, 1–9.

Zuiker, V.S., Katras, M.J., Montalto, C.P., and Olson, P.D. (2003). Hispanic self-employment: Does gender matter? *Hispanic Journal of Behavioral Sciences*, 25(1), 73–94.

32

Entrepreneurial Venturing for Family Business Research

Frank Hoy

INTRODUCTION

Both entrepreneurship and family business are prehistoric in origin. Archaeologists have discovered evidence worldwide of commerce, venture creation, and the involvement of family members that predates written records. Yet both fields have only recently received attention in academia. (Hoy and Verser, 1994: 9)

In the years since those words were published, entrepreneurship courses have been introduced in thousands of colleges and universities worldwide. Family business courses have proliferated, though not to the extent of entrepreneurship. There are now dozens of journals specializing in entrepreneurship for research publication. In recent years, *Family Business Review*, launched in 1988, has been joined by the *Electronic Journal of Family Business Studies* (2007), the *Journal of Family Business Strategy* (2010), and the *Journal of Family Business Management* (2011). Despite these advances, many scholars in business schools and other disciplines still consider entrepreneurship and family business to be emerging fields.

The title of this essay conveys multiple meanings. First, it indicates that I am approaching family business research from an entrepreneurship perspective. I came to entrepreneurship from an organization theory education and remain primarily an entrepreneurship educator.

Second, the inclusion of the word 'venturing' implies that future directions for family business research may involve and should involve some risk taking by scholars. In other words, investigations must go beyond safely building on prior studies and established theories. The choice of 'venturing' also reflects an argument that I made years ago that the word 'venture' has particular application to entrepreneurship, whereas we associate 'firm' with economics and finance and 'organization' with organization theory (Hoy, 1995). A venture is an entity distinct from an individual entrepreneur. It could be a business firm or an organization with an alternative purpose. It involves organizing, but may not in fact result in an organization.

Third, an early and continuing concern of entrepreneurship scholars has been a maturing of a field that should, by its nature, be innovative and disruptive. Will future research streams be characterized by incremental contributions to dominant themes, or will scholars venture down paths less taken? This essay proposes approaches to scholarly contributions to the family business literature that interrelate with entrepreneurship with a call for studies that provide value to practice.

Trudy Verser and I (Hoy and Verser, 1994) proposed interrelationships between entrepreneurial venturing and behavior and the governance and strategy formulation and implementation of family firms. Specifically, we contended that leadership, culture, boards of directors, life cycles, strategic management processes, and ethics and values offered particular promise for researchers and practitioners. Advances have been made in each of these areas. Leadership has, of course, long been one of the most studied subjects in management. Along with boards of directors and strategic management processes, attention has been given to leadership associated with succession, habitual entrepreneurship, growth strategies and numerous other issues in the family business literature (Yu et al., 2012; and in this *Handbook*, McKelvie et al., 2014; Rosa et al., 2014). There is much yet to be learned on these subjects, but the research streams are well established.

Culture, life cycles, and ethics and values have similarly been investigated over the intervening years. They are not generally included among the lists of most frequently studied nor most influential topics. Yet there are aspects of each that suggest exciting and productive paths for investigation for teaching and practice as well as research. Within culture, the application of business history research methods offers great potential, while from a practical perspective, documenting the organizational culture may serve as a tool for infusing guiding beliefs. Life cycles have been examined in numerous ways, and various authors have devised models applicable to family firms. Yet evidence of value is elusive, arguably a function of the low number of longitudinal studies. Life cycle analyses typically focus on single,

relatively limited stage models, for products or for organizations or for individuals. Gersick et al. (1997) anticipated that their more complex interactive model would stimulate further research, but report being discouraged that they have not observed such results (Hoy, 2012). Ethics and values seem to get more attention in the practitioner literature than in scholarship. The *Journal of Ethics & Entrepreneurship* was introduced in 2011, perhaps indicative of greater interest in the subject. Although advisors to family businesses discuss ethical issues with their clients, there has been little research into the daily events that arise for entrepreneurs and family business owners that are not necessarily illegal, but which may diminish trust in business and personal relationships.

THOUGHTS ON FUTURE DEVELOPMENT

There are a variety of approaches to recommending new directions for family business research. Chrisman et al. (2010) identified a set of articles that they felt established the dominant research themes in family business, suggesting high potential future directions. Some of the most respected scholars in the field have laid out alternative agendas for research (Brockhaus, 2004; Heck et al., 2008; Sharma, 2004; Zahra et al., 2006; Uhlaner et al., 2012). One conclusion that may be drawn from these various reviews and summaries is that 'new' trends tend to be logical, often incremental, extensions of prior research to learn something new about the issues that continue to be important to family business practitioners.

It is obviously possible to develop a lengthy set of trends and directions. As indicated above, there are three subject areas that I would like to advocate for future development: life cycles, histories, and ethics. Each of these areas can be examined from a multitude of disciplinary perspectives. I find them especially applicable to this essay because they adhere to the Aldrich and Cliff notion of *family embeddedness*. In 2003, Aldrich and

Cliff argued that family embeddedness was an overlooked dimension in entrepreneurship studies. They acknowledged that serious attention was being given to the social relationships of entrepreneurs, but faulted scholars for ignoring the social institution to which all entrepreneurs belong: the family. The chapters in this *Handbook* provide ample evidence that any understanding of family business demands a grasp of embeddedness, whether entrepreneurship, accounting, anthropology, economics, marketing, or other disciplines. The perspective of embeddedness is especially attractive to certain fundamentals of entrepreneurship: venture creation and innovation. Adding depth to the body of knowledge in these three areas selected for this essay offers direct value to practitioners and students regarding starting, growing, and sustaining family ventures.

Life cycles and ethics have appeared on earlier lists of topics needing further research in family business. Nevertheless, I consider them legitimate 'new' trends in that they have only recently begun to receive the attention they deserve in ways that can prove useful to practitioners. Histories can be approached in a variety of ways. In this *Handbook*, for example, Colli and Fernández Pérez (2014) conduct a business history investigation into family firms. Alternatively, what I have in mind is closely related to *culture* as the term has been used by authors. Recording histories of family enterprises, however, is a more practical mechanism for sustaining and even instilling culture in organizations and families than prior prescriptions. Let us turn now to each of these developments

Life Cycles

Early applications of the life cycle as a tool for business analysis addressed the introduction and acceptance of products in the marketplace. This draws a biological analogy of an organism's life cycle, applied to the explanation of the birth or introduction of a product, its growth in sales, maturity through a leveling off period, and subsequent decline and death or disappearance. Assuming validity to this theory, product managers could select promotion and distribution tactics to fit each stage of development and could predict customer response. As with any behavioral theory, there are many exceptions and aberrations to the product life cycle pattern. The product life cycle has received general acceptance in the marketing literature.

Organizational theorists and strategic management scholars have similarly concluded that organizations also follow life cycles, progressing naturally from conception to death. Early contributions to the understanding of the life cycles of organizations were made by Chandler (1962) and Scott (1971). Churchill and Lewis (1983) tailored a model to smaller firms. Day, among others, declared that 'life cycle stages may be one of the single most important variables to consider' in strategy (1987: 105). Why have life cycle models achieved this prominence? Primarily because they have been found to have both predictive and explanatory value.

One of the first studies to tie life cycles to family firms was by Navin (1971). Navin identified five stages of development based on the leadership exhibited in the firm: initiator, founder, founder's heirs, technicians, and professional managers. Hollander and Elman (1988) reported that phase and stage models offered predictability and highlighted interactive influences of the individual, family and business life cycles. From this perspective, the growth and transitions of family firms are seen as normal and predictable rather than pathological. A recurring theme in the entrepreneurship literature is the question of whether a founding entrepreneur can mature through organizational life stages into a professional manager. Demonstrating the difficulty of maturing, Pascarella and Frohnan (1990) listed the following clashes that occur as firms grow:

- The founder's autonomy vs reporting systems and controls.
- Tolerance for uncertainty vs reduction of uncertainty.

- Independent and unstructured vs interdependent and coordinated.
- Personal energy and efforts vs ability to work with and through others.
- Ideas and individuality vs policies and procedures.

It should be evident that life cycle analysis may contribute findings to the professionalization debates that have long been going on both in entrepreneurship (Hofer and Charon, 1984) and family business (Hall and Nordqvist, 2008). The stereotype of the entrepreneur is the controlling visionary, good at launching and growing the new venture, but lacking the skills to manage it for long-term sustainability. With family firms, this perception has been transferred to the patriarch who may be unwilling to surrender control to a succeeding generation, whether or not they are prepared. This has led some scholars to reexamine the idea of professionalization. Hall and Nordqvist contend that professionalization encompasses formal competence associated with education, training, and experience, but should also perpetuate family values and norms. Similarly, Stewart and Hitt (2012) question whether we have even developed a vocabulary to articulate what professionalization is in an entrepreneurial family firm. Such concerns call out for longitudinal investigations of the interactions among the life cycles of generational participants of their organizations.

The most comprehensive description of family business life cycles to date is the book by Gersick et al., *Generation to Generation: Life Cycles of the Family Business* (1997). Gersick et al. offered an important contribution to the literature by adding development over time to the three circle model. Their three-dimensional development model adds a sequence of stages to each of the subsystems: ownership, family, and business. They contend that each of the evolutionary progressions is independent of, yet influences the other two. They ultimately derived two lessons from their analysis:

1   Treat the business like a business, the family like a family, and ownership with respect (p. 274).
2   Keep in mind the inevitable, constant nature of developmental change (p. 276).

The arguments of Gersick et al. introduce us to the interactions of multiple life cycles. My inclusion of life cycles as a trend in family business research to watch resulted from an interview with Gersick (Hoy, 2012), in which he observed that he and his co-authors were gratified by the attention their work received, but disappointed that their model did not lead to a breakthrough by others in the use of life cycle analysis as a tool for scholars and practitioners. We see from the family business literature that the developmental stages of owners, families, and businesses are independent yet interactive. We began this discussion with the life cycles of products. That would add a fourth dimension to the Gersick et al. model. Suppose the model also included the life cycle of the industry in which the firm competes. Consider the evolution of the transportation industry, or health care, or consumer electronics. Each of those encompasses much more than a single product, yet each follows a development stage model. Then add life cycles for technology, for the market being served, for key employees, etc. Clearly, a typical business owner will, at any point in time, find some of the life cycles to be compatible and others to be in conflict in terms of appropriate strategies and behaviors for success of the business and harmony of the family.

One of the underlying assumptions of scholarship is that it is desirable to be parsimonious in our models. The amount of information available to business owners and managers is overwhelming. They must, therefore, make decisions under the constraints of bounded rationality. Family business is a complex domain. Life cycle analysis can be an extremely valuable tool to help founders, successors, and others understand the inherent conflicts of the enterprise and move toward more optimal solutions.

Histories

Years ago, the second generation owner of a family enterprise told me that there was a key reason why his firm would not be a family business after his retirement, even though it might still be managed by his son. The son did not possess the same commitment or emotional attachment to the business that the current owner did or his father before him. The owner could recall the struggles his father went through in founding the business and building it into a thriving enterprise. The business was, in some sense, another child to the father. The owner grew up working beside his father, making the company a major competitor in its industry. His son did not have the same appreciation for the sacrifices that his progenitors had made. In the opinion of the owner, by the third generation, memories of what had made the company and why it existed were lost. The third generation, as a result, would not seek to continue the firm as a family enterprise.

Many corporations have commissioned biographers to write histories of their companies. Some may see this as an egotistical exercise designed to glorify a founder or a management team. Others may interpret authorized histories as efforts to counter criticisms or rationalize actions. Family businesses can benefit from the capture of historical events, however, by documenting what are often amazing achievements. A business that survives long enough to transfer from one generation to another may have prevailed against tremendous odds.

In an early, seminal contribution to the family business literature, Dyer (1986) emphasized the guiding beliefs of organizational members, explaining how critical such beliefs can be to sustaining the culture of an organization and gaining commitment from new entrants. Sharing the history of the venture has the effect of ensuring that the culture will be maintained in some form over the years. Shared vicarious experiences bring the group together in times of celebration and in times of trauma. Similarly, a shared knowledge of the family business can bind family members together and even encourage commitment from non-family employees who may feel they are part of an epic saga. As mentioned in the life cycle section, Hall and Nordqvist (2008) and Stewart and Hitt (2012) envisioned guiding beliefs to be essential in the professionalization of family firms, thus increasing the prospects for survival and growth.

One purpose of histories is to document the emotional origins of a family firm. This is especially relevant to the entrepreneurial context. What gave the founder the 'fire in the belly' to start the business? Was the venture born a family firm with family members acknowledged as direct participants or indirectly involved through financing and other support? Or do they evolve into family businesses with family members participate in ownership and management (Chua et al., 2004; Welsch et al., 1995). Humanizing the process, rather than a simple litany of facts and dates, brings the history to life for those who follow. The history should include the key factors that led to the company's survival and success. Major forces, both internal and external, that influenced how the company developed should be included.

In 2005, six universities, one in the United States and five in Europe, created a research consortium in recognition of the need to gather and analyze enterprise survival across generations. The underlying assumption of the organizers of the Successful Transgenerational Entrepreneurship Practices (STEP) project was that growth and continuity involved more than simply passing a business from one generation to the next. They hypothesized that the fire in the belly was as important to successors as to founders, thus requiring entrepreneurial mindsets and capabilities on the part of those successors (STEP, 2010; Babson College, 2012). STEP researchers compile histories of multi-generational enterprises examining whether the entrepreneurial orientation of firms results in growth and wealth creation. The potential impact of the in-depth case studies being conducted attracted the interest of family business scholars from around the world. There are now four regional consortia with over 40 universities designated as members of STEP.

In their chapter on business history and family firms in this *Handbook*, Colli and

Fernández Pérez (2014) emphasize an additional dimension regarding how historical analyses add value to our understanding of dominant themes in family business. They criticize traditional analyses for attempting to separate ownership and management in historical investigations and call for including family embeddedness into studies, which could be seen as a charge to the STEP researchers. Colli and Fernández Pérez explain that research into family business histories can add to theory and model development, which I would argue will further our understanding of the family business/entrepreneurship relationship.

Research is needed not just into family business histories, but also to determine whether a company history can be used to chart a course for the future. A history may have both internal and external uses. It may motivate both family and nonfamily staff members and can be a sales tool with prospective customers. It informs and encourages future generations. It may enable successors to move up the learning curve more rapidly, rather than having to learn solely through experience as their predecessors did. The history can articulate a set of principles or values for both the business and the family.

Ethics

As with the two prior directions I have discussed, the notion of ethics is not new. Yet I believe it is appropriate to include in a call for venturing in family business research. Partially, this is because I concur with others that the subject of ethics has received insufficient empirical research attention in the family business literature to date (O'Boyle et al., 2010). But primarily, I include ethics because I believe in this era of global enterprise and expanded communication ability, the price of unethical behavior is higher than ever before. And there are unique threats and opportunities for family businesses regarding ethical practices. There is some evidence that family-owned businesses, on average, behave more ethically than nonfamily-owned

businesses as a result of two driving forces (Aronoff and Ward, 1995):

1 People who think longer term tend to be more ethical.
2 The more relationships matter, the more ethical people will be.

Thus, the strength of family relationships and the tendency to think of the firm surviving transitions from one generation to another support ethical behavior.

Prior research has observed cultural differences in attitudes toward ethics in cross-country comparisons. Other studies have reported that entrepreneurs are more similar across cultures than they are to non-entrepreneurs within their own countries (Thomas and Mueller, 2000). If perceived ethical behavior influences the ability to initiate and grow trade relationships both within a country and internationally, are family enterprises able to achieve competitive advantages through building trust derived from consistent representation of family values with business partners?

Eddleston et al. (2010) called for further research into trust, described as a willingness to be vulnerable with the expectation that a partner will not engage in opportunistic behavior, in family business. Their focus was on governance of the enterprise and trust within the firm and family. In their chapter on trust in this *Handbook*, Steier and Muethel (2014) approach families as social organizations, along the lines of Aldrich and Cliff (2003). They propose metaphors that facilitate understanding how trust may be engendered or diminished. Their theoretical frameworks should encourage examining how trust and distrust arise and are manifested in family enterprises. Family ethical issues arise frequently in the practitioner literature with examples such as employing and promoting family members who lack qualifications for their positions, compensating family members who do not perform assigned responsibilities, allocating organizational resources to non-business-related family activities, etc. Accepting the concept of embeddedness suggests that these behaviors will be observed within the firm potentially communicated to external parties.

Extending the notion of trust beyond organization boundaries, in the entrepreneurship literature start-up ventures are often found to suffer liabilities of newness. Because the firms lack resources, experience, and reputation, they are at a competitive disadvantage in obtaining customers, suppliers, and sources of financing. Actions taken by entrepreneurs may be ethically questionable regarding efforts to represent themselves as longer established or better financed (Pivoda et al., 2011). Entrepreneurs have been found to intentionally engage in misleading actions to present images of their firms as more stable than their track records can document. Compromising on ethical values in early stages of the venture's life cycle may set a pattern for further compromises. If relationships matter, however, are the founding entrepreneurs jeopardizing trust that might otherwise be established with prospective alliance partners? This may help us answer questions such as, do organizational cultures serve to foster higher standards or authorize lower ethical standards by family members and employees?

CONCLUSION

This essay proposes areas in which more and better research is needed, literally globally. As much as they may have in common, family business practices are not identical from one country to another, or even within countries. Family-owned firms are a relatively recent subject of research and education. We have much to confirm in and add to the literature to be sure that we are offering useful principles and models to students and practitioners. Studies specific to the life cycles of family firms, the writing and use of company histories, and the influence of ethics on firm survival are needed to confirm or revise what we currently treat as common knowledge.

For the first recommended direction, I concur with the conclusion reached by many of my academic colleagues: life cycle stage models are among the most useful tools for explaining and predicting strategic management behavior currently available. My caution at this point relates to the interactions of multiple life cycles. The simple model is indeed too simple. Understanding the complexity of interacting life cycles can give the family business manager not only insight into what strategies might be most effective at a point in time, but also can help explain conflict among family members and within the firm.

Second, recording the history of the firm can add value in many ways. In the short term the history can be a useful sales tool and can motivate employees. In the longer term, it can establish a culture that can contribute to the survival of the firm across generations. Historical analysis is a methodology that has been underutilized in entrepreneurship and family business scholarship. It provides a depth of penetration that can contribute new approaches to model building and to explanations that offer value to practitioners.

Third, ethical practices will only become more important to business success in the global economy. In the information age, reputation is more important than ever. Research has demonstrated the multitude of undesirable downside effects of unethical behavior by family members. We need to learn much more about the interconnectedness of ethics and trust and the implications for marketing, human resource management, and strategic alliance issues in family enterprises.

REFERENCES

Aldrich, H.E. and Cliff, J.E. (2003) 'The pervasive effects of family on entrepreneurship: Toward a family embeddedness perspective', *Journal of Business Venturing*, 18(5): 573–596.

Aronoff, C.E. and Ward, J.L. (1995) 'Family-owned businesses: A thing of the past or a model for the future?', *Family Business Review*, 8(2): 121–130.

Babson College (2012) 'Successful entrepreneurship transgenerational practices (STEP)', available at: http://www.babson.edu/Academics/centers/blank-center/global-research/step/Pages/home.aspx.

Brockhaus, R. (2004) 'Family business succession: Suggestions for future research', *Family Business Review*, 17(2): 165–177.

Chandler, A.D. (1962) *Strategy and Structure: Chapters in the History of the Industrial Enterprise*. Cambridge, MA: MIT Press.

Chrisman, J.J., Chua, J.H., and Steier, L.P. (2003) 'An introduction to theories of family business', *Journal of Business Venturing*, 18(4): 441–448.

Chrisman, J.J., Kellermanns, F.W., Chan, K.C., and Liano, K. (2010) 'Intellectual foundations of current research in family business: An identification and review of 25 influential articles', *Family Business Review*, 23(1): 9–26.

Chua, J.H., Chrisman, J.J., and Chang, E.P.C. (2004) 'Are family firms born or made? An exploratory investigation', *Family Business Review*, 17(1): 37–54.

Churchill, N.C. and Lewis, V.L. (1983) 'The five stages of small business growth', *Harvard Business Review*, 61(3): 30–51.

Colli, A. and Fernández Pérez, P. (2014) 'Business history and family firms', in L. Melin, M. Nordqvist, and P. Sharma (eds), *The SAGE Handbook of Family Business*. London: Sage.

Day, D.L. (1987) 'A contingency theory of product life cycle, relatedness and resulting synergies', in N.C. Churchill, J.A. Hornaday, B.A. Kirchhoff, O.J. Krasner, and K.H. Vesper (eds), *Frontiers of Entrepreneurship Research*. Wellesley, MA: Babson College.

Dyer, W.G. Jr. (1986) *Cultural Change in Family Firms: Anticipating and Managing Business and Family Transitions*. San Francisco, CA: Jossey-Bass.

Eddleston, K.A., Chrisman, J.J., Steier, L.P., and Chua, J.H. (2010) 'Governance and trust in family firms: An introduction', *Entrepreneurship: Theory and Practice*, 34(6): 1043–1056.

Gersick, K.E., Davis, J.A., Hampton, M.M., and Lansberg, I.S. (1997) *Generation to Generation: Life Cycles of the Family Business*. Cambridge, MA: Harvard Business School Press.

Hall, A. and Nordqvist, M. (2008) 'Professional management in family businesses: Toward an extended understanding', *Family Business Review*, 21(1): 51–69.

Heck, R.K.Z., Hoy, F., Poutziouris, P.Z., and Steier, L.P. (2008) 'Emerging paths of family entrepreneurship research', *Journal of Small Business Management*, 46(3): 317–330.

Hofer, C.W. and Charon, R. (1984) 'The transition to professional management: Mission impossible?', *American Journal of Small Business*, 9(1): 1–11.

Hollander, B.S. and Elman, N.S. (1988) 'Family-owned businesses: An emerging field of inquiry', *Family Business Review*, 1(2): 145–164.

Hoy, F. (1995) 'Researching the entrepreneurial venture', in J.A. Katz and R.H. Brockhaus, Sr., (eds), *Advances in Entrepreneurship, Firm Emergence, and Growth*, Vol. 2. Greenwich, CT: Jai Press, pp. 145–174.

Hoy, F. (2012) 'Book review: *Generation to Generation: Life Cycles of the Family Business*', *Family Business Review*, 25(1): 117–120.

Hoy, F. and Verser, T.G. (1994) 'Emerging business, emerging field: Entrepreneurship and the family firm', *Entrepreneurship: Theory and Practice*, 19(1): 9–23.

McKelvie, A., McKenny, A., Lumpkin, G.T., and Short, J. (2014) 'Corporate entrepreneurship in family businesses: Past contributions and future opportunities', in L. Melin, M. Nordqvist, and P. Sharma (eds), *The SAGE Handbook of Family Business*. London: Sage.

Navin, T.R. (1971) 'Passing on the mantle', *Business Horizons*, 14(5): 83–93.

O'Boyle, E.H., Jr., Rutherford, M.W., and Pollack, J.M. (2010) 'Examining the relation between ethical focus and financial performance in family firms: An exploratory study', *Family Business Review*, 23(4): 310–326.

Pascarella, P. and Frohnan, M.A. (1990) *The Purpose-Driven Organization*. San Francisco, CA: Jossey-Bass.

Pivoda, M., Hoy, F., Todorov, K., and Vojtko, V. (2011) 'Entrepreneurial tricks and ethics surveyed in different countries', *International Journal of E-Entrepreneurship and Innovation*, 2(3): 46–63.

Rosa, P., Howorth, C., and Discua Cruz, A. (2014) 'Habitual and portfolio entrepreneurship in the family contexts: Longitudinal perspectives', in L. Melin, M. Nordqvist, and P. Sharma (eds), *The SAGE Handbook of Family Business*. London: Sage.

Scott, B.R. (1971) 'Stages of corporate development – Part I', Boston, MA: Intercollegiate Case Clearinghouse, Harvard University.

Sharma, P. (2004) 'An overview of the field of family business studies: Current status and directions for the future', *Family Business Review*, 17(1): 1–36.

Steier, L. and Muethel, M. (2014) 'Trust and family businesses', in L. Melin, M. Nordqvist, and P. Sharma (eds), *The SAGE Handbook of Family Business*. London: Sage.

STEP Project for Family Enterprising (2010) 'STEP enlistment packet', Babson College.

Stewart, A. and Hitt, M.A. (2012) 'Why can't a family business be more like a nonfamily business? Modes of professionalization in family firms', *Family Business Review*, 25(1): 58–86.

Thomas, A.S. and Mueller, S.L. (2000) 'A case for comparative entrepreneurship: Assessing the relevance of culture', *Journal of International Business Studies*, 31(2): 287–301.

Uhlaner, L., Kellermanns, F., Eddleston, K., and Hoy, F. (2012) 'The entrepreneuring family: A new paradigm for family business research', *Small Business Economics*, 38(1): 1–11.

Welsch, H., Hills, G., and Hoy, F. (1995) 'Family impacts on emerging ventures in Poland', *Family Business Review*, 8(4): 293–300.

Yu, A., Lumpkin, G.T., Sorenson, R.L., and Brigham, K.H. (2012) 'The landscape of family business outcomes: A summary and numerical taxonomy of dependent variables', *Family Business Review*, 25(1): 33–57.

Zahra, S.A., Klein, S.B., and Astrachan, J.H. (2006) 'Theory building and the survival of family firms: Four promising research directions', in P.Z. Poutziouris, K.X. Smyrnios, and S.B. Klein (eds), *Handbook of Research on Family Business*. Cheltenham: Edward Elgar, pp. 196–214.

33

A Look into the Future: What is the Next Generation of Family Business Scholars Focusing on?

Alexandra Dawson

INTRODUCTION

Although motivations and objectives may vary significantly, many of us representing the next generation of family business scholars (henceforth next-gen FB scholars, defined as individuals who are currently PhD candidates, research assistants/fellows, or assistant professors) strive to be first-class scholars advancing the family business discipline. In today's universities, scholarship can be thought of as having two key functions referring to discovery and integration (Boyer, 1990; Sharma, 2010). First, scholarship of discovery is about research, that is pursuing knowledge for its own sake through freedom of inquiry and efforts of investigation. Scholars engaged in discovery enjoy not only the outcomes, but also the process and the passion that are associated with that effort. 'Scholarly investigation … is at the very heart of academic life' and 'the probing mind of the researcher is an incalculably vital asset to the academy and the world' (Boyer, 1990: 18). As next-gen FB scholars, we are often drawn to the family business field by interest and passion. In their survey of family business scholars, Litz et al. (2012) found that one of the strongest motivations for undertaking family business research was 'because family businesses are intrinsically interesting'. Second, scholarship of integration is closely related to discovery and entails making connections among isolated facts – even across disciplines – and giving them perspective and meaning. Scholars writing review articles, meta-analyses, or essays for handbooks such as this one can be considered as being engaged in this type of interpretative scholarship (Sharma, 2010). This form of scholarship is more challenging for next-gen FB scholars, because it requires specialized skills to link, bridge, and connect to current and prior work (Rindova, 2008). Although it may be easy to find a topic that seems conducive to writing a review article, for example one that has generated equivocal findings in the past or that has not been synthesized for a certain amount of time, the actual 'art of writing' a review is not easy (Short, 2009).

As well as analyzing relevant works, integrating prior knowledge entails presenting strengths and weaknesses, highlighting general themes, evaluating trends, providing novel explanations, and, most importantly, encouraging new theoretical insights and indicating new areas of research. These skills are best developed over time, often through collaborations with more senior scholars (Rindova, 2008).

As they focus on scholarship of discovery and integration, next-gen FB scholars need to find the right balance between joining the academic conversation on topics of interest and developing new avenues of research or ways of thinking about such topics (Rindova, 2008). The aim of this essay is to explore the research areas that next-gen FB scholars are interested in and to compare these to the prevalent topics – as well as the gaps – in family business research. The rest of the essay is structured as follows. First, I present how I identified next-gen FB scholars and present an analysis of their published articles. The analysis is based on a comparison with the main areas, as well as gaps, in family business research (Chrisman et al., 2003a; Debicki et al., 2009). Second, I discuss three main themes that emerge from the analysis. Finally, I present concluding remarks offering ideas for future research.

METHOD AND RESULTS

The data for this survey was gathered in two steps. First, I identified next-gen FB scholars by searching websites listing the main academic awards in the family business field (see Table 33.1). I only considered next-gen FB scholars who were first or second author, because I took this as an indication that the individual played a key role in the research project. Two award winners were excluded (one is a family business consultant who is not engaged in an academic career and the other has previously held a position as associate professor). The search included awards that went back to 2006, in order to capture individuals (such as myself) who were in the early or middle stages of their PhD dissertation at the time. This search resulted in 39 award winners, including 19 PhD candidates, 4 research assistants/fellows, and 16 assistant professors, who won a total of 48 awards.

The second step was to identify articles written by next-gen FB scholars. This was done through a Google Scholar search, including the individuals identified in step one as authors and using 'family' as a keyword in the title. The search was limited to peer-reviewed articles, therefore book chapters, conference proceedings, and discussion and working papers were excluded. Online resumes for award winners were also checked, to capture forthcoming articles (for 2012). This search resulted in 48 articles, authored or co-authored by 22 next-gen FB scholars (see Table 33.2). Because of the inclusion criteria, the list does not include articles published on topics outside the family business area. Out of the 39 award winners identified in step one, 17 did not have any peer-reviewed publications with the word 'family' in the title. Almost half of the articles appeared in dedicated journals: *Family Business Review* (18, or 38%) and *Journal of Family Business Strategy* (5, or 10%).

Table 33.1   Next-gen FB award winning scholars

Year	Award*	Next-gen FB scholars
2011	AoM Best Family Business Paper Award	Bammens, Yannick
	FBN Asia/IFERA Asia Pacific Research Grant	Guerra, Archimedes David
	FBN-I/IFERA Honors to next generation	Binz, Claudia

Year	Award*	Next-gen FB scholars
	FBR Best Paper Winner	Block, Jörn
	FERC Doctoral Award	Barbera, Francesco; Hasso, Tim; Kammerlander, Nadine
	FOBI Award	Boers, Börje; Holt, Daniel T.; Joshi, Mahendra
2010	FBR Best Paper Winner	Hsu, Wen-Tsung
	FERC Best Paper Award	Jaskiewicz, Peter
	FERC Doctoral Award	Gunn, Frances; Joseph, Alexandra; Lindow, Corinna; Litchfield, Shanan R.; McKee, D'Lisa N.; Parada, Maria Jose
	FOBI Award	Barbera, Francesco; Dawson, Alexandra; Giudice, Rebecca M.; Gottschall, Richard; Hanisch, David; Hasso, Tim; Pieper, Torsten M.
2009	FBN-I/IFERA Honors to next generation	Woodfield, Paul
	FBR Best Paper Winner	Sciascia, Salvatore
	FERC Doctoral Award	Funk, Jeremy; Greidanus, Nathan; James, Albert E.; Niedermeyer, Christian
	FERC Honorable Mention Award	Blombäck, Anna; Singal, Manisha; Wigren, Caroline
	FOBI Award	Chirico, Francesco; Memili, Esra; Misra, Kaustav; Perry, John
2008	FBN-I/IFERA Best policy-oriented research paper	Block, Jörn
	FBN-I/IFERA Doctoral Research Competition	Björnberg, Åsa
	FERC Best Paper Award	Chirico, Francesco
	FOBI Award	Singal, Manisha
2007	FERC Best Paper Award	Bammens, Yannick; Berent-Braun, Marta; Jaskiewicz, Peter; Pieper, Torsten M.
2006	Babson College Best Paper on the Topic of Family Business	Dawson, Alexandra
	FERC Best Paper Award	Loy, Teik-Cheok Johnben

* AoM=Academy of Management; FBN=Family Business Network; FERC=Family Enterprise Research Conference; FOBI=Family Owned Business Institute; IFERA=International Family Enterprise Research Academy.

Table 33.2   Articles by next-gen FB scholars

Article*	Title	Topic(s)**
Astrachan, J. and *Jaskiewicz, P.* (2008)	Emotional returns and emotional costs in privately held family businesses: advancing traditional business valuation	Nonstrategic management
Bammens, Y., Voordeckers, W., and Van Gils, A. (2008)	Boards of directors in family firms: a generational perspective	Corp. governance

(Continued)

Table 33.2 (Continued)

Article*	Title	Topic(s)**
Bammens, Y., Voordeckers, W., and Van Gils, A. (2011)	Boards of directors in family businesses: a literature review and research agenda	Corp. governance
Barbera, F. and Moores, K. (2013)	Firm ownership and productivity: a study of family and non-family SMEs	Economic performance
Berent-Braun, M.M. and Uhlaner, L.M. (2012)	Family governance practices and teambuilding: paradox of the enterprising family	Corp. governance; economic performance
Björnberg, A. and Nicholson, N. (2007)	The family climate scales – development of a new measure for use in family business research	Culture and values
Block, J. (2010)	Family management, family ownership, and downsizing: evidence from S&P 500 firms	Business strategy; leadership and ownership
Block, J. (2011)	How to pay non-family managers in large family firms: a principal–agent model	Professionalization
Block, J. (2012)	R&D investments in family and founder firms: an agency perspective	Entrepreneurship and innovation
Chang, E.P.C., *Memili, E.,* Chrisman, J.J., Kellermanns, F.W., and Chua, J.C. (2009)	Family social capital, venture preparedness, and start-up decisions. A study of Hispanic entrepreneurs in New England	Resources and comp. advantage
Chen, H.L. and *Hsu, W.T.* (2009)	Family ownership, board independence, and R&D investment	Corporate governance; entrepreneurship and innovation
Chirico, F. (2008a)	Knowledge accumulation in family firms: evidence from four case studies	Systems, processes, and networks
Chirico, F. (2008b)	The creation, sharing and transfer of knowledge in family business	Systems, processes and networks
Chirico, F., Ireland, R.D., and Sirmon, D.G. (2011a)	Franchising and the family firm: creating unique sources of advantage through 'familiness'	Functional strategy
Chirico, F. and Nordqvist, M. (2010)	Dynamic capabilities and trans-generational value creation in family firms: the role of organizational culture	Culture and values
Chirico, F., Nordqvist, M., Colombo, G., and Mollona, E. (2012)	Simulating dynamic capabilities and value creation in family firms: is paternalism an 'asset' or a 'liability'?	Business strategy
Chirico, F. and Salvato, C. (2008)	Knowledge integration and dynamic organizational adaptation in family firms	Evolution and change
Chirico, F., Sirmon, D.G., *Sciascia, S.,* and Mazzola, P. (2011b)	Resource orchestration in family firms: investigating how entrepreneurial orientation, generational involvement, and participative strategy affect performance	Business strategy; resources and comp. advantage

Article*	Title	Topic(s)**
Danes, S.M., *Loy, T.J.*, and Stafford, K. (2008)	Business planning practices of family-owned firms within a quality framework	Strategic planning; economic performance
Danes, S.M., Stafford, K., and *Loy, T.J.* (2007)	Family business performance: the effects of gender and management	Economic performance
Dawson, A. (2011)	Private equity investment decisions in family firms: the role of human resources and agency costs	Non strategic management; succession
Dawson, A. (2012)	Human capital in family businesses: focusing on the individual level	Resources and competitive advantage
Dawson, A. and Hjorth, D. (2012)	Advancing family business research through narrative analysis	Succession
Granata, D. and *Chirico, F.* (2010)	Measures of value in acquisitions: family versus non-family firms	Non strategic management; succession
Greidanus, N. (2011)	Corporate venturing in family firms: a strategic management approach	Corporate strategy
Gudmunson, C.G., Danes, S.M., Werbel, J.D., and *Loy, T.J.* (2009)	Spousal support and work – family balance in launching a family business	Behavior and conflict
Holt, D.T., Rutherford, M.W., and Kuratko, D.F. (2010)	Advancing the field of family business research: further testing the measurement properties of the F-PEC	Other
James, A.E., Jennings, J.E., and Breitkreuz, R.S. (2012)	Worlds apart? Rebridging the distance between family science and family business research	Other
Jaskiewicz, P., González, V.M., Menéndez, S., and Schiereck, D. (2005)	Long-run IPO performance analysis of German and Spanish family-owned businesses	Economic performance
Jaskiewicz, P. and Klein, S. (2007)	The impact of goal alignment on board composition and board size in family businesses	Non-ec. goals; corporate governance
Lindow, C.M., Stubner, S., and Wulf, T. (2010)	Strategic fit within family firms: the role of family influence and the effect on performance	Resources and comp. advantage; environment threats and opportunities
Litz, R., Pearson, A.W., and *Litchfield, S.R.* (2012)	Charting the future of family business research: a report from the field	Other
Marchisio, G., Mazzola, P., *Sciascia, S.*, Milesc, M., and Astrachan, J. (2010)	Corporate venturing in family business: the effects on the family and its members	Corporate strategy
Memili, E., Chrisman, J.J., and Chua, J.H. (2011a)	Transaction costs and outsourcing decisions in small- and medium-sized family firms	Functional strategy

(Continued)

Table 33.2   (Continued)

Article*	Title	Topic(s)**
Memili, E., Chrisman, J.J., Chua, J.H., Chang, E.P.C., and Kellermanns, F.W. (2011b)	The determinants of family firms' subcontracting: a transaction cost perspective	Functional strategy
Memili, E., Eddleston, K.A., Kellermanns, F.W., Zellweger, T.M., and Barnett, T. (2010)	The critical path to family firm success through entrepreneurial risk taking and image	Entrepreneurship and innovation; economic performance
Niedermeyer, C., Jaskiewicz, P., and Klein, S. (2010)	'Can't get no satisfaction?' Evaluating the sale of the family business from the family's perspective and deriving implications for new venture activities	Corporate strategy; succession
Parada, M.J., Nordqvist, M., and Gimeno, A. (2010)	Institutionalizing the family business: the role of professional associations in fostering a change of values	Non strategic management
Parada, M.J. and Viladás, H. (2010)	Narratives: a powerful device for values transmission in family businesses	Culture and values
Perry, J.T., Pett, T.L., and Buhrman, A. (2010)	Participation in business associations and performance among family firms	Non strategic management; Economic performance
Pieper, T.M. (2010)	Non solus: toward a psychology of family business	Other
Pieper, T.M. and Klein, S.B. (2007)	The bulleye: a systems approach to modeling family firms	Goals and objectives
Pieper, T.M., Klein, S.B., and *Jaskiewicz, P.* (2008)	Impact of goal alignment on board existence and top management team composition: evidence from family-influenced businesses	Non-economic goals; leadership and ownership
Rutherford, M.W., Kuratko, D.F., and *Holt, D.T.* (2008)	Examining the link between 'familiness' and performance: can the F-PEC untangle the family business theory jungle?	Other; economic performance
Salvato, C., *Chirico, F.,* and Sharma, P. (2010)	A farewell to the business: championing exit and continuity in entrepreneurial family firms	Succession
Sciascia, S. and Mazzola, P. (2008)	Family involvement in ownership and management: exploring nonlinear effects on performance	Economic performance; leadership and ownership
Sciascia, S., Mazzola, P., Astrachan, J.H., and *Pieper, T.M.* (2012)	The role of family ownership in international entrepreneurship: exploring nonlinear effects	International strategy; leadership and ownership
Singal, M. and Singal, V. (2011)	Concentrated ownership and firm performance: does family control matter?	Economic performance

* Next-gen FB scholars are indicated in italics.
** Based on Chrisman et al. (2003a).

Table 33.3 Topic areas in family business research

Strategic Management primary topics	Chrisman et al. (2003a), 1999–2003 (n = 190)		Debicki et al. (2009), 2001–2007 (n = 291)		Δ% between studies	Next-gen FB scholars awards, 2006–2012 (n = 40[a])		Next-gen FB scholars' articles, 2006–2012 (n = 48)	
Most researched	%	Ranking	%	Ranking		%	Ranking	%	Ranking
Succession	22%	1	15%	3	−32%	3%	12	10%	2
Economic performance	15%	2	n/a[b]	n/a	n/a	20%	1	21%	1
Corporate governance	10%	3	19%	1	103%	13%	3	10%	2
Leadership and ownership	7%	4	16%	2	114%	10%	4	8%	6
Behaviors and conflict	6%	5	7%	5	4%	0%	–	2%	15
Resources and competitive advantage	6%	6	9%	4	48%	10%	4	8%	6
Gaps	%	Ranking	%	Ranking		%	Ranking	%	Ranking
Goal formulation process	1%	23	0%	21	−100%	0%	–	0%	–
Business strategy	1%	22	2%	16	56%	3%	12	6%	8
Corporate strategy	2%	19	1%	18	−14%	8%	6	6%	8
Structure	2%	19	4%	9	158%	0%	–	0%	–
Evolution and change	2%	19	5%	6	222%	0%	–	2%	15
Environment opportunity and threats	2%	16	1%	18	−35%	3%	12	2%	15
Stakeholders, ethics, social responsibility	2%	16	3%	11	31%	3%	12	0%	–
Professionalization	2%	16	3%	11	31%	5%	10	2%	15
Noneconomic goals	3%	13	1%	20	−60%	0%	–	4%	13

[a] Eight (out of 48) awards were shared.
[b] Not included in Debicki et al. (2009).

In order to analyze what next-gen FB scholars are focusing on, the 48 articles were coded according to their primary topics of research using the categories that were first identified by Chrisman et al. (2003a) and then used by Debicki et al. (2009) for their content analysis of family business research. These authors identified seven main research categories – goals and objectives, strategy formulation and content, strategy implementation and control, management, organizational performance, as well as other and nonstrategy – which were further divided into 23 subcategories (see Chrisman et al., 2003a, for a complete list and description). The top half of Table 33.3 shows the percentage and ranking of primary topics in family business research that received most interest in 1999–2003 (Chrisman et al., 2003a); the percentage and ranking for the same topics for 2001–2007 (Debicki et al., 2009); the percentage change from one period to the next; and the percentage and ranking for the research topics based on awards received and articles written by next-gen FB scholars in 2006–2012. The bottom half of Table 33.3 includes the same information referred to gaps in family business research.

Next-gen FB scholars are focusing on some of the most researched, and growing, topics in family business. These include economic performance (e.g., Barbera and Moores, 2013; Danes et al., 2007; Jaskiewicz et al., 2005; Perry et al., 2010; Sciascia and Mazzola, 2008; Singal and Singal, 2011) and corporate governance (e.g., Bammens et al., 2008; Berent-Braun and Uhlaner, 2012; Chen and Hsu, 2009). Other major topics, such as behaviors and conflict, are not attracting much attention by next-gen FB scholars. Next-gen FB scholars are also interested in topics categorized as 'other': for example, the definition of family business (e.g., Holt et al., 2010), methodologies (e.g., Dawson and Hjorth, 2012), theories of family business (e.g., Pieper, 2010), and trends in family business research (e.g., James et al., 2012; Litz et al., 2012). Among award winners, culture and values (particularly organizational identity) are, together

with economic performance, the topics that attracted most interest.

With regard to gaps in the literature, some next-gen FB scholars are addressing business strategy, which was identified by Debicki et al. (2009) as a gap being filled (e.g., Block, 2010, on downsizing; Chirico et al., 2011b, on participative strategy). Although it showed declining interest in Debicki et al.'s (2009) study, corporate strategy is attracting some interest by next-gen FB scholars who are focusing, for example, on corporate venturing (Greidanus, 2011; Marchisio et al., 2010).

DISCUSSION

Three main considerations emerge from this study. First, with regard to topics researched, although family business research has increasingly focused on a variety of issues (Bird et al., 2002; Chrisman et al., 2003b), succession has remained a dominant theme (Chrisman et al., 2005; Zahra and Sharma, 2004), even among next-gen FB scholars. Interestingly, next-gen FB scholars focusing on succession are considering nonfamily routes such as the sale of the family business (Granata and Chirico, 2010; Niedermeyer et al., 2010) or investment by private equity firms (Dawson, 2011). Furthermore, next-gen FB scholars are mostly focused on topics relating to economic performance (as discussed above) and not only on 'softer' topics such as culture (e.g., Björnberg and Nicholson, 2007) or image (e.g., Memili et al., 2010), thus addressing the concern raised by Habbershon and Pistrui (2002) about the family business field being excessively skewed towards 'soft' topics. Whilst both succession and economic performance are key components of the strategic management process (Sharma et al., 1997), there are still important gaps with regard to goal formulation, strategy formulation (other than succession), strategy implementation, and organizational performance concerning family goals. This suggests opportunities to advance the family business field by moving towards 'the primary goals of business research: the improvement of management practice and organizational performance' (Sharma et al., 1997: 17). Indeed incorporating a strategic management perspective could allow next-gen FB scholars to move our field closer towards developing a theory of the family firm (Chrisman et al., 2005).

Second, with regard to types of scholarship that next-gen FB scholars are engaging in, scholarship of discovery is prevalent. This is where these researchers can make most difference by contributing to the intellectual advancement of the family business field through new insights into established topics of research (such as economic performance or corporate governance) and into new areas (such as culture and values). Scholarship of discovery may actually be easier for next-gen FB scholars because they are less 'socialized in the paradigms' of our field and can bring novel ways of thinking to the family business discipline (Rindova, 2008: 300). However, the discovery activities that next-gen FB scholars are embarking on are mostly puzzle solving and incremental. This type of detailed analysis, aimed at analyzing, operationalizing, and measuring, is indeed what most research focuses on (Morgan, 1980). However, this should not become an end in itself and next-gen FB scholars should grasp the opportunity to make theoretical contributions to the field of family business, albeit within the realm of middle-range (or propositional) theory (Reay and Whetten, 2011). Next-gen FB scholars can push themselves more in terms both of theory building, by identifying new mediating or moderating variables and exploring more nuanced relationships or processes (delving not only into the 'what' but also into the 'how'), and of theory testing, by including not only causal connections in their models and diagrams, but also the underlying processes and phenomena that explain such connections (Colquitt and Zapata-Phelan, 2007; Whetten, 1989). With regard to theory building, the introduction of new constructs, such as familiness or socio-emotional wealth, is probably a greater challenge for next-gen

FB scholars, as it 'requires a considerable amount of skillful linking, bridging, and connecting to the current work in a given area' (Rindova, 2008: 300), which is developed with time and experience. This is also a riskier activity, as efforts towards theory building need to be reconciled with 'playing it safe', as the latter may be viewed as increasing chances of success in publishing.

To a lesser extent, next-gen FB scholars are also engaging in the more challenging scholarship of integration, helping to consolidate prior knowledge and showing new directions (Sharma, 2010). For example, James et al. (2012) review trends in family business research in the period 1985–2010, comparing them to family science research.

Third, with regard to approaches and methodologies, next-gen FB scholars have embraced the trend towards rigorous empirical studies with large samples (Zahra and Sharma, 2004). However, studies by next-gen FB scholars continue to be generally based on functionalist approaches, which assume that organizations and organizational phenomena are objective (Gioia and Pitre, 1990), and rely on 'familiar research methods and analytical tools that essentially give published research a mechanical quality' (Zahra and Sharma, 2004: 336), as is made evident by the predominance of regression analysis. Writing about the management field, Hambrick lamented that:

> [the] field's theory fetish … prevents the reporting of rich detail about interesting phenomena for which no theory yet exists. And it bans the reporting of facts – no matter how important or competently generated – that lack explanation, but that, once reported, might stimulate the search for an explanation. (2007: 1346)

A couple of articles by next-gen FB scholars (Dawson and Hjorth, 2012; Parada and Viladás, 2010), however, offer new directions towards the adoption of new, and richer, methods that can broaden the way we understand family business phenomena. By supplementing functionalist approaches, interpretive methods, such as narrative analysis, can generate insights and explain phenomena and processes by focusing on understanding human behavior and the complex, dynamic and relational quality of social interactions (Cope, 2005; Leitch et al., 2010). This can be done through the use of rigorous and in depth case studies, interviews, observations and documents (including biographies and autobiographies) providing new, and sometimes critical, interpretations (Nordqvist et al., 2009). In this regard, the Successful Transgenerational Entrepreneurship Practices (STEP) Project (Sharma et al., 2012) is building a database of rich case studies of family firms used, for example, by Salvato et al. (2010) in their longitudinal analysis of the entrepreneurial renewing of a family firm. Another way of broadening our understanding of family businesses is by addressing the multifaceted and complex nature of family business through multilevel models. This is being done both on a theoretical level – Pieper and Klein (2007) proposed a model of family business with multiple levels of analysis and dynamic interdependencies among subsystems – and on a methodological level – Dawson (2011) employed a multilevel data analysis method.

CONCLUSION

Given that next-gen FB scholars are the future of our field, which directions are they moving towards and what are the opportunities available to them? First, the scholarship of discovery that next-gen FB scholars are engaging in is very much incremental. While this is comprehensible, especially in light of publish or perish pressures, future efforts in this area might focus on stressing one of the strengths, and sources of interest, of the family business field, i.e., its eclectic nature, offering opportunities for multidisciplinary (e.g., integrating psychology or family studies) and multimethod (e.g., adopting interpretive approaches) research. Second, activities directed at scholarship of integration can benefit from incorporating insights and frameworks from

other disciplines. Whilst there has been regular stocktaking in the family business field (Zahra and Sharma, 2004), it may be interesting to compare the state of the art of our field with other fields (both inside and outside the business domain) at various stages of their emergence and development, as similarities and differences could yield helpful insights. Third, future research can be enriched by recognizing the natural affinity between family business research on the one hand and entrepreneurship and strategic management research on the other. Opportunity- and advantage-seeking behaviors (Hitt et al., 2001) are idiosyncratic in family firms because the desired outcome is not only wealth but also value creation. Whilst next-gen FB scholars are addressing some of the topics stemming from the integration between entrepreneurship and strategic management, such as resources, organizational learning, innovation and internationalization (Hitt et al., 2001; Lounsbury and Glynn, 2001), other fruitful avenues of research include exploring external networks as sources of information and resources, managerial practices favoring innovation, learning traps hindering innovation, as well as storytelling by family firms as a means to increase legitimacy and shape (organizational but also familial) identity. Fourth, there are untapped opportunities for next-gen FB scholars to give back to other disciplines (Zahra and Sharma, 2004). For example, are there conditions under which the positive outcomes of the 'family effect' on firm performance, such as kinship ties reducing agency costs or unique assets such as human and social capital (Dyer, 2006), can be successfully replicated in nonfamily firms? Or, conversely, can we apply what we have learnt about conflict in family firms – for example, that altruism and paternalism among members of the same family can generate agency conflicts (Kellermanns et al., 2008; Schulze et al., 2001) – to nonfamily firms in which managers have comparable altruistic and paternalistic attitudes towards their employees? Finally, whilst around half of the articles by next-gen

FB scholars have appeared in dedicated family business outlets, greater integration with other business disciplines, leading to publishing in more general outlets, can be fruitful (Zahra and Dess, 2001) and also increase the legitimacy and reputation of the family business field.

ACKNOWLEDGEMENTS

I am grateful to Guido Corbetta who first opened the doors to the family business world for me and then guided me with his challenging and insightful ways; to Carlo Salvato who showed me what the life of a generous and tireless scholar is like; and to Pramodita Sharma who has opened new avenues, and has given me direction and inspiration. Also, thank you to the editors, and especially Leif Melin, for their helpful comments.

REFERENCES

Astrachan, J. and Jaskiewicz, P. (2008) 'Emotional returns and emotional costs in privately-held family businesses: advancing traditional business valuation', *Family Business Review*, 21(2): 139–149.

Bammens, Y., Voordeckers, W., and Van Gils, A. (2008) 'Boards of directors in family firms: a generational perspective', *Small Business Economics*, 31(2): 163–180.

Bammens, Y., Voordeckers, W., and Van Gils, A. (2011) 'Board of directors in family businesses: a literature review and research agenda', *International Journal of Management Reviews*, 13(2): 134–152.

Barbera, F. and Moores, K. (2013) 'Firm ownership and productivity: a study of family and non-family SMEs', *Small Business Economics*, 40(4): 953–976.

Berent-Braun, M.M. and Uhlaner, L.M. (2012) 'Family governance practices and teambuilding: paradox of the enterprising family', *Small Business Economics*, 38(1): 103–119.

Bird, B., Welsch, H., Astrachan, J.H., and Pistrui, D. (2002) 'Family business research: the evolution of an academic field', *Family Business Review*, 15(4): 337–350.

Björnberg, A. and Nicholson, N. (2007) 'The family climate scales: development of a new measure for use in family business research', *Family Business Review*, 20(3): 229–246.

Block, J. (2010) 'Family management, family ownership, and downsizing: evidence from S&P 500 firms', *Family Business Review*, 23(2): 109–130.

Block, J. (2011) 'How to pay nonfamily managers in large family firms: a principal–agent model', *Family Business Review*, 24(1): 9–27.

Block, J. (2012) 'R&D investments in family and founder firms: an agency perspective', *Journal of Business Venturing*, 27(2): 248–265.

Boyer, E.L. (1990) *Scholarship Reconsidered: Priorities of the Professoriate*. Princeton, NJ: The Carnegie Foundation for the Advancement of Teaching.

Chang, E.P.C., Memili, E., Chrisman, J.J., Kellermanns, F.W., and Chua, J.C. (2009) 'Family social capital, venture preparedness, and start-up decisions: a study of Hispanic entrepreneurs in New England', *Family Business Review*, 22(2): 279–292.

Chen, H.L. and Hsu, W.T. (2009) 'Family ownership, board independence, and R&D investment', *Family Business Review*, 22(4): 347–362.

Chirico, F. (2008a) 'Knowledge accumulation in family firms: evidence from four case studies', *International Small Business Journal*, 26(4): 433–462.

Chirico, F. (2008b) 'The creation, sharing and transfer of knowledge in family business', *Journal of Small Business & Entrepreneurship*: 21(4): 413–433.

Chirico, F., Ireland, R.D., and Sirmon, D.G. (2011a) 'Franchising and the family firm: creating unique sources of advantage through "familiness"', *Entrepreneurship: Theory and Practice*, 35(3): 483–501.

Chirico, F. and Nordqvist, M. (2010) 'Dynamic capabilities and transgenerational value creation in family firms: the role of organizational culture', *International Small Business Journal*, 28(5): 487–504.

Chirico, F., Nordqvist, M., Colombo, G., and Mollona, E. (2012) 'Simulating dynamic capabilities and value creation in family firms: is paternalism an "asset" or a "liability"?', *Family Business Review*, 25(3): 318–338.

Chirico, F. and Salvato, C. (2008) 'Knowledge integration and dynamic organizational adaptation in family firms', *Family Business Review*, 21(2): 169–181.

Chirico, F., Sirmon, D.G., Sciascia, S., and Mazzola, P. (2011b) 'Resource orchestration in family firms: investigating how entrepreneurial orientation, generational involvement, and participative strategy affect performance', *Strategic Entrepreneurship Journal*, 5(4): 307–326.

Chrisman, J.J., Chua, J.H., and Litz, R.A. (2003b) 'A unified systems perspective of family firm performance: an extension and integration', *Journal of Business Venturing*, 18(4): 467–472.

Chrisman, J.J., Chua, J.H., and Sharma, P. (2003a) *Current Trends and Future Directions in Family Business Management Studies: Toward a Theory of the Family Firm*. Coleman Foundation White Paper Series, available at: http://www.usasbe.org/knowledge/whitepapers/ index.asp.

Chrisman, J.J., Chua, J.H., and Sharma, P. (2005) 'Trends and directions in the development of a strategic management theory of the family firm', *Entrepreneurship: Theory and Practice*, 29(5): 555–576.

Colquitt, J.A. and Zapata-Phelan, C.P. (2007) 'Trends in theory building and theory testing: a five-decade study of Academy of Management Journal', *Academy of Management Journal*, 50(6): 1281–1303.

Cope, J. (2005) 'Researching entrepreneurship through phenomenological inquiry: philosophical and methodological issues', *International Small Business Journal*, 23(2): 163–189.

Danes, S.M., Loy, J.T., and Stafford, K. (2008) 'Business planning practices of family-owned firms within a quality framework', *Journal of Small Business Management*, 46(3): 395–421.

Danes, S.M., Stafford, K., and Loy, T.J. (2007) 'Family business performance: the effects of gender and management', *Journal of Business Research*, 60(10): 1058–1069.

Dawson, A. (2011) 'Private equity investment decisions in family firms: the role of human resources and agency costs', *Journal of Business Venturing*, 26(2): 189–199.

Dawson, A. (2012) 'Human capital in family businesses: focusing on the individual level', *Journal of Family Business Strategy*, 3(1): 3–11.

Dawson, A. and Hjorth, D. (2012) 'Advancing family business research through narrative analysis', *Family Business Review*, 25(3): 339–355.

Debicki, B.J., Matherne III, C.F., Kellermanns, F.W., and Chrisman, J.J. (2009) 'Family business research in the new millennium: an overview of the who, the where, the what, and the why', *Family Business Review*, 22(2): 151–166.

Dyer, D.G. Jr. (2006) 'Examining the "family effect" on firm performance', *Family Business Review*, 29(4): 253–273.

Gioia, D.A. and Pitre, E. (1990) 'Multiparadigm perspectives on theory building', *Academy of Management Review*, 15(4): 584–602.

Granata, D. and Chirico, F. (2010) 'Measures of value in acquisitions: family versus nonfamily firms', *Family Business Review*, 23(4): 341–354.

Greidanus, N. (2011) 'Corporate venturing in family firms: a strategic management approach', *International Journal of Entrepreneurial Venturing*, 3(2): 125–148.

Gudmunson, C.C., Danes, S.M., Werbel, J.D., and Loy, J.T. (2009) 'Spousal support and work–family balance in launching a family business', *Journal of Family Issues*, 30(8): 1098–1121.

Habbershon, T.G. and Pistrui, J. (2002) 'Enterprising families domain: family-influenced ownership groups in pursuit of transgenerational wealth', *Family Business Review*, 15(3): 223–238.

Hambrick, D.C. (2007) 'The field of management's devotion to theory: too much of a good thing?', *Academy of Management Journal*, 50(6): 1346–1352.

Hitt, M.A., Ireland, R.D., Camp, S.M., and Sexton, D.L. (2001) 'Strategic entrepreneurship: entrepreneurial strategies for wealth creation', *Strategic Management Journal*, 22(6–7): 479–491.

Holt, D.T., Rutherford, M.W., and Kuratko, D.F. (2010) 'Advancing the field of family business research: further testing the measurement properties of the F-PEC', *Family Business Review*, 23(1): 76–88.

James, A.E., Jennings, J.E., and Breitkreuz, R.S. (2012) 'Worlds apart? Rebridging the distance between family science and family business research', *Family Business Review*, 25(1): 7–108.

Jaskiewicz, P., González, V.M., Menéndez, S., and Schiereck, D. (2005) 'Long-Run IPO performance analysis of German and Spanish family-owned businesses', *Family Business Review*, 18(3): 179–202.

Jaskiewicz, P. and Klein, S.B. (2007) 'The impact of goal alignment on board size and board composition in family-owned businesses', *Journal of Business Research*, 60(10): 1080–1089.

Kellermanns, F.W., Eddleston, K.A., Barnett, T., and Pearson, A. (2008) 'An exploratory study of family member characteristics and involvement: effects on entrepreneurial behavior in the family firm', *Family Business Review*, 21(1): 1–14.

Leitch, C.M., Hill, F.M., and Harrison, R.T. (2010) 'The philosophy and practice of interpretivist research in entrepreneurship: quality, validation, and trust', *Organizational Research Methods*, 13(1): 67–84.

Lindow, C., Stubner, S., and Wulf, T. (2010) 'Strategic fit within family firms: the role of family influence and the effect on performance', *Journal of Family Business Strategy*, 1(3): 167–178.

Litz, R.A., Pearson, A.W., and Litchfield, S. (2012) 'Charting the future of family business research: perspectives from the field', *Family Business Review*, 25(1): 16–32.

Lounsbury, M. and Glynn, M.A. (2001) 'Cultural entrepreneurship: stories, legitimacy, and the acquisition of resources', *Strategic Management Journal*, 22(6–7): 545–564.

Marchisio, G., Mazzola, P., Sciascia, S., Milesc, M., and Astrachan, J. (2010) 'Corporate venturing in family business: the effects on the family and its members', *Entrepreneurship & Regional Development*, 22(3–4): 349–377.

Memili, E., Chrisman, J.J., and Chua, J.H. (2011a) 'Transaction costs and outsourcing decisions in small- and medium-sized family firms', *Family Business Review*, 24(1): 47–61.

Memili, E., Chrisman, J.J., Chua, J.H., Chang, E.P.C., and Kellermanns, F.W. (2011b) 'The determinants of family firms' subcontracting: a transaction cost perspective', *Journal of Family Business Strategy*, 2(1): 26–33.

Memili, E., Eddleston, K.A., Kellermanns, F.W., Zellweger, T.M., and Barnett, T. (2010) 'The critical path to family firm success through entrepreneurial risk taking and image', *Journal of Family Business Strategy*, 1(4): 200–209.

Morgan, G. (1980) 'Paradigms, metaphors, and puzzle solving in organization theory', *Administrative Science Quarterly*, 25(4): 605–622.

Niedermeyer, C., Jaskiewicz, P., and Klein, S. (2010) '"Can't get no satisfaction?" Evaluating the sale of the family business from the family's perspective and deriving implications for new venture activities', *Entrepreneurship & Regional Development*, 22(3–4): 293–320.

Nordqvist, M., Hall, A., and Melin, L. (2009) 'Qualitative research on family businesses: the relevance and usefulness of the interpretive approach', *Journal of Management & Organization*, 15(3): 294–308.

Parada, M.J., Nordqvist, M., and Gimeno, A. (2010) 'Institutionalizing the family business: the role of professional associations in fostering a change of values', *Family Business Review*, 23(4): 355–372.

Parada, M.J. and Viladás, H. (2010) 'Narratives: a powerful device for values transmission in family businesses', *Journal of Organizational Change Management*, 23(2): 166–172.

Perry, J.T., Pett, T.L., and Buhrman, A. (2010) 'Participation in business associations and performance among family firms', *International Journal of Entrepreneurship and Small Business*, 11(3): 367–378.

Pieper, T.M. (2010) 'Non solus: toward a psychology of family business', *Journal of Family Business Strategy*, 1(1): 26–39.

Pieper, T.M. and Klein, S.B. (2007) 'The bulleye: a systems approach to modeling family firms', *Family Business Review*, 20(4): 301–319.

Pieper, T.M., Klein, S.B., and Jaskiewicz, P. (2008) 'Impact of goal alignment on board existence and top management team composition: evidence from family-influenced businesses', *Journal of Small Business Management*, 46(3): 372–394.

Reay, T. and Whetten, D.A. (2011) 'What constitutes a theoretical contribution in family business?', *Family Business Review*, 24(2): 105–110.

Rindova, V.P. (2008) 'Editor's comments: publishing theory when you are new to the game', *Academy of Management Review*, 33(2): 300–303.

Rutherford, M.W., Kuratko, D.F., and Holt, D.T. (2008) 'Examining the link between "familiness" and performance: can the F-PEC untangle the family business theory jungle?', *Journal of Small Business Management*, 46(3): 372–394.

Salvato, C., Chirico, F., and Sharma, P. (2010) 'A farewell to the business: championing exit and continuity in entrepreneurial family firms', *Entrepreneurship & Regional Development*, 22(3–4): 321–348.

Schulze, W.S., Lubatkin, M.H., Dino, R.N., and Buchholtz, A.K. (2001) 'Agency relationship in family firms: theory and evidence', *Organization Science*, 12(9): 99–116.

Sciascia, S. and Mazzola, P. (2008) 'Family involvement in ownership and management: exploring nonlinear effects on performance', *Family Business Review*, 21(4): 331–345.

Sciascia, S., Mazzola, P., Astrachan, J.H., and Pieper, T.M. (2012) 'The role of family ownership in international entrepreneurship: exploring nonlinear effects', *Small Business Economics*, 38(1): 15–31.

Sharma, P. (2010) 'Advancing the 3Rs of family business scholarship: rigor, relevance, reach', in A. Stewart, G.T. Lumpkin, and J.A. Katz (eds), *Advances in Entrepreneurship, Firm Emergence and Growth*. Bingley, UK: Emerald Group Publishing, pp. 383–400.

Sharma, P., Chrisman, J.J., and Chua, J.H. (1997) 'Strategic management of the family business: past research and future challenges', *Family Business Review*, 10(1): 1–35.

Sharma, P., Chrisman, J.J., and Gersick, K.E. (2012) '25 Years of Family Business Review: reflections on the past and perspectives for the future', *Family Business Review*, 25(1): 5–15.

Short, J. (2009) 'The art of writing a review article', *Journal of Management*, 35(6): 1312–1317.

Singal, M. and Singal, V. (2011) 'Concentrated ownership and firm performance: does family-control matter?', *Strategic Entrepreneurship Journal*, 5(4): 373–396.

Whetten, D. (1989) 'What constitutes a theoretical contribution?', *Academy of Management Review*, 14(4): 490–495.

Zahra, S.A. and Dess, G.G. (2001) 'Entrepreneurship as a field of research: encouraging dialogue and debate', *Academy of Management Review*, 26(1): 8–10.

Zahra, S.A. and Sharma, P. (2004) 'Family business research: a strategic reflection', *Family Business Review*, 17(4): 331–346.

34

Developing the Field of Family Business Research: Legitimization, Theory and Distinctiveness

David G. Sirmon

Like many scholars conducting research in the family business domain, my interests were primed by close personal experience. My older brothers formed a firm with expectations that their children would be involved and encouraged to assume leadership overtime. But the complexity of mixing family(ies) and business objectives proved insurmountable to this vision. Despite increasing, and indeed high, profitability, along with strong support from extended family members not involved with the actual enterprise, my brothers dissolved the business after many years. This ending, unfortunately, involved emotional trauma that continues to affect my extended family.

After my exposure to the unique resources and troubling complexities of family business, I was quite surprised and disappointed by the lack of theoretical coverage of this ownership structure in the major journals I was exposed to in my early doctoral program (around Fall, 2000). However, with broader reading I found that research pertaining to family firms had been flourishing and was just beginning to be placed more consistently in mainstream strategy and entrepreneurship journals. This growth was assisted by many individuals and endeavors. For instance, the *Family Business Research* journal, which was founded only 12 years before I began my doctoral studies, was advancing swiftly. The work of Professors Chua, Chrisman, and Steier was also very important. Their series of special issues in *Entrepreneurship: Theory and Practice* (*ET&P*) exposed many scholars to the field of family business. In fact, in a fortunate stroke of luck, they happened to ask Michael Hitt, my advisor, to consider writing about family firms for the initial family business special issue in *ET&P* in 2003 (Sirmon and Hitt, 2003). It took little time for us to develop a paper, based on my experiences and framed with resource-based logic, discussing the unique resources found in family firms and how these resources can be managed. While the special issues in *ET&P* continue, a reflection of the growth of the field can be found in the placement of family business special issues in other journals such as in the *Journal of Management Studies* (Schulze and Gedajlovic, 2010), *Strategic Entrepreneurship Journal* (Lumpkin et al., 2011), and *Small Business Economics* (Uhlaner et al., 2012).

While several excellent reviews of the family business literature exist, I find that reviewing these special issues offers a unique catalogue of how family business research has evolved in recent years. From my vantage point, these special issues suggest three issues related to the development of family business research. They are legitimization, theory, and distinctiveness.

First, a prominent goal for family business research, as echoed in many sources (e.g., see Sharma et al., 2012, in *Family Business Review*) over the past 20 years, has been to expand the role of family business research. Special issues remain a key driver for this strategy as they draw accomplished scholars to the family business research domain and with them younger scholars. This was clearly the case for Mike and me. Mike's credibility as a world-class scholar has helped in some ways to draw attention to the domain by raising awareness of family business research as well as increase the domain's sophistication in terms of theory development. Indeed, perusing the author list of the many family business special issues indicates that editors have been successful in drawing the attention of numerous world-class scholars to the phenomena of family business. Engaging these scholars provided strong impetus to the recent and rapid development of family business research. But as important, this strategy also drew many junior scholars from strategy, organizational theory, organizational behavior and entrepreneurship to family business of which many have maintained a continued interest. The efforts to draw senior and junior scholars to the field have worked to legitimize the domain (Melin and Nordqvist, 2007).

Indeed, the legitimization process is an ongoing one, but I would argue that most management scholars and scholars from allied fields are now familiar with family business and its growing importance to organizational studies. For example, several prominent authors whose family business research was first seen in a special issue continue to publish family business research in other outlets. Today, these outlets include the most prestigious journals such as *Administrative Science Quarterly*, *Academy of Management Journal*, and *Strategic Management Journal*.

Thus legitimization has occurred via the co-opting of scholars from allied areas and the development of junior scholars focused on family business research. Strengthening the field is ongoing via increased quality and relevance of research.

The second theme present in the recent development of family business research is related to theory. This comes in two parts. Early on the field seemed to be in a search for relevant theory. Arguably the two most prominent theories introduced recently have been agency and resource-based theory. Both theories have helped frame the unique context of family business. For example, my first work drew upon resource-based theory to identify the unique resources potentially available to family businesses and how the management or orchestration of those resources provide the family firm a potential competitive advantage and thereby a reason for the organizational form to exist in the competitive landscape. Agency theory, on the other hand, has been used to describe two different viewpoints pertaining to family businesses – one positive and the other negative. In this regard, Carney's (2005) agency-based work is tremendously useful. In debating the value of family firm governance, this model demonstrates how the unique governance elements of family firms could provide an advantage. However, not all family firms experience such an advantage because of differences in their alignment of three dominant propensities: parsimony, personalism, and particularism. Parsimony is the careful resource conservation and allocation resulting from family involvement. Personalism describes the personalization of authority in the family that can project its own vision onto the business. Particularism means that the family can use 'particularistic' criteria in making decisions. Importantly, neither the agency nor the resource-based approaches suggests a family firm will always have an advantage. Instead they provide a broader understanding of how and when family involvement could provide advantage.

To develop more specific representation of family business, recent work has begun to draw upon additional theories. For example, identity, socio-political, and multiple-agency theories, among others, are being presented and expanded on these special issues. However, of important note is the role that *Family Business Review* is playing in the flourishing of the family research agenda. An area of inquiry can be highlighted with special issues, but its sustainability requires ongoing, dedicated resources. The critical work being published in *Family Business Review* provides the ongoing development needed to extend our knowledge of family business. For example, in this journal we see work that extends our knowledge across a myriad of issues, including how the governance choices made by family firms affects firm performance (Miller and Le Breton-Miller, 2006), the role of family member characteristics in determining the firm's entrepreneurial behavior (Kellermanns et al., 2008), how family involvement in management and ownership differ (Sciascia and Mazzola, 2008), and how the management of social relationships over time (generations) is a key driver for family firm success (Salvato and Melin, 2008).

Thus in total, drawing theories into the family business domain has been very useful. While theory importation is useful, I would argue that 'home-grown' theories, such as socio-emotional wealth (e.g., Gomez-Mejia et al., 2011), offer the greatest advancements for the field. A focus on such family-focused theories will be critical for the fields continued development.

The third and last theme I see is distinctiveness. That is an effort in creating a field that possesses a unique focus thereby creating a complementary difference to other areas of inquiry. If a domain is not unique then, of course, it does not require dedicated resources such as dedicated journals, like *Family Business Review*; shepherding behaviors as demonstrated by the ongoing work of our senior scholars; nor special conferences, associations or the development of new family-focused divisions within existing associations – all of which are factors that help create and support the field distinctiveness. However, paradoxically, if a domain is too distinct then cross fertilization between domains is minimized, the intellectual richness of the field grows dull, and new scholars are less likely to focus their attention on the domain, all of which could lead the field to weaken and reverse the gains we have experienced in the past few decades.

Thus, the strong efforts to create and support the field of family business research were vital to the domain's rapid growth. However, we need to guard against becoming isolated as a field so that the pursuit of distinctiveness does not become ill-formed.

There is no doubt I have strong feelings toward the field and a keen interest in the future of family business research. My desire is for the field's continued ascension in terms of rigor, relevance, and reach; for family business research to influence academics, practitioners, and policy makers. It is my opinion that by maintaining a healthy tension in the literature, this future will be realized.

By tension, I mean a healthy debate among participants. Much like a healthy political system requires, at least, two capable groups or parties to develop robust initiatives, our field needs to embrace tensions in the literature. So, for example, while some may see value in proposing greater distinctiveness between family business research and other research, I argue for vigilance to prevent isolation. Family involvement – being intertwined with other ownership structures, cultures, political arrangements, and objectives – is simply too prevalent around the globe to encourage a narrow focus. Indeed, Sharma et al. (2012) identified how efforts by editors in *Family Business Review* worked to create a large domain for research pertaining to family business. Thus, in step to maintain this vision, preventing isolation may mean allowing tension to exist in our definition of family business.

Any reader versed in the family firm literature has seen many different definitions related to family involvement. In fact, some research shows that the performance benefits often attributed to family involvement is largely dependent on the chosen definition. We have also seen debate related to an essence- versus component-based definitional approach. This debate and tension is healthy. While, a consensus definition may sound appealing, it may encourage rigidness that prevents future extensions of our understanding.

I understand that such ambiguity slows the accumulation of findings and generally adds complexity to the literature stream. But as I have developed as a scholar, I have realized the benefits of such tension. For example, I clearly remember my frustration as a new PhD student as I searched for *the* definition of a firm 'resource'. It was not to be found. Many existed, each had strengths and deficiencies – some too narrow and others too inclusive. That *one* definition just did not exist in the literature and senior scholars in the area would not offer clear guidance. I wondered what could be gained by such ambiguity, but with time and a more broad understanding of the literature and the different perspectives of other scholars engaged in the stream – be it based on their current scholarly area (organizational theory, strategy, entrepreneurship, or international business) or an affiliation with a different discipline (economics, sociology, etc.) – I have begun to see that a vibrant area requires some level of tension.

I argue that only when authors, reviewers, and editors demand an *appropriate* definition of family business per research question instead of pushing for '*the*' definition, can true contributions spring forth. So, my hope is for family business researchers to require a thoughtful definition of the focal

organizations in each paper, but that a single definition is not allowed to become dominant. Such an approach will help retain the area's distinctiveness while providing for creative and inspiring work to propel our field. In fact, such an approach may encourage our theoretical knowledge to affect scholars in related areas. For example, insights from family firms help scholars understand other closely knit organizations such as religious or focused-nonprofit organizations. So, my first hope for the future of family business research is to promote tension. Here, I discuss tension in terms of definitions, but I would extend that to suggest tension in primary theories as well.

Another hope I have for future family business research is that our theories improve. From my vantage point the field's search for theory has been positive; however, despite the theoretical advancements we still do not capture the complexities that family involvement in business provides. The current state of theory portrays a 'clear but shallow' view of family business, while the integration of theories is needed to deepen understanding. To allow such integration, we should all accept, to the appropriate amount, the 'water to be muddied'. That is, we need to encourage the creative integration of theories. For example, how could Sirmon's resource-based (Sirmon and Hitt, 2003) work and Carney's agency-based (Carney, 2005) work be integrated to provide a more complete picture of potential advantage in family firms? Please note the work of these scholars both point to different, yet complementary elements which can support advantage. However, neither suggests all family firms will enjoy any such advantage. Do certain combinations of parsimony, personalism, and particularism affect the accumulation of certain unique resources? Or their bundling and deployment? Or does the initial resource portfolio of a family firm affect the development of the firm's governance element?

Likewise, the integration of entrepreneurial orientation and family firms may be promising. As Nordqvist and colleagues (Nordqvist and

Zellweger, 2010) have suggested, we simply do not yet understand why and how some family firms act entrepreneurially and others do not. What configurations of attributes lead to such behaviors? How fragile or robust are these combinations? Another series of questions that may hold important relevance examines how family involvement affects the sustainability of a firm's advantage, a community's vibrancy or even a nation's economy?

In fact, sustainability is an important interface with allied fields. While sustainability in strategy has often been focused on competitive advantage, in architecture the focus is on the sustainability of communities, and in science the focus is on the sustainability of ecosystems. But what does family business research bring to discussions of sustainability? I argue that much is offered. Not only do we focus on value creation, but also value retention across time and in the context of communities.

Family business research draws on two of the most basic mechanisms likely to affect any sustainability efforts – economic and familial. Thus, hybrid ownership structures, where different types of owners have input, may reconcile conflicting objectives (e.g., short- and long-term profits, the location of manufacturing facilities, treatment of employees, etc.). I suspect that balancing ownership structures (e.g., family and public ownership) will prevent systematic failures in industries and regions and the different objectives of the owners will burnish each other whereby some combination will promote sustainability. Of course, this is an optimistic perspective. The data may offer evidence to the contrary. But in either direction, we offer a unique academic voice, with rigor and relevance, to a debate with enormous policy implications. Thus, I hope that the field supports and encourages the integration of theories to address the many important topics that these few examples reflect.

It is important that my desire to allow the 'water to be muddied' not be misrepresented. I wholly support the creative integration of theories and know that this approach may lead to periods where our understanding may

even seem obfuscated, but that over time such efforts should provide greater clarity with increased depth of understanding. However, to accomplish this goal, as a field we need to increase the support we offer the research scholar.

This support may come in many forms. We already have specialized journals and associations. However, interest groups in our more general associations, such as the Strategic Management Society and the Academy of Management, may be worthwhile objectives. Moreover, the field may want to reconsider where such an interest group would first be sponsored. Family business research is often lodged with entrepreneurship. However, it may be better situated within a governance division, or altogether separate from other divisions.

Creating a division or interest group would offer support for Ph.D. students and young scholars as they begin their dissertation research and move on to publishing such work. Also, a division could enhance efforts to obtain empirical support for the field. For example, several special issues in *Organizational Research Methods* have been focused on strategy and/or entrepreneurship. It is high time for the application of sophisticated analytical tools be aimed at the family business researcher with treatment of the issues unique to this context. For example, as the family firm is inherently multi-level, our empirical treatment should reflect this reality. Thus, questions related to the decomposition of performance variance to the family versus other nested levels within the family firm may be worthwhile. However, is the current presentation of multi-level modeling adequately addressing the family business context such that scholars in the field can apply the tool effectively? In total, a division or interest groups in a major association could help focus support for the field's continued development.

I look forward to being a co-producer with you in the mutual objective of increasing our knowledge of family involvement. I think we are in for a very rewarding ride!

REFERENCES

Carney, M. 2005. Corporate governance and competitive advantage in family-controlled firms. *Entrepreneurship: Theory and Practice*, 29: 249–265.

Gomez-Mejia, L.R., Cruz, C., Berrone, P., and De Castro, J. 2011. The bind that ties: Socioemotional wealth preservation in family firms. *The Academy of Management Annals*, 5: 653–707.

Kellermanns, F.W., Eddleston, K.A., Barnett, T. and Pearson, A. 2008. An exploratory study of family member characteristics and involvement: Effects on entrepreneurial behavior in the family firm. *Family Business Review*, 21: 1–14.

Lumpkin, G.T., Steier, L., and Wright, M. 2011. Strategic entrepreneurship in family business. *Strategic Entrepreneurship Journal*, 5: 285–306.

Melin, L. and Nordqvist, M. 2007. The reflexive dynamics of institutionalization: The case of the family business. *Strategic Organization*, 5: 321–333.

Miller, D. and Le Breton-Miller, I. 2006. Family governance and firm performance: Agency, stewardship, and capabilities. *Family Business Review*, 19: 73–87.

Nordqvist, M. and Zellweger, T.M. 2010. *Transgenerational Entrepreneurship: Exploring growth and performance in family firms across generations*. Edward Elgar: Cheltenham, UK.

Salvato, C. and Melin, L. 2008. Creating value across generations in family-controlled businesses: The role of family social capital. *Family Business Review*, 21: 259–276.

Schulze, W.S. and Gedajlovic, E.R. 2010. Whither family business? *Journal of Management Studies*, 47: 191–204

Sciascia, S. and Mazzola, P. 2008. Family Involvement in ownership and management: Exploring nonlinear effects on performance. *Family Business Review*, 21: 331–345.

Sharma, P., Chrisman, J.J., and Gersick, K.E. 2012. 25 Years of *Family Business Review*: Reflections on the past and perspectives for the Future. *Family Business Review*, 25: 5–15.

Sirmon, D.G. and Hitt, M.A. 2003. Managing resources: Linking unique resources, management and wealth creation in family firms. *Entrepreneurship: Theory and Practice*, 27(4): 339–358.

Uhlaner, L.M., Kellermanns, F.W., Eddleston, K.A., and Hoy, F. 2012. The entrepreneuring family: A new paradigm for family business research. *Small Business Economics*, 38:1–11.

35

Toward a Paradox Perspective of Family Firms: The Moderating Role of Collective Mindfulness in Controlling Families

Thomas Zellweger

INTRODUCTION

Despite numerous attempts to establish the link between family involvement and firm performance, research findings are alarmingly inconsistent. Some researchers, mostly drawing from traditional economics, depict a very pessimistic picture, suggesting that family involvement is a source of fundamental inefficiency because of owner–owner agency conflicts, resource constraints, and family utility maximization that detracts from firm value maximization (Dharwadkar et al., 2000; La Porta et al., 2002; Morck and Yeung, 2003; Peng and Jiang, 2010). Other researchers, however, referring to reduced owner–manager agency conflicts, concerns for long-term organizational prosperity, and the provision of unique resources such as patient financial capital, suggest that family-owned firms outperform nonfamily firms (Anderson and Reeb, 2003; Barontini and Caprio, 2005; McConaughy et al., 1998; Villalonga and Amit, 2006). This favorable

perspective has found support in a recent meta-analysis of studies on family firm performance in the US stock market, which indicate a systematic outperformance of family firms (Carney et al., 2011). While inconsistent empirical findings on fundamental questions are not uncommon in management research, the theoretical inconsistencies are particularly worrying and raise fundamental concerns about the adequacy of our linear reasoning on the (in)efficiency of family involvement. What is noteworthy is that the concerns for tensions and theoretical inconsistencies have been very prominent in earlier family business writings (e.g., Tagiuri and Davis, 1996; Whiteside and Brown, 1991). Unfortunately, however, and most likely as a consequence of the shift towards empiricist research methodologies that are best suited to uncover linear relationships, the attention of academics over the last few years has moved away from how family firms deal with tensions and competing forces.

PARADOX AS A FRESH LENS TO INVESTIGATE THE EFFICIENCY OF FAMILY INVOLVEMENT

Whether one adheres to the negative or positive view as depicted, we must acknowledge that the link between family involvement and performance may be less straightforward than expected. Both views hold some level of incontestable truth, reflected in succinct theoretical reasoning and wide empirical evidence. When taken alone, these two perspectives are fundamentally juxtaposed and incompatible. When taken together, however, they form a tradition of theoretical discourse potentially richer than either perspective by itself. Building on paradox and systemic management research, I suggest that linear approaches, such as those advocated by agency theory (heightened principal–principal conflicts versus reduced owner–manager conflicts), are biased toward consistency, thereby overlooking the management of tensions, paradoxes, and inconsistencies (Achtenhagen and Melin, 2003; Cameron, 1986; Farjoun, 2010; Gibson and Birkinshaw, 2004; Leonard-Barton, 1992; Luhmann, 1992; March, 1991; Miller, 1993; Smith and Lewis, 2011; Sundaramurthy and Lewis, 2003; Van de Ven and Poole, 1995).

Paradox thinking has a long tradition in management theory and has been applied to dilemmas such as stability and change, exploration and exploitation, centralization and decentralization, short-term and long-term focus, and structural determination and purposive action (for an overview refer to Poole and Van de Ven, 1989; Smith and Lewis, 2011). The paradox perspective assumes that tensions persist within complex and dynamic systems. It shifts attention asked by contingency theorists from identifying the factors/conditions that drive organisations"? (e.g., stability versus change orientation; family versus business interests) to examining how firms engage in these competing factors simultaneously (Smith and Lewis, 2011). It moves away from the original meaning of paradox (i.e., the simultaneous existence of incompatible dimensions), whereby managers are urged to overcome disjunctions, and toward seeking synergies between the dimensions and striving to harness efficiency advantages arising from complexity.

THE NECESSITY AND PROMISE OF A PARADOX PERSPECTIVE

The paradox perspective seems to impose itself on the study of family firms, for two reasons: (1) the inextricable and axiomatic tie between family and firm that defines the very nature of this type of organization; and (2) the challenge related to the combination of such seemingly competing demands for unconditional love, long-term focus, stability (often attributed to the family sphere) and meritocracy, short-term focus, and adaptation (often attributed to the business sphere). Recent family business studies have started building on this perspective (Basco and Perez-Rodriguez, 2009; Frank, Lueger, Nose, and Suchy, 2010; James et al., 2012; Litz et al., 2012; Nordqvist and Melin, 2010; Plate and von Schlippe, 2010; Schuman et al., 2010; Stewart and Hitt, 2010; Zellweger et al., 2012a; Zellweger and Nason, 2008). I adhere to Smith and Lewis' (2011: 382) definition of paradox: 'contradictory yet interrelated elements that exist simultaneously and persist over time. This definition highlights two components of paradox: (1) underlying tensions – that is, elements that seem logical individually but inconsistent and even absurd when juxtaposed – and (2) responses that embrace tensions simultaneously.' This perspective of paradox alludes to the recent work by Farjoun (2010) on duality, which emphasizes the simultaneous existence of two essential elements (doubleness), which are contradictory and complementary at the same time, where one enables the other and is a constituent of the other. Without overstating the compatibility of the aforementioned demands of the family and business spheres, and following Whiteside and Brown (1991), I propose four critiques of this dual systems approach to family firms and advocate a paradox perspective to overcome the resulting limitations.

First, there seems to be a largely overlooked common ground between family and business systems. While certain social rules and norms, such as support, commitment, cohesiveness, and interdependence, are particularly pronounced in the family context, they are neither absent nor incompatible with the efficient functioning of the business sphere. Indeed, relationships characterized by these norms are often depicted as highly desirable in the business context. For instance, the literature on affective commitment and team building depicts a very favorable picture of humane interactions, which stand out from mechanistic tit-for-tat relationships (Allen and John, 1990; Menz, 2012). Just as importantly, certain attributes that are ascribed to the business sphere, such as efficient use of resources, are found in familial norms such as parsimony (Carney, 2005) and the family's provision of economic goods such as shelter and education. Many family firm studies are undermined by flawed ontological assumptions about the nature of family and business social systems, because each is defined as the opposite of the other. This juxtaposition of family and business systems is misleading, because even stability-providing systems, a role often attributed to families, are essential grounds for organizational change (Feldman and Pentland, 2003). Neglecting these findings assigns a negative and inertial role to families, thereby disregarding the role of families in not only absorbing, but also enabling, change. Consequently, I suggest that family and business systems are not orthogonal and that the incompatibility of social norms in family and business spheres is overstated.

Second, the overwhelming relevance of family firms in economies across the world, both emerging and otherwise (Shanker and Astrachan, 1996), challenges the trade-off perspective between family and business goals. If most family firms pursue socioemotional goals accruing at the family level, such as dynastic control, benevolent ties, positive affect, and reputation (Berrone et al., 2010; Gomez-Mejia et al., 2007, 2011; Zellweger et al., 2012b), it is impossible that these nonfinancial goals only detract from financial performance. Otherwise, the family firm would have disappeared long ago. The combined family business system is thus not inevitably undermined by the seemingly opposing goals of the subsystems. On the contrary, and as tentatively addressed in Tagiuri and Davis' article (1996) on the bivalent attributes of family firms, there must be 'economies of synergy' between socioemotional and financial goals, which have been largely overlooked to date.

Third, and as epitomized in the owner–owner agency writings alluded to previously, families do not uniformly deprive their firms of necessary resources. As depicted in the familiness literature, families often provide unique resources to their firms, such as patient capital, survivability capital, and tacit knowledge, which serve as the basis for competitive advantage (Habbershon and Williams, 1999; Sirmon and Hitt, 2003). Also, because not only financial but also socioemotional wealth is at stake in many family firms, it seems unlikely that families systematically exploit the firm's resource base. In addition, because family firm owners are concerned not only about money but also about resources such as reputation and social capital, the family and the firm do not systematically compete for the same resources. Thus, families cannot be seen as systematic resource 'extractors', but as critical resource providers to their firms.

Fourth, and on a more general basis, a dual systems approach that assigns a defective role to the family sphere advocates a simplified, mono-dimensional approach to management that systematically excludes the family. Such a reductionist approach to the management of family firms neglects the opportunities related to the combination of family and business in avoiding dysfunctionalities that undermine organizational effectiveness. In fact, Bateson (1973, 1979) and Cameron (1986) suggest that without the tension that exists between simultaneous opposites in organizations, entropy and unproductive schismogenesis occur, whereby schismogenesis is defined as a 'process of self-reinforcement where one action or attribute in the organization perpetuates itself until it becomes extreme and therefore dysfunctional' (Cameron, 1986: 546). According to Cameron (1986), it is not the presence of mutually exclusive opposites that makes for effectiveness, but the creative leaps, the flexibility, and the unity made possible by them that leads to excellence. Interestingly enough, family business practitioners have started to actively explore the benefits of a paradox perspective. For example, in their recent book, emblematically entitled *Family Business as Paradox*, Schuman et al. (2010) present the case of Beretta, an Italian family firm founded in 1526, which seeks to maintain systematic creativity by managing paradoxes. At Beretta, paradox thinking is ingrained in corporate culture and is, for example, perceptible in the company's motto: 'prudence and audacity'. Prudence thereby represents wisdom in practical matters; audacity stands for fearlessly daring. This line of thinking alludes to the ongoing debate about the synchronous pursuit of explorative and exploitative actions (Gavetti and Levinthal, 2000; Gupta et al., 2006; March, 1991). These streams of research converge on the idea that resolving all simultaneous contradictions and pursuing logical consistency may, in fact, inhibit excellence by eliminating the creative tension that paradoxes produce.

COLLECTIVE MINDFULNESS OF THE CONTROLLING FAMILY

From a theoretical standpoint, the promise of such a paradox perspective applied to the management of family firms largely depends on our ability to define the mindset and behaviors required for paradox thinking. I suggest that *collective mindfulness*, defined as the controlling family's ability to use paradox thinking to seek synergies between family and firm, plays a decisive role in the positive or negative effectiveness consequences arising from family involvement (Farjoun, 2010;

Levinthal and Rerup, 2006; Weick and Roberts, 1993; Weick et al., 1999).

In partial adaptation of and extension to existing mindfulness writings, collective mindfulness of controlling families comprises an awareness of the bivalent nature of many aspects of family involvement, such as those described by Tagiuri and Davis (1996). For instance, Tagiuri and Davis (1996) mention the issue of shared identities of family and firm, and shared identities of family members being involved in the firm. While this may create a stifling sense of being overwatched, and resentment toward family and business, it may at the same time imply heightened family and company loyalty and a strong sense of mission. Similarly, a lifelong common history between family members may imply that family members can point out weaknesses. Also, early disappointments can reduce trust in work interactions. At the same time however, because of a common history relatives can draw out relatives' strengths and complement their weaknesses. And it may form a strong foundation to weather adversity. Mindful families are hence reluctant to simplify interpretations; they appreciate multiple interpretations and perspectives and are open to ambiguity stemming from the family and business interaction (Farjoun, 2010; Langer, 1989). As a consequence of the greater reluctance to simplify, mindful families hesitate to separate the humane from the mechanistic, and are hesitant to assign strict priority to the family or to the firm. Mindful families thus resist pressures to implement generally accepted quasi-solutions such as business first *or* family first and follow their own uniquely successful way to combine family *and* business. To a certain degree, such families deinstitutionalize the solution to the paradoxical situation, and disregard the force of habit, history, and tradition being either respectful of the family or business domain (Oliver, 1992). Trapped in previously created categories, less-mindful families easily confuse the stability of their emotionally rigid, rule-based assumptions with stability in the world, thus obtaining a false reading of their surroundings (Langer, 1989).

Building on Miller's (1993) suggestions of threats posed by simplicity and automatism, collective mindfulness is just as much pre-occupied with failure and affordable loss as it is concerned about success (Fiol and O'Connor, 2003; Sarasvathy, 2001). I suggest that collective mindfulness of the controlling family is also characterized by a concern for reliability and effectiveness of the firm, and hence about going concern as well as commitment to resilience and hence the capability to rebound from setbacks (Wildavsky, 1991). Also, collective mindfulness in the context of controlling families considers the long-term perspective. The family would not put its own interests behind those of the firm as suggested in stewardship writings; but the firm, in particular its future prosperity, is an integral part of the family's utility function. In consequence, mindful families will be less likely to seek immediate financial return and more willing to accept a future and, hence, more uncertain payback (Bazerman et al., 1998). They are less likely to fall prey to fallacies such as inappropriately high discounting of future returns (Loewenstein and Thaler, 1989). This includes the absence of a sense of entitlement vis-à-vis the firm. Instead, mindful families are more likely to develop a sense of responsibility and will care about the firm's long-term success.

My theorizing on collective mindfulness of controlling families could be considered a moderator that splits family involvement in a firm into an upside and a downside (Fiol and O'Connor, 2003). These considerations on possible components of collective mindfulness among controlling families and its moderating impact on organizational effectiveness are depicted in Figure 35.1.

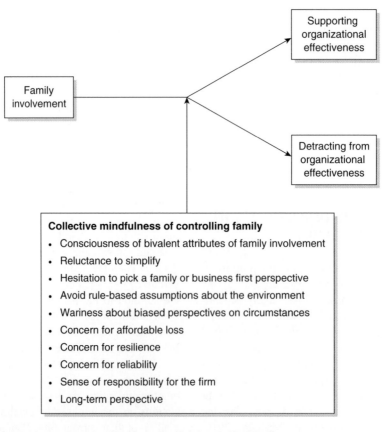

Figure 35.1   Components of collective mindfulness in family firms

SOME CONSIDERATIONS ABOUT MEASUREMENT

Recent case study evidence suggests that what I bulkily label collective mindfulness of the controlling family may be a very natural way for families to manage their business activities (e.g., see the case studies in Nordqvist and Zellweger, 2010). Controlling families may 'simply have it', consciously or unconsciously. It is perhaps rather we as researchers who have made things – more complex – too simplistic in light of our different research traditions. Nevertheless, empirical evidence and ultimately measurement will become an issue if we want to examine the usefulness of the paradox perspective and in particular the concept of collective mindfulness of the controlling family. Given the theoretical novelty of the concepts, qualitative case study research seems appropriate to untangle the processes and structures that are put in place to deal with dilemmas such as unconditional acceptance (born) and conditional acceptance (hired), socialistic and capitalistic regimes, cooperative and competitive behavior, emotionality and rationality, equality and merit, to mention a few.

At the same time, however, I believe there is space to quantitatively explore the effectiveness of a paradox perspective. To this end researchers could adhere to the empirical methodologies applied in ambidexterity literature. One way of advancing along this path is to investigate how various degrees of family emphasis – measured via the presence of the first elements in the above dilemmas – combined with various degrees of business emphasis – measured, for instance, via the presence of the second elements in the above dilemmas – affect the effectiveness of the controlled firm(s). Just as we proposed in Zellweger et al. (2012a), researchers could investigate how a dominant family coalition that scores high on both logics affects value creation, in which case the product (family emphasis * business emphasis) would be a good proxy for collective mindfulness. Alternatively, a family may

be regarded as ambidextrous if it displays relatively equal emphasis on both logics. In this balanced approach, one would have to take the difference (family emphasis − business emphasis) as the proxy for collective mindfulness. In this case, even a firm that puts low emphasis on both dimensions would be classified as ambidextrous (Andriopoulos and Lewis, 2009; He and Wong, 2004; Raisch and Birkinshaw, 2008).

CONCLUSION

I have tried to advance our thinking beyond the dualism perspective of family firms by drawing attention to the power of anomalies and paradoxes. The fundamental assumption here is that the combination of family and firm, through the management of paradoxes ingrained in the collective mindfulness of the family, can generate a positive outcome. Collectively mindful families display an ongoing wariness of the synergies between family and firm and move away from one-dimensional representations, simplifications, and inertial tendencies, and try to uncover the double-sided nature of family and business practices and their conjoint operations, complementarities, and, ultimately, synergies. This strand of thinking is underlined by the simple observation that in family firms a one-sided specialization on either family or business is illogical, because – for better or worse – these systems coincide in family organizations. In light of this observation I suggest that the stronger the collective mindfulness of the controlling family, the more likely the firm will exhibit effectiveness advantages arising from family involvement. The question then becomes how best to combine competing demands and to 'live' collective mindfulness, not as a matter of necessity but as a matter of opportunity. I hope that the present text makes a small step toward answering this important question and has raised readers' interest in an underexplored strand of family business research.

REFERENCES

Achtenhagen, L. and Melin, L. 2003. Managing the homogeneity-heterogeneity duality. In A. Pettigrew, R. Whittington, L. Melin, C. Sanchez-Runde, F. Van den Bosch, W. Ruigrok, and T. Numagami (eds), *Innovative Forms of Organizing*: 301–328. Thousand Oaks, CA: Sage.

Allen, N.J. and John, P.M. 1990. The measurement and antecedents of affective, continuance and normative commitment to the organization. *Journal of Occupational Psychology*, 63(1): 1–18.

Anderson, R.C. and Reeb, D.M. 2003. Founding-family ownership and firm performance: Evidence from the S&P 500. *Journal of Finance*, 58(3): 1301–1328.

Andriopoulos, C. and Lewis, M. 2009. Exploitation-exploration tensions and organizational ambidexterity: Managing paradoxes of innovation. *Organization Science*, 20(4): 696–717.

Barontini, R. and Caprio, L. 2005. The effect of family control on firm value and performance – evidence from continental Europe. *European Financial Management*, 12(5).

Basco, R. and Perez-Rodriguez, M.J. 2009. Studying the family enterprise holistically. *Family Business Review*, 22(1): 82–95.

Bateson, G. 1973. *Steps to an Ecology of Mind*. London: Paladin.

Bateson, G. 1979. *Mind and Nature: A Necessary Unity*. New York: Bantam Books.

Bazerman, M.H., Tenbrunsel, A.E., and Wade-Benzoni, K. 1998. Negotiating with yourself and losing: making decisions with competing internal preferences. *Academy of Management Review*, 23(2): 225–241.

Berrone, P., Cruz, C., Gomez-Mejia, L.R., and Larraza-Kintana, M. 2010. Socioemotional wealth and corporate responses to institutional pressures: Do family-controlled firms pollute less? *Administrative Science Quarterly*, 55(1): 82–113.

Cameron, K.S. 1986. Effectiveness as paradox: Consensus and conflict in conceptions of organizational effectiveness. *Management Science*, 32: 539–553.

Carney, M. 2005. Corporate governance and competitive advantage in family-controlled firms. *Entrepreneurship Theory & Practice*, 29(3): 249–265.

Carney, M., Gedajlovic, E., and van Essen, N. 2011. Do US publicly listed family firms outperform? A meta-analysis. *Academy of Management Conference*, San Antonio.

Dharwadkar, R., George, G., and Brandes, P. 2000. Privatization in emerging economies: an agency theory perspective. *Academy of Management Review*, 25: 650–669.

Farjoun, M. 2010. Beyond dualism: Stability and change as a duality. *Academy of Management Review*, 35(2): 202–225.

Feldman, M.S. and Pentland, B.T. 2003. Reconceptualizing organizational routines as a source of flexibility and change. *Administrative Science Quarterly*, 48: 94–118.

Fiol, C.M. and O'Connor, E. 2003. Waking up! Mindfulness in the face of bandwagons. *Academy of Management Review*, 28: 54–70.

Frank, H., Lueger, M., Nose, L., and Suchy, D. 2010. The concept of 'familiness': Literature review and systems theory-based reflections. *Journal of Family Business Strategy*, 1(3): 119–130.

Gavetti, G. and Levinthal, D. 2000. Looking forward and looking backward: Cognitive and experiential search. *Administrative Science Quarterly*, 45: 113–137.

Gibson, C.B. and Birkinshaw, J. 2004. The antecedents, consequences, and mediating role of organizational ambidexterity. *Academy of Management Journal*, 47(2): 209–226.

Gomez-Mejia, L.R., Cruz, C.C., Berrone, P., and De Castro, J. 2011. The ties that bind: Socioemotional wealth preservation in family firms. *Academy of Management Annals*: 1–55.

Gomez-Mejia, L.R., Haynes, K.T., Nunez-Nickel, M., Jacobson, K.J.L., and Moyano-Fuentes, J. 2007. Socioemotional wealth and business risks in family-controlled firms: Evidence from Spanish olive oil mills. *Administrative Science Quarterly*, 52(1): 106–137.

Gupta, A.K., Smith, K.G., and Shalley, C.E. 2006. The interplay between exploration and exploitation. *Academy of Management Journal*, 49(4): 693–706.

Habbershon, T.G. and Williams, M.L. 1999. A resource-based framework for assessing the strategic advantages of family firms. *Family Business Review*, 12(1): 1–25.

He, Z. and Wong, P. 2004. Exploration vs. exploitation: An empirical test of the ambidexterity hypothesis. *Organization Science*, 15: 481–494.

James, A.E., Jennings, J.E., and Breitkreuz, R. 2012. Worlds apart? Rebridging the distance between family science and family business research. *Family Business Review*, 25(1): 87–108.

La Porta, R., Lopez-De-Silanes, F., Shleifer, A., and Vishny, R. 2002. Investor protection and corporate valuation. *Journal of Finance*, 57(3): 1147–1170.

Langer, E.J. 1989. *Mindfulness*. Reading, MA: Addison-Wesley.

Leonard-Barton, D. 1992. Core capabilities and core rigidities: A paradox in managing new product development. *Strategic Management Journal*, 13: 111–125.

Levinthal, D.A. and Rerup, C. 2006. Crossing an apparent chasm: Bridging mindful and less-mindful perspectives on organizational learning. *Organization Science*, 17: 502–513.

Litz, R.A., Pearson, A.W., and Litchfield, S. 2012. Charting the future of family business research: Perspectives from the field. *Family Business Review*, 25(1): 16–32.

Loewenstein, G. and Thaler, R.H. 1989. Anomalies: Intertemporal choice. *Journal of Economic Perspectives*, 3(Fall): 181–193.

Luhmann, N. 1992. *Social Systems*. Stanford, CT: Stanford University Press.

March, J.G. 1991. Exploration and exploitation in organizational learning. *Organization Science*, 1(1): 71–87.

McConaughy, D.L., Walker, M.C., Henderson, G.V., and Mishra, C.S. 1998. Founding family controlled firms: Efficiency and value. *Review of Financial Economics*, 7(1): 1–19.

Menz, M. 2012. Functional top management team members: A review, synthesis, and research agenda. *Journal of Management*, 38(1): 45–80.

Miller, D. 1993. The architecture of simplicity. *Academy of Management Review*, 18(1): 116–138.

Morck, R. and Yeung, B. 2003. Agency problems in large family business groups. *Entrepreneurship Theory & Practice*, 27(4): 367–382.

Nordqvist, M. and Melin, L. 2010. Entrepreneurial families and family firms. *Entrepreneurship & Regional Development*, 22(3): 1–29.

Nordqvist, M. and Zellweger, T. (eds). 2010. *Transgenerational Entrepreneurship: Exploring Growth and Performance in Family Firms across Generations*. Cheltenham, UK and Brookfield, WI: Edward Elgar.

Oliver, C. 1992. The antecedents of deinstitutionalization. *Organization Studies*, 13(4): 563–588.

Peng, M.W. and Jiang, Y. 2010. Institutions behind family ownership and control in large firms. *Journal of Management Studies*, 47(2): 253–273.

Plate, M. and von Schlippe, A. 2010. Organizational paradoxes and paradox management in family firms, *WIFU working paper series*.

Poole, M.S. and Van de Ven, A.H. 1989. Using paradox to build management and organization theories. *Academy of Management Review*, 14(4): 562–578.

Raisch, S. and Birkinshaw, J. 2008. Organizational ambidexterity: Antecedents, outcomes and moderators. *Journal of Management*, 34: 375–409.

Sarasvathy, S. 2001. Causation and effectuation: Toward a theoretical shift from economic inevitability to entrepreneurial contingency. *Academy of Management Review*, 26(2): 243–263.

Schuman, S., Stutz, S., and Ward, J. 2010. *Family Business as Paradox*. New York: Palgrave.

Shanker, M.C. and Astrachan, J.H. 1996. Myths and realities: Family businesses' contribution to the U.S. economy: A framework for assessing family business statistics. *Family Business Review*, 9(2): 107–118.

Sirmon, D.G. and Hitt, M.A. 2003. Managing resources: Linking unique resources, management, and wealth creation in family firms. *Entrepreneurship Theory & Practice*, 27(4): 339–358.

Smith, W.K. and Lewis, M.W. 2011. Toward a theory of paradox: A dynamic equilibrium model of organizing. *Academy of Management Review*, 36(2): 381–403.

Stewart, A. and Hitt, M.A. 2010. The yin and yang of kinship and business: Complementary or contradictory forces? (And can we really say?). *Advances in Entrepreneurship, Firm Emergence and Growth*, 12: 243–276.

Sundaramurthy, C. and Lewis, M. 2003. Control and collaboration: Paradoxes of governance. *Academy of Management Review*, 28(3): 397–415.

Tagiuri, R. and Davis, J. 1996. Bivalent attributes of the family firm. *Family Business Review*, 9(2): 199–208.

Van de Ven, A.H. and Poole, M.S. 1995. Explaining development and change in organizations. *Academy of Management Review*, 20(3): 510–540.

Villalonga, B. and Amit, R. 2006. How do family ownership, control and management affect firm value? *Journal of Financial Economics*, 80(2): 385–417.

Weick, K. and Roberts, K. 1993. Collective mind in organizations: Heedful interrelating on flight decks. *Administrative Science Quarterly*, 38: 357–381.

Weick, K., Sutcliffe, K., and Obstfeld, D. 1999. Organizing for high reliability: Processes of collective mindfulness. In B. Staw and R. Sutton (eds), *Research in Organizational Behavior*. Stamford, CT: JAI Press Inc.

Whiteside, M.F. and Brown, F.H. 1991. Drawbacks of a dual systems approach to family firms: Can we expand our thinking? *Family Business Review*, 4(4): 383–395.

Wildavsky, A. 1991. *Searching for Safety*. New Brunswick: Transaction Books.

Zellweger, T.M., Nason, R., and Nordqvist, M. 2012a. From longevity of firms to transgenerational entrepreneurship of families. *Family Business Review*, 25(2): 136–155.

Zellweger, T., Kellermanns, F., Chrisman, J., and Chua, J. 2012b. Family control and family firm valuation by family CEOs: The importance of intentions for transgenerational control. *Organization Science*, 23(3): 851–868.

Zellweger, T.M. and Nason, R.S. 2008. A stakeholder perspective on family firm performance. *Family Business Review*, 21(3): 203–216.

Index